Freedom in the World
2005

The findings of *Freedom in the World 2005* include events from December 1, 2003, through November 30, 2004.

Freedom in the World 2005

THE ANNUAL SURVEY
OF POLITICAL RIGHTS & CIVIL LIBERTIES

EDITED BY
AILI PIANO AND ARCH PUDDINGTON

FREEDOM HOUSE
New York • Washington, DC

ROWMAN & LITTLEFIELD PUBLISHERS, INC.
Lanham • Boulder • New York • Toronto • Oxford

ROWMAN & LITTLEFIELD PUBLISHERS, INC.

Published in the United States of America
by Rowman & Littlefield Publishers, Inc.
A wholly owned subsidiary of The Rowman & Littlefield Publishing Group, Inc.
4501 Forbes Boulevard, Suite 200, Lanham, Maryland 20706
www.rowmanlittlefield.com

P.O. Box 317, Oxford OX2 9RU, United Kingdom

British Library Cataloguing in Publication Information Available

Library of Congress Cataloging-in-Publication Data

Freedom in the world / —1978–
New York : Freedom House, 1978–
v. : map; 25 cm.—(Freedom House Book)
Annual.
ISSN 0732-6610=Freedom in the World.
1. Civil rights—Periodicals. I. R. Adrian Karatnycky, et al. I. Series.
JC571 .F66 323.4'05—dc 19 82-642048
AACR 2   MARC-S
Library of Congress [84101]

ISBN 0-7425-5050-8 (alk. paper)—ISBN 0-7425-5051-6 (pbk. : alk. paper)
ISSN 0732-6610

Printed in the United States of America

The paper used in this publication meets the minimum requirements of American
National Standard for Information Sciences—Permanence of Paper for Printed Library
Materials, ANSI/NISO Z39.48-1992.

Contents

Acknowledgments

Freedom in the World 2005 could not have been completed without the contributions of numerous Freedom House staff and consultants (please see the section titled "The Survey Team" at the end of the book for a detailed list of these contributors). Several other Freedom House staff members took time out of their schedules to read and provide valuable feedback on the country reports, including Mike Staresinic and Sanja Pesek of the Belgrade office; Stuart Kahn of the Bishkek office; Zvonko Zinrajh of the Dushanbe office; Scott Charlesworth and Claire Mason of the Mexico City office; and Margarita Assenova, Sandy Acosta, and Xavier Utset of the Washington, DC office. Amy Phillips and Sanja Tatic of the New York office supplied critical administrative support. Jennifer Windsor, the executive director of Freedom House, provided overall guidance for the project.

Generous financial support for the survey was provided by the Lynde and Harry Bradley Foundation, the Smith Richardson Foundation, the Lilly Endowment, and the F. M. Kirby Foundation.

Civic Power
and Electoral Politics

Adrian Karatnycky

Russia entered the ranks of Not Free countries in 2004 for the first time since the breakup of the Soviet Union, according to the findings of *Freedom in the World 2005*, the survey of global political rights and civil liberties published annually by Freedom House. This setback for freedom represented the year's most important political trend.

Russia's steady drift toward authoritarian rule under President Vladimir Putin saw increased Kremlin control of national television content and growing influence over radio and print media, the use and manipulation—bordering on outright control—of "alternative" political parties with leaders linked to the country's security services, growing encroachments against local government, and elections that were neither free nor fair. The extent of Russia's long-term decline is suggested by the country's political rights rating of 3 and civil liberties rating of 4 for the year 1997 (toward the end of the presidency of Putin's predecessor, Boris Yeltsin), as compared to its rating of 6 for political rights and 5 for civil liberties today. Such a precipitous drop during that time frame is relatively rare—in that same time period, only Haiti has seen comparable declines.

While Russia became increasingly authoritarian, in neighboring Ukraine, fraudulent elections and other widespread violations of political rights and civil liberties led millions of Ukraine's citizens into the streets to defend their democratic rights. Although Ukraine's presidential election is to be re-run on December 26, its nonviolent Orange Revolution has already led to the widespread expansion of media freedoms, with most newspapers and national television networks now reporting freely. Ukraine's "people power" has contributed to greater independence of the legal system, particularly the Supreme Court, which annulled fraudulent election results and ordered a revote. Furthermore, civic ferment has helped increase academic freedom. All these developments have improved the state of the country's civil liberties, according to the survey findings.

These diametrically opposite trends were echoed in the growing differentiation between democratizing and increasingly authoritarian states throughout the former U.S.S.R. While the year saw important progress for freedom in Ukraine and Georgia, the erosion of freedoms in Russia was matched by ongoing repression in Belarus, Uzbekistan, and Turkmenistan, as well as authoritarian consolidation in Armenia. All this suggests that the post-Communist East-West divide (which formerly separated the countries of Central and Eastern Europe from those of the former Soviet Union) is gradually migrating eastward, as liberal values make gains in key post-Soviet states.

3

Freedom in the World—2005 Survey

The population of the world as estimated in mid-2004 is 6,395.4 million persons, who reside in 192 sovereign states. The level of political rights and civil liberties as shown comparatively by the Freedom House Survey is:

Free: 2,819.1 million (44.08 percent of the world's population) live in 89 of the states.

Partly Free: 1,189.0 million (18.59 percent of the world's population) live in 54 of the states.

Not Free: 2,387.3 million (37.33 percent of the world's population) live in 49 of the states.

A Record of the Survey
(population in millions)

Year under Review	FREE	PARTLY FREE	NOT FREE	WORLD POPULATION
Mid-1992	1,352.2 (24.83%)	2,403.3 (44.11%)	1,690.4 (31.06%)	5,446.0
Mid-1993	1,046.2 (19.00%)	2,224.4 (40.41%)	2,234.6 (40.59%)	5,505.2
Mid-1994	1,119.7 (19.97%)	2,243.4 (40.01%)	2,243.9 (40.02%)	5,607.0
Mid-1995	1,114.5 (19.55%)	2,365.8 (41.49%)	2.221.2 (38.96%)	5.701.5
Mid-1996	1,250.3 (21.67%)	2,260.1 (39.16%)	2,260.6 (39.17%)	5,771.0
Mid-1997	1,266.0 (21.71%)	2,281.9 (39.12%)	2,284.6 (39.17%)	5,832.5
Mid-1998	2,354.0 (39.84%)	1,570.6 (26.59%)	1,984.1 (33.58%)	5,908.7
Mid-1999	2,324.9 (38.90%)	1,529.0 (25.58%)	2,122.4 (35.51%)	5,976.3
Mid-2000	2,465.2 (40.69%)	1,435.8 (23.70%)	2,157.5 (35.61%)	6,058.5
Mid-2001	2,500.7 (40.79%)	1,462.9 (23.86%)	2,167.1 (35.35%)	6,130.7
Mid-2002	2,717.6 (43.85%)	1,293.1 (20.87%)	2,186.3 (35.28%)	6,197.0
Mid-2003	2,780.1 (44.03%)	1,324.0 (20.97%)	2,209.9 (35.00%)	6,314.0
Mid-2004	2,819.1 (44.08%)	1,189.0 (18.59%)	2,387.3 (37.33%)	6,395.4

* The large shift in the population figure between 1997 and 1998 is due to India's change in status from Partly Free to Free.

As 2004 drew to a close, 89 countries worldwide were judged as Free (possessing a high degree of political rights and civil liberties in an environment of strong rule of law), one more than in 2003. The gain was represented by progress in Antigua and Barbuda, which entered the ranks of Free countries in the wake of the electoral defeat of corrupt Prime Minister Lester Bird, whose departure from government created significant opportunities to promote democratic practices and the rule of law. Liberia entered the ranks of Partly Free states as a result of greater political freedom that developed through the establishment of a broad-based, transitional government. This gain was offset by the decline in the status of Russia, which moved from Partly Free to Not Free. (Additionally, the territory of Kosovo declined from Partly Free to Not Free in the wake of a significant increase in ethnic violence that led to the nonparticipation of the Serbian minority in parliamentary elections.) As a result of these offsetting trends, the year ended with 54 countries rated as Partly Free, one fewer than in the previous year. The number of Not Free countries, where political rights are severely constricted amid widespread civil liberties problems and a weak rule of law, stood at 49, the same as in 2003.

In 2004, 44 percent of the globe's population (2.819 billion) lived in Free countries and territories, 19 percent (1.189 billion) lived in Partly Free settings, while 37 percent (2.387 billion) lived in Not Free polities—of these, 1.3 billion (nearly three-fifths) lived in China. As a result of shifts in population and changes in freedom status, the number of people living in Free countries and territories increased by 39 million. The number of those living in Partly Free polities dropped by 136 million, while the number of those living in Not Free countries climbed by 177 million, largely due to Russia's entry into this category.

A deeper analysis of Freedom House data suggests that Free, Partly Free, and Not Free societies differ somewhat in comparative performance with regard to the four broad categories of civil liberties examined by the survey. An assessment of these differences helps to illuminate some of the underlying historical trajectories and political trends within types of countries. These main categories of civil liberties evaluated in the survey are: Freedom of Expression and Belief, Associational and Organizational Rights, Rule of Law, and Personal Autonomy and Individual Rights.

Overall, countries in all three types of societies show their weakest performance in Associational and Organizational Rights and the Rule of Law, while Freedom of Expression and Belief

The Global Trend

	Free	Partly Free	Not Free
1974	41	48	63
1984	53	59	55
1994	76	61	54
2004	89	54	49

Tracking Elecoral Democracy

Year under Review	Number of Electoral Democracies
1994	114
1999	120
2004	119

rankings are highest. However, Free and Partly Free societies rank considerably higher than Not Free polities in their median Associational and Organizational Rights ratings. This is hardly surprising, as it suggests that authoritarian regimes place great emphasis on controlling and limiting the ability of individuals to organize, associate, and engage in collective action, as this may prove highly threatening to entrenched authority and power.

In 2004, 119 out of 192 countries (62 percent) qualified as electoral democracies, two more than in 2003. The designation of electoral democracy is based on whether a country's last major national elections qualified under established international standards as "free and fair." All electoral democracies are not liberal democracies (or Free countries), as states with democratically elected leaders may still have serious problems in terms of human rights, the rule of law, and corruption. Out of 119 electoral democracies, 89 (75 percent) are Free, liberal democracies, while 30 (25 percent) are rated Partly Free. While Russia exited from the ranks of electoral democracies this year, new electoral democracies included Antigua and Barbuda, Comoros, and Georgia.

REGIONAL TRENDS

At year's end, the Middle East and North Africa continued to lag behind other world regions when overall levels of freedom are measured. In this region, only 1 country, Israel, is rated as Free, with 5 rated as Partly Free and 12 rated as Not Free. It is important to note that according to the survey's long-standing methodology, the rating for Israel only reflects events that occur within its territorial boundaries. The state of freedom in the Israeli Occupied Territories (and in areas formally administered under the Palestinian Authority) are rated separately, and both are rated Not Free given the significant human rights abuses and restrictions that are placed on Palestinian residents.

Comparable year-end figures for the Americas were 24 Free, 9 Partly Free, and 2

(Cuba and Haiti) Not Free countries. In Central and Eastern Europe and the former Soviet Union, 12 countries were Free, 7 were Partly Free, and 8 were Not Free (all five of the countries of Central Asia are rated Not Free, with two—Turkmenistan and Uzbekistan—among the most repressive states in the world). In the Asia-Pacific region, the survey found 17 countries are Free, 11 Partly Free, and 11 Not Free. In Sub-Saharan Africa, there were 11 Free, 21 Partly Free, and 16 Not Free states. And in Western Europe, 24 countries were rated Free; one country in the region, Turkey, was rated as Partly Free, although it made measurable strides in civil liberties this year, improving its score from 4 to 3.

Beyond these broad regional trends, in addition to the two countries (Antigua and Barbuda and Liberia) that registered status improvements in 2004, 24 countries showed numerical gains in freedom, although they were insufficient to produce a change in the overall freedom designation: Afghanistan, Bosnia-Herzegovina, Central African Republic, Comoros, Costa Rica, Czech Republic, Dominican Republic, Egypt, Estonia, Georgia, Guinea-Bissau, Hungary, Jordan, Malaysia, Mauritius, Morocco, Niger, Poland, Qatar, Slovakia, South Korea, Taiwan, Turkey, and Ukraine.

Meanwhile, in addition to a decline in freedom status in Russia, ten other countries experienced a decline in their numerical rankings that did not lead to a status change: Armenia, Belarus, Burkina Faso, Cote d'Ivoire, Haiti, Lithuania, Malawi, Nepal, Romania, and Zimbabwe.

GAINS IN FREEDOM

This year's survey registered modest trends in improved civil liberties in the Middle East and North Africa specifically, and in Muslim majority countries in general. While Muslim majority countries constitute 24 percent of the world's states, they accounted for over a third (9 of 25) of the states that made measurable progress this year, mainly as a result of improved civil liberties. This trend was matched by growing discourse in many Islamic states about the need for political reform, as well as growing attention to the absence of fundamental rights for women in many Islamic—and particularly Arab—societies.

While in Iraq, progress toward stability and the creation of civic life was stalled by a brutally violent insurgency that increasingly made targets of innocent civilians, the survey reflected modest, but positive, trends in the Arab countries of the Middle East and North Africa. Although no Arab country gave evidence of improvement sufficient to merit a status change, modest gains were registered in Egypt, Jordan, Morocco, and Qatar. In Egypt, the civil liberties score increased from 6 to 5 because of greater civic activism, particularly by women's advocacy groups. Jordan's civil liberties score increased from 5 to 4 because of improvements in women's rights and press freedom. In Morocco, the civil liberties rating improved from 5 to 4 due to the adoption of one of the most liberal family codes in the Arab world. Qatar's civil liberties rating increased from 6 to 5 on the basis of improvements in academic freedom. It is noteworthy that the gains in the Arab world were concentrated in the civil liberties area; many of the changes stem from increased civic activism, which is factored in along with governmental actions and policies in overall evaluations. No country in the Arab Middle East has yet adopted significant liberalization of its political system.

Other majority-Muslim states registering gains included Malaysia, whose political rights rating improved as a result of more openly contested national elections. Comoros saw increased political contestation in its national legislative elections. Niger saw both political rights and civil liberties improvements due to increased representation of minorities in government and because of efforts to improve the status of women. Turkey's civil liberties strengthened due to the passage of another round of major reforms this year, including a complete overhaul of the penal code that makes it much more democratic. The Turkish government also increased civilian control of the military and started broadcasts in minority languages, including an increase in Kurdish language broadcasting. As Turkey awaited a decision concerning its consideration for European Union (EU) membership, the severest forms of torture decreased, and there were other improvements in human rights practices. In Afghanistan, reasonably free and fair presidential elections led to improved political rights despite obstacles to open contestation in regions where violence remained a significant factor.

The gains are spread relatively evenly across the main geographic regions. In Central and Eastern Europe, the Czech Republic, Estonia, Hungary, Poland, and Slovakia all made modest improvements in freedom as a result of their incorporation of European Union rights standards in the past year. These new EU states now enjoy the survey's highest numerical ranking for both political rights and civil liberties. At the same time, civic and political organizations in Bosnia-Herzegovina exercised significant influence in successful municipal elections throughout the country in October 2004, revealing a deepening maturity of civil society.

Improvements in Latin America included the strengthening of the rule of law in Costa Rica due to the indictment and detention of two former presidents, Rafael Calderon and Miguel Angel Rodriguez, for corruption, coercion, and illegal enrichment. This progress was matched by improvements in free press coverage and freedom of expression. In the Dominican Republic, political rights improved due to improvements in the country's electoral climate that occurred during the election of President Leonel Fernandez.

In Sub-Saharan Africa, gains included the Central African Republic, whose political rights improved as a result of increased political activism in preparation for democratic elections in 2005. Guinea-Bissau's political rights were strengthened by legislative elections that international observers pronounced as largely free and fair. Mauritius further increased its civil liberties score through the consolidation of associational rights and social equalities.

South Korea's political rights improved after the strengthening of the democratic process in free and fair elections, following last year's highly politicized presidential impeachment process. Taiwan's civil liberties registered steady gains due to gradual improvements in the rule of law, including the consolidation of judicial independence. In the territory of Hong Kong, despite the government of China's decision to rule out direct elections of the full legislature and Chief Executive, civil liberties improved modestly due to unparalleled civic activism, which led to incremental gains in associational rights and the rule of law.

As indicated above, positive developments also took place in Ukraine (civil liberties) and in Georgia (political rights). In Georgia, President Edward Shevardnadze was forced from office after fraudulent legislative elections in 2003 spurred nationwide protests. Mikhail Saakashvili was later elected president in polling in January 2004 that international observers asserted was honest and professionally conducted.

In Ukraine, a surge in civic activism and a major improvement in press freedom emerged during that country's presidential campaign and the protest movement that ignited in the wake of widespread ballot fraud.

DECLINES IN FREEDOM

In addition to Russia's entry into the ranks of Not Free states, three other former Soviet republics suffered measurable declines in freedom. Belarus, which ranks as the least free country in Europe, saw a further deepening of harassment of opposition political forces. In Armenia, the government responded violently to peaceful civic protests during the year amidst a broader pattern of increasingly unresponsive and undemocratic governance. Lithuania's political rights suffered a modest setback due to the determination by parliament that impeached President Rolandas Paksas had been under the influence of a foreign security service and organized crime elements while president. During the special election for his successor, a series of official raids was also perpetrated against parties supporting Paksas's replacement, Valdas Adamkus. Despite Paksas's removal from office, the fact of significant infiltration of high state offices by a foreign government raised worrying questions about the full autonomy of Lithuania's political leadership.

In Romania, political rights declined due to flaws in the first round of the country's presidential and parliamentary election process. One territory under international supervision, Kosovo, registered a setback in its political rights and saw its status decline from Partly Free to Not Free due to a Serbian community boycott of parliamentary elections following an increase in ethnic violence.

In Sub-Saharan Africa, Burkina Faso saw an increase in corruption and reports of illegal arms trafficking, resulting in a decline in civil liberties. Cote d'Ivoire's civil liberties decreased due to the deterioration in security and civil freedoms resulting from an upsurge in hostilities emanating from an unresolved civil conflict. Malawi's political rights declined due to flawed political elections. Despite the acquittal of opposition leader Morgan Tsangvirai on trumped-up charges of treason and attempted assassination, Zimbabwe's political rights declined further due to increased government repression of the political opposition.

Although an increasingly authoritarian President Jean-Bertrand Aristede left the country in 2004, overall Haiti's political rights declined in the absence of democratically derived sovereign authority and the imposition of an ineffective interim government after the deployment of an international security force.

Nepal continues its downward trend with a decline this year in civil liberties due to a violent Maoist insurgency, the government's increasingly brutal response to that conflict, further deterioration in the rule of law, and increased pressures on economic activity.

THE RELATIONSHIP BETWEEN FREEDOM AND TERRORISM

Despite the increase in global terrorism, freedom and democracy have shown a demonstrable resilience and progress—even if incremental and tentative—continues in many regions. Unfortunately, in some cases, the war on terrorism has been used by some states to justify the reduction of personal and political freedoms by unscrupulous regimes that are drifting further toward authoritarian rule. Among these is Russia, where President Vladimir Putin has cynically exploited the terrorist attacks in Beslan this September to dismantle local elected authority. Uzbekistan's authoritarian ruler, Islam Karimov, has similarly used the war on terror as a justification for repressing peaceful civic movements while maintaining a ban on moderate opposition political parties.

The threat of terrorism has put a strain on established democracies as well. Democratic leaders are naturally under pressure from their publics to respond effectively and vigorously to emerging terrorist threats. However, at times, such responses may lead in directions which put a strain on a country's traditional patterns of tolerance and respect for civil liberties. In the aftermath of the murder of Dutch film documentarian Theo Van Gogh, there was a wave of arson attacks against both Christian and Muslim houses of worship. These events contributed to heightened fears of a wider network of potential terrorists in the country's growing Muslim immigrant community. In France, concern about the spread of Muslim fundamentalism has led to restrictions on the display of religious symbols in state schools. While not threatening the broadly based and well-secured rights and liberties of these EU member states, these trends nevertheless are capable of putting at risk some civil liberties and suggest that even well-established democracies must be vigilant against encroachments on their own freedoms.

Similarly, in the United States, there has been a thoroughgoing debate about the civil liberties implications of the USA PATRIOT Act, some provisions of which are believed by civil libertarian and some human rights groups to pose a potential threat to freedom of expression, freedom of religion, and the spread of government surveillance capability. In addition, serious questions have been raised by prisoner abuse in Abu Ghraib prison in Iraq and in Afghanistan, and by the detention without judicial oversight of accused terrorists in Guantanamo. During 2004, American courts issued several decisions that chipped away at the PATRIOT Act and challenged the government's claim to exclusive authority over terrorism detainees.

No aspect of freedom has been the subject of greater commentary than its relationship to the global threat presented by terrorist movements. This year, studies by Harvard Professor Alberto Abadie and Professor John Mearsheimer of the University of Chicago found statistically significant correlations between levels of freedom and terrorism, reinforcing similar studies by Alan Krueger of Princeton.

Freedom House's own research into the relationship between democracy and terrorism bears out these academic conclusions. In an ongoing research initiative, Freedom House has correlated data from all recorded terrorist acts from the period 1999-2003 with data from the *Freedom in the World* survey.[1] First, our research finds that the targeting of liberal democratic societies has increased dramatically after September 11, 2001. In the 32 months before the 9/11 attacks, 16 percent of all terrorist fatalities occurred in the democratic world. Post-9/11, this proportion rose to 27 percent, and the number of terrorist casualties occurring in democracies rose from 9.3 to 37.8 per month, an increase of over 400 percent.

In part, of course, this can be explained as radical Islamist rage over the attacks by U.S.-led coalitions against Afghanistan's Taliban and Saddam Hussein's Iraq. But this pattern also reflects a calculus by terrorists that at root even powerful democracies are weak and susceptible to terrorist pressure. Revolutionary Islamist terrorists are specifically targeting the democratic world. As a result, including the victims of September 11, 62 percent of all casualties (deaths and injuries) caused throughout the world since 1999 by radical Islamist terrorists have occurred in liberal, democratic societies (countries rated Free by Freedom House). Such radicals are responsible for seven out of every eight deaths from terrorism that have occurred in the democratic world in the last five years, and for 32 percent of all terrorist attacks on open, democratic societies. Even when the single-day death toll from September 11 is not included, revolutionary Islamist terror is still responsible for over 55 percent of the terrorist fatalities that have occurred in the democratic world in the last five years.

Freedom House's findings—which will be released in a detailed report in 2005—reinforce Krueger and Mearsheimer's findings about the correlations between terror and levels of freedom. Between 1999 and 2003, 70 percent of all deaths from terrorism were caused by terrorists and terrorist groups originating in Not Free societies, while only 8 percent of all fatalities were generated by terrorists and terror movements with origins in Free societies. Moreover, terrorists from dictatorial and repressive societies that brutalize their inhabitants are themselves significantly more brutal than terrorists born and acculturated in democratic societies. Over the last five years, terrorists who came from societies that are rated Not Free by Freedom House and in which most basic rights are denied, on average, killed some 11 and injured 15 people per attack,[2] whereas those perpetrated by organizations and individuals from Free societies on average claimed two lives and injured seven. Even if we exclude 9/11's fatalities, terrorists from closed societies are over twice as lethal as their counterparts from less repressive states. All terrorism is morally reprehensible and odious, but this difference in degree must be better understood.

No society and no political system can guarantee that it will not produce terrorists, just as no society can guarantee that it will not generate violent criminals. Still, as the data in this study indicate, stable democracies generate fewer and less lethal terrorists and terrorist movements than tyrannies. In order to successfully wage a war of ideas against such a lethal enemy, the human benefits of greater political, civil, and economic freedom must be consistently encouraged. This makes urgent the priority of bringing democracy and human rights reforms to Central Asia and the Arab world. Such an agenda of promoting democracy and reform requires a long-term approach and a long-term commitment; a military and intelligence driven war on terror is not enough. Even if the war on terror scores significant intelligence, security, and military achievements, long-term success can be best secured if it is accompanied by democratic reform and liberalization of the world's most repressive and politically closed regimes.

This effort to promote democratic change will be most effective if it is waged by democrats from closed societies themselves, and augmented by international cooperation that engages moderate and reformist governments from majority-Muslim states. A corollary of this approach should include efforts to engage respected religious leaders who oppose the cynical manipulation of religious faith on behalf of extremist political agendas. Finally, the United States and other established democracies must ensure that they maintain the highest standards of conduct in in their own actions to combat the scourge of terrorism.

THE FATE OF ILLIBERAL DEMOCRACIES: DO ELECTIONS REALLY NOT MATTER?

While no one doubts the correlation between democratic political processes and broad-based freedoms, in recent years, the relationship between elections and freedom has been subjected to significant criticism. Fareed Zakaria, Thomas Carothers, Larry Diamond and others have warned about the rise of "illiberal democracies" in which elections are held but leaders remain unaccountable and engage in actions that undermine political rights and civil liberties.

Recently—amid rising domestic pressures and international standards—one-party states and other monolithic authoritarian systems have collapsed and been replaced by multiparty systems. In the last 15 years alone, the number of competitive electoral democracies has risen from 69 out of 167 (41 percent) to 119 out of 192 (62 percent). This process means that each year, on average, 3.3 additional states have adopted minimal standards of free and fair elections. As noted before, however, only 89 of these 119 electoral democracies are Free, while over a quarter lag behind in terms of their civil liberties.

Many of these new multiparty systems have become open and competitive democracies, often with significant gains for the rule of law. But in other post-transition systems, truly competitive multiparty elections have often been supplanted by dominant party states which employ a wide array of authoritarian techniques. While there were some examples of dominant party states in the post-World War II era (including Mexico under the seven-decade rule of the Institutional Revolutionary Party (PRI), the Philippines under Marcos, Indonesia under Suharto, and Peru under Fujimori), a large number arose in the aftermath of the collapse of one-party Marxist-Leninist systems. The development of dominating institutions in these states has been so widespread that some scholars have pointed to the rise of pseudo-democracies and "hybrid states," which contain the false trappings of democratic processes and opposition political parties. These "dominant party" states use a variety of means to preserve a façade of electoral contestation while maintaining unchallenged political power, including the financial resources of crony-capitalist oligarchic elites to back party campaigns, pro-government media dominance, use of state administrative resources in campaigns, and political harassment of independent media and opposition groups. Among such states, scholars have pointed to Armenia, Azerbaijan, Belarus, Kazakhstan, Kyrgyzstan, Russia, and Ukraine—all of which possess to one degree or another a political party opposition that participates in electoral processes, however constrained or fraudulent.

In each of these pseudo-democracies, dominant parties maintain control in semi-authoritarian systems that retain the external trappings of democracy while real political power remains in the hands of an unchallenged, entrenched elite. Scholars have suggested that these trends presage a new stable polity, not a mid-point in the evolution toward authentic democracy.

Freedom House data continue to show that a considerable proportion of electoral democracies (25 percent this year) are rated Partly Free. Fareed Zakaria, in an influential essay, has pointed to this discrepancy in Freedom House data to suggest that, in the absence of strong constitutional and legal frameworks, elections often empower illiberal majorities that persecute minority groups. Zakaria dubbed this phenomenon illiberal democracy.

Some political scientists also have suggested that this discrepancy is the result of an overemphasis on the part of donors on the formality of elections and have urged a greater emphasis on the rule of law, independent media, and civil society. In fact, donor strategies have generally incorporated this more multidimensional approach.

With the people power movements this year in Ukraine, in Georgia (2003), and in Serbia (2000) fresh in our memories, there is good reason to reexamine and reevaluate the thesis that the electoral process is merely a formality. As each of these pivotal transitions indicates, an important factor in leading to political openings has been the evidence of growing civic ferment generated by electoral processes themselves. Indeed, it can be said that the very fact of voter fraud and electoral manipulation has proven a catalyst for massive civic opposition that has led to a free and fair electoral result.

To the Ukrainian, Georgian, and Serbian examples of civic mobilizations revolving around electoral processes, we can add the 1986 people power revolution in the Philippines and civic activism in Chile in 1988 around a plebiscite that helped force General Augusto Pinochet from office and launched a democratic transition. Civic protests around tainted elections in Mexico in 1988 and long-term civic and political mobilization paved the way to a more open and contested process, resulting 12 years later in the defeat of the ruling party's candidate. In Slovakia, widespread civic mobilization around elections in 1998 created a broad-based left-right coalition that defeated the party of the authoritarian Prime Minister Vladimir Meciar and ushered in more liberal rule.

There are several important reasons why electoral processes in pseudo-democracies and illiberal democracies have a catalytic effect on more deeply rooted democratic change.

First, elections concentrate civic energy and activity around a culminating focal point—the date of the election. This allows opposition parties and movements to mobilize their resources for deployment in a concentrated period of political contestation.

Second, despite state media dominance in many pseudo-democracies, some alternative media—in the form of the Internet, local radio, local cable television, and independent newspapers—manage to emerge in the cracks of the edifice of state control.

Third, if there is some limited space for electoral contestation, there is equally some space for freedom of assembly and associational rights that enable opposition civic life.

Fourth, corruption and crony capitalism—frequent characteristics of these less-than-fully democratic regimes—often become a source of civic anger and mobilization.

Fifth, because pseudo-democracies adopt their political model to be acceptable to the growing democratic world, they are often open to external donor activity, cross-border cooperation among civic groups, and extensive external election monitoring.

As importantly, because the formal legal basis for multiparty systems and civic and media pluralism is already in place, changes in such part-democratic/part-authoritarian hybrid settings usually occur within constitutional bounds. Indeed, many nonviolent "people power revolutions" do not topple existing constitutional systems, but instead make it possible for state and civic institutions to begin functioning according to the spirit and letter of the basic law.

FOREIGN AID: CREATING INCENTIVES FOR LIBERALIZATION

In March 2002, President George W. Bush announced the Millennium Challenge Account, a new foreign aid initiative that would reward developing countries that "rule justly." A set of criteria was crafted that included absence of corruption, support for market liberalization, greater investment in health and education, and respect for political rights and civil liberties as reflected in Freedom House's ratings.

The new paradigm for foreign aid was put into practice this year, and it is useful to evaluate its performance to date.

On balance, the countries selected and rewarded with $1 billion in cumulative new foreign aid include seven that are rated Free and nine that are rated Partly Free.[3] Seven of the nine Partly Free states had combined Freedom House scores of 3.5 or above and were thus some of the better performing Partly Free countries. Only two states that received support under the program, Armenia and Morocco, were ranked at the lower end of Partly Free states.

By contrast, the cohort that qualified for inclusion but was not given MCA enhanced foreign aid included three Free and nine Partly Free countries, of which six had lower-end Partly Free ratings. While Freedom House is appreciative of the Millennium Challenge Corporation Board using its discretion not to reward a number of potentially eligible poor performers—including Vietnam, Mauritania, and Bhutan— it urges the board to reexamine the criteria to ensure that the rule of law criteria adequately consider issues of due process and judicial independence.

On balance, the first year's decisions by the Millennium Challenge Corporation, while not fully according with levels of freedom as reflected in Freedom House's ranking, nevertheless incorporated enough of these factors to ensure that the foreign aid initiative does not reward those developing countries that practice widespread political suppression or massively violate most fundamental rights. However, Freedom House urges the administration to ensure that policy dialogue and assistance continue to be provided to participating countries, as many, especially the poorer performing qualifiers, have significant deficits in respect for political rights and civil liberties.

CONCLUSIONS: THE LESSONS OF 2004

The year brought with it many important lessons and reminders of relevance to policymakers, civic activists, and donors.

First, people power—that is, nonviolent civic protest—was yet again revealed to be a potent force for political change. It was a reminder that support for nonpartisan civic life through aid and training for membership organizations, labor unions, student and youth groups, election monitoring organizations, rights groups, and think tanks focused on the development of reform agenda deserve significant donor investment.

Second, international democratic solidarity by the world's economically powerful democracies was shown to be a positive force for change. From U.S.-EU joint action to press Ukraine's authorities to ensure free and fair elections, to the improvements in the freedom rankings of Turkey and Central and East European states, occasioned by their efforts to integrate into the EU, coalitions of democracies helped advance freedom.

Third, positive incentives to reward developing countries taking the democratic path should be strengthened and enhanced with the participation of other prosperous democracies, particularly the member states of the EU and Japan.

These three factors, if employed cohesively and comprehensively, may help propel further liberalization in states formerly thought stuck in a semi-authoritarian no man's land. They will also offer measured hope to democracy activists in closed societies.

Adrian Karatnycky is Counselor and Senior Scholar at Freedom House.

NOTES

1. The *Freedom in the World* data used here do not include the 2004 scores detailed in this essay. The research encompasses terrorist acts that took place January 1, 1999 through December 31, 2003. The three freedom status changes in 2004 do not affect the statistical conclusions of the research. (Chechnya, which has been both a target of and a source for terrorists, is rated separately from Russia, and has been rated Not Free throughout the five-year period.)

2. While several of the 9/11 terrorists, including Mohammed Atta, lived for years in open societies, they all had grown up in repressive and closed societies. Despite living abroad in the environment of democracy, they were integrated into insular ethno-religious environments and terror networks in which exiles from closed societies predominated. This insular cultural environment—which is widespread in many liberal Western societies—unquestionably contributed to their radicalization and contributed to their pitiless commitment to the mass murder of innocents.

3. The MCA aid will be distributed in 2005, and the countries listed are either eligible or on the threshold for 2005 aid.

Introduction

The *Freedom in the World 2005* survey contains reports on 192 countries and 14 related and disputed territories. Each country report begins with a section containing basic political, economic, and social data arranged in the following categories: **population, gross national income per capita (GNI/capita), life expectancy, religious groups, ethnic groups, capital, political rights** [numerical rating], **civil liberties** [numerical rating], and **status** [Free, Partly Free, or Not Free]. Each territory report begins with a section containing the same data, except for GNI/capita and life expectancy figures.

The **population** and **life expectancy** figures are from the *2004 World Population Data Sheet* of the Population Reference Bureau. **GNI/capita figures** are from the World Bank's *World Development Indicators 2004* and www.internetworld stats.com. Information about **religious groups** and **ethnic groups** are derived primarily from the CIA *World Factbook 2005*. Population figures and information about religious and ethnic groups for territories are from sources including the CIA *World Factbook 2005, The World Almanac and Book of Facts 2005*, the BBC, World Gazetteer, and the Unrepresented Nations and Peoples Organization (UNPO).

The **political rights** and **civil liberties** categories contain numerical ratings between 1 and 7 for each country or territory, with 1 representing the most free and 7 the least free. The **status** designation of Free, Partly Free, or Not Free, which is determined by the combination of the political rights and civil liberties ratings, indicates the general state of freedom in a country or territory. The ratings of countries or territories that have improved or declined since the previous survey are indicated by asterisks next to the ratings. Positive or negative trends that do not warrant a ratings change since the previous year may be indicated by upward or downward trend arrows, which are located next to the name of the country or territory. A brief explanation of ratings changes or trend arrows is provided for each country or territory as required. For a full description of the methods used to determine the survey's ratings, please see the chapter on the survey's methodology.

Following the section on political, economic, and social data, each country and territory report is divided into two parts: an **overview** and an analysis of **political rights and civil liberties**. The overview provides a brief historical background and a description of major recent events. The political rights and civil liberties section summarizes each country or territory's degree of respect for the rights and liberties which Freedom House uses to evaluate freedom in the world.

Afghanistan

Population: 28,500,000   **Political Rights:** 5*
GNI/capita: $700   **Civil Liberties:** 6
Life Expectancy: 43   **Status:** Not Free
Religious Groups: Sunni Muslim (80 percent),
Shi'a Muslim (19 percent), other (1 percent)
Ethnic Groups: Pashtun (42 percent), Tajik (27 percent),
Hazara (9 percent), Uzbek (9 percent), other (13 percent)
Capital: Kabul
Ratings Change: Afghanistan's political rights rating improved from 6 to 5 due to the holding of a reasonably free and fair presidential election in October.

Ten-Year Ratings Timeline (Political Rights, Civil Liberties, Status)

1995	1996	1997	1998	1999	2000	2001	2002	2003	2004
7,7NF	7,7NF	7,7NF	7,7NF	7,7NF	7,7NF	7,7NF	6,6NF	6,6NF	5,6NF

Overview:

Afghanistan made measurable progress towards establishing the framework for an inclusive democratic state during 2004. A new constitution providing for a presidential system of government with a bicameral parliament and guaranteeing equal rights to women was adopted in January. Despite concerns over threats to candidates and voters and minor irregularities in the voting process, an unexpectedly successful presidential election was held in October in which incumbent president Hamid Karzai won 55 percent of the vote. Nevertheless, the government continued to face a number of hurdles, the most pressing of which is an environment of pervasive insecurity throughout much of the country, which has hampered the work of local and international humanitarian organizations in rebuilding Afghanistan's shattered infrastructure and institutions and the efforts of the central government to exert its authority over the provinces. Although the level of personal autonomy has substantially increased since the fall of the ultraconservative Taliban regime in 2001, numerous human rights abuses, including attacks on humanitarian aid workers and violations of women's rights, were reported during the year.

Located at the crossroads of the Middle East, Central Asia, and the Indian subcontinent, Afghanistan has for centuries been caught in the middle of great power and regional rivalries. After besting Russia in a contest for influence in Afghanistan, Britain recognized the country as an independent monarchy in 1921. King Zahir Shah ruled from 1933 until he was deposed in a 1973 coup. Afghanistan entered a period of continuous civil conflict in 1978, when a Communist coup set out to transform this highly traditional society. The Soviet Union invaded in 1979, but faced fierce resistance from U.S.-backed mujahideen (guerrilla fighters) until its troops finally withdrew in 1989.

The mujahideen factions overthrew the Communist government in 1992 and then battled each other for control of Kabul, killing more than 25,000 civilians in the capital by 1995. The Taliban militia, consisting largely of students in conservative Islamic religious schools, entered the fray and seized control of Kabul in 1996. Defeating or buying off mujahideen commanders, the Taliban soon controlled most of the country except for parts of northern and central Afghanistan, which remained in the hands of the Tajik-dominated Northern Alliance coalition.

In response to the terrorist attacks of September 11, 2001, the United States launched a military campaign in October 2001 aimed at toppling the Taliban regime and eliminating Saudi militant Osama bin Laden's terrorist network, al-Qaeda. Simultaneously, Northern Alliance forces engaged the Taliban from the areas under their control. The Taliban crumbled quickly, losing Kabul to Northern Alliance forces in November and surrendering the southern city of Kandahar, the movement's spiritual headquarters, in December.

As a result of the Bonn agreement of December 2001, an interim administration enjoying the nominal support of Afghanistan's provincial leaders and headed by Karzai, a Pashtun tribal leader, took office. The UN-brokered deal that put Karzai in office sought to balance demands for power by victorious Tajik, Uzbek, and Hazara military commanders with the reality that many Pashtuns, who are Afghanistan's largest ethnic group, would not trust a government headed by ethnic minorities. In June 2002, the United Nations administered an emergency *loya jirga* (gathering of representatives), presided over by the formerly exiled King Zahir Shah, which appointed a Transitional Administration (TA) to rule Afghanistan for a further two years. Karzai won the votes of more than 80 percent of the delegates to become president and head of the TA, decisively defeating two other candidates. The Tajik-dominated Northern Alliance filled more than half the cabinet positions, including the key positions of ministers of defense and the interior, while the remainder were given to Pashtuns and representatives of other ethnic groups.

The UN-mandated International Security Assistance Force (ISAF), over which NATO assumed command in August 2003, is responsible for providing security in Kabul, but many areas outside the capital remain unstable and lawless. Military commanders, tribal leaders, rogue warlords, and petty bandits continue to hold sway. Bolstered by arms, money, and support from the United States and neighboring governments, some warlords maintain private armies and are reluctant to submit to the leadership of the central administration. Nearly 1,000 civilians, officials, and foreign aid workers were killed and injured during 2004 by an increasing number of bombings, rocket attacks, and other sporadic violence by suspected Taliban sympathizers, as well as recurrent fighting between various factional militias.

Seeking to curb the power of regional strongmen, Karzai signed a decree in December 2002 banning political leaders from taking part in military activity; he has also undertaken several reshuffles of provincial governors and other key officials in the past two years. The TA initiated a voluntary program of disarmament, demobilization, and reintegration (DDR) in October 2003, and heavy weapons began to be removed from Kabul in January 2004. In a significant victory, the central government managed to oust regional strongman Ismael Khan from his position as governor of Herat in September.

In December 2003, a 502-member constitutional loya jirga (CLJ) met to debate a draft constitution, which had been prepared by a constitutional commission earlier in the year and widely circulated in order to elicit feedback from Afghan citizens. Because of disagreements among the delegates over issues such as the system of government and national languages, proceedings stretched on for three weeks before the amended draft was ratified in January 2004. It describes Afghanistan as an Islamic republic in which no law should contravene the beliefs and practices of Islam, and provides for a presidential system of government and a National Assembly composed of two houses. Equal rights for women and men are guaranteed, as is the right to practice minority religions, although human rights advocates expressed concern that inadequate mechanisms were put in place to guarantee the provision of these and other rights.

For most of 2004, the focus was on preparing for Afghanistan's first elections since 1969, a process that was overseen by the Joint Electoral Management Body (JEMB). While a decision was taken to postpone legislative elections until 2005 because of logistical complications and security concerns, on October 9 more than 75 percent of registered Afghans voted in a delayed presidential poll contested by 17 candidates, including one woman. Karzai, the incumbent, won 55 percent of the vote, while main challengers Yunus Qanooni, Haji Mohammed Mohaqeq, and Abdul Rashid Dostum won 16, 11, and 10 percent, respectively. Initially, a group of opposition candidates contested the result, but in deference to public opinion, they agreed to respect the findings of a panel established to investigate their complaints. On November 3, the panel concluded that the shortcomings with the electoral process would not have affected the overall result, thereby confirming Karzai's victory. Despite several assassination attempts and other attacks, the Taliban were unable to significantly disrupt the election as they had threatened, thus raising questions about their level of support.

Political Rights and Civil Liberties:

The political rights and civil liberties of most Afghans remained circumscribed in 2004, although the adoption of a new, moderate constitution and the holding of a relatively free and fair presidential election were key positive improvements. The constitution and electoral law passed in June provide for a directly elected president who has the power to appoint ministers (subject to parliamentary approval) and a bicameral National Assembly composed of a directly elected 249-seat Wolesi Jirga (House of the People) and a 102-seat Meshrano Jirga (House of Elders). Legislative elections originally scheduled for 2004 were postponed until 2005 to allow more time for the government to map out district boundaries, enact election laws, and improve the security situation. However, despite allegations of intimidation by militias and insurgent groups, multiple voter registrations, partisanship within the JEMB, and other irregularities such as ballot stuffing and the improper use of indelible ink on voting day, the presidential election held in October 2004 was judged to be reasonably free and fair.

In the run-up to legislative elections, restrictions on political activity remain a concern. A law passed in October 2003 prohibits the registration of political parties that are backed by armed forces or which oppose Islam or promote racial, religious, or sectarian hatred and violence, but this provision has not been strictly enforced. Some delegates to the December 2003 CLJ complained that warlords and Islamic fundamentalists had threatened them during the proceedings. The Afghan Independent Human Rights Commission (AIHRC) noted in July that levels of political freedom were higher in Kabul and the eastern provinces, but that extremist violence and widespread self-censorship were prevalent in the south and west of the country and could be a significant factor in limiting people's political choices. According to a November International Crisis Group report, nonmilitarized and opposition political parties have found it difficult to campaign openly because of the security situation and pressure from factional militias.

The TA functioned as a central government with both executive and legislative authority, but its writ over areas outside Kabul remained limited. While two women and a broad range of ethnic groups held positions in the cabinet, concerns were raised about the domination of the Northern Alliance over state structures, particularly the security apparatus. In the absence of a legislature, input from Afghans into decision-making processes has taken the form of participation in the indirectly elected loya jirgas that have met to choose the main officeholders in the TA and, more recently, to debate and ratify the new constitution.

Widespread corruption, nepotism, and cronyism are growing issues of concern, although the TA has professed a commitment to improving transparency and accountability, particularly in the disbursement of foreign aid, which makes up a significant part of the national budget.

Afghanistan's media environment remained fragile although some improvements were seen in 2004. A new press law adopted in May guarantees the right to freedom of expression and prohibits censorship, but does retain certain restrictions such as registration requirements and overly broad guidelines on content. Authorities have granted more than 250 licenses to independent publications, and several dozen private radio stations and a number of television stations are now broadcasting. Media diversity and freedom are markedly higher in Kabul, and some warlords do not allow independent media in the areas under their control. However, pressures on journalists in Herat eased considerably following the ouster of local strongman Ismael Khan in September. A number of journalists were threatened or harassed by government ministers and others in positions of power as a result of their reporting. Many practice self-censorship or avoid writing about sensitive issues such as Islam, national unity, or crimes committed by specific warlords. The two employees of the Kabul-based newspaper *Aftab* who were charged with blasphemy in 2003 fled the country and remain abroad. In September, U.S. military personnel seized a BBC reporter from his house and took him to Bagram air base, where he was interrogated for 24 hours before being released with an apology.

Religious freedom improved following the fall of the ultraconservative Taliban movement in late 2001, as the TA attempted to pursue a policy of greater religious tolerance despite some pressure from Islamic fundamentalist groups. The minority Shia population, particularly those from the Hazara ethnic group, has traditionally faced discrimination from the Sunni majority, and relations between the two groups remain somewhat strained. The small numbers of non-Muslim residents in Afghanistan are now generally able to practice their faith, although Hindus and Sikhs have had difficulty in obtaining cremation grounds and building new houses of worship. The constitution ratified in January 2004 establishes Islam as the official state religion but does not prohibit the practice of other religions, according to the U.S. State Department's International Religious Freedom Report.

Academic freedom is not restricted. However, government regulations prohibit married women from attending high school, and in 2003, several thousand young women were expelled from school. In some provinces, schools have also been the target of threats and violent attacks by fundamentalist groups.

With the fall of the Taliban, residents of Kabul and most other cities were able to go about their daily lives with fewer restrictions and were less likely to be subjected to harassment from the authorities. Rights to assembly, association, and free speech were formally restored, but are applied erratically in different regions. In addition, police and security forces have occasionally used excessive force when confronted with demonstrations or public protests. In May 2003, police arrested and beat students protesting nepotism at Kabul University, according to the U.S. State Department's 2003 human rights report. Both international and Afghan nongovernmental organizations (NGOs) are able to operate freely, but their effectiveness is impeded by the poor security situation in much of the country. The incidence of attacks against foreign humanitarian organizations has increased since mid-2003; in June, Medecins Sans Frontieres (Doctors without Borders) decided to pull out of Afghanistan after five of its staff were killed by unidentified gunmen. Despite broad constitutional protections for workers, labor rights are not well defined, and there are currently no enforcement or resolution mechanisms.

The new administration faced the question of whether to bring to justice, co-opt, or simply ignore perpetrators of past abuses. There is no functioning, nationwide legal system, and justice in many places is administered on the basis of a mixture of legal codes by judges with minimal training. In addition, outside influence over the judiciary remains strong; in many areas, judges and lawyers are frequently unable to act independently because of threats from local power brokers or armed groups, and bribery is also a concern. The Supreme Court, stacked with 150 religious scholars who have little knowledge of jurisprudence and headed by an 80-year-old conservative, is particularly in need of reform. The Karzai administration's plans to rebuild the judiciary have proceeded slowly, although a new criminal procedure code was promulgated in early 2004 and some progress has been made with the construction of courts and correctional facilities.

While the Bonn agreement recognized the need to create a national army and a professional police force, progress on both fronts has been limited. By August, only 13,700 recruits to the Afghan National Army (ANA) had been trained, out of a proposed force of 70,000, and attrition levels have been high. Nevertheless, ANA forces were deployed during the year to prevent factional clashes in Herat and Maimana, and also helped to provide security around polling centers during the election. In October 2003, the TA initiated a voluntary DDR program that is eventually intended to target an estimated 100,000 armed men in Afghanistan, but by November 2004, only 22,000 militiamen had been demobilized.

In a prevailing climate of impunity, government ministers as well as warlords in some provinces sanctioned widespread abuses by the police, military, and intelligence forces under their command, including arbitrary arrest and detention, torture, extortion, and extrajudicial killings. The AIHRC, which was formed in August 2002 and focuses on raising awareness of human rights issues in addition to monitoring and investigating abuses, received more than 2,000 complaints of rights violations during the second half of 2004, including torture, land-grabbing and forced migration, kidnapping, and forced marriage. A Human Rights Watch report released in March documents numerous cases of abuse of Afghan detainees by U.S. forces, and eight detainees are confirmed to have died while in custody. However, in September, the U.S. military brought charges against a serviceman accused of mistreating Afghan prisoners at Bagram air base in December 2002.

Hundreds of civilians have been killed as a result of bombings, rocket attacks, and other acts of terror by unknown assailants; during localized fighting between ethnic factions, particularly in the North; or during skirmishes between Taliban supporters on one side and government forces and the U.S. military on the other. Both the foreign and Afghan staff of a number of international organizations and nongovernmental aid agencies have been targeted for attack, particularly in provinces with an active Taliban presence, and dozens were killed during the year. In October 2003, the United Nations voted that the ISAF should expand its operations beyond Kabul, but because of continued reluctance on the part of the international community to significantly expand these forces, ISAF's total strength was estimated at only 6,500 in July 2004. Despite the establishment of over a dozen Provincial Reconstruction Teams (PRTs) consisting of mixed groups of U.S. and NATO military forces and development personnel in various regional centers, the security situation in much of the country continued to be extremely poor.

Several hundred thousand Afghans returned to their homes during 2004, but well over a million refugees remain in both Pakistan and Iran, and in addition, more than 150,000 civilians continue to be displaced within the country. Humanitarian agencies and Afghan authorities have been ill-equipped to deal with the scale of the repatriation, while the poor security situation compounded by widespread land-grabbing meant that many refugees were unable to return to their homes and instead congregated in and around major urban centers.

The end of Taliban rule freed women from harsh restrictions and punishments that had kept them veiled, isolated, and, in many cases, impoverished. Women's formal rights to education and employment were restored, and in some areas they were once again able to participate in public life. Several hundred female delegates took part in the CLJ, and the constitution that was ratified contained the significant provisions of guaranteeing equal rights for women and reserving a quarter of the seats in the Wolesi Jirga for women. Record numbers of women were registered to vote—an average 41 percent of all registered voters were women—and took part in the October elections. However, an October Human Rights Watch report noted that women in the public sphere, particularly those who advocate for women's rights, continue to face threats and harassment from armed factions and conservative religious leaders.

Women's choices regarding marriage and divorce, particularly their ability to choose a marriage partner, remain circumscribed by custom and discriminatory laws, and the forced marriage of young girls to older men or of widows to their husband's male relation is a problem, according to Amnesty International. To the extent that it functions, the justice system discriminates against women, and they are unable to get legal redress for crimes committed against them. A March BBC report noted that the incidence of cases of self-immolation by women seeking to escape abusive marriages, particularly in the province of Herat, was a growing concern. As a result of continued lawlessness, women and children are increasingly subjected to abduction, trafficking, and sexual violence. In certain areas, ruling warlords impose Taliban-style dress and behavioral restrictions on women. While record numbers of children have returned to school, a number of girls' schools were subject to arson and rocket attacks from Islamic fundamentalists during the year.

Albania

Population: 3,200,000   **Political Rights:** 3
GNI/capita: $1,450   **Civil Liberties:** 3
Life Expectancy: 74   **Status:** Partly Free
Religious Groups: Muslim (70 percent), Albanian
Orthodox (20 percent), Roman Catholic (10 percent)
Ethnic Groups: Albanian (95 percent), Greek (3 percent),
other (2 percent)
Capital: Tirana

Ten-Year Ratings Timeline (Political Rights, Civil Liberties, Status)

1995	1996	1997	1998	1999	2000	2001	2002	2003	2004
3,4PF	4,4PF	4,4PF	4,5PF	4,5PF	4,5PF	3,4PF	3,3PF	3,3PF	3,3PF

Overview:

Large and mostly peaceful protests took place against the government in February 2004. A dispute about electoral reform required intervention from the Organization for Security and Cooperation in Europe (OSCE). Albania also saw its first terrorist bombings.

From World War II until 1990, former dictator Enver Hoxha's xenophobic Communist regime turned Albania into the most isolated country in Europe. The Communist government collapsed in 1990, and in March 1992, multiparty elections brought the Democratic Party (DP), led by Sali Berisha, to power. Continuing poverty and corruption weakened Berisha's government, and in 1997, the collapse of several popular pyramid investment schemes resulted in widespread looting and violence. The prior progress made by the country was destroyed.

In the years since the unrest of 1997, Albania has been ruled by the Socialist Party (SP), led by Prime Minister Fatos Nano. After the 2001 parliamentary elections, Berisha's DP announced a boycott of parliament to protest alleged electoral irregularities. The party returned in January 2002. However, the truce between Berisha and Nano proved fragile, and by the beginning of 2003, Albania's short-lived national political unity again broke down. More signs of the continued turmoil within Albanian politics came with the resignation of Foreign Minister (and former prime minister) Ilir Meta, a bitter Nano rival, in July 2003. Disagreements within ruling factions in the government prevented the nomination of a replacement for the rest of the year. In December, Nano was reelected chairman of the SP, after which he reshuffled his cabinet; the Meta faction was sidelined.

Because of such infighting, little serious progress has been made to combat organized crime and promote economic reform. Although in February 2003 the European Union (EU) opened negotiations with Albania for a Stabilization and Association Agreement—generally seen as the first step toward full EU membership—realistic analyses of the country's situation suggest that it has far to go before joining the EU. As one sign of this, in March the EU accused Albania's leaders of lacking the political will to meet preconditions for concluding the agreement.

Huge protests took place in early 2004 against the Nano government amid opposition claims that he manipulated the October 2003 elections and has not done enough to improve the standard of living. The rallies were the largest in seven years, and although there was some violence, they were generally peaceful.

Albania experienced its first terrorist acts in 2004 when a chemical bomb exploded in Tirana in January. Such violence had not previously been a problem.

Political Rights and Civil Liberties:

Albanians can change their government democratically. The last elections to the 140-seat Kuvend Popullor (People's Assembly) were held in 2001. One hundred seats are filled in elections for single-member districts; the remaining seats use proportional voting for party lists. Socialists are the largest party and rule as part of a majority coalition. Although international monitoring groups admitted that there were "serious flaws" in the election process, the polls were nevertheless deemed valid. The president, who holds a largely symbolic post, is chosen by parliament. Prime Minister Fatos Nano is the most powerful government leader.

Parliament passed a new electoral code in June 2003 that sought to ensure a more balanced election process. However, two major flaws remain: the Central Election Commission currently has five ruling coalition members and only two opposition members, and voter lists are in dispute. After municipal elections were held in October 2003, elections were repeated in 130 out of 346 precincts because of irregularities. Although the opposition claimed that the Socialists had manipulated the voting lists, largely the same lists were used in the second round of elections. In fall 2004, the OSCE intervened in an effort to improve voting procedures before 2005 parliamentary elections, but no resolution was reached.

A number of political parties operate throughout the country. The most important political organizations are the DP and the SP; the differences between the parties are more a matter of the personalities leading them than of serious programmatic or ideological approaches. Albanian society remains clan-based; in very general terms, Sali Berisha's DP commands the allegiance of the Gheg clans in the north, while Nano's SP has the support of the Tosk clans in the south. Except for the 1992 elections, all multiparty elections in Albania since the end of Communism have been controversial, having been contested or boycotted by some party.

The Greek minority is mostly represented through the Party of the Union for Human Rights, which has three seats in parliament. Other minorities are less directly (and less well) represented. Muslim leaders were prevented from registering a party called Motherland in 2004 because religiously or ethnically based parties are illegal in Albania, although supporters denied that the proposed party was Islamic.

In December 2003, an SP congress decreed that all party members must vote according to party decisions or give up their mandates. The measure was intended to curb the power of the party faction led by Ilir Meta.

Considerable anticorruption legislation is in place, but little progress has been made. Petty corruption is rife, as is corruption in business. Government regulations are not excessive, but implementation is unpredictable. There are also international concerns that some Albanian politicians are linked to organized crime. A further problem is that the state does not pursue accusations of official corruption, except in the case of low-level officials. A law was passed in 2003 requiring public officials to publish their assets. In June, Nano was the first to declare his wealth. Albania was ranked 108 out of 146 countries surveyed in the 2004 Transparency International Corruption Perceptions Index.

The constitution guarantees freedom of expression, and freedom of the press has improved since the fall of communism, although considerable harassment of journalists persists. The intermingling of powerful business, political, and media interests inhibits the development of independent media. The government controls crucial subsidies that are doled out to those outlets providing sympathetic coverage. The number of libel suits is rising as well. In May, the prime minister filed a lawsuit against the publisher of *Koha Jone* that resulted in a fine of 2 million *leks* (almost $20,000, or more than 100 times the average monthly wage in Albania). Journalists and press groups protested, alleging irregularities in the court procedure. The government does not limit Internet access, although poverty means that most people cannot afford it regardless.

The constitution provides for freedom of religion and religious practice, and Albania has not seen the inter-religious turmoil typical of its neighbors. However, there has been a rise in tensions in northern parts of the country between rival Muslim sects, as well as between Roman Catholics and Muslims. The restitution of church properties confiscated during the Communist period remains unresolved. Albania's small Greek Orthodox minority has intermittently been subjected to various forms of discrimination.

The government does not significantly limit academic freedom, but some educational institutions have had to accept political appointments.

Freedom of association is generally respected, but problems remain. In the huge protests that took place in February 2004, groups attempted to storm official buildings and at some points were dispersed by police using gunshots and tear gas. However, the protests were largely peaceful. About 200 independent nongovernmental organizations (NGOs) are active, and while locating funding for NGOs can be difficult, these groups have had an effect on national politics at times. In contrast, trade groups tend to be weak.

The constitution provides for an independent judiciary. However, the judiciary, along with law enforcement agencies, remains inefficient and prone to corruption, and judges are often inexperienced and untrained. The combination of a weak economy and the growth of powerful organized crime syndicates makes judges susceptible to bribery and intimidation. The structure of the judiciary also leaves room for government pressure. Amnesty International published a report in February describing inhumane and degrading conditions for detainees. Violence by police does occur, although it is generally investigated and perpetrators are disciplined.

Widespread lawlessness plagues large parts of Albania. Weak state institutions have augmented the power of crime syndicates, and international law enforcement officials claim that Albania has become an increasingly important transshipment point for drug smugglers. The weakness of state institutions in northern Albania has also resulted in the resurgence of traditional tribal law in these areas, most importantly the tradition of blood feuds between different families and clans. Revenge killings continue to take place.

Parliament passed a bill in 2004 on property restitution and compensation for pre-Communist property owners. The opposition did not take part in the vote.

The constitution places no legal impediments on women's role in politics and society, although women are vastly under-represented in most governmental institutions. The labor code mandates that women are entitled to equal pay for equal work, but data are lacking on whether this is respected in practice. Traditional patriarchal social mores pose significant problems for the position of women. Many segments of society, particularly in northern Albania, still abide by a medieval moral code according to which women are considered chattel property and may be treated as such. The trafficking of women and girls remains a significant problem, although, with the help of advisers from abroad, Albania has seriously reduced its role as a transit country.

Algeria

Population: 32,300,000   **Political Rights:** 6
GNI/capita: $1,720   **Civil Liberties:** 5
Life Expectancy: 73   **Status:** Not Free
Religious Groups: Sunni Muslim (99 percent), Christian and Jewish (1 percent)
Ethnic Groups: Arab-Berber (99 percent), other (1 percent)
Capital: Algiers

Ten-Year Ratings Timeline (Political Rights, Civil Liberties, Status)

1995	1996	1997	1998	1999	2000	2001	2002	2003	2004
6,6NF	6,6NF	6,6NF	6,5NF	6,5NF	6,5NF	6,5NF	6,5NF	6,5NF	6,5NF

Overview: Algerians held presidential elections in April 2004, and incumbent Abdelaziz Bouteflika won a landslide victory against five challengers in a process that international observers pronounced free of serious problems. The violence in Algeria continued to claim lives, but it was considerably diminished and Bouteflika's triumph was attributed largely to a "civil harmony" program he introduced when he first took office in 1999. After his reelection, Bouteflika promised to resolve the Berber crisis and free women from a restrictive family code.

Algeria gained independence in 1962 following 132 years of French colonial rule. Algeria's current problems can be traced to the 1986 oil market collapse, which reduced its key source of foreign exchange. Unemployment, housing shortages, and other social ills fed growing popular resentment. With no political outlet, young men took to the streets in violent riots during October 1988.

Once peace was restored, President Chadli Bendjedid legalized political parties after more than 30 years of single-party rule under the National Liberation Front (FLN). The Islamic Salvation Front (FIS) was formed in 1989 as an umbrella organization of

Islamist opposition groups, with significant grassroots support. In January 1992, the FIS was poised to win a commanding parliamentary majority when the army intervened, forced Bendjedid to resign, and canceled the vote. The FIS was banned and its leaders imprisoned. The country was placed under a state of emergency that remains in effect.

Violence ensued as Islamist militants took up arms against the regime. The FIS splintered into rival armed factions and a guerrilla-style insurgency erupted in the countryside, while urban-based extremists resorted to terrorism. An estimated 150,000 were killed in a series of massacres perpetrated by Islamic extremists and in mass killings attributed to government-backed militias. Human rights groups have accused the Algerian security forces of responsibility for thousands of "disappearances."

In 1997, the Islamic Salvation Army (AIS), the least radical of the armed groups, announced a unilateral ceasefire and laid down its arms. However, extremist offshoots such as the Armed Islamic Group (GIA) and the Salafist Group for Preaching and Combat (GSPC) continued to conduct terrorist attacks on civilian and government targets.

A presidential election held in 1999 was severely flawed. Citing government fraud and manipulation, opposition candidates withdrew, leaving Bouteflika to run unopposed. After Bouteflika took office, the government introduced a "civil harmony" law that granted amnesty to Islamist rebels who renounced violence. By January 2000, some 5,500 members of the armed groups had surrendered, but the GIA and the GSPC continued to wage attacks, killings thousands in 2003. The attacks diminished in 2004, but instances of weekly clashes with security forces and ambushes against civilians continued. In June, the army said it had killed the leader of the GSPC, Nabil Sahraoui; the group quickly appointed a new leader. Another GSPC member, who was one of Algeria's most wanted terror suspects, was handed over to the government in late October. Caught in Chad, Amar Saifi (Abderrezak El Para) was accused of being behind kidnappings of 32 German and European tourists in 2003. A massive earthquake in May 2003 left 2,200 dead and thousands homeless. The government responded slowly, and the only rapid assistance came from Islamic charitable networks. In 2004, tens of thousands of people still lived in temporary housing, which contributes to Algeria's festering social ills. A lighter earthquake hit Algiers in February 2004, causing injuries and the destruction of more houses.

The 2004 presidential election marked a difference from previous votes. Bouteflika ran against five other candidates, but his strongest opponent was his former right-hand man, Ali Benflis, a prime minister whom he fired in 2002. The army, long at the political helm of the country, announced its neutrality. Although government control of the broadcast media gave Bouteflika a clear advantage, he and the other candidates ran strong campaigns around the country, using new campaigning techniques to grab voters. Candidates included a woman, Trotskyite Worker's Party leader Louisa Hanoune; the head of a Berber party; an Islamist leader popular in the poor districts of Algiers; and the chief of a nationalist party. Public apathy and a low turnout combined with support for Bouteflika by Islamists, nationalist parties, and Algerian workers to give him a resounding 84.99 percent of the vote. Opposition candidates denounced discrepancies and irregularities, but international monitors from the Organization for Security and Cooperation in Europe declared the electoral process to be free of serious problems.

Bouteflika seemed to take steps in 2004 to reinforce his strength in the small circle of powerful generals. He reshuffled senior military positions and, in August, accepted the resignation for health reasons of the army chief, General Mohammed Lamari, long at the center of the war against the Islamists. The daily *Al Watan* hailed the move by saying "The time has come for the military to...go back to the barracks."

As a result of increased security and political stability in Algeria, the World Bank and France, Turkey, and other countries started talks in 2004 on economic growth programs and structural reforms. Algeria suffers a 30 percent unemployment rate as well as housing shortages, and a significant proportion of the population lives below the poverty level.

Political Rights and Civil Liberties: The right of Algerians to choose their government freely is restricted. While the last presidential elections may signal a cautious new start, the fact remains that Abdelaziz Bouteflika was endorsed by the army for his first term. Algeria's civilian president is generally the nominal head of state, but the president wields minimal leverage with the small group of generals who retain ultimate power. Parliamentary elections have been largely free of systematic fraud.

Algeria was ranked 97 out of 146 countries surveyed in the 2004 Transparency International Corruption Perceptions Index. In late 2004, President Bouteflika promised to fight corruption. In recent years, a number of scandals involving bribery, embezzlement and fraud have been brought to light in both the private and public sectors. Such corruption is partly to blame for continued poverty in Algeria despite the country's oil wealth.

The press in Algeria is relatively vibrant, with more than 40 newspapers, but the government often enforces strict defamation laws and influences content through the state-owned printing press and advertising company. Activists and journalists claimed that following the reelection of Bouteflika in 2004, the government moved to stem reports revealing corruption or human rights violations. The International Federation of Journalists opened a branch office in Algiers in November to campaign for improved press freedom. Reporters without Borders, a press freedom watchdog, said 2004 was "an especially hard year for the news media in Algeria," because of the number of newspapers suspended and of journalists arrested and given prison sentences. A local correspondent served a six-month jail sentence for defamation after he reported on police abuse and a local hospital scandal in the southern town of Djelfa. In June, Mohammed Benchicou, publisher of the daily *Le Matin*, received a two-year prison sentence for violating foreign currency controls. Benchicou was strongly critical of Bouteflika and other officials during the election campaign. Around ten other journalists were detained or sentenced on similar charges. In July, the authorities temporarily suspended the work of the Arab satellite station Al-Jazeera, and a court sentenced the editors of a press group to two months in jail for insulting an official figure. They had published articles critical of local officials in Oran. Access to the Internet is almost completely open, despite potentially restrictive legislation demanding Internet service providers monitor their sites for material harmful to the public order and morality.

Religious freedom is generally respected. Islam is the state religion, although the government rarely interferes in the practice of non-Muslim faiths. The government monitors mosques closely, to prevent political activities. The government does not restrict academic freedom.

Algerian authorities have exploited the state of emergency, in effect since 1992, to curtail freedom of assembly. Government permits, sometimes difficult to obtain, are required for public meetings and a decree bans demonstrations in Algiers. In other areas of the country, security forces dispersed peaceful demonstrations in 2004, sometimes violently. Emergency laws have also impeded Algerians' right of association as well as their right to form political parties and nongovernmental organizations. The Algerian workers unions are largely thought to be allied with the government. Other professional associations maintain relative independence, but have been subjected to government harassment.

While the human rights situation has improved, torture has not ended, thousands arrested remain "disappeared," and investigations into human rights abuses are rarely carried out. Human rights activists say that the judiciary is not independent except for a few judges who are subject to disciplinary or other repressive measures. FIS leaders Abassi Madani and Ali Belhadj were released in July 2003 at the end of their 12-year sentences. Belhadj was briefly re-arrested in the summer of 2004 while attending the wedding of the daughter of a deceased FIS founder.

The government in late 2003 established an ad hoc mechanism to look into the issue of the more than 7,000 "disappearances," mostly dating to the mid-1990s, and to serve as an interface with the families of the victims. The committee lacked the power to investigate the cases or end the impunity enjoyed by those responsible for the violations. In 2004, Amnesty International called on the government to conduct full investigations of human rights abuses by armed groups, security forces, and state-armed militias. It also asked for the investigation of mass graves believed to contain the bodies of victims killed by armed groups or by state-sponsored militia during the mid-1990s. In November 2004, President Bouteflika said a general amnesty covering all those implicated in the sectarian violence of the past decade would be considered. It would include armed Islamists as well as members of the security forces accused of torture and summary executions.

Berbers comprise approximately 20 percent of the population. However, their cultural identity and language are not fully recognized, and riots have erupted over the last few years, leaving scores dead. In his acceptance speech, Bouteflika called for a return to the negotiating table, but in September 2004, police clashed with Berber activists protesting that Bouteflika was not meeting their demands.

The law provides for freedom of domestic and foreign travel, and freedom to emigrate; however, the government at times restricted these rights, especially concerning former FIS leaders. The government also does not allow draft-age men to leave the country without a special permit. Under the State of Emergency, the Interior Minister and the provincial governors may deny residency in certain districts to persons regarded as threats to public order.

Women face discrimination in several areas. The 1984 Family Code, based largely on Sharia (Islamic law), places women under the legal guardianship of a husband or male relative. The code allows men to have up to four wives and makes divorce easy for men but nearly impossible for women. After Bouteflika promised to focus on reform, in September 2004 the government said it would press ahead with a bill reversing many of the code's articles, despite protests by Islamic political parties and clerics. However, by the end of the year no change had taken place. Some feminist groups have asked for the family law to be scrapped altogether.

Andorra

Population: 100,000 **Political Rights:** 1
GNI/capita: $16,990 **Civil Liberties:** 1
Life Expectancy: na **Status:** Free
Religious Groups: Roman Catholic (predominant)
Ethnic Groups: Spanish (43 percent),
Andorran (33 percent), Portuguese (11 percent),
French (7 percent), other (6 percent)
Capital: Andorra la Vella

Ten-Year Ratings Timeline (Political Rights, Civil Liberties, Status)

1995	1996	1997	1998	1999	2000	2001	2002	2003	2004
1,1F	1,1F	1,1F	1,1F	1,1F	1,1F	1,1F	1,1F	1,1F	1,1F

Overview:

Andorra remained in 2004 on the list of "uncooperative tax-havens" maintained by the Organization for Economic Co-operation and Development (OECD). However, it is expected to follow a European Union (EU) directive that will most likely reduce investments in the country's offshore banking centers.

As a co-principality, Andorra has been ruled jointly for 716 years by the president of France and the Spanish bishop of Urgel, who, as of May 12, 2003, was Monsignor Joan Enric Vives Sicilia. The 1993 constitution modified this feudal system, keeping the titular heads of state but transforming the government into a parliamentary democracy. Andorra became a member of the United Nations in 1993 and a member of the Council of Europe in 1994.

In March 2001, the country held elections and returned Marc Forne of the conservative Liberal Party of Andorra (PLA) as head of the government. The PLA won an absolute majority with 15 out of the 28 seats in the Counsell General, while the Andorran Democratic Center Party (ADCP, formerly the Democratic Party) won 5 seats, the Socialist Party (PS) captured 6 seats, and the Unio Laurediana party won 2 seats.

Tourism is the mainstay of the economy and accounts for 90 percent of its gross domestic product. In the 1990s, the country began attracting foreign investment with secret banking laws that are now under attack by the transparency initiatives championed by the OECD and the EU.

A new EU directive passed in early 2003 threatens Andorra's status as a major tax-haven. The new directive calls for EU members with secret banking laws to impose a withholding tax on revenue from interest-bearing accounts. After negotiations with the EU, Andorra and other key non-EU countries have agreed to adopt similar measures. The country, which has no personal income tax and no value-added tax, relies a great deal on banking as a financial resource.

The OECD has also put additional pressure on the country's tax-haven status. During the OECD Global Forum on Taxation in Berlin in June 2004, most member countries agreed to participate in a number of actions to achieve the high standards of transparency sought by the organization. The OECD proposes to hold dialogues with uncooperative members and to review the transparency and information exchange practices applied by financial centers.

Political Rights and Civil Liberties: Andorrans can change their government democratically. More than 80 percent of eligible voters participated in elections in 2001 to choose the members of the Counsell General, which then selects the Executive Council president, who is the head of government. Popular elections to the 28-member parliament are held every four years. Fourteen members are chosen in two-seat constituencies known as "parishes," and 14 are chosen by a national system of proportional representation. The people have a right to establish and join different political parties, and an opposition vote exists. However, more than 65 percent of the population consists of noncitizens, who have no right to vote and face a number of hurdles that bar them from becoming citizens. As a result, there is little participation by non-Andorrans in government and politics.

Because of a lack of available information, Transparency International did not review and rank Andorra in its 2004 Corruption Perceptions Index.

Freedom of speech and religion are respected across the country. There are two independent daily newspapers (*Diari d'Andorra* and *El Peridico de Andorra*), access to broadcasts from neighboring France and Spain, and unlimited Internet access.

Although Roman Catholicism is the predominant religion (90 percent of the whole population is Catholic) and the constitution recognizes a special relationship with the Roman Catholic Church, the state has ceased providing the Church with subsidies. There are no restrictions on proselytizing, and Mormons and members of Jehovah's Witnesses continue to do so unimpeded. Despite the presence of close to 2,000 Muslims, there is no proper mosque in the country. The Muslim community's 2003 request to convert some public buildings into a mosque was turned down by the government. Similar requests made to the Catholic Bishop to use a former church were not received well. Academic freedom is respected.

Freedom of assembly and association are generally respected. Although the government recognizes that both "workers and employers have the right to defend their own economic and social interests," there is neither an explicit right to strike nor legislation penalizing anti-union discrimination. A law regulating collective bargaining has been expected from parliament for some time. There have been few advances in labor rights in the country since the creation of a registry for associations in 2001, which has enabled trade unions to gain the legal recognition that they had lacked previously.

The country's judicial system, which is based on Spanish and French civil codes, does not have the power of judicial review of legislative acts. The country does not maintain a military force and depends on France and Spain for the defense of its borders. Prison conditions met international standards. However, the police can detain suspects for up to 48 hours without charging them with a crime.

The European Commission against Racism and Intolerance (ECRI) criticized Andorra in its 2003 report on the country for having restrictive naturalization criteria. Despite the fact that a majority of those living in Andorra are noncitizens, a person can become a citizen only by marrying an Andorran or by residing in the country for more than 25 years. Prospective citizens are also required to learn Catalan, the national language. Although noncitizens receive most of the social and economic benefits of citizens, they lack the right to vote.

Immigrant workers, primarily from North Africa, complain that they lack the same rights as citizens. Although the law gives legal status to 7,000 immigrants, many immigrants hold only "temporary work authorizations." Temporary workers are in a precarious position, as they have to leave the country when the job contract expires.

Citizens have the right to own property, but noncitizens can own only a 33 percent share of a company unless they have lived in the country for 20 years or more.

Women enjoy the same legal, political, social, and professional rights as men, although they are under-represented in government. Today, only four women occupy seats in parliament. There are no specific laws addressing violence against women, which remains a problem across the country. There are no government departments for women's issues or government-run shelters for battered women.

Angola

Population: 13,300,000
GNI/capita: $710
Life Expectancy: 40
Political Rights: 6
Civil Liberties: 5
Status: Not Free
Religious Groups: Indigenous beliefs (47 percent), Roman Catholic (38 percent), Protestant (15 percent)
Ethnic Groups: Ovimbundu (37 percent), Kimbundu (25 percent), Bakongo (13 percent), mestico (2 percent), European (1 percent), other (22 percent)
Capital: Luanda

Ten-Year Ratings Timeline (Political Rights, Civil Liberties, Status)

1995	1996	1997	1998	1999	2000	2001	2002	2003	2004
6,6NF	6,6NF	6,6NF	6,6NF	6,6NF	6,6NF	6,6NF	6,5NF	6,5NF	6,5NF

Overview:
Angola saw signs of greater stability in 2004, two years after the death of rebel leader Jonas Savimbi ended three decades of civil war. Civil society debate is growing as the country approaches general elections planned for 2006. However, the ruling Popular Movement for the Liberation of Angola (MPLA) is still wary of critics, and independent media and opposition parties find it hard to thrive outside the capital.

Angola was at war continually for nearly three decades following independence from Portugal in 1975. During the Cold War, the United States and South Africa backed Savimbi's National Union for the Total Independence of Angola (UNITA), while the former Soviet Union and Cuba supported the Marxist MPLA government.

A 1991 peace accord that led to general elections in 1992 disintegrated when Savimbi lost the presidency and resumed fighting. A subsequent peace agreement in 1994 also fell apart. The UN Security Council voted in February 1999 to end the UN peace-keeping mission in Angola following the collapse of the peace process and the shooting down of two UN planes.

A 2002 ceasefire between UNITA and the ruling MPLA has held. However, the resettlement of 4 million refugees and internally displaced people has exposed the collapse in social services. With peace, the government can no longer use the war as an excuse for lack of delivery in housing, education, and health. Civic groups are increasingly urging the government to become more accountable for violations of human rights, slow political reform, and non-transparency in oil transactions. The United Nations, now a lead actor in the humanitarian effort, is shifting its focus from emergency relief to sustainable development. Nonetheless, more than 2.5 million Angolans depend on food aid, which poses a threat to social stability.

UNITA appears committed to peace. About 80,000 former rebel soldiers have been demobilized; 5,000 of them have been integrated into the armed forces and the police. However, the MPLA and UNITA disagree about how rapidly political and economic reforms can occur, and both sides need to demonstrate a commitment to rebuilding Angola rather than simply dividing up its diamond and oil riches.

The conflict claimed 500,000 to 2 million lives, displaced 4 million people, and sent 500,000 fleeing to neighboring countries. The majority of resettled people today remain without land, proper shelter and food, health care, jobs, education, and even identification documents. They commonly lack transport to return to places of origin or were coerced to resettle elsewhere. Women are vulnerable to sexual abuse and rarely receive demobilization benefits. Former child soldiers—estimates vary from 7,000 to 11,000—have also remained outside the disarmament process. The United Nations expects the return and resettlement process to continue until 2006.

The resettlement process has been slowed by the presence of an estimated 700,000 land mines and by a war-ruined infrastructure, which make large tracts of the country inaccessible to humanitarian aid. At least 70,000 people have lost limbs to mines over the years. Rebuilding roads, bridges, and communications networks will take years.

Angola is Africa's second-largest oil producer. Petroleum accounts for up to 90 percent of government revenues, but corruption and war have prevented the average Angolan from benefiting from the wealth. More than $1 billion in oil revenue goes missing each year. The country's rich diamond areas have been carved up between MPLA and UNITA elites. Subsistence agriculture supports 85 percent of the population. The government has failed to make significant progress in reforms recommended by the IMF.

Accusations continue of human rights abuses against civilians in the oil enclave of Cabinda, perpetrated mainly by government soldiers sent in to crush a low-intensity separatist conflict that has simmered for decades. Two factions of the insurgent Front for the Liberation of the Enclave of Cabinda (FLEC) merged in 2004 to strengthen their negotiating position, should the government wish to continue dialogue begun the previous year.

Political Rights and Civil Liberties: Angolans freely elected their own representatives only once, in the September 1992 UN-supervised presidential and legislative elections. International observers pronounced the vote generally free and fair despite some irregularities. However, Jonas Savimbi rejected his defeat to President Jose Eduardo dos Santos in the first round of presidential voting and resumed fighting.

The two factions of the former rebel group UNITA merged into one party in 2002. Eighty-seven other opposition groups have formed a coalition with negligible weight. The National Assembly has little power, but members engage in heated debates, and legislation proposed by the opposition is sometimes adopted. The MPLA dominates the 220-member National Assembly; UNITA holds 70 seats. General elections planned for 1997 were put off until 2006. In May 2004, opposition parties walked out of parliament's Constitutional Commission, which is charged with laying the groundwork for the poll, accusing dos Santos of delaying work on a new constitution. UNITA and six other opposition parties have threatened to boycott the vote unless an independent electoral commission is created.

About 125 parties are registered in Angola. Although political debate is lively, opposition parties blame the MPLA for attacks on their members and offices, especially in the provinces of Huambo and Moxico where UNITA has traditionally claimed strong support. Recently, unidentified gangs have burned down homes of UNITA members and ransacked the party's offices. An opposition member of parliament was murdered in Luanda in July 2004 and several other MPs were beaten in June. The ruling party denies responsibility and says harassment is not official policy. However, the MPLA has not fostered the participation of civil society in reconstruction.

Corruption and patronage are endemic in the government. Angola was ranked 133 out of 146 countries surveyed in the 2004 Transparency International Corruption Perceptions Index.

Severe repression of the media by UNITA and the MPLA eased following the 2002 ceasefire. However, despite constitutional guarantees of freedom of expression, journalists often practice self-censorship or are subjected to intimidation by the authorities. The detention of journalists still occurs, especially outside the capital. Defamation of the president or his representatives is a criminal offense, punishable by imprisonment or fines. Private media outlets are often denied access to official information and events, and they report problems with funding. There are several independent weekly newspapers and radio stations in Luanda, but the government dominates media elsewhere. Authorities have prevented the outspoken Roman Catholic radio, Radio Ecclesia, from broadcasting outside Luanda. The only daily newspaper and the sole television station are state-owned, although the government announced plans in 2003 to open up the sector to private broadcasters. Internet access is limited to a small elite, as most citizens lack computers or even electricity.

Religious freedom is widely respected. The educational system barely functions. More than 50 percent of rural children do not attend school. Only 3 out of 10 rural women older than 15 years of age can read and write.

Hundreds of nongovernmental organizations and civic groups have formed in peacetime, demanding political reform and greater government accountability in human rights, and churches especially have grown more outspoken with peace. However, civil society organizations require greater coherence to be effective. The constitution guarantees freedom of assembly, and increasingly authorities are allowing opposition groups to hold demonstrations in Luanda. However, crackdowns are common in the interior of the country. Human Rights Watch reports that in April 2004, armed men believed to be police fired on protestors, killing nine people including three children.

The right to strike and form unions is provided by the constitution, but the MPLA dominates the labor movement and only a few independent unions exist. The lack of a viable economy has hindered labor activity.

The government has yet to establish a Constitutional Court, as mandated by the constitution. Local courts rule on civil matters and petty crime in some areas, but an overall lack of training and infrastructure inhibit judicial proceedings, which are heavily influenced by the government. Only 23 of the 168 municipal courts are operational. Prisoners are commonly detained for long periods in overcrowded and unsanitary conditions while awaiting trial. Often, prisoners must rely on outsiders for food.

Severe human rights abuses—including torture, abduction, rape, sexual slavery, and extrajudicial execution—were perpetrated during the war by both sides. Such actions, though their frequency has subsided, still occur in the provinces. Displaced Angolans returning home have faced harassment, and police and security forces are rarely held accountable for shakedowns, muggings, rapes, or beatings. An estimated 4 million weapons in civilian hands threaten to contribute to lawlessness.

Angolans have the right to own property. However, the government dominates the economy and the war discouraged the development of a private sector. Prospects look better with peace, and the government in 2003 passed legislation aimed at facilitating private investment.

Women occupy cabinet positions and National Assembly seats. Nevertheless, despite legal protections, de facto discrimination against women remains strong, particularly in rural areas. Spousal abuse is common, and the war spawned rape and sexual slavery. Women are often the victims of land mines as they forage for food and firewood.

Antigua and Barbuda

Population: 100,000
GNI/capita: $9,190
Life Expectancy: 71
Religious Groups: Anglican (predominant)
Ethnic Groups: Black, British, Portuguese, Lebanese, Syrian
Capital: St. John's

Political Rights: 2*
Civil Liberties: 2
Status: Partly Free

Ratings Change: Antigua and Barbuda's political rights rating improved from 4 to 2, and its status from Partly Free to Free, due to free and fair parliamentary elections that brought an end to the political dynasty of the tainted Bird family, providing significant opportunities for the promotion of democratic practices and the rule of law.

Ten-Year Ratings Timeline (Political Rights, Civil Liberties, Status)

1995	1996	1997	1998	1999	2000	2001	2002	2003	2004
4,3PF	4,3PF	4,3PF	4,3PF	4,3PF	4,2PF	4,2PF	4,2PF	4,2PF	2,2F

Overview:
The defeat of Prime Minister Lester Bird by opposition figure Baldwin Spencer in free and fair parliamentary elections in March 2004 ended the political dynasty of the tainted Bird family, which had dominated politics in Antigua and Barbuda for decades.

Antigua and Barbuda, a member of the British Commonwealth, gained independence in 1981. In 1994, the elder Vere Bird stepped down as prime minister in favor of his son Lester. In the run-up to the 1994 election, three opposition parties united to form the United Progressive Party (UPP), which campaigned on a social-democratic platform emphasizing rule of law and good governance. Parliamentary seats held by Bird's Antigua Labour Party (ALP) fell from 15 in 1989 to 11, while the number for the UPP rose from 1 to 5.

After assuming office, Lester Bird promised a less corrupt, more efficient government. Yet the government continued to be dogged by scandals, and in 1995, one of the prime minister's brothers, Ivor, received only a fine after having been convicted of cocaine smuggling. In the March 1999 elections, the ALP won 12 parliamentary seats; the UPP, 4; and the Barbuda People's Movement (BPM), 1.

On March 23, 2004, after a hard-fought, and at times vitriolic, campaign, the UPP, led by Baldwin Spencer, defeated the ALP. The vote was deemed to be generally free and fair by Commonwealth observers, and the election's results, which were not contested, were a crushing defeat for the ALP, which retained only 4 out of the 17 seats in parliament. The UPP won 12 seats, while the BPM, an ally of the UPP, won the Barbuda seat in a runoff election. Both the prime minister and his brother, Vere Bird Jr., lost their seats in parliament.

The endemic corruption of state institutions continues unabated. Only 4 of the 14 people named in a 2002 Royal Commission of Inquiry, which concluded there were serious instances of fraud in the medical-benefits program, had been indicted before Bird left office. The Medical Association has alleged official obstruction and emphasizes that improprieties continue. One of the former prime minister's brothers, Vere Bird Jr., continued to serve until the 2004 elections as minister of agriculture despite an arms-trafficking inquiry that concluded he should be barred from government service.

Political Rights and Civil Liberties:

Citizens of Antigua and Barbuda can change their government democratically. The 1981 constitution establishes a parliamentary system: a bicameral legislature is composed of the 17-member House of Representatives (16 seats go to Antigua, 1 to Barbuda), in which members serve five-year terms, and an appointed Senate. Of the senators, 11 are appointed by the prime minister, 4 by the parliamentary opposition leader, 1 by the Barbuda Council, and 1 by the governor-general.

Political parties can organize freely. However, the ruling party's monopoly on patronage makes it difficult for opposition parties to attract membership and financial support. The government has been planning to reform the electoral system by establishing an Independent Electoral Commission to review electoral law and redraw constituency boundaries, creating a new voter registry, and introducing voter identification cards; however, the relevant legislation has not yet been introduced. The Electoral Office of Jamaica commission was contracted to prepare a new voter list, deceased and absent voters have not been removed from the list since 1975.

Although the government introduced anticorruption and integrity legislation in parliament in October 2002, no significant action had been taken as of November 2004. The Integrity of Public Life Bill passed parliament and immediately caused outcries by the Antigua Labour Party because of a clause interpreted to sanction same-sex relationships; the country has an anti-sodomy law. The Integrity Bill requires that public officials make an annual declaration of assets, with failure to comply becoming a punishable offense. In January, the country became the fourth member of the Organisation of Eastern Caribbean States to ratify the Inter-American Convention against Corruption, which requires public officials to declare their assets and liabilities, improves cooperation on the collective fight against corruption, and strengthens corporate accounting practices. Antigua and Barbuda was not ranked by Transparency International in its 2004 Corruption Perceptions Index.

The family of former prime minister Lester Bird continues to control television, cable, and radio outlets. The government owns one of three radio stations and the television station. One of the Bird brothers owns a second station, and another brother owns the cable company. Opposition parties complain of receiving limited coverage from, and having little opportunity to present their views on, the government-controlled electronic media. There is free access to the Internet. The Declaration of Chapultepec on press freedoms was signed in September 2002.

The government respects religious and academic freedom.

Nongovernmental organizations and labor unions can organize freely. The Industrial Court mediates labor disputes, but public sector unions tend to be under the sway of the ruling party. Demonstrators are occasionally subject to police harassment.

The country's legal system is based on English common law. The ALP had manipulated the nominally independent judicial system, which had been powerless to address corruption in the executive branch. The islands' security forces are composed of the police and the small Antigua and Barbuda Defence Forces. The police generally respect human rights; basic police reporting statistics, however, are confidential. The country's prison is in primitive condition and has been criticized for the abuse of inmates, though visits are permitted by independent human rights groups.

An increasing level of crime led to calls in August to post police officers at gas stations; the police commissioner declined to honor the requests citing insufficient personnel. Increased patrols and the reintroduction of roadblocks and stiffer fines for firearms violations were offered as a response. The crime wave has been used by the UPP to attack the mixed economic record of the Bird administration, while the ALP has accused the administration of Prime Minister Baldwin Spencer of pursuing poor economic policies that have increased unemployment and crime.

A resolution to ratify the International Labour Organisation Convention Concerning Equal Remuneration for Men and Women Workers for Work of Equal Value was presented to parliament in late 2002. Social discrimination and violence against women are problems. The governmental Directorate of Women's Affairs has sought to increase awareness of women's legal rights.

⬆Argentina

Population: 37,900,000 **Political Rights:** 2
GNI/capita: $4,220 **Civil Liberties:** 2
Life Expectancy: 74 **Status:** Free
Religious Groups: Roman Catholic (92 percent),
Protestant (2 percent), Jewish (2 percent), other
(4 percent)
Ethnic Groups: White [mostly Spanish and Italian]
(97 percent), other [including mestizo and Amerindian] (3 percent)
Capital: Buenos Aires
Trend Arrow: Argentina received an upward trend arrow due to reforms in the country's judicial system.

Ten-Year Ratings Timeline (Political Rights, Civil Liberties, Status)

1995	1996	1997	1998	1999	2000	2001	2002	2003	2004
2,3F	2,3F	2,3F	3,3F	2,3F	1,2F	3,3PF	3,3PF	2,2F	2,2F

Overview: The government of Peronist president Nestor Kirchner appeared in 2004 to confound the forecasts of international financial experts. Kirchner negotiated successfully with foreign investors in restructuring the country's debt, taking advantage of the IMF's admission that its policies had helped to cripple the Argentine economy. He also made good on promises to reform the politicized judiciary, even as his government was criticized for backsliding on other aspects of his anticorruption agenda.

The Argentine Republic was established after independence from Spain in 1816. Democratic rule was often interrupted by military coups. The end of Juan Peron's authoritarian regime in 1955 led to a series of right-wing military dictatorships that spawned left-wing and nationalist violence. Argentina returned to elected civilian rule in 1983, after seven years of vicious and mostly clandestine repression of leftist guerrillas and other dissidents in what is known as the "dirty war."

As a provincial governor, Carlos S. Menem, running an orthodox Peronist platform of nationalism and state intervention in the economy, won a six-year presidential term in 1989, amidst hyperinflation and food riots. As president, he implemented, mostly by decree, an economic liberalization program and firmly allied the country with U.S. foreign policy.

In the October 1997 elections, voter concerns about rampant corruption and unemployment resulted in the first nationwide defeat of Menem's Peronists, whose macroeconomic stabilization stalled as a result of international economic strife and popular disenchantment due to his own government's growing corruption. Buenos Aires mayor and Radical Party leader Fernando De la Rua was chosen as the nominee of the center-left Alliance for presidential elections to be held in October 1999. Menem's long-running feud with his former vice president, Eduardo Duhalde, the Peronist Party presidential nominee and governor of Buenos Aires province, sealed the latter's fate. Duhalde was defeated by De la Rua, 48.5 to 38 percent.

Weak, indecisive, and facing an opposition-controlled congress, De la Rua sought to cut spending, raise taxes, and push forward an anticorruption agenda and unpopular labor reforms.

Unable to halt the economic crisis, De la Rua called on Menem's former economy minister to restore credibility to the government's economic program and to stave off default on Argentina's $128 billion in public sector debt. Record unemployment, reduced and delayed wages to federal and provincial workers, and the closing of public schools created the kind of social mobilization and protest unseen for nearly a generation. In the October 2001 congressional by-elections, the Peronist Party bested the ruling Alliance coalition. However, citizen anger resulted in an unprecedented 21 percent of the votes being spoiled or nullified.

In December 2001, government efforts to stop a run on Argentina's banking system sparked widespread protests. Middle-class housewives—the bulwark of the government coalition—turned out in massive street protests. At the same time, riots and looting of supermarkets in poorer districts erupted, some of which appeared to have been organized by rivals within the opposition Peronists and by disaffected serving or former members of the intelligence services. As the death toll reached 27, De la Rua resigned. He was replaced by an interim president, who himself was forced to quit less than a week later.

On December 31, 2001, Duhalde was selected as Argentina's new president. A decade-old law prohibiting the use of the military for internal security, a sizable reduction in military strength carried out by the Menem government, and continuing civilian abhorrence of the recent legacy of the dirty war helped keep the military from intervening in politics during the weeks-long transition.

The steep devaluation of the peso and a debilitating default on its $141 billion foreign debt left Argentina teetering on the brink of political and economic collapse throughout 2002, as the restrictive fiscal policies urged by the IMF and pursued by the government were not matched by increases in foreign investment. An attempt by Congress to impeach a highly politicized Supreme Court loyal to Menem was dropped, after international financial institutions said the move would endanger the country's access to foreign credit, and the legislature itself was the target of persistent accusations of bribery. Unemployment soared to levels unheard of since the founding of the republic, and violent crime spiraled out of control.

Kirchner, a relatively unknown governor from the Patagonian region, succeeded in getting into a runoff in the first round of the April 2003 presidential election, winning 22 percent to Menem's 24.3 percent. Menem's high negative poll ratings convinced him to drop out of the contest.

Upon taking office on May 25, 2003, as Argentina's sixth president in 18 months, Kirchner promised that his government would act as "the great repairer of social inequities" in what was once Latin America's most developed country. He quickly moved to purge the country's authoritarian military and police leadership. The new head of the Federal Police was fired a few months after the election in a corruption scandal—a first in the country's history. Kirchner also took steps to remove justices from the highly politicized Supreme Court, considered the country's most corrupt institution, and signed a decree that permitted the extradition of former military officials accused of human rights abuses. A former sympathizer of leftist guerrillas active in the country three decades ago, the populist Kirchner also moved Argentina into closer alliances with Venezuelan strongman Hugo Chavez and Cuba's Fidel Castro.

After making some efforts to put a break on government spending, Kirchner presided over a long-hoped-for economic recovery after the country's worst-ever depression. The 2004 admission by the IMF that it has significantly contributed to the Argentine economic crisis, and the role the international financial institutions played in financing the hated military, allowed the Kirchner government unaccustomed room to maneuver on how to repay nearly $88 billion owed to foreign creditors.

Lawlessness among the country's law enforcement institutions continued to be a major problem, particularly in Buenos Aires province, as did that of indigent street protestors. In August, an Argentine investigative television program aired a secret video tape that a leftist activist had made of a medical supply company executive trying to bribe him into using his influence to obtain a state medical care contract. In October, a Buenos Aires court revoked the acquittal of Menem on charges of illegal arms running, adding to his judicial predicament, as did the prosecution and conviction of top aides on other corruption charges. Meanwhile, Menem returned from his self-exile in Chile, where he had sought refuge from prosecution on corruption charges, and threatened to retake the presidency in 2007.

Political Rights and Civil Liberties: Citizens can change their government democratically. As amended in 1994, the 1853 constitution provides for a president elected for four years with the option of reelection for one term. Presidential candidates must win 45 percent of the vote to avoid a runoff. The legislature consists of the 257-member Chamber of Deputies elected for six years, with half the seats renewable every three years, and the 72-member Senate nominated by elected provincial legislatures for nine-year terms, with one-third of the seats renewable every three years. Two senators are directly elected in the autonomous Buenos Aires federal district. The 2003 elections were considered to be free and fair, despite claims made by former president Carlos Menem—and considered false by outside observers—that he was withdrawing from the presidential contest out of fear that he would be fraudulently denied the election.

The government of President Nestor Kirchner initially made anticorruption pledges a central theme, and Decree 1172/03 established the public's right to information and other transparency guarantees. In 2004, however, leading anticorruption activists accused the Kirchner government of having stalled on its good-government agenda, particularly in not ensuring the effective functioning of administrative controls. For example, there are no specific legal protections offered to either government or private sector whistle-blowers, who are forced to seek redress in inadequate administrative or judicial remedies such as the Public Employees Law or the Work Contract Law. Argentina was ranked 108 out of 146 countries surveyed in the 2004 Transparency International Corruption Perceptions Index.

The press, which was frequently under attack during Menem's presidency, continues to enjoy broad credibility and influence, the latter due in part to the continued discredit of public institutions and the major political parties, although less so than in other years. The Kirchner government, whose officials were increasingly accused of verbally mistreating independent journalists, boosted the amount of official advertising in the media and channeled the advertising disproportionately in favor of news outlets it considers friendly. In a negative development, the pro-Kirchner daily, *Pagina/12,* censored one of its own journalists, who was preparing an investigative report on government corruption. The ensuing scandal ended with the dissolution of the decade-old free press group, *Periodistas*, which split between pro-government and anticensorship factions.

The constitution guarantees freedom of religion. Nevertheless, the 250,000-strong Jewish community, the largest in Latin America, is a frequent target of anti-Semitic vandalism. Neo-Nazi organizations and other anti-Semitic groups, often tied to remnants of the old-line security services, remain active. In 2004, a federal court acquitted five men of being accessories in the 1994 car bombing of the Argentine Jewish Mutual Association (AMIA) community center, which resulted in 85 deaths. At the end of the three-year trial, not a single person was convicted for responsibility for the attack. The case languished in part because of sloppy police work at the crime scene and the anti-Semitic views of members of the security forces in charge of investigating the crime. During the trial, the investigating judge deliberately sidetracked the probe by bribing key witnesses with funds from a secret slush fund. Two prosecutors were removed for alleged irregularities, increasing already strong suspicions that complicity in the attack extended into Menem's inner circle.

Academic freedom is a cherished Argentine tradition and is largely observed in practice.

The right to organize political parties, civic organizations, and labor unions is generally respected. Labor is dominated by Peronist unions. Union influence, however, has diminished dramatically in the past decade because of corruption scandals, internal divisions, and restrictions on public sector strikes decreed by Menem to pave the way for his privatization program.

Menem's manipulation of the judiciary resulted in the undermining of the country's separation of powers and the rule of law. Although the tenure of scores of incompetent and corrupt judges remains a serious problem, some positive steps have been taken. In June 2004, Kirchner took an unprecedented step toward creating an independent judicial system by issuing a decree that limited the president's powers to appoint Supreme Court judges while widening the selection process to include the views of a number of nongovernmental organizations. By September 2004, four Supreme Court justices who formed an "automatic" pro-Menem majority had died or resigned, and Kirchner appointed two women in their place in an unprecedented move to give them representation in a body from which they had been excluded. However, the Magistrates' Council, responsible for choosing judges, remained a virtually moribund institution, seemingly incapable of even disciplining judicial misconduct in the AMIA case.

Public safety is a primary concern for Argentines, much of it fueled by a marked increase in illegal drug consumption that began during the Menem years. Within a decade, crime in Argentina has doubled, and in Buenos Aires, tripled, including a 50 percent increase in the murder rate in the past five years.

In May 2002, the Argentine penal code was changed, and the penalty for being convicted of killing a police officer became a life sentence without the possibility of parole. Police misconduct includes growing numbers of allegedly extrajudicial executions by law enforcement officers. The Buenos Aires provincial police have been involved in drug trafficking, extortion, and vice. Arbitrary arrests and abuse by police are rarely punished in civil courts owing to intimidation of witnesses and judges, particularly in Buenos Aires province. The torture of detainees in police custody in the province is widespread. Prison conditions are generally substandard throughout the country. In May 2004, law enforcement minister Gustavo Beliz resigned after denouncing "judicial and police mafias" who, along with renegade state intelligence agents, sought to undermine his work.

Argentina's estimated 700,000 to 1.5 million indigenous people are largely neglected. Approximately 70 percent of the country's rural indigenous communities lack title to their lands.

Women actively participate in politics in Argentina. However, domestic abuse remains a serious problem, and child prostitution is reported to be on the rise. In 2002, the city of Buenos Aires significantly expanded the legal rights of gay and lesbian couples.

Armenia

Population: 3,200,000
GNI/capita: $790
Life Expectancy: 73
Religious Groups: Armenian Apostolic (94 percent),
other Christian (4 percent), Yezidi (2 percent)
Ethnic Groups: Armenian (93 percent), Azeri (1 percent),
Russian (2 percent), other [including Kurd] (4 percent)
Capital: Yerevan

Political Rights: 5*
Civil Liberties: 4
Status: Partly Free

Ratings Change: Armenia's political rights rating declined from 4 to 5 due to the government's violent response to peaceful civic protests in April, a broader pattern of political repression, and the authorities' increasingly unresponsive and undemocratic governance.

Ten-Year Ratings Timeline (Political Rights, Civil Liberties, Status)

1995	1996	1997	1998	1999	2000	2001	2002	2003	2004
4,4PF	5,4PF	5,4PF	4,4PF	4,4PF	4,4PF	4,4PF	4,4PF	4,4PF	5,4PF

Overview:

Politics in Armenia in 2004 featured an ongoing, sometimes even violent, struggle between the ruling coalition and the country's opposition forces. A campaign of street demonstrations in April by Armenia's main opposition parties, whose demands were based on the government's failure to redress the flawed 2003 presidential elections, was met with a brutal response from the authorities. These events took place within a wider context of a closing of political space in Armenia, where independent voices, including news media, were further marginalized.

Following a brief period of independence from 1918 to 1920, a part of the predominantly Christian Transcaucasus republic of Armenia became a Soviet republic in 1922, while the western portion was ceded to Turkey. Armenia declared its independence from the Soviet Union in September 1991.

The banning of nine political parties prior to the 1995 parliamentary elections ensured the dominance of President Levon Ter Petrosian's ruling Armenian National Movement (ANM) coalition. In February 1998, Petrosian stepped down following the resignation of key officials in protest of his gradualist approach to solving the conflict over Nagorno-Karabakh, the disputed enclave in Azerbaijan. Prime Minister Robert Kocharian, the former president of Nagorno-Karabakh, was elected president in March of that year with the support of the previously banned Armenian Revolutionary Federation–Dashnaktsutiun.

Parliamentary elections in May 1999 resulted in an overwhelming victory for the Unity bloc, a new alliance of Defense Minister Vazgen Sarkisian's Republican Party and former Soviet Armenian leader Karen Demirchian's People's Party, which campaigned on a political platform of greater state involvement in the economy and increased social spending. In June, Sarkisian was named prime minister and Demirchian became Speaker of Parliament.

The country was plunged into a political crisis on October 27, 1999, when five gunmen stormed the parliament building and assassinated Sarkisian, Demirchian, and several other senior government officials. The leader of the gunmen, Nairi Hunanian, maintained that he and the other assailants had acted alone in an attempt to incite a popular revolt against the government. Meanwhile, allegations that Kocharian or members of his inner circle had orchestrated the shootings prompted opposition calls for the president to resign. However, because of an apparent lack of evidence, prosecutors did not press charges against Kocharian, who gradually consolidated his power during the following year. In May 2000, Kocharian named Republican Party leader Andranik Markarian as prime minister, replacing Vazgen Sarkisian's younger brother, Aram, who had served in the position for only five months following the parliament shootings.

In 2003, Kocharian was reelected in a presidential vote that was widely regarded as flawed. He defeated Stepan Demirchian, son of the late Karen Demirchian, in a second round run-off with 67 percent of the vote. The Organization for Security and Cooperation in Europe (OSCE) described the elections as falling "short of international standards for democratic elections," and asserted that "voting, counting, and tabulation showed serious irregularities, including widespread ballot-box stuffing." The second round of voting, which was held on March 5, saw the authorities place more than 200 opposition supporters under administrative detention for over 15 days; the detainees were sentenced on charges of hooliganism and participation in unsanctioned demonstrations. The Constitutional Court rejected appeals by opposition leaders to invalidate the election results, although it did propose holding a "referendum of confidence" in Kocharian within the next year to allay widespread doubts about the validity of the election returns. Kocharian indicated that he would not comply with the proposal. In response to the problems associated with the election, a standoff emerged between Kocharian and the political opposition, formed by two major groups—the Artarutiun (Justice bloc) and the National Unity Party—with opposition parties choosing not to attend sessions of the National Assembly.

Protest rallies were organized in Yerevan from April 2004 into June over the failure of the government to redress the 2003 presidential vote. The authorities responded with violence, using police to disperse demonstrators in Yerevan with water cannons, batons, and stun grenades. Following the crackdown by the authorities in April, these demonstrations grew ever smaller. Perhaps as a testament of the opposition's inability to coordinate and settle on an effective strategy, no meaningful movement on the political scene was apparent as of November.

The Parliamentary Assembly of the Council of Europe (PACE) adopted a resolution in October 2004 expressing concern about the lack of investigation into the flawed 2003 elections and calling for steps to end pretrial administrative detention, physical ill-treatment, and other abuses.

A resolution to the long-standing Nagorno-Karabakh conflict came no closer during the year, and there were reports of some heavy fighting along the ceasefire line.

Political Rights and Civil Liberties: Armenians cannot change their government democratically. The 1995 and 1999 parliamentary and 1996 presidential elections were marred by serious irregularities. The most recent presidential and parliamentary polls, in February-March and May 2003, respectively, were strongly criticized by international election monitors, who cited widespread fraud, particularly in the presidential vote. The 1995 constitution provides for a weak legislature and a strong, directly elected president who appoints the prime minister. Most parties in Armenia are dominated by government officials or other powerful figures, suffer from internal dissent and division, and tend to be weak and ineffective. President Robert Kocharian, whose term expires in 2008, does not belong to any political party and relies on a three-party coalition to rule the country.

Bribery and nepotism are reported to be common among government bureaucrats, and government officials are rarely prosecuted or otherwise removed for abuse of office. Corruption is also believed to be serious in law enforcement. Armenia was ranked 82 out of 146 countries surveyed in the 2004 Transparency International Corruption Perceptions Index.

There are limits on press freedom, and in 2004 the Armenian media continued to exist on a landscape where independent television and radio news content was effectively nonexistent. There are a number of private television stations, and most radio stations are privately owned. While most newspapers are in private hands, the majority operate with limited resources and have small circulations and consequently are dependent on economic and political interest groups for their survival. Newspapers in impoverished Armenia are often out of the economic reach of many Armenians. A media law adopted in 2003 abolishes the requirement that media organizations register with the Ministry of Justice, but the criminal code still includes libel as a criminal offense. A high level of political intimidation also leads to considerable self-censorship by journalists.

In 2002, the independent television station A1+ lost its license after the national television and radio broadcasting commission granted a tender for its broadcasting frequency to another channel. Journalists and opposition politicians criticized the closure of A1+, which had a reputation for balanced reporting, as a politically motivated decision to control media coverage in the run-up to the 2003 presidential and parliamentary elections. Following the decision, thousands of people demonstrated in a series of weekly protests over the station's closure and to demand Kocharian's resignation. In 2003, additional bids by A1+ for a broadcast frequency were rejected. In 2004, A1+ won the right to take its case to the European Court of Human Rights. According to the U.S. Department of State 2004 human rights report, Armenia did not restrict access to the Internet.

Freedom of religion is somewhat respected. The Armenian constitution provides for freedom of religion, but the law specifies some restrictions on the religious freedom of adherents of minority faiths. The Armenian Apostolic Church, to which 90 percent of Armenians formally belong, enjoys a privileged status and has advocated for restrictions on nontraditional denominations. While 50 religious groups are officially registered, the Jehovah's Witnesses have been denied registration repeatedly because of the group's strong opposition to compulsory military service.

The government generally does not restrict academic freedom. In September 2002, the Ministry of Education ordered the compulsory display of the portraits of Kocharian and the head of the Armenian Apostolic Church in secondary schools. The history of the Apostolic Church is a required school subject.

Registration requirements for nongovernmental associations are cumbersome and time-consuming. The authorities abused administrative detention regulations to intimidate and punish peaceful demonstrators and political activists following the 2003 presidential election. This issue remained a bone of contention in 2004, with the PACE condemning the use of violence by the Armenian authorities in April and criticizing them for the continued application of the administrative code to arrest protesters. Opposition activist Eduard Arakelian was given an 18-month jail sentence in May for hitting a policeman with a plastic mineral water bottle during the April rally. Arakelian pleaded guilty but said that he had struck the policeman after the official had hit him with a truncheon in the face. In May, parliament banned rallies not approved in advance on virtually all public squares in Yerevan and other major cities.

While the constitution enshrines the right to form and join trade unions, in practice, labor organizations are weak and relatively inactive.

The judiciary is subject to political pressure from the executive branch and also suffers from violations of due process. Police frequently make arbitrary arrests without warrants, beat detainees during arrest and interrogation, and use torture to extract confessions. A Human Rights Watch report concluded that police denied access to legal counsel to those opposition supporters who were given short prison terms for participating in unauthorized rallies after the 2003 presidential vote.

Although members of the country's tiny ethnic minority population rarely report cases of overt discrimination, they have complained about difficulties in receiving education in their native languages.

Freedom of travel and residence is largely respected. However, registering changes in residency is sometimes complicated by the need to negotiate with an inefficient or corrupt government bureaucracy. According to a Human Rights Watch report, in March and April of 2004, the police restricted the movement of opposition supporters seeking to travel to Yerevan by setting up roadblocks, stopping cars, and questioning the passengers.

Citizens have the right to own private property and establish businesses, but an inefficient and often corrupt court system and unfair business competition hinder operations. Key industries remain in the hands of oligarchs and influential clans who received preferential treatment in the early stages of privatization.

Domestic violence and trafficking in women and girls for the purpose of prostitution are believed to be serious problems.

Australia

Population: 20,100,000
GNI/capita: $19,530
Life Expectancy: 80
Political Rights: 1
Civil Liberties: 1
Status: Free
Religious Groups: Anglican (26.1 percent), Roman
Catholic (26 percent), other Christian (24.3 percent),
non-Christian (11 percent), other (12.6 percent)
Ethnic Groups: White (92 percent), Asian (7 percent), other
[including Aboriginal] (1 percent)
Capital: Canberra

Ten-Year Ratings Timeline (Political Rights, Civil Liberties, Status)

1995	1996	1997	1998	1999	2000	2001	2002	2003	2004
1,1F	1,1F	1,1F	1,1F	1,1F	1,1F	1,1F	1,1F	1,1F	1,1F

Overview:

Prime Minister John Howard called for a new election in October 2004 to fend off challenges from the Labor Party's Mark Latham, who took over the party leadership in December 2003. Latham's vocal attacks against the government's decision to send troops to join the U.S.-led Operation Iraqi Freedom in Iraq and the government's close relationship with U.S. president George W. Bush and his administration found considerable resonance with public sentiments. The Howard government's close alliance with the United States became the major difference between Labor and the Liberal Party.

Britain claimed Australia as a colony in 1770. The country became independent in 1901 as a commonwealth of six states. In 1911, the government adopted the Northern Territories and the capital territory of Canberra as territorial units. Since World War II, political power has alternated between the center-left Labor Party and a conservative coalition of the Liberal Party and the smaller, rural-based National Party. The Liberal and National Parties capitalized on discontent with high unemployment and an economic recession to oust Labor in the 1996 parliamentary elections; Howard, of the ruling Liberal Party/National Party coalition, has been prime minister since that year. In the November 2001 parliamentary poll, the Liberal Party won 68 seats and the National Party took 13 seats, while Labor managed to secure 65 seats.

The government has tightened immigration laws in recent years to curb illegal immigration. There is considerable public support for these new measures despite international criticism and challenges by some human rights advocates. The government affirmed its "Pacific Solution" policy of using detention centers in neighboring states to hold illegal immigrants and screen those eligible for refugee status. In May 2004, the government announced that it will continue to use detention centers in Nauru to hold Afghans and other nationals who tried to enter Australia illegally by stowing away on merchant ships and using human traffickers. Nevertheless, the government granted refugee status to a number of persons who do not have third-country options and gave permanent residency to about 700 East Timorese asylum seekers in 2003. Concerns about the threat of rising sea levels as a result of global climate change on Nauru, a former Australian trust territory, led the government to commission a paper in December 2003 to consider offering Australian citizenship to Nauru's 10,000 people.

Australia has been active regionally in promoting peace, restoring rule of law, and strengthening democratic governance. The government is worried that weakened states in the South Pacific, where corruption and abuse are widespread and governments unstable, would be vulnerable to terrorist activity. This "arc of instability" north of Australia includes Papua New Guinea, Vanuatu, and Fiji. Australia signed antiterrorism accords with Fiji, the Philippines, Indonesia, Malaysia, and Thailand in 2002 and 2003. The treaties commit these countries to increasing cooperation in law enforcement, intelligence, and information sharing, and in other initiatives to disrupt terrorists and their financial backers.

Since a ceasefire was reached in Bougainville in 1998, Australia has sent 3,500 military personnel and 300 monitors to Papua New Guinea. Australia also sent troops, police, and other personnel to the Solomon Islands in July 2003 to lead a multinational force to restore law and order after years of ethnic warfare. The Australia-funded Pacific Transnational Crime Center opened in Fiji in June 2004 to provide police and judicial training for several Pacific island nations.

Political Rights and Civil Liberties: Australia is a constitutional democracy with a federal parliamentary form of government. Citizens participate in free and fair multiparty elections to choose representatives to the parliament. However, Aboriginal people are under-represented at all levels of political leadership.

Australia is regarded as one of the least corrupt societies in the world and was ranked 9 out of 146 countries surveyed in the 2004 Transparency International Corruption Perceptions Index.

The constitution does not provide for freedom of speech and of the press, but citizens and the media freely criticize the government without reprisal. In a rare instance of government intervention, the government announced in March 2003 that it monitored and blocked e-mail messages sent to its troops in Iraq. Electronic mail messages that were "negative, inappropriate, and not supportive" were blocked to protect the morale of Australian troops involved in the U.S.-led military action to oust the Iraqi regime.

Freedom of religion is respected, as is academic freedom.

The rights of assembly and association are not codified in law, but the government respects these rights in practice. Canberra's decision to send 2,000 troops to Iraq sparked sharp public debates and antiwar protests in many larger cities. Workers have the right to organize and bargain collectively, but the Federal Workplace Relations Act of 1996 abolished closed shops and union demarcations among other restrictions. Critics say this law makes it more difficult for unions to get into workplaces and organize workers.

The judiciary is independent, and prison conditions are generally good by international standards. Allegations of abuse by guards at the Port Hedland Detention Center in Western Australia after a riot there in November 2003 will be investigated by Australia's Commonwealth Ombudsman.

Australia began to tighten its immigration policy following a marked increase in illegal immigrants, mostly from the Middle East, between 1998 and 2001. In one instance, more than 430 mainly Afghan refugees tried to sail to Australia in 2001. Canberra refused to grant them entry when a Norwegian commercial freighter that had rescued them in the Indian Ocean tried to turn them over to Australia. Canberra transferred the refugees to Australian-funded refugee holding facilities in Nauru and Papua New Guinea.

Many people, particularly legal immigrants, complained that such boat refugees are "queue jumpers." The government cited this complaint as a reason for the Migration Amendment Bill in 2001. This law bars noncitizens from applying for a "permanent protection visa"—which allows a person to live and work permanently in Australia as a refugee—if entry was unlawful and occurred in one of several "excised" territories along the country's northern arc: Christmas Island, Ashmore and Cartier Islands, the Cocos Islands, and resource installations designated by the government. All such foreign nationals would be detained and only released pending full adjudication of their asylum claim.

The Aboriginal population suffers general discrimination, reflected by a disproportionately high level of unemployment (three times that of the general population), inferior access to medical care and education, imprisonment rates 15 times higher than that of the general population, and a life expectancy 20 years shorter than that for the non-indigenous population. They complain of routine mistreatment and discrimination by police and prison officials.

Aboriginal groups have called for an official apology for the "Stolen Generation" of Aboriginal children who were taken from their parents by the government from 1910 until the early 1970s and raised by foster parents and in orphanages. Government officials have stood firm against such an apology, reasoning that the present generation has no responsibility to apologize for the wrongs of a previous generation.

In 2004, the government announced abolishment of the Aboriginal and Torres Strait Islander Commission (ATSIC). Canberra said that ATSIC, the representative organization for Aborigines, was a failure and that advisors will instead be appointed to advise the government.

Although women enjoy equal rights and freedoms, violence against women is a problem, particularly within the Aboriginal population.

Austria

Population: 8,100,000 **Political Rights:** 1
GNI/capita: $23,860 **Civil Liberties:** 1
Life Expectancy: 79 **Status:** Free
Religious Groups: Roman Catholic (73.6 percent),
Protestant (4.7 percent), Muslim and other (17 percent)
Ethnic Groups: German (88.5 percent), indigenous
minorities [includes Croatians, Slovenes, Hungarians,
Czechs, Slovaks, Roma] (1.5 percent), recent immigrant groups
[includes Turks, Bosnians, Serbs, Croatians] (10 percent)
Capital: Vienna

Ten-Year Ratings Timeline (Political Rights, Civil Liberties, Status)

1995	1996	1997	1998	1999	2000	2001	2002	2003	2004
1,1F	1,1F	1,1F	1,1F	1,1F	1,1F	1,1F	1,1F	1,1F	1,1F

Overview:

In 2004, Austria's government pushed economic reforms, which contributed to a modest economic recovery from 2003 but also cost the government somewhat in popularity. The Freedom Party, a far-right party involved as a junior partner in government, continued its moderating trend at the national level but did poorly in local and European Parliament elections.

Modern Austria emerged at the end of World War I, when the Austro-Hungarian Empire was dismembered. It was voluntarily annexed to Nazi Germany in 1938 and suffered the defeat of Hitler's regime. Postwar Austria, by consent of the World War II Allies, remained neutral between the Cold War blocs. Focusing instead on economic growth, Austria has developed one of the wealthiest economies in Europe.

From 1986 until 2000, the two biggest political parties—the center-left Social Democratic Party of Austria (SPO) and the center-right People's Party of Austria (OVP)—governed together in a grand coalition. Members of the two parties shared in the administration of cabinet ministries as well as in many other government functions. Labor relations were corporatist, with management and unions both represented not only in individual firms' decision making, but also in national policy making.

The election of October 1999 saw the emergence of the first government since 1970 not to include the SPO. Instead, the OVP formed a coalition with the Freedom Party, a far-right nationalist party with vestigial Nazi sympathies. The Freedom Party had grown steadily in the polls as voters became disaffected with the power sharing of the two big parties and the near impossibility of major political change. The Freedom Party won its biggest ever share of the vote, 27 percent, in that election, and was thus included in a coalition with the OVP's Wolfgang Schuessel as chancellor.

The reaction among fellow members of the European Union (EU) was immediate and dramatic. In 2000, the EU officially suspended ties with Austria. Though this move had little practical effect, technically it meant that the other 14 EU countries had to deal with Austria on a bilateral basis rather than through the EU. Moreover, support in Austria for the Freedom Party jumped, as Austrian voters resented the EU's attempts to interfere with the choice they had expressed at the polls. Later in 2000, the EU reinstated Austria.

One effect of the EU sanctions was that Joerg Haider, the Freedom Party's leader, withdrew from that post and contented himself with the governorship of the state of Carinthia. Haider had been both Freedom's biggest vote-winner and the source of its major controversies. For example, he referred to Nazi death camps as "punishment camps" and once told a rally of former SS officers that they were worth "honor and respect," though he also referred to the Nazi regime as a "cruel and brutal dictatorship." With Haider's official withdrawal, Austrian politics returned to near-normality and Freedom was forced to moderate its far-right stances as it dealt with the day-to-day reality of governing.

However, Haider did not remain absent from the national stage for long, and his meddling in a national Freedom Party leadership struggle caused the party to withdraw from the coalition in September 2002. The parliamentary elections of November 2002 saw Freedom's vote share fall from 27 percent in 1999 to 10 percent. In subsequent cabinet negotiations, the Freedom Party rejoined the coalition with the OVP, but this time clearly as the junior partner.

In his second term, Schuessel has sought to tackle several thorny economic issues, including pushing privatizations, trimming pensions, and generally keeping a tight rein on the budget. Economic growth, which was just 0.7 percent in 2003, was forecast to improve somewhat, though not spectacularly, in 2004 as Europe's economies rebounded generally.

Perhaps as a result of the ongoing struggle with these economic issues, the Freedom Party continued to lose support in 2004. Though Haider was reelected governor of Carinthia in a March 2004 state election, the party fared worse in another state election that same day and did especially badly in the European Parliament elections in June. Having captured 23 percent of the vote in those elections in 1999, the Freedom Party received just 6 percent in 2004. The SPO, in opposition at the national level, did best at the European poll, winning 33 percent of the vote, benefiting from a general anti-incumbent trend across Europe.

Relations with the EU remained Austria's most important foreign affairs issue. Austria supported the draft EU constitution signed in June. The enlargement of the EU to former Soviet bloc countries shortly afterward was also particularly important, as Austria borders four of them (the Czech Republic, Slovakia, Hungary, and Slovenia). However, Austria is skeptical about Turkey's application, which it was expected to oppose at the December 2004 EU summit meeting.

Political Rights and Civil Liberties: Austrians can change their government democratically. Perhaps ironically, the participation of the Freedom Party in government emphasized this basic right when other European countries tried in 2000 to induce Austrians to forgo their democratic choice. Though there are competitive political parties and free and fair elections, the traditional practice of grand coalitions in Austria has disillusioned many with the political process. Frustration with the cozy relationship between the OVP and the SPO helped lead to the rise of the Freedom Party as a protest party. However, Freedom's participation in government brought it closer to the mainstream right.

Austria is less corrupt than during the 1980s, when campaign donation laws were tightened somewhat. Austria was ranked 13 out of 146 countries surveyed in the 2004 Transparency International Corruption Perceptions Index.

The media are free, though not highly pluralistic. The end of the monopoly by the state broadcaster ORF has not brought significant competition to the broadcast market, and print media ownership is concentrated in a few hands, particularly the News and the Print-Medien groups. Harassment and libel lawsuits by politicians (notably from the Freedom Party) against investigative and critical journalists have hampered reporters' work. There are no restrictions on Internet access.

Religious freedom is respected in Austria and enshrined in the constitution. However, there are only 12 officially recognized religions, and these have the ability to draw on state funds for religious education. Joining that group of state-recognized religions requires a period of ten years of observation. The Jehovah's Witnesses have complained that this practice violates their freedom of religion, although they are recognized as a "confessional community." Academic freedom is generally respected.

The rights to freedom of assembly and association are protected in the constitution, and trade unions have traditionally been powerful. They not only are free to organize and strike, but have been considered an essential partner in national policy making. Strikes held in May 2003 against the government's controversial pension reforms did not stop those reforms from going through.

The judiciary is independent, and the Constitutional Court examines the compatibility of legislation with the constitution. Austria is a member of the Council of Europe, and its citizens have recourse to the European Court of Human Rights in Strasbourg, France. The quality of prisons and police generally meet high European standards, though isolated incidences of police brutality and harsh prison conditions are reported.

Residents generally are afforded equal protection under the law. However, immigration has fueled some resentment towards minorities and foreigners—Austria has the highest number of asylum seekers per capita in Europe. Since a tightening in December 2003, the asylum law is among the strictest in the developed world. Under that law, criticized by the UN High Commissioner for Refugees, some asylum seekers could be deported while appeals of their cases are held. New arrivals will be asked for full statements within 72 hours.

A 1979 law guarantees women freedom from discrimination in various areas, especially the workplace. A 1993 law sought to increase women's employment in government agencies where women were underrepresented.

Azerbaijan

Population: 8,300,000   **Political Rights:** 6
GNI/capita: $710   **Civil Liberties:** 5
Life Expectancy: 72   **Status:** Not Free
Religious Groups: Muslim (93.4 percent), Russian
Orthodox (2.5 percent), Armenian Orthodox (2.3 percent),
other (2.3 percent)
Ethnic Groups: Azeri (90 percent), Dagestani (3.2 percent),
Russian (2.5 percent), Armenian (2 percent), other (2.3 percent)
Capital: Baku

Ten-Year Ratings Timeline (Political Rights, Civil Liberties, Status)

1995	1996	1997	1998	1999	2000	2001	2002	2003	2004
6,6NF	6,5NF	6,4PF	6,4PF	6,4PF	6,5PF	6,5PF	6,5PF	6,5NF	6,5NF

Overview:

The year 2004 saw President Ilham Aliyev, who ascended to the presidency in late 2003, attempt to put his mark on Azerbaijani politics and consolidate his power base among the country's ruling elite. However, Aliyev's rule did not reflect any significant change in governance or the adoption of notable political reforms. Meanwhile, no credible investigation of the violent police crackdown against opposition protestors following the 2003 presidential election had been conducted by year's end.

After having been controlled by the Ottoman Empire since the seventeenth century, Azerbaijan entered the Soviet Union in 1922 as part of the Transcaucasian Soviet Federal Republic, becoming a separate Soviet republic in 1936. Following a referendum in 1991, Azerbaijan declared independence from the disintegrating Soviet Union.

In 1992, Abulfaz Elchibey, leader of the nationalist opposition Azerbaijan Popular Front, was elected president in a generally free and fair vote. A military coup one year later ousted him from power and installed the former first secretary of the Azerbaijan Communist Party, Heydar Aliyev, in his place. In the October 1993 presidential elections, Aliyev reportedly received almost 99 percent of the vote. Azerbaijan's first post-Soviet parliamentary elections, held in November 1995, saw five leading opposition parties and some 600 independent candidates barred from the vote in which Aliyev's Yeni Azerbaijan Party (YAP) won the most seats. In October 1998, Aliyev was chosen president with more than 70 percent of the vote in an election marred by serious irregularities.

In November 2000, the ruling YAP captured the majority of seats in the parliamentary election. The Azerbaijan Popular Front and the Communist Party came in a distant second and third, respectively. International monitors from the Organization for Security and Cooperation in Europe (OSCE) and the Council of Europe cited mass electoral fraud, including the stuffing of ballot boxes and a strong pro-government bias in state-run media. Despite widespread criticism of the elections, the Council of Europe approved Azerbaijan's application for membership just days after the vote, a decision widely criticized by international human rights groups.

An August 2002 national referendum led to the adoption of a series of constitutional amendments, some of which critics charged would further strengthen the ruling party's grip on power. One particularly controversial amendment stipulates that the prime minister become president if the head of state resigns or is incapacitated. Critics charged that the aging and ailing Aliyev would appoint his son, Ilham, prime minister in order to engineer a transfer of power. Opposition groups and the OSCE charged that the referendum was marred by fraud, including ballot-box stuffing, intimidation of election monitors and officials, and inflated voter-turnout figures of nearly 90 percent.

Throughout 2002, a number of public demonstrations demanded various political and economic changes, including Aliyev's resignation. In June, an unarmed protestor was shot and killed by police in the town of Nardaran, the first time that such a tragedy had occurred since Azerbaijan's independence more than a decade earlier. The government blamed the riots on radical Islamic groups, although residents insisted that the authorities used these accusations as a pretext to repress dissent. In April 2003, 15 individuals arrested in Nardaran in 2002 were found guilty of fomenting the unrest and given prison terms or suspended sentences; during the year, the four defendants who had been imprisoned were pardoned and released.

In the months preceding the October 15, 2003, presidential election, the political environment was marked by uncertainty over Aliyev's declining health and its implications for his reelection bid. The elder Aliyev, who had a history of heart trouble, collapsed during a live television broadcast in April and left Azerbaijan that summer to receive medical treatment abroad. At the same time, government officials continued to deny that his health problems were serious, and he remained the official YAP candidate for the presidential election. In June, Aliyev's son, Ilham, was officially nominated as a presidential candidate, and the elder Aliev withdrew his candidacy in favor of his son's on October 2.

Final figures election results released by the Central Election Commission showed Ilham Aliyev defeating seven challengers with nearly 77 percent of the vote. His closest rival, opposition Musavat Party leader Isa Gambar, received only 14 percent of the vote, while six other candidates received less than 4 percent each. According to OSCE observers, the election was marred by widespread fraud and failed to meet international standards for democratic elections. Meanwhile, during violent clashes between security forces and demonstrators in Baku on October 15 and 16, in which at least one person was reportedly killed and several hundred were injured, the authorities unleashed a crackdown against the opposition in which more than 600 people were detained. Among those arrested were opposition party leaders and supporters who had not been directly involved in the preceding days' violence, along with many election officials who refused to certify fraudulent election results.

Heydar Aliyev, who had long dominated the country's political life, died on December 12, 2003. Throughout 2004, Ilham attempted to put his stamp on Azerbaijani politics and consolidate his position among the country's ruling elite, but his rule did not reflect any significant change in governance. The level of official control of key institutions remained high, while the political opposition, which was weak and splintered, provided little serious challenge to the country's leadership. This political landscape thus offers scant prospect that Aliyev will face meaningful competition before the parliamentary election scheduled to be held in 2005. The absence of observable reform over the last year raises the question of whether the country will be reoriented in a more open, democratic direction under Aliyev's leadership, as was hoped for by many in advance of his taking the reigns of power.

In the fall of 2004, stiff prison sentences were handed down to a number of opposition leaders who were arrested during the aftermath of the 2003 presidential poll. As of November 30, there still had not been a credible investigation of the violence surrounding the election.

A lasting settlement for the disputed territory of Nagorno-Karabakh, over which Armenia and Azerbaijan fought in the early 1990s, did not materialize during the year. The region, which is formally part of Azerbaijan, is now predominantly ethnically Armenian and effectively under Armenian control.

Political Rights and Civil Liberties:

Citizens of Azerbaijan are not able to change their government democratically. The country's constitution provides for a strong presidency, and in practice parliament exercises little independence from the executive branch. The 1993, 1998, and 2003 presidential and 1995 and 2000 parliamentary elections were considered neither free nor fair by international observers. Amendments to the constitution adopted in a 2002 referendum included a provision replacing the proportional-representation system, under which one-fifth of the members of parliament were elected, with single-mandate constituency races, under which the remaining four-fifths of parliament were already chosen. Opposition parties argued that the proportional system was the only way for them to participate in elections, since most lack nationwide organizations.

More than 40 political parties are registered. However, most opposition parties are weak and are based on personalities rather than political platforms, and they have been unable to unite in lasting alliances to challenge the government. Hundreds of opposition activists and leaders were detained by police in the weeks surrounding the October 2003 presidential election. The repressive posture of the authorities continued throughout 2004.

Corruption is deeply entrenched throughout society, with government officials rarely held accountable for engaging in corrupt practices. Azerbaijan was ranked 140 out of 146 countries surveyed in the 2004 Transparency International Corruption Perceptions Index.

While Azerbaijan's constitution guarantees freedom of speech and the press, journalists who publish articles critical of the president or other prominent state officials are routinely harassed and prosecuted, and self-censorship is common. State-owned newspapers and broadcast media reflect the position of the government. Independent and opposition papers struggle financially in the face of low circulation, limited advertising revenues, and heavy fines or imprisonment of their staff. Libel is a criminal offense.

During the run-up to and aftermath of the 2003 presidential election, journalists suffered increased intimidation. Rauf Arifoglu, editor of the opposition *Yeni Musavat* newspaper, was arrested for allegedly organizing public demonstrations following the October 2003 elections and was given a five-year prison sentence in November 2004. Under the pressure of $160,000 in fines applied against it in the aftermath of the 2003 elections, *Yeni Musavat* was forced to suspend publication in November 2004. Other restrictions on the non-state media included editorial interference and lawsuits for criticizing government officials. In 2004, the authorities exerted considerable pressure on what remained of the independent print media, including the publications *Zerkalo* and *Ekho*. According to the U.S. Department of State 2004 human rights report, the government required Internet service providers to have licenses and formal agreements with the Ministry of Communications and Information Technologies. At the end of 2004, there were 21 licensed providers.

The government restricts some religious activities of members of "nontraditional" minority religious groups through burdensome registration requirements and interference in the importation and distribution of printed religious materials. Islam, Russian Orthodoxy, and Judaism are considered traditional religions, and their members can generally worship freely. The Juma Mosque community, which was the object of an eviction by the Azerbaijani authorities in June, challenged the court-ordered eviction at the European Court of Human Rights. The Juma Mosque community has sought to function independently, rather than as part of the state-approved Caucasian Muslim Board.

The government generally does not restrict academic freedom, and several tenured professors are active in opposition parties, according to the 2003 U.S. State Department human rights report, released in 2004. However, some faculty and students have experienced political pressure; after the October 2003 election, some professors and teachers said they were dismissed because of their membership in opposition parties, the State Department report said.

The government often restricts freedom of assembly, especially for political parties critical of the government. Registration with the Ministry of Justice is required for a nongovernmental organization (NGO) to function as a legal entity, and the registration process has been described as cumbersome and nontransparent. Amendments adopted in 2003 to NGO laws further complicated requirements for registering grants, presenting an obstacle that continued into 2004. There are some 1,600 NGOs registered in Azerbaijan, but only 200 or so of them work actively. Although the law permits the formation of trade unions and the right to strike, the majority of trade unions remain closely affiliated with the government and most major industries are state owned.

The judiciary, corrupt and inefficient, is subservient to the executive branch. Arbitrary arrest and detention are common, particularly for members of the political opposition. Detainees are often held for long periods before trial, and their access to lawyers is restricted. Police abuse of suspects during arrest and interrogation reportedly remains commonplace, with torture sometimes used to extract confessions. Prison conditions are reportedly severe, with many inmates suffering from overcrowding and inadequate medical care.

Some members of ethnic minority groups, including the small Armenian population, have complained of discrimination in areas including education, employment, and housing. Hundreds of thousands of ethnic Azeris who fled the war in Nagorno-Karabakh have been prevented by the Armenian government from returning to their homes and remain in Azerbaijan, often living in dreadful conditions.

Significant parts of the economy are in the hands of a corrupt elite, which severely limits equality of opportunity. Supporters of the political opposition face job discrimination, demotion, or dismissal.

Traditional societal norms and poor economic conditions restrict women's professional roles. Domestic violence is a problem, and there are no laws regarding spousal abuse. In 2004, Azerbaijan adopted a new national program to combat human trafficking. According to the U.S. State Department's annual report on human trafficking, issued in 2004, Azerbaijan is both a country of origin and a transit point for the trafficking of women for prostitution.

Bahamas

Population: 300,000
GNI/capita: $16,700
Life Expectancy: 72
Religious Groups: Baptist (32 percent), Anglican (20 percent), Roman Catholic (19 percent), other Protestant (24 percent)
Ethnic Groups: Black (85 percent), white (12 percent), Asian and Hispanic (3 percent)
Capital: Nassau

Political Rights: 1
Civil Liberties: 1
Status: Free

Ten-Year Ratings Timeline (Political Rights, Civil Liberties, Status)

1995	1996	1997	1998	1999	2000	2001	2002	2003	2004
1,2F	1,2F	1,2F	1,2F	1,1F	1,1F	1,1F	1,1F	1,1F	1,1F

Overview:

In 2004, the ruling Progressive Liberal Party (PLP) denied allegations of having received illegal contributions during the 2002 parliamentary election. On the international front, the Bahamas worked to balance closer relations with both the United States and Cuba.

The Bahamas, a 700-island archipelago in the Caribbean, gained independence in 1973 and is part of the British Commonwealth. Lynden Pindling served as the country's first prime minister and head of the PLP for 25 years. After years of allegations of corruption and involvement by high officials in narcotics trafficking, Pindling was defeated by the Free National Movement (FNM) in 1992. His successor, Prime Minister Hubert Ingraham promised honesty, efficiency, and accountability in government. The FNM captured 32 seats in the House of Assembly, while the PLP took 17 seats.

In the 1997 legislative elections, Ingraham took credit for revitalizing the economy by attracting foreign investment and his FNM won 34 seats to the PLP's 6. In April 1997, Pindling resigned as opposition leader and was replaced by Perry Christie.

In the May 2002 parliamentary poll, the PLP won 29 seats, while the FNM received only 8. Ingraham retired from politics, fulfilling a promise he had made prior to the elections. He was replaced as prime minister by Christie who, while not as popular as Ingraham, was able to capitalize on the large majority of the PLP. Christie and Ingraham are close personal friends and business partners, a possible indication of why the new prime minister's economic and political policies do not diverge much from those of his predecessor's.

Rising crime rates in the late 1990s, which undermined the early accomplishments of the Ingraham government, were linked to illegal trafficking in narcotics and gunrunning. Ingraham is credited with having subsequently improved the country's international reputation with policies that reduced money laundering and improved counternarcotics cooperation with the United States. His administration established a new anti-drug intelligence unit and announced plans to bring the financial sector into full compliance with international standards and practices by strengthening requirements to report suspicious and unusual transactions. The Bahamas has promoted tourism and allowed the banking industry to grow; both practices have made the country's economy one of the Caribbean's most affluent.

However, the Christie administration has not been able to effectively curb narcotics trafficking, and the incidence of violent crime associated with drug-gang activity has escalated. In addition, the offshore financial system, despite having undergone reforms, continues to be used for illicit purposes. Several banks have been named in U.S. fraud cases, while at least two individuals have been convicted on fraud and forgery charges.

In August 2004, Christie was urged to disclose his knowledge of illegal contributions to the PLP coffers in the 2002 race. The Coalition for Democratic Reform (CDR) and the FNM—the main opposition parties—have joined in this call. The PLP responded with a statement indicating that the political donations were not illegal or improper and that neither the party nor its leaders were for sale.

A confrontation with the U.S. ambassador over counternarcotics policies was resolved when the issues were largely addressed. The Bahamas continued to make efforts at building closer ties with the United States, responding positively to a request from the U.S. Department of Homeland Security to place armed sky marshals on selected flights. At the same time, the country was under pressure from the U.S. government to reduce existing ties with Cuba. Bahamians are, however, sensitive to the perception that their international policy is determined by Washington and have continued to maintain independent foreign relations, including upgrading relations with Cuba by announcing that a Bahamian consul general will be appointed to Havana in 2004-2005.

The year 2004 witnessed the destructiveness of the hurricane season, which caused more than $125 million in damages to the islands' infrastructure.

Political Rights and Civil Liberties: Citizens of the Bahamas can change their government democratically. There is a 49-member House of Assembly, directly elected for five years, and a 16-member Senate. The prime minister appoints 9 members; the leader of the parliament opposition, 4; and the governor-general, 3. The assembly was subsequently reduced to 40 members, in keeping with a campaign promise by the FNM. Political parties can organize freely.

The Bahamas was not ranked by Transparency International in its 2004 Corruption Perceptions Index.

Daily and weekly newspapers, all privately owned, express a variety of views on public issues, as do the government-run radio station and four privately owned radio broadcasters. Opposition politicians claim that the state-run television system, the Broadcasting Corporation of the Bahamas, gives preferential coverage to the ruling party. Full freedom of expression is constrained by strict libel laws. There is free access to the Internet.

Rights to religious and academic freedom are respected.

Constitutional guarantees of the right to organize civic organizations are generally respected, and human rights organizations have broad access to institutions and individuals. Labor, business, and professional organizations are generally free from governmental interference. Unions have the right to strike, and collective bargaining is prevalent.

The judicial system is headed by the Supreme Court and a court of appeals, with the right of appeal under certain circumstances to the Privy Council in London. Some progress has been reported in reducing both the length of court cases and the backlog of criminal appeals. Nevertheless, some murder suspects have been held for up to four years before being brought to trial.

Violent crime is a continuing concern and a focus of Prime Minister Perry Christie's government. Nongovernmental organizations have documented the occasional abuse of prisoners, arbitrary arrest, and lengthy pretrial detention. The Royal Bahamas Police Force has made progress in reducing corruption in the force, including introducing new procedures to limit unethical or illegal conduct. While the police have been recognized for their key role in regional efforts to stem the drug trade, coordination with the Royal Bahamas Defence Force (RBDF) has presented difficulties that reflect general ambivalence about the RBDF's role in law enforcement.

Although the Ingraham administration made important efforts to relieve prison overcrowding, there are persistent reports that it continues, and poor medical facilities are still the norm. Children continue to be housed with adults, and there have been reports of sexual abuse.

The Bahamas is an accessible transit area for illegal aliens seeking entrance to the United States. No laws specifically address trafficking in persons, but there are also no reports of such activity. The Bahamian government forcibly repatriates most asylum seekers, including Haitians and Cubans.

Discrimination against persons of Haitian descent persists, and between 30,000 and 40,000 Haitians reside illegally in the Bahamas. Strict citizenship requirements and a stringent work permit system leave Haitians with few rights. There is no legislation regulating the processing of asylum seekers, whose influx has created social tension because of the strain on government services.

Violence against women is a widespread problem, and child abuse and neglect remain serious issues of concern.

Bahrain

Population: 700,000
GNI/capita: $11,130
Life Expectancy: 74
Religious Groups: Shi'a Muslim (70 percent), Sunni
Muslim (30 percent)
Ethnic Groups: Bahraini (63 percent), Asian (19 percent),
other Arab (10 percent), Iranian (8 percent)
Capital: Manama

Political Rights: 5
Civil Liberties: 5
Status: Partly Free

Ten-Year Ratings Timeline (Political Rights, Civil Liberties, Status)

1995	1996	1997	1998	1999	2000	2001	2002	2003	2004
6,6NF	7,6NF	7,6NF	7,6NF	7,6NF	7,6NF	6,5NF	5,5PF	5,5PF	5,5PF

Overview:

After several years of political reform culminating in the restoration of the national parliament in 2002, Bahrain reversed course in 2004, taking steps that raised questions about its commitment to political rights and civil liberties. The government arrested numerous opposition activists critical of government policy and democracy advocates calling for more reform, closed a leading independent human rights organization, and cracked down on public protests.

The Al Khalifa family, which has ruled Bahrain for more than two centuries, comes from Bahrain's minority Sunni Muslim population in this mostly Shia Muslim country. Bahrain gained independence in 1971 after more than a hundred years as a British protectorate. The country's first constitution provided for a national assembly with both elected and appointed members, but the king dissolved the assembly in 1975 because it attempted to end Al Khalifa rule; the Al Khalifa family ruled without the national assembly until 2002.

In 1993, the king established a consultative council of appointed notables, although this advisory body had no legislative power and did not lead to any major policy shifts. In 1994, Bahrain experienced protests sparked by arrests of prominent individuals who had petitioned for the reestablishment of democratic institutions such as the national assembly. The unrest left more than 40 people dead, thousands arrested, and hundreds either imprisoned or exiled.

Shaikh Hamad bin Isa Al Khalifa's March 1999 accession to the throne following his father's death marked a turning point in Bahrain. Hamad released political prisoners, permitted the return of exiles, and eliminated emergency laws and courts. He also introduced the National Charter, which set a goal of creating a constitutional monarchy with an elected parliament, separation of powers with an independent judicial branch, and rights guaranteeing women's political participation.

In February 2001, voters overwhelmingly approved the National Charter. However, the process of political reform ultimately disappointed many Bahrainis by the time of the holding of local elections in May 2002 and parliamentary elections in October 2002. Leading Shia groups and leftists boycotted these elections, protesting restrictions on political campaigning and electoral gerrymandering aimed at diminishing the power of the Shia majority. Sunni Muslim groups ended up winning most of the seats in the new National Assembly. Despite the boycott, opposition groups fared well at the polls, and the new cabinet included opposition figures.

Throughout 2004 the Bahraini government took steps to stifle rising criticisms of its resistance to further political reforms from independent and opposition figures. During a conference held in February, four leading opposition groups renewed demands for a new constitution, contending that the 2002 constitution was illegitimately issued by a decree from Shaikh Hamad bin Isa Al Khalifa without meaningful public input. The government, displeased with the conference, denied entry to three Kuwaiti members of parliament and to democracy activists from Great Britain, France, Kuwait, and Jordan. In April and May, the government arrested 20 democratic activists for allegedly organizing an "illegal" petition for constitutional changes that would give greater political authority to Bahrain's parliament.

Political reform took a backseat to economic reform and rising security concerns during the year. Bahrain pushed forward on privatization in 2004 and signed a free trade agreement with the United States in September. Increasing violence and instability in Saudi Arabia led Bahrain to step up security on the causeway linking Bahrain to Saudi Arabia.

Political Rights and Civil Liberties:

Bahraini citizens do not have the ability to choose the leader with the most power in Bahrain, the king. Bahrain's 2002 constitution gives the king power over the executive, legislative and judicial authorities. He appoints cabinet ministers and members of the Consultative Council. The National Assembly consists of 40 popularly elected members of the Council of Deputies and 40 members of the Shura Council appointed by the king. The National Assembly may propose legislation, but the cabinet must draft the laws. A July 2002 royal decree forbids the National Assembly from deliberating on any action taken by the executive branch before December 2002—the date the new National Assembly was inaugurated.

The Council of Deputies has shown signs of assertiveness in checking the power of the government. In January, the Council of Deputies issued a report on an eight-month parliamentary probe into alleged financial and administrative irregularities at the General Organization for Social Insurance and the Pension Fund Commission, two leading pension funds. Parliamentary committees questioned three government ministers and eventually cleared them of any wrongdoing in May.

Formal political parties are illegal in Bahrain, but the government allows political societies or groupings to operate and organize activities in the country. The National Assembly's legislative and legal affairs committee rejected a proposal in 2004 to legalize political parties.

Although Bahrain has some anticorruption laws, enforcement is weak, and high-ranking officials suspected of corruption are rarely punished. Bahrain was ranked 34 out of 146 countries surveyed in Transparency International's 2004 Corruption Perceptions Index.

Freedom of expression is limited in Bahrain, which in 2004 received a low ranking of 143 out of 167 countries in press freedom by the media watchdog group Reporters Sans Frontieres. The government owns all broadcast media outlets. In August, the government announced plans to eliminate the Information Ministry and establish the Bahrain

Radio and Television Commission as a new regulatory commission for the media. There is a stronger degree of freedom in the print media; the country's three main newspapers are privately owned. Though Internet and e-mail access has generally been unrestricted, there are reports of government monitoring of e-mail communications.

Islam is the state religion. However, non-Muslim minorities are generally free to practice their religion. According to the law, all religious groups must obtain a permit from the Ministry of Justice and Islamic affairs to operate, although the government has not punished groups that have operated without this permit. Although Shiites constitute a majority of the citizenry, they are underrepresented in government and face discrimination in the workplace.

Bahrain has no formal laws or regulations that limit academic freedom, but teachers and professors tend to avoid politically sensitive topics and issues in the classroom and their research. The constitution provides for freedom of assembly, and the government generally allows demonstrations. In December 2003, political opposition leaders organized a mass demonstration to mark what they called the day of martyrs, to commemorate those who were killed by Bahraini security forces during the 1994 protests. In March, at the U.S. Embassy, hundreds of Bahrainis protested the Israeli assassination of Hamas founder Shaikh Ahmad Yasin. Protests in May against military actions in the Iraqi cities of Najaf and Karbala, American abuses of Iraqi prisoners, and Israeli mistreatment of Palestinians resulted in numerous clashes between police and protestors. However, in the face of recent criticisms of government policy, Prime Minister Shaikh Khalifa bin Salman Al Khalifa signaled new legal changes that would impose more regulations on rallies and public gatherings.

Bahrain has seen strong growth in the number of nongovernmental organizations (NGOs) working in charitable activities, human rights, and women's rights, but restrictions remain on these groups. In July, the Ministry of Labor and Social Affairs sent letters to more than 80 of Bahrain's estimated 360 registered NGOs threatening them with closure for technical violations of the 1989 Associations Law, including failing to have permanent headquarters and to convene annual meetings.

The government closed and dissolved the Bahrain Center for Human Rights (BCHR) in September, raising serious questions about its commitment to political reform and freedom for civil society. The government arrested 'Abd al-Hadi al-Khawaja, executive director of the BCHR, who criticized the prime minister and government's performance during a September conference on poverty and economic rights. Al-Khawaja was convicted of inciting hatred against the government and sentenced to jail for one year. However, in late November, Shaikh Hamad intervened to suspend the sentence.

Bahrainis have the right to establish independent labor unions without government permission. A royal decree giving workers the right to form labor unions also imposes limits, including a two-week notice to the company before a strike and a prohibition on strikes in vital sectors such as security, civil defense, transportation, hospitals, communications, and basic infrastructure. The law includes workers' rights to strike after approval by three-quarters of union members in a secret ballot. In January, Bahraini labor leaders announced the formation of the country's first general federation of labor unions, the second such body in the Gulf region.

The judiciary is not independent of the executive branch of government. The king appoints all judges, and courts have been subject to government pressure. The

Ministry of the Interior is responsible for public security within the country and oversees the police and internal security services, and members of the royal family hold all security-related offices. The constitution provides rule-of-law protections, and government authorities generally respect these protections.

Over the past five years, Bahrain has taken steps to integrate stateless persons, known as bidoon and mostly consisting of Shi'a of Persian origin, into the country, offering citizenship to several thousand. Nevertheless, bidoon and citizens who speak Farsi as their first language continue to face some social discrimination and special challenges finding employment.

Although women have the right to vote and participate in local and national elections, they are underrepresented politically. No woman has been elected to office in municipal or legislative elections. The king appointed six women to the Consultative Council. Women are generally not afforded equal protections under the law. In September, a group of women's rights activists announced plans to sue the government over the refusal of the Ministry of Labor and Social Affairs to grant them a license to form the Bahrain Women's Union, an independent women's organization.

⬇ Bangladesh

Population: 141,300,000
GNI/capita: $380
Life Expectancy: 60
Religious Groups: Muslim (83 percent), Hindu (16 percent), other (1 percent)
Ethnic Groups: Bengali (98 percent), other [including Bihari] (2 percent)
Capital: Dhaka

Political Rights: 4
Civil Liberties: 4
Status: Partly Free

Trend Arrow: Bangladesh received a downward trend arrow due to a further deterioration in the rule of law and an increase in political violence during the year.

Ten-Year Ratings Timeline (Political Rights, Civil Liberties, Status)

1995	1996	1997	1998	1999	2000	2001	2002	2003	2004
3,4PF	2,4PF	2,4PF	2,4PF	3,4PF	3,4PF	3,4PF	4,4PF	4,4PF	4,4PF

Overview: Bangladesh continued to be plagued by lawlessness, rampant corruption, and violent political polarization, all of which impede the efficacy of its democratic institutions. Although the opposition Awami League (AL) ended its parliamentary boycott in June, it remained reliant on national strikes to impede the effective functioning of the coalition government led by the Bangladesh Nationalist Party (BNP). For its part, the BNP continues to deploy army personnel to maintain law and order as part of an anticrime drive in which a number of human rights violations have taken place. Official harassment of journalists, human rights advocates, and leaders and perceived supporters of the political opposition persisted throughout the year. In addition, analysts are concerned that the increased strength and influence of Islamist groups pose a long-term threat to Bangladesh's traditionally moderate interpretation of Islam.

With the partition of British India in 1947, what is now Bangladesh became the eastern part of the newly formed state of Pakistan. Bangladesh won independence from Pakistan in December 1971 after a nine-month war during which Indian troops helped defeat West Pakistani forces stationed in Bangladesh. The 1975 assassination of Prime Minister Sheikh Mujibur Rahman by soldiers precipitated 15 years of military rule and continues to polarize Bangladeshi politics. The country's democratic transition began with the resignation in 1990 of the last military ruler, General H. M. Ershad, after weeks of pro-democracy demonstrations. Elections in 1991 brought the BNP to power under Khaleda Zia.

The political deadlock began in 1994, when Sheikh Hasina Wajed's center-left AL began boycotting parliament to protest alleged corruption in Zia's BNP government. The AL and the BNP differ relatively little on domestic policy. Many disputes reflect the personal animosity between Hasina, the daughter of independence leader Sheikh Mujibur Rahman, and Zia, the widow of a former military ruler allegedly complicit in Mujibur's assassination. The AL boycotted the February 1996 elections, which the BNP won, but then forced Zia's resignation in March and triumphed in elections held in June. The BNP marked its time in opposition by boycotting parliament and organizing periodic nationwide strikes.

In October 2001, the AL was voted out of office in elections marred by political violence and intimidation. A new four-party coalition, dominated by the BNP and including two hard-line Muslim parties, the Jamaat-e-Islami and the Islami Oikyo Jote, was sworn into power with a convincing majority of 214 of the 300 seats in parliament. The AL initially refused to accept the election results and since then has intermittently boycotted parliament. Reneging on a pledge she made during the election campaign, Hasina has also organized countrywide *hartals* (general strikes) in order to pressure the government to step down.

Faced with a continuing deterioration in law and order, the government deployed nearly 40,000 army personnel in an anticrime drive in October 2002. Although the policy was initially popular among Bangladeshis weary of rising crime rates and a general climate of impunity for criminals, both domestic and international groups criticized police and army excesses committed during operations in which thousands were arrested.

Despite these measures, lawlessness coupled with the growing threat of Islamist extremism continues to plague most of the country; a bomb planted at a shrine in Sylhet injured the British High Commissioner in May 2004, while further explosions targeted cinemas in the same town in August. Analysts have voiced concern that the reluctance of the government to crack down on radical Islamist groups poses a long-term threat to Bangladesh's stability as well as its tradition of tolerance.

A series of crippling AL-sponsored demonstrations and hartals held in February and March failed to dislodge the government from power, as have the party's ultimatums that the government step down. The AL returned to parliament in June, ending a 20-month periodic boycott. Meanwhile, frustration with the unwillingness of the two major parties to address lawlessness and corruption rose. In March, a national convention of politicians, journalists, lawyers, and civic leaders endorsed a 17-point charter calling for an end to "criminalized politics," violence, and corruption, and in May former president Badruddoza Chowdhury announced the formation of a new political party aimed at tackling corruption.

In August, a series of grenades exploded at an AL rally in Dhaka, leaving at least 18 people dead and several hundred injured, including several top party leaders. In the atmosphere of heightened political antagonism following the blasts, the government announced that an independent commission would investigate the attacks, as well as increasing security measures, conducting mass arrests, and enlisting the armed forces to help fight terrorism. The AL's predictable response was to call for a fresh series of strikes and street agitation, but the party has also attempted to forge alliances with smaller left-leaning parties in order to strengthen its position versus the BNP.

Political Rights and Civil Liberties: Bangladeshis can change their government through elections. A referendum held in 1991 transformed the powerful presidency into a largely ceremonial head-of-state position in a parliamentary system. Elections to the 300-member unicameral parliament are held in single-member districts under a simple-plurality rule. The 1996 vote was the first under a constitutional amendment requiring a caretaker government to conduct elections. The most recent national elections, held in October 2001, were described as generally free and fair despite concerns over polling irregularities, intimidation, and violence. More than 140 people were killed throughout the campaign period in what was Bangladesh's most violent election to date. In July, European Union (EU) representatives as well as local nongovernmental organizations (NGOs) raised concerns about the validity of a by-election held in the Dhaka-10 constituency that was marred by fraud and intimidation.

Both major parties have undermined the legislative process through lengthy parliamentary boycotts while in opposition. In recent years, political violence during demonstrations and general strikes has killed hundreds of people in major cities and injured thousands, and police often use excessive force against opposition protesters. Party leaders are also targeted, and several died during the year after being attacked. Odhikar, a local NGO, claimed that during the first half of 2004, there were 287 people killed in political violence. Student wings of political parties continue to be embroiled in violent campus conflicts.

Analysts blame endemic corruption, a weak rule of law, limited bureaucratic transparency, and political polarization for undermining government accountability. In October, Transparency International again listed Bangladesh at the bottom of a 146-country list on its 2004 Corruption Perceptions Index and noted that corruption was perceived to be "acute." An Anti-Corruption Commission, which is authorized to conduct investigations and try corruption cases in special courts, was launched in November. However, critics remain concerned that the new body will not be truly independent either politically or financially.

Media continued to face a number of pressures in 2004, the most striking of which was the high level of violence directed against members of the press and the impunity enjoyed by those who attack them. Journalists are regularly harassed and violently attacked by organized-crime groups, political parties and their supporters, government authorities, the police, and extremist groups. In August, *Prothom Alo,* Bangladesh's largest Bengali-language daily, was targeted after it published a series of investigative reports on militant Islamist activities in the southeastern region of Chittagong. Five journalists were killed during the year, and numerous others received death threats. As a result, many journalists practice self-censorship when reporting on topics such as corruption, criminal activity, electoral violence, the rise of Islamic fundamentalism, or human rights abuses. Although the print media are diverse, the state owns most broadcast media, whose coverage favors the ruling party. Political considerations influence the distribution of government advertising revenue and subsidized newsprint, on which most publications are dependent. Access to the Internet is generally unrestricted.

Islam is the official religion. Hindus, Christians, and other minorities have the right to worship freely but face societal discrimination and remain under-represented in government employment. Violence against the Hindu minority flared up after the 2001 elections, when BNP supporters attacked Hindus because of their perceived support for the rival AL party. Atrocities, including murder, rape, destruction of property, and kidnapping, forced hundreds of Hindus from their homes, some across the border into India. Hindus continue to face harassment and violence at the hands of orthodox Islamist political parties and their supporters. During the year, the 100,000-strong Ahmadiya Muslim sect also faced increased attacks from Islamist groups; in addition, in January 2004, the government announced a ban on the publication and distribution of the sect's publications.

While authorities largely respect academic freedom, research on sensitive political and religious topics is forbidden, according to the U.S. State Department's 2003 human rights report. Political polarization at many public universities, which occasionally erupts into protests and clashes between students and security forces, inhibits the ability of some students to receive an education. In March, leading author and lecturer Humayun Azad was stabbed by suspected Islamist extremists on the Dhaka University campus.

The constitution provides for freedom of assembly, but the government frequently limits this right in practice. Demonstrators are occasionally killed or injured during clashes with police. Numerous NGOs operate in Bangladesh and fulfill a variety of basic needs in fields such as education, health care, and microcredit programs. However, those that are perceived to have links to the opposition or that criticize the government, particularly on human rights issues, are subject to intense official scrutiny. Proshika, a poverty-reduction NGO, was subjected to politically motivated harassment during the year; in May, the national anticorruption agency accused the group of financial irregularities, and in June, the government brought sedition charges against the president and six other members of the organization.

Union formation is hampered by a 30 percent employee approval requirement and restrictions on organizing by unregistered unions. Employers can legally fire or transfer workers suspected of union activities. The law prohibits many civil servants from joining unions; these workers can form associations but are prohibited from bargaining collectively. Child labor is widespread.

The Supreme Court displays a "significant degree of independence" and often rules against the executive, according to the U.S. State Department. However, lower-level courts remain subject to executive influence and are rife with corruption. The government continues to delay implementing the separation of the judiciary from the executive as ordered by a 1999 Supreme Court directive. The judicial system is severely backlogged, and pretrial detention is lengthy. Many defendants lack counsel, and poor people have limited recourse through the courts. Prison conditions are extremely poor, and severe overcrowding is common. According to the New Delhi–based Asian Centre for Human Rights (ACHR), hundreds of juveniles are illegally detained in prisons in contravention of the 1974 Children's Act. Prisoners are routinely subjected to physical abuse and demands for bribes from corrupt law enforcement officials. In a 2003 report, Amnesty International expressed concern that police frequently detain people without an arrest warrant and that detainees are routinely subjected to torture and other forms of abuse. The majority of police abuses go unpunished, which contributes to a climate of impunity.

As part of Operation Clean Heart, a government-initiated anticrime drive of questionable constitutional legality that began in October 2002, the army detained nearly 11,000 people, over 40 of whom died while in police custody. Legislation passed in February 2003 granted members of the security forces immunity from prosecution in civilian courts for the abuses committed during the operation. Further efforts were made to tackle criminal activity with the formation and deployment of the Rapid Action Battalion (RAB), composed of approximately 4,500 members of the armed forces and police, in March 2004. However, an ACHR briefing issued in November alleged that 43 people had been extrajudicially executed by the RAB from June to October.

Many of these forms of abuse are facilitated by the existence of legislation such as the 1974 Special Powers Act, which permits arbitrary detention without charge, and Section 54 of the Criminal Procedure Code, which allows individuals to be detained without a warrant. Authorities regularly detain thousands of political opponents and ordinary citizens, and use serial detentions to prevent the release of political activists. Amnesty International in 2002 highlighted a continuing pattern of politically motivated detentions, noting that senior opposition politicians, academics, journalists, and human rights activists critical of government policies were particularly at risk of prolonged detention and ill treatment in custody. According to a 2002 UN Development Program report, almost 90 percent of "preventative detention" cases that reach the courts are judged to be unlawful. In April 2004, the high court directed the government to amend certain sections of the code within six months, but this directive had not been acted upon by November 30.

Tribal minorities have little control over land issues affecting them, and Bengali-language settlers continue to illegally encroach on tribal lands in the Chittagong Hill Tracts (CHT) with the reported connivance of government officials and the army. A 1997 accord ended a 24-year insurgency in the CHT that had sought autonomy for indigenous tribes and had resulted in the deaths of 8,500 soldiers, rebels, and civilians. However, in December 2003, demonstrators blocked roads and held general strikes in order to protest the continued presence of army camps and the government's perceived failure to implement the terms of the 1997 accord. Tribal inhabitants of the area remain subject to attacks from Bengali settlers, including killings, rapes, and the destruction of houses and other property, according to a March report issued by Amnesty International, as well as to human rights violations at the hands of security forces; and impunity for past abuses continues.

Roughly 260,000 Rohingyas fleeing forced labor, discrimination, and other abuses in Burma entered Bangladesh in the early 1990s; some 22,000 Rohingya refugees and 100,000 other Rohingyas not formally documented as refugees remain in the country. Bangladesh also hosts some 300,000 Urdu-speaking Biharis who were rendered stateless at independence in 1971, many of whom seek repatriation to Pakistan. In May 2003, a landmark high court ruling gave citizenship and voting rights to 10 Bihari refugees.

Rape, dowry-related assaults, acid throwing, and other violence against women occur frequently. A law requiring rape victims to file police reports and obtain medical certificates within 24 hours of the crime in order to press charges prevents most rape cases from reaching the courts. Police also accept bribes not to register rape cases and rarely enforce existing laws protecting women. The Acid Survivors Foundation, a local NGO, recorded 410 acid attacks in 2003, with the majority being carried out against women. While prosecution for acid-related crimes remains inadequate, under the stringent Acid Crime Prevention Act passed in 2002, one attacker was sentenced to death early in 2003. In rural areas religious leaders occasionally issue fatwas (religious edicts) that impose floggings and other punishments on women accused of violating strict moral codes. Women also face some discrimination in health care, education, and employment, and are underrepresented in politics and government. However, in May, parliament amended the constitution to provide for 45 reserved seats in parliament for women.

Barbados

Population: 300,000   **Political Rights:** 1
GNI/capita: $15,700   **Civil Liberties:** 1
Life Expectancy: 72   **Status:** Free
Religious Groups: Protestant (67 percent), Roman
Catholic (4 percent), other (29 percent)
Ethnic Groups: Black (90 percent), white (4 percent),
other (6 percent)
Capital: Bridgetown

Ten-Year Ratings Timeline (Political Rights, Civil Liberties, Status)

1995	1996	1997	1998	1999	2000	2001	2002	2003	2004
1,1F	1,1F	1,1F	1,1F	1,1F	1,1F	1,1F	1,1F	1,1F	1,1F

Overview:

In 2004, Barbados faced conflicts with Trinidad and Tobago over maritime borders and fishing rights, and this small island country continued to suffer from crime linked to narcotics trafficking throughout the Caribbean region.

Barbados gained its independence in 1966 and is a member of the British Commonwealth. By 1994, after a recession, the economy appeared to be improving, but unemployment still stood at nearly 25 percent. Prime Minister Erskine Sandiford's popularity suffered, and he was increasingly criticized for his authoritarian style of government. He lost a no-confidence vote in parliament when four backbenchers from the opposition Democratic Labor Party (DLP) and one independent legislator who had quit the DLP joined nine Barbados Labor Party (BLP) legislators. David Thompson, the young finance minister, replaced Sandiford.

In the 1994 elections, the BLP won 19 seats; the DLP won 8 seats; and the New

Democratic Party (NDP), a splinter of the DLP established in 1989, gained 1 seat. Prime Minister Owen Seymour Arthur, an economist elected in 1993 to head the BLP, promised to build "a modern, technologically dynamic economy," create jobs, and restore investor confidence. The BLP retained power in 1999 by winning 26 parliamentary seats, leaving Arthur firmly in control of the country.

In the May 23, 2003, elections, the BLP won 23 seats in the House of Assembly, ratifying Arthur's administration. Meanwhile, the DLP was strengthened under the uncontested leadership of Clyde Mascoll. In June, the Public Accounts Committee's independent oversight of government accounts was enhanced, giving the DLP the ability to better monitor official expenditures.

In 2004, Barbados and Trinidad and Tobago became embroiled in a bitter struggle over their maritime boundary and associated fishing rights. Barbados has decided to submit the issue to binding arbitration by the United Nations. The dispute arose out of the 1990 Maritime Delimitation Treaty that Trinidad and Tobago signed with Venezuela.

Barbados has not escaped the increase in crime experienced by much of the Caribbean region. Joint patrols of the Royal Barbados Police Force and the all-volunteer Barbados Defence Force have been initiated to patrol the island as violent crimes, many linked to narcotics trafficking, have been on the rise. Narcotics seizures have increased and there is evidence that drug crime is better organized, primarily in the form of patronage, than in the past.

The Arthur government has made efforts to reduce dependence on tourism—a sector which was badly hurt after the September 2001 terrorist attacks in the United States—and sugar production through diversification into the financial and computer services industries.

Political Rights and Civil Liberties: Citizens of Barbados can change their government democratically. The 30-member House of Assembly is elected for a five-year term; the governor-general appoints the 21 members of the Senate: 12 on the advice of the prime minister, 2 on the advice of the leader of the opposition, and the remaining 7 at the discretion of the governor-general. The prime minister is the leader of the political party with a majority in the House. Power has alternated between two centrist parties—the DLP and the BLP. The May 2003 parliamentary elections were free and fair.

Political parties are free to organize. In addition to the parties holding parliamentary seats, there are other political organizations, including the small, left wing Workers' Party of Barbados.

Barbados was ranked 21 out of 146 countries surveyed in the 2004 Transparency International Corruption Perceptions Index.

Freedom of expression is fully respected. Public opinion expressed through the news media, which are free of censorship and government control, has a powerful influence on policy. Newspapers are privately owned, and there are two major dailies. Four private and two government radio stations operate. The single television station, operated by the government-owned Caribbean Broadcasting Corporation, presents a wide range of political viewpoints. There is free access to the Internet.

The constitution guarantees freedom of religion. Academic freedom is fully respected.

The right to organize civic organizations and labor unions is respected. There are two major labor unions and various smaller ones are active.

The judicial system is independent, and the Supreme Court includes a high court and a court of appeals. Lower-court officials are appointed on the advice of the Judicial and Legal Service Commission. The prison system is overcrowded and outdated, with more than 800 inmates held in a building built for 350. There are separate facilities for female prisoners and children. The government allows private groups to visit prisons. Although the authorities have made significant efforts to discharge prison personnel alleged to have beaten inmates, their prosecution has not made significant progress.

In October 2002, Attorney-General Mia Mottley announced that a National Commission on Law and Order would be established to reduce lawlessness. The Commission published a Plan on Justice, Peace and Security in June 2004 that included sixty-eight recommendations on constitutional support for social institutions, governance and civil society, cultural values, law enforcement, and criminal courts, among others. Mottley strongly voiced reservations about the Inter-American Convention against Corruption, claiming that it did not sufficiently regulate private sector corruption; Barbados signed the convention in April 2001, but has not yet ratified, accepted or acceded to it.

The high crime rate, fueled by an increase in drug abuse and narcotics trafficking, has given rise to human rights concerns. The number of murders has remained constant, and a constitutional change allows convicts to be hanged as soon as possible after their appeals are exhausted. There are occasional reports and complaints of excessive force used by the Royal Barbados Police Force to extract confessions, along with reports that police do not always seek warrants before searching homes. The Caribbean Human Rights Network was disbanded because of a lack of funds.

Barbados has refused to agree to the immunity of U.S. military personnel from proceedings in the International Criminal Court. The United States responded by suspending military education programs and military equipment sales. The impasse has dampened efforts to control drug trafficking in the region. Barbados is likely to continue to remain a strong supporter of Trinidad and Tobago, whose former president helped to set up the court.

Women make up roughly half of the workforce. A domestic violence law was passed in 1992 to give police and judges greater power to protect women. Violence against and abuse of women and children continue to be major social problems.

Belarus

Population: 9,800,000
GNI/capita: $1,360
Life Expectancy: 69
Political Rights: 7*
Civil Liberties: 6
Status: Not Free
Religious Groups: Eastern Orthodox (80 percent), other (20 percent)
Ethnic Groups: Byelorussian (81.2 percent), Russian (11.4 percent), Polish, Ukrainian and other (7.4 percent)
Capital: Minsk
Ratings Change: Belarus's political rights rating declined from 6 to 7 due to massive falsifications in the country's October parliamentary election and referendum on the presidency and an unrelenting campaign against independent media, political parties, and civic groups.

Ten-Year Ratings Timeline (Political Rights, Civil Liberties, Status)

1995	1996	1997	1998	1999	2000	2001	2002	2003	2004
5,5PF	6,6NF	6,6NF	6,6NF	6,6NF	6,6NF	6,6NF	6,6NF	6,6NF	7,6NF

Overview:

Belarus saw the further consolidation of authoritarian rule under the personal dictatorship of President Alyaksandr Lukashenka in 2004. The October legislative elections and a parallel national referendum that lifted the constitution's two-term restriction on the presidency saw voter irregularities, tight state control of the mass media in favor of the government candidates and the government's referendum position, and intense pressure on opposition and civic activists. The year also witnessed a widespread, systematic campaign of state-directed legal pressures on newspapers, punishments meted out to opposition civic leaders and demonstrators, the disbanding of human rights and civic organizations, and efforts at total state control over independent schools.

Belarus declared independence in 1991, ending centuries of foreign control by Lithuania, Poland, Russia, and, ultimately, the Soviet Union. Stanislau Shushkevich, a reform-minded leader, served as head of state from 1991 to 1994. That year, voters made Lukashenka, a member of parliament with close links to the country's security services, the first post-Soviet president. Lukashenka has pursued efforts at reunification with Russia and subordinated the government, legislature, and courts to his political whims while denying citizens basic rights and liberties.

In a 1996 referendum, Belarusian citizens backed constitutional amendments that extended Lukashenka's term through 2001, broadened presidential powers, and created a new bicameral parliament. When the president ignored a court ruling that the referendum was nonbinding, Prime Minister Mikhail Chyhir resigned in protest.

In October 2000, Belarus held deeply flawed elections to the Chamber of Representatives, parliament's lower house. State media coverage of the campaign was limited and biased, and approximately half of all opposition candidates were denied registration. Nongovernmental organizations (NGOs) reported irregularities such as ballot-box stuffing and tampering with voter registration lists. Seven opposition parties boycotted the elections when the government failed to ensure a fair campaign and to give parliament more substantial duties. Some opposition candidates participated in the election, but only three were elected.

Lukashenka won a controversial reelection in September 2001 amid accusations from former security service officials that the president was directing a government-sponsored death squad aimed at silencing his opponents. Formally, citizens had three presidential candidates from whom to choose. However, the outcome was predetermined and Western observers judged the election to be neither free nor fair. During the campaign, the government and its supporters harassed would-be candidates and independent media outlets, and state television was used as an instrument for propaganda on behalf of Lukashenka. On election day, Lukashenka declared himself the victor with 78 percent of the vote over opposition candidate Vladimir Goncharik (12 percent). However, independent nongovernmental exit polls showed that Lukashenka had received 47 percent of the vote and Goncharik 41 percent—an outcome that by law should have forced a second round. While opposition parties and civil society were active in the election process, by 2002, Lukashenka had launched a campaign of political retribution against those who opposed him during the presidential campaign.

In 2004, the Lukashenka regime intensified its policy of systematic legal persecution and physical intimidation of its democratic opponents. Courts banned or liquidated NGOs and imposed prohibitive fines against independent media, and the Information Ministry ordered the suspensions of independent newspapers critical of the Lukashenka government. Other government actions included harassment of independent civic activists and arrests of scores of peaceful protestors. On April 26, the former minister of foreign economic affairs and member of parliament Mikhail Marynich was arrested and later sentenced to five years' imprisonment on trumped-up charges arising from his opposition activities. On June 9, a Minsk court sentenced a pregnant opposition activist, Aksana Novikava, to two and a half years of deprivation of freedom for "defamation of the President of the Republic of Belarus" arising from her distribution of leaflets. In October, two opposition leaders, Valery Levaneuski and Alyaksandr Vasilyew, were sentenced to two years in a work colony on charges of "public slander" against Lukashenka.

Parliamentary elections and a parallel referendum on the presidency were held in October 2004. The Central Election Commission claimed 89.73 percent of voters took part in the plebiscite and some 86 percent of them voted in favor of the government's proposal that would allow President Alyaksandr Lukashenka to run for a third term in 2006. According to the announced election results, not a single candidate fielded by opposition parties entered the parliament.

An OSCE monitoring effort that deployed 270 international observers from 38 countries in Belarus declared on October 17 that the parliamentary elections fell "significantly short" of Belarus's OSCE commitments. "We were concerned by police raids in campaign offices, the detention of a candidate, campaign workers and domestic observers, as well as numerous reports of coercion on certain groups, particularly students, to vote," OSCE Parliamentary Assembly vice president Tone Tinsgaard observed. An NGO called Partnership, which fielded 3,500 monitors for the parliamentary elections and presidential referendum, declared the election marred by massive falsification and widespread violations of the electoral law. Despite efforts by NGOs, the vote count at virtually all polling stations in the country was conducted in the absence of independent monitors. An exit poll conducted by the Gallup Organization/Baltic Surveys that collected data during the weeklong voting process found that just 48.4 percent of all eligible voters in the country said yes to the referendum as compared with the government results that showed more than 77 percent of eligible voters supporting the referendum question. Thus, according to independent poll data, the referendum actually failed to amend the Belarusian constitution or give Lukashenka the right to run for reelection, as claimed by Belarus authorities.

According to the European Bank for Reconstruction and Development, the country's private sector share of gross national income is the lowest of all the post-Communist countries. World Bank data also show that more than a quarter of the population lives below the national poverty line.

Political Rights and Civil Liberties: Despite a constitutional guarantee of universal, equal, and direct suffrage, citizens of Belarus cannot change their government democratically. The 2001 presidential vote, in which Lukashenka was declared to have been reelected by a wide majority, was neither free nor fair. Independent exit polls found the results were significantly altered, and domestic supporters of opposition candidate Vladimir Goncharik accused the government of massively falsifying the results. The OSCE report on the election indicated it was conducted in a "manner that actively sought to exclude candidates representing a diversity of interests." The October 2004 parliamentary elections and a parallel referendum on the presidency were marred by serious and widespread irregularities.

Belarus was ranked 74 out of 146 countries surveyed in the 2004 Transparency International Corruption Perceptions Index.

The Lukashenka regime systematically curtails press freedom. State media are subordinated to the president, and harassment and censorship of independent media are routine. Libel is both a civil and a criminal offense. The State Press Committee can issue warnings to publishers for unauthorized activities such as changing a publication's title or distributing copies abroad. It also can arbitrarily shut down publications without a court order. The country's Information Ministry has promulgated regulations that required the heads of all FM radio stations to provide a complete daily printout of news bulletins and daily playlists to ensure monitoring of content. Russian television is occasionally subject to suspensions, and some Russian newscasts that are rebroadcast in Belarus are censored. Belarusian national television is completely under the control and influence of the state and does not provide coverage of alternative and opposition views.

Harassment and legal attacks against independent newspapers and broadcast media were widespread in 2004. Journalists, including the chief editor of *Narodnaya Volya,* were regularly fined for their reporting. On February 5, the Information Ministry suspended the independent newspaper *Zgoda* for one month. On June 3, the ministry suspended the newspaper *Rabochaya Solidarnasts* for three months on the technicality that it failed to report its new address. In October, the journalist Veronika Cherkasova of the opposition newspaper *Solidarnasts* was murdered in Minsk in what opposition groups regard as a possible political killing.

Internet sites within the country are under the control of the government's State Center on Information Security, which is part of the Security Council of Belarus. Independent information is posted by some opposition groups and journalists in Belarus and abroad. The government at times censors and blocks independent Web sites, particularly during preelection periods. In February, an opposition Web site— www.Charter97.org—accused state authorities of a wave of kicker attacks that flooded the site with requests and prevented normal access. The impact of independent Internet sites is limited. According to the International Telecommunications Union, fewer than 10 percent of the population has some access to the Internet, while other estimates suggest that only 2 percent of the population enjoy regular Internet access.

Despite constitutional guarantees that "all religions and faiths shall be equal before the law," government decrees and registration requirements have increasingly restricted the life and work of religious groups. Amendments in 2002 to the Law on Religions provide for government censorship of religious publications and prevent foreign citizens from leading religious groups. The amendments also place strict limitations on religious groups that have been active in Belarus for fewer than 20 years. The government pressures and intimidates members of the independent Autocephalous Orthodox Christian Church, harasses Hindus for public meditation, and represses Baptists for singing hymns in public. In 2004, the Union of Evangelical Christian Faiths reported a growing number of actions by government authorities that prevented students from attending evangelical religious services. In February 2004, authorities shut down the International Institute for Humanities, the only higher education institution in the country that offered Jewish studies.

Academic freedoms are subject to intense state ideological pressures. In 2003, the entire staff of the Modern Studies Institute's journalism faculty, some of them active in an independent journalists' association, were dismissed after criticism leveled at them by a presidential commission and the Ministry of Education. The leader of the country's most highly regarded secondary school, the National State Humanities Lyceum, was dismissed, and a Lukashenka loyalist was appointed in his place; the move prompted a walkout by students and faculty. In 2004, state pressure to implement curriculum reform that reduced academic freedom resulted in an end to Jewish studies in state institutions. The year also saw the establishment of a new higher education course based on Lukashenka "ideas." Titled "Foundations of Ideology," it is to be mandatory for students in all of Belarus' colleges and universities. Textbooks are being rewritten under political pressure from the authorities.

Freedom of association is severely restricted. In 2004, independent civic groups were subject to surveillance by the country's security service, the KGB. Leaders of the Strike Committee of Entrepreneurs were sentenced to long terms of imprisonment in 2004. Among the organizations whose activists and officials were harassed and impeded were the youth group Zubr, the Batskaushchyna Cultural and Educational Foundation, the Leu Sapaha Foundation, the Belarusian Popular Front, and the Viasna Human Rights Center. The Belarus Helsinki Committee, a human rights group, was ordered to pay $176,000 in back taxes in a step regarded as an effort to shut down and cripple the monitoring organization, although a court later struck down the decision. Independent trade unions are subject to harassment and their leaders are frequently arrested and prosecuted for peaceful protests and dismissed from employment. In November, a 200-page report, drawn up by an International Labor Organization commission, accused Belarus' authorities of interference in the activities of trade unions.

The Lukashenka government limits freedom of assembly by groups independent of and critical of his regime. Protests and rallies require authorization from local authorities, who can arbitrarily withhold or revoke permission. When public demonstrations do occur, police typically break them up and arrest participants.

Although the country's constitution calls for judicial independence, courts are subject to heavy government influence. During the year, numerous independent civic leaders, opposition political activists, independent journalists, and other persons who oppose government policies experienced arbitrary persecution, arrest, and imprisonment. The right to a fair trial is often not respected in cases with political overtones. Human rights groups continue to document instances of beatings, torture, and inadequate protection during detention in cases involving leaders of the democratic opposition.

An internal passport system, required for domestic travel and securing permanent housing, controls freedom of movement and choice of residence. Wiretapping by state security agencies limits the right to privacy. The country's command economy severely limits economic freedom.

Women are not specifically targeted for discrimination, but there are significant discrepancies in incomes between men and women, and women are poorly represented in leading government positions. As a result of extreme poverty, many women have become victims of the international sex-trafficking trade.

Belgium

Population: 10,400,000　**Political Rights:** 1
GNI/capita: $22,940　**Civil Liberties:** 1
Life Expectancy: 79　**Status:** Free
Religious Groups: Roman Catholic (75 percent),
other [including Protestants] (25 percent)
Ethnic Groups: Fleming (58 percent), Walloon (31 percent),
other (11 percent)
Capital: Brussels

Ten-Year Ratings Timeline (Political Rights, Civil Liberties, Status)

1995	1996	1997	1998	1999	2000	2001	2002	2003	2004
1,1F	1,2F	1,2F	1,2F	1,2F	1,2F	1,2F	1,1F	1,1F	1,1F

Overview:　The country's highest court ruled in November that the far-right Vlaams Blok party, whose platform is based on Flemish independence and opposing immigration, was guilty of violating anti-racism laws. In June, the party garnered considerable support during local and European Parliament elections. A number of concerns were raised over the year about human rights abuses in the country, especially the ill-treatment of criminal suspects in police custody.

Modern Belgium dates from 1830, when the territory broke away from the Netherlands and formed a constitutional monarchy. Today the monarchy is largely ceremonial. Belgium was one of the founding members of the European Economic Community and still hosts the central administration of the European Union (EU) in Brussels.

Ethnic and linguistic conflicts broke out between the different communities in the country during the 1960s, prompting a number of constitutional amendments in 1970, 1971, and 1993 that devolved considerable central government power to the three regions in the federation: French-speaking Wallonia in the South, Flemish-speaking Flanders in the North, and Brussels, the capital, where French and Flemish share the same status. The small German minority in Wallonia, which consists of around 70,000 persons, has also been accorded cultural autonomy. Another 1993 amendment granted the three regional assemblies primary responsibility in a number of important policy areas, including housing, education, and the environment, while keeping issues like foreign policy, defense, justice, and monetary policy in the hands of the central state. In 2002, Belgium became the second country in the world after the Netherlands to partially legalize euthanasia.

During parliamentary elections in May 2003, the two main political parties—the Liberals and the Socialists—both gained at the expense of the Greens, which dropped from 20 to 4 seats in the lower house and were forced out of the ruling coalition. The Socialists led with 27 percent of the vote compared with 26 percent for the Liberals. Altogether, the coalition holds 97 of the 150 seats in the lower house.

In mid-June 2004, the Vlaams Blok gained a quarter of the vote during regional and European elections in Flanders, affirming its continuing support in the region. In addition to maintaining its anti-immigrant and law-and-order stance, the party also argues that the wealthier Flanders is bolstering the burden of the less-well-off French-speaking Wallonia in the South. The highest court in the country ruled that the Vlaams Blok had breached anti-racism legislation. The ruling, which prevents the party from accessing state funding and bans it from public media, forced it to re-form under a new name and platform.

The year was also marked by an increase in racial tensions. An Antwerp senator went into hiding after she had received death threats for her comments about Muslims. The senator, who is of Moroccan descent, was targeted after suggesting that prominent Muslims in the country erred in not condemning the murder of the controversial Dutch filmmaker Theo Van Gogh, who was killed in the Netherlands by an alleged Islamic extremist in November.

According to the Economist Intelligence Unit, the country's strong opposition to the U.S.-U.K.–led war in Iraq is the primary reason why Prime Minister Guy Verhofstadt failed to win in his bid to be the next president of the European Commission. His candidacy was strongly opposed by Britain, Italy, and other supporters of the war.

In a well-publicized case, Marc Dutroux, the convicted pedophile and child killer, was sentenced to life in prison in June for kidnapping, raping, and killing young girls in the mid-1990s.

Political Rights and Civil Liberties: Belgians can change their government democratically. In February, parliament granted non-EU immigrants who have been living in the country for at least five years the right to vote in local elections. More than 91 percent of all registered voters turned out at the polls during the last elections in 2003. Voting, however, is compulsory for those eligible. The party system is highly fragmented, with the two leading parties each gaining little more than 20 percent of the vote. In addition, political parties are generally organized along ethno-regional lines, with separate organizations in Flanders and Wallonia, a factor that makes for difficult coalitions.

Belgium was ranked 17 out of 146 countries surveyed in the 2004 Transparency International Corruption Perceptions Index.

Freedom of speech and the press is guaranteed by the constitution and generally respected by the government. The parliament adopted a draft law in March that guarantees the protection of journalistic sources, except when issues dealing with state security, the royal family, or spying are involved. In addition, newspapers have gone through increasing concentration in ownership since the 1960s as corporations have steadily been buying up papers. As a result, today a handful of corporations run most of the country's newspapers. The government does not limit access to the Internet.

Freedom of religion is protected in Belgium, where the state grants subsidies to Christian, Jewish, and Muslim institutions. About half of the population identifies itself with the Roman Catholic religion. A number of minority religions have complained of discrimination by the government, which has been criticized for its characterization of some non-Catholic religious groups as "sects." The government does not restrict academic freedom.

Freedom of association is guaranteed by law, except for membership in groups that practice discrimination "overtly and repeatedly." Freedom of assembly is also respected. A gentleman's agreement between workers and employers was reached in 2002 that bolstered the right to strike. Up to that point, employers were able to use the courts to ban strikes. About 63 percent of the Belgian work force is unionized. Employers found guilty of firing workers because of union activities are required to reinstate the worker or pay an indemnity. According to the International Commission for Free Trade Unions, the fines are probably too low to act as a deterrent, as Belgian employers prefer to pay the fines rather than reinstate dismissed employees active in union affairs.

The judiciary is independent in Belgium, and the rule of law generally prevails in civil and criminal matters. The United Nations Human Rights Committee issued a report in July that expressed concerns about a number of human rights abuses, including acts of abuse and racial discrimination committed by the police forces in the country. The report also expressed concerns about the treatment of rejected asylum seekers and illegal immigrants awaiting deportation who, after being released from detention centers for aliens, were often placed in unsanitary conditions in the transit zone of Brussels national airport, sometimes for several months at a time.

There are specific anti-racism laws in the country that prohibit and penalize the incitement of discrimination, hate, or violence based on race, ethnicity, or nationality.

Equality of opportunity for foreigners is undermined by a relatively high degree of racial and ethnic intolerance in society. Despite recent court rulings against it, the xenophobic Vlaams Blok party continues to maintain considerable support in Flanders, the region where it is based.

The country passed a law in 1994 that stipulates that two-thirds of each party's candidates must be of a different sex. Women won more than 35 percent of the seats in the lower house of parliament during elections in 2003, a 10 percent increase since prior elections in 1999. The government actively promotes equality for women. In 2003, the government created the Institute for the Equality of Men and Women. The Institute, which was formerly the Ministry of Labor's Division of Equal Opportunity, is empowered to initiate sex-discrimination lawsuits.

Belize

Population: 300,000   **Political Rights:** 1
GNI/capita: $2,960   **Civil Liberties:** 2
Life Expectancy: 70   **Status:** Free
Religious Groups: Roman Catholic (49.6 percent),
Protestant (27 percent), other (23.4 percent)
Ethnic Groups: Mestizo (48.7 percent), Creole (24.9 percent),
Maya (10.6 percent), Garifuna (6.1 percent), other (9.7 percent)
Capital: Belmopan

Ten-Year Ratings Timeline (Political Rights, Civil Liberties, Status)

1995	1996	1997	1998	1999	2000	2001	2002	2003	2004
1,1F	1,1F	1,1F	1,1F	1,1F	1,1F	1,2F	1,2F	1,2F	1,2F

Overview: In 2004, Belize continued to become more active with regional and international political and economic initiatives seeking to better integrate the country into the global economy, while still trying to tackle violent crime, corruption, and drug trafficking problems.

Belize achieved independence in 1981 and is a member of the British Commonwealth. The government has changed hands three times, alternating between the center-right United Democratic Party (UDP) and the center-left People's United Party (PUP). In 1993, the UDP and the National Alliance for Belizean Rights (NABR) formed a coalition, winning 16 of the 29 seats in the House of Representatives.

The August 1998 parliamentary elections, in which the PUP won 26 of 29 seats, proved to be a referendum on Prime Minister Manuel Esquivel's largely unfulfilled pledge that his UDP would create jobs. Musa, the new prime minister and former attorney general, promised adherence to international treaties on indigenous and women's rights. However, his government later blocked efforts by Indian groups to make claims of their land rights before the Inter-American Commission on Human Rights.

Belize's ruling PUP returned to power with an overwhelming victory in the March 2003 parliamentary election. The PUP captured 22 seats in the House of Representatives, ratifying Musa's mandate.

In December 2004, Prime Minister Said Musa of the PUP reshuffled his cabinet, affecting all but the deputy prime minister and the finance minister. According to a government press release, the changes were made "in keeping with government's commitment to good governance and the streamlining of operations."

In September 2002, the government proposed a constitutional amendment to end appeals to the Judicial Committee of the Privy Council in the United Kingdom. The Belize Court of Appeals would be established as the final court of appeals for cases carrying a mandatory death sentence. Despite a moratorium on executions since 1985, there is concern that a change in the law could lead to a resumption of capital punishment. The legislation had not been passed by the end of November 2004, and appeals to the Privy Council continue to be possible. In July 2004, the government failed to get parliamentary approval for constitutional changes that would allow Belize to fully participate in the Caribbean Court of Justice.

In recent years, Belize has experienced increases in the rates of violent crime, drug trafficking, and money laundering. Soldiers of the Belize Defence Force routinely participate in joint patrols with the police in an effort to reduce violent crime. Corruption and fraud involving nationality applications and passport processing continue to haunt the Immigration and Nationality Department. In August 2004, the prime minister announced full disclosure for all public sector loans, loan guarantees and obligations for government, and statutory boards. The Minister of Home Affairs and Investment announced the introduction of machine-readable passports by January 2005, along with heightened visa requirements in order to prevent illegal entry into the country.

In February 2004, the U.K.'s Privy Council approved the construction of the Chalillo dam, opposed by indigenous and environmental groups.

Political Rights and Civil Liberties: Citizens of Belize can change their government democratically. The 29-seat House of Representatives is elected for a five-year term. Members of the Senate are appointed: 5 by the governor-general on the advice of the prime minister, 2 by the leader of the parliamentary opposition, and 1 by the Belize Advisory Council. There are no restrictions on the right to organize political parties, and there are Mestizo, Creole, Maya, and Garifuna parties in parliament.

Belize was ranked 60 out of 146 countries surveyed in the 2004 Transparency International Corruption Perceptions Index.

The mostly English-language press is free to publish a variety of political viewpoints, including those critical of the government, and there are Spanish-language media. However, there are certain judicial restrictions on freedom of the press, including prison terms for those who question the validity of financial disclosure statements submitted by public officials. Belize has 10 privately owned newspapers, 3 of which are subsidized by major political parties. There are 11 private commercial radio stations and two private television stations, along with several cable systems. An independent board oversees operations of the government-owned outlets.

Belizeans enjoy freedom of religion. There is full academic freedom in Belize.

A large number of nongovernmental organizations are active in social, economic, and environmental areas. Freedom of assembly is generally respected. Labor unions are independent and well organized and have the right to strike, but the percentage of the workforce that is organized has declined. Official boards of inquiry adjudicate disputes, and businesses are penalized for failing to abide by the labor code.

The judiciary is independent and nondiscriminatory, and the rule of law is generally respected. In the past, judges and the director of public prosecutions negotiated the renewal of their employment contracts, which made them vulnerable to political influence. Judges now serve until their mandatory retirement at 65. Lengthy backlogs of trials are due, in part, to the high turnover of judges, which is the result of their low pay. Cases often continue for years while defendants are free on bail. Reports of police misconduct are investigated by the department's internal affairs office or by an ombudsman's office. Extrajudicial killing and use of excessive force are the country's primary rights concerns.

Prisons do not meet minimum standards, although the Hattieville Prison was privatized and is run by a nonprofit foundation that has made some progress in improving the physical conditions of inmates. Drug trafficking and gang conflicts have contributed to an increase in crime. An antinarcotics agreement was signed with the United States in September 2002. Projects aimed at suppressing the cultivation, processing, and trafficking of drugs, curbing violent crime, and eliminating money laundering are priorities. The United States has provided Belize with counter-narcotics and law enforcement assistance, including equipment and training for the police department's counter-narcotics unit, and training for the Department of Immigration, the Customs and Excise Department, and the magistrate and supreme courts. In June 2004, the government announced the introduction of legislation formalizing a Mutual Legal Assistance Treaty with the United States that was signed four years ago.

The government actively discourages racial and ethnic discrimination. Although the Maya claim to be the original inhabitants of Belize, the government has designated only 77,000 acres as Mayan preserves out of the 500,000 acres claimed. Most of the indigenous population lives in the South, the poorest part of the country. The Belize Human Rights Commission is independent and effective. Human rights concerns include the conditions of migrant workers and refugees from neighboring countries and charges of labor abuses by Belizean employers. Most of the estimated 40,000 Spanish speakers who have immigrated to the largely English-speaking country since the 1980s do not have legal status. Undocumented Guatemalan, Honduran, and Salvadoran workers, especially in the service and agricultural sectors, continue to be exploited. Chinese and Indian nationals have been found to be working as bonded labor.

The majority of women working in brothels are from Guatemala, Honduras, and El Salvador. In May 2003, the U.S. State Department listed Belize as a candidate for sanctions because of its failure to control human trafficking. Violence against women and children is a serious problem. In September 2004, the government introduced an 11-year Plan of Action for Children and Adolescents aimed at promoting education, health, child protection, HIV/AIDS education, family, and culture.

Benin

Population: 7,300,000
GNI/capita: $380
Life Expectancy: 51
Religious Groups: Indigenous beliefs (50 percent),
Christian (30 percent), Muslim (20 percent)
Ethnic Groups: African [42 ethnic groups, including
Fon, Adja, Bariba, Yoruba] (99 percent), other (1 percent)
Capital: Porto-Novo

Political Rights: 2
Civil Liberties: 2
Status: Free

Trend Arrow: Benin received a downward trend arrow due to harsh, punitive measures carried out against members of the press.

Ten-Year Ratings Timeline (Political Rights, Civil Liberties, Status)

1995	1996	1997	1998	1999	2000	2001	2002	2003	2004
2,2F	2,2F	2,2F	2,2F	2,3F	2,2F	3,2F	3,2F	2,2F	2,2F

Overview:

In a departure from what has been a good record for press freedom in recent years, courts in Benin jailed two journalists and two others faced the prospect of imprisonment in 2004. The government continued efforts to fight child trafficking and corruption. About 80 judges faced trial on charges of embezzlement.

Benin was once the center of the ancient kingdom of Dahomey, the name by which the country was known until 1975. Six decades of French colonial rule ended in 1960, and Mathieu Kerekou took power 12 years later, ending successive coups and countercoups. He imposed a one-party state under the Benin People's Revolutionary Party and pursued Marxist-Leninist policies. However, by 1990, economic hardships and rising internal unrest had forced Kerekou to agree to a national conference that ushered in democracy. The transition culminated in his defeat by Nicephore Soglo in the 1991 presidential election, and the country's human rights record subsequently improved. Kerekou made a comeback in the 1996 presidential poll.

Presidential elections in 2001 were marred by technical and administrative problems, as well as a boycott by the second- and third-place finishers in the second round of voting. Former president Soglo and Adrien Houngbedji claimed fraud after they won 29 percent and 14 percent, respectively, in the first round of voting, compared with incumbent president Kerekou's 47 percent. The boycott gave Kerekou a solid victory, with 84 percent of the vote in the second round of voting, in which he ended up running against an obscure fourth-place candidate. Several members of the Autonomous National Electoral Commission had stepped down in protest before the second round of voting, citing a lack of transparency and poor administration of the election.

In March 2003, Benin held National Assembly elections that gave the ruling-party coalition a majority in parliament for the first time since multiparty democracy was introduced more than a decade ago. The ruling party and its allies hold 65 seats, compared with 18 seats for opposition parties. Fourteen political parties participated in the elections. Voter turnout was low, and there were some logistical problems, but the polls were considered free and fair. Opposition party members had accused the ruling party of intimidation ahead of the elections, and the government banned "anti-fraud brigades" that had been organized by the opposition.

The legislative polls followed local elections that represented the last step in Benin's decentralization process and helped reinstate voter confidence following the flawed presidential elections in 2001. Pro-Kerekou parties came out ahead in the local polls.

As part of an investigation into misused government funds, more than 20 judges were put on trial in January on charges of embezzling millions of dollars. About 80 court and Finance Ministry officials were charged in the scandal. For their part, judges went on strike during the year after accusing the government of interfering in judicial matters.

Child trafficking continued to be a problem in Benin in 2004, although the government set up a national child protection committee to oversee the fight against the practice. Authorities during the year intercepted a number of children on their way to being smuggled to work abroad, and repatriated others who had been sent to Benin to work as laborers.

Benin is a poor country whose economy is based largely on subsistence agriculture. An economic crisis gripped the nation in 2004 with prices of staple goods skyrocketing. Some blame trade restrictions imposed by neighboring Nigeria, while others accuse the government of corruption and incompetence.

Political Rights and Civil Liberties: Citizens of Benin can change their government democratically. Benin held its first genuine multiparty elections in 1991 and now has dozens of political parties.

Historically, Benin has been divided between northern and southern ethnic groups, which are the main roots of current political parties; the South has enjoyed more advanced development. Northern ethnic groups enlisted during President Mathieu Kerekou's early years in power still dominate the military, although efforts have been made in recent years to rectify this situation.

Benin was ranked 77 out of 146 countries surveyed in the 2004 Transparency International Corruption Perceptions Index.

Harsh libel laws have been used against journalists, but constitutional guarantees of freedom of expression are largely respected in practice. An independent and pluralistic press publishes articles highly critical of both government and opposition leaders and policies. Benin has dozens of daily newspapers, magazines, and private radio stations. It also has at least two private television stations.

Press freedom, however, suffered a setback in 2004. In August, Patrick Adjamonsi, publication director of the independent daily newspaper *L'Aurore* was arrested on defamation charges and imprisoned. The charges stem from an article he wrote in 2003, which suggested that corruption might have been involved when the state communications authority disbursed government subsidies for the private press. Adjamonsi was initially sentenced to six months in jail and won an appeal for a retrial. Jean-Baptiste Hounkonnou, publication director of the daily newspaper *Le Nouvel Esor*, was jailed in March after being sentenced to six months in prison for defamation. He was released in May on appeal. Two other journalists with the private newspaper *La Pyramide* were scheduled to go to trial in October. John Akintola and Christophe Hodonou are being charged with defamation. The New York–based Committee to Protect Journalists said the punitive measures were troubling because the government had generally been tolerant of criticism and there had been a growing and vibrant media in the country.

The government respects religious and academic freedom.

Freedom of assembly is respected in Benin, and requirements for permits and registration are often ignored. Numerous nongovernmental organizations (NGOs) and human rights groups operate without hindrance. The right to organize and join unions is constitutionally guaranteed and respected in practice. Strikes are legal, and collective bargaining is common.

The judiciary is generally considered to be independent, but it is inefficient and susceptible to corruption. The executive retains important powers but generally respects court decisions. The Constitutional Court has demonstrated independence, but was accused of bias in favor of the president during the 2001 presidential elections. Prison conditions are harsh, marked by poor diet and inadequate medical care. Human rights are largely respected, although concern has been raised about the operation of anticrime vigilante groups and the failure of the police to curb vigilantism. Smuggling children into neighboring countries for domestic service and meager compensation is reportedly widespread. Many, especially young girls, suffer abuse. Efforts are under way in Benin to fight child abuse and child trafficking through media campaigns and education.

Although the constitution provides for equality for women, they enjoy fewer educational and employment opportunities than men, particularly in rural areas. In family matters, in which traditional practices prevail, their legal rights are often ignored. After much debate, a family code that in part strengthened property and inheritance rights for women was approved by the National Assembly in 2002. The law was reviewed in 2004 after judges declared certain aspects of it too harsh and unconstitutional. The revised law tolerates the practice of polygamy, but monogamy remains the only legal form of marriage. The National Assembly passed a law against female genital mutilation in 2003, and NGOs have been working to raise awareness about the health dangers of the practice.

Bhutan

Population: 1,000,000
GNI/capita: $590
Life Expectancy: 66
Religious Groups: Lamaistic Buddhist (75 percent), Hindu (25 percent)
Ethnic Groups: Drukpa (50 percent), Nepalese (35 percent), indigenous or migrant tribes (15 percent)
Capital: Thimphu

Political Rights: 6
Civil Liberties: 5
Status: Not Free

Ten-Year Ratings Timeline (Political Rights, Civil Liberties, Status)

1995	1996	1997	1998	1999	2000	2001	2002	2003	2004
7,7NF	7,7NF	7,7NF	7,6NF	7,6NF	7,6NF	7,6NF	6,5NF	6,5NF	6,5NF

Overview:

The ongoing process of political reform undertaken by King Jigme Singye Wangchuk, which is expected to lead to Bhutan's emergence as a constitutional monarchy, continued in 2004. A new Royal Advisory Council was elected in October, and a draft of the constitution was presented to the cabinet in November. However, little further progress was made on resolving the thorny issue of repatriating a significant proportion of the Bhutanese refugees currently residing in camps in Nepal.

Britain began guiding this Himalayan land's affairs in 1865 and, in 1907, installed the Wangchuk monarchy. However, a 1949 treaty gave India control over Bhutan's foreign affairs. In 1972, the current monarch succeeded his father to the throne.

Reversing a long-standing policy of tolerating cultural diversity in the kingdom, the government, in the 1980s, began requiring all Bhutanese to adopt the dress of the ruling Ngalong Drukpa ethnic group. Authorities said that they feared for the survival of Drukpa culture because of the large number of Nepali speakers, also known as Southern Bhutanese, in the South. The situation worsened in 1988, when the government began using a strict 1985 citizenship law to arbitrarily strip thousands of Nepali speakers of their citizenship. The move came after a census showed Southern Bhutanese to be in the majority in five southern districts.

Led by the newly formed Bhutanese People's Party (BPP), Southern Bhutanese held demonstrations in September 1990 against the new measures. Arson and violence that accompanied the protests led authorities to crack down on the BPP. As conditions worsened, tens of thousands of Southern Bhutanese fled to Nepal in the early 1990s, many of them forcibly expelled by Bhutanese forces. Credible accounts suggest that soldiers raped and beat many Nepali-speaking villagers and detained thousands as "anti-nationals."

In early 2001, a bilateral team began certifying citizenship documents and interviewing family heads of the estimated 102,000 Bhutanese refugees currently in Nepal. After a number of delays in the process, in October 2003, the Nepalese and Bhutanese governments agreed to repatriate approximately 70 percent of the refugees from the first of the seven camps to undergo the verification procedure. However, following an incident where refugees at one of the camps injured three Bhutanese inspectors in December of that year, progress ground to a virtual halt in 2004, while inconclusive investigations into the incident were conducted. In July, the UN High Commissioner for Refugees offered to take a lead role in the process if Nepal and Bhutan agreed that they were unable to solve the problem bilaterally.

After facing diplomatic pressure from India regarding the presence in Bhutan of a number of militant Indian separatist groups, the Bhutanese government held talks with the United Liberation Front of Assam (ULFA) in 2001. When the ULFA did not honor its commitment to reduce its presence within the country, the National Assembly authorized the Bhutanese army to initiate operations against ULFA and two other insurgent groups. In December 2003, with support from Indian forces, the army expelled about 3,000 insurgents and destroyed many of their camps. However, the security situation in much of southern Bhutan remains poor; in September 2004, a bomb blast in the border town of Gelephu killed or injured several dozen people. Later that month, 111 Bhutanese citizens were convicted of providing assistance to various militant groups and were sentenced to terms ranging from four years to life imprisonment.

During the past several years, the government has made further progress on the issue of political reform. The 39-member constitutional drafting committee submitted a second draft of the constitution to the king in 2003, and after being reviewed by legal experts throughout 2004, it was presented to the cabinet in November for their comments. Local government structures have been granted greater executive authority and now are headed by elected chairpersons. A new Royal Advisory Council, which is now expected to play a role similar to that of an upper house of parliament, was elected in October.

Political Rights and Civil Liberties: Bhutanese cannot change their government through elections, and they enjoy few basic political rights. King Jigme Singye Wangchuk and a small group of elites make key decisions and wield absolute power, although the king did take several steps in 1998 to increase the influence of the National Assembly. He removed himself as chairman of Bhutan's Council of Ministers; in addition, he gave the National Assembly the power to remove the king from the throne and to elect cabinet members from among candidates nominated by the king. In July, the assembly resolved that it would meet biannually in order to take a more active role in approving legislation or official policy.

The government discourages the formation of political parties, and none exist legally. The 150-member National Assembly has little independent power, although some analysts note that debate within the assembly has become more lively and critical in recent years. Every three years, village headmen choose 105 National Assembly members, while the king appoints 35 seats and religious groups choose 10 seats. For the 105 district-based seats, each village nominates one candidate by consensus, with votes being cast by family heads rather than by individuals. Human rights activists say that in reality, authorities suggest a candidate to the headman in each village and the headman asks families to approve the candidate. Members of all major ethnic groups are represented in the National Assembly, although ethnic Nepalese remain under-represented.

The Bhutanese government operates with limited transparency or accountability, although steps have been taken in recent years to improve both, with among other measures efforts to strengthen the powers of local government bodies. In June, 16 men involved in a local election bribery case were sentenced to prison terms. Bhutan was not ranked by Transparency International in its 2004 Corruption Perceptions Index.

Bhutanese authorities restrict freedom of expression. The government prohibits criticism of King Wangchuk and Bhutan's political system. Bhutan's only regular publication, the weekly *Kuensel*, generally reports news that puts the kingdom in a favorable light, although it does provide occasional coverage of criticism of government policies during assembly meetings. Similarly, state-run broadcast media do not carry opposition positions and statements. Cable television services, which carry uncensored foreign programming, thrive in some areas but are hampered by a high sales tax and the absence of a broadcasting law. Internet access is growing and is unrestricted, and the online edition of *Kuensel* provides a somewhat lively forum for discussion and debate.

While Bhutanese of all faiths generally can worship freely, government policy favors the Drukpa Kagyupa school of Mahayana Buddhism, which is the official religion. The government helps fund the construction of Drukpa monasteries and shrines and subsidizes some monks, according to the U.S. State Department's 2004 Report on International Religious Freedom. Drukpa monks also wield political influence. Some members of the country's small Christian minority are reportedly subject to harassment by local authorities. No restrictions on academic freedom have been reported, although the country's first university opened only in 2003.

Freedom of assembly and association is restricted. Citizens may participate in a peaceful protest only if the government approves of its purpose. Nongovernmental groups that work on human rights or other overtly political issues are not legally allowed to operate inside the country. In recent years, security forces have arrested Bhutanese for taking part in peaceful pro-democracy demonstrations. They have also arrested and deported Southern Bhutanese refugees living in Nepal who entered and demonstrated inside Bhutan for the right to return home.

The government prohibits independent trade unions and strikes. In any case, some 85 percent of the workforce is engaged in subsistence agriculture. Draft labor legislation would prohibit forced labor, discrimination, sexual harassment, and child employment in the private sector.

Bhutan's judiciary is not independent of the king, and legal protections are incomplete as a result of the lack of a fully developed criminal procedure code and deficiencies in police training. However, litigants' rights were bolstered by legislation that provided for legal counsel in court cases. In addition, in 2003, the king approved the establishment of a five-member National Judicial Commission to oversee the appointment of judges and other judicial staff. Capital punishment was abolished in March 2004, and a new penal code was enacted in August.

Arbitrary arrest, detention, and torture remain areas of concern. According to Amnesty International, approximately 60 political prisoners from southern and eastern Bhutan continue to serve lengthy prison sentences. In April, the BBC reported that police had detained 46 members of banned political parties. However, the government's human rights record has improved since the early 1990s, when soldiers and police committed grave human rights abuses against Nepali-speaking Bhutanese.

Conditions for Nepali speakers living in Bhutan have improved somewhat, but several major problems remain. According to a 2003 report by the Human Rights Council of Bhutan, a consortium of Bhutanese human rights organizations based in Nepal, ethnic Nepalese are still required to obtain official "security clearance certificates" to enter schools, receive health care, take government jobs, or travel within Bhutan or abroad. At the same time, the government has eased some cultural restrictions that specifically targeted Southern Bhutanese. For example, in recent years, enforcement of a 1989 royal decree forcing all Bhutanese to adopt the national dress and customs of the ruling Drukpas has been sporadic.

The government's expulsion of tens of thousands of Nepali-speaking Bhutanese in the early 1990s, and recent bilateral efforts to repatriate them, have underscored the tentative nature of citizenship in the kingdom. Prior to the expulsions, the government stripped thousands of Southern Bhutanese of their citizenship under a 1985 law that tightened citizenship requirements. The new law required both parents to be Bhutanese citizens in order for citizenship to be conferred on a child. In addition, Bhutanese seeking to verify citizenship had to prove that they or both of their parents were residing in Bhutan in 1958.

While the UN High Commissioner for Refugees asserts that the overwhelming majority of refugees who entered camps in Nepal have documentary proof of Bhutanese nationality, the Bhutanese government continues to maintain that many of the refugees either left Bhutan voluntarily or were illegal immigrants. A deal to repatriate a first batch of 9,000 refugees was brokered in October 2003 under considerable international pressure, but bilateral efforts to continue the repatriation process remained stalled in 2004. In addition, approximately 20,000 refugees currently reside in India.

However, since 1998, the government has been resettling Bhutanese from other parts of the country on land in southern Bhutan vacated by those who fled to Nepal. A 2002 Habitat International Coalition report documented specific cases of the appropriation of houses and land and noted that this policy will considerably complicate the refugee repatriation process.

Women participate freely in social and economic life, but continue to be underrepresented in government and politics despite some recent gains. The application of religious or ethnically based customary laws regarding inheritance, marriage, and divorce sometimes results in discrimination against women.

Bolivia

Population: 8,800,000
GNI/capita: $900
Life Expectancy: 63
Religious Groups: Roman Catholic (95 percent), other [including Protestant (Evangelical Methodist)] (5 percent)
Ethnic Groups: Quechua (30 percent), Mestizo (30 percent) Aymara (25 percent), European (15 percent)
Capital: La Paz (administrative), Sucre (judicial)

Political Rights: 3
Civil Liberties: 3
Status: Partly Free

Ten-Year Ratings Timeline (Political Rights, Civil Liberties, Status)

1995	1996	1997	1998	1999	2000	2001	2002	2003	2004
2,4PF	2,3F	1,3F	1,3F	1,3F	1,3F	1,3F	2,3F	3,3PF	3,3PF

Overview:

Interim president Carlos Mesa spent 2004 trying to consolidate his presidency in Latin America's poorest country following the forced resignation of his predecessor, Gonzalo Sanchez de Losada, the year before. Mesa seemed to achieve a popular consensus by winning a vaguely worded referendum over the politically charged issue of the extraction and export of natural gas. However, other polarizing issues festered, including demands by the majority indigenous peoples for greater rights and representation.

After achieving independence from Spain in 1825, the Republic of Bolivia endured recurrent instability and military rule. However, the armed forces, responsible for more than 180 coups in 157 years, have stayed in their barracks since 1982.

In 1993, Sanchez de Losada, a wealthy U.S.-educated businessman, was elected president. During his first term in office, he initiated a sweeping privatization program, and, under U.S. pressure, stepped up eradication of the country's illegal coca production. The measures provoked widespread public protests and, together with unhappiness over growing official corruption, caused a decline in his popularity, as well as that of his party, the center-right Revolutionary Nationalist Movement (MNR). Former dictator Hugo Banzer Suarez succeeded Sanchez de Losada in presidential elections in 1997, but the terminally ill Banzer resigned for health reasons in 2001. He was succeeded by Vice President Jorge Quiroga, who finished the remaining year of Banzer's term in office.

The June 2002 presidential election was held in the midst of growing social unrest and a continuing economic downturn. With no candidate winning a majority of the popular vote, members of the Bolivian Congress were tasked with deciding the outcome of the election. They selected Sanchez de Losada over Evo Morales, a radical Indian leader of the country's coca growers. Parliamentary elections, which were held concurrently with the presidential vote, resulted in the MNR-led coalition winning 17 seats in the Senate and 71 in the Chamber of Deputies. The opposition, dominated by Morales' Movement Towards Socialism, won 10 seats in the upper house, as well as 59 deputy seats.

Although in 1997, as the world's largest exporter of coca, Bolivia produced 270 metric tons of the leaf used to make cocaine, by 2002, U.S.-sponsored antidrug efforts had resulted in that figure dropping to 20 metric tons. However, not only did the country lose an estimated $500 million in revenues from the sales of the leaf, more than 50,000 coca growers and their families were left without viable alternatives for their support. Morales's showing in the 2002 polls was evidence of how unpopular these policies were among the country's majority Indian population, who use the coca leaf for traditional medicine and have been shut out from the benefits of U.S.-backed economic reforms.

An anti-coca expeditionary task force paid for by the U.S. Embassy and made up of 1,500 former Bolivian soldiers was the subject of frequent charges of the use of excessive force and human rights violations ranging from torture to murder. Critics claimed that the creation of a military force paid for by foreign funds violated both the Bolivian constitution and military regulations. Defenders of the force pointed out that the coca growers, who demanded respect for their own property rights, worked closely with narcotics traffickers, and claimed that the traffickers include snipers and experts in booby traps. In 2004, security forces killed at least three persons and injured dozens of others during violent social unrest; several law enforcement officers were also killed.

In September and October 2003, Bolivian indigenous groups, workers, students, and coca growers engaged in a revolt over the planned construction of a $5 billion pipeline, once heralded as Latin America's largest infrastructure development project, and the sale of natural gas supplies through long-time rival Chile to the United States and Mexico. The mass protests against Sanchez de Losada were fueled by resentment over the failure of nearly two decades of democratic reform and economic restructuring to improve the lot of Bolivia's Indian majority, who speak Spanish as a second language. Sanchez de Losada's own cabinet had become irreparably fractured over the brutal repression practiced by the security forces, whose use of large-caliber combat ammunition appeared excessive. A crackdown during the protests left some 56 people dead; it followed a bloody shootout in February between soldiers and police that killed 30. In October, the violence culminated in the forced resignation of Sanchez de Losada, who fled to Miami. Vice President Mesa, a nonpartisan former media personality and historian, assumed office and immediately appointed a cabinet that had no representative from the country's traditional parties, but included two indigenous Indian members.

On July 18, 2004, Mesa, in need of shoring up his fragile political base, prevailed overwhelmingly in a national referendum that had split the country between its Indian majority and European descended elites. The vote, which posed five questions about the disposition of the country's oil and gas reserves—the country's most important legal economic asset—permitted natural gas exports while exerting greater control over the oil-and-gas industry. It revived the state-owned oil-and-gas company, raised taxes on exports from as low as 18 percent to 50 percent, and revised previous hydrocarbons law. The outcome was hailed by some as a step toward greater political stability, but questioned by others, who wondered whether the move to squeeze foreign capital out of the energy sector through strong state controls and higher taxes would not, in fact, cripple it. Meanwhile, a dispute between Mesa and the Congress over how to implement the referendum brought opposition charges that he was exercising dictatorial powers.

In October, the Bolivian Congress brought criminal charges against Sanchez de Losada, in self-exile in a Washington, DC, suburb, and his cabinet, for their alleged responsibility in the deaths during protests the previous year. Sanchez de Losada said that he would fight extradition.

Bolivia remains a hemisphere leader in unequal distribution of wealth, with about 80 percent of its people living in poverty. Official statistics put unemployment at 12 percent. Crime in La Paz and other major cities is increasing steadily, and the national police are considered to be both inefficient and corrupt.

Political Rights and Civil Liberties:

Citizens can change their government through elections. The 2002 presidential elections were generally free and fair, although U.S. government officials say they had evidence that Colombian drug lords financed some of Evo Morales's political organization. Evidence abounds that drug money has been used to buy the favor of government officials, including that of police and military personnel.

As a result of reforms that were enacted in 1993-1994 and began in 1997, presidential terms in office were extended from four to five years. Congress consists of a 130-member House of Representatives and a 27-member Senate. Bolivians have the right to organize political parties. The principal traditional parties are the conservative National Democratic Action (ADN), the social-democratic Movement of the Revolutionary Left (MIR), and Gonzalo Sanchez de Losada's center-right Revolutionary Nationalist Movement (MNR). In 2002, the Socialist Movement (MAS) and the Pachacutti Indian Movement (MIP) gained significant electoral support as well.

The broad immunity from prosecution enjoyed by legislators is a serious stumbling block in the fight against official corruption. Bolivia was ranked 122 out of 146 countries surveyed in the 2004 Transparency International Corruption Perceptions Index.

Although the constitution guarantees freedom of expression, it is subject to some limitations in practice. Journalists covering corruption stories are occasionally subjected to verbal intimidation by government officials, arbitrary detention by police, and violent attacks. During mass public protests in 2003, reporters suffered physical assaults both from demonstrators and from law enforcement officers. The press, radio, and television are mostly private, and the government does not restrict access to the Internet.

Freedom of religion is guaranteed by the constitution. The government does not restrict academic freedom, and the law grants public universities autonomous status.

The right to organize civic groups and labor unions is guaranteed by the constitution. Government-sponsored, as well as independent, human rights organizations exist, and they frequently report on security force brutality. The congressional Human Rights Commission is active and frequently criticizes the government. However, rights activists and their families are subject to intimidation.

Bolivian law provides for the rights of peaceful assembly and freedom of association. While the authorities generally respected this practice, security forces killed several people during violent social protests in 2004. The government requires nongovernmental organizations to register with the appropriate departmental government, although the rule was only episodically enforced.

The judiciary, headed by the Supreme Court, remains the weakest branch of government and is corrupt, inefficient, and the object of intimidation by drug traffickers, as are Bolivia's mayoral, customs, and revenue offices. In recent years, the government has made serious efforts to improve the administration of justice, including making it more accessible. However, the selection of Supreme Court judges and members of the Judicial Council by a two-thirds vote of the national Congress—a measure adopted to prevent the majority party from filling all vacancies—has instead resulted in a political quota system that also violates the principles of independence and impartiality. In a positive development, in 2004, the process of judicial appointment included allowing citizens to have access to the professional and academic backgrounds of the nominees, with the objective of strengthening the judicial branch and avoiding "party quota" distortions.

Efforts to reform the judiciary have not included meaningful efforts to codify and incorporate customary law—a system still practiced semi-clandestinely—into national legislation, at least for minor crimes, as a means of reaching out to the indigenous majority. In 2004, the lack of a codified system resulted in at least one act of "communal justice"—the lynching of a highland mayor accused of corruption—that violated international human rights norms and brought the total number of lynchings in Bolivia to 27 since 2001. Prison conditions are harsh, with some 5,500 prisoners held in facilities designed to hold half that number, and nearly three-quarters of prisoners are held without formal sentences.

More than 520 indigenous communities have been granted legal recognition under the 1994 Popular Participation Law, which guarantees respect for the integrity of native peoples. The languages of the indigenous population are officially recognized. However, Indian territories are often neither legally defined nor protected, and coca growers and timber thieves exploit Indian lands illegally. Some Indians are kept as virtual slaves by rural employers through the use of debt peonage, with employers charging workers more for room and board than they earn. The observance of customary law by indigenous peoples is common in rural areas. In the remotest areas, the death penalty, forbidden by the constitution, is reportedly sometimes used against those who violate traditional laws or rules. In the 2002 presidential campaign, Indian advocates demanded that the constitution be amended to explicitly grant them greater participation in government and clearer land rights.

Violence against women is pervasive. However, no system exists to record the incidence of cases, and rape is a serious but under-reported problem. Women generally do not enjoy a social status equal to that of men. Many women do not know their legal rights.

Bosnia-Herzegovina

Population: 3,900,000   **Political Rights:** 4
GNI/capita: $1,310   **Civil Liberties:** 3*
Life Expectancy: 74   **Status:** Partly Free
Religious Groups: Muslim (40 percent), Orthodox
(31 percent), Roman Catholic (15 percent),
other (14 percent)
Ethnic Groups: Serb (37.1 percent), Bosniak (48 percent),
Croat (14.3 percent), other (0.6 percent)
Capital: Sarajevo
Ratings Change: Bosnia-Herzegovina's civil liberties rating improved from 4 to 3 due
to the deepening maturity of civic and political organizations, including the holding
of successful municipal elections throughout the country in October, the first postwar
elections completely organized and financed by Bosnian institutions themselves.

Ten-Year Ratings Timeline (Political Rights, Civil Liberties, Status)

1995	1996	1997	1998	1999	2000	2001	2002	2003	2004
6,6NF	5,5PF	5,5PF	5,5PF	5,5PF	5,4PF	5,4PF	4,4PF	4,4PF	4,3PF

Overview:
Nine years after the end of a brutal civil war, Bosnia-Herzegovina held its first postwar elections in 2004 that were organized entirely by the country's authorities themselves. At the same time, the lack of an internal consensus in Bosnia on both the nature of the state and how it should function continued to retard the country's development. In June, Bosnia was denied membership in NATO's Partnership for Peace program. Nevertheless, Bosnia's government still managed to make some progress on several pieces of legislation important for its integration into Europe. Significantly, this legislation was passed by Bosnian authorities themselves and was not forced on them by international officials.

Bosnia-Herzegovina became one of six constituent republics of Yugoslavia in 1945. As Yugoslavia began to disintegrate in the early 1990s, Bosnia-Herzegovina was recognized as an independent state in April 1992. A 43-month-long civil war immediately ensued, resulting in the deaths of tens of thousands of individuals and the "ethnic cleansing" and forced resettlement of approximately half of Bosnia-Herzegovina's population. In November 1995, the Dayton peace accords brought an end to the civil war by creating a loosely knit state composed of the Bosniac-Croat "Federation of Bosnia-Herzegovina" and the largely Serbian Republika Srpska (RS). The Dayton accords also gave the international community a decisive role in running post-Dayton Bosnia-Herzegovina, manifested in the significant powers and authorities (known as the "Bonn powers") granted to international civilian agencies such as the Office of the High Representative (OHR). Peace and security in post-Dayton Bosnia-Herzegovina is provided by the NATO-led Stabilization Force (SFOR). Despite these considerable efforts by the international community to integrate Bosnia, however, most aspects of political, social, and economic life remain divided along ethnic lines.

Bosnia-Herzegovina's latest presidential and parliamentary elections were held in October 2002. Contrary to the hopes of many members of the international community, Bosnian voters across the ethnic divide mainly gave their votes to nationalist parties. The most important ethnically based parties—the Bosniac Party of Democratic Action (SDA), the Serbian Democratic Party (SDS), and the Croatian Democratic Union (HDZ)—took control of the joint state presidency, the joint state parliament, and both entities' governments.

In October 2004, the country held local elections in 142 municipalities. Importantly, these were the first elections since the war funded and organized entirely by the country itself. Voter turnout for the elections was 45.5 percent, and the three main ethnically based parties that have dominated the country's politics since 1990 were again victorious, continuing a pattern that has persisted throughout the postwar period.

Bosnia-Herzegovina's central government made some progress in 2004 toward passing several pieces of legislation crucial to its plan for European integration, but not without prodding from outsiders. In March, the European Union (EU) reported that Bosnia's progress in fulfilling Stabilization and Association Process agreements was disappointing, but by the summer, Bosnian institutions had passed 21 of 40 laws on the EU agenda, and 19 were still under debate in parliament. Importantly, Bosnian authorities had passed these laws on their own, breaking a postwar pattern in which international authorities had imposed laws on deadlocked institutions. Over the past several years, international officials had in this fashion imposed more than 470 pieces of legislation on recalcitrant local authorities.

Overall, however, there is growing concern among international observers and Bosnians themselves over the slow pace of progress in the country and the resulting international isolation in which Bosnia finds itself. Bosnia-Herzegovina remains one of the few countries in Europe (together with Serbia-Montenegro) that is not a member of NATO's Partnership for Peace, to which it was denied membership in June largely because the RS has failed to apprehend any suspected war criminals on its territory. Bosnia also has not joined the World Trade Organization.

In July, perhaps one of the most serious critiques of the way the international community is running Bosnia came in the form of a report published by the Parliamentary Committee of the Council of Europe, one of the few regional organizations Bosnia has managed to enter. The report questioned how compatible Bosnia's membership in that body is given the High Representative's near dictatorial Bonn powers to dismiss elected officials from office and freeze their assets, without any requirement to show the basis on which such decisions are made. Prospects now also appear bleak for Bosnia's request to the EU to open negotiations on a Stabilization and Association Agreement.

All of this uncertainty has an impact on the economy as well; less than a third of Bosnia's working-age population is currently in the labor force, compared to an EU average of 64 percent. On a more positive note, however, in 2004, the World Bank announced that it was officially reclassifying Bosnia from a "post-conflict" to a "transitional" country.

At the end of the year, the SFOR ended its mission, turning over responsibilities for maintaining security and enforcing the Dayton accords to an EU-led force popularly known as EUFOR.

Political Rights and Civil Liberties: In general, voters can freely elect their representatives and can form political parties insofar as party programs are compatible with the Dayton peace accords. The High Representative, however, has the authority to remove publicly elected officials from office if they are deemed to be obstructing the peace process. In June, the current international High Representative, Sir Paddy Ashdown, removed 59 Bosnian Serb officials from their posts in government and state-owned enterprises, allegedly for obstructing implementation of the Dayton accords and aiding fugitive Radovan Karadzic's support network; 49 of the 59 dismissed officials were from the leading Bosnian Serb party, the SDS.

Many analysts believe that as a consequence of such policies, the Bosnian electorate has increasingly lost interest in the electoral process. Turnout has dropped consistently for postwar elections: in 1998, turnout was 71 percent; in 2000, it was 64 percent; and in 2002, it sank to 54 percent. Electoral turnout for the October 2004 municipal elections declined to 45.5 percent.

Corruption remains a major problem in the country, especially because it is widely believed that a direct link exists between organized crime groups and extremist political forces. Bosnia-Herzegovina was ranked 82 out of 146 countries surveyed in the Transparency International 2004 Corruption Perceptions Index.

A plethora of independent electronic and print media organizations operate in Bosnia-Herzegovina. However, journalism in Bosnia continues to be plagued by a relatively low standard of professional ethics, a reliance on foreign donations for survival, and the consideration that most media outlets appeal only to narrow ethnic constituencies. Serious investigative journalism remains a dangerous activity for Bosnian journalists. In October, a journalist in the RS known for his exposés on organized crime and war criminals was badly beaten near the town of Bosanko Grahovo. Another problem for the media has been a growing division in Bosnian society between secularists and more religiously oriented segments of the population. The leader of the Bosnian Muslim community, for instance, appealed to Bosnian Muslim business owners to join an advertising boycott against the Sarajevo newsweekly *Dani* after the magazine had attacked him and the policies of the official Islamic Community in the country. In July, the HDZ demanded that Bosnian Croats be allowed to create a separate public broadcasting network for their community, despite plans by the international community to implement a reform of the state broadcasting system that would be nonethnic. There were no reports of denial of access to the Internet.

Individuals enjoy freedom of religious belief and practice in areas dominated by members of their own ethnic group, but members of local ethnic minorities often face various forms of discrimination or harassment. In January, a new Law on Religious Freedom was passed granting churches and religious communities legal status akin to those enjoyed by nongovernmental organizations (NGOs). In March, partly as a result of a spillover effect of the violence in nearby Kosovo, a Serbian Orthodox Church was burned in the Bosniac-majority town of Bugojno, and a mosque was then vandalized in the town of Gradiska. Other relatively minor acts of vandalism against various holy sites associated with all three major religions occurred throughout the year as well. The three major religious organizations in the country—Islamic, Roman Catholic, and Orthodox—have claims against the government for property confiscated during the Communist period.

While the various governments in Bosnia-Herzegovina do not restrict academic freedom, ethnic favoritism in appointments to academic positions, and the politicization of such appointments, remain a continuing problem.

The constitution provides for freedom of assembly and association, and the various entity and cantonal governments generally respect these rights. However, ethnic or religious minorities in a particular area often find it more difficult to exercise these rights than the local majority population. Although there are no legal restrictions on the right of workers to form and join labor unions, which many workers do, unions are mainly divided along ethnic lines.

Corruption in the judiciary, police forces, and civil service forms a considerable obstacle to establishing the rule of law in Bosnia-Herzegovina. International officials claim that there is an "imbalance between the components of the rule of law." The judiciary is still considered to be unduly influenced by nationalist political parties and executive branches of government. Judges who show some independence are reported to have come under various forms of intimidation. A new criminal code was introduced in March 2003, along with a new Bosnian State Court and State Prosecutor's office. Initial reports suggest, however, that legal officials in Bosnia are having some difficulty making the transition from the earlier system, used in the former Yugoslavia and based on European-style code law, to the Anglo-American approach adopted in the new system.

One of the most significant provisions of the new criminal code allows Bosnian authorities to prosecute individuals who aid or abet persons indicted for war crimes by the International Criminal Tribunal for the Former Yugoslavia (ICTY). The code also contains provisions allowing for the dismissal of public officials who fail to arrest, detain, or extradite those so charged and for the imposition of a prison sentence of up to 10 years for such individuals. Nevertheless, cooperation with the ICTY is often strained, especially in the RS. In June, however, Bosnian Serb officials accepted the results of an official local inquiry into the Srebrenica massacres, where thousands of Bosnian Muslims were killed in 1995. The most sought-after indicted war criminals from Bosnia-Herzegovina's civil conflict—former Bosnian Serb political leader Radovan Karadzic and former Bosnian Serb military leader Ratko Mladic—remain at large.

In 2004, the UN High Commissioner for Refugees announced that 1,000,000 Bosnian refugees and displaced persons had returned to their homes since the end of the war, roughly half the total number driven from their homes during the fighting. The vast majority of property restitution cases left over from the war have now been resolved. Despite these relative successes, however, many people are returning to their prewar homes only to sell their property and move back to areas in which they are members of the local ethnic majority. Consequently, Bosnia-Herzegovina is now divided into three relatively ethnically homogenous Bosniac, Croat, and Serb areas. Nevertheless, there have been some large-scale, permanent returns, particularly in the northern RS in and around the town of Kozarac.

Women are legally entitled to full equality with men. However, they are significantly underrepresented in politics and government and are frequently discriminated against in the workplace in favor of demobilized soldiers. To compensate for the absence of women in public life, political parties have to list three women among the top 10 names on their lists of candidates. A significant problem in postwar Bosnia-

Herzegovina has become its emergence as a destination country for trafficked women, and UN reports claim that the large international civil and military presence in the country provides considerable demand for such services. The new Bosnian criminal code that went into effect in March 2003 specifically makes trafficking in human beings a crime and increases penalties available to law enforcement officials for such offenses.

Botswana

Population: 1,700,000   **Political Rights:** 2
GNI/capita: $3,010   **Civil Liberties:** 2
Life Expectancy: 36   **Status:** Free
Religious Groups: Indigenous beliefs (85 percent),
Christian (15 percent)
Ethnic Groups: Tswana (79 percent), Kalanga (11 percent),
Basarwa (3 percent), other (7 percent)
Capital: Gaborone

Ten-Year Ratings Timeline (Political Rights, Civil Liberties, Status)

1995	1996	1997	1998	1999	2000	2001	2002	2003	2004
2,2F	2,2F	2,2F	2,2F	2,2F	2,2F	2,2F	2,2F	2,2F	2,2F

Overview:

Africa's longest-lasting multiparty democracy continued to demonstrate stability in 2004, with general elections held in October that were deemed generally free and fair. President Festus Mogae and his Botswana Democratic Party (BDP) soundly extended their reign. However, AIDS continued to tear at the country's social and economic fabric, and members of the indigenous San group took the government to court for forcing the minority group off ancestral lands.

Elected governments have ruled the country since it gained independence from Britain in 1966. A referendum on whether the president should be directly elected, rather than chosen by the elected National Assembly, was withdrawn shortly before a scheduled vote in late 1997. Mogae, a former central bank chief, succeeded Ketumile Masire as president in 1998 and was confirmed as the country's leader in 1999. The ruling BDP won by a wide majority in legislative elections in October 1999. Polling was deemed free and fair, although the BDP enjoyed preferential access to state-run media.

In the October 30, 2004, legislative poll, the BDP firmly defeated a fractured opposition, sweeping 44 of the 57 contested seats in the National Assembly and securing President Mogae a second term in office. International observers declared polling free and fair, but recommended measures to strengthen the democratic process. These included giving the opposition equal access to state-run media and setting the date for elections well in advance.

In July, some 240 San, an indigenous group that traditionally lives by hunting and gathering, challenged in court the government's 2002 policy to evict them from traditional lands in the Central Kalahari Game Reserve. They claim the government acted unlawfully by cutting off essential services to force them from their homes and are asserting their right to return. The resettled San say they are worse off in villages with scant job prospects.

Economic progress in Botswana has been built on sound fiscal management and low rates of corruption, and privatization is progressing slowly. Efforts are under way to diversify an economy where diamonds account for 75 percent of export earnings. However, unemployment is an estimated 40 percent, and AIDS has taken a toll on the economy. More than one-third of the population is infected with HIV. The government has taken a pioneering regional role in combating the pandemic, including offering free anti-retroviral drugs.

Political Rights and Civil Liberties: Citizens of Botswana can change their government democratically. The National Assembly, elected for five years, chooses the president to serve a concurrent five-year term. The courts confirm the assembly's choice when the winning party receives more than half the seats in parliament. The Independent Election Commission, created in 1996, has helped consolidate Botswana's reputation for fairness in voting. President Festus Mogae has said that he will not serve a full five-year term and plans to hand over the presidency in 2008, a year before the next elections, to his vice president, Ian Khama.

The House of Chiefs represents the country's eight major tribes and some smaller ones, and mainly serves in an advisory role to parliament and the government. Critics say it favors the Setswana-speaking tribes. Groups outside the eight majority tribes tend to be marginalized from the political process, especially the San, who live in extreme poverty, having lost their fertile ancestral lands. Under the Chieftainship Act, land in ethnic territory is distributed under the jurisdiction of majority groups. A lack of representation in the House has imposed Tswana patriarchal customary law on minority groups, which often have different rules for inheritance, marriage, and succession than the laws.

The government passed a bill in 1994 that set up an anticorruption body with special powers for investigation, arrest, and search and seizure; the conviction rate has been more than 80 percent. Transparency International has rated Botswana the least corrupt country in Africa for more than five years. Botswana was ranked 31 out of 146 countries surveyed in the organization's 2004 Corruption Perceptions Index.

A free and vigorous press thrives in cities and towns, and political debate is open and lively. Several independent newspapers and magazines are published in the capital. The opposition and government critics, however, receive little access to the government-controlled broadcast media. Botswana easily receives broadcasts from neighboring South Africa. The private Gaborone Broadcasting Corporation television system has a limited reach. There are two private radio stations, but state-run radio is the main source of news for much of the rural population, which also lacks Internet access.

Freedom of religion is guaranteed, although all religious organizations must register with the government. Academic freedom is respected.

The government generally respects freedom of assembly and association, which are guaranteed by the constitution. Civic and nongovernmental organizations, including human rights groups, operate openly without government harassment. However, concentration of economic power has hindered labor organization. While independent unions are permitted, workers' rights to strike and bargain collectively for wages are restricted.

The courts are generally considered to be fair and free of direct political interference. Trials are usually public, and those accused of the most serious violent crimes are provided with public defenders. Civil cases, however, are sometimes tried in customary courts, where defendants have no legal counsel. Prisons are overcrowded, but the government has been making moves to address the problem by building new facilities.

Botswana has an excellent record in Africa for human rights, although there are occasional reports of police misconduct and poor treatment of the San. Since 1985, authorities have relocated about 5,000 San to settlements outside the Central Kalahari Game Reserve. The last 530 left in 2002 after the government cut off water, food, health, and social services. The government said the cost of keeping them there was prohibitive. Officials deny that the government forced the San to move and insist it is providing decent education and health facilities. Government officials also have rejected assertions by critics that the government wanted to protect diamond reserves in the region from potential claims by the San, who had lived there for 30,000 years. The San tend to be marginalized educationally and thus do not enjoy the same employment opportunities as more privileged groups.

Women enjoy the same rights as men under the constitution, but customary laws limit their property rights. Women married under traditional laws are deemed legal minors. Progress in improving women's rights has been slow, but analysts see the participation of more women in parliament and the cabinet as important steps. Domestic violence is rampant, but law enforcement officers rarely intervene in domestic affairs, especially in rural areas.

Brazil

Population: 179,100,000 **Political Rights:** 2
GNI/capita: $2,830   **Civil Liberties:** 3
Life Expectancy: 71   **Status:** Free
Religious Groups: Roman Catholic (80 percent), other (20 percent)
Ethnic Groups: White (55 percent), mixed (38 percent), black (6 percent), other (1 percent)
Capital: Brasilia

Ten-Year Ratings Timeline (Political Rights, Civil Liberties, Status)

1995	1996	1997	1998	1999	2000	2001	2002	2003	2004
2,4PF	2,4PF	3,4PF	3,4PF	3,4PF	3,3PF	3,3PF	2,3F	2,3F	2,3F

Overview: In October 2004, President Luiz Inacio "Lula" da Silva's Worker's Party (PT) expanded its sphere of influence and consolidated its power in nationwide municipal elections.

However, the PT's losses of the powerhouse Sao Paulo and Porto Alegre mayoralties meant that da Silva, a former labor leader and political prisoner, ultimately was denied the boost in political capital that would have helped push through his legislative agenda and better position him for a run for reelection in 2006. Festering corruption scandals, a slow economic recovery, and high levels of violence in many of the country's urban and rural districts further dampened the president's popularity.

After gaining independence from Portugal in 1822, Brazil retained a monarchical system until a republic was established in 1889. Democratic governance has been interrupted by long periods of authoritarian rule, most recently under the military regime that was in control from 1964 to 1985, when elected civilian rule was reestablished.

Civilian rule has been marked by frequent corruption scandals. The scandal with the greatest political impact eventually led the Congress to impeach President Fernando Collor de Mello, who was elected in 1989 and removed from office in 1992.

In early 1994, Fernando Henrique Cardoso, a former socialist and critic of capitalist development who became a market-oriented, centrist finance minister in the interim government that followed Collor de Mello's resignation, forged a three-party, center-right coalition around Cardoso's Brazilian Social Democratic Party (PSDB). In October 1994, Cardoso won the presidency with 54 percent of the vote, against 27 percent for da Silva, the leader of the leftist PT and an early front-runner. However, Cardoso's coalition did not have a majority in either house of the Congress.

Cardoso embarked on an ambitious plan of free-market reforms, including deep cuts in the public sector and massive privatizations of state enterprises. He also ushered in a new era of dialogue with international human rights organizations and good government groups. These measures were popular enough that Cardoso sought, and obtained, a constitutional amendment permitting presidential reelection.

In 1998, Cardoso's first-ballot reelection victory (nearly 52 percent of the votes cast) over da Silva, his nearest rival, was tempered somewhat by a less convincing win at the congressional and gubernatorial levels. His win was also overshadowed by published accounts of corruption among senior government officials. The PSDB's legacy of reform was further tarnished by a 2001 energy crisis, which drove a wedge between it and its fractious coalition partners, although the causes of the crisis went beyond the critics' allegations of lack of government foresight and managerial talent.

Already faced with rampant street crime, urban sprawl, rural lawlessness, and the devastation of the Amazon basin, Brazilians increasingly voiced concerns that political corruption severely limited the government's ability to address difficult problems. At the same time, violence in several major Brazilian cities, most notably Rio de Janeiro, involving rival drug gangs and the sometimes outgunned police was fueled by the volume of cocaine and its cheaper derivatives consumed locally. For some years a transshipment country for cocaine produced in the Andean region, Brazil had become the world's second-largest consumer of the illegal drug after the United States by the beginning of the twenty-first century.

During the 2002 presidential campaign, as the economy staggered under the weight of some $260 billion in foreign debt, unemployment soared and the country's currency lost more than 40 percent of its value against the U.S. dollar. Da Silva campaigned by attacking both the government's economic record and the effects of globalization while abandoning his party's previous anti-free-market stands and its willingness to default on Brazil's foreign debt. After far outdistancing his rivals in a first-round ballot on October 6, da Silva received 52.5 million votes in the runoff election held three weeks later, besting Jose Serra, a center-left former PSDB health minister, 61 to 39 percent. The PT, however, won fewer than 20 percent of the seats in both houses of Congress, while all important governorships in the 5 largest of Brazil's 27 states were won by other parties.

On January 1, 2003, da Silva was inaugurated as president of Brazil, breaking a historic monopoly on power by members of a small southern elite, military rulers, and local political bosses in a country with one of the worst income distributions in the world and 50 million people living in poverty. After taking office, da Silva focused throughout the year on tackling the country's economic crisis, including the huge foreign debt, corruption, and racial inequality. With a mandate for change conditioned by his coalition's lack of a congressional majority, da Silva defied expectations by controlling inflation through fiscal discipline and tight monetary policies, which in turn boosted investor confidence and resulted in a $30 billion credit line from the IMF. He also instituted anticorruption measures, maintained cordial relations with the United States despite his independent foreign policy, and quickly established himself as one of the world's foremost voices for developing nations. As part of this effort, the country stepped up its campaign for a permanent seat on the UN Security Council. Brazil's progress, however, was marred by frequent police abuses, including torture and murder, and marked increases in the use of narcotics and their illegal sale by heavily armed gangs.

In 2004, the top two executives of the Brazilian Central Bank were accused of tax evasion and fraud, a claim that forced the No. 2 official to resign. The air of scandal grew to include da Silva's health minister and his vice president, the latter of whom was accused by a federal prosecutor of stock manipulation.

The October 2004 municipal elections saw the PT win in nearly 400 cities, double the number it won four years earlier, including in rural areas where the party has been weakest. The victories were overshadowed by the losses in the party strongholds of Sao Paulo, which with 10 million people is South America's largest city, and Porto Alegre, where it had ruled for 16 years. The victor in the Sao Paulo mayoral contest was former presidential candidate Jose Serra, whose centrist PSDB also won a total of five state capitals. The anemic PT victory portended continued problems for da Silva's legislative agenda at a time when observers said he needed to stimulate greater economic growth, as well as to overhaul antiquated labor laws and excessively high taxes that form part of the so-called Brazilian cost—those expenses to business that make the country less attractive to foreign investors.

In the international arena, da Silva won continued respect on Wall Street for his government's tight fiscal policies, even while he maintained his crusade against what he called U.S. and European protectionism.

Political Rights and Civil Liberties: Citizens of Brazil can change their government democratically, and the October 2004 municipal elections were free and fair. A new constitution, which went into effect in 1985 and was heavily amended in 1988, provides for a president to be elected for four years and a bicameral Congress consisting of an 81-member Senate elected for eight years and a 513-member Chamber of Deputies elected for four years. A constitutional amendment adopted in 1997 permits presidential reelection, a measure that was touted as enhancing presidential accountability. Despite a constitutionally proclaimed right to access to public information, Brazil does not have specific laws to regulate and guarantee the principle of transparency provided for in the constitution.

Corruption remains a serious problem in Brazil, which was ranked 59 out of 144 countries surveyed in the 2004 Transparency International Corruption Perceptions Index.

The constitution guarantees freedom of expression. The press is privately owned, but foreigners can acquire only a 30 percent share of a media company and are restricted in their ability to influence editorial decisions or management selection. There are dozens of daily newspapers and numerous other publications throughout the country. In recent years, TV Globo's near-monopoly over the broadcast media has been challenged by its rival, Sistema Brasileiro de Televisao (STB). The print media have played a central role in exposing official corruption. At the same time, reporters are frequently the target of threats, assaults, and occasionally even killings, especially those who focus on organized crime, corruption, or impunity issues. In 2004, a proposal floated by the government-allied National Federation of Journalists sought to regulate who could work as a journalist, but the measure was the object of heated criticism from free speech advocates and even members of da Silva's own party. Earlier, the government had threatened to expel a *New York Times* reporter over an article alleging heavy drinking by the president, but it later withdrew the threat. Although the government does not impose restrictions on the use of the Internet, federal and state police have begun to monitor the Internet to detect online recruitment by sex traffickers and to check on the activities of hate groups.

The constitution guarantees freedom of religion, and the government generally respects this right in practice. Evangelical Christian communities have grown significantly in recent years, from 9 percent of the population in 1991 to 15 percent in 2000. The government does not restrict academic freedom.

The right to organize political parties and civic organizations is recognized, as is the right to strike. Industrial labor unions are well organized and politically connected, although they are more autonomous of political party control than is true in most other Latin American countries. There are special labor courts. Hundreds of strikes have taken place in recent years against attempts to privatize state industries.

The climate of lawlessness is reinforced by a weak judiciary, which, though largely independent of the executive branch, is overtaxed, plagued by chronic corruption, and virtually powerless in the face of organized crime. Because the judiciary uses its independence above all to resist reforms and stop outside investigations of judicial corruption, judicial reform has progressed less than in any other large country of the region. In addition, judges regularly employ legal formalisms to overturn government modernization efforts, including those aimed at privatizing state-owned industries and reforming the ineffective but expensive system of public welfare. Public distrust of the judiciary and ineffective policing in the neighborhoods has resulted in poor citizens taking the law into their own hands, with hundreds of reported lynchings.

Recently, however, some judicial improvements have been made. The National

Coordination for the Protection of Human Rights Defenders, made up of government officials and civil society representatives, was established in 2003, and in 2004 it put into place a telephone hotline service that people can use to report rights abuses. In 2004, da Silva created the new position of secretary for judicial reform within the Ministry of Justice in hopes of providing fresh impetus to reform proposals that have languished in the Congress for over a decade. The government was also on its way to signing judicial cooperation agreements with dozens of countries as part of an effort to fight corruption, including drug-money laundering. In addition, a bill was approved by the Senate that would amend the constitution to establish the principle of binding precedent for high court decisions and allow for external control of the judiciary. The national security law permitting the shooting down by the air force of aircraft suspected of being involved in the drug trade went into effect on October 17; only neighboring Colombia has a similar law in the region.

Brazil has the highest rate of homicide caused by firearms of any country not at war—more than 70 percent. Police say that most violent crime in the country, perhaps as much as 70 to 80 percent, is directly or indirectly related to the illegal drug trade, including most of the 37,000 annual murders. An estimated 200,000 Brazilians are employed in the narcotics business, with at least 5,000 heavily armed gang members working for various drug-trafficking groups in Rio de Janeiro alone. Since 1994, the federal government has deployed the army to quell police strikes and bring order to Rio de Janeiro's 400 slums, most of which are ruled by gangs in league or in competition with corrupt police and local politicians.

Brazil's police are among the world's most violent and corrupt, and they systematically resort to torture to extract confessions from prisoners. Extrajudicial killings are usually disguised as shootouts with dangerous criminals. "Death squads" operating in at least 15 of Brazil's 26 states, often composed of off-duty state police, terrorize shantytown dwellers and intimidate human rights activists attempting to investigate abuses. In the rare instances when police officers are indicted for such abuses, convictions are not obtained; typically such indictments are dismissed for "lack of evidence." In May, Brazilian human rights secretary Nilmario Miranda admitted that an Amnesty International report accusing the police of torturing and killing thousands the previous year "reflects the truth." The prison system in Brazil is anarchic, overcrowded, and largely unfit for human habitation; human rights groups charge that torture and other inhumane treatment common to most of the country's detention centers turn petty thieves into hardened criminals. Some 200,000 people are incarcerated in Brazil, nearly half of them in Sao Paulo.

Racial discrimination, long officially denied as a problem in Brazil, began to receive both recognition and remediation from the da Silva government. Afro-Brazilians earn more than 50 percent less than other citizens, and on average, Afro-Brazilian university graduates earn less than others with only high school diplomas. In a precedent-setting series of actions, on taking office da Silva named four Afro-Brazilians to his cabinet, appointed the country's first Afro-Brazilian Supreme Court justice, and pressed for the adoption of a Racial Equality Statute to redeem his pledge that Afro-Brazilians would make up at least one-third of the federal government within five years.

Large landowners control nearly 60 percent of the country's arable land, while the poorest 30 percent share less than 2 percent. In rural areas, violence linked to land invasions organized by the MST, the landless peasants' movement, continues to be a sporadic problem; courts have increasingly supported the eviction of such land invaders. Although Brazil abolished slavery in 1888, in 2004 the government acknowledged that at least 25,000 Brazilians work under "conditions analogous to slavery," with other estimates putting that figure as high as 50,000. Many slaves work in the forest industry in the state of Para. Landowners who enslave workers face two to eight years in prison, in addition to fines. However, the latter are minimal and few, if any, of the modern-day slavers ever spend a day in jail.

Violence against Brazil's 250,000 Indians mirrors generalized rural lawlessness. A decree issued by former president Cardoso opened Indian land to greater pressure from predatory miners and loggers. In some remote areas, Colombian drug traffickers have been using Indians to transport narcotics. In September 2003, the new head of Brazil's Indian agency promised that the government was serious about demarcating wide swaths of ancestral lands as the first step in converting the land into indigenous reserves. Suicide is common among Indian youths. In April 2004, members of the Cinta-Larga tribe were blamed for killing 29 diamond prospectors who were illegally trespassing on their lands in the state of Rondonia. The former head of the country's indigenous affairs agency, Apoena Meireles, was murdered by unknown assailants in the city of Porto Velho.

In August 2001, Congress approved a legal code that for the first time in the country's history makes women equal to men under the law. In January 2003, a new civil code took effect, formally replacing a 1916 text that contained myriad sexist provisions concerning social behavior in government, in business, and at home; the new code gave women the same rights in marriage as men. Nevertheless, violence against women and children is a common problem, and protective laws are rarely enforced. Forced prostitution of children is widespread. Child labor is prevalent, and laws against it are rarely enforced. In June 2001, a decree granted same-sex partners the same rights as married couples with respect to pensions, social security benefits, and taxation. Brazil is a source country for victims of both domestic and international trafficking of human beings, the majority of whom are women and girls. Occasionally, women are employed as domestic servants in conditions tantamount to slavery.

✦ Brunei

Population: 400,000
GNI/capita: $13,724
Life Expectancy: 76
Religious Groups: Muslim (67 percent), Buddhist (13 percent), Christian (10 percent), other [including indigenous beliefs] (10 percent)
Ethnic Groups: Malay (67 percent), Chinese (15 percent), other (18 percent)
Capital: Bandar Seri Begawan

Political Rights: 6
Civil Liberties: 5
Status: Not Free

Trend Arrow: Brunei received an upward trend arrow due to the announcement of the reconsitution of the legislative council after 20 years.

Ten-Year Ratings Timeline (Political Rights, Civil Liberties, Status)

1995	1996	1997	1998	1999	2000	2001	2002	2003	2004
7,5NF	7,5NF	7,5NF	7,5NF	7,5NF	7,5NF	7,5NF	6,5NF	6,5NF	6,5NF

Overview:

Although Sultan Hassanal Bolkiah Mu'izzaddin Waddaulah took a landmark step in announcing the revitalization of Brunei's parliament in 2004, he shows no signs of fully liberalizing this Southeast Asian nation's political system. His action most likely represents a small concession in the face of ongoing problems such as the growing number of foreign workers in the country and the possibility of declining oil revenues.

Consisting of two tiny enclaves on the northern coast of Borneo, Brunei is an oil-rich, hereditary sultanate that has been under the absolute rule of Sultan Hassanal Bolkiah four nearly four decades. The 1959 constitution vested full executive powers in the sultan while providing for five advisory councils, including the Legislative Council (parliament). In 1962, Sultan Omar Ali Saifuddin annulled legislative election results after the leftist Brunei People's Party (BPP), which sought to end the sultanate, won all 10 elected seats in the 21-member council. The BPP then mounted an insurgency that was crushed by British troops but whose legacy is still felt. Sultan Omar invoked constitutionally granted emergency powers, which are still in force, and began ruling by decree. That practice was continued by his son, Sultan Hassanal Bolkiah, who became the twenty ninth ruler in a family dynasty that has spanned six centuries, when his father abdicated the throne in 1967. The British granted full independence in 1984.

Oil and natural gas exports to Japan and other countries have given Brunei a per capita income rivaling that of many Western societies. Food, fuel, housing, schooling, and medical care are either free or subsidized, and there is virtually no poverty except for small pockets in tiny, remote villages. Energy reserves are dwindling, however, and the government has had limited success in diversifying the economy. The oil and gas sector's contribution to gross domestic product was 39.8 percent in 2003, up from 37.1 percent in 2002 because of higher oil prices. The ongoing dispute with Malaysia over the contested oil- and gas-rich Baram Delta waters off the northern Borneo coast took on a new urgency with the discovery in March 2004 of deepwater oil at Gumusut, near the disputed territory. Negotiations with Malaysia may be more successful under that country's new prime minister, Abdullah Badawi.

In July, the sultan announced that he would reconvene Brunei's Legislative Council as part of a set of measures designed to "engage the citizens." The council, which has been suspended since 1984, will not be elected; Sultan Hassanal Bolkiah appointed the first 21 members in September 2004.

Political Rights and Civil Liberties: Bruneians cannot change their government through elections. The sultan wields broad powers under a state of emergency that has been in effect since 1962, and no legislative elections have been held since then. Lacking a more open political system, citizens often convey concerns to their leaders through a traditional system under which government-vetted, elected village chiefs meet periodically with top government officials. Citizens generally avoid political activity altogether, apparently because they know that the government disapproves of it. Their docility is explained by the lavish benefits the government grants them, including free health care, free education, generous pensions, and housing subsidies.

Now 58 years old and one of the world's richest men, Sultan Hassanal Bolkiah has done little to reform the ossified political system that he inherited. Although the sultan decided in July to reconvene the Legislative Council, members continue to be appointed by the sultan rather than elected, and the only two legal political parties are largely inactive. Both the Brunei People's Awareness Party and the Brunei National Solidarity Party (BNSP) publicly support the sultan. The BNSP is an offshoot of one of two parties banned in 1988.

Although hard data indicating high levels of corruption are scarce, the sultanate's vast wealth lends itself easily to profligacy among officials. The settlement of a major corruption scandal, involving the misappropriation of state funds by the Sultan's brother, made headlines across the world in 2000. In October 2004, Brunei's former minister of development pleaded not guilty to 12 counts of corruption; his trial is set for February 2005. Brunei was not ranked by Transparency International in its 2004 Corruption Perceptions Index.

Bruneian journalists face considerable restrictions. Legislation introduced in 2001 allows officials to shut down newspapers without showing cause and to fine and jail journalists who write or publish articles deemed "false and malicious." The largest daily, the *Borneo Bulletin*, practices self-censorship, though it does publish letters to the editor criticizing government policies. Another daily, the *News Express*, closed in 2002 after being sued successfully by a private law firm for defamation. Brunei's only television station is state-run, although Bruneians also can receive Malaysian television and satellite channels. The Internet is becoming widespread. In addition to restricting the media, the government has in previous years detained several Bruneians for publishing or distributing antigovernment materials.

The Shafeite sect of Islam, Brunei's official religion, permeates all levels of society in this predominantly Muslim country. In schools, Islamic study is mandatory, and the teaching of other religions is prohibited. The sultan promotes a combination of Islamic values, local Malay culture, and allegiance to the hereditary monarchy through a national ideology called "Malay Muslim Monarchy." Critics say that the ideology, which is taught in schools, is used in part to legitimize an undemocratic system. While promoting Islam, Brunei's secular government has also voiced concern over religious fundamentalism, and one Islamist group, Al-Arqam, is banned. The government also restricts religious freedom for non-Muslims. It prohibits proselytizing, bans the importation of religious teaching materials and scriptures such as the Bible, and ignores requests to build, expand, or repair temples, churches, and shrines, according to the U.S. State Department's human rights report for 2003, released in February 2004.

Freedom of assembly is restricted under emergency powers that have been in effect since 1962. Membership in political parties is highly restricted, and those parties that exist remain largely inactive. Most nongovernmental organizations and civil groups are locally based professional or business organizations. All such organizations must receive permission to operate in Brunei under the Companies Act. All trade unions must be registered with the government. Brunei's three trade unions are all in the oil sector, and their membership makes up less than 5 percent of that industry's workforce. Strikes are illegal in Brunei, and collective bargaining is not recognized. There was no union activity of any sort in the country in 2004.

Courts in Brunei generally "appeared to act independently," according to the U.S. State Department report, despite the fact that the constitution does not specifically provide for an independent judiciary. The legal system is based on British common law, although Sharia (Islamic law) takes precedence in areas including divorce, inheritance, and some sex crimes. Sharia does not apply to non-Muslims.

While the government has faced few overt threats since the 1960s, authorities occasionally detain suspected antigovernment activists under Brunei's Internal Security Act. The act permits detention without trial for renewable two-year periods. Recent detainees include a prominent citizen said to have committed treason by providing classified government documents to an unnamed foreign country, two others deemed subversive for posting classified information on a Hong Kong-based Web site, 16 people involved in selling and distributing counterfeit Brunei currencies to the public, and six people who attempted to revive the proscribed Al-Arqam group (these six were released in July 2004).

Freedom of movement of persons other than former political persons is not restricted. Most citizens enjoy reasonable personal autonomy, but many "stateless" people—mostly ethnic Chinese—are not accorded full citizenship status and thus lack rights such as the right to own land and to have access to subsidized medical care. Foreign workers, especially female domestic servants, are the persons most likely to be subjected to economic exploitation.

Women remain unequal to men in areas such as divorce and inheritance, in accordance with Islamic law. Nevertheless, the number of women entering the workforce has increased substantially over the past several years. Women in government-run institutions must wear the *tudong* (a traditional head covering); many educational institutions also pressure non-Muslim students to wear it as part of a uniform.

Bulgaria

Population: 7,800,000 **Political Rights:** 1
GNI/capita: $1,770 **Civil Liberties:** 2
Life Expectancy: 72 **Status:** Free
Religious Groups: Bulgarian Orthodox (82.6 percent),
Muslim (12.2 percent), other (5.2 percent)
Ethnic Groups: Bulgarian (82.6 percent), Turk (9.4 percent),
Roma (4.7 percent), other (2 percent)
Capital: Sofia

Ten-Year Ratings Timeline (Political Rights, Civil Liberties, Status)

1995	1996	1997	1998	1999	2000	2001	2002	2003	2004
2,2F	2,3F	2,3F	2,3F	2,3F	2,3F	1,3F	1,2F	1,2F	1,2F

Overview:
Bulgaria joined NATO in March 2004 and concluded its membership negotiations with the European Union (EU). Its troop presence in Iraq made it a target for a double kidnapping in July.

Bulgaria became independent from the Ottoman Empire in 1878. After originally siding with Germany in World War II, Communist Todor Zhivkov ultimately persuaded a none-too-reluctant army to side with the Russians. A Communist government was established in Bulgaria after the Soviet Red Army swept through the country toward the end of 1944. From 1954 to 1989, Zhivkov ruled the country. His 35-year reign ended when a massive pro-democracy rally in Sofia was inspired by the broader political changes sweeping across Eastern Europe at the end of the 1980s.

In the post-Communist period, the main political actors in the country have been the Union of Democratic Forces (UDF) and the Bulgarian Socialist Party (BSP). The BSP dominated parliament from 1989 to 1997, and the UDF was in power from 1997 to 2001. The UDF was credited with significant success in privatizing and restructuring most of the state economy as well as winning an invitation for EU membership talks.

In 2001, Bulgaria's former king, Simeon II, returned from exile and formed the National Movement for Simeon II (NDSV). Promising quicker integration into Europe, Simeon attracted a large segment of the electorate. In the 2001 elections to Bulgaria's parliament, the NDSV won 120 of the 240 seats; the UDF, 51; the Coalition for Bulgaria (which includes the BSP), 48; and the Movement for Rights and Freedoms (MRF), 21. The NDSV formed a coalition with the MRF after failing to gain an outright majority. By 2003, however, there were signs that Simeon's popularity was beginning to wane, with his NDSV winning only 7 percent of the votes cast in that year's local elections.

Despite the weakness of the government, Bulgaria has made substantial progress toward joining the EU. It completed its formal negotiations in 2004, and a positive report from the EU in October 2004 confirmed a target date of 2007 for admission.

Bulgaria joined NATO in March. Although it does not have a large defense program, it has almost 500 troops in Iraq. Two Bulgarian civilians were kidnapped and beheaded in Iraq in July, but the government maintained its troop presence there.

Political Rights and Civil Liberties: Bulgarians can change their government democratically. The unicameral National Assembly, composed of 240 members, is elected every four years. Georgi Parvanov of the BSP was elected in November 2001 to a five-year term as president, defeating incumbent Petar Stoyanov. Prime minister and former king Simeon II leads the NDSV, the largest party in government.

The constitution forbids political groups that act against national integrity, call for ethnic or religious hostility, or create secret military structures. In the 2001 elections, 54 parties and coalitions were registered, most representing local interests. The NDSV, the UDF, the BSP (which is trying to move away from its Communist past), and the centrist MRF were the only parties with enough votes to be represented in the National Assembly. However, in March a new party, called New Time, was formed by 10 NDSV defectors.

The Turkish minority in Bulgaria is almost exclusively represented by the MRF. In contrast, no party represents the Roma (Gypsy) minority, despite attempts to create one.

Although the government has attempted to build a framework against corruption, overall levels have not changed significantly. Organized crime and corruption in government and business continue to be problems, and deficiencies in the legal system prevent the government from effective prosecution of perpetrators. Bulgaria was ranked 54 out of 146 countries surveyed in the 2004 Transparency International Corruption Perceptions Index. At the same time, the government operates with relative openness.

The constitution guarantees freedom of the press, although international observers believe that the government still exerts undue influence over the media, and many journalists complain of feeling harassed about their reporting. Defamation is a criminal offense, and sentences can be severe. A Romanian journalist was arrested in Bulgaria in November for filming with a concealed camera, which is a crime. The head of Bulgarian National TV was dismissed in March after being accused of allowing biased reporting on state broadcasts. Internet access is not restricted.

Freedom of religion is generally respected in Bulgaria. The government has in recent years made it difficult for "nontraditional" religious groups to obtain registration permits allowing them to be active. Those groups considered traditional are the Orthodox, Roman Catholic, Islamic, and Jewish communities. The Bulgarian Orthodox Church has been divided for 12 years between those who support Bishop Maxim, appointed by the Bulgarian Communist Party 30 years ago, and those who support Bishop Inokentii, who was canonically elected. The Bulgarian government favors the former, and it further institutionalized this preference through the 2002 Confessions Act—essentially a law on religion that makes Bishop Maxim the only representative of the Bulgarian Orthodox Church and thereby withdraws the right of Bishop Inokentii's priests to preach. The Council of Europe and others have criticized the act for restricting freedom of religion. Moreover, in July, Bulgarian police raided as many as 250 churches of the synod of Bishop Inokentii, expelling and arresting their priests and in some cases appointing priests from Bishop Maxim's synod in their place. Technically, the Inokentii priests were illegally occupying the property, which had been granted to the other synod.

The government does not restrict academic freedom.

The constitution provides for freedom of assembly and association, and the government generally respects these rights. The government prohibits the formation of groups that propagate ethnic, religious, or racial hatred, or that advocate achieving their goals through the use of violence. There have been reports that the government has denied ethnic Macedonians and other groups less favorable to the government the right to hold public gatherings. The rights of trade unions are respected.

The judiciary is legally guaranteed independence and equal status with the executive and legislative branches of government. Rights groups claim that the judicial system suffers from problems including corruption, inadequate staffing, low salaries for magistrates, and a perceived unwillingness to prosecute crimes against ethnic minorities, charges that the government denies. In 2003 and 2004, parliament passed amendments to the constitution designed to improve judicial independence and effectiveness.

Torture and inhumane treatment are reportedly less common than before, but they remain problems in Bulgaria and are allegedly not investigated thoroughly. The election by the Supreme Judicial Council of Konstantin Penchev to the Supreme Administrative Court in March raised criticism; Penchev is a legislator for the ruling party, and there were reports of interference by the prime minister. In 2004, the Council of Europe reported an improvement in treatment of minorities in Bulgaria. However, the Roma population remains subjected to discrimination, police violence, and segregation.

Women hold about one-quarter of the seats in parliament. Trafficking of women for the purpose of prostitution remains a serious problem, although the Act for Combating Trafficking in People became effective in January. Domestic violence is a continual concern. A 2004 poll found that one man in four beats his wife, while a local nongovernmental organization published a separate survey showing that one in five Bulgarian women is the victim of some form of spousal abuse.

Burkina Faso

Population: 13,600,000
GNI/capita: $250
Life Expectancy: 45
Religious Groups: Indigenous beliefs (40 percent), Muslim (50 percent), Christian (10 percent)
Ethnic Groups: Mossi (over 40 percent), other [including Gurunsi, Senufo, Lobi, Bobo, Mande and Fulani] (60 percent)
Capital: Ouagadougou

Political Rights: 5*
Civil Liberties: 4
Status: Partly Free

Ratings Change: Burkina Faso's political rights rating declined from 4 to 5 due to an increase in corruption and reports of arms trafficking.

Ten-Year Ratings Timeline (Political Rights, Civil Liberties, Status)

1995	1996	1997	1998	1999	2000	2001	2002	2003	2004
5,4PF	5,4PF	5,4PF	5,4PF	4,4PF	4,4PF	4,4PF	4,4PF	4,4PF	5,4PF

Overview:

Burkina Faso's political opposition feared that President Blaise Compaore would run for a third term as the country geared up for presidential elections to be held in 2005.

Changes to the electoral code in 2004 essentially return the country to a proportional representation system of voting. Meanwhile, Burkina Faso had strained relations with its neighbors and was dealing with internal dissent as well.

After gaining independence from France in 1960 as Upper Volta, Burkina Faso suffered a succession of army coups. In 1983, Compaore installed himself as president in a violent coup against members of a junta that had seized power four years earlier and had pursued a watered-down Marxist-Leninist ideology. The populist, charismatic President Thomas Sankara and 13 of his closest associates were murdered. More Sankara supporters were executed two years later.

The presidential poll of December 1991, in which Compaore was reelected by default, was marred by widespread violence and an opposition boycott by all five candidates challenging the incumbent. Compaore was returned to office for a second seven-year term in November 1998 with nearly 88 percent of the vote.

The 2002 National Assembly elections were overseen by the reconstituted Independent National Electoral Commission and were considered among the most free and fair polls in Burkina Faso to date. The commission includes representatives from the government, civil society, and the opposition. The 2002 polls marked the first time that a simple ballot was used in voting, a measure that opposition parties had urged for several years. The ruling Congress for Democracy and Progress Party won 57 of the 111 National Assembly seats, compared with 101 during the 1997 polls. Opposition parties fared better than they had during any time previously.

Although Compaore has served two consecutive, elected seven-year terms, his supporters say that he is eligible to contest the presidency in 2005. They base their argument on a 2001 constitutional amendment that stipulated that the presidential term of office be five years, renewable once, starting in 2005. This term limit cannot be enforced retroactively. However, although the constitution allows Compaore to run for another term, the opposition would view a choice to do so as an attempt to cling to power, and his candidacy could set off protests or trigger an opposition boycott.

Changes to Burkina Faso's electoral code in 2004 designated the country's 45 provinces, instead of its 15 regions, as electoral units. Opposition members insisted that this gives the government an unfair advantage because they claim it will be impossible for them to field candidates and polling observers in all 45 electoral units. The changes are in effect a return to the proportional representation system that existed prior to 2002.

The government tackled internal dissent in 2004 when it sacked the defense minister, who had been questioned in connection with an alleged coup plot. A military court sent several officers to prison for their role in the alleged plot. However, Compaore appears to retain the loyalty of the military. The prosecutor in the case accused Cote d'Ivoire and Togo of backing the plot, which they deny.

The Burkinabe government in August denied being behind a plot to topple Mauritania's president. Mauritania accused Burkina Faso of conspiring with Libya to destabilize the region; Burkina Faso denied the charges.

Relations between Burkina Faso and Cote d'Ivoire have been strained since civil war broke out in Cote d'Ivoire in 2002. Burkinabe, Muslims, and members of northern Ivorian ethnic groups were among those targeted after Cote d'Ivoire accused

Burkina Faso of supporting mutinous Ivorian soldiers in a coup attempt that triggered the civil war. Many families in Burkina Faso depend on remittances from relatives working in Cote d'Ivoire; about 350,000 Burkinabe have returned home. However, peace is not assured in Cote d'Ivoire, and Burkina Faso could experience further economic and political turbulence.

Burkina Faso has been cited in reports by New York–based Human Rights Watch as a transshipment point for arms from Eastern Europe destined for Liberia and Sierra Leone. Burkina Faso has denied this, as well as reports that it has supported Ivorian rebels fighting against the government in Ivory Coast.

Political Rights and Civil Liberties: Although the 1991 constitution guarantees citizens of Burkina Faso the right to elect their government freely through periodic multiparty elections, this right has not been fully realized in practice. The 1998 presidential election was marked by heavy use of state patronage, resources, and media by the ruling party. The 2002 legislative elections were considered among the most free and fair polls in Burkina Faso to date, and opposition parties in 2002 fared better than they had any time previously. However, the opposition maintains that changes to the country's electoral code made in 2004 will provide the government with an unfair advantage in future polls.

Corruption is a problem in Burkina Faso. Despite the creation of two anticorruption bodies in 2001, such efforts to reduce graft have been largely cosmetic. A nongovernmental organization (NGO) in the country that focuses on corruption says that public perception is that graft is getting worse because of low salaries, poverty, and the low risk of detection. Burkina Faso was not ranked by Transparency International in its 2004 Corruption Perceptions Index.

Burkina Faso has a vibrant free press, and freedom of speech is protected by the constitution and generally respected in practice. At least 50 private radio stations, a private television station, and numerous independent newspapers and magazines function with little governmental interference. The media, which are often highly critical of the government, play an important role in public debate. There is liberal Internet access.

Burkina Faso is a secular state, and religious freedom is respected. The government does not restrict academic freedom.

Freedom of assembly is constitutionally protected and generally respected, with required permits usually issued routinely. However, demonstrations are sometimes violently suppressed or banned. Many NGOs, including human rights groups, which have reported detailed accounts of abuses by security forces, operate openly and freely. Labor union rights are provided for in the constitution. Unions are a strong force in society and routinely stage strikes over wages, human rights abuses, and the impunity of security forces.

The judiciary is subject to executive interference in political cases and is hampered by a lack of resources and lengthy delays. A military court in April sentenced an army captain to 10 years in prison for leading a plot to overthrow President Blaise Compaore; other military officers received lighter sentences.

National security laws permit surveillance and arrest without warrants. Police routinely ignore prescribed limits on detention, search, and seizure. Security forces commit abuses with impunity, including torture and occasional extrajudicial killing.

Harsh prison conditions are characterized by overcrowding, poor diet, and minimal medical attention.

Various ethnic groups are represented in Burkina Faso's government, and official decisions do not favor one group over another.

Burkina Faso is one of the world's poorest countries, with more than 80 percent of the population relying on subsistence agriculture. Burkina Faso's economy has suffered as a result of the war in neighboring Cote d'Ivoire, and there has been an increased cost of routing trade via the ports of Ghana, Togo, and Benin.

Constitutional and legal protections for women's rights are nonexistent or poorly enforced. Customary law sanctions discrimination against women. Female genital mutilation is still widely practiced, even though it is illegal and a government campaign has been mounted against it. Burkina Faso is used as a transit point for the trafficking of women and children for purposes of forced labor and prostitution, but the government has made an effort to stop this criminal activity.

Burma (Myanmar)

Population: 50,100,000 **Political Rights:** 7
GNI/capita: $105 **Civil Liberties:** 7
Life Expectancy: 57 **Status:** Not Free
Religious Groups: Buddhist (89 percent),
Christian (4 percent), other (7 percent)
Ethnic Groups: Burman (68 percent), Shan (9 percent),
Karen (7 percent), Rakhine (4 percent), Chinese (3 percent),
Mon (2 percent), Indian (2 percent), other (5 percent)
Capital: Rangoon

Ten-Year Ratings Timeline (Political Rights, Civil Liberties, Status)

1995	1996	1997	1998	1999	2000	2001	2002	2003	2004
7,7NF	7,7NF	7,7NF	7,7NF	7,7NF	7,7NF	7,7NF	7,7NF	7,7NF	7,7NF

Overview:
Following the crackdown on the opposition National League for Democracy (NLD) party in mid-2003, the collapse of a halting process of national reconciliation, and a leadership purge within the military junta, Burma remained under the firm grip of the hardliners in the military junta during 2004. Although the National Convention, tasked with drafting a new constitution, was reconvened by the regime in May 2004, it was boycotted by the main opposition parties; it thus failed to provide a veneer of legitimacy for the junta's strategy of positioning it as a first step on a planned "road map to democracy." Meanwhile, the regime maintained its hold on virtually all levers of power and showed few signs of being willing to consider meaningful positive reform. NLD leader Aung San Suu Kyi remained under house arrest, and the activities of the NLD were severely curtailed, while a wide range of human rights violations against NLD members and other political opponents, as well as members of ethnic and religious minority groups, continued unabated throughout the year. With the ouster of prime minister and head of military intelligence Khin Nyunt in October, followed by

a purge of his allies, hardliners within the junta had firmly reasserted their control by year's end, and prospects of reform seemed dimmer than ever.

After being occupied by the Japanese during World War II, Burma achieved independence from Great Britain in 1948. The military has ruled since 1962, when the army overthrew an elected government buffeted by an economic crisis and a raft of ethnic-based insurgencies. During the next 26 years, General Ne Win's military rule helped impoverish what had been one of Southeast Asia's wealthiest countries.

The present junta, currently led by General Than Shwe, dramatically asserted its power in 1988, when the army opened fire on peaceful, student-led, pro-democracy protesters, killing an estimated 3,000 people. In the aftermath, a younger generation of army commanders created the State Law and Order Restoration Council (SLORC) to rule the country. The SLORC refused to cede power after it was defeated in a landslide election by the NLD in 1990. The junta jailed dozens of members of the NLD, which won 392 of the 485 parliamentary seats in Burma's first free elections in three decades.

Than Shwe and several other generals who headed the junta refashioned the SLORC as the State Peace and Development Council (SPDC) in 1997. The generals appeared to be trying to improve the junta's international image, attract foreign investment, and encourage an end to U.S.-led sanctions linked to the regime's grim human rights record. In late 2000, encouraged by the efforts of UN special envoy Razali Ismail, the regime began holding talks with Suu Kyi, which led to an easing of restrictions on the NLD by mid-2002. Suu Kyi was released from house arrest and was allowed to make several political trips outside the capital, and the NLD was permitted to reopen a number of its branch offices.

Suu Kyi's growing popularity and her revitalization of the NLD during the first half of 2003, especially in the sensitive ethnic minority areas, apparently rattled hardliners within the regime. On May 30, a deadly ambush on an NLD convoy in northern Burma by SPDC supporters, in which an unknown number of people were killed or injured, illustrated the lengths to which hardliners within the SPDC would go to limit an NLD challenge. Suu Kyi and dozens of other NLD officials and supporters were detained, many in undisclosed locations, following the attack. NLD offices were once again shut down, and universities and schools were temporarily closed in a bid to suppress wider unrest. Her detention and the junta's subsequent crackdown evoked outrage: Japan, the country's largest aid donor, temporarily suspended its aid programs, while the U.S. government tightened sanctions by imposing a ban on all Burmese imports into the United States.

A cabinet reshuffle in August 2003 left hard-liner Than Shwe as head of state, while the more pragmatic intelligence chief, Khin Nyunt, was promoted to prime minister. Around the same time, the junta announced that the National Convention (NC), which has the responsibility for drafting principles for a new constitution but which had not met since 1996 after being boycotted by the opposition, would be reconvened in May 2004 as part of its new "road map to democracy" announced in 2003. However, heavy restrictions on its format and operations—authorities hand-picked most of the delegates and limited the scope of permissible debate from the outset—led to a boycott of the proceedings by both the NLD and some of the ethnic parties, who remain wary that the NC is being used as a means of legitimizing the junta's rule and enshrining the military's role in government. The National Convention was adjourned indefinitely in July 2004 and had not been reconvened by year's end, although the leadership had reaffirmed its commitment to do so.

Meanwhile, authorities also maintained their focus on containing the popularity of the NLD party. Aung San Suu Kyi was released from prison in September 2003 but remained under house arrest, as did other senior NLD leaders. Periodic arrest and detention of political activists and other perceived threats to the regime, including journalists and students, remained the norm in 2004. Talks between the SPDC and several rebel groups still at war with the junta continued for most of the year. However, although the SPDC had verbally agreed to an informal ceasefire with the Karen National Union (KNU) in late 2003, skirmishes between the two sides have continued, as have human rights violations in the Karen and other ethnic-minority states.

On October 19, Khin Nyunt, the prime minister and head of military intelligence (MI), was removed from office and placed under house arrest amid conflicting reports that he was retiring for health reasons or had been "involved in corruption." However, his dismissal was followed by a widespread purge of his key allies, the dismantlement of the MI ministry itself, and takeovers of Khin Nyunt's extensive business interests, thus confirming that hardliners in the regime intended to reassert their control over government policy making. A relative moderate, Nyunt had advocated limited dialogue with both the NLD and Burma's armed ethnic factions. His replacement by hardliner Lieutenant-General Soe Win—who has been accused by the U.S. government and others of masterminding the May 2003 attack on Suu Kyi's motorcade—suggests that the junta will continue to resist all pressure to reform, although it publicly reaffirmed its commitment to continuing with its road map in November.

Political Rights and Civil Liberties:

Burma continues to be ruled by one of the world's most repressive regimes. The SPDC rules by decree; controls all executive, legislative, and judicial powers; suppresses nearly all basic rights; and commits human rights abuses with impunity. Military officers hold most cabinet positions, and active or retired officers hold most top posts in all ministries, as well as key positions in both the administration and the private sector.

Since rejecting the results of the 1990 elections and preventing the elected parliament from convening, the junta has all but paralyzed the victorious NLD party. Authorities have jailed many NLD leaders, pressured thousands of party members and officials to resign, closed party offices, harassed members' families, and periodically detained hundreds of NLD supporters at a time to block planned party meetings. After being allowed somewhat greater freedom during 2002, the NLD was subjected to another crackdown in 2003, which largely continued throughout 2004. Although the party's main office was allowed to reopen in April, its branch offices remained closed and several key party leaders, including Aung San Suu Kyi, remain under house arrest. In the run-up to the National Convention held in May, opposition party leaders and members faced heightened surveillance, intimidation, and arrest as they attempted to engage in peaceful political activities, according to an Amnesty International report. An NLD campaign calling for the release of political prisoners begun in July was countered with increased harassment of party members; in September, four were jailed for seven years following a secret trial after being charged with sending information to overseas groups.

Besides the NLD, there are more than 20 ethnic political parties that remain suppressed by the junta. An International Crisis Group report published in 2003 notes that ethnic-minority groups feel that they are denied a role in national political life and do not have a chance to influence policy decisions that affect their lives.

In a system that lacks both transparency and accountability, official corruption is reportedly rampant at both the high and local levels. Burma was ranked 142 out of 146 countries surveyed in the 2004 Transparency International Corruption Perceptions Index.

The junta sharply restricts press freedom, owning or tightly controlling all daily newspapers and radio and television stations. It also subjects private periodicals to prepublication censorship and restricts the importation of foreign news periodicals. After the purge, the new hardline leadership took control of the censorship bureau (which previously had been controlled by associates of Khin Nyunt in the MI ministry) and suspended seventeen publications, most of them indefinitely. According to the Committee to Protect Journalists, although some people have access to international shortwave radio or satellite television, those caught accessing foreign broadcasts can be arrested. In May, authorities moved to limit coverage of the National Convention, refusing to grant visas to foreign correspondents and imposing advance censorship on the dissemination of the proceedings. Although several journalists and writers were released from jail throughout the year, a number remained imprisoned as a result of expressing dissident views. The sentence of journalist Zaw Thet Htwe, editor of a sports magazine, who was detained in June 2003, accused of involvement in a "conspiracy" against the government, and sentenced to death in November for treason, was reduced in May 2004 to three years' imprisonment. The Internet, which operates in a limited fashion in the cities, is tightly regulated and censored.

Ordinary Burmese generally can worship relatively freely. However, the junta shows preference for Theravada Buddhism, discriminating against non-Buddhists in the upper levels of the public sector and coercively promoting Buddhism in some ethnic-minority areas. The regime has also tried to control the Buddhist clergy by placing monastic orders under a state-run committee, monitoring monasteries, and subjecting clergy to special restrictions on speech and association. A number of monks remain imprisoned for their pro-democracy and human rights work. Burma was once again designated a "country of particular concern" in the 2004 report by the U.S. Commission on International Religious Freedom, which noted severe and systematic official discrimination against members of minority religious groups. A 2002 Human Rights Watch (HRW) report alleged that the government had failed to protect Muslims from a significant increase in anti-Muslim violence and that it had imposed restrictions on Muslim religious activities and travel. Violence against the Muslim minority continues to be a problem, with deadly flare-ups in Yangon and Mandalay divisions being reported in late 2003. According to a 2004 report by the Chin Human Rights Organization, the regime has targeted the predominantly Christian Chin ethnic minority, destroying churches, intimidating and assaulting members of the clergy, and supporting coerced conversions to Buddhism.

Academic freedom is severely limited. Teachers are subject to restrictions on freedom of expression and publication and are held accountable for the political activities of their students. Since the 1988 student pro-democracy demonstrations, the junta has sporadically closed universities, limiting higher education opportunities for a generation of young Burmese. Most campuses were relocated to relatively isolated areas as a measure to disperse the student population. Following the May 2003 clashes, the junta, fearing student unrest, once again temporarily closed some schools and universities, but two students were killed when the military violently suppressed a student demonstration held to protest the attack on Suu Kyi, according to Amnesty International.

Authorities continued to infringe on citizens' privacy rights by arbitrarily searching homes, intercepting mail, and monitoring telephone conversations. Laws and decrees criminalize the possession and use of unregistered electronic devices, including telephones, fax machines, computers, modems, and software.

Freedom of association and assembly is restricted. An ordinance prohibits unauthorized outdoor gatherings of more than five people, and authorities regularly use force to break up peaceful demonstrations and prevent pro-democracy activists from organizing events or meetings. Since the May 2003 crackdown, an increasing number of people have been detained for attempting to exercise their rights to freedom of association and expression. However, nearly all public sector employees, as well as other ordinary citizens, are induced to join the pro-junta mass mobilization organization, the Union Solidarity and Development Association. Domestic human rights organizations are unable to function independently, and the regime generally dismisses critical scrutiny of its human rights record from international nongovernmental organizations and journalists. Although Amnesty International was given permission to make two trips to Burma in January and December 2003, it was not allowed back into the country during 2004.

Independent trade unions, collective bargaining, and strikes are illegal, and several labor activists are serving long prison terms for their political and labor activities. The regime continues to use forced labor despite formally banning the practice in October 2000. The International Labor Organization (ILO) and other sources report that soldiers routinely force civilians, including women and children, to work without pay under harsh conditions. Laborers are commandeered to construct roads, clear minefields, porter for the army, or work on military-backed commercial ventures. Forced labor appears to be most widespread in states dominated by ethnic minorities. Although the ILO's plans to work with the junta to eradicate the practice were put on hold after the attack on the NLD in May 2003, it continues to monitor the situation on the ground.

The judiciary is not independent. Justices are appointed or approved by the junta and adjudicate cases according to the junta's decrees. Administrative detention laws allow people to be held without charge, trial, or access to legal counsel for up to five years if the SPDC feels that they have threatened the state's security or sovereignty. Some basic due process rights are reportedly observed in ordinary criminal cases, but not in political cases, according to the U.S. State Department's 2003 human rights report. Corruption, the misuse of overly broad laws, and the manipulation of the courts for political ends continue to deprive citizens of their legal rights.

Detailed reports issued recently by Amnesty International have raised a number of concerns regarding the administration of justice, including laws and practices regarding detention, torture, trial, and conditions of imprisonment. Political prisoners are frequently held incommunicado in pretrial detention, which facilitates the use of torture and other forms of ill treatment, and are denied access to family members, legal counsel, and medical care. In addition, political trials are conducted summarily and do not meet international standards of fairness. Prisons and labor camps are overcrowded, although conditions in some facilities have reportedly improved gradually since the regime began allowing the International Committee of the Red Cross access to prisons in 1999.

The junta has periodically released some of those people arrested in the aftermath of the May 2003 violence, and following Khin Nyunt's removal, thousands of prisoners were released in November, of which several dozen were being held on politicized charges. However, more than 1,350 political prisoners remained incarcerated in 2004, according to Amnesty International. Most prisoners are held under broadly drawn laws that criminalize a range of peaceful activities. These include distributing pro-democracy pamphlets and distributing, viewing, or smuggling out of Burma videotapes of Suu Kyi's public addresses. The frequently used Decree 5/96 of 1996 authorizes jail terms of up to 20 years for aiding activities "which adversely affect the national interest." After the October 2004 purge, jails were also filled with suspected allies of General Khin Nyunt within the MI ministry; several thousand were arrested, and in November, the BBC reported that three senior army intelligence officers had been sentenced to 22 years in prison.

The UN Commission on Human Rights in Geneva condemns the regime each year for committing grave human rights abuses. Annual resolutions commonly highlight a systematic pattern of extrajudicial, summary, or arbitrary executions; arrests, incommunicado detention, and "disappearances"; rape, torture, inhuman treatment, and forced labor, including the use of children; and forced relocation and the denial of freedom of assembly, association, expression, religion, and movement. Police and security forces that commit such abuses operate in a climate of impunity, as such incidents are not commonly investigated and prosecutions are rare.

Some of the worst human rights abuses take place in the seven states dominated by ethnic minorities. In these border states, the *tatmadaw*, or Burmese armed forces, reportedly kill, beat, rape, and arbitrarily detain civilians. For example, a report issued in April 2004 by the Karen Women's Organization documents numerous cases of rape committed against Karen women by members of the army as part of a strategy to intimidate, control, and shame ethnic-minority populations. Soldiers also routinely destroy property and seize livestock, cash, property, food, and other goods from villagers.

Tens of thousands of ethnic minorities in Shan, Karenni, Karen, and Mon states remain in squalid and ill-equipped relocation centers set up by the army. The army has forcibly moved the villagers to the sites since the mid-1990s as part of its counterinsurgency operations. Press reports suggest that the army continues to forcibly uproot villagers and that at least one million people have been internally displaced by these and other tactics. In addition, according to Refugees International, an estimated several million Burmese have fled to neighboring countries, including Thailand, India, and Bangladesh. Thailand continues to host at least 135,000

Karen, Mon, and Karenni in refugee camps near the Burmese border, as well as hundreds of thousands more who have not been granted refugee status.

A number of ethnic-minority groups complain of systematic discrimination at the hands of the regime, including a lack of representation in the government and military, economic marginalization, and the suppression of their cultural and religious rights. The junta has committed particularly serious abuses against the Muslim Rohingya minority in northern Rakhine state. A report published by Amnesty International in May noted that the vast majority of Rohingyas are denied citizenship and face severe restrictions on their freedom of movement, their right to own land, and their ability to marry. In addition, they are regularly subjected to arbitrary taxation and other forms of extortion, as well as forced eviction and land confiscation, at the hands of Burmese security forces. More than 250,000 Rohingyas remain in neighboring Bangladesh, where they fled in the 1990s to escape extrajudicial execution, rape, forced labor, and other abuses.

The junta continues to face low-grade insurgencies waged by the KNU and at least five other ethnic-based rebel armies. The junta agreed to an informal ceasefire with the KNU in December 2003, but hostilities reportedly continue. A number of rebel groups, however, have reached ceasefire deals with the junta since 1989, under which they have been granted effective administrative authority of the areas under their control. While army abuses are the most widespread, some rebel groups forcibly conscript civilians, commit extrajudicial killing and rape, and use women and children as porters, according to the U.S. State Department's annual human rights report. A 2002 HRW report documented the widespread use of children as soldiers by 19 different armed opposition groups, as well as by the Burmese army, where at least 20 percent of active-duty soldiers are estimated to be under the age of 18. Although authorities announced the formation of a committee to prevent the recruitment of child soldiers in late 2003, the practice has continued unabated, according to HRW.

Burmese women have traditionally enjoyed high social and economic status, but domestic violence is a growing concern, and they remain under-represented in the government and civil service. A September 2004 report by the Women's League of Burma detailed an ongoing nationwide pattern of sexual violence against women by SPDC military personnel and other authorities, including rape, sexual slavery, and forced marriage. Criminal gangs have in recent years trafficked thousands of women and girls, many from ethnic-minority groups, to Thailand and other destinations for prostitution, according to reports by HRW and other groups.

♠ Burundi

Population: 6,200,000   **Political Rights:** 5
GNI/capita: $100   **Civil Liberties:** 5
Life Expectancy: 43   **Status:** Partly Free
Religious Groups: Christian (67 percent), Indigenous
beliefs (23 percent), Muslim (10 percent),
Protestant (5 percent)
Ethnic Groups: Hutu [Bantu] (85 percent), Tutsi (14 percent),
Twa [Pygmy] (1 percent)
Capital: Bujumbura
Trend Arrow: Burundi received an upward trend arrow due to agreement on the constitutional basis for restoration of a democratic political system.

Ten-Year Ratings Timeline (Political Rights, Civil Liberties, Status)

1995	1996	1997	1998	1999	2000	2001	2002	2003	2004
6,7NF	7,7NF	7,7NF	7,6NF	6,6NF	6,6NF	6,6NF	6,5NF	5,5PF	5,5PF

Overview:
Burundi continued its very slow progress in 2004 toward resolving the multifaceted crisis that has plagued the country since 1993. A broad-based agreement was reached regarding the specifics of renewed democratic institutions that would balance the interests of the majority Hutu and minority Tutsi populations. National elections are due in 2005, but this process could be delayed since a planned constitutional referendum had not taken place by the end of 2004. Sporadic violence in the country and in the region continued to threaten the process.

With few exceptions, the minority Tutsi ethnic group has largely governed this small African country since independence from Belgium in 1962. The military, judiciary, educational system, business sector, and news media have also been dominated by the Tutsi. Violence between the country's two main ethnic groups—the Tutsi and the majority Hutu—has occurred repeatedly since independence. However, the assassination of the newly elected Hutu president, Melchoir Ndadaye, in 1993 resulted in sustained and widespread carnage. Since 1993, an estimated 200,000 Burundi citizens, out of a population of 5.5 million, have lost their lives.

Ndadaye's murder fatally weakened the hold on power of the mainly Hutu Front for Democracy in Burundi (FRODEBU). Negotiations on power sharing took place over the succeeding months, as ethnically backed violence continued to wrack the country. Ndadaye's successor was killed, along with Rwandan president Juvenal Habyarimana, in 1994 when their plane was apparently shot down while approaching Kigali airport in Rwanda. This event triggered the Rwandan genocide and intensified killings in Burundi.

Under a 1994 power-sharing arrangement between the main political parties—FRODEBU and Unity for National Progress (UPRONA)—Hutu politician Sylvestre Ntibantunganya served as Burundi's new president until his ouster in a 1996 military coup led by former president Pierre Buyoya. Buyoya claimed to have carried out the coup to prevent further human rights abuses and violence. Peace and political stability within the country continued to be elusive, as armed insurgents sporadically staged attacks and the government security forces pursued an often ruthless campaign of intimidation. The search for peace eventually led to an agreement to allow a measure of political space for parliament, which has a FRODEBU majority, and the beginning of negotiations in Arusha, Tanzania, in 1998.

In 2000, the negotiations, mediated by former South African president Nelson Mandela, resulted in agreement in principle by most parties on a future democratic political solution to the conflict. Nineteen organized groups from across the political spectrum agreed to recommendations from committees on the nature of the conflict, reforms in the nation's governing institutions, security issues, and economic restructuring and development.

The form of the political institutions through which power would be shared and the reform of the military proved to be especially sensitive and difficult issues. In October 2001, the National Assembly adopted the transitional constitution, and a transition government was installed the next month, with President Buyoya temporarily remaining chief of state and Domitien Ndayizeye vice president. The failure of key elements of the Hutu-dominated Forces for the Defense of Democracy (FDD) and National Liberation Front (FNL) to participate in the transition resulted in both continued negotiations and violence.

As a result of the South African–mediated negotiations, by the end of 2002, most of the factions had agreed to stop the violence and participate in transitional arrangements leading to national elections to be held in late 2004. In April 2003, Buyoya stepped down and was replaced as president by FRODEBU secretary-general Ndayizeye. In October, the FDD, one of the two remaining rebel groups that had refused to participate in the peace process, reached an agreement with the government. Although hopes were raised that Burundi's civil strife could be nearing an end, the FNL continued to engage in guerilla activities.

In 2004, the security situation remained relatively calm in most of the country. Demobilization of former combatants continued, and some refugees returned, especially from Tanzania. Sporadic fighting continued, however, near the capital of Bujumbura. In August 2004, agreement was reached on the shape of new democratic institutions and the holding of elections. Continued political infighting, as well as delayed logistical preparations, resulted in a delay in the first scheduled poll, a constitutional referendum. By the end of November 2004 there was yet to be a date determined for this election.

Political Rights and Civil Liberties:

Citizens of Burundi cannot change their government democratically. Political rights continue to be circumscribed, although parties and civic organizations do function. Burundi does not have an elected president or parliament. As part of the negotiated political agreement, which entered into force in November 2001, President Pierre Buyoya was replaced in April 2003 by Domitien Ndayizeye for the subsequent 18 months until presidential and parliamentary elections, originally scheduled for November 2004, are held. The National Assembly is to be 60 percent Hutu and 40 percent Tutsi, with three additional deputies from the Twa ethnic minority and a minimum of 30 percent of the deputies being women.

Delays in the electoral process have been a highly sensitive issue. Many protagonists have insisted that they be held as soon as possible, but others emphasized the technical problems inherent in organizing legitimate elections within a short time frame and the need for inclusiveness. Tasks to be performed include conducting an electoral census, registering voters, adopting the post-transition texts on the constitution, disarming combatants, and presenting parties' political programs.

In June 1998, a transitional constitution reinstituted and enlarged the parliament through the appointment of additional members and created two vice presidents. The parliament's membership was subsequently changed to reflect the entry of additional opposition parties into the political process. Its powers remain limited in practice, although it provides an outlet for political expression and remains an important player in determining the nation's future.

There are more than two dozen active political parties, ranging from those that champion radical Tutsi positions to those that hold extremist Hutu positions. Most are small in terms of membership. FRODEBU and the Tutsi-dominated UPRONA remain leading political parties.

Some government revenues and expenditures have not been regularly listed on the budget, contributing to corruption problems. Burundi was not ranked by Transparency International in its 2004 Corruption Perceptions Index.

Some different viewpoints are expressed in the media, although media outlets operate under significant self-censorship and the opposition press functions only sporadically. The government-operated radio station allows a measure of diversity. The European Union has funded a radio station. The press group Reporters Sans Frontiers placed Burundi 92 out of 116 countries in its 2003 press freedom rankings.

Freedom of religion is generally observed. The ongoing civil strife and the predominant role of the Tutsi have impeded academic freedom by limiting educational opportunities for Hutus.

There is a modest but important civil society with a key area of focus on the protection of human rights. The Transitional Constitution provides for freedom of assembly; however, the transitional government occasionally restricted this right in practice. Constitutional protections for unionization are in place, and the right to strike is protected by the labor code. The Organization of Free Unions of Burundi is the sole labor confederation and has been independent since the rise of the multiparty system in 1992. Most union members are civil servants and have bargained collectively with the government.

The judicial system is seriously burdened by a lack of resources. Not surprisingly, given Burundi's recent history, there are far more existing and potential cases than can easily be handled by the current judiciary, and many of them are highly sensitive politically. Many crimes go unreported. Conditions in prisons continued to be poor and at times life-threatening.

Burundians continue to be subjected to arbitrary violence, whether from the government or from guerrilla groups. Detailed, specific figures on the number of dead or injured are difficult to obtain. However, the continuation of widespread violence in parts of the country in 2004 has been documented by respected independent organizations inside and outside Burundi, including Amnesty International, Human Rights Watch, and the ITEKA Human Rights League.

According to statistics published by the Central Bank in Bujumbura, most economic indicators have sharply declined since civil war broke out in 1993. The gross domestic product has dropped by 50 percent, and about 67 percent of the population are currently living below the poverty line. Access to basic social and health services has been severely diminished.

Women have limited opportunities for advancement in the economic and political spheres, especially in the rural areas. As part of the negotiated political agreement, parties also agreed that parliament would be composed of 30 percent women. Only 5 percent of females are enrolled in secondary school. Widespread sexual violence, including rape, against women occurs, according to Amnesty International.

⬆ Cambodia

Population: 13,100,000   **Political Rights:** 6
GNI/capita: $300   **Civil Liberties:** 5
Life Expectancy: 57   **Status:** Not Free
Religious Groups: Theravada Buddhist (95 percent), other (5 percent)
Ethnic Groups: Khmer (90 percent), Vietnamese (5 percent), Chinese (1 percent), other (4 percent)
Capital: Phnom Penh
Trend Arrow: Cambodia received an upward trend arrow due to the formation of a new coalition government that brought an end to a year-long political stalemate.

Ten-Year Ratings Timeline (Political Rights, Civil Liberties, Status)

1995	1996	1997	1998	1999	2000	2001	2002	2003	2004
6,6NF	6,6NF	7,6NF	6,6NF	6,6NF	6,6NF	6,5NF	6,5NF	6,5NF	6,5NF

Overview:

A new coalition government consisting of the Cambodian People's Party (CPP) and royalist Funcinpec in September 2004 brought an end to a year-long political stalemate. King Norodom Sihanouk, who turned 82 years old on October 31, abdicated and was succeeded by his son, Prince Sihamoni. On October 4, the Cambodian parliament unanimously approved plans for a special war-crimes tribunal to try surviving leaders of the Khmer Rouge.

Cambodia won independence from France in 1953. King Sihanouk ruled in the 1950s and 1960s until he was ousted by the U.S.-backed Lon Nol regime in the early 1970s. The Chinese-supported Khmer Rouge seized power in 1975. Under its dictatorship, at least 1.7 million of Cambodia's 7 million people died of disease, overwork, starvation, or execution. In 1979, Vietnam toppled the Khmer Rouge and installed a Communist regime. Civil strife continued in the 1980s, with the Hanoi-backed government fighting the allied armies of Sihanouk, the Khmer Rouge, and other political contenders. Hun Sen, a one-time Khmer Rouge cadre, emerged as the regime's strongman in the early 1980s. The Paris peace accords of 1991 mandated democratic elections and a ceasefire, but the Khmer Rouge continued to wage a low-grade insurgency from the jungle until its disintegration in the late 1990s.

Cambodia had its first free parliamentary elections in 1993. The royalist party, known as Funcinpec after its French acronym, won the largest number of seats with a campaign that stirred nostalgia among voters for the stability that Cambodia had enjoyed under the monarchy in the 1960s. However, Hun Sen used his control over the security forces to coerce Funcinpec, led by Prince Norodom Ranariddh, a son of King Sihanouk's, into sharing power with the CPP. Hun Sen also harassed and intimidated opposition groups and the press before finally ousting Ranariddh in a bloody coup in 1997.

During the campaign for the July 27, 2003, parliamentary elections, opposition candidates held dozens of rallies but faced restrictions on access to radio and television. Several political killings occurred, and local officials were also alleged to have intimidated voters and activists in the countryside. After the CPP failed to obtain the required two-thirds majority to form its own government, Prime Minister Hun Sen and the CPP formed a coalition government with Funcinpec in November, which quickly broke down because of intense political rivalry.

In September 2004, the CCP and Funcinpec agreed on the formation of a new coalition government. Foreign donors, who provide more than half of the government's annual budget and had become tired of the chronic lack of progress in legal, economic, and administrative reforms, put additional pressure on the parties to reach an agreement. The CPP took control of a large number of the important ministries in the new coalition government, and Hun Sen remained the prime minister. Sihanouk gave his blessings from Beijing, China, where he has stayed since January in protest of the breakup of the first coalition government he had helped to create in November 2003. With the new coalition government in place, the national assembly is expected to ratify Cambodia's accession to the World Trade Organization.

In past political negotiations, King Sihanouk had used the threat of abdication, which was also his condition for returning to Cambodia from Beijing. However, the 1993 constitution, which included no provision for abdication, states that the monarch rules for life and that a nine-member royal throne council must choose a successor within a week of the king's death. Although the monarchy is not hereditary, the king must be descended from certain bloodlines. A new law was quickly adopted requiring the royal throne council to elect a successor within seven days if the king "dies, retires, or abdicates." The council chose Prince Sihamoni, Sihanouk's son and favored choice as successor, as the new king on October 30. Sihamoni, who was educated in Czechoslovakia and North Korea after his family fled from the Khmer Rouge in 1975, had lived in France for two decades.

In January, union leader Chea Vichea was killed in a downtown thoroughfare. His funeral three days later attracted the largest crowd in the capital since antigovernment protests following the 1998 general election. Police put the number of mourners at 10,000; organizers and journalists estimated at least 30,000 people.

On October 4, parliament approved a plan agreement with the United Nations to establish a special tribunal in Phnom Penh to try surviving leaders of the Khmer Rouge. The special tribunal will be a mixed panel of Cambodian and international justices. Most judges will be Cambodian, but no majority can be taken without a vote by an international judge. As many as ten surviving Khmer Rouge leaders will be tried, including Ieng Sary, who had received a royal pardon for genocide but not for other crimes. Lack of resources may be the main obstacle to the functioning of this special court, which will require $57 million to run for the three years planned; all of the funding depends on voluntary contributions from UN member states. Under a Cambodian law adopted in 2001, no Khmer Rouge leader is exempt from prosecution.

Political Rights and Civil Liberties: Citizens of Cambodia cannot change their government democratically. Cambodia is a constitutional monarchy with a bicameral legislature consisting of a National Assembly and a Senate. The constitution was adopted on September 21, 1993, and promulgated by King Norodom Sihanouk, who served as the head of state, on September 24, 1993. The king, currently King Sihamoni, has no power under the constitution, but he is highly revered and exercises considerable influence as a symbol of unity for the nation.

The government, led by the prime minister and a council of ministers, must be approved via a two-thirds vote of confidence by the National Assembly, which has 123 seats. Members are elected by popular vote to serve five-year terms. The Senate has 61 members, 2 of whom are appointed by the king, 2 elected by the National Assembly, and 57 chosen by functional constituencies. Senate members serve five-year terms.

Policy debates are becoming more common in the National Assembly, but actual powers to scrutinize government actions are limited. Prime Minister Hun Sen and the CPP dominate national and local politics with their control of the security forces, officials at all levels of government, and the state-owned media.

Cambodia's 2003 parliamentary elections were marred by restrictions on opposition access to radio and television and allegations of intimidation of voters and activists in the countryside. Local officials, most of whom are CPP members, threatened opposition supporters with violence, expulsion from villages, and denial of rice rations and other goods. Funcinpec and the Sam Rainsy Party were also reported to have violated election laws, though less seriously.

Corruption is a problem in Cambodia. A World Bank report released in August cited that "unofficial payments" are "frequent, mostly, or always required" for business transactions. About 600 of the 800 companies surveyed across Cambodia for this study reported that bribes represent on average about 5.2 percent of their total sales revenue. The IMF estimated that economic growth would slow to 1.9 percent in 2005, down from the earlier estimates of 4.3 percent, because of corruption and bureaucratic red tape. Cambodia was not ranked by Transparency International in its 2004 Corruption Perceptions Index.

Radio and television journalists reportedly practice self-censorship, and broadcast news coverage favors the CPP. Authorities have denied repeated requests from opposition politician Sam Rainsy for a radio station license. Meanwhile, unknown assailants killed an editor with a pro-Funcinpec radio station in Phnom Penh in October 2003. Cambodia's print journalists are freer than their broadcast counterparts and routinely criticize government policies and senior officials, including the prime minister. However, authorities used the country's press law to suspend several newspapers for 30-day periods for criticizing the government or monarchy. Mobile phone service is expanding rapidly across the country, and there are more than 30,000 Internet users.

Religious freedom is generally respected in this country, where over 90 percent of the population are Theravada Buddhists. However, discrimination against the ethnic Cham Muslims is widespread. Many Chams complain of harassment by officials and ethnic Khmers. The Khmer Rouge almost annihilated this minority group, and the Chams have come under new suspicion from the Khmer majority in the wake of Islamic terrorist attacks in Southeast Asia, the United States, and elsewhere. Wider Khmer suspicion of the Chams is further fueled by rumors that the Chams are plotting to secede and reestablish the Cham kingdom of Champa.

Extreme poverty and the lack of government assistance have compelled many within the Cham community to seek help from overseas donors, many of which are advocates of orthodox forms of Islam. Much of the money donated to the Chams is coordinated through nongovernmental organizations (NGOs). The most prominent of these groups are the Cambodian Islamic Development Foundation and the Cambodian Islamic Youth Association, which receive funds from Saudi Arabia, Kuwait, Malaysia, Brunei, Indonesia, and Iran. Education—choosing between the new orthodox Islamic schools that focus on the Koran and Arabic language instruction and the government-run schools—has turned into a flashpoint in debates within the Cham community and with Cambodian society at large.

Workers, students, political activists, and others held numerous protests throughout 2004 with little interference, although police or pro-government thugs were reported to have broken up some demonstrations. Cambodia's 40-odd nongovernmental human rights groups investigate and publicize abuses and carry out training and other activities.

The few independent trade unions are active, but they are small, have limited resources and experience, and generally have little clout in negotiating with management. Factory workers frequently stage strikes in Phnom Penh to protest low wages, forced overtime, and poor and dangerous working conditions. However, union leaders are reported to face dismissal and other harassment at some factories, and hired thugs at times intimidate or physically attack union members and other workers. With some 80 percent of Cambodians relying on subsistence farming, union membership is estimated at less than 1 percent of the workforce. In April 2004, 300 workers of the Raffles Hotel La Royal in the capital and the Raffles Grand Hotel d'Angkor in Siem Reap were fired for demanding payment to them of the 10 percent service charge collected from customers. Cambodian courts declared the strike illegal and ordered the workers to return to work. The Cambodian Tourism and Service Workers Federation called for a boycott of these hotels, and international hotel workers unions backed this call.

Cambodia's judiciary is not independent and is marred by inefficiency and corruption. These problems reflect, in part, the court system's limited resources, severe shortage of lawyers, and poorly trained and underpaid judges. Security forces and local officials at times illegally detain suspects, while the accused frequently spend lengthy periods in detention before their trials. Police also routinely conduct searches without warrants.

Investigators often torture criminal suspects to extract confessions, and defendants frequently lack lawyers and must bribe judges to gain favorable verdicts. Delays or corruption allow many suspects to escape prosecution, leading to impunity for some government officials and members of their families who commit crimes. Despite recent reforms, jails remain dangerously overcrowded and inmates often lack sufficient food, water, and health care, human rights groups say. In a further sign that the rule of law is fragile in Cambodia, police, soldiers, and government officials are widely believed to often tolerate, or even take part in, gunrunning, drug trafficking, prostitution rings, and money laundering.

Six years of negotiations between Cambodia and the United Nations finally resulted in an agreement in 2003 to create an internationally backed tribunal for former Khmer Rouge leaders. Many observers complained that the tribunal will have a majority of Cambodian judges, who are widely believed to lack independence.

With the courts largely unable to enforce property rights, and the land registration system a shambles, military and civilian officials have in recent years forcibly evicted several thousand families from their land. Observers say that the local committees set up to settle land disputes render inconsistent decisions, operate with limited transparency, and are undermined by conflicts of interest among committee members.

The estimated 200,000 to 500,000 ethnic Vietnamese in Cambodia face widespread discrimination. Meanwhile, several hundred Montagnards, a predominantly Christian, mountain-dwelling ethnic group in Vietnam, who fled to Cambodia to escape repression, were forcibly returned to Vietnam in 2001 and 2002.

Women enjoy the same access to education as men, but suffer economic and social discrimination, and few are active in politics or hold senior government posts. Rape and domestic violence are common. Trafficking of women and girls within and outside Cambodia for prostitution continues despite some recent prosecutions of traffickers and sporadic crackdowns on Phnom Penh brothel owners.

Cameroon

Population: 16,100,000   **Political Rights:** 6
GNI/capita: $550   **Civil Liberties:** 6
Life Expectancy: 48   **Status:** Not Free
Religious Groups: Indigenous beliefs (40 percent),
Christian (40 percent), Muslim (20 percent)
Ethnic Groups: Cameroon Highlander (31 percent),
Equatorial Bantu (19 percent), Kirdi (11 percent),
Fulani (10 percent), Northwestern Bantu (8 percent),
Eastern Nigritic (7 percent), other (14 percent)
Capital: Yaounde

Ten-Year Ratings Timeline (Political Rights, Civil Liberties, Status)

1995	1996	1997	1998	1999	2000	2001	2002	2003	2004
?,5NF	7,5NF	7,5NF	7,5NF	7,6NF	7,6NF	6,6NF	6,6NF	6,6NF	6,6NF

Overview:
As was widely expected, President Paul Biya won another seven-year term in elections in October 2004 that international observers reported lacked credibility but nevertheless reflected the will of a majority of Cameroonians. The opposition denounced the results as fraudulent and took legal action to have the results annulled. Meanwhile, a dispute between Cameroon and Nigeria over the Bakassi Peninsula continued during the year.

Cameroon was seized during World War I, in 1916, and divided between Britain and France after having been a German colony from 1884. Distinct Anglophone and

Francophone areas were reunited as parts of an independent country in 1961. For three decades after independence, Cameroon was ruled under a repressive one-party system.

Prime Minister Biya succeeded Ahmadou Ahidjou as president in 1982. In 1996, the constitution extended the presidential term to seven years and allowed Biya to run for a fourth term. His reelection in 1997, with 93 percent of the vote, was marred by serious procedural flaws and a boycott by the three major opposition parties.

The ruling Cameroon People's Democratic Movement (CPDM) dominated legislative and municipal elections in 2002 that were no more free and fair than previous polls, despite the creation of the National Observatory of Elections. In the June 2002 parliamentary elections, the ruling CPDM increased the number of its seats in the 180-member National Assembly from 116 to 149. The main opposition, the Social Democratic Front, won 22 seats, down from 43 it had held previously. Smaller parties won the remainder. Municipal elections, which had been postponed from January 2001, were also dominated by the CPDM. The Supreme Court ordered a rerun of municipal elections in six constituencies where massive fraud was proven in 2002, but that vote, conducted in June 2004, proved to be equally flawed, according to observers, with the ruling CPDM winning the same five seats.

Biya easily won presidential elections in October 2004 with 75 percent of the vote, although the polling was marred by low voter registration and allegations of multiple voting by supporters of the CPDM. The two opposition candidates charged fraud and appealed to the country's Constitutional Council for the election to be annulled. Although turnout approached 80 percent, only 4.6 million of the estimated 8 million Cameroonians over the age of 20 who are eligible to vote were registered, and many others attempted to cast ballots but were turned away because their names did not appear on the voter rolls. Cameroon does not have an independent electoral commission.

Wrangling between Nigeria and Cameroon over the oil-rich Bakassi Peninsula dragged on in 2004 despite a ruling by the International Court of Justice awarding the territory to Cameroon. The two countries have occasionally clashed militarily over the region, and Nigeria maintains a troop presence there. At the last minute, Nigeria postponed the formal handover set for September 15, citing logistical problems. Most Bakassi residents consider themselves Nigerian and have staged public protests over the court ruling. A lawsuit filed in Nigeria by Bakassi natives to declare the handover unconstitutional promises to further delay any resolution.

Privatization and economic growth in Cameroon have progressed, with the government renewing its commitment to the IMF to sell off the state-owned water and telephone companies, and the country near to qualifying for significant debt relief. However, graft and the absence of independent courts inhibit business development.

Political Rights and Civil Liberties: Although Cameroon's constitution provides for a multiparty republic, citizens have not been allowed to choose their government or local leaders by democratic means. Presidential elections have been devalued by rampant intimidation, manipulation, and fraud, and legislative elections have also been fraudulent. However, some observers say the peaceful conduct of the most recent presidential election, in 2004, indicates that the country is on a more democratic track. Approximately one-fourth of Cameroonians are Anglophone. The administration of President Paul Biya remains largely Francophone, and the government's main opposition is from Anglophone Cameroonians. The linguistic distinction constitutes the country's most potent political division.

Cameroon was ranked 129 out of 146 countries surveyed in the 2004 Transparency International Corruption Perceptions Index. A survey by the group found that more than 50 percent of Cameroonians admitted to paying a bribe in 2003, the highest figure in the world. During the campaign, President Biya vowed to crack down on official graft, which would be a condition for Cameroon's entry into the Highly Indebted Poor Countries initiative.

The constitution provides for freedom of the press, but criminal libel laws have often been used to silence regime critics. Several private newspapers publish regularly. Eleven years after the National Assembly passed a bill liberalizing broadcast media, Biya signed the legislation in 2001. However, the government continued to drag its feet in granting broadcasting licenses, forcing many stations to operate illegally. There are at least six national Internet service providers, some of which are privately owned. The government has not tried to restrict or monitor Internet communication.

Repression of the media remains a serious problem. In December 2003, the government shut down 12 independent radio and television stations on the grounds that they were operating without licenses. Radio Veritas, a Catholic station founded by Cardinal Christian Tumi, an outspoken critic of the government, was closed in November 2003 but was allowed to resume broadcasting the following month under a license restricting its content to religious programming. In July 2004, two journalists from the BBC were detained and placed under house arrest by Cameroonian security forces in Bakassi, where they had traveled to report on the handover by Nigeria. They were accused of spying, but were released without charge five days later.

Freedom of religion is generally respected. Although there are no legal restrictions on academic freedom, state security informants reportedly operate on university campuses, and many professors fear that participation in opposition political parties could harm their careers.

Numerous nongovernmental organizations generally operate without hindrance. Trade union formation is permitted, but is subject to numerous restrictions. Workers have the right to strike but only after arbitration, the final decisions of which the government can overturn. In April, the government arrested six trade unionists, including the president of the Confederation of Cameroon workers, on sabotage charges.

The courts remain highly subject to political influence and corruption. The executive controls the judiciary and appoints provincial and local administrators. Military tribunals may exercise jurisdiction over civilians in cases involving civil unrest or organized armed violence. In the North, powerful traditional chiefs known as *lamibee* run their own private militias, courts, and prisons, which are used against the regime's political opponents. Torture and ill-treatment of prisoners and detainees are routine. Indefinite pretrial detention under extremely harsh conditions is permitted either after a warrant is issued or in order to "combat banditry." Inmates routinely die in prison.

Various intelligence agencies operate with impunity, and opposition activists are often held without charge or disappear while in custody. Security forces routinely impede domestic travel, repress demonstrations, and disrupt meetings. Cameroonian political and civil society groups have taken steps in Belgium, under its universal jurisdiction law, to institute legal proceedings against Biya for crimes against humanity.

The London-based human rights group Amnesty International called for an investigation into reports that dozens of extrajudicial executions were carried out in 2002 as part of an anticrime campaign. A military court in July 2002 acquitted six of eight gendarmes accused of killing nine young men who disappeared in January 2001 after having been detained by an anticrime squad called the Operational Command; two others were given suspended sentences.

Cameroon's population consists of nearly 200 ethnic groups. Slavery reportedly persists in parts of the North, and discrimination exists against indigenous Pygmies and other ethnic minorities. The Beti and Bula dominate the civil service and state-run businesses.

Violence and discrimination against women are widespread. Women are often denied inheritance and landownership rights, even when these are codified, and many other laws contain unequal gender-based provisions and penalties. Cameroon is a transit center and market for child labor and traffickers.

Canada

Population: 31,900,000   **Political Rights:** 1
GNI/capita: $22,390   **Civil Liberties:** 1
Life Expectancy: 79   **Status:** Free
Religious Groups: Roman Catholic (46 percent),
Protestant (36 percent), other (18 percent)
Ethnic Groups: British Isles origin (28 percent),
French (23 percent), other European (15 percent),
Amerindian (2 percent), other (32 percent)
Capital: Ottawa

Ten-Year Ratings Timeline (Political Rights, Civil Liberties, Status)

1995	1996	1997	1998	1999	2000	2001	2002	2003	2004
1,1F	1,1F	1,1F	1,1F	1,1F	1,1F	1,1F	1,1F	1,1F	1,1F

Overview: The year 2004 was marked by a national parliamentary election in which the long-dominant Liberal Party suffered major setbacks. In another important development, same-sex marriage was made legal in four provinces during the year, bringing to seven the number of provinces to legalize such marriages.

Colonized by French and British settlers in the seventeenth and eighteenth centuries, Canada came under the control of the British Crown under the terms of the Treaty of Paris in 1763. After granting home rule in 1867, Britain retained a theoretical right to overrule the Canadian Parliament until 1982, when Canadians established complete control over their own constitution.

The war against terrorism has been a leading item on the government's agenda since the September 11, 2001 attacks on the United States. Shortly after those attacks, Canada implemented a series of measures to combat international terrorism, including stopping funds for foreign terror groups. Canada also reached a comprehensive bilateral agreement with the United States on improving cross-border security.

Of the measures the government has adopted in the name of curbing terror organizations, several have drawn criticism on civil liberties grounds, with two measures in an omnibus antiterrorism bill evoking particular concern. One allows police to make preventive arrests of those suspected of planning a terrorist act. Another requires suspects to testify before a judge, even if they have not been formally accused of a crime.

Concern about terrorism was behind passage in 2002 of the Public Safety Act, which became law in 2004. The law's sections on data sharing—transportation, police, and intelligence officials have access to airline passenger information—drew criticism from civil liberties groups and from the country privacy commissioner, who expressed concern over the possible retention of data on private citizens for long periods of time and for the possibility that information could be used for purposes other than terrorism investigations.

In addition, as part of the antiterrorism bill, the government adopted the Security of Information Act, a revised version of the Official Secrets Act. The federal police used the Security of Information Act to raid the house of a newspaper reporter who allegedly had leaked classified information relating to Maher Arar. Arar, a dual citizen of Canada and Syria, was detained by U.S. authorities while transiting the United States and was deported to Syria, where he claims to have been tortured. In January 2004, the government announced a judicial inquiry into the Arar matter. The antiterrorism law itself is slated for review in 2005.

National elections in June 2004 dealt a setback to the long-dominant Liberal Party. Under the leadership of Prime Minister Paul Martin, who succeeded Jean Chretien on his retirement in late 2003, the Liberals had managed to retain governing power. However, they lost their status as a majority party and were compelled to depend on support from smaller parties, in particular the New Democratic Party (NDP), a social democrat-oriented party with ties to organized labor. With 135 seats in the House of Commons, the Liberals remain the single largest party, followed by the Conservatives with 99, the Bloc Quebecois with 54, and the NDP with 19. In the previous parliament, the Liberals enjoyed an outright majority with 168 seats, followed by the Conservatives with 73.

An important factor in the Liberals' electoral setback was a major scandal stemming from allegations of payoffs and kickbacks to Liberal supporters, particularly in Quebec province. Martin responded by pledging a package of reforms, including protections for whistle-blowers and new measures to ensure transparency in the awarding of contracts. Canada was also shaken by charges of serious misconduct by police in Toronto. Police were accused of beating drug suspects, extorting money from business people, and other offenses.

A foreign policy controversy with political implications emerged over U.S. pressure on Canada to join its planned missile defense system. The NDP declared itself opposed to Canada's participation in the plan during the election campaign, and a number of demonstrations were held prior to the election by peace organizations that opposed the missile defense

Canada continued to move gradually toward the enactment of legislation that would legalize same-sex marriage throughout the country. During 2004, courts in four provinces issued decisions that found that denying homosexuals the right to marry violated the constitution. These decisions bring to seven the number of provinces that permit same-sex marriage. The Liberal government was said to be planning to push for passage of a national law in Parliament in fall 2005.

Political Rights and Civil Liberties: Canadians can change their government democratically. The country is governed by a prime minister, a cabinet, and Parliament. The Parliament consists of an elected 301-member House of Commons and an appointed 104-member Senate. The British monarch remains nominal head of state, represented by a ceremonial governor-general appointed by the prime minister. As a result of government canvassing, Canada has nearly 100 percent effective voter registration. Prisoners have the right to vote in federal elections, as do citizens who have lived abroad for fewer than five years. The turnout of eligible voters for the 2004 election was slightly over 60 percent. During 2003, the Supreme Court issued a ruling that compels the federal government to adopt legislation to make it easier for small parties to raise money and appear on the ballot. In May, the Supreme Court issued a decision that validated legislation that places a limit on the amount lobbying groups can spend on advertisements that support or oppose political candidates.

Civil liberties have been protected since 1982 by the federal Charter of Rights and Freedoms, but have been limited by the constitutional "notwithstanding" clause, which permits provincial governments to exempt themselves by applying individual provisions within their jurisdictions. Quebec has used the clause to retain its provincial language law, which restricts the use of languages other than French on signs. The provincial governments exercise significant autonomy.

Canada is regarded as one of the least corrupt societies in the world, having been ranked 12 out of 146 countries surveyed in the 2004 Transparency International Corruption Perceptions Index.

The media are generally free, although they exercise self-censorship in areas such as violence on television. Limitations on freedom of expression range from unevenly enforced "hate laws" and restrictions on pornography to rules on reporting. Some civil libertarians have expressed concern over an amendment to the criminal code that gives judges wide latitude in determining what constitutes hate speech in material that appears online. In 2004, the government conducted investigations of Internet chat rooms and Web sites that are alleged to preach hatred against minority groups and advocate violence against political leaders.

Religious expression is free and diverse. Academic freedom is respected.

Freedom of assembly is respected, and many political and quasi-political organizations function freely. Trade unions and business associations enjoy high levels of membership and are free and well organized.

The judiciary is independent. Recently, there have been complaints that the judiciary has become overly activist and has issued decisions that effectively usurp the powers of the legislature. This debate has been inflamed by provincial court rulings permitting same-sex marriages. Canada's criminal law is based on British common law and is uniform throughout the country. Civil law is also based on the British system, except in Quebec, where it is based on the French civil code.

Canada maintains relatively liberal immigration policies. However, concern has mounted over the possible entry into Canada of immigrants who were involved in terrorist missions. In 2002, the Immigration and Refugee Protection Act was passed. It seeks to continue the tradition of liberal immigration by providing additional protection for refugees while making it more difficult for potential terrorists, people involved in organized crime, and war criminals to enter the country. Recently, human rights organizations have charged that Canada has deported immigrants to countries that practice torture. The Canadian government contends that in such cases, assurances have been made by the receiving country that the deported individual will not be subjected to torture.

Canada boasts a generous welfare system that supplements the largely open, competitive economy. A major problem is unemployment, which even under high-growth conditions remains at more than 7 percent of the workforce.

Canada has taken important steps to protect the rights of native groups, although some native groups contend that indigenous peoples remain subject to discrimination. During 2003, the federal government reached an agreement whereby it ceded control of a tract of land the size of Switzerland to the Tlicho First Nation.

Women's rights are protected in law and in practice. Women have made major gains in the economy and have strong representation in such professions as medicine and law. Women's rights advocates report high rates of violence against women in aboriginal communities.

Cape Verde

Population: 500,000 **Political Rights:** 1
GNI/capita: $1,290 **Civil Liberties:** 1
Life Expectancy: 69 **Status:** Free
Religious Groups: Roman Catholic, Protestant
Ethnic Groups: Creole [mulatto] (71 percent),
African (28 percent), European (1 percent)
Capital: Praia

Ten-Year Ratings Timeline (Political Rights, Civil Liberties, Status)

1995	1996	1997	1998	1999	2000	2001	2002	2003	2004
1,2F	1,2F	1,2F	1,2F	1,2F	1,2F	1,2F	1,2F	1,1F	1,1F

Overview: The ruling African Party for the Independence of Cape Verde (PAICV) faced a tough challenge from the opposition Movement for Democracy (MPD) in local elections held in March 2004. The International Monetary Fund (IMF) praised Cape Verde for its economic reform measures, which have pushed up prices on staple goods and services.

After achieving independence from Portugal in 1975, Cape Verde was governed for 16 years under Marxist, one-party rule by the African Party for the Independence of Guinea and Cape Verde, now the PAICV. The MPD won a landslide 1991 victory in the first democratic elections after Cape Verde became the first former Portuguese colony in Africa to abandon Marxist political and economic systems. In 1995, the MPD was returned to power with 59 percent of the vote. Antonio Mascarenhas Monteiro's mandate ended in 2001 after he had served two terms as president.

Cape Verde had a spectacularly close presidential election in 2001. In the second round of voting, opposition candidate Pedro Verona Rodrigues Pires defeated ruling party contender Carlos Alberto Wahnon de Carvalho Veiga by 12 votes in an election that overturned a decade of rule by the MPD; both presidential candidates had served as prime ministers. It was a test for Cape Verde's democracy that despite the closeness of the election, trust remained in the country's institutions and the results were accepted.

The PAICV also defeated the MPD in the 2001 legislative polls. The change in voting appeared to be a reflection of the popular attitude that the MPD had grown complacent. The PAICV won 40 seats compared with 30 for the MPD and 2 for the Democratic Alliance for Change. Disagreements within the MPD in 2000 resulted in a split and the formation of a new party, the Democratic Renewal Party, which won no assembly seats.

The MPD made a strong showing in local elections held in March 2004, defeating the ruling party in several of its traditional strongholds. The MPD's president, Agostinho Lopes, claimed there had been irregularities in the voters' rolls of some polling stations, but international observers said the elections were free and fair.

The government has undertaken unpopular measures as part of its move toward a market economy. Prices for water, electricity, and transportation soared after officials privatized state utilities in 2003. The country's stagnant economy has been bolstered somewhat by increased exports and tourism, but infrastructure improvements are still needed to assist in private sector development. Cape Verde is one of Africa's smallest and poorest lands. Foreign aid and remittances by Cape Verdean expatriates provide a large portion of national income.

The IMF approved a loan of $13 million to Cape Verde in April 2004 and praised the country's efforts at controlling inflation and improving its trade balance. It called on officials to implement regulatory reforms to improve conditions for the private sector. Consumers, trade unions, and other civil society groups have strongly protested the effects of privatization, in particular increases in the price of water, electricity, and transportation.

Political Rights and Civil Liberties: Since the 1991 transition to multiparty democracy, Cape Verdeans have changed their government three times by democratic means. The president and members of the National People's Assembly are elected through universal suffrage in free and fair elections. The 2001 presidential and legislative elections were declared free and fair, and those who were later found guilty of "election crimes" had apparently acted on a local level. Delegates of both candidates were found guilty of violations such as stuffing ballot boxes and were given light prison sentences.

Freedom of expression and of the press is guaranteed and generally respected in practice. No authorization is needed to publish newspapers and other publications. Broadcasts are largely state-controlled, but there is a growing independent press. There are six independent radio broadcasters and one state-run radio broadcaster, in addition to one state-run television station and two foreign-owned stations. Criticism of the government by state-run media is limited by self-censorship resulting from citizens' fear of demotion or dismissal. There is liberal access to the Internet.

Cape Verde was not ranked by Transparency International in its 2004 Corruption Perceptions Index.

The constitution requires the separation of church and state, and religious rights are respected in practice. However, the vast majority of Cape Verdeans belong to the Roman Catholic Church, and followers of the Catholic faith enjoy privileged status. Academic freedom is respected.

Freedom of peaceful assembly and association is guaranteed and respected. Human rights groups, including the National Commission on the Rights of Man and the Ze Moniz Association, operate freely. The constitution also protects the right to unionize, and workers may form and join unions without restriction. Collective bargaining is permitted, but it occurs rarely.

The judiciary is independent, although cases are frequently delayed. Judges must bring charges within 24 hours of arrest. Prison conditions are poor and are characterized by overcrowding. There were some reports that police continued to beat persons in custody or detention. Although the government investigated the allegations, no legal action was taken against the alleged perpetrators.

Ethnic divisions are not a problem.

Discrimination against women persists despite legal prohibitions against gender discrimination, as well as provisions for social and economic equality. Many women do not know their rights or do not possess the means to seek redress, especially in rural areas. At the encouragement of the government and civil society, more women are reporting criminal offenses such as spousal abuse or rape. Violence against women has been the subject of extensive public service media coverage in both government- and opposition-controlled media. The Women Jurists Association sought legislation in 2004 to establish a special family court to address crimes of domestic violence and abuse. Although women do not receive equal pay for equal work, they have made modest gains in various professions, especially in the private sector.

Central African Republic

Population: 3,700,000   **Political Rights:** 6*
GNI/capita: $250   **Civil Liberties:** 5
Life Expectancy: 42   **Status:** Not Free
Religious Groups: Indigenous beliefs (35 percent),
Protestant (25 percent), Roman Catholic (25 percent),
Muslim (15 percent)
Ethnic Groups: Baya (33 percent), Banda (27 percent),
Mandjia (13 percent), Sara (10 percent), Mboum (7 percent), other (10 percent)
Capital: Bangui
Ratings Change: Central African Republic's political rights rating improved from 7 to
6 due to preparations for democratic elections in 2005.

Ten-Year Ratings Timeline (Political Rights, Civil Liberties, Status)

1995	1996	1997	1998	1999	2000	2001	2002	2003	2004
3,4PF	3,5PF	3,5PF	3,4PF	3,4PF	3,4PF	5,5PF	5,5PF	7,5NF	6,5NF

Overview:

The Central African Republic (CAR) edged closer toward restoring democratic rule in 2004, with a referendum on the new constitution set for December and the start of voter registration for parliamentary and presidential polls that are scheduled for January 2005. The current leader of the CAR, General Francois Bozize, who seized power in a March 2003 coup, has said repeatedly that he has no plans to enter the presidential race, although supporters have been organizing rallies around the country urging him to run.

The CAR, a sparsely populated country, gained independence from France in 1960 after a period of particularly brutal colonial exploitation. Colonel Jean-Bedel Bokassa seized power in 1967 and, as self-declared emperor, imposed an increasingly bizarre personal dictatorship on the CAR, which he renamed Central African Empire. After Bokassa began to murder schoolchildren, French forces finally ousted him in 1979. A French-installed successor was deposed by General Andre Kolingba in 1981, who assumed the presidency in a bloodless coup.

Kolingba accepted a transition to a multiparty system that led to democratic presidential elections in 1993 and 1999, both of which were won by Ange-Felix Patasse, leader of the Movement for the Liberation of the Central African People. Although international observers judged the 1999 vote to be free, there were reports of irregularities such as ballot shortages in some areas with a strong opposition following, and Kolingba and other candidates claimed fraud. Until the elections, members of Kolingba's Yakoma ethnic group had occupied a disproportionate number of positions in the government, security forces, and state-owned businesses. The 1998 National Assembly elections produced a nearly even split between supporters of Patasse and those of his opponents.

UN peacekeepers withdrew in February 2000 following the elections and were replaced by a peace-building office. In May 2001, a failed coup attempt led by Kolingba left at least 250 people dead in the capital, Bangui, and forced 50,000 others to flee their homes.

In the country's fourth coup since independence, Patasse was deposed in March 2003 after six months of fighting between government troops and renegade soldiers loyal to General Bozize. Patasse, who had ruled the CAR for 10 years, fled to exile in Togo, and the new government has sought his arrest on corruption charges. Following the coup, Bozize created a National Transitional Council with delegates from the country's 16 provinces, as well as from all political, social, religious, and professional associations. Bozize lifted a 2002 death sentence imposed in absentia on Kolingba (who had fled to Uganda) and issued a general amnesty for the participants in the 2001 failed coup.

Once the referendum on the proposed constitution is completed in December 2004, the country's new electoral commission plans to authorize the start of political campaigning. Several parties have declared candidates, including a coalition led by Kolingba, of the Rassemblement Democratique Centrafricain party. Election day is set for January 30, 2005, with a second round of voting scheduled for February 27. UN-backed voter registration efforts are ongoing.

Bozize reshuffled the government in September following the resignation of Finance Minister Jean-Pierre Lebouder, who had accused the general of corruption. Although the cabinet was reduced from 28 to 24 posts, most key portfolios were unchanged.

Following clashes in the capital that left seven people dead, the CAR agreed to pay off former Chadian rebels who had fought for Bozize but were never integrated into the national army. The former fighters have been accused of abuses against the civilian population that caused many to flee their homes, which compounded the existing refugee crisis created by years of political instability.

After freezing all assistance following the coup that installed Bozize, the IMF and World Bank restored ties with the CAR in July 2004, approving $8.5 million in post-conflict emergency aid. More than one-third of the money will be used to pay government debts, including months of back salaries for civil servants.

The CAR signed an agreement in September to repatriate some 10,000 refugees from the Democratic Republic of Congo, marking a thaw in relations. The two countries are in talks to completely reopen their common border, which Bozize ordered closed after a Congolese rebel group crossed into the CAR in 2002 to assist Patasse in putting down the insurrection that eventually led to Bozize's seizure of power. It has since been opened only intermittently.

Most of the CAR's people are subsistence farmers, while diamonds and forestry are the government's main source of foreign exchange. In 2003, the CAR joined the Kimberley Process, a global initiative aimed at ending trade in so-called blood diamonds by establishing that exported gems have not come from conflict areas.

Political Rights and Civil Liberties: Citizens of the Central African Republic cannot change their government democratically. Presidential and legislative elections held in 1993, in line with the 1986 constitution—now suspended by General Francois Bozize—gave the CAR's people their first opportunity to choose their leaders in an open and democratic manner. A military coup in March 2003 ousted the civilian president, Ange-Felix Patasse, and suspended the National Assembly. An independent electoral commission, funded chiefly by France, Germany, Japan, and the United States, was appointed in May 2004 to oversee elections set for early 2005. The commission consists of 10 representatives of political parties, 10 from civil society, and 10 from the administration.

Bozize has pledged to root out the rampant corruption that prevailed under Patasse, and has targeted reforms at the country's lucrative mining sector. The Central African Republic is the world's fifth-largest producer of diamonds, but its actual exports of the precious gem are nearly double the official number reported. The Central African Republic was not ranked by Transparency International in its 2004 Corruption Perceptions Index.

Broadcast media are dominated by the state, but there are several independent newspapers. The only licensed private radio stations are music- or religion-oriented, although some carry programming on human rights and peace-building issues. Legislation enacted in 1998 rescinded the government's authority to censor the press, but authorities have occasionally been restrictive and have used draconian criminal libel laws to prosecute journalists. Several journalists fled the country following the May 2001 coup attempt; some journalists were tortured. The government does not restrict Internet access.

Despite promises by Bozize to respect press freedom and decriminalize media laws, several journalists were jailed in 2004 for slander. In March, a court sentenced Jude Zosse, publisher of the privately owned newspaper *L'Hirondelle*, to six months in prison for slandering Bozize by calling him a "state tax-collector." Zosse was released under a presidential pardon after serving two months of his sentence. On July 8, Maka Gbossokotto, publisher of the daily newspaper *Le Citoyen*, was arrested after Jean-Serge Wanfio, a relative of Bozize's and head of the state-owned electricity company, filed a court complaint. After more than a month of pretrial detention, Gbossokotto received a one-year suspended sentence and $1,000 fine for "publicly insulting" the official in an article that alleged misappropriation of funds. Religious freedom is generally respected, but the government occasionally infringes on this right. University faculty and students generally belong to many political parties and are able to express their views without fear of reprisal. Open public discussion is permitted.

Some 200 human rights and other nongovernmental organizations operate unhindered, although the constitutionally guaranteed freedom of assembly is not always honored by the authorities. The CAR's largest single employer is the government, and government employee trade unions are especially active. Worker rights to form or join unions are legally protected. The law does not provide for collective bargaining specifically, but workers are protected from employer interference.

Corruption, political interference, and lack of training hinder the efficiency and impartiality of judicial institutions. Limitations on searches and detention are often ignored. Conditions for prisoners, including many long-term pretrial detainees, are extremely difficult and sometimes life threatening. Juveniles are not separated from adults. Police brutality is also a serious problem, and security forces act with impunity.

Discrimination against indigenous Pygmies exists, although the government has taken steps to legalize their status by issuing birth certificates to Pygmy children.

Societal discrimination in many areas relegates women to second-class citizenship, especially in rural areas, and constitutional guarantees for women's rights are generally not enforced. However, women have made some gains in the political sphere. Female genital mutilation is still practiced, but it was made illegal in 1996 and is reportedly diminishing. Human rights groups said more than 100 women were raped during the October 2002 military uprising.

Chad

Population: 9,500,000
GNI/capita: $210
Life Expectancy: 49
Religious Groups: Muslim (51 percent), Christian (35 percent), animist (7 percent), other (7 percent)
Ethnic Groups: 200 distinct groups, including Arabs, Gorane, Sara, and Moundang
Capital: N'Djamena

Political Rights: 6
Civil Liberties: 5
Status: Not Free

Ten-Year Ratings Timeline (Political Rights, Civil Liberties, Status)

1995	1996	1997	1998	1999	2000	2001	2002	2003	2004
6,5NF	6,5NF	6,5NF	6,4NF	6,5NF	6,5NF	6,5NF	6,5NF	6,5NF	6,5NF

Overview:

President Idriss Deby secured passage of a constitutional amendment, subject to ratification by a referendum, allowing him to seek a third term in office amid an opposition boycott. The humanitarian crisis in neighboring Sudan brought increasing instability, as armed militias staged raids across the border into villages and clashed with Chadian troops.

Chad has been in a state of almost constant war since achieving its independence from France in 1960. Deby gained power in 1990 by overthrowing Hissein Habre, who had been president since 1981. The country was a militarily dominated, one-party state until Deby lifted the ban on political parties in 1993. A national conference that included a broad array of civic and political groups then created a transitional parliament, which was controlled by Deby's Patriotic Salvation Movement (MPS).

In May 2001, Deby was reelected president with more than 67 percent of the vote. The six opposition candidates, who alleged that the election was marred by fraud and called for the result to be annulled, undertook a civil disobedience campaign and were briefly arrested. The government subsequently banned gatherings of more than 20 people, although political protests continued.

Parliamentary elections in May 2002 increased the dominance of the MPS in the National Assembly, with the MPS capturing 110 of the 155 seats. Its parliamentary ally, the Rally for Democracy and Progress, won 12 seats; the Federation Action for the Republic, nine; the National Rally for Development and Progress, five; the Union for Renewal and Democracy, five; and the National Union for Renewal and Democracy, three. Other independents won 11 seats. The elections were boycotted by several opposition parties that claimed the electoral process lacked transparency.

In 2004, Deby pursued his campaign for a third term of office by pushing through a constitutional amendment that eliminated presidential term limits; opposition legislators boycotted the parliamentary vote. The move prompted outrage from the country's opposition parties, as well as labor unions and human rights groups, who have accused Deby of wanting to install himself in the presidency for life. The amendment will not become official until it is approved in a national referendum, set to take place by the end of 2004. Having lost its court challenge of the constitutional amendment, an opposition coalition has threatened to boycott future elections unless the government ensures greater electoral transparency.

As the crisis in Sudan grew increasingly urgent during the year, Deby assumed the role of mediator between the Sudanese government and two rebel movements in the Darfur region of Sudan, the Sudan Liberation Army and the Justice and Equality Movement. However, relations soured with an influx of armed groups into eastern Chad. The Chadian government charged that the Arabic-speaking Janjawid militias were collaborating with the Renewed National Front of Chad rebel movement, which had stopped fighting the Chadian government in 2002. Chad is currently hosting 190,000 Sudanese refugees and 27,000 refugees from the Central African Republic. France has deployed 200 troops along the eastern border with Sudan to augment Chadian and African Union security forces.

Millions of dollars in oil revenues began flowing into government coffers in 2004. Unlike in most other oil-rich African countries, however, the money is being closely monitored by the World Bank and a citizens' oversight group. Chad promised to spend 80 percent of oil revenues on schools, clinics, roads, and other basic needs. However, the oversight committee has complained that it is underfunded and lacks adequate information from the government and its oil company partners, predominantly the Exxon Mobil Corporation. Most Chadians are mired in extreme poverty. The country ranked 167 out of 177 on the UN Development Program's Human Development Index for 2004.

France, which remains highly influential in Chad, maintains a 1,000-member garrison in the country and, despite a sometimes rocky bilateral relationship, serves as Deby's main political and commercial supporter. Brutality by Chadian soldiers and rebels alike marked insurgencies in the vast countryside, but the large-scale abuses of the past have abated somewhat.

Political Rights and Civil Liberties: Citizens of Chad cannot change their government democratically. Chad has never experienced a peaceful, fair, and orderly transfer of political power. Recent legislative and presidential elections have been marred by serious irregularities and indications of outright fraud. The National Assembly, whose members are directly elected for four-year terms, is the country's sole legislative chamber. In a referendum held in March 1996, voters approved a new constitution based on the French model and providing for a unified and presidential state. A law establishing an ostensibly independent election commission was passed in 2000, despite significant opposition. The law gives the predominance of seats to government representatives and representatives of parties in the ruling coalition. Scores of political parties are registered.

Chad's army and political life are largely in the hands of members of the small Zaghawa and Bideyat groups from Deby's northeastern region, whose elite are often treated as being above the law. This is a source of ongoing resentment among the more than 200 other ethnic groups in the country. The formal exercise of deeply flawed elections and democratic processes has produced some opening of Chadian society, but real power remains with Deby.

Human rights groups have expressed concern that despite a World Bank monitoring program, the country's oil revenues would be diverted from national development. In 2000, Deby admitted that he had spent $4.5 million of the government's first oil receipts to buy weapons instead of bolstering social programs. Chad was ranked 142 out of 146 countries surveyed in the 2004 Transparency International Corruption Perceptions Index.

Newspapers critical of the government circulate freely in the capital, N'Djamena, but have little impact among the largely rural and illiterate population. According to the BBC, radio is the medium of mass communication, but state control over broadcast media allows few dissenting views. Despite high licensing fees for commercial radio stations, a number of private stations are on the air, some operated by nonprofit groups including human rights groups and the Roman Catholic Church. These broadcasters are subject to close official scrutiny.

In February, the authorities in southern Chad shut down a small independent radio station, Radio Brakos, after it aired an interview with an opposition politician. Police physically assaulted its director, Vatankah Tchanguis, detained him for three days, and then released him without charge. In a move applauded by press freedom groups, FM Radio Liberte was awarded some $11,000 by Chad's Supreme Court for damages sustained when the station was shut down by authorities for airing statements critical of Deby's third-term bid. The country's sole Internet service provider is a state-owned telecommunications monopoly.

Although religion is a source of division in society, particularly between Christians and Muslims, Chad is a secular state, and freedom of religion is generally respected. The government does not restrict academic freedom.

Despite harassment and occasional physical intimidation, the Chadian Human Rights League, Chad Nonviolence, and several other human rights groups operate openly and publish findings critical of the government. Workers' right to organize and to strike is generally respected, but the formal economy is small. Union membership is low. Most Chadians are subsistence farmers.

The rule of law and the judicial system remain weak, with courts heavily influenced by the executive. Security forces routinely ignore constitutional protections regarding search, seizure, and detention. Independent human rights groups have credibly charged Chadian security forces and rebel groups with killing and torturing with impunity. Overcrowding, disease, and malnutrition make prison conditions life threatening, and many inmates spend years in prison without being charged.

In recent years, tens of thousands of Chadians have fled their country to escape politically inspired violence. Several of the 20 or more other armed factions have reached peace pacts, but many of these agreements have failed. Chad's long and porous borders are virtually unpoliced. Trade in weapons among nomadic Sahelian peoples is rife, and banditry adds to the pervasive insecurity.

Turmoil resulting from ethnic and religious differences is exacerbated by clan rivalries and external interference: the country is divided between Nilotic and Bantu Christian farmers, who inhabit the country's South, and Arab and Saharan peoples, who occupy arid deserts in the North.

Women's rights are protected by neither traditional law nor the penal code, and few educational opportunities are available. Female genital mutilation is commonplace.

Chile

Population: 16,000,000 **Political Rights:** 1
GNI/capita: $4,250 **Civil Liberties:** 1
Life Expectancy: 76 **Status:** Free
Religious Groups: Roman Catholic (89 percent),
Protestant (11 percent)
Ethnic Groups: White and mestizo (95 percent),
Amerindian (3 percent), other (2 percent)
Capital: Santiago

Ten-Year Ratings Timeline (Political Rights, Civil Liberties, Status)

1995	1996	1997	1998	1999	2000	2001	2002	2003	2004
2,2F	2,2F	2,2F	3,2F	2,2F	2,2F	2,2F	2,1F	1,1F	1,1F

Overview:

The October 2004 municipal elections, in which results favored the governing Concertacion coalition, were regarded as an important gauge for the forthcoming 2005 presidential vote. Meanwhile, the remnants of former dictator Augusto Pinochet's military regime were diminished further with the lifting of his immunity from prosecution for his role in mass murders committed in the 1970s, the restoration of the president's right to fire his military commanders, and the discovery of secret bank accounts held by Pinochet.

The Republic of Chile was founded after independence from Spain in 1818. Democratic rule predominated in the twentieth century until the 1973 overthrow of President Salvador Allende by the military under General Pinochet. An estimated 3,000 people were killed or "disappeared" during his regime. The 1980 constitution provided for a plebiscite in which voters could reject another presidential term for Pinochet. In the 1988 vote, 55 percent of voters said no to eight more years of military rule, and competitive presidential and legislative elections were scheduled for the following year.

In 1989, Christian Democrat Patricio Aylwin, the candidate of the center-left Concertacion for Democracy, was elected president and the Concertacion won a majority in the Chamber of Deputies. However, with eight senators appointed by the outgoing military government, the coalition fell short of a Senate majority. Aylwin's government was unsuccessful in its efforts to reform the constitution and was stymied by a right-wing Senate bloc in its efforts to prevent Pinochet and other military chiefs from remaining at their posts until 1997.

Eduardo Frei, a businessman and the son of a former president, carried his Concertacion candidacy to an easy victory in the December 1993 elections. Frei promised to establish full civilian control over the military, but he found he lacked the votes in Congress, as the 48-seat Senate included a senator-for-life position for Pinochet and nine designated senators mandated by the 1980 constitution. Frei was also forced to retreat on his call for full accountability for rights violations that had occurred under military rule.

The October 1998 detention of Pinochet in London as the result of an extradition order from Spain, where he was wanted for alleged rights crimes against Spanish citizens living in Chile, was viewed as a reaffirmation of the rule of law, even though it was the result of foreign intervention.

In the December 1999 presidential election, Ricardo Lagos, a moderate socialist, faced right-wing Alliance for Chile candidate Joaquin Lavin, the mayor of a Santiago suburb and a former advisor to Pinochet, winning 47.96 percent to Lavin's 47.52 percent; Lagos won the January 16, 2000, runoff vote. Although the Concertacion coalition had 70 seats to the opposition's 50 in the lower house, it held just 20 seats in the Senate to 18 held by the opposition. A bloc of 11 others were either senators-for-life or had been designated under Pinochet's rules. Lagos's strong early performance appeared, by late 2000, to be threatened by soaring unemployment, price increases, and charges of government corruption.

In December 2000, a judge indicted Pinochet on homicide and kidnapping charges, in a year that saw the judiciary rule that allegations of crimes against humanity, including torture, kidnapping, and genocide, fell within its purview and were not subject to amnesty decrees. In July 2001, an appeals court in Santiago dropped the charges against Pinochet after it found that he suffered from dementia. In December legislative elections, Pinochet supporters made big gains, although they failed to win control of congress from the governing center-left coalition.

Political corruption scandals dominated the headlines in 2003 in Chile, a country long viewed as a regional leader in clean government and transparency. Incidents of influence peddling, insider trading, and kickbacks resulted in the head of the central bank and two cabinet members—one a presidential confidant—leaving their jobs. Dozens of lower-ranking officials and several members of Congress from the ruling coalition were indicted. In response to the corruption scandals, Lagos forged a working alliance with the opposition's strongest party, the Union Democrata Independiente, to push for reforms to eliminate what he said were the causes of the high-profile cases.

In July 2003, the Supreme Court ruled that Pinochet was unfit to undergo trial in the infamous "Caravan of Death" case involving the murder of 57 political prisoners following the 1973 coup. A week later, Pinochet resigned his honorary lifetime seat in the Senate.

In the October 31, 2004, municipal elections, the Concertacion coalition secured 45 percent of the vote, compared to the Alliance for Chile coalition, which captured 39 percent. More than a referendum on Lagos' government, the results of the elections were seen by many observers as an indication of the chances of the country's right wing to return to power in the December 2005 presidential contest after 15 years in the opposition. Although Concertacion has won a majority of votes in every municipal, congressional, and presidential election since the 1988 plebiscite, Alliance has gained increasing support, especially after divorcing itself from Pinochet and his regime's legacy of massive rights abuses. Lagos's continued popularity in 2004 was due largely to his deft handling of Chile's civil-military divide and the fact that the country continued to enjoy the longest period of economic growth in its history, the result in part of the state's involvement in the free-market economy. A multiparty agreement to undo what remains of the authoritarian elements of Pinochet's constitution appeared to allow Lagos the chance to claim that he had redeemed his campaign pledge to usher in "a constitution that passes the full test of democracy."

Facing possible prosecution for massive human rights crimes committed under his regime, Pinochet found he also had to fight a judicial rearguard action after it was revealed in July by a U.S. congressional committee that the former dictator had up to $8 million in personal funds stashed in secret accounts in the Riggs Bank of Washington, DC. The Chilean Chamber of Deputies initiated an investigation about the possible illegal origin of the secret fortune, and the Internal Tax Service filed a criminal complaint against him for failing to report the funds. The very fact of their existence appeared to finally cause Chilean conservatives—and even the head of the Chilean army—to distance themselves from Pinochet. His legal situation also worsened in August, when the Supreme Court ruled that Pinochet was not immune from prosecution for his role in mass murders carried out by Operation Condor, a secret framework for mutual cooperation against dissidents between six South American military dictatorships in the 1970s. In October, the Senate largely repealed the last vestiges of Pinochet's legacy, moving to abolish authoritarian curbs on the legislative branch and agreeing to restore the president's right to remove the commanders in chief of the country's armed services.

Political Rights and Civil Liberties: Citizens of Chile can change their government democratically. The 1999, 2000, and 2001 elections were considered free and fair, although low registration rates among young voters is a cause for concern. In 2004, a report from the Chilean Youth Institute said that the registry of young Chileans in the country's electoral rolls dropped by 50 percent between 1997 and 2003.

In response to public outcry over the political corruption scandals, congress passed laws in 2003 to prevent political patronage in high-level civil service jobs, increase government workers' salaries to reduce their susceptibility to bribes, create public funding for political campaigns, and require private campaign contributors names to be listed publicly. Chile was ranked 20 out of 146 countries surveyed in Transparency International's 2004 Corruption Perceptions Index.

The Chilean media generally operate without constraint, although some Pinochet-era laws, such as the anti-defamation statutes, remain in effect and some self-censorship continues. Chile has no law guaranteeing access to public information. In August, the director of the government-owned daily *La Nacion* was fired, apparently because of his paper's coverage of a pedophile scandal in which senior figures in both ruling and opposition parties were implicated.

The constitution provides for freedom of religion, and the government generally respects this right in practice. The government does not restrict academic freedom.

The right to assemble peacefully is largely respected, although police occasionally use force against demonstrators. The constitution guarantees the right of association, which the government has also generally respected. Workers may form unions without prior authorization as well as join existing unions. Approximately 12 percent of Chile's 5.7 million workers belong to unions. In October, a violent government crackdown on dock workers—in which navy troops attacked picketing union members—led to the temporary closure of nine Chilean ports.

The constitution provides for an independent judiciary, and the government generally respects this provision in practice. Most sitting judges come from the career judiciary, and all judges are appointed for life. The constitution provides for the right to legal counsel, but indigent defendants, who account for the majority of the cases in the Santiago region, have not always received effective legal representation.

Chile has two national police forces: a uniformed force, the Carabineros, one of Latin America's best law enforcement institutions with a history of popular support and respect; and a smaller, plainclothes investigations force. However, in recent years, the Carabineros have been the subject of complaints about the inadequate number of uniformed police patrolling the streets and allegations of increasing narcotics-related corruption. Continued problems exist with police use of excessive force against demonstrators, brutality, and the lack of due process rights for detainees. In 2001, courses in human rights became part of the core curriculum in police academies for both rank-and-file police and officers, and similar courses were introduced at the academy for prison guards and officials. Prisons are overcrowded and antiquated, with facilities nationally running at about 163 percent of capacity.

In 1990, the Truth and Reconciliation Commission was formed to investigate rights violations committed under military rule. Its report implicated the military and secret police leadership in the death or forcible disappearance of 2,279 people between September 1973 and March 1990. Chilean courts have recently convicted several former military officers of heinous crimes, ruling that a 1978 amnesty decree set down by the Pinochet government was inapplicable to cases of forced disappearance, which, they have held, is an ongoing crime. More than 200 former and serving military members now face trial. At the same time, the army, the military branch most implicated in rights crimes, has extended limited cooperation to judicial investigations. In mid-2003, President Ricardo Lagos announced a series of measures relating to the criminal prosecution of former members of the military—including transfer of human rights cases currently under review in military tribunals to the jurisdiction of the civilian court system—and to reparations for victims of past rights crimes and their relatives. In 2004, army commander General Juan Emilio Cheyre, who previously had made speeches distancing the institution from the military regime, claimed that the country's political class "still owes a debt" to the country's armed forces—a position challenged even by the head of the Chilean air force.

Native American groups in the country's southern region are increasingly vocal about their rights to ancestral lands that the government and private industry seek to develop. Chile has some 1.2 million indigenous people, two-thirds of them Mapuches. On taking office, Lagos began to make good on a campaign promise that the "Indian question" would receive priority attention. In October 2003, Lagos proposed constitutional recognition for the country's indigenous people.

Violence and discrimination against women and violence against children remain problems. In March, Congress passed a law that legalized divorce; Chile had been one of only a handful of countries in the world, and the only one in the Americas, to prohibit divorce. In 2000, Lagos appointed five women to his 16-person cabinet. One, Defense Minister Michelle Bachelet Jeria, is the daughter of a Chilean general tortured to death for his opposition to the 1973 coup. In late 2004, polls showed that Bachelet, who had resigned from the cabinet in September, appeared to have the greatest chances of becoming the ruling coalition's candidate for the December 2005 presidential election.

China

Population: 1,300,100,000
GNI/capita: $960
Life Expectancy: 71
Religious Groups: Daoist (Taoist), Buddhist, Muslim (1-2 percent), Christian (3-4 percent)
Ethnic Groups: Han Chinese (92 percent), other, [including Tibetan, Mongol, Korean, Manchu, and Uighur] (8 percent)
Capital: Beijing

Political Rights: 7
Civil Liberties: 6
Status: Not Free

Ten-Year Ratings Timeline (Political Rights, Civil Liberties, Status)

1995	1996	1997	1998	1999	2000	2001	2002	2003	2004
7,7NF	7,7NF	7,7NF	7,6NF	7,6NF	7,6NF	7,6NF	7,6NF	7,6NF	7,6NF

Overview:

The new generation of Chinese leaders, led by President Hu Jintao and Prime Minister Wen Jiabao, continued its monumental task of transforming the country's economy from a centrally controlled, state-planned model to an open one run by market forces. In 2004, the most significant economic challenge faced by the government was a controlled slowing of the rapidly expanding economy. Ongoing and substantial economic reform did not lead to many significant political changes, however, as the country remains an authoritarian state under the complete control of the Chinese Communist Party (CCP).

The CCP took power in 1949 under Mao Zedong after defeating the Kuomintang, or Nationalists, in a civil war that began in the 1920s. Aiming to tighten party control, Mao led several brutal mass-mobilization campaigns that resulted in millions of deaths and politicized nearly every aspect of daily life. Following Mao's death in 1976, Deng Xiaoping emerged as China's paramount leader. Over the next two decades, Deng oversaw China's transformation from a hermetic, agrarian, and often tumultuous Communist society into an authoritarian state with a market-led economy, eager to sell its products abroad and expand its role in global affairs even as it trampled on internationally recognized human rights.

Deng and other leaders signaled their intent to maintain power at all costs with the 1989 massacre of hundreds of student protesters in Beijing. Following the crackdown, the party tapped Jiang Zemin, then Shanghai mayor and party boss, to replace the relatively moderate Zhao Ziyang as party secretary-general. Jiang became state president in 1993 and was widely recognized as China's new paramount leader following Deng's death in 1997.

Jiang continued Deng's policies of selling off state firms, encouraging private enterprise, and rolling back China's social welfare system. China's leaders appeared to agree that continued market reforms would be needed in order to boost living standards and stave off broad calls for political reform. They feared, however, that freeing up the economy too fast could increase social hardship in the near term and create a groundswell against the party.

A new generation of leaders took control during the two-stage succession process of November 2002 and March 2003. At the CCP's 16th party congress in November 2002, Hu replaced Jiang, and in March of the following year, Wen took day-to-day charge of the economy by replacing Prime Minister Zhu Rongji. The succession had been vetted by the outgoing leaders. The new government pledged to improve conditions for rural Chinese, who remain disproportionately unaffected by the rapid growth of the economy; privatize the state-owned firms that still dominate the economy; and carry out a reform of the welfare system, among many other tasks.

Rural China's woes have contributed to a "floating population," officially tallied at 80 to 130 million people, who have left their rural homes in search of work in cities. Urbanization is transforming this historically agricultural society by providing many rural migrants with modest but unprecedented opportunities, though their shaky legal status often makes migrants vulnerable to abuse by police and employers.

In 2004, the government took several regulatory and administrative measures to cool investment-led growth in several sectors. However, these steps were undermined by noncompliance from local-level officials, whose authority has increased in line with the ongoing decentralization of the economy, and growth was still strong in the last quarter of the year. In addition, the government remained under pressure from the United States and other countries to revalue its currency, the *renminbi*, which is allegedly undervalued to boost Chinese exports. The government is open to the idea of a revaluation, but is highly unlikely to bow to this pressure as quickly as foreign governments would prefer.

Political Rights and Civil Liberties: Chinese citizens cannot change their government democratically or express their opposition to its policies. The CCP holds all political power, and party members hold almost all top national and local government, police, and military posts. Direct elections of officials above the village level is expressly forbidden. The parliament—the National People's Congress (NPC)—elects the top officials, but the NPC itself is controlled by the CCP. There is one opposition party, the China Democratic Party, but the government suppresses its activities, and it exists, for all practical purposes, in theory only. The only competitive elections in China are for village committees, which are not in any case considered government bodies; even these are tightly controlled by the CCP.

Corruption within the CCP is rampant; embezzlement and bribery are particularly serious problems. China was ranked 71 out of 146 countries surveyed in the 2004 Transparency International Corruption Perceptions Index.

Press freedom is severely limited. The government bars the media from criticizing senior CCP leaders or their policies, challenging CCP ideology, and discussing "sensitive topics"—in particular, constitutional reform, political reform, and reconsideration of the 1989 Tiananmen movement. Journalists violating these restrictions may be harassed, detained, and/or jailed. The government owns all television and radio stations and most print media outlets, and uses these organs to promote its ideology. According to the U.S. State Department's 2003 human rights report, released in February 2004, "All media employees were under explicit, public orders to follow CCP directives and 'guide public opinion' as directed by political authorities." Because of this, most journalists practice a high degree of self-censorship. The government also directly censors both the domestic and foreign media.

The government promotes use of the Internet, but regulates access, monitors use, and restricts and regulates content. According to the U.S. State Department report, China's Internet control system employed some 30,000 people and was the world's largest such system. Authorities target and punish Internet publishers and essayists far more frequently than journalists affiliated with more conventional media.

There is little respect in China for religious freedom, though it is recognized in the constitution. All religious groups and spiritual movements must register with the government, which judges the legitimacy of religious activity. The government also monitors the activities of the official religions (Buddhism, Taoism, Islam, Protestantism, and Catholicism). It targets leaders of unauthorized religious groups for harassment, interrogation, detention, and abuse, and destroys or seizes unregistered places of worship. The extent to which such actions are taken or rules are enforced, though, varies widely by region. Religious controls remain particularly tight in Xinjiang and other areas that have seen ethnic unrest. In Xinjiang, the government continues to censor imams' sermons, discourage overt religious attire and religious wedding ceremonies, and restrict the building of mosques. Religious believers are denied the ability to hold public office not by law, but by a logical extension of the fact that most government positions go to CCP members, and that CCP membership and religious belief are said to be incompatible.

The government also continues to strongly repress traditional meditation groups and religious groups accused of propagating beliefs that contradict or go beyond the CCP line. Practitioners of Falun Gong receive the harshest treatment, being subjected to criminal, administrative, and extrajudicial punishment on the grounds of "endangering state security." Punishment is triggered for mere refusal to denounce the movement or its founder, even without public manifestations of its tenets. Police and other security authorities are believed to use excessive force when dealing with Falun Gong practitioners. Authorities at times also crack down on folk religions, unorthodox religious sects, and movements considered to be cults.

The government teaches atheism in schools. Academic freedom is also restricted, as universities and research institutions must also follow the CCP line. Therefore, academics also engage in self-censorship.

Freedom of assembly and association is severely restricted. Protests against political leaders or the political system in general are banned, and the constitution stipulates that assemblies may not challenge "Party leadership" or go against the "interests of the State." Security forces are known to use excessive force against demonstrators. All nongovernmental organizations must be registered with and approved by the government. Though the formation of political parties is not specifically discussed in any laws or regulations, the one opposition party that has formed, the China Democrat Party, has been targeted and suppressed by the government and has no real political power.

Independent trade unions are illegal, and enforcement of labor laws is poor. All unions must belong to the state-controlled All China Federation of Trade Unions, and several independent labor activists have been jailed for their advocacy efforts. Collective bargaining is legal in all industries, but it does not occur in practice. Despite the fact that workers lack the legal right to strike, there has been a growing wave of strikes over layoffs, dangerous working conditions, or unpaid wages, benefits, or unemployment stipends. The reaction of local officials has been mixed, with strike leaders often arrested, while other strikers are given partial concessions. Chinese labor law mandates that labor disputes be addressed first in the workplace, then by a mediation committee, then through a local government-sponsored arbitration committee, and finally, if still unresolved, through the court system; however, this procedure is rarely followed in practice.

The government controls the judiciary. The CCP directs verdicts and sentences, particularly in politically sensitive cases. Despite some recent criminal procedure reforms, trials—which in any case are often mere sentence hearings—are often closed; few criminal defendants have access to counsel. Officials often subject suspects to "severe psychological pressure" to confess, and coerced confessions are frequently admitted as evidence. Police frequently conduct searches without warrants and at times monitor telephone conversations and other personal communications to use as evidence against suspected dissidents. Many political prisoners and ordinary alleged criminals lack trials altogether, detained instead by bureaucratic fiat in "reeducation through labor" camps. The U.S. State Department claimed that some 250,000 people were serving sentences in these camps in 2003. Endemic corruption further exacerbates the lack of due process in the judicial system. According to the U.S. State Department, judicial conditions are worst in capital punishment cases. Sixty-five crimes carry the death penalty, and perpetrators are often executed within days of their arrest.

Although security forces are generally under civilian control, serious human rights abuses are widespread. These include extrajudicial and politically motivated killings, torture, physical abuse of prisoners, coercion, arbitrary arrest and detention, and lengthy incommunicado detention. For example, police can detain a person for up to 37 days before releasing or formally arresting him. Arrests to thwart political dissent are frequent. Moreover, the government does not permit independent observation of prisons or of reeducation-through-labor camps.

Although antidiscrimination laws exist, Muslims and other minorities and people with HIV/AIDS face discrimination in mainstream society, hampered in their access to jobs and other benefits. The government did pass a new law in August 2004 specifically banning discrimination against people with HIV/AIDS, and though the move was applauded by institutions like Human Rights Watch, it remains to be seen whether it will have any practical impact. Minorities in border regions, who tend to have lower levels of education, suffer the most. The majority Han Chinese population has reaped an outsized share of benefits from government programs and economic growth, despite government initiatives to improve minority living standards. Tensions between ethnic groups occasionally flare up; in November 2004, for example, a minor incident in Henan province escalated into a full-scale riot involving hundreds of Han Chinese and Hui Muslims. The violence left at least seven people dead and resulted in the government declaring martial law in the area.

The gradual implementation of reforms over the past several decades has freed millions of Chinese from CCP control of their day-to-day lives. Nevertheless, citizens require permission from the government and from their employer to move from city to city, and special restrictions are imposed on people in rural areas who wish to move to urban areas, as a massive rural-urban migration has already occurred, straining cities' infrastructures to capacity. Urban redevelopment and city planning have also resulted in forced relocations. Human Rights Watch reported that in December

2003, a Shanghai court of appeals upheld the prison sentence of a lawyer who had been charged with "circulating state secrets"—he had in fact been an advocate for residents who had been forcibly relocated. Freedom of movement within the country is still restricted during visits to China by foreign leaders and on other politically sensitive occasions. Legal emigration and foreign travel, however, are not highly restricted.

Recent reforms have allowed Chinese to marry, divorce, and sell their state-assigned housing without their employer's permission. A highly significant step taken in late 2002 allowed private entrepreneurs to become members of the CCP. A landmark property rights law aimed at protecting private property and income is under consideration. However, authorities continue to ignore citizens' constitutionally guaranteed "freedom of privacy," routinely monitoring phone conversations, facsimile transmissions, and e-mail and Internet communications. They also open and censor domestic mail and enter residences and offices.

China's population control policy is another significant area of personal life that has not been deregulated. Officially, Chinese couples may have no more than one child, though this is more strictly enforced in the cities. The Population and Family Planning Law requires couples to employ birth control measures and requires that couples who have an unapproved child pay "social compensation fees." The government gives preferential treatment to couples who abide by the birth limits and, in some areas, still requires couples to apply for official permission before having a child. Furthermore, it is illegal in most areas for a single woman to have a child. The use of forced abortion or sterilization by local officials trying to keep within county birth quotas is believed to occur in occasional, isolated cases, though less frequently than in the past.

Chinese women reportedly face serious discrimination in education and employment and are far likelier than men to be laid off when state firms are downsized or privatized. Despite government crackdowns, trafficking in women and children for marriage, to provide sons, and for prostitution remains a serious problem.

↓ Colombia

Population: 45,300,000 **Political Rights:** 4
GNI/capita: $1,820 **Civil Liberties:** 4
Life Expectancy: 72 **Status:** Partly Free
Religious Groups: Roman Catholic (90 percent),
other (10 percent)
Ethnic Groups: Mestizo (58 percent), white (20 percent),
mulatto (14 percent), black (4 percent), other [including
Amerindian] (4 percent)
Capital: Bogota
Trend Arrow: Colombia received a downward trend arrow due to new revelations of widespread paramilitary infiltration of government institutions in the country, including the attorney general's office.

Ten-Year Ratings Timeline (Political Rights, Civil Liberties, Status)

1995	1996	1997	1998	1999	2000	2001	2002	2003	2004
4,4PF	4,4PF	4,4PF	3,4PF	4,4PF	4,4PF	4,4PF	4,4PF	4,4PF	4,4PF

Overview: In 2004, Colombia's President Alvaro Uribe Velez retreated from his earlier promises to maintain a hard-line approach with right-wing paramilitaries, a move that appeared to falter as the demobilization of these groups began haltingly. Meanwhile, left-wing guerrilla groups were in retreat in several parts of the country. New revelations of paramilitary infiltration of state institutions, including the office of the attorney general, surfaced during the year. Also in 2004, Uribe was named in a U.S. State Department report alleging his connection with a major drug cartel a decade earlier.

Following independence from Spain in 1819, the former "Gran Colombia" broke up into the present-day states of Venezuela, Ecuador, and the Republic of Colombia. The 1904 succession of Panama, engineered by the United States, left Colombia with its present boundaries. Modern Colombia, Latin America's third most populous country, has been marked by the corrupt machine politics of the Liberals and the Conservatives, whose leadership has largely been drawn from the traditional elite, as well as by left-wing guerrilla insurgencies, right-wing paramilitary violence, the emergence of vicious drug cartels, and gross human rights violations committed by all sides.

In the June 21, 1998, election, Conservative candidate Andres Pastrana won the presidency in an impressive victory over the Liberal Party candidate, Interior Minister Horacio Serpa. In an effort to consolidate the peace process, in November, Pastrana arranged for the leftist Revolutionary Armed Forces of Colombia (FARC) guerrillas to regroup and peacefully occupy a so-called demilitarized zone consisting of five southern districts, from which a dispirited military was withdrawn. The move, which had been strongly resisted by the military, gave the guerrillas de facto control over a territory the size of Switzerland.

The gamble failed, however, although Pastrana did achieve some success in severing ties between the armed forces and right-wing death squads known as the United Self-Defenses of Colombia (AUC). Colombia's most notorious death squad leader admitted what had long been an open secret—not only do the paramilitary groups earn large revenues from the drug trade, as do the guerrillas, but they are also financed by local and foreign private enterprise. In 2001, it became clear that the FARC's "demilitarized zone" was actually a state within a state that the guerrillas used as a sanctuary for coordinating military operations, as a rest area for battle-weary insurgents, and as a base for criminal activities such as drug trafficking and the warehousing of hostages.

In the March 2002 parliamentary elections, the Liberal Party secured the largest number of seats in both the Senate and House of Representatives, followed by the Conservative Party; both parties have long dominated politics in Colombia. In May 2002, war-weary Colombians gave Uribe, a hard-line former provincial governor who ran independently of the country's two dominant parties, an unprecedented first-round victory that was a referendum on how best to end Colombia's decades-long civil strife. He had run on a platform of no concessions to leftist guerrillas and the implacable use of the military to eliminate them. Uribe, the victim of an assassination attempt by leftist guerrillas just a month before the election, emerged from a six-candidate field with 52 percent of the vote. Serpa, running again as the Liberal candidate, received 32 percent.

Uribe's inauguration in August was marred by guerrilla attacks that left 19 people dead. In response, he decreed a state of emergency, stepped up anti-guerrilla efforts in urban areas, and created "special combat zones" in 27 municipalities in which the U.S.-backed military was allowed to restrict civilian movement and conduct searches without a warrant. He also established a "war tax" to finance thousands of additional troops and tightened restrictions on the foreign press.

At the end of its first year in office, the Uribe government continued to be popular as it made limited gains in delivering on promises of peace and prosperity for Latin America's most violent nation. Some improvements were made in 2003 in the fight to dismantle the world's biggest cocaine industry, and civilian casualties in Colombia's four-decades-long civil war were reduced. However, the country continued to be wracked by massacres—the work of both the guerrillas and right-wing paramilitary death squads—and drug trafficking, and by the highest rate of kidnapping in the Western Hemisphere. Uribe created a firestorm when he proposed to grant amnesty to the paramilitaries that would entail reduced prison sentences, or the payment of reparations in lieu of jail time, for leaders found guilty of such crimes; this was seen as a controversial move even in Washington, where several death squad leaders have been indicted as terrorists and narcotics traffickers.

In 2003, Uribe won high marks for his hands-on, take-charge style and his personal courage in traveling to the country's most violent regions. In his first 10 months in office, Uribe allowed the extradition of 64 accused drug traffickers to the United States, more than his predecessor had allowed during his entire four-year term. Meanwhile, Colombia's highest tribunal dealt Uribe a surprise political setback, stripping him of the emergency powers he had assumed in 2002 to fight leftist rebels. The decision by the Constitutional Court, which annulled the special militarized zones he had created and took away his ability to issue special decrees, signaled the court's willingness to intervene if Uribe tried to overstep his powers.

In November, more than 850 members of a right-wing paramilitary group, part of an illegal army responsible for some of the country's bloodiest massacres, laid down their arms and were allowed to return to civilian life. Many had past careers as common criminals, and human rights groups said the move made a mockery of justice. That same month, the commander of the Colombian National Police and his four closest deputies were cashiered in a corruption scandal just days after Uribe replaced three cabinet ministers, including the defense minister, who had taken a hard line on corruption within the military. On a positive note, Uribe publicly denounced what he called the "collusion" between the police and the paramilitaries in various regions of the country.

Also in November, Colombian troops defeated an unprecedented effort by 14 FARC combat units to encircle Bogota and to cut off major roads leading to the capital city of 7 million people. The previous month, Colombians voted down key referendum proposals supported by Uribe that had been intended to freeze government spending in order to provide more funds to wage war against the guerrillas, fight corruption, and streamline a top-heavy political structure.

In 2004, Uribe found himself forced to seek to bring the AUC into the political arena and to bargain with them. Uribe's move, however, generated protests from human rights groups and the United States, which receives 90 percent of its cocaine from Colombia. Washington pointed out that several chiefs of the AUC, blacklisted as a terrorist organization, were also wanted in the United States for narcotics-related crimes. Uribe's initiative appeared to falter as the demobilization of the paramilitaries began fitfully, with right-wing squads active in 26 of Colombia's 32 departments and more than a third of its municipalities during the year. At the same time, the once seemingly unstoppable leftist guerrillas appear to be on the run in several areas of the country, and the largest leftist group, itself rent by internal divisions and ever more steeped in narcotics and common crime, appeared determined to hold out on the battlefield, even as it appeared to retreat. In August, Uribe made a dramatic turnabout by offering to release about 50 leftists accused of lesser crimes in exchange for an equal number of hostages in insurgent hands. Meanwhile, the country's military, which, although better equipped and trained and increasingly possessing more useful intelligence, retained much of its inefficient and almost feudal structure, continued to rely on mostly peasant conscripts and lacked the manpower and equipment needed to carry out its mission. In a positive development, nearly 3,000 combatants from five separate AUC paramilitary blocs were demobilized after negotiations with government representatives.

During the year, there were new revelations of widespread paramilitary infiltration of government institutions around the country, including the attorney general's office. On July 28, three chiefs of the death squads were allowed to speak before a special session of Congress, demanding that they should not be imprisoned for their crimes. These appearances were justified by the government as being part of ongoing negotiations to demobilize the paramilitary factions.

Considered to be one of the United States' closest allies in Latin America, particularly in the "war on drugs." Uribe was embarrassed in 2004 by a 1991 U.S. Defense Intelligence Agency report, declassified in July, that suggested he collaborated with Pablo Escobar's Medellin drug cartel in the early 1990s and described him as a "close personal friend" of Escobar's. Uribe, whose government claimed to have extradited a record of more than 170 suspected drug traffickers, denied the report, which was also disavowed by a U.S. State Department spokesman.

Despite these developments, Uribe enjoyed 70 percent popularity ratings during most of the year. Uribe, who has survived more than a dozen assassination attempts, including two since taking office as president, also pushed for a change in the constitution that would allow him to run for reelection in 2006.

Political Rights and Civil Liberties: Citizens of Colombia can change their government democratically. Although in 2002 Colombians were largely able to express their preferences by voting, electoral participation was inhibited by threats of death squads operating with impunity as well as guerrilla violence, particularly in rural areas where the latter engaged in an explicit campaign of intimidation. More than 200,000 soldiers, police, and security agents were deployed during the voting in a largely successful attempt to keep the peace. The October 2003 municipal elections were generally free of violence on election day. Although dozens of political parties are registered, politics is dominated by the Liberal Party and Conservative Party.

Corruption affects virtually all aspects of public life and extends far beyond the narcotics trade. For example, foreign business executives with military procurement contracts complain that the armed forces sometimes do not honor their contracts and that the executives are subjected to intimidation if they protest. Anticorruption activists claim that the annual cost of systemic problems exceeds $2.2 billion and that corruption may be a greater threat to the country's institutional survival than is the internal war. Colombia was ranked 60 out of 146 countries surveyed in Transparency International's 2004 Corruption Perceptions Index.

The constitution guarantees freedom of expression. However, media ownership is concentrated in the hands of wealthy families, large national conglomerates, or groups associated with one or the other of the two dominant political parties. In 2003, the Spanish media conglomerate Prisa acquired majority ownership of the country's largest radio network, thus becoming the first foreign media owner in the country. Media dependency on government advertising may account for a recent reduction in criticism of official actions and policies. Journalists are frequently the victims of political and revenge violence, and the Committee to Protect Journalists ranks Colombia as the second most dangerous country in the world for the media. More than 120 journalists have been murdered in the past decade, many of whom were killed for reporting on drug trafficking and corruption; most of the cases remain unresolved by the legal authorities. According to the Columbia Foundation for Press Freedom, in the first 10 months of 2004 three journalists were murdered, one tortured, at least two kidnapped, and 37 the recipients of death threats. In a positive development, two former soldiers were convicted in 2002 of the assassination of two TV cameramen; each defendant was sentenced to 19 years in prison. The government does not limit or block access to the Internet or censor Web sites.

The constitution provides for freedom of religion, and the government generally respects this right in practice. It also does not restrict academic freedom, although threats and harassment have caused many professors and students to adopt lower profiles and avoid discussing controversial topics, with some academics opting for voluntary exile. Paramilitary groups and guerrillas maintained a presence on many university campuses in order to generate political support and to undermine their adversaries through both violent and nonviolent means.

Constitutional rights regarding the freedom to organize political parties, civic groups, and labor unions are restricted in practice by politically motivated and drug-related violence and by the government's inability to guarantee the security of its citizens. Human rights workers in Colombia are frequently murdered by the military and by rightist paramilitary forces. Uribe has called rights workers "terrorist sympathizers" and cowards and claimed that many Colombian nonofficial human rights organizations are "spokespeople" for terrorism.

The murder of trade union activists has made Colombia the most dangerous country in the world for organized labor. Only about 6 percent of the country's workforce is unionized, one of the lowest percentages in Latin America. More than 2,500 trade union activists and leaders have been killed in little more than a decade, although the killings reported went down by 25 percent in 2004. Labor leaders are frequently targeted for attack by paramilitary groups, guerrillas, narcotics traffickers, and other union rivals. In August, three labor leaders were killed in the Arauca region in what an army commander claimed was a gun battle. Initially, Vice President Francisco Santos suggested that the three were involved in guerrilla activity, but he was later forced to reverse his position.

The justice system remains slow and compromised by corruption and extortion. In 2002, a new chief of the national police was named after a corruption scandal involving 71 officers—including the head of anti-narcotics operations—who were accused of stealing more than $2 million in U.S. aid. Previously, the 85,000-strong force had been considered to be a bulwark against corruption. In August, the Supreme Court overturned Uribe-sponsored antiterrorism legislation from June 2003 that gave the military and police sweeping powers to search homes, tap phones, and detain suspected terrorists without warrant for up to 36 hours.

The civilian-led Ministry of Defense is responsible for internal security and oversees both the armed forces and the national police. Since Uribe took office, defense expenditures have increased 46 percent. Civilian management of the armed forces, however, is limited; cadres of army "informants" and "collaborators" have been organized and a separate army of peasant soldiers, led by professional soldiers, was recruited and trained, all without civilian authorization.

Colombia's 165 prisons, which were built for 32,000 people but hold more than 47,000, are frequent sites of murders and riots. A penal code approved by Congress in June 2001 was designed to relieve the strain on prisons and allowed convicts to be released after serving 60 percent of their sentences, rather than the 80 percent previously required.

Colombia is one of the most violent countries in the world. More than 3,000 people are kidnapped each year—although the government claimed that in the 12 months ending in May 2004, that number fell 44 percent, to 1,737. Political violence in Colombia continues to take more lives than in any other country in the Western Hemisphere, and civilians are prime victims. In the past decade, an estimated 40,000 have died and more than 1.5 million have been displaced from their homes. More than 90 percent of violent crimes go unsolved. Government figures comparing 2002 and 2003 that show marked decreases in most types of violence and rights abuse were challenged by the country's most prestigious human rights organizations. In a positive development, the government said that more than 3,000 paramilitary fighters were captured in 2003, even as it entered into peace talks with the AUC leadership.

Left-wing guerrillas, some of whom also protect narcotics-production facilities and drug traffickers, also systematically violate human rights. The FARC guerrillas also regularly extort payments from hundreds of business people throughout the country. In 2004, the FARC increasingly used dozens of hostages—politicians, police, soldiers, and others—as "human shields" as they sought to escape from pursuit by the security forces. Another problem concerns "social cleansing," or the elimination of drug addicts, street children, and other marginal citizens by vigilante groups often linked to police.

There are approximately 80 distinct ethnic groups among Colombia's more than 800,000 indigenous inhabitants, who live on more than 50 million acres granted to them by the government, often located in resource-rich, strategic regions fought over by the warring armed groups. Despite their seeking to remain neutral in the armed conflict, these Native Americans are frequently the targets of forced recruitment by the guerrillas and selective assassination by the paramilitary forces. Human rights groups charge that more than 1,500 Indians were forced into service with the guerrillas in a three-year period. The Colombian National Indigenous Organization reported that in the first six months of 2004, Native American groups suffered 313 armed attacks—49.7 percent by the paramilitaries, 34.5 percent by the military and police, and 15.9 percent by the leftist guerrillas. In August, Indian leaders rejected Uribe's demands that they name tribal members as "contact officials" with the army. That same month, Fredy Arias, the spokesman and human rights coordinator for the Kankuamo tribe, was murdered by suspected paramilitaries. Indian claims to land and resources are under challenge from government ministries and multinational corporations. In 2004 there were four indigenous senators—two of whom occupied seats reserved for indigenous people—and two Afro-Colombian members of the upper house; there was also one Native American and three Afro-Colombians members of the House of Representatives. Neither group, however, was represented in Uribe's cabinet nor on any of the nation's high courts.

According to the United Nations, some 948,000 children under the age of 14 work in "unacceptable" conditions. An estimated 60 percent of FARC fighters are believed to be under the age of 15, and female child-soldiers were reported to be subject to sexual abuse. Child-soldiers attempting to leave without permission are executed by firing squad.

Sexual harassment, violence against women, and the trafficking of women for sexual exploitation remain serious problems. In 2004, Amnesty International reported that soldiers, leftist rebels, and rightist paramilitaries treat women as "trophies of war," and that the crimes committed by the paramilitaries—the main offenders—include rape, mutilation, and murder. Women are active in politics and community organizations.

Comoros

Population: 700,000
GNI/capita: $390
Life Expectancy: 56
Religious Groups: Sunni Muslim (98 percent),
Roman Catholic (2 percent)
Ethnic Groups: Antalote, Cafre, Makoa, Oimatsaha,
Sakalava
Capital: Moroni

Political Rights: 4*
Civil Liberties: 4
Status: Partly Free

Ratings Change: Comoros' political rights rating improved from 5 to 4 due to the holding of legitimate parliamentary elections.

Ten-Year Ratings Timeline (Political Rights, Civil Liberties, Status)

1995	1996	1997	1998	1999	2000	2001	2002	2003	2004
4,4PF	4,4PF	5,4PF	5,4PF	6,4PF	6,4PF	6,4PF	5,4PF	5,4PF	4,4PF

Overview: Successful legislative elections that took place in 2004 reenforced the regional governmental power of Comoros's three constituent islands vis-à-vis that of the central government. Internal strains and rivalries, however, between the leaders of the islands and the federation president resulted in continued political tension.

Two mercenary invasions and at least 18 other coups and attempted coups have shaken the Indian Ocean archipelago of Comoros since its independence from France in 1975. In 1990, in the country's first contested elections, Supreme Court Justice Said Mohamed Djohara won a six-year term as president. French soldiers reversed a 1995 attempted coup by elements of the Comoros security forces, who were aided by foreign mercenaries. President Mohamed Taki Abdoulkarim was elected in 1996 in internationally monitored elections that were considered free and fair. Tadjidine Ben Said Massonde became the interim ruler when Taki died suddenly in November 1998.

Three islands comprise Comoros: Grande Comore, Anjouan, and Moheli. Anjouan voted for self-determination in a 1997 referendum, repulsed an attempted military takeover by the government, and then dissolved into violence as rival separatist groups took up arms against one another. Separatists on Moheli also declared independence. The federal government is located in Grande Comore, but even there serious tensions exist between the federal and regional governments.

Mayotte Island, the fourth island of the Comorian archipelago, had voted to remain a French overseas territory in a 1974 referendum and today enjoys a far higher, French-subsidized standard of living than do the other islands.

Efforts to end the separatist crisis began with the 1999 Antananarivo agreement. Anjouan's refusal to sign the agreement led to violence on Grande Comore and a subsequent coup by Colonel Assoumani Azali. A reconciliation agreement, known as the Fomboni Declaration, was signed in 2000 between the Azali government and Anjouan separatists. A national referendum was approved in December 2001 for a new constitution that gave greater autonomy to the three islands of Comoros within the framework of a confederation and provided for a rotating executive presidency among the islands every four years.

In 2002, while elections for the president of each of the three islands that make up the new federation appeared to have been largely free and fair, the poll for the executive leader of the federation was not. Azali, who won the executive presidency, was the only candidate, as his two opponents had claimed fraud and dropped out of the race. Lengthy negotiations occurred over minimum conditions for holding postponed legislative elections. In September 2002, an agreement was reached that would result in legislative polls, which were subsequently postponed until 2004. Key terms of the accord had the central government maintaining control over the country's army, while the police were to be administered by the local presidents. Another key compromise was the decision to set up a provisional customs council to facilitate the fair distribution of revenue among the three islands.

Comorans are among the world's poorest people. The country relies heavily on foreign aid and earns a small amount through exports of vanilla, ylang-ylang, and cloves. The political troubles have affected the country's economic relations with the outside world. In March 2003, for example, two of the island presidents signed a resolution calling on the European Union to "temporarily delay" its payments to the central government for fishing rights. They also asked ComoreTel, the largest telecommunications company on the island, to suspend its revenue payments. This tense political situation created confusion among Comorans who did not know whether to pay their taxes to their island government or to the central government. Legislative elections took place in April 2004. Despite concerns that the government would attempt to rig the elections, Comoran and international observers assessed them as legitimate, and the government suffered a serious setback. Candidates supporting the three autonomous islands came out victorious after obtaining 41 out of the 55 contested seats, while backers of Azali won only 12. Since the elections the various opposition and government authorities have sought to manage their differences, and relative calm has prevailed.

Political Rights and Civil Liberties: Comorans have the constitutional right to change their government democratically, although this right has not been fully realized. The 2004 legislative and 2002 presidential elections for the presidency of each of the country's three main islands were considered to be largely fair. The vote for the executive presidency, however, lacked legitimacy. After the country's electoral commission concluded that the vote for the executive presidency was not fair, the commission was dissolved and a body of five magistrates ruled that the election would stand.

Comorans exercised their constitutional right to change their government in open elections for the first time in the 1996 parliamentary and presidential elections. Mohamed Taki Abdoulkarim won the presidency in a runoff election with more than 60 percent of the vote. Prior to the 2004 elections, the parliament had not met since Colonel Azali's 1999 coup. Political discourse is focused mainly on the question of relations between the central government and the governments of the various islands. A wide range of political parties and protagonists exists.

Comoros was not ranked in Transparency International's 2004 Corruption Perceptions Index. In previous years there have been complaints of corruption among the security forces and unpaid salaries for teachers and other government workers. Freedom of expression is generally, but not fully, respected. The semiofficial weekly *Al-Watwan* and several private newspapers sharply critical of the government are published in the capital, but they appear only sporadically because of limited resources. All are believed to exercise extensive self-censorship. Two state-run radio stations broadcast, and about 20 regional radio stations and five local private television stations operate without overt government interference.

Islam is the official state religion. Non-Muslims are legally permitted to practice, but there were reports of restrictions, detentions, and harassment. Detainees are sometimes subjected to attempts to convert them to Islam. Christians are not allowed to proselytize. Academic freedom is generally respected.

The government generally respects the rights of freedom of assembly and association. The former is explicitly recognized in the constitution, although the latter is not. Occasionally, the police have violently dispersed protesters. Unions have the right to bargain collectively and strike, but collective bargaining is rare in the country's small formal business sector.

The Comorian legal system is based both on Sharia (Islamic law) and on parts of the French legal code and is subject to influence by the executive and other elites. Most minor disputes are settled by village elders or a civilian court of first instance. Harsh prison conditions are marked by severe overcrowding and the lack of adequate sanitation facilities, medical attention, and proper diet.

Women possess constitutional protections. In practice, however, they enjoy little political or economic power and have far fewer opportunities for education or salaried employment than do men. Economic hardship has forced growing numbers of young girls into domestic servitude. They receive room and board, but little or no pay.

Congo, Democratic Republic of (Kinshasa)

Population: 58,300,000 **Political Rights:** 6
GNI/capita: $100 **Civil Liberties:** 6
Life Expectancy: 49 **Status:** Not Free
Religious Groups: Roman Catholic (50 percent), Protestant (20 percent), Kimbanguist (10 percent), Muslim (10 percent), other (10 percent)
Ethnic Groups: More than 200 tribes, mostly Bantu
Capital: Kinshasa

Ten-Year Ratings Timeline (Political Rights, Civil Liberties, Status)

1995	1996	1997	1998	1999	2000	2001	2002	2003	2004
7,6NF	7,6NF	7,6NF	7,6NF	7,6NF	7,6NF	6,6NF	6,6NF	6,6NF	6,6NF

Overview:
Recent gains made in the Democratic Republic of Congo (DRC), chiefly the inauguration of a still-tenuous national power-sharing government, were threatened in 2004 by po-

litical infighting, halting progress in preparing for national elections in July 2005, and violence in the volatile eastern region bordering Burundi, Rwanda, and Uganda. The instability and violence aggravated ethnic rivalries within the transitional government, which appeared increasingly fragile and incapable of extending its authority throughout the country. Meanwhile, the United Nations authorized the expansion of its forces in the country, and the International Criminal Court launched an investigation into war crimes in the DRC.

As the Congo Free State, and then the Belgian Congo, the vast area of Central Africa that is today the DRC was exploited with a brutality that was extreme even by colonial standards. The country became a center for Cold War rivalries on Belgium's withdrawal in 1960 and remained so until well after Colonel Joseph Mobutu seized power with CIA backing in 1964; Mobutu soon renamed Congo as Zaire, and himself Mobutu Sese Seko. Western governments chose to ignore Mobutu's severe repression of his people and the financial excesses that made him one of the world's richest men and contributed to making his countrymen among the world's poorest people.

Domestic agitation for democratization and a post-Cold War loss of Western support forced Mobutu to open up the political process in 1990. In 1992, his Popular Revolutionary Movement, the sole legal party after 1965, and the Sacred Union of the Radical Opposition and Allied Civil Society, a coalition of 200 groups, joined scores of others in a national conference to establish the High Council of the Republic to oversee a democratic transition. However, Mobutu delayed and manipulated the transition.

More than the widespread opposition to his rule, it was the 1994 genocide of the Tutsi people in neighboring Rwanda that triggered Mobutu's demise. He had allowed the Hutu Interahamwe—a Rwandan Hutu militia responsible for the massacre of about 800,000 Tutsis and moderate Hutus—to base themselves in his country, then still known as Zaire. In 1996, Rwanda and Uganda easily tapped into popular hatred for Mobutu in their seven-month advance on Kinshasa. They installed Laurent Kabila, who at the time was a semi-retired guerrilla fighter, as the head of their rebellion and toppled the Mobutu regime in May 1997; the country was subsequently renamed the Democratic Republic of Congo. Mobutu fled to Morocco and died of cancer there a few months later.

A subsequent armed conflict erupted in late 1998 after Kabila fell out with Uganda and Rwanda. However, a peace agreement in 1999, the Lusaka accord, obliged Rwanda to withdraw its troops, which had entered the DRC in 1996 to pursue the Interahamwe. After Kabila was assassinated in January 2001, his son Joseph revived the 1999 Lusaka peace accord and furthered the consolidation of a ceasefire. The war at some point had drawn forces from at least eight countries into the fighting: Angola, Chad, Namibia, Sudan, and Zimbabwe on the side of Kabila; and Burundi, Rwanda, and Uganda on the side of the rebels. By the end of 2002, Angola, Burundi, Chad, Namibia, Sudan, and Zimbabwe had all withdrawn their troops from the DRC, while Uganda and Rwanda officially withdrew their forces in 2003.

Under an accord reached in December 2002 in Pretoria, South Africa, the DRC is now run by a two-year transitional government headed by President Joseph Kabila. Multiparty elections are mandated by July 2005, although the government will be hard-pressed to adhere to this timetable unless security conditions improve. During the last two years, the transitional government has been troubled by serious internal divisions. In October 2003, the Mayi-Mayi militia and the Congolese Rally for Democracy (RCD) former rebel movement signed a ceasefire agreement. Until then, fighting had continued unabated between their troops, even though both are signatories to the national power-sharing accord. In 2004, the RCD briefly suspended its participation in the government following the massacre of 160 ethnic Tutsis at a refugee camp in Burundi, in which Rwandan and Congolese rebel groups were accused of collaborating, a claim that was later discredited by Human Rights Watch. In June 2004, the government faced another crisis when Rwandan-backed rebels and renegade army officers seized the strategic town of Bukavu and other locations, occupying the area for a week until UN peacekeepers convinced them to withdraw.

Moreover, none of the militias operating in the northeastern Ituri region are signatories to the national power-sharing agreement, and they have complained of being excluded from the transition process. Despite assurances of cooperation by these armed groups, the killing, torture, rape, and abduction of civilians to forced labor camps continue to be reported. Human Rights Watch estimates that at least 5,000 civilians were killed in Ituri between July 2002 and early 2003, with hundreds more having died over the past year. There are some 4,500 UN peacekeepers deployed in the Ituri region, and that number will be increased with the imminent expansion of the DRC mission. A UN arms embargo remains in effect, although all armed factions seem to face no shortage of weaponry.

In September 2004, the UN Security Council authorized the expansion of the UN force in the DRC from 10,800 to 16,700, including the rapid deployment of another 3,300 peacekeepers to the troubled eastern provinces. A UN-led disarmament and reintegration program for the estimated 15,000 rebel fighters (including child-soldiers) in the Ituri region got off to a slow start in September, with most of the Congolese militias operating in the area failing to honor earlier commitments to lay down their arms. Although the leaders of seven armed groups in Ituri had agreed in May to end hostilities, clashes and the killings of civilians persist.

A UN panel investigating the plunder of natural resources in the DRC confirmed that the war evoked competition to control the DRC's vast diamond and other mineral wealth, and this illicit economic exploitation persists through proxy militias controlled by neighboring countries and government officials. The UN peacekeeping mission warned in an August 2004 report that violence in the Ituri region would persist until the government assumed control of the extraction of natural resources there. At the request of the DRC government, the International Criminal Court launched an investigation into war crimes and crimes against humanity in the DRC in June.

Diplomatic efforts to ease tensions among the Great Lakes countries culminated in September with the governments of the DRC, Rwanda, and Uganda signing agreements pledging to resolve their differences peacefully and to disarm all rebel groups operating in their territories and that threaten the security of neighboring states. The DRC and Rwanda also signed a deal to establish a joint verification mechanism to improve security along their common border. However, the DRC government's ability to impose its will in many areas of the country remains tenuous, at best.

Most people live marginal lives as subsistence farmers, even though the country contains vast natural resources. Despite rampant corruption and smuggling, the

DRC's economy continued to recover in 2004, posting growth of 6 percent, albeit from a very low base. The IMF and World Bank, as well as foreign donors and the African Development Bank, stepped up assistance to the country in the form of grants, loans, and debt forgiveness.

Political Rights and Civil Liberties:

The people of the DRC cannot change their government through democratic means. There are no elected representatives in the entire country. Large portions of the DRC remain essentially ungoverned, subject to local warlords or militia. Former leader Mobutu Sese Seko's successive, unopposed presidential victories and legislative polls were little more than political theater. Infrastructure and institutions to support a free and fair election are almost entirely absent, although the United Nations and South Africa are working with the government and the Independent Electoral Commission to provide support for the presidential and legislative polls slated for 2005.

President Joseph Kabila heads a two-year transitional government of national unity that consists of 4 vice presidents, 36 ministers, and 24 vice ministers shared among various factions. Extensive executive, legislative, and military powers are vested in the president and vice presidents. Key ministries are shared among the government and the two main former rebel groups—the RCD and the Uganda-backed Movement for the Liberation of Congo (MLC).

In accordance with a transitional constitution adopted in April 2003, the National Assembly and the Senate convened later that year in the capital, Kinshasa. The National Assembly consists of 500 appointed members from the parties to the intra-Congolese dialogue: namely, the former Kinshasa government, the unarmed political opposition, civil society, and former rebel movements. The Senate is made up of 120 appointees from the various parties to the national power-sharing accord. Its first task will be to draft legislation in line with the transitional constitution, such as laws on nationality, the functioning and organization of political parties, electoral law, and institutional management, as well as enacting a general amnesty for all former combatants. Civil society representatives head five other constitutionally mandated bodies on human rights, the media, truth and reconciliation, elections, and the fight against corruption.

At least 400 political parties registered after their 1990 legalization, but they were later banned under Laurent Kabila. Following the passage, in April 2004, of new electoral laws, 34 of 239 existing political parties were dissolved for failing to register with the government before a six-month deadline. Most former rebel groups are now authorized to act as political parties.

Corruption is rampant throughout the country. The DRC was ranked 133 out of 146 countries surveyed in Transparency International's 2004 Corruption Perceptions Index.

Freedom of expression is limited. Defamation carries a prison sentence of up to five years, and journalists are often jailed as soon as they are accused, under a policy of preventive detention. However, the new constitution contains several articles intended to guarantee free expression, and the government has created a national law reform commission tasked with amending legislation that curtails the media. The UN broadcaster, Radio Okapi, has expanded its coverage of the country to include several local languages. The Catholic Church operates the Elikya radio network throughout most of the country. At least 30 independent newspapers are published regularly in Kinshasa but are not widely circulated beyond the city. Although the government does not restrict access to the Internet, very few people can afford the connection costs or have computers and reliable electricity.

Despite some statutory protections, independent journalists are frequently threatened, arrested, or attacked by both rebel groups and government officials. A June mutiny in the town of Bukavu prompted a government crackdown on the press, with authorities issuing several directives restricting coverage and jailing at least four journalists. Attackers allegedly led by an army officer severely beat another journalist, according to the Committee to Protect Journalists, which led an investigation to the area. Rebels also shut down Bukavu's three leading community radio stations and threatened at least four journalists.

The transitional constitution provides for freedom of religion, and this right is generally respected in practice, although religious groups must register with the government to be recognized. Academic freedom is restricted in practice. Fears of government harassment often lead university professors to engage in self-censorship.

Freedom of assembly and association allowed by law is limited in practice. Numerous nongovernmental organizations, including human rights groups, operate despite intimidation and arrest. The June unrest in Bukavu, including looting and attacks on humanitarian agencies, forced almost 200 aid workers, working in more than 30 international organizations, to leave the area and brought critical assistance operations to a virtual halt. Humanitarian workers have also been attacked in many of the country's larger cities.

More than 100 new independent unions were registered after the end of one-party rule in 1990, but they remained largely an urban phenomenon. Previously, all unions had to affiliate themselves with a confederation that was part of the ruling party. Some unions are affiliated with political parties, and labor leaders and activists have faced harassment. There is little union activity, owing to the breakdown of the country's formal (business) economy and its replacement by the black market.

Despite guarantees of independence, in practice the judiciary remains subject to corruption and manipulation by both official and non-state actors. However, there are some indications that the nearly defunct legal system is beginning to revive. A court in Ituri resumed hearing cases after suspending work in 2003 because of poor security conditions, although it has generally avoided investigating the most serious human rights abuses. In its highest-profile conviction so far, the court sentenced the former security chief of the Union of Congolese Patriots, blamed for numerous abuses in the region, to 20 years in prison for condoning torture and arbitrary arrests; the UPC is currently recognized as a legal political party. Prison conditions are often harsh and life threatening.

The conflict in the DRC has directly and indirectly claimed the lives of an estimated 3.3 million people, according to the International Rescue Committee; this makes it the most deadly conflict since World War II. By UN estimates, another 2.7 million people were displaced. The UN Special Rapporteur of the Commission on Human Rights on the Situation of Human Rights in the DRC confirmed that genocide may have occurred in the Ituri region and reported extrajudicial executions in South Kivu province and throughout the eastern parts of the country. Humanitarian agencies say that up to 150,000 people have been displaced by the latest round of fighting. Recruitment of child-soldiers remains a serious problem. International human rights groups say that 30,000 children are serving in government and rebel groups, accounting for about 10 percent of the total combatants in the DRC. Ethnic societal discrimination is practiced widely among the country's 200 ethnic groups.

Despite constitutional guarantees, women face de facto discrimination, especially in rural areas, where there is in any case little government presence. They also enjoy fewer employment and educational opportunities than men and often do not receive equal pay for equal work. Violence against women, including rape and forced sexual slavery, has soared since the onset of armed conflict in 1996. Children continue to face forced conscription by all sides in the conflict, although the government appeared to be scaling back this practice. The Save the Children organization has ranked the DRC among the world's five worst conflict zones in which to be a woman or child.

Congo, Republic of (Brazzaville)

Population: 3,800,000
GNI/capita: $610
Life Expectancy: 48
Religious Groups: Christian (50 percent), animist (48 percent), Muslim (2 percent)
Ethnic Groups: Kongo (48 percent), Sangha (20 percent), Teke (17 percent), M'Bochi (12 percent), other (3 percent)
Capital: Brazzaville

Political Rights: 5
Civil Liberties: 4
Status: Partly Free

Ten-Year Ratings Timeline (Political Rights, Civil Liberties, Status)

1995	1996	1997	1998	1999	2000	2001	2002	2003	2004
4,4PF	4,4PF	7,5NF	7,5NF	6,5NF	6,4PF	5,4PF	6,4PF	5,4PF	5,4PF

Overview:

Following years of intermittent civil war, the Republic of Congo saw improvements in human rights and political stability in 2004 with the consolidation of a 2003 peace deal between the government and the Ninja rebel group in the northeastern Pool region. However, reports persisted of occasional abuses by both sides. More than 20 opposition political parties formed a new alliance to pressure the government to institute reforms before the next round of legislative and presidential polls.

A decade after Congo's independence from France, a 1970 coup established a Marxist state in the country. In 1979, General Denis Sassou-Nguesso seized power and maintained one-party rule as head of the Congolese Workers' Party. Domestic and international pressure forced his acceptance of a national conference leading to open, multiparty elections in 1992. Pascal Lissouba won a clear victory over former prime minister Bernard Kolelas in a second-round presidential runoff that excluded Sassou-Nguesso, who had run third in the first round.

Disputes over the 1993 legislative polls led to armed conflict. The fighting subsided but flared once again among ethnic-based militias in 1997. Sassou-Nguesso, who has had military support from Angola and political backing from France, built a private army in his native northern Congo and forcibly retook the presidency in

October 1997. Peace agreements signed in late 1999 included an amnesty for combatants who voluntarily disarmed. A new constitution was adopted by referendum in January 2002, providing for a multiparty system and establishing wide-ranging powers for the president, who would be directly elected for a seven-year term.

The March 2002 presidential poll was marred by irregularities, and there was no independent electoral commission, but international observers hailed the peaceful nature of the vote. Sassou-Nguesso was virtually assured a victory when his main challenger, former prime minister Andre Milongo, dropped out of the race just before the election, claiming irregularities. Sassou-Nguesso won the election with 89 percent of the vote. Elections for the 137-member National Assembly in May and June were dominated by Sassou-Nguesso's Congolese Workers' Party and other parties affiliated with it.

In August 2004, the political opposition, including supporters of Kolelas, formed a new party, the Coordination de l'Opposition pour une Alternance Democratique. They pledged to boycott government initiatives until Sassou-Nguesso took steps to ensure that parliamentary elections set for 2007 and presidential polls scheduled for 2009 are free and fair, including reviewing Congo's electoral code and creating a genuinely independent electoral commission.

Since the signing of a ceasefire agreement with Ninja militias in early 2003, peace has gradually returned to the northeast Pool region. Train service to the capital resumed after a six-year hiatus, and most of those internally displaced by the fighting returned to their villages. The government is working with international donors to rebuild the Pool region's shattered infrastructure. However, unidentified armed elements remained active, restricting citizens' freedom of movement, and there were reports that government security forces killed civilians in the region.

A major stumbling block to improved relations with the neighboring Democratic Republic of Congo (DRC) was lifted with an agreement to repatriate 4,000 former combatants of the now disbanded Zairean Armed Forces. The former fighters' presence in Congo had fueled tensions, particularly following attacks against targets in the DRC that were apparently launched from Brazzaville. Former fighters living in the DRC, who had served under ousted Congolese president Pascal Lissouba, are also covered by the agreement.

In July 2004, Congo was suspended from the Kimberly Process, a global diamond certification initiative seeking to end the trade in so-called blood, or conflict, diamonds—which are used by rebel movements to finance wars against legitimate governments—when Congo was unable to account for large discrepancies in the number of diamonds it exports and the number it actually produces. The disparities raised concerns that Congo was a transshipment point for illicit diamonds from the DRC and other neighboring countries. The government said that it would institute new oversight measures and temporarily halted all diamond exports.

Although Congo is the fifth-largest producer of oil in sub-Saharan Africa, poverty remains widespread, affecting some 70 percent of the population. After several years of shrinking oil revenues, which account for 95 percent of Congo's export earnings, the economy is expected to rebound as new oil fields come on-line. The government has proceeded with privatization plans under the direction of the IMF and complied with requirements that it disclose government audits of oil revenues and other transparency measures.

Political Rights and Civil Liberties: Since the outbreak of civil war in 1997, Congolese have been only partly able to exercise their constitutional right to change their leaders through democratic elections. Competitive multiparty elections were held for the first time in 1992 and 1993. Presidential and legislative elections held in 2002 were not deemed fair, in part because of irregularities and the absence of an independent electoral commission.

The Republic of Congo was ranked 114 out of 146 countries surveyed in Transparency International's 2004 Corruption Perceptions Index. There were media reports of government bribery and corruption, particularly regarding oil revenues.

The government generally respects press freedom, but continues to monopolize the broadcast media. In 2000, the government abolished censorship and sharply reduced penalties for defamation. About 10 private newspapers appear weekly in Brazzaville, and they often publish articles and editorials that are critical of the government. There are approximately 10 domestic Internet service providers and no government restrictions on Internet use.

Religious freedom is guaranteed and respected. Academic freedom is restricted, and university professors often exercise self-censorship to conform to the views of the government. However, there were no reports of students or professors being overtly censored.

Freedom of assembly and association is constitutionally guaranteed, and this right is generally respected in practice, although public demonstrations are rare. Nongovernmental organizations (NGOs) generally operate freely. Workers' rights to join trade unions and to strike are legally protected, and collective bargaining is practiced freely. Most workers in the formal business sector are union members, and unions have made efforts to organize informal sectors, such as those of agriculture and retail trade.

The judiciary is subject to corruption and political influence. The court system was generally considered to be politically independent until the civil war, although the judiciary was ranked fourth in a 2004 government survey of the most corrupt public bodies. Scarce resources and understaffing have created a backlog of court cases and long periods of pretrial detention. In rural areas, traditional courts retain broad jurisdiction, especially in civil matters. Prison conditions are life threatening, with reports of beatings, overcrowding, and other ill-treatment. Women and men, as well as juveniles and adults, are incarcerated together. Human rights groups and the International Committee of the Red Cross have been allowed access.

During a trip to France in April 2004, Congo's chief of police, Jean-Francois Ndengue, was arrested in connection with the disappearance of 353 Congolese refugees who had returned from exile in the Democratic Republic of Congo (DRC) in 1999. Ndengue was released shortly afterward when a French court ruled that he had diplomatic immunity. The detention stemmed from a lawsuit filed in France by human rights groups and survivors against Ndengue, President Denis Sassou-Nguesso, and other high-ranking government officials for alleged crimes of torture, forced disappearance, and crimes against humanity. The Congolese government contends that France does not have jurisdiction over incidents occurring in Congo and has sued France in The Hague-based International Court of Justice to suspend the prosecutions. The Congolese government is currently conducting its own parallel hearings into the disappearances before a tribunal in Brazzaville, although relatives of the missing have denounced the legal proceedings as biased.

In accordance with the country's new constitution, a human rights commission consisting of members from civil society organizations, professional associations, and public institutions was formed in August 2003. While its establishment has been hailed by local rights groups as a positive development, the commission's powers are limited. Members are named by presidential decree and have no authority to summon accused parties. The president also appointed the members of a social and economic council and freedom-of-speech council, completing the range of constitutionally required bodies. In September 2003, the government ratified the UN Convention against Torture and Other Cruel, Inhuman or Degrading Treatment or Punishment, although local human rights groups say police abuse of detainees remains a serious problem. Human rights violations against the civilian population abated with the 2003 ceasefire between the government and Ninja militias.

Ethnic discrimination persists. Pygmy groups suffer discrimination, and many are effectively held in lifetime servitude through customary ties to Bantu "patrons." According to local human rights groups, rape of Pygmy women by Bantu men is widespread. Members of virtually all ethnic groups practice discrimination in hiring practices.

Legal and societal discrimination against women is extensive, despite constitutional protection. Access to education and employment opportunities, especially in the countryside, are limited, and civil codes regarding family and marriage formalize women's inferior status. Violence against women is reportedly widespread. After declining in 2000 and 2001, incidents of rape increased in 2002 with the renewed outbreak of hostilities. NGOs have drawn attention to the issue and provided counseling and assistance to victims.

Costa Rica

Population: 4,200,000
GNI/capita: $4,070
Life Expectancy: 79
Religious Groups: Roman Catholic (76.3 percent), Evangelical (13.7 percent), other (10 percent)
Ethnic Groups: White and mestizo (94 percent), black (3 percent), Amerindian (1 percent), other (2 percent)
Capital: San José

Political Rights: 1
Civil Liberties: 1*
Status: Free

Ratings Change: Costa Rica's civil liberties rating improved from 2 to 1 due to the indictment of three former presidents for corruption, along with free press coverage of the processes.

Ten-Year Ratings Timeline (Political Rights, Civil Liberties, Status)

1995	1996	1997	1998	1999	2000	2001	2002	2003	2004
1,2F	1,2F	1,2F	1,2F	1,2F	1,2F	1,2F	1,2F	1,2F	1,1F

Overview:

The year 2004 saw the indictment on corruption charges of three former presidents of Costa Rica, one of whom was serving as secretary-general of the Organization of American States (OAS).

Costa Rica achieved independence from Spain in 1821 and became a republic in 1848. In the 1994 elections, Jose Maria Figueres, son of the legendary president Jose "Pepe" Figueres, defeated Miguel Angel Rodriguez of the Social Christian Unity Party (PUSC). The outgoing president, Rafael A. Calderon Jr., also of the PUSC, had promoted neoliberal economic policies, against which Figueres campaigned. Despite his campaign pledges, Figueres's last two years in office saw the adoption of free market policies. In the 1998 elections, Rodriguez bested Jose Miguel Corrales of the National Liberation Party (PLN).

For many years, there has been a consistent flow of Nicaraguans searching for employment in Costa Rica. There are more than 400,000 Nicaraguans in Costa Rica, many of whom work without papers on farms where they are paid subsistence wages. In 1998, Costa Rica declared a temporary amnesty for these and other illegal Central American immigrants, and more than 200,000 Nicaraguans legalized their status. Simmering tensions with Nicaragua were exacerbated in 2001 when the Costa Rican government began to build a seven-foot-high fence along the Penas Blancas border crossing on the Pan-American Highway along the Pacific Coast. Claims that the wall was being built to control heavy traffic in goods in a region that has become a favored route for drug smuggling were dismissed in Nicaragua.

When no single candidate received the constitutionally required 40 percent of the vote in the February 2002 presidential election, a second round runoff was held in April. Although Abel Pacheco of the PUSC was victorious in the second round, improprieties in the financing of his election tarnished his image. After increasing voter dissatisfaction with the two traditional parties—the PUSC and the PLN—two smaller upstarts, the Citizens Action Party (PAC) and the Libertarian Movement (ML), received significant support in the February legislative poll. PUSC candidates won 19 of the assembly's 57 seats, while the PLN captured 17, followed by the PAC with 14, the ML with 6, and the Costa Rican Renovation Party with 1.

Although Costa Rica is usually seen as a paragon of law and order, the political waters have been muddied since the presidential elections by continuing allegations of illegal funding of Pacheco's campaign. Nevertheless, his problems appeared to pale in comparison to the successive indictments, on charges of corruption, of two of his recent predecessors—Rodriguez (1998–2002) and Calderon (1990–1994)—in 2004. Rodriguez, moreover, abruptly resigned as head of the OAS. Similar accusations against former PLN president Jose Maria Figueres (1994–1998) forced his resignation as managing director of the World Economic Forum. Pacheco's own government has been singularly unstable, having lost 14 ministers since his coming to office.

Costa Rica's once stable economy has been buffeted by a decline in the value of its agricultural exports and a growing gap between the earnings of this traditional sector and the income gains of workers in high-tech production. Continuing efforts to limit and reduce the public debt, along with relatively high inflation, have led to numerous labor actions, many of which have paralyzed the economy.

Despite the relative calm, the increase in gang-related violent crime has led public security forces to coordinate actions with Costa Rica's neighbors since September 2003. While not yet as dangerous or numerous as in neighboring countries, the gangs active in the country have increased the levels of violence faced by the now beleaguered Costa Ricans.

Political Rights and Civil Liberties: Democratic government change takes place with free and fair elections. The president and the 57-member Legislative Assembly are elected for a four-year term and were banned from seeking a second term until the Supreme Court overturned this law in 2003. There are guarantees for the right to organize political parties. In response to allegations of drug money financing the elections, new campaign laws have been passed to make party funding more transparent.

Following the indictments on charges of corruption of three former presidents in 2004, the most popular public figure is Francisco Dall'Anese, the public prosecutor who has taken on all of the major cases of official corruption. According to Dall'Anese, "Here [in Costa Rica] there are no untouchables." Costa Rica was ranked 41 out of 146 countries surveyed in Transparency International's Corruption Perceptions Index.

The press, radio, and television are generally free. Ninety percent of the population is literate, and there are six major privately owned dailies. Television and radio stations are both public and commercial, with at least four private television stations and more than 90 private radio stations. Article 309 of the criminal code, which had allowed up to two years in prison for anyone damaging the reputation or insulting the rank of a government official, was repealed in February 2002. However, other similar laws are still on the books, including one allowing people who feel that their reputation was impugned by an item of news to sue. Article 149 of the criminal code places the burden on journalists to prove their innocence, and Article 152 punishes anyone who repeats offensive remarks. The unrestrained outcry of the media over the recent accusations of corruption in government have not been restricted by either the government or the individuals accused of malfeasance.

Freedom of religion is recognized, and there is complete academic freedom.

The constitution provides for the right to organize civic organizations. Numerous nongovernmental organizations are active in all parts of society and the country. Labor can organize freely, but there has been a noticeable reluctance to expand labor rights. Frequent labor actions, ranging from local to nationwide protests, take place with a minimum of governmental restraints. Minimum wage and social security laws are often ignored, and the consequent fines are insignificant.

The judicial branch is independent, with members elected by the legislature. The legal system includes a Supreme Court, courts of appeals, and district courts. The Supreme Court can rule on the constitutionality of laws and chooses an independent national election commission. There are long delays in the justice system, partly as a result of budget cuts. Prisons are notoriously overcrowded, but generally meet international standards.

A 1994 Police Code and the 2001 Law for Strengthening the Civilian Police were designed to depoliticize and professionalize the police in order to create a permanent career path within the institution. The law replaced military ranks with civilian titles and required the police academy to develop a course and diploma in police administration. The Ministry of Public Security and the Ministry of the Presidency share responsibility for law enforcement and national security. Several entities, including the Border Guard, the Rural Guard, and the Civil Guard, were merged into a single "public force." The 1949 constitution bans the formation of a national army. Independent rights monitors report increases in allegations of arbitrary arrest and brutality. Human rights complaints are investigated by an ombudsman who has the authority to issue recommendations for rectification, including sanctions against government bodies, for failure to respect rights. Corruption is not considered a serious problem in the public security forces and, when discovered, is usually dealt with in a decisive manner.

The country is a regional leader in the enactment of progressive antidrug statutes, including the use of wiretaps, controlled deliveries, and undercover agents. Financial institutions must report any transactions involving more than $10,000. In 1999, the Legislative Assembly passed legislation allowing for U.S. antidrug patrols to operate in Costa Rican waters.

Indigenous rights are not a priority, but in general, conditions for native peoples are better than those in neighboring countries.

The government is making significant efforts to combat human trafficking; Costa Rica is a transit and destination country for trafficked persons. Often, women workers are sexually harassed, made to work overtime without pay, and fired when they become pregnant. Violence against women and children is a problem, although the government has shown concrete support for programs and policies to combat it. A law criminalizing sex with minors was passed in 1999 in an attempt to crack down on the country's growing sex tourism industry.

Cote d'Ivoire

Population: 16,900,000 **Political Rights:** 6
GNI/capita: $620 **Civil Liberties:** 6*
Life Expectancy: 42 **Status:** Not Free
Religious Groups: Christian (20-30 percent),
Muslim (35-40 percent), indigenous beliefs (25-40 percent)
Ethnic Groups: Akan (42.1 percent), Voltaiques,
or Gur (17.6 percent), Northern Mandes (16.5 percent),
Krous (11 percent), Southern Mandes (10 percent), other (2.8 percent)
Capital: Yamoussoukro (official); Abidjan (de facto)
Ratings Change: Cote d'Ivoire's civil liberties rating declined from 5 to 6 due to a deterioration in security and civil freedoms resulting from ongoing hostilities emanating from an unresolved civil war.

Ten-Year Ratings Timeline (Political Rights, Civil Liberties, Status)

1995	1996	1997	1998	1999	2000	2001	2002	2003	2004
6,5NF	6,5NF	6,4NF	6,4NF	6,4PF	6,5PF	5,4PF	6,6NF	6,5NF	6,6NF

Overview:

Cote d'Ivoire remained split near the end of 2004, as ethnic and political divisions became more entrenched and the prospect of elections in 2005 looked increasingly uncertain. Members of the political opposition and rebel New Forces suspended their participation in the government during the year. Human rights groups said the killing of civilians continued throughout the year. The government attempted to crush the New Forces with a bombing campaign that killed nine French peacekeepers in November.

France responded by destroying the Ivorian air force, triggering rioting and looting in the commercial capital, Abidjan. French citizens and businesses were targeted; thousands of French nationals fled the country.

Cote d'Ivoire gained independence from France in 1960, and President Felix Houphouet-Boigny ruled until his death in 1993. Henri Konan Bedie assumed power and won fraudulent elections in 1995, with 95 percent of the vote. Alassane Ouattara, the opposition's most formidable candidate, was barred from the contest, demonstrations were banned, and the media were intimidated.

General Robert Guei seized power in December 1999 and stood for election in October 2000. When initial results showed Guei was losing to Laurent Gbagbo, he sacked the electoral commission, detained its officers, and declared himself the winner. Tens of thousands of people took to the streets in a popular uprising that toppled Guei from power. Clashes followed between supporters of Gbagbo's Ivorian Popular Front (FPI), who claimed electoral victory, and Ouattara's Rally of Republicans (RDR), who called for new elections. Supported by security forces, Gbagbo refused to call for new polls. The political violence, in which hundreds of civilians died, led to a deepening division between the largely Muslim north and mainly Christian south, although the conflict is not strictly rooted in a north-south, Muslim-Christian divide. Gbagbo was eventually declared the winner of the election, with 59 percent, compared with 33 percent for Guei.

The FPI won 96 seats in the December 2000 legislative elections, while 4 went to the Democratic Party of Cote d'Ivoire and 5 to the RDR. Twenty-four seats went to smaller parties and independents, and 2 seats in Ouattara's district went unfilled.

Civil war erupted in September 2002 when the government attempted to demobilize and retire some 700 soldiers. In what appeared to be either a coup attempt or a mutiny, Guei was killed. An insurgent group—the Patriotic Movement of Cote d'Ivoire, now part of the rebel New Forces—emerged in the north, calling for Gbagbo to step down and for new elections. The insurgents quickly seized control of more than half of the country. Fighting erupted in the west, and African immigrants were targeted.

Gbagbo's government and the New Forces signed a ceasefire brokered by France in January 2003 that provided for a broad-based coalition government that would rule until elections in 2005. New Forces representatives and opposition members began a boycott of the government in September 2003, saying Gbagbo was failing to implement the French-brokered peace deal. They rejoined the government in January 2004 and withdrew again in March after security forces violently suppressed an opposition demonstration in Abidjan. The United Nations said at least 120 people were killed in the political violence that followed. After talks in Ghana, New Forces and political opposition members again rejoined the government.

Several challenges lie ahead, including tackling controversial laws on nationality and eligibility to run for president. Disarmament of an estimated 30,000 fighters did not begin in March 2004 as scheduled. Cote d'Ivoire's relationship with neighboring Burkina Faso remained strained during the year, although Burkina Faso denies supporting Ivorian rebels.

The International Crisis Group (ICG) reported in July that government officials, rebels, businessmen, and members of the security forces were profiting from the civil war. The ICG said profits from cocoa, cotton, and weapons, and informal taxes made resolving the Ivorian conflict a less attractive option than continuing the political stalemate. The World Bank in 2004 suspended aid to Cote d'Ivoire following an accumulation of debt arrears, and the United Nations has hinted at sanctions unless genuine progress is made at ending the civil war.

Cote d'Ivoire retains strong political, economic, and military backing from France, which has maintained a military garrison near Abidjan for years, mainly to protect French nationals who live in Cote d'Ivoire. Many French, however, fled after the war erupted. Some 4,000 French peacekeepers are monitoring the ceasefire line across the middle of the country, with some 6,000 more UN troops deployed there as well. Following the death of nine French peacekeepers in a government bombing campaign to crush the New Forces movement, France destroyed the Ivorian air force, and—with the backing of the African Union—persuaded the UN Security Council to impose an arms embargo on the country.

Political Rights and Civil Liberties: The people of Cote d'Ivoire cannot change their government democratically. The 1995 presidential election was neither free nor fair and was boycotted by all the major opposition parties. Voting in the October 2000 presidential election appeared to be carried out fairly, but only 5 of 19 potential candidates were allowed to contest the vote. The FPI of President Laurent Gbagbo won an overwhelming number of seats in the December 2000 legislative election.

Cote d'Ivoire was ranked 133 out of 145 countries surveyed in the 2004 Transparency International Corruption Perceptions Index. According to a July 2004 report by the Brussels-based ICG, "the political impasse is exceptionally lucrative for almost everyone except ordinary citizens. Major government figures have been accused of using state monies, especially from the Enron-like maze of interlinked institutions within the cocoa marketing system, for personal enrichment, purchasing weapons, and hiring mercenaries."

Press freedom is generally not respected in practice. State-owned newspapers and a state-run broadcasting system are usually unreservedly pro-government. The Paris-based Reporters Sans Frontieres said in June that the government had tightened its grip on the national radio and television station following the announcement by the information minister of a series of new measures aimed at bringing the news coverage in line with "government interests." Authorities will now be able to exert complete control over state-run news.

Several private radio stations and a cable television service operate, but only the state broadcasting system reaches a national audience. In August 2004, the United Nations launched its own radio station to promote peace and reconciliation in Cote d'Ivoire, despite negative pressure by the ruling party. Dozens of independent newspapers are published, many of which are linked to political parties.

Despite the reconciliation process, most Ivorian media remain partisan and provocative. Some human rights groups have characterized some of the commentary as "incitement to violence." In the north, the circulation of newspapers printed in Abidjan is heavily restricted, and local radio and television stations remain under the tight control of the rebel authorities. There is liberal access to the Internet.

The New York–based Committee to Protect Journalists (CPJ) said several journalists were attacked or arrested during opposition demonstrations in March, and several news outlets were censored during and after the protests. Michel Legre, a brother-in-law of the first lady, was formally charged in June 2004 as an accessory in the kidnapping, confinement, and murder of freelance journalist Guy-Andre Kieffer, who was last seen in April 2004. Kieffer, who had both French and Canadian citizenship, was also a commodities consultant specializing in the cocoa and coffee sectors. Gaston Bony, publication director of the weekly newspaper *Le Venin* and a host at the radio station La Voix de l'Agneby, was provisionally released in July after serving more than four months of a six-month sentence for criminal defamation. A military tribunal in January found a police sergeant guilty of murdering French radio journalist Jean Helene in October 2003. The sergeant was sentenced to 17 years in prison. Helene was shot outside a police station as he was waiting for opposition figures to be released from custody. In a positive development, Gbagbo in 2004 announced a draft law that would eliminate prison sentences for press offenses.

Religious freedom is guaranteed but is not respected in practice. The government openly favors Christianity, and Muslims have been targeted as a result of worsening economic conditions and growing xenophobia during the past few years of political unrest. The government, which owns most of the educational facilities in the country, inhibits academic freedom by requiring authorization for all political meetings held on college campuses. Security forces reportedly use students as informants at the University of Abidjan.

Human rights groups generally operate freely in Cote d'Ivoire, and a ministry of human rights has been created. Union formation and membership are legally protected, although only a small percentage of the workforce is organized. Workers have the right to bargain collectively.

According to a 2004 UN report, more than 120 people were killed during and after opposition demonstrations in March. The report said suspected opposition supporters were killed as part of a "carefully planned and executed" crackdown by the Ivorian security forces that was sanctioned by the "highest state authorities." The report further stated that people were targeted according to their names and ethnic groups.

Cote d'Ivoire does not have an independent judiciary. Judges are political appointees without tenure and are highly susceptible to external interference. In many rural areas, traditional courts still prevail, especially in the handling of minor matters and family law. Security forces generally operate with impunity, and prison conditions are harsh.

The New York–based Human Rights Watch (HRW) has reported that pro-government militias kill, torture, and harass civilians with impunity. Most of the militia members are from Gbagbo's Bete tribe in south-central Cote d'Ivoire. HRW said both the government and rebels were responsible for summary executions and sexual violence against women and girls that were rooted in ethnic discrimination occurring in a climate of impunity.

The United Nations reported that northern rebels were responsible for killings in 2004. Three mass graves containing about 100 bodies total were found near the northern rebel-held town of Korhogo, which was the scene of fighting between rival factions in June. In the north, freedom of movement is curtailed, and there is forced conscription, including conscription of many child-soldiers.

HRW has accused officials of deliberately encouraging a culture of violent xenophobia in Cote d'Ivoire, whose economy has long attracted workers from neighboring countries. More than one-quarter of the country's population is estimated to be African expatriates. Land-use disputes, aggravated by political tension, often trigger violence against African foreigners. At least 500,000 Africans have returned to their respective countries, mainly Mali and Burkina Faso, because of the civil war and another 500,000 people have been displaced.

New tough rules that cut the length of time foreigners can work in Cote d'Ivoire were announced in March. A decree stipulates that in order to gain a work permit for a non-national, an employer must indicate how the job will ultimately be transferred to an Ivorian within two years. The Economic Community of West African States criticized the rules, saying they violate existing agreements on freedom to travel and work within the region. Ivorian officials denied that West African workers would be affected.

Child labor and child trafficking are problems, although Cote d'Ivoire has made efforts to stem both practices. Tens of thousands of West African children are believed to be working on Ivorian plantations in hazardous conditions.

Women suffer widespread discrimination, despite official encouragement for respect for constitutional rights. Equal pay for equal work is offered in the small formal business sector, but women have few chances to obtain, or advance in, wage employment. In rural areas that rely on subsistence agriculture, education and job opportunities for women are even scarcer. Female genital mutilation is still practiced, although it has been a crime since 1998, and violence against women is reportedly common.

◆ Croatia

Population: 4,400,000
GNI/capita: $4,540
Life Expectancy: 75
Religious Groups: Roman Catholic (87.8 percent), Orthodox (4.4 percent), Muslim (1.3 percent), Protestant (0.3 percent), other and unknown (6.2 percent)
Ethnic Groups: Croat (89.6 percent), Serb (4.5 percent), Bosniak (0.5 percent), Hungarian (0.4 percent), Slovene (0.3 percent), Czech (0.2 percent), Roma (0.2 percent), Albanian (0.1 percent), Montenegrin (0.1 percent), other (4.1 percent)
Capital: Zagreb

Political Rights: 2
Civil Liberties: 2
Status: Free

Trend Arrow: Croatia received an upward trend arrow due to the second smooth transition of power since 1999 and the improved cooperation of the new government with the International Criminal Tribunal for the Former Yugoslavia (ICTY).

Ten-Year Ratings Timeline (Political Rights, Civil Liberties, Status)

1995	1996	1997	1998	1999	2000	2001	2002	2003	2004
4,4PF	4,4PF	4,4PF	4,4PF	4,4PF	2,3F	2,2F	2,2F	2,2F	2,2F

Overview:

Croatia marked an important success in its foreign policy in June 2004 when it was invited to begin negotiations on entering the European Union (EU). The invitation was issued after the winner of Croatia's November 2003 parliamentary elections, the right-of-center Croatian Democratic Union (HDZ), convinced European diplomats and officials of the International Criminal Tribunal for the Former Yugoslavia (ICTY) that it was making serious progress in cooperating with the court, creating a more hospitable environment for refugee return, and repairing relations with its neighbors.

As part of the Socialist Federal Republic of Yugoslavia, Croatia held its first multiparty elections in 1990, electing Franjo Tudjman, a former Communist general turned nationalist politician, as president in May 1990. Tudjman's HDZ ruled Croatia from 1990 to 1999. As rival nationalisms competed with each other in Croatia during 1990 and 1991, Croatia's Serb population in the region known as Krajina declared independence from Croatia, even as Croatia itself was declaring its independence from the former Yugoslavia. The result was a de facto partition of the country between 1991 and 1995. In May and August 1995, a majority of the Serb population of Croatia either fled or was forcibly expelled from Krajina during Croatian military offensives to establish control over the contested territory.

On December 11, 1999, Tudjman died, and in the subsequent extraordinary presidential elections in January 2000, Stjepan Mesic of the Croatian People's Party (HNS) was elected president. In legislative elections that also took place in January 2000, a center-left coalition wrested control of parliament from the HDZ. The leader of the SDP (the former League of Communists of Croatia), Ivica Racan, was named prime minister.

In Croatia's latest parliamentary elections, held on November 23, 2003, the HDZ, together with its new leader, Dr. Ivo Sanader, gained 66 seats, making the HDZ the strongest party in the new 152-member parliament and ending three years of a relatively weak SDP-led coalition government. Because of international objections to the formation of a coalition majority government with extreme right-wing nationalist parties, Sanader decided to lead a minority government with the support of the Independent Democratic Serb Party, the Croatian Party of Pensioners (HSU), the Croatian Peasants Party (HSS), and representatives of Croatia's Italian minority.

The HDZ's return to power was viewed with caution because of the party's history of engaging in nationalist demagogy, its meddling in neighboring Bosnia-Herzegovina, and its poor record in dealing with Croatia's ethnic minorities. Prime Minister Sanader has claimed that the party is now "reformed" and has evolved into a normal European Christian-democratic party purged of extremists, but many of its more controversial figures from the past remain in influential positions. It is widely believed, however, that only a party with strong nationalist credentials such as the HDZ will have the strength to extradite Croatian citizens indicted by the ICTY, one of the most important preconditions for Croatia's entry into the EU.

In June 2004, Croatia's application for EU membership was accepted. The decision was viewed as a major victory for the Sanader government, which, immediately on coming to office, embarked on a series of initiatives intended to assure the EU that despite its nationalist past, the HDZ would back up its promises and prove itself to be a more moderate force. Sanader, for instance, immediately began reaching out to the Serbian community in Croatia, visiting the former World War II concentration camp of Jasenovac (where tens of thousands of Serbs, Jews, and Roma were killed), and unequivocally denouncing the crimes that had been committed there—a move unimaginable for his more extreme nationalist predecessors in the

HDZ, and even too politically dangerous for the left-center leaders of the previous coalition government. Nevertheless, quick accession to the EU is not guaranteed for Croatia; EU leaders continue to demand numerous potentially painful reforms and initiatives from the Croatian government, including full cooperation with the ICTY, more action on facilitating the return of Serb refugees, and more effort on the part of Croatia to improve regional cooperation, accelerate judicial reform, and fight against corruption. It is unclear whether Croatia can satisfactorily complete all these requirements in time to catch up with Bulgaria and Romania when they are scheduled to join the EU in 2007.

Political Rights and Civil Liberties: Croatian voters can change their government democratically. Since 2000, there have been two peaceful transfers of power in the country. The parliamentary elections of November 2003 were contested by a record 34 candidates competing for each of the 152 seats in parliament. Although the elections were generally free and fair, the Organization for Security and Cooperation in Europe (OSCE) expressed concern over the short time frame available for election administration, the lack of accessibility for out-of-country voters, particularly for refugees in Serbia and Montenegro and Bosnia-Herzegovina, and the lack of transparency in campaign financing. Respect for the separation of powers in the Croatian political system remains problematic, and there have been numerous cases in recent years in which the executive or legislative branches of government have failed to abide by or implement decisions made by the Constitutional Court.

Croatia was ranked 67 out of 146 countries surveyed in Transparency International's 2004 Corruption Perceptions Index. During the course of the year, Sanader's government was plagued by corruption scandals affecting the deputy prime minister and the foreign minister, both old-guard HDZ officials from the 1990s. As in other parts of the Balkans, a nexus of official security institutions, networks supporting fugitive war criminals, and "legitimate" businesspeople is often at the center of many corruption cases.

Croatia's constitution guarantees freedom of expression and the press. On the whole, freedom of the media is respected in Croatia, but more reform of government media regulations is needed. The most important media outlet, HRT (Croatian Radio and Television), is still under substantial political control, despite long-running efforts to transform it into a European-style public service broadcaster. Most observers regard the 2003 Law on Croatian Radio and Television to be a step backward in terms of promoting the institution's independence. Journalistic freedom also remains weak; in a 2003 survey, half of the journalists questioned claimed that they do not feel free in their work. The penal code still allows for prison sentences for journalists found guilty of defamation and libel. There are no governmental restrictions with respect to Internet access.

Respect for freedom of religion has increased in Croatia in the post-Tudjman period, although ethnic and religious minorities enjoy these rights to a significantly lesser degree than do ethnic Croatians. The overwhelming majority of Croatians are Roman Catholic. Consequently, the Roman Catholic Church has a considerable degree of power and influence in the country and enjoys a favored position in many respects; for example, the state-run HRT provides up to 10 hours a month of coverage of Catholic events. The Catholic Church in Croatia also has considerable influence over social policies in the country, and in recent years has campaigned against a variety of proposals, ranging from school plans to introduce yoga classes into school curriculums (for fear of spreading Buddhist practices) to campaigns against Sunday business hours. Restitution of properties confiscated during the Communist period for the Orthodox and Jewish communities is believed to lag behind settlement of such problems with the Roman Catholic Church. There were also numerous reports of vandalism against Serbian Orthodox sites during the year. There were no reports of restrictions on academic freedom.

The constitution provides for freedom of association and assembly. A wide variety of both international and domestic nongovernmental organizations (NGOs) operate in Croatia, and there were no reported instances of governmental harassment of NGOs during the year. The constitution allows workers to form and join trade unions, and they do so freely. Approximately 64 percent of the workforce is unionized.

Croatia's judicial system suffers from numerous problems, including a large number of judicial vacancies and a shortage of experienced judges, both of which have led to a huge backlog of cases (estimated at 1.4 million in 2003); excessive trial length; and a lack of enforcement of judicial decisions, especially in cases relating to the repossession of property owned by Serbs. The judicial system also faces considerable intimidation in the always difficult field of war crimes prosecutions. Nevertheless, in June, ICTY chief prosecutor Carla del Ponte announced that she was satisfied with the cooperation she was receiving from the Croatian government.

In July, Human Rights Watch reported that "bias and a lack of legal professionalism" are characteristic of Croatian war crimes trials. However, there are indications that Croatia has become more willing to honor international obligations to prosecute and/or apprehend individuals accused of war crimes. In October, a judge in Split ordered the arrest of eight police officers who had previously been accused of killing and abusing Serb prisoners in the Lora prison, but had been released after controversial court proceedings in 2002. Prison conditions generally meet acceptable international standards, and the police are considered to act professionally. However, there are reports that police treat ethnic minorities more harshly than they do ethnic Croatians.

According to international monitoring organizations, Croatia continues to fail to live up to obligations, stemming from its accession to the Council of Europe in 1996, to adopt nondiscriminatory laws relating to ethnic minorities. A U.S. State Department report released in 2003 said, "A pattern of often open and severe discrimination continues against ethnic Serbs and, at times, other minorities in a wide number of areas, including the administration of justice, employment, housing, and freedom of movement."

The constitution prohibits discrimination on the basis of gender. Domestic violence against women is believed to be a widespread and under-reported phenomenon. In July 2003, parliament passed a Law on Gender Equality intended to further empower women in the workplace and public life. Women currently make up 27 of the 152 members of parliament, and there are 4 women in the 15-member cabinet. Trafficking in women for the purposes of prostitution continues to be a problem. Croatia is considered to be primarily a transit country for most trafficked women sent to Western Europe.

Cuba

Population: 11,300,000 **Political Rights:** 7
GNI/capita: $2,900 **Civil Liberties:** 7
Life Expectancy: 76 **Status:** Not Free
Religious Groups: Roman Catholic, Protestant, other
Ethnic Groups: Mulatto (51 percent), white (37 percent),
black (11 percent), Chinese (1 percent)
Capital: Havana

Ten-Year Ratings Timeline (Political Rights, Civil Liberties, Status)

1995	1996	1997	1998	1999	2000	2001	2002	2003	2004
7,7NF	7,7NF	7,7NF	7,7NF	7,7NF	7,7NF	7,7NF	7,7NF	7,7NF	7,7NF

Overview:

Cuba's leader Fidel Castro marked his 45th year in power in 2004, amid signs that the 78-year-old's health continued to decline. His second fall in public in three years raised questions about his physical vulnerability and about his capacity to continue to govern. Meanwhile, his Communist government steadily reasserted its control over the limited opening in the economy legalized by the regime in 1993. On the international front, there was growing tension between the government in Washington and the Castro regime, including efforts by the United States to increase broadcasts to and economic restrictions against Cuba.

Cuba achieved independence from Spain in 1898 as a result of the Spanish-American War. The Republic of Cuba was established in 1902, but remained under U.S. tutelage as a result of the Platt Amendment until 1934. In 1959, Castro's July 26th Movement—named after an earlier, failed insurrection—overthrew the U.S.-supported dictatorship of Fulgencio Batista, who had ruled for 18 of the previous 25 years.

Following the 1991 collapse of the Soviet Union and the end of some $5 billion in annual Soviet subsidies, Castro sought Western foreign investment. The legalization of the U.S. dollar in Cuba in 1993 heightened social tensions, as the minority with access to dollars from abroad or through the tourist industry emerged as a new moneyed class, while the majority without access became increasingly desperate. Under Castro, cycles of repression have ebbed and flowed depending on the regime's need to keep at bay the social forces set into motion by his post–Cold War economic reforms. In February 1999, the government introduced tough legislation against sedition, with a maximum prison sentence of 20 years. It stipulated penalties for unauthorized contacts with the United States and the import or supply of "subversive" materials, including texts on democracy and by news agencies and journalists. Castro's collapse at a long outdoor rally near Havana in June 2001 raised questions about the Cuban leader's health and focused attention on a possible post-Castro future.

In November 2001, Hurricane Michelle, the most powerful tropical storm to hit Cuba in a half-century, left a low death toll but also a trail of physical destruction, devastating Cuba's crops. In the wake of the storm, the United States permitted the first direct food trade with Cuba since the beginning of an economic embargo in 1962.

In 2002, the Varela Project, a referendum initiative seeking broad changes in the four-decades-old socialist system, achieved significant support domestically. Its leader, Oswaldo Paya, was showered with international recognition, including the European Union's Andrei Sakharov Prize for Freedom of Thought. In May, project organizers submitted more than 11,000 signatures to the National Assembly demanding that a referendum be held in which Cubans could vote for fundamental reforms such as freedom of expression, the right to own private businesses, and electoral reform. A June visit by former U.S. president Jimmy Carter also added status and visibility to the protest movement. After Carter mentioned the project on Cuban television that month, the regime held its own "referendum" in which 8.2 million people supposedly declared the socialist system to be "untouchable." In October, more than 300 dissident organizations joined together as the Assembly to Promote Civil Society in preparation for a post–Fidel Castro Cuba. Composed of 321 dissident organizations ranging from human rights groups and independent libraries to labor unions and the independent press, the civil society assembly announced that it would prepare for a post–Castro transition rather than seek reforms from the regime. Meanwhile, Castro faced serious popular discontent, particularly because of the country's failing sugar industry; in June, the government closed 71 of Cuba's 156 sugar mills.

In early 2003, the government initiated a crackdown against the pro-democracy opposition. Seventy-five people, including 27 independent journalists, 10 independent librarians, and signature collectors for the Varela Project, were sentenced to an average of 20 years in prison following one-day trials held in April. (At the end of 2004, 61 of the activists who were arrested remained in prison.) Later that year, Paya delivered more than 14,000 signatures to the National Assembly demanding a referendum for sweeping changes; these demands have yet to be met by the Cuban government.

Castro suffered another fainting spell in Buenos Aires in May 2003 as he exited an inauguration event for Argentina's new president. However, there were few palpable signs during the year that his regime was any closer to collapsing, even though recovery from a 1990s economic depression faltered and discontent increased. Castro also continued his attempts to enlist the assistance of U.S. farm state congressional delegations to break the economic embargo by diverting $250 million from paying old debts to buy American agricultural products; in 2001, the embargo had been relaxed to allow direct sales of food and medicine on a cash basis only. Meanwhile, Castro appeared to shrug off a decision by the European Union to review its policies toward Cuba because of human rights concerns.

In May 2004, Bush announced that the United States would intensify pressure on the Cuban regime by increasing broadcasts designed to break through the island's information blockade, by aiding dissidents, and by limiting the amount of money Cuban-Americans could bring with them on family visits or through remittances.

Castro had another much-publicized tumble in October, resulting in a fractured right knee and right arm. His fall raised further questions about his health and his ability to continue to govern the country.

Cuba's economy continued to show limited growth during the year—GDP is expected to grow only 2.6 percent in 2004, while foreign debt totals more than $12 billion—as the government backtracked on its timid economic reforms of the early 1990s. Despite Venezuelan oil subsidies, the country is mired in an acute energy crisis that has led to the closure of over 100 factories and an indefinite national plan of blackouts. Tourism remains the primary source of hard currency, followed closely by remittances from family members living abroad. In an effort to re-centralize the availability of hard currency in the state's coffers, the government has adopted new laws ending the use of the dollar for basic economic transactions and restricting its use by state companies.

Political Rights and Civil Liberties: Cubans cannot change their government through democratic means. Fidel Castro dominates the political system, having transformed the country into a one-party state with the Cuban Communist Party (PCC) controlling all governmental entities from the national to the local level. Communist structures were institutionalized by the 1976 constitution installed at the first congress of the PCC. The constitution provides for a National Assembly, which designates the Council of State. It is that body which in turn appoints the Council of Ministers in consultation with its president, who serves as head of state and chief of government. However, Castro is responsible for every appointment and controls every lever of power in Cuba in his various roles as president of the Council of Ministers, chairman of the Council of State, commander in chief of the Revolutionary Armed Forces (FAR), and first secretary of the PCC.

In October 2002, some eight million Cubans voted in tightly controlled municipal elections. On January 19, 2003, an election was held for the Cuban National Assembly, with just 609 candidates—all supported by the regime—vying for 609 seats. All political organizing outside the PCC is illegal. Political dissent, spoken or written, is a punishable offense, and those so punished frequently receive years of imprisonment for seemingly minor infractions. In early 2003, the government cracked down on the opposition movement, imprisoning 75 of its most active members. Few have been released despite international condemnation by many of Cuba's allies and diplomatic sanctions from trade partners such as the European Union.

Official corruption remains a serious problem, with a "culture of illegality" shrouding the mixture of private and state-controlled economic activities allowed on the island. In late 2003, Juan Jose Vega, the president of Cubanacan, a state-run enterprise controlling over $600 million in foreign investment in Cuba's tourism industry, was dismissed on charges of corruption. Cuba was ranked 62 out of 146 countries surveyed in the 2004 Transparency International Corruption Perceptions Index.

The press in Cuba is the object of a targeted campaign of intimidation by the government, which uses Ministry of Interior agents to infiltrate and report on the independent media. Independent journalists, particularly those associated with five small news agencies established outside state control, have been subjected to continued repression, including jail terms of hard labor and assaults by state security agents while in prison. Foreign news agencies must hire local reporters only through government offices, which limits employment opportunities for independent journalists. In 2004, 22 independent journalists arrested in March 2003 remained imprisoned in degrading conditions, which included physical and psychological abuse; acts of harassment and intimidation were also directed against their families. In April, two journalists held without trial since March 2002 were finally tried by a court in Ciego de Ávila on charges of insulting Castro and the police and public disorder; one received a three-year prison sentence and the other a sentence of three and a half years.

In 1991, Roman Catholics and other believers were granted permission to join the Communist Party, and the constitutional reference to official atheism was dropped the following year. However, in October 2002, the U.S. State Department issued a report saying that Cuba was one of six countries that engaged in widespread repression of religion. Security agents frequently spy on worshippers, the government continues to block construction of new churches, the number of new foreign priests is limited, and most new denominations are refused recognition. An estimated 70 percent of all Cubans on the island practice some form of Afro-Cuban religion. In a positive development, the regime now tolerates the Baha'i faith.

The government restricts academic freedom. Teaching materials for courses such as mathematics or literature must have an ideological content. Affiliation with official Communist Party structures is generally needed to gain access to educational institutions, and students' report cards carry information regarding their parents' involvement with the Communist Party. In 2003, state security forces raided 22 independent libraries and sent 10 librarians to jail with terms of up to 26 years.

Limited rights of assembly and association are permitted under the constitution; however, these are subject to the stipulation that they may not be "exercised against the existence and objectives of the Socialist State." The unauthorized assembly of more than three persons, including those for private religious services in private homes, is punishable by law by up to three months in prison and a fine. This prohibition is selectively enforced and is sometimes used as a legal pretext to imprison human rights advocates.

Workers do not have the right to bargain collectively or to strike. Members of independent labor unions, which the government considers illegal, are often harassed or dismissed from their jobs and subsequently barred from future employment.

The executive branch controls the judiciary. In practice, the Council of State, of which Castro is chairman, serves as a de facto judiciary and controls both the courts and the judicial process as a whole.

There are some 300 prisoners of conscience in Cuba, most held in cells with common criminals and many convicted on vague charges such as "disseminating enemy propaganda" or "dangerousness." Members of groups that exist apart from the state are labeled "counterrevolutionary criminals" and are subject to systematic repression, including arrest, beatings while in custody, and intimidation by uniformed or plainclothes state security agents. During the year, authorities arrested 22 human rights activists, including three Varela Project organizers and an independent librarian, the latter seized on the charge of "contempt for authority" for having shouted "Down with Fidel." By year's end, 13 of the 22 had been tried and sentenced. In a positive development, dissident Martha Beatriz Roque and six other detainees of the 75 arrested in the March 2003 sweep were released from prison for health reasons in 2004.

Since 1991, the United Nations has voted annually to assign a special investigator on human rights to Cuba, but the Cuban government has refused to cooperate. Cuba also does not allow the International Red Cross or other humanitarian organizations access to its prisons.

Freedom of movement and the right to choose one's residence and place of employment are severely restricted. Attempting to leave the island without permission is a punishable offense. In the post-Soviet era, the rights of Cubans to own private property and to participate in joint ventures with foreigners have been recognized by law, and non-Cuban businesses have also been allowed. However, PCC membership is still required to obtain good jobs, serviceable housing, and real access to social services, including medical care and educational opportunities. In 2004, a Labor Ministry decree halted the issuance of all new licenses for 40 categories of self-employment that were legalized in 1993. Roughly 150,000 Cubans are self-employed, approximately 2 percent of the workforce. The government systematically violates international salary standards, the terms of contract, and other labor codes for workers employed on the island by foreign-owned firms.

About 40 percent of all women work, and they are well represented in most professions. However, violence against women is a problem, as is child prostitution. According to the 2004 U.S. State Department Trafficking in Persons Report, Cuba is a country of internal trafficking for sexual exploitation and a destination for sex tourists, including foreigners searching for underage prostitutes.

Cyprus

Population: 900,000
GNI/capita: $12,320
Life Expectancy: 78
Religious Groups: Greek Orthodox (78 percent), Muslim (18 percent), other (4 percent)
Ethnic Groups: Greek (77 percent), Turkish (18 percent), other (5 percent)
Capital: Nicosia

Political Rights: 1
Civil Liberties: 1
Status: Free

Ten-Year Ratings Timeline (Political Rights, Civil Liberties, Status)

1995	1996	1997	1998	1999	2000	2001	2002	2003	2004
1,1F	1,1F	1,1F	1,1F	1,1F	1,1F	1,1F	1,1F	1,1F	1,1F

Overview:

In 2004, the Greek and Turkish communities of Cyprus came the closest yet to reaching a settlement after months of intervention and a proposed reunification plan by UN Secretary-General Kofi Annan. However, amid accusations that the proposed plan favored the Turkish side, the Greek side voted against it in a referendum on April 24. Thus, the island remained divided, and only the Greek part of the island joined the European Union (EU) on May 1.

Annexed by Britain in 1914, Cyprus gained independence in 1960 after a 10-year guerrilla campaign by partisans demanding union with Greece. In July 1974, Greek Cypriot National Guard members, backed by the military junta in power in Greece, staged an unsuccessful coup aimed at such unification. Five days later, Turkey invaded northern Cyprus, seized control of 37 percent of the island, and expelled 200,000

Greeks from the north. Today, the Greek and Turkish communities are almost completely separated in the south and north, respectively.

A buffer zone, called the "Green Line," has divided Cyprus since 1974. The capital, Nicosia, is similarly divided. Tensions and intermittent violence between the two populations have plagued the island since independence. UN resolutions stipulate that Cyprus is a single country in which the northern third is illegally occupied. In 1983, Turkish-controlled Cyprus declared its independence, a move recognized only by Turkey.

A major change occurred with the election in November 2002 of a new Turkish government. This government has been much less indulgent of Turkish Cypriot president Rauf Denktash's opposition to reunification because Turkey's own chances of EU membership have been linked to a resolution of the island's division. This, combined with significant pressure from the EU and the United States as well as UN intervention, has moved the two sides closer to settlement.

The latest and as yet most promising round of reunification negotiations began after the parliamentary elections in northern Cyprus in December 2003. These elections brought to power a new coalition led by the new prime minister, Mehmet Ali Talat. Talat's party, the Republican Turkish Party (CTP), partnered with its former rival, the Democratic Party, to form a pro-unification government. With the subsequent sidelining of Denktash, the way was cleared for UN Secretary-General Annan to propose a new path toward a settlement.

Annan led a series of negotiations that included the leaders of the Greek and Turkish Cypriot communities, followed by the inclusion of Greece and Turkey. When no consensus was reached, Annan himself proposed a plan that was put to a vote in simultaneous, separate referendums in northern and southern Cyprus on April 24, 2004. Prior to the Turkish Cypriot parliamentary elections, the international community had taken it for granted that the Turkish side would always be the one to delay a settlement. However, with the Turkish Cypriot government fully on board, the Greek Cypriots began to express severe reservations about the plan, especially concerning security and international guarantees that the Turkish side would comply. After Greek Cypriot president Tassos Papadopoulos expressed his opposition to the Annan plan in a speech less than a month before the referendum, it became clear that the plan would not be implemented. Ultimately, 76 percent of Greek Cypriots voted against the plan, while 65 percent of Turkish Cypriots voted in favor. With the island still divided, only Greek Cyprus joined the EU as planned on May 1. Subsequently, the Greek Cypriot government was accused of inappropriate involvement in the campaign process, including through influence of the media.

The overwhelming approval of the Turkish Cypriots for reunification sparked profound efforts on the part of the international community to reward them by ending their isolation. The Greek Cypriots have opposed the most far-reaching proposals, such as direct trade between the north and the rest of the world. Meanwhile, trade has increased between the two sides, and Greek Cypriots no longer need to show a passport to cross into the north. As a sign that the tide may be turning back, the pro-reunification opposition enjoyed an overwhelming victory over the ruling party in the European parliamentary elections in Greek Cyprus on June 14.

Political Rights and Civil Liberties: Greek Cypriots can change their government democratically. Suffrage is universal, and elections are free and fair.

The 1960 constitution established an ethnically representative system designed to protect the interests of both Greek and Turkish Cypriots, and from the Greek Cypriot point of view, the constitution still applies to the entire island. There is a clear separation of powers between the executive and legislature through a presidential system. The unicameral House of Representatives has 80 seats filled through proportional representation. Of these, 24 seats are reserved for the Turkish Cypriot community; however, it has not been represented since 1964, when the Turkish Cypriot representatives withdrew. (The Turkish Cypriots currently have a separate parliament in the northern part of the island.) President Tassos Papadapoulous of the Democratic Party (DIKO) was elected in 2003 for a five-year term. The two major parties are the Progressive Party of the Working People (AKEL) and the Democratic Party (DISY), but six other parties are represented in the house. Voting is compulsory, although there is no penalty for those who do not vote.

The government was accused of many irregularities with regards to the referendum campaign for the reunification plan of UN Secretary-General Kofi Annan. Accusations were made that civil servants were pressured to vote "no" through insinuations that they might lose their benefits if the referendum passed, that teachers were encouraged to push a "no" vote in schools, and that the government interfered with independent media to skew coverage against the referendum. Some campaigners in favor of the plan faced verbal and physical harassment.

A bill passed in January allowed Turkish Cypriots to vote along with their Greek counterparts in the European parliamentary elections, although only 97 did. In June, Turkish Cypriot Sener Levent filed a case with the Greek Cypriot Supreme Court, arguing that he should not have been barred from standing in the European parliamentary elections; the government had denied his candidacy because he had not registered to vote. In that same month, the European Court of Human Rights ruled that all Turkish Cypriots must be allowed to register to vote in all Greek Cypriot elections.

Corruption is not a significant problem in Cyprus. A new anticorruption law that went into effect in September addresses the unlawful acquisition of property by public officials and institutes compulsory asset declaration by state officials. Cyprus was ranked 36 out of 146 countries surveyed in Transparency International's 2004 Corruption Perceptions Index.

Freedom of speech is generally respected, and a vibrant independent press frequently criticizes authorities. Several private television and radio stations in the Greek Cypriot community compete effectively with government-controlled stations. However, during the referendum campaign, the media showed a marked bias against the Annan plan. Opponents of the Annan plan were given nearly two times as much television airtime on public and private channels combined as those who supported it. The state-owned Cyprus Broadcasting Corporation declined to interview members of the international community who were in favor of the Annan plan in the days leading up the referendum, despite these parties' requests to appear. Meanwhile, Papadapoulous, who was openly against the plan, gave a televised interview that was broadcast by all channels only one hour before a ban on political campaigning took effect, two days before the referendum.

Freedom of religion is provided for by the constitution and is protected in practice. Around 99 percent of the inhabitants of Greek-controlled Cyprus are Greek Orthodox Christians. The government does not restrict academic freedom.

Nongovernmental organizations, including human-rights groups, operate without government interference. Workers have the right to strike and to form trade unions without authorization.

The independent judiciary operates according to the British tradition, upholding the presumption of innocence and the right to due process. Standard procedure calls for trial before a judge, although requests for trial by jury are regularly granted. Non-Greek-Cypriot inmates at Nicosia's central prison smuggled out a petition in July accusing prison authorities of violence against them.

A 1975 agreement between the Greek and Turkish sides of the island governs treatment of minorities. In practice, Turkish Cypriots in the South have reported difficulty obtaining identity cards and other documents, and have complained of surveillance by the police. The Pontian Greek population, which immigrated from the former Soviet Union, has had difficulty integrating into the rest of the population. In June, violence erupted between Pontian Greeks and police after allegations of police mistreatment of two Pontian suspects.

Disabled people staged a protest in June, accusing the government of failing to implement measures to ensure their basic human rights. A disabilities law to aid integration and rehabilitation has never been implemented.

Since Cypriot accession to the EU in May, all citizens can move freely throughout the island. Those attempting to enter the Greek part of the island illegally are now fined and turned back instead of imprisoned, as had previously been the case. A landmark Supreme Court ruling in September gave a Turkish Cypriot man the right to return immediately to his property on the Greek side, which he had deserted after the Turkish invasion, because his recent move to the Greek-controlled territory made him no longer a "Turkish Cypriot" (a 1991 law stated that property left by "Turkish Cypriots" belonged to the state). At the end of November, an appeal in the case was still pending. This ruling could have profound effects on the status of property abandoned in 1974.

In 2003, 45 percent of the labor force was female. The first female Supreme Court judge was appointed in May. However, men make up a greater share of all professions except the administrative and secretarial. Trafficking in women for the purposes of prostitution became a major issue in 2004 after both the Council of Europe and the U.S. State Department called attention to the situation in Cyprus. The police set up a new Human Trafficking Prevention Bureau to address the problem.

Czech Republic

Population: 10,200,000
GNI/capita: $5,480
Life Expectancy: 75
Religious Groups: Roman Catholic (39.2 percent),
Protestant (4.6 percent), other (57.2 percent)
Ethnic Groups: Czech (81.2 percent), Moravian (13.2 percent),
Slovak (3.1 percent), other (3.5 other)
Capital: Prague

Political Rights: 1
Civil Liberties: 1*
Status: Free

Ratings Change: The Czech Republic's civil liberties rating improved from 2 to 1 due to the deepening of EU integration trends, resulting in greater conformity with EU human rights standards.

Ten-Year Ratings Timeline (Political Rights, Civil Liberties, Status)

1995	1996	1997	1998	1999	2000	2001	2002	2003	2004
1,2F	1,2F	1,2F	1,2F	1,2F	1,2F	1,2F	1,2F	1,2F	1,1F

Overview:

On May 1, 2004, the Czech Republic joined the European Union (EU), fulfilling a long-standing goal. However, like most incumbent parties of countries in the EU, the main party in the coalition government suffered badly in the June elections to the European Parliament. The result was the replacement of the prime minister, Vladimir Spidla, by his deputy, Stanislav Gross.

Czechoslovakia was created in 1918 following the collapse of the Austro-Hungarian empire. Soviet troops helped establish the Communist People's Party of Czechoslovakia in 1948, renamed the Czechoslovak Socialist Republic in 1960. In 1968, Soviet tanks crushed the so-called Prague Spring led by reformist leader Alexander Dubcek.

In December 1989, an anti-Communist opposition led by dissident Vaclav Havel and the Civic Forum brought down the Czechoslovak government. The country's first post-Communist elections were held the following year. In 1992, a new constitution and Charter of Fundamental Rights and Freedoms were adopted and the country began an ambitious program of political and economic reform under Finance Minister Vaclav Klaus. A leading figure in the ruling center-right Civic Democratic Party (ODS), Klaus became prime minister the same year. In 1993, the state dissolved peacefully into the Czech and Slovak republics and Havel became president of the new Czech Republic. In 1997, Klaus resigned amid allegations of corruption in the ODS.

Close parliamentary elections in 1998 brought about Czech Social Democratic Party (CSSD) control of the government, although the ODS managed to negotiate control of key government positions. This so-called opposition agreement between the CSSD and the ODS drained meaningful political competition and brought about several years of political gridlock. The last parliamentary election to the Chamber of Deputies (lower house) was held in June 2002, and a by-election to the Senate (upper house) took place in November 2002. The CSSD secured the most votes, and Spidla, the party's chairman, became the new prime minister.

In the February 2003 presidential poll, Klaus was elected on the third round of voting following two inconclusive ballots. Klaus obtained 142 votes, a single vote more than the 141 needed from the 281-member joint parliamentary session. In March, Spidla's cabinet asked the Chamber of Deputies for a vote of confidence, which it received.

In May 2004, the Czech Republic joined the EU, fulfilling one of the government's most important goals. This had required years of work to meet tough EU standards, such as the creation of a stable market economy, a consolidated democracy, a cleaner environment, and the protection of minority rights, and most Czechs took pride in "returning" to Europe's mainstream after the Communist era. The Czech Republic was one of the richest countries from Central Europe to join the EU in 2004.

In the country's first elections for the European Parliament, the government was soundly trounced: the CSSD took just 9 percent of the vote. The unreformed Communist Party of Bohemia and Moravia surged to 20 percent. The humiliated Spidla stepped down in favor of Gross, his deputy. Gross formed a new government including the same parties and many key figures from the old one. Despite their strong results, the Communists were shut out of government again. Gross's government has a bare majority and will struggle to pass his ambitious agenda of pension and health care reform, as well as help for small and medium-sized businesses.

Although progress has been made in the Czech Republic toward establishing the mechanisms and institutions of a full market economy—and EU membership will help further with this—the economic sector requires further reform. A substantial part of state-owned property was privatized during the early to middle-1990s on the basis of a "voucher" program, under which Czech citizens were permitted to buy vouchers entitling them to bid for shares in selected companies. Power stations, oil and gas networks, banks, and the social and pension insurance sectors were among the strategic holdings exempt from the privatization program. Greater strides were made after 1999, when the government initiated an effort to revitalize Czech industry that sought to prepare public enterprises for privatization through internal reform and debt restructuring. The economy grew by 3.1 percent in 2003 and was forecast to do somewhat better in 2004. The Czech Republic is required by its EU membership to adopt the euro as its currency, and to do so it must bring down its budget deficit to the EU-mandated limit of 3 percent of gross domestic product, which the government has proposed to do by 2008.

Political Rights and Civil Liberties: Czech citizens can change their government democratically. Since shedding the Soviet yoke more than a decade ago, the Czech Republic has had a sound record of free and fair elections. Voters elect members of the Senate and the Chamber of Deputies, which comprise the National Assembly. The Chamber of Deputies (lower house) has 200 members who are elected for four years, and the Senate (upper house) has 81 members, elected for six years with one-third of the senators being replaced every two years. The president, elected by the National Assembly for a five-year term (with a maximum of two subsequent terms), appoints judges, the prime minister, and other cabinet members.

The Czech Republic continues to confront some difficult remnants of the Soviet legacy, including significant corruption that affects many sectors of Czech society.

The Czech Republic was ranked 51 out of 146 countries surveyed in the 2004 Transparency International Corruption Perceptions Index.

Freedom of expression is honored in the Czech Republic, although the Charter of Fundamental Rights and Freedoms prohibits threats against individual rights, state and public security, public health, and morality. Libel can be prosecuted as a criminal offense. The country's print and electronic media are largely in private hands. In 2000, the Law on Free Access to Information took effect and the National Assembly amended broadcasting laws to meet EU standards. In 2001, the assembly passed an important bill designed to limit political influence over Czech Television (CT), the state broadcaster. Passage of the legislation helped end a standoff at CT between journalists and management. Under this law, nongovernmental groups, rather than politicians, make nominations for membership to CT's governing council, the body that controls the selection of CT's director. In January, an editor for *Respekt*, a weekly newspaper known for its investigative work, was attacked, beaten, and sprayed with tear gas. Police closed the case without finding the perpetrators of the attack, which may have been connected to *Respekt*'s investigations into criminal gangs in northern Bohemia.

The government generally respects freedom of religion. A 2002 law that provides for the registration and regulation of churches, including pay for clergy, has been criticized by the Roman Catholic Church as unduly restrictive of its activities. In 2003, the Church won a judgment against a government decision to deny registration to a Church-run medical center. The Catholic leadership continues to complain that the registration law makes its activities difficult. Academic freedom is widely respected in the Czech Republic.

Czech citizens may assemble peacefully, form associations, and petition the government. Trade unions and professional associations function freely. Judges, prosecutors, and members of the armed forces and police may not strike. In 2003, the government's proposed fiscal reform measures generated considerable opposition from the country's trade unions, including a major one-day strike in September by the teacher's union, in which more than 70,000 teachers reportedly took part.

The Czech Republic's independent judiciary consists of a Supreme Court, a Supreme Administrative Court, and high, regional, and district courts. There is also a Constitutional Court. In December 2001, President Vaclav Havel signed a bill on judicial reform but suggested he might challenge aspects of the law, which he expected to "more widely and consistently separate judicial and executive power."

Property ownership, choice of residence, and fair wages are legally protected, and citizens generally enjoy all of these rights.

The Charter of Fundamental Rights and Freedoms gives minorities the right to help resolve matters pertaining to their group. A 1999 law restored citizenship to many residents, including Roma (Gypsies), who continue to experience discrimination. In 2001, the National Assembly approved legislation for the protection of ethnic minority rights. The law's provisions include the creation of a governmental minority council. A number of anti-Semitic attacks were committed in 2003. Holocaust denial and inciting religious hatred are illegal.

Gender discrimination is legally prohibited. Nevertheless, sexual harassment in the workplace appears to be fairly common. In May 2003, the government amended a resolution setting priorities and procedures for enforcing gender equality in the workplace.

Denmark

Population: 5,400,000
GNI/capita: $30,260
Life Expectancy: 77
Religious Groups: Evangelical Lutheran (95 percent), Muslim (2 percent), other (3 percent)
Ethnic Groups: Scandinavian, Inuit, Faroese, German, Turkish, Iranian, Somali
Capital: Copenhagen

Political Rights: 1
Civil Liberties: 1
Status: Free

Ten-Year Ratings Timeline (Political Rights, Civil Liberties, Status)

1995	1996	1997	1998	1999	2000	2001	2002	2003	2004
1,1F	1,1F	1,1F	1,1F	1,1F	1,1F	1,1F	1,1F	1,1F	1,1F

Overview:

Denmark's right-of-center coalition government maintained its hold on power in 2004 despite experiencing stringent criticism of Danish involvement in the U.S.-led war in Iraq and a significant setback in June's European Parliament elections. The government initiated legislation to reform radically the country's administrative structure of counties and municipalities. The government also continued to enforce and strengthen strict immigration laws in spite of domestic and European protestations.

Denmark has been a monarchy since the fourteenth century, but the monarch's power became ceremonial with the first democratic constitution, written in 1849. The country was occupied by Germany during World War II, yet its sizable resistance movement earned it recognition as part of the Allied powers. In 1949, Denmark abandoned its traditional neutrality and joined NATO, and in 1973, it joined the European Economic Community, forerunner to the European Union (EU).

After World War II, Danish politics were dominated by the Social Democrats. However, in the November 2001 elections, popular concerns with increased immigration brought a right-of-center government to power. The ruling coalition of Prime Minister Anders Fogh Rasmussen's Liberal Party and the Conservative People's Party, which together hold 40 percent of the seats, is supported by the populist, euroskeptic Danish People's Party (DPP).

Denmark has a conflicted relationship within the EU. When the Treaty of Maastricht was written in 1992, extending the EU's competence into justice, foreign, and monetary policy, Denmark's population rejected the treaty in a referendum. Since then, Denmark has opted out of participation in these areas. In 2003, the EU constructed a constitutional treaty, and polls indicate the Danish population is slowly moving in favor of participating in EU defense and judicial cooperation, although support for the euro is less clear. The prime minister is committed to holding a referendum on both the new constitution and the "opt-outs" in September 2005.

Danish citizens vote in European Parliamentary elections. The June 14 poll saw the opposition Social Democrats garner 32.7 percent of the vote, compared to 19.4 percent for the Liberal Party. In addition, the euroskeptic parties suffered a significant defeat.

Government-sponsored administrative reform, expected to be implemented in January 2007, will replace the country's 13 counties with 5 federally funded regions responsible for health and transportation but unable to levy taxes. In addition, Denmark's 271 municipalities will be consolidated into 100 with a variety of new public service mandates.

Denmark has an active foreign policy that includes 500 troops stationed in Iraq. Unsubstantiated intelligence on Iraqi weapons of mass destruction and the recall of several senior commanders amid allegations of prisoner abuse have fueled criticism of Rasmussen's decisions to support the 2003 U.S.-led invasion of Iraq and maintain the Danish troop presence until Iraqi elections, scheduled for January 2005.

Political Rights and Civil Liberties: Danes can change their government democratically. The current Danish constitution, which established a single-chamber parliament, was adopted in 1953. Denmark is a constitutional monarchy, in which Queen Margrethe II has mostly ceremonial duties. The 179 representatives are elected to the unicameral parliament, called the Folketing, at least once every four years in a system of modified proportional representation. Danish governments are most often minority administrations, governing with the aid of one or more supporting parties. Since 1909, no single party has held a majority of seats, a history that has helped create a tradition of interparty compromise.

The semiautonomous territories of Greenland and the Faeroe Islands each have two representatives in the Folketing. They also have their own elected home rule governments that have power over almost all areas of governance. In February, a new, cross-party governing coalition was formed in the Faeroe Islands, agreeing to continue devolution from Denmark while remaining firmly within the Danish North Atlantic Commonwealth.

Levels of corruption in Denmark are very low. Denmark was ranked 3 out of 146 countries surveyed in Transparency International's 2004 Corruption Perceptions Index.

The constitution guarantees freedom of expression, and the media reflect a wide variety of political opinions and are frequently critical of the government. The state finances radio and television broadcasting, but state-owned television companies have independent editorial boards. Independent radio stations are permitted, but tightly regulated. In April, two journalists from the conservative daily *Berlingske Tidende* were charged with publishing confidential military information after quoting Danish military intelligence reports in a series of articles.

Freedom of worship is guaranteed to all. However, the Evangelical Lutheran Church is subsidized by the government as the official state religion. The faith is taught in public schools, although students may withdraw from religious classes with parental consent. In February, the government introduced plans to monitor Muslim imams' Friday sermons to prevent the preaching of anti-Western propaganda and to institute strict Danish language requirements for imams who wish to perform marriages. Academic freedom is ensured for all, and consistent efforts are made to ensure that local policies of segregating bilingual children into separate classes are repudiated by the state.

The constitution provides for freedom of assembly and association, and workers are free to organize. The labor market is mainly regulated by agreements between employers' and employees' organizations, and membership in trade unions is around 80 percent. In April, a Council of Europe expert subcommittee ruled that union exclusivity agreements are a violation of the right to free organization. Government efforts to ban exclusivity agreements have been opposed by the DPP and the Social Democrats.

The judiciary is independent, and citizens enjoy full due process rights. The court system consists of 100 local courts, two high courts, and the 15-member Supreme Court, with judges appointed by the queen on government recommendation.

In March, Danish police staged a massive raid into the communal Copenhagen enclave of Christiania, aimed at rooting out the neighborhood's infamous cannabis industry and instituting a legal system of property rights. After almost 50 arrests and resistance from residents, lawmakers in June agreed on a new law allowing an independent committee to take charge of Christiania, reform the housing market, and make residents pay for utilities such as gas and electricity.

Discrimination is prohibited under the law. Although Denmark has not seen the kind of neo-Nazi movements that have emerged elsewhere in Scandinavia, human rights groups have noted an increase in hate speech in Denmark and in harassment of Muslims and Jews. According to the Vienna-based European Monitoring Centre on Racism and Xenophobia, anti-Semitic attacks and rhetoric are increasingly common in Denmark.

The rise of the anti-immigrant DPP since its strong electoral showing in 2001 has sparked more public examination of the position in Denmark of citizens and residents of non-Danish descent. The Alien Act, which took effect in 2002, has continued a trend of tightening immigration and asylum laws, particularly in the area of family unification. Despite the easing of such restrictions in September 2003 due to advocacy group pressure, Danish family reunification laws were harshly criticized in July 2004 by the Council of Europe's Human Rights Commissioner, who specifically cited the country's 24-year age minimum and financial requirements for foreign spousal residency permits. The Danish Institute for Human Rights echoed these concerns in a publicly funded report, released in October, which also took issue with the stipulation that a reunified family's husband and wife must both prove "close ties to Denmark." In February, the government announced plans to increase fines for individuals found harboring rejected asylum seekers and to restrict the entry of radical Muslim imams by way of strict educational and financial qualifications. In addition, members of Rasmussen's Liberal Party have called for a zero-tolerance policy on immigrant crime.

The law requires equal pay for equal work, but men in Denmark earn about 14 percent more than women in blue-collar jobs and 20 percent more in professional positions, according to the Confederation of Danish Labor Unions and the Danish Employer Association. Trafficking in women and children for the purposes of prostitution is a problem in Denmark, and the government introduced legislation in 2002 defining and criminalizing trafficking. However, the fact that prostitution is legal in Denmark limits the legal tools available. Strict immigration rules limiting residence permits for foreign-born sex trade workers, some of whom are children, have been severely criticized by women's advocacy groups.

Djibouti

Population: 700,000
GNI/capita: $900
Life Expectancy: 46
Religious Groups: Muslim (94 percent),
Christian (6 percent)
Ethnic Groups: Somali (60 percent), Afar (35 percent),
other (5 percent)
Capital: Djibouti

Political Rights: 5
Civil Liberties: 5
Status: Partly Free

Ten-Year Ratings Timeline (Political Rights, Civil Liberties, Status)

1995	1996	1997	1998	1999	2000	2001	2002	2003	2004
5,6NF	5,6NF	5,6NF	5,6NF	4,6PF	4,5PF	4,5PF	4,5PF	5,5PF	5,5PF

Overview:

The government of President Ismail Omar Guelleh used Djibouti's strategic importance to generate both international support and development assistance in 2004. Djibouti has allowed foreign armed forces, particularly those of the United States, access to its port and airport facilities. President Guelleh has also taken a proactive position among Arab League members in support of actions taken by the U.S. and other countries to combat terrorism. The country's limited political opening continued, with presidential elections scheduled for 2005 but with little prospect for significant competition. Meanwhile, the government maintained its effective control over the country's media.

Djibouti was known as the French Territory of the Afar and Issa before gaining independence from France in 1977. Djibouti's people are deeply divided along ethnic and clan lines, with the majority Issa (Somali) and minority Afar peoples holding most political power. In 1991, Afar rebels of the Front for the Restoration of Unity and Democracy (FRUD) launched a three-year guerrilla war against Issa domination. In 1994, the largest FRUD faction agreed to end its insurgency in exchange for inclusion in the government and electoral reforms. However, sporadic attacks by a radical wing of the group continued.

President Gouled controlled a one-party system until 1992, when a new constitution adopted by referendum authorized four political parties. In 1993, Gouled was declared the winner of a fourth six-year term in Djibouti's first contested presidential elections. Both the opposition and international observers considered the poll fraudulent. In the 1997 legislative elections, which were also considered unfair, the Popular Rally for Progress (RPP), in coalition with the legalized arm of the FRUD at the time, won all 65 National Assembly seats.

Gouled stepped down in 1999 after 22 years in power, opening the way for the country's first change in presidential leadership. The RPP's Ismael Omar Guelleh won the presidential poll that year with 74 percent of the vote, while Moussa Ahmed Idriss, of the Unified Djiboutian Opposition (ODU), received 26 percent. Guelleh, who was Gouled's nephew and a former head of state security, had long been considered the de facto head of government and the president's probable successor.

For the first time since elections began in 1992, no group boycotted the vote, which was regarded as generally fair.

In 2001, the government followed up a peace agreement it had signed with the radical wing of the FRUD in 2000 with a more extensive accord. Like the previous agreement, this one was aimed at putting an end to the ethnic Afar insurgency that began a decade earlier.

In the January 2003 parliamentary elections, a pro-government bloc of four parties under the umbrella Union for the Presidential Majority (UMP) ran against the opposition Union for Democratic Alternance (UAD) bloc of four parties. The ruling UMP captured all 65 seats despite the UAD receiving 37 percent of the votes in a low voter turnout of 48 percent. In addition, although the coalition won 62 percent of the vote, the election law stipulates that the majority victor in each of the country's five electoral constituencies (in this election, the UMP) wins all seats in that district.

The polls came at a time of increasing U.S. interest in Djibouti, which is strategically located on the Red Sea. In 2004, some 2,000 U.S. Army and Special Forces troops were stationed in Djibouti in support of U.S. foreign policy objectives. These troops are especially focused on limiting terrorist activities in the region, as neighboring Somalia has particularly identified as an area of activity for Al Qaeda and other terrorist groups. In addition, approximately 2,700 French troops are among 8,000 French residents.

Djibouti has little industry and few natural resources, although its strategic position has long proved to be an important asset. Services provide most of the national income.

Political Rights and Civil Liberties:

Citizens of Djibouti cannot change their government democratically. The trappings of representative government and formal administration have had little relevance to the real distribution and exercise of power in Djibouti. Although international observers declared the 1999 presidential poll generally fair, the ruling party had the advantage of state resources to conduct its campaign. President Guelleh announced in September 2002 that Djibouti would have a full multiparty system, as opposed to a four-party system.

The unicameral parliament, the National Assembly, has 65 members directly elected for a five-year term. In the 2003 legislative election, opposition parties were significantly disadvantaged by electoral rules and by the government's use of the power of its incumbency, including its dominance over the government administrative apparatus. The opposition UAD subsequently alleged widespread voter fraud, but its case was rejected by the Constitutional Council. The country's political opposition has suffered from significant divisions and had previously been unable to achieve any successes in elections that were controlled by the government. Presidential elections are due in mid-2005.

Efforts to curb the country's rampant corruption have met with little success. Djibouti was not ranked by Transparency International in its 2004 Corruption Perceptions Index.

Despite constitutional protection, freedom of speech is not guaranteed. The government owns the principal newspaper, *La Nation*, as well as Radiodiffusion-Television de Djibouti (RTD), which operates the national radio and TV. Journalists generally have to avoid covering sensitive issues, including human rights, the army, the FRUD, relations with Ethiopia, and French financial aid. In 2004, a journalist from *Le Renouveau* newspaper was arrested after police ordered him to stop his vehicle during a motorcade escorting the president's wife. Press watchdog groups, such as the International Federation of Journalists, condemned his detention. The journalist's brother, who is the editor-in-chief of *Le Renouveau,* has frequently been jailed by the authorities. Legal action aimed at closing the paper is currently under way in the Supreme Court. Djibouti has been identified by Reporters Sans Frontieres as a country in which freedom of speech is significantly limited. There is only limited Internet access.

Islam is the official state religion, but freedom of worship is respected, although the government discourages proselytizing. While academic freedom is generally respected, education choices are limited and Djibouti has no university.

Freedom of assembly and association are nominally protected under the constitution, but the government has demonstrated little tolerance for political protest. There are complaints of harassment of political opponents and union leaders. Local human rights groups do not operate freely. However, women's groups and other nongovernmental organizations operate without hindrance. Workers may join unions and strike, but the government routinely obstructs the free operation of unions and has in the past reorganized labor unions.

The judiciary is not independent. Sharia (Islamic law) prevails in family matters. Security forces arrest Djiboutians without proper authority, despite constitutional requirements that arrests may not occur without a decree presented by a judicial magistrate. The former chief of police, General Yacin Yabel Galab, was sentenced to 15 years in prison in 2002 on charges related to an attempted coup in December 2000. Eleven other police, including eight senior officers, received sentences ranging from 3 to 10 years. Prison conditions are harsh, with reports of beatings, torture, and the rape of female inmates.

The right to own property is respected. Djibouti is a major food importer, and more than 40 percent of its people lived in extreme poverty in 2002. The IMF noted a significant delay in adopting certain structural reforms, particularly a new labor code and an investment code, which were to have been adopted by mid-2004.

Although women in Djibouti enjoy a higher public status than in many other Islamic countries, women's rights and family planning face difficult challenges, many stemming from poverty. Few women hold senior government positions; a record number of seven women were elected to parliament in January 2003. Education of girls still lags behind that of boys, and because of the high unemployment rate, employment opportunities are better for male applicants. Despite equality under civil law, women suffer serious discrimination under customary practices in inheritance and other property matters, in divorce, and regarding the right to travel. Female genital mutilation is widespread, and legislation forbidding mutilation of young girls is not enforced; women's groups are engaged in efforts to curb the practice.

Dominica

Population: 100,000   **Political Rights:** 1
GNI/capita: $3,360   **Civil Liberties:** 1
Life Expectancy: 74   **Status:** Free
Religious Groups: Roman Catholic (77 percent),
Protestant (15 percent), other (8 percent)
Ethnic Groups: Mostly black and mulatto, Carib Amerindian
Capital: Roseau

Ten-Year Ratings Timeline (Political Rights, Civil Liberties, Status)

1995	1996	1997	1998	1999	2000	2001	2002	2003	2004
1,1F	1,1F	1,1F	1,1F	1,1F	1,1F	1,1F	1,1F	1,1F	1,1F

Overview: Following the sudden death of Prime Minister Pierre Charles in January 2004, parliament appointed Roosevelt Skerrit to succeed him.

Dominica has been internally self-governing since 1967 and an independent republic within the Commonwealth since 1978. The centrist opposition Dominica Labour Party (DLP) swept to victory for the first time in 20 years in the January 30, 2000, parliamentary elections, winning 10 of 21 seats and forming a coalition with the right-wing Dominica Freedom Party (DFP). DLP leader Roosevelt "Rosie" Douglas was named prime minister, but died of a heart attack in October 2000. Douglas was replaced by Pierre Charles, who was Douglas' communications and works minister.

On January 6, 2004, Prime Minister Charles, 49, collapsed and died of heart failure. He was succeeded by Roosevelt Skerrit, also of the DLP, who had been serving as education and youth affairs minister.

Skerrit's government, which has only a slender majority in parliament, inherits tremendous financial troubles, compounded by a loss of his party's popular support as a result of the implementation of austerity measures; the recent global economic downturn hurt the agriculturally based economy especially hard and contributed to the imposition of an unpopular program of stabilization and adjustment. Despite facing these difficulties, in April 2004, the DLP won a by-election by a landslide, ratifying Skerrit's popularity. In addition, on April 10, China promised $122 million in return for the revocation of the recognition of Taiwan, bringing in more than a third of the government's normal revenue for five years.

Dominica's economy is primarily agricultural, though there have been efforts to build the infrastructure required to promote tourism and high-technology investment. Because of the island's volcanic geology, rugged terrain, and few beaches, most tourist activity is limited to cruise ship visits. Destruction caused by hurricanes, at times devastating, has further strained the banana industry, which has also been affected by changing market forces, especially increasing competition. Unemployment continues to hover around 20 percent. A major escape valve is the continuing emigration of residents of Dominica to the United States and the francophone Caribbean.

The offshore business sector includes several thousand international companies, banks, and Internet gambling companies. Offshore banking interests continue to raise concerns about penetration by international organized crime, particularly Russian organizations. Despite the announcement in January 2000 that the practice will end, Dominica continues to raise money by selling passports and "economic citizenship."

Political Rights and Civil Liberties: Citizens of Dominica are able to change their government through free and fair elections. Dominica is headed by a prime minister and the House of Assembly, with 21 members elected to five-year terms. Nine senators are appointed—five by the prime minister and four by the opposition leader. The house elects the president for a five-year term. There are three major political parties and one minor one.

The press is free, and there is no censorship or government interference. There are four private newspapers and an equal number of political party journals. Although the main radio station is state-owned, there is also an independent station. Citizens have unimpeded access to cable television and regional radio broadcasts, as well as to the Internet.

Freedom of religion is recognized. While a majority of the population is Roman Catholic, some Protestant churches have been established. In the past, members of the small Rastafarian community charged that their religious rights were violated by a policy of cutting off the dreadlocks of prisoners, and that Rastafarian women are singled out for drug searches. Academic freedom is respected.

Advocacy groups are free to operate and include the Association of Disabled People, the Dominican National Council of Women, and a women and children's self-help organization. Workers have the right to organize, strike, and bargain collectively. Though unions are independent of the government and laws prohibit anti-union discrimination by employers, less than 10 percent of the workforce is unionized.

There is an independent judiciary, and the rule of law is enhanced by the court's subordination to the inter-island Eastern Caribbean Supreme Court. However, the judicial system is understaffed, which has led to a large backlog of cases. The only prison on Dominica is overcrowded and has sanitation problems. In addition, minors are housed with adults. Prison visits by independent human rights monitors are permitted.

The Commonwealth of Dominica Police Force (CDPF) became responsible for security after the Dominica Defense Force (DDF) was disbanded in 1981. The DDF had been implicated in an attempted coup staged by supporters of former Prime Minister Patrick John, who was convicted in 1986 for his role and given a 12-year prison sentence. He was released by executive order in 1990, became active in the trade union movement, and lost as a DLP candidate in the 1995 election.

Occasional instances of excessive use of force by police are among the few human rights complaints heard. In 1997, the commissioner and deputy commissioner of police were forced to retire as a result of recommendations by a commission of inquiry that investigated allegations of mismanagement, corruption, and police brutality. Under new leadership, the police created the Internal Affairs Department late that year to investigate public complaints against the police and to provide officers with counseling. There were continuing allegations of corruption relating to document falsification. Narcotics traffickers use the country as a transshipment point.

Of the 3,000 indigenous Carib Indians, many live on a 3,783-acre reservation on the northeast coast created in 1903 and expanded in 1997. The reservation is governed by the 1978 Carib Constitution.

There are no laws mandating equal pay for equal work for men and women in private sector jobs. Inheritance laws do not fully recognize women's rights. When a husband dies without a will, the wife cannot inherit their property, though she may continue to inhabit their home.

Dominican Republic

Population: 8,800,000   **Political Rights:** 2*
GNI/capita: $2,070   **Civil Liberties:** 2
Life Expectancy: 69   **Status:** Free
Religious Groups: Roman Catholic (95 percent), other (5 percent)
Ethnic Groups: Mixed (73 percent), white (16 percent), black (11 percent)
Capital: Santo Domingo
Ratings Change: The Dominican Republic's political rights rating improved from 3 to 2 due to improvements in the country's electoral climate with the election of President Leonel Fernandez Reyna.

Ten-Year Ratings Timeline (Political Rights, Civil Liberties, Status)

1995	1996	1997	1998	1999	2000	2001	2002	2003	2004
4,3PF	3,3PF	3,3PF	2,3F	2,3F	2,2F	2,2F	2,2F	3,2F	2,2F

Overview: Former president Leonel Fernandez, whose previous term in office, from 1996 to 2000, was accompanied by the biggest period of economic growth in the country's recent history, swept back into the presidency in the May 16, 2004, elections amid the country's worst economic crisis in decades. At the head of the Dominican Liberation Party (PLD), Fernandez retook the office from incumbent Rafael Hipolito Mejia Dominguez of the Dominican Revolutionary Party (PRD) in a generally free and fair election.

After achieving independence from Spain in 1821 and from Haiti in 1844, the Dominican Republic endured recurrent domestic conflict. The assassination of General Rafael Trujillo in 1961 ended 30 years of dictatorship, but a 1963 military coup led to civil war and U.S. intervention. In 1966, under a new constitution, civilian rule was restored with the election of the conservative Joaquin Balaguer.

In the May 16, 2000, presidential elections, Mejia Dominguez, a former agriculture minister and a PRD outsider, struck a chord among those who felt left out of the economic prosperity, particularly the 20 percent who were then living below the poverty level. Mejia won 49.87 percent of the vote, compared with 24.9 percent for ruling party candidate Danilo Medina and 24.6 percent for Balaguer, who was running for his eighth term in office. In the May 2002 legislative elections, the PRD captured the largest number of seats in both houses of parliament.

The largest bank scandal in the history of the Dominican Republic exploded onto the political landscape in May 2003, as the powerful Banco Intercontinental collapsed amid accusations of a $2.2 billion fraud. The scandal was estimated to cost the Dominican Republic the equivalent of 60 to 80 percent of the national budget. The government bailout of the bank, which primarily benefited the 1 percent of the bank's customers holding nearly 80 percent of its deposits, was linked in the public mind to the millions of dollars Intercontinental officials had paid to generals, government officials, and political figures.

According to the Central Bank, the country's gross domestic product fell from $21.7 billion in 2002 to $16.8 billion in 2003. Following the collapse of Banco Intercontinental, the government entered into urgent talks with the IMF for help with the crisis, which cost the national treasury at least $2.2 billion. Opposition to the proposed deal with the IMF and to increased prices for fuel and other basic necessities, as well as continued energy blackouts, led to months of protests in which at least 13 people were killed, frequently as the result of alleged use of excessive force by the police. The scandal also undercut Mejia's lobbying campaign to get the Dominican Republic included in the free trade pact that the United States negotiated with five Central American countries, the Central American Free Trade Agreement (CAFTA). In August, the Dominican Republic entered into a free trade agreement with the countries included in the CAFTA: Costa Rica, El Salvador, Guatemala, Honduras, Nicaragua, and the United States.

In the May 2004 presidential election, Fernandez won 57.1 percent of the vote to 33.7 percent garnered by discredited incumbent Mejia. Because Fernandez won more than 50 percent of the vote, a second round was unnecessary. In an effort to diffuse tensions in the run-up to the poll, the Central Election Board opened the electoral registry to inspection by all political parties and to observers from the Organization of American States (OAS) before sending copies on to the voting districts. Some 6,000 citizen volunteers and hundreds of OAS observers helped to keep the election free and fair. The contest also marked the first time that Dominicans living abroad—mainly in the United States and Spain—were able to vote by absentee ballot, although bureaucratic snafus contributed to keeping the actual number of registered expatriates low. Inaugurated August 16, Fernandez faced the huge task of combating a ballooning $6 billion foreign debt, a 16 percent unemployment rate, yearly inflation of some 32 percent, and a decrepit and indebted energy sector that left much of the country without electricity for as much as 20 hours a day.

In 2004, the UN Development Program concluded that at least one million Dominicans slipped below the poverty line in three years—putting the total number of people living in poverty at nearly five million, or almost 60 percent of the population. The increasingly desperate situation of the island nation's poor was reflected in the fact that the thousands of Dominicans intercepted by U.S. authorities while trying to reach Puerto Rico by boat far outstripped the numbers of Haitians and Cubans intercepted by the Coast Guard at sea. Fernandez, who first term in office was marred by a scandal involving the disappearance of $100 million in government funds, nonetheless made fighting corruption a central theme in his election campaign. In his inauguration address, he pledged austerity for his government and promised large cuts in the borrowing, government hiring, and heavy spending that had characterized Mejia's term in office.

Political Rights and Civil Liberties: Citizens of the Dominican Republic can change their government democratically, and the 2004 presidential election was free and fair. The constitution provides for a president and a congress elected for four-year terms. The bicameral National Congress consists of the 30-member Senate and, as a result of a recent census, a Chamber of Deputies that in 1998 went from 120 members to 149. At the end of 2001, the Dominican legislature approved constitutional changes allowing presidents to serve consecutive terms, as part of a package of electoral changes that also included reducing from 50 to 45 percent the minimum vote required to win presidential elections in the first round. The reforms also established direct election of the president, eliminating an electoral college system in which representative sectors chose the president on the basis of popular votes.

Official corruption remains a serious problem. The Dominican Republic was ranked 87 out of 146 countries surveyed in Transparency International's 2004 Corruption Perceptions Index.

The media are mostly private. On May 15, 2003, in response to the collapse of the Banco Intercontinental, a court ordered the takeover of several media companies, whose main stockholders the government accused of major money-laundering fraud. Two newspapers, *Ultima Hora* and *El Financiero*, were ultimately shut down, and two others, plus four television channels, a cable television company, and more than 70 radio stations, were placed under government control. Some of the media assets were then used to publicize political activity of the then-ruling party, and radio programs of government opponents were suppressed. In September 2004, radio commentator Euri Cabral was attacked by men who fired 10 gunshots at him as he returned home from work; Cabral and a colleague escaped unharmed. Earlier that month, journalist Juan Andujar of *Listín Diario* was shot and killed in the town of Azua.

Constitutional guarantees regarding religious and academic freedom are generally respected.

The government generally respects the right to organize political parties and civic groups. Civil society organizations in the Dominican Republic are some of the most well organized and effective in Latin America. Labor unions are well organized. Although legally permitted to strike, they are often subject to government crackdowns. On August 6, 2003, police raided a local trade union and opened fire on those inside, reportedly to prevent them from carrying out a protest later that day. Peasant unions are occasionally targeted by armed groups working for large landowners.

The judiciary, headed by the Supreme Court, is politicized and riddled with corruption, although less so in recent years. The courts offer little recourse to those without money or influence, although reforms implemented of late, including those aimed at promoting greater efficiency and due process, show some promise in increasing citizen access to the courts. In September a new Criminal Procedures Code took effect that gave suspects additional protections. The following month, a new Code for Minors was inaugurated that provided for more protection and stiffer penalties in cases of sexual or commercial exploitation. Extrajudicial killings by police remain a problem, although the government has begun to refer cases of military and police abuse to civilian courts, instead of to nontransparent police or military tribunals. Police salaries are low, and there is a high level of corruption throughout the country's law enforcement institutions. Prisons, in which 9 out of 10 inmates have not been convicted of a crime, suffer from severe overcrowding, poor health and sanitary conditions, and routine violence that results in a significant number of deaths. Homosexual and transvestite detainees report frequent incidents of police brutality, including rape, while in detention.

A major transit country for South American drugs to the United States, the Dominican Republic serves local, Puerto Rican, and Colombian drug smugglers as both a command-and-control center and a transshipment point, mostly for cocaine. The government estimates that some 20 percent of the drugs entering the country remain there as "payment in kind." This phenomenon has contributed to increasing drug abuse and street crime.

The migration of Haitians, some legally but the vast majority without legal documents, to the Dominican Republic in search of economic opportunity has long been a source of tension between the two countries. Some of the illegal migration was assisted by the authorities, who profit from it. Human rights groups report that children born of Haitian parents in the Dominican Republic, generally denied registration as citizens, frequently were among the thousands of people deported each year as illegal aliens.

Violence and discrimination against women is a serious problem, as are trafficking in women and girls, child prostitution, and child abuse. The Dominican Republic is primarily a source country for trafficked women between the ages of 18 and 25, and girls as young as 15, and an estimated 100,000 Dominican women work overseas as prostitutes. Only 25 representatives in the lower house of congress and 2 senators are women.

East Timor

Population: 800,000
GNI/capita: $520
Life Expectancy: 49
Religious Groups: Roman Catholic (90 percent), Muslim (4 percent), Protestant (3 percent), other (3 percent)
Ethnic Groups: Austronesian (Malayo-Polynesian), Papuan, small Chinese minority
Capital: Dili

Political Rights: 3
Civil Liberties: 3
Status: Partly Free

Ten-Year Ratings Timeline (Political Rights, Civil Liberties, Status)

1995	1996	1997	1998	1999	2000	2001	2002	2003	2004
--	--	--	--	6,4PF	6,3PF	5,3PF	3,3PF	3,3PF	3,3F

Overview:

Two years after gaining independence, the world's newest nation continued in 2004 the arduous task of constructing effective state institutions, promoting social reconciliation, and developing the economy. However, the euphoria that greeted independence has given way to concern over economic growth, unemployment, and corruption. Acknowledging that the East Timor government still lacked capacity in numerous fields, the

United Nations extended its Mission in Support of East Timor (UNMISET), which had been scheduled to end in 2004, until May 2005.

The Portuguese colonized East Timor in the sixteenth century but did little to develop the territory. After Portugal abruptly abandoned East Timor in 1975, the leftist Revolutionary Front for an Independent East Timor (Fretilin) and the right-wing Democratic Union of Timor (UDT) fought for control of the territory. Fearing that a left-wing East Timor would emerge in the midst of the Indonesian archipelago, the staunchly anti-Communist regime of Indonesia's General Suharto covertly supported right-wing groups in East Timor. Indonesia responded to Fretilin's November 1975 declaration of independence by invading East Timor in December 1975 and formally incorporating it as Indonesia's twenty-sixth province in 1976. The United Nations condemned both actions.

Over the next two decades, Fretilin's armed wing, Falintil, waged a low-grade insurgency against the Indonesian army (TNI), which ruled East Timor with few civilian checks on its power. As Indonesian forces consolidated their control over East Timor, they committed widespread abuses against the local population. Civil conflict and famine may have killed up to 200,000 Timorese during Indonesian rule.

When the TNI fired on a peaceful funeral demonstration in the presence of foreign cameramen in 1991, killing more than 200, foreign governments increasingly conditioned their relations with Indonesia on the latter's treatment of East Timor. The 1996 Nobel Peace Prize was awarded to two leading East Timorese, exiled activist Jose Ramos-Horta and the Catholic bishop of Dili, Carlos Belo. Negotiations on autonomy for East Timor conducted with jailed resistance leader Jose Alexendre "Xanana" Gusmao and others went nowhere, owing to Suharto's opposition.

Suharto's successor, Habibie, approved a referendum on East Timor's status. After 78.5 percent of the electorate in East Timor voted for independence in August 1999, elements of the TNI and their pro-integrationist East Timor allies embarked on a scorched-earth policy. By the time an Australian-led multinational force arrived to restore order, up to 1,000 civilians had been killed, more than 250,000 others had been driven into Indonesian West Timor, and approximately 80 percent of East Timor's buildings and infrastructure had been destroyed.

In October 1999, The UN Security Council authorized the UN Transitional Authority for East Timor (UNTAET), charged to provide security, oversee reconstruction, and prepare for independence. In August 2001, East Timor elected an 88-member Constituent Assembly to draft a constitution. In an election contested by 16 political parties, Fretilin won 57 percent of the vote, significantly less than the 80 percent that its leader, Mari Alkatiri, had predicted. Many attribute this result to statements by Gusmao that a Fretilin landslide would not be good for democracy. Gusmao had been chairman of Fretilin until 1988, when he left the party with a stinging critique, rejected violence, and created a broad resistance coalition. Gusmao was directly elected president for a five-year term, with 87 percent of the vote, in May 2002.

Little controversy surrounded the political substance of the constitution, which came into effect upon independence on May 20, 2002. However, the designation of November 28, 1975, the day of the Fretilin takeover in Dili, as independence day; the choice of its previous term for the territory, Republica Democratica de Timor Leste as the official name of the new country; and the close resemblance of the national flag to the old Fretilin party flag all generated dissent. The opposition claimed that the use of Fretilin symbols and conventions for the new state was an attempt to conflate the ruling party with the state itself. Fretilin also inserted a clause into the constitution to transform the Constituent Assembly into the country's first postindependence parliament. This action was opposed by President Gusmao, Bishop Belo, and most of the non-Fretilin political leaders, who all favored fresh elections. The designation of Portuguese, the language of the elite spoken by only 5 percent of Timorese, as the national language alongside Tetum, a language understood by approximately 82 percent of the population, also triggered opposition.

UNTAET was disbanded upon independence. Mindful of the severe dearth of trained personnel in virtually all public sectors, as well as the cross-border threat from Indonesian West Timor, the United Nations authorized UNMISET, which retained responsibility for security and continued UN programs in economic recovery, reconstruction, and capacity building. On May 20, 2004, UNMISET officially handed over responsibility for external defense and internal security to East Timor. Concerned over the immaturity of the country's security and civil institutions, however, the United Nations voted to extend UNMISET's mandate for an additional year, until May 2005, although significantly reducing its presence. Security personnel fell from 3,000 civilian police, troops, and military observers to 604, while the number of experts serving in the country's civil administration was cut from 100 to 60.

East Timor has made extensive progress in implementing the national development plan launched in 2002, which prioritizes health, education, infrastructure, and agriculture in that order. According to the *Far Eastern Economic Review*, more than 700 of the 900 schools burnt during the postreferendum violence have been rebuilt, health centers have spread across the country, and 80 percent of a budgeted 13,100 civil service positions have been filled. Nevertheless, the country only has 20 doctors, roads in many part of the country are impassable, and only Dili can count on a stable power supply.

Poverty hampers East Timor's nation-building efforts. East Timor is Asia's poorest country, with an average per capita income of less than $500, and 41 percent of the population live below the national poverty line of 55 cents per day, according to Oxfam. Up to 80 percent of the country's working-age population is unemployed. After experiencing an unsustainable boom in 2000-2001, when the economy, driven by massive international presence in the country and postreferendum reconstruction spending, expanded 15 percent, East Timor sustained a contraction of 3 percent in 2003. Prospects for 2004 are limited.

Income from oil and gas is the economic lifeline that the Timorese and international donors are counting on to help the country achieve self-sufficiency. For most of 2004, East Timor was locked in a bitter dispute with Australia over the maritime border in the Timor Sea that divides the two countries. At stake are proceeds from rich oil and gas deposits that would give East Timor an estimated additional $8 billion over the next two decades, according to *The Economist*. Australia adopted formidable tactics toward this issue, withdrawing from the International Court of Justice's jurisdiction on law of the sea issues two months before East Timor became independent. Not until mid-2004, when the oil consortium involved threatened to abandon its project unless an agreement was reached by year's end, did Australia return to the negotiating table.

An estimated 16,000 of the 250,000 East Timorese who fled or were pushed across the border to Indonesian West Timor are still there. Fewer than 100 returned to East Timor in the first three months of 2004, leading the United Nations to conclude that the majority of those remaining had decided to stay in Indonesia, at least for now. Although there has been no major cross-border violence since late 2003, the mere presence of the refugee camps along the Indonesian–East Timor border and of an unknown number of militia members in them remains a security threat.

Political Rights and Civil Liberties: East Timor's directly elected president plays a largely symbolic role, with his formal powers limited to the right to veto legislation and make appointments. Governing power resides with the prime minister, Fretilin leader Mari Alkatiri, and parliament, both holdovers from the directly elected Constituent Assembly. The Democratic Party (PD) and the Social Democratic Party (SDT) each won slightly more than 8 percent of the vote in the August 2001 elections, and form the nucleus of a parliamentary opposition that numbers around 25 of the 88 members. In contrast to Fretilin, which derives its legitimacy from its role in the independence struggle, PD is run by a younger generation of university graduates and intellectuals.

Elections for village leaders, which were scheduled to take place in successive rounds beginning in late 2004, have been pushed back. There are fears that Fretilin will attempt to limit the power and activities of political opposition groups. Following a March 6 opposition rally, a number of civil servants faced investigations, disciplinary actions, and job loss, measures that have been questioned in the press. The administration claims that those disciplined violated laws prohibiting civil servants from attending political rallies during business hours; those involved claim they were off duty.

There is great concern that corruption, largely as a product of bad habits learned from Indonesia, will explode once the UN presence finally ends. Many welcome the fact that Western experts effectively run the Finance Ministry and keep a tight reign on spending. East Timor was not ranked by Transparency International in its 2004 Corruption Perceptions Index.

East Timor's press legislation is one of the most liberal in Asia, according to Reporters Sans Frontieres. However, anecdotal evidence indicates that there have been more than a few instances in which reporters have been seriously rebuked or fired for writing investigative articles on public officials. A recent proposal to create an independent TV station as an alternative to the state-owned one was rejected by the prime minister. Draft legislation is currently being considered by the government that would make defamation a criminal act.

East Timor is a secular state, but the Roman Catholic Church plays a central role in the life of the country. Church rules prohibit persons living under religious vows from holding political office, so some politically active priests and nuns have been barred from government office. No significant threats to religious freedom exist, and the prime minister, a member of the country's small Arab minority, is a practicing Muslim.

Although the government generally respects freedom of assembly and association, there were a few cases in which these rights were violated. In March, PNTL officers raided a house in the village of Uatulari where an opposition party was holding a public meeting. Although a permit is not necessary for a meeting in a private home, police claimed that the party had not obtained a permit.

East Timor has a labor code based on the International Labor Organization's standards. The law permits workers to form and join worker organizations without prior authorization. However, attempts to organize workers generally have been slowed by inexperience and a lack of organizational skills. During the year, the government established official registration procedures for trade unions and employer organizations.

The country's legal system is fragile. With only two functioning courthouses in the country, communities are frequently left with the responsibility of adjudicating their own disputes. The rights to due process and an expeditious fair trial are often restricted or denied, largely because of shortages of resources and lack of trained personnel. The establishment of the National Judicial Training Center by the UNDP in September 2004 to provide standardized, postgraduate legal training for judges, prosecutors, and public defenders is a significant step toward alleviating the human capacity problems and lack of standardization currently plaguing the legal system.

Neither the police (PNTL) nor the military (FDLT) are perceived to have the trust of the population or the capacity to provide adequate security and order. Infighting between the PNTL and FDLT erupted into a public confrontation between members of the two security forces on January 25 in Los Palos. Tensions between the two organizations are attributable to a recruitment process that resulted in a large number of former Falintil members being incorporated into the defense force while police officers were drawn largely from the Indonesian-era police force. Insufficient clarity in the division of labor between the two security forces, as well as PNTL resentment that FDLT has garnered the lion's share of foreign training resources, exacerbate relations. The fact that the FDLT falls under President Jose Alexendre "Xanana" Gusmao's control, while the PNTL reports to Alkatiri, has further deepened social mistrust of the political independence and neutrality of these bodies.

An April 2004 report by UN Secretary-General Kofi Annan stated that the PNTL had been the subject of "continuing, disturbing reports of excessive use of force, assault, negligent use of firearms, criminal activities, corrupt practices and violations of human rights." The creation of two special units within the security forces—a bodyguard unit of the Internal Administrative Ministry and a police rapid-intervention unit supplied with submachine guns and assault rifles—are also worrisome signs.

Like other postconflict societies, East Timor faces the vexing question of how to balance the desire for justice for past abuses with the need for reconciliation. In 2001, UNTAET created an independent Commission for Reception, Truth, and Reconciliation (CAVR) with the mandate to investigate human rights violations committed between April 1974 and October 1999, and to facilitate community reconciliation. CAVR is scheduled to issue its final report in October 2004. In May 2004, parliament debated an amnesty law that would extend to crimes such as genocide, as well as to war crimes, murder, sexual offenses, and torture. International human rights organizations have lobbied against this move, arguing that the proposed pardons would preempt any serious judicial followup to the CAVR's final report.

The UN Serious Crime Unit (SCU) was established in 2000 to investigate serious incidents, including murder, rape, and torture, that were committed between January 1, 1999, and October 15, 1999. The SCU, which is housed within the East Timor Attorney General's office, has filed charges against approximately 400 people, including many high-ranking Indonesians such as General Wiranto, head of the TNI at the time of the 1999 referendum and the third-place finisher in Indonesia's 2004 presidential election. In the midst of the election campaign, the SCU issued an arrest warrant for Wiranto, but East Timor's attorney general refused to process it.

The latest UN resolution did not extend the mandate of the SCU, which was required to complete all of its investigations by November 2004, with all trials and other activities completed no later than May 2005. The widespread belief that the majority of those responsible for serious crimes will not be brought to justice by this time, combined with Indonesia's unwillingness to prosecute those responsible for the 1999 violence under its jurisdiction, has led many in the human rights community to call for a UN tribunal. East Timor's leaders have rejected such proposals in the name of reconciliation with Indonesia.

At least 275 Indonesians who have been denied citizenship by East Timor and lack Indonesian papers are stateless and have been targets of violence in the past. Many Timorese claim that their country's brutal history has led to a "culture of violence" in society, including widespread domestic violence. With the assistance of the UN Population Fund, East Timor has helped draft new domestic violence legislation to protect women and children that is to be reviewed and implemented as part of the country's new penal code.

Ecuador

Population: 13,400,000 **Political Rights:** 3
GNI/capita: $1,490 **Civil Liberties:** 3
Life Expectancy: 71 **Status:** Partly Free
Religious Groups: Roman Catholic (95 percent), other (5 percent)
Ethnic Groups: Mestizo (65 percent), Amerindian (25 percent), white (7 percent), black (3 percent)
Capital: Quito

Ten-Year Ratings Timeline (Political Rights, Civil Liberties, Status)

1995	1996	1997	1998	1999	2000	2001	2002	2003	2004
2,3F	2,4PF	3,3PF	2,3F	2,3F	3,3PF	3,3PF	3,3PF	3,3PF	3,3PF

Overview: President Lucio Gutierrez spent 2004 trying, unsuccessfully, to establish his presidency's legitimacy following the rupture the previous year of his ruling coalition and his party's disastrous electoral showing in the October regional and municipal elections. Before the elections, Gutierrez, who had won the presidency on an anticorruption platform, faced serious questions about his commitment to transparency and honest government. Despite the election results, Gutierrez did not accede to pressure to resign and appeared to be trying to outmaneuver his many opponents.

Established in 1830 after achieving independence from Spain in 1822, the Republic of Ecuador has endured many interrupted presidencies and military governments. The last military regime gave way to civilian rule when a new constitution was approved by referendum in 1978.

In January 2000, Vice President Gustavo Noboa took over as president after demonstrators had forced his predecessor to step down. The protests by indigenous groups, reportedly manipulated by putschist senior army commanders, were joined by those of significant numbers of mid-level military officers led by Gutierrez, an army colonel. Despite the protestors' acclamation of a three-person "junta" that included Gutierrez, congress met in emergency session in Guayaquil to ratify Noboa, who did not belong to any political party, as the new constitutional president.

In the October 2002 legislative elections, the Social Christian Party secured the largest number of seats. Gutierrez, who was inspired by another coup plotter, Venezuela's Hugo Chavez, won a surprise first-round victory in the concurrent presidential election, defeating two former presidents who stood as standard-bearers for Ecuador's traditional political parties. He emerged in the hard-fought campaign as a advocate for the elimination of the country's infamous corruption and the alleviation of its extraordinary rural poverty. Gutierrez, who had never held political office, went on to best populist banana magnate Alvaro Noboa in the November 24 runoff, heading a leftist coalition sustained by the country's increasingly empowered Indian groups. Gutierrez was sworn into office on January 15, 2003. His election constituted the first time that Ecuador's chief executive shared the humble background and dark-skinned complexion of the country's majority.

Despite the unprecedented incorporation of indigenous peoples in Gutierrez's government, by the end of 2003, the conflicting demands placed on the country's still fragmented political system by his heterogeneous coalition and the need for economic reform resulted in the withdrawal of key political support by Indian and peasant communities. After initiating a few reforms, such as an overhaul of the corrupt customs service and the introduction of some tough fiscal policies, including increases in bus fares and in oil and electricity prices, the Gutierrez government quickly became mired in internal disputes. Dissent over the fiscal reforms as well as over government plans to encourage private investment in the oil industry and controversial labor reforms boiled over into the streets, as one-time Gutierrez supporters expressed their frustration that the cash-strapped government had not done more to fight poverty.

Despite government successes in fighting inflation and making vast improvements in Ecuador's balance of payments situation, the decision by the powerful indigenous Pachakutik movement to withdraw support for Gutierrez portended serious social tensions. In November 2003, a scandal erupted over the alleged ties of Vice President Alfredo Palacio to a businessman detained on drug-trafficking charges who had contributed $30,000 to the Gutierrez-Palacio campaign.

During the 2004 campaign, Gutierrez met in Panama with self-exiled former president Abdala Bucaram, who was forced from office in 1997 on the grounds of "mental incapacity" amid rampant corruption scandals. The meeting with Bucaram, whose small political party was considered a key potential ally in the upcoming elections, triggered charges that the president was attempting to interfere with the judicial process; his spokesman denied the charge. The meeting, however, pointed to the virtual absence of support for Gutierrez in parliament, where he was forced to govern by means of temporary alliances. Gutierrez's political standing was also hurt when he dismissed the head of the national tax agency, who had won fame for temporarily closing business tax scofflaws and who had raised the country's tax collection. Another cause for concern was the increasing territorial reach and political influence of drug traffickers from neighboring Colombia.

In the October 2004 regional and municipal elections, Gutierrez's Patriotic Society failed to receive even the 5 percent of the vote required for official recognition as a political party. Following the rout in the polls, the country's largest opposition party and several others across ideological lines pressed for Gutierrez's removal. However, as of November 30, Gutierrez had refused either to resign or to hold early elections and was reported to be looking to change the alignment of political forces by judicial manipulation.

Political Rights and Civil Liberties:

Citizens of Ecuador can change their government democratically. The 2004 regional and municipal elections were generally considered to be free and fair, although the Supreme Electoral Tribunal admitted it was incapable of regulating campaign spending, and questions were raised about the registration of candidates as well as the geographic distribution of elected offices. The 1978 constitution provides for a president elected for four years, with a runoff between two front-runners if no candidate wins a majority in the first round. The 77-member unicameral congress (National Chamber of Deputies) is composed of 65 members elected on a provincial basis every two years and 12 elected nationally every four years. In 1998, the national Constituent Assembly decided to retain Ecuador's presidential system. It also mandated that in the year 2002, a presidential candidate would need to win 40 percent of valid votes in first-round balloting and exceed by 10 percent those received by the nearest rival in order to avoid a runoff.

A government report published in 2000 said that corruption costs Ecuador more than $2 billion a year. In July 2003, former president Gustavo Noboa was given asylum in the Dominican Republic, becoming the latest in a long line of politicians, including other former presidents, who opted for exile rather than face corruption charges. Ecuador was ranked 112 out of 146 countries surveyed in Transparency International's 2004 Corruption Perceptions Index.

Constitutional guarantees regarding freedom of expression are generally observed, and the media, which are mostly private, are outspoken. However, journalists were the targets of violence during the year. In April, a Quito doctor assaulted two journalists from Ecuavisa who had happened upon two policemen acting as "facilitators" (taking money to speed up the processing of paperwork). Two weeks later, a reporter from *El Universo*, who was investigating a botched police operation in which both suspects and innocent bystanders were killed, filed a criminal complaint saying that he had been threatened by unidentified persons. The Transparency and Access to Information Law enacted in May 2004 was hailed by journalists' organizations as a step forward in freedom of the press and freedom of expression. By the end of the year, the law, which an increasing number of critics said may be unenforceable, was still awaiting the issuance of implementation regulations by Gutierrez.

The constitution provides for freedom of religion, and the government generally respects this right in practice. The government does not require religious groups to be licensed or registered unless they form nongovernmental organizations (NGOs) that engage in commercial activity. The government allows missionary activity and religious demonstrations by all religions. The government does not restrict academic freedom.

The right to organize political parties, civic groups, and unions is generally respected. Labor unions are well organized and have the right to strike, although the labor code limits public sector strikes. Ecuador has numerous human rights organizations, and despite occasional acts of intimidation, they report on arbitrary arrests and instances of police brutality and military misconduct.

The judiciary, generally undermined by the corruption afflicting the entire political system, is headed by a Supreme Court that, until 1997, was appointed by the legislature and thus subject to political influence. In reforms approved by referendum in May 1997, power to appoint judges was turned over to the Supreme Court, with congress given a final chance to choose that 31-member body on the basis of recommendations made by a special selection commission. A new criminal justice procedural code that fundamentally changes Ecuador's legal system entered into force in July 2001. The new code empowers prosecutors to investigate and prosecute crimes, and alters the role of the judge to that of neutral arbiter presiding over oral trials. In 2003, an Ecuadoran court initiated a case against ChevronTexaco, alleging that a subsidiary of the California-based multinational oil company polluted the rain forest with billions of gallons of waste from 1971 to 1992.

Torture and ill-treatment of detainees and prisoners remain widespread. Police courts that are neither impartial nor independent continue to try members of security forces accused of human rights violations.

Ecuador is a transshipment point for cocaine passing from neighboring Colombia to the United States, as well as a money-laundering haven. Widespread corruption in Ecuador's customs service led the government to privatize it in May 1999. The dollarization of the Ecuadoran economy appears to have had the unintended effect of making the country more attractive for money laundering and other financial criminal activity.

A growing number of incursions from both Colombian guerrilla groups and their paramilitary enemies into Ecuadoran territory added to regional concern about the extent to which the neighboring country's civil war would affect public safety and the survival of democratic institutions. Violent crime has undermined public faith in the police to maintain order.

Despite their growing political influence, indigenous people continue to suffer discrimination at many levels of society and are the frequent victims of abuse by military officers working in league with large landowners during disputes over land. In the Amazon region, indigenous groups have attempted to win a share of oil revenues and a voice in natural resources and development decisions. Although the government tends to consult indigenous communities on natural resources matters, their wishes are not always granted.

After the 2002 elections, women held 17 of 100 seats in congress, the largest proportion in the country's history. Gutierrez initially named four female cabinet ministers, including the first female minister of foreign affairs. At year's end, there were two female cabinet ministers, following turnover in the cabinet. Violence against women, particularly in indigenous areas where victims are reluctant to speak out against other members of their community, is common.

Egypt

Population: 73,400,000   **Political Rights:** 6
GNI/capita: $1,470   **Civil Liberties:** 5*
Life Expectancy: 68   **Status:** Not Free
Religious Groups: Muslim [mostly Sunni] (94 percent),
other [including Coptic Christian] (6 percent)
Ethnic Groups: Eastern Hamitic stock [Egyptian, Bedouin,
Berber] (99 percent), other (1 percent)
Capital: Cairo
Ratings Change: Egypt's civil liberties rating improved from 6 to 5 due to the government's relaxation of restrictions on the media and increased tolerance of public criticism.

Ten-Year Ratings Timeline (Political Rights, Civil Liberties, Status)

1995	1996	1997	1998	1999	2000	2001	2002	2003	2004
6,6NF	6,6NF	6,6NF	6,6NF	6,6NF	6,5NF	6,5NF	6,6NF	6,6NF	6,5NF

Overview:

The government took two steps forward and one step back in its respect for civil liberties in 2004. While no far-reaching political reforms were on the horizon, President Hosni Mubarak eased restrictions on independent print media and tolerated an increasingly vibrant public discussion of controversial political issues, such as constitutional reform and presidential succession, that would have been unimaginable a few years ago. However, the authorities also launched the most sweeping crackdown on the Muslim Brotherhood since the mid-1990s and continued to severely restrict the activities of human rights organizations.

Egypt formally gained independence from Great Britain in 1922 and acquired full sovereignty following the end of World War II. After leading a coup that overthrew the monarchy in 1952, Colonel Gamel Abdel Nasser established a repressive police state that he ruled until his death in 1970. The constitution adopted in 1971 under his successor, Anwar al-Sadat, established a strong presidential political system with nominal guarantees for most political and civil rights that were not fully respected in practice.

Following the assassination of Sadat in 1981, Mubarak became president and declared a state of emergency (which he has since renewed every three years, most recently in February 2003). Despite receiving billions of dollars in U.S. and other foreign financial aid, the government failed to implement comprehensive economic reforms, and a substantial deterioration in living conditions for many Egyptians fueled an Islamist insurgency in the early 1990s. The authorities arrested thousands of suspected militants and cracked down on political dissent. Although the armed infrastructure of Egyptian Islamist groups had been largely eradicated by 1998, the government continued to restrict political and civil liberties.

High levels of economic growth in the late 1990s temporarily alleviated Egypt's dire socioeconomic problems, particularly poverty and high unemployment among college graduates. However, the country experienced an economic slowdown after the September 11, 2001, attacks in the United States, with tourism revenue, Suez Canal receipts, expatriate remittances, and foreign direct investment declining substantially. Popular disaffection with the government spread palpably, and demands for political change became more vocal. Anti-war protests during the U.S.-led invasion of Iraq in March 2003 quickly changed into mass antigovernment demonstrations, which sparked a harsh crackdown by security forces that left hundreds injured.

In the face of both rising internal discontent and growing Western pressure for political and economic liberalization, the government embarked on a high-profile effort to cast itself as a champion of reform in 2004. In July, Mubarak appointed a new prime minister, Ahmed Nazif, a 52-year-old engineer and former minister of communications and information technology, charged with reviving the stalled economic liberalization process, and he replaced nearly half of the cabinet with younger technocrats, most of them under the age of 50. During his first two months in office, Nazif introduced a major overhaul of customs regulations, reduced import tariffs, and cut subsidies on fuel and water, but it remains to be seen whether he has the political clout to tackle more critical economic problems. The removal of several "old guard" ministers who had built extensive patronage networks over the past two decades was interpreted by some analysts as an indication that Mubarak is committed to major economic reforms. However, the fact that all key economic portfolios were awarded to associates of his 41-year-old son, Gamal, raised concerns that the president is paving the way for a hereditary transition.

Talk of succession has been rife since November 2003, when Mubarak nearly collapsed during a televised speech and was abruptly whisked away by bodyguards. Officials claimed that the 76-year-old president was suffering from a stomach flu, but he has made far fewer public appearances since then. In June 2004, he abruptly canceled several high-level meetings with foreign dignitaries and left for medical treatment in Germany (ostensibly to treat a slipped disk). Since Mubarak never appointed a vice president, these incidents sparked vigorous public debate over who will come next—a hitherto taboo topic in Egypt. Gamal's equivocal denials of presidential ambitions have most Egyptians wagering that he will make a run for the presidency in 2005 if his father is unable to pursue a fifth term.

A broad consensus emerged in 2004 among leftist, liberal, and Islamist political forces as to the components of desired political reform: direct multicandidate presidential elections, the abrogation of emergency law, full judicial supervision of elections, the lifting of restrictions on the formation of political parties, and an end to government interference in the operation of nongovernmental organizations (NGOs). However, the opposition remained deeply polarized between licensed and unlicensed political groups, which formed rival reform coalitions—the Alliance of National Forces for Reform and the Popular Movement for Change, respectively—during the year. Although the National Democratic Party's policy committee, headed by Gamal Mubarak, repeatedly declared its commitment to sweeping political reform, the reform plan unveiled at its annual conference in September was largely cosmetic.

Political Rights and Civil Liberties: Egyptians cannot change their government democratically. As a result of government restrictions on the licensing of political parties, state control over television and radio stations, and systemic irregularities in the electoral process, the 454-seat People's Assembly (*Majlis al-Sha'b*), or lower house of parliament, is perpetually dominated by the ruling NDP, as is the partially elected upper house, the Consultative Council (*Majlis al-Shura*), which functions only in an advisory capacity. There is no competitive process for the election of the president; the public is entitled only to confirm in a national referendum the candidate nominated by the People's Assembly for a six-year term. The assembly has limited influence on government policy, and the executive initiates almost all legislation. The president directly appoints the prime minister, the cabinet, and the governors of the country's 26 provinces. NDP candidates won 87 of the 88 Shura Council seats contested in the June 2004 elections.

Political opposition remains weak and ineffective. A ban on religious parties prevents the Muslim Brotherhood and other Islamist groups from organizing politically, although their members typically compete in elections as independents. Political parties cannot be established without the approval of the Political Parties Committee (PPC), an NDP-controlled body affiliated with the Shura Council. Since 1977, the PPC has approved the formation of only four new political parties (the most recent being the Free Social Constitutional Party in November 2004), while issuing more than 60 rejections.

Corruption in Egypt is a serious problem; investors frequently complain that red tape and bureaucratic inertia make bribery essential to doing business. Egypt was ranked 77 out of 146 countries surveyed in Transparency International's 2004 Corruption Perceptions Index.

Freedom of the press is limited. The government owns and operates all terrestrial broadcast television stations. Although several private satellite television stations have been established, their owners have ties to the government and their programming is subject to state influence. A few private radio stations have recently been established, but their programming is restricted to entertainment. The three leading daily newspapers are state controlled, and their editors are appointed by the president.

The government encourages legal political parties to publish newspapers and exercises indirect control over the publications through its monopoly on printing and distribution, but it has long restricted the licensing of nonpartisan newspapers. Only foreign publications are subject to direct government censorship, but some privately owned Egyptian publications have been forced to register abroad (usually in Cyprus) and are therefore subject to censorship. Two independent private newspapers—the daily *Al-Masri Al-Yom* (*Egypt Today*) and the weekly *Nahdet Misr* (*Egyptian Renaissance*)—were recently established.

Freedom of expression is restricted by vaguely worded statutes in the Press Law, the Publications Law, the penal code, and libel laws. Direct criticism of the president, his family, or the military, as well as discussions of Christian-Muslim tensions and expressions of views regarded as anti-Islamic, can result in the imprisonment of journalists and the closure of publications. In February, President Hosni Mubarak pledged to end prison sentences for press offenses, but this promise remained unfulfilled. In June, journalist Ahmed Ezzedine was sentenced to two years' imprisonment on libel charges for writing an article accusing the agriculture minister of perjury. Days earlier, four men involved in printing and distributing a bumper sticker that read "Cairo Traffic Rules: Green = Stop, Red = Go, Yellow = Go Faster" were arrested on charges of harming the country's reputation (Egypt has one of the world's highest motor vehicle mortality rates in the world), but the charges were quickly dropped. In November, the editor of the Arab nationalist weekly *Al-Arabi*, Abdel-Halim Qandil, was beaten by unidentified assailants.

The government does not significantly restrict or monitor Internet use, but publication of material on the Internet has been prosecuted under the same statutes as regular press offenses. The Muslim Brotherhood claimed in 2004 that the government pressured the country's main Internet service providers to block access to its Web site.

Islam is the state religion, and the government directly controls most mosques, appoints their preachers and other staff, and closely monitors the content of sermons. It is implementing a plan to establish control over thousands of small, unauthorized mosques (known as *zawaya*) located in residential buildings. Most Egyptians are Sunni Muslim, and there are small numbers of Jews, Shiite Muslims, Baha'is, and Coptic Christians. Although non-Muslims are generally able to worship freely, the government has seized church-owned property and frequently denies permission to build or repair churches. Muslim extremists have carried out several killings of Coptic villagers in recent years and frequently burn or vandalize Coptic homes, businesses, and churches.

Academic freedom is generally respected in Egypt, though professors have been prosecuted for political and human rights advocacy outside of the classroom.

Freedom of assembly and association is heavily restricted. Organizers of public demonstrations, rallies, and protests must receive advance approval from the Ministry of the Interior, which is rarely granted. A new law regulating NGOs went into effect in 2003. The Law of Associations prohibits the establishment of associations "threatening national unity [or] violating public morals," prohibits NGOs from receiving foreign grants without the approval of the Ministry of Social Affairs (which generally blocks funding to human rights defenders and advocates of political reform), requires members of NGO governing boards to be approved by the ministry, and allows the ministry to dissolve NGOs without a judicial order. Some groups have avoided the new NGO restrictions by registering as law firms or civil companies. In July, the authorities raided the Cairo offices of the Nadim Center for the Psychological Treatment and Rehabilitation of Victims of Violence, an NGO that is registered as a medical clinic but engages in extensive human rights activities, and subsequently threatened to close it down.

The 2003 Unified Labor Law limits the right to strike to "non-strategic" industries and requires workers to first obtain approval for a strike from the government-controlled Egyptian Trade Union Federation—the country's only legal labor federation. Only a handful of strikes occurred in 2004. Egyptian law establishes a minimum wage and requires companies to provide social security insurance, but off-the-record employment is widespread, especially in the agricultural sector.

The regular judiciary is widely considered the most independent and impartial in the Arab world. The Supreme Judicial Council, a supervisory body of senior judges, nominates and assigns most judges. However, political and security cases are usually placed under the jurisdiction of exceptional courts that are controlled by the executive branch and deny defendants many constitutional protections. The Emergency State Security Courts, empowered to try defendants charged with violating decrees promulgated under the Emergency Law, issue verdicts that cannot be appealed and are subject to ratification by the president. Although judges in these courts are usually selected from the civilian judiciary, they are appointed directly by the president. Since 1992, civilians charged with terrorism and other security-related offenses have often been referred by the president to military courts. Since military judges are appointed by the executive branch to short, renewable, two-year terms, these tribunals lack independence. Verdicts by military courts are subject to review only by a body of military judges and the president. Moreover, evidence produced by the prosecution in cases before the military courts often consists of little more than the testimony of security officers and informers. Allegations of forced confessions by defendants are routine.

In March, 23 Egyptians and 3 British Muslims were sentenced by an emergency court to between one and five years' imprisonment on charges of membership in the illegal Hizb al-Tahrir al-Islami (Islamic Liberation Party), although their alleged activities were peaceful. Egyptian officials said in 2003 that only terrorism and other security-related offenses would henceforth be tried in emergency courts, but this pledge has not been upheld. Opposition activist Ashraf Ibrahim was arrested in April 2003 for videotaping police beatings of peaceful demonstrators and charged in the emergency courts with "weakening the prestige of the state by disseminating false information." After 11 months in detention, he was acquitted in March 2004 and released from prison.

The Emergency Law restricts many basic rights. It empowers the government to wiretap telephones, intercept mail, and search persons and places without warrants. Its provisions also allow for the arrest and prolonged detention without charge of suspects deemed a threat to national security. In November 2002, the UN Committee against Torture concluded that there is "widespread evidence of torture and ill-treatment" of suspects by the State Security Intelligence (SSI) agency. According to Human Rights Watch, 17 people died as a result of suspected torture in police or SSI custody in 2002 and 2003. At least six such deaths occurred in 2004. Local and international human rights organizations estimate that more than 10,000 people are currently detained without charge on suspicion of security or political offenses, and that several thousand who have been convicted are serving sentences on such charges. Following the October 2004 terrorist attacks in Sinai by alleged al-Qaeda operatives, according to local human rights groups, the Egyptian authorities arrested some 5,000 residents of the area, some of whom claimed to have been tortured.

Although the constitution provides for equality of the sexes, some aspects of the law and many traditional practices discriminate against women. Unmarried women under the age of 21 are not permitted to obtain passports without permission from their fathers. A Muslim female heir receives half the amount of a male heir's inheritance (Christians are not subject to provisions of Islamic law governing inheritance matters). Domestic violence is common, and there are no laws against marital rape. Job discrimination is evident even in the civil service. The law provides for equal access to education, but the adult literacy rate of women lags well behind that of men (34 and 63 percent, respectively). Female genital mutilation is practiced, despite government efforts to eradicate it. The year 2004 also witnessed the first appointment of a woman to Egypt's Constitutional Court and the first appointment of a woman as director-general of Egypt's national museum.

El Salvador

Population: 6,700,000
GNI/capita: $2,110
Life Expectancy: 70
Religious Groups: Roman Catholic (83 percent),
other (17 percent)
Ethnic Groups: Mestizo (90 percent), white (9 percent),
Amerindian (1 percent)
Capital: San Salvador

Political Rights: 2
Civil Liberties: 3
Status: Free

Ten-Year Ratings Timeline (Political Rights, Civil Liberties, Status)

1995	1996	1997	1998	1999	2000	2001	2002	2003	2004
3,3PF	3,3PF	2,3F	2,3F	2,3F	2,3F	2,3F	2,3F	2,3F	2,3F

Overview:

Elias Antonio "Tony" Saca, representing the National Republican Alliance (ARENA), won El Salvador's March 2004 presidential election, the fourth since the country's civil war ended in 1991. Meanwhile, high levels of crime, particularly gang violence, continued to plague El Salvador throughout the year.

The Republic of El Salvador was established in 1859, and more than a century of civil strife and military rule followed. The civil war that raged from 1979 to 1991, and left more than 80,000 dead and 500,000 displaced ended with the Chapultepec accords.

In the 1999 presidential election, the ARENA party's candidate, Francisco Flores Perez, was chosen with 52 percent of the votes, avoiding a second-round runoff. However, the election was marked by a low voter turnout of only 39 percent.

The two earthquakes of 2002, the collapse of coffee prices, and the slowdown of the U.S. economy, where many of the country's exports go, made governance in El Salvador a challenge a decade after the end of the civil war. High levels of crime—especially on the part of gangs (*maras*)—corruption, and government incompetence have led to popular distrust of national political leaders. More than 70 percent of public officials are perceived to be corrupt.

In 2002, two former generals, Jose Guillermo Garcia and Carlos Eugenio Vides Casanova, were on trial in Florida for torture and extrajudicial killings. After a general amnesty was granted to the armed forces in 1993, legal action for human rights abuses committed during the civil war moved to the United States. A case against the generals, accusing them of bearing ultimate responsibility for the killings of three nuns and a lay worker and for covering up the role of senior officers, had been dismissed by a U.S. appeals court. Former U.S. ambassador Robert White, who served in El Salvador at the time of the murders, testified that he long believed that there was a cover-up of the killings by both the Salvadoran and the U.S. governments.

President Flores Perez canceled the 10-year anniversary celebrations of the end of the civil war, set for March 15, 2002, and after the Frente Farabundo Marti (FMLN) threatened a boycott, and he declared the Chapultepec accords completed.

In the March 16, 2003, parliamentary elections, the FMLN captured 31 seats, the largest number, in the 84-seat Legislative Assembly. ARENA lost 2 seats, down to 27. The Partido de Conciliacion Nacional (PCN) gained 2 seats, up to 16, and moved quickly to establish an alliance with the FMLN to pass legislation.

The months before the March 2004 election were tense with threats of violence and intervention from both within the country and abroad. However, the polls were relatively peaceful and free of major irregularities. ARENA candidate Saca captured 58 percent of the vote, while Shafik Handal, of the FMLN, received 36 percent of the votes. The conclusive results validated ARENA's hold on the presidency, while also exposing the FMLN's poor choice of candidate. On June 1, Saca was sworn into office, along with the first Salvadoran woman to be elected vice president, Ana Vilma de Escobar. Saca has been mostly generous in victory, a reality that reflects the divided legislative assembly, where ARENA and the FMLN hold roughly the same number of seats.

El Salvador's greatest challenge is the ever-increasing violence from gangs who are thought to be responsible for half of each day's murders in the country. Among Saca's electoral promises was the vow to implement a "super-hard-hand plan," a more draconian policy than the "hard-hand plan," already passed by the legislature in 2003, which criminalizes membership in gangs. Also a priority is the economy, held afloat in part by the $2 billion in remittances, by now the largest source of foreign exchange, received from the more than two million Salvadorans living in the United States. ARENA is a strong backer of the regional free-trade agreement with the United States.

Political Rights and Civil Liberties:

Citizens of El Salvador can change their government democratically. The 2004 presidential and 2003 legislative elections were free and fair. The 1983 constitution and subsequent reforms provide for a president elected for a five-year term and the 84-member, unicameral National Assembly elected for three years. Four political parties are represented in the assembly, and five more are recognized.

Corruption is regarded to be a serious problem in the country's judicial system. El Salvador was ranked 51 out of 146 countries surveyed in the 2004 Transparency International Corruption Perceptions Index.

The media are privately owned. There are five daily newspapers and 16 television stations. One government and five private television stations reach most of the country. Two cable television systems cover much of the capital, and other cable companies operate in major cities. All carry major local stations and a wide range of international programming. There are approximately 20 small cable-television companies across the country, serving limited local areas. There are some 150 licensed radio stations, and broadcasts from neighboring countries are available. A national defense bill approved by the assembly in August 2002 raised concerns that reporters would have to reveal their sources. The law that was passed includes a requirement that public officials provide information related to national defense. Books, magazines, films, and plays are not censored. There is free access to the Internet.

The government abstains from any intervention in religious freedom. Although the country is overwhelmingly Roman Catholic, evangelical Protestantism has made substantial inroads, leading to friction among the faithful. Academic freedom is respected.

Freedom of assembly and association is respected. Many nongovernmental organizations (NGOs) are active and represent diverse interests. There are 133 unions, 16 federations, and 3 confederations representing labor. Public employees are not allowed to have unions; they are represented by professional and employee organizations that engage in collective bargaining.

The judicial system continues to be ineffectual and corrupt, and a climate of impunity is pervasive, especially for those politically, economically, or institutionally well connected. Poor training and a lack of sustained disciplinary action for judges, as well as continued corruption, a lack of professionalism, and a slow system of processing cases, greatly undermine public confidence in the justice system. The Office of the Human Rights Ombudsman, who is elected by the National Assembly for a three-year term, was created by the 1992 peace accords with an amendment to the constitution defining its role. The office has been accused of corruption and is hampered by staffing problems, including a 17-month period when there was no ombudsman.

The peace accords led to a significant reduction in human rights violations. Nevertheless, political expression and civil liberties are still circumscribed by sporadic political violence, repressive police measures, a mounting crime wave, and right-wing death squads, including "social cleansing" vigilante groups. Random killings, kidnappings, and other crimes, particularly in rural areas, have reinforced the country's reputation as one of the most violent in Latin America. The crime wave has also been fed by the deportation of hundreds of Salvadorans with criminal records from the United States; gang violence is pronounced.

In response, the government introduced a controversial state security offensive against the extreme violence of youth street gangs in 2003. The law, which makes membership in a gang illegal, received strong public support. More than 7,000 young adults have been imprisoned, and the already overburdened legal system has been overwhelmed. Most of the detained have been released by judges who found insufficient cause to support charges of "illicit association." While the measure raises constitutional questions over rights and due process, the Supreme Court refused to rule on the law. Meanwhile, violent crime, especially armed assaults and kidnapping, has not diminished.

El Salvador is one of the few Latin American countries to formally restrict military involvement in internal security, but the army occasionally joins the police in patrolling San Salvador and some rural districts in crackdowns on gang violence. The National Civilian Police, which incorporated some former FMLN guerrillas into its ranks, has been unable to curb the country's crime while protecting human rights. Complaints of police brutality and corruption are widespread; scores of police have been imprisoned on human rights charges. Prisons are overcrowded, and up to three-quarters of the prisoners are waiting to be charged and tried. The anti-gang police actions have further strained the judicial and prison system.

Research conducted in 2003 determined that there were three different indigenous groups in El Salvador: Nahua-Pipiles, Lencas, and Cacaoperas. The research project concluded that indigenous people have lost their relationship with the land and that they are generally considered to be peasants. Urban populations do not believe the country to have an indigenous population. Nevertheless, some small NGOs represent these peoples' interests. There are no national laws regarding indigenous rights.

Violence against women and children is widespread and common. Human trafficking for prostitution is a serious problem, and up to 40 percent of victims are children. Child labor is a major problem in the country.

Equatorial Guinea

Population: 500,000
GNI/capita: $700
Life Expectancy: 49
Religious Groups: Roman Catholic (predominant)
Ethnic Groups: Bioko [primarily Bubi, some Fernandinos], Rio Muni [primarily Fang], other
Capital: Malabo

Political Rights: 7
Civil Liberties: 6
Status: Not Free

Ten-Year Ratings Timeline (Political Rights, Civil Liberties, Status)

1995	1996	1997	1998	1999	2000	2001	2002	2003	2004
7,7NF	7,7NF	7,7NF	7,7NF	7,7NF	7,7NF	6,6NF	7,6NF	7,6NF	7,6NF

Overview:

An apparent coup attempt against President Teodoro Obiang Nguema Mbasogo involving suspected foreign mercenaries was derailed in March 2004 with the arrests of 19 men in Equatorial Guinea and 70 others in Zimbabwe. A government crackdown on foreigners ensued, and hundreds of immigrants, mostly West Africans, were deported or fled. Obiang's ruling Democratic Party and its allies won a landslide victory in parliamentary elections in April that were criticized by the opposition and foreign observers as seriously flawed.

Equatorial Guinea achieved independence in 1968 following 190 years of Spanish rule. It has since been one of the world's most tightly closed and repressive societies. Obiang seized power in 1979 by deposing and murdering his uncle, Francisco Macias Nguema. Demands from donor countries for democratic reforms prompted Obiang to proclaim a new "era of pluralism" in January 1992. Political parties were legalized and multiparty elections announced, but in practice, Obiang and his clique wield all power. Obiang won the 1996 presidential election, which was marred by official intimidation, a near total boycott by the political opposition, and very low voter turnout. In the 1999 parliamentary elections, which were tainted by intimidation and fraud, the ruling Democratic Party of Equatorial Guinea (PDGE) won 75 of 80 seats. Many opposition candidates were arrested or confined to their villages prior to the polls.

Citing irregularities, the four main opposition challengers withdrew from the December 2002 presidential election. The candidates said soldiers, police, and electoral officials were present at polling stations and were opening ballot envelopes after votes were cast. Obiang was declared the winner of his third seven-year term with 99.5 percent of the vote. Following the election, the administration of Equatorial Guinea announced the formation of a "government of national unity" that brought members of eight small parties, all considered close to the PDGE, into the cabinet.

Despite an extensive reshuffle in 2004, key cabinet positions continue to be held by presidential relatives and loyalists.

The expansion of parliament to 100 seats in 2004 did little to break the dominance of the PDGE. Parliamentary elections in April were swept by a coalition headed by the PDGE, which captured 68 of the 100 seats. The party's allies won another 30 seats. The opposition Convergence for Social Democracy, which complained of numerous irregularities and voter intimidation by the ruling party, won the remaining two seats.

The trial of 19 suspected coup plotters began in August 2004 in the capital, with a separate trial for 70 others under way in Zimbabwe, where authorities had detained a group of men in March allegedly en route to Equatorial Guinea. Amnesty International has expressed concern over the likely use of torture in extracting confessions from the defendants in Malabo, particularly in the case of a German suspect who died in custody. Many of the accused plotters, who hail from various African and European nations, have ties to the defunct mercenary firm Executive Outcomes, founded by apartheid-era South African military officers. The Equatorial Guinea government has accused Severo Moto, an opposition figure living in exile in Spain, South African financier and oil broker Eli Calil, and Mark Thatcher, son of former British Prime Minister Margaret Thatcher, of being behind the scheme to oust Obiang. Hundreds of West Africans left or were expelled from the country in late March as the government rounded up foreigners in the wake of the coup attempt, jailing many for alleged visa violations.

Equatorial Guinea is the continent's third-largest oil producer and boasts one of the highest figures for per capita gross domestic product in Africa. The expanding oil sector has led to more jobs, but the lives of most people have yet to change. U.S. oil companies have invested at least $5 billion in Equatorial Guinea since the mid-1990s. Although Obiang has declared the disposition of the country's oil revenues a "state secret," a U.S. Senate investigation found in July 2004 that at least $35 million has been siphoned from accounts in a Washington, DC, bank by Obiang, his family, and senior officials of his regime. A presidential decree issued in February ordered all civil servants and members of the armed forces to declare their assets to a national public ethics commission, but failed to specify whether the order included Obiang.

A long-running dispute with Gabon over exploration rights in the potentially oil-rich Corisco islands was temporarily resolved in 2004 with an agreement that the two countries would conduct joint exploration pending a UN-brokered mediation process.

Thanks to surging oil revenues, Equatorial Guinea currently has the world's fastest-expanding economy, and the IMF predicts further growth of 45.1 percent in 2005. However, few benefits have trickled down to the population. Equatorial Guinea ranked 109 out of 177 countries on the UN Human Development Index in 2004.

Political Rights and Civil Liberties: Equatorial Guinea's citizens are unable to change their government through peaceful, democratic means. The 1999 and 2004 parliamentary and 1996 and 2002 presidential elections have not been credible. Obiang wields broad decree-making powers and effectively bars public participation in the policy-making process. After his overwhelming electoral victory of 2002, most opposition parties joined a coalition with the ruling party, although several remain officially banned or operate in exile.

Equatorial Guinea was not ranked by Transparency International in its 2004 Corruption Perceptions Index. However, charges of corruption and human rights violations by Equatorial Guinea's government led the United States to close its embassy in Malabo in 1995, although this was reopened in 2002 as U.S. interest in the region grew.

Press freedom is constitutionally guaranteed, but the government restricts these rights in practice. Nearly all print and broadcast media are state run and tightly controlled. The 1992 press law authorizes government censorship of all publications. Mild criticism of infrastructure and public institutions is allowed, but nothing disparaging about the president or security forces is tolerated. Publications that irk the government are banned from the newsstands without explanation.

Foreign publications have become more widely available in recent years. The shortwave programs of Radio France Internationale and Radio Exterior (the international shortwave service from Spain) can be heard. A few small independent newspapers publish occasionally, but they exercise self-censorship, and all journalists must be registered. Journalists, political leaders, and association heads have complained of increasing difficulties in accessing the Internet. They charge that illegal wiretapping has increased and that the country's sole Internet service provider allegedly monitors e-mail traffic closely.

The constitution guarantees religious freedom, and government respect for freedom of individual religious practice has generally improved. About 80 percent of the population is Roman Catholic. The government does not restrict academic freedom.

Freedom of association and assembly is restricted. Authorization must be obtained for any gathering of 10 or more people for purposes the government deems political. There are no effective domestic human rights organizations in the country, and the few international nongovernmental organizations operating in Equatorial Guinea are prohibited from promoting or defending human rights. Dozens of opposition activists remain in prison.

Steps have been taken to reform the labor sector. The country's first labor union, the Small Farmers Syndicate, received legal recognition in 2000 and is independent. The government has ratified all International Labor Organization conventions. However, there are many legal steps required prior to collective bargaining.

The judiciary is not independent, and laws on search and seizure—as well as detention—are routinely ignored by security forces, which act with impunity. Unlawful arrests remain commonplace, and government security forces routinely use torture and excessive force. Civil cases rarely go to trial. A military tribunal handles cases tied to national security. Prison conditions are extremely harsh.

Monopoly political power by the president's Mongomo clan of the majority Fang ethnic group persists. Differences between the Fang and the Bubi are a major source of political tension that often has erupted into violence. Fang vigilante groups have been allowed to abuse Bubi citizens with impunity.

Constitutional and legal protections of equality for women are largely ignored. Traditional practices discriminate against women, and few women have educational opportunities or participate in the formal (business) economy or government. Violence against women is reportedly widespread.

Eritrea

Population: 4,400,000
GNI/capita: $190
Life Expectancy: 53
Religious Groups: Muslim, Coptic Christian,
Roman Catholic, Protestant
Ethnic Groups: Tigrinya (50 percent), Tigre and
Kunama (40 percent), Afar (4 percent), Saho (3 percent),
other (3 percent)
Capital: Asmara

Political Rights: 7
Civil Liberties: 6
Status: Not Free

Ten-Year Ratings Timeline (Political Rights, Civil Liberties, Status)

1995	1996	1997	1998	1999	2000	2001	2002	2003	2004
6,4PF	6,4PF	6,4PF	6,4PF	7,5NF	7,5NF	7,6NF	7,6NF	7,6NF	7,6NF

Overview:

The government of President Isaias Afwerki continued in 2004 its repressive policy of allowing no opposition or independent organizations in the political or civil sphere. A group of political dissidents and journalists imprisoned in 2001 remain in jail despite widespread international calls for their release. Tensions with neighboring Ethiopia over their disputed border continued.

In 1950, after years of Italian occupation, Eritrea was incorporated into Ethiopia. Eritrea's independence struggle began in 1962 as a nationalist and Marxist guerrilla war against the Ethiopian government of Emperor Haile Selassie. The seizure of power by a Marxist junta in Ethiopia in 1974 removed the ideological basis of the conflict, and by the time Eritrea finally defeated Ethiopia's northern armies in 1991, the Eritrean People's Liberation Front (EPLF) had discarded Marxism. Internationally recognized independence was achieved in May 1993 after a referendum supervised by the United Nations produced a landslide vote for statehood.

War with Ethiopia broke out in 1998. In May 2000, an Ethiopian military offensive succeeded in making significant territorial gains. Eritrea signed a truce with Ethiopia in June 2000, and a peace treaty was signed in December 2000. The agreement provided for a UN-led buffer force to be installed along the Eritrean side of the contested border and further negotiations to determine the final boundary line. The war had dominated the country's political and economic agenda and reflected deeper issues of nationalism and political mobilization by a government that has long used the threat of real or perceived enemies to generate popular support and unity.

In May 2001, a dissident group of 15 senior ruling-party members (the "Group of 15") publicly criticized Isaias and called for "the rule of law and for justice, through peaceful and legal ways and means." Eleven members of this group were arrested in September 2001, allegedly for treason (three members who were out of the country at the time escaped arrest and one withdrew his support of the group). The small independent media sector was also shut down, and 18 journalists were imprisoned. An increasingly unpopular policy of obligatory national service for extended and open-ended periods of time and with no conscientious objector clause has also heightened tension. Critics have called it "forced labor."

In 2004, the Eritrean government showed no sign of altering its repressive policy of allowing no opposition or independent organizations in the political or civil sphere. International criticism has been muted, perhaps because of Eritrea's support in the war against terror.

During the year, the Eritrean government claimed that Ethiopians were not respecting the border agreement, and it did not rule out the possibility of renewed conflict. In addition to the war with Ethiopia, since 1993, Eritrea has engaged in hostilities with Sudan and Yemen, and has also had strained relations with Djibouti.

Political Rights and Civil Liberties: Eritreans have never had the opportunity to choose their leaders through open elections. Created in February 1994 as a successor to the EPLF, the Popular Front for Democracy and Justice (PFDJ) maintains a dominance over the country's political and economic life that is unlikely to change in the near or medium-term future. Instead of moving toward creating a framework for a democratic political system, since the end of the war with Ethiopia, the PFDJ has taken significant steps backward. The 2001 crackdown against those calling for greater political pluralism has chilled the already tightly controlled political atmosphere.

In 1994, a 50-member Constitutional Commission was established. In 1997 a new constitution authorizing "conditional" political pluralism with provisions for a multiparty system was adopted. The constitution provides for the election of the president from among the members of the National Assembly by a vote of the majority of its members.

In 2000, the National Assembly determined that the first elections would be held in December 2001 and appointed a committee that issued draft regulations governing political parties. These draft regulations have not been enacted, and independent political parties authorized by the constitution do not exist. National elections have been postponed indefinitely. In 2004, regional assembly elections were conducted, but they were carefully orchestrated by the PFDJ and offered no real choice. Eritrea was ranked 102 out of 146 countries surveyed in the 2004 Transparency International Corruption Perceptions Index.

Government control over all broadcasting and pressures against the independent print media have seriously constrained public debate. In its September 2001 crackdown, the government banned all privately owned newspapers while claiming that a parliamentary committee would examine conditions under which they would be permitted to re-open. The newspapers were accused of contravening the 1996 Press Law, but their alleged offenses were not specified. Ten leading journalists were arrested by the police in the capital of Asmara. They had protested in writing to the minister of information concerning the arrest of members of the Group of 15 and the closure of the newspapers. Other journalists were arrested in 2002, and the independent media in Eritrea has in effect ceased to exist. Internet use remains limited, with an estimated 9,500 users in 2003 out of a population of over 4 million.

Religious persecution of minority Christian faiths has escalated in recent years, particularly against Jehovah's Witnesses (who were stripped of their basic civic rights in 1994) and evangelical and Pentecostal churches. The government does not recognize the right to conscientious objection. Members of other minority churches have been jailed and tortured or ill-treated to make them abandon their faith. Muslims have been targeted too, some held in secret incommunicado detention for years on suspicion of links with an Islamist armed opposition group operating from Sudan. Academic freedom is constrained, and high school students are required to spend their 12th-grade year at a high school based at a military camp in Sawa, in the far western part of the country, near the Ethiopian border.

The government continues to maintain a hostile attitude toward civil society. Independent nongovernmental organizations (NGOs) are not allowed, and the legitimate role of human rights defenders is not recognized. International human rights NGOs are barred from the country. The civil service, the military, the police, and other essential services have some restrictions on their freedom to form unions. In addition, groups of 20 or more persons seeking to form a union require special approval from the Ministry of Labor.

A judiciary was formed by decree in 1993 and has yet to adopt positions that are significantly at variance with government perspectives. A low level of training and resources limits the courts' efficiency. Constitutional guarantees are often ignored in cases relating to state security. The provision of speedy trials is limited by a lack of trained personnel, inadequate funding, and poor infrastructure, and the use of a special court system limits due process.

According to a 2004 report by Amnesty International, torture, arbitrary detentions, and political arrests are widespread. Religious persecution and ill-treatment of those trying to avoid military service are increasing, and torture is systematically practiced by the army. Political prisoners and members of minority churches are said to be particularly singled out. Prison conditions are poor, and prison monitors such as the International Committee of the Red Cross have been denied access to detainees. There have been reports of government and societal discrimination against the Kunama, one of nine ethnic groups, who reside primarily in the west.

Official government policy is supportive of free enterprise, and citizens generally have the freedom to choose their employment, establish private businesses, and function relatively free of government harassment. Until recently, at least, government officials have enjoyed a reputation for relative probity.

Women played important roles in the guerrilla movement, and the government has worked in favor of improving the status of women. In an effort to encourage broader participation by women in politics, the PFDJ named three women to the party's executive council and 12 women to the central committee in 1997. Women participated in the Constitutional Commission (filling almost half of the positions on the 50-person committee) and hold senior government positions, including the positions of minister of justice and minister of labor. Equal educational opportunity, equal pay for equal work, and penalties for domestic violence have been codified. However, traditional societal discrimination persists against women in the largely rural and agricultural country.

Estonia

Population: 1,300,000
GNI/capita: $4,190
Life Expectancy: 71
Religious Groups: Evangelical Lutheran, Russian
Orthodox, Estonian Orthodox, other
Ethnic Groups: Estonian (65 percent), Russian (28 percent),
other (7 percent)
Capital: Tallinn

Political Rights: 1
Civil Liberties: 1*
Status: Free

Ratings Change: Estonia's civil liberties score improved from 2 to 1 due to the effective
implementation of judicial reforms and greater economic freedom.

Ten-Year Ratings Timeline (Political Rights, Civil Liberties, Status)

1995	1996	1997	1998	1999	2000	2001	2002	2003	2004
2,2F	1,2F	1,2F	1,2F	1,2F	1,2F	1,2F	1,2F	1,2F	1,1F

Overview:

Estonia achieved two of its main foreign policy goals in 2004
when it became a member of NATO in April and joined the
European Union (EU) in May. The next month saw a low voter
turnout for the country's first European parliamentary elections, in which the ruling
coalition suffered a stern rebuke. Frequently strained relations with neighboring
Russia deteriorated throughout the year. On the domestic front, judicial reforms
enacted in 2002 continued to be implemented successfully, fortifying judicial independence and competence.

After gaining its independence from Russia in 1918, Estonia was occupied and
annexed by the U.S.S.R. during World War II. Under Soviet rule, approximately one-
tenth of Estonia's population was deported, executed, or forced to flee abroad. Subsequent Russian immigration substantially altered the country's ethnic composition, with ethnic Estonians constituting just over 61 percent of the population in
1989. Estonia regained its independence with the disintegration of the Soviet Union
in 1991.

The last few months of 2001 witnessed several dramatic political developments,
including the September victory of former Soviet Estonian leader Arnold Ruutel to
the largely ceremonial post of president. Prime Minister Mart Laar announced in late
December that he would resign in January 2002 because of growing infighting among
the national ruling coalition members, particularly after the Reform Party's break with
the same coalition partners in Tallinn's City Council. On January 8, 2002, Laar fulfilled his pledge to step down; he was replaced on January 22 by Reform Party leader
and former central bank president Siim Kallas.

In the March 2003, parliamentary elections, the Center Party and Res Publica, a
newly formed right-of-center party, each garnered 28 seats in the 101-seat parliament. Despite his party's having received fewer votes than the Center Party, Res Publica
chairman Juhan Parts outmaneuvered Center Party leader Edgar Savisaar to form a
ruling coalition with the neoliberal Reform Party and the left-of-center People's Union.

Estonian participation in the June 13, 2004, elections to the European Parliament was the third lowest in the EU at 26.8 percent. Those that did vote voiced their disapproval of the ruling coalition by giving three out of six seats (36.8 percent) to the opposition Social Democratic Party (SDP). The Reform Party was the only coalition member to win a seat (12.2 percent), with the Center Party (17.5 percent) and Pro Patria Union (10.5 percent) earning a seat each. The contest was unique in that while Estonians voted for individual candidates, seats were distributed by party on the basis of their candidates' proportion of the overall vote. Toomas Hendrik Ilves of the SDP led all candidates and will serve as the deputy chairman of the parliament's foreign affairs committee. Former prime minister Siim Kallas of the Reform Party joined the 25-member European Commission on November 1, where he is one of five vice presidents and the only one from a country recently admitted to the EU. On September 3, the government decided to rule out a popular referendum on the new EU constitution, opting instead to ratify it in parliament.

In September, the minister of economy and communication, Meelis Atonen, resigned after failing to secure cabinet support for a new service agreement for a ferry company operating between the mainland and Estonia's two largest islands. Reform Party leader Andrus Ansip replaced him.

Estonian relations with Russia deteriorated significantly in 2004, perhaps worsened by Estonia's recent membership in the EU and NATO. Moscow has continued to accuse Tallinn of explicitly discriminating against Estonia's ethnic Russian minority, increasingly through international bodies like the Organization for Security and Cooperation in Europe (OSCE) and the Council of Europe. Russia has warned against the presence of NATO bases or troops in Estonia and has repeatedly violated Estonian airspace. For its part, in March, Estonia expelled two Russia diplomats accused of spying. Following the completion of a 12-year study by a government commission in May, Estonia called for financial compensation from Russia for the damage caused by almost 50 years of Soviet occupation, and some leaders have urged the European Parliament to investigate and condemn Soviet communism. At a June conference about the Baltic Sea, the Russian prime minister refused to hold separate talks with his Estonian counterpart, signifying a recent nadir in Estonian-Russian relations.

Estonia, one of the world's most economically free countries, was ranked 4 out of the 155 countries surveyed in the Heritage Foundation's 2005 *Index of Economic Freedom*, the result of the country's successful efforts at maintaining a low inflation rate.

Political Rights and Civil Liberties: Estonians can change their government democratically. The 1992 constitution established a 101-member unicameral legislature (Riigikogu) elected for four-year terms, with a prime minister serving as head of government and a president in the largely ceremonial role of head of state. After the first president was chosen by popular vote in 1992, subsequent presidential elections reverted to parliamentary ballot. However, the current governing parties have agreed to endorse direct presidential elections, with a referendum on the necessary constitutional changes to be held along with local elections in October 2005. The March 2003 parliamentary elections were free and fair and were conducted in accordance with the comprehensive dictates of the recently implemented Riigikogu Election Act.

While progress has been made to combat corruption, it is still a concern. Prime Minister Juhan Parts has made his anticorruption election platform a priority of his administration. Estonia was ranked 31 out of 146 countries surveyed in Transparency International's 2004 Corruption Perceptions Index. Estonia is among the world's leaders in e-government and features an impressively transparent system in which government decisions are almost instantly made available on the Internet, where Estonians may comment and exchange views.

The government respects freedom of speech and the press. There are three national television stations, including two in private hands, which broadcast both Estonian- and Russian-language programs. Dozens of independent newspapers and radio stations offer diverse viewpoints, and Estonia is one of the most Internet-friendly countries in the world. According to the U.S. State Department, the Law on Language prohibits the use of any foreign language on public signs, advertisements, and notices, including election posters.

Religious freedom is respected in law and practice in this predominantly Lutheran country. While Estonia has very few restrictions on academic freedom, both officials in Moscow and ethnic Russians living in Estonia have opposed legislation that mandates the use of Estonian as the language of instruction in what are currently Russian-language schools by 2007.

The constitution guarantees freedom of assembly, and the government respects this provision in practice. Political parties are allowed to organize freely, although only citizens may become members. Workers have the right to organize freely, to strike, and to bargain collectively. In December 2003, Estonia saw its first major strike since independence, where some 20,000 workers participated in a one-day strike coordinated by the Organization of Employee Unions and aimed at greater benefits for teachers and cultural workers.

The judiciary is independent and generally free from governmental interference. A courts act adopted in June 2002 intended to restrict executive influence over the judiciary continued to be successfully implemented, and a new criminal procedure code adopted in February 2003 took effect in the summer of 2004. As a result, the arbitrary, legally weak court decisions that were a feature of post-Soviet Estonia have become increasingly rare, according to the European Bank for Reconstruction and Development, the Heritage Foundation, and the U.S. and Canadian governments. There have been reports that some police officers physically or verbally abuse suspects. Despite ongoing improvements in the country's prison system, overcrowding, a lack of financial resources, and inadequately trained staff remain problems.

Of Estonia's population of 1.4 million, more than 1 million are Estonian citizens, of which some 120,000 have been naturalized since 1992. Approximately 170,000 people are noncitizens, the majority of whom are ethnic Russians. Estonia's Citizenship Law has been criticized for effectively disenfranchising many Russian speakers through an excessively difficult naturalization process. Many ethnic Russians arrived in Estonia during the Soviet era and are now regarded as immigrants who must apply for citizenship, a process that requires Estonian language capability, five years' residency, and knowledge of the constitution and Citizenship Law. Although noncitizens may not participate in national elections, they can vote (but not serve as candidates) in local elections. The OSCE and other international organizations have found Estonia's citizenship laws to be satisfactory. In December 2003, the government passed legislation that allowed for reimbursement of 50 percent of the costs related to language and citizenship examinations for successful examinees; the EU reimburses the other 50 percent.

In May 2001, parliament adopted legislation setting out specific requirements of Estonian-language proficiency for private-sector employees, such as pilots, rescue workers, and teachers; the law built upon a previous amendment to the language law passed in June 2000 requiring that Estonian be used in areas of the private sector deemed to be in the public interest, such as health or safety. Despite allegations of discrimination against ethnic Russians in the workplace, education, housing, and social services, a July OSCE resolution on national minorities was not critical of Estonia. That same month, the Dutch ambassador to Russia, Tiddo Hofstee, affirmed Estonia's compliance with the Copenhagen criteria on the protection of ethnic minorities.

Although women enjoy the same legal rights as men, they continue to be underrepresented in senior-level business positions and in the government. Parliament has yet to pass a gender-equality act proposed in 2002. A study conducted in October by the Praxis Center for Policy Studies, an independent Estonian think tank, revealed that while the gender salary gap was decreasing, Estonian women earn an average of 73 percent of men's salaries. Trafficking in people is a problem, with many Estonian and Russian women trafficked from Estonia to Nordic countries and Western Europe.

Ethiopia

Population: 72,400,000   **Political Rights:** 5
GNI/capita: $100   **Civil Liberties:** 5
Life Expectancy: 46   **Status:** Partly Free
Religious Groups: Muslim (45-50 percent), Ethiopian Orthodox (35-40 percent), animist (12 percent), other
Ethnic Groups: Oromo (40 percent), Amhara and Tigrean (32 percent), Sidamo (9 percent), other (19 percent)
Capital: Addis Ababa

Ten-Year Ratings Timeline (Political Rights, Civil Liberties, Status)

1995	1996	1997	1998	1999	2000	2001	2002	2003	2004
4,5PF	4,5PF	4,5PF	4,4PF	5,5PF	5,5PF	5,5PF	5,5PF	5,5PF	5,5PF

Overview:

In 2004, increasing focus was paid to national elections due to take place in Ethiopia during the first half of 2005. The dominance of the ruling Ethiopian People's Revolutionary Democratic Front (EPRDF), regional strife, internal unrest in parts of the country, and a threat of boycott by opposition parties characterized the preelection environment.

On the international front, tension continued with Eritrea in a bloody border dispute that lasted from 1998 until 2000. Draft press and nongovernmental organization (NGO) laws pending during the year were criticized by press freedom and civil society groups as threats to civil liberties.

One of the few African countries never to have been colonized, Ethiopia saw the end of a long tradition of imperial rule in 1974, when Emperor Haile Selassie was overthrown in a Marxist military coup. Colonel Mengistu Haile Mariam subsequently became the leader of a brutal dictatorship that was overthrown by a coalition of guerrilla groups in 1991. These groups were spearheaded by the EPRDF, itself an alliance of five parties.

The EPRDF government instituted a transition period that resulted in the establishment of formal democratic institutions. As expected, the EPRDF gained a landslide victory against a weak and divided opposition in the most recent national elections, in May 2000, after which parliament reelected Prime Minister Meles Zenawi to another five-year term. Opposition parties and some observers criticized the government's conduct of the vote, stating that the polls were subject to government interference, that media coverage was significantly tilted in the EPRDF's favor, and that opposition supporters were subjected to harassment and detention. However, the opposition was able to engage in some criticism of the government in the media during the official election campaign, and a series of unprecedented public debates were broadcast over state-run radio and television during the electoral campaign.

A dispute over borders with neighboring Eritrea resulted in open warfare from 1998 until 2000. In the wake of the bloody conflict, the Eritrea-Ethiopia Boundary Commission (EEBC), a mediating body established to draw up a new border, announced its decision, which included assigning the town of Badme to Eritrea in April 2002. The boundary commission's decisions were supposed to be binding on both sides, but Ethiopia formally rejected the EEBC decision. The result is an indefinite postponement of the physical demarcation of the new border.

Considerable focus in 2004 was centered on upcoming national elections in 2005. Critics of the government, who argued that the playing field was seriously imbalanced in favor of the ruling coalition, cited draft press and NGO laws that raised concerns that they could be used by the government to further inhibit the NGO sector. A leading NGO in restive Oromia province was closed by the government. In addition, guerrilla activity continued by the Oromo Liberation Front and other groups amid intimidation of regime opponents, especially in the southern Oromo-dominated region.

Political Rights and Civil Liberties: Ethiopians cannot change their government democratically. The EPRDF has been in power since 1991, although six other major parties and numerous smaller ones participate in the political system. The country's legislature is bicameral, and executive power is vested in a prime minister, who is selected by the House of People's Representatives. The 1995 constitution has a number of unique features, including decentralization based on ethnicity and the right to secession. The government has devolved some power to regional and local governments. However, the reality differs from what is constitutionally mandated, in practice seriously limiting the right of the people to select their government. In 2003, the central government acquired additional powers to intervene in states' affairs in situations where public security was deemed to be at risk.

Ethiopia is preparing for its third national election since 1991. Previous elections have included polling for local officials (1992), a Constituent Assembly (1994), and regional and national legislatures (1995 and 2000). Previous elections resulted in allegations from opposition parties and civil society that serious irregularities had existed, including unequal access to media, biased election officials, lack of transparent procedures, a flawed election law, and a partisan National Electoral Board. The ruling EPRDF proclaimed the 2000 elections "free and fair" and used its overwhelming victory to consolidate power. Regional elections in 2001 were marred by killings, candidate harassment, voter intimidation, and allegations of ballot box stuffing.

There are currently more than 60 legally recognized political parties active in Ethiopia, although the political scene continues to be dominated by the EPRDF. While opposition parties claim that their ability to function is seriously impeded by government harassment, observers note that these parties are often reluctant to take part in the political process. Some parties have supported, either directly or indirectly, armed resistance to the government.

Ethiopia was ranked 114 out of 146 countries surveyed in Transparency International's 2004 Corruption Perceptions Index. The government has taken a number of initiatives to limit corruption, although it has also been accused of participating in corrupt practices.

The press is dominated by the state-owned broadcast media and government-oriented newspapers. Opposition and civic organizations criticize slanted news coverage. Prime Minister Meles Zenawi has officially pledged that opposition parties will receive fair coverage during the upcoming elections in 2005, but it is not yet clear how this would be ensured. A number of privately owned newspapers exist, but they struggle to remain financially viable and also face intermittent government harassment.

A draft press law has been widely criticized by press freedom groups as further chilling the press environment. Issues of concern include restrictions on who may practice journalism; government-controlled licensing and registration systems; harsh sanctions for violations of the law, including up to five years' imprisonment; excessively broad exceptions to the right to access information held by public authorities; and the establishment of a government-controlled press council with powers to engage in prior censorship.

The government announced in 1999 that private FM radio stations with a range of approximately 150 kilometers around Addis Ababa would be permitted, but to date no licenses have been issued. Under the draft press law, cross ownership of newspapers and FM stations would not be permitted. This provision has drawn criticism from the independent media, which argue that, in practical terms, the ruling party currently owns both. There is extremely limited Internet usage, mainly in the major urban areas.

Constitutionally mandated religious freedom is generally respected, although religious tensions have risen in recent years. The Ethiopian Coptic Church is influential, particularly in the North. In the South, there is a large Muslim community, made up mainly of Arabs, Somalis, and Oromos.

Academic freedom is restricted. In recent years, students have gone on strike to protest the government's repressive policies and to seek an end to police brutality.

These strikes have resulted in scores of deaths and injuries and hundreds of arrests, including arrests of prominent human rights leaders. Student grievances include perceived government repression of the Oromo ethnic group.

Freedom of association is limited, although a large and increasing number of NGOs are active. However, NGOs generally continue to be reluctant to energetically discuss issues and advocate policies that may bring them into conflict with the government. A draft NGO law, which includes a provision permitting the government to arbitrarily close NGOs at any time, is opposed by much of the civil society sector. In 2004, some NGOs were harassed or shut down by the government.

The freedom of trade unions to bargain and strike has not yet been fully tested. The law governing trade unions states that a trade organization may not act in an overtly political manner. Some union leaders have been removed from their elected office or forced to leave the country. All unions must be registered, and the government retains the authority to cancel union registration.

The judiciary is officially independent, although there are no significant examples of decisions at variance with government policy. The competencies of police, judicial and administrative systems at the local level are highly uneven. Some progress has been made in reducing a significant backlog of court cases.

There are more than 80 ethnic groups in Ethiopia, of which the Oromo is the largest. There were continued incidents of ethnic conflict during 2004. Security forces were involved in some ethnic clashes, including with the Oromo, and, most prominently, in disturbances in the Gambella Region that began in December 2003.

Women traditionally have few land or property rights and, especially in rural areas, few opportunities for employment beyond agricultural labor. Violence against women and social discrimination are reportedly common, despite legal protections.

Fiji

Population: 800,000
GNI/capita: $2,360
Life Expectancy: 67
Religious Groups: Christian (52 percent), Hindu (38 percent), Muslim (8 percent), other (2 percent)
Ethnic Groups: Fijian [Melanesian-Polynesian] (51 percent), Indian (44 percent), other (5 percent)
Capital: Suva

Political Rights: 4
Civil Liberties: 3
Status: Partly Free

Ten-Year Ratings Timeline (Political Rights, Civil Liberties, Status)

1995	1996	1997	1998	1999	2000	2001	2002	2003	2004
4,3PF	4,3PF	4,3PF	4,3PF	2,3F	6,3PF	4,3PF	4,3PF	4,3PF	4,3PF

Overview:
A lengthy stalemate between Fiji's ruling and opposition parties over the formation of a multiparty cabinet was finally resolved in late 2004. However, ethnic tensions between indigenous Fijians and Indo-Fijians continued throughout the year. On the international front, the Pacific Transnational Crime Center opened in Suva in June

to manage, coordinate, and support law enforcement intelligence among Pacific Island countries.

After colonizing Fiji in 1874, the British began bringing Indian laborers to work on sugar plantations. Fiji gained full independence in 1970, by which time Indians comprised nearly half of the total population. The Indo-Fijians became active participants in all spheres of Fijian society, and the Indo-Fijian Alliance Party ruled until 1987 when Sitiveni Rabuka, a senior army officer of Fijian extract, overthrew the government.

Intense ethnic rivalry between the indigenous Fijians and Indo-Fijians has become the main source of political tension in the country. In a May 2000 coup that overthrew an elected government, George Speight, an indigenous Fijian, held Prime Minister Mahendra Chaudhry, an Indo-Fijian, and his cabinet hostage in the parliament house. President Ratu Mara was ousted from office. Speight and his followers surrendered after a 56-day standoff. After defusing the crisis, the military installed Laisenia Qarase, a banker and indigenous Fijian, to lead an interim government and arrested Speight and more than 300 of his supporters. Following the coup, ethnic Fijians engaged in a campaign of violence to destroy Indo-Fijian homes and businesses. In 2002, Speight pleaded guilty to treason and was given the mandatory death sentence, which was later commuted to life imprisonment.

In the August-September 2001 elections to the House of Representatives, Prime Minister Qarase's Duavata ni Lewenivanua (SDL) party captured the largest number of seats, 32, followed by former Prime Minister Chaudhry's Fiji Labour Party (FLP), with 27. Qarase formed a new government without the FLP, despite a constitutional requirement that any party receiving more than 10 percent of seats be offered cabinet posts. After Qarase defied the court's orders, the Supreme Court ruled in July 2003 that the prime minister must offer cabinet seats to the FLP. Subsequent negotiations between Qarase and Chaudhry broke down over the exact number of FLP parliamentarians to be admitted into Qarase's cabinet. On November 26, 2004, Qarase and Chaudhry finally ended the lengthy stalemate by agreeing not to pursue the dispute any further.

Meanwhile, the recovery from the effects of the coup has been slow and arduous. The opposition has criticized as too lenient the sentences for others implicated in the coup. So far, 92 soldiers have gone to prison, and another 42 have been remanded for their alleged involvement. Those brought to trial included Vice President Ratu Jope Seniloli, who was sentenced to four years in jail in August 2004 for his involvement in the coup.

In January 2004, President Ratu Josefa Iloilo extended the appointment of Commodore Voreqe (Frank) Bainimarama as army commander for another term. Despite strong public support for Bainimarama's reappointment—people feared the possibility of another military coup without his firm leadership of the military—differences between Bainimarama and some senior politicians over prosecution of soldiers involved in the May 2000 coup was a major political issue throughout the year. Following his contract renewal, Bainimarama replaced several of his top aides and senior officers.

In July 2004, Qarase named Ratu Rakavo Lalabalavu to succeed Ratu Epeli Ganilau as a member of the Great Council of Chiefs, a traditional indigenous Fijian body. Ratu Epeli, who was the council's chair, argued that his term does not expire until 2006 and that his removal was due to his strong criticism of government policies. The Great Council appointed Ratu Ovini Bokini as chair for a one-year term to allow time for resolution of the dispute between Ratu Epeli and the government.

The Ministry of Education introduced a controversial plan in early 2004 to provide a free high school education only to indigenous Fijian students. Qarase distanced himself from the proposal, but welcomed the idea of a grand indigenous Fijian coalition proposed by former coup leader Rabuka. On the Indo-Fijian side, Chaudhry, the leader of the opposition Labour Party, chose not to attend a reconciliation ceremony, in which traditional chiefs were to offer an apology on behalf of the indigenous Fijians for damage done to Indo-Fijian homes and businesses in the aftermath of the May 2000 coup.

Australia is a major sponsor of the Pacific Transnational Crime Center, an effort to improve Fiji's police, justice, and prison systems over the next several years, which opened in June. Canberra hopes restoring the rule of law will help revive the Fijian economy and curb money laundering, drug trafficking, arms smuggling, and terrorist activities in and around the country.

Political Rights and Civil Liberties:

Fiji returned to elected civilian rule in 2001. The bicameral parliament consists of the 32-seat Senate and the 71-seat House of Representatives. In the House, 25 seats are open to all races and ethnicities, 23 are reserved for Fijians, 19 for Indo-Fijians, 3 for other ethnic groups (mainly citizens of Caucasian and East Asian extraction), and 1 for voters on Rotuma Island. A new constitution introduced in 1997 ended the guarantee of parliamentary majority by indigenous Fijians but continued to give them many political advantages. For example, indigenous Fijians hold more reserved seats than do Indo-Fijians in the House of Representatives.

The constitution empowers the Great Council of Chiefs, a traditional indigenous Fijian body, to name the largely ceremonial president, who in turn approves the nominations of the Senate. Successive governments have used this provision to place indigenous Fijians and Rotumans in at least half of all public-sector jobs at all levels, including the most senior positions. In 2003, the Great Council of Chiefs tried to expand its powers into the legislative domain.

Official corruption and abuses are widespread. A series of financial scandals rocked the Fijian economy and continue to hinder its economic recovery following the May 2000 coup. Past anticorruption efforts have not produced significant improvement. In 2004, the government endorsed measures that could lead to the creation of an anticorruption agency, but critics see a lack of resources and political will to bring about real changes.

The government exercises considerable authority in censoring the media and restricting freedom of speech. Politicians frequently threaten journalists for reporting "negative" stories about the country. The Television Act grants the government powers to influence programming content. The Press Correction Act authorizes officials to arrest anyone who publishes "malicious" material and to order a publication to print a "correcting statement" to an allegedly false or distorted article. A proposed Fiji Media Bill, intended to regulate the content and conduct of the media, is the latest addition to these controls. The bill has received widespread public opposition. If adopted, a government media company will replace the current self-regulating body. The government justified the need for the Fiji Media Bill on the grounds of alleged inaccurate reporting by some media outlets.

The government has a dominant place in the local media through its ownership of Fiji Television, which until 2004 held a monopoly license. The government ended the monopoly in 2004, but granted the station tax exemption. Community Television Fiji, a noncommercial and nondenominational group, produces and broadcasts educational and informational programs in English, Fijian, and Hindustani. The government also owns stake in several newspapers, and fully acquired the *Daily Post* in October 2003. The government-owned Fiji Broadcasting Corporation operates four radio stations and broadcasts in English, Fijian, and Hindustani. There are no government controls on the Internet. Access is primarily limited by cost and connectivity constraints outside the capital.

The constitution provides for freedom of religion. Religious affiliation runs largely along ethnic lines, with indigenous Fijians being Christians and Indo-Fijians being mostly Hindus. The number of attacks on Hindu and Muslim places of worship has increased in recent years. All religious organizations must register under the Registration of the Religions Act. In 2004, the government announced a review of this law—the first time since it came into effect in 1881—in response to expressions of concern by traditional chiefs that more than 1,214 different religious bodies are now registered.

Academic freedom is generally respected. Fiji, as host to the University of South Pacific, is a center for higher education for the South Pacific region.

Freedom of assembly is guaranteed in the Bill of Rights of the 1997 constitution. However, civic groups must file petitions for proposed meetings, a requirement since 2000, and approval is granted on a case-by-case basis. In particular, civil rights groups criticize the Emergency Powers Act of 1998, a security law that restricts civil liberties during a state of emergency, as being too expansive. The law allows parliament to censor the press, ban public meetings, authorize searches without warrants, and seize private property. Workers can organize, and several trade unions exist but they face considerable restrictions in their activities. In September, the police removed striking workers at a teacher's college seeking back pay from their employer.

The judiciary is independent, and trials are generally free and fair. Many politicians and soldiers have been found guilty of treason or other crimes committed during and after the coup in 2000. However, the courts are severely backlogged due to a lack of funds, and suspects are frequently held for long periods before trials. Inadequate funding for law enforcement also contributes to poor prison conditions and abuse and corruption among law enforcement officers, who are poorly trained. In October, poor prison conditions were grounds for a high court release of two robbery suspects.

Political, economic, and social debates are frequently divided along ethnic lines, and race-based discrimination is pervasive. The main rivalry is between the indigenous Fijians, who dominate government and the armed forces, and the Indo-Fijians, who control much of the economy. Affirmative action programs for indigenous Fijians in education and training, housing and land, and employment are not open to other ethnic groups. More than 120,000 Indo-Fijians have left in recent years as anti–Indo-Fijian sentiments have grown and crimes targeting Indo-Fijian homes and businesses have increased. The large number of illegal Chinese immigrants and a growing Chinese business community that is estimated to control 5 percent of the economy, while making up less than 1 percent of the population, have become a source of widening anti-Chinese sentiments among indigenous Fijians.

Discrimination and violence against women are widespread. The number of rape, child abuse, and incest cases continues to rise. An amendment to the Penal Code in 2003 raised the minimum sentence for rape from 7 to 10 years, and incest is punishable by a maximum of 20 years. Women groups have expressed concern that many offenders use traditional reconciliation mechanisms to avoid felony charges.

Finland

Population: 5,200,000
GNI/capita: $23,890
Life Expectancy: 79
Political Rights: 1
Civil Liberties: 1
Status: Free
Religious Groups: Evangelical Lutheran (89 percent),
Russian Orthodox (1 percent), other (10 percent)
Ethnic Groups: Finnish (93 percent), Swedish (6 percent),
other, [including Lapp (Saami)] (1 percent)
Capital: Helsinki

Ten-Year Ratings Timeline (Political Rights, Civil Liberties, Status)

1995	1996	1997	1998	1999	2000	2001	2002	2003	2004
1,1F	1,1F	1,1F	1,1F	1,1F	1,1F	1,1F	1,1F	1,1F	1,1F

Overview:

In March 2004, former prime minister Anneli Jaatteenmaki, who had resigned amid political scandal just two months after Finland's March 2003 general elections, was acquitted of charges of inciting or assisting in the breach of official secrets. Her successor, Matti Vahhanen, ruled out the possibility of a referendum of the proposed European Union (EU) constitution in August, as the treaty is uncontroversial in Finland.

Finland was ruled by Sweden until the early eighteenth century and then became a Grand Duchy of Russia until its independence in 1917. The country is traditionally neutral, but its army has enjoyed broad popular support ever since it fended off a Russian invasion during World War II. Finland joined the EU in 1995 after its friendship treaty with the Soviet Union became void. It has been an enthusiastic member state and is the only Nordic country to have adopted the euro.

In the 2000 presidential election, Tarja Halonen of the Social Democratic Party (SDP) was chosen as the country's first woman president. She defeated four other female candidates—from a total field of seven—from across the political spectrum to serve a six-year term.

The Center Party came to power after winning 55 seats in the parliamentary elections held on March 16, 2003. The second-largest party, the SDP, had led the ruling coalition since 1995. It remains part of the new ruling coalition, which also includes the Center Party and the Swedish People's Party (representing the Swedish-language minority). Jaatteenmaki replaced the SDP's Paavo Lipponen as prime minister, becoming the first woman to hold the post. However, just two months after she was chosen, Jaatteenmaki stepped down when it was alleged that she had leaked information from classified foreign policy documents and then lied about having done so. Jaatteenmaki had used evidence from the documents, which included details of Lipponen's confidential discussions with U.S. president George W. Bush, in her public attacks against Lipponen's pro-U.S. stance on the war in Iraq. After Jaatteenmaki's resignation just two months after the election, Vanhanen, of the Center Party, succeeded her.

A Helinski court unanimously acquitted Jaatteenmaki of breaching official secrets in March 2004. However, Martti Manninen, a presidential aide who had given her the documents, was found guilty of violating the Official Secrets Act and fined 3,600 euros. Jaatteenmaki subsequently drew the most votes in the Finnish elections for the European Parliament.

Finland emerged as a leader of the smaller states within the EU during the 2003 drafting of the EU constitution. Unlike in other EU member states, the proposed constitution is uncontroversial in Finland, and Prime Minister Vanhanen ruled out a possible referendum on the treaty in August 2004. Finns continued to debate abandoning their traditional neutrality and seeking membership in NATO, an issue of particular relevance given the recent inclusions of the Baltic States in the alliance. Finnish citizens vote in European Parliament elections. In the June 13 poll, 41.1 percent of voters turned out, and the conservative National Coalition Party led all parties by garnering 23.7 percent of the vote (4 seats). The Center Party won 23.3 percent (4 seats); the SDP, 21.3 percent (3 seats); the Green League, 10.4 percent (1 seat); the Left Wing Alliance, 9.1 percent (1 seat); and the Swedish People's Party, 5.7 percent (1 seat).

Because of its combination of traditional and modern industries, the World Economic Forum ranked Finland the most competitive economy in the world in 2004. In addition to timber and metals industries, the country has a strong telecommunications sector, and the Finnish firm Nokia is the top mobile-phone maker worldwide. Still, unemployment is above the average for the EU.

Political Rights and Civil Liberties: Citizens of Finland can change their government democratically. The prime minister in Finland has primary responsibility for running the government. Representatives in the 200-seat unicameral parliament, called the Eduskunta, are elected to four-year terms. The Aland Islands—an autonomous region that is located off the southwestern coast of Finland and whose inhabitants speak Swedish—have their own 29-seat parliament and have one seat in the national legislature. The indigenous Saami of northern Finland also have their own parliament.

Finland has been rated the least-corrupt country in the world in Transparency International's Corruption Perceptions Index since 2000. However, in September, the chief of the country's Security Police, Seppo Nevala, was suspended from office amid allegations of illegal procurement of telecommunications log data. Later that month, Finland sent a team of specialists to Costa Rica to investigate an embezzlement scandal involving the sale of medical equipment from Instrumentarium, a Finnish company, to the Costa Rican health authorities. The allegedly corrupt deal was financed by a $32 million loan from the Finnish bank Sampo, a loan guaranteed and subsidized by the Finnish government.

Finland has a large variety of newspapers and magazines. Newspapers are published privately owned but publicly subsidized, and many are controlled by or support a particular political party. Finnish law gives every citizen the right to publish and guarantees the right of reply. In February, the Eduskunta substantially liberalized a controversial media law that placed burdensome restrictions on Internet publishers and service providers. As a result, Internet traffic logging is no longer required, and online discussion groups are beyond the scope of the law. However, Web publications must name a responsible editor in chief and archive published materials for at least twenty-one days.

Finns enjoy freedom of religion. Both the predominant Lutheran Church and the smaller Orthodox Church are financed through a special tax, from which citizens may exempt themselves. Other religious groups are eligible for tax relief if they register and are recognized by the government. Religious education is part of the curriculum in all public schools, but students may opt out of these classes in favor of more general education in religion and philosophy. The government respects academic freedom.

Freedom of association and assembly is respected in law and in practice. Workers have the right to organize, bargain collectively, and strike. More than 70 percent of workers belong to a trade union.

The constitution provides for an independent judiciary, which consists of the Supreme Court, the supreme administrative court, and the lower courts. The president appoints Supreme Court judges, who in turn appoint the lower court judges. The Ministry of Interior controls police and Frontier Guard forces. While ethnic minorities and asylum seekers report occasional police discrimination, there were no reports of human rights abuses, according to the U.S. State Department.

The rights of ethnic and religious minorities are protected in Finland. Since 1991, the indigenous Saami, who make up less than 1 percent of the population, have been heard in the Eduskunta on relevant matters. The constitution guarantees the Saami cultural autonomy and the right to their traditional means of livelihood, which include fishing and reindeer herding. Their language and culture are also protected through financial support. However, representatives of the community have complained that they cannot exercise these rights in practice and that they do not have the right to self-determination in land use.

While Roma (Gypsies) also make up a very small percentage of the population, they are more widely disadvantaged and marginalized. According to the U.S. State Department, a recent academic study found that nearly one-third of surveyed immigrants (primarily Arabs, Kosovar Albanians, Somalis, Vietnamese, Russians, Estonians, and Ingrians) reported experiencing racism in the previous 12 months. The Ministry of Justice has engaged in an action plan for combating racism.

The government, under pressure from international human rights bodies, has commissioned a prominent historian to advise whether a study reevaluating Finnish collaboration with Nazi Germany during World War II is warranted.

Women enjoy a high degree of equality with men. In 1906, Finland became the first country in Europe to grant women the vote and the first in the world to allow women to become electoral candidates. In the current parliament, 38 percent of the delegates and 8 of 18 government ministers are women. Tarja Halonen was the first woman to be elected president in Finland. However, women continue to make 10 percent less than men of the same age, education, and profession, and they are generally employed in lower-paid occupations.

Trafficking in women and girls for prostitution is a problem in Finland, and the government has taken significant steps to address it. In September, a conference on human trafficking, held in Helsinki and sponsored by the Organization for Security and Cooperation in Europe, called on member countries to do more to stop the smuggling and exploitation of people. Finland is both a destination and a transit country for trafficked people.

France

Population: 60,000,000 **Political Rights:** 1
GNI/capita: $22,240 **Civil Liberties:** 1
Life Expectancy: 79 **Status:** Free
Religious Groups: Roman Catholic (83-88 percent),
Protestant (2 percent), Muslim (5-10 percent),
Jewish (1 percent)
Ethnic Groups: Celtic and Latin with Teutonic, Slavic,
North African, Indochinese, Basque minorities
Capital: Paris

Ten-Year Ratings Timeline (Political Rights, Civil Liberties, Status)

1995	1996	1997	1998	1999	2000	2001	2002	2003	2004
1,2F	1,2F	1,2F	1,2F	1,2F	1,2F	1,2F	1,1F	1,1F	1,1F

Overview:

In 2004, France pushed for the creation of a strongly "federalist"—or centralized—constitution for the European Union (EU), in which it has long been a key member. However, these views were largely thwarted in the draft constitution. Domestically, difficult reforms cost the center-right ruling party in both regional and EU polls, despite an economy that gathered strength over the course of the year.

After the French Revolution of 1789, democratic development was uneven. Republics alternated with Bonapartist and Bourbon monarchies until 1871, with the creation of the Third Republic. Invaded and defeated by Germany in World War II, France was split into an occupied northern part and the collaborationist Vichy regime in the South. After the war, democracy was restored and Charles de Gaulle, Free France's wartime leader, became president with the creation of the presidential system of the Fifth Republic, which stands today.

President Jacques Chirac was first elected in 1995. In the first round of the May 2002 presidential election, it was expected that he and Lionel Jospin, the prime minister and head of the rival Socialist Party, would receive the most votes and move to the second round. However, Jean-Marie Le Pen, the head of the far-right, xenophobic National Front, stunned France and the world by receiving more votes than Jospin. Chirac defeated Le Pen overwhelmingly in the second round, and in subsequent June parliamentary elections, the newly created Union for a Presidential Majority (UMP) won a comfortable majority of seats in parliament for Chirac.

In late 2002, France supported UN Security Council Resolution 1441, which threatened "serious consequences" against Iraq if it did not comply with weapons inspectors. However, France clearly never supported an early war and fought to prolong inspections. When the United States sought a second resolution explicitly declaring Iraq in breach of its obligations and paving the way to war, France stated that it would veto any such resolution. Along with the opposition of Russia, another permanent veto-holder on the Security Council, France effectively blocked UN authorization for the war in early 2003, in a move that severely strained French relations with the United States but which bolstered Chirac's popularity at home.

Since the war, Chirac has sought to strengthen the EU as a counterweight to American power, including proposing in early 2003 an EU-only military planning cell with Belgium, Germany, and Luxembourg. In negotiations during 2003 and 2004, France also sought to include a strong "common foreign and security policy" in the EU's new draft constitution. However, in the final draft document, EU foreign policy will be subject to a veto by each EU member. Ten countries joined the EU on May 1, which brought the membership to 25, and made it unlikely that France will easily be able to rally Europe around any controversial foreign policy, including any that is hostile to the United States.

With the economy fairly weak after the 2002 polls, the government, led by Prime Minister Jean-Pierre Raffarin, had begun a bold series of reforms aimed at trimming pensions, loosening labor-market restrictions, and shaking up health care. These moves quickly disillusioned the voting public, and Chirac and his party suffered in elections in 2004. In March, the UMP was humiliated at regional elections, losing 20 of 21 mainland regions. This was followed in June with a drubbing at the European Parliament elections. Like most ruling parties across the EU, the UMP did badly, winning just 16 percent of the vote; the opposition Socialist Party took 29 percent. Unexpectedly, Raffarin survived in his post as prime minister.

In 2004, the attention of voters was also on the position of Nicolas Sarkozy. Long a rival to Chirac in the UMP, he had become highly popular in his crime-fighting role as interior minister, and had even maintained this popularity through a stint as finance minister, a difficult job given that France's deficits have exceeded EU limits for several years. He is known to have his eyes on the presidency, and his way seemed to be cleared when Chirac's own protégé, Alain Juppe, was convicted of corruption in January. In the fall, Sarkozy agreed with Chirac that he would quit the government; in exchange, Chirac did not fight Sarkozy's successful bid to take over the UMP, making him the obvious center-right candidate for the 2007 presidential election. This year's strengthening economic growth may, correctly or not, be attributed by voters to Sarkozy's work as finance minister and boost his prospects.

Political Rights and Civil Liberties:

French citizens can change their government democratically. The president is elected for a five-year term (reduced from seven years as of the 2002 election). The key house of parliament, the lower National Assembly, is also elected to a five-year term. The prime minister must be able to command a majority in parliament. For most of the Fifth Republic's history, the president and prime minister have been of the same party; as a consequence, the president was the most powerful figure in the country. However, there have been several periods, like that which preceded the 2002 elections, in which the president and prime minister are of rival parties. Under these circumstances, the prime minister has the dominant role in domestic affairs, while the president retains control over the armed forces and largely guides foreign policy.

Parties organize and compete on a free and fair basis. Political parties with significant support range from the largely unreformed French Communist Party on the left to the anti-immigrant and anti-EU National Front on the right. France remains a relatively unitary state, with some administrative powers devolved to regions and smaller prefectures, but with key decisions being made in Paris. The issue of Corsica continues to fester. In December 2001, the government devolved some legislative autonomy to the island and allowed teaching in the Corsican language in public schools. However, voters on the island, which hosts a sometimes violent separatist movement, rejected a government proposal for devolution of more power to local Corsican institutions in June 2003.

President Jacques Chirac has used his office to head off allegations of corruption stemming from his time as mayor of Paris, claiming immunity as head of state to prevent prosecutions so long as he remains president. However, his protégé, Alain Juppe, was convicted in January of allowing UMP party workers to be paid out of Paris's municipal treasury when Juppe was the city's treasurer and Chirac was its mayor. Members of the French elite, trained in a small number of prestigious schools, often move between politics and business, increasing opportunities for corruption. France was ranked 22 out of 146 countries surveyed in Transparency International's 2004 Corruption Perceptions Index.

The French media operate largely freely and represent a wide range of political opinion. An 1881 law forbids "offending" various personages, including the president and foreign heads of state, but the press remains lively and critical. However, they are not entirely free of harassment. Journalists covering events involving the National Front have been attacked by supporters of the party. Seven reporters had their phones tapped between 2000 and 2002 as part of a government investigation into Corsican separatist violence. Two reporters were arrested on December 30, 2002, after filming the deportation of a Malian immigrant.

Freedom of religion is protected by the constitution, and strong antidefamation laws prohibit religiously motivated attacks. However, 2004, like previous years, was marred by numerous incidents of anti-Semitic vandalism believed to be connected to the ongoing Palestinian intifada (uprising) in Israel, and Ariel Sharon, Israel's prime minister, caused controversy by recommending that French Jews emigrate to Israel. Not all branches of the Church of Scientology and the Jehovah's Witnesses are recognized as religious associations for tax purposes. A new law took effect in 2004 banning "ostentatious" religious symbols in schools. Believed by most to be aimed at the *hijab* (headscarf worn by Muslim women and girls), the controversial ban was supported by most voters. Militants kidnapped two French journalists in Iraq in August 2004, demanding unsuccessfully that the ban be overturned (the journalists were freed in December). Academic freedom is generally respected.

Freedom of assembly and association is respected. Trade unions are strong in France, although their memberships have declined over the past two decades.

France has a well-qualified judiciary, and the rule of law is well established. The legal system is based on Roman code law, and French citizens are treated equally under the law. However, the police are frequently criticized for aggressiveness in random personal checks, which often target youths of North African and African descent. This has deepened resentment between minorities and the authorities. A Council of Europe delegation reported in 2004 that French prisons suffer from over-crowding and poor conditions, though no prisoner maltreatment was found.

The rise of the National Front has tempted the government to tighten immigra-tion and asylum rules, which are perceived to be abused by economic migrants. The governing UMP (though not the president) opposes Turkish membership in the EU, largely because of fears of Muslim economic migration.

Gender equality is protected by law. A law governing the 2002 legislative elec-tion threatened to reduce public funding for political parties that ran fewer than 50 percent women candidates for the National Assembly. No party fully complied; the Socialists, who introduced the parity bill, ran 37 percent women. Despite equal legal status and well-established social liberty, women earn about three-quarters of what men earn. Gay rights are protected, and a type of nonmarriage civil union, the PACS, or civil solidarity pact, is recognized.

Gabon

Population: 1,400,000 **Political Rights:** 5
GNI/capita: $3,060 **Civil Liberties:** 4
Life Expectancy: 57 **Status:** Partly Free
Religious Groups: Christian (55-75 percent),
animist (25-45 percent)
Ethnic Groups: Bantu, other Africans, Europeans
Capital: Libreville

Ten-Year Ratings Timeline (Political Rights, Civil Liberties, Status)

1995	1996	1997	1998	1999	2000	2001	2002	2003	2004
5,4PF	5,4PF	5,4PF	5,4PF	5,4PF	5,4PF	5,4PF	5,4PF	5,4PF	5,4PF

Overview:

President Omar Bongo remained firmly in power in 2004 despite Gabon's poor economic prospects, including the long-term decline of its oil wealth. Meanwhile, Bongo agreed to a series of reform measures to obtain much-needed aid from the IMF.

Straddling the equator on Central Africa's West Coast, Gabon gained indepen-dence from France in 1960. Bongo, whom France raised from soldier to president in 1967, completed the consolidation of power begun by his predecessor, Leon Mba, by officially outlawing the opposition. France, which maintains marines in Gabon, has intervened twice to preserve Bongo's regime. In 1990, protests prompted by economic duress forced Bongo to accept a conference that opposition leaders hoped would promote a peaceful democratic transition. However, Bongo retained power in rigged 1993 presidential elections that sparked violent protests, which were repressed by his presidential guard. The 1996 parliamentary elections were also seriously flawed. Following 1996 local government polls, which gave the opposition several victories, the government transferred key electoral functions from the electoral commission to the Interior Ministry. Bongo's electoral victory in 1998, with 61 percent of the vote, followed a campaign that made profligate use of state resources and state media. The polling, which was partially boycotted by the opposition, was marked by serious irregularities, while the National Election Commission proved neither autonomous nor competent.

The Gabonese Democratic Party (PDG), which Bongo created in 1968, won parliamentary elections in December 2001. A divided opposition and low voter turnout, as well as government interference in the polls, helped assure the PDG victory. Ruling party candidates won 88 seats compared with 32 for independent and opposition candidates. Some opposition parties boycotted the vote.

Led by the ruling PDG, parliament in 2003 removed a 1997 constitutional amendment that imposed term limits on the head of state, allowing Bongo to seek reelection indefinitely. The move also replaced the country's runoff system with a single round of voting in all elections. These changes, fiercely opposed by most opposition parties, are widely viewed as an attempt to make Bongo, whose current term ends in 2005, president for life. It marked the sixth time the constitution has been amended since the introduction of a multiparty system in 1990. Bongo is adept at the use of patronage in undermining the opposition. In April 2004, six more parties joined his 27-party ruling alliance, further bolstering Bongo's future electoral ambitions.

Throughout the year, Gabon faced dwindling oil production, heavy debt, and a stagnant economy, although high oil prices have provided a temporary cushion; oil accounts for some 80 percent of the country's exports. In a bid to secure assistance from the IMF, Gabon agreed to a series of economic reforms, including reducing spending and increasing non-oil revenues, and forming an anticorruption body, the National Commission against Illicit Enrichment. The commitment to the IMF paved the way for the rescheduling of Gabon's unmanageable foreign debt burden in June. A compromise deal with neighboring Equatorial Guinea to jointly explore disputed islands, pending the outcome of UN mediation, could boost Gabon's shrinking oil reserves. The government has also taken steps to strengthen relations with countries other than France, signing its first-ever oil exploration deal with China

Three decades of autocratic and corrupt rule have made Bongo among the world's richest men, although some money has trickled down to rural areas and contributed to education. State institutions are influenced or controlled by Bongo and a small elite, with strong backing by the Gabonese army and France.

Political Rights and Civil Liberties: Despite a gradual political opening since 1990, Gabon's citizens have never been able to exercise their constitutional right to change their government democratically. With the 2003 lifting of term limits on the presidency and the continued co-optation and marginalization of the political opposition, President Omar Bongo is poised for another landslide victory in the 2005 elections. Although there are numerous political parties, the PDG has ruled since Bongo created it in 1968 and is the only one with national reach.

A special government ministry to fight corruption was established in 2003. However, it issued no reports and took no action against corrupt officials during 2004. Meanwhile, a revelation during high-profile corruption trials in France involving the TotalFinaElf oil company, that tens of millions of dollars in bribes were paid to Bongo, had negligible fallout for the president at home. Gabon was ranked 74 out of 146 countries surveyed in Transparency International's 2004 Corruption Perceptions Index.

Press freedom is guaranteed in law, but often restricted in practice. The state is authorized to criminalize civil libel suits. A government daily and at least 10 private weeklies, which are primarily controlled by opposition parties, are published. Almost all Gabonese private newspapers are printed in Cameroon because of the high costs at the only local printing company. At least six private radio and television broadcasters have been licensed and operate, but their viability is tenuous and most of the programming is nonpolitical. At the end of 2002, there were three Internet service providers in the country, two of which are privately owned. The government did not restrict access to or use of the Internet.

State censorship of the press escalated in early 2004, with publications printed outside of the country subjected to review before distribution. Several independent newspapers critical of the government were temporarily shuttered, and a new commission was formed with wide powers to decide who qualifies for accreditation as a professional journalist.

Religious freedom is constitutionally guaranteed and respected. The government does not restrict academic freedom.

The rights of assembly and association are constitutionally guaranteed, but permits required for public gatherings are sometimes refused. Freedom to form and join political parties is generally respected, but civil servants may face harassment because of associations. Nongovernmental organizations operate openly, but local human rights groups are weak and not entirely independent. Virtually the entire formal private sector workforce is unionized. Collective bargaining is allowed by industry, not by firm.

The judiciary suffers from political interference. Rights to legal counsel and a public criminal trial are generally respected. However, judges may deliver summary verdicts, and torture is sometimes used to produce confessions. Prison conditions are marked by beatings and insufficient food, water, and medical care. Arbitrary arrest and long periods of pretrial detention are common.

While no legal restrictions on travel exist, harassment on political and ethnic bases has been reported. Discrimination against African immigrants, including harassment by security forces and arbitrary detention, is a problem. Most of Gabon's several thousand indigenous Pygmies live in the forest and are largely independent of the formal government.

Gabon has come under scrutiny for the exploitation of thousands of child laborers who are sent from other Central or West African countries to work as domestic servants. The government has cooperated with international organizations to fight child trafficking, but says it lacks sufficient funds and resources to tackle the problem.

Legal protections for women include equal-access laws for education, business, and investment. In addition to owning property and businesses, women constitute more than 50 percent of the salaried workforce in the health and trade sectors, and women hold high-ranking positions in the military and judiciary. Government ministries must appoint at least four women as advisers, that is, more than 150 women for the whole government. Women continue to face legal and cultural discrimination, however, particularly in rural areas, and domestic violence is reportedly widespread.

The Gambia

Population: 1,500,000 **Political Rights:** 4
GNI/capita: $270 **Civil Liberties:** 4
Life Expectancy: 54 **Status:** Partly Free
Religious Groups: Muslim (90 percent), Christian
(9 percent), indigenous beliefs (1 percent)
Ethnic Groups: Mandinka (42 percent), Fula (18 percent),
Wolof (16 percent), Jola (10 percent), Serahuli (9 percent),
other (5 percent)
Capital: Banjul

Ten-Year Ratings Timeline (Political Rights, Civil Liberties, Status)

1995	1996	1997	1998	1999	2000	2001	2002	2003	2004
7,6NF	7,6NF	7,6NF	7,5NF	7,5NF	7,5NF	5,5PF	4,4PF	4,4PF	4,4F

Overview:

The Gambia's anticorruption commission began hearings in 2004 as part of President Yahya Jammeh's "Operation No Compromise."

After gaining independence from Britain in 1965, The Gambia functioned as an electoral democracy under President Sir Dawda Jawara and his People's Progressive Party for almost 30 years. A 1981 coup by leftist soldiers was reversed by intervention from Senegal, which borders The Gambia on three sides. The two countries formed the Confederation of Senegambia a year later, but it was dissolved in 1989. Senegal declined to rescue the Jawara government again when Jammeh struck in 1994. The leaders of the 1994 coup denounced the ousted government's alleged corruption, promising transparency, accountability, and early elections. Instead, they quickly imposed draconian decrees curtailing civil and political rights and the free media. A new constitution, adopted by a closely controlled 1996 referendum, allowed Jammeh to transform his military dictatorship into a nominally civilian administration.

Jammeh secured a victory in the October 2001 presidential poll, defeating opposition leader Ousainou Darboe. Jammeh won 53 percent of the vote compared with 33 percent for Darboe, a human rights lawyer who headed a three-party opposition coalition. Three other candidates won a combined total of 14 percent. While the Independent Electoral Commission was under some pressure by the ruling party, it generally operated freely. However, there were lingering concerns about President

Yahya Jammeh's commitment to democracy when several opposition supporters, human rights workers, and journalists were detained after the polls. Allegations surfaced after the vote that Jammeh's party had brought in members of his ethnic group living in neighboring Senegal and had issued them voter cards.

The ruling Alliance for Patriotic Reorientation and Construction (APRC) won all but three seats in the January 2002 National Assembly elections. The elections showed signs of improvement over the previous, highly flawed, legislative vote in 1997, although there were some administrative problems with voter registration and the major opposition coalition boycotted the polls.

An anticorruption commission, which is chaired by a Nigerian judge, is probing the acquisition of assets by active and retired ministers and senior military officials during Jammeh's decade in power. No elected lawmaker will have to appear, and neither will the president. Jammeh launched the anticorruption campaign in 2003 as part of an effort to win foreign investment. The National Assembly supported his "Operation No Compromise" by passing legislation against corruption and money laundering. A number of officials faced charges of financial impropriety, including some officials from Jammeh's inner circle. Among them was the majority leader of the ruling APRC in the National Assembly. In July 2004, the anticorruption commission began hearings as part of "Operation No Compromise."

In December 2003, opposition leader Lamine Waa Juwara of the national Democratic Action Movement was rearrested after a judge revoked his bail order. He has been awaiting trial on sedition charges. He was charged after calling for mass protests against the government in September 2003 and has been in and out of jail several times since Jammeh came to power.

The Gambia is a poor, tiny country, with few natural resources, that depends on exports of peanuts and other commodities. However, oil has been discovered offshore.

Political Rights and Civil Liberties:

The Gambia's citizens were granted their right to choose or change their government for the first time in several years in the 2001 presidential election, despite sporadic violence preceding the polls.

An anticorruption campaign was launched in 2003, and a number of officials have faced corruption charges. The Gambia was ranked 90 out of 146 countries surveyed in Transparency International's 2004 Corruption Perceptions Index.

Press freedom is guaranteed, but harassment and self-censorship sometimes inhibit free expression by the country's independent print media. The National Assembly passed the National Media Commission Bill in 2002, which provided for the creation of a commission that has the power to decide who is and is not a journalist and to deny the right to confidentiality of sources. The commission can issue arrest warrants for journalists and can jail journalists for contempt for up to six months. Offenses can include the publication or broadcast of "language, caricature, cartoon, or depiction, which is derogatory, contemptuous, or insulting against any person or authority," according to the New York-based Committee to Protect Journalists. Fearing that the commission would not be impartial, private media in May 2004 declared a temporary news blackout in protest. The Gambia Press Union has taken the commission to court over some of its powers.

Private broadcasters and newspapers in The Gambia struggle to pay high licensing fees. State-run Radio Gambia broadcasts only tightly controlled news that is also relayed by private radio stations. A single, government-run television station operates. Citizen FM broadcasts in a number of indigenous languages and is an important source of independent information for rural Gambians. Authorities shut it down in October 2001, and it remained closed in 2004.

In April, armed men stormed a building that housed the printing press of the private biweekly newspaper, *The Independent*. The men fired shots into the building before dousing equipment with gasoline and setting it ablaze. Three employees were injured in the fire. In August, there was an arson attack on the home of BBC correspondent Ebrima Sillah, who was able to escape without injury. Several days before the attack, Demba Jawo, president of the Gambia Press Union, received an anonymous threatening letter at his home. Internet access is unrestricted.

Freedom of religion is guaranteed, and the government respects this right. Academic freedom is guaranteed and respected.

Freedom of assembly is guaranteed, but this right is not always respected. Security forces often crack down violently on demonstrators. Human rights groups and other nongovernmental organizations generally operate freely, although human rights workers, opposition members, and journalists occasionally face harassment. Gambians, except for civil service employees and members of the security forces, have the right to form unions, strike, and bargain for wages. There are two main labor unions, and about 10 percent of the workforce is unionized.

The constitution provides for an independent judiciary. While lower courts are sometimes subject to executive influence, the judiciary has demonstrated its independence on several occasions, at times in significant cases. There are a number of judges from Nigeria, Ghana, and other African countries who tend to operate fairly and vigorously. Local chiefs preside over courts at the village level. The judicial system recognizes customary law, or Sharia (Islamic law), primarily in marriage matters.

Although the Jammeh government has made some steps toward political openness, it still has extensive repressive powers. A 1995 decree allows the National Intelligence Agency to cite "state security" to "search, arrest, or detain any person, or seize, impound, or search any vessel, equipment, plant, or property without a warrant." In such cases, the right to seek a writ of habeas corpus is suspended. Torture of prisoners in jails has been reported, although conditions in some of the country's prisons have improved.

Impunity for the country's security forces is a problem. Parliament passed a law in 2001 giving amnesty "for any fact, matter or omission of act, or things done or purported to have been done during any unlawful assembly, public disturbance, riotous situation or period of public emergency." The legislation was backdated to April 2000, when security forces had cracked down on demonstrators, killing 16 people. Military decrees still existed that give authorities broad power to detain individuals indefinitely without charge "in the interest of national security."

Ethnic groups in The Gambia live harmoniously. The constitution prohibits discrimination based on religion, language, ethnicity, gender, and other factors, and the government generally enforced these provisions.

Religious and traditional obstacles to the advancement of women are being addressed by both the government and women's organizations. Higher education and wage employment opportunities are still far fewer for women than for men, especially in rural areas. However, the government has waived school fees for girls, and women occupy senior government posts, including those of the vice president and minister of education. Sharia provisions regarding family law and inheritance restrict women's rights. Female genital mutilation is not banned and is widely practiced, but women's groups are working to eliminate the practice, and the government supports these efforts.

Georgia

Population: 4,500,000   **Political Rights:** 3*
GNI/capita: $650   **Civil Liberties:** 4
Life Expectancy: 72   **Status:** Partly Free
Religious Groups: Georgian Orthodox (65 percent),
Muslim (11 percent), Russian Orthodox (10 percent),
Armenian Apostilic (8 percent), other (6 percent)
Ethnic Groups: Georgian (70 percent), Armenian (8 percent),
Russian (6 percent), Azeri (6 percent), Ossetian (3 percent),
Abkhaz (2 percent), other (5 percent)
Capital: Tbilisi
Ratings Change: Georgia's political rights rating improved from 4 to 3 due to the holding of free and fair presidential and parliamentary elections.

Ten-Year Ratings Timeline (Political Rights, Civil Liberties, Status)

1995	1996	1997	1998	1999	2000	2001	2002	2003	2004
4,5PF	4,4PF	3,4PF	3,4PF	3,4PF	4,4PF	4,4PF	4,4PF	4,4PF	3,4PF

Overview:

Following Georgia's "Rose Revolution," in which President Eduard Shevardnadze stepped down in November 2003 in the face of a popular uprising against his rule, Mikhail Saakashvili was overwhelmingly elected to replace him in January 2004. Elections for a new parliament held in March saw Saakashvili's party capture the majority of seats. While Saakashvili received praise for trying to rein in the country's rampant corruption, there were concerns over new constitutional amendments that increased the powers of the president at the expense of parliament and of judges, and over possible growing restrictions against the country's media. During the year, the new president sought to reassert central government control over a number of regions and territories, including Abkhazia, Ajaria, and South Ossetia, that have operated outside the reach of Tbilisi.

Absorbed by Russia in the early nineteenth century, Georgia gained its independence in 1918. In 1922, it entered the U.S.S.R. as a component of the Transcaucasian Federated Soviet Republic, becoming a separate union republic in 1936. An attempt by the region of South Ossetia in 1990 to declare independence from Georgia and join Russia's North Ossetia sparked a war between rebels and Georgian forces. Although a ceasefire was signed in June 1992, the territory's final political status remains unresolved.

Following a national referendum in April 1991, Georgia declared its independence from the Soviet Union, which then collapsed in December of that year. Nationalist leader and former dissident Zviad Gamsakhurdia was elected president in May. The next year, he was overthrown by opposition forces and replaced with former Georgian Communist Party head and Soviet foreign minister Eduard Shevardnadze. Parliamentary elections held in 1992 resulted in more than 30 parties and blocs gaining seats, although none secured a clear majority.

In 1993, Georgia experienced the violent secession of the long-simmering Abkhazia region and armed insurrection by Gamsakhurdia loyalists. Although Shevardnadze blamed Russia for arming and encouraging Abkhazian separatists, he legalized the presence of 19,000 Russian troops in Georgia in exchange for Russian support against Gamsakhurdia, who was defeated and reportedly committed suicide. In early 1994, Georgia and Abkhazia signed an agreement in Moscow that called for a ceasefire, the stationing of Commonwealth of Independent States troops under Russian command along the Abkhazian border, and the return of refugees under UN supervision. In parliamentary elections in November and December 1995, the Shevardnadze-founded Citizens' Union of Georgia (CUG) captured the most seats, while Shevardnadze was elected with 77 percent of the vote in a concurrent presidential poll.

The ruling CUG repeated its victory four years later, in the October 1999 parliamentary election. Election observers from the Organization for Security and Cooperation in Europe (OSCE) concluded that, despite some irregularities, the vote was generally fair. In the April 2000 presidential poll, Shevardnadze easily won a second five-year term with a reported 81 percent of the vote. While Shevardnadze's win was widely anticipated, the large margin of his victory led to accusations of electoral fraud. Election monitors noted numerous and serious irregularities, including the stuffing of ballot boxes, inflated voter turnout figures, and a strong pro-Shevardnadze bias in the state media.

Following the parliamentary elections, various competing factions developed within the CUG, which had dominated Georgian politics for much of the 1990s. Shevardnadze himself faced growing opposition from prominent members, including Speaker of Parliament Zurab Zhvania and Justice Minister Mikhail Saakashvili, who criticized the president's failure to contain widespread corruption throughout the country. While Shevardnadze resigned as CUG chairman in September 2001, Saakashvili left the CUG to form his own party, the National Movement, and a formal party split was ratified in May 2002. Local elections held in June saw the CUG lose its long-standing dominance to several rival parties, including the New Rights Party, which was formed by many prominent businessmen, the National Movement, and the Labor Party. Subsequently, Saakashvili was named to the influential post of chairman of the Tbilisi City Council.

A flawed parliamentary vote on November 2, 2003, served as the catalyst for the civic action that ultimately led to the Shevardnadze resignation from office. According to official Central Election Commission results, the For New Georgia pro-presidential coalition—led by Shevardnadze and composed of the CUG, Socialist Party, National Democratic Party (NDP), and Great Silk Road movement—received 21 percent of the vote. The Union of Democratic Revival (UGR), a party led by Aslan Abashidze, the leader of the republic of Ajaria, won almost 19 percent of the vote.

Saakashvili's National Movement came in a close third with 18 percent, followed by the Labor Party with 12 percent. The only other two parties to pass the 7 percent threshold to enter parliament were the opposition Burjanadze-Democrats alliance formed by Zhvania and Speaker of Parliament Nino Burjanadaze, which captured almost 9 percent of the vote, and the New Rights, which secured 7 percent.

A domestic monitoring organization, the International Society for Fair Elections and Democracy, conducted a parallel vote tabulation, concluding that the National Movement had won the election with nearly 27 percent of the vote, with For New Georgia placing second with about 19 percent. Monitors from the OSCE reported that the elections fell short of international standards for democratic elections. Among the violations noted were ballot-box stuffing, inaccurate voter lists, biased media coverage, harassment of some domestic election monitors, and pressure on public employees to support pro-government candidates.

A series of mass public protests took place in the aftermath of the flawed vote. On November 22, protesters led by Mikhail Saakashvili broke into the parliament building and forced Shevardnadze, who was addressing the new legislature's opening session, to flee the building. Shevardnadze resigned the following day, and Burjanadze was named interim president. Meanwhile, the supreme court cancelled the results of the parliamentary election.

Snap presidential elections were called for January 4, 2004, with Saakashvili effectively facing no opposition. Capitalizing on mass dissatisfaction with corruption, cronyism, and poverty, Saakashvili won the poll with an overwhelming 96 percent of the vote. In new parliamentary elections held on March 28, 2004, the National Movement-Democrats bloc (composed of Saakashvili's National Movement and the Burjanadze-Democrats) captured about two-thirds of the seats, followed by the Rightist Opposition bloc (composed of the Industrialists and New Rights Party) with nearly 10 percent; seven other parties received 8 percent or fewer of the total number of seats.

Saakashvili took office amid extremely high expectations that his political program would help solve Georgia's considerable challenges, including entrenched corruption and a weak economy. Over the course of 2004, Saakashvili attempted to rein in corrupt officials, bring in the rule of law, and make a dent in the oligarchic system that had long dominated the country. At the same time, the constitution was amended to further strengthen the powers of the executive at the expense of the legislature and judiciary, a move criticized by international and domestic observers.

In the southwestern region of Ajaria, Saakashvili in May engineered the overthrow of Aslan Abashidze, the president of the semiautonomous region, who until that time had exercised almost complete control over the territory. Saakashvili's party won a decisive victory in pre-term parliamentary elections in Ajaria, which solidified his position in the autonomous republic after the ouster of pro-Moscow leader Abashidze the month before. The president's party, Saakashvili–Victorious Ajaria, gained 77 percent of the vote in the June 20 balloting.

On November 26, 2004, Abkhazia's parliament officially decreed the October 3 Abkhazian presidential elections valid "despite certain electoral violations" and declared Sergei Bagapsh president-elect. This was the latest development in an ongoing political battle in Abkhazia that pitted the two candidates from the breakaway region's presidential election, Prime Minister Raul Khadjimba and Bagapsh, against each other. Some 80,000 voters took part in the polls. The two candidates were separated by only several hundred votes.

In South Ossetia, which has maintained de facto independence from Tbilisi since 1992, Saakashvili has sought deeper involvement of the OSCE in resolving the conflict.

Political Rights and Civil Liberties: Citizens of Georgia can change their government democratically. The November 2003 parliamentary elections, which led to President Eduard Shevardnadze's ouster, fell short of international standards for democratic elections. According to the International Election Observer Mission, the January 2004 presidential and March 2004 parliamentary elections represented "commendable progress in relation to previous elections." The report went on to say, however, that "the consolidation of the democratic election process will only be fully tested in a more competitive environment, once a genuine level of political pluralism is re-established."

In February, parliament passed a number of constitutional amendments that strengthened the power of the executive relative to the parliament and judiciary. The amendments also gave the president power to dismiss parliament if it fails to approve the state budget, or the appointment of the prime minister or other ministers or in times of crisis. The constitutional amendments themselves and the fashion in which they were adopted were problematic, according to local watchdog groups and international observers. For example, authorities ignored the constitutional provision for a one-month debate period prior to adoption.

Although the former government initiated a high-profile anticorruption campaign in 2000, corruption remains endemic throughout all levels of Georgian society. Given the profound levels of corruption, President Mikhail Saakashvili has made anticorruption efforts a centerpiece of his administration. Over the course of 2004, a number of officials accused of corruption or embezzlement during the Shevardnadze era have been arrested. In a number of these instances, these former officials have paid substantial fines as part of the adjudication of their cases. More than $50 million is believed to have been collected in this fashion. This approach has raised questions about the soundness of a process by which lump-sum contributions paid by a suspect can simply be transferred to the Georgian treasury, or if criminal charges can actually be dropped on the basis of this sort of payment. Georgia was ranked 133 out of 146 countries surveyed in Transparency International's 2004 Corruption Perceptions Index.

Before the Georgian leadership change, the country's independent press was able to publish discerning and critical political analyses, although economic difficulties limited the circulation of most newspapers, particularly outside Tbilisi. During 2004, some critics of the new government leveled charges that media outlets unfriendly to Saakashvili were pressured and that a new round of self-censorship had begun. There were also some indications that a wider effort to manage news media was being undertaken by the authorities, in instances as part of an effort to establish financial order and fight corruption. The authorities do not restrict access to the Internet.

In July, the government passed a new law on defamation. It provides that statements made in parliament, in the courts, and during political debates are not considered libel. The law also moves the burden of proof to the accuser, and places entire companies, rather than individual reporters, as defendants. The authorities did not use libel laws to inhibit journalism in 2004.

Freedom of religion is respected for the country's largely Georgian Orthodox population and some minority religious groups traditional to the country, including Muslims and Jews. However, members of nontraditional religious minority groups, including Baptists, Pentecostals, and Jehovah's Witnesses, face harassment and intimidation by law enforcement officials and certain Georgian Orthodox Church extremists.

Although the government does not restrict academic freedom, the quality of the country's educational system has been compromised by widespread corruption. Students frequently pay bribes to receive high marks or pass entrance examinations. In 2004, the government proposed draft education legislation designed to move away from a Soviet model to one more in line with European structures.

The authorities generally respect freedom of association and assembly, although the government dispersed several peaceful demonstrations and arrested participants for disrupting the peace in 2004. Nongovernmental organizations (NGOs), including human rights groups, are able to register and operate without arbitrary restrictions. In the absence of a strong political opposition, the NGO community began to fill this void during the year. In October, 14 prominent legal experts and journalists published an open letter that stated that Saakashvili was marginalizing all forms of opposition or alternative opinion. The authors of the letter said that "intolerance towards people with different opinions is being implanted in Georgian politics and in other areas of political life."

The constitution and the Law on Trade Unions allow workers to organize and prohibit anti-union discrimination. The Amalgamated Trade Unions of Georgia, the successor to the union that existed during the Soviet period, is the principal trade union confederation. It is not affiliated with, and receives no funding from, the government.

The judiciary is not fully independent, with courts influenced by pressure from the executive branch. The payment of bribes to judges is reported to be common. As part of the effort to reduce corruption and improve the performance of law enforcement, the government dismissed half of the police force in August. Despite recent reform efforts, the law enforcement community continues to face accusations of torture. Interior Minister Irakli Okruashvili and the general prosecutor, Zurab Adeishvili, promised to work to eradicate human rights abuses within law enforcement agencies. They announced that monitoring groups would be created under the ombudsman's office to control the activities of the police and other law enforcement bodies.

The government generally respects the rights of ethnic minorities in nonconflict areas of the country. Freedom of residence, as well as the freedom to travel to and from the country, is generally respected.

Societal violence against women was a problem. While there are no laws that specifically criminalize spousal abuse or violence against women, the Criminal Code classifies rape, including spousal rape, and sexual coercion as crimes. Georgian law prohibits trafficking in persons; however, the country was a source, transit point, and destination for trafficked persons

Germany

Population: 82,600,000 **Political Rights:** 1
GNI/capita: $22,740 **Civil Liberties:** 1
Life Expectancy: 78 **Status:** Free
Religious Groups: Protestant (34 percent),
Roman Catholic (34 percent), Muslim (3.7 percent),
other (28.3 percent)
Ethnic Groups: German (92 percent), Turkish (2 percent),
other (6 percent)
Capital: Berlin

Ten-Year Ratings Timeline (Political Rights, Civil Liberties, Status)

1995	1996	1997	1998	1999	2000	2001	2002	2003	2004
1,2F	1,2F	1,2F	1,2F	1,2F	1,2F	1,2F	1,1F	1,1F	1,1F

Overview:

Germany's government, led by the Social Democratic Party (SDP) with the Green Party as a junior partner, remained unpopular in 2004, owing mainly to a poor economy. The government did poorly in regional elections, several of which saw extreme left- and right-wing parties do better than expected. However, they did not pose any threat to stable governance at either the state or the federal level.

The modern German state emerged in 1871 out of the fragmented Germanic states that existed until then. Defeated in World War I, and again more devastatingly in World War II, Germany was divided into two states—the capitalist and democratic Federal Republic in the west and the Communist German Democratic Republic in the east—during the ensuing Cold War. In 1989, the Berlin Wall keeping East Berliners from fleeing west was opened, and in 1990, East Germany was absorbed into the Federal Republic. Despite more than a decade of massive subsidies, eastern Germany remains considerably poorer than the rest of the country, with higher levels of unemployment. This economic situation is seen to have contributed to higher levels of support for political groups on the far right and far left in the former East.

The current government, a coalition of the SPD and the Green Party, was first elected in 1998, with the SPD's Gerhard Schroeder as chancellor. The government's first term was marked by slow economic growth (just 0.6 percent and 0.2 percent in 2001 and 2002), and the SPD's poll ratings languished late in 2002. However, Schroeder's vocal opposition to the war in Iraq played well with voters, and the coalition parties bested the opposition alliance of the Christian Democratic Party and Christian Social Union (CDU/CSU) in the September 2002 legislative elections.

Poll ratings sank quickly again after the election, and the SPD has struggled since. The primary reason may be dissatisfaction with the economy, which shrank slightly in 2003. The unemployment rate remains stubbornly high, at around 10 percent. Schroeder began to tackle this issue in earnest with labor-market reforms in 2002. His proposals have included making it easier for firms to fire workers, encouraging the creation of part-time and lower-wage "mini-jobs," and cutting benefits to the unemployed if they prove unwilling to move to take a job or to take an available job.

However, piecemeal reforms have both irritated labor unions, a key component of the SPD's electoral base, and failed to ignite the economy quickly enough for voters (although 2004 was forecast to be an improvement on 2003, with positive, if modest, growth.) While the SPD was trounced in several state elections in September 2004, its only comfort was that its main rival, the CDU/CSU, failed to do significantly better. The CDU/CSU largely cooperated with the government on the reforms, and thus seemed to be at least partly responsible for them in the eyes of voters.

The state elections received attention for the success of extreme parties. In Saxony, the neo-Nazi National Democratic Party (NDP) took 9 percent of the vote, almost as much as the SPD. Another far-right wing party, the German People's Union (DVU), did well in Brandenburg, with 6 percent. The former Communist Party of Democratic Socialism (PDS) also did well. Both elections took place in the former East Germany, where unemployment—and hence voter disaffection—is higher. However, these parties pose no serious threat to German democracy or governability. Though the PDS remains committed to state ownership and strongly socialist policies, it has been included in state government before and has behaved responsibly. The two far-right parties are shunned by the vast majority of the population and are not candidates for inclusion in government coalitions, even at the state level.

Germany remains in conflict with some of its European Union partners over its budget deficit. A condition of accepting the euro as its currency, which Germany did in 1999, is keeping the deficit below 3 percent of gross domestic product. Germany has breached this ceiling in 2002 and 2003, was certain to do so again in 2004, and was on track to do so in 2005. Because it was Germany that insisted on the 3-percent rule when the euro was created, this has given rise to some animosity from Germany's fellow EU countries, particularly the Netherlands.

Political Rights and Civil Liberties:

Germans can change their government democratically. The constitution provides for a lower house (Bundestag) elected by a 50-50 mixture of proportional representation and single-member districts, to be reelected at least every four years. The chancellor must control a majority in the Bundestag. The upper house, the Bundesrat, represents the states, and it must approve much key legislation, including economic bills. Its members are delegates from the individual state governments, and each state's delegation must vote as a block. The head of state is a largely ceremonial federal president, chosen by the parliament. Germany is strongly federal; state governments have considerable authority over areas such as education and policing, as well as substantial powers to tax and spend.

Political pluralism in Germany has been constrained by laws restricting the far left and far right. The Communist Party of Germany was banned in the Federal Republic in 1956. However, the former ruling East German Communist Party, now the PDS, is a legal and democratic, if far-left, party that has participated in state governments. The two main far-right parties, the NDP and the DVU, are hostile to immigration and the EU and sometimes receive a small share of the vote, but they are routinely kept out of government. Moreover, the alteration of asylum laws has undercut basic support for such parties, which together won less than 3 percent of the vote in 2002 and no seats in parliament. Nazism is illegal, but the government's attempts to ban the NDP were hung up in court when it was revealed that many of those testifying against the party were government agents.

Germany's government is accountable through open debates in parliament that are widely covered in the media. The government is free of pervasive corruption and was ranked 15 out of 145 countries surveyed in the 2004 Transparency International Corruption Perceptions Index.

Freedom of expression is protected in the Basic Law (the constitution), and the media are largely free and independent. However, it remains illegal to advocate Nazism or deny the Holocaust. Germany authorities have sought to prosecute Internet users outside Germany posting Nazi propaganda aimed at Germany, although this will be technically impossible to prosecute. The Constitutional Court ruled in March 2003 that surveillance of journalists' phone calls could be deemed legal in "serious" cases (on a case-by-case basis) by judges. The lack of a definition of "serious" is a cause for concern to reporters, who fear that the vagueness of the word invites abuse.

Freedom of belief is protected under law. Religions that fulfill certain requirements have the status of a "corporation under public law," and the government collects taxes from church members on the churches' behalf, for a fee. However, Germany has taken a strong stance against the Church of Scientology, which it deems an economic organization rather than a religion. Major parties deny membership to Scientologists, and the group has been under surveillance by government intelligence agencies. The Jehovah's Witnesses were denied public law corporation status in 1997 for failing to demonstrate "indispensable loyalty" to the democratic state, but this ruling was overturned on church-state separation grounds by the high court in 2000. However, as of November 2004, the case was still under review by the courts, which have expressed concern that the Jehovah's Witnesses' child-rearing practices do not conform to international human rights law. Two states, Bavaria and Baden-Wuerttemberg, have passed laws prohibiting Muslim female teachers from wearing headscarves on duty. Academic freedom is respected.

Civic groups and NGOs may operate without hindrance, and the right of peaceful assembly is not infringed, except in the case of outlawed groups such as those advocating Nazism or opposing Germany's democratic order. Trade unions, farmers' groups, and business confederations are free to organize, and they have traditionally played a strong role in Germany's consensus-based policy-making system. However, unions have weakened in recent years.

The judiciary is independent, and the rule of law prevails. The Federal Constitutional Court vets the compatibility of laws with the Basic Law. In addition to having its own provisions, Germany is a party to the European Convention on Human Rights. Prison conditions are adequate. Anti-immigrant sentiment have led to attacks on members of ethnic minorities.

Women's rights are strongly protected, with generous maternity policies and antidiscrimination laws, though the latter do not prevent some wage discrimination. There are six women in the 14-member federal cabinet. Limited gay partnership rights are permitted.

➤Ghana

Population: 21,400,000   **Political Rights:** 2
GNI/capita: $270   **Civil Liberties:** 2
Life Expectancy: 58   **Status:** Free
Religious Groups: Indigenous beliefs (21 percent),
Muslim (16 percent), Christian (63 percent)
Ethnic Groups: Akan (44 percent), Moshi-Dagomba
(16 percent), Ewe (13 percent), Ga (8 percent), other (19 percent)
Capital: Accra
Trend Arrow: Ghana received an upward trend arrow due to efforts to improve the rule of law, including the conclusion of hearings of the National Reconciliation Commission, and to improve freedom of the press.

Ten-Year Ratings Timeline (Political Rights, Civil Liberties, Status)

1995	1996	1997	1998	1999	2000	2001	2002	2003	2004
4,4PF	3,4PF	3,3PF	3,3PF	3,3PF	2,3F	2,3F	2,3F	2,2F	2,2F

Overview:

Ghanaians were preparing for a likely close race for the presidency in December 2004 between President John Kufuor and former vice president John Atta Mills. The country's National Reconciliation Commission, which held hearings on human rights abuses committed at various times since independence, concluded its hearings during the year.

Once a major slaving center and long known as the Gold Coast, Ghana, a former British possession, became black Africa's first colony to achieve independence in 1957. After the 1966 overthrow of its charismatic independence leader, Kwame Nkrumah, the country was wracked by a series of military coups for 15 years. Successive military and civilian governments vied with each other in both incompetence and deception.

In 1979, Flight Lieutenant Jerry Rawlings led a coup against the ruling military junta and, as promised, returned power to a civilian government after a purge of corrupt senior army officers. However, the new civilian administration did not live up to Rawlings's expectations, and he seized power again in December 1981 and set up the Provisional National Defense Council (PNDC). The radically socialist, populist, and brutally repressive PNDC junta banned political parties and free expression. Facing a crumbling economy, Rawlings, in the late 1980s, transformed Ghana into an early model for the structural adjustment programs urged by international lenders. A new constitution adopted in April 1992 legalized political parties, and Rawlings was declared president after elections that were neither free nor fair. Rawlings's victory in the 1996 presidential poll, which was generally regarded as free and fair, was assured by the then-ruling party's extensive use of state media and patronage, as well as by opposition disunity.

In the December 2000 presidential elections, the opposition, led by Kufuor of the New Patriotic Party (NPP), alleged intimidation and other irregularities as the second round of voting began. However, those claims dissipated as the polling proceeded and Kufuor's looming victory became apparent. He won soundly with 57 percent of the vote in the second round of polling, compared with 43 percent for Atta Mills, who was vice president under Rawlings. The elections were hailed as having been conducted both freely and fairly.

During concurrent legislative elections, the opposition also broke the stranglehold of Rawlings's National Democratic Congress (NDC) on parliament. The NPP captured 99 of the 200 seats available, compared with 92 for the NDC, which had previously held 133 seats. Smaller opposition parties and independents won the remainder of the seats. The NPP won a majority in parliament in 2003 through by-elections, finishing with 103 seats.

The presidential election in December 2004 is likely to be a close race between Mills and Kufuor, but Kufuor has four years of solid economic achievement behind him. World prices have been good for cocoa and gold, two of Ghana's main exports, and the country's growth rate has exceeded 5 percent. The reputation of the Kufuor government for good governance has won aid from Western donors. Ghana qualified in June for debt relief under the World Bank's Highly Indebted Poor Countries initiative, which will slash the $6 billion external debt in half over 20 years and reduce debt service payments each year.

Political Rights and Civil Liberties:

Citizens of Ghana can change their government democratically. The December 1996 presidential and parliamentary elections conducted under the 1992 constitution allowed Ghanaians their first opportunity since independence to choose their representatives in genuine elections. The 2000 presidential and parliamentary polls were hailed in Africa and abroad as a successful test of Ghana's democracy. The presidential poll marked the first time in Ghana's history that one democratically elected president was succeeded by another.

A coalition of 25 civil society groups, the Coalition of Domestic Election Observers, plans to deploy nearly 5,000 monitors across the country for the December 2004 presidential and parliamentary elections. In March, the Electoral Commission (EC) began a two-week voter listing exercise in 21,000 registration centers to prepare a new voter's register and supply all voters with a photo identity card for the polls. The government shelved a bid to fast-track a bill seeking to allow all Ghanaians abroad to register for the elections. Political opposition members protested the fast-track effort, saying Ghana lacked the infrastructure and resources to transparently register all Ghanaians abroad ahead of the December election. The EC accredits political parties and requires that they show evidence of a "national character," such as official representation in all 10 of the country's regions.

The government of President John Kufuor has made efforts to improve transparency and reduce corruption. Ghana was ranked 64 out of 146 countries surveyed in the 2004 Transparency International Corruption Perceptions Index.

Freedom of expression is constitutionally guaranteed and generally respected. Numerous private radio stations operate, and several independent newspapers and magazines are published in Accra. State media sometimes criticizes government policies, but avoids direct criticism of the president. Fulfilling a campaign promise, the Kufuor government repealed Ghana's criminal libel law and otherwise eased pressure on the press in 2001. The president appointed a new chairman of the National Communications Authority in 2003, which is responsible for granting media licenses. Previously, the chairman was also the minister of communications, which raised questions of conflict of interest. Internet access is unrestricted.

Religious freedom is respected, and the government has increased its prosecution of perpetrators of religious violence.

Academic freedom is guaranteed and respected. A ban on campus demonstrations has not been enforced or challenged.

The right to peaceful assembly and association is constitutionally guaranteed, and permits are not required for meetings or demonstrations. Numerous nongovernmental organizations operate openly and freely. Kufuor signed into law new labor legislation in 2003 that conformed with International Labor Organization (ILO) conventions. Under the new laws, every worker has the right to form or join a trade union. A National Labor Commission, which is comprised of government, employer, and organized labor representatives, was created to help resolve labor disputes, first through mediation, and then through arbitration.

Ghanaian courts have acted with increased autonomy under the 1992 constitution, but are still occasionally subject to corruption. The government has made efforts to reduce corruption in the justice system. Traditional courts often handle minor cases according to local customs that fail to meet constitutional standards. Scarce judicial resources compromise the judicial process, leading to long periods of pretrial detention under harsh conditions.

Ghana's National Reconciliation Commission finished hearing testimony from more than 2,000 people in 2004. The reconciliation panel is based on South Africa's Truth and Reconciliation Commission, and its hearings covered Ghana's history since independence, although much of the focus was on the early years of rule under Rawlings in the 1980s. The proceedings were seen as a test of the flexibility of the country's democracy and how well Ghana could look into its past, acknowledge its failings, and continue to move democratically into the future. Former president Jerry Rawlings testified before the commission live on national television. It was significant for Ghana and Africa that a former head of state was publicly questioned about his human rights record. Rawlings was asked about the 1982 murders of three high court judges and a retired army major; although he was not asked if he had ordered their killings, he was questioned about various videotapes that might shed light on the circumstances of the killings.

Communal and ethnic violence occasionally flares in Ghana. In August, the government lifted a state of emergency and evening curfew in the Dagbon region of northern Ghana, more than two years after the Dagbon king was beheaded and his palace razed during clashes between rival clans. The Andani and the Abudu have been vying for the chieftaincy for more than half a century.

Ghana has been coordinating with regional countries and the ILO to create a comprehensive plan to address the growing problem of child trafficking and child labor.

Despite women's equal rights under the law, Ghanaian women suffer societal discrimination that is particularly serious in rural areas, where opportunities for education and wage employment are limited. Women's enrollment in universities, however, is increasing. Domestic violence against women is said to be common, but often remains unreported. Legislation in 1998 doubled the prison sentence for rape, and efforts were under way in 2004 to further extend sentences for sexual violence. Efforts were also being made to abolish the *tro-kosi* system of indefinite servitude to traditional priests in rural areas and the practice of sending young girls to penal villages as prisoners in the North after they are accused of practicing witchcraft. Female genital mutilation was made illegal in Ghana in 1994, and those who perform the operation face a prison sentence of at least three years.

Greece

Population: 11,000,000 **Political Rights:** 1
GNI/capita: $11,660 **Civil Liberties:** 2
Life Expectancy: 78 **Status:** Free
Religious Groups: Greek Orthodox (98 percent),
Muslim (1.3 percent), other (0.7 percent)
Ethnic Groups: Greek (98 percent), other [including
Macedonian, Turkish] (2 percent)
Capital: Athens

Ten-Year Ratings Timeline (Political Rights, Civil Liberties, Status)

1995	1996	1997	1998	1999	2000	2001	2002	2003	2004
1,3F	1,3F	1,3F	1,3F	1,3F	1,3F	1,3F	1,2F	1,2F	1,2F

Overview:

After being in power almost continuously for 23 years, the Pan Hellenic Socialist Movement (PASOK) lost to the conservative New Democracy party in parliamentary elections in March 2004. Despite fears over security, no major terrorist attacks occurred during the Olympic Games in Athens in August. The games—the most expensive in 100 years, thanks largely to security arrangements—left the country in massive debt.

Modern Greece began in 1830, when the country gained its independence from the Ottoman Empire. The ensuring century brought continued struggle between royalists and republican forces. During World War II, Greece fell to Germany in 1941 after a failed invasion by Italy the year before. From 1942 to 1944 local Communist and royalist forces put up a strong resistance against the Nazis, which were eventually defeated with the help of British forces in 1944. National solidarity broke down in the early postwar period, when royalists won national elections and eventually defeated the Communists in a civil war. In 1967 a group of army officers staged a military coup, suspending elections and arresting hundreds of political activists. A referendum in 1974 rejected the restoration of the monarchy, and a new constitution in 1975 declared Greece a parliamentary republic.

PASOK won more than half of the seats in the 2000 parliamentary elections, while the more conservative New Democracy party came in a close second. Other parties winning seats include the Communist Party of Greece and Synaspismos (SYN), a coalition of smaller left parties. Of those eligible to vote, 89 percent turned out at the polls.

During parliamentary elections in March 2004, the New Democracy party received

45 percent of the vote, winning 165 of the 300 seats in the unicameral parliament. New Democracy beat PASOK, which won 117 seats, and the Communist Party of Greece, which won 12 seats. A coalition of leftist and environmentalist movements (the former SYN) won 6 seats. PASOK had governed the country since 1981, except for a brief period from 1990 to 1993, when New Democracy was in power.

A three-year-old nationalist and xenophobic party, the far-right People's Orthodox Rally (LAOS), won 4.1 percent of the vote during European Parliament elections in June. LAOS, which had failed to pass a 3 percent threshold to win seats during the national parliamentary elections in March, is led by a populist journalist, Yiorgos Karatzaferis, who has been accused by various human rights groups of holding racist and anti-Semitic views. Support for LAOS represents the largest increase in support for the far-right in the country in 20 years.

The first task of the new prime minister, Costas Karamanlis, was to revive a number of stalled construction projects for the Olympic Games that took place in Athens in August. In November, the government announced that the costs of the games, not including major projects like the new airport, roads, and railways, had run up to $11.5 billion, close to double the original estimate. More than $1 billion was spent on security alone in anticipation of a possible major terrorist attack, which did not occur. NATO assisted by securing the coastlines and air space and by providing special assistance for possible chemical, biological, or nuclear attacks.

The December 2003 trial of 15 members of the urban guerrilla group, November 17, ended with convictions on a number of crimes, including homicide. The group, which had committed a series of murders, bombings, and robberies since its formation in 1975, had begun to unravel after the arrest of one of its members in June 2002.

Greek-Turkish relations improved during the year. The Turkish prime minister, Recep Tayyip Erdogan, made a landmark visit to Greece, the first of its kind in 16 years. During the visit, Greece's Prime Minister Karamanlis publicly stated that his government would support Turkey's bid to join the European Union (EU). The Greek government also pledged economic aid to Turkish-controlled northern Cyprus after they voted overwhelmingly in favor of unifying the Turkish and Greek sides of the island.

Political Rights and Civil Liberties: Greeks are free to change their government democratically. All 300 members of the unicameral parliament are elected according to a system of proportional representation. The president is elected by parliament to a five-year term. The country generally has fair electoral laws, equal campaigning opportunities, and a system of compulsory voting that is weakly enforced. Some representatives of the Roma (Gypsy) community complain that certain municipalities failed to register Romanies who did not fulfill basic residency requirements.

Corruption continues to be a problem in Greece. Despite disciplinary measures by the Bureau of Internal Affairs of the Ministry of Public Order, corruption continued to be a problem within the police forces. Greece was ranked 49 out of 146 countries surveyed in the 2004 Transparency International Corruption Perceptions Index, the lowest among all EU members.

The constitution includes provisions for freedom of speech and the press. There are, however, some limits to speech that incites fear, violence, and disharmony among the population, as well as publications that offend religious beliefs, that are obscene, or that advocate the violent overthrow of the political system. Despite these limitations, there are many independent newspapers and magazines, including those that are critical of the government.

In June, police entered the premises of a private radio station, Makedonikos Ichos ("Macedonian Sound") in Naoussa, seized transmitting equipment and arrested the owner. Although the official explanation for the seizures and arrest was that the station lacked a proper operation license, there was concern that the station was signaled out because it broadcasts in the Slavo-Macedonian language.

The Eastern Orthodox Church of Christ is considered the "prevailing" religion of the country in the constitution, which, however, also guarantees the right of all citizens to practice the religion of their choice. Despite this, members of some minority religions face social discrimination as well as legal barriers. For example, some religious groups have encountered legal restrictions to inheriting property as a religious entity. Although all religions, including the Orthodox Church, have to pay taxes, the government subsidizes the Orthodox Church. In addition, "known" religious groups are required to obtain permits from the Ministry of Education and Religion in order to open houses of worship. The law prohibits proselytizing, and consequently, Mormons and members of the Jehovah's Witnesses are routinely arrested and have reported abuse by police officers for their religious beliefs. The government does not restrict academic freedom.

Although the constitution allows for freedom of association, ethnic and religious minority groups face a number of barriers. The government does not officially recognize the existence of any non-Muslim minority groups, particularly Slavophones. In addition, the government does not recognize Macedonian as a language, as officials fear the secessionist aspirations of this group. Using the term *Turkos* or *Tourkikos* ("Turk" and "Turkish," respectively) in the title of an association is illegal and may lead to persecution. The right to freedom of assembly is guaranteed by the constitution and generally protected by the government.

The constitution and laws provide workers with the right to join and form unions. Twenty-six percent of all nonagricultural salaried workers are union members.

The judiciary is independent, and the constitution provides for public trials. However, a number of nongovernmental organizations (NGOs) have raised concerns about the ill-treatment of detainees by law enforcement officials, especially concerning immigrants and members of religious minorities. Concerns have also been raised about the overcrowding of prisons.

Although military service is compulsory, conscientious objectors (for religious and ideological reasons) can participate in an alternative national service—to work in state hospitals or municipal services for 36 months in lieu of military service. However, the law has been criticized, in part, for imposing a punitive length of time: alternative service is double the 18 months required for military service. In February, a naval court ruled that it did not have the jurisdiction to try the case of a conscientious objector, Lazaros Petromelidis, who had been convicted in 2003 of insubordination for not fulfilling his civilian service. In addition to Petromelidis, a number of other conscientious objectors have been convicted of insubordination for refusing to perform military or national service.

During the year, the country made progress toward improving its human rights record by announcing plans for legislative action to mandate the equal treatment between persons irrespective of race or ethnicity and to banish discrimination based on race, religion, sex, disability or nationality in the workplace. If eventually passed, such laws will bring Greece in line with EU standards of human rights. In addition, efforts have been made to provide police officers with sensitivity training with respect to human rights and the prohibition of racial discrimination. However, racial intolerance is still pervasive in society and is often expressed by people in the media, in politics, and in the Orthodox Church. In addition, noncitizens face bureaucratic difficulties when renewing their residency permits. The immigration process is slow and, as a result, makes the position of immigrants unstable, as they never know whether, pending a renewal, they might face expulsion before they obtain a new permit.

The Roma community continues to face considerable discrimination. In preparation for the 2004 Olympic Games, more than a hundred Roma were evicted in 2002 from a construction site in Athens near the Olympic stadium. Amnesty International has reported that the government has yet to honor its agreement to effectively provide these individuals with rent subsidies to live in alternative accommodations.

Women lack specific legislation to deal with domestic violence and, in addition, face sex-based discrimination in the workplace. Progress, however, has been made for women in politics. During the 2004 elections, women gained 14 percent of the seats in parliament, almost double the 8.7 percent they held after previous elections.

Trafficking in women and children for prostitution remains a problem, despite efforts by the government over the past few years to address the issue. Some law enforcement officials, who are on the payroll of organized crime gangs, aid traffickers. A number of NGOs are working in the country to combat trafficking and have received financial and other assistance from the government. A presidential decree in the summer of 2003 established the creation of shelters for trafficking victims.

Grenada

Population: 100,000
GNI/capita: $3,790
Life Expectancy: 71
Political Rights: 1
Civil Liberties: 2
Status: Free
Religious Groups: Roman Catholic (53 percent), Anglican (13.8 percent), other Protestant (33.2 percent)
Ethnic Groups: Black (82 percent), mulatto (13 percent), European and East Indian (5 percent)
Capital: St. George's

Ten-Year Ratings Timeline (Political Rights, Civil Liberties, Status)

1995	1996	1997	1998	1999	2000	2001	2002	2003	2004
1,2F	1,2F	1,2F	1,2F	1,2F	1,2F	1,2F	1,2F	1,2F	1,2F

Overview:
In 2004, Prime Minister Keith Mitchell continued to be the focus of a corruption scandal alleging that that he accepted money from a German citizen in return for awarding the

latter a government post. Meanwhile, the sentences of 14 members of the so-called Grenada 17 were ruled unconstitutional by the country's High Court.

Grenada, a Commonwealth member that gained independence from Britain in 1974, includes the islands of Carriacou and Petite Martinique. Maurice Bishop's Marxist New Jewel Movement seized power in 1979. In 1983, Bishop was murdered by New Jewel hard-liners Bernard Coard and Hudson Austin, who took control of the country in the name of the People's Revolutionary Government (PRG). A joint U.S.-Caribbean military intervention removed the PRG. In 1986, Coard and 18 others were sentenced to death; subsequently, 2 were pardoned, and 17—who became known as the "Grenada 17"— had their sentences commuted to life imprisonment.

In the run-up to the November 7, 2003, elections, the Mitchell government was accused of garnering voter support by paying public workers retroactive payments. The opposition also reported discrepancies in voter lists. The elections, which were nevertheless deemed to be generally free and fair, were called seven months early. Mitchell's New National Party (NNP) won 8 seats, down from the 15-seat sweep of the 1999 elections, while the National Democratic Party (NDP), headed by Tillman Thomas, won 7 seats. The Grenada United Labor Party (GULP), the Good Old Democracy Party (GODP), and the Grenada Renaissance Party (GRP) were unsuccessful in securing any seats. Mitchell retained his position as prime minister. After opposition parties suffered a crushing defeat in the 1999 elections, their role as alternatives in future elections was seen as seriously in doubt.

A formal investigation began in 2004 into allegations that Mitchell received $500,000 from German-born Eric E. Resteiner in exchange for Resteiner's appointment as trade counselor for Grenada. Mitchell maintained that the money had been approved by the cabinet and was for legitimate expenses regarding trade promotion.

In March, the Grenada High Court ruled unconstitutional the sentences given to 14 members of the Grenada 17. The High Court was set to re-sentence and possibly free the 14 until the government appealed the decision to the Eastern Caribbean Supreme Court; a decision was pending as of November 30. The Truth and Reconciliation Commission—which was formally inaugurated in September 2001 and has a mandate to investigate violence from the mid-1970s to the late 1980s—is expected to review the convictions of the Grenada 17. As of November 2004, the commission had not yet presented its final report to the government; the report was due to be delivered in June.

Political Rights and Civil Liberties: Citizens are able to change their government through democratic elections. The 2003 parliamentary elections were considered generally free and fair, with some allegations of voter list manipulation and government pandering. The bicameral parliament consists of the 15-seat House of Representatives and the 13-seat Senate, to which the prime minister appoints 10 senators and the opposition leader 3. A governor-general represents the British monarchy.

Grenada was not ranked by Transparency International in its 2004 Corruption Perceptions Index. After suspending the Economic Citizenship Program that allowed the purchase of Grenadian nationality following September 11, 2001, allegations surfaced in August 2004 that some passports had been issued without following appropriate procedures and that the records of these documents were missing from the Immigration Department. By the end of November, no further information on these charges was available.

The right to free expression is generally respected. The media, including three weekly newspapers and several other publications, are independent and freely criticize the government. A privately owned corporation, with a minority government share, owns the principal radio and television stations. In addition, there are nine privately owned radio stations, one privately owned television station, and a privately owned cable company. All media outlets are independent of the government and regularly report on all political views. There is free access to the Internet.

Citizens of Grenada generally enjoy the free exercise of religious beliefs. There are no official restrictions on academic freedom.

Constitutional guarantees regarding the rights of freedom of assembly and association are respected. Workers have the right to organize and to bargain collectively. Numerous independent labor unions include an estimated 20 to 25 percent of the workforce. All unions belong to the Grenada Trades Union Council (GTUC), which is represented in the Senate. A 1993 law gives the government the right to establish tribunals empowered to make "binding and final" rulings when a labor dispute is considered of vital interest to the state; the GTUC claimed that the law was an infringement on the right to strike.

The independent and prestigious judiciary has authority generally respected by the 782-member Royal Grenada Police Force. There are no military courts. In 1991, Grenada rejoined the Organization of Eastern Caribbean States court system, with the right of appeal to the Privy Council in London. Detainees and defendants are guaranteed a range of legal rights that the government respects in practice. However, a lack of judges and facilities results in a substantial backlog of six months to one year for cases involving serious offenses.

Amnesty International has advocated that the government carry out an independent judicial review of the convictions of the Grenada 17, arguing that there were numerous irregularities and violations of international standards in the trial of the accused. In 2003, Amnesty International classified the Grenada 17 as political prisoners based on its findings that their original trial was unfair and subsequent appeals manipulated for political reasons.

Like many Caribbean island nations, Grenada has suffered from a rise in violent, drug-related crime, particularly among increasingly disaffected youth. Prison conditions are poor, although they meet minimum international standards, and the government allows human rights monitors to visit. With Hurricane Ivan causing severe damage in 2004 to the country's only prison, it is expected that the new facility will address some of the shortcomings of the old one. Flogging is still legal but rarely used, and then primarily as a punishment for sex crimes and theft cases.

There are no significant minority issues in Grenada.

Women are represented in the government, though in greater numbers in the ministries than in parliament. Women generally earn less than men for equal work. Domestic violence against women is common, and police say that most instances of abuse are not reported, while others are settled out of court.

Guatemala

Population: 12,700,000   **Political Rights:** 4
GNI/capita: $1,760   **Civil Liberties:** 4
Life Expectancy: 66   **Status:** Partly Free
Religious Groups: Roman Catholic, Protestant,
indigenous beliefs
Ethnic Groups: Mestizo (55 percent), Amerindian
(43 percent), other (2 percent)
Capital: Guatemala City

Ten-Year Ratings Timeline (Political Rights, Civil Liberties, Status)

1995	1996	1997	1998	1999	2000	2001	2002	2003	2004
4,5PF	3,4PF	3,4PF	3,4PF	3,4PF	3,4PF	3,4PF	4,4PF	4,4PF	4,4PF

Overview:

Oscar Berger, representing the Great National Alliance (GANA), defeated Alvaro Colom of the National Unity for Hope (UNE) in the December 2003 presidential runoff election. Guatemala's governance problems are on the rise as corruption and lawlessness increase with impunity.

The Republic of Guatemala, which was established in 1839, has endured a history of dictatorship, coups, and guerrilla insurgency. Civilian rule followed the 1985 elections, and a 36-year civil war, which claimed the lives of more than 200,000 people, ended with the signing of a peace agreement in 1996. The peace accords led to the successful demobilization of the Guatemalan National Revolutionary Unity (URNG) guerrillas and their political legalization, the retirement of more than 40 senior military officers on corruption and narcotics charges, and the reduction of the army's strength by one-third. A truth commission mandated by the peace accords began receiving complaints of rights violations committed during the conflict. However, in a May 1999 referendum, voters rejected a package of amendments to the constitution, approved by Congress a year earlier that had been prepared in accordance with the peace plan.

The former guerrillas of the URNG, seriously divided and unable to make electoral gains, offered a blunt assessment of the peace accords in early 2002: "Genocide is no longer state policy." There was consensus that with the failure to implement substantive reforms redressing social and economic inequalities, the peace process was dead. This failure included the government's inability to end the military's political tutelage and impunity, to fully recognize the rights of the Maya Indians, and to reform taxation to pay for health, education, and housing programs for the poor. Late in the year, the government of President Alfonso Portillo signed an agreement to provide victims of the civil war with $400 million in compensation under a National Compensation Program.

In July 2003, the constitutional court ruled that retired General Efrain Rios Montt could stand for the presidency. He was later chosen as the candidate for the National Guatemalan Republican Front (FRG). The court's decision was condemned at home and abroad. On July 24 and 25, violent demonstrations were staged in Guatemala City as the FRG brought armed supporters to intimidate the court's justices and critics.

In November 9, 2003, parliamentary elections, the FRG lost its congressional majority, but it still captured 44 seats, with GANA holding 49 and UNE 34. At the local level, the FRG was the most successful party, having won over 100 municipalities; GANA won 69 and UNE, 33. This outcome made governability a serious concern, as the FRG still enjoyed significant support at the grassroots level. The FRG's appeal was based partly on a message of law and order appealing to segments of the population exposed to high levels of lawlessness and violence. While UNE is identified as left of center, as a whole the left did not fare well, with the URNG capturing two seats in Congress.

Presidential elections held concurrently with the legislative polls were marked with less than the expected violence, although voting was suspended in seven municipalities because of violence. GANA candidate Oscar Berger, a former mayor of Guatemala City, received 34 percent of the vote. The UNE's Alvaro Colom obtained 26 percent of the ballot, and Montt came in a distant third with 19 percent. Since no candidate polled more than 50 percent, a runoff election was held on December 28 between Berger, who won with 54 percent of the vote, and Colom.

Berger was sworn into office on January 14, 2004, and will have to govern with a seriously divided Congress, and in a country where the FRG won a majority of the mayoral races. Former president Alvaro Arzu, of the National Advancement Party (PAN), who had negotiated the peace agreement with the guerrillas, was elected mayor of Guatemala City. After a first electoral round characterized by intimidation and uncertainty, especially around the role of Montt and his supporters in the FRG, the outcome of the second round reassured Guatemalan and international observers about the integrity of the electoral system. Later in 2004, Montt was placed under house arrest for inciting peasant militia units (PACs) to riot.

Nevertheless, the challenges faced by the new president have only increased since the controversial presidency of his predecessor, Portillo. Of special concern has been the role of the PACs, which had supported Montt's failed candidacy and were most active in the 36-year-long civil war during the period from 1990 to 1996. In an effort to preclude outbursts of violence, Berger met with Maya representatives during the year and promised to enforce anti-racism laws. He also assured representatives of the PACs that he would continue with the compensation process initiated by Portillo.

While the civil war is over, assassinations, kidnappings, beatings, break-ins, and death threats are still common. Death squads have reappeared, and hundreds of street children continue to be murdered and mutilated. In response to a dramatic increase in gang-related violence, the government has implemented a controversial jail-based program targeting gangs (*maras*) called "The Sweep-up Plan," modeled after Honduras's draconian anti-gang efforts. Portillo had admitted that clandestine groups with military ties exist, but claimed to be powerless to combat them. Berger faces an uphill battle in trying to reduce rampant violence, while also reining in what Guatemalans call "parallel powers," which include gangs, drug traffickers, rogue retired and active-duty police and armed forces, and sundry government officials. Portillo, wanted on charges of money laundering and embezzlement in both Guatemala and the United States, disappeared on leaving office.

A final complication has been the failure to move toward a final resolution of the border dispute with Belize, an early hope during the Portillo administration that was dashed in 2004 without much explanation.

Political Rights and Civil Liberties: Citizens of Guatemala can change their government through democratic means. The 1985 constitution, amended in 1994, provides for a four-year presidential term and prohibits reelection. A unicameral Congress consisting of 113 members is elected for four years. The 2003 presidential and legislative elections were regarded by international observers as generally free and fair.

Corruption is widespread, and efforts to promote transparency have made little progress. Guatemala was ranked 122 out of 146 countries surveyed in Transparency International's 2004 Corruption Perceptions Index.

While freedom of speech is protected by the constitution, those who loudly condemn injustice or past human rights abuses can become targets for persecution. The press and most broadcast media outlets are privately owned. Seven dailies are published in the capital, and six are local. There are several radio stations, most of them commercial. Four of the six television stations are commercially operated and are owned by the same financial interest. Reporters Sans Frontieres (RSF), a Paris-based organization, has repeatedly noted that journalists and human rights activist were targets of intimidation, including death threats. Several journalists lost their lives during the 2004 presidential campaign. Access to the Internet is not limited.

The constitution guarantees religious freedom. The government does not interfere with academic freedom. However, academics have been targets of death threats for raising questions about past human rights abuses or continuing injustice.

The constitution guarantees the right to organize civic organizations and political parties. Nevertheless, human rights groups are the targets of frequent death threats and the victims of acts of violence. In January 2003, the Guatemalan human rights prosecutor's office (PDH) pushed for a UN-appointed commission to curb threats and attacks against human rights activists. The resulting entity, the Commission for the Investigation of Illegal Bodies and Clandestine Security Apparatus (CICIACS), was created on January 7, 2004, and received a pledge of support from President Oscar Berger.

Trade unions are targets of intimidation, physical attacks, and assassination, particularly in rural areas during land disputes. Workers are frequently denied the right to organize and are subjected to mass firings and blacklisting, particularly in export-processing zones, where the majority of workers are women.

The judicial system remains ineffectual for most legal and human rights complaints. In general, it suffers from corruption, intimidation, insufficient personnel, lack of training opportunities, and lack of transparency and accountability. The indigenous population continues to be shut out from the national justice system. Although indigenous languages are now being used in courtrooms around the country, Guatemalan authorities mostly dismiss traditional justice systems. Cursory recruitment efforts have resulted in only a handful of indigenous recruits for the National Civilian Police (PNC).

Despite increasing freedom, Guatemala has yet to end a tradition of military dominance. The demobilization of the presidential bodyguard and military intelligence, the two units held most accountable for human rights abuses, mandated by the peace accords has finally taken place. Berger reduced the armed forces from 27,000 to 15,500 troops. Guatemala remains one of the most violent countries in Latin America. During the first seven months of 2004, more than 2,000 murders took place. The closing of military barracks throughout the country—the armed forces were the one Guatemalan institution that had a truly national presence—while the PNC was being created and deployed created a vacuum in which criminal activity escalated. One result was an upsurge of vigilantism and lynchings. Neighborhood patrols, some armed with automatic weapons, have sprung up in an attempt to arrest the spiraling crime wave. More than 60,000 private security guards far outnumber the PNC. Former president Alfonso Portillo had called out army troops to assist the PNC, whose 22,000 members are overtasked, undertrained, and frequently corrupt, in patrolling urban areas. Drug trafficking is a serious problem, and Guatemala remains a transit point for drugs going to the United States.

Eighty percent of the population lives below poverty levels, and infant mortality rates among the Maya are among the highest on the continent.

Violence against women and children is widespread and common. Street children and women, especially those believed to be engaged in prostitution, are the most common victims of murder. Women and children are drawn into prostitution both locally and in neighboring countries. Guatemala has a murder rate of 101 per 100,000, which is almost twice the Central American rate and three times that of Latin America. Guatemala has the highest rate of child labor in the Americas, with one-third of school-aged children forced to work on farms or in factories. There is extensive human trafficking, especially of illegal aliens from Asia en route to the United States.

⬇ Guinea

Population: 9,200,000 **Political Rights:** 6
GNI/capita: $410 **Civil Liberties:** 5
Life Expectancy: 49 **Status:** Not Free
Religious Groups: Muslim (85 percent), Christian (8 percent), indigenous beliefs (7 percent)
Ethnic Groups: Peuhl (40 percent), Malinke (30 percent), Soussou (20 percent), other (10 percent)
Capital: Conakry
Trend Arrow: Guinea received a downward trend arrow due to the poor conduct of the December 2003 presidential elections.

Ten-Year Ratings Timeline (Political Rights, Civil Liberties, Status)

1995	1996	1997	1998	1999	2000	2001	2002	2003	2004
6,5NF	6,5NF	6,5NF	6,5NF	6,5NF	6,5NF	6,5NF	6,5NF	6,5NF	6,5NF

Overview: President Lansana Conte won a third term in the December 2003 election that was boycotted by the country's major opposition parties and that international observers criticized as neither free nor fair. Concern mounted over Conte's health and the potential for unrest if he were to die while in office without a clear successor.

Under Ahmed Sekou Toure, Guinea declared independence from France in 1958. Alone among France's many African colonies, Guinea rejected continued close ties with France. Paris retaliated quickly, removing or destroying all "colonial property" and enforcing an unofficial but devastating economic boycott. Sekou Toure's one-party rule became highly repressive, and Guinea was increasingly impoverished under his Soviet-style economic policies. Conte seized power in a 1984 coup and was nearly toppled by a 1996 army mutiny. In the midst of general looting in Conakry, he rallied loyal troops and reestablished his rule.

Conte was returned to office in a 1998 presidential election that was marked by state patronage, media that strongly backed the incumbent, broad manipulation of the electoral process, and opposition disunity. Although the polls were an improvement over past elections, hundreds of people were arrested after the vote, including the official third-place finisher, Alpha Conde. The June 2002 National Assembly elections, in which the ruling Progress and Unity Party easily won a two-thirds majority, were not considered fair because of an opposition boycott and the government's control of the electoral process.

In the December 2003 presidential election, Conte, who reportedly captured more than 90 percent of the vote, faced only one relatively unknown opponent in the poll; a Supreme Court panel had disqualified six other presidential hopefuls for reasons ranging from a failure to pay the application fee to questionable dates of birth. Main opposition parties boycotted the election, and members of the opposition accused Conte of taking control of the electoral commission and of using state funds to finance his campaign. Although the government said turnout was more than 80 percent, human rights groups estimated that it was less than 15 percent and cited several instances of blatant vote rigging. The European Union declined to help finance the election or send observers because of doubts over the fair conduct of the poll.

The Brussels-based International Crisis Group (ICG) reported that the political process in Guinea remained blocked by manipulation of the electoral system and by divisions and weaknesses within the political opposition. It warned that squabbling for power among Guinea's three main tribes—the Soussou, the Peuhl, and the Malinke—and among the country's different political and military factions could plunge Guinea into the kind of chaos seen in neighboring Liberia, Sierra Leone, and Cote d'Ivoire. The ICG said that Guinea's stability depends on the capacity of the army to reach an internal understanding and present a candidate who would be able to impose legitimacy after the departure of Conte.

In April 2004, the Paris-based International Federation for Human Rights harshly criticized Guinea as a "caricature of democracy" where basic freedoms are enshrined in law but not respected by the government. The group warned that Conte's death in office would lead to "a high risk period of transition," which could easily take the form of "a military coup followed by possible violence." Poor health cast doubts during the year on whether Conte would be able to carry out a full seven-year term, and concern is mounting as to whether Guinea can have a peaceful transition of leadership.

In April, authorities charged opposition leader and former prime minister Sidya Toure of plotting a coup; he was cleared of the charges in July. Prime Minister Francois Fall resigned in April and went into exile. Fall, a respected former foreign minister, said that the government was blocking his attempts at political and economic reform.

The country is the world's second-largest producer of bauxite and is also rich in gold, diamonds, and iron ore. However, corruption, mismanagement, and conflict have negatively affected the economy. In 2004, the government struggled to stem mounting public discontent over high prices for rice, which have been blamed on corruption. The World Bank in 2004 halted the disbursement of further loans to Guinea and suspended field projects following the government's failure to pay off debt-servicing arrears. The IMF has also withdrawn from Guinea. Both lenders have cited Guinea for bad governance, lack of transparency, corruption, and improper economic practices.

Political Rights and Civil Liberties:

Citizens of Guinea cannot change their government democratically. A referendum held in 2001 proposed to extend presidential terms from five to seven years, allow for unlimited terms in office, and eliminate presidential age limits. The provisions in the referendum were approved in a flawed vote that was boycotted by members of the opposition and marked by low turnout. The referendum also granted President Lansana Conte the power to appoint local officials and Supreme Court judges. The cabinet and armed forces leadership include members of all major ethnic groups in Guinea, but there are a disproportionate number of senior military officers from Conte's Soussou ethnic group. Politics and parties are largely defined along ethnic lines. The government controls the national election commission, as well as registration and election procedures, including the casting and counting of votes.

Corruption, which has had a detrimental effect on Guinea's economy, has been cited as a serious problem in the country by both the IMF and World Bank. Guinea was not ranked by Transparency International in its 2004 Corruption Perceptions Index.

The government has wide powers to bar any communications that insult the president or disturb the peace, and defamation and slander are considered criminal offenses. A restrictive press law allows the government to censor or shutter publications on broad and ill-defined bases. All broadcasting outlets, as well as the country's largest and only daily newspaper, are state controlled and offer little coverage of the opposition and scant criticism of government policy. Although the law permits private electronic media, the government has never approved license requests for private radio and television stations, on the grounds of national security. Several newspapers in Conakry offer sharp criticism of the government despite frequent harassment. Internet access is unrestricted. The print media have little impact in rural areas, where incomes are low and illiteracy is high.

Constitutionally protected religious rights are respected in practice, although the main body representing the country's Muslims, who constitute a majority of the population, is government controlled. Academic freedom is generally respected, but the government influences hiring and the content of curriculums.

Several statutes restrict freedom of association and assembly in apparent contravention of constitutional guarantees. The government may ban any gathering that "threatens national unity." Authorities arrested more than a dozen student leaders at Gamal Abdel Nasser University after its 14,000 students went on strike in February. Nevertheless, several human rights groups and many other nongovernmental groups operate openly in Guinea. The constitution provides for the right to form and join unions. Several labor confederations compete and have the right to bargain collectively. Unions in rural areas sometimes face harassment and government interference.

While nominally independent, the judicial system remains affected by corruption, nepotism, ethnic bias, and political interference, and lacks resources and training. Minor civil cases are often handled by traditional ethnic-based courts. Arbitrary arrests and detention are common, and there are reports of persistent maltreatment and torture of detainees. Prison conditions are harsh and sometimes life-threatening, although conditions in at least one prison improved in 2003. Security forces commit abuses, including torture and extrajudicial execution, with impunity. Prior to the December 2003 presidential election, about a dozen people were arrested in connection with an alleged coup plot.

Ethnic identification is strong in Guinea, and there is widespread societal discrimination by members of all major ethnic groups. The ruling party is more ethnically integrated than opposition parties, which have clear regional and ethnic bases. In addition to the tens of thousands of refugees from Liberia and Sierra Leone that Guinea hosts, more than 100,000 Guinean migrants returned from Cote d'Ivoire after the outbreak of hostilities there at the end of 2002. Most of the returnees have been hosted by communities along the border, increasing competition for scant resources. Human rights groups say an influx of arms and idle gunmen from Liberia threatens the stability of southeastern Guinea. In addition, many local youths were armed by the government as militiamen when insurgents backed by former Liberian president Charles Taylor unsuccessfully tried to invade Guinea in 2000 and 2001.

Women enjoy far fewer educational and employment opportunities than men, and many societal customs discriminate against women. Constitutionally protected women's rights are often unrealized. Women have access to land, credit, and business, but inheritance laws favor men. Violence against women is said to be prevalent. Spousal abuse is a criminal offense, but security forces rarely intervene in domestic matters. Women's groups are working to eradicate the illegal, but widespread, practice of female genital mutilation.

Guinea-Bissau

Population: 1,500,000   **Political Rights:** 4*
GNI/capita: $130   **Civil Liberties:** 4
Life Expectancy: 45   **Status:** Partly Free
Religious Groups: Indigenous beliefs (50 percent),
Muslim (45 percent), Christian (5 percent)
Ethnic Groups: Balanta (30 percent), Fula (20 percent),
Manjaca (14 percent), Mandinga (13 percent), Papel (7 percent),
other (16 percent)
Capital: Bissau
Ratings Change: Guinea-Bissau's political rights rating improved from 6 to 4 due
to legislative elections that international observers described as largely free and fair.

Ten-Year Ratings Timeline (Political Rights, Civil Liberties, Status)

1995	1996	1997	1998	1999	2000	2001	2002	2003	2004
3,4PF	3,4PF	3,4PF	3,5PF	3,5PF	4,5PF	4,5PF	4,5PF	6,4PF	4,4PF

Overview:

With the holding of legislative elections in March 2004, Guinea-Bissau took one of the first steps in its pledged return to democratic rule following a coup in 2003 that toppled elected president Kumba Yala. However, a military mutiny in October, during which the head of the armed forces, General Verissimo Correia Seabre, who had led the 2003 coup, was killed, threatened to derail the transition.

Guinea-Bissau won independence from Portugal in 1973, after a 12-year guerrilla war. The African Party for the Independence of Guinea-Bissau and Cape Verde (PAIGC) held power for the next 18 years. Luis Cabral became president in 1974 and made Joao Bernardo Vieira his prime minister, but Vieira toppled Cabral in 1980. Constitutional revisions in 1991 ended the PAIGC's repressive one-party rule. Vieira won the country's first free and fair presidential election in 1994, but he eventually came to be seen as the leader of a corrupt ruling class.

An army mutiny broke out in 1998 after Vieira sacked General Ansumane Mane, accusing him of smuggling arms to rebels in the southern Casamance region of neighboring Senegal, which for years had complained that Guinea-Bissau was backing the rebels. Encouraged by France, Senegal and Guinea sent about 3,000 troops to intervene on behalf of Vieira. The troops were eventually replaced by fewer than 600 unarmed West African peacekeepers, which made Vieira vulnerable to his overthrow in May 1999 by Mane.

In the November 1999 presidential elections, the populist Yala, of the Social Renewal Party (PRS), won a January 2000 second-round runoff over Malam Bacai Sanha of the PAIGC. However, fighting broke out in 2000 between military supporters of Yala and those of Mane after Mane declared himself the head of the armed forces; Mane was subsequently killed. In November 2002, Yala dissolved the National Assembly. He failed to promulgate a constitution approved in 2001, and Guinea-Bissau was governed by decree.

By the time the military, led by Seabre, stepped in, in 2003, civil servants had not been paid for nearly a year, there was no constitution, strikes were rampant, and parliamentary elections had been postponed four times. As a result of consultations with a spectrum of political groups, a Transitional National Council (TNC) was established to oversee a pledged return to elected government. A businessman, Henrique Rosa, was named interim president.

After the coup, a blanket amnesty was granted to all those involved. Nonetheless, in October 2004, soldiers staged a mutiny, killing Seabre. The outcome of his killing was not immediately clear, but it could deepen divisions within the military. Several other military officers went into hiding. The mutinous soldiers, who were demanding payment of outstanding wages, and better pay and living conditions in the barracks, denied staging a coup.

In March 2004 legislative elections, the PAIGC won 45 of the 102 seats, compared with 35 seats for the PRS. Smaller parties took the remainder. Presidential elections are to be held in 2005. Prime Minister Carlos Gomes Jr.'s cabinet is dominated by young technocrats. Yala, who spent nearly six months under house arrest, was barred from taking part in any political activity for the next five years.

Despite the successful conduct of the March legislative polls, Guinea-Bissau's stability is by no means guaranteed. The United Nations said in a report in June that the process of democratization remained fragile. The report highlighted the persistence of ethnic imbalances and pay arrears in the armed forces and the poor condition of the military barracks, and it also expressed concern at the human rights situation, particularly the continued detention without trial of 20 people arrested in December 2002 in connection with a coup attempt.

The vast majority of Guinea-Bissau's one million citizens survive on subsistence farming. Cashew nuts are a key export. There are hopes for substantial oil reserves offshore. An emergency budget was drawn up in 2004 with the support of the IMF, the World Bank, and the African Development Bank.

Political Rights and Civil Liberties: The people of Guinea-Bissau were able to choose their government freely for the first time in 1994, and both direct presidential polls and legislative elections were judged free and fair by international observers. Voting in the 1999 legislative and presidential elections was declared free and fair by international observers despite widespread delays, isolated cases of violence, and other voting irregularities. The March 2004 legislative elections were marked by strong turnout, and international observers declared the polls largely free and fair despite some administrative problems such as ballot shortages and polling booths opening late. President Kumba Yala was overthrown in a military coup in September 2003, and Henrique Rosa was named interim president pending elections; presidential elections are scheduled to be held in 2005.

Guinea-Bissau was not ranked in Transparency International's 2004 Corruption Perceptions Index. Official graft, however, has been a serious problem. Hopes were raised after Yala's ouster that new leaders would make efforts to reduce corruption.

Freedom of speech and the press is guaranteed, but journalists practice self-censorship and face some harassment. Repression of the press eased after Yala's ouster. There are several private and community radio stations. Few private newspapers publish, and the lack of vibrant, independent media outlets may be due more to financial constraints than to government interference. Internet access is unrestricted.

Religious freedom is protected and is usually respected in practice. Academic freedom is guaranteed and respected.

The right to peaceful assembly and association is guaranteed and usually respected in practice. Several hundred students rioted in the capital in March 2004 after police used batons and tear gas and fired into the air to break up a demonstration by secondary school pupils protesting a strike by their teachers; several dozen students were arrested.

Nongovernmental organizations and human rights groups operate openly. The right to strike is guaranteed. Collective bargaining rights are not guaranteed, but a National Council for Social Consultation has been established, including the government, workers, and employers, to deal with labor issues. Most wages are established in bilateral negotiations.

The judiciary has operated independently of the government, but its freedom was increasingly limited by Yala. Judicial performance is often unpredictable owing to political interference, poor training, and scant resources. The transitional government reinstated Supreme Court judges previously barred or arrested. Traditional law usually prevails in rural areas. Police routinely ignore privacy rights and protections against search and seizure. Prison conditions are harsh.

Women face some legal and significant traditional and societal discrimination, despite legal protection. They generally do not receive equal pay for equal work and have fewer opportunities for education and jobs in the small formal sector. Domestic violence against women is common, and female genital mutilation is legal and widespread. The government has formed a national committee to discourage the practice.

⬇ Guyana

Population: 800,000   **Political Rights:** 2
GNI/capita: $881   **Civil Liberties:** 2
Life Expectancy: 63   **Status:** Free
Religious Groups: Christian (50 percent), Hindu (35 percent), Muslim (10 percent), other (5 percent)
Ethnic Groups: East Indian (50 percent), black (36 percent), Amerindian (7 percent), other (7 percent)
Capital: Georgetown
Trend Arrow: Guyana received a downward trend arrow due to the failure of the government to effectively reform a police force facing credible accusations of extrajudicial killings.

Ten-Year Ratings Timeline (Political Rights, Civil Liberties, Status)

1995	1996	1997	1998	1999	2000	2001	2002	2003	2004
2,2F	2,2F	2,2F	2,2F	2,2F	2,2F	2,2F	2,2F	2,2F	2,2F

Overview: Guyanese political life was dominated in 2004 by public allegations by a self-confessed police informant about the existence of death squads that included current and former police officers. The charges spilled over into the political arena, when the main opposition party announced it was breaking off a "constructive engagement" dialogue with the government begun in May 2003.

From independence in 1966 until 1992, Guyana was ruled by the autocratic, predominantly Afro-Guyanese, People's National Congress (PNC). Descendants of indentured workers from India—known as Indo-Guyanese—make up about half of the population, while about 36 percent are Afro-Guyanese descended from African slaves.

Finance Minister Bharrat Jagdeo, of the PPP/C, an alliance of the predominantly Indo-Guyanese People's Progressive Party (PPP) and the Civic Party, replaced the alliance's Janet Jagan as president after she resigned, because of ill health, in August 1999. Jagdeo was reelected on March 19, 2001, after 90 percent of eligible voters turned out to cast their ballots in voting that showed the country's continuing deep divisions along racial lines. Jagdeo's first initiative on being declared the winner was to make a televised national appeal to his countrymen to begin a process of national healing. In mid-2001, violence erupted in several small towns in protest against crime, poverty, and poor public services.

A rising crime rate and a parliamentary impasse dominated Guyana's political scene throughout 2002. The PPP/C and the main opposition People's National Congress/Reform (PNC/R) traded bitter words over the issue of payment for opposition members engaged in a boycott of parliament that began in March 2002 and lasted for 14 months.

From February to September 2002, nearly a dozen police officers and more than 50 civilians were killed in an outbreak of violent crime that exacerbated uneasy relations between the two main races. In September, the PPP/C-dominated parliament passed four anticrime initiatives. However, PNC/R representatives who boycotted the legislative session claimed that the measures would not solve Guyana's crime problem, but rather were meant "to arm the regime with the draconian powers of dictatorship."

In January 2003, Amnesty International called recently adopted anticrime legislation "draconian" and said that its mandatory death penalty provisions for those committing a "terrorist act" were "in breach of international law." The organization was also particularly concerned that "the broad and vague definition of 'terrorist act'...could be interpreted so as to encompass activities which involve the legitimate exercise of rights guaranteed under international law," including the right to strike.

In September, a new controversy erupted with the publication of a draft of a June World Bank report that claimed there was a "crisis of governance" in Guyana and that the government in Georgetown, which had yet to demonstrate a "real commitment to political reform," was unable to promote growth and development or to manage the challenges of endemic crime and corruption. The crisis, the report said, "discouraged investments, severely compromised good governance and fuelled migration." The World Bank report warned that increasing racial tension would result in violent conflict. Also, that month, Jagdeo asked U.S. president George Bush for help in combating cocaine trafficking, saying he feared that the Colombian drug trade was gaining a foothold in Guyana.

The political climate appeared to improve, however briefly, in early 2004, when the two main parties announced that they had reached agreement on a wide variety of issues, including tax reform, procurement, and the composition of the commissions that control appointments, promotions, and discipline in the judiciary, the police, public administration, and public education.

Then, in January 2004, a police informant brought public accusations of the existence of death squads whose members included current and former police officials who, he said, enjoyed official sanction and had killed some 64 people. Investigations involving gun licenses and telephone records revealed alleged links to Guyana's home affairs minister, and both the United States and Canada revoked the minister's visa without publicly stating their reasons. However, efforts to probe the charges, which created both a domestic and international outcry, ground to a standstill when the informant himself was murdered in June and the chief magistrate heading the inquiry quit, following reports that she herself was on a death squad "hit list."

After accusations concerning the existence of the alleged death squads was heard, three "rule of law" marches were held in the nation's capital. Officials admitted that following the death of the former police informant who revealed the alleged existence of the death squads, potential witnesses were afraid to come forward. In protest of the alleged involvement of the home affairs minister with the death squads, the main opposition party, the PNC/R, began boycotting most sessions of parliament for several weeks, including the presentation and debate of the 2004 budget. The breakdown occurred just after the two parties announced agreement on a wide range of issues.

Political Rights and Civil Liberties:

Citizens of Guyana can change their government democratically. The 2001 elections generated a broader consensus about the importance of election reform to the democratic process. The 1980 constitution provides for a strong president and a 65-seat National Assembly elected every five years. The leader of the party winning the plurality of parliamentary seats becomes president for a five-year term, and the president appoints the prime minister and cabinet.

Guyana was not ranked by Transparency International in its 2004 Corruption Perceptions Index. However, the U.S. State Department's March 2004 International Narcotics Control Strategy Report, which declares the country to be a transshipment point for South American cocaine destined for North America and Europe, also says that "counter-narcotics efforts are undermined by corruption," and that "allegations of corruption are widespread, and reach to high levels of government, but continue to go uninvestigated."

Several independent newspapers operate freely, including the daily *Stabroek News*. However, a growing number of journalists charged the government with failure to respect freedom of the electronic media. The government owns and operates the country's sole radio station, which broadcasts on three frequencies. There are no private radio stations. Seventeen privately owned television stations freely criticize the government. However, opposition party leaders complain that they lack access to the state media.

Guyanese generally enjoy freedom of religion, and the government does not restrict academic freedom.

The freedom to organize political parties, civic organizations, and labor unions is generally respected. Labor unions are well organized. However, companies are not obligated to recognize unions in former state enterprises sold off by the government.

The judicial system is independent, although due process is undermined by shortages of staff and funds. Guyana was the only former British colony in the Caribbean to have cut all ties to the Privy Council of London, the court of last resort for other former colonies in the region. A Trinidad-based Caribbean Court of Justice, which will open its doors in 2005, will become Guyana's highest appellate court. Prisons are overcrowded, and conditions are poor.

The Guyana Defence Force and the Guyana Police Force are under civilian control, the latter invested with the authority to make arrests and maintain law and order throughout the country. Racial polarization has seriously eroded Guyana law enforcement: Many Indo-Guyanese say they are victims of Afro-Guyanese criminals at the same time that they are largely ignored by the predominantly Afro-Guyanese police; many Afro-Guyanese claim that the police are manipulated by the government for its own purposes. Although official inquiries have repeatedly pointed to the need for improved investigative techniques, more funding, community-oriented policing, better disciplinary procedures, and greater accountability, as well as a better ethnic balance, in the police, the government has given mostly lip service to the proposed reforms. The March 2004 State Department narcotics control report noted that "the swearing-in by the Guyana Police Force of a reputed drug lord and several of his cohorts as special constables raises serious questions about the integrity of the Force."

The Guyana Human Rights Association, an autonomous and effective group backed by independent civic and religious groups, reported that security forces killed 39 civilians during 2003, compared with 28 in 2002. Although authorities have taken some steps to investigate extrajudicial killings, and charges against some officers have been brought, the numbers are further evidence that abuses are still committed with impunity.

Racial clashes have diminished within the last decade. However, long-standing animosity between Afro- and Indo-Guyanese remains a deep concern. A Racial Hostility Bill passed in September 2002 increased the penalties for race-based crimes. In May 2003, the government appointed an ethnic relations commission to help combat discrimination and reduce social tensions.

There are nine groups of indigenous peoples in Guyana numbering approximately 80,000, or 10 percent of the population, and they constitute the country's fastest-growing ethnic group. Human rights violations against them are widespread and pervasive, particularly concerning the failure of the state to adequately respect indigenous land and resource rights. Indigenous peoples' attempts to seek redress through the courts have been met with unwarranted delays by the judiciary. On a positive note, two large Amerindian communities, the Konashen and the Baramita, recently received absolute grants to their lands that will allow their villages the permanent right to their property.

Violence against women, including domestic violence, is common in Guyana. There are no legal protections against sexual harassment in the workplace. In a positive development, in 2004, a group, Men of Purpose, was created to combat domestic violence. In 2003, the government shelved a constitutional amendment that would have outlawed discrimination against gays and lesbians.

Haiti

Population: 8,100,000 **Political Rights:** 7*
GNI/capita: $440 **Civil Liberties:** 6
Life Expectancy: 51 **Status:** Not Free
Religious Groups: Roman Catholic (80 percent),
Protestant (16 percent), other (4 percent)
Ethnic Groups: Black (95 percent), mulatto and white
(5 percent)
Capital: Port-au-Prince
Ratings Change: Haiti's political rights rating declined from 6 to 7 due to the lack
of a democratically derived sovereign authority resulting from the ouster of President
Jean Bertrand Aristide, the imposition of an ineffective interim government, and the
deployment of an international security force.

Ten-Year Ratings Timeline (Political Rights, Civil Liberties, Status)

1995	1996	1997	1998	1999	2000	2001	2002	2003	2004
5,5PF	4,5PF	4,5PF	5,5PF	5,5PF	6,5NF	6,6NF	6,6NF	6,6NF	7,6NF

Overview:
On February 29, 2004, Jean-Bertrand Aristide resigned from the presidency and went into initial exile in the Central African Republic. Despite efforts to maintain a constitutional façade, the government continued to govern through force and intimidation, as Haiti became a dictatorship in all but name.

Since gaining independence from France in 1804 following a slave revolt, the Republic of Haiti has endured a history of poverty, violence, instability, and dictatorship. A 1986 military coup ended 29 years of rule by the Duvalier family, and the army ruled for most of the next eight years. Under international pressure, the military permitted the implementation of a French-style constitution in 1987.

Aristide was first elected in 1990. After having called on his supporters to use force in defending his government, he was deposed by a military triumvirate after only eight months in office and sent into exile. While paramilitary thugs terrorized the populace, the regime engaged in blatant narcotics trafficking. The United States and the United Nations imposed a trade and oil embargo. In September 1994, facing an imminent U.S. invasion, the officers stepped down. U.S. troops took control of the country, and Aristide was reinstated. Aristide dismantled the military before the June 1995 parliamentary elections got under way. International observers questioned the legitimacy of the June election, and Aristide's supporters fell out among themselves. The more militant Lavalas Family (FL) party remained firmly behind him, while the National Front for Change and Democracy (FNCD), a leftist coalition that had backed him in 1990, claimed fraud and boycotted the runoff elections. The FL won an overwhelming parliamentary majority.

The FL nominated Rene Preval, who had been Aristide's prime minister in 1991, as its presidential candidate in the fall. In the December 17, 1995, election, marred by irregularities and fraud, Preval won about 89 percent of the vote with a turnout of less than one-third of those eligible; he took office on February 7, 1996. The United

Nations had planned to withdraw its troops by the end of the month. The new U.S.-trained Haitian National Police (HNP), however, lacked the competence to fill the void. At Preval's urging, the United Nations extended its stay, but by June cut its presence to 1,300; the final U.S. combat force had withdrawn two months earlier.

Aristide, previously revered as a defender of the powerless, was swept to victory again in November 2000. The elections were boycotted by all major opposition parties and held amid widespread civil unrest and voter intimidation. Aristide ran on a populist platform of economic reactivation; opponents claimed he was bent on establishing a one-party state. Aristide's nearly 92 percent of the vote in the presidential election was mirrored in contests for nine Senate seats—all won by his FL party—giving his new government all but one seat in the upper house. In parliamentary elections, which opponents claimed were rigged, the FL won 80 percent of the seats in the lower house.

Although constitutionally elected, Aristide ultimately lacked the domestic legitimacy and international backing to stay in power. Seeking to prevent chaos and the taking of power by the armed opposition, the United States and France landed a peacekeeping force. Aristide's troubled government, unable to overcome the fraudulent elections of 2000, which had given it a stranglehold over power, found itself alone in power as the mandates of 4 senators and all 83 deputies expired on January 12, 2004.

With no possibility for popular elections to be held in January and left with only 15 sitting senators—9 had already resigned—Aristide would be forced to govern by decree. The opposition, united under the Democratic Convergence (DC), remained unwilling to negotiate a political solution that kept Aristide in office. In the meantime, an armed insurrection led by the Front de Resistance, that had gradually taken shape in the previous months, crystallized on February 5. This development raised the prospect that the country could fall to an organized group of armed ruffians, many of whom had been Aristide supporters, previously known as the Cannibal Army (AC).

On Aristide's resignation in February, in line with constitutional procedures, Boniface Alexandre, head of the Supreme Court, was sworn into office as president. Yvon Neptune, an Aristide loyalist, agreed to remain in office to help the transition process. Political decay continued throughout the rest of the country. By March 1, the National Resistance Front for the Liberation of Haiti, led by the controversial Guy Philippe, a former soldier and the U.S.-trained chief of police of Cap Haitien, rolled into Port-au-Prince. Without a mandate to disarm the new arrivals, the peacekeeping force limited itself to patrols, while generalized looting took place.

On March 10, a commission of elder statesmen announced that Gerard Latortue, who had been in exile in Miami, would become the country's new prime minister. The multinational peacekeeping force gradually extended its reach from the capital and was renewed by the leadership of Brazil and forces from Chile, Argentina, and Uruguay, as well as others. These forces, however, continued to be spread thin, and violence still erupted around the country. Destructive floods that took more than 2,000 lives in May exacerbated the political chaos. In September, gangs of former soldiers challenged the by-now UN-led peacekeeping force. A protracted struggle led to an uneasy peace, with the peacekeepers holding nominal control over the country, but having a continuous presence only in major cities.

Political stability has not followed the anarchy that coincided with the departure of Aristide. After leaving the Central African Republic, his brief presence in neighboring Jamaica (before long-term exile in South Africa) fueled the discontent of his many followers, some of whom remain unconvinced that he departed of his own will. The government of Prime Minister Latortue, lacking a strong political base, continues to try to establish order, primarily through the use of a retrained police force. Negotiations with the opposition have not yet led to a clear indication of when parliamentary elections will take place, or if the presidential elections to be held in February 2005 can go on as scheduled.

Haiti has the lowest life expectancy and highest infant mortality rates in the Western Hemisphere. Haiti's people are among the poorest in the Western Hemisphere and have the lowest levels of human development, including a literacy rate of less than 50 percent. In August 2004, the UN Food and Agriculture Organization announced that 50 percent of Haiti's population lacks "food security," the food needed to live a healthy and active life.

Political Rights and Civil Liberties: Citizens of Haiti cannot change their government democratically. Haiti's 1987 constitution provides for a president elected for five years, an elected parliament composed of the 27-member Senate and the 83-member Chamber of Deputies, and a prime minister appointed by the president. Credible charges of irregularities and fraud have beset every election since 1990. The FL party has manipulated most elections, including the presidential poll of 2000. Until the departure of President Jean-Bertrand Aristide, the FL controlled the presidential, legislative, and judicial branches, while most local and regional elected leaders were members of the same party.

Haiti received the dubious distinction of being ranked with Bangladesh as the most corrupt country in the world by Transparency International in its 2004 Corruption Perceptions Index.

Freedom of speech and the press continues to be limited, and violence against journalists is common. International observers find that media outlets still tend to practice self-censorship over fear of violent retribution. There are a variety of newspapers, including two French-language ones, with a combined circulation of less than 20,000 readers. Many newspapers include a page of news in Creole. While opposition to the government can be found in the written press, access to such views is beyond the reach of most, primarily because of illiteracy and cost. There are 275 private radio stations, including 43 in the capital. Most stations carry news and talk shows, which many citizens regard as their only opportunity to speak out with some freedom. Television is state run and strongly biased toward the government. There are five television stations, and although satellite television is available, it has a minimal impact, as most Haitians cannot afford access to television. The few stations carrying news or opinion broadcasts express a range of views. There is no censorship of books or films, and access to the Internet is free.

There is freedom of religion. The official educational system was hostage to patronage and pressure from the FL.

Freedom of assembly and association, including labor rights, are not respected. Unions are too weak to engage in collective bargaining, and their organizing efforts are undermined by the country's high unemployment rate.

The judicial system continues to be corrupt, inefficient, and dysfunctional. The legal system is burdened by a large backlog, outdated legal codes, and poor facilities; business is conducted in French rather than Creole, Haiti's majority language. Prison conditions are harsh, and the ponderous legal system guarantees lengthy pretrial detention periods. International reform efforts ended in 2000 following allegations of corruption involving the U.S. Agency for International Development, U.S. Justice Department contractors, and others.

The 5,200-member Haitian National Police (HNP) force has been politicized by the FL, is inexperienced, and lacks resources. The HNP has been accused of using excessive force and mistreating detainees, and accusations of corruption are frequent. The HNP was increasingly used against protesters attacking the government. Police brutality is still on the rise, and there is credible evidence of extrajudicial killings by members of the HNP.

Mob violence and armed gangs pose serious threats in urban areas. Former soldiers and others linked to the former military regime, as well as common criminals, are responsible for much of the violence, including political assassinations. Break-ins and armed robberies are commonplace, and many observers tie the growing violence directly to increases in the drug trade and local narcotics consumption. Haitian officials also say that the rise in crime is due to the repatriation of convicted criminals from other countries, particularly the United States. Turf wars between rival drug gangs have resulted in the killing of scores of people, including several policemen. Private security forces that carry out extralegal search and seizure are flourishing.

Trafficking of drugs and people is a serious problem. There is widespread violence against women and children. Up to 300,000 children serve in *restavec* ("live with" in Creole), a form of unpaid domestic labor with a long national history.

Honduras

Population: 7,000,000
GNI/capita: $930
Life Expectancy: 71
Religious Groups: Roman Catholic (97 percent), other [including Protestant] (3 percent)
Ethnic Groups: Mestizo (90 percent), Amerindian (7 percent), black (2 percent), white (1 percent)
Capital: Tegucigalpa

Political Rights: 3
Civil Liberties: 3
Status: Partly Free

Ten-Year Ratings Timeline (Political Rights, Civil Liberties, Status)

1995	1996	1997	1998	1999	2000	2001	2002	2003	2004
3,3PF	3,3F	2,3F	2,3PF	3,3PF	3,3PF	3,3PF	3,3PF	3,3PF	3,3PF

Overview:

Election campaigning for Honduras' November 2005 presidential elections already began during 2004, despite a law prohibiting such early campaigning. Meanwhile, a large prison fire in which more than 100 inmates, mostly gang members, were killed was the latest incident in serious gang-related violence in the country.

The Republic of Honduras was established in 1839, eighteen years after independence from Spain. It has endured decades of military rule and intermittent elected government, with the last military regime giving way to elected civilian rule in 1982. The 1969 armed conflict between Honduras and El Salvador over land, sometimes known as the "Soccer War," ended with a peace treaty in 1980. In 1992, the International Court of Justice ruled that 69 percent of the territory in dispute should go to Honduras, and the court ruled further, in late 2003, against El Salvador's latest appeal. Nonetheless, in 2004, El Salvador again appealed the judgment, citing new evidence.

In the November 25, 2001, parliamentary election, the center-left National Party of Hondruas (PN) captured the largest number of seats, followed closely by the conservative Liberal Party (PL). After winning the concurrent presidential election, the PN's Ricardo Maduro Joest took office on January 27, 2002. Elected on a "zero tolerance" pledge aimed at ending crime, Maduro defeated PL candidate Rafael Pineda Ponce by 8 percent of the vote. The elections, the sixth held since military rule came to an end, were characterized by international observers as mostly free, fair, and peaceful. On the eve of the election, however, congressional candidate Angel Pacheco, of the PN, was gunned down outside his house. Police arrested three employees of the PL, an indication that the crime might have been politically motivated.

Although the next national elections are not scheduled until November 27, 2005—and a new electoral law passed in May 2004 limits the length of campaigns to 90 days for primary and 120 days for general elections—campaigning already began during the year. The campaigns are subject to new disclosures and media limitations, but limitations on the media have already failed as unofficial campaigns by presidential hopefuls are in full swing. Maduro's approval rating of 37 percent leads political analysts to predict that the PN is not likely to break the cycle of failed reelection efforts characteristic of the country. The PL's two main factions have established an alliance that seeks to counter Maduro's decline in popularity with a show of unity by the opposition. Most of Maduro's woes come from the country's weak economic performance as well as a host of austerity measures the government implemented in 2004 to receive favorable terms from the IMF and others to reduce its debt burden.

Gang violence has escalated in Honduras in recent years and includes apparently random attacks against both civilians and the police. In response, Congress unanimously approved a law in August 2003 banning gangs and stiffening the penalties for membership. Membership in a gang is now punishable by up to 12 years in prison, and the law also provides for fines of up to $12,000 for gang leaders. The national commissioner of human rights is questioning the constitutionality of the law. Though controversial, support for the tough stand taken against the gangs has not diminished among average Hondurans. The Ministry of Security has reported that of the estimated 70,000 gang members in Central America, 65 percent can be found in Honduras. There are some 36,000 gang members and 65,000 others who associate with gang members in the country, with 129 gangs active in the capital alone. By September 2003, in Operation Freedom, 300 people had been arrested under the new law.

Several severe outbursts of violence, including mass murders on buses, have been attributed to gangs. On May 17, 2004, a large fire at the San Pedro Sula prison killed 104 inmates, most of them members of the Salvatrucha gang. This followed an April 2003 fire where 68 inmates, also gang members, died in a prison near La Ceiba on the Caribbean coast. A study of the 2003 fire that Maduro commissioned concluded that most of the dead had been killed by prison guards working with other gang members; to date there have been no prosecutions in the La Ceiba incident.

The aftereffects of Hurricane Mitch, which devastated the country's economy and infrastructure in 1998, continued to be felt in 2004. About two-thirds of households live in poverty, and 40 percent of the population live on less than one dollar a day.

Political Rights and Civil Liberties: Citizens of Honduras are able to change their government through regularly scheduled elections, and the 2001 contest was considered generally free and fair. The constitution provides for a president and a 130-member, unicameral Congress elected for four-year terms. The number of votes received by a party's presidential candidate determines the proportional representation of each party.

Official corruption and the lingering power of the military have dominated the political scene since the return to democracy. Honduras was ranked 114 out of 146 countries surveyed in Transparency International's 2004 Corruption Perceptions Index.

Authorities generally respect constitutional guarantees of freedom of speech and of the press. Newspapers circulate freely, numerous radio and television stations broadcast freely, and there is free access to the Internet. There are, however, important exceptions, including credible reports of repression against journalists. Journalists have admitted to self-censorship when they uncover reports that threaten the political or economic interests of media owners. In 2004, Reporters Sans Frontieres reported that repressive laws restricting the media were still enforced. The group cited the case of Renato Alvarez, who was sentenced to two years and eight months for slander (suspended for five years on condition of "good behavior") and deprived of some civil rights. His crime involved questioning Security Minister Oscar Alvarez and revealing the names of public figures accused of involvement in corrupt practices. While intimidation of the media, especially through the use of slander laws, is relatively common, the death of a journalist is not, and the murder of the journalist German Antonio Rivas late in 2003 caused great upheaval; as of late 2004, his violent death has not been solved.

Freedom of religion is respected. Academic freedom is generally honored.

Constitutional guarantees regarding the right to form political parties and civic organizations are generally respected, and citizens have the right to assembly freely. Labor unions are well organized and can strike, although labor actions often result in clashes with security forces. Labor leaders and members of religious groups and indigenous-based peasant unions pressing for land rights remain vulnerable to repression and have been killed.

The judicial system is weak and open to corruption, and due process is generally not followed. Changes introduced early in the administration of President Ricardo Maduro Joest, including increasing the number of Supreme Court justices to 15, have not borne fruit. Death threats and violent attacks continue against judges who take on human rights cases. Prison conditions are deplorable, and prisoners awaiting trial are housed with convicted inmates. Two deadly fires (in 2003 and 2004) have highlighted the appalling conditions in prisons. Generalized lawlessness has allowed private and vigilante security forces to commit a number of arbitrary and summary executions, including the murders of hundreds of street children. Drug trafficking through Honduras is on the rise, and drug-related corruption is pervasive.

The police are underfunded, ill trained, understaffed, and highly corrupt. The military controlled the police since 1963, but civilian control was reestablished beginning in 1997. In the past, the military was for internal security tasks—suppressing labor unrest, quelling street protests, and combating street crime. Extrajudicial killings, arbitrary detention, and torture by the police still take place. There is open talk of social cleansing by off-duty law enforcement officials and private citizens in groups known as "death cars." Several hundred youth gangs engage in murder, kidnapping, and robbery, as well as drug trafficking. The need to strengthen and professionalize the poorly equipped civilian police is hampered by a lack of public confidence.

At the invitation of the government, the UN Special Rapporteur on Extrajudicial, Summary, or Arbitrary Executions visited Honduras in 2001 and noted evidence that 66 minors were killed by police and private security forces from January to June 2001 and that the government was negligent in investigating or preventing extrajudicial and summary executions. Casa Alianza, which works with street children, has calculated that from January 1998 to March 2004, more than 2,190 youths were killed; in 2003 alone, 557 were killed, up from 93 in 1998. In November 2002, after being shamed by international publicity over the murders of hundreds of children, the government announced the formation of a special security force, in addition to the 6,000 new police officers already put on the streets.

The military exerts considerable, if waning, influence over the government. A constitutional amendment established a civilian minister of defense in direct control over the armed forces and replaced the position of armed forces commander in chief with that of chief of the joint staff. Congress also passed the Organic Law of the armed forces to solidify civilian control over the military. Former president Carlos Roberto Reina (1993–1997) defied the military and abolished compulsory military service. The armed forces made public its budget for the first time in 2001. Most criminal cases against the military remained under military court jurisdiction, and charges were usually dismissed, even though since 1999, military personnel have no longer been immune from prosecution in civilian courts. Military officers have been found guilty of drug trafficking, including taking sides in cartel turf wars and protecting drug shipments in transit through Honduras.

The government of President Carlos Flores Facusse (1997–2001) had made efforts to give the concerns of indigenous and black peoples in Honduras a more prominent place in the public agenda. The current wave of violent crime, some of which is directed against the indigenous community, has pushed such efforts into the background.

Some 85,000 workers, mostly women, are employed in the low-wage *maquiladora* (assembly plant) export sector. Child labor is a problem in rural areas and in the informal economy. Prostitution is a serious problem, involving local women and children as well as sex workers from neighboring countries.

Hungary

Population: 10,100,000
GNI/capita: $5,290
Life Expectancy: 73
Religious Groups: Roman Catholic (67.5 percent), Calvinist (20 percent), Lutheran (5 percent), other (7.5 percent)
Ethnic Groups: Hungarian (90 percent), Roma (4 percent), German (3 percent), other (3 percent)
Capital: Budapest

Political Rights: 1
Civil Liberties: 1*
Status: Free

Ratings Change: Hungary's civil liberties rating improved from 2 to 1 due to the deepening of EU integration trends, resulting in greater conformity with EU human rights standards.

Ten-Year Ratings Timeline (Political Rights, Civil Liberties, Status)

1995	1996	1997	1998	1999	2000	2001	2002	2003	2004
1,2F	1,2F	1,2F	1,2F	1,2F	1,2F	1,2F	1,2F	1,2F	1,1F

Overview:

In May 2004, Hungary finally achieved its long-standing goal of joining the European Union (EU). However, after removing a minister belonging to the junior coalition party, Prime Minister Peter Medgyessy was deposed in August by the two parties in his coalition government; he was replaced by former businessman Ferenc Gyurcsany.

King Stephen I, who ruled from 1001 to 1038, is credited with founding the Hungarian state. In the centuries that followed, Hungarian lands passed through Turkish, Polish, and Austrian hands. In the mid-nineteenth century, Hungary established a liberal constitutional monarchy under the Austrian Hapsburgs, but two world wars and a Communist dictatorship in the twentieth century forestalled true independence. In the late 1980s, the country's economy was in sharp decline, and the Hungarian Socialist Worker's Party came under intense pressure to accept reforms. Ultimately, the party congress dissolved itself, and Hungary held its first free, multiparty parliamentary election in 1990. Since that time, government control in Hungary has passed freely and fairly between left- and right-leaning parties. The country has followed an aggressive path of reform and pursued the very popular cause of European integration.

The current political landscape reflects the thin margin of power enjoyed by the governing coalition since a closely contested 2002 parliamentary election. After two rounds of voting, Prime Minister Viktor Orban's ruling coalition of the Hungarian Civic Party-Hungarian Democratic Forum (Fidesz-MDF) garnered just over 44 percent of the vote (188 mandates) and was unable to retain control of parliament. The Hungarian Socialist Party (MSZP) won 42.8 percent (178 mandates), and the Alliance of Free Democrats (SZDSZ) narrowly exceeded the 5 percent threshold (19 mandates). Voters elected one candidate on a joint MSZP-SZDSZ ticket. Following the election, the MSZP formed a majority government in partnership with the SZDSZ. The new Socialist-Liberal government elected Medgyessy as prime minister.

Medgyessy focused on fiscal consolidation. He also sent Hungarian troops into

Iraq, an unpopular move for many voters. After years of negotiation, and an 84 percent "yes" vote in a referendum in 2003, Hungary entered the EU on May 1, 2004, as one of 10 mostly formerly Communist countries joining the bloc. However, shortly afterward, the MSZP, like most governing parties in the EU, did badly in elections to the European Parliament, winning just 9 of 24 seats.

In August, Medgyessy initiated a cabinet reshuffle, removing the SZDSZ economy and transport minister, Istvan Csillag. When the SZDSZ refused to accept the decision, Medgyessy offered to resign as a way of pressuring the party to accede. However, the MSZP accepted his resignation. After appearing ready to back Peter Kiss to replace Medgyessy, the party decided instead to back Ferenc Gyurcsany, a former businessman and sports minister. In office, Gyurcsany must balance the effort to bring Hungary's budget deficit down (it must be less than 3 percent of gross domestic product for Hungary to adopt the euro) with placating the left wing of his party, which advocates more expensive, economically interventionist policies.

Political Rights and Civil Liberties: Citizens of Hungary can change their government democratically. Voters elect representatives to the 386-seat unicameral National Assembly under a mixed system of proportional and direct representation. The Hungarian parliament elects both the president and the prime minister. Parliamentary elections are held every four years.

Post-Communist elections in Hungary have been generally free and fair, although some problems persist. During the heated 2002 parliamentary elections, few parties respected campaign spending caps. The Organization for Security and Cooperation in Europe observed that state media coverage frequently favored the ruling Fidesz party and that government-sponsored "voter education" advertisements appeared to mirror Fidesz-sponsored campaign ads.

Prior to the 2002 election, Fidesz and Lungo Drom, a national Roma (Gypsy) party, concluded a political cooperation agreement. Despite this development, only four Roma candidates were elected to the National Assembly (two from Fidesz and two from the MSZP), the same number as in the previous election. Toward the end of 2002, the European Commission reported that Hungary was not meeting its constitutional obligation to ensure direct parliamentary representation of minorities. Hungary's constitution guarantees national and ethnic minorities the right to form self-governing bodies, and all 13 recognized minorities have exercised this right.

While challenges still remain, previous and current governments have taken measures to introduce stronger penalties for bribery and implement a long-term anticorruption strategy. However, some corruption persists. In 2003-2004 a major corruption scandal involving Hungary's second-biggest bank touched Prime Minister Peter Medgyessy and Laszlo Csaba, the finance minister. Csaba was a director of K&H, the bank involved in the scandal, and Medgyessy was the chairman of Inter-Europa, another bank involved in the affair. There were allegations of questionable public tenders in 2004, and a deputy speaker of parliament resigned after his personal vineyard received large state subsidies. Hungary was ranked 42 out of 146 countries surveyed in Transparency International's 2004 Corruption Perceptions Index.

Freedom of speech is respected, and independent media operate freely in Hungary, although within a highly polarized atmosphere. However, political controversy continues to trouble state television and radio. A 1996 media law requires both ruling and opposition parties to share appointments to state media oversight boards. Left-leaning opposition parties had previously accused the Fidesz party of stacking the oversight boards with supporters. After losing power in the parliamentary elections, Fidesz leaders accused the new Socialist-Liberal government of attempting to inappropriately influence state television and radio. A large number of libel suits in 2004, some resulting in suspended prison sentences for journalists, contributed to the tense media atmosphere. Foreign ownership of Hungarian media (7 of 10 national daily newspapers) is high, but the successful launch of a private Hungarian television station has challenged the argument that state-supported media are necessary for balanced coverage.

The constitution guarantees religious freedom and provides for the separation of church and state. While adherents of all religions are generally free to worship in their own manner, the state provides financial support and tax breaks to large or traditional religions, such as the Roman Catholic Church. Some critics have charged that these practices effectively discriminate against smaller denominations. The state does not restrict academic freedom.

The constitution provides for freedom of assembly, and the government respects these rights in practice. NGOs are active in Hungary, and operate without restrictions. The government respects citizens' rights to form associations, strike, and petition public authorities. Trade unions account for less than 30 percent of the workforce.

Hungary has a three-tiered, independent judiciary in addition to the Supreme Court and a constitutional court. The constitution guarantees equality before the law, and courts are generally fair. Limited budget resources leave the system vulnerable to outside influence, but this is being improved, as required by EU membership, with new spending. The police have been criticized for racist attitudes toward the Roma minority despite a government campaign against anti-Roma racism. Prisons suffered from overcrowding but generally are approaching Western European standards.

Hungary implemented a legal rights protection network in 2001 to provide legal aid to the Roma community, and passed an antidiscrimination law introduced in 2003 as a requirement of EU membership. The government has also created the Roma Coordination Council, appointed special commissioners in the Ministry of Education and Employment and the Ministry of Labor to specifically oversee Roma issues, and named a minister-without-portfolio in the prime minister's office to promote equal opportunity. However, the Roma population continues to face widespread discrimination in many respects.

In 2001, parliament passed the controversial Status Law granting special health and educational benefits to ethnic Hungarians residing outside the country, causing concern in Romania and Slovakia, which have large Hungarian minorities. In 2003, Hungary modified the application of the law to address these concerns, as well as those of the EU. In December 2004, a referendum was to be held on extending citizenship to Hungarians abroad, reawakening some concern among Hungary's neighbors. Though a majority voted in favor, turnout was insufficient for the referendum to pass.

Women possess the same legal rights as men, although they face hiring and pay discrimination and tend to be under-represented in senior-level business and government positions. Hungary is primarily a transit point, but also a source and destination country, for trafficked persons.

Iceland

Population: 300,000
GNI/capita: $27,970
Life Expectancy: 81
Political Rights: 1
Civil Liberties: 1
Status: Free
Religious Groups: Evangelical Lutheran (87.1 percent), other Protestant (4.1 percent), Roman Catholic (1.7 percent), other (7.1 percent)
Ethnic Groups: Homogeneous mixture of descendants of Norse and Celts (94 percent), population of foreign origin (6 percent)
Capital: Reykjavik

Ten-Year Ratings Timeline (Political Rights, Civil Liberties, Status)

1995	1996	1997	1998	1999	2000	2001	2002	2003	2004
1,1F	1,1F	1,1F	1,1F	1,1F	1,1F	1,1F	1,1F	1,1F	1,1F

Overview:

President Olafur Ragnar Grimsson spurred a constitutional crisis in May 2004 when he vetoed a law, sponsored by then prime minister David Oddson and passed by parliament, restricting media ownership. Grimsson was reelected by a wide margin in presidential elections held the same month. In September, Oddson swapped portfolios with Foreign Minister Halldor Asgrimsson in accordance with an agreement struck after the 2003 parliamentary elections.

After being dominated for centuries by Denmark and Norway, Iceland gained independence in 1944. It became a founding member of NATO in 1949, and two years later, it entered into a defense agreement with the United States that has allowed it to keep no military forces of its own. In 1985, Iceland declared itself a nuclear-free zone. Although the United States had proposed a withdrawal from Iceland, it was decided in fall 2003 that the U.S. Air Force base will remain, at least in the short term.

In general elections held on May 10, 2003, Oddsson's right-of-center Independence Party won 34 percent of the votes, gaining only two seats more than the left-leaning Social Democratic Alliance. As a result, the Independence Party formed a ruling coalition with the Progressive Party, acceding to the condition that Oddsson would hand over the post of prime minister to Progressive Party leader Asgrimsson the following year. This condition was fulfilled on September 15, 2004, with Oddsson taking Asgrimsson's previous post as foreign minister.

In May, Grimsson vetoed a law placing limits on media ownership—the first time an Icelandic president had done so in the republic's 60-year history. The veto will force Icelanders to vote on the issue in an upcoming referendum and catalyzed a constitutional controversy, as many felt that Grimsson had overstepped the traditionally apolitical bounds of the presidency. The controversy was exacerbated by the fact that the legislation was sponsored by then prime minister Oddson. Nevertheless, Grimsson was reelected by a wide margin in the June 26 presidential election, capturing more than 85 percent of the vote.

Iceland began whale hunting in 2003 after not having done so since 1989. Although the program was set up for scientific purposes only, it has been severely criticized by environmentalists and Iceland's own tourism sector, which fears that the hunting could damage the country's booming whale-watching industry. In response, the Fisheries Ministry announced in June 2004 that it would cull only 25 minke whales that year, a substantial decrease from the ministry's previous projections. Countries such as the United States and the United Kingdom have formally condemned the practice, but a majority of Iceland's population supports it.

While Iceland has strong historical, cultural, and economic ties with Europe, Icelanders are hesitant to join the European Union (EU), primarily because of the EU's Common Fisheries Policy, which Icelanders believe would threaten their own fishing industry, upon which Iceland's economy is predominantly dependent. While Oddsson ruled out joining the EU, Asgrimsson is more EU-friendly and has expressed willingness to compromise on fisheries issues. The largest opposition party, the Social Democrats, favors EU membership for Iceland. In the meantime, the country has access to European markets as a member of the European Economic Area.

The 2004 UN Development Program's Human Development Index ranked Iceland seventh worldwide in quality of life. The country's abundant hydrothermal and geothermal resources make it one of the cleanest environments in the world.

Political Rights and Civil Liberties: Icelanders can change their government democratically. The constitution, adopted in 1944, vests power in a president, whose functions are mainly ceremonial, a prime minister, a unicameral legislature (the Althingi), and a judiciary. The president is directly elected for a four-year term. The legislature is also elected for four years (subject to dissolution). The prime minister, who performs most executive functions, is appointed by the president but is responsible to the legislature. Elections are free and fair.

Five political movements are represented in the Althingi. The largest is the Independence Party, whose leader, David Oddsson, was Europe's longest-serving prime minister until handing power to Progressive Party leader Halldor Asgrimsson in September 2004. Although the Independence Party has dominated Icelandic politics since the country's independence, elections are competitive. Of the 63 members of the Althingi, about 30 percent are women.

Corruption is not a problem in Iceland. Transparency International ranked Iceland the third least corrupt country of the 146 countries surveyed in its 2004 Corruption Perceptions Index.

The constitution provides for freedom of speech and of the press. A wide range of publications includes both independent and party-affiliated newspapers. An autonomous board of directors oversees the Icelandic National Broadcasting Service, which operates a number of transmitting and relay stations. There are both private and public television stations. However, media ownership is concentrated, with the Northern Lights Corporation controlling television networks, most radio stations, and two out of three of the country's national newspapers. A proposed law to restrict media ownership has been the cause of one of the country's most severe political crises.

The constitution provides for the right to form religious associations and to practice any religion freely, although nearly 90 percent of Icelanders belong to the Evangelical Lutheran Church. The state financially supports and promotes the church, both through a church tax and through religious instruction in schools.

However, citizens who do not belong to a recognized religious organization may choose to give the tax to the University of Iceland and have their children exempted from religious instruction.

Academic freedom is widely respected and enjoyed, and the education system is free of excessive political involvement.

Freedom of association and peaceful assembly are respected. About 85 percent of all eligible workers belong to labor unions, and all enjoy the right to strike. Many domestic and international nongovernmental organizations operate freely in Iceland and enjoy extensive government cooperation. In November, the government cut all direct funding to the Icelandic Human Rights Center starting in 2005, a move that elicited protest from public figures and civic actors.

The judiciary is independent. The law does not provide for trial by jury, but many trials and appeals use panels consisting of several judges. All judges, at all levels, serve for life. Since amendments made in 1996, the constitution states that all people shall be treated equally before the law, regardless of sex, religion, opinion, ethnic origin, race, property, or other status. However, there is no constitutional provision specifically prohibiting racial discrimination.

In May, the Act on Foreigners, which specifies the government's powers with regard to foreigners, including refugees and asylum seekers, was amended to close perceived loopholes in the legislation. Foreign spouses must now be at least 24 years of age, and those suspected of fraud are subject to house searches or DNA tests without a court order. These new provisions led to criticism for human rights organizations, which claimed the law was discriminatory and violated privacy rights.

In 2002, Iceland agreed to give its citizens' genetic data to a private, U.S.-backed medical research company to create a national medical record database, an action that has raised fears over privacy issues. Objections from patients and doctors and security considerations have stymied the completion of the database.

Women enjoy equal rights in Iceland, and more than 80 percent participate in the workforce. However, there has been some concern about women of immigrant origin, who may not have the opportunity to learn the Icelandic language and customs and may be unaware of their rights and status under the law. The European Commission against Racism and Intolerance has also criticized Iceland over immigrant women who become sex-trade workers in the country after being caught by traffickers.

♠ India

Population: 1,086,600,000
GNI/capita: $470
Life Expectancy: 62
Religious Groups: Hindu (81.3 percent), Muslim
(12 percent), Christian (2.3 percent), other (4.4 percent)
Ethnic Groups: Indo-Aryan (72 percent), Dravidian
(25 percent), other (3 percent)
Capital: New Delhi

Political Rights: 2
Civil Liberties: 3
Status: Free

Trend Arrow: India received an upward trend arrow due to improvements in the climate for religious freedom, as well as the new government's efforts to amend anti-terrorism legislation and review the content of school textbooks.

Ten-Year Ratings Timeline (Political Rights, Civil Liberties, Status)

1995	1996	1997	1998	1999	2000	2001	2002	2003	2004
4,4PF	2,4PF	2,4PF	2,3F	2,3F	2,3F	2,3F	2,3F	2,3F	2,3F

Overview:

In a surprise result, India's ruling coalition government, headed by the Hindu nationalist Bharatiya Janata Party (BJP), was defeated in an early general election held in May 2004. The main opposition Congress Party assumed power as the lead partner in a minority coalition government, and former finance minister Manmohan Singh was appointed prime minister. The new government pledged to rescind several elements of the BJP's program, including controversial antiterrorism legislation. Despite the sustained efforts of local activists and lawyers and of India's Supreme Court and the National Commission for Human Rights, justice for the 2002 killings in Gujarat continued to be elusive during the year. The BJP-dominated state government of Gujarat remained reluctant to provide an adequate level of rehabilitation for the victims of the violence or to bring those accused of crimes to trial.

India achieved independence in 1947 with the partition of British India into a predominantly Hindu India, under Prime Minister Jawaharlal Nehru, and a predominantly Muslim Pakistan. The centrist, secular Congress Party ruled almost continuously at the federal level for the first five decades of independence. After winning the 1991 elections, the Congress government responded to a balance-of-payments crisis by initiating gradual economic reforms. However, even as the economic crisis receded, the party lost 11 state elections in the mid-1990s, with regional parties making gains in southern India and low-caste parties and the BJP gaining in the northern Hindi-speaking belt. Congress's traditional electoral base of poor, low-caste, and Muslim voters appeared disillusioned with economic liberalization and, in the case of Muslims, the government's failure to prevent communal violence. In December 1992, India experienced some of the worst communal violence since independence after Hindu fundamentalists destroyed a sixteenth-century mosque in the northern town of Ayodhya. Some 2,000 people, mainly Muslims, died in riots and police gunfire.

After the 1996 elections, a series of minority coalitions tried unsuccessfully to form a stable government. Infighting among centrist and leftist parties enabled the BJP to form a government under Atal Behari Vajpayee in 1998, but it faced frequent threats from small but pivotal coalition members. The government fell after a regional party defected, but it won reelection in 1999 as the lead partner in the 22-party National Democratic Alliance.

In February 2002, at least 58 people were killed in Godhra, Gujarat, when a fire broke out on a train carrying members of a Hindu extremist group. A Muslim mob was initially blamed for the fire, and in the anti-Muslim riots that followed throughout Gujarat, more than 1,000 people were killed and roughly 100,000 were left homeless and dispossessed. The violence was orchestrated by Hindu nationalist groups, who organized transportation and provisions for the mobs and provided printed records of Muslim-owned property. Evidence that the BJP-headed state government was complicit in the carnage led to calls for Chief Minister Narendra Modi's dismissal, but he retained the support of the party leadership. In state elections held later that year in which Modi campaigned on an overtly nationalistic and anti-Muslim platform, the BJP won a landslide reelection victory.

The rehabilitation of those displaced by the violence, as well as the prosecution of those responsible for murder, rape, and destruction of property, made little headway during 2004. Some arrests have been made, and a dozen cases are making their way through the judicial system. However, witnesses in the few cases that have been brought to trial, as have lawyers and activists working on their behalf, continue to face threats and intimidation at the hands of local authorities and Hindu nationalist sympathizers. In March 2004, the Supreme Court, responding to petitions from witnesses in several cases, ordered that they be given protection by national forces rather than by Gujarat state police. Further condemnation of the state government's prosecution record was implicit in an April Supreme Court order that the Best Bakery case be retried outside of Gujarat, and an August directive that the state government review more than 2,000 closed riot cases and reexamine acquittals to determine the possibility of filing appeals.

Relations between India and Pakistan worsened in December 2001 following an attack on the Indian parliament building by a Pakistan-based militant group, and the two countries came close to war in 2002, which prompted a flurry of diplomatic activity on the part of the United States. Individuals with connections to Pakistan-based militant groups continued to carry out terrorist attacks within India. Nevertheless, there was some easing of tensions between the two countries by the end of 2003, and formal talks over the disputed territory of Kashmir were held in February 2004 with follow-up discussions continuing in June and September. A number of confidence-building measures, such as improved nuclear safeguards, reopened transport links, and an increased diplomatic presence, were also agreed upon.

Buoyed by improving relations with Pakistan and victories in several key state elections held in late 2003, as well as high levels of economic growth, the government decided to call an early general election. However, in a surprise result, it was defeated—final results announced in May gave the BJP only 137 seats out of 545, and its allies also performed poorly—and the main opposition Congress Party was able to form a minority coalition government with additional parliamentary support from a group of leftist parties. In a further surprise, Congress leader Sonia Gandhi declined the position of prime minister and instead appointed former finance minister Manmohan Singh to the post. However, in a unique power-sharing arrangement, she remains party leader and wields considerable leverage over official policy.

The new United Progressive Alliance (UPA) government is perceived by some analysts as unstable and will need to balance demands from a range of disparate coalition partners. Its effectiveness was also tested by a BJP parliamentary boycott called in protest at the government's appointment of several ministers who are facing criminal charges, as well as increasing civil unrest and violence in several northeastern states. However, the Common Minimum Program (CMP) agreed to by the coalition partners promised a renewed focus on effective governance, a social-democratic budget, and the reversal of several policies initiated by the previous government, including the repeal of controversial antiterrorism legislation and the removal from state-run schools of school textbooks that had been imbued with Hindu nationalist ideology.

Political Rights and Civil Liberties:

Indian citizens can change their government through elections. The 1950 constitution provides for a lower house, the 545-seat Lok Sabha (House of the People), whose members are directly elected for five-year terms (except for 2 appointed seats for Indians of European descent). Members of the 245-seat upper house, the Rajya Sabha (Council of States), are either elected by the state legislatures or nominated by the president; they serve staggered six-year terms. Executive power is vested in a prime minister and a cabinet, while an indirectly elected president serves as head of state.

India is a mature democracy that has held regular and reasonably free elections since independence. A large number of regional and national parties participate, and sitting governments are thrown out of office with increasing regularity. Under the supervision of the vigilant Election Commission of India (ECI), recent elections have generally been free and fair. National elections held in April and May saw a decline in levels of election-related violence. However, some vote fraud and other minor irregularities were apparent in several districts of Bihar despite the introduction of new electronic voting machines throughout the country. Badly maintained voters' lists and the intimidation of voters are also matters of concern. Women and religious and ethnic minorities are well represented in national and local government (there are reserved seats for "scheduled castes" and "scheduled tribes"), and in May, Manmohan Singh, a Sikh, became India's first prime minister from a minority group.

Despite the vibrancy of the Indian political system, effective and accountable rule continues to be undermined by political infighting, pervasive criminality in politics, decrepit state institutions, and widespread corruption. Transparency International's 2004 Corruption Perceptions Index ranked India 90 out of 145 countries. The electoral system depends on black money that is obtained though tax evasion and other means. Politicians and civil servants are regularly caught accepting bribes or engaging in other corrupt behavior, but are rarely prosecuted. Moreover, criminality is a pervasive feature of political life, with a number of candidates with criminal records being elected, particularly in the state legislatures. In 2002, the ECI was able to implement a Supreme Court directive requiring candidates seeking election to declare their financial assets, criminal records, and educational backgrounds. However, in June, *The Economist* reported that 100 of the 545 recently elected members of the national legislature were facing criminal charges.

India's private press continues to be vigorous, although journalists face a number of constraints. In recent years, the government has occasionally used its power under the Official Secrets Act to censor security-related articles. Intimidation of journalists by a variety of actors continues; Hindu nationalist activists connected with the BJP attacked the premises of the Bombay daily *Mahanagar* in June, and reporters in several states face pressure from separatist militant groups or from local or state-level authorities. The broadcast media are predominantly in private hands, but the state-controlled All India Radio enjoys a dominant position, and its news coverage favors the government. Potentially inflammatory books and films are occasionally banned or censored by the national or state governments. Internet access is unrestricted, although some states have proposed legislation that would require the registration of customers at Internet cafes.

The right to practice one's religion freely is generally respected, but violence against religious minorities remains a problem and prosecution of those involved in such attacks continues to be inadequate. Attacks on Christian targets, including the murder and rape of clergy and the destruction of property, dramatically increased after the BJP came to power in 1998, mainly in the predominantly tribal regions of Orissa, Gujarat, Bihar, and Madhya Pradesh. Members of the *sangh parivar*, a group of Hindu nationalist organizations including the BJP, and some local media outlets promote anti-minority propaganda. Legislation on the books in several states, including Orissa, Madhya Pradesh, Tamil Nadu, and Gujarat, criminalizes conversions that take place as a result of "force" or "allurement." These laws have been opposed by human rights activists and religious groups, who argue that the vague provisions of these statutes could be misused.

The promotion of Hindu nationalist ideology by the BJP government also affected the educational system. According to the U.S. State Department's International Religious Freedom Report for 2004, textbooks that had been rewritten to favor a Hindu extremist version of history were introduced in late 2002, despite protests from academics, minority leaders, and advocates of secular values. However, the new Congress-headed government pledged to reverse the "saffronization" of education, and the content of the textbooks is currently under revision. Academic freedom is also occasionally threatened by intimidation of and attacks on professors and institutions: in January, Hindu activists vandalized a research institute in Pune, according to the BBC.

There are some restrictions on freedom of assembly and association. Section 144 of the criminal procedure code empowers state-level authorities to declare a state of emergency, restrict free assembly, and impose curfews. Officials occasionally use Section 144 to prevent demonstrations, and police sometimes use excessive force against demonstrators. Human rights groups say that police and hired thugs have occasionally beaten, arbitrarily detained, or otherwise harassed villagers and members of nongovernmental organizations who protest forced relocation from the sites of development projects.

Human rights organizations generally operate freely. However, Amnesty International's 2004 report noted that the intimidation of human rights defenders by state officials and other actors, including threats, legal harassment, the use of excessive force by police, and occasionally lethal violence, remains a concern. In Gujarat, activists and organizations that have taken an active role in pushing for justice following the February 2002 riots have faced harassment from state authorities, including targeted investigations by income tax authorities or the police, according to Human Rights Watch. The work of rights activists may also be hindered by a Home Ministry order issued in 2001 that requires organizations to obtain clearance before holding international conferences or workshops if the subject matter is "political, semi-political, communal or religious in nature or is related to human rights."

Workers regularly exercise their rights to bargain collectively and strike. The Essential Services Maintenance Act enables the government to ban strikes in certain key industries and limits the right of public servants to strike. It is estimated that there are roughly 55 million child laborers in India. Many work in the informal sector in hazardous conditions, and several million are bonded laborers.

The judiciary is independent of the executive. Judges have exercised unprecedented activism in response to public interest litigation over official corruption, environmental issues, and other matters. However, in recent years, courts have initiated several contempt-of-court cases against activists and journalists, raising questions about their misuse of the law to intimidate those who expose the behavior of corrupt judges or who question their verdicts. Corruption in the judiciary is reportedly rife, and access to justice by the socially and economically marginalized sections of society remains limited. The court system is severely backlogged and understaffed, which results in the detention of a large number of persons who are awaiting trial. In April 2003, the government-appointed Malimath Committee recommended an overhaul of the Indian criminal justice system. However, rights groups expressed concern that its proposals would weaken the rights of the accused and of women while increasing the power of judges and the police.

Police routinely torture or otherwise ill-treat suspects to extract confessions or bribes. Custodial rape of female detainees continues to be a problem, as does routine abuse of ordinary prisoners, particularly minorities and members of the lower castes. Police brutality appears to be especially prevalent in the northern Indian state of Uttar Pradesh, which has high levels of custodial deaths and extrajudicial executions, according to a 2003 briefing paper released by the New Delhi–based Human Rights Documentation Centre. The National Human Rights Commission (NHRC), whose profile has grown since its creation in 1993, is headed by a retired Supreme Court judge and handles roughly 75,000 complaints each year. However, while it monitors abuses, initiates investigations, and makes independent assessments, its recommendations are often not implemented and it has few enforcement powers. Reports by the NHRC, Human Rights Watch, and a number of other groups alleged that police in Gujarat had been given orders by the state government not to intervene during the communal violence that engulfed the state in 2002 and that police have been reluctant to register complaints against those accused of murder, rape, and other crimes, or arrest those known to have played a role in the rioting. Since the riots, scores of Muslim men in Gujarat have been illegally detained and interrogated about their involvement in subsequent attacks such as the killing of former minister Haren Pandya in March 2003, according to Amnesty International. More generally, the failure of the Indian criminal justice system to protect the rights of, and provide equal protection under the law to, minorities, *dalits* (untouchables), and other underprivileged groups remains a concern.

Police, army, and paramilitary forces continue to be implicated in disappearances, extrajudicial killing, rape, torture, arbitrary detention, and destruction of homes, particularly in the context of insurgencies in Kashmir, Andhra Pradesh, Assam, and several other northeastern states. The Armed Forces Special Powers Act (AFSPA) and the Disturbed Areas Act remain in effect in several states, and these grant security forces broad powers of arrest and detention. Security forces also continued to detain suspects under the broadly drawn National Security Act, which authorizes detention without charge for up to one year. The criminal procedure code requires the central or state governments to approve prosecution of security force members, which is rarely granted. As a result, impunity for security forces implicated in past human rights abuses remains a concern. After the alleged custodial rape and killing of civilian Thangjam Manorama in July, antigovernment protests erupted in the northeastern state of Manipur, with protestors demanding that the AFSPA be lifted.

In March 2002, the Prevention of Terrorism Act (POTA) was passed by a special joint session of parliament, amid protests by journalists, human rights groups, and some members of the government and judiciary. In addition to widening the definition of terrorism and banning a number of terrorist organizations, the bill also increased the state's powers of investigation and allowed for up to 90 days of preventive detention without charge. Since its enactment, the act has been used in a number of states to detain political opponents, members of minority groups (including tribal members, dalits and Muslims), and other ordinary citizens, as well as against terrorist suspects. Of the 287 cases registered in Gujarat under POTA as of December 2003, there were 286 against Muslims, according to a September 2004 report by Human Rights Watch. However, in September, the new government announced its decision to repeal POTA.

In India's seven northeastern states, more than 40 mainly tribal-based insurgent groups, who seek either greater autonomy or complete independence for their ethnic or tribal groups, sporadically attack security forces and engage in intertribal violence. The rebel groups have also been implicated in numerous bombings, killings, abductions, and rapes of civilians. Rebel positions were weakened by an operation launched by Bhutan in December 2003 to drive a number of groups out of its territory; during the raids, more than 1,000 rebels were either killed or taken into custody by Indian forces. However, violence continued throughout 2004; a series of bombs planted by various groups in early October killed at least 46 people. In a number of states, left-wing guerrillas called Naxalites control some rural areas and kill dozens of police, politicians, landlords, and villagers each year. Police also continued to battle the People's War Group (PWG), a guerrilla organization that aims to establish a Communist state in the tribal areas of Andhra Pradesh, Orissa, West Bengal, Jharkhand, Bihar, and Chhattisgarh. Nevertheless, in October, the Andhra Pradesh state government held a first set of direct talks with the PWG aimed at ending the decades-old conflict.

The constitution bars discrimination based on caste, and laws set aside quotas in education and government jobs for members of the so-called scheduled tribes, scheduled castes (dalits), and other backward castes (OBCs). However, members of the lower castes, as well as religious and ethnic minorities, continue to routinely face unofficial discrimination and violence. The worst abuse is experienced by the 160 million dalits, who are often denied access to land or other public amenities, abused by landlords and police, and forced to work in miserable conditions. In July,

Human Rights Watch criticized the use of excessive police force against dalits who tried to participate in a religious ceremony in Tamil Nadu. Tension between different ethnic groups over land, jobs, or resources occasionally flares into violent confrontation, and sporadic Hindu-Muslim violence remains a concern. Other forms of discrimination against Muslims are sometimes excused in the context of ongoing tensions with Pakistan as well as the global campaign against terrorism. Although India hosts several hundred thousand refugees from various neighboring states, it has no national refugee law, and, according to Refugees International, the treatment of displaced people varies widely.

Each year, several thousand women are burned to death, driven to suicide, or otherwise killed, and countless others are harassed, beaten, or deserted by husbands, in the context of dowry and other disputes. Despite the fact that making demands for dowry is illegal and that hundreds are convicted each year, the practice continues to spread. Rape and other violence against women remain serious problems, with lower-caste and tribal women being particularly vulnerable to attacks. Muslim women and girls were subjected to horrific sexual violence during the communal violence that engulfed Gujarat in 2002, and there has been no official attempt to provide rehabilitation for those victims still alive or to prosecute their attackers, according to a 2003 Amnesty International report. Muslim personal status laws as well as traditional Hindu practices discriminate against women in terms of inheritance rights. The malign neglect of female children after birth remains a concern. An increasing use of sex-determination tests during pregnancy, after which female fetuses are more likely to be aborted, and the practice of female infanticide by those who cannot afford the tests have contributed to a growing imbalance in the male-female birth ratios in a number of states, particularly in the northwest.

⬆ Indonesia

Population: 218,700,000 **Political Rights:** 3
GNI/capita: $710 **Civil Liberties:** 4
Life Expectancy: 68 **Status:** Partly Free
Religious Groups: Muslim (88 percent), Protestant
(5 percent), Roman Catholic (3 percent), other (4 percent)
Ethnic Groups: Javanese (45 percent), Sundanese
(14 percent), Madurese (7.5 percent), Malay (7.5 percent),
other (26 percent)
Capital: Jakarta
Trend Arrow: Indonesia received an upward trend arrow due to the holding of three free and fair elections during the year.

Ten-Year Ratings Timeline (Political Rights, Civil Liberties, Status)

1995	1996	1997	1998	1999	2000	2001	2002	2003	2004
7,6NF	7,5NF	7,5NF	6,4PF	4,4PF	3,4PF	3,4PF	3,4PF	3,4PF	3,4PF

Overview: Indonesia consolidated its position as the world's third largest democracy in 2004 with three separate free and fair elections. In April, Indonesia held what some have called the world's most complicated one-day elections in which over 100 million Indonesians went to the polls and completed highly complicated ballots to elect the parliament. The first round of Indonesia's first-ever direct presidential election followed in July and was carried out peacefully, although some administrative problems with the distribution and layout of ballots persisted. In the September runoff, Susilo Bambang Yudhoyono, commonly known as SBY, defeated incumbent Megawati Sukarnoputri by a wide margin. SBY and his cabinet were sworn in on October 20 with promises of reform, including pledges to tackle some of Indonesia's long-standing problems, such as rebellions in Aceh and Papua, corruption, and legal reform. Some analysts believe that SBY has the political will to tackle these problems, but whether he will have the capability to overcome entrenched interests remains to be seen.

Indonesia won full independence in 1949 following a four-year, intermittent war against its Dutch colonial rulers. After several parliamentary governments collapsed, the republic's first president, Sukarno, took on authoritarian powers in 1959 under a system that he called "Guided Democracy." Sukarno retained his political supremacy by balancing the country's two most powerful groups, the conservative military (TNI) and the Communist Party of Indonesia (PKI), against one another. This unstable political triad came apart in 1965, when the army, led by General Suharto, crushed an apparent coup attempt that it blamed on the PKI. In the aftermath, the TNI and its conservative Muslim allies engaged in mass acts of violence against suspected PKI members that ultimately left an estimated 500,000 dead. With the backing of the TNI, Suharto eased aside the populist Sukarno and formally became president in 1968.

Having eliminated the PKI, Suharto's "New Order" regime engineered both the merger of the "old order" political parties into two unwieldy ones and also the creation of Golkar, a pro-government political party based on bureaucratic and military interests. In the elections Suharto held every five years, restrictions on civil liberties and the coercive power of the state ensured that Golkar always won with impressive margins. During his 32 years in power, Suharto created a patrimonial political system that rewarded supporters, including his family and close friends, and punished his opponents.

In part to sustain his power, Suharto embarked on an economic development program that led the Indonesian economy to grow by an annual average of 7 percent for three decades, helping to lift millions of Indonesians out of poverty. In the 1990s, Suharto's children and cronies were the major beneficiaries of state privatization schemes and also often ran large business monopolies that operated with little oversight. When Indonesia was hit by the Asian financial crisis, which devalued the currency by more than 5,000 percent over six months, Suharto agreed to a $43 billion IMF bailout in October 1997. In 1998, the country's economy shrank by 13.8 percent; it was the largest single-year contraction for any country since the Great Depression.

Soaring prices and rising unemployment led many Indonesians to demonstrate against the corruption, collusion, and nepotism of the Suharto regime that they blamed for the crisis. In the midst of devastating urban riots in May 1998, Suharto resigned and was succeeded by Vice President B. J. Habibie, a long-time Suharto loyalist. Habibie responded to the *reformasi* movement that had helped topple

Suharto by freeing the press, labor unions, and political parties in an attempt to shore up his political legitimacy.

In June 1999, Indonesia held its first free parliamentary elections since 1955. The Indonesian Democratic Party–Struggle (PDI-P), led by Sukarno's daughter Megawati, won 154 of the 462 contested seats. Golkar won 120 seats, and smaller parties the remainder. In October 1999, the People's Consultative Assembly (MPR), a body that then consisted of the Parliament (DPR), plus another 195 appointed members held its first competitive vote and elected Muslim leader Abdurrahman Wahid president and Megawati vice president.

Hopes that this team of two reformist leaders—representing moderate Islam and Indonesian nationalism, respectively—would have the political credibility to tackle many of Indonesia's deep-seated political, economic, and social issues went unfulfilled. Wahid's credentials as a democratic reformer and champion of religious freedom gave him the moral authority to call for an end to the insurgency in Aceh and the deadly ethnic and sectarian violence raging in the Moluccas, Sulawesi, and Kalimantan, but he chose not to do so. Moreover, Wahid did little to revive the economy, and his administration was dogged by corruption allegations. Facing impeachment charges, Wahid made a mockery of his initial attempts to exert civilian control over the TNI when he called on the armed forces to declare a state of emergency in an effort to prevent his political demise. The TNI refused, Wahid was impeached, and Megawati become president in July 2001.

Megawati generally is credited with stabilizing Indonesia's volatile post-1997 economy, which only returned to pre-crisis per capita income levels in 2004. However, critics charge that she has largely failed to rein in what is widely seen as a corrupt elite whose unchecked self-interest has sapped the economy and stunted political development. Many observers say that corruption has increased since Megawati took office, in part because of both the recent decentralization of government—which has expanded the power of local officials without improving their oversight—and a lack of enforcement.

Investors remain wary of sinking capital into Indonesia because of government corruption as well as fickle courts, inadequate laws, and a poor regulatory environment. Economists say that Indonesia's recent economic growth rate is only about half that needed to keep pace with new entrants in the labor market and to substantially reduce poverty. Investors made no secret of their preference for SBY in the presidential election, and many are hoping that he will address these obstacles to growth.

Megawati took a tough line against Jemaah Islamiyah, a network of Islamic militants in Southeast Asia allegedly linked to al-Qaeda, the terrorist network. Although she was initially reluctant to tackle homegrown Islamic militancy for fear of offending powerful Muslim constituencies, her government arrested scores of suspected terrorists following the 2002 bombing on the resort island of Bali that killed 202 people. However, Megawati's hard-line approach to the insurgencies in Aceh and Papua did not lead to peace. In May 2004, the government lifted the martial law decree it had issued a year earlier in Aceh, an oil-rich province of 4.6 million people in northern Sumatra. Nevertheless, the military continued to launch fresh offensives against separatist rebels. Voters punished Megawati for these perceived failures by giving the PDI-P less support in the April parliamentary elections. The big surprise was the strong showing for Partai Demokrat (PD), the electoral vehicle for SBY, who resigned from Megawati's cabinet as coordinating minister for political and security affairs in March.

On September 20, SBY won 61 percent of the vote and claimed a mandate for change. However, to implement his agenda, SBY will need the cooperation of parliament, and the standoff between the president and parliament that followed his October 20 inauguration illustrates how difficult that task may be. SBY's PD holds only 55 out of 550 seats, while the two other parties that formally support SBY can muster 111 votes. The People's Coalition, which will probably support the president most of the time, commands 233 seats, but it is opposed by the Nationhood coalition that supported Megawati and includes parliament's two largest parties, Golkar and PDI-P.

Golkar former chairman Akbar Tandjung has made no secret of his desire to bring down the SBY government within two years. However, Tandjung, whose 2002 corruption conviction was overturned, faces a fierce challenge for the Golkar chairmanship in December 2004, and some of the candidates favor a closer working relationship with SBY's administration.

Courts have convicted several suspects in the 2002 Bali bombing, though a court in September acquitted Muslim cleric Abu Bakar Bashir, 65, of being the spiritual head of Jemaah Islamiyah. Though the cleric was jailed for four years on other charges pending appeal, the acquittal was seen as a setback for Indonesia's antiterrorism campaign. Regardless of Bashir's fate, many analysts say that the government must take the sensitive step of investigating the handful of Islamic boarding schools allegedly linked to Jemaah Islamiyah and further professionalize the gathering and sharing of intelligence in order to better curb terrorism.

Political Rights and Civil Liberties:

Citizens of Indonesia can change their government democratically. In 2004, Indonesians directly elected their president and all of the members to parliament, DPR, as well as representatives to a new legislative body, the Regional Representatives Council (DPD). The DPD is tasked with proposing, discussing, and monitoring laws related to regional autonomy. Together with the DPR, it will form the reconstituted MPR. All elections were free, fair, and remarkably peaceful. New parties, such as SBY's electoral vehicle, the PD, and the rise in support of the Prosperous Justice Party (PKS), indicate the ability of new parities to capture seats. However, some of the new electoral rules favor larger, more established parties and may reduce access to new parties. For example, independent candidates cannot contest elections—they must be nominated by political parties—and voters choose parties, not candidates, in the voting booth. Parties, in turn, must prove they have a nationwide network of members and offices before they can make nominations. Parties that fail to win 3 percent of the vote will not be allowed to contest future elections. Although the president will continue to be directly elected, beginning in 2009 the presidential candidate must be nominated by at least 15 percent of the members of parliament. Similarly, when direct elections for provincial governors and regents begin in 2005, candidates will need 15 percent of the vote in local assemblies to secure a nomination.

The military formally withdrew from politics when it lost its 38 appointed seats in the MPR in 2004. However, the army also maintains a "territorial network" of soldiers in every district and village, which gives it influence at the local level. Discussions to disband the territorial structure were on the agenda early in the reformasi era, when the military was discredited because of its shooting of pro-democracy advocates and its links to Suharto. The military's stock in the eyes of the public increased, however, as a result of its decision to remain impartial during the Wahid impeachment process, and because of the legitimacy Megawati bestowed upon it. The appointment to the post of defense minister of Juwono Sudarsono, a respected civilian who served in this position during the Wahid administration, is a positive sign. Juwono has proposed a major reorganization that would fold the TNI into the civilian-led Ministry of Defense and the police into the Interior Ministry, but whether Parliament approves the reorganization remains to be seen. A key obstacle to civilian control over the military has long been the fact that the TNI receives only 30 percent of its funding from the state budget and has relied on military-run charities and businesses for the bulk of its financing. In an effort to rein in these activities and enhance civilian control, Juwono had proposed disbanding all military-run charities and bringing the military businesses into the state apparatus. Whether he is able to accomplish these objectives remains to be seen, as the military still wields considerable influence in politics and business.

Corruption is endemic in Indonesia, including throughout the judiciary. The government acknowledged the judicial system's inability to police itself when it created the Corruption Eradication Commission, a group of special prosecutors with the power to investigate any suspected misconduct involving government officials who are believed to have cost the state more than one billion rupiah, approximately $10,500. The government has no formal right to intervene with the work of this body. To date, the commission has completed only two investigations, a fact many attribute to the Megawati administration's foot-dragging over the nomination of judges to a special anticorruption court that will hear the commission's cases. The Megawati administration also ignored the commission's order to suspend an official under investigation. Indonesia was ranked 133 out of 146 countries surveyed in Transparency International's 2004 Corruption Perceptions Index.

Press freedom eroded sharply in Indonesia during Megawati's tenure: the country dropped from its 57th place ranking in the Reporters Sans Frontieres 2002 global survey of press freedom to a 117th place ranking in 2004. The sharp drop is a function of attacks on and the killing of journalists, the use of criminal defamation charges to prosecute journalists, and the effective closure of strife-torn Aceh to independent media. In October, one of Indonesia's most respect journalists, Bambang Harymurti, editor of *Tempo*, was sentenced to a year in jail for suggesting that a businessman with ties to the Megawati administration might have committed arson.

Indonesians of all faiths can generally worship freely in this predominantly Muslim nation, although officials monitor and have outlawed some extremist Islamic groups. Indonesia officially recognizes five faiths—Islam, Protestantism, Catholicism, Hinduism, and Buddhism—and although Islamic holidays predominate, holy days such as Good Friday, Waisak (a Buddhist holiday), and Nyepi (a Balinese/Hindi festival) are public holidays. Animists, Confucians, Baha'is, and others whose faith is not among Indonesia's five officially recognized religions have difficulty obtaining national identity cards, which are needed to register births, marriages, and divorces.

Indonesia has many effective, outspoken human rights groups, including

Imparsial, Humanika and the Indonesian Legal Aid Foundation, that aid victims and vigorously promote rights. However, they face "monitoring, abuse, and interference by the government," the U.S. State Department report said. At least 39 Indonesians have been detained or jailed for peacefully criticizing the government since Megawati took office in 2001, the human rights group Amnesty International reported in July. They include independence activists in Aceh, Papua, and Malaku and labor and political activists in Java and Sulawesi. Many were charged under colonial-era defamation laws. In September, Munir, one of Indonesia's most prominent rights activists, died from arsenic poisoning while on a flight to Amsterdam. Indonesia has launched an investigation and SBY received Munir's widow. Whether Munir's killing was related to his human rights advocacy or a corruption case he was investigating is unclear. However, the way in which this case is investigated and prosecuted will send a strong signal regarding the new government's commitment to civil rights.

Indonesian workers can join independent unions, bargain collectively, and, except for civil servants, stage strikes. Government enforcement of minimum-wage and other labor laws is weak, however, and there are credible reports of employers dismissing or otherwise exacting retribution from union organizers. Moreover, unions allege that factory managers at times use youth gangs or plainclothes security forces—often off-duty soldiers and police—to intimidate workers or break strikes. Roughly 10 to 15 percent of Indonesia's 80 million industrial workers are unionized.

SBY has made legal reform a key objective of his new government and has appointed well-known reformers to the positions of attorney general and chief justice of the Supreme Court. Indonesia's judicial system, according to its new attorney general, Abdul Rahman Saleh, is mired in corruption so that justice typically is awarded to the highest bidder. Bribes influence prosecution, conviction, and sentencing in countless civil and criminal cases. Courts often limit defendants' access to counsel and allow forced confessions to be used as evidence in criminal cases. Saleh attributes the problem in part to extremely low salaries for judicial officials as well as to the traditional lack of punishment for illegal activity. Over the past year, a number of steps have been taken to rectify this problem. In July, the DPR passed a law creating a Judicial Appointments Commission to nominate candidates for the Supreme Court (subject to DPR approval) and monitor the conduct of all judges. The current chief justice of the Supreme Court successfully lobbied parliament for the power to appoint non-career judges, who are considered less corrupt. At the same time, the Supreme Court has been disciplining judges in an unprecedented manner, with five dismissed in the second half of 2004 alone.

The new Constitutional Court, only a year old, has infuriated some in the government and in other countries with its ruling that the government's attempt to apply new antiterrorist laws retroactively were unconstitutional. Hailed as the correct decision by legal authorities, it nevertheless caused consternation in many quarters.

The judiciary's weakness has helped perpetuate human rights abuses by the security forces. In Aceh, the army has been implicated in summary killings, "disappearances," rapes, illegal detentions, and other abuses against suspected GAM guerrillas or sympathizers, according to Amnesty International and the New York–based Human Rights Watch. For their part, GAM forces have routinely summarily killed both soldiers and civilians, while intimidating and extorting money from ordinary

Acehnese, these groups say. Army abuses also continue in Papua, and questions remain about whether the military and Kopassus, the intelligence service, were involved in a 2002 ambush in the province that killed two Americans. The government denies any official involvement in the deaths.

Indonesian forces also enjoy near impunity in encounters with ordinary criminal suspects. Meanwhile, Amnesty International said in an October report that it continued to receive reports of torture by soldiers and police not only of suspects in conflict zones but also of criminal suspects, peaceful political activists, and Indonesians involved in land and other disputes with authorities. In addition, guards routinely mistreat and extort money from inmates in the country's overcrowded prisons.

Efforts to curb military impunity were dealt a setback by the acquittals or relatively short jail terms handed down in the recent trials of 18 suspects, including senior army officials, in the 1999 violence in East Timor that killed more than 1,000 civilians. In a series of trials that ended in August 2004, a Jakarta court acquitted 12 defendants and handed down jail terms of between three and ten years to six found guilty. Amnesty International said that prosecutors failed to present credible cases and gave a sanitized version of the 1999 violence.

Ethnic Chinese continue to face some harassment and violence, though far less than in the late 1990s, when violent attacks killed hundreds and destroyed many Chinese-owned shops and churches. Unlike other Indonesians, ethnic Chinese must show a citizenship card to obtain a passport, credit card, or business license or to enroll a child in school, a requirement that makes them vulnerable to extortion by bureaucrats. Ethnic Chinese make up less than 3 percent of the nation's population, but are resented by some Indonesians for holding the lion's share of private wealth. A few ethnic Chinese have amassed huge fortunes in business, though most are ordinary traders or merchants.

Ethnic Dayaks in Kalimantan and other members of Indonesia's tiny indigenous minority face considerable discrimination. The government at times fails to stop mining and logging companies from encroaching on indigenous land in Kalimantan and other areas—often in collusion with local military and police—and appropriates land claimed by indigenous Indonesians for development projects without fair compensation.

In a positive development, peace is slowly returning to areas of the archipelago that recently have been torn by violence along ethnic or sectarian lines, including the Moluccas, central Sulawesi, and Kalimantan. But setbacks continue to occur. On April 25, 2004, the anniversary of a short-lived Republic of the South Moluccas supported by the local Christian organization Front for Moluccan Sovereignty, snipers killed dozens of people in orchestrated attacks. Despite poor police preparations, the killings did not trigger the wisespread violence the snipers apparently sought to ignite. In Kalimantan and other areas, many disputes between ethnic groups are said to be linked in part to the government's decades-old policy of resettling tens of thousands of Indonesians to remote parts of the archipelago from overcrowded areas such as Java.

Indonesian women face considerable discrimination. They are often steered by factory employers into low-level, low-paying jobs, and female university graduates reportedly receive salaries that are 25 percent lower, on average, than those paid to their male counterparts. Female household servants at times are forced to work without pay, for extremely low wages, or in situations of debt bondage. Female genital mutilation is reportedly still practiced in some areas, although the more extreme forms of the practice apparently are becoming less common. Trafficking of women for prostitution, forced labor, and debt bondage reportedly continues unabated, often with the complicity or involvement of police, soldiers, and officials, despite the recent passage of a child-trafficking bill and of stiffer provisions against trafficking of women.

⬇ Iran

Population: 67,400,000 **Political Rights:** 6
GNI/capita: $1,720 **Civil Liberties:** 6
Life Expectancy: 69 **Status:** Not Free
Religious Groups: Shi'a Muslim (89 percent),
Sunni Muslim (9 percent), other (2 percent)
Ethnic Groups: Persian (51 percent), Azeri (24 percent),
Gilaki and Mazandarani (8 percent), Kurd (7 percent),
Arab (3 percent), other (7 percent)
Capital: Tehran
Trend Arrow: Iran received a downward trend arrow due to the hard-line clerical establishment's obstruction of the electoral process and increased restrictions on freedom of expression.

Ten-Year Ratings Timeline (Political Rights, Civil Liberties, Status)

1995	1996	1997	1998	1999	2000	2001	2002	2003	2004
6,7NF	6,7NF	6,7NF	6,6NF	6,6NF	6,6NF	6,6NF	6,6NF	6,6NF	6,6NF

Overview:
The regression of political and civil liberties in Iran accelerated in 2004 as the hard-line clerical establishment seized control of parliament from reformers through sham elections and launched heavy-handed campaigns to combat "social corruption" and to silence dissent. Although widespread public apathy and record oil receipts enabled Iran's theocratic regime to impose its authority without sparking significant political unrest, its power play was squarely out of step with popular opinion and some Iranians remained cautiously optimistic that this attempt to turn back the clock on reform would not stand in the long run. Tensions between Iran and the West increased substantially after Tehran reneged on an October 2003 agreement with the International Atomic Energy Agency (IAEA) to suspend key components of its suspected nuclear weapons program.

In 1979, Iran witnessed a tumultuous revolution that ousted a hereditary monarchy marked by widespread corruption and brought into power the exiled cleric Ayatollah Ruhollah Khomeini. The constitution drafted by Kohmeini's disciples provided for a president and parliament elected through universal adult suffrage, but non-elected institutions controlled by hard-line clerics were empowered to approve electoral candidates and certify that the decisions of elected officials are in accord with Sharia (Islamic law). Khomeini was named Supreme Leader and invested with control over the security and intelligence services, armed forces, and judiciary. After his death in 1989, the role of Supreme Leader passed to Ayatollah Ali Khamenei, a middle-ranking cleric who lacked the religious credentials and popularity of his predecessor. The constitution was changed to consolidate his power and give him final authority on all matters of foreign and domestic policy.

Beneath its veneer of religious probity, the Islamic Republic gave rise to a new elite that accumulated wealth through opaque and unaccountable means. By the mid-1990s, dismal economic conditions and a demographic trend toward a younger population had created widespread hostility to clerical rule. A coalition of reformers began to emerge within the ruling elite, advocating a gradual process of political reform, economic liberalization, and normalization with the outside world that was designed to legitimize, not radically alter, the current political system.

Representing this coalition, former culture minister Mohammed Khatami was elected president in 1997 with nearly 70 percent of the vote. Khatami's administration made considerable strides over the next few years in expanding public freedoms. More than 200 independent newspapers and magazines representing a diverse array of viewpoints were established during his first year in office, and the authorities relaxed the enforcement of strict Islamic restrictions on social interaction between unmarried men and women. Reformists won 80 percent of the seats in the country's first nationwide municipal elections in 1999 and took the vast majority of seats in parliamentary elections the following year, gaining the power, for the first time, to legislate major changes in the political system.

The 2000 parliamentary elections prompted a backlash by hard-line clerics that continues to this day. Over the next four years, the conservative-controlled judiciary closed more than 100 reformist newspapers and jailed hundreds of liberal journalists and activists, while security forces cracked down ruthlessly on student protests against these measures. Critical pieces of reform legislation were overwhelmingly approved by parliament, only to be vetoed by the Council of Guardians, an appointed clerical body. Gridlock between government moderates and hard-liners also obstructed much-needed economic reforms.

Khatami was reelected in 2001 with 78 percent of the vote, but this popular mandate did not lead him to challenge the country's ruling theocrats. He ignored recurrent pleas by reformist members of parliament to call a national referendum to approve vetoed reform legislation, while repeatedly imploring citizens to refrain from demonstrating in public. Khatami's failure to carry out further reforms (or even to preserve the progress made during his first three years in office) led many Iranians to abandon hopes that the political system can be changed from within. Within the broader reform movement, Khatami and other government "moderates" came under accusations of not just being ineffective, but of willingly serving as a democratic façade for an oppressive regime. Record low turnout for the February 2003 municipal elections resulted in a landslide victory by hard-liners and showed that the ability of reformist politicians to mobilize the public had deteriorated markedly.

The February 2004 parliamentary elections marked a watershed in the country's political regression. Prior to the elections, the Council of Guardians rejected the candidacies of over 2,000 reformist politicians, including scores of incumbent deputies, while the government-backed Ansar-i Hezbollah and Basij vigilante groups "repeatedly attacked political gatherings" of the opposition, according to the U.S. State Department's annual report on human rights practices. Consequently, hard-liners won the overwhelming majority of seats in an election marked by a record-low turnout.

Emboldened by this electoral triumph, the clerical establishment quickly moved to further restrict public freedom. Several major reformist newspapers were closed, while dozens of journalists and civil society activists were arrested during the year as the authorities attacked the country's last refuge of free expression—the Internet. In October, the head of the judiciary, Ayatollah Mahmoud Shahroudi, announced that "anyone who disseminates information aimed at disturbing the public mind through computer systems" would be jailed.

The government also launched a crackdown on "social corruption," sending thousands of morality police and vigilantes into the streets to enforce Islamic dress codes and laws prohibiting public mingling of unmarried men and women. During one two-day period in October, at least 150 Iranian youths were arrested for infractions such as dancing and eating in public during the Ramadan fast. In the summer, the government banned the widespread and popular smoking of water pipes in public places (a measure intended to discourage social gatherings of young people) and arrested dozens of alcohol smugglers. Earlier in the year, in March, Islamist vigilantes had stormed four factories in eastern Tehran in March and seized 40,000 illegally manufactured satellite dishes.

The hard-liners' electoral triumph was also followed by an increasingly salient role played by the Islamic Revolutionary Guards Corps (IRGC). Within weeks of the election, IRGC checkpoints began sprouting up in on main roads in the capital, ostensibly to combat the drug trade. In May, IRGC units forced the newly built Imam Khomeini International Airport to shut down on its opening day, claiming that involvement of a Turkish company in the airport constituted a threat to national security. In June, the IRGC arrested eight British servicemen who had strayed from southern Iraq into Iranian waters and paraded them blindfolded on national television before releasing them three days later.

In September, the hard-liner–dominated parliament approved legislation enabling it to veto government contracts with international companies, paralyzing the Khatami administration's efforts to attract international investment (at least three foreign companies canceled investment agreements shortly after the bill was passed). When shares in state companies valued at $570 million were offered for sale on the Tehran stock exchange in October, less than 10 percent were sold, and the only buyers were finance companies affiliated with state banks.

Tensions between Iran and the West escalated during the year after Tehran announced that it was resuming uranium-enrichment activities it had agreed to halt in 2003, further raising suspicions that it is pursuing a nuclear weapons program. Although Iran agreed again to temporarily freeze its enrichment programs in November 2004, efforts by Britain, France, and Germany to convince Iran to permanently halt its uranium-enrichment and plutonium-reprocessing programs and allow intrusive IAEA inspections, in return for trade agreements and other incentives, remained inconclusive at year's end.

Since the Council of Guardians is not expected to permit any credible opposition candidates to stand for election when Khatami leaves office in 2005, conservatives are likely to monopolize political power in Tehran for several years to come. While record oil receipts in 2004 (nearly double those projected) temporarily blunted the socioeconomic impact of declining investor confidence and tensions with the West, the government will eventually face mounting social unrest if it does not further liberalize the economy and shore up relations with Europe.

Political Rights and Civil Liberties: Iranians cannot change their government democratically. The most powerful figure in the Iranian government is the Supreme Leader (Vali-e-Faghih), currently Ayatollah Ali Hoseini-Khamenei; he is chosen for life by the Assembly of Experts, a clerics-only body whose members are elected to eight-year terms by popular vote from a government-screened list of candidates. The Supreme Leader is commander in chief of the armed forces and appoints the leaders of the judiciary, the heads of state broadcast media, the commander of the IRGC, the Expediency Council, and half the members of the Council of Guardians. Although the president and parliament are responsible for designating cabinet ministers, the Supreme Leader exercises de facto control over appointments to the ministries of Defense, the Interior, and Intelligence.

All candidates for election to the presidency and 290-seat unicameral parliament are vetted for strict allegiance to the ruling theocracy and adherence to Islamic principles by the 12-person Council of Guardians, a body of 6 clergymen appointed by the Supreme Leader and 6 laymen selected by the head of the judiciary chief (the latter are nominally subject to parliamentary approval). The Council of Guardians also has the power to reject legislation approved by parliament (disputes between the two are arbitrated by the Expediency Council, another non-elected conservative-dominated body, currently headed by former president Ali Akbar Rafsanjani). Corruption is pervasive. The hard-line clerical establishment has grown immensely wealthy through its control of tax-exempt foundations (*bonyads*) that monopolize many sectors of the economy, such as cement and sugar production. Iran was ranked 87 out of 146 countries surveyed in Transparency International's 2004 Corruption Perceptions Index.

Freedom of expression is limited. The government directly controls all television and radio broadcasting and, since 2003, has reportedly had some success in jamming broadcasts by dissident overseas satellite stations. The Press Court has extensive procedural and jurisdictional power in prosecuting journalists, editors, and publishers for such vaguely worded offenses as "insulting Islam" and "damaging the foundations of the Islamic Republic." In recent years, the authorities have issued ad hoc gag orders banning media coverage of specific topics and events. Since 1997, more than 100 publications have been shut down by the judiciary and hundreds of journalists and civil society activists have been arrested, held incommunicado for extended periods of time, and convicted in closed-door trials.

As in years past, many reformist newspapers were suspended or closed by the authorities in 2004. In February, the weekly *Hadith-e Kerman* and the dailies *Sharq* and *Yas-e Nau* were closed down. In May, the Azeri-language daily *Nedai Azarabadegan* was suspended for two months and the weekly *Gorgan e Emrouz* was banned. The newspapers *Jumhuriyat* and *Vaqa-yi Itifaqi-yi* were closed in July. By year's end, the few reformist newspapers that remained open had been intimidated into practicing self-censorship.

Most liberal journalists are forced to publish their work on the Internet. However, the government systematically censors Internet content. Since 2003, the government has forced Internet service providers (ISPs) to block access to a list of "immoral sites and political sites that insult the country's political and religious leaders." The authorities stepped up Internet censorship in 2004, blocking access to hundreds of additional Web sites. In September, the authorities launched a massive crackdown on free expression, arresting at least 25 journalists, civil society activists, and computer technicians involved in Internet publishing, on charges ranging from defamation to "acts against national security." According to Human Rights Watch, many were coerced by interrogators to sign written confessions saying they had taken part in an "evil project" directed by "foreigners and counter-revolutionaries."

Religious freedom is limited in Iran, which is largely Shia Muslim with a small Sunni Muslim minority. Shia clerics who dissent from the ruling establishment are frequently harassed. In May, an aide to Ayatollah Hossein Ali Montazeri was arrested for publishing a book that described the ayatollah's experiences under house arrest. Sunnis enjoy equal rights under the law, but there are some indications of discrimination, such as the absence of a Sunni mosque in the Iranian capital and the paucity of Sunnis in senior government offices. The constitution recognizes Zoroastrians, Jews, and Christians as religious minorities and generally allows them to worship without interference so long as they do not proselytize. However, they are barred from election to representative bodies (though a set number of parliamentary seats are reserved for them), cannot hold senior government or military positions, and face restrictions in employment, education, and property ownership. Some 300,000 Baha'is, Iran's largest non-Muslim minority, enjoy virtually no rights under the law and are banned from practicing their faith. Hundreds of Baha'is have been executed since 1979. Iranian security forces raided two major evangelical Christian religious gatherings in May and September 2004, arresting scores of people, most of whom had been released by year's end.

Academic freedom in Iran is limited. Scholars are frequently detained for expressing political views, and students involved in organizing protests often face suspension or expulsion by university disciplinary committees. In November, members of the Basij militia reportedly assaulted and briefly detained the head of Elm-o-Sanaat University after the school hosted a lecture by a prominent dissident.

The constitution permits the establishment of political parties, professional syndicates, and other civic organizations, provided they do not violate the principles of "freedom, sovereignty and national unity" or question the Islamic basis of the republic. In 2002, the 44-year-old Iran Freedom Movement was banned on such grounds and 33 of its leading members imprisoned. In 2004, at least four prominent human rights activists were prevented by the authorities from traveling abroad.

The 1979 constitution prohibits public demonstrations that "violate the principles of Islam," a vague provision used to justify the heavy-handed dispersal of assemblies and marches. Hard-line vigilante organizations unofficially sanctioned by the conservative establishment, most notably the Basij and Ansar-i Hezbollah, play a major role in dispersing public demonstrations. In sharp contrast to recent years, hardly any public demonstrations took place in 2004 following the hardliners' electoral victory in February. Because of the public's deepening political apathy and fear of reprisals by vigilantes, even the fifth anniversary of the regime's harsh July 1999 crackdown on students passed quietly.

Iranian law does not allow independent labor unions to exist, though workers' councils are represented in the government-sanctioned Workers' House, the country's only legal labor federation. While strikes and work stoppages are not uncommon, the authorities often ban or disperse demonstrations that criticize national economic policies. In January, security forces in the village of Khatunabad in southeastern Kerman province attacked striking copper factory workers, killing at least four people and injuring many others. In May, at least 40 workers were arrested by security forces during a Labor Day march in the city of Saqez.

The judiciary is not independent. The Supreme Leader directly appoints the head of the judiciary, who in turn appoints senior judges. Civil courts provide some procedural safeguards, though judges often serve simultaneously as prosecutors during trials. Political and other sensitive cases are tried before Revolutionary Courts, where detainees are denied access to legal counsel and due process is ignored. Clerics who criticize the conservative establishment can be arrested and tried before the Special Court for the Clergy. The penal code is based on Sharia and provides for flogging, stoning, amputation, and death for a range of social and political offenses. In February, Mohsen Mofidi died in a Tehran hospital shortly after receiving 80 lashes on charges including possession of a medicine containing alcohol, possession of a satellite dish, and aiding his sisters' "corruption." In July, an Iranian court acquitted a government intelligence agent on charges of beating Canadian-Iranian freelance photographer Zahra Kazemi to death in July 2003 after she was detained while taking photos of Evin prison. The court refused to call to the witness stand six senior judicial officials present during Kazemi's interrogation.

Iranian security forces subjected hundreds of citizens to arbitrary arrest and incommunicado detention in 2004. Suspected dissidents are often held in unofficial, illegal detention centers, and allegations of torture are commonplace. Although legislation banning the use of torture in interrogations was approved by parliament and the Council of Guardians in May, allegations of torture persisted throughout the year. In August, according to local human rights groups, a prisoner who had been left hanging by his wrists had to have his hands amputated.

There are few laws that discriminate against ethnic minorities, who are permitted to establish community centers and certain cultural, social, sports, and charitable associations. However, Kurdish demands for more autonomy and a greater voice in the appointment of a regional governor have not been met, and some Kurdish opposition groups are brutally suppressed. The opposition Democratic Party of Iranian Kurdistan (KDPI) alleged that two of its members were executed in December 2003. In June 2004, security forces reportedly arrested 80 ethnic Azeris for allegedly "spreading secessionist propaganda."

Although women enjoy the same political rights as men and currently hold several seats in parliament and even one of Iran's vice presidencies, they face discrimination in legal and social matters. A woman cannot obtain a passport without the permission of a male relative or her husband, and women do not enjoy equal rights under Sharia (Islamic law) statutes governing divorce, inheritance, and child custody. A woman's testimony in court is given only half the weight of a man's. Women must conform to strict dress codes and are segregated from men in most public places. In August, a 16-year-old girl was executed after being sentenced to death for "acts incompatible with chastity."

⬆ Iraq

Population: 25,900,000
GNI/capita: $1,090
Life Expectancy: 60
Political Rights: 7
Civil Liberties: 5
Status: Not Free
Religious Groups: Muslim (97 percent) [Shi'a Muslim (60-65 percent), Sunni Muslim (32-37 percent)], other [including Christian] (3 percent)
Ethnic Groups: Arab (75-80 percent), Kurd (15-20 percent), other [including Turkmen and Assyrian] (5 percent)
Capital: Baghdad
Trend Arrow: Iraq received a downward trend arrow due to an increase in violence and a lack of general security.

Ten-Year Ratings Timeline (Political Rights, Civil Liberties, Status)

1995	1996	1997	1998	1999	2000	2001	2002	2003	2004
7,7NF	7,7NF	7,7NF	7,7NF	7,7NF	7,7NF	7,7NF	7,7NF	7,5NF	7,5NF

Overview:

Iraq's transition from an authoritarian past to a democratic future progressed significantly in 2004, but an escalating campaign of extremist violence severely hampered reconstruction efforts and obstructed preparations for nationwide elections. While Iraqis faced relatively few government restrictions on civil liberties, thousands were brutally massacred by Islamist terrorists for practicing their religion, exercising their right to work, or expressing their political beliefs.

The modern state of Iraq, consisting of three former Ottoman provinces, was established after World War I as a British-administered League of Nations mandate. Britain installed a constitutional monarchy in which Sunni Arabs came to dominate most political and administrative posts at the expense of Kurds and Shiite Arabs. Sunni political dominance in Iraq, which formally gained independence in 1932, continued after the monarchy was overthrown in a 1958 military coup. Following a succession of weak leftist regimes, the pan-Arab Baath (Renaissance) party seized power in 1968. The Baathist regime's de facto strongman, Saddam Hussein, formally assumed the presidency in 1979.

Hussein brutally suppressed all political opposition and sought to establish Iraq as a regional superpower by invading Iran in 1980. During the eight-year war, his regime used chemical weapons against both Iranian troops and rebellious Iraqi Kurds. Iraqi troops invaded Kuwait in 1990 and were ousted the following year by a U.S.-led coalition. After the war, the UN Security Council imposed economic sanctions on Iraq, pending the destruction of its weapons of mass destruction. Because of Iraq's refusal to fully cooperate with UN weapons inspectors, however, the sanctions remained in place for over a decade.

Following the withdrawal of Iraqi military forces and administrative personnel from northern Iraq and the establishment of a U.S.-enforced no-fly zone north of the 36th parallel in 1991, most of the three northern provinces of Erbil, Duhok, and Suleimaniyah came under the control of Massoud Barzani's Kurdistan Democratic

Party (KDP) and Jalal Talabani's Patriotic Union of Kurdistan (PUK). Northern Iraq experienced rapid development during the 1990s. With their 13 percent share of Iraqi revenue from the UN oil-for-food program, and customs duties from Iraqi-Turkish trade, the Kurdish authorities built schools, roads, hospitals, and sewage systems and engaged in other development projects. Anxious to win international support for long-term Kurdish self-governance, both the KDP and the PUK allowed a flourishing of political and civil liberties not seen elsewhere in the Arab world.

In the aftermath of the September 11, 2001, attacks on the United States, U.S. president George W. Bush designated Iraq's weapons of mass destruction a salient threat to American national security and committed his administration to engineering Hussein's ouster. In March 2003, a U.S.-led military coalition invaded Iraq, captured Baghdad within three weeks, and established a Coalition Provisional Authority (CPA) to run the country temporarily. In July, after extensive and often contentious negotiations with leading Iraqi political and religious leaders, the CPA appointed a 25-member Iraqi Governing Council (IGC) and granted it limited law-making authority.

The initial euphoria felt by many Iraqis in the immediate aftermath of the regime's collapse was quickly tempered by the security vacuum, widespread looting, and acute electricity and water shortages that followed. Unemployment soared as a result of the CPA's dismissal of Baath party loyalist from government posts, which left around 35,000 civil servants out of work, and the disbanding of Iraq's 400,000-man army.

While Iraq's interim governing bodies reflected the country's confessional and ethnic demography, Sunnis viewed the diminution of their political supremacy with trepidation. Exploiting these fears, loose networks of former regime officials and foreign Islamist militants organized an insurgency in the "Sunni triangle" (the triangular region, bounded by Baghdad, Ramadi, and Tikrit, in which the bulk of Iraqi Sunnis live) that rapidly gained strength in 2003—coalition combat fatalities rose from 7 in May to 94 in November. Several prominent Iraqi political and religious leaders who supported the U.S.-led occupation were assassinated during the year, while outbreaks of violence between Kurds and Turkmen occurred in and around the northern city of Kirkuk.

Iraq's political transition progressed substantially in 2004. In March, the IGC adopted a Transitional Administrative Law (TAL) to serve as the country's interim constitution. In June, the CPA and the IGC transferred authority to an Iraqi Interim Government (IIG), formed after weeks of UN-mediated negotiations among the main (noninsurgent) political groups. The IIG received widespread diplomatic recognition abroad. In November, the world's leading industrial nations agreed to cancel 80 percent of Iraq's nearly $39 billion foreign debt.

In spite of Saddam Hussein's capture in December 2003, the insurgency escalated dramatically in 2004. With financial backing from exiled former Baathist regime elements in Syria and Syrian-occupied Lebanon, radical foreign and Iraqi Islamist groups carried out a sophisticated, multipronged campaign of deadly terrorist attacks. Thousands of security personnel, civilian government employees, and other Iraqi citizens viewed as collaborators were killed or injured during the year (the number of police officers killed since the fall of Baghdad surpassed 1,500 in late 2004), while hundreds of Iraqi Shiite and Kurdish civilians were massacred in suicide bombings aimed at inflaming ethnosectarian hatred. In an effort to frighten away non-

Iraqis with expertise needed for the country's reconstruction, terrorists abducted scores of humanitarian aid workers, civilian contractors, and other foreigners; dozens were executed, some in gruesome videos distributed on the Internet.

The insurgency hampered the ability of coalition and Iraqi security forces to combat ordinary crime (kidnappings for ransom by organized criminal syndicates became a daily occurrence in 2004) and quell an uprising launched by radical Shiite cleric Muqtada al-Sadr in April, which continued intermittently until a truce was reached in August. The insurgency also slowed progress in many critical areas of Iraq's reconstruction. By the latter half of 2004, an estimated one-fifth of all reconstruction funds flowing into Iraq was being used to provide security for foreign contractors—a diversion of billions of dollars from other projects. Throughout the year, oil production remained well below its pre-March 2003 level as a result of insurgents' sabotage of the petroleum infrastructure, while essential public services, such as power and water, were repeatedly disrupted in most areas of the country. Unemployment remained, by most estimates, well over 50 percent; nearly two-thirds of Iraqi families were dependent on food rations.

Residents of northern Iraq, where Kurdish militia forces (*peshmerga*) were allowed to maintain security much as they had since the early 1990s, were spared most of these tribulations. With a few exceptions—most notably the simultaneous terrorist bombings of KDP and PUK headquarters on February 1 that left 56 people dead—Kurdish areas remained secure and experienced few shortages.

In early November, coalition and Iraqi forces launched a major military operation against radical Islamist forces, capturing Falluja after days of bloody fighting that reduced much of the city to rubble. Islamist forces quickly regrouped and counterattacked elsewhere, particularly Mosul. In an effort to derail the January 2005 elections, Islamist insurgents attacked election workers, obstructing voter registration in many areas of the Sunni triangle, while threatening to murder those who venture to the polls. With most Sunni political and religious leaders calling for a boycott (some very reluctantly), prospects for the formation of a transitional government viewed as legitimate by all main ethnic and religious groups appeared limited.

Estimates of the total number of Iraqi civilians killed between March 2003 and the end of 2004 vary widely. The Web site Iraqbodycount.org, which compiles media-reported casualties in Iraq, put the number at roughly 17,000, while a British medical journal, *Lancet*, estimated the number to be 100,000.

Political Rights and Civil Liberties:

Iraqis cannot change their government democratically. The IIG (Iraqi Interim Government) is unelected and, in light of its heavy dependence on U.S. financial and military support, is fully sovereign in name only. UN-mediated negotiations among political groups supporting the American-led occupation led to the appointment of Iyad Allawi, a Shiite, as IIG prime minister in June 2004; Ghazi al-Yawar, a Sunni, assumed the largely ceremonial post of president.

The 100-member Interim National Council (INC), an unelected body established in August 2004 and representing the country's main pro-government political groups, does not have legislative powers, but can veto cabinet decisions and appointments and override executive orders with a two-thirds majority. The IIG will govern the country until the formation of an Iraqi Transitional Government (ITG) after elections are held for the 275-seat Transitional National Assembly (TNA) in January 2005. The ITG is expected to draft a permanent constitution and hold elections for a permanent government by the end of 2005.

Although the Baath Party is banned, political parties representing a wide range of viewpoints are allowed to organize and campaign freely.

Corruption is rampant in transitional government institutions. An October 2004 report by the UN International Advisory and Monitoring Board highlighted numerous irregularities in expenditures, such as lack of competitive bidding for lucrative contracts, that facilitate corruption. Iraq was ranked 129 out of 146 countries surveyed in Transparency International's 2004 Corruption Perceptions Index.

Freedom of expression in Iraq is generally respected by the authorities. Around a dozen private television stations had been established by year's end. Although most are affiliated with particular religious or political groups, the first privately owned nonpartisan station, Al-Sharqiya, was launched in March 2004; a second, Nahrain TV, was established a few months later (but had not begun broadcasting by year's end). Major Arab satellite stations are easily accessible in Iraq, as roughly one-third of Iraqi families own a satellite dish. More than 130 print publications established since the fall of Saddam Hussein were allowed to operate without significant government interference. Internet access remained limited to roughly one-tenth of 1 percent of the population.

CPA Order 14 (June 2003) prohibited media organizations from publishing or broadcasting material that incites violence or civil disorder. In March, the CPA accused *Al-Hawza*, a weekly newspaper controlled by Muqtada al-Sadr, of publishing false information intended to incite attacks against coalition forces and suspended the paper for 60 days. In July, the IIG created a Higher Media Commission with the authority to sanction media outlets for similar infractions. In August, the IIG accused the Qatar-based Al-Jazeera satellite channel of inciting violence and banned it from working in the country for 30 days; in September, the ban was extended indefinitely.

Iraq remained the most dangerous country in the world for journalists. In 2004, according to the Committee to Protect Journalists, 15 Iraqi and foreign journalists, as well as 16 media workers (drivers, bodyguards, and translators—all but one Iraqis), were deliberately killed by extremist groups. In addition, five journalists died while covering live combat, while three journalists and one media worker were killed near checkpoints by coalition forces because of mistaken identity. Many of these latter nine deaths could probably have been avoided had more adequate safeguards (for example, improved military communication regarding the presence of journalists in conflict areas) been in place. In addition, 22 journalists were abducted during the year by insurgent groups or for ransom by professional kidnappers.

Many journalists and media workers were detained, most of them briefly, by coalition forces and Iraqi police in 2004. Three Iraqi employees of Reuters news agency who were detained in January later claimed to have been subjected to sexual abuse by U.S. soldiers. In August, Iraqi police ordered all journalists not embedded with coalition forces battling Sadr's militia in Najaf to leave the city and briefly detained 60 who ignored the order.

The TAL designates Islam as the state religion and "a source of legislation" in Iraq, while guaranteeing freedom of religious belief and practice. With the lifting of

Baathist-era controls over religious institutions, mosques and churches in Iraq operate with virtually no formal government oversight. Religious and ethnic groups in Iraq were represented in the IIG and civil service in rough proportion to their demographic strength.

Iraqi Christians were targeted by Islamist terrorist groups in 2004. Between August and November, 12 churches were bombed in Baghdad and Mosul; at least 15 people were killed. Roughly 5 percent of Iraq's 900,000-strong Christian community had left the country by year's end. Hundreds of Shiites were also killed in terrorist attacks by suspected Sunni Islamist operatives. In November, a prominent Sunni cleric was assassinated.

Baathist-era restrictions on academic freedom were abolished in 2003, and faculties at most universities are allowed to elect administrators. However, university professors are frequently targeted by extremist groups. According to the Iraqi Ministry of Human Rights, at least 80 professors were killed during the year.

Freedom of assembly and association are recognized by the TAL and were generally respected in practice. Domestic and international human rights groups were able to operate without restrictions, though security constraints limited their activities in many areas of the country. Peaceful demonstrations occurred frequently during the year without interference from coalition forces or the Iraqi government, except when they were in violation of curfews.

The TAL guarantees the right to "form and join unions" and to "strike peaceably in accordance with the law." While Iraq's 1987 labor law has remained in force, technically prohibiting unionization in the public sector—where the vast majority of Iraqi workers are employed—union activity has flourished in nearly all industries since 2003 and strikes have not been uncommon. In December 2003, coalition forces raided the headquarters of the newly established Iraqi Federation of Trade Unions and arrested eight union officials, but all were quickly released without charge (faulty intelligence was reportedly to blame). In early 2004, the CPA increased wages for workers in power plants and oil production facilities after they threatened to strike.

The TAL provides for an independent judiciary, but in practice judges come under immense political pressure. In 2003, a Judicial Review Committee was established to screen judges and prosecutors for past links to the Baath party, involvement in human rights violations, and corruption, and to appoint replacements. The head of Iraq's Central Criminal Court, Zuhair al-Maliky, who had launched investigations into alleged corruption and abuse of power by several senior officials in the IIG, was dismissed in October 2004.

Iraq's newly amended Criminal Procedure Code stipulates that suspects cannot be held more than 24 hours without an examining magistrate's ruling of sufficient evidence. However, lengthy pre-arraignment detention was common. According to the U.S. State Department's 2004 human rights country report, "coerced confessions and interrogation continued to be the favored method of investigation by police." Most criminal trials are summary; a majority of cases examined by Human Rights Watch monitors lasted less than thirty minutes.

Thousands of people suspected of security offenses were detained without charge by coalition troops during the year. In April, the American media published photographs of U.S. soldiers subjecting detainees at Abu Ghraib prison to various forms of physical and sexual abuse or torture. The following month, Pentagon officials acknowledged that 32 detainees had died while in U.S. custody. Two of the deaths were classified as unjustifiable homicides, and several others remained under investigation.

The National Security Order passed by the IIG in July enables the prime minister to declare martial law for a 60-day period (renewable every 30 days with the endorsement of the president and both vice presidents) in areas of the country where violence against citizens poses a "danger of grave proportions." Under martial law, the government can restrict freedom of movement and assembly, detain suspects and search homes without warrants, and impose curfews. On the eve of the November military offensive in Falluja, the government announced a 60-day state of emergency in the city and the nearby town of Ramadi and imposed nighttime curfews on several other cities.

The Iraq Special Tribunal (IST) was created in 2003 to try former officials of the Baathist regime. The IST statute does not explicitly prohibit confessions extracted by torture or require that guilt be proven beyond a reasonable doubt. More than 90 "high value detainees" awaiting trial before the IST were in detention at an undisclosed U.S. military facility in late 2004; only 12, including Saddam Hussein, had been formally arraigned.

Iraq's Baathist-era Personal Status Law remains in force and guarantees equal rights for women, as does the TAL. In December 2003, the IGC issued a decree to repeal the Personal Status Law and impose Sharia (Islamic law) restrictions on women's rights in matters such as divorce and inheritance, but the decision was reversed under pressure from the United States and secular Iraqi political groups. The TAL guarantees Iraqi women at least 25 percent of the seats in the January 2005 elections. There were six female ministers in the IIG.

Public security for Iraqi women remained a major problem in 2004. Women who hold jobs, attend university, or go out in public unveiled were frequently harassed by radical Islamist groups (both Sunni and Shiite). In March, an American women's rights coordinator for the CPA, Fern Holland, and her Iraqi assistant, Salwa Oumashi, were murdered. In November, women's rights activist Nisreen Mustafa al-Burawari was killed, along with her secretary, bodyguard, and driver.

Ireland

Population: 4,100,000 **Political Rights:** 1
GNI/capita: $23,030 **Civil Liberties:** 1
Life Expectancy: 77 **Status:** Free
Religious Groups: Roman Catholic (91.6 percent),
Church of Ireland (2.5 percent), other (5.9 percent)
Ethnic Groups: Celtic, English minority
Capital: Dublin

Ten-Year Ratings Timeline (Political Rights, Civil Liberties, Status)

1994	1995	1996	1997	1998	1999	2000	2001	2002	2003	2004
1,2F	1,1F	1,1F	1,1F	1,1F	1,1F	1,1F	1,1F	1,1F	1,1F	1,1F

Overview:
The government coalition, led by the Fianna Fail party, continued to lose popularity over the course of 2004, and Fianna Fail did poorly in local and European Parliament elections. However, the government did win respect for its successful presidency of the European Union (EU) during the first six months of 2004.

The Irish Free State emerged from the United Kingdom after the Anglo-Irish Treaty of 1921. (Six Protestant-majority counties in the province of Ulster remained within the United Kingdom.) A short civil war followed, ending in 1923. In 1937, the Irish Free State adopted a new constitution and a new name—Ireland, or Eire.

Ireland has been independent in its foreign policy, staying out of World War II and out of NATO. It joined the European Community (now the EU) along with Britain and Denmark in 1973. As a member, thanks in part to large subsidies for poorer regions within the EU, Ireland has enjoyed high rates of economic growth and has gone from being one of the poorest countries in Europe to being richer than Britain by some measures. It adopted the euro on its launch (as an electronic currency only) in 1999 and introduced euro notes and coins in 2001.

Ireland has resisted any EU moves that would impinge on its neutrality, including the idea of setting up an EU military capability. Partly for this reason, Irish voters rejected the EU's Treaty of Nice in June 2001, temporarily blocking the enlargement of the EU into Eastern Europe. In a second referendum, in October 2002, Irish voters approved the treaty.

Growth in the gross domestic product (GDP) averaged an outstanding 8.6 percent from 1998 through 2002. The growth led to inflation and wage increases, which eroded Ireland's competitiveness. That erosion, compounded by a strong euro, which depressed exports, slowed GDP growth sharply, to 3.7 percent in 2003. The slower growth hit the government's budget, forcing the country to take a step back from the highly generous fiscal policies of previous years.

Though the economy was forecast to pick up again in 2004, the budget tightening caused by the general slowdown of 1998–2002 led to voter disillusionment. This was further fed by a perception that the governing coalition—Fianna Fail, with its junior coalition partner, the Progressive Democratic Party—which has been in power since 1997, had begun to grow arrogant, increasing taxes after having promised not to before the 2002 general election. As a result, Fianna Fail did poorly in local elections in June 2004, despite the fact that the elections coincided with a popular government-sponsored referendum on tightening Irish citizenship laws. The voters' verdict was reconfirmed with another poor showing for Fianna Fail in European Parliament elections later that month. Prime Minister Bertie Ahern reshuffled his cabinet in September, hoping to shore up the coalition for elections that must be held by 2006.

Ireland did win praise for its diplomacy in 2004, particularly for its success holding the EU's rotating six-month presidency for the first half of the year. The biggest event was the enlargement of the EU by 10 new countries, mostly formerly Communist countries of Central and Eastern Europe. However, Irish diplomacy also helped bring about a draft constitution for the EU that will fundamentally change how the 25-member bloc is run—if the draft is ratified by each country, not a forgone conclusion. Ahern, representing the Irish presidency, helped broker compromises between big countries and small, as well as between those who want deeper European integration and more sceptical countries. He also helped EU leaders through the bitter negotiations that led to the selection of Jose Manuel Durao Barroso of Portugal as head of the European Commission (the EU's executive).

Political Rights and Civil Liberties: The Irish can change their government democratically. The legislature consists of a lower house (the Dail), whose 166 members are elected by proportional representation, and an upper house (the Seanad, or Senate) of 60 members, some appointed, some elected by a body representing various interest groups. The Senate is mainly a consultative body. The president, whose powers are largely ceremonial, is directly elected for a seven-year term.

The political party system is open to the rise and fall of competing groupings. The two largest parties—Fianna Fail and Fine Gael—do not differ widely in ideological orientation, but mainly represent the opposing sides of the 1920s civil war. The smaller parties are the Labour Party, the Progressive Democrats, Sinn Fein, and the Greens.

Corruption has been an ongoing issue, with many of the scandals having involved members of Fianna Fail. A former prime minister, Charles Haughey, who headed several governments from 1979 to 1992, was discovered in 1997 to have received up to one million euros from an owner of a food and textile retailer. Though there is no direct connection of corruption to Prime Minister Bertie Ahern, he was found to have signed blank checks as party leader. Ireland was ranked 17 out of 146 countries surveyed in Transparency International's 2004 Corruption Perceptions Index.

The media are free and independent, and Internet access is unrestricted. The print media present a variety of viewpoints. Television and radio are dominated by the state broadcaster, RTE, but the growth of cable and satellite television is weakening its influence. The state maintains the right to censor pornographic and violent material, which critics charge is an anachronism and possibly in contravention of the European Convention on Human Rights. Government plans to reduce media access to government information have been criticized, as have plans to introduce a Press Council to regulate media conduct.

Freedom of religion is provided for in the constitution, and discrimination on the basis of religion is illegal. Though the country is overwhelmingly Roman Catholic, there is no state religion. Adherents of other faiths face little trouble with religious expression. Religious education is provided in most primary and secondary schools, on whose boards sit officials of the Catholic Church. However, parents may exempt their children from religious instruction, and the constitution requires equal funding for students wishing instruction in other faiths. Academic freedom is respected.

There is freedom of assembly and association, and nongovernmental organizations can operate freely. Collective bargaining is legal and unrestricted and unions operate without hindrance. The right of public assembly and demonstration is not infringed.

The legal system is based on common law, and the judiciary is independent. In a 2003 visit, the Council of Europe found evidence of some ill-treatment, including beatings, of detainees by police, mostly at the time of their detention, but stated that the prisons are on the whole well run. Despite equal protection for all under the law, the Irish Travellers, a nomadic group of about 25,000, face social discrimination in housing, hiring, and other areas.

Inequality persists in the pay of men and women, but discrimination in employment on the basis of sex and sexual orientation is forbidden under national and EU law. The past two presidents have been women: Mary McAleese (elected in 1997 and re-elected in 2004) and Mary Robinson (1990-1997). Abortion is legal only when the life of the mother is threatened.

Israel

Population: 6,800,000
[Note: includes about 220,000 Israeli settlers in the West Bank, about 20,000 in the Golan Heights, and 5,000 in the Gaza Strip. Approximately 177,000 Jews and 174,000 Arabs live in East Jerusalem.]
GNI/capita: $16,020
Life Expectancy: 79
Religious Groups: Jewish (80.1 percent), Muslim [mostly Sunni] (14.6 percent), Christian (2.1 percent), other (3.2 percent)
Ethnic Groups: Jewish (80 percent), non-Jewish [mostly Arab] (20 percent)
Capital: Jerusalem

Political Rights: 1
Civil Liberties: 3
Status: Free

Note: The numerical rating and status reflect the state of political rights and civil liberties within Israel itself. Separate reports examine political rights and civil liberties in the Israeli-occupied territories and in the Palestinian administered areas.

Ten-Year Ratings Timeline (Political Rights, Civil Liberties, Status)

1995	1996	1997	1998	1999	2000	2001	2002	2003	2004
1,3F	1,3F	1,3F	1,3F	1,3F	1,3F	1,3F	1,3F	1,3F	1,3F

Overview: A sharp reduction in terrorist attacks in 2004 fostered a greater sense of public security among Israelis. The drop in attacks came with a price, however, as Israel became the target of intense international opprobrium, diplomatic isolation, and sanctions threats over its antiterrorism tactics, which included further construction of a West Bank security barrier and ongoing killings of Palestinian terror suspects. Prime Minister Ariel Sharon proposed a plan to withdraw Jewish settlers and Israeli armed forces from the Gaza Strip by 2005, causing a significant political shakeup; by the summer, Sharon was presiding over a minority government and was later fending off no-confidence motions and parliamentary revolts. Members of the Jewish Orthodox establishment appealed to Israeli soldiers to disobey settlement evacuation orders. Sharon spent much of the year engulfed in potentially destabilizing bribery and corruption scandals.

Israel was formed in 1948 from less than one-fifth of the original British Mandate of Palestine. Arab nations rejected a UN partition plan that would also have created a Palestinian state. Immediately following Israel's declaration of independence, its neighbors attacked. While Israel maintained its sovereignty, Jordan seized East Jerusalem and the West Bank, and Egypt took control of the Gaza Strip.

In the 1967 Six-Day War, Israel came to occupy the Sinai Peninsula, the West Bank, Gaza, East Jerusalem, and the Golan Heights. Syria had previously used the Golan to shell towns in northern Israel. Israel annexed East Jerusalem in 1967 and the Golan Heights in 1981. It returned the Sinai to Egypt in 1982 as part of a peace agreement between the two countries.

In 1993, Prime Minister Yitzhak Rabin's Labor-led coalition government secured a breakthrough agreement with the Palestine Liberation Organization (PLO). The Declaration of Principles, negotiated secretly between Israeli and Palestinian delegations in Oslo, Norway, provided for a phased Israeli withdrawal from the Israeli-occupied West Bank and Gaza Strip and for limited Palestinian autonomy in those areas, and for Palestinian recognition of Israel and a renunciation of terrorism. On November 4, 1995, a right-wing Jewish extremist, opposed to the peace process, assassinated Rabin in Tel Aviv.

At Camp David in July 2000 and at Taba, Egypt, in the fall and in early 2001, Prime Minister Ehud Barak and U.S. president Bill Clinton engaged the Palestinian leadership in the most far-reaching negotiations ever. The Palestinian leadership ultimately rejected the Israeli offers, leading some analysts to suggest that Yasser Arafat, chairman of the Palestinian Authority, was not satisfied that Palestinian territory in the West Bank would be contiguous or that Israel would recognize a "right of return" allowing Palestinian refugees to live in Israel. Following a controversial visit by then Likud Party leader Ariel Sharon to the Temple Mount in Jerusalem in September 2000, the Palestinians launched an armed uprising, effectively ending the peace process.

Sharon, first elected in 2001, was reelected in national elections in January 2003, against a backdrop of continuing Palestinian violence in Israel, characterized mainly by devastating suicide bombings on buses, and in cafés, restaurants, bars, and marketplaces.

While Palestinian suicide bombers succeeded in carrying out some attacks in 2004, terrorist strikes inside Israel declined markedly, which allowed for unusual stretches of calm and a return to relative normality for Israeli citizens. Israeli intelligence operations, combined with the construction of a security barrier in the West

Bank and targeted killings of suspected Palestinian terrorist operatives and leaders, helped reduce the overall level of terrorism inside Israel. According to the Israeli security establishment, nearly three-quarters of suicide bombers were intercepted before reaching their targets. A twin suicide bombing in August aboard buses in the southern city of Beersheba killed 16 people. The attack's success was attributed to the incomplete section of the security barrier along the southern edge of the West Bank, from where the bombers were thought to have originated.

Palestinians in the Gaza Strip launched increasing numbers of crude, short-range Qassam rockets into Israel. Most rockets struck the town of Sderot, where three people were killed, including two children. Israeli officials voiced fears that Qassams might eventually be fired from the West Bank, where the largely inaccurate rockets would be within ideal firing range of dense Israeli population centers.

Israeli Defense Forces (IDF) retaliated for many terrorist attacks throughout the year. The IDF carried out targeted killings of terrorist suspects in the West Bank and Gaza, where it also staged air strikes, demolished private homes, and imposed curfews. The United States and many other countries, along with the United Nations, criticized Israel over its tactics and for the deaths of innocent Palestinians during antiterrorism operations.

Sharon weathered political storms throughout the year, brought on primarily by his announced plan to unilaterally withdraw Israeli settlers and troops from Gaza. In June, two right-wing members of Sharon's cabinet resigned over the plan, reducing the government to a minority coalition composed of 59 of 120 Knesset (parliament) seats. The resignations followed the dismissals of seven other cabinet officers opposed to the Gaza pullout plan. Likud Party members also voted in a nonbinding poll to reject the plan, setting the stage for a contentious debate over the withdrawal proposal. According to polls, at least two-thirds of Israelis back the plan, but it was strenuously opposed by some in the settler community and among the right-wing establishment. Some members of the Orthodox community publicly urged soldiers to disobey evacuation orders. This tactic elicited sharp denunciations from political and military leaders, distressed over the apparent undermining of Israel's democracy by segments of the religious establishment. Sharon prevailed at the end of October, when the Knesset voted to approve the Gaza withdrawal plan by a vote of 67 to 45.

Tensions remained high along Israel's northern border with Lebanon during the year. In January, Hezbollah, a radical Shiite Muslim group backed by Iran and Syria and based in southern Lebanon, fired across the border at an Israeli soldier clearing mines, killing him. Hezbollah reportedly has taken delivery of rockets capable of striking Israeli population and industrial centers. The group has in the past attacked Israeli positions patrolling near the Shebba Farms area. Hezbollah considers the area occupied Lebanese territory, despite UN confirmation in June 2000 that Israel had withdrawn fully from a "security zone" in southern Lebanon it had occupied for 18 years. Israel had held the zone to protect its northern flank from attacks, which included repeated Hezbollah rocketing of Israeli towns and farms.

In January, Israel conducted a prisoner swap with Hezbollah, releasing more than two dozen Lebanese and Arab prisoners and 400 Palestinian prisoners. Hezbollah released an Israeli businessman kidnapped in 2000 and the bodies of three Israeli soldiers. The soldiers had gone missing near the border with Lebanon in October

2000. Hezbollah is still believed to be holding or at least have information about missing Israeli airman Ron Arad, thought to be held in Lebanon or Iran since his plane was shot down over Lebanon in 1986.

The Israeli economy, especially its tourism sector, rebounded slightly during the year as terrorist attacks abated.

Political Rights and Civil Liberties: Israeli citizens can change their government democratically. Although Israel has no formal constitution, a series of basic laws has the force of constitutional principles. A largely ceremonial president serves as chief of state while the prime minister, appointed by his or her party, serves as head of government. The unicameral Knesset (parliament) is composed of 120 seats, and members are elected by popular vote for four-year terms. Israel features a wide range of political parties.

Arab residents of East Jerusalem, while not granted automatic citizenship, were issued Israeli identity cards after the 1967 Six-Day War. However, by law, Israel strips Arabs of their Jerusalem residency if they remain outside the city for more than three months. Arab residents have the same rights as Israeli citizens, except the right to vote in national elections. They do have the right to vote in municipal elections and are eligible to apply for citizenship. Many choose not to seek citizenship out of solidarity with Palestinians in the West Bank and Gaza Strip and because they believe East Jerusalem should be the capital of an independent Palestinian state. East Jerusalem's Arab population does not receive a share of municipal services proportionate to its numbers. Arabs in East Jerusalem do have the right to vote in Palestinian Authority elections.

Israel was ranked 26 out of 146 countries surveyed in Transparency International's 2004 Corruption Perceptions Index. Sharon was cleared of involvement in a bribery and corruption scandal that emerged early in the year. Sharon and his son Gilad, were allegedly bribed by an Israeli businessman seeking Greek government approval to develop property on a Greek island. Although Israel's state prosecutor recommended in March that Sharon be indicted, the attorney general dropped the case in June out of lack of evidence.

Press freedom is respected in Israel. While media reports on security matters are subject to a military censor, the scope of permissible reporting is wide. Editors may appeal a censorship decision to a three-member tribunal that includes two civilians. Publishing the praise of violence is prohibited under the Counter-terrorism Ordinance. Israeli authorities prohibit expressions of support for groups that call for the destruction of Israel.

Arabic-language publications are censored more frequently than are Hebrew-language ones. Newspapers are privately owned and freely criticize government policy. Internet access is widespread and unrestricted. In March, the Organization of Arab Journalists in Israel called for the creation of an Arabic-language television channel, claiming that Israel's Arab community is underserved by the national media.

In May, Israeli police arrested British journalist Peter Hounam who allegedly violated a court order barring interviews of Mordechai Vanunu, an Israeli citizen released from jail in April after serving an 18-year sentence for spying and discussing Israel's reputed nuclear capability. Hounam was freed shortly after his arrest. In August, the Supreme Court denied a government appeal to uphold a ban on granting Palestinians Israeli press credentials. Israel's Government Press Office earlier ceased issuing press cards to Palestinians on security grounds; the government claimed some Palestinians posing as journalists used the cards to gain entry into Israel to carry out or abet terrorist attacks. In September, Israel deported a British freelance journalist who had been prevented from entering the country because of her political activities with the International Solidarity Movement (ISM), a group sympathetic to Palestinians. According to Israel, ISM members obstruct Israeli operations in the West Bank and Gaza strip, endangering themselves and others.

Freedom of religion is respected. Christian, Muslim, and Baha'i communities have jurisdiction over their own members in matters of marriage, burial, and divorce. In the Jewish community, the Orthodox establishment generally handles these matters. As a result, the law does not allow civil marriages, which prevents Jews and non-Jews from marrying. Many Israelis choose to marry in civil ceremonies outside the country, rather than submit to a religious ceremony. In February 2002, the Supreme Court for the first time formally recognized Jewish conversions performed by Reform and Conservative rabbis in Israel. While the ruling allows those converted by non-Orthodox rabbis to be listed as Jews in the official population registry, the Orthodox establishment can still refuse services—such as weddings—to Reform and Conservative converts.

In 2003, the Sharon cabinet disbanded the Religious Affairs Ministry, effectively putting rabbinic courts under the control of the Justice Ministry. The decision cleared the way for increased allocations of state resources to non-Orthodox religious institutions, including those attached to the Reform and Conservative movements. The move was seen as a further erosion of the Orthodox monopoly on Israel's religious affairs.

Freedom of assembly and association is respected. Israel features a vibrant civic society that includes a diverse array of nongovernmental organizations. Demonstrations, including those outside government buildings and the official residence of the prime minister, are permitted. Demonstrations by Jewish protestors in or near the West Bank are sometimes treated differently, and usually draw a greater security force. In December, Israeli troops fired on Israeli demonstrators protesting at a section of the West Bank security barrier, wounding one person in the leg. In September a state prosecutor opened a criminal investigation into a right-wing activist thought to have caused incitement by making threatening remarks toward Sharon.

Workers may join unions of their choice and enjoy the right to strike and to bargain collectively. Three-quarters of the workforce either belong to unions affiliated with Histadrut (the national labor union) or are covered under its social programs and collective bargaining agreements. Foreign workers in the country legally enjoy wage protections, medical insurance, and guarantees against employer exploitation. Illegal workers are often at the mercy of employers, and many are exploited.

The judiciary is independent, and procedural safeguards are generally respected. Security trials, however, may be closed to the public on limited grounds. The Emergency Powers (Detention) Law of 1979 provides for indefinite administrative detention without trial. The policy stems from emergency laws in place since the creation of Israel. Most administrative detainees are Palestinian. In September, thousands of Palestinian prisoners staged an 18-day hunger strike to protest prison conditions. Israel insisted conditions were satisfactory and that the prisoners were demanding extra privileges such as telephone calls, which Israel was refusing. There are approximately 7,000 Palestinians in Israeli jails.

While extended full political rights, some one million Arab citizens of Israel (roughly 19 percent of the population) receive inferior education, housing, and social services relative to the Jewish population. Israeli Arabs are not subject to the military draft, though they may serve voluntarily. Those who do not join the army are not eligible for financial benefits—including scholarships and housing loans—available to Israelis who have served.

In 2003, an independent commission issued its findings of a public inquiry into the shooting deaths of 13 Arab Israelis by police in October 2000. The police opened fire on rioters demonstrating in support of the Palestinian uprising. The report identified discrimination against Israel's Arab minority as the primary cause of the riots and led to the initiation of criminal investigations of several of the police officers who had opened fire, labeling them "prejudiced." While the 800-plus-page report was criticized by some for not going far enough—and by others for excusing Arab violence—it was generally regarded as an important breakthrough in addressing the social and economic disparities between Jewish and Arab Israelis. In January 2004, Sharon declared that every state-run company must have at least one Arab-Israeli on its board of directors. Salah Tarif, an Arab-Israeli, is a member of Sharon's cabinet. An Arab-Israeli judge also sits on the Supreme Court.

Some Israeli analysts, including supporters of Arab minority rights, cautioned against the radicalization of segments of Israel's Arab population and of Arab residents of East Jerusalem. Several Arab-Israelis and East Jerusalem residents were arrested in 2004 for involvement in terrorism.

While the state protects wide personal autonomy, the Law of Citizenship, passed in 2003, bars citizenship to Palestinians from the West Bank and Gaza who marry Arab-Israelis. The law, extended for six months in July 2004, would ostensibly lead to the separation of families or to their relocation from Israel. As the law is not retroactive, it does not affect Palestinians previously granted citizenship. Some human rights groups characterized the law as racist. Israel maintained the law was necessary because some Palestinians have opportunistically married Arab citizens of Israel so they can move to the country to more easily carry out terrorist attacks or to slowly shift the demographic reality in their favor.

Most Bedouin housing settlements are not recognized by the government and are not provided with basic infrastructure and essential services.

Freedom of movement is sometimes affected by security alerts and emergency measures that can subject Israelis to delays at roadblocks and public places. Israeli security forces and police sometimes carry out random, spot identity checks of civilians. By law, all citizens must carry national identification cards.

Women have achieved substantial parity at almost all levels of Israeli society. Women are somewhat under-represented in public affairs; 18 women sit in the 120-seat Knesset. In the May 1999 election, an Arab-Israeli woman, Husaina Jabara, was elected to the Knesset for the first time. Arab women citizens and residents face some societal pressures and traditions that negatively affect their professional, political, and social lives. The trafficking of women for prostitution has become a problem in recent years.

Italy

Population: 57,800,000
GNI/capita: $19,080
Life Expectancy: 80
Religious Groups: Roman Catholic (predominant)
Ethnic Groups: Italian, small minorities of German, French, Slovenian, and Albanian
Capital: Rome

Political Rights: 1
Civil Liberties: 1
Status: Free

Ten-Year Ratings Timeline (Political Rights, Civil Liberties, Status)

1995	1996	1997	1998	1999	2000	2001	2002	2003	2004
1,2F	1,2F	1,2F	1,2F	1,2F	1,2F	1,2F	1,1F	1,1F	1,1F

Overview:
Italy's parliament approved a controversial media law in April 2004 that, critics argue, consolidates Prime Minister Silvio Berlusconi's hold over the media. In July 2004, parliament passed a conflict-of-interest law that seeks to address Berlusconi's dual role as the country's leading media magnate and prime minister. During European Parliament and local elections held in June, the ruling coalition of parties, the Casa delle Liberta (House of Liberties), suffered a defeat, leading to a government crisis. The country continued its steadfast support of the U.S.-led war in Iraq, keeping its 3,000 plus troops on the ground there, despite opposition at home and a number of kidnappings of Italians in Iraq.

Modern Italy begins with the mid-nineteenth century Risorgimento that brought together the various regions of the peninsula under the control of the northwestern region of Piedmont. Italy's liberal period ended abruptly with the rise to power of Benito Mussolini and the Fascist Party, which ruled the country for 20 years starting in 1922. During World War II, the country, under Mussolini, joined Germany and Japan as an Axis power, declaring war on France, Britain, and the Soviet Union and invading Greece. The Allied invasion in the South, along with the help of the anti-Fascist resistance in the North, led to Italy's eventual defeat in 1945. A referendum in 1946 replaced the monarchy with a republican form of government.

The "Clean Hands" corruption trials in the early 1990s led to the collapse of the major political parties that had dominated postwar Italian politics—the Christian Democrats, the Communists, and the Socialists. Since that time, many new parties and coalitions have emerged.

In the late 1990s, Italy began a number of institutional reforms to address a list of pressing issues, including revolving-door governments: Italy has had more than 50 governments since 1945. In 1993, a new electoral law switched the country from a pure system of proportional representation to a (mostly) plurality system in an attempt to reduce the number of political parties that can obtain seats. Other reforms have included efforts to modernize the judiciary by streamlining the prosecution of cases in the courts and reduce unnecessary legislation.

The Casa delle Liberta coalition, which won the last national elections, in May 2001, includes Berlusconi's Forza Italia, as well as the post-Fascist Allianza Nazionale and the regionalist Lega Nord. During those elections, about 85 percent of eligible voters went to the polls—a turnout that was lower than the postwar average of over 90 percent. The main opposition to the Casa delle Liberta is the leftist Ulivo (Olive Tree) coalition, which includes the former Communist Party, now called the Party of the Democratic Left (DS), as well as different Green formations and former leftist Christian Democrats. The constitution forbids the reemergence of the Fascist Party. In December 2003, President Carlo Azeglio Ciampi invoked his little-used veto powers to stop the passage of an earlier version of the media law in parliament that allowed Berlusconi to expand his media and publishing interests. Ciampi's veto was eventually overruled, and the Gasparri law was passed in late April.

Parliament passed a controversial conflict-of-interest law in July 2004 that is intended to deal with the prime minister's dual role as a media magnate and the country's top legislator. The law, which forces politicians to hand over managerial control of their companies while in office, has been criticized by the opposition because it does not compel Berlusconi to sell off any part of his huge media empire.

A corruption trial against Berlusconi resumed in April 2004 after the prime minister's immunity from prosecution was removed by the Constitutional Court in January 2004. The law granting Berlusconi and other top government officials immunity was seen by critics as simply an attempt to disrupt pending trials against the prime minister. The Constitutional Court argued that the law violated the constitution. A verdict was expected in December 2004.

Shortly after suffering losses during the local and European Parliament elections in June 2004, the members of the governing coalition held talks to avoid a government crisis. The coalition had become increasingly fractious due to the diverging interests of its members and resentment by some of them toward Berlusconi's continuing conflict-of-interest problems. Since the 2001 elections, Berlusconi's Casa delle Liberta coalition has suffered losses at every election. Despite these losses, Berlusconi heads the longest-serving government since the end of World War II.

At the end of September 2004, the parliament approved legislation that will devolve control over education, health, and local policing from Rome to the country's 20 regions. The legislation will have to go through more parliamentary hurdles and might face a national referendum.

Italy kept its 3,000 troops in Iraq in the face of demands by kidnappers who seized a number of Italian citizens, killing one, a journalist. A ransom of $1 million was allegedly paid to gain the release of two Italian women hostages in September. Hundreds of illegal immigrants arrived on coastal areas during the year. In response, the government tightened immigration restrictions that had come into force two years prior. However, in July, the Constitutional Court ruled that the restrictive immigration law violated fundamental rights guaranteed by the constitution. After suffering a serious heart attack, Umberto Bossi, the leader of the anti-immigrant Lega Nord party, quit his parliamentary post for a seat in the European Parliament.

Political Rights and Civil Liberties: Italians can change their government democratically. Although the role of the president—who is chosen by parliament and representatives of the regions—is largely ceremonial, Italian presidents, like Mr. Ciampi, have not shied from taking sides on national political issues. The president chooses the prime minister, who is often, but not always, a member of the largest party in the lower house, the Chamber of Deputies. The constitution also provides for 20 subnational administrative districts. Currently, 75 percent of the 630 seats in the Chamber of Deputies are elected in single-member districts; the other 25 percent are elected by proportional representation, with a 4 percent threshold. The new electoral law limits the chances of smaller parties to attain seats on their own, forcing them to align with other parties in large coalitions on the left and right. In 2000, parliament approved a constitutional change that gives the estimated four million Italians abroad the right to vote, effective with the next national elections.

Corruption remains an issue in politics despite the changes in government coalitions over the past decade. Transparency International ranked Italy 42 out of 146 countries surveyed in its 2004 Corruption Perceptions Index, one of the worst rankings in Western Europe. The head of Parmalat, the Italian food conglomerate, and five other top executives were taken into police custody in late December 2003 following an investigation into large gaps in the company's accounting. A late January 2004 investigation in the case uncovered that the company had debts of around 14 billion euros in September of the previous year, close to eight times what the company's management had claimed at that time.

Freedom of speech and the press is constitutionally guaranteed. However, in *Freedom of the Press 2004*, Freedom House ranked the country as being only "partly free," due to the continued concentration of media power in the hands of Prime Minister Silvio Berlusconi, who, through his private media holdings and political power over the state television networks, controls 90 percent of the country's broadcast media.

In April, the Senate adopted the Gasparri law on broadcasting, which ostensibly introduces a number of reforms, like the preparation for the switchover from analogue to digital broadcasting that is due to take place in 2006. However, the law has been heavily criticized for providing measures that serve the interests of Berlusconi's media holdings. The law was initially vetoed in December by the Italian president, Carlo Azeglio Ciampi, who sent a five-page commentary on the law to parliament, pointing out that it undermined news pluralism by allowing the creation of "dominant positions" in the media. Crucial for Berlusconi, the law removes a previous restriction on one person owning more than two national broadcasting stations. This provision allows Retequattro, one of three television stations owned by Berlusconi's Mediaset group, to continue terrestrial broadcasting. The law runs contrary to a Constitutional Court ruling in 2002 that demanded that Retequattro switch to satellite by January 2004 to ensure competition. The shift to satellite would have led to a considerable loss in the station's market value.

In response to the new law, a number of high-profile media people quit the state-run radio and television network, RAI, including its head, Lucia Annunziata, and a star television broadcaster, Lili Gruber. In addition, questions continue to be raised about the political impact of Berlusconi's control of the media. The Osservatorio di Pavia, an independent watchdog group that focuses on media issues, reported that in one month, February 2004, Berlusconi's presence on television accounted for 42 percent of the time dedicated to politicians.

A 2001 high court ruling gave the government the power to block foreign-based Internet sites if they contravene national laws. The government, however, has yet to restrict access to the Internet.

Freedom of religion is respected and guaranteed by the constitution. A revised

Concordat in 1984 established the secular state in Italy. Although Roman Catholicism is the dominant religion, and the Catholic Church is granted some privileges by the state, there is no state religion. In addition, the state provides support, if requested, to other religions represented in the country. To date, the state has signed agreements with a number of religious groups and is currently finalizing an omnibus religious freedom law.

However, a new fertility law that was strongly supported by the Vatican and Catholic politicians has been criticized for being overly restrictive. The law, passed in the spring, prohibits sperm or egg donation, surrogacy, embryo research, and the screening or freezing of pre-implanted embryos. Italy's nominee to the new European Commission, Rocco Buttiglione, had to withdraw his name after controversy emerged about his conservative views on gays and women. A devout Catholic, Buttiglione had stated in October 2004 that he thought homosexuality was a "sin." Academic freedom is respected and protected.

Italians are free to organize into social and political associations. However, a bill introduced into parliament by the conservative majority seeks to ban child protests. The new law, if it goes into effect, will fine parents up to $2,500 if they allow their minor children to participate in street protests. Between 35 and 40 percent of the workforce is unionized.

The independence of the country's judiciary continues to be undermined by long trial delays and the influence of organized crime. However, the government has vowed to institute a number of reforms, including establishing a merit system for judicial advancement (it is now based on seniority) and having parliament set priorities for the categories of crimes to be prosecuted. The opposition parties and magistrates themselves oppose these reforms.

The law prohibits torture; however, there were reports of excessive use of force by the police. In February, a number of senior police officers were indicted on perjury, conspiracy, or assault charges in connection with a 2001 police raid at the headquarters of the Genoa Social Forum during the G-8 summit protests. Many prisons continue to be overcrowded and antiquated, lacking, for example, adequate medical care.

The country is a major port of entry for undocumented immigrants. Large numbers of people from North Africa, the Middle East, China, and South Asia continue to arrive on the country's shores. A German captain of a ship was arrested during the summer for aiding and abetting illegal immigration. The Constitutional Court in Rome deemed that new rules in the country's two-year-old immigration law regarding the arrest and expulsion of illegal immigrants are in violation of the fundamental rights guaranteed by the constitution.

A Moroccan teacher trainee was denied a job at a private nursery because she wore a headscarf. The conservative interior minister, Giuseppe Pisanu, supported the teacher and ordered the school to reverse its decision.

Women benefit from liberal maternity-leave provisions and government efforts to ensure parity in the workforce. However, violence against women continues to be a problem. In addition, there are no quotas for women in either house of parliament, although some parties do maintain them. Around 11 percent of the 630 members of the Chamber of Deputies are women. Italy is a transit point and country of destination for trafficked persons. Women are trafficked from Africa and Eastern Europe for sexual exploitation, and children from China for sweatshop labor.

⬇Jamaica

Population: 2,600,000   **Political Rights:** 2
GNI/capita: $2,690   **Civil Liberties:** 3
Life Expectancy: 75   **Status:** Free
Religious Groups: Protestant (61.3 percent),
Rastafari (34.7 percent), Roman Catholic (4 percent)
Ethnic Groups: Black (91 percent), other [including white,
Chinese, and East Indian] (9 percent)
Capital: Kingston
Trend Arrow: Jamaica received a downward trend arrow due to the failure of the government to successfully prosecute police officers for extrajudicial killings.

Ten-Year Ratings Timeline (Political Rights, Civil Liberties, Status)

1995	1996	1997	1998	1999	2000	2001	2002	2003	2004
2,3F	2,3F	2,3F	2,2F	2,2F	2,2F	2,3F	2,3F	2,3F	2,3F

Overview: Jamaica continued to suffer from rampant crime, high levels of unemployment, and a lack of investment in social development in 2004. The government's failure to fully extend the rule of law over its police force was evidenced by a five-year record of failure to successfully prosecute any officers on charges of extrajudicial killings, despite the force's having one of the highest per capita rates of police killings in the world. Meanwhile, a contentious succession struggle wracked the country's main opposition party.

Jamaica, a member of the Commonwealth, achieved independence from Great Britain in 1962. Since independence, power has alternated between the social-democratic People's National Party (PNP) and the conservative Jamaica Labor Party (JLP). In 1992, the PNP elected P. J. Patterson to replace Michael Manley as party leader and prime minister. In the 1993 legislative elections, which were marred by irregularities and violence, the PNP won 52 parliamentary seats and the JLP 8 seats. The parties differed little on continuing the structural adjustment designed to bring economic stability and growth to the country that was begun in the 1980s, although the JLP was hurt by long-standing internal rifts.

The Patterson government confronted labor unrest and an increase in violent crime carried out largely by gangs operating a lucrative drug trade only loosely tied to local party bosses. In 2000, Patterson promised to stanch Jamaica's "rampant criminality" by introducing new efforts to control guns, creating a new police strike force targeting organized crime, and reintroducing the death penalty. The promises came after criticisms from key leaders of the vital tourism industry joined complaints from Jamaicans of all walks of life demanding an end to the mostly drug-related street crime that had been spiraling upward over the previous two decades. The fierce crime wave crippled local businesses and created an exodus of middle-class Jamaicans overseas. Gang fighting in West Kingston erupted in May 2001, leaving a toll of 71 dead; 28 others, including at least 3 police officers and 1 soldier, were killed in several days of gunfights as police and soldiers moved into opposition-held communities.

In 2002, Patterson became the only prime minister in Jamaican history to be elected to three consecutive terms. His PNP won 34 of 60 parliamentary seats and retained the office of prime minister for an unprecedented fourth term; the JLP took 26 seats. An observer delegation led by former U.S. president Jimmy Carter said that despite measures taken to restrain voter fraud, such activity remained high in areas controlled by politically linked gangs. Patterson also became the first chief executive to swear allegiance to the Jamaican people and constitution, rather than to the Queen of England.

A national crime plan, hammered out with the support of the JLP and the country's business community, helped to bring about large cocaine seizures. The plan included increased training for police, stronger criminal intelligence planning, and greater ties to foreign law enforcement agencies. In May 2003, the government announced that it was putting 1,000 new police officers on the streets.

In June 2003, the JLP won a landslide victory in bitterly contested local elections that appeared to be a referendum on the PNP's fiscal policies. The JLP secured control of 11 of the 13 municipal councils contested; 23 percent of the candidates were women. Following the vote, 27 people, including 2 police officers, were killed during security force operations in western Kingston, and 16 others died in gun battles in the eastern part of the city, as gangs loyal to the country's two major political parties battled. The JLP announced in November that it was refusing to support a new antiterrorism bill that it claimed gave the government "draconian powers" to confiscate private property and to suppress antigovernment protests, and it continued its dissent through 2004. The PNP also pushed to give the military the power to effect searches and make arrests even in the absence of the police.

In 2004, the Patterson government remained trapped by the vicious cycle in which violent crime helped to depress tourism and investment, while the country's economic conditions kept it from alleviating unemployment or making expenditures on social development. Edward Seaga's 30-year leadership of the JLP grew increasingly tenuous, in part because of the party's four consecutive national election defeats. However, a bitter succession struggle appeared to sustain Seaga's position at least for the short term, after the annual party conference scheduled for November was delayed by a judicial order issued on behalf of one of the candidates, who claimed that hundreds of his main challenger's delegates were chosen illegally. Potential successors to Patterson within the PNP increased their own maneuvering for position within the party, as the prime minister signaled his intention to retire as PNP leader before the 2006 elections.

Political Rights and Civil Liberties: Citizens of Jamaica are able to change their government democratically. The British monarchy is represented by a governor-general, who is appointed by the monarch on the recommendation of the prime minister, the country's chief executive. Following legislative elections, the leader of the majority party or the leader of the majority coalition in the House of Representatives is appointed prime minister by the governor-general, with the deputy prime minister recommended by the prime minister. The bicameral parliament consists of the 60-member House of Representatives elected for five years and the 21-member Senate, with 13 senators appointed by the prime minister and 8 by the leader of the parliamentary opposition. In October 2003, the government announced that it was considering a proposal to allow Jamaicans residing oversees to vote in the island's national elections.

The Access to Information Act of 2002 implements the constitutionally guaranteed right to information; however, it has not been fully implemented. Government whistle-blowers who ethically dissent over official acts of waste, fraud, or abuse of power are not well protected by Jamaican law, as required under the Inter-American Convention against Corruption. Jamaica was ranked 74 out of 146 countries surveyed in Transparency International's 2004 Corruption Perceptions Index. The constitutional right to free expression is generally respected. Broadcast media are largely public but are open to pluralistic points of view. There are an estimated 1.9 million radios in Jamaica—the highest per capita ratio in the Caribbean—but only 330,000 television sets. Newspapers are independent and free of government control, although newspaper readership is generally low. Journalists are occasionally intimidated during election campaigns. Public opinion polls play a key role in the political process, and election campaigns feature debates on state-run television. The government does not restrict access to the Internet.

The constitution provides for freedoms of religion, assembly, and association, and the government generally respects these rights in practice. The government does not restrict academic freedom. The right to organize political parties, civic organizations, and labor unions is generally respected. Labor unions are politically influential and have the right to strike. The Industrial Disputes Tribunal mediates labor conflicts.

The judicial system is headed by the Supreme Court and includes several magistrates' courts and a court of appeals, with final recourse to the Privy Council in London. A Trinidad-based Caribbean Court of Justice, which will open its doors in 2005, will become Jamaica's highest appellate court, replacing the Privy Council, whose recent rulings against the death penalty have angered many in Jamaica.

Despite government efforts to improve penal conditions, a mounting backlog of cases and a shortage of court staff at all levels continue to undermine the judicial system, which is slow and inefficient, particularly in addressing police abuses and the violent conditions in prisons. Before the government announced in October 2003 that it was adding 1,000 new police officers, Jamaica had just 2.9 officers per 100,000 people, compared with regional averages ranging from 3.2 to 6.9. Although there has been some willingness by authorities to charge police for extrajudicial killings, the system for investigating such abuses lacks personnel dedicated to probing abuses, an ability to protect crime scene evidence and to take statements from officers concerned in a timely manner, and adequate autopsies of victims of alleged police misconduct.

There are continuing concerns over criminal justice practices, particularly the shooting of suspects by police. Officially, police are allowed to use lethal force if an officer's life is threatened or a dangerous felon is escaping, but in practice, its use is more widespread, and officials have promised to adopt a stricter use-of-force policy. Other disputed practices include the imposition of death sentences following trials of questionable fairness, corporal punishment, alleged ill-treatment by police and prison wardens, and appalling detention centers and prisons. Deaths of detainees are also a problem. A mounting crime rate in recent years led the government to take controversial steps toward restoring capital punishment and flogging; rights groups protested both measures. Critics charge that flogging is unconstitutional because it can be characterized as "inhuman or degrading punishment," which the constitution prohibits. In July 2004, the Privy Council struck down a law, the Offences against the Person Act, that imposed a mandatory death sentence for certain crimes, saying that it amounted to inhuman and degrading punishment.

Jamaica is a main transit point for cocaine being shipped from Colombia through the Caribbean to U.S. markets, and the drug trade is now largely controlled by Colombian organized crime syndicates. Violence is the major cause of death in Jamaica, and the murder rate is one of the highest in the world. Much of the violence is the result of warfare between drug gangs known as "posses." Jamaican-born criminal deportees from the United States and a growing illegal weapons trade are major causes of the violence. Mobs have been responsible for numerous vigilante killings of suspected criminals. Inmates frequently die as a result of prison riots. Jamaican officials complain that the United States was flagrantly applying a double standard by demanding a full effort by Jamaica to help stop the flow of drugs into the United States, while at the same time failing to stem the flow of guns into Jamaica. On a positive note, in February 2004, Jamaica and the United States signed a new accord that increased U.S. authority to pursue suspected drug smugglers in the island's waters and airspace.

Persecution against homosexuals is rampant, with same-sex intercourse punishable by 10 years' imprisonment with hard labor. In recent years, several gay Jamaicans have been grated asylum in Britain on the grounds that they were in danger in Jamaica because of their homosexuality. In 2004, there was a growing debate over the anti-gay lyrics of Jamaican entertainers, particularly reggae singers. Many gays and lesbians do not report acts of violence committed against them because of police hostility. In June 2004, Brian Williamson, a spokesperson for J-FLAG (Jamaica Forum for Lesbians, All-Sexuals and Gays), a leading advocacy group, was brutally murdered in his New Kingston apartment, although the motive for the attack was unclear.

In 1998, a woman was for the first time elected Speaker of Parliament. Violence against women is widespread, but social and cultural traditions that work against its acknowledgment and reporting made estimates about its prevalence unreliable. Although the constitution and the country's employment laws give women full legal equality, in practice workplace discrimination, including lower pay, is common. On a positive note, in February, parliament passed the Family Property (Rights of Spouses) Act that provides for the equitable division of property following a divorce.

Japan

Population: 127,600,000 **Political Rights:** 1
GNI/capita: $34,010 **Civil Liberties:** 2
Life Expectancy: 82 **Status:** Free
Religious Groups: Shinto and Buddhist (84 percent),
other [including Christian] (16 percent)
Ethnic Groups: Japanese (99 percent), other (1 percent)
Capital: Tokyo

Ten-Year Ratings Timeline (Political Rights, Civil Liberties, Status)

1995	1996	1997	1998	1999	2000	2001	2002	2003	2004
1,2F	1,2F	1,2F	1,2F	1,2F	1,2F	1,2F	1,2F	1,2F	1,2F

Overview: The Democratic Party of Japan (DPJ), the main opposition party, was the best performer in the elections to the upper house of the Diet (parliament) held in July 2004. The result indicated general public dissatisfaction with the vaguely defined reformist agenda of Prime Minister Junichiro Koizumi—and, in particular, with necessary but very unpopular reforms to the pension sector.

Japan has been a parliamentary democracy since its defeat in World War II. The conservative Liberal Democratic Party (LDP) has dominated postwar Japanese politics, winning all but one election since it was created in 1955. During the Cold War, the LDP presided over Japan's spectacular economic ascent while maintaining close security ties with the United States. In what became known as Japan's Iron Triangle—the close nexus of the LDP, banks, and big business representatives—LDP governments more or less mandated that corporations, particularly construction firms in charge of major public works projects—rely on banks for capital, and the banks in turn took large equity stakes in the companies. All the while, the government maintained centralized control through its influence over the banking sector and its ability to direct lending—often to debt-laden companies engaged in politically expedient but financially unviable projects.

Current economic woes stem from the collapse of Japan's stock and real estate markets in the early 1990s. The crash saddled Japanese banks with tens of billions of dollars worth of problem loans, and successive LDP-led governments in the 1990s have largely failed to contain the fallout.

Under a turnout of less than 60 percent, the LDP won 237 seats in the 480-seat house in the November 9, 2003, snap elections for the lower house. After the vote, it gained a simple majority by welcoming three independents into its ranks and merging with the tiny New Conservative Party, which won four seats. The DPJ gained 40 seats to finish with 177. This was the largest tally for any opposition party since 1958, though changes in the size and electoral structure of parliament make comparisons difficult. Most of the DPJ's gains came at the expense of smaller, leftist parties rather than the LDP. The LDP's victory was helped by Koizumi's high personal popularity among Japanese voters.

The DPJ won 50 seats—a gain of 12 seats—out of the 121 being contested in the upper house of parliament in elections in July 2004. The LDP won 49, two seats short of its target of 51 seats. Nevertheless, the LDP's grip on power was not going to be threatened regardless of the outcome. The DPJ's strong performance reflected the voting public's displeasure with the government, and primarily with its controversial pension reform bill, which would reduce benefits and increase premiums paid by workers. Public sentiment against the reform program ran particularly high since the elections were held shortly after it had come to light that several senior officials had been shirking their own payments into the national pension system.

Under Koizumi, Japan has continued to expand its role in international peacekeeping and security. Japanese troops have participated in several UN peacekeeping missions since 1992, Japanese warships provided logistical support to U.S.-led forces during the war in Afghanistan, and in 2003, parliament approved the dispatch of 1,000 troops to Iraq to provide logistical support to U.S.-led troops and humanitarian aid. The ongoing crisis over North Korea's nuclear weapons program has increased debate about the need to boost the capacity of Japan's already formidable military, which is limited to a self-defense role by the country's pacifist constitution.

Japan's relations with its neighbors, while generally stable, are marked by periodic tensions. China and South Korea both object to Koizumi's continued visits to the Yasukuni shrine, which honors Japan's war dead—including its war criminals—and which the two nations see as symbolizing Japan's historical militarism. In 2004, Japan made stronger efforts to engage North Korea, both to improve relations between the two countries and to persuade North Korea to participate in multiparty talks about its nuclear capabilities.

Political Rights and Civil Liberties:

Japanese citizens change their government through free and fair elections. As in other parliamentary systems of government, the prime minister heads a cabinet of ministers. The emperor is head of state, but has only a ceremonial role. There are numerous political parties, and the current government is a coalition of the leading LDP and the smaller New Komeito party.

Despite recent reforms aimed at curbing the power of the bureaucracy, senior civil servants, rather than elected politicians, largely shape policy, generally with little transparency. Japan was ranked 24 out of 146 countries surveyed in Transparency International's 2004 Corruption Perceptions Index—the country's best ranking in years. Corruption most often takes the form of bribery or bid-rigging in the country's numerous large public works projects.

Japan's press is free and independent, though not always outspoken. Reporters Without Borders ranks the country 26 (tied with Austria and South Africa) out of 139 countries in its index of press freedom. The press operates independently of the government, and censorship is not a concern. The Japan Broadcasting Corporation operates broadcast media, which comprises hundreds of television and radio broadcasters as well as numerous foreign, cable, and satellite broadcasters. Homogeneity, especially in political news, is facilitated in part by a system of press clubs, or *kisha kurabu*, in which major media outlets have cozy relationships with bureaucrats and politicians.

Japanese of all faiths can worship freely, though Buddhism and Shintoism have the most followers. Religious groups are not required to be licensed, but registering with government authorities as a "religious corporation" brings tax benefits and other advantages.

There are no restrictions on academic freedom, though China, South Korea, and other countries in the region frequently lodge protests against passages in Japanese history textbooks that try to justify the country's occupation of other Asian nations before and during World War II and downplay the imperial army's wartime atrocities in occupied lands.

Freedom of assembly and association is guaranteed by the constitution and protected in practice. Japan has many well-funded and active civic, human rights, social welfare, and environmental groups. Trade unions are independent and vigorously promote workers' interests. Only some public employees, such as police and firefighters, are not allowed to form unions or strike. The Japanese Trade Union Confederation is the largest labor organization, representing some 6.8 million workers. Collective bargaining is widespread.

Japan's judiciary is independent. There are several levels of courts, and suspects are generally given fair public trials by an impartial tribunal (there are no juries) within three months of being detained. Arbitrary arrest and imprisonment are not practiced. Prison conditions comply with international standards, although some human rights groups have criticized them for being overly disciplined. Prison officials sometimes use physical and psychological intimidation to enforce discipline or elicit confessions. The government restricts human rights groups' access to prisons. In November 2004, the Ministry of Justice reported that the number of prisoners in Japan topped 60,000 for the first time in 43 years. The National Police Agency is under civilian control and is highly disciplined, though reports of human rights abuses committed by police persist.

Japan's organized crime network, the Yakuza, is one of the largest in the world, and is closely linked with drug-trafficking, prostitution, gambling, and money laundering. Though the Yakuza were active in buying land and stock shares in the 1990s, today they are broadly tolerated by both the police and the public, and have a negligible effect on business activity or personal freedom. The government took a somewhat tougher stance in 2004, however: in April, the National Police Agency established a department in charge of organized crime in the Criminal Investigation Bureau, and in October, it compiled a comprehensive manual to guide police nationwide in dealing with organized crime.

Although the constitution prohibits discrimination based on race, creed, sex, and social status, certain groups of people continue to face unofficial discrimination. Japan's three million Burakumin, who are descendants of feudal-era outcasts, and the indigenous Ainu minority suffer from entrenched societal discrimination that prevents them from having equal access to housing and employment opportunities. Foreigners generally, and Koreans in particular, suffer the same disadvantage.

Privacy rights are respected in Japan, and there are no restrictions on travel within the country or abroad.

Women have full access to education but face employment discrimination. In addition, sexual harassment on the job is widespread. Violence against women is a problem that often goes unreported because of "social and cultural concerns about shaming one's family or endangering the reputation of one's spouse or children," according the U.S. State Department's 2003 human rights report, released in February 2004. The trafficking of persons is not specifically forbidden by law.

Jordan

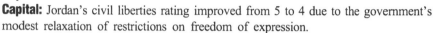

Population: 5,600,000
GNI/capita: $1,760
Life Expectancy: 72
Religious Groups: Sunni Muslim (92 percent), Christian (6 percent), other (2 percent)
Ethnic Groups: Arab (98 percent), other [including Armenian] (2 percent)
Capital: Amman

Political Rights: 5
Civil Liberties: 4*
Status: Partly Free

Capital: Jordan's civil liberties rating improved from 5 to 4 due to the government's modest relaxation of restrictions on freedom of expression.

Ten-Year Ratings Timeline (Political Rights, Civil Liberties, Status)

1995	1996	1997	1998	1999	2000	2001	2002	2003	2004
4,4PF	4,4PF	4,4PF	4,5PF	4,4PF	4,4PF	5,5PF	6,5PF	5,5PF	5,4PF

Overview:

Despite growing popular anger over the U.S.-led occupation of Iraq and continuing Israeli-Palestinian violence, Jordan witnessed a limited expansion of civil liberties in 2004, owing mainly to an informal understanding between the government and opposition groups on the boundaries of acceptable public discourse. Buoyed by substantially increased foreign aid, subsidized petroleum supplies, and a booming export sector, economic conditions in the kingdom improved markedly.

The Hashemite Kingdom of Jordan, known as Transjordan until 1950, was established as a League of Nations mandate under the control of Great Britain in 1921 and granted full independence in 1946. Following the assassination of King Abdullah in 1951, the crown passed briefly to his mentally unstable eldest son, Talal, and then to his grandson, Hussein. King Hussein's turbulent 46-year reign witnessed a massive influx of Palestinian refugees (who now comprise a majority of the population), the loss of all territory west of the Jordan River in 1967, and numerous assassinations and coup attempts by Palestinian and Arab nationalists. Although the 1952 constitution provided for a directly elected parliament, political parties were banned in 1956, and parliament was either suspended entirely or emasculated by government intervention in the electoral process for over three decades. While political and civil liberties remained tightly restricted, Hussein proved adept at co-opting, rather than killing, jailing, or exiling, his political opponents. As a result, Jordan avoided the legacy of brutal repression characteristic of other authoritarian regimes in the Arab world.

As a result of the decline of oil revenues in 1980s, which translated into reduced aid and worker remittances from the Arab Gulf countries, Jordan borrowed heavily throughout the decade and was eventually forced to implement economic austerity measures in return for IMF assistance. In 1989, price increases for fuel and other subsidized commodities provoked widespread rioting and mounting internal pressure for greater freedom and representation. In response, the government launched a rapid process of political liberalization and progressively eased restrictions on civil liberties. However, the reform process ground to a halt in the mid-1990s and suffered some reversals.

By the time of Hussein's death in 1999 and the ascension of his son, Abdullah, the kingdom was again faced with severe economic problems. The "peace dividend" expected to follow from Jordan's 1994 peace treaty with Israel, in the form of improved trade with the West Bank and increased investment from Western Europe, had not filtered down to the population at large. Faced with a crippling public debt and 27 percent unemployment, Abdullah launched economic reforms needed to attract international investment and signed one of the Arab world's first free-trade agreements with the United States.

The September 2000 outbreak of the al-Aqsa *intifada* (uprising) in the West Bank and Gaza had an enormous impact on the country, inflaming anti-Israeli sentiments among Jordanians of Palestinian descent, leftists, and Islamists, who dominate much of civil society. As the violence next door continued unabated, the Professional Associations Council (PAC) formed an anti-normalization committee to spearhead mass demonstrations demanding the annulment of Jordan's peace treaty with Israel.

The government reacted by suppressing criticism of Jordanian relations with Israel and banning all demonstrations. In 2001, Abdullah dissolved parliament, postponed general elections scheduled for November, and replaced elected municipal councils with state-appointed local committees. For more than two years, Abdullah ruled by decree, issuing over 200 "temporary laws" that imposed new restrictions on freedom of expression and assembly, weakened due process protections, and promulgated economic policies that would probably have been rejected by the outgoing parliament.

Although the U.S.-led invasion of Iraq further inflamed popular opposition to the kingdom's foreign policy, Abdullah quickly moved to restore the country's limited democratic institutions and relax restrictions of freedom of expression. Reasonably free and transparent, though not fair, parliamentary and municipal elections were held in 2003. An informal understanding was reached between the palace and dissident leftist and Islamist groups. In return for limited freedom to express themselves and participate in the political system, the latter agreed to curtail their efforts to mobilize public opinion against Jordan's pro-American alignment as long as progress was being made at the economic level. Buoyed by an infusion of "oil grants" from the Arab Gulf states and a dramatic increase in economic assistance from the United States, Jordan's economy picked up steam and achieved 7 percent growth in 2004.

This compromise between the palace and opposition made possible a further expansion of civil liberties in 2004. While dozens of Jordanians were jailed during the year for security offenses (for example, conspiring to carry out terrorist attacks on American or Israeli targets in Jordan, attempting infiltration into Israel or Iraq, smuggling weapons, or collecting donations for the Zarqawi terrorist network in Iraq), no journalists were sent to prison, and only one major demonstration was forcibly dispersed by police. This new climate of freedom clearly rested on negotiated tradeoffs rather than on institutionalized civil rights protections—prominent Jordanian public figures would not have been able to issue a petition in July declaring the government's Iraq policy against "the will of the Jordanian people" without repercussions had they been engaged in more proactive efforts to undermine it.

This political arrangement appeared to come undone in September, when security forces raided the homes of numerous Islamist clerics and detained at least nine of them on charges of preaching without a license. A tense standoff ensued, with Muslim Brotherhood leader Abdul Majeed Thneibat warning that the movement would go underground if his colleagues were not released. After a lengthy meeting with senior Muslim Brotherhood officials, however, Prime Minister Faisal al-Fayez agreed to release the detained clerics and allow them to continue preaching in exchange for the group's commitment to tone down its rhetoric.

Political Rights and Civil Liberties:

Jordanians cannot change their government democratically. King Abdullah holds broad executive powers and may dissolve parliament and dismiss the prime minister or cabinet at his discretion. The 110-seat lower house of parliament, elected through universal adult suffrage, may approve, reject, or amend legislation proposed by the cabinet, but is restricted in its ability to initiate legislation and cannot enact laws without the assent of the 55-seat upper house of parliament, which is appointed by the king. Regional governors are appointed by the central government, as are half of all municipal council seats.

The electoral system is heavily skewed toward the monarchy's traditional support base. The single-member-district system, introduced in 1993, favors tribal and family ties over political and ideological affiliations, while rural districts with populations of Transjordanian origin are over-represented relative to urban districts, where most Jordanians of Palestinian descent reside. (According to the *Financial Times*, Amman has a member of parliament for every 52,255 voters, while the small town of Karak has one MP for every 6,000 voters.) In 2003, only 27 percent of registered voters went to the polls in Amman, a possible indication that many Palestinian Jordanians still feel excluded from the political system.

Jordan was ranked 37 out of 146 countries surveyed in Transparency International's 2004 Corruption Perceptions Index. Several high profile cases of embezzlement and abuse of authority by government employees were prosecuted in 2004.

Freedom of expression is restricted. Although the government officially relinquished its monopoly on television and radio outlets and issued several private broadcasting licenses in 2004, all broadcast news media remain under state control. The government has broad discretionary powers to close print publications. In 2003, the government repealed Article 150 of the Penal Code, which made the publication of information deemed harmful to national unity or the reputation of the state punishable by up to three years in prison, and pledged that journalists would no longer be sent to prison for their writings. However, other vaguely worded laws criminalizing expression are still in force and journalists remain subject to detention. In May 2004, the authorities detained Fahd Rimawi, the editor of the weekly *Al-Majd*, for over 24 hours on charges of publishing an article "harming ties with a neighboring state," releasing him only after he agreed to retract, in the paper's next issue, allegations he had made about Saudi Arabia. A new independent daily, *Al-Ghad*, was established in 2004 and earned widespread praise for its investigative reporting and editorial critiques of government policies.

There is no official advance censorship in Jordan, but the authorities are routinely tipped off about the contents of potentially offensive articles by informers at printing presses, and editors frequently come under pressure to remove such material. In September, the authorities blocked an issue of *Al-Majd* from going to press after Rimawi refused to remove objectionable material. The government has not attempted to censor Internet content.

Islam is the state religion. The government appoints all Islamic clergy, pays their salaries, and monitors sermons at mosques, where political activity is banned under Jordanian law. Sunni Muslims constitute 92 percent of the population, but Christians and Jews are officially recognized as religious minorities and allowed to worship freely. In November, a Christian was named deputy prime minister for the first time. Baha'is and Druze are allowed to practice their faiths, but are not officially recognized. Academic freedom is generally respected in Jordan.

Freedom of assembly is heavily restricted. A new Public Rallies Law, issued by decree in 2001 and approved by parliament in February 2004, bans demonstrations lacking written consent from the government. Although opposition groups complained that most of their requests were denied, the government allowed several licensed anti-Israeli and anti-American demonstrations to take place during the year. In May, police forcibly dispersed an unlicensed anti-Israeli protest in a Palestinian refugee camp and arrested 60 people on minor charges, but only after demonstrators began burning the Jordanian flag and destroying property.

While dozens of licensed nongovernmental organizations (NGOs) addressing numerous political and social issues are allowed to operate freely, the government occasionally withholds licenses from NGOs led by people it deems subversive. In October, prominent human rights activist Fawzi al-Samhouri said that the authorities had denied a license to his newly established Jordanian Organization for Human Rights (Samhouri contends that the refusal to grant him a license was politically motivated, although the government denies this charge). Professional associations have come under pressure to abstain from political activities. Workers have the right to bargain collectively but must receive government permission to strike. More than 30 percent of the workforce is organized into 17 unions.

The judiciary is subject to executive influence through the Justice Ministry and the Higher Judiciary Council, whose members are appointed by the king. While most trials in civilian courts are open and procedurally sound, proceedings of the State Security Court (SSC) are occasionally closed to the public. A temporary law promulgated in 2001 allows the prime minister to refer any case to the SSC and denies the right of appeal to people convicted of misdemeanors, which can carry short prison sentences.

Jordanian citizens enjoy little protection from arbitrary arrest and detention. Under the constitution, suspects may be detained for up to 48 hours without a warrant and up to 10 days without formal charges being filed, but courts routinely grant prosecutors 15-day extensions of this deadline. Even these minimal protections are denied to suspects referred to the SSC, who are often held in lengthy pretrial detention and refused access to legal council until just before trial. Many defendants charged with security-related offenses in 2004 claimed to have been tortured in custody.

Jordanians of Palestinian descent face discrimination in employment by the government and the military and in admission to universities. Labor laws do not protect foreign workers. Abuse of mostly South Asian domestic servants is widespread.

Women enjoy equal political rights, but face legal discrimination in matters of inheritance and divorce, which fall under the jurisdiction of Sharia (Islamic law) courts, and in the provision of government pensions and social security benefits. Although women constitute only 14 percent of the workforce, the government has made efforts to increase the number of women in the civil service. Women are guaranteed a quota of six seats in parliament and occupy several cabinet positions. Although the government issued a draft law ending lenient treatment of those convicted of "honor crimes" (the murder or attempted murder of women by relatives for alleged sexual misconduct) in 2003, the newly elected lower house of parliament has repeatedly rejected the law. A royal decree granting women the right to initiate divorce proceedings was also rejected by parliament in 2004 (the law, which was upheld by the upper house, was still being implemented by Sharia courts; a joint legislative session will be held in 2005 to amend, uphold, or reject the law).

Kazakhstan

Population: 15,000,000
GNI/capita: $1,520
Life Expectancy: 64
Religious Groups: Muslim (47 percent), Russian
Orthodox (44 percent), Protestant (2 percent),
other (7 percent)
Ethnic Groups: Kazakh (53 percent), Russian (30 percent),
Ukrainian (4 percent), Uzbek (3 percent), German (2 percent), other (8 percent)
Capital: Astana

Political Rights: 6
Civil Liberties: 5
Status: Not Free

Ten-Year Ratings Timeline (Political Rights, Civil Liberties, Status)

1995	1996	1997	1998	1999	2000	2001	2002	2003	2004
6,5NF	6,5NF	6,5NF	6,5NF	6,5NF	6,5NF	6,5NF	6,5NF	6,5NF	6,5NF

Overview:

Political parties loyal to President Nursultan Nazarbayev continued to dominate parliament following the September 2004 legislative elections, which were criticized by international monitors for failing to meet basic democratic standards. Only one opposition deputy was elected, although he refused to take his seat in protest over the flawed nature of the polls. Meanwhile, the resignations of key senior officials raised questions about internal power struggles and dissension within Nazarbayev's government.

This sparsely populated, multiethnic land stretching from the Caspian Sea to the Chinese border was gradually conquered by Russia during the eighteenth and nineteenth centuries. After a brief attempt at independence in 1917 in the wake of the Russian Revolution, Kazakhstan became an autonomous Soviet republic in 1920 and a union republic in 1936.

The former first secretary of the Communist Party, Nazarbayev was elected president on December 1, 1991, just two weeks before Kazakhstan declared independence from the U.S.S.R. The country's first national legislative elections, in March 1994, were invalidated by the Constitutional Court a year later because of numerous irregularities. Nazarbayev subsequently dissolved parliament and called for a referendum on April 29, 1995, in which a reported 95 percent of voters supported the extension of his term until December 2000. An additional referendum in August of that year, which was boycotted by the main opposition parties, approved a new constitution strengthening the powers of the presidency. In the December 1995 elections for a new bicameral parliament, Nazarbayev supporters captured most of the seats in the legislature.

In October 1998, parliament approved Nazarbayev's call for presidential elections to be held in January 1999, almost two years before their scheduled date, as well as an amendment to the constitution extending the presidential term of office from five to seven years. The key challenger, former prime minister Akezhan Kazhegeldin, was banned from competing on a legal technicality, while two other candidates were known supporters of the incumbent. Nazarbayev was reelected with a reported 80 percent of the vote.

Otan (Fatherland), a newly formed party loyal to Nazarbayev, won the single largest number of seats in the September 1999 parliamentary vote, which was the first multiparty election in Kazakhstan's history and in which four opposition deputies captured seats. Despite some improvement since the controversial presidential ballot in January, the parliamentary poll remained deeply flawed. In June 2000, parliament overwhelmingly approved giving Nazarbayev lifetime privileges after the end of his second term in office in 2006, including formal access to key government officials to advise them on policy matters, as well as a permanent place on the Security Council.

Signs of a deepening split within the country's ruling elite became evident following the November 18, 2001, founding of a new political movement, the Democratic Choice of Kazakhstan (DCK). Established by prominent business leaders, some of whom held positions in Nazarbayev's administration, the DCK proclaimed its commitment to democratization, rule of law, and anticorruption efforts. However, some observers questioned the sincerity of its stated goals and maintained that the group's primary purpose was to safeguard its members' substantial political and economic interests while countering those of the president's family and close associates.

Apparently sensing that the DCK posed a growing political threat to his regime, Nazarbayev cracked down increasingly on the group throughout 2002. In what critics charged were politically motivated cases, two of the DCK's cofounders—former minister of energy Mukhtar Abliyazov and former Pavlodar governor Galymzhan Zhakiyanov—were subsequently arrested, convicted of abuse of power and corruption during their tenure in government, and sentenced to prison. Abliyazov was freed from prison in 2003 after receiving an amnesty from Nazarbayev; as of late 2004, he was living in exile in Russia. Abliyazov announced that he would cease political activity to concentrate on his business interests, leading to widespread speculation that his release was made conditional on his leaving politics. Zhakiyanov was transferred from prison to a minimum security settlement colony in northern Pavlodar in August 2004. In May 2004, the DCK was formally registered as a political party.

In the September 19, 2004, parliamentary elections and October 3 runoff vote, pro-government parties secured an even larger number of seats than in the previous legislative poll. The election was contested by 12 parties, of which 9 supported the president. The three opposition parties that had been able to register for the vote—the DCK, Communist Party, and Ak Zhol—faced intense government pressure, including detentions of party activists, interference in campaign events, and unfair allocation of public space for advertising. The DCK, which was formally registered as a political party in May, formed an electoral bloc with the Communist Party in July. Otan captured 42 of 77 total seats, while nominally independent candidates—most of whom were reportedly associated with one of the pro-government parties—won 18. The Agrarian Party–Civic Party Bloc (AIST) secured 11 seats, followed by Asar, led by the president's daughter Dariga, with 4 seats, and the Democratic Party of Kazakhstan with 1 seat. The only opposition candidate to win a seat, Alikhan Baymenov of Ak Zhol, announced that he refused to take up his seat in protest over the conduct of the elections. None of the opposition parties recognized the outcome of the elections.

Although international monitors from the Organization for Security and Cooperation in Europe (OSCE) noted some improvements over previous polls, they criticized the election for failing to meet international standards for democratic elections. Among the problems noted were lack of political balance on election commissions; media bias in favor of pro-presidential candidates; the exclusion of certain candidates for politically motivated reasons; a lack of integration between electronic and paper voter lists, which increased the possibility of multiple voting; and the presence of unauthorized personnel in polling stations.

The flawed elections heightened political tensions and, despite the overwhelming victory of pro-government parties, raised questions about dissension within Nazarbayev's support base. In October, Nazarbayev's primary economic advisor, Grigory Marchenko, resigned and called for the removal of the country's prime minister. In the same month, Zharmakhan Tuyakbai announced his resignation as both Speaker of the lower house of parliament and vice chairman of Otan, citing massive election irregularities as his reason for stepping down. Some observers speculated that his decision may have been prompted by his having lost a political fight within the ruling establishment. Tuyakbai subsequently announced that he had joined an opposition group.

Speaking to the new parliament on November 3, Nazarbayev accused wealthy businessmen of preventing competition in the economy; many observers maintained that the president's remarks were directed at key financial backers of opposition parties. On November 28, two bombs exploded in Otan's offices in the former capital of Almaty, injuring one person slightly. Although Otan party leaders did not directly accuse the political opposition of responsibility for the attacks, they characterized the bombings as an attempt to undermine the stability of the state. Meanwhile, the opposition maintained that the incident could have been conducted by the authorities as a pretext for further crackdowns against opponents of the regime.

Kazakhstan is the leading economy in Central Asia, with petroleum and gas exports contributing to an expected growth of nearly 10 percent in gross domestic product in 2004. However, the government's focus on the oil sector, which constitutes approximately half of state budget revenues, has led to concerns of overreliance on a potentially volatile industry. In addition, much of this wealth has not benefited the majority of the population, who suffer from high levels of unemployment and low wages.

Political Rights and Civil Liberties:

Citizens of Kazakhstan cannot change their government democratically. The constitution grants the president considerable control over the legislature, the judiciary, and local governments, and President Nursultan Nazarbayev continues to enjoy sweeping executive powers and governs virtually unchallenged. The bicameral parliament is composed of an upper house (Senate), whose 39 members are chosen by regional councils, whose members are directly elected; and a lower house (Majilis), whose 77 members are elected by popular vote (67 in single-mandate constituency contests and 10 from party lists on the basis of proportional representation). A second-round vote is held if no candidate in a single-mandate contest receives more than 50 percent of the vote. The country's presidential and parliamentary elections have been neither free nor fair.

In April, Nazarbayev signed a series of amendments to the country's election law that had been the focus of intense and lengthy debate. According to representatives from the OSCE, although the amendments represented progress over previous legislation, further improvements would be necessary—including greater guarantees for pluralistic representation of political parties on election commissions—for the law to meet fully OSCE commitments for democratic elections .

The country's law on political parties prohibits parties based on ethnic origin, religion, and gender. Opposition parties have complained of harassment, surveillance, denial of access to the state-run media, and arbitrary bans on registering candidates. A 2002 law raised from 3,000 to 50,000 the number of members that a party must have to register. In addition, there must be at least 700 members in each of the country's regions (*oblasts*). In September 2003, Dariga Nazarbayeva announced her intention to turn her Asar political movement into a political party. Many observers believed that this move was designed to provide an additional base of support for the Nazarbayev family, help Dariga gain a seat in the 2004 parliamentary election, and position her as an eventual presidential successor to her father.

Corruption is widespread throughout all levels of government, and businesses are forced to pay bribes in order to deal with the government bureaucracy. The U.S. Justice Department is continuing to investigate the so-called Kazakhgate scandal, in which Western oil companies allegedly paid millions of dollars to top Kazakh officials, including Nazarbayev, in exchange for lucrative contracts. Kazakhstan was ranked 122 out of 146 countries in Transparency International's 2004 Corruption Perceptions Index.

While the constitution provides for freedom of the press, the government has repeatedly harassed or shut down many independent media outlets. Libel is a criminal offense, and the country's criminal code prohibits insulting the honor and dignity of the president; self-censorship is widespread. Most media outlets, including publishing houses, are controlled or otherwise influenced by members of the president's family, including Nazarbayev's daughter Dariga, and trusted government officials. Although Dariga resigned her position as head of the state-run Khabar television station before the 2004 parliamentary election campaign because of the involvement of her political party, Asar, in the election, many observers maintain that she continued to direct the station from behind the scenes. Most local media outlets are not willing to report on the Kazakhgate story. The content of Web sites has been subject to libel laws, and the government at times has prevented clients of the country's two largest Internet service providers from gaining direct access to several opposition Web sites.

Harassment of and attacks against journalists and media outlets critical of the regime continued during the year. In January, Radio Free Europe/Radio Liberty journalist Zhuldyz Toleuova was beaten by unknown assailants, an attack that her colleagues believed was connected to her work, including reporting on the activities of the political opposition. Later that month, police beat journalist Svetlana Rychkova of the opposition paper *Assandi Times*—formerly known as *Respublika*—which had printed articles about government corruption, politics, and media rights. In March, unknown men attacked *Vremya* sports journalist Maxim Khartashov, who had frequently exposed corruption scandals in the country's sports sector. Independent journalist Ashkat Sharipzhan, who had interviewed leading opposition figures and reported on government corruption scandals, died of injuries he sustained in a suspicious car accident in July. In June, a fake special edition of the *Assandi Times* was published that contained false statements by opposition politicians. The newspaper charged that the government was behind the printing of the fake issue in an effort to discredit the opposition in advance of the September parliamentary elections. The authorities responded with a libel suit against the *Assandi Times*, which they won in July, and the paper was ordered to pay nearly $370,000 in damages.

In April, Nazarbayev rejected a draft media law, which had been adopted by the lower house of parliament in December 2003 and by the upper house in March. The draft had been criticized by international and domestic observers for further restricting media freedom. A new draft proposed in August by Information Minister Altynbek Sarsenbayev contained more guarantees for journalistic freedoms; the bill had not been adopted as of November 30. In a legal case that attracted international attention, journalist Sergei Duvanov was sentenced in January 2003 to three and a half years in prison on charges of raping a 14-year-old girl. His supporters insisted that the case against Duvanov, who wrote articles accusing Nazarbayev and other political figures of corruption, including the Kazakhgate scandal, was politically motivated. He was transferred from prison to house arrest in January 2004 and granted early release in August for what the authorities said was good behavior; many observers believe that his release was due to international pressure.

The constitution guarantees freedom of worship, although local officials sometimes harass certain nontraditional groups. Religious organizations must register with the Ministry of Justice to receive legal status, without which they cannot engage in legal transactions, including buying or renting property or hiring employees. Religious groups reportedly did not experience lengthy delays registering, as in previous years, because of a law that went into effect in September 2004 that simplified registration procedures.

The government reportedly permits most academic freedom, except for criticisms of the president and his family. During the 2004 parliamentary elections, there were credible reports that teachers and professors were pressured by local officials to join certain parties and vote for particular candidates. Schoolchildren and university students are often forced to participate in staged official celebrations or face poor grades or other penalties. Corruption in the educational system is widespread, with students frequently paying bribes to professors to earn passing grades.

Despite constitutional guarantees, the government imposes restrictions on freedom of association and assembly. The government harasses nongovernmental organizations (NGOs) that address sensitive issues through measures including investigations by tax police and surveillance by law enforcement and security agencies. A new law that went into effect in September 2004 simplified and shortened the registration process for NGOs and other legal entities, which is required for them to operate. Complicated procedures to obtain necessary permits for public demonstrations include a requirement that organizations must apply to local authorities 10 days in advance. In September, police broke up an unsanctioned rally that was held in front of the state-controlled Khabar television station in protest over biased media coverage of the parliamentary election campaign; nine people were arrested and briefly detained.

Workers have the legal right to form and join trade unions and participate in collective bargaining, and a number of unions operate throughout the country. Workers have engaged in strikes, primarily over the nonpayment of wages. However, the government exercises considerable influence over organized labor, and the largest trade union association is affiliated with the state. Some union members have been dismissed, transferred to lower-paying jobs, and threatened for their union activities.

The constitution significantly constrains the independence of the judiciary, which is subservient to the executive branch. Judges are subject to bribery and political bias, and corruption is evident throughout the judicial system. Police at times abuse detainees during arrest and interrogation, often to obtain confessions, and arbitrary arrest and detention remain problems. Conditions in pretrial facilities and prisons are harsh. Following a moratorium on the death penalty ordered in December 2003, Nazarbayev issued a decree in January introducing life imprisonment as an alternative to the death penalty. As part of the government's measures against Islamist groups that it considers a threat for advocating extremist views, parliament in October 2004 adopted a law on extremism which defined the term very vaguely.

Since Kazakhstan's independence, much of the country's large ethnic Russian population has emigrated, in part because of the enhanced role granted to the Kazakh language. Many of the remaining Russians, most of whom do not speak Kazakh, have complained of discrimination in employment and education.

While the rights of entrepreneurship and private property are legally protected, bureaucratic hurdles and the control of large segments of the economy by clan elites and government officials loyal to Nazarbayev limit equality of opportunity and fair competition. In June 2003, parliament adopted a Land Code allowing for private ownership of the country's vast tracts of agricultural land. Critics charged that the law will primarily benefit those wealthy individuals with close ties to government officials.

Traditional cultural practices and the country's economic problems limit professional opportunities for women, and women's rights experts regard current legislation addressing sexual harassment as inadequate. Nine women were elected to parliament in the 2004 election, an increase of one since the 1999 election. Domestic violence is a problem, with police often reluctant to intervene in what are regarded as internal family matters. Despite legal prohibitions, the trafficking of women for purposes of prostitution remains a serious problem, with Kazakhstan a place of origin, transit point, and destination country for victims of trafficking. During the year, an anti-trafficking commission developed a National Plan to Combat Trafficking, and amendments to the criminal and administrative codes were drafted to strengthen legislative provisions against trafficking; parliament is scheduled to vote on the amendments in 2005.

Kenya

Population: 32,400,000   **Political Rights:** 3
GNI/capita: $360   **Civil Liberties:** 3
Life Expectancy: 51   **Status:** Partly Free
Religious Groups: Protestant (45 percent), Roman
Catholic (33 percent), Muslim (10 percent), indigenous
beliefs (10 percent), other (2 percent)
Ethnic Groups: Kikuyu (22 percent), Luhya (14 percent),
Luo (13 percent), Kalenjin (12 percent), Kamba (11 percent), Kisii (6 percent), Meru
(6 percent), other African (15 percent), other [including Asian, European, and Arab]
(1 percent)
Capital: Nairobi

Ten-Year Ratings Timeline (Political Rights, Civil Liberties, Status)

1995	1996	1997	1998	1999	2000	2001	2002	2003	2004
7,6NF	7,6NF	6,6NF	6,5NF	6,5NF	6,5NF	6,5NF	4,4PF	3,3PF	3,3PF

Overview: Kenya continued its ambivalent reform process throughout 2004. The efforts at political, economic, and social reforms undertaken by the administration of President Mwai Kibaki were highlighted by a lively press and public investigative commissions. At the same time, political tensions, entrenched corruption, lack of specific reform results, and questions regarding the depth of the government's commitment to reform raised concerns about the extent of progress toward democratic consolidation.

Britain conquered Kenya in the late eighteenth century in order to open and control a route to the Nile River headwaters in Uganda; in 1963, Kenya achieved its independence. The nationalist leader Jomo Kenyatta was president until his death in 1978, when Daniel arap Moi succeeded him. Moi's ascent to the presidency kept the Kenyan African National Union (KANU) in power, but gradually diminished the power of the previously dominant Kikuyu ethnic group.

In 1992, after a lengthy period of de facto single-party rule, domestic unrest and pressure from international aid donors forced Moi to hold multiparty elections. Moi was reelected president in controversial polling. In December 1997 presidential and parliamentary elections took place, and Moi again secured victory over a divided opposition. Moi's reelection was ensured by his massive use of state patronage and the official media to promote his candidacy and by harassment of the divided opposition.

KANU's election victories were achieved through political repression, media control, and dubious electoral procedures. Physical violence, an often-docile judiciary, police powers, and executive decrees were used against political opponents and in efforts to undermine the wider civil society. Moi's rule was associated with poor governance. Limits on political and civil rights were common, as was corruption in the ruling party and government. In the 1990s, the government sponsored ethnic violence, which heightened political polarization. Despite these problems, political space continued to open up. Over time, many of the core elements necessary for the growth of a democratic political system developed.

In 2002, the opposition succeeded in uniting behind Kibaki in national elections. He was elected president, defeating Uhuru Kenyatta, the son of Kenya's first president and Moi's chosen successor. In addition, the National Rainbow Coalition (NARC), which supported Kibaki, won the majority of seats in parliament. These elections raised the prospect of a sea change in Kenyan politics: the new leadership's ambitious reform program included tackling corruption and economic and social issues, as well as undertaking institutional reforms designed to promote democracy. To date, reform efforts have been complicated by the fragility of the governing NARC coalition; an ongoing, complex constitutional reform process; significant resource constraints; the threat of terrorism; and ambiguous attitudes on the part of major donor countries.

A drawn-out constitutional review process has included the participation of a wide range of civic groups and associations. Under consideration are the creation of a senate and an executive prime minister to be elected by parliament; presidential and parliamentary electoral reform; decentralization; and other changes designed to limit the power of the presidency, including giving parliament the power to impeach the president. In 2004, the commission was hamstrung by political infighting and was unable to reach decisions on a number of sensitive and politically charged issues. The question of whether parliament is to participate in the process, and at what stage, has also bogged down the proceedings.

The press, parliament, and the judiciary are increasingly highlighting examples of government corruption and malfeasance. President Kibaki established an independent anticorruption commission, which has been investigating over 3,000 cases of alleged corruption since its inception in 2003, although its track record of initiating successful prosecutions has been modest. One of President Kibaki's early appointments was to place John Githongo, the widely respected head of Transparency International's (TI) Kenya chapter, in charge of the government's Office of Ethics and Governance. A number of commissions are investigating particular scandals, such as the Goldenberg and Euro Bank affairs.

The failures of governance in the Moi era present the Kibaki administration with a challenge of whether, and how, to deal with the past. Debate is under way over the extent to which the government should actively seek to right past wrongs and to actively pursue alleged wrongdoers, up to and possibly including former president Moi. In 2003 a presidential task force solicited views from the public and recommended that a truth commission be established to probe injustices perpetrated since 1963, but such a commission has yet to be constituted.

Political Rights and Civil Liberties: With the 2002 elections, Kenyans were able for the first time to choose their leaders in genuinely open and competitive elections. The general domestic and international view was that the elections were legitimate. However, the country is far from consolidating its nascent and fragile democracy, including its electoral processes. Nevertheless, political parties are active and vocal, and parliament is the setting for much of the nation's political discourse. A varied and energetic civil society plays an important role in public policy debates.

TI's 2004 Corruption Perceptions Index suggests that corruption is beginning to fall in many significant areas, and the Kenya Bribery Index states that the incidence of corruption has dropped significantly compared with that of 2002. In 2004, the government raised police salaries to reduce incentives for corruption; according to TI, police are still the most frequently bribed public officials. There have been meager results to date from investigations such as the Goldenberg inquiry, emphasizing the magnitude of the challenge to reduce corruption in Kenya. In addition, Kibaki's increasing reliance on the "Mount Kenya Mafia"—powerful businessmen from the president's majority Kikuyu ethnic group—has raised increasing concerns. In mid-2004, European donors suspended aid over concerns about corruption, but the IMF provided a more positive assessment. Kenya was ranked 129 out of 146 countries surveyed in TI's 2004 Corruption Perceptions Index.

The constitution provides for freedom of speech and of the press, rights that the Moi government had restricted in practice. Despite a hostile government attitude, the print media remained fairly free in the latter years of Moi's rule, and the electronic media began to show some signs of independence. This trend has been accentuated under the Kibaki government, although the Kenya Union of Journalists has criticized the government for failing to expand media freedom in the country. The government does not restrict access to the Internet.

In general, the government has respected freedom of religion. According to the 2004 U.S. State Department's Report on International Religious Freedom, "there is generally a great level of tolerance among religious groups." The report concluded that Kenya was one of the least repressive African states in this regard. However, disputes occur between Muslims and Christians, and Muslim leaders often criticize the government. Religion-based tension has risen in recent years, as terrorist acts associated with Islamic fundamentalism have been committed on Kenyan soil. In June 2004, the Council of Imams and Preachers of Kenya accused the government of persecuting Muslims and cited the arrest of some 30 Muslims on terrorism charges as proof.

Reflecting Kenya's generally positive record on freedom of thought issues, academic freedom is the norm. The constitution explicitly permits freedom of assembly, and the Kibaki government, unlike its predecessor, has generally respected this right, although there have been cases of unnecessary use of force. In July, security forces, for example, killed and injured a number of demonstrators in Nairobi and Kisumu following the cancellation of public rallies demanding a new constitution.

One of the core strengths of Kenya's political culture is its energetic and robust civil society. The success of the 2002 elections was due in large part to the ability of nongovernmental organizations (NGOs) in Kenya to pry open political space and greater freedom. In recent years, public policy has achieved significant elements of transparency, especially when compared with many other countries wrestling with the legacy of decades of authoritarian rule. The role of civil society in the ongoing constitutional reform process is a good example, as has been the ability of NGOs to undertake voter education and election monitoring.

All workers other than the police are legally free to join unions of their choice. The government also may deregister a union, but the Registrar of Trade Unions must give the union 60 days to challenge the deregistration notice. The Trade Union Act makes provision for a registrar of trade unions, who is appointed by the minister of labor. Historically, most of the trade union movement has been at least partially subservient to the governing authorities.

Although Kenya's judicial system is based on the British model, for much of the independence period its actions reflected the primacy of the executive branch. In 2002, a panel of Commonwealth judicial experts from Africa and Canada examined the court system and found it to be among the most incompetent and inefficient in Africa. Judges commonly accepted bribes, and many were subject to political influence.

The Kibaki government came into power promising that the rule of law would be upheld and judicial independence strengthened. Kibaki has criticized the extent of corruption in the judiciary and instructed the minister of justice to establish a process to identify corrupt judges. The president has appointed new high court judges to replace those tainted by corruption. Senior judges have also been suspended while they are investigated for alleged corruption and misconduct.

The courts are understaffed and underfinanced, and Kenyans awaiting trial face long delays that violate their right to due process. The country has officially recognized "Kadhi" Islamic courts that administer Sharia (Islamic law) for such issues as marriage and inheritance disputes, located in areas with a predominantly Muslim population. Controversy exists over whether these courts should be explicitly included in the new Kenyan constitution.

While checks against arbitrary arrest exist in the legal system, they are not uniformly respected. In 2003, the Kibaki government introduced into parliament controversial draft legislation, the Suppression of Terrorism Bill, aimed at combating terrorism. The bill was re-drafted following protests from a wide range of advocacy and human rights organizations, but concerns remain over the extent to which the final bill may restrict civil liberties.

Police still use force to extract information from suspects and deny them an opportunity to get legal representation. The Kenya Human Rights Network claims to have recorded 485 cases of torture and extrajudicial shootings in 2003. The upward trend may partly be because human rights campaigns have prompted more citizens to report violations. Generally, prisons are congested, some holding five times their capacity. This congestion is in some measure caused by the large number of prisoners awaiting trial. Courts often set bail beyond the means of the accused, and overworked prosecutors are slow in preparing for trial.

Kenya's population is divided into more than 40 ethnic groups, among which there were frequent allegations of discrimination and occasional violence. Land disputes frequently form the basis of ethnic tension and violence. Members of the Nubian community, most of whom are Muslim, claimed that the government discriminated against them by trying to eliminate their ethnic identity. The continued presence of and, at times, criminal activities by Somali refugees have exacerbated the problems faced by that minority. Factors contributing to this tension include widespread firearms possession, the commercialization of traditional cattle rustling, poor economic conditions, drought conditions, and ineffective security forces.

Women in Kenya continue to face serious obstacles in the exercise of their freedom. In 2002, a draft gender equity bill created considerable public controversy, with some Muslims protesting that it was too sweeping in scope, but the government announced in 2004 that a revised bill would be introduced in parliament. There is evidence of widespread violence against women; one report determined that more than 50 percent of women had been victims of domestic violence. Traditional attitudes limit the role of women in politics, although there are no legal restrictions and some change is occurring. The 2002 elections increased the number of women in parliament to eight elected and seven nominated, along with three cabinet ministers. The Kibaki government has explicitly targeted improving women's rights as a key policy goal. This issue is also the focus of considerable attention and discussion in the constitutional review process.

Kiribati

Population: 100,000
GNI/capita: $810
Life Expectancy: 63
Religious Groups: Roman Catholic (52 percent), Protestant (40 percent), other (8 percent)
Ethnic Groups: Micronesian, some Polynesian
Capital: Tarawa

Political Rights: 1
Civil Liberties: 1
Status: Free

Ten-Year Ratings Timeline (Political Rights, Civil Liberties, Status)

1995	1996	1997	1998	1999	2000	2001	2002	2003	2004
1,1F	1,1F	1,1F	1,1F	1,1F	1,1F	1,1F	1,1F	1,1F	1,1F

Overview:

In December 2003, China closed its embassy and removed its satellite-tracking facility in Kiribati at the request of newly elected president Anote Tong.

Kiribati, a constitutional republic, gained independence from Britain in 1979. The country consists of 33 small islands scattered across nearly 1.5 million square miles of the central Pacific Ocean and Banaba island in the western Pacific. In 1998, the incumbent president, Teburoro Tito, won a second four-year term, defeating opposition candidates Harry Tong and Amberoti Nikora.

A major issue in the February 2003 presidential election—in which President Teburoro Tito was reelected to a third and final term in office over Taberannang Timeon, a former secretary to the cabinet—was the presence of a Chinese satellite-tracking facility on the capital atoll of Tarawa. Beijing claimed that the facility was part of its civilian space program, but others suspected that its purpose was to monitor U.S. missile tests in the Pacific. Before the vote, opposition party member Anote Tong pledged to review the 15-year Chinese lease and "to take the appropriate action at the right time." China's influence became an issue when parliament member Harry Tong asked Tito to release details about the lease and Tito refused.

The controversy led to a no-confidence vote of 40 to 21 against the Tito government in March 2003. Parliament was dissolved and fresh parliamentary and presidential polls were called. In two rounds of parliamentary elections, held on May 9 and 14, the government secured 24 seats against the opposition's 14, with two independent members. However, in July 4 presidential elections, opposition candidate Anote Tong was elected president with 47.4 percent of the vote, defeating rivals Harry Tong (Anote's elder brother) of the ruling Maurin Maneaba Party with 43.5 percent and Banuera Berina with 9.1 percent. Opposition candidates complained that they did not have sufficient access to the government-owned Radio Kiribati station and *Te Uekara* newspaper during the election campaign.

Tong kept his promise to review the 15-year lease to China and decided in November 2003 to cut ties with China and restore relations with Taiwan. China closed its embassy and dismantled the satellite facility in December 2003. In addition to development assistance, Taiwan sent medical doctors to replace vacancies left when China pulled out of Kiribati.

Political Rights and Civil Liberties:

Citizens of Kiribati can change their government democratically. The 2003 presidential and parliamentary elections were considered free and fair. The president is popularly elected in a two-step process. Forty of the representatives to the 42-member parliament (Maneaba ni Maungatabu) are chosen by universal adult suffrage, one is nominated by the Rabi Island Council in Fiji, and the attorney general holds an assembly position ex officio. (Rabi Island is a part of Fiji, but many residents there are of Kiribati origin. They were forced to move there from Banaba island by the British when phosphate mining made Banaba uninhabitable.) Parliament then selects three or four candidates for the presidential round. The president, vested with executive authority by the constitution, is limited to serving three 4-year terms.

In 2004, the government decided to stop issuing investor passports in response to pressure from donor countries to improve immigration control following reports of fake passports and illegal passport sales. Official corruption is a considerable problem, and the government has yet to take real steps to improve transparency and provide a more competitive environment for big and small businesses.

Freedom of speech is generally respected. However, the government has powers to shut down any newspaper that is subject to complaint and bar publication of any article that offends good taste or decency, or is likely to incite crime or disorder. The government owns *Te Uekera*, one of the country's two newspapers. Churches also put out several newsletters and other periodicals. The *Kiribati Newstar*, the only private newspaper, is owned by Ieremia Tabai, a former president and member of the parliament. Tabai launched the newspaper after the government blocked his efforts to set up a radio station, Newair FM 101, in 1999. The government closed the station and fined Tabai and other directors of the station for attempting to import broadcasting equipment without a license. In December 2002, the government granted Newair FM 101 a license to broadcast, and the station went into operation in January 2003. Until then, the government had owned the only radio station in Kiribati. There is one television station.

Opposition candidates have criticized the Newspaper Registration Act for its vaguely worded restrictions on the printing of offensive materials. The law allows officials to censor articles that could incite or encourage crime or disorder and to shut down any publication against which a complaint has been filed. A single Internet service provider supports about 1,000 users. The main constraints to broader Internet access are costs and limited bandwidth.

There were no reports of religious suppression or restrictions on academic freedom.

Freedom of association and the right to organize and bargain collectively are generally respected. A number of nongovernmental groups are involved in development assistance, education, health, and advocacy for women and children. Only about 10 percent of the labor force belongs to unions, the largest of which is the Kiribati Trade Union Congress with about 2,500 members. The law provides for the right to strike, but strikes are rare; the last strike took place in 1980.

The judicial system is modeled on English common law and provides adequate due process rights. It consists of the high court, a court of appeal, and magistrates' courts; appeals may go to the Privy Council in London. The president makes all judicial appointments. Internal security is maintained by a police force of about 260 sworn officers who perform law enforcement and paramilitary functions under the leadership of a civilian commissioner, who reports directly to the office of the president. The country has no armed forces. Australia and New Zealand provide defense assistance under bilateral security agreements. Traditional customs permit corporal punishment, and island councils on some outer islands occasionally order such punishment for petty theft and other minor offenses.

Citizens enjoy freedom of movement. The government does not use forced exile, but village councils have used this punishment.

The government is the main employer in this largely subsistence agricultural economy. The economy also depends considerably on foreign assistance and generates a small sum from selling fishing licenses to foreign fishing fleets. The main exports are copra (dried coconut meat) and fish. Interest from a well-managed trust fund built from royalties from phosphate sales have balanced the national budget and kept the country debt free.

Economic opportunities for women are limited. Discrimination against women is severe in the traditional, male-dominant culture. Spousal abuse and other forms of violence against women and children are not uncommon and are often associated with alcohol abuse. Prostitution and sexual harassment are illegal, but neither was reported as widespread. Of concern is the growing number of HIV/AIDS cases, which reached 42 by the beginning of 2004.

Kuwait

Population: 2,500,000
GNI/capita: $16,340
Life Expectancy: 78
Political Rights: 4
Civil Liberties: 5
Status: Partly Free
Religious Groups: Muslim (85 percent) [Sunni 70 percent, Shi'a 30 percent], other (15 percent)
Ethnic Groups: Kuwaiti (45 percent), other Arab (35 percent), South Asian (9 percent), Iranian (4 percent), other (7 percent)
Capital: Kuwait City

Ten-Year Ratings Timeline (Political Rights, Civil Liberties, Status)

1995	1996	1997	1998	1999	2000	2001	2002	2003	2004
5,5PF	5,5PF	5,5PF	5,5PF	4,5PF	4,5PF	4,5PF	4,5PF	4,5PF	4,5PF

Overview:

Kuwait took modest steps to introduce political reforms in 2004, including proposing a measure that would grant Kuwaiti women the right to vote and run for office. The government also legally recognized the first independent Kuwaiti human rights organization. However, the government did not succeed in implementing any significant political reforms in 2004, achieving no progress on passing a new proposed election law and a draft law that would grant women full political rights.

For more than 200 years, the Al-Sabah family has played a role in ruling Kuwait. A year after Kuwait gained its independence from Britain in 1961, a new constitution gave broad powers to the emir and created the National Assembly. In August 1990, Iraq attacked and invaded Kuwait. A coalition force mandated by the United Nations and led by the United States liberated Kuwait using military force in February 1991.

The emir has suspended the National Assembly two times, from 1976 to 1981 and from 1986 to 1992. After its restoration in 1992, parliament played an active role in monitoring the emir and the government, forcing government ministers out of office and blocking legislation proposed by the royal family. Parliament, however, has also served as an impediment to progressive political change, rejecting measures that would have granted women the right to vote and accelerated economic reforms.

The 2003 legislative elections did not meet minimal international standards, tainted by the exclusion of women from voting and allegations of widespread government-subsidized vote buying. Following the elections, Sabah al-Ahmad Al-Sabah, half-brother of Emir Jaber al-Ahmad Al-Sabah, became prime minister, taking over for ailing Saad al-Abdallah Al-Sabah, who remains the crown prince. Sabah al-Ahmad Al-Sabah's appointment as prime minister marked the first time since Kuwait's independence that the prime minister has not been the crown prince. The Al-Sabah ruling dynasty is currently led by aging family members; the emir and crown prince, both in their seventies, spent several weeks overseas for medical treatment in the fall of 2004.

By the end of the year, Kuwait's National Assembly was poised to debate a bill that would give women full political rights, six years after a previous attempt to grant women the right to vote and run for office was rejected by the legislature.

Enjoying its best economic growth in 30 years and its sixth consecutive year of budget surpluses, the results of record-high oil prices, Kuwait saw a relatively calm year, after 2003, when a U.S.-led coalition staged most of its ground troops for the Iraq War in Kuwait. In January 2004, the United States designated Kuwait a major non-NATO ally, signaling a closer relationship between the two countries.

Political Rights and Civil Liberties: Freely elected representatives do not determine the government's policies. The royal family of Kuwait, which is a hereditary emirate, largely sets the policy agenda, dominates political life, and controls meaningful power. The emir has overriding power in the political system and appoints the prime minister and cabinet. Members of the ruling family hold key cabinet posts, such as those for defense, the interior, foreign affairs, and oil.

Under the constitution, the emir shares legislative power with the 50-member National Assembly (parliament), which is elected by a limited popular vote involving only about 15 percent of the country's 900,000 citizens. The emir has the power to dissolve parliament at will but must call elections within 60 days. Parliament is granted powers to overturn decrees from the emir issued during a period when it is not in session, and it has exercised this power in a number of cases. Parliament can veto the appointment of the country's prime minister, but then it must choose from three alternates put forward by the emir. It also has the power to remove government ministers with a majority vote of elected members.

Formal political parties are banned, but political groupings, such as parliamentary blocs, have been allowed to emerge. The National Assembly showed signs of becoming increasingly assertive throughout the year, questioning numerous government ministers in investigations into financial mismanagement and corruption.

Members of Kuwait's National Assembly questioned the deputy prime minister and minister of state for cabinet and National Assembly affairs Mohammad Dhaifallah Sharar on allegations of corruption, including mismanagement and negligence resulting in the loss of $260 million to the Kuwait Municipality. Sharar was not found guilty of wrongdoing and remained in office by the end of the year. Kuwait was ranked 44 out of 146 countries surveyed in Transparency International's 2004 Corruption Perceptions Index.

The government allows some open criticism and debate on politics in the press. In 2004, Kuwait approved the establishment of private television channels to transmit from Kuwait, a first for the country. All major newspapers are privately owned, and foreign broadcasts are available. Limitations on freedom of press and expression remain, with the Ministry of Information imposing restrictions from time to time. In August, the government banned *Fahrenheit 9/11*, a documentary film by American filmmaker Michael Moore, for being critical of Saudi Arabia's royal family. Ministry of Information officials justified the decision by saying that Kuwaiti law prohibits insulting friendly nations. Kuwaitis have access to the Internet, though Internet service providers have blocked access to certain sites.

Islam is the state religion; nevertheless, religious minorities are generally permitted to practice their religion freely in private. The Roman Catholic, Anglican,

National Evangelical, Greek Orthodox, Armenian Orthodox, Coptic Orthodox, and Greek Catholic churches operate freely. Kuwaiti law bans missionaries from proselytizing Muslims. Academic freedom is generally respected, though some academics exercise self-censorship. Kuwait has a tradition of allowing relatively open and free private discussions, often conducted in traditional gatherings and usually only including men, called *diwayniyas*.

The government restricts freedom of assembly, and public gatherings require government approval. The Kuwaiti government licensed the first independent human rights organization in August. The Ministry of Social Affairs and Labor officially recognized the existence of the Kuwait Human Rights Society, which was founded ten years ago but previously operated without legal standing. Workers have the right to join labor unions, but the government restricts freedom of association by mandating that there be only one union per occupational trade.

Kuwait lacks a truly independent judiciary. The emir appoints all judges, and the executive branch of government approves judicial promotions and renewals of judicial appointments. According to Kuwaiti law, authorities may detain suspects for four days without charge. The Ministry of the Interior supervises the main internal security forces, including the national police, the Criminal Investigation Division, and Kuwait State Security. Four Kuwaiti Islamists accused government authorities of torturing them to extract confessions in a case in which they were accused of conspiring to attack foreign forces in Kuwait and Iraq. The government permitted visits to prisons by human rights activists, who report adherence to international standards, though with some concern about overcrowding.

An estimated 80,000 stateless residents, known as *bidoon*, are considered illegal residents and do not have full citizenship rights.

Both male and female citizens have the right to own property and establish businesses. Oil dominates the economy, accounting for nearly 90 percent of public revenues. The National Assembly debated Project Kuwait, a proposed $8 billion investment by foreign oil companies to develop the country's oil fields close to the Iraqi border. The National Assembly stalled legislative action on the proposed project, with some members of the National Assembly seeking assurances that control of natural resources would not be given to foreigners.

The 1962 constitution provides men and women with equal rights. Nevertheless, women face discrimination in several areas of society and remain under represented in the workforce, although they have made recent gains. Women have been fighting for full political participation for decades, but have been blocked by conservative male political leaders and Islamist groups. However, in 2004, the government took steps to grant women political rights when the emir opened the new session of the National Assembly in October with a call for giving women the right to vote and run for office. Women constitute more than 60 percent of the student body at several leading universities in Kuwait.

Kyrgyzstan

Population: 5,100,000
GNI/capita: $290
Life Expectancy: 68
Religious Groups: Muslim (75 percent), Russian
Orthodox (20 percent), other (5 percent)
Ethnic Groups: Kyrgyz (64.9 percent), Russian (12.5 percent),
Uzbek (13.8 percent), Ukrainian (1 percent), other (8 percent)
Capital: Bishkek

Political Rights: 6
Civil Liberties: 5
Status: Not Free

Ten-Year Ratings Timeline (Political Rights, Civil Liberties, Status)

1995	1996	1997	1998	1999	2000	2001	2002	2003	2004
4,4PF	4,4PF	4,4PF	5,5PF	5,5PF	6,5NF	6,5NF	6,5NF	6,5NF	6,5NF

Overview:

With presidential and parliamentary elections scheduled for 2005, Kyrgyzstan's political opposition began preparations in 2004 to challenge the authoritarian rule of President Askar Akayev at the polls. Meanwhile, growing discord within the legislature, including two failed no-confidence votes against the prime minister and a scandal over listening devices discovered in the offices of several opposition deputies, was visible during the year. On the international front, Kyrgyzstan continued to juggle its relations with the United States and Russia over strategic matters, while border and water resource issues contributed to tensions with neighboring Central Asian countries.

Having been populated by nomadic herders and ruled by tribal leaders for centuries, Kyrgyzstan was conquered by Russia in the mid-1800s and incorporated into the Soviet Union in 1924. The country declared independence from the U.S.S.R. in August 1991. After Akayev, a respected physicist, was elected president in the country's first direct presidential vote two months later, he introduced multiparty elections and pursued economic reforms.

In the 1995 parliamentary elections, no single party won a clear majority, with a mix of governing officials, intellectuals, and clan leaders capturing most of the seats in the legislature. Later that year, Akayev was reelected president in early elections with more than 70 percent of the vote. In a February 1996 referendum, 94 percent of voters endorsed constitutional amendments that substantially increased the powers of the presidency.

Opposition parties, including the Democratic Movement of Kyrgyzstan (PDMK), El Bei-Bechora (The People's Party), and Ar-Namys (Dignity), were barred from competing in the February 2000 parliamentary elections over minor technicalities in rulings that were widely regarded as politically motivated. Ar-Namys chairman Feliks Kulov, who ran as an independent candidate, lost in the runoff by a suspiciously large margin despite having enjoyed a secure lead in the first round. According to official election results, the Communist Party received the largest percentage of votes, followed by the pro-government Union of Democratic Forces. International election observers, including representatives from the Organization for Security and Cooperation in Europe, noted serious irregularities such as attempts to bribe voters, violations in vote tabulations, and a state media bias in favor of pro-government parties.

The October 29, 2000, presidential poll was contested by six candidates, including the heavily favored incumbent, who received nearly 75 percent of the vote. Kulov, who was widely regarded as Akayev's main challenger, was denied registration as a candidate for refusing to take a mandatory Kyrgyz language exam, which he charged violated election laws and the constitution. As with the parliamentary elections, international monitors and opposition figures cited widespread irregularities, including the exclusion of candidates for political purposes, the stuffing of ballot boxes, and biased state media coverage.

For the second successive year, Islamic militants conducted armed incursions in August 2000 into the southern region of Kyrgyzstan. The rebels were members of the Islamic Movement of Uzbekistan (IMU), a group seeking the overthrow of the secular government of Uzbekistan and its replacement with one based on Islamic law. After several months of battles between the rebels and Uzbek and Kyrgyz troops, the fighting ceased with the onset of winter, with many of the rebels fleeing back to their bases in neighboring Tajikistan.

Following the September 11, 2001, terrorist attacks against the World Trade Center and the Pentagon, Kyrgyzstan offered its support for the U.S.-led war in Afghanistan, including the use of its air bases. For the cash-strapped Kyrgyz economy, U.S. troop deployments promised to be a valuable source of income. Meanwhile, human rights groups expressed concern that the government would use its increased cooperation with the United States to crack down further on sources of domestic dissent, including independent media outlets and opposition political groups.

Years of simmering frustrations in the economically depressed and politically marginalized south culminated in an unprecedented series of public protests in 2002. The demonstrations were sparked by the January arrest of parliament member Azimbek Beknazarov on abuse-of-power charges, although critics maintained that he had been detained because of his public criticism of a controversial 1999 border agreement ceding land to China. On March 17 and 18, a few days after his trial began, thousands of pro-Beknazarov demonstrators marched in the southern district of Aksy. In the first outbreak of deadly political violence since Kyrgyzstan's independence, several protestors were killed and more than a dozen were wounded when police fired into the crowd. In an apparent effort to quell the protests, the authorities released Beknazarov from prison the following day. However, on May 24, he was convicted of abuse of office, given a one-year suspended sentence, and stripped of his seat in parliament.

Thousands of Beknazarov supporters continued to hold rallies, demanding that the charges against him be dismissed and that those responsible for the killings in Aksy be punished. The demonstrators adopted additional demands, including Akayev's resignation and the overturning of a May 8 conviction of Kulov for embezzlement. Kulov was already serving a seven-year prison term, which he had received in January 2001, for abuse of power while national security minister in 1997 and 1998. Most analysts maintained that the cases against him were politically motivated and were intended to exclude him from further activities in politics.

The crisis eased somewhat after an appeals court annulled Beknazarov's sentence on June 28, 2002, allowing him to retain his seat in parliament. On December 28, four former regional prosecutors and police officials were sentenced to two to three years in prison in connection with the Aksy shootings. However, critics charged that senior officials who had authorized the use of force had not been prosecuted and brought to justice. The government subsequently made certain conciliatory gestures toward the southern regions of the country by designating the city of Osh the "southern capital" and awarding it special budgetary privileges.

Disquiet in parliament and underlying divisions within the political elite were evident throughout 2004. In January, several opposition members of parliament announced that they had discovered listening devices in their offices. A parliamentary commission created to examine the case issued a critical report in May that concluded that the National Security Service (SNB) had planted the devices. The SNB responded by presenting a videotape of a former SNB employee confessing to having passed classified documents to two of the opposition deputies, charges that the deputies denied. As a result of the report, the lower house of parliament adopted a resolution calling on Akayev to hold the SNB officials accountable; by November 30, no actions had been taken to follow up on the resolution.

In April, Prime Minister Nikolai Tanayev narrowly survived a no-confidence vote in the upper house of parliament. Tanayev, who had the president's declared support, had been accused of financial abuses and corruption. Although a second vote of no confidence, this time in the lower house of parliament in May, also failed, parliament's attempts to remove the prime minister were indications of genuine discontent within the legislature over government policies. The year also saw the defection to the opposition of Misir Ashirkulov, former secretary of the Kyrgyz Security Council and a long-standing ally of the president.

In the October 10 local elections, candidates representing the pro-government parties Alga, Kyrgyzstan and Adilet captured the largest number of seats. Although the elections took place without significant government interference, some domestic observers reported irregularities, including multiple voting and vote tampering. In a positive step, a new electoral code provision provided for the participation of opposition parties and nongovernmental organizations (NGOs) on local electoral commissions. While recent legislation somewhat enhanced the responsibilities of local councils—including the right to control local budget expenditures—the councils remain relatively powerless compared with the presidential-appointed regional governors.

With the next parliamentary and presidential elections scheduled for February and October 2005, respectively, opposition parties and groups began positioning themselves throughout 2004 to challenge pro-government candidates in the upcoming polls. Several political blocs and tactical coalitions were established during the year in an attempt to improve their chances of gaining seats in parliament and to strengthen their position for the subsequent presidential election. With prominent opposition figure Kulov incarcerated and ineligible for parole until November 2005—and recent electoral code amendments denying people with a criminal record the right to contest elections—a number of opposition groups declared their support for former prime minister Kurmanbek Bakiyev, who announced his candidacy for president in June. Meanwhile, speculation continued over whether Akayev will seek another term in office. Although he is constitutionally barred from running again—and despite his repeated pledges that he will step down after his current term ends—

some analysts believe that the country's constitution will be reinterpreted to allow Akayev to become a candidate.

Kyrgyzstan continued to balance its strategic and economic relations with Russia, China, and the United States throughout the year. In August, Russia and Kyrgyzstan announced an expansion of a military base in the town of Kant near Bishkek that was established in 2003 under the auspices of the Commonwealth of Independent States Collective Security Treaty Organization. Although Kyrgyz and Russian officials have insisted that Russian and U.S. military bases in Kyrgyzstan will serve complementary, rather than competing, strategic roles, the Kant air base is widely seen as an attempt by Moscow to counter the growing U.S. influence in Central Asia after September 11, 2001. The economic benefits of a continued U.S. presence in the country are likely to lead Kyrgyzstan to maintain good relations with both Washington and Moscow. Meanwhile, the Kyrgyz government held discussions with neighboring China during the year to broaden trade and investment opportunities.

Kyrgyzstan's border with Uzbekistan continued to be a source of tension between the two countries. Following the 1999 and 2000 IMU incursions into Kyrgyzstan, Uzbekistan placed land mines along the Kyrgyz-Uzbek border to prevent renewed IMU invasions. Tashkent has refused most demands by Bishkek to remove the mines, which have killed a number of Kyrgyz civilians. In one of the latest issues of concern, in September 2004, Kyrgyz members of parliament called for the return of the primarily ethnic Kyrgyz enclave of Shakhimardan, which was transferred to Uzbekistan in the 1930s in a move that Bishkek described as illegal. Disputes over the region's critical water supply also strained Kyrgyzstan's relations with both Kazakhstan and Uzbekistan, to which Bishkek provides water in exchange for supplies of coal, oil, and natural gas.

Political Rights and Civil Liberties:

Citizens of Kyrgyzstan cannot change their government democratically. International election observers described the 2000 parliamentary and presidential elections as neither free nor fair. The constitution codifies strong presidential rule and a weak parliament, and the post of prime minister is largely ceremonial. Although the constitution limits the president to only two terms in office, President Askar Akayev was allowed to run in 2000 after the Constitutional Court ruled that his first term had begun in 1995, after the country's first post-Soviet constitution was adopted (in 1993), rather than in 1991, when he was first elected.

The current bicameral legislature is composed of a 45-member People's Assembly (upper house) and a 60-seat Legislative Assembly (lower house). Constitutional amendments adopted in a February 2003 referendum will create a unicameral legislature with 75 deputies after the 2005 parliamentary poll. Other amendments adopted during the referendum further strengthened the authority of the president at the expense of parliament and included the abolition of party-list voting in parliamentary elections in favor of the first-past-the-post system (which could further weaken political parties) and the granting of immunity to former presidents and their families. Voters also approved a proposal that Akayev should serve out the remainder of his term until December 2005. Election observers noted various irregularities during the referendum, including multiple voting, forged voting results, and polling officials hampering independent observers from monitoring the vote. In addition, the role of the Constitutional Council, which was composed of government officials and civil society representatives and tasked with proposing the amendments, was marginalized, as the final government-prepared text differed significantly from what had been offered by the Constitutional Council. Furthermore, the time frame from the selection of the various proposals for the referendum until the holding of the referendum was extremely short.

A new election code regarded as an improvement over previous legislation was signed into law in January. While the new code contains provisions to improve transparency and NGO and political party participation in the electoral process, concerns remain about certain elements, including some that could be used to restrict the rights of candidates and the media.

The government harassed some members of opposition political groups during the year, including Ar-Namys party deputy chairman Emil Aliyev, who was arrested in July on embezzlement charges that were suspected of being politically motivated. In August 2003, Kyrgyzstan's Supreme Court upheld the 2002 guilty verdict against Ar-Namys party leader Feliks Kulov that had resulted from a politically motivated prosecution. Twelve months later, a district court denied Kulov parole. Most political parties are weak, poorly organized, and centered around a specific leading figure.

Corruption is widespread throughout Kyrgyz society, and bribes are frequently required to obtain lucrative government positions. As part of the country's anticorruption campaign, parliament in 2004 adopted a law on income declarations for high-level officials; the first declarations are to be presented in May 2005. Kyrgyzstan was ranked 122 out of 146 countries in Transparency International's 2004 Corruption Perceptions Index.

Both state and private media are vulnerable to government pressure, which causes many journalists to practice self-censorship. Libel is a criminal offense punishable by up to three years in prison. Most of the country's media outlets are owned or controlled by individuals with close ties to the government and the president's family. All media outlets are required to register with the Ministry of Justice and wait for formal approval before commencing operations; the registration process is often lengthy and includes background checks on owners and sources of financing. The state printing house, Uchkun, which is the country's primary newspaper publisher, has at times refused to print some independent and opposition newspapers. An internationally funded printing press operated by the nongovernmental Media Support Center Foundation provides services to more than 60 local and regional papers without fear of censorship. There are no credible reports of government interference in or censorship of the Internet.

Journalists and media outlets faced harassment, and even violence, during the year. Chingiz Sydykov, the son of Zamira Sydykova, who is the editor of the *Respublica* newspaper, received serious injuries during an attack in April. His mother believed that the assault was in retaliation for a recent series of articles that she wrote in the paper criticizing the government. *Kyrgyz Ruhu* newspaper journalist Ernis Nazalov was found dead in September 2003 in a canal in the southern town of Osh; the fact that Nazalov was investigating government corruption at the time increased suspicion that his death was politically motivated. In February 2004, police closed the investigation into his death after an official inquiry concluded that he died of drowning. In September, the *MSN* newspaper was found guilty of monopolistic practices for allegedly setting low prices designed to restrict competition. Critics charged that the ruling against *MSN*, which had published controversial articles about socioeconomic conditions in the country, was politically motivated. The independent television station Pyramida was prevented from broadcasting for more than a month in early 2004 because of alleged technical problems. However, the station's director maintained that Pyramida's weekly political program might have angered the authorities because it featured opposition leaders. In August, the telecommunications company Aeropag, with reported ties to the president's family, announced the purchase of shares in Pyramida.

The government generally respects freedom of religion in this predominantly Muslim country. To obtain legal status, all religious organizations must register with the Ministry of Justice, a process that is often cumbersome. The government has increased efforts to monitor and restrict Islamic groups that it regards as extremist and a threat to national security, particularly Hizb-ut-Tahrir, an international movement calling for the creation of an Islamic caliphate throughout the Muslim world. There have been reports of some alleged Hizb-ut-Tahrir members being tortured while in police custody. In May, Uzbek and Kyrgyz secret services conducted joint surveillance of a mosque in Karasuu near Osh during prayers. The mosque is led by Imam Muhammad Rafik Kamalov, whom a member of parliament accused the same month of being associated with Hizb-ut-Tahrir.

Teachers have been forced to subscribe to government newspapers, and municipal authorities in some cities require schoolchildren to perform during national holidays and visits by government officials. Corruption is widespread throughout the educational system, with bribes often required to obtain admission to schools or universities.

Freedom of assembly is respected with some restrictions. Numerous protests and rallies took place across the country in 2004, most without interference from the authorities. However, on April 15, police detained more than a dozen demonstrators, including prominent human rights activists, who were protesting Kulov's continued imprisonment. The protestors were given small fines for violating public order and released. In October, the Constitutional Court ruled that a law on assembly was not in compliance with the constitution, which requires only that organizers of public gatherings inform the authorities in advance, rather than seek their permission, to hold such meetings and demonstrations.

Freedom of association is generally respected, although some NGOs have faced harassment and intimidation, sometimes perpetrated by the authorities. On July 3, the daughter of Ramazan Dyryldaev, head of the Kyrgyz Committee for Human Rights, was beaten by unknown assailants. On November 16, Tursunbek Akunov, head of the Human Rights Movement of Kyrgyzstan, disappeared. On the day he went missing, he was gathering signatures for a petition calling for the president's resignation and was in the process of organizing a large protest, to be held the next morning, calling for Akayev to step down. As of November 30, Akunov's whereabouts and the circumstances surrounding his disappearance remained unknown. During the year, Akayev and the state media accused foreign NGOs, including the Soros Foundation and National Democratic Institute, of trying to foment popular unrest to overthrow the government.

The law provides for the formation of trade unions, and unions generally are able to conduct their activities without obstruction. Although the right to strike is not specifically codified in law, it is not prohibited. The Federation of Trade Unions is the only union umbrella organization in the country, but unions are not required to join it.

Despite various legislative reforms in the court system, the judiciary is not independent and remains dominated by the executive branch. Corruption among judges, who are underpaid, is reportedly widespread. Defendants' rights, including the presumption of innocence until proven guilty, are not always respected. Police at times use violence against suspects during arrest and interrogation and to extract confessions. In November 2003, Akayev signed a decision outlawing torture; police will face criminal charges and up to ten years in prison if convicted. During 2004, numerous Ministry of Internal Affairs officials were dismissed and prosecuted for offenses including police brutality, according to the 2004 U.S. State Department human rights report. In March 2004, the president signed a law limiting the crimes that carry the death penalty to aggravated murder, rape of underage children, and genocide. On November 16, eighteen prisoners in a detention center in Osh slashed their wrists to protest alleged ill-treatment and a lack of basic services. The incident highlighted persistent reports of poor prison conditions, including severe overcrowding, a high prevalence of infectious diseases, shortage of medicine, and inadequate nutrition.

Ethnic minority groups, including Uzbeks, Russians, and Uighurs, have complained of discrimination in employment and housing. Members of the country's sizable ethnic Uzbek minority have been demanding more political and cultural rights, including greater representation in government and more Uzbek language schools. In April, Akayev signed a new language law requiring that students applying to universities and state and local government officials be proficient in Kyrgyz and stipulating that at least one-third of news broadcasts and advertisements be in Kyrgyz. Some critics charge that the law will lead to further discrimination against the country's large minority population, particularly Uzbeks, and exclude them from political participation.

The government of Kyrgyzstan, which abolished the Soviet-era exit-visa system in 1999, generally respects the right of free travel to and from the country. However, certain policies complicate internal migration, including a requirement for citizens to obtain official permits to work and settle in particular areas of the country.

Personal connections, corruption, organized crime, and widespread poverty limit business competition and equality of opportunity. Conscript soldiers are commonly rented out to civilian employers under illegal arrangements, and some are forced to work for no pay.

Cultural traditions and apathy by law enforcement officials discourage victims of domestic violence and rape from seeking legal help. The trafficking of women and girls into forced prostitution abroad is a serious problem, and some victims report that the authorities are involved in trafficking. In response, the criminal code was amended in 2003 to punish trafficking with up to 20 years in prison, and the Ministry of Internal Affairs opened an anti-trafficking police unit in 2004. The tradition of bride kidnapping and forcing women into marriage persists despite being illegal, and few are prosecuted for the crime. Although women are well represented in the workforce and in institutions of higher learning, declining economic conditions in the country have had a negative impact on women's professional and educational opportunities.

Laos

Population: 5,800,000
GNI/capita: $310
Life Expectancy: 54
Religious Groups: Buddhist (60 percent), other [including animist] (40 percent)
Ethnic Groups: Lao Loum [lowland] (68 percent), Lao Theung [upland] (22 percent), Lao Soung [highland] including the Hmong and the Yao (9 percent), ethnic Vietnamese/Chinese (1 percent)
Capital: Vientiane

Political Rights: 7
Civil Liberties: 6
Status: Not Free

Ten-Year Ratings Timeline (Political Rights, Civil Liberties, Status)

1995	1996	1997	1998	1999	2000	2001	2002	2003	2004
7,6NF	7,6NF	7,6NF	7,6NF	7,6NF	7,6NF	7,6NF	7,6NF	7,6NF	7,6NF

Overview:

In 2004, government harassment of the Christian minority in Laos continued, as did repressive actions against those seeking political reform. Laotian dissidents outside the country charged that the government denied food and medicine to thousands of civilians caught up in a military campaign against Hmong rebels in a northeastern province since 2003. In October, a court in southern Laos sentenced 16 alleged rebels to prison for attacking a checkpoint on the Thai-Laotian border in July 2000.

Laos, a landlocked and mountainous country, won independence in 1953 after six decades of French rule and Japanese occupation during World War II, and a constitutional monarchy was established. Backed by Vietnam's Viet Minh rebels, Communist Pathet Lao (Land of Lao) guerrillas quickly tried to topple the royalist government in Vientiane, which began a civil war involving the Communist, royalist, and "neutralist forces" in 1960. Amid continued internal fighting, Laos was drawn into the Vietnam War in 1964, when the United States began bombing North Vietnamese forces operating inside Laos. The Pathet Lao finally seized power in 1975, shortly after the Communist victory in neighboring Vietnam. A one-party Communist state was set up under Prime Minister Kaysone Phomvihane's Lao People's Revolutionary Party (LPRP).

By the 1980s, the Laotian economy was in tatters after years of civil war and the inept economic policies of the LPRP. Seeing the success of China's economic opening, the LPRP began to relax control on prices, encourage foreign investment, and privatize farms and some state-owned firms. These actions spurred much needed economic growth, but the government rejected deeper economic reform for fear of losing its grip on the nation. Moreover, those who called for political reform—however minor the proposed change—were jailed or faced other forms of suppression.

Ethnic Hmong rebels, who are remnants of an army once backed by the U.S. CIA during the Vietnam War, are today a fractious and poorly equipped group. Critics charge that the government exaggerates the Hmong threat and contend that many civilians have been killed by the Laotian military in its campaign against the Hmong rebels. Laotian exiles also maintain that the government had starved 3,000 civilians to death in its blockade targeting rebels in Khouang Province since 2003.

In 2004, about 35 Christian families in Luang Prabang province were ordered to renounce their faith by district government officials. All Christians in a village in Savannakhet province were asked to renounce their faith or face arrest. In some cases, local governments ordered their agents to live in Christian homes and forced these impoverished families to bear the living costs of these agents.

Laos remains one of the poorest and least developed countries in the world. More than three-quarters of Laos's 5.3 million people live on less than $2 a day, and about four-fifths of Laotians are subsistence farmers contributing about 53 percent of the gross domestic product. Trade, tourism, and sales of hydroelectric power to neighboring Thailand are key sources of foreign revenue. A recent decision to expand hydroelectric power generation in southern Laos is expected to displace more subsistence farmers. The economy has yet to recover from the regional financial crisis that began in 1997, and the government's refusal to deepen reform discourages foreign investment.

Political Rights and Civil Liberties: Laotians cannot change their government democratically. The 1991 constitution makes the ruling LPRP the sole legal political party and gives it a leading role at all levels of government. The LPRP vets all candidates for election to the rubber-stamp National Assembly; elections are held once every five years. In the last election, held in 2002, only 1 of 166 candidates fielded for the assembly's 109 seats was not a LPRP cadre. Kaysone Phomvihane was prime minister and head of the LPRP from 1975 until his death in 1992. Khamtay Siphandone succeeded Kaysone as both head of the LPRP and chief executive.

Corruption and abuses by government officials are widespread. Official announcements and new laws to curb corruption have little real impact. Government regulation of virtually every facet of life provides corrupt officials with many opportunities to demand bribes. High-level officials in government and the military are also frequently involved in commercial logging and mining, as well as other enterprises aimed at exploiting Laotian natural resources. Laos was not ranked by Transparency International in its 2004 Corruption Perceptions Index.

Laotian media are controlled by the state and parrot the party line. For example, the party paper *Paxoxon* bans criticisms of "friendly" countries like Vietnam and Burma. Any journalists who criticize the government or discuss controversial political topics, such as questioning the authority of LRLP, are subject to punishment. Two European journalists investigating conditions for the Hmong minority were arrested in June 2003 for the alleged killing of a village guard. They were sentenced to long prison terms but were quickly released and expelled. Although the state controls the country's television and radio stations, residents within frequency range of Radio Free Asia and other foreign broadcasts from Thailand can pick up these foreign broadcasts. Internet access is severely limited, and Web sites critical of the government are blocked. The government is the only Internet service provider.

Religious freedom is tightly restricted. Dozens of Christians have been detained on religious grounds, and several have been jailed for proselytizing or for other religious activities. A campaign was launched in some provinces in 1999 to shut churches and force Christians to renounce their faith. While the national campaign has eased, local officials have continued to harass Christians—from forcing them to renounce their faith to barring them from celebrating major religious holidays and withholding permission to build places of worship. For the majority of the population who are Buddhists, the LPRP controls training for the Buddhist clergy and oversees temples and other religious sites.

Academic freedom is highly restricted. University professors cannot teach or write about democracy, human rights, and other politically sensitive topics. However, a small but increasing number of young people have been allowed to travel overseas, including to the United States, for university and graduate-level training.

Laos has some nongovernmental welfare and professional groups, but they are prohibited from having political agendas and are subjected to strict state control. All unions must belong to the official Federation of Lao Trade Unions. Strikes are not expressly prohibited, but workers rarely stage walkouts and do not have the right to bargain collectively. Laotian trade unions have little influence also because the vast majority of people are subsistence farmers and fishermen.

The courts are corrupt and are controlled by the LPRP. Long delays in court hearings are common, particularly for cases dealing with public grievances and complaints against government abuses. Security forces often illegally detain suspects, and some Laotians have allegedly spent more than a decade in jail without trial. Hundreds of political activists have also been held for months or years without trial. Prisoners are often tortured and must bribe prison officials to obtain better food, medicine, visits from family, and more humane treatment. The most recent controversy involves 16 men accused by the Laotian government of attacking a Thai-Laotian border checkpoint in July 2000. These men escaped to Thailand. In December 2003, a Thai appeals court threw out an extradition order from the Laotian government and ordered the men released within 48 hours. The United Nations High Commission on Refugees said these 16 men were eligible for consideration of asylum or resettlement in a third country. However, they were removed to a detention center, and the Thai government decided in July 2004 to repatriate them to Laos, where a local court handed them long prison sentences soon after their return.

Ordinary Laotians enjoy somewhat greater freedom in their daily lives today. Subsistence farmers and fishermen now work for themselves, and many also run small businesses or are employed by private enterprises. Government surveillance of the population has been scaled back in recent years but searches without warrants still occur.

Discrimination against members of minority tribes is common at many levels. An estimated 15,000 to 20,000 Laotian women and girls, mainly highland ethnic minorities, are trafficked each year for prostitution.

Latvia

Population: 2,300,000   **Political Rights:** 1
GNI/capita: $3,480   **Civil Liberties:** 2
Life Expectancy: 72   **Status:** Free
Religious Groups: Lutheran, Roman Catholic,
Russian Orthodox
Ethnic Groups: Latvian (57 percent), Russian (30 percent),
Byelorussian (4 percent), Ukrainian (3 percent), Polish (3 percent),
other (3 percent)
Capital: Riga

Ten-Year Ratings Timeline (Political Rights, Civil Liberties, Status)

1995	1996	1997	1998	1999	2000	2001	2002	2003	2004
2,2F	2,2F	1,2F	1,2F	1,2F	1,2F	1,2F	1,2F	1,2F	1,2F

Overview:

In 2004, Latvia accomplished two long-standing goals by joining NATO on April 2 and the European Union (EU) on May 1. The year was marked by significant political turbulence, as two coalition governments collapsed in an eight-month period. Elections to the European Parliament, held on July 13, drew only 41 percent of Latvian citizens to the polls and resulted in a resounding defeat for the governing coalition. In February, the parliament passed a law mandating Latvian as the primary language of instruction in all public schools; the ethnic Russian community protested the law. Relations with Moscow continued to deteriorate.

After having been ruled for centuries by Germany, Poland, Sweden, and Russia, Latvia gained its independence in 1918, only to be annexed by the U.S.S.R. during World War II. More than 50 years of Soviet occupation saw a massive influx of Russians and the deportation, execution, and emigration of tens of thousands of ethnic Latvians. In 1991, Latvia regained its independence in the wake of the disintegration of the Soviet Union.

In parliamentary elections held on October 5, 2002, the newly formed center-right New Era party, led by Einars Repse, garnered the most votes. Repse was named the new prime minister to lead a majority coalition government composed of the New Era party, Union of Greens and Farmers (ZZS), Latvia First Party (LFP), and For Fatherland and Freedom/LNNK (FF/LNNK). Latvia's Way, the longest-serving party in parliament, failed to win enough votes to enter the legislature. Voter turnout was estimated at more than 70 percent. Running unopposed, President Vaira Vike-Freiberga was reelected to a second four-year term in June 2003 by an overwhelming majority in the Latvian parliament.

Almost 73 percent of Latvian voters participated in a September 2003 referendum on EU accession, with 67 percent voting to join the body. Repse hailed the vote as one of the three most important events in the country's history, along with the brief spate of independence between the two world wars and the collapse of the U.S.S.R. in 1991. Shortly after referendum polling stations closed, however, deep fissures were exposed in Repse's coalition, most conspicuously over the appointment of the head of the new Corruption Prevention Bureau. Latvia became a member of NATO in April 2004 and the EU the following month.

Political tensions continued to fester in 2004, and in February, Repse and his ruling coalition resigned after the LFP withdrew its support of the government. Repse had sacked LFP leader and deputy prime minister Ainars Slesers a week earlier, after Slesers backed the establishment of a parliamentary committee to probe Repse's allegedly corrupt real estate purchases. In March, parliament voted in a new coalition government led by ZZS head Indulis Emsis, who become Europe's first ever Green prime minister. The coalition included the LFP, the People's Party, and one rebel New Era deputy. However, Emsis's government was forced to resign in October after parliament's rejection of its draft 2005 budget, regarded as a no-confidence vote by parliamentary rules. President Vaira Vike-Freiberga was scheduled to nominate a new prime minister in December 2004.

Only 41 percent of Latvian voters turned out for the country's first-ever elections to the European Parliament. Those who did vote issued a stern rebuke to the then-governing coalition by voting overwhelmingly for the conservative opposition. FF/LNNK garnered 29.8 percent of the vote and 4 of Latvia's 9 seats in the European Parliament, while New Era picked up 2 seats (19.7 percent) and Latvia's Way, 1 seat (6.5 percent). The People's Party, with 6.6 percent of the vote, was the only governing party to earn a seat. For Human Rights in a United Latvia, a leftist party supported by Latvia's ethnic Russian minority, also earned a seat, with 10.7 percent.

Latvian relations with Russia worsened in 2004, a situation exacerbated by the debate over the status of ethnic Russians in Latvia. In December 2003, a Latvia court decision finding 82-year-old former Soviet security agent Nikolai Tess guilty of genocide and crimes against humanity elicited condemnations from Moscow. Russian officials have repeatedly expressed their opposition to the new Latvian education language law and raised the issue with the Organization for Security and Cooperation in Europe, the EU, and the Council of Europe. Moscow has also considered economic sanctions and has already stopped sending crude oil through Latvia's pipeline system. In April, Riga expelled a Russian diplomat for allegedly trying to access NATO military secrets. The next month, the parliament voted to make public thousands of KGB files left in the country after the collapse of the Soviet Union, a controversial decision vociferously opposed by the Russian minority. Also in May, Repse joined the Estonian prime minister, Juhan Parts, in signing a declaration calling for the European Parliament to condemn the totalitarian Communist regimes of the Soviet era.

Political Rights and Civil Liberties: Latvians can change their government democratically. The constitution provides for a unicameral, 100-seat parliament (Saeima), whose members are elected for four-year terms by proportional representation, and who in turn select the country's president. The prime minister is nominated by the president and must be approved by an absolute parliamentary majority. According to international observers, the most recent national legislative elections in 2002 and the European Parliament elections on July 13, 2004, were free and fair.

Transparency International (TI) regularly cites Latvia as the most corrupt of the

Baltic states. Latvia was ranked 57 out of 146 countries surveyed in TI's 2004 Corruption Perceptions Index. The government, however, has adopted various anticorruption measures, including the establishment of a Corruption Prevention Bureau (KNAB) and laws to prevent conflict of interest among state officials. In January, parliament established a commission to investigate a series of then prime minister Repse's real estate purchases in 2003, allegedly financed by loans with artificially low interest rates. (LFP support for this investigation led to the resignation of Repse and his governing coalition.) In February, parliament voted unanimously to amend the political party funding law, disallowing corporate donations for politicians, setting a tight spending limit for preelection campaigns, and restricting private donations to funds acquired in the past three years. Nevertheless, in March the KNAB found 12 political parties guilty of finance violations and ordered them to transfer all dubious funds to the state treasury. After an almost two-year search fraught with political infighting, the parliament approved Alexei Loskutov as the head of the KNAB in May.

The government respects freedom of speech and the press. Private television and radio stations broadcast programs in both Latvian and Russian, and newspapers publish a wide range of political viewpoints. However, a recent survey by the Public Opinion Research Center revealed that only 24 percent of Latvians polled believed the press to be free, while 47 percent believed the Latvian press to be partially free and 10 percent considered it not free. Internet access is unrestricted.

Freedom of worship and academic freedom are generally respected. In February, the parliament passed the controversial Education Law mandating that at least 60 percent of public school classes be taught in Latvian, even in schools that cater to the approximately 120,000 ethnic Russian students. Having already provoked widespread protests from the Russian community when it was proposed, passage of the law sparked the largest demonstrations in Latvia since independence. On May 1, the day of Latvian accession to the EU, at least 20,000 ethnic Russians marched peacefully through Riga in opposition to the law.

Freedom of assembly and association is protected by law, and gatherings occur without governmental interference. Generally, the government does not restrict the activities of nongovernmental organizations. Workers have the right to establish trade unions, strike, and engage in collective bargaining. However, only 17 percent of the workforce is unionized.

While the government generally respects constitutional provisions for an independent judiciary, reform of the courts has been slow and judges continue to be inadequately trained and prone to corruption. Severe backlogs in the court system have led to lengthy delays in reviewing cases and to lengthy pretrial detention for large numbers of persons. However, the government has taken significant steps to address these problems. According to the U.S. State Department's 2004 Country Report on Human Rights Practices, a clear majority of criminal cases were adjudicated within three months, and 80.5 percent were adjudicated within six months. Incarceration facilities remain severely overcrowded, and cases of excessive force by security officials have been reported. A reformed criminal code is awaiting parliamentary approval.

Naturalization applications have increased significantly since accession to the EU, and the government has actively promoted the process by reducing financial and lingual requirements. Nearly one-fifth of Latvia's residents are noncitizens. Latvia's citizenship laws have been criticized for disenfranchising those who immigrated to Latvia during the Soviet period and who must now apply for citizenship, the majority of whom are ethnic Russians. Noncitizens are barred from participating in state and local elections and from holding some civil service jobs. They are also not allowed to hold some private sector jobs; for example, jobs as lawyers, notaries, and commercial pilots. Alleged political, social, and economic discrimination suffered by the Russian-speaking community is a subject of much debate both in Latvia and the wider region. In December 2003, the European Court of Human Rights charged Riga with restricting the rights of an ethnic Russian family and ordered the state to pay compensation of 20,000 euros, forcing the Supreme Court to review a previous expulsion order.

Women possess the same legal rights as men, although they frequently face hiring and pay discrimination. Trafficking in persons, mostly women in the sex industry, is a problem, and the government has undertaken an increasingly robust effort to address it.

Lebanon

Population: 4,500,000   **Political Rights:** 6
GNI/capita: $3,990   **Civil Liberties:** 5
Life Expectancy: 73   **Status:** Not Free
Religious Groups: Muslim [Mostly Shi'a] (60 percent),
Christian (39 percent), other (1 percent)
Ethnic Groups: Arab (95 percent), Armenian (4 percent),
other (1 percent)
Capital: Beirut

Ten-Year Ratings Timeline (Political Rights, Civil Liberties, Status)

1995	1996	1997	1998	1999	2000	2001	2002	2003	2004
6,5NF	6,5NF	6,5NF	6,5NF	6,5NF	6,5NF	6,5NF	6,5NF	6,5NF	6,5NF

Overview:
The year 2004 witnessed the rapid and decisive erosion of tacit international support for Syria's control of Lebanon, culminating in an unprecedented UN Security Council resolution calling for the immediate departure of Syrian forces. While the unconstitutional extension of Lebanese president Emile Lahoud's tenure in September underscored that Syrian resolve to continue dominating its smaller neighbor had not wavered, the rapid growth of a broad-based, pro-democracy movement during the year, fed by a steady stream of defections within the country's once-quiescent postwar governing elite, left the world's sole remaining satellite state teetering on the brink of political collapse.

For more than a thousand years, the rough terrain of Mount Lebanon attracted Christian and heterodox-Muslim minorities fleeing persecution in the predominantly Sunni Muslim Arab world. After centuries of European protection and relative autonomy under Turkish rule, Mount Lebanon and its surrounding areas were established as a French mandate in 1920. After winning its independence in 1943, the new state of Lebanon maintained a precarious democratic system based on the division of parliamentary seats, high political offices, and senior administrative positions among the country's 17 officially recognized sectarian communities. As emigration transformed Lebanon's slight Christian majority into a minority, Muslim leaders demanded amendments to the fixed 6 to 5 ratio of Christian-to-Muslim parliamentary seats and to exclusive Maronite Christian control of the presidency. In 1975, war erupted between a coalition of Lebanese Muslim and leftist militias aligned with Palestinian guerrilla groups on one side and an array of Christian militias bent on preserving Christian political privileges on the other.

After the first few years of fighting, a loose consensus emerged among Lebanese politicians regarding a new power-sharing arrangement. However, following the entry of Syrian and Israeli troops into Lebanon in 1976 and 1978, the various militias and their foreign backers had little interest in disarming. The civil war lost much of its sectarian character over the next decade, with the bloodiest outbreaks of fighting taking place mainly within the Shiite, Christian, and Palestinian communities. Outside forces played a more direct role in the fighting. The Syrians battled Israeli forces in 1982, attacked a Palestinian-Islamist coalition in the mid-1980s, and fought the Lebanese army in 1989 and 1990, while the Israelis combated Palestinian and Shiite groups.

In 1989, the surviving members of Lebanon's 1972 parliament convened in Taif, Saudi Arabia, and agreed to a plan put forward by the Arab League that weakened the presidency, established equality in Christian and Muslim parliamentary representation, and mandated close security cooperation with occupying Syrian troops. After the ouster of General Michel Aoun from East Beirut by Syrian forces in October 1990, a new Syrian-backed government extended its writ throughout most of the country.

In the years that followed, Syria consolidated its control over Lebanese state institutions, particularly the presidency, the judiciary, and the security forces. However, in return for tacit Western acceptance of its control of Lebanon, Damascus permitted a degree of political and civil liberties in Lebanon that exceeded those in most other Arab countries. While those who openly condemned the occupation risked arbitrary arrest and imprisonment, criticism of the government was largely tolerated. The motley assortment of militia chiefs, traditional elites, and nouveaux riches who held civilian political positions in postwar Lebanon were persuaded to accept continued Syrian hegemony, primarily through a system of institutionalized corruption fueled by massive deficit spending on reconstruction during the 1990s. By the end of the decade, Lebanon's government debt far exceeded its gross domestic product and the economy was in deep recession. Consequentially, public disaffection with the postwar political establishment rose to an all-time high and demonstrations against the occupation, primarily by secular nationalist university students, grew steadily in size and frequency.

In 2000, following the death of Syrian president Hafez Assad and Israel's withdrawal from south Lebanon (which invalidated a frequently cited official rationale for the occupation), vocal opposition to the Syrian presence rapidly spread from university campuses to the editorial pages of leading Lebanese newspapers and began to span the political and sectarian spectrum. After the September 2001 terrorist attacks on the United States, Western pressure to preserve civil liberties subsided for a time, in exchange for Syrian and Lebanese cooperation in the war against al-Qaeda (the terrorist network), and the Lebanese authorities cracked down harshly on dissent. In 2002, the government closed an independent television station that had given voice to political dissidents, invalidated an opposition victory in a parliamentary by-election, and placed several leading opposition figures under investigation for alleged ties to Israel and other foreign powers. At the end of the year, many Lebanese political leaders who had joined the opposition were inching their way back into Syria's political fold.

In 2003, as Syrian-American relations rapidly deteriorated amid allegations of Syrian meddling in Iraq, the U.S. government began openly criticizing the Syrian occupation of Lebanon, a policy reversal that inspired the opposition movement in Lebanon to reassert itself. By early 2004, France had also ended its official silence on the occupation and both Western powers were openly calling for a Syrian withdrawal, leading most other European governments to follow suit. Defying these calls, Damascus moved to consolidate its control by pressing the Lebanese parliament to approve a constitutional amendment extending (on dubious legal ground) the tenure of President Lahoud, a staunch Syrian ally, beyond his six-year term. In September, on the eve of the parliamentary vote, the UN Security Council approved a resolution calling for a constitutional presidential election and the withdrawal of all foreign forces. Syria's decision to push ahead with the amendment provoked an unprecedented international outcry and veiled threats by Western governments to take "further measures."

Inspired by the international community's long overdue attention to Lebanon, many politicians who had long been loyal to Syria began defecting to the opposition. In October, former minister for economy and trade Marwan Hamadeh was severely wounded by a car bomb just weeks after resigning in protest over the extension of Lahoud's term in office—an attack that dampened public calls for a Syrian withdrawal within the political elite, but failed to subjugate it. Three weeks later, Prime Minister Rafiq Hariri resigned. A new cabinet of staunchly pro-Syrian loyalists, headed by Omar Karami, was narrowly approved with only 59 out of 128 votes in parliament (23 members abstained).

Notwithstanding the multitude of factors that skew the electoral process in favor of candidates backed by Damascus, opposition leaders remained confident at year's end that this "rump" pro-Syrian coalition will face a resounding defeat in the spring 2005 parliamentary elections.

Political Rights and Civil Liberties:

The Lebanese people cannot change their government democratically. The president is formally selected every six years by the 128-member parliament. In practice, however, this choice is made after Syrian authorization, known as "the password" in the Lebanese media. Many members of parliament who had publicly declared their opposition to an extension of President Emile Lahoud's term in office (including Prime Minister Rafiq Hariri, who famously remarked in 2003 that he would rather shoot himself) were pressured by Damascus to vote for it in September 2004.

Syria and its allies also influence parliamentary and municipal elections more indirectly. The distribution of parliamentary seats is skewed in favor of regions where Syrian forces have been stationed the longest, such as the Beqaa Valley, and electoral districts are blatantly gerrymandered to ensure the election of pro-Syrian politicians. There has also been widespread interference during the elections themselves, with Lebanese security forces often present inside the polls. Prior to a June 2002 parliamentary by-election, Interior Minister Elias Murr declared that using voting booth curtains to ensure secrecy was "optional," a remarkably blatant move to facilitate vote buying.

Political corruption in Lebanon is widely considered to be the most egregious in the Arab world. Lebanon was ranked 97 out of 146 countries surveyed in Transparency International's 2004 Corruption Perceptions Index.

Freedom of expression is limited in some critical respects, but is far more substantial than elsewhere in the Arab world. Lebanon has a long tradition of press freedom, though nearly all media outlets are owned by prominent political and commercial elites. Five independent television stations and more than 30 independent radio stations operate in Lebanon, as well as dozens of independent print publications, reflecting a diverse range of views.

A number of vaguely worded laws criminalize critical reporting on Syria, the Lebanese military, the security forces, the judiciary, and the presidency. Although journalists are frequently questioned and occasionally indicted for such infractions, imprisonment of journalists is uncommon; most, however, practice some degree of self-censorship. Permanent closures of licensed media outlets were rare until 2002, when the authorities closed Murr Television (MTV), a station sympathetic to the opposition. The closing generated palpable anxiety among media owners of all political persuasions. In December 2003, the owner of New Television (NTV) was arrested and briefly detained. In July 2004, a reporter for NTV discovered three hand grenades, and a death threat warning him to stop reporting, on the windshield of his car.

The General Security Directorate (GSD) has the authority to censor all foreign magazines and non-periodical media. In September, authorities pulled a best-selling American novel, *The Da Vinci Code*, by Dan Brown, from shelves after Christian religious leaders objected to the book. In March, the GSD pressured popular Lebanese singer Najwa Karam to cut out portions of a music video that showed footage of clashes between security forces and student demonstrators. Internet access is not restricted.

Freedom of religion is guaranteed in the Lebanese constitution and protected in practice, though sectarianism is formally enshrined in the political system. Religious leaders frequently come under political pressure from Syrian officials in Lebanon. Shortly before the parliament voted on Lahoud's term extension in 2004, according to the U.S. State Department's annual report on human rights practices in Lebanon, Syrian officials pressured Lebanese clerics to delete from an official press release a clause calling for respect for the constitution.

Academic freedom is long-standing and firmly entrenched. The country's universities are the region's most open and vibrant.

Freedom of association and assembly is restricted. Although political parties are legal, a 1994 ban on the Christian Lebanese Forces (LF) party remains in place. Nongovernmental organizations, including human rights groups, are permitted to operate openly, though the authorities occasionally impose ad hoc restrictions. In

June, security officials pressured the owner of a Beirut hotel to back out of hosting a major pro-democracy gathering. Public demonstrations are not permitted without prior approval from the Interior Ministry, which does not rule according to uniform standards, and security forces routinely beat and arrest those who demonstrate against the Syrian occupation. Police and army troops forcibly dispersed several peaceful demonstrations in 2004 and briefly detained dozens of protestors during the year.

All workers except those in government may establish unions, and all have the right to strike and to bargain collectively. Several major strikes occurred in 2004. In May, Lebanese soldiers opened fire on a demonstration called by the General Confederation of Labor to protest fuel price increases, killing five people. Forty-eight people were arrested on charges of inciting a riot and sentenced to short prison terms. In October, two postal service employees were fired for involvement in union activities.

The judiciary is strongly influenced by Syria, which directly appoints key prosecutors and investigating magistrates. Consequentially, trials of dissidents are heavily tainted by political pressure, and acts of violence by Syrian-backed groups in Lebanon are rarely investigated. The judicial system consists of civilian courts, a military court, and a judicial council. International standards of criminal procedure are not observed in the military court, which consists largely of military officers with no legal training, and cases are often tried in a matter of minutes. In recent years, the nominally independent Beirut Bar Association (BBA) has become less willing to confront the judiciary, allegedly because of widespread corruption.

Arbitrary arrest and detention by Lebanese security forces (and, occasionally, Syrian troops and Syrian-backed paramilitary groups) are commonplace, and the use of torture to extract confessions is widespread. According to a 2004 report by Lebanon's Parliamentary Commission on Human Rights, there are more than 1,500 people in prison who have never been convicted of a crime. In July, the militant Shiite organization Hezbollah seized a resident of Nabatieh, Fouad Mazraani, on charges of "collaborating with Israel" and held him for at least a week before turning him over to the authorities. Dozens of Islamist militants were arrested during the year on national security grounds. One of them, the leader of an alleged al-Qaeda cell, Ismail al-Khatib, died in the custody of security forces shortly after his arrest in September. It is widely known that the Syrian-controlled security agencies monitor the telephones of both cabinet ministers and political dissidents.

Nearly 350,000 Palestinian refugees living in Lebanon are denied citizenship rights and face restrictions on working, building homes, and purchasing property—restrictions that reflect Lebanese sensitivities about the impact of mostly Muslim Palestinian assimilation on the country's precarious sectarian balance.

Women enjoy many of the same rights as men, but suffer social and some legal discrimination. Since family and personal status matters are adjudicated by the religious authorities of each sectarian community, Muslim women are subject to discriminatory laws governing marriage, divorce, inheritance, and child custody. Women are under-represented in politics, holding only three parliamentary seats (and, until the appointment of two female ministers in October, no cabinet positions), and do not receive equal social security provisions. Men convicted of so-called honor crimes against women usually receive lenient sentences. Foreign domestic workers are routinely exploited and physically abused by employers.

Lesotho

Population: 1,800,000   **Political Rights:** 2
GNI/capita: $550   **Civil Liberties:** 3
Life Expectancy: 38   **Status:** Free
Religious Groups: Christian (80 percent), indigenous
beliefs (20 percent)
Ethnic Groups: Sotho (99.7 percent), other [including
European and Asian] (0.3 percent)
Capital: Maseru

Ten-Year Ratings Timeline (Political Rights, Civil Liberties, Status)

1995	1996	1997	1998	1999	2000	2001	2002	2003	2004
4,4PF	4,4PF	4,4PF	4,4PF	4,4PF	4,4PF	4,4PF	2,3F	2,3F	2,3F

Overview:
The tiny mountain kingdom of Lesotho faced its third year
of drought and poor harvests in 2004, with half a million
people remaining reliant on food aid through November.

Lesotho's status as a British protectorate saved it from incorporation into South
Africa. King Moshoeshoe II reigned from independence in 1966 until the installation of his son as King Letsie III in a 1990 military coup. Democratic elections in 1993
did not lead to stability. After violent military infighting, assassinations, and a suspension of constitutional rule in 1994, King Letsie III abdicated to allow his father's
reinstatement. He resumed the throne following the accidental death of his father in
January 1996.

In 1998, troops from South Africa and Botswana were sent to this mountain
kingdom at the request of Prime Minster Pakalitha Mosisili, under the mandate of
the 14-country Southern African Development Community (SADC), to quell army-
backed violence and a potential overthrow of the government. The violence was
touched off by the results of National Assembly elections. Although international
observers described the voting as free and fair, the appearance of irregularities and
the absence of opposition voices in government prompted demonstrators to reject
the results that gave the ruling Lesotho Congress for Democracy (LCD) 79 of 80
National Assembly seats. At least 100 people were reportedly killed before order
was restored. An agreement, drafted by the Commonwealth in 1998, allowed the
elected, but highly unpopular, government to retain power, but stipulated that new
elections be supervised by an independent election commission.

The 2002 legislative election was marked by a turnout of 68 percent. The ruling
LCD captured 55 percent of votes cast, winning 77 of 78 constituency seats. The
Lesotho People's Congress (LPC) won one seat. There are 80 constituency seats,
but elections in two constituencies failed. The Basotho National Party (BNP) won
22 of the 40 seats chosen by proportional representation, while the National Independent Party won 5 and the LPC won 4. Smaller parties won the remainder. The BNP
assumed its seats but has refused to formally accept the election results, filing numerous legal challenges and boycotting several by-elections.

After the Canadian construction conglomerate Acres International was convicted in September 2002 in Lesotho's High Court for corrupt practices in a multibillion-dollar dam and watershed project, the World Bank banned the company from new contracts for a three-year period. Other multinational companies also face possible sanctions from the bank.

Lesotho's 2003 winter harvest failed, and rains in early 2004 came too late to save the maize crop, estimated at 68 percent below average. Drought has plagued the country since 2001. Following the food security crisis and a dramatic rise in HIV/AIDS cases, the government declared a state of emergency in February 2004.

Entirely surrounded by South Africa, Lesotho is highly dependent on its powerful neighbor. Its economy is sustained by remittances from its many citizens who work in South African mines. Retrenchments at the mines, however, have contributed to high unemployment in Lesotho. Increased growth in the textile industry has party offset these losses, although some 40 percent of the population remains in absolute poverty. Lesotho's economic problems are compounded by one of the world's highest HIV/AIDS rates, which has lowered average life expectancy to less than 38 years.

Political Rights and Civil Liberties:

The people of Lesotho are guaranteed the right to change their leaders through free and fair elections. The mixed-member voting system introduced in the May 2002 parliamentary elections expanded the number of National Assembly seats by 40, to 120. The additional seats were chosen by proportional representation, while the others continued to be chosen by the first-past-the-post system of awarding seats to whoever gets the most votes. The Senate, the upper house of the bicameral legislature, includes royal appointees and Lesotho's 22 principal traditional chiefs, who still wield considerable authority in rural areas. Any elected government's exercise of its constitutional authority remains limited by the autonomy of the military, the royal family, and traditional clan structures. Parliamentary elections take place every five years. Under the constitution, the leader of the majority party in the Assembly automatically becomes prime minister.

Lesotho was not ranked by Transparency International in its 2004 Corruption Perceptions Index. However, the government has aggressively pursued criminal charges against state officials and multinational corporations engaging in corrupt practices, as seen in the landmark trials connected to the Lesotho Highlands Water Project.

The government generally respects freedom of speech and the press, but journalists have suffered occasional harassment or attack. The several independent newspapers routinely criticize the government. There are four private radio stations, and extensive South African radio and television broadcasts reach Lesotho.

Freedom of religion in this predominantly Christian country is generally respected. The government does not restrict academic freedom.

Freedom of assembly and association is generally respected, and several nongovernmental organizations operate openly. While labor rights are constitutionally guaranteed, the labor and trade union movement is weak and fragmented. Approximately 10 percent of the country's labor force is unionized. Of the remainder, most are engaged in subsistence agriculture or employed in South African mines.

Courts are nominally independent, but higher courts are especially subject to outside influence. The large backlog of cases often leads to lengthy delays in trials. Mistreatment of civilians by security forces reportedly continues. Prisons are dilapidated and severely overcrowded, and lack essential health services. Between 2001 and 2003, 90 prisoners died at Lesotho's biggest prison, according to a government commission of inquiry.

The textile industry has become crucial to the economy as a result of the U.S.'s African Growth and Opportunity Act. The industry now provides nearly half of all foreign exchange and has attracted foreign investors, notably Taiwan, which employs an estimated 25 percent of all workers. In May, Lesotho successfully lobbied the United States to extend the preferential trade regime until 2015.

The constitution bars gender-based discrimination, but customary practice and law still restrict women's rights in several areas, including property rights and inheritance. Lesotho's constitution perpetuates the minority status of Basotho women married under customary law. A woman is considered a legal minor while her husband is alive. Domestic violence is reportedly widespread but is becoming increasingly socially unacceptable. Women's rights organizations have highlighted the importance of women's participation in the democratic process as part of a broader effort to educate women about their rights under customary and common law. Out of 120 parliamentary seats, just 13 are held by women.

Liberia

Population: 3,500,000
GNI/capita: $140
Life Expectancy: 42
Religious Groups: Indigenous beliefs (40 percent), Christian (40 percent), Muslim (20 percent)
Ethnic Groups: Indigenous tribes (95 percent), other [including Americo-Liberians] (5 percent)
Capital: Monrovia

Political Rights: 5*
Civil Liberties: 4*
Status: Partly Free

Ratings Change: Liberia's political rights rating improved from 6 to 5, its civil liberties rating from 6 to 4, and its status from Not Free to Partly Free, due to greater political freedom brought about through the broad-based, transitional government, and to improvements in press freedom and human rights.

Ten-Year Ratings Timeline (Political Rights, Civil Liberties, Status)

1995	1996	1997	1998	1999	2000	2001	2002	2003	2004
7,6NF	7,6NF	4,5PF	4,5PF	4,5PF	5,6PF	6,5PF	6,6NF	6,6NF	5,4PF

Overview:

Political freedoms expanded in Liberia in 2004 as officials of the country's Transitional National Government were making preparations to hold elections in October 2005, and former president Charles Taylor remained living in exile in Nigeria. Press freedom and other civil liberties also improved compared with the previous year. Sporadic rioting broke out in Liberia's capital, Monrovia, during the year.

Liberia was settled in 1821 by freed slaves from the United States and became an independent republic in 1847. Americo-Liberians, descendants of the freed slaves, dominated the country until 1980, when army sergeant Samuel Doe led a bloody coup and murdered President William Tolbert. Doe's regime concentrated power among members of his Krahn ethnic group and suppressed others. Forces led by Taylor, a former government minister, and backed by Gio and Mano ethnic groups that had been subjected to severe repression, launched a guerrilla war from neighboring Cote d'Ivoire against the Doe regime on Christmas Eve 1989. In 1990, Nigeria, under the aegis of the Economic Community of West African States (ECOWAS), led an armed intervention force, preventing Taylor from seizing the capital but failing to protect Doe from being captured and tortured to death by a splinter rebel group. A peace accord in 1996 led to elections in 1997 that Taylor won.

The peace accord, however, was not entirely effective. Long-standing grievances were not resolved, and Taylor made little effort to seek genuine reconciliation. Many of his rivals were forced to flee the country. Some formed the rebel Liberians United for Reconciliation and Democracy (LURD) and used neighboring Guinea as a staging ground from which to launch their rebellion against Taylor. With rebels poised to overrun the capital and the United States calling for him to step down, Taylor resigned in August 2003 and accepted Nigeria's offer of asylum.

Taylor's departure from Liberia almost immediately stopped the war. ECOWAS helped negotiate an end to the fighting between Taylor's forces, LURD, and the rebel Movement for Democracy in Liberia (MODEL). The West African peacekeepers became part of a 15,000-strong UN-led force that is overseeing disarmament and demobilization. Human rights abuses abated following the ceasefire, but some violations have continued, especially in the countryside.

Delegates to the peace talks in 2003 chose businessman Gyude Bryant as Liberia's interim president. The delegates allocated posts in the transitional parliament to the former ruling National Patriotic Party (NPP), LURD, MODEL, other political parties, and civil society groups. Under the terms of the peace deal, the NPP and the two rebel groups could each name five ministers to the cabinet.

Fourteen years of intermittent civil war in Liberia brought fighting to three neighboring countries and claimed 200,000 lives in Liberia alone. Peacekeeping troops have been deployed to neighboring Sierra Leone and Cote d'Ivoire, as fighters have routinely crossed the borders into those two countries, as well as into Guinea. Liberia lacks electricity, running water, a functioning educational system, and proper medical facilities. More than 80,000 people turned up at disarmament and demobilization sites in 2004, but many of them lacked a weapon; the former fighters receive a payment of $300 as part of the demobilization process. Rioting broke out at least three times in Monrovia between December 2003 and October 2004, and a riot in October claimed at least 14 lives and turned into clashes between Christians and Muslims.

Members of a spectrum of political parties now operate openly and freely in Liberia. There were no political prisoners at the end of 2004, unlike in previous years. Freedom of assembly is respected, and political discourse has replaced armed conflict. A National Election Commission was laying the foundation for polls to be held in 2005. The legislative branch of government operated with much greater independence from the executive branch in 2005 compared with previous years under Taylor.

Press freedom improved in 2004, and journalists faced far less harassment than they had during Taylor's administration. Private radio stations began broadcasting, including the shortwave radio station of the Roman Catholic Church in Liberia, Radio Veritas.

A team from the IMF, the World Bank, and the U.S. Treasury warned the transitional government in October 2004 that it must account for public funds in a more transparent manner if the UN is to lift sanctions on timber and diamond exports, and if donors are to release funds for the country's reconstruction. The sanctions had been imposed to prevent the former Taylor government from using the resources to finance arms purchases in violation of a UN arms embargo. In October, the transitional government froze the assets of several relatives and former associates of Taylor, an action the UN Security Council had urged in March.

Political Rights and Civil Liberties: Citizens of Liberia cannot change their government democratically. President Charles Taylor and his party assumed power after the 1997 elections. The votes for the presidency and the National Assembly, on the basis of proportional representation, were held under provisions of the 1986 constitution. The polls constituted Liberia's most genuine electoral exercise in decades but were conducted in an atmosphere of intimidation. Taylor's victory was more reflective of a vote for peace than for a particular ideology, as many people believed that the only way to stop the war was to elect him as president. After Taylor fled to Nigeria in August 2003, a transitional government was installed to lead the country to elections in 2005.

Liberia was not ranked in Transparency International's 2004 Corruption Perceptions Index. International lending institutions have urged the transitional government to crack down on corruption and operate with more transparency to secure donor funding.

Liberia's independent media have survived at the cost of extensive self-censorship. Employees have suffered from constant surveillance, harassment, threats, detentions, and beatings. Criminal charges were brought against journalists working for the private weekly newspaper *Telegraph* in January. Editor in chief Philip Moore Jr., managing editor Adolphus Karnuah, and subeditor Robert Kpadeh Jr. were charged with "criminal malevolence" in connection with a story alleging that the country's national security minister embezzled about $15,000; they were released the same day. Internet access is not impeded, but Liberia suffers from poor communications infrastructure.

Press freedom improved markedly in 2004 compared with the situation in the previous year. Several private newspapers are published, and there are at least five new FM radio stations, including Radio Veritas, the shortwave station of the Roman Catholic Church.

Religious freedom is respected in practice, but Muslims have been targeted because many Mandingos, who were a key ethnic component of the rebel group LURD, follow Islam. Religious freedom suffered a setback in October when a property dispute that triggered rioting in Monrovia dissolved into religious fighting. Several churches and mosques were attacked. Authorities arrested up to 250 people in connection with the violence, which claimed about 14 lives. The unrest was the worst seen in the city since Taylor was forced into exile in 2003.

Academic freedom was restricted under the Taylor government, as students feared expressing political views opposed to the government. Exiled student leaders returned to the country after the transitional government was installed. Security forces were sent to the University of Liberia in Monrovia in March after students protested the school's continued closure.

Numerous civil society groups, including human rights organizations, operate in the country. Human rights workers have been allowed access to prisons, where conditions are harsh and torture is used to extract confessions. The transitional government generally respects freedom of assembly. There were reports of brutality by police and members of the UN peacekeeping force during violent demonstrations in Monrovia in 2004. The right to strike, organize, and bargain collectively is permitted by law, but there is little union activity because of the lack of economic activity. Two umbrella unions cover some 60,000 workers, but most of them are unemployed. Forced labor exists in rural areas, and child labor is widespread.

The judiciary is subject to executive influence, corruption, and intimidation by security forces, which operate with impunity. International human rights groups have urged Nigeria to hand Taylor over to the UN-backed Special Court for Sierra Leone, which has indicted him for war crimes linked to his alleged involvement in the arms-for-diamonds trade that helped sustain Sierra Leone's civil war. Liberia's Justice Ministry in October froze the assets of several Taylor associates and relatives in line with a UN resolution. The Supreme Court ordered the suspension of the sanctions against two associates after their lawyers argued that only the courts had the authority to impose such measures. Prison conditions are harsh and sometimes life threatening. However, there was no evidence that the government operated unofficial detention facilities where prisoners were tortured, as in previous years. Arbitrary detention and brutality by the police, former members of Taylor's security forces, and former rebel groups are problems. Violations were less frequent in 2004 than in previous years.

Societal ethnic discrimination is rife, and the Taylor government discriminated against indigenous ethnic groups that opposed Taylor during the civil war, especially the Mandingo and Krahn ethnic groups. Ethnic clashes erupted sporadically during 2004.

Treatment of women varies by ethnic group, religion, and social status. Many women continue to suffer from physical abuse and traditional societal discrimination, despite constitutionally guaranteed equality. Rape, including gang rape, was rampant during the civil war. Women and girls were often abducted as laborers and sex slaves, while others joined rebel groups or militias to protect themselves.

Libya

Population: 5,600,000
GNI/capita: $5,944
Life Expectancy: 76
Religious Groups: Sunni Muslim (97 percent),
other (3 percent)
Ethnic Groups: Arab-Berber (97 percent), other [including
Greek, Italian, Egyptian, Pakistani, Turkish, Indian] (3 percent)
Capital: Tripoli

Political Rights: 7
Civil Liberties: 7
Status: Not Free

Ten-Year Ratings Timeline (Political Rights, Civil Liberties, Status)

1995	1996	1997	1998	1999	2000	2001	2002	2003	2004
7,7NF	7,7NF	7,7NF	7,7NF	7,7NF	7,7NF	7,7NF	7,7NF	7,7NF	7,7NF

Overview:

Although Libyan leader Colonel Mu'ammar al-Qadhafi introduced sweeping changes in 2004 with the aim of enabling the country to join the international community, these did not translate into reforms that affected political rights and civil liberties. Nevertheless, his announcement in 2003 to abandon weapons of mass destruction and his subsequent cooperation with international arms inspectors have earned him international favor and, this year, an end to U.S. trade and diplomatic sanctions. Libya also agreed to pay $35 million in compensation to victims of a Berlin nightclub bombing 18 years ago, blamed on Libya's intelligence agents. A number of Western countries established economic ties with the oil-rich state, and European leaders paid visits to the once-ostracized country, while oil companies announced their return to Libya.

Following centuries of Ottoman rule, Libya became an Italian colony after an invasion in 1912. French and British forces occupied Libya during World War II. The country's independence dates to 1951, when King Idris assumed power following a UN resolution establishing Libya as an independent and sovereign state.

In 1969, Qadhafi, at the age of 25, seized power in a military coup that deposed the staunchly pro-West King Idris. Qadhafi railed against Western control of Libya's oil fields and the presence of foreign military bases in Libya. He ushered in a highly personalized style of rule that combines elements of pan-Arabism with Islamic ideals and rejects both Western-style democracy and communism.

In the years following Qadhafi's rise to power, Libya became a pariah state with its sponsorship of various acts of terrorism, as well as its support of insurgencies throughout sub-Saharan Africa. Libyan involvement in the 1988 bombing of Pan Am flight 103 over Lockerbie, Scotland, led to UN sanctions on Libya in 1992, including an air embargo and a ban on the import of arms and oil production equipment. The United States had maintained its own sanctions against Libya since 1981, citing Libyan sponsorship of terrorism.

In 1999, Qadhafi embarked on a strategy to end Libya's international isolation. He surrendered two Libyan nationals suspected in the Pan Am 103 bombing and agreed to compensate families of victims of the 1989 bombing of a French airliner over Niger. The Libyan government also accepted responsibility for the 1984 death of British police officer Yvonne Fletcher, killed by shots fired from the Libyan Embassy in London.

In response, the United Nations suspended sanctions against Libya in 1999, and the United States eased some trade restrictions. Britain re-opened its embassy in Tripoli in March 2001. The European Union (EU) followed suit by lifting sanctions, but maintained an arms embargo.

The two Pan Am terrorism suspects went on trial in March 2000 at the International Court of Justice in The Netherlands, but under Scottish law. One of the suspects was found guilty of murder and sentenced to life imprisonment in January 2001, while the other suspect was acquitted and freed. In August 2003, the Libyan government offered to pay $2.7 billion in compensation to the families of the Pan Am bombing victims, roughly $10 million for each family. In response, the United Nations lifted sanctions on Libya. French families of the victims of the 1989 UTA airliner bombing over Niger sought a higher compensation package than that offered.

In 2004, Libya agreed to increase the UTA compensation to $170 million, about $1 million per family, and to pay $35 million to relatives of the victims of a 1986 attack on a discotheque in West Berlin. Qadhafi flew to Brussels in April 2004—his first visit to Europe in 15 years—for preliminary talks on joining an EU-Mediterranean association agreement. British Prime Minister Tony Blair, Italian Prime Minister Silvio Berlusconi, and French President Jacques Chirac were among European dignitaries who visited Libya in 2004. In September, pressured by Italy to help Libya control illegal migrants crossing over to Europe from its shores, the EU agreed to lift its arms embargo on Tripoli.

In response to Libya's decision in December 2003 to renounce weapons of mass destruction, Washington suspended trade and economic sanctions against Libya in April 2004, and the U.S. Assistant Secretary of State for Near East Affairs, William Burns, visited Tripoli, in the first visit by a U.S. government official in more than 30 years. The United States lifted the sanctions in September, and a White House statement said Libya had removed virtually all of its declared nuclear weapons program, destroyed its chemical munitions, and provided "excellent cooperation and support" to international inspectors. Tripoli had threatened to cancel its Pan Am payments unless sanctions were lifted by mid-September. The change allowed U.S. oil companies to do business in Libya and ended a travel ban on Americans. The United States, however, kept Libya on the list of countries supporting terrorism, maintaining a ban on military-related exports and on full resumption of diplomatic ties. Reports in 2004 of Libyan involvement in an assassination plot against Saudi Arabia's Crown Prince Abdullah and of its support of a foiled coup attempt in Mauritania raised concerns in Washington; Libya has denied both accusations.

Despite its oil wealth, the Libyan economy remained hobbled by its years of isolation and corruption. Libya introduced wide-ranging economic reforms in 2003, liberalizing the exchange rate, privatizing companies, and opening up the country to foreign investment. In 2004, the government announced plans to cut $5 billion worth of subsidies in fuel, food, and electricity as part of its liberalization drive. Tripoli has also introduced a transparent bidding process for foreign oil companies seeking exploration rights in the country and offshore.

Political Rights and Civil Liberties: Despite recent dramatic diplomatic developments, Libyans still cannot change their government democratically, and Colonel Mu'ammar al-Qadhafi rules by decree with little accountability or transparency. Libya is officially known as a *jamahiriyah*, or state of the masses, conceived as a system of direct government through popular organs at all levels of society. In reality, an elaborate structure of revolutionary committees and people's committees serves as a tool of repression. Real power rests with Qadhafi and a small group of close associates who appoint civil and military officials at every level. Libya's governing principles stem from Qadhafi's Green Book, a treatise that combines Islamic ideals with elements of socialism and pan-Arabism.

Libyans do not have the right to organize into different political parties. Extra-governmental bodies, including the revolutionary committees and people's committees, serve as tools of repression, and the multiple security services rely on an extensive network of informers.

Libya was among the poorest performing countries in the 2004 annual report by the corruption watchdog group Transparency International, which ranked Libya 108 of 146 countries surveyed.

Free media do not exist in Libya. The government severely limits freedom of speech and of the press, particularly any criticism of Qadhafi, and in 2004 suspended the publication of a number of papers and banned the distribution of a magazine from Egypt. The state owns and controls all print and broadcast media outlets, and thereby maintains a monopoly on the flow of information. Satellite television is widely available, although foreign programming is censored at times. Internet access increased in 2004.

The government restricts religious freedom and controls mosques and Islamic institutions. It is tolerant of other faiths and allows Christian churches to operate openly, according to the U.S. State Department's 2004 International Religious Freedom Report.

The government restricts academic freedom, and professors and teachers who discuss politically sensitive issues face the risk of reprisals.

Freedom of assembly is severely restricted, as are the rights to hold public demonstrations and open public discussions. The government prohibits the right to form independent trade unions and professional associations, but workers can join the National Trade Unions federation, a quasi-governmental body.

The judiciary is not independent. Security forces have the power to pass sentence without a trial. Special People's Courts and the government have used summary judicial proceedings to suppress domestic dissent. Political trials are held in secret. Arbitrary arrest and torture are commonplace. In May 2004, a criminal court sentenced five Bulgarian nurses and a Palestinian doctor to death by firing squad after convicting them of deliberately contaminating some 400 hospital children with AIDS. The six medics, who are appealing the verdict, said they were tortured in order to extract a confession, which they later retracted in court. Amnesty International highlighted the case of Fathi al-Jahmi, a member of the General People's Congress, Libya's indirectly elected legislative branch, who was arrested and sentenced to one year in jail for demanding democratic reforms. He was released in March 2004, but was beaten after he gave interviews to Arabic satellite channels. Subsequently, he and his immediate family disappeared. The case of some 150 alleged members of the Muslim Brotherhood remains open as the prosecution has appealed the acquittal of 66 of them and the rest are appealing verdicts against them.

In February 2004, a team from Amnesty International visited Libya for the first time in 15 years. Later, in April, Qadhafi referred in a speech to their recommendations for the improved treatment of prisoners and a reduction in the imposition of the death penalty. However, these changes were not discussed in the annual General People's Congress, and that, taken together with the AIDS case, signaled Tripoli's rejection of international pressure. A Libyan human rights society headed by Qadhafi's son, Saif al-Islam, initiated investigations into death in custody and torture allegations, but these were largely overshadowed by continued severe violations and an atmosphere of impunity. In April, Amnesty issue a strongly worded press release accusing Qadhafi of maintaining a "climate of fear," with a consistent pattern of violations.

The Berber and Tuareg minorities face discrimination. While women's status has improved in some areas, such as education and employment, discrimination continues in other areas where local traditions predominate. Female genital mutilation is still practiced in remote rural areas. Violence against women also continues to be a problem.

Liechtenstein

Population: 40,000
GNI/capita: $30,000
Life Expectancy: 80
Religious Groups: Roman Catholic (76.2 percent), Protestant (7 percent), other (16.8 percent)
Ethnic Groups: Alemannic (86 percent), other [including Italian and Turkish] (14 percent)
Capital: Vaduz

Political Rights: 1
Civil Liberties: 1
Status: Free

Ten-Year Ratings Timeline (Political Rights, Civil Liberties, Status)

1995	1996	1997	1998	1999	2000	2001	2002	2003	2004
1,1F	1,1F	1,1F	1,1F	1,1F	1,1F	1,1F	1,1F	1,1F	1,1F

Overview: In 2004, Prince Hans-Adam II handed over power to his son, Crown Prince Alois. Both refrained during the year from abusing the wide latitude to which they were entitled by a 2003 constitutional reform, which strengthened the monarch's powers considerably.

Liechtenstein was established in its present form in 1719 after being purchased by Austria's Liechtenstein family. Native residents of the state are primarily descendants of the Germanic Alemanni tribe, and the local language is a German dialect. From 1938 to 1997, the principality was governed by a coalition of the Progressive Citizens' Party (FBP) and the Fatherland Union (VU, now the Patriotic Union). The FBP was the senior coalition partner for most of this period. Otmar Hasler of the FBP became leader of his party and prime minister after the FBP won a majority of seats in parliament in February 2001 elections.

In 2000, the Organization for Economic Co-operation and Development's Financial Action Task Force labeled the principality "noncooperative" on money laundering because of Liechtenstein's traditional banking secrecy laws. Under pressure, Liechtenstein passed a law ending anonymity for account holders. It was removed from the list of noncooperative states in June 2001, but after the terrorist attacks in the United States on September 11, 2001, concerns reemerged that Islamic terrorists could be laundering money there. The IMF reported in September 2003 that Liechtenstein had made progress updating its banking regulations, but worried that there might not be enough staff to enforce regulations fully.

An amendment legislating major constitutional reform was passed by referendum in March 2003, with just over 64 percent of voters approving. It concentrated a good deal more power in the hands of the monarch, currently Prince Hans-Adam II. The prince had threatened to leave Liechtenstein for Austria if the measure were not passed.

The amendment, which makes Liechtenstein's monarchy the most powerful in Europe, gives the prince the power to dismiss the government, veto legislation, and appoint judges. However, it removes the prince's right to rule by emergency decree. The Council of Europe, which monitors democracy among its member countries, expressed concern and considered placing the democratic standards of Liechtenstein's political system under formal monitoring. It decided against doing so, instead merely entering into formal dialogue with Liechtenstein's parliament.

On August 15, 2004, Prince Hans-Adam handed his constitutional powers to his son, Crown Prince Alois, though Hans-Adam retained his title as head of state. Alois, 36, studied at Britain's Royal Military Academy at Sandhurst and has training in law and accounting (the latter is especially important, as his country is a major financial center). He is expected to be somewhat less confrontational with Leichtenstein's other political institutions than his father.

Political Rights and Civil Liberties: The people of Liechtenstein can change their government democratically, but the unelected monarchy won greater powers in 2003; Leichtenstein's ruling family is now perhaps the most politically powerful in Europe. The legislature consists of 25 deputies chosen in fair elections carried out under proportional representation every four years. These freely elected representatives determine the policies of the government, but the monarch, currently Crown Prince Alois, now has the power to veto legislation, dismiss the government, and appoint judges.

Political parties are able to freely organize. While two parties have dominated Liechtenstein's politics over the last half-century, there are a few independents in the legislature. Switzerland and Austria, the two countries that surround Liechtenstein, have a good measure of influence on the tiny principality.

Liechtenstein's politics and society are largely free of corruption; however, concerns about abetting the corruption of others continue, as Liechtenstein works to build sufficient capacity to fight money laundering in its banking system.

The constitution guarantees freedom of expression and of the media. There is one private television station competing with the state broadcaster, and the only radio station is in private hands. The two daily newspapers are aligned roughly with the two major political parties. Austria's and Switzerland's broadcasts are available and popular in the country, as are foreign newspapers and magazines. Internet access is unfettered.

The constitution establishes Roman Catholicism as the state religion but protects freedom of belief. Catholic or Protestant religious education is mandatory, but exceptions are routinely granted. All religious groups are tax-exempt. The government respects academic freedom.

The right of association is protected, and the principality has one small trade union. The right to assembly and demonstration is not infringed.

Judges are appointed by the prince. Due process is respected, and conditions in prisons are acceptable. After the controversy over the monarch's new powers, the Council of Europe's secretary-general sought to reassure those concerned about democracy that "Liechtenstein's status as a law-based state is unarguable." The IMF rated the financial-services regulators, important to a country so reliant on banking, as capable but too few to police all banks and account holders fully. Crime is rare and the police are professional. Switzerland is responsible for Liechtenstein's defense.

Liechtenstein is a member of the European Economic Area, a free-trade area of countries that are not members of the European Union. Liechtenstein's currency is the Swiss franc. Living standards are high, with a large number of small businesses and a strong financial sector.

A restrictive abortion law allows the procedure only when the life or health (including mental health) of the woman is threatened. A 2003 court decision upheld the principle of equal pay for equal work for women, but Liechtenstein's society remains socially conservative, and practice lags behind principle.

Lithuania

Population: 3,400,000   **Political Rights:** 2*
GNI/capita: $3,670   **Civil Liberties:** 2
Life Expectancy: 72   **Status:** Free
Religious Groups: Roman Catholic, Lutheran,
Russian Orthodox, other
Ethnic Groups: Lithuanian (81 percent), Russian
(9 percent), Polish (7 percent), Byelorussian (2 percent),
other (2 percent)
Capital: Vilnius
Ratings Change: Lithuania's political rights rating declined from 1 to 2 due to circumstances surrounding the impeachment of President Rolandas Paksas, including the findings of parliament that he was under the influence of foreign security service and organized crime elements while president, as well as a series of official raids on the offices of parties supporting Paksas' replacement, Valdas Adamkus.

Ten-Year Ratings Timeline (Political Rights, Civil Liberties, Status)

1995	1996	1997	1998	1999	2000	2001	2002	2003	2004
1,2F	1,2F	1,2F	1,2F	1,2F	1,2F	1,2F	1,2F	1,2F	2,2F

Overview:
Lithuania became a member of the European Union (EU) on May 1, 2004, and joined NATO the month before. However, these accomplishments were marred by a series of high-profile political corruption scandals, including the impeachment of President Rolandas Paksas. In June, Lithuanians voted in the country's first election to the European Parliament and elected former president Valdas Adamkus to replace Paksas. Parliamentary elections in October resulted in a left-wing ruling coalition including the newly formed Labor Party and its leader, Russian-born Viktor Uspaskich. Lithuania's relations with Russia deteriorated in 2004.

Lithuania merged with Poland in the sixteenth century and was subsequently absorbed by Russia in the eighteenth century. After gaining its independence at the end of World War I, Lithuania was annexed by the Soviet Union in 1940 under a secret protocol of the 1939 Hitler-Stalin pact. The country regained its independence with the collapse of the U.S.S.R. in 1991.

Parliamentary elections held in October 2000 resulted in a resounding defeat for the ruling Homeland Union/Lithuanian Conservatives (TS), apparently because of the public's dissatisfaction over the government's economic austerity policies. While the Social Democratic Coalition secured the most votes, the informal New Policy electoral bloc, composed of an ideologically diverse cohort of right- and left-wing parties, bypassed the Social Democratic Coalition to form a bare-majority centrist government. Rolandas Paksas was chosen to be prime minister for the second time since 1998.

After only eight months in power, this unstable ruling coalition collapsed following disagreements over the budget and privatization plans for the country's energy sector. Paksas was replaced in July by Algirdas Brazauskas, the chairman of the Lithuanian Social Democratic Party (LSDP). The more ideologically compatible LSDP and New Union (Social Liberals) subsequently formed a new ruling coalition government.

In presidential elections held on December 22, 2002, Adamkus, the incumbent, received 35 percent of the vote, not enough for a first-round victory, which requires a candidate to receive more than 50 percent. Adamkus faced Paksas, the second-place winner with 20 percent of the vote, in a January 5, 2003, runoff election. Surprisingly, Paksas defeated Adamkus, who had successfully secured Lithuania invitations to both the EU and NATO. In May 2003, Lithuanians voted overwhelmingly to join the EU in a national referendum. Lithuania became a member of NATO in April 2004 and the EU the following month.

Paksas was impeached by parliament in April on three charges of violating the Lithuanian constitution, becoming the first European head of state to be successfully impeached. Paksas's troubles began in October 2003 with the leaking of a security services report alleging that the main financial backer in his presidential campaign, a Russian named Jurijus Borisovas, sold illegal arms to Sudan and that Borisovas, along with some of Paksas's close advisors, was linked with organized crime and foreign intelligence services. Subsequently, Paksas was charged with illegally granting Borisovas Lithuanian citizenship.

The parliamentary committee investigating Paksas confirmed the allegations in December and ruled Paksas vulnerable to criminal interests and a threat to state security; in February 2004, the committee found Paksas guilty of six charges of violating the constitution. The following month, the Constitutional Court deemed Paksas guilty of three of these charges (unlawfully granting citizenship, leaking classified information, and meddling in private business affairs), clearing the way for the decisive parliamentary impeachment vote. Arturas Paulauskas, the parliamentary chairman, took over as acting president following the impeachment. While Paskas was barred from running in another presidential election in May, a Lithuanian court later cleared him of the charge of leaking state secrets to Borisovas. In October, Paksas filed suit against his country at the European Court of Human Rights, alleging his rights to a fair trial and defense during the impeachment proceedings were violated.

In June, 48 percent of voters turned out for Lithuania's first elections to the European Parliament. The new populist Labor Party, led by Russian-born millionaire Viktor Upaskich, topped all parties by garnering 5 of Lithuania's 13 seats with 30.4 percent of the vote. The right-leaning Liberal and Center Union and TS won 2 seats each, as did the left-leaning LSDP. The Liberal Democrats and the Union of Farmers and New Democracy (VNDPS) each earned a seat in the European Parliament. Lithuania became the first country to ratify the new EU constitution when the parliament approved the text in October.

Elections to select a new president were held simultaneously with the European Parliament vote. Adamkus defeated Kazimira Prunskiene, the leader of the Union of Farmers' and New Democracy parties, in a tight runoff contest later that month by winning 52.1 percent of the vote and was sworn in as president in July.

Parliamentary elections were conducted in October over two rounds, with the second round limited to single-mandate constituencies where no candidate won 50 percent of the vote in the first round. The second-round election was inaugurated in 2004 and pushed through parliament by the governing SDP and New Union (Social

Liberals) parties, a development the Economic Intelligence Unit attributed to the rise of the Labor Party in opinion polls. After both rounds, a right-wing coalition of the TS and the Liberal and Center Union won 43 seats (25 for TS and 18 for the Liberal and Center Union), Labor won 39 seats, the ruling leftist coalition of LSDP and New Union (Social Liberals) won 31 seats (20 seats and 11 seats, respectively), the VNDPS won 10 seats, and the Election Action of Lithuania's Poles won 2 seats. After negotiations between left- and right-wing parties broke down, a ruling center-left coalition emerged in November, with the Labor Party joining the LSDP and New Union (Social Liberals).

Relations with Russia became tenser in 2004. In February, Lithuania expelled three Russian diplomats for spying and claimed they posed a threat not only to Lithuania but also to the EU and NATO. Russia warned Lithuania it viewed the expulsions as an "unfriendly act" and retaliated a month later by expelling three Lithuania diplomats. In addition, the Lithuanian parliament adopted a resolution backing an Estonian call for compensation from Russia for almost 50 years of Soviet occupation. The two countries also clashed over the Russian proposal to establish a "free transit corridor" between Russia and Kaliningrad via Lithuanian soil.

Political Rights and Civil Liberties: Lithuanians can change their government democratically. The 1992 constitution established a 141-member parliament (Seimas), in which 71 seats are selected in single-mandate constituencies and 70 seats are chosen by proportional representation, all for four-year terms. The president is directly elected for a five-year term. All permanent residents are allowed to run for office and vote in local government elections, while only citizens can participate in national elections. In 2004, the national legislative election, presidential election, and election to the European Parliament were all conducted freely and fairly.

Corruption scandals continued to haunt Lithuanian politics in 2004, the most prominent being the April impeachment of President Rolandas Paksas for violating the constitution. In June, anticorruption authorities from the Special Investigation Service (STT) raided the office of four main political parties (Liberal and Center Union, New Union [Social Liberals], TS, and LSDP) a few days before the presidential run-off election. The raids aroused the suspicion of political motivation, as all four parties supported Paksas's impeachment and three of the four were supporting Adamkus in the presidential election. (In September, STT chief Valentinas Junokas resigned amidst allegations that the raids and subsequent actions were attempts to influence the country's political process.)

Also, in July, prosecutors accused three members of parliament of taking bribes from the Rubicon energy company. While the parliament deemed the evidence insufficient to strip the accused of their immunity from prosecution, Deputy Speaker Vytenis Andriukatis (LSDP), Vytautas Kvietkauskas (New Union [Social Liberals]), and Arvydas Vidziunas (TS) had all resigned their mandates by the end of the month and agreed to cooperate with investigators. In October, another MP, Virginijus Martisauskas, resigned amid allegations of corruption. Lithuania was ranked 44 out of 146 countries surveyed in Transparency International's 2004 Corruption Perceptions Index.

The government generally respects freedom of speech and of the press. There is a wide variety of privately owned newspapers, and several independent, as well as state-run, television and radio stations broadcast throughout the country. In February, a LNK television reporter was stripped of his credentials by the President's Office after reporting critically on events at the office, a move decried by the opposition party LCS and the LNK news service. In September, Lithuania shut down the pro-Chechen rebel Web site Kavkaz-Center, hosted on a Lithuanian server, a decision that had been stalled by a September 2003 Vilnius court ruling. The closure of the site was spurred by repeated complaints from Moscow, an influence that elicited sharp criticism from the opposition party TS.

Freedom of religion is guaranteed by law and largely enjoyed in practice in this predominantly Roman Catholic country. Academic freedom is respected.

Freedom of assembly and association is generally respected. Workers have the right to form and join trade unions, to strike, and to engage in collective bargaining. According to the U.S. State Department's 2004 Country Report on Human Rights Practices, approximately 10 percent of the workforce is unionized.

The judiciary is largely independent of the executive branch, and the recently revised Law of Courts has fortified its autonomy. However, the lack of qualified judges and lawyers often undermines the right to a fair trial. In November, an ad hoc commission charged with investigating the June SST raids (and some related cases of wiretapping) concluded that authorities had acted unlawfully by failing to secure the appropriate court orders; the Seimas accepted these conclusions. There have been credible reports of police abuse of suspects and detainees. Prison overcrowding and prolonged pretrial detention remain serious problems. New legislation, including a Criminal Procedures Code, has led to an improvement in prison conditions, and in May the government approved a program for the Renovation and Humanization of Prisons aimed at bringing Lithuanian prisons in line with EU standards.

The rights of the country's ethnic minorities are protected in practice. In 1992, Lithuania extended citizenship to all those born within its borders, and more than 90 percent of nonethnic Lithuanians, mostly Russians and Poles, became citizens. In October 2003, the Seimas ratified Protocol 13 of the Convention for the Protection of Human Rights and Fundamental Freedoms, abolishing capital punishment in all cases. Anti-Semitic incidents are on the rise in Lithuania.

Women are under-represented in upper-level management positions and earn lower average wages than men for the same work. However, party lists for the 2004 parliamentary elections included 2.5 times more female candidates than did lists for the 2000 polls. Trafficking in persons, particularly women and girls for purposes of prostitution, is a problem, and the government has taken steps to address it.

Luxembourg

Population: 500,000
GNI/capita: $38,830
Life Expectancy: 78
Religious Groups: Roman Catholic (87 percent),
Protestant (13 percent), other [including Jewish and Muslim]
(10 percent)
Ethnic Groups: Celtic, Portuguese, Italian, Slavs, other
Capital: Luxembourg

Political Rights: 1
Civil Liberties: 1
Status: Free

Ten-Year Ratings Timeline (Political Rights, Civil Liberties, Status)

1995	1996	1997	1998	1999	2000	2001	2002	2003	2004
1,1F	1,1F	1,1F	1,1F	1,1F	1,1F	1,1F	1,1F	1,1F	1,1F

Overview:

In June 2004, the main party in Luxembourg's governing coalition did well at a general election, assuring the reelection as prime minister of Jean-Claude Juncker. However, the center-right junior party did poorly and was replaced by a center-left party in the new governing coalition. Juncker was also widely considered to be a strong candidate for president of the European Commission, the executive of the European Union (EU). However, having promised that he would stay on if he won the election, Juncker remained the Grand Duchy's prime minister.

The Grand Duchy of Luxembourg was established in 1815, after the Napoleonic wars. Following a brief merger with Belgium, it reemerged with its current borders in 1839. The country has always faced the possibility of domination by its neighbors—it was occupied by Germany during both world wars—and it abandoned neutrality in favor of joining NATO in 1949. After joining in an economic union with Belgium and The Netherlands in 1948, Luxembourg became one of the six founding members of the European Community (now the EU) in 1957. Because it has a small, open economy, Luxembourg's relationship with the EU is highly important in its politics; it adopted the euro as its currency in 1999. A former prime minister, Jacques Santer, served as president of the EU's commission from 1995 to 1999.

Over the course of 2003, the opinion-poll ratings of the center-right Democratic Party (PD) fell, while the opposition Socialist Worker Party of Luxembourg's (POSL) rose. It was therefore little surprise when the PD did poorly in the general election of June 2004, losing 5 of its 15 seats in parliament. The POSL gained a seat, holding 14 seats in the new parliament, and joined Juncker's Christian Social Party in government as a junior partner.

Luxembourg is a strong proponent of greater European integration through the EU. In 2004, the 25 member states of the EU finalized a new draft constitution for the EU and simultaneously chose a new president for the European Commission, which serves as the EU's executive and civil service. Negotiations over both were difficult and sometimes bitter, but shortly after Luxembourg's own election, a text was completed that would strengthen European cooperation in many areas.

In the fraught negotiations over the choice of a new commission president,

Juncker's name was often mentioned as a potential compromise candidate, as he is widely respected and offensive to none of the EU's biggest members. However, he had promised to remain prime minister if his party won the general election and kept that promise. Nonetheless, the new constitution, if ratified, would also create a new presidency of the European Council (representing the member states rather than the EU itself). Juncker has also been spoken of as a candidate for this job.

Political Rights and Civil Liberties: Luxembourgers can change their government democratically. The head of state is the unelected Grand Duke Henri, but his powers are largely ceremonial. The unicameral legislature consists of 60 deputies elected by proportional representation. Voting is compulsory for all who are registered. (Residents from EU countries may vote after six years' residence but are not obliged to do so; non-EU residents may not vote. Foreigners comprise a third of Luxembourg's population.)

The political party system is open to the rise of new parties, as seen by the growth of the Action Committee for Democracy and Pension Reform, originally a one-issue party focusing on higher pensions, which first had deputies elected in 1989 and is now a significant party. There are three traditionally strong parties in Luxembourg's politics: the Christian Social Party (PCS), traditionally aligned with the Catholic Church; the Democratic Party (PD), which favors free-market economic policies and a smaller welfare state; and the Socialist Worker Party (POSL), a formerly radical but now center-left party representing the working class. The current government, elected in 2004, is a coalition of the PCS, which has taken part in almost all governments in Luxembourg's modern history, and the POSL.

The government is largely free from corruption; Transparency International, a corruption watchdog, ranked Luxembourg the thirteenth cleanest of the 146 countries it surveyed in 2004.

Freedom of expression is guaranteed by the constitution, and Luxembourg has a vibrant media environment. A single media conglomerate, RTL, dominates the broadcast radio and TV market, and its broadcasts are popular in Luxembourg's neighboring countries. Newspapers represent a broad range of opinion. Internet access is unrestricted.

Roman Catholicism is the dominant religion, but there is no state religion and the state pays the salaries of ministers from a variety of religions. Students may choose to study either the Roman Catholic religion or ethics; most choose the former. Protestant education is available on demand.

Freedom of assembly and association is protected. Civic groups and NGOs may operate freely, and Luxembourgers may organize in trade unions. The right to strike is constitutionally guaranteed.

The judiciary is independent, but its judges are appointed by the grand duke. Prisoners are humanely treated in police stations and prisons. Luxembourg's Muslim minority, mainly of Bosnian origin, faces no official hostility but does experience some mild social racism.

In part because of its conservative social mores, women comprise just under 40 percent of the labor force, and there remains a significant gap between men's and women's wages. Though abortion law does not technically provide for abortion on demand, a woman who has had an abortion while under "distress" is considered not to have violated the law, and "distress" is interpreted liberally.

⬇ Macedonia

Population: 2,000,000   **Political Rights:** 3
GNI/capita: $1,710   **Civil Liberties:** 3
Life Expectancy: 73   **Status:** Partly Free
Religious Groups: Macedonian Orthodox (70 percent),
Muslim (29 percent), other (1 percent)
Ethnic Groups: Macedonian (64 percent),
Albanian (25 percent), Turkish (4 percent), Roma (3 percent),
Serb (2 percent), other (2 percent)
Capital: Skopje
Trend Arrow: Macedonia received a downward trend arrow due to increasing ethnic tensions related to difficulties in passing a local governmental decentralization plan, forcing a delay in local elections, as well as an increase in the harassment of leaders of various religious groups.

Ten-Year Ratings Timeline (Political Rights, Civil Liberties, Status)

1995	1996	1997	1998	1999	2000	2001	2002	2003	2004
4,3PF	4,3PF	4,3PF	3,3PF	3,3PF	4,3PF	4,4PF	3,3PF	3,3PF	3,3PF

Overview:

In 2004, one of the last—but perhaps most important—aspects of the 2001 Ohrid accords, which had barely averted a civil war in the country, faced considerable public opposition after ethnic Macedonian citizens called for a referendum on controversial aspects of the decentralization proposal. Although the referendum to defeat the government's plans did not succeed, it forced a delay in local elections. In the aftermath of the referendum, the prime minister resigned, throwing the country into a period of considerable political uncertainty.

Macedonia, a republic in the former Yugoslav Communist federation, was recognized as an independent state in 1992. Since gaining independence, Macedonia has suffered from disputes with most of its neighbors over a number of issues: the name "Macedonia" with Greece, the status of the Macedonian language with Bulgaria, and Macedonia's northern border with Serbia and Montenegro. Most of these external disputes have been successfully resolved. The international community has tried in a number of ways to support Macedonia's fragile existence, most notably in April 2002, when the European Union (EU) signed a Stabilization and Association Agreement (considered the first step toward full EU membership) with Skopje. In November 2004, just days before a tension-filled referendum on the government's decentralization plans, the United States announced it would recognize Macedonia under its constitutional name to bolster confidence in the country and reassure Macedonian voters that the international community would continue to support its existence.

Parliamentary elections in 1998 resulted in the first peaceful transfer of power from the left-of-center governmental coalition that had ruled Macedonia since independence to a grouping of right-of-center parties led by the Internal Macedonian Revolutionary Organization–Democratic Party of Macedonian National Unity (VMRO-DPMNE).

Relations between the country's two primary ethnic groups—Macedonian Slavs and ethnic Albanians—deteriorated precipitously after the 1999 Kosovo war. By 2000, ethnic Albanian guerrillas who had participated in the Kosovo conflict were operating in Macedonia, often using NATO-occupied Kosovo as their base. Among the guerrillas' political demands were changes to the Macedonian constitution endorsing greater use of the Albanian language in official institutions, an increase in the number of ethnic Albanians in the civil services, and a decentralization of governmental powers to local municipalities. In August 2001, an agreement reached in the town of Ohrid produced a temporary lull in the conflict, which was estimated to have cost the fragile Macedonian economy more than $800 million.

In mid-September 2002, Macedonia held its latest set of parliamentary elections. The elections returned to power the left-of-center Social Democratic Alliance of Macedonia (SDSM), led by Branko Crvenkovski, which succeeded in ousting former prime minister Ljubco Georgievski's right-of-center coalition. As in previous governments, ethnic Albanian parties were included in the governing coalition. After the 2002 elections, the Democratic Union for Integration (BDI), led by the leader of the ethnic Albanians' armed uprising, Ali Ahmeti, became Crvenkovski's main coalition partner.

Implementation of the 2001 Ohrid accords has proceeded in fits and starts. Three of the five signatories to the 2001 agreement repudiated it in 2003, and two have called for an outright partition of the country. A further blow to the Ohrid accords came in February, when the man most associated with the agreement, President Boris Trajkovski, died in a plane crash while on an official state visit to Bosnia-Herzegovina. Presidential elections called after Trajkovski's death were held in April. The leading candidate for the position, Prime Minister Crvenkovski, scored a comfortable second-round victory in the election, winning 62 percent of the votes against the 37 percent gained by his leading challenger, VMRO-DPMNE leader, Sasko Kedev. In a sign of how contentious the election had been, however, VMRO-DPMNE officials boycotted Crvenkovski's inauguration ceremony. Upon Crvenkovski's assumption of the presidency, the prime minister's post was assumed by Hari Kostov, an economic expert unaffiliated with any political party.

Nevertheless, most of the measures called for in the Ohrid accords had been passed by parliament and implemented by 2004. The last remaining major reform legislation—a decentralization plan intended to devolve powers from the central government in Skopje to local municipalities, along with a redrawing of the capital's boundaries to increase the number of ethnic Albanians living in the city—has proved to be the most controversial. Macedonian Slavs reacted to the proposed changes by calling for a referendum on the issue; although the referendum, held in November, did not pass (only 26 percent of a required 50 percent of the electorate turned out), ethnic tensions in the country increased significantly during the political debates preceding the referendum. Ethnic Albanian politicians warned that canceling the government's decentralization plan could lead to a renewal of ethnic violence, while opposition leaders from ethnic Macedonian parties claimed that the decentralization plans were a sellout to the Albanians and would eventually lead to the country's breakup. Given the heightened political tensions in the country resulting from the decentralization debates, local elections scheduled for October had to be postponed. In the aftermath of the referendum, Prime Minister Kostov resigned, throwing Macedonia into another period of political uncertainty.

Political Rights and Civil Liberties: Citizens of Macedonia can choose their political representatives in free and fair elections. The last elections to the 120-seat, unicameral Sobranie (Assembly), held in September 2002, were deemed by international organizations to be 'largely in accordance with...international standards for democratic elections." Voter turnout was approximately 70 percent of the electorate. In April's two rounds of presidential elections, called after the death of President Boris Trajkovski, international organizations again deemed the elections "generally consistent" with international standards, but both domestic opposition parties and some international organizations, such as the Organization for Security and Cooperation in Europe, reported important irregularities with the elections. There are 64 registered political parties in Macedonia.

As throughout the region, corruption remains a serious problem hampering economic growth and political transparency. Within days of assuming the presidency, Crvenkovski authorized a number of high-profile arrests of individuals in the defense ministry and the police forces on charges of accepting bribes, and, in some cases, complicity in the murder of six Pakistani migrant workers. Macedonia was ranked 97 out of 146 countries surveyed in Transparency International's 2004 Corruption Perceptions Index.

Although the constitution provides for freedom of the press, the media are often aligned with particular political interests that render them less than independent. Many senior positions in state-owned media, from which the majority of the population gets its information, are filled by political appointees rather than by professional journalists. The media in Macedonia are frequently criticized for their lack of professionalism and unwillingness to uphold recognized journalistic standards. Macedonia has been fairly open about providing ethnic minorities in the country with media in their own languages. According to one recent report, Macedonian Radio Television (MRTV) provides broadcasts in Albanian, Turkish, Vlach, Romany, and Serbian for the different ethnic groups in the country. One of the most notable developments in the media in 2004 was the purchase by the German WAZ media group of the country's three major dailies, which together account for 90 percent of the print newspapers in circulation in the country. There were no reports of restrictions of access to the Internet during the year.

The constitution guarantees freedom of religious belief and practice. A number of religious sites were destroyed or damaged in the fighting in 2001, although vandalism against religious sites has decreased significantly since then. In 2002, a serious rift developed within the Orthodox Church in Macedonia, when part of the church split off from the so-called "Macedonian Orthodox Church," which remains unrecognized by any other church in the Orthodox world, and agreed to come under the jurisdiction of the Serbian Orthodox Church. The leader of the pro-Serbian branch, Bishop Jovan Vraniskovski, was arrested several times in 2004, and in August he was given an 18-month sentence for allegedly inciting "ethnic or religious intolerance." Amnesty International has declared him a prisoner of conscience. Bishop Vraniskovski and his followers were also physically attacked on a number of occasions during the year, and churches they have built or served in have been destroyed. There are considerable tensions in Macedonia's Islamic community as well. The leader of Macedonia's Muslims, Hadzi Arif Efendi Emini, was taken hostage on two occasions during the year by other Muslim clerics unhappy with policies within that community. There were no reports of restrictions on academic freedom.

The constitution provides for freedom of assembly and association, and there were no reports that the government infringed on these rights in 2004. The constitution also recognizes worker's rights to organize and to bargain collectively, although given the poor state of the Macedonian economy, workers generally have little leverage. Nevertheless, strikes and work stoppages are frequent occurrences. More than 50 percent of the legal workforce is unionized.

The judicial system is widely seen as composed of corrupt and incompetent officials. In January, Macedonia's public prosecutor noted that in recent years, 47 judges, 10 prosecutors, and 41 Interior Ministry officials have been formally charged with a variety of offenses, but that over half the cases had to be dropped because of lack of evidence. Nevertheless, some of the abuses have been egregious; in the town of Strumica, a judge released from custody a well-known dealer of arms and illegal drugs who was the subject of an international arrest warrant. There is also a large backlog of cases in the judicial system, and some judges maintain that reform is needed to allow petty offenses to be dealt with by administrative officials rather than by criminal courts. A number of international watchdog groups have charged Macedonian police forces with serious cases of ill-treatment and torture of prisoners.

A serious blow to the reputation of Macedonia's official institutions came in March, when it was alleged that the former interior minister, Ljube Boskovski, had been involved in a plot in 2002 in which a group of Pakistani and Indian migrant workers were lured into the country and subsequently killed by Macedonian security forces. At the time, Macedonian officials had claimed that the workers were members of an al-Qaeda cell traveling through Macedonia, and the setup was meant to portray Macedonian as a loyal ally in the war on terrorism. After an arrest warrant was issued for Boskovski, he fled the country.

Macedonia's most important political and societal problem remains satisfying the demands of the ethnic Albanian minority for a more privileged status within the country. In accordance with the Ohrid accords, references in the constitution to Macedonia as the "land of the Macedonian people" have been eliminated, and the Albanian language has been made an "official" language in municipalities where ethnic Albanians constitute at least 20 percent of the population. The constitutional reforms envisioned by the Ohrid accords include granting more self-government to local municipalities, increasing the number of ethnic Albanians in the police force, devolving some of the powers of the central government from Skopje to local municipalities, and granting amnesty to ethnic Albanian insurgents.

Women in Macedonia enjoy the same legal rights as men, although lingering patriarchal social attitudes limit women's participation in nontraditional social roles in the economy and in government. Twenty-two of the 120 members of parliament are women (21 ethnic Macedonians and an ethnic Albanian). Violence against women is considered a particular problem within the ethnic Albanian and Roma (Gypsy) communities. Domestic violence and trafficking of women from former Soviet republics remain serious problems. In Muslim areas, many women are effectively disenfranchised because proxy voting by male relatives is common.

Madagascar

Population: 17,500,000   **Political Rights:** 3
GNI/capita: $230   **Civil Liberties:** 3
Life Expectancy: 55   **Status:** Partly Free
Religious Groups: Indigenous beliefs (52 percent),
Christian (41 percent), Muslim (7 percent)
Ethnic Groups: Malayo-Indonesian tribes, Arab, African,
Indian, French
Capital: Antananarivo

Ten-Year Ratings Timeline (Political Rights, Civil Liberties, Status)

1995	1996	1997	1998	1999	2000	2001	2002	2003	2004
2,4PF	2,4PF	2,4PF	2,4PF	2,4PF	2,4PF	2,4PF	3,4PF	3,3PF	3,3PF

Overview: Madagascar was buffeted by continuing social and political
unrest in 2004. In addition, President Marc Ravalomanana's
government was the focus of growing frustration from army
reservists demanding better compensation for their role in quelling the country's
2002 political crisis after disputed elections.

Madagascar, the world's fourth-largest island, lies 220 miles off Africa's south-eastern coast. After 70 years of French colonial rule and episodes of severe repression, Madagascar gained independence in 1960. A leftist military junta seized power from President Philbert Tsiranana in 1972. A member of the junta, Admiral Didier Ratsiraka, emerged as leader in 1975 and maintained power until his increasingly authoritarian regime bowed to social unrest and nonviolent mass demonstrations in 1991.

Under the new, 1992 constitution, opposition leader Albert Zafy won the presidency with more than 65 percent of the vote. Zafy failed to win reelection after being impeached by the Supreme Court in 1996. Ratsiraka won a narrow victory in a December 1996 presidential runoff election that was deemed generally legitimate by international and domestic observers.

In the 1990s, a weak party system complicated efforts at governance. Legislative elections in May 1998 were viewed as more problematic than preceding polls since Madagascar's transition to multiparty politics in 1992. The Council of Christian Churches and several political groups, for example, noted that the elections were marred by fraud and other abuses. The ruling Association for the Rebirth of Madagascar (AREMA) party won 63 of 150 parliamentary seats and emerged as the leading force in a coalition government.

A decentralization plan was narrowly approved in a 1998 referendum that was boycotted by the country's increasingly fractious opposition. November 1999 municipal polls resulted in overall success for independents who did not have close identification with a particular party. Elections were held in December 2000 for provincial councils, as the next step in the government's decentralization policy. In 2001, the first-ever Senate elections, part of a policy to extend democratic governance, finally took place after a long delay.

A presidential election was held in December 2001. Insisting that he had been denied an outright victory by polling irregularities and refusing to take part in a postponed second round, Ravalomanana declared himself president in February 2002. After considerable violence between supporters of the two rival candidates, the High Constitutional Court announced in April that Ravalomanana had indeed won the election in the first round, and he was sworn into office in May. Ratsiraka refused to acknowledge this result. Fighting continued until July 2002, when Ratsiraka left the country and the last of his forces surrendered. The extended crisis had a seriously negative effect on the Malagasy economy.

Parliamentary elections took place in December 2002. Ravalomanana's I Love Madagascar Party (TIM) won a large majority, gaining 131 out of 160 seats. Observers from the European Union said the conduct of the poll was "generally positive" despite a few reported "lapses," while the International Francophone Organization said it was "credible and transparent." Local elections that were held in 2003 further strengthened the Ravalomanana's position.

In 2004, army reservists demanded better compensation for their efforts during the country's political crisis in 2002. A series of grenade attacks that resulted in numerous injuries and arrests are believed to be linked to growing frustration over continued economic problems.

A heated debate continued on a proposed amnesty law for people who were detained following the 2002 political unrest; an attempt by opposition parties to have the law adopted had failed in November 2003.

Political Rights and Civil Liberties:

Citizens of Madagascar have the right to change their government democratically, although the most recent presidential election demonstrates that this right is not yet fully enshrined in the country's political culture. The head of state is a president, directly elected to a five-year term by universal adult suffrage. The National Assembly, the lower chamber of the bicameral legislature, has 150 members directly elected to five-year terms. The upper chamber, the Senate, has 90 members—two-thirds of them elected by an electoral college and the remainder nominated by the president—serving six-year terms. A 1998 constitutional referendum gave the president the power to appoint or dismiss the prime minister, who may come from a party that has a minority of seats in the assembly; formerly, the National Assembly had this power. Approximately 150 parties are registered amid a welter of shifting political alliances. A variety of parties are active, but they suffer from internal divisions and a lack of clear ideology and resources.

Madagascar was ranked 82 out of 146 countries in Transparency International's 2004 Corruption Perceptions Index.

Madagascar's 16 million people have six daily newspapers and a number of weeklies and monthlies, as well as TV and radio stations. Because of the low literacy rate, the print media are mostly aimed at the French-educated urban elite. Some formerly pro-Ratsiraka radio stations, which operated like "hate radios" during the crisis, have switched to more mainstream forms of broadcasting. Internet use, although not widespread, is becoming more popular.

While there are constitutional provisions for press freedom, the government has limited these in practice. Some government officials reportedly sought to limit critical media coverage of alleged government malfeasance. The division of the country into two political camps following the disputed December 2001 presidential elections is apparent in the press. In February 2004, a private radio station, Radio Sava, was ordered closed. Reporters Sans Frontieres criticized the government's decision in June to close Radio Say, a private radio station known for its independent editorial stance, for "broadcasting false news, defamation and insults against the speaker of the National Assembly and a member of the government, and breach of operating terms and conditions." Radio Say was ordered to cease broadcasting following violence during Independence Day celebrations. No link has been made between the attack and the station's activities.

The government does not interfere with religious rights. More than half of the population adhere to traditional Malagasy religions and coexist with Christians and Muslims. In 1997, the Rally for Madagascar's Muslim Democrats was registered as the country's first Islamic political party. There are no limitations on academic freedom.

The right to freedom of assembly is generally respected, and hundreds of nongovernmental organizations, including lawyers' and human rights groups, are active. As has been evidenced by various interest group advocacy efforts over a wide variety of issues, political and civic organizations do exercise their right to affect the public policy process. These activities are usually permitted by the government; however, the chairman of a group named the Organization of Families of People Detained Following the Current Political Crisis was arrested on suspicion of having participated in election-related violence in 2002.

Workers' rights to join unions and to strike are exercised frequently. Some of the country's labor organizations are affiliated with political groups. More than four-fifths of the labor force is employed in agriculture, fishing, and forestry at subsistence wages.

A lack of training, resources, and personnel hampers judicial effectiveness, and case backlogs are prodigious. Most of the 20,000 people held in the country's prisons are pretrial detainees, who suffer extremely harsh conditions. In many rural areas, customary law courts that follow neither due process nor standardized judicial procedure often issue summary and severe punishments.

With the stated intent of reestablishing a rule of law, President Marc Ravalomanana has sought to arrest and prosecute individuals who were involved in acts of "terrorism" and killings during the 2002 crisis. Most of these people were pro-Ratsiraka and *cotiers*—coastal peoples mostly of mixed (Malayo-Polynesian, Arab, and African) descent or of black African origin.

Ravalomanana's opponents say the government is cracking down on them for political motives and that the legal system is biased against them. A report by Amnesty International has identified some instances of detention without trial and arbitrary arrest. Pro-government supporters say, however, that those who sought to undermine the country's democracy and promote ethnic and regional discord should not be immune from legal sanctions.

Race and ethnicity are important factors in Madagascar's politics. Its mostly very poor population is divided between highland Merina people of Malay origin and the *cotiers*. Approximately 45 percent of the workforce is female. Malagasy women hold significantly more government and managerial positions than women in continental African countries. At the same time, they still face societal discrimination and enjoy fewer opportunities than men for higher education and official employment.

Malawi

Population: 11,900,000
GNI/capita: $160
Life Expectancy: 44
Religious Groups: Protestant (55 percent), Roman Catholic (20 percent), Muslim (20 percent), indigenous beliefs (3 percent), other (2 percent)
Ethnic Groups: Chewa, Nyanja, Lomwe, Ngonde, Tumbuku, Yao, Sena, Tonga, Ngoni, Asian, European
Capital: Lilongwe

Political Rights: 4*
Civil Liberties: 4
Status: Partly Free

Ratings Change: Malawi's political rights rating declined from 3 to 4 due to flawed presidential elections.

Ten-Year Ratings Timeline (Political Rights, Civil Liberties, Status)

1995	1996	1997	1998	1999	2000	2001	2002	2003	2004
2,3F	2,3F	2,3F	2,3F	3,3PF	3,3PF	4,3PF	4,4PF	3,4PF	4,4PF

Overview:

Bingu wa Mutharika, the hand-picked successor to long-time president Bakili Muluzi, won controversial elections in May 2004 that opposition parties and international observers described as peaceful but flawed.

After the country gained independence from Britain in 1963, President (later President-for-Life) Hastings Kamuzu Banda ruled Malawi for nearly three decades. Banda exercised dictatorial and often eccentric rule through the Malawi Congress Party (MCP) and its paramilitary youth wing, the Malawi Young Pioneers. Facing a domestic economic crisis and strong international pressure, he accepted a referendum approving multiparty rule in 1993. Muluzi won the presidency in an election in 1994 beset by irregularities, but seen as largely free and fair. The army's violent December 1993 dispersal of the Young Pioneers had helped clear the way for the polls.

In the June 1999 presidential poll, Muluzi won 51 percent, compared with 44 percent for leading opposition candidate Gwanda Chakuamba, of the MCP and the Alliance for Democracy (MCP-AFORD). Three presidential contenders sued the electoral commission, contending that Muluzi failed to win votes from more than half of the eligible electorate. The Supreme Court upheld the results of the election. In polls for the National Assembly in 1999, the ruling United Democratic Front (UDF) managed to retain a narrow majority. Violence erupted in opposition strongholds of northern Malawi after the 1999 election results indicated wins for the UDF. Supporters of MCP-AFORD attacked mosques, shops, and homes of suspected UDF supporters.

An unpopular campaign to amend the constitution to allow Muluzi to run for a third term was effectively ended when the UDF chose Mutharika, a relative political outsider, as his successor for the May 2004 elections. Mutharika went on to win the presidency on an anticorruption platform with 35 percent of the vote. The MCP won a majority in the 193-seat parliament, with 56 seats, and the UDF finished second with 49. A seven-party coalition and independent candidates won the remainder.

Observers said the polls were tainted by registration problems and biased campaign coverage by the state-run radio and television stations. A parliamentary inquiry into voting irregularities led to the resignation in August of the chairman of the Malawi Electoral Commission, Justice James Kalaile. In July, the UDF regained its majority status in parliament when 26 independent legislators defected to the ruling party, giving it a total of 75 seats. The UDF had previously merged with one of its fiercest rivals, the National Democratic Alliance (NDA), raising concerns that the political opposition was being co-opted. Under a deal reached with Muluzi, who remains the UDF chairman, two other opposition parties also allied themselves with the UDF and dropped legal challenges to the election results.

Vowing "zero tolerance" of corruption, Mutharika has aggressively gone after senior officials of the old government. The Office of Public Prosecutions is investigating 10 former ministers over $93 million that reportedly vanished during Muluzi's decade-long tenure. Several others were arrested in separate corruption cases, including the current director-general of TV Malawi.

While the food crisis that gripped the region in 2002 has eased, the government says that more than a million people will continue to rely on food aid through March 2005.

Agriculture in Malawi employs 80 percent of the labor force, and the economy is dependent on tobacco, which accounts for more than half of exports. Wealth is concentrated in the hands of a small elite. Foreign donors accused the government of corruption and mismanagement in 2002, in part because of the $38 million sale of the country's strategic grain reserves. In 2003, the IMF approved its first loan disbursements to the country since aid was frozen two years earlier. The World Bank has also resumed aid, but other key donors, such as the European Union, are waiting to assess the performance of the new president before following suit.

Political Rights and Civil Liberties: The citizens of Malawi can change their government democratically, although there were irregularities in the 2004 presidential elections. The unicameral National Assembly is composed of 193 seats. Members are elected by popular vote to five-year terms. Suffrage is universal except for serving members of the military. The 1994 presidential elections were considered Malawi's first generally free and fair multiparty elections. The country's electoral commission has shown bias in favor of the ruling party on several occasions, and there have been problems with voter registration.

Malawi was ranked 90 out of 146 countries surveyed in Transparency International's 2004 Corruption Perceptions Index. The political opposition has repeatedly charged that the government uses bribery and intimidation to exploit opposition party divisions and encourage defections. However, President Mutharika has moved to fulfill campaign promises to crack down on state corruption, and the Anti-Corruption Bureau (ACB) made several arrests and indictments of former high-level government officials during the year.

Freedom of speech and of the press is legally guaranteed and generally respected in practice. Despite occasional restrictions and harassment, a broad spectrum of opinion is presented in Malawi's two dozen newspapers. Nevertheless, there were a number of attacks on the press in 2002 and 2003, allegedly committed by members of the Young Democrats, who are linked to the ruling UDF. After signs that the government was becoming increasingly intolerant of coverage of opposition activities, particularly relating to Muluzi's third-term bid, the situation improved somewhat in 2004. However, in May, just three days after the presidential polls, police arrested four journalists from the community radio station MIJ 90.3 after host Arthur Chokotho interviewed an opposition spokeswoman who accused the ruling party of stealing the elections. All four were released without charge within 24 hours. The station was shut down for a week, until the country's high court ordered it reopened. The Malawi Institute of Journalism has since sued the government for loss of income resulting from the closure. There are no restrictions on access to the Internet, although it is not widely used.

Religious freedom is usually respected, but Muslims were targeted in post-election violence in 1999 in protest against the ruling party. President Bingu wa Mutharika is a Catholic, and his vice president is Muslim. The government does not restrict academic freedom.

The government generally respects freedom of association and assembly. Many human rights organizations and other nongovernmental organizations operate openly and without interference. The right to organize and to strike is legally protected, with notice and mediation requirements for workers in essential services. Unions are active but face harassment and occasional violence during strikes. Collective bargaining is widely practiced.

The judiciary has demonstrated broad independence in its decisions, but due process is not always respected by an overburdened court system that lacks resources and training. Police brutality is still said to be common, either while detainees are in custody or when they are just released. In April 2004, police shot dead two youths protesting the death of an opposition sympathizer who had allegedly committed suicide while in custody. Police said the youths had attacked the station house with stones. Arbitrary arrest and detention are common. Appalling prison conditions lead to many deaths, including suffocation from overcrowding. Lengthy pretrial detention is a serious problem.

There are no laws limiting the participation of ethnic minorities in the political process. The constitution prohibits discrimination based on language or culture.

Despite constitutional guarantees of equal protection, customary practices maintain de facto discrimination against women in education, employment, and business. Traditional rural structures deny women inheritance and property rights, and violence against women is reportedly routine. The Malawi Human Rights Commission issued a report in 2003 charging that a sex-slave trade flourishes in remote areas of the north, with young girls sold by their parents to pay off debts. However, there has been increased attention to domestic violence and a greater effort to improve the rights of widows. Women employees recently won the right to maternity leave.

Malaysia

Population: 25,600,000   **Political Rights:** 4*
GNI/capita: $3,540   **Civil Liberties:** 4
Life Expectancy: 73   **Status:** Partly Free
Religious Groups: Muslim, Buddhist, Daoist,
Hindu, other
Ethnic Groups: Malay and other indigenous (58 percent),
Chinese (24 percent), Indian (8 percent), other (10 percent)
Capital: Kuala Lumpur
Ratings Change: Malaysia's political rights rating improved from 5 to 4 due to the
holding of reasonably free parliamentary elections.

Ten-Year Ratings Timeline (Political Rights, Civil Liberties, Status)

1995	1996	1997	1998	1999	2000	2001	2002	2003	2004
4,5PF	4,5PF	4,5PF	5,5PF	5,5PF	5,5PF	5,5PF	5,5PF	5,4PF	4,4PF

Overview:
By promising improvements in governance, Malaysia's prime minister, Abdullah Ahmad Badawi, succeeded in shoring up support for the ruling coalition ahead of general elections held in March 2004, which were reasonably free. Abdullah confirmed onlookers' faith in him in September when, under his rule, the Supreme Court overturned the six-year-old politicized sodomy conviction of former deputy prime minister Anwar Ibrahim, a case that had become the benchmark for human rights and political freedom in Malaysia.

Malaysia gained independence from Britain in 1957 and in 1963 merged with the British colonies of Sarawak, Sabah, and Singapore (Singapore left in 1965). The ruling Barisan National (BN) coalition has won at least a two-thirds majority in all 11 general elections since 1957. The BN consists of 14 mainly ethnic-based parties, dominated by the conservative, Malay-based United Malays' National Organization (UMNO).

Modern Malaysia has been shaped by Dr. Mahathir Mohamed, who became Malaysia's fourth prime minister in 1981. During his tenure, he transformed Malaysia from a sleepy backwater, dependent on tin, rubber, and palm oil exports, to a hub for multinationals and local firms exporting high-tech goods. However, he also stunted democratic institutions, weakened the rule of law by curtailing the press and political opponents, and fostered allegations of cronyism with his state-led industrial development. In addition, he was a polarizing figure at home and abroad, criticizing Malaysia's conservative Muslim leaders for failing to promote a more modern brand of Islam while rankling outsiders with anti-Western and anti-Semitic views.

In October 2003, Mahathir stepped down as the nation's leader after more than two decades in office, paving the way for his deputy, Abdullah, who sought to distance himself from his predecessor. Many countries and international organizations with hopes of reform looked on the subsequent appointment of Abdullah as prime minister with enthusiasm.

In the March 2004 election, the BN, led by Abdullah, won 198 of the 219 available seats in parliament. The elections were conducted in a generally transparent manner. However, the three main opposition parties—the Democratic Action Party, the Parti Islam Se-Malaysia and the Parti Keadilan Rakyat—challenged the results on the grounds that the BN had engaged in vote rigging and other irregularities; most specific challenges were rejected in court or withdrawn. Despite a strong popular mandate, reforms slowed over 2004, as Abdullah faced resistance within UMNO, especially in the September party elections. Abdullah's softer approach, however, has opened the regime and is working to strengthen political institutions.

On the economic front, Malaysia faces the challenge of finding new economic niches now that low-cost manufacturers in China are increasingly attracting the foreign investment that helped fuel Malaysia's roaring, electronics-led, economic growth in the 1980s and 1990s. Malaysia retains good relations with China. However, in May, Abdullah paid his first visit to China since taking office and discussed the promotion of economic and political ties with his Chinese counterpart. Abdullah has followed Mahathir's recent policies of emphasizing the role of small firms in driving economic growth and reducing the country's need for external demand and foreign direct investment.

Political Rights and Civil Liberties: Malaysians choose their leaders in elections that are free but not fair. Malaysia has a parliamentary government within a federal system. Executive power is vested in a prime minister and cabinet. Mahathir's 22-year tenure was marked by a steady concentration of power in the prime minister's hands; parliament's role as a deliberative body has deteriorated over the years, as legislation proposed by opposition parties tends not to be given serious consideration. Opposition parties face serious obstacles, such as unequal access to the media and restrictions on campaigning and on freedom of assembly, that leave them unable to compete on equal terms with the BN.

Malaysia was ranked 39 out of 146 countries surveyed in Transparency International's 2004 Corruption Perceptions Index. Corruption is marked in the police force; political corruption, particularly bribery and cronyism, is common in the ruling BN coalition. This may be changing under Abdullah's leadership, however. In November 2004, for example, the UMNO suspended several of its members on charges of vote buying in party elections. In reiterating his commitment to fighting corruption, Abdullah noted in October 2004 that 359 graft-related arrests had been made in the first eight months of the year, compared to 331 for full-year 2003. Earlier in the year, the government established a National Institute for Ethics and implemented a National Integrity Plan, both designed to help combat corruption.

The constitution provides for freedom of expression, but the government restricts this right in practice. Because all publications must obtain an operating permit every year from the government, most print media outlets practice self-censorship and downplay investigative journalism. Printers must also obtain government permits and are thus reluctant to print publications that are critical of the government. Internet editions of newspapers, however, are not required to obtain permits. Both privately owned television stations have close ties to the BN, so news and analysis related to opposition parties is restricted and slanted. The government directly censors books and films for profanity, nudity, and violence, as well as for certain political or religious material; television stations censor programming according to government guidelines.

Although the constitution guarantees freedom of religion, the government's official policy is to "infuse Islamic values" into the administration of the country. Nevertheless, Sikhs, Hindus, Christians, Buddhists, and other religious minorities worship freely in Malaysia, although the government tightly controls building and land allocation for their religious needs. The government restricts the practice of Islamic sects other than Sunni Islam and forbids proselytizing of Muslims by other religious groups. Muslim children are required to receive religious education that conforms with a government-approved curriculum, and Muslim civil servants must take Islamic classes taught by government-approved teachers.

The government restricts academic freedom to the extent that teachers or students espousing overtly antigovernment views may be subject to disciplinary action.

Freedom of assembly and association is limited on the grounds of maintaining security—particularly reducing ethnic conflict—and public order. A police permit is required for all public assemblies except for picket lines, and the granting of permits is sometimes politically influenced. The Societies Act of 1996 defines a society as any club, company, partnership, or association of seven or more people (excluding schools, businesses, and trade unions). Societies must be approved and registered by the government, and the government has refused to register organizations or revoked the registration of an existing society, generally for political reasons. Nonetheless, numerous nongovernmental organizations operate in Malaysia, but some international human rights organizations are not allowed to form Malaysian branches.

Most Malaysian workers can join trade unions, but Malaysian law contravenes International Labor Organization (ILO) guidelines by restricting trade unions to representing workers in a single, or similar, trade, industry, or occupation, thus preventing the formation of broad-based unions. Unions may organize workplaces and associate with national federations, of which there are currently two. Collective bargaining is widespread in sectors with organized labor. Labor laws restrict strikes by requiring that unions in "essential" services—the government's list of such services includes several not deemed essential by the ILO—give advance notice of planned strikes, and by imposing requirements so stringent that strikes are in practice impossible.

Judicial independence has been severely compromised over the past two decades in line with the increasing influence of the executive over the judiciary. Many examples of arbitrary or politically motivated verdicts, selective prosecution, and preferential treatment of lawyers and litigants have occurred. The most prominent of these, which had become the bellwether case for human rights and political freedom in Malaysia, was the conviction of Anwar Ibrahim in 1999 and 2000 for corruption and sodomy. Anwar was arrested in 1998, beaten while in custody, held under the Internal Security Act, and sentenced in two trials to consecutive prison terms of six and nine years. The move was widely regarded as having been entirely politically motivated, as Anwar, then the deputy prime minister, had been having political differences with then-prime minister Mahathir Mohamad; both trials, as well as Anwar's appeals, exhibited serious violations of due process.

In a landmark step in September 2004, however, Malaysia's High Court accepted the appeal on Anwar's sodomy conviction and released him from prison. The corruption charge was upheld, but since he had he had completed the sentence in 2003 after it was reduced to four years for good behavior, he was released. His release signaled changes in the governance under Abdullah. Human Rights Watch called the occasion "an historic moment for the rule of law in Malaysia" and expressed the hope that the acquittal might signal "a renewed commitment to judicial independence." It is too early to determine, however, whether this one instance reflects a wholesale change in the government's attitude toward human rights and the rule of law.

Malaysia's secular legal system is based on English common law. However, Muslims are subject to Sharia (Islamic law), which varies from state to state. Law enforcement is the responsibility of the Royal Malaysia Police, which are under the jurisdiction of the Home Ministry. Individuals may be arrested without a warrant for some offenses, and they may be held for 24 hours without being charged. There is no constitutional provision specifically banning torture, and the police have been known to torture prisoners and abuse detainees. There have also been reports of police killing individuals in the course of apprehending them. The creation of a Police Commission to review the force in 2004 has led to improvements in detention centers. Nevertheless, in November 2004 hundreds of prison inmates went on a hunger strike to protest poor prison conditions.

The Internal Security Act (ISA), in force since 1960, gives the police sweeping powers to hold any person acting "in a manner prejudicial to the security of Malaysia" for up to 60 days (extendible to two years). It has been used in recent years to jail mainstream politicians, alleged Islamic militants, trade unionists, suspected Communist activists, ordinary criminal suspects, and members of "deviant" Muslim sects, among others. In May 2004, Human Rights Watch released a report documenting systematic abuse of detainees held under the ISA at the Kamunting Detention Center; it also asserted that detainees had been denied their rights to due process. Later that month, the government opened the center for the first time ever to a tour by selected journalists. While they welcomed the gesture, observers at Human Rights Watch did not believe this step alone would end abuse under the ISA.

Although the constitution provides for equal treatment of all citizens, Malaysia maintains an official affirmative action policy intended to boost the economic status of ethnic Malays and other indigenous people known as *bumiputras*. Bumiputeras receive preferential treatment in many areas, including property ownership, higher education, civil service jobs, and business affairs.

Foreign domestic workers are not covered under the Workmen's Compensation Act and so are subject to economic exploitation and abuse by their employers and are extorted by the police. Malaysians officially employ about 240,000 domestic workers, 90 percent of whom are from Indonesia, although the actual number is much larger. There are an estimated two million illegal workers in Malaysia, who are seen to contribute to crime. The government initiated a series of programs to expel workers in 2004, although it offered an amnesty for Indonesian workers. In general, Malaysian citizens may travel, live, and work without restrictions; however, the government occasionally infringes on these rights.

Despite government initiatives and continued gains, women are still underrepresented in politics, the professions, and the civil service. Violence against women also remains a serious problem. Muslim women, whose grievances on family matters are heard in Islamic courts, receive unequal treatment because Islamic law favors men in matters such as inheritance and divorce, and does not give equal weight to the testimony of women.

⬇Maldives

Population: 300,000 **Political Rights:** 6
GNI/capita: $2,090 **Civil Liberties:** 5
Life Expectancy: 73 **Status:** Not Free
Religious Groups: Sunni Muslim
Ethnic Groups: South Indian, Sinhalese, Arab
Capital: Male
Trend Arrow: The Maldives received a downward trend arrow due to the imposition of a state of emergency and a continuing crackdown on opposition activists.

Ten-Year Ratings Timeline (Political Rights, Civil Liberties, Status)

1995	1996	1997	1998	1999	2000	2001	2002	2003	2004
6,6NF	6,6NF	6,6NF	6,5NF	6,5NF	6,5NF	6,5NF	6,5NF	6,5NF	6,5NF

Overview:

Political unrest continued to plague the Maldives in 2004, as President Maumoon Abdul Gayoom faced sustained pressure from pro-reform Maldivians who desire greater political freedom. Although Gayoom has promised to undertake reform of both the constitution and of existing political institutions, his government continues to severely restrict basic rights to freedom of speech and assembly and to commit various human rights violations, including arbitrary arrest, detention, and torture. Following a large antigovernment protest in August, authorities imposed a state of emergency and the halting reform process was put on hold indefinitely.

Consisting of a 500-mile-long string of nearly 1,200 islands in the Indian Ocean, the Maldives achieved independence in 1965 after 78 years as a British protectorate. A 1968 referendum set up a republican government, ending 815 years of rule by the Ad-Din sultanate. The Maldives's first president, Amir Ibrahim Nasir, introduced a number of changes to the political system, abolishing the post of prime minister in 1975.

Gayoom has held power since 1978, when he won his first five-year term under the country's tightly controlled presidential referendum process. The most serious threat to Gayoom's survival came in 1988, when Indian commandos crushed a coup attempt by a disgruntled businessman reportedly backed by Sri Lankan mercenaries. In the aftermath, the autocratic Gayoom strengthened the National Security Service (NSS) and named several relatives to top government posts.

Following an altercation at Maafushi prison in which prison guards beat an inmate to death, unrest erupted in September 2003. Security forces opened fire on other prisoners, killing three more and wounding over a dozen. Meanwhile, protesters attacked government buildings in the capital, setting several on fire. In response, Gayoom ordered the arrest of a number of NSS personnel and an inquiry into the circumstances of the initial killing was conducted, although an uncensored version of the report was not made public.

Gayoom's reelection was approved in an October 2003 referendum by just over 90 percent of participating voters. After being sworn in for a sixth presidential term, he promised to reform national institutions. In May 2004, elections were held to a People's Special Majlis that was tasked with amending the current constitution, and in June, Gayoom presented proposals for constitutional reform to the parliament.

However, in August, several thousand people demonstrated against the slow pace of democratic reforms and the continued detention of four political activists. In the violent unrest that followed, four police officers were stabbed and hundreds of protestors, including several reformist former members of parliament and government officials, were arrested and detained. On August 13, Gayoom declared a state of emergency, during which a number of civil liberties were suspended, and imposed an indefinite curfew on the capital city of Male. Although some of these rights were restored in October, the ban on public meetings and criticism of the government remains in place and at least 78 of the arrested protesters remain in jail, according to the BBC.

Political Rights and Civil Liberties:

Maldivians cannot change their head of government through elections. Under the 1968 constitution, the Majlis (parliament) chooses a single presidential nominee from among a list of candidates. The nominee is then approved or rejected by a national referendum held every five years. A 1998 constitutional amendment allowed citizens to declare their candidacies, but not campaign for the presidential nomination. The constitution grants the president—currently Maumoon Abdul Gayoom—broad executive powers and allows him to appoint 8 of the Majlis's 50 members (the remainder are directly elected) as well as the Speaker and Deputy Speaker. Nevertheless, in recent years, the Majlis has rejected some governmental legislation and has held livelier policy debates.

In addition to making arrests prior to the 1999 parliamentary elections, authorities also banned public campaign events, permitting only small meetings on private premises. Political parties are officially discouraged, and candidates for the Majlis run as individuals. After making an unsuccessful application for permission to register in 2001, the pro-reform Maldivian Democratic Party (MDP) operates in exile from Sri Lanka. Activists and supporters who took part in MDP internal elections were arrested ahead of a planned protest rally in February 2004.

Government accountability is limited by the fact that the executive exercises almost complete control over both the legislative and judicial branches. In such an atmosphere, nepotism and corruption are reportedly rampant, with other prominent official positions being filled by Gayoom's relatives and friends, according to a report by the New Delhi–based South Asia Human Rights Documentation Centre. The Maldives was not ranked by Transparency International in its 2004 Corruption Perceptions Index.

The law allows authorities to shut newspapers and sanction journalists for articles containing unfounded criticism of the government. Moreover, regulations make editors responsible for the content of material they publish. In 2002, four writers for *Sandhaanu*, an Internet magazine, were arrested; after they were held in detention and charged with defamation, three were sentenced to life imprisonment, although the sentences were later reduced. In this environment, many journalists practice self-censorship and do not scrutinize official policies. All broadcast media are government owned and operated, while close associates of the president control the main daily newspapers. The Web sites of the MDP and other antigovernment groups have been blocked by the government and are inaccessible from Internet cafés in Male, and Internet connectivity was suspended entirely during the August disturbances.

Freedom of religion is severely restricted by the government's requirement that all citizens be Sunni Muslims, a legal ban against the practice of other religions, and a constitutional provision making Islam the state religion. Non-Muslim foreigners are allowed to practice their religion privately, according to the U.S. State Department's 2004 Report on International Religious Freedom. There were no reported restrictions on academic freedom.

The government limits freedom of assembly and association. The penal code bans speech or actions that could "arouse people against the government," while a 1968 law prohibits speech considered libelous, inimical to Islam, or a threat to national security. In recent years, authorities have imprisoned political dissidents under broadly drawn laws, and police occasionally use excessive force against demonstrators. The Maldives has no known nongovernmental human rights groups.

Workers lack the legal rights to form trade unions, stage strikes, or bargain collectively. In practice, no unions exist, although some workers have established informal associations that address labor issues. The Maldives has about 27,000 foreign workers out of a total workforce of 70,000 to 75,000. Most workers are in the informal (unorganized) sector, although some work in the country's high-end tourism industry, which provides 70 percent of foreign exchange revenues.

Because Gayoom can review high court decisions and appoint and dismiss judges, "the judiciary is subject to executive influence," according to the U.S. State Department's human rights report for 2003. Civil law is generally used in civil and criminal cases, although it is subordinate to Sharia (Islamic law), which is used in matters not covered by civil law as well as in cases involving divorce or adultery. Under Sharia, the testimony of two women is equal to that of one man, and men are favored in divorce and inheritance matters. Punishments such as flogging and banishment to a remote island, which are provided for under the country's interpretation of Sharia, are occasionally carried out. With international donor assistance, a new criminal code is currently being drafted.

The NSS functions as the police, army, and intelligence services, and human rights groups allege that it acts with virtual impunity. Incidents of torture or other forms of ill-treatment of detainees held at police stations or prison facilities continue to be reported, according to Amnesty International. Arbitrary arrest and prolonged detention remain a concern, although judges must authorize the continued detention of suspects on a monthly basis. In response to the September 2003 disturbances, the government did establish a Human Rights Commission in December. However, as its members are appointed by the president and are to report directly to him, observers fear that its investigations of cases of abuse may not be impartial.

The government has in recent years detained or kept several political prisoners under house arrest, and some have been sentenced to long prison terms after being convicted in trials in which they have been denied legal representation. After the September 2003 civil protests, authorities arrested more than 100 people; although most were eventually released, Amnesty International alleged that over a dozen remained in detention at year's end. Authorities carried out a wave of preventive arrests prior to a planned MDP-sponsored rally in February and arrested several hundred protesters during the August 2004 demonstrations.

More women are entering the civil service, increasingly receiving equal pay to that of men for equal work. Women enjoy a 98 percent literacy rate, compared with 96 percent for men. However, traditional norms that oppose letting women lead independent lives outside their homes continue to limit educational and career opportunities for many women. The government has in recent years sponsored programs to help make women aware of their rights. Children's rights are incorporated into law, and government policy provides for equal access to educational and health programs for both male and female children.

Mali

Population: 13,400,000   **Political Rights:** 2
GNI/capita: $240   **Civil Liberties:** 2
Life Expectancy: 48   **Status:** Free
Religious Groups: Muslim (90 percent), indigenous
beliefs (9 percent), Christian (1 percent)
Ethnic Groups: Mande (50 percent), Peul (17 percent),
Voltaic (12 percent), Tuareg and Moor (10 percent),
Songhai (6 percent), other (5 percent)
Capital: Bamako

Ten-Year Ratings Timeline (Political Rights, Civil Liberties, Status)

1995	1996	1997	1998	1999	2000	2001	2002	2003	2004
2,3F	2,2F	3,3F	3,3F	3,3F	2,3F	2,3F	2,3F	2,2F	2,2F

Overview:
The government of President Amadou Toumani Toure was reshuffled in 2004. Nearly 100 political parties competed for control of more than 700 communes across the country in elections in May.

Following independence from France in 1960, Mali was ruled by military or one-party dictators for more than 30 years. After soldiers killed more than 100 demonstrators demanding a multiparty system in 1991, President Moussa Traore was overthrown by his own military. Traore and his wife, Mariam, were sentenced to death in January 1999 for embezzlement. Traore had also received the death sentence in 1993 for ordering troops to fire on demonstrators two years earlier. Sentences for both Traore and his wife have been commuted to life imprisonment.

After the 1991 coup, a national conference organized open elections that most observers judged to be free and fair, with Alpha Oumar Konare of the Alliance for Democracy in Mali (ADEMA) party winning the presidency in 1992. In 1997, a little more than a quarter of registered voters participated as Konare was overwhelmingly reelected against a weak candidate who alone broke an opposition boycott of the presidential contest.

Konare's ADEMA party suffered a split in 2001, adding more competition to the

May 2002 presidential election, in which 24 candidates participated. Toure, a former general who led Mali during the transition period to multiparty politics in the early 1990s, ran as an independent. After the first round of voting, the Constitutional Court canceled more than 500,000 ballots cast, citing voting by nonregistered voters and missing election reports as some of the irregularities. Several presidential candidates had petitioned the court to annul the results entirely, alleging fraud and vote rigging. Toure and Soumaila Cisse, of ADEMA, went to a second round of voting, with Toure securing 64 percent of the vote compared with 36 percent for Cisse. International observers said the polls were well managed and conducted in a spirit of transparency, although they also noted several logistical and administrative irregularities.

The Hope coalition dominated voting for National Assembly elections in July 2002, gaining 66 seats, while a coalition led by ADEMA won 51 seats. Smaller parties captured the remainder of the seats.

A government reshuffle in 2004 followed Toure's dissatisfaction with his prime minister. The new cabinet, like the previous one, was ethnically and politically broad based. The cabinet was expanded from 18 posts to 28.

The conduct of communal elections held in May 2004 was orderly and transparent. It was the first time the government had organized the simultaneous urban and communal elections. ADEMA won nearly 30 percent of seats in the more than 700 communes.

Toure, like his predecessor, has a strong international profile for having been active in regional peace and humanitarian efforts as a UN envoy. (In 2003, Konare took office as chairman of the African Union, which was formerly the Organization of African Unity.) Mali was working closely with the United States in 2004 as part of the Pan-Sahel Initiative to stem the growth of terrorist organizations across the vast Sahel region.

Despite steady economic growth, Mali remains desperately poor. About 65 percent of its land is desert or semi-desert, and about 80 percent of the labor force is engaged in farming or fishing. Hundreds of thousands of Malians are economic migrants across Africa and Europe.

Political Rights and Civil Liberties: Citizens of Mali can choose their government democratically. Since the end of military rule, Mali's domestic political debate has been open and extensive. Despite some irregularities noted by international observers, the 2002 presidential elections were regarded as well managed and conducted in a spirit of transparency. The president is elected for a five-year term. Elections for 147 National Assembly seats in 2002 were also regarded as being free and fair despite some administrative irregularities.

In 2004, some larger opposition political parties formed a coalition with the aim of boosting their chances in subsequent parliamentary and presidential elections.

Decentralization, which began in 1999, remained controversial. The process changed traditional power relationships between government and the governed and relieved formerly powerful civil servants of their authority. The government has passed many laws that allow greater financial autonomy in the areas of education, health, and infrastructure. The government has established a special commission to help eradicate corruption. Mali was ranked 77 out of 146 countries surveyed in Transparency International's 2004 Corruption Perceptions Index.

Although libel is still considered a criminal offense and press laws include punitive presumption-of-guilt standards, Mali's media are among Africa's most open. At least 40 independent newspapers operate freely, and more than 100 independent radio stations, including community stations broadcasting in regional languages, broadcast throughout the country. The government controls one television station and many radio stations, but all present diverse views, including those critical of the government. Three reporters from a private radio station were jailed for two weeks in 2003 on charges of defaming an attorney, in what was essentially a contempt-of-court proceeding. The government does not impede access to the Internet.

Mali is predominantly Muslim. However, it is a secular state, and minority and religious rights are protected by law. Religious associations must register with the government, but the law is not enforced. Sectarian violence occasionally flares between Muslim groups. Academic freedom is guaranteed and respected.

Many civic groups and nongovernmental organizations, including human rights groups, operate without interference. Freedom of assembly is guaranteed and respected. Workers are guaranteed the right to join unions, and nearly all salaried employees are unionized. The right to strike is guaranteed, with some restrictions. Public school teachers in December 2003 went on strike for two days to press for better working conditions and higher salaries.

Although the judiciary is not independent of the executive, it has shown considerable autonomy in rendering anti-administration decisions, which the government has in turn respected. The UN Human Rights Committee praised Mali in 2003 for its progress in improving human rights, citing the country's extensive legislative reform and a moratorium on capital punishment. Local chiefs, in consultation with elders, decide the majority of disputes in rural areas. Detainees are not always charged within the 48-hour period set by law, and there are often lengthy delays in bringing people to trial. Mali's human rights record is generally good, although there are reports of police brutality. The government permits visits by human rights monitors to prisons, which are characterized by overcrowding and inadequate medical care and food.

No ethnic group predominates in the government or the security forces, and political parties are not based on ethnicity. Long-standing tensions between the marginalized Moor and Tuareg pastoralist groups on the one hand and the more populous nonpastoralist groups on the other have been a main cause of political instability and violence, including the Tuareg rebellions of the early 1990s. A 1995 agreement ended the brutal, multisided conflicts between Tuareg guerrillas, black ethnic militias, and government troops.

Although the constitution prohibits forced labor, thousands of Malian children have been sold into servitude on coffee and cocoa plantations in neighboring Cote d'Ivoire by organized traffickers. Mali now requires children under 18 to carry travel documents; a law that made child trafficking punishable by up to 20 years in prison was enacted in 2001.

The UN Human Rights Committee concluded in 2003 that further work needs to be done to improve women's rights, specifically regarding marriage, divorce, inheritance, land ownership, and domestic violence. Most formal legal advances in the protection of women's rights have not been implemented, especially in rural areas. Societal discrimination against women persists, and social and cultural factors continue to limit their economic and educational opportunities. Legislation gives women property rights, but traditional practices and ignorance prevent many from taking advantage of the laws. Violence against women, including spousal abuse, is tolerated and common. Female genital mutilation remains legal, although the government has conducted educational campaigns against the practice. Numerous groups promote the rights of women and children.

Malta

Population: 400,000
GNI/capita: $9,200
Life Expectancy: 78
Religious Groups: Roman Catholic (98 percent), other [including Muslim, Jewish, and Protestant] (2 percent)
Ethnic Groups: Maltese [mixed Arab, Norman, Spanish, Italian, and English]
Capital: Valletta

Political Rights: 1
Civil Liberties: 1
Status: Free

Ten-Year Ratings Timeline (Political Rights, Civil Liberties, Status)

1995	1996	1997	1998	1999	2000	2001	2002	2003	2004
1,1F	1,1F	1,1F	1,1F	1,1F	1,1F	1,1F	1,1F	1,1F	1,1F

Overview:

Malta's legislature chose a new president, Eddie Fenech Adami, in March 2004. In May, the country joined the European Union (EU) along with nine other European countries in the largest expansion of the organization's history.

Malta is a small island nation with ties to both the European and Arab worlds. After gaining independence from the British in 1964, the country joined the Commonwealth and became a republic in 1974. From 1964 to 1971, Malta was ruled by the Nationalist Party (PN), which pursued a pro-Western alliance. In 1971, the European alliance broke down when the Labour Party (MLP) took power and moved the country toward nonalignment and a special friendship with leftist governments in Libya and Algeria. The PN returned to power in 1987, and in 1990 the country submitted its application for full membership in the EU (then the European Community).

After a brief interlude with the return to power of the MLP from 1996 to 1998, Malta continued in a pro-European direction that culminated on March 8, 2003, in a national referendum on EU accession. Malta was the first among the 10 current candidate countries to hold a referendum on the issue of EU membership, which was approved by a vote of 54 percent. The country formally joined the EU in May 2004 in the organization's largest expansion since its founding in the early years after World War II.

On March 29, 2004, the Chamber of Representatives elected a new president of the republic, Eddie Fenech Adami, the former prime minister and veteran leader of the ruling Nationalist Party. Lawrence Gonzi, the former deputy prime minister, took over the post of prime minister.

Political Rights and Civil Liberties: The Maltese are free to change their government democratically. The country has a unicameral legislature with 65 seats that are decided by a national system of proportional representation with an additional single-transferable-vote (STV) arrangement. STV is different from the traditional "list" proportional representation systems because it allows the voter not only to choose a party but also to rank-order the candidates running for office. Parliament is elected for a five-year term, and members of parliament, in turn, elect the president to serve five years. The prime minister is selected by a vote of party delegates.

National elections in 2003 returned the incumbent PN into power with around 52 percent of the vote and 35 seats. The MLP came in second with around 48 percent of the vote and 30 seats. The smaller Alternattiva Demokratika (AD) lost support compared with the elections in 1998.

The EU, in its 2003 monitoring report, which seeks to determine whether candidate countries are adopting its body of law, criticized Malta for lacking a specific anticorruption program. The issue of corruption emerged in the country after a chief justice in 2003 had to resign because of a bribery scandal over a prison sentence appeal. Malta was ranked 25 out of 146 countries surveyed in Transparency International's 2004 Corruption Perceptions Index.

The constitution guarantees freedom of speech and of the press. There are several newspapers and weeklies in both Maltese and English, as well as radio and television stations. The island also has access to Italian television, which many Maltese watch. The government does not block Internet access.

The constitution establishes Roman Catholicism as the state religion, and the state grants subsidies only to Catholic schools. However, although the population is overwhelmingly Roman Catholic, other religious groups are tolerated and respected. There are small communities of Muslims, Jews, and Protestants, the latter being mostly British retirees. There is one Muslim private school in the country. The government had also approved a site for a 500-grave Muslim cemetery, although by the end of the year work on this project had not yet begun.

Academic freedom is respected, and there is generally free and open discussion in the country. However, an amendment to the criminal code makes incitement to racial hatred a crime punishable by a prison term of six to eight months.

The constitution provides for freedom of assembly and association, and the government generally respected these rights. International and domestic NGOs investigating human rights issues were able to operate without government interference. The law recognizes the right to form and join trade unions, and limits on the right to strike were eased in 2002. However, the country's compulsory arbitration clause in its Employment and Industrial Relations Act allows the government to force a settlement on striking workers. This clause, which permits compulsory arbitration to be held even if it is requested by only one of the parties involved, contravenes the International Labor Organization's Convention 87. According to the International Confederation of Free Trade Unions, the government insists that it rarely invokes this clause as it is used only when all other channels for arbitration have been exhausted.

The judiciary is independent, and the rule of law prevails in civil and criminal matters. The Police Ordinance Act, which took effect in 2003, provides a number of reform measures related to policing and criminal justice, including the establishment of a witness protection program and a mechanism for handling both internal and external complaints directed toward the police. Prison conditions generally met international standards.

A magisterial inquiry commenced in May to investigate the deportation of 220 Eritrean citizens in 2002, who subsequently disappeared and are believed to have been killed. According to the U.S. State Department, the inquiry concluded that officials did not use irregular or illegal practices and had "exercised due discretion and diligence throughout the entire deportation process and had provided the Eritrean nationals full information about their rights."

The government respects personal autonomy and freedom. However, divorce is illegal and violence against women continues to be a problem on the island. Additionally, of the 65 seats in parliament, women occupy only 6. Progress, though, has been made. Women now occupy two government posts, the Minister of Gozo (the second island in the archipelago) and the Minister for Family and Solidarity. The women are the first to occupy government positions of such high standing.

Marshall Islands

Population: 100,000
GNI/capita: $2,270
Life Expectancy: 69
Religious Groups: Christian (mostly Protestant)
Ethnic Groups: Micronesian
Capital: Majuro

Political Rights: 1
Civil Liberties: 1
Status: Free

Ten-Year Ratings Timeline (Political Rights, Civil Liberties, Status)

1995	1996	1997	1998	1999	2000	2001	2002	2003	2004
1,1F	1,1F	1,1F	1,1F	1,1F	1,1F	1,1F	1,1F	1,1F	1,1F

Overview:
Landowners in Kwajalein Island, the U.S. government's most important missile-testing site in the Marshall Islands, refused in 2004 to accept a proposed agreement to extend the American presence through 2066, demanding payment of $19.1 million a year instead of the $15 million being offered. However, their view had not significantly swayed the governments of either the Marshall Islands or the U.S. in their negotiations.

The atolls and islands that constitute the present-day Republic of the Marshall Islands were under Spanish and German rule before being occupied by Japan during World War II. They were placed under U.S. trusteeship in 1947, and in 1986, the island republic, 4,200 miles southwest of California, gained full independence. The country continues to maintain close relations with the United States through the Compact of Free Association, an agreement that provides the Marshall Islands with U.S. defense protection and development assistance in exchange for rights to establish U.S. missile bases. (The Federated States of Micronesia and the Republic of Palau have similar agreements with the United States.) The compact provides nearly half of the country's national budget.

Kessai Note was chosen president by parliament in January 2000 after his United Democratic Party (UDP) won general elections in December 1999. The first commoner to hold the post, Note succeeded Imata Kabua, whom opponents accused of misusing government funds and running an administration that lacked openness and accountability. Many also criticized Kabua's proposal to rent remote, uninhabited islands to foreign countries as nuclear waste dumps.

In the November 2003 parliamentary elections—the seventh national election since independence—the UDP won a majority in the 33-seat House of Representatives (Nitijela). Note was elected to a second term in the subsequent presidential elections held in the same month.

Since 1964, Kwajalein has been the primary U.S. testing ground for long-range nuclear missiles and antimissile defense. Between 1946 and 1958, 67 nuclear weapons tests were conducted in the Marshall Islands. Activities at the testing range have increased since 2000. Negotiations in 2002 and 2003 resulted in an amended compact that was entered into force on May 1, 2004. The amended compact provides for a transfer of $57 million from the United States to the Marshall Islands over the next 10 years and another $62 million over the following 10 years. Marshallese will also have access to U.S. education and medical programs and services throughout these next two decades. Rent payments to landowners in Kwajalein have been raised to $15 million, plus $5.1 million in annual development funding. Marshallese will also retain visa-free entry to the United States to live, work, and study, but lose $800,000 in annual college scholarships.

In exchange for increased funds, the Marshallese government has agreed to crack down on illegal passport sales. The illegal sale of passports has been a problem since the mid-1990s, when about 2,000 people, mainly from China, Taiwan, and Hong Kong, were found to have purchased fake documents. In addition, a Joint Economic Management and Financial Accountability Committee (JEMFAC), composed of representatives of both governments, has been set up to ensure that the funds are spent effectively. The United States is interested in negotiating a new compact to extend U.S. use of the Kwajalein missile-testing range through 2066, in exchange for $2.3 billion and the establishment of an $800 million trust fund to replace direct U.S. assistance after the expiration of the recently amended compact.

Political Rights and Civil Liberties: Citizens of the Marshall Islands can change their government democratically. The president is the head of state and chief executive, and is chosen by the House of Representatives (Nitijela) from among its members. The members of the 33-seat Nitijela are directly elected to four-year terms. The upper house—the Council of Chiefs (Iroji)—consists of 12 traditional leaders who advise on customary law. Political parties are legal, but there are none. The UDP of President Kessai Note is more of a loose caucus than a formal party. Note, the only commoner to have held the office of president, was first elected to the post in January 2000.

After the country was placed on the European Union's watch list, the government took action against tax evasion and money laundering. Corruption is a considerable problem. Public dissatisfaction with political corruption and abuses by government officials has led to calls for change. However, international watch groups and domestic critics report little progress on reform and improved transparency.

Freedom of speech is respected. A privately owned newspaper publishes articles in English and Marshallese. Two radio stations, one government owned and one church-owned, carry news broadcasts from overseas. The government station carries public service announcements and live broadcasts of legislative sessions, and cable television offers foreign news and entertainment programs and occasional videotaped local events. The government does not restrict Internet access, but penetration rates are low due to cost and technical access issues outside the capital.

Freedom of religion and academic freedom are respected in practice. College education is rare among Marshall Islanders. Of its 55,000 people, fewer than 130 currently attend four-year colleges in the country and elsewhere in the Pacific region and the United States.

Non-government organizations (NGOs) operate freely in the country, many of which are involved in women's rights and children's welfare. NGOs sponsored by or affiliated with Christian church organizations help provide social services. The government broadly interprets constitutional guarantees of freedom of assembly and association to cover trade unions. There is no formal right to strike or engage in collective bargaining, but there are no formal prohibitions against such activities.

The constitution provides for an independent judiciary, although past governments have tried to influence the judiciary. Three former chief justices either resigned or were fired by the government in the late 1990s. Chief Justice Charles Henry, a U.S. citizen, was tried in August 2003 on 29 charges of alleged misuse of government funds, cheating and criminal libel. Nearly all judges, prosecutors, and public defenders are foreigners because few Marshallese have law degrees. The government raised judges' salaries in recent years to better attract and retain more qualified judges.

There were no reports of police abuse of suspects or prisoners. Detention centers and prisons provide a basic level of comfort. Domestic and foreign human rights groups have not been barred from visiting these facilities or reporting their observations.

Social and economic discrimination against women is widespread despite this being a matrilineal society, where traditional rank and property are passed through female bloodlines. Domestic violence against women is often alcohol-related. The government has taken a stronger stand in prosecuting rapes: five cases went to court in 2003 compared with just one in 2002.

Mauritania

Population: 3,000,000
GNI/capita: $280
Life Expectancy: 54
Religious Groups: Muslim (100 percent)
Ethnic Groups: Mixed Maur and black (40 percent),
Maur (30 percent), black (30 percent)
Capital: Nouakchott

Political Rights: 6
Civil Liberties: 5
Status: Not Free

Ten-Year Ratings Timeline (Political Rights, Civil Liberties, Status)

1995	1996	1997	1998	1999	2000	2001	2002	2003	2004
6,6NF	6,6NF	6,6NF	6,5NF	6,5NF	6,5NF	5,5PF	5,5PF	6,5NF	6,5NF

Overview:

Authorities in Mauritania announced that they had foiled two coup plots, one at the end of 2003 by the incumbent's main challenger who was defeated in the 2003 presidential election, and another in 2004 allegedly backed by Burkina Faso and Libya.

After nearly six decades of French colonial rule, Mauritania's borders as an independent state were formalized in 1960. A 1978 military coup ended a civilian one-party state led by Moktaar Ould Daddah. Another coup, in 1984, installed Colonel Maaouya Ould Sid'Ahmed Taya as Mauritania's leader. The absence of an independent election commission, state control of broadcasts, harassment of independent print media, and the incumbent's use of state resources to promote his candidacy devalued Taya's presidential victories in 1992—the country's first, and deeply flawed, multiparty poll—and again in 1997. Taya's Democratic and Social Republican Party (PRDS) ruled the country as a de facto one-party state after the main opposition parties boycotted National Assembly elections in 1992 and 1996.

In the 2001 municipal and National Assembly elections, Mauritanians were, for the first time, permitted to exercise their constitutional right to choose their representatives in relatively open, competitive elections. More than a dozen parties participated in the elections to choose 81 members of the National Assembly. However, the ruling PRDS was the only party to present candidates in every constituency, and the electoral law was modified to ban independent candidates, whose seats went mainly to the PRDS. The PRDS won 64 assembly seats, while opposition parties won 17.

In June 2003, the Taya government weathered a coup attempt that triggered two days of fighting in the capital. Some of the leaders of the uprising escaped and announced the formation of an armed rebel movement called the Knights of Change.

The November 2003 presidential election saw the issuance of new voter cards that were difficult to falsify, the publication of a list of registered voters, and the use of transparent ballot boxes. However, although the six candidates were each allocated equal time on state-run broadcast media, Taya received more than his share. Civil society groups were barred from forming an independent body to monitor the poll, and many foreign observers declined to participate after Taya's main challenger, Mohamed Khouna Ould Haidalla, was briefly detained on the eve of the election.

Police raided the home of Haidalla, whom Taya had overthrown nearly two decades ago, reportedly on suspicion that he and his supporters were plotting to overthrow Taya if Haidalla lost the election. Opposition members said some voters were allowed to cast ballots without proper identification and that opposition representatives were barred from polling stations. They also reported double voting, voting by proxy, and vote buying.

Taya was reelected to another six-year term with 67 percent of the vote compared with 19 percent for Haidallah. The day after the election, authorities detained Haidallah, and he and more than a dozen of his supporters were to go on trial for allegedly threatening state security. Although opposition candidates disputed the results of the election, they did not choose to take their complaints to court. Haidallah received a five-year suspended prison sentence in December 2003 after being found guilty of planning a coup to seize power immediately after the November presidential poll. An appeals court in April 2004 confirmed that he would be stripped of his political rights for five years.

In September 2004, the government announced that it had foiled a new coup plot and accused Burkina Faso and Libya of backing disgruntled soldiers. Both countries denied the charges. Three leading opposition leaders, including former president Haidallah, were detained in November 2004 and charged with scheming to overthrow the government. They were among the nearly 200 people, including about 170 military personnel, who were put on trial at the end of November 2004 for coup plotting. The government accuses some of the suspects of belonging to an Islamist group that is dissatisfied with Taya's pro-Israel and pro-U.S. policies. Some opposition supporters say the charges are a convenient way for the government to silence its political opposition.

Mauritania has been cultivating closer ties with the United States and is undergoing free market reform. The country is one of three Arab League states, along with Egypt and Jordan, that has diplomatic relations with Israel, despite domestic criticism. Diplomatic ties were established in 1999. Mauritania is working with the United States as part of the Pan-Sahel Initiative to promote security and stem the growth of terrorist organizations across the vast Sahel region.

Mauritania is one of the world's poorest countries, although recently oil has been discovered offshore. Much of the country's wealth is concentrated in the hands of a small elite that controls an economy based on iron ore exports and fishing. In 2004, Mauritania was faced with agricultural devastation, as swarms of locusts threatened to destroy the country's agricultural production and trigger famine.

Political Rights and Civil Liberties:

Mauritanians cannot choose their government democratically. The National Assembly exercises little independence from the executive. The country's narrowly based, authoritarian regime has gradually become liberalized, but most power remains in the hands of the president and a very small elite. The November 2003 presidential poll lacked transparency and was held in an atmosphere of intimidation. The president is elected for a six-year term and appoints the prime minister. The ruling party dominates the bicameral legislature. Members of the 81-seat National Assembly are elected by popular vote every five years. Polls for some of the Senate seats are held every two years; the remainder of senators, who are elected by municipal leaders, serve six-year terms.

In 2004, the government denied a request to legalize the Party for Democratic Convergence. Authorities say the party includes Islamic radicals and fugitives. The party was formed from the broad coalition of opposition forces that backed Mohamed Khouna Ould Haidalla for the 2003 presidential election.

Mauritania was not ranked by Transparency International in its 2004 Corruption Perceptions Index. Authorities in 2004 promised sweeping anticorruption measures after prosecutors broke a rare case against five officials of the rural development ministry accused of stealing more than $1 million.

Prepublication censorship, arrests of journalists, and seizures and bans of newspapers devalue constitutional guarantees of free expression. The state monopolizes all broadcast media. Independent publications openly criticize the government, but all publications must be submitted to the Interior Ministry prior to distribution. The constitution forbids dissemination of reports deemed to "attack the principles of Islam or the credibility of the state, harm the general interest, or disturb public order and security." The government does not impede Internet access.

Police in June 2004 detained and interrogated Aidahy Ould Saleck, regional correspondent of the independent *L'Eveil Hebdo* weekly newspaper, for four hours in connection with a story about police abuses.

Mauritania is an Islamic state in which, by statute, all citizens are Muslims who may not possess other religious texts or enter non-Muslim households. Among foreigners, however, non-Muslims are permitted to worship privately, and some churches operate openly. President Maaouya Ould Sid Ahmed Taya has targeted Muslim extremism. Academic freedom is guaranteed and is not restricted, although security forces have cracked down violently on student demonstrations in the past.

Freedom of association is restricted, and infrequent demonstrations are often violently suppressed. The law requires all recognized political parties and nongovernmental organizations (NGOs) to apply to the local prefect for permission to hold large meetings or assemblies. While numerous NGOs, including human rights and antislavery groups, operate, a handful of black African activist groups and Islamist parties are banned.

The constitution provides for the right of citizens to unionize and bargain for wages. All workers except members of the military and police are free to join unions. Approximately one-fourth of Mauritania's workers serve in the small formal (business) sector. The right to strike is limited by arbitration.

Mauritania's judicial system is heavily influenced by the government. Many decisions are shaped by Sharia (Islamic law), especially in family and civil matters. A judicial reform program is under way. Prison conditions in Mauritania are harsh, but conditions have slightly improved. There were several reports in 2004 of arbitrary arrest and detention. Security forces suspected of human rights violations operated with impunity.

Mauritania's people include the dominant Beydane (white Maurs) of Arab extraction and Haratine (black Maurs) of African descent. Other, non-Muslim, black Africans inhabiting the country's southern frontiers along the Senegal River valley constitute approximately one-third of the population. For centuries, black Africans were subjugated and taken as slaves by both white and black Maurs. In 2003, the government passed a law that makes slavery a crime and provides for punishment of violators. Although the government does not officially sanction slavery, a few thousand blacks still live in conditions of servitude. A government campaign against the mainly black southern part of the country in the late 1980s culminated with a massive deportation of blacks to Senegal, and relations between the two countries remain strained.

The Mauritanian Committee for the Elimination of Racial Discrimination issued a report in 2004 that said slavery was an ongoing and widespread practice, as was discrimination against Mauritania's black minority. The government denied the allegations.

Societal discrimination against women is widespread, but is improving. In 2003, for the first time, a female candidate participated in the presidential election and the first Haratine female was appointed to the cabinet. Under Sharia, a woman's testimony is given only half the weight of a man's. Legal protections regarding property and equality of pay are usually respected only in urban areas among the educated elite. At least one-quarter of girls undergo female genital mutilation; the government has intensive media and education campaigns against this practice.

Mauritius

Population: 1,200,000 **Political Rights:** 1
GNI/capita: $3,860 **Civil Liberties:** 1*
Life Expectancy: 72 **Status:** Free
Religious Groups: Hindu (52 percent), Roman Catholic
(26 percent), Protestant (2.3 percent), Muslim
(16.6 percent), other (3.1 percent)
Ethnic Groups: Indo-Mauritian (68 percent), Creole
(27 percent), Sino-Mauritian (3 percent), Franco-Mauritian (2 percent)
Capital: Port Louis
Ratings Change: Mauritius' civil liberties rating improved from 2 to 1 due to the consolidation of associational rights.

Ten-Year Ratings Timeline (Political Rights, Civil Liberties, Status)

1995	1996	1997	1998	1999	2000	2001	2002	2003	2004
1,2F	1,2F	1,2F	1,2F	1,2F	1,2F	1,2F	1,2F	1,2F	1,2F

Overview:

Although Mauritius was generally peaceful throughout 2004, hundreds of civil servants stormed the a government building in August to protest a decision to set up a body to oversee revenue collection. The country's economy continued to grow steadily throughout the year.

Mauritius's ethnically mixed population is primarily descended from immigrants from the Indian subcontinent who were brought to the island as laborers during its 360 years of Dutch, French, and British colonial administration. Since gaining independence from Britain in 1968, Mauritius has maintained one of the developing world's most successful democracies. In 1992, the island became a republic within the Commonwealth, with a president as head of state.

In a surprise move, in August 2000 President Cassam Uteem dissolved the National Assembly and called early elections, in large part because of a series of corruption scandals that had led to the resignation of several cabinet ministers. Some 80 percent of eligible voters went to the polls. The outgoing prime minister, Dr. Navin Rangoolam, had served since 1995. In the 2000 elections, the victorious opposition alliance was led by the Militant Socialist Movement (MSM). Its leader, Sir Anerood Jugnauth, returned to the prime minister's office, a position he had previously held between 1982 and 1995. The MSM is allied with the Mauritian Militant Movement (MMM).

Mauritius has achieved a stable democratic and consolidated constitutional order, a level of political development enjoyed by few other African states. The political process is used to maintain ethnic balance and economic growth rather than dominance by any single group. In addition, according to the *Political Handbook of the World*, political parties are divided more by personality and pragmatic considerations than by ideology or ethnicity.

The country's political stability has been underpinned by steady economic growth and improvements in the island's infrastructure and standard of living. Per capita income is $3,860, one of the highest in Africa. Adult literacy is 84 percent. Mauritius's integrated, multinational population has provided a capable and reliable workforce that, along with preferential European and U.S. market access for sugar and garment exports, is attracting foreign investment.

According to IMF figures, real growth in gross domestic product for 2004 was projected to be approximately 4.5 percent in 2004, following a disappointing 2.5 percent the previous year. This was predicated on the recovery of tourism and sugar production, the latter due to favorable weather, and continued strong construction and transportation activity. However, high domestic production costs and increasing competition have continued to affect adversely the export processing zone (EPZ) sector, which registered negative growth for the second consecutive year. In addition, significant environmental degradation has occurred as the economy has developed.

In a planned power shift, Paul Berenger assumed the prime minister's position in September 2003, becoming the first person from outside the island's Indian-origin majority to hold the post. As part of the same pact, former prime minister Jugnauth moved up to the largely symbolic presidency. Although 2004 was generally a peaceful year in Mauritius, in August about 1,000 civil servants stormed the government building to protest a decision to set up a body to oversee revenue collection. The demonstrators feared that this would lead to the retrenchment of 2,000 civil servants.

On the international front, Berenger threatened to pull the country out of the Commonwealth because of a dispute with Britain over the sovereignty of the Chacos Islands, which include the strategically important island of Diego Garcia.

Political Rights and Civil Liberties: Citizens of Mauritius have the right to change their government democratically. The head of state is a president, elected by the National Assembly for a five-year term. Executive power resides in the prime minister. The National Assembly is unicameral; it has 62 members who are directly elected by universal adult suffrage and a maximum of 8 (currently 4) members appointed from unsuccessful parliamentary candidates who gained the largest number of votes. The members serve for a five-year term, and the next elections are due in 2005. There is considerable debate taking place over election law reform. Two proposals are being considered in parliament on the introduction of a mixed majoritarian-proportional representation system.

Since independence, Mauritius has regularly chosen its representatives in free, fair, and competitive elections. In 2002, the National Assembly appointed two separate committees to examine recommendations submitted by a constitutional and electoral reform commission. In 2003, constitutional amendments that modestly strengthened presidential powers were passed. These deal with the duties of the president, the appointment of the president and members of the electoral commission, the dissolution of the National Assembly, and the exercise of the prerogative of clemency. Decentralized structures govern the country's island dependencies. The largest of these is Rodrigues Island, which has its own government and local councils, and two seats in the National Assembly.

In recent years, there have been a number of corruption cases, and recent efforts to market Mauritius as an international financial center have been impeded by a number of domestic banking market scandals. Mauritius was ranked 54 out of 146 countries surveyed in Transparency International's 2004 Corruption Perceptions Index.

According to the BBC, the constitution guarantees freedom of expression and of the press. The state-owned Mauritius Broadcasting Corporation (MBC) operates radio and TV services and generally reflects government thinking. A small number of private radio stations have been authorized, but the state-run media enjoy a monopoly in broadcasting local news. A special committee chaired by the prime minister has been set up to review the Independent Broadcasting Act. The prime minister has criticized private radio stations, stating that they should be more responsible. The government consequently asked the Independent Broadcasting Authority to implement measures to control the radio stations. Opponents of greater government control emphasize that the independent media are a vital arena in which ordinary citizens can voice their opinions on the government's performance.

Several private daily and weekly publications, however, are often highly critical of both government and opposition politicians and their policies. Four daily newspapers and eight weeklies offer balanced coverage in several languages and are often critical of both the government and the opposition parties. Internet access is available.

Freedom of religion is respected, as is academic freedom.

The rights to freedom of assembly and association are also respected, although police occasionally refuse to issue permits for demonstrations. Numerous nongovernmental organizations operate. Nine labor federations include 300 unions.

The generally independent judiciary is headed by the Supreme Court. The legal system is an amalgam of French and British traditions. Civil rights are generally well respected, although cases of police brutality have been reported. There are no known political prisoners, reports of political or extrajudicial killings, or significant criticisms of prison conditions.

Various cultures and traditions flourish in peace, though Mauritian Creoles, descendents of African slaves who make up a third of the population, live in poverty and complain of discrimination. In addition, tensions between the Hindu majority and Muslim minority persist, despite the general respect for constitutional prohibitions against discrimination. These tensions constitute one of the country's few potential political flashpoints.

Women constitute approximately 20 percent of the paid labor force and generally occupy a subordinate role in society, although the constitution guarantees that all Mauritians are equal before the lawWomen can now form part of a jury. Professional women can be assessed separately from their husbands for tax purposes. In 1997, Mauritius became the first country in the region to have passed a Protection from Domestic Violence Act. In 2000, only 4 women were elected to the 562-member parliament. Only 5 percent of women occupy senior positions in the 100 top companies.

Mexico

Population: 106,200,000 **Political Rights:** 2
GNI/capita: $5,920 **Civil Liberties:** 2
Life Expectancy: 75 **Status:** Free
Religious Groups: Roman Catholic (89 percent),
Protestant (6 percent), other (5 percent)
Ethnic Groups: Mestizo (60 percent), Amerindian
(30 percent), white (9 percent), other (1 percent)
Capital: Mexico City

Ten-Year Ratings Timeline (Political Rights, Civil Liberties, Status)

1995	1996	1997	1998	1999	2000	2001	2002	2003	2004
4,4PF	4,3PF	3,4PF	3,4PF	3,4PF	2,3F	2,3F	2,2F	2,2F	2,2F

Overview: The year 2004 marked a resurgence of hard-line sectors of the Institutional Revolutionary Party (PRI) that ruled Mexico for more than seven decades, as the PRI swept to power in the states of Oaxaca, Veracruz, and Baja California and took the mayoralty in Tijuana by running as its candidate a highly controversial gambling tycoon linked in the press to drug lords. President Vicente Fox's National Action Party (PAN) continued to fight, mostly unsuccessfully, an electoral and parliamentary rearguard action, hampered by public discontent with poverty, corruption, and crime that appeared to finally dent the chief of state's own popularity. Meanwhile, attention focused increasingly on the 2006 presidential elections, with the mayor of Mexico City the apparent front-runner throughout 2004.

Mexico achieved independence from Spain in 1810 and established itself as a republic in 1822. Seven years after the Revolution of 1910, a new constitution was promulgated under which the United Mexican States became a federal republic consisting of 31 states and a federal district (Mexico City). From its founding in 1929 until 2000, the PRI dominated the country by means of its corporatist, authoritarian structure, which was maintained through patronage, corruption, and repression. The formal business of government took place mostly in secret and with little legal foundation. In 1999, the PRI nominated, in first-ever open-party competition, former interior minister Francisco Labastida, hailed by some as the politician's return to the helm of a party ruled during the three previous administrations by technocrats. In September, the PAN nominated Fox, governor of Guanajuato. Cuauhtemoc Cardenas took leave of the Mexico City mayoralty and announced he would again lead the national ticket of the Democratic Revolution Party (PRD). Despite election-eve polls suggesting Fox would lose, on July 2, 2000, he won Mexico's presidency with 42.5 percent of the vote. Labastida won 36 percent, and Cardenas, just 16.6 percent. By becoming almost the largest party in the lower house of congress, the PAN won enough state governorships to put the long-ruling PRI in danger, momentarily at least, of becoming a regional party.

Following his election, Fox selected an eclectic cabinet whose new faces signaled an end to the revolving door of bureaucrats in top positions and included businessmen and leftist intellectuals. However, his choice for attorney general, a serving general, was bitterly opposed by human rights groups. Fox announced plans to overhaul the notoriously corrupt and inefficient law enforcement agencies, breaking political ties between the police and the presidency. In his inaugural address, Fox pledged to make Mexico an international leader in human rights.

As Fox reached the halfway mark of his six-year presidency in 2003, his greatest achievements remained having bested the long-ruling PRI in the 2000 presidential contest and decapitating the country's vicious drug cartels. The most popular decision of his presidency—to oppose the U.S.-led Iraq war—nonetheless did little to enhance his party's standing with the electorate. Washington's refusal to engage Fox on migration issues, despite early assurances that it would, deprived the president of a policy win on the most important issue in U.S.-Mexico bilateral relations.

Most Mexicans saw little progress in addressing the problems of poverty, corruption, crime, and unemployment that the charismatic rancher-politician had promised to fix. Elections held in July 2003, which shook up Mexico's congress in the first major federal election in three years, not only were the most expensive in recent memory, but also yielded a record low voter turnout. The results of the vote, in which the PAN lost the governorship in the prosperous industrial state of Nuevo Leon, long a party stronghold, reaffirmed the dominant roles of opposition parties in both houses of congress as well as increased the PRI's representation in many state legislatures and governorships. The PAN's congressional vote dropped from 38 percent in 2000 to 30.5 percent, while the PRI won 38 percent and the PRD received 18 percent. The PRD not only increased its own congressional representation, but also consolidated its hold on Mexico City, the Western Hemisphere's largest urban area, winning the presidency of 14 of the city's 16 boroughs.

Despite Fox's post-election promises to work harder to collaborate with the opposition on a reform agenda, the PAN's bickering with the president over indigenous rights and fiscal reform, combined with jockeying within the unreformed PRI for the party's 2006 presidential nomination, made that possibility seem increasingly remote. By 2004, a perceived power vacuum—brought about in part by a long-standing partisan logjam in congress—resulted in greater attention to the next presidential contest, even though it was still two years away. Through much of the year, popular Mexico City mayor Andres Manuel Lopez Obrador of the PRD appeared to be the runaway front-runner for the 2006 elections, despite having been tainted by several corruption scandals involving top aides. In June and July, Fox faced several high-level resignations from his government in a crisis that was only resolved when his wife publicly denied planning to run to replace him in 2006. In addition, Fox had to fend off charges that he was behind efforts to impeach the mayor of Mexico City in a legal dispute involving an obscure land case that the leftist opposition party called "a technical coup d'etat."

During 2004, 14 state-level elections were held, including 10 gubernatorial races, with a major surprise in the near-loss by the PRI of the governorship of Veracruz, long a party stronghold. Legal challenges to how gubernatorial contests in Oaxaca and Veracruz and the mayoral election in Tijuana were conducted were issued and subsequently denied, with the three victors taking their posts on December 1. In June, half a million people protested in Mexico City against rampant kidnappings and crime in general. In November, anger over the seemingly unstoppable crime wave gripping much of the country appeared to have been at least partly responsible for the lynching by an angry mob of three federal police officers in Mexico City in November.

In October, a unanimous decision by the Supreme Court to review a case seeking to charge former president Luis Echeverria (1970–1976) and 13 other former government officials with genocide for a 1971 student massacre was hailed by rights and legal experts as a significant step toward accountability for a "dirty war" against leftist dissidents in which no public officials were ever convicted. It was the first time a former president of Mexico had been charged with any crime.

Political Rights and Civil Liberties:

Mexicans can choose their government democratically. In four consecutive elections, opposition parties made gains in state and municipal contests in elections that were generally considered to be free and fair. The president is elected to a six-year term and cannot be reelected. A bicameral congress consists of the 128-member Senate elected for six years, with at least one minority senator from each state, and the 500-member Chamber of Deputies elected for three years, 300 directly and 200 through proportional representation. Members of Congress are also barred from reelection. Each state has an elected governor and legislature.

A series of high-profile cases of prominent politicians caught on videotape while taking illegal cash earlier in the year had led the political parties to pledge support for an overhaul of elections rules in order to limit corruption. However, there continued to be credible reports of misuse of power and resources by incumbent parties to favor their candidates in the 2004 elections, with numerous complaints lodged with Mexico's Special Prosecutor for Electoral Crimes.

According to a recent study by the Mexico chapter of Transparency International, some $2.3 billion (approximately 1 percent) of the country's economic production goes to officials in bribes, with the poorest families paying nearly 14 percent of their income in bribes. Corruption at the state-owned petroleum giant Pemex alone is estimated to cost the company more than $1 billion a year. The U.S. Drug Enforcement Administration estimates that between $25 billion and $30 billion of illegal drug money is laundered each year in Mexico and says that the country's financial, political, military, and judicial institutions facilitate those crimes. In November 2003, the Mexican Senate approved a legislative package designed to prevent and detect terrorist financing by clamping stricter reporting requirements on financial institutions and setting down strict penalties for violations of those rules. Mexico was ranked 64 out of 146 countries surveyed in Transparency International's 2004 Corruption Perceptions Index.

The media, while mostly private, largely depend on the government for advertising revenue. In 2000, President Vicente Fox Quesada pledged to end the PRI practice of buying favorable stories and vowed to respect media independence, a promise that he has largely kept. Reporters investigating police issues, narcotics trafficking, and public corruption remain at particular risk, and in 2004, five journalists were killed. In 2002, Mexico enacted its first freedom of information law, which expressly prohibits the government from withholding for any reason information about crimes against humanity or gross human rights violations; the law went into effect in June 2003. The government does not restrict Internet access, which is widely available across the nation, although much less so among the poor and the elderly, because of economic constraints or lack of computer literacy.

The constitution provides for religious freedom and in practice the government generally respects this right. However, the free practice of religion is limited in some areas of the country's south, particularly in Chiapas state, and there are frequent reports of harassment of Jehovah's Witnesses. In order to operate legally, religious associations must register with the Under Secretariat of Religious Affairs of the Federal Secretariat (SSAR), although the registration process has been routine. The constitution was amended in 1992 to restore the legal status of the Roman Catholic Church and other religious institutions. Priests and nuns were allowed to vote for the first time in nearly 80 years. The government does not restrict academic freedom.

Constitutional guarantees regarding political and civic organizations are generally respected in the urbanized northern and central parts of the country. Political and civic expression, however, is restricted throughout rural Mexico, in poor urban areas, and in poor southern states. Civil society participation has grown in recent years; human rights, pro-democracy, women's, and environmental groups are active. In June 2003, Fox signed legislation that banned all forms of discrimination, including those based on ethnic origin, gender, age, or religion.

The justice system is based on the cumbersome nineteenth-century Napoleonic code, in which judges decide cases by reading documentary evidence. There is virtually no body of law governing juvenile justice. In most rural areas, respect for laws by official agencies is still tenuous at best. Lower courts and law enforcement in general are undermined by widespread bribery, despite efforts at reform by the Fox administration. Torture, arbitrary arrest, and abuse of prisoners persist in many areas, although somewhat less so than just a decade ago. In November 2003, the Supreme Court ruled that the "disappearances" of leftist activists in the 1960s and 1970s were kidnappings not subject to the statute of limitations. The decision paved the way for the arrest of former senior officials implicated in the rights crimes. In 2004, the court itself became the object of controversy when it was revealed that its head and Fox had met secretly at a time when the president's rival, Lopez Obrador, was being threatened with dismissal from office for disobeying a questionable lower-court order.

In Mexico City, approximately 80 percent of crimes go unreported because the notoriously underpaid police are viewed as either inept or in league with the wrongdoers; only about 6 percent of reported crimes are solved. Ten percent of all extortive kidnappings in Mexico are believed to be carried out by former or serving police officers. In early 2001, Fox announced a crusade to clean up the law enforcement system, urging Mexicans to report common crimes and announcing a citizen program to make the police more accountable by making their files more accessible to the public. In 2002, the mayor of Mexico City announced the hiring of former New York mayor Rudolph Giuliani as a security consultant, a move questioned by rights activists familiar with the New York City Police Department's record during the 1990s. Two years later, Giuliani's recommendations on "zero tolerance" measures, panic buttons on city buses, and surveillance cameras in high-crime areas had been adopted.

Because Mexico has no foreign enemies, the military, which operates largely beyond public scrutiny, serves mainly as an auxiliary police force and acts as the country's main antinarcotics force. In places such as the states of Chiapas and Guerrero, army counterinsurgency units, moving through local civilian populations like an occupying force, continue to cause numerous rights violations. Human rights groups say more than 100 people have "disappeared," and hundreds more tortured, by the Mexican army in the conflict-ridden state of Guerrero in the past decade. The military justice system allows for soldiers accused of rights violations to be tried in secret, and the outcomes of their trials are only occasionally made public. In 2004, the role of a vicious northern Mexico gang known as the Zetas—former Mexican army commandos in league with the drug traffickers they were trained to capture—received much media attention.

Although civil-military relations are in a state of flux, presidential authority over the armed forces is extensive. However, in a February 19, 2004, Army Day address, Defense Secretary General Gerardo Vega Garcia broke with long-standing tradition by directly speaking about domestic politics at a time when civilian authorities were trying to exercise greater oversight of the secretive armed forces.

Dozens of labor and peasant leaders have been killed in recent years in ongoing land disputes, particularly in the southern states, where Indians constitute close to half the population. Most Native Americans are relegated to extreme poverty in rural villages lacking roads, running water, schools, and telephones. Indian groups said that a 2001 constitutional reform designed to strengthen their rights fell far short of addressing their concerns.

The *maquiladoras* (export-processing zones) have fostered substantial abuses of workers' rights. Most maquiladora workers are young, uneducated women who accept lower pay more readily, with annual labor turnover averaging between 200 and 300 percent. Workers have no medical insurance, paid holidays, or profit sharing, and female employees are frequently the targets of sexual harassment and abuse. Domestic violence and sexual abuse remain serious problems, although the Fox government has pledged to fight a problem that some experts say affects 50 to 70 percent of women. Mexico is a source country for trafficked persons to the United States, Canada, and Japan, and a transit country for persons from various places, especially Central America and China. Internal trafficking is also a problem. In 2004, Amalia Garcia of the PRD won the governorship of Zacatecas, becoming the first democratically elected woman governor in Mexican history.

Micronesia

Population: 100,000
GNI/capita: $1,980
Life Expectancy: 67
Religious Groups: Roman Catholic (50 percent), Protestant (47 percent), other (3 percent)
Ethnic Groups: Micronesian, Polynesian
Capital: Palikir

Political Rights: 1
Civil Liberties: 1
Status: Free

Ten-Year Ratings Timeline (Political Rights, Civil Liberties, Status)

1995	1996	1997	1998	1999	2000	2001	2002	2003	2004
1,1F	1,1F	1,2F	1,2F	1,2F	1,2F	1,2F	1,2F	1,1F	1,1F

Overview:

The Federated States of Micronesia (FSM) ratified its amended Compact of Free Association with the United States in May 2004. As with previous compacts, the United States agreed to provide financial assistance and external defense in exchange for the right to maintain military bases in FSM. In January 2004, the proposal of a bill that would grant amnesty to "certain classes who are being accused, or yet to be accused, or who have been prosecuted of certain types of crimes" was met with broad public criticism.

The United States administered the FSM between 1947 and 1979 as a UN Trusteeship Territory. The FSM adopted a constitution in 1979 and reached full independence in 1984. The FSM's four states—Chuuk (formerly Truk), Kosrae, Pohnpei, and Yap—represent a total of 607 islands in the Pacific Ocean.

Micronesian voters in August 2002 rejected a proposed constitutional amendment that would have introduced direct elections for president and vice president. Under the current system, Congress chooses the two top officeholders from among its ranks.

In May 2003, Congress elected Joseph Urusemal over former president Leo Falcam to be the sixth president of the FSM. Redley Killion was chosen as the vice president. Urusemal is a former governor of Yap, one of the constituent states of the federation, while Killion was vice president in Falcam's administration.

The new Compact of Free Association, which came into effect in December 2003, will cover the next 20 years. In the first three years, the FSM will receive $76 million in economic assistance grants for education, health, capacity building, private sector development, the environment, and infrastructure. Another $16 million will go to a trust fund that will be overseen by a joint board of U.S. and FSM trustees to ensure good management of U.S. assistance to curb widespread corruption and abuse. Beginning in the fourth year, an annual decrement of $800,000 from the sectoral grants would be re-allocated to the trust fund until 2023. FSM citizens will continue to enjoy visa-free access to the United States, work in the United States without work visa requirements, and access U.S. health services.

Compact funds represent a third of the country's national income, and the division of those funds has been a source of serious tension in federal-state relations. In 2003, the people of Faichuk in the state of Chuuk threatened to leave the federation and proposed a separate bilateral treaty with the United States unless Chuuk receives a larger share of the compact funds. This complaint resonated with people in the other states and spurred debates on federal-state relations. In November of that year, the federal government announced it would increase the share of compact funds to the four states.

Political Rights and Civil Liberties:

Citizens of Micronesia can change their government democratically. A unicameral, 14-member legislature has one representative each from the four constituent states directly elected for four-year terms and 10 representatives from single-member districts directly elected for two-year terms. As Chuuk, the largest of the four states, has nearly half the country's population, it holds a proportionate number of congressional seats; this has been a source of resentment among the three smaller states. The president and vice president are chosen from among the four state representatives in the legislature to serve four-year terms. By informal agreement, these two top offices are rotated among the representatives of the four states. There are no formal political parties, although there are no restrictions against their formation.

Each state has its own constitution, elected legislature, and governor. State governments have considerable power, particularly in budgetary matters. Traditional leaders and institutions exercise significant influence in society, especially at the village level.

A bill proposed in January 2004 would grant amnesty to any FSM citizen charged with the misuse and misappropriation of any government funds over the past 17 years. Current charges for such crimes would also be dropped against all defendants. Just months prior to the bill's introduction, 14 people were named in an indictment for stealing $1.2 million in government funds, and a congressman was charged in 1992 with misappropriation of funds. Several other congressmen have also been charged with misuse of public funds. Intense public reaction to the bill forced the government to send it to a subcommittee for further study rather than pushing it through the parliament.

The media operate freely. In addition to government-published newsletters, there are several small private newspapers, and television stations operate in three of the four states. Each state government runs its own radio station, and a religious group runs a fifth station. Satellite television is increasingly common. Internet access is small but growing. However, the small populations and limited income in the FSM do not generate sufficient revenue for Internet service providers to reduce fees and expand bandwidth—a problem shared by most other Pacific Island countries.

Religious freedom is respected in this mainly Christian country. There were no reports of restrictions of academic freedom.

Citizens are free to organize civic groups, and there are a few student and women's groups. No labor unions exist, but there are no laws against their formation. The economy is dependent on fishing, tourism, assistance from the United States, and subsistence agriculture. No specific laws regulate work hours, recognize the right to strike or bargain collectively, or set workplace health and safety standards.

The judiciary is independent, but lack of funds hinders improvements in the functioning of the courts and prison condition. Cultural resistance to using the courts, particularly for sex crimes, means many offenders are not brought to justice.

Women suffer significant social and economic discrimination in the male-dominated culture of these islands. Domestic violence is common, and cases often go unreported because of family pressure, fear of further assault, or an expectation of inaction by the authority. Offenders rarely go to trial and those found guilty usually receive light sentences. In October 2003, the government ratified the UN Convention on the Elimination of All Forms of Discrimination against Women, but took exception to certain parts, including an article requiring employers to give women full pay and benefits when they take maternity leave.

Moldova

Population: 4,200,000
GNI/capita: $460
Life Expectancy: 68
Religious Groups: Eastern Orthodox (98 percent),
Jewish (1.5 percent), other [including Baptist] (0.5 percent)
Ethnic Groups: Moldovan/Romanian (64.5 percent),
Ukrainian (13.8 percent), Russian (13 percent),
Bulgarian (2 percent), Jewish (1.5 percent), other [including Gaguauz] (5.2 percent)
Capital: Chisinau

Political Rights: 3
Civil Liberties: 4
Status: Partly Free

Ten-Year Ratings Timeline (Political Rights, Civil Liberties, Status)

1995	1996	1997	1998	1999	2000	2001	2002	2003	2004
4,4PF	3,4PF	3,4PF	2,4PF	2,4PF	2,4PF	2,4PF	3,4PF	3,4PF	3,4PF

Overview:

Press freedom continued to be a problem in Moldova in 2004, with protests against the allegedly politically motivated dismissals of journalists during the state broadcaster's transformation into an independent public broadcaster. The European Union (EU) and Moldova agreed in June on an Action Plan to increase economic and political cooperation.

The Soviet Socialist Republic of Moldova declared independence from the Soviet Union in 1991. The country's first free and fair popular election took place in 1994. While the Communist Party of Moldova (PCM) won a plurality of votes in the 1998 parliamentary elections, three centrist parties united to form a majority coalition. Subsequently, Moldova undertook much-needed economic reforms and drafted a new constitution. In 2000, constitutional changes made Moldova a parliamentary republic, with the president chosen by parliament instead of by popular vote.

In the February 2001 parliamentary elections, the PCM won a landslide victory on the promise of a return to Soviet-era living standards. In April of that year, PCM leader Vladimir Voronin was elected president. Moldova thus became the first former Soviet republic to elect a Communist Party member as president.

Moldova has not made the kind of substantial progress toward stable democracy seen in some of its Western neighbors. Frequent changes in political leadership have impeded the development of consistent and effective policies. Local elections held nationwide in 2003 were declared by the Organization for Security and Cooperation in Europe (OSCE) to be in line with international standards, but some observers expressed concerns about intimidation of opposition candidates, bias among the media, and irregularities during the poll.

Unemployment rates in Moldova, one of Europe's most impoverished countries, are very high. By the government's own estimates, some 80 percent of the population subsists on less than the officially designated minimum, and the shadow economy accounts for between 30 and 70 percent of all economic activity. Harsh economic conditions have led a substantial number of people to emigrate. However, Moldova has had strong economic growth since 2000, reaching 6.3 percent in 2003.

Separatist elements have declared a "Dniester Republic" in Transnistria—situated between the Dniester River and Ukraine—in which Russian troops continue to maintain a presence. Transnistria is home to approximately 750,000 of Moldova's 4.35 million people. During 2004, five-party talks that included Russia, Ukraine, the authorities of Moldova and of Transnistria, and the OSCE produced no resolution.

In June, the EU and Moldova agreed on an Action Plan. The first of its kind between the EU and a neighbor, the plan is designed to increase economic integration and deepen political cooperation between the two sides.

Political Rights and Civil Liberties:

Citizens of Moldova can change their government democratically. In 2000, Moldova ended direct presidential elections. Today voters elect members to the 101-seat unicameral parliament by proportional representation for four-year terms; parliament then elects the prime minister and president. The president remains dominant on the political scene; important policy decisions are made by a political board of the PCM—President Vladimir Voronin's party—reporting directly to the president. Although international observers believe that Moldova's Electoral Code provides a sound framework for the conduct of free and fair elections, accuracy of voter lists and transparency of the tabulation of election results could be improved.

More than 30 political parties are registered and competed in the last elections. However, the 2000 constitutional changes appear to have provided the conditions for a single party to establish dominance. Only three parties are represented in the parliament: the PCM has 71 seats, while the Our Moldova Alliance and the Christian Democratic Popular Party have 12 and 11 seats, respectively. The remaining seats are held by independents. Government security forces are believed to monitor opposition political figures and to conduct unauthorized wiretaps. Moreover, opposition groups have difficulty pursuing their agendas in face of the dominant ruling party. The opposition has accused the PCM of trying to establish a dictatorship.

The self-declared government in Transnistria severely limits the ability of voters in that region to participate in Moldova's national elections. In contrast, the Gagauz-Yeri region in the south of Moldova, populated by a Christian Turkic minority, has been granted autonomy and has abandoned separatist aspirations. In 2003, the region was also given the right to initiate legislation in the national parliament. Corruption is a major concern in Moldova. Anticorruption efforts have failed in the past and have been used as weapons against political opponents. Despite laws to promote governmental transparency, access to governmental information remains limited. Moldova was ranked 114 out of 146 countries surveyed in Transparency International's 2004 Corruption Perceptions Index.

Although the constitution guarantees freedom of expression and of the press, media freedom is somewhat restricted. Electronic media are the most widely accessed news sources, and only the former state broadcaster, Teleradio Moldova, has national reach. The government has been accused of using Teleradio Moldova against the opposition and pressuring independent media through financial and legal means. For example, in February, the audiovisual council suspended the broadcast licenses of one radio and one television station that were often critical of the government. These were reinstated in April. In March, the state-owned telecommunications company cut off the country's main Internet service provider, allegedly for political reasons. In contrast, prison sentences for libel were abolished in 2004, although journalists can still be subject to very large fines.

In 2003, parliament passed legislation transforming Teleradio Moldova into an independent company. Still, a June 2004 study by two nongovernmental organizations (NGOs) found that Teleradio Moldova's coverage had a heavy pro-government bias. After all journalists were dismissed prior to the change, critics claimed that rehiring procedures were used to get rid of journalists for political reasons. Police used force against peaceful protesters of the procedures in August.

In June, a journalist for the weekly *Timpul* was beaten by unknown assailants in Chisinau, allegedly with government backing. The reporter had investigated official corruption, and she was attacked the day before she was due to testify in a libel case against her publication.

Moldova's constitution guarantees religious freedom, although there have been some legal impediments to the functioning of various religious groups and sects. All religious groups are required to register with the government, and unregistered groups are not allowed to buy property or obtain construction permits. The Moldovan Orthodox Church receives some favored treatment from the government. Both the Moldovan Orthodox Church and the Bessarabian Orthodox Church claim to be the lawful successors of the pre–World War II Romanian Orthodox Church, whose property is still in dispute. In February, the Supreme Court ruled illegal a 2001 decision by the Moldovan government that the Moldovan Orthodox Church was the lawful successor.

The government does not restrict academic freedom.

Citizens may participate freely in NGOs and political parties. Private organizations must register with the state, and demonstrations require permits from local authorities. Some NGOs have complained of government interference. In addition, lack of funding limits NGO activities. Workers are allowed to strike, petition the government, and form and join trade unions. The law allows collective bargaining but prohibits strikes by government employees and essential workers.

Moldova's constitution provides for an independent judiciary. It also guarantees equality before the law and the presumption of innocence. However, there is evidence that some prosecutors, judges, and law enforcement officials accept bribes and are subject to official pressure from governmental figures. Prison conditions are exceptionally poor, and levels of malnutrition and disease are high in penal institutions. The central court in Chisinau ruled against the Ministry of the Interior in March in a case of detainment in what were judged to be inhuman and degrading conditions. Torture by police against suspects and prisoners reportedly takes place and is rarely investigated.

Although ethnic minorities constitute some 30 percent of the population, specific legislation makes it difficult for them to organize politically. Nevertheless, ethnic minority representation in parliament after the 2001 elections rose from 16 percent to 30 percent. The Roma (Gypsy) community is the victim of particular discrimination in Moldovan society. With no opposition support, parliament approved a controversial Nationalities Policy in December 2003 that designates the promotion of the Russian language alongside Moldovan as a national priority. In July 2004, parliament approved an amendment to the citizenship law allowing anyone who lived on Moldovan territory before independence to have automatic citizenship. The law targets Transnistrians who previously had difficulty obtaining Moldovan citizenship.

There are no official restrictions on women's rights in Moldova, although women are considerably under-represented in public life. Women are discriminated against in employment, and they currently hold only 13 of 101 seats in parliament. Domestic violence against women is believed to be widespread. Although the law prohibits trafficking in human beings, Moldova remains a major source for women and girls trafficked to other countries for purposes of forced prostitution. The police have attempted to crack down on perpetrators, but the problem continues.

Monaco

Population: 30,000
GNI/capita: $26,900
Life Expectancy: na
Religious Groups: Roman Catholic (90 percent), other (10 percent)
Ethnic Groups: French (47 percent), Italian (16 percent), Monegasque (16 percent), other (21 percent)
Capital: Monaco

Political Rights: 2
Civil Liberties: 1
Status: Free

Ten-Year Ratings Timeline (Political Rights, Civil Liberties, Status)

1995	1996	1997	1998	1999	2000	2001	2002	2003	2004
2,1F	2,1F	2,1F	2,1F	2,1F	2,1F	2,1F	2,1F	2,1F	2,1F

Overview: Prince Rainier, the 80-year-old ruler of the country, was hospitalized in the early part of the year with acute heart problems caused by general fatigue. The country joined the Council of Europe as the forty-sixth member state in October. The European Court of Human Rights ruled that German tabloids had wrongly invaded the private life of Princess Caroline by showing pictures of her sunbathing, cycling, and shopping.

The Principality of Monaco is an independent and sovereign state, although it remains closely associated with neighboring France. The royal Grimaldi family has ruled the principality for the past 700 years, except for a brief period of French colonial rule from 1789 to 1814. Under a treaty ratified in 1919, France pledged to protect the territorial integrity, sovereignty, and independence of the principality in return for a guarantee that Monegasque policy would conform to French political, military, and economic interests.

Prince Rainier III has led the country since 1949 and is often credited for the country's impressive economic growth. Since his ascension, the country has ended its dependence on gambling and increased other sources of revenue—principally tourism, financial services, and banking. In August 2002, the country added a huge new floating pier to its harbor, the Port of Monaco, which is well known as a major port for expensive yachts and fancy cruisers. The pier, the largest in the world, cost almost $250 million and doubles the capacity of the country's port. In February 2002, Monaco adopted the euro despite that fact that it is not a member of the European Union (EU).

Elections in February 2003 led to a major upset for the National and Democratic Union (UND), which lost after dominating national politics in the country for the past several decades. The opposition Union for Monaco (UPM) received 58.5 percent of the vote and 21 of the 24 seats in the Conseil National, while the UND received 41.5 percent of the vote. The UPM's victory represented widespread support for Monaco's bid for membership in the Council of Europe, an issue the party had promoted strongly.

Rainier was hospitalized in January for heart problems related to general fatigue. His doctors said that he had been suffering from bronchial conditions connected with exhaustion. Rainier, who has led the country for 55 years, is the world's second-longest reigning monarch after the king of Thailand. He has also ruled the country longer than any of his predecessors since the eighteenth century. His only son, Prince Albert, is his likely successor.

The country is one of five uncooperative tax havens listed by the Organization for Economic Cooperation and Development (OECD). A new EU directive passed in early 2003 threatens Monaco's status as a major tax haven. The directive calls for EU members with secret banking laws to impose a withholding tax on revenue from interest-bearing accounts. After negotiations with the EU, Monaco and other key non-EU countries have agreed to adopt similar measures.

Political Rights and Civil Liberties: Citizens of Monaco can elect their parliamentary representatives democratically. However, the prince has the sole authority to initiate laws and change the government. The 24 members of the Conseil National are elected every five years: 16 are elected by a majority electoral system and 8 by proportional representation. The head of state is not elected but inherits the position. Prince Rainier III, who has ruled the country for the past 55 years, fell gravely ill with a heart condition and is expected to be succeeded in the near future by Prince Albert, his only son with the late American actress Grace Kelly.

The head of government—the minister of state—is traditionally appointed by the monarch from a list of three candidates who are French nationals presented by the French government. The current minister of state, Patrick Leclercq, has held the post since 2000. In addition to the minister of state, the prince also appoints three other ministers (counselors) who collectively make up the government. All legislation and the budget, however, require the assent of the Conseil National.

Because of a lack of available financial information, the country's level of corruption is difficult to measure. Monaco remains on the OECD's list of uncooperative tax havens. However, Monaco is one of five non-EU tax havens that are negotiating with the EU to adopt measures to combat harmful tax competition. The country is expected to agree either to provide information to EU member states about the interest paid to individual savers from those member states, or to levy a withholding tax.

The media in Monaco are free and independent. The constitution provides for freedom of speech and the press, although the penal code prohibits denunciations of the ruling family. Internet access is not restricted.

In June, the European Court of Human Rights ruled unanimously in favor of Princess Caroline von Hannover of Monaco, who had filed a suit against German tabloids arguing that they have transgressed her rights to privacy. The tabloids had published pictures of her on vacation and other aspects of her private life.

The constitution provides for freedom of religion. However, Roman Catholicism is the state religion, and Catholic ritual plays a role in state festivities. There are no laws against proselytizing by formally registered religious organizations, although to do so is strongly discouraged. There are no restrictions on academic freedom. The country has only one institution of higher education, the University of Monaco, a private university that only offers degrees in business administration.

The government does not impose restrictions on the formation of civic and human rights groups. Workers have the legal right to organize and bargain collectively, although they rarely do so. Only 10 percent of the workforce is unionized. All workers except those in the government have the right to strike. The constitution provides for the freedom of assembly and the government respected this right. Although outdoor meetings require police authorizations, there were no reports that the government withheld authorization for political reasons.

The legal right to a fair public trial and an independent judiciary is generally respected. The constitution requires that the prince delegate his judicial powers to the judiciary. Prisons generally met international standards.

The constitution differentiates between the rights of nationals and those of noncitizens. Of the estimated 32,000 residents in the principality, only about 7,000 are actual Monegasques, who alone may participate in the election of the Conseil National. Monegasques also benefit from free education, unemployment assistance, and the right to hold elective office.

A woman can lodge criminal charges against a husband for domestic violence, and women generally receive equal pay for equal work. Although naturalized male citizens in Monaco can transfer citizenship, naturalized women cannot. Also, women who become naturalized citizens by marriage cannot become an elector or eligible to be a candidate in elections until five years after the marriage. There were no reports of trafficking in persons into, from, or within Monaco over the year.

Mongolia

Population: 2,500,000 **Political Rights:** 2
GNI/capita: $430 **Civil Liberties:** 2
Life Expectancy: 65 **Status:** Free
Religious Groups: Tibetan Buddhist Lamaism (50 percent),
Muslim (4 percent), other [including Shamanist and
Christian] (46 percent)
Ethnic Groups: Mongol [predominantly Khalkha] (94.9 percent),
Turkic [predominantly Kazakh] (5 percent), other [including Chinese
and Russian] (0.1 percent)
Capital: Ulaanbaatar

Ten-Year Ratings Timeline (Political Rights, Civil Liberties, Status)

1995	1996	1997	1998	1999	2000	2001	2002	2003	2004
2,3F	2,3F	2,3F	2,3F	2,3F	2,3F	2,3F	2,2F	2,2F	2,2F

Overview:

In June 2004, Mongolians voted in their country's fifth parliamentary elections since the fall of communism. The ruling Mongolian People's Revolutionary Party (MPRP) lost more than 30 seats in parliament, and the elections resulted in a political stalemate, as neither the MPRP nor the main opposition party, the Motherland Democracy Coalition (MDC), controlled the 39 seats required to form a government. The two parties only formed a coalition government in August.

Once the center of Genghis Khan's sprawling empire, Mongolia was dominated for much of the past three centuries by its neighbors. China controlled Mongolia for two centuries, until 1921. A Soviet-backed, Marxist revolt that year led to the creation in 1924 of a single-party Communist state, the world's second ever, under the MPRP.

Mongolia's transition from Soviet satellite to democratic republic began in 1990, when the MPRP responded to antigovernment protests by legalizing opposition parties and holding the country's first multiparty elections. Facing an unprepared and underfunded opposition, the MPRP easily won parliamentary elections that year and again in 1992. The MPRP was swept out of parliamentary power, after 72 years, in the 1996 elections. However, the policies of the reformist coalition that came into office, combined with steep drops in world prices for two of Mongolia's biggest foreign exchange earners (copper and cashmere), sent inflation and unemployment soaring. As a consequence, the MPRP regained power with victories in the 1997 election for the largely ceremonial presidency and the more important 2000 parliamentary vote.

General elections held in June 2004 resulted in a political impasse, as neither the ruling MPRP party nor the main opposition, the MDC, holds the 39 seats required to form a government. The MDC was accused of bribing voters and engaging in improper polling procedures in some constituencies, leading to demands for a recount of the votes. President Natsagiin Bagabandi called the first session of parliament in early July, but the MPRP refused to attend because the final election results had not been decided; the session was cancelled. Parliament finally met later in July, but not all members of parliament were sworn in because confirmation of the election results in the disputed constituencies were still being awaited. In August, the MPRP finally agreed to form a coalition government with the MDC, and Tsakhilganiin Elbegdorj, a former journalist, began his second term as prime minister.

The key political issue in post-Communist Mongolia has been the pace and extent of economic reform. Market reforms have helped create a fledgling private sector, but also have contributed to soaring unemployment and other social miseries. MPRP governments in the early 1990s privatized small businesses and ended collectivized herding, but had difficulty retooling the economy to survive the loss of Soviet subsidies. Many large firms went bankrupt, and thousands of Mongolians were thrown out of work. Despite strong economic growth in the first half of 2004, poverty is still widespread. Poverty and unemployment remain prime concerns for Mongolians.

Mongolia is actively trying to shore up its foreign relations. In July 2004, the president, Natsagiin Bagabandi, visited neighboring China and spoke with the Chinese prime minister and vice president on furthering diplomatic relations and increasing cooperation on both the international and the regional levels. The two countries also signed agreements on cooperation in trade and banking. Later that month, Bagabandi visited the United States to talk with President George W. Bush about international security, foreign aid to Mongolia, and increased bilateral cooperation. To further this last goal, the two countries signed a trade and investment framework agreement. U.S. Assistant Secretary of State James Kelly visited Mongolia in November, demonstrating the U.S.'s growing awareness of the country—situated between Russia and China and with cordial relations with North Korea—as strategically important.

In January 2004, Russia's foreign minister visited Mongolia and discussed regional security and integration with his Mongolian counterpart, Luvsangiin Erdenechuluun. Bagabandi said in July that he planned to visit Russia by the end of 2004, though this had not occurred as of December. The biggest problem concerning friendly relations between the two countries, Mongolia's huge Soviet-era debt to Russia, has been resolved: Russia agreed in December 2003 to write off most of the debt, and Mongolia repaid the remaining $250 million in January 2004.

Political Rights and Civil Liberties: Mongolians can change their government through elections. The 1992 constitution created a hybrid presidential-parliamentary system. Most executive powers are vested in a prime minister, who is chosen by the party or coalition with the most seats in parliament. The president, however, must approve parliament's choice of prime minister and can veto legislation, subject to a two-thirds parliamentary override. Both the president and the 76-seat parliament, known as the Great Hural, are directly elected for four-year terms.

Mongolia was ranked 85 out of 146 countries surveyed in Transparency International's 2004 Corruption Perceptions Index. The index shows a decline in Mongolia's standing over the past five years; the country was ranked 43 out of 99 countries in the 1999 survey. Luvsandendev Sumati, the head of the Mongolian good-governance organization Sant Maral Foundation, attributed the decline to increased levels of poverty. The U.S. Department of Commerce cites "corruption in the bureaucracy" as an impediment to business.

Mongolia's press is largely free but faces some government pressure. The 1999 media law banned the censorship of public information, and newspapers and magazines carry a wide range of party and independent views that often criticize the government. The government, however, has at times filed libel suits and launched tax audits against publications in the wake of critical articles. Libel charges are hard to defend against because Mongolian law places the burden on the defendant to prove the truth of the statement at issue. In this environment, many journalists practice some degree of self-censorship. In April 2004, a journalist with an independent newspaper was fined and given a three-month prison sentence for libel against a member of parliament and a former police chief. The local independent press as well as international organizations such as Reporters Sans Frontieres protested, and the journalist was released after serving just 23 days of her sentence.

While newspapers are popular in cities, the main source of news in the vast countryside is the state-owned Radio Mongolia. Although most radio and television stations remained state owned, they are generally free of political control. For example, following the June 2004 general elections, the ruling party used the media to convince the electorate that the opposition, the MDC, had bribed voters and otherwise engaged in unfair electioneering. In response, the MDC demanded media access to put forward its own case and was granted 20 minutes of free air time per day. The government has, however, been slow to comply with a 1999 law requiring state broadcast media to be transformed into public corporations.

Besides the state broadcast services, Mongolians have access to local private television, English-language broadcasts of the BBC and Voice of America on private FM stations, and, in the capital city of Ulaanbaatar, foreign television on cable and commercial satellite systems. Political reporting by both print and broadcast journalists is hampered by limited access to official information and a lack of transparency in government. Internet access is available and is not hampered by government interference.

In an effort to further Mongolia's "strengthening democratic parliament" project, the government began broadcasting parliamentary meetings directly to the public on cable television in May 2004.

Mongolians of all faiths worship freely in this mainly Buddhist nation, although proselytizing is limited by law. Some religious groups seeking to fulfill mandatory registration requirements, however, have faced demands for bribes by local officials, according to the U.S. State Department's human rights report for 2003, released in February 2004. Mongolian professors and other teachers generally can write and lecture freely.

The country has many active environmental, human rights, and social welfare groups, though most depend on foreign donors. Freedom of assembly is respected in law and in practice. Mongolian trade unions are independent and active, though the government's slimming down or sale of many state factories has contributed to a sharp drop in union membership, to less than half the workforce. Collective bargaining is legal, but with Mongolia's poor economy, employers enjoy considerable leverage and often set wages unilaterally. The government prohibits strikes in sectors that it considers essential, including utilities, transportation, and law enforcement. Laws on child labor and workplace health and safety are poorly enforced. Private land ownership is not permitted, although the law allows land to be leased for up to 100 years.

The judiciary is independent, but corruption among judges persists, according to the U.S. State Department report. In a holdover from the country's Communist past, defendants are not presumed innocent.

Although the constitution prohibits unlawful arrest and detention, Mongolia's police force, under the jurisdiction of the Ministry of Justice and Home Affairs, has been known to make arbitrary arrests, keep detainees for long periods of time, and beat prisoners and detainees. Such actions were more prevalent in rural areas. Corruption in the police force remains a problem. The military, which has been downsized because of budgetary constraints, is under the aegis of the Ministry of Defense. Prisons have in recent years been outfitted with video monitoring systems, decreasing the incidence of beatings by guards. Nevertheless, deaths in prisons continue to be reported; these are due largely to disease—often tuberculosis—exacerbated by poor conditions like insufficient food, heat, and medical care. A prison reform program centering on training guards and upgrading facilities is ongoing.

The constitution prohibits arbitrary interference with privacy, family, home, or correspondence, and these provisions are generally respected. In addition, the government respects all citizens' rights to travel freely within the country and abroad.

Men and women have equal rights in all areas under the constitution. Although women are well-integrated in the workforce, domestic violence continues to be a serious problem, affecting as much as one-third of the female population, according to the U.S. State Department report.

Morocco

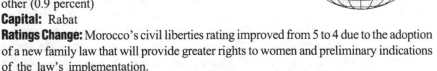

Population: 30,600,000 **Political Rights:** 5
GNI/capita: $1,170 **Civil Liberties:** 4*
Life Expectancy: 70 **Status:** Partly Free
Religious Groups: Muslim (98.7 percent),
Christian (1.1 percent), Jewish (0.2 percent)
Ethnic Groups: Arab-Berber (99.1 percent),
other (0.9 percent)
Capital: Rabat
Ratings Change: Morocco's civil liberties rating improved from 5 to 4 due to the adoption of a new family law that will provide greater rights to women and preliminary indications of the law's implementation.

Ten-Year Ratings Timeline (Political Rights, Civil Liberties, Status)

1995	1996	1997	1998	1999	2000	2001	2002	2003	2004
5,5PF	5,5PF	5,5PF	5,4PF	5,4PF	5,4PF	5,5PF	5,5PF	5,5PF	5,4PF

Overview: As Morocco slowly recovered from the 2003 Casablanca suicide bombings, it moved ahead in 2004 with a new family code providing women with more rights and initiated fresh attempts at addressing past human rights violations. Activists generally welcomed these developments, but an antiterrorism law in place since the bombings continued to erode human rights protection as thousands of Islamists suspected of ties to the 2003 bombings were still detained and hundreds of people from the Western Sahara territory remained "disappeared." An attack in Spain in March 2004 by a group of mostly young Moroccans drew attention again to the threat of homegrown terrorists.

Moroccan independence dates from 1956, when power passed to King Muhammad V following 44 years of French colonial rule. King Hassan II ascended the throne five years later on the death of his father. In 1975, Morocco laid claim to the Western Sahara following the withdrawal of Spanish forces from the territory; the status of the territory remains in dispute and is a source of tension in the country. Hassan II oversaw much of Morocco's modern development, but power remained concentrated entirely in the hands of the king. He introduced political reform in the 1990s, establishing a directly elected lower house of parliament, and moved to improve the human rights situation.

King Muhammad VI came to power in July 1999 after the death of his father. While Morocco had made tentative steps toward political and economic liberalization, Muhammad inherited a country with severe social and economic problems. More than 20 percent of the population was unemployed, nearly half remained illiterate, and a third lived below the poverty line. Mounting public debt hampered the government's ability to provide social services. Islamist charitable networks quickly filled the gap, providing services and gaining support at the grassroots level.

King Muhammad has continued to pursue political openings. Soon after he ascended the throne, he dismissed Interior Minister Driss Basri, long considered one of the most powerful men in Morocco and the embodiment of the corruption and repression that marked the monarchy. Thousands of prisoners were released, and the king allowed exiled opposition figures to return home.

In 2002, Morocco held parliamentary elections that were widely considered to be the most representative in the country's history. The elections led to a parliament with a significant Islamist presence and in which 10 percent of members were women.

Five suicide bombings in May 2003 that killed 45 people and injured another 100 shattered Morocco's sense of stability. Victims were primarily Moroccans, and the targets included visible symbols of Morocco's Jewish community. The 14 attackers were Casablanca residents, with suspected links to al-Qaeda, the terrorist network. The Moroccan government's response to the attacks was swift and harsh: thousands were arrested and courts handed down death sentences and long prison terms.

Less than a year later, a series of bombs exploded on passenger trains in Madrid in March 2004 focused international attention on North Africa. The attacks killed nearly 200 people and wounded almost 2,000. Most of the attackers were Moroccans, apparently linked to the Casablanca bombers and to al-Qaeda. Spain's new prime minister, Jose Luis Rodriguez Zapatero, who took office days after the blasts, visited Morocco in April, and the two countries agreed to fight terrorism, drug trafficking, and illegal immigration. In the summer of 2004, France proposed the formation of a defense partnership between Europe and Morocco, Algeria, and Tunisia. In addition, U.S. president George W. Bush designated Morocco a major non-NATO ally in the fight against terrorism.

The king expanded efforts at improving the country's human rights record. In December 2003, he announced the creation of the Equity and Reconciliation Commission to document abuses perpetrated under the previous regime and to compensate victims. The commission is headed by Driss Benzikri, a former political prisoner. Most human rights activists welcomed the move, but critics said it did not provide for bringing past violators to justice.

In early 2004, Morocco enacted reforms to its personal status law, known as the *Mudawana* and based in Islamic law. The new code aimed at rectifying gender inequality by raising the marriage age to 18 and strengthening women's rights to divorce. A similar effort was suspended in 2000 when Islamists organized massive protests, but since the 2003 attacks, Moroccan Islamists have kept a low profile.

Political Rights and Civil Liberties:

Moroccans' right to change their government democratically is limited. The monarch retains ultimate authority and may appoint or dismiss cabinet members, dissolve parliament, and rule by decree. Legislative powers are shared by the king and a bicameral legislature that includes a directly elected lower house. The 2002 parliamentary elections and municipal elections held in 2003 were regarded as the most representative in the country's history.

Opposition parties remain weak. The government crackdown on Islamic extremists has deterred moderate Islamist elements from political participation. The single most effective opposition party, the Islamist Justice and Development Party (PJD), was pressured by the government into running only a few candidates in the municipal elections. In an effort to improve its image, the party elected a new leader in 2004, known for his moderate views. Secular opposition parties have yet to make significant inroads at the grassroots level.

Morocco was ranked 77 out of 146 countries surveyed in the 2004 Transparency International Corruption Perceptions Index. In a July 2004 report, Transparency Morocco, a network of civil society organizations, described instances of bribery of officials, including the judiciary. Proceedings were subsequently initiated against 14 judges, two of whom were dismissed and six retired.

Press freedom remains somewhat restricted. There is a lively press, but under a 2002 law, journalists are subject to prison sentences and fines for defamation and libel, especially regarding the royal family, Islam, and the Western Sahara. In January 2004, the king pardoned six journalists, two of whom had been sentenced to up to three years in jail. Notable among them was Ali Lmrabet, editor of a French-language weekly, *Demain,* and an Arabic weekly, *Douman,* convicted of insulting the king and challenging the territorial integrity of the state. Government prosecution of journalists resumed, however, and in April 2004, Anas Guennoun, editor of the weekly *Al Ahali,* was sentenced to 10 months in jail for defamation. In June, two Norwegian journalists were expelled for attempting to meet a Western Sahara activist. In September 2004, a court sentenced Anas Tadili, the editor of the weekly *Akhbar al-Ousbouaa,* to one year in jail for libel after he wrote about a government minister's homosexuality. Broadcast media are mostly government controlled. Foreign broadcasting is available via satellite. The government did not generally impede Internet access, but blocked the Web site of the Justice and Charity Organization, a religious group barred from political activity.

Islam is the official religion of Morocco, and almost 99 percent of the population is Sunni Muslim. Morocco's Jewish community, while quite small (approximately 5,000), has been able to worship freely. However, the 2003 bombings largely targeted Jewish community sites.

Academic freedom was somewhat restricted, with no open debates allowed on the monarchy, Islam, or the status of the Western Sahara. Government informers monitored Islamist activity on campuses, and the Interior Ministry approved the appointment of rectors.

Freedom of association is somewhat limited. Nongovernmental organizations (NGOs) need government permission to operate, but in practice few groups have been rejected or subjected to funding controls in place. A royal pardon in January 2004 included some 20 political prisoners and detainees, among them activists working on human rights in the Western Sahara. Freedom of assembly is limited, and public gatherings require Interior Ministry permission, although peaceful protests are generally tolerated.

The law allows workers to establish and join trade unions. A new labor law enforced in June 2004 prohibits anti-union discrimination and prescribes the government's authority to intervene in strikes, which are allowed by the constitution but subject to a subsequent law requiring compulsory arbitration of disputes. Most strikes during 2004 were of 24 to 48 hours duration and involved, among others, the teachers' unions, bank officers, and health professionals.

The judiciary lacks independence and is subject to corruption and bribery. The current antiterrorism law allows suspects to be held for up to 12 days without being charged, broadens the definition of terrorism, and expands the number of crimes punishable by death. The justice minister said in May 2004 that more than 2,000 people had been charged, some 900 convicted, and 17 sentenced to death. Amnesty International reported that the practice of torture had widened in Morocco as part of the antiterrorism campaign and charged that the trials of terror were not conducted fairly.

While the new Equity and Reconciliation Commission is to investigate and document disappearances and other abuses that occurred between 1956 and 1999, it lacks the authority to take to court alleged perpetrators and can only provide information and recommend compensation to the victims or their relatives. It also cannot compel government institutions to cooperate with it. Further complicating its mandate is the fact that most of the "disappeared" are from the Western Sahara; it is consequently difficult for their relatives to trust an officially appointed body. Nevertheless, the commission has consulted international experts on truth and reconciliation and is to present a record of the cases by April 2005.

Moroccan women are guaranteed equal rights under the constitution, but the reality has been one of marked inequality. The 2004 amendment to the family code fueled hopes for improvement. The amendment raises the marriage age from 15 to 18 for women, cedes greater rights to women in the areas of marriage and divorce, and makes polygamy difficult. However, women's rights groups warned that in order for the changes to succeed, judges needed to be trained and women must be informed about their new rights. Many NGOs and government departments had begun mobilizing to adopt the new Mudawana. Domestic violence is common, but the Mudawana may make it easier for women to obtain a divorce. A new labor code makes it illegal for children under age 15 to be employed. Child labor has been common, especially the employment of young girls as unpaid domestics or as prostitutes.

Mozambique

Population: 19,200,000
GNI/capita: $200
Life Expectancy: 40
Religious Groups: Indigenous beliefs (50 percent), Christian (30 percent), Muslim (20 percent)
Ethnic Groups: Indigenous tribal groups [Makhuwa, Tsonga, Lomwe, Sena, and others] (99.7 percent), other (0.3 percent)
Capital: Maputo

Political Rights: 3
Civil Liberties: 4
Status: Partly Free

Ten-Year Ratings Timeline (Political Rights, Civil Liberties, Status)

1995	1996	1997	1998	1999	2000	2001	2002	2003	2004
3,4PF	3,4PF	3,4PF	3,4PF	3,4PF	3,4PF	3,4PF	3,4PF	3,4PF	3,4PF

Overview:

Presidential and parliamentary elections planned for December 2004, the third since civil war ended a decade ago, were expected to extend the dominance of the ruling Mozambique Liberation Front (FRELIMO). Corruption continued to tarnish the government, especially after the second escape from prison of a man charged with killing the country's foremost investigative journalist.

Portuguese traders and settlers arrived in Mozambique in the late fifteenth century, and full-scale colonization began in the seventeenth century. FRELIMO was established in 1962 and launched a guerrilla campaign to oust the Portuguese, and in 1975, Mozambique gained independence. FRELIMO was installed as the sole legal party, and its leader, Samora Machel, as president. Independence was followed by 16 years of civil war waged by the Mozambique National Resistance (RENAMO), which was supported first by Rhodesia (Zimbabwe) and later by South Africa.

In 1986, Machel died in an airplane crash, and Joachim Chissano became president. In 1989, FRELIMO formally abandoned Marxism-Leninism for democratic socialism and a market economy. In 1992, a ceasefire was signed, followed by a full peace agreement. RENAMO agreed to operate as an opposition political party.

The first multiparty elections, which were held in 1994, attracted a 90 percent turnout. The elections were judged a resounding success by the international community, despite a brief preelection boycott called by RENAMO, which accused FRELIMO of fraud. RENAMO leader Alphonse Dhlakama captured 33.7 percent of the presidential vote, versus 53.3 percent for Chissano. FRELIMO won a narrow, but workable, majority in parliament in concurrent legislative polls.

Chissano and FRELIMO were reelected in general elections in 1999, despite a strong showing by the opposition. The polls were marred by logistical and administrative difficulties, and RENAMO complained of fraud. However, many Mozambicans and the international community viewed the elections as expressing the people's will. In protest of alleged fraud, RENAMO deputies repeatedly walked out of parliament or interrupted proceedings in 2000 and 2001. At one point, RENAMO threatened to form its own government in six northern and central provinces.

Widespread corruption has damaged the standing of Chissano's government. In January 2003, six men were found guilty of murdering journalist Carlos Cardoso, who died in 1990 while investigating bank scandals. While the convictions were a triumph of judiciary independence, no charges were lodged against the president's son, Nyimpine Chissano, who was alleged by some of the accused to have ordered the assassination. Suspicions of high-level complicity flared in May 2004 with the second escape from prison of Anibal Antonio dos Santos, who was sentenced to 28 years in prison for the murder; he had previously escaped in 2002. Dos Santos was captured later that month at Toronto's Pearson International Airport, and sought asylum in Canada. The Mozambican government is currently seeking his extradition.

FRELIMO maintains dominance of government institutions, but Chissano's announcement that he would not run in the December 2004 presidential elections appears to reflect an acceptance of democratic practice. Armando Guebeza, a former interior minister and hard-line Marxist, was FRELIMO's nominee for president and widely expected to win.

Meanwhile, deep political divisions remain, with occasional violence. August 2004 saw two incidents in Sofala province, a RENAMO stronghold. Political rivals clashed in the town of Inhaminga, and then a gun battle erupted between the police and Dhlakama's security guards in nearby Maringue.

Mozambique boasts one of Africa's best-performing economies, thanks partly to extensive foreign aid. Nevertheless, the country remains among the world's poorest. With some 14 percent of Mozambicans stricken with HIV/AIDS, the economy faces challenges ahead, including a contracting agricultural labor force in subsistence farming.

Political Rights and Civil Liberties: Mozambicans can change their government democratically, although this freedom is constrained by the economic legacy of war and unfamiliarity with democratic practices. The president, who is elected to a five-year term by popular vote, appoints the prime minister. The unicameral Assembly of the Republic comprises 250 seats; FRELIMO holds 160 and RENAMO 90. The next legislative and presidential elections are scheduled for December 2009. Parliament plays an important role in the political process, although the executive branch overshadows its power. The influence of smaller opposition parties is negligible, which leaves RENAMO the only viable electoral challenge to the status quo.

Parliament agreed in 2002 to change electoral law provisions regarding settling disputes, deploying observers, and naming members to the electoral commission. In parliament, procedural changes undertaken in 2001 have resulted in that body's increased effectiveness, although partisan tensions sometimes impede work.

Corruption is pervasive, although the government is taking steps, such as compelling high-ranking civil servants, as the result of a law passed in 2003, to declare their incomes on assuming their posts. Mozambique's attorney general admitted in a 2002 report to parliament that corruption plagued the legal system. He cited incompetence and abuse of power at all levels of the administration of justice, including police, attorneys, judges, lawyers, and prison personnel. He also blamed prosecuting attorneys for failing to press charges against suspects despite sufficient evidence. Mozambique was ranked 90 out of 146 countries surveyed in Transparency International's 2004 Corruption Perceptions Index.

The constitution provides for media freedom, but the state controls nearly all broadcast media and owns or influences the largest newspapers. The independent media have enjoyed moderate growth, but publications in the capital of Maputo have little influence in the largely illiterate rural population. The most important media company to arise is the cooperative Mediacoop, which owns *Mediafax* (which is faxed to hundreds of subscribers but read very widely), the periodical *Mozambique Interview*, and the weekly *Savana*. Criminal libel laws deter open expression. The more than a dozen licensed private radio and television stations exercise some self-censorship. The opposition receives inadequate coverage in state-run media, especially radio and television. Only a fraction of the population has access to the Internet because of a scarcity of electricity and computers.

The constitution provides for freedom of religion. There was no reported government interference with religious practice or academic freedom.

Freedom of assembly is broadly guaranteed, but limited by notification and timing restrictions. Nongovernmental organizations, including the Mozambican Human Rights League, operate openly, as do international human rights and humanitarian groups. FRELIMO's grip on the labor movement is loosening. The Organization of Mozambican Workers, the major trade confederation, is now nominally independent. The Organization of Free and Independent Unions, a more independent group, was formed in 1994. All workers in nonessential services have the right to strike. The right to bargain collectively is legally protected.

The judicial system is hobbled by a dire shortage of judges, magistrates, and defense lawyers. Bribery of judges by lawyers is alleged to be common. Detainees often wait months, sometimes years, before appearing in court without any formal defense. They are tried only in Portuguese, which many Mozambicans speak poorly. The Constitutional Council, entrusted with deciding whether laws and governmental decisions are constitutional, made its debut in late 2003. Abuses by security forces still occur. Prisons are severely overcrowded with appalling health conditions.

The government and organized crime influence the business elite. Western donors praise Mozambique's privatization drive, although it has slowed in recent years and major sectors remain in state hands.

Women occasionally pierce the male-dominated political arena; in February, Luisa Dias Diogo was named the country's first female prime minister. However, women generally suffer from legal and societal discrimination, and domestic violence is common. Only formally married women have full rights.

Namibia

Population: 1,900,000
GNI/capita: $1,790
Life Expectancy: 47
Religious Groups: Christian (80-90 percent),
indigenous beliefs (10-20 percent)
Ethnic Groups: Black (87.5 percent), white (6 percent),
mixed (6.5 percent)
Capital: Windhoek

Political Rights: 2
Civil Liberties: 3
Status: Free

Ten-Year Ratings Timeline (Political Rights, Civil Liberties, Status)

1995	1996	1997	1998	1999	2000	2001	2002	2003	2004
2,3F	2,3F	2,3F	2,3F	2,3F	2,3F	2,3F	2,3F	2,3F	2,3F

Overview:

Hifikepunye Pohamba, the successor to Namibia's founding president Sam Nujoma, won national elections held in November, and the ruling South West Africa People's Organization party (SWAPO) maintained its overwhelming majority in parliament. The government completed the crucial first stage of its land reform program, paving the way for the purchase of white-owned farms and the resettlement of landless blacks.

Namibia was seized by German imperial forces in the late 1800s. Thousands of people were massacred by German troops in efforts to crush all resistance to colonial settlement and administration. The territory became a South African protectorate after German forces were expelled during World War I and was ruled under the apartheid system for 42 years after 1948. After 13 years of violent guerrilla war, Namibia achieved independence in 1990. During a UN-supervised democratic transition, Sam Nujoma was chosen president that year by a freely and fairly elected National Assembly.

SWAPO scored a sweeping victory, and Nujoma was reelected in 1994. Nujoma, the leader of the country's struggle against apartheid, adopted an increasingly authoritarian governing style. He was easily returned to power with 77 percent of the vote for a third five-year term in the 1999 presidential election. The party had succeeded in passing a bitterly contested constitutional amendment to allow Nujoma to seek a third term.

Legislative polls in 1999 saw SWAPO retain its two-thirds majority in the 72-member National Assembly, increasing its number of seats from 53 to 55. The ruling party's main base is among the country's largest ethnic group, the Ovambo, whose prominence within SWAPO has evoked allegations of ethnic discrimination.

In April 2002, the Angolan government and the National Union for the Total Independence of Angola (UNITA) signed a ceasefire agreement. Fighting in Namibia's Caprivi region had flared in October 1998 and in August 1999, and UNITA was accused of supporting Caprivi insurgents. Under a 1999 mutual defense pact, the governments of Angola and Namibia agreed that each could pursue suspected rebels into the other's territory. Caprivi, a finger of land poking eastward out of northern Namibia along its borders with Angola and Botswana, differs geographically, politically, and in its ethnic makeup from the rest of Namibia; it was used by South Africa in that country's operations against SWAPO guerrillas.

In November 2004 elections for the National Assembly, SWAPO won 55 seats (the same number it won in 1999), the Congress of Democrats won 5, the Democratic Turnhalle Alliance won 4, the United Democratic Front took 3, and other parties took the remaining 5. SWAPO's Hifikepunye Pohamba easily beat out six other presidential candidates, taking 76 percent of the vote. Turnout was approximately 85 percent, compared to 61 percent in 1999.

Whites, who make up about 6 percent of the population, owned just under half of Namibia's arable land in 2003. The government has since assessed the value of more than 12,000 commercial farms and plans to implement a land tax that will help pay for the land reform program. Farm owners who contest the valuations may appeal in court; some 285 objections have been lodged so far. Nujoma also announced plans to expropriate 192 farms belonging to foreign absentee landlords. The government says it has resettled more than 6,000 black families and remains in negotiations with the commercial farmers' union to fully implement its "willing-seller, willing-buyer" land redistribution strategy. The program has won praise from Germany, which has agreed to fund part of the plan, for proceeding in an orderly and peaceful manner.

Capital-intensive extractive industries, such as diamond and uranium mining, have drawn significant foreign investment and are the centerpiece of Namibia's economic growth. In 2004, the government embarked on a massive power project that would quadruple Namibia's electricity production by developing gas fields. Most Namibians, however, continue to live as subsistence farmers, and many lack basic services.

Political Rights and Civil Liberties: Namibians can change their government democratically. The 1999 elections were judged to be largely free and fair, although there were some instances of government harassment of the opposition, as well as unequal access to media coverage and campaign financing. The legislature consists of the 26-seat National Council, whose members are appointed by regional councils for six-year terms, and the 72-seat National Assembly, whose members are elected by popular vote to serve five-year terms. Observer missions from the Electoral Institute of Southern Africa and the Southern African Development Community said the 2004 elections were free and fair, although opposition parties complained that they only got access to the full voters' roll four days before the polls and vowed to go to court to demand a recount.

Namibia was ranked 54 out of 146 countries surveyed in Transparency International's 2004 Corruption Perceptions Index. An anticorruption bill was signed into law by President Sam Nujoma in 2003, but a long-awaited autonomous Anti-Corruption Commission with investigative and arrest powers has yet to come into existence.

The constitution guarantees the right to free speech and a free press, and the country's press in considered one of the freest on the continent. Private radio stations and critical independent newspapers usually operate without official interference, but reporters for state-run media have been subjected to indirect and direct pressure to avoid reporting on controversial topics. There are at least eight private radio stations and one private television station. The state-run Namibia Broadcasting Corporation has regularly presented views critical of the government. There are no government restrictions on the Internet, and several publications have popular Web sites.

Freedom of religion is guaranteed and respected in practice. The government does not restrict academic freedom.

Freedom of assembly is guaranteed by law and permitted in practice, except in situations of national emergency. Local and international human rights groups operate freely without government interference. Constitutionally guaranteed union rights are respected. Although collective bargaining is not practiced widely outside the mining and construction industries, informal collective bargaining is increasingly common. Essential public sector workers do not have the right to strike. Domestic and farm laborers remain the country's most heavily exploited workers, in part because many are illiterate and do not know their rights.

The constitution provides for an independent judiciary, and the government respects this right. However, in rural areas, local chiefs use traditional courts that often ignore constitutional procedures. Allegations of police brutality persist. After nearly five years of delays, the mass trial of 120 defendants accused of high treason and other crimes in relation to the separatist rebellion in Caprivi opened in June 2004. A judge had freed 13 of the defendants in February, but the men were immediately rearrested and the Supreme Court later upheld their detention. The trial of another 12 alleged Caprivi separatists has been set for March 2005. Human rights groups have called for independent investigations into the deaths of 13 Caprivi suspects in police custody since 1999. Authorities have dismissed allegations of torture. Conditions in prisons and military detention facilities generally meet international standards.

Respect for human rights in Namibia is good, and the country's National Society for Human Rights (NSHR) said that the overall civil and political situation in the formerly volatile Caprivi, Kavango, and Ohangwena regions has improved considerably. Nevertheless, Caprivians accuse the government of neglect in the province, which is among the country's poorest.

The Herero and Damara peoples are among the minority ethnic groups demanding larger government allocations for development in their home areas. Herero leaders have filed a $2 billion lawsuit in the United States to demand reparations for abuses they suffered at the hands of German colonists. The Herero were nearly wiped out during colonialism. In 2004, the German government apologized for atrocities committed against the Herero people, but ruled out reparations, instead promising increased development aid. The Namibian government has made efforts to end discrimination of indigenous San (Bushmen), although the NSHR says that the San remain marginalized and subject to rights abuses.

Despite constitutional guarantees, women continue to face discrimination in customary law and other traditional societal practices. Violence against women is reportedly widespread, and the UN Human Rights Committee criticized the government in 2004 for failing to prosecute the majority of cases or provide compensation to the victims, despite the existence of a domestic violence act. Women are increasingly involved in the political process, but remain under-represented in government and politics.

Nauru

Population: 10,000
GNI/capita: $3,540
Life Expectancy: 61
Political Rights: 1
Civil Liberties: 1
Status: Free
Religious Groups: Christian (two-thirds Protestant, one-third Roman Catholic)
Ethnic Groups: Nauruan (58 percent), other Pacific Islander (26 percent), Chinese (8 percent), European (8 percent)
Capital: Yaren

Ten-Year Ratings Timeline (Political Rights, Civil Liberties, Status)

1995	1996	1997	1998	1999	2000	2001	2002	2003	2004
1,3F	1,3F	1,3F	1,3F	1,3F	1,3F	1,3F	1,2F	1,1F	1,1F

Overview: Intense political rivalry continued unabated in Nauru in 2004, bringing the government to a virtual standstill and adversely affecting an already dire economy. In June, a no-confidence vote ousted President Rene Harris and his cabinet, and Ludwig Scotty was selected by parliament to succeed Harris. October parliamentary elections resulted in a legislative majority for Scotty supporters and a political mandate for much-needed economic reforms.

Nauru, a tiny Pacific island state located 1,600 miles northeast of New Zealand, was a German protectorate from 1888 until the close of World War I, in 1917, when Australia began administering it under a League of Nations mandate. The Japanese occupied Nauru during World War II, but Australian administrators returned to Nauru after the war under a UN mandate. Nauru gained independence in 1968, adopting a modified form of parliamentary democracy.

Severe party and factional competition have produced several leadership changes in recent years. The use of no-confidence votes has been a common tool to oust the president and his cabinet. Such intense political rivalry has been a hindrance to sustaining various policies, including those supporting economic development.

On January 8, 2003, Harris was ousted by a parliamentary vote of no confidence following opposition allegations of economic mismanagement and corruption. Just days after, Nauru's chief justice ruled that the 8 to 3 no-confidence vote was invalid without an absolute majority in the 18-member parliament and ordered that Harris be reinstated. Parliament voted Bernard Dowiyogo to replace Harris, but the Supreme Court barred Dowiyogo from claiming the presidency. The Speaker of parliament resigned in protest over the Supreme Court ruling. The parliament then refused to nominate a new speaker, without whom a new parliament session cannot convene to pass legislation or a new budget.

This impasse ended with Dowiyogo's death in March 2003 in Washington, DC, following heart surgery. Derog Gioura was appointed acting president to lead the caretaker administration until new elections were held in May 2003. Scotty was elected as the new president, but was ousted by a no-confidence vote just four months later. The parliament again chose Harris to lead the government.

Just months after he resumed power, another no-confidence vote was cast in February 2004. Harris held onto power when a tie resulted, but he was ousted by another no-confidence vote in June 2004. Again, parliament elected Scotty to succeed Harris; Riddel Akua was elected Speaker of parliament. However, parliament's deadlock over the budget caused Scotty to dissolve parliament in early October and to declare a state of emergency. A new election on October 23 produced a clear parliamentary majority for Scotty, giving his government a strong mandate to push for tough reforms to restore the island nation's economic health.

Nevertheless, economic improvement remained illusive throughout the year. Phosphate, once plentiful and mined by Australia for use as fertilizer, is almost entirely exhausted, and the mining industry has left behind broken lands and other environmental problems. More than 80 percent of this 8-square-mile island republic is uninhabitable. At one time, phosphate mining made Nauru one of the richest in the world in per capita income, but financial mismanagement by the government squandered much of this wealth. A trust fund built on phosphate mining royalties is likely to be depleted in a few years. Nauru is highly dependent on foreign aid, and the country is also saddled with a large foreign debt relative to its size.

Recent administrations have been seeking new ways to generate income—including passport sales and offshore banking operations—but with varying results. Since 2001, Nauru has served as a refugee-processing and detention center for Australia in exchange for financial aid; the country provides temporary housing for hundreds of mainly Middle Easterners seeking asylum in Australia. Nauru also obtained U.S. agreement for additional financial aid in exchange for the establishment of an intelligence listening post in the country. The country switches diplomatic recognition between China and Taiwan to secure the most financial aid from the two competitors. Nauru switched recognition from Taiwan to Beijing in July 2002. In 2003, Nauru resumed official ties with Taiwan in exchange for Taiwanese assistance to settle Nauru's outstanding loans of $2.7 million for a Boeing 737 jet aircraft owed to the Export-Import Bank of the United States.

Political Rights and Civil Liberties: Citizens of Nauru can change their government democratically. The 18-member unicameral legislature is elected from 14 constituencies by popular vote for three-year terms. Members of parliament choose from among themselves the president and vice president. The president is the head of state and chief executive. Suffrage is universal and compulsory for all citizens 20 years and older.

As an offshore banking center, Nauru has been implicated in international money laundering. The country was also under international pressure, particularly from the United States, to crack down on passport sales when two alleged al-Qaeda operatives were arrested in Malaysia carrying Nauruan passports. In 2003, the government announced that it would close its offshore banking operation, suspend its investor passport program, and update its banking laws and financial sector legislation that year. Political rivalry, however, has kept the government from moving forward with any of these plans. Nauru was not ranked by Transparency International in its 2004 Corruption Perceptions Index.

There have been no reports of government monitoring or censorship of any media. The country has no regular print media, but foreign publications, the majority in English, are freely admitted and widely available. The government publishes occasional bulletins a,nd the opposition publishes its own newsletters. The government owns and operates the only radio station and Nauru TV. However, a private network provides sports news coverage. Internet connection began in 1998, and the government is the sole provider of Internet services. Internet use is constrained by cost and the lack of reliable infrastructure outside the capital. Nauru's communication system is fragile: television service was unavailable for nearly two months in 2003 when a frequency amplifier broke.

The constitution provides for freedom of religion, and the government generally respects this right in practice. There were no reports of government suppression of academic freedom.

The government respects the right of assembly and association in practice. There are a few advocacy groups for women, development-focused groups, and religious organizations. No trade unions or labor protection laws exist in this largely agriculture-based, subsistence economy.

The judiciary is independent, and defendants generally receive fair trials and representation. The Supreme Court is the highest court when addressing constitutional issues, and the parliament cannot overturn court decisions. Appeals in civil and criminal cases can be lodged with the high court of Australia under the terms of a bilateral agreement. Nauru has no armed forces. Traditional reconciliation mechanisms rather than the formal legal process are used in many cases, usually by choice but sometimes under communal pressure. Defense is the responsibility of Australia under an informal agreement. A civilian head controls the 100-person police force. Police abuse is rare; however, foreign workers complain that the police are slow to act on cases filed against native employers.

Strict immigration rules govern foreign workers. Those who leave Nauru without their employer's permission cannot reenter, and immigrant workers must leave Nauru within 60 days of termination of employment.

The law provides equal freedom and protection for men and women, but societal pressures limit opportunities for women to fully exercise these rights. Prostitution is illegal and not widespread. Sexual harassment is a crime, but spousal rape is not. Domestic violence is frequently associated with alcohol abuse. Although the government and judiciary generally respond to cases filed, most incidents are reconciled informally within the family or communally by traditional leaders. As a result, reliable figures for domestic abuse and sex crimes are not available.

Nepal

Population: 24,700,000 **Political Rights:** 5
GNI/capita: $230 **Civil Liberties:** 5*
Life Expectancy: 59 **Status:** Partly Free
Religious Groups: Hindu (86.2 percent), Buddhist
(7.8 percent), Muslim (3.8 percent), other (2.2 percent)
Ethnic Groups: Brahman, Chetri, Newar, Gurung, Sherpa,
Magar, Tamang, Bhotia, Rai, Limbu
Capital: Kathmandu
Ratings Change: Nepal's civil liberties rating dropped from 4 to 5 due to a further deterioration in the rule of law and in free economic activity under the Maoist insurgency.

Ten-Year Ratings Timeline (Political Rights, Civil Liberties, Status)

1995	1996	1997	1998	1999	2000	2001	2002	2003	2004
3,4PF	3,4PF	3,4PF	3,4PF	3,4PF	3,4PF	3,4PF	4,4PF	5,4PF	5,5PF

Overview:

Conditions in Nepal worsened in 2004 as the standoff between King Gyanendra and the political parties showed few signs of resolution and the ongoing Maoist insurgency continued to destabilize much of the country. In the wake of the collapse of a ceasefire in August 2003, the incidence of extrajudicial murders, abductions, and other human rights violations by both sides once again rose dramatically, with several thousand soldiers, rebels, and civilians being killed during the year. Maoist strikes, blockades, and violence directed at key business targets caused added hardship for civilians and further crippled the economy. Although a new interim prime minister and government with somewhat more legitimacy than the king's previous appointments took power in June, the relationship between the palace and the main political parties remained unproductive. Meanwhile, the Maoists continued to reject official invitations to resume negotiations unless their primary demand—the convening of a constituent assembly mandated to write a new constitution—was on the agenda.

King Prithvi Narayan Shah unified this Himalayan land in 1769. Following two centuries of palace rule, the left-leaning Nepali Congress (NC) party won Nepal's first elections in 1959. King Mahendra abruptly dissolved parliament and banned political parties in 1960, and in 1962 began ruling through a repressive *panchayat* (village council) system. Many parties went underground until early 1990, when the NC and a coalition of Communist parties organized pro-democracy rallies that led King Birendra to re-legalize political parties. An interim government introduced a constitution that vested executive power in the prime minister and cabinet, and turned Nepal into a constitutional monarchy.

In Nepal's first multiparty elections in 32 years, Giraja Prasad Koirala, a veteran dissident, led the NC to victory and formed a government in 1991. Riven by intraparty conflicts, the NC was forced in 1994 to call early elections, which it lost to the Communist Party of Nepal/United Marxist-Leninist, or CPN-UML. The Communists, however, failed to win a majority in parliament. Hopes for a more stable government rose after the NC won a majority in elections held in 1999. The campaign centered on the problems of rampant official corruption, stagnant economic growth, and the Maoist insurgency. Led by Baburam Bhattarai and Pushpa Kamal Dahal, the Communist Party of Nepal/Maoist (CPN-M, or Maoists) insurgent group has said that it wants an end to the constitutional monarchy and the feudal structure that persists in many parts of the country.

In June 2001, Gyanendra ascended the throne after a palace massacre in which the crown prince apparently shot to death the king and nine other members of the royal family before killing himself. After Sher Bahadur Deuba became interim prime minister in July, the rebels agreed to a ceasefire, but when they broke the ceasefire in November, Gyanendra declared a state of emergency. The government's subsequent decision to use the army to fight the Maoists marked a sharp escalation in the conflict; an estimated 5,000 people were killed in 2002, and Nepal's infrastructure and economy were severely damaged.

Political instability heightened in May 2002, when the prime minister dissolved parliament and called for fresh elections to be held in November. When caretaker prime minister Deuba, citing the worsening security situation, asked the king in October to postpone the elections, Gyanendra dismissed Deuba and assumed executive powers himself. While postponing elections indefinitely, he also installed an interim administration headed by Lokendra Bahadur Chand, a former prime minister and the leader of a small royalist party. Mainstream parties termed his decision undemocratic and have intermittently organized antigovernment protests calling for a return to the democratic process. The subsequent installation of Surya Bahadur Thapa, a member of a right-wing royalist party, as prime minister by royal decree in June 2003 also lacked legitimacy, and in June 2004, Deuba, who enjoys somewhat more support than his predecessors, was reappointed as prime minister and formed a coalition government. However, the NC and three other parties refused to join the government and parliament remained dissolved. Deuba was also charged with holding an election before April 2005, and restoring peace.

The latter task proved virtually impossible during the second half of 2004. A ceasefire between the rebels and government forces, which had been in effect from January to August 2003, collapsed following disagreements that emerged at a third round of peace talks about the possible formation of a constituent assembly. After that, the rate of killings on both sides once again escalated dramatically. During 2004, the Maoists continued their policy of bombing, assassinating government officials, particularly at the local level, and attacking key targets such as an Indian-owned five-star hotel and the America Center in Kathmandu. Periodic strikes and blockades called throughout the year crippled the economy and caused further hardship for Nepali civilians and business interests. In August, the Maoists announced that they were preparing for a "strategic offensive." The cabinet formally invited the Maoists to negotiate in September 2004, but they appear unwilling to engage in sustained and serious negotiations unless the government will agree to convene a constituent assembly to write a new constitution.

Political Rights and Civil Liberties: The Nepalese cannot change their government democratically. The 1990 constitution provides for a 205-seat lower house of parliament that is directly elected for a five-year term and a 60-seat upper house whose members are either elected by national or local government bodies or appointed by the king. During 2004, these constitutional provisions remained suspended, and polls that would have elected a new parliament in November 2002 have been indefinitely postponed. King Gyanendra rules through an interim prime minister and cabinet; since October 2002, he has appointed three such puppets who have had limited powers and little legitimacy. The king's influence is bolstered by his authority to wield emergency powers and suspend many basic freedoms. He also serves as commander in chief of the army.

A wide range of political parties have been allowed to operate since 1990, although the constitution bans political parties that are formed along religious, caste, ethnic, tribal, or regional lines. Recent elections have been free, though not entirely fair. In the 1999 elections, interparty clashes led to several election-related deaths, and Maoist violence caused balloting to be postponed in dozens of districts.

As a result of the escalation in the insurgency, government institutions have all but fallen apart in much of rural Nepal. Elected governments have made few reforms to Nepal's bloated, inefficient civil service, and ministries operate with little openness or accountability. Corruption is perceived to be endemic in politics and government administration. Legislation passed in 2002 disqualified those convicted on corruption charges from contesting political elections for five years and placed the burden of proof in corruption cases on the accused. However, compliance with anticorruption regulations remains weak, and the prosecution of high-level officials is rare, which contributes to a climate of impunity. Representation of ethnic minorities, lower castes, and women in state institutions is negligible. Nepal was ranked 90 out of 146 countries surveyed in Transparency International's 2004 Corruption Perceptions Index.

Both the constitution and the Press and Publications Act broadly suppress speech and writing that could undermine the monarchy, national security, public order, or interethnic or intercaste relations. The government owns both the influential Radio Nepal, whose political coverage favors the ruling party, and Nepal's main television station. Although access to the Internet is generally unrestricted, in February the government instructed privately run Internet Service Providers (ISPs) to block access to the Maoists' Web site.

Conditions for the media, which deteriorated sharply as the Maoist insurgency escalated in late 2001, have remained poor. Journalists who are suspected of pro-Maoist leanings or who produce material critical of the government are regularly arrested and detained by police and security forces, and a number have reportedly been subjected to harassment, torture, and occasionally death. During the daily pro-democracy demonstrations that engulfed Kathmandu in April, hundreds of reporters who were attempting to cover unfolding events were arrested, and several were beaten or otherwise injured by police. While many private publications continue to criticize government policies, self-censorship is a growing concern.

Media professionals are also under increasing pressure from the Maoists. Rebels killed Dakendra Raj Thapa, a journalist with the state-owned Radio Nepal, in August, and other reporters have been abducted and threatened as well as being expelled from rebel-held areas. In November, the Maoists imposed a reporting ban in five western districts and put into place provisions that required journalists to obtain permission from local Maoist leaders before reporting from the area.

Although the constitution describes Nepal as a Hindu kingdom, there is a considerable Buddhist minority. The constitution provides for freedom of religion, but proselytizing is prohibited, and members of religious minorities occasionally complain of official harassment. Although the government does not restrict academic freedom, more than 100 teachers have been killed both by security forces and by Maoists, and Maoists regularly target private schools in the rural areas. A strike called by a pro-Maoist student union in June affected more than 33,500 schools and forced an estimated six million students to stay home, according to the Economist Intelligence Unit.

Freedom of assembly and association is occasionally restricted, and police sometimes use excessive force against peaceful protestors. In April, the government declared Kathmandu to be a riot zone and banned the assembly of more than five people after the main parliamentary parties organized daily demonstrations calling for a return to democracy. Protestors defied the ban, and more than 900 were arrested on April 9 alone, while dozens were injured by police during the course of the demonstrations.

The government generally allows nongovernmental organizations (NGOs) to function freely. However, Amnesty International and others reported that human rights activists faced increasing harassment from both police and Maoist guerrillas during 2004, including threats, torture and detention, and occasional violence. The insurgency has forced a number of NGOs working in rural Nepal to curb substantially their activities, as the Maoists require NGOs to seek their permission to function in many districts and have expressed hostility towards international development organizations, according to Human Rights Watch. In May, three major Western donor organizations announced that they were indefinitely suspending their operations in western Nepal, citing persistent intimidation and extortion by the Maoists.

Trade unions are independent, but they have notched up few real gains for workers. By law, workers in certain essential services cannot stage strikes, and 60 percent of a union's membership must vote in favor of a strike for it to be legal. In March, the government expanded the list of "essential industries" to cover entire sectors such as transport, tourism, telecommunications, and public utilities. While export-oriented carpet factories have reduced their use of child workers, smaller carpet factories and several other industries continue to depend on child labor. Although bonded labor was outlawed in 2000, it persists in rural areas.

The Supreme Court is viewed as largely independent of the executive. However, lower-level courts are subject to political pressure and endemic corruption, and effective access to justice for many Nepalese remains limited. Because of heavy case backlogs and a slow appeals process, suspects often spend longer in pretrial detention than they would if convicted of the crimes for which they stand accused. Prison conditions are poor, with overcrowding common and detainees sometimes handcuffed or otherwise fettered.

In ordinary criminal cases, police at times commit extrajudicial killings and cause the disappearance of suspects in custody. They also occasionally torture and beat suspects to punish them or to extract confessions. The government generally has refused to conduct thorough investigations and take serious disciplinary measures against officers accused of brutality. Nevertheless, BBC reports in January and March 2004 quoted an official spokesman as saying that a number of soldiers had been imprisoned or dismissed from the army after having committed human rights abuses. Set up in 2000, the National Human Rights Commission (NHRC) has a mandate to investigate alleged human rights violations, such as the extrajudicial killing of 19 people in Ramechhap district by the army in August 2003. However, both the government and the Maoists have refused to sign a Human Rights Accord prepared by the NHRC that would give it greater powers to monitor violations with technical assistance from the United Nations.

Both the government and the Maoists have been accused of increased human rights violations in the context of the insurgency, which now affects the entire country and has claimed more than 10,500 lives since 1996. The army and poorly equipped police force have been implicated in extrajudicial killings, disappearances, arbitrary arrests and detentions, rapes, and the torture of suspected Maoists and alleged supporters. The NHRC has recorded several thousand extrajudicial executions since 2001 and several hundred disappearances in each of the last few years, a situation that confers on Nepal the dubious honor of having the highest number of unexplained political disappearances worldwide. In November 2003, then-prime minister Surya Bahadur Thapa announced plans to arm civilians to help defend villages against the Maoists, a move that was criticized by the International Crisis Group and others.

Domestic human rights groups accuse the government of using tough security laws such as the Public Security Act (PSA) and the Terrorism and Disruptive Activities Act (TADA), promulgated in April 2002, to deter civilians from supporting the Maoists. Both laws allow officials to detain suspects for up to six months without filing charges. The government detained dozens of civilians under TADA, including journalists, teachers, lawyers, and political activists. TADA expired in April 2004, but had been kept in force as an ordinance (TADO), and in October, the government amended TADO, extending the period during which suspects could be detained without trial to one year.

The Maoists have killed, tortured, or kidnapped civilians, including suspected informers, landowners, local officials, teachers, and members of mainstream political parties. The rebels, estimated to consist of approximately 5,000 well-trained guerrillas supported by some 15,000 fighters who control perhaps 45 percent of Nepal's territory, have also set up "people's courts" in some districts that hand down summary justice and "people's governments" that levy taxes on inhabitants' income and landholdings. Villagers are regularly coerced into providing food and lodging for traveling Maoist cadres and have been forced to attend political programs in which they are indoctrinated in Maoist ideology. Adding to civilian hardship, the guerrillas fund themselves in part through extortion and looting, and they ordered a number of strikes and blockades throughout the year that paralyzed major urban centers. The Maoists also use forcibly recruited children as soldiers, human shields, and couriers. An intensified campaign of abductions during 2004 caused thousands of students to flee to other parts of Nepal and even to India, according to the Economist Intelligence Unit.

Members of the Hindu upper castes dominate government and business, and low-caste Hindus, ethnic minorities, and Christians face discrimination in the civil service, courts, and government offices. Despite constitutional provisions that ban caste-based discrimination, *dalits* (untouchables) continue to be subjected to particularly severe exploitation, violence, and social exclusion. Nepalese officials at times extort money from, or otherwise harass, Tibetan asylum seekers who cross the border into Nepal, and occasionally hand Tibetans back to Chinese authorities, according to the U.S. State Department's human rights report for 2003. Some 2,000 to 3,000 Tibetans escape into exile via Nepal each year, with most ending up in India. Nepal also provides asylum to more than 100,000 Bhutanese refugees. International organizations estimate that several hundred thousand Nepalese have been internally displaced as a result of the Maoist insurgency.

Women rarely receive the same educational and employment opportunities as men, and there are relatively few women in government and civil service. Although a 2002 law legalized abortion and broadened women's property rights, several dozen women remain in jail on abortion offenses, and many other laws relating to property, divorce, and several other areas discriminate against women. Domestic violence and rape continue to be serious problems. The government has taken few steps to curb violence against women or to assist victims, and authorities generally do not prosecute domestic violence cases. Organized gangs traffic some 5,000 to 12,000 Nepalese girls to work in Indian brothels each year, according to estimates by local NGOs. Because the majority of prostitutes who return to Nepal are HIV-positive, nearly all returnees are shunned and are unable to obtain help to rebuild their lives.

Netherlands

Population: 16,300,000
GNI/capita: $23,390
Life Expectancy: 79
Religious Groups: Roman Catholic (31 percent), Protestant (21 percent), Muslim (4.4 percent), unaffiliated (43.6 percent)
Ethnic Groups: Dutch (83 percent), other [including Turks, Moroccans, Antilleans, Surinamese and Indonesians] (17 percent)
Capital: Amsterdam

Political Rights: 1
Civil Liberties: 1
Status: Free

Ten-Year Ratings Timeline (Political Rights, Civil Liberties, Status)

1995	1996	1997	1998	1999	2000	2001	2002	2003	2004
1,1F	1,1F	1,1F	1,1F	1,1F	1,1F	1,1F	1,1F	1,1F	1,1F

Overview:

In November 2004, Dutch filmmaker Theo Van Gogh was murdered a few months after his controversial film on the position of women in Islamic society was aired on Dutch television and more than two years after the death of the far-right politician Pim Fortuyn. Van Gogh's murder led to protest demonstrations in which thousands took part and sparked fears of increased racial tensions. In October, thousands protested a new austerity plan that will cut welfare support and health coverage, among other reforms. Parliament approved a new asylum bill that will forcibly remove thousands of failed asylum seekers over the next few years.

After the Dutch won their independence from Spain in the sixteenth century, the House of Orange assumed sovereignty over the United Provinces of the Netherlands. A constitutional monarchy emerged in the 1800s with a representative government. The Netherlands remained neutral in both world wars, but was invaded by Nazi Germany in 1940. The occupation ended in 1945, after five years of harsh rule during which Dutch workers were forced to work in German factories and Dutch Jews were deported to concentration camps. The Netherlands ended its neutrality when it joined NATO in 1949; it then became, in 1952, one of the founding members of the European Coal and Steel Community, the precursor to the European Union (EU).

Following the shooting death in May 2002 of far-right politician Pim Fortuyn, his newly formed party, the Pim Fortuyn List (LPF), went on to win second place on an anti-immigrant platform in national elections that same month. The fortunes of the LPF were short-lived, however, when infighting within the party led to a collapse of the new government in October and new elections were called for 2003. In November 2004, Dutch television viewers voted Fortuyn the greatest Dutchman of all times, beating William of Orange, the seventeenth century founder of the modern Dutch state, and Anne Frank, the diarist.

During the January 2003 election, 80 percent of those registered voted and nine parties won seats in parliament. The Christian Democrats (CDA) received more than 28 percent of the vote and 44 seats, just above the Labor Party (PvdA), which received around 27 percent and 42 seats, and the People's Party for Freedom and Democracy (VVD), which received 18 percent and 28 seats. The LPF dropped to fifth place with only around 6 percent of the vote and 8 seats. Following four months of talks and a failed attempt to form a broad center-left coalition with the PvdA, the CDA brought the VVD and Democrats-66 (D66) into a center-right coalition with a slim majority of only six seats. Jan Peter Balkenende was named prime minister for a second term.

In April 2003, an animal rights activist, Volkert van der Graaf, was sentenced to 18 years in prison for the murder of Pim Fortuyn.

An all-party parliamentary report issued in January 2004 concluded that the country had failed to create an integrated, multiethnic society. The report further made an about-face from the country's 30-year-old policy of multiculturalism, arguing that Muslims resident in The Netherlands should "become Dutch." In addition, parliament adopted a government proposal to forcibly deport as many as 26,000 failed asylum seekers over the next three years, including many who have been in the country for years. Human Rights Watch has criticized the country for sending people back to places where they could be in danger.

The murder of Theo Van Gogh in November led to heightened racial tensions in the country. Twenty incidents of vandalism at Muslim buildings, including arson at an Islamic school, took place during the two-week period after the murder.

On the international front, the Dutch took over the rotating EU presidency in July just after the largest expansion of the organization since its founding in the early postwar period.

A new government austerity plan sparked the largest public demonstrations in Amsterdam in two decades. The plan would extend the workweek from 36 to 40 hours, cut health care benefits, and end financial benefits that make early retirement possible. The austerity measures were introduced to help reduce the costs of the country's aging population. The number of people over 65 in the country is expected to double over the next 35 years.

Political Rights and Civil Liberties: The Dutch can change their government democratically. The 150-member lower house, or Second Chamber, is elected every four years by proportional representation and passes bills on to the 75-member upper house, or First Chamber, for approval. During elections in 2003, 80 percent of those registered voted, and nine parties won seats in parliament. Foreigners resident in the country for five years or more are legally eligible to vote in local elections. Uniquely among the EU member countries, mayors are not elected in The Netherlands but appointed from a list of candidates submitted by the municipal councils. The monarch, currently Queen Beatrix, appoints the Council of Ministers (cabinet) and the governor of each province on the recommendation of the majority in parliament.

The country has few issues with political corruption. The Netherlands was ranked 10 out of 146 countries surveyed in Transparency International's 2004 Corruption Perceptions Index.

The country's media are free and independent. Restrictions against insulting the monarch and royal family exist but are rarely enforced. Despite a high concentration of newspaper ownership, a wide variety of opinion is expressed in the print media. Internet access is not restricted.

The Dutch constitution provides for freedom of religion. Religious organizations that provide educational facilities can receive subsidies from the government. Members of the country's Muslim population have encountered an increase in racist incidents in the recent past, including vandalism, arson, defacing of mosques or other Islamic institutions, harassment, and verbal abuse. The LPF won significant support in 2002 running on a platform that characterized Islam as a backward and intolerant culture that oppressed women and homosexuals. Membership is decreasing among all religious denominations, except Islam.

In order to counter undesired foreign influence in the affairs of Dutch Muslim groups, the government has decided to require all imams and other spiritual leaders recruited in Islamic countries to take a one-year integration course before practicing in the country.

The government does not restrict academic freedom.

People have the right to assemble, demonstrate, and generally express their opinions. National and international human rights organizations operated freely without government intervention during the year. Workers have the right to organize, bargain collectively, and strike. In October, more than 200,000 people took to the streets in Amsterdam to protest a government austerity plan that will lead to the biggest cutbacks in public spending in the country's history. The demonstration was organized by a broad coalition of Dutch trades unions and represented a wide spectrum of workers.

The judiciary is independent, and the rule of law prevails in civil and criminal matters. The police are under civilian control, and prison conditions meet international standards. The population is generally treated equally under the law, although human rights groups have criticized the country's recent asylum policies for being unduly harsh and violating international standards. Early in the year, parliament approved a bill that will lead to the deportation of as many as 26,000 failed asylum seekers. A Dutch court sentenced a former colonel from the Democratic Republic of Congo to 30 months in prison for torturing people there in the 1990s.

The Dutch are known for their liberal values and laws; among these are tolerant attitudes toward so-called soft drugs, such as marijuana, and the legalization of euthanasia and same-sex marriage. However, the country passed a law in June that abolished anonymity in sperm donations so that the children of artificially inseminated women can trace their fathers.

The country is a significant destination and transit point for trafficking in persons, particularly women for sexual exploitation. The Dutch government, however, has made efforts in recent years to confront the problem, cracking down on illegal employment of prostitutes in the 2000 Prostitution Law and making trafficking in persons a priority issue during its 2003 chairmanship of the Organization for Security and Cooperation in Europe. During the country's 2003 elections, 37 percent of the seats in parliament were won by women.

New Zealand

Population: 4,100,000
GNI/capita: $13,260
Life Expectancy: 78
Religious Groups: Anglican (24 percent), Presbyterian (18 percent), Roman Catholic (15 percent), other (43 percent)
Ethnic Groups: New Zealand European (74.5 percent), Maori (9.7 percent), other European (4.6 percent), Pacific Islander (3.8 percent), other [including Asian] (7.4 percent)
Capital: Wellington

Political Rights: 1
Civil Liberties: 1
Status: Free

Ten-Year Ratings Timeline (Political Rights, Civil Liberties, Status)

1995	1996	1997	1998	1999	2000	2001	2002	2003	2004
1,1F	1,1F	1,1F	1,1F	1,1F	1,1F	1,1F	1,1F	1,1F	1,1F

Overview:

The focal issue in New Zealand in 2004 was the Maori claim to the country's foreshores (the land between high-water and low-water marks) and seabed. The opposition National Party capitalized on the dissatisfaction of the non-Maori population over this matter to attack the government. Faced with growing pressure to defend its majority in parliament, the Labour Party–led government passed a bill declaring all foreshores and seabed state property, leading a Maori cabinet member to resign in protest. Meanwhile, a new Maori political party was established during the year.

New Zealand became self-governing before World War II and gained full independence from Britain in 1947, establishing itself as a parliamentary democracy. The Labour Party, in office since 1999, was reelected in the 2002 general election, retaining its 52 seats in the 120-seat parliament. Labour, headed by Prime Minister Helen Clark, formed a minority government with the populist Progressive Coalition Party, which had won 2 parliamentary seats, and received a pledge of support from the centrist United Future Party, which had won 8 seats. The National Party, the conservative opposition, won only 27 seats, its worst finish ever.

The Maori population has been more assertive in its claims for land, resources, and compensation from the government. The Waitangi Tribunal, which hears Maori claims for land and compensation, supported a multimillion dollar claim in a report issued in May 2003. The government said the report's findings were "useful information," but not legally binding. Recent claims for rights to gas and oil fields in the Marlborough Sounds on the South Island, in particular, spawned ill will among the non-Maori population. In June 2003, the court of appeal ruled that Maori tribes could pursue their claim of the Marlborough Sounds, which currently are used for commercial operations, including marine farms and tourism.

The year 2004 saw a watershed in New Zealand politics, as the national consensus on how to deal with Maori matters was shattered, and ethnicity became the defining matter in many political issues. In January, the new National Party leader, Don Brash, made Maori access to the foreshores and seabed the focus of his first major speech in the parliament. He attacked, in particular, the Maori tribes that made claims for land and other compensation and charged that Maori use the Treaty of Waitangi, the country's founding document, to demand special treatment. This exacerbated the race debate and put the government in a difficult situation before its Maori and non-Maori constituents. In February, the Labour government of Prime Minister Clark underscored that all foreshores and seabeds are held in perpetuity by the state for all New Zealand citizens. It also announced a review of assistance for the Maori population, indicating that policies have to be based on need, not privilege. These decisions brought thousands of Maori to the streets to protest and alienated Maori members within her party. In April, the minister for labor, Tariana Turia, a Maori, resigned when the government passed the Foreshore and Seabed Bill, which put the ownership of the foreshore and seabed in Crown hands.

A new Maori political party emerged to push for self-determination. Turia was a co-leader, and 250 of the country's Maori leaders and academics declared support. The Maori Party easily won a by-election in 2004, taking more than 90 percent of the vote in the North Island seat of Te Tai Hauauru. The party aims to take all seven parliamentary seats reserved for Maori in the 2005 general election.

The government is moving to tighten immigration requirements. A new law, expected to be in effect in 2005, will require residents to live for five years in New Zealand before they are eligible to apply for citizenship. Another measure to restrict automatic citizenship for persons born in Samoa from 1924 to 1948 spurred 50,000 people to protest before the New Zealand Embassy in Samoa. In August, the government relaxed immigration for Pacific Islanders after failing to fill half the spaces allocated to them under a special quota.

Political Rights and Civil Liberties: Citizens of New Zealand can change their government democratically. The prime minister and a 20-member cabinet are elected by universal suffrage. A mixed-member electoral system combines voting in geographic districts with proportional representation balloting. As New Zealand is a member of the Commonwealth, Queen Elizabeth II is the chief of state and is represented by the governor-general. The two main political parties are the center-left Labour Party and the mildly conservative National Party. Prime Minister Helen Clark of the Labour Party was elected in 1999 and has been in power since. For more than 130 years, the native Maori population has held seven reserved seats in the 120-member parliament. In the current legislature, 18 members identified themselves as Maori or part-Maori. Maori constitute 11 percent of the voting population and just over 10 percent of the country's four million people.

New Zealand was ranked second out of 146 countries surveyed in Transparency International's 2004 Corruption Perceptions Index.

The media are free and competitive. A number of papers are published nationally and locally in English and, as New Zealand's ethnic minority population increases, other languages such as Filipino, Hindi, and Chinese. The number and diversity of radio and television stations broadcasting in English and other languages for general and target audiences are equally great. The first Maori-language television station was launched in March 2004. A stronger movement among the Maori population to celebrate their language, arts, and history have increased demand for Maori-language media products. There is no government control of Internet access, and competitive rates are offered by a number of Internet service providers.

Freedom of religion is provided by law and respected in practice. Religious organizations do not need to register with the government unless they intend to collect donations. Christianity is the dominant religion: some 55 percent of the population identify themselves as Christians or affiliated with a Christian church. Although a secular state, the government has fined businesses that operate on the official holidays of Christmas Day, Good Friday, and Easter Sunday. A new law passed in 2001 granted exemptions to several categories of stores in response to demands from the small but growing non-Christian population. Academic freedom is enjoyed at all levels of instruction in the country.

The government respects freedom of assembly and association. Various nongovernmental and civil society groups are active throughout the country, working to promote community health, minority rights, education, children's welfare, and other issues. Many receive considerable financial support from the government, in addition to private donations.

The New Zealand Council of Trade Unions is the main labor federation. Fewer than 20 percent of the country's wage earners are members of trade unions. Trade union membership began to decline almost 15 years ago with the passage of the Employment Contracts Act of 1991 (ECA), which ended compulsory unionism and prohibited certain strikes. In 2000, the Labour-led government replaced the ECA with the Employment Relations Act (ERA), which promotes collective bargaining and emphasizes good faith bargaining. A 2004 revision of the ERA provides additional protections for workers in the event of company ownership changes. It also allows unions to charge bargaining fees to non-union workers who enjoy union-negotiated wages and conditions, although workers can opt out of paying the fee if they negotiate their own contracts.

The judiciary is independent, and defendants can appeal to the Privy Council in London. Police discrimination against Maoris, who comprise more than half of the prison population, has been an issue.

A special tribunal hears Maori tribal claims to land and other resources stemming from the European settlement of New Zealand. The 1850 Treaty of Waitangi between the Maori and the British leased Maori land in perpetuity to the white "settlers." Maoris now seek higher "rents" for their land and compensation from the government, and these claims have become a source of tension with the non-Maori population. Successive governments have introduced programs to boost the social and economic status of Maoris and Pacific Islanders, but most appear to have enjoyed only marginal success.

Violence against women remains a major issue, with reports by the U.S. State Department and civil society groups in New Zealand noting an increase in the number of assaults against women in recent years. The problem had been particularly serious among the Maori population. Although Maori women and children make up less than 10 percent of New Zealand's population, half of them have reported abuse. The number of abuse cases is also disproportionately high among Pacific Islanders, who make up about 5 percent of the population. Many governmental and nongovernmental programs attempt to prevent domestic violence and provide support to victims, and special programs target the Maori community. However, these efforts have not significantly improved the situation. The Domestic Violence Act of 1995 broadened the definition of "violence" to include psychological abuse, threats, intimidation, harassment, and allowing children to witness psychological abuse. It also expanded police powers to address these cases and provided legal assistance.

Nicaragua

Population: 5,600,000　**Political Rights:** 3
GNI/capita: $710　**Civil Liberties:** 3
Life Expectancy: 69　**Status:** Partly Free
Religious Groups: Roman Catholic (85 percent), other [including Protestant] (15 percent)
Ethnic Groups: Mestizo (69 percent), white (17 percent), black (9 percent), Amerindian (5 percent)
Capital: Managua

Ten-Year Ratings Timeline (Political Rights, Civil Liberties, Status)

1995	1996	1997	1998	1999	2000	2001	2002	2003	2004
4,4PF	3,4PF	3,4PF	2,3PF	3,3PF	3,3PF	3,3PF	3,3PF	3,3PF	3,3,PF

Overview:　The Sandinista National Liberation Front (FSLN) enjoyed a resounding victory in the November 2004 local elections. A UN report issued in August confirmed that much of the country's population suffers from a lack of basic nutritional requirements.

The Republic of Nicaragua was established in 1838, 17 years after independence from Spain. Its history has been marked by internal strife and dictatorship. The Sandinistas overthrew the authoritarian Somoza regime in 1979. Subsequently, the FSLN attempted to establish a Marxist government, which led to a civil war. The United States intervened indirectly, using Argentine military veterans of that country's "dirty war" on behalf on the right-wing irregular army known as the Contras. The FSLN finally agreed in 1987 to a new constitution.

In 1990, the newspaper publisher Violeta Chamorro easily defeated the incumbent, President Daniel Ortega, a Sandinista leader. Her 14-party National Opposition

Union (UNO) won a legislative majority in the National Assembly. In February 1995, after passage of a law ensuring the military's autonomy, Humberto Ortega—Daniel's brother—turned over command of the military to General Joaquin Cuadra. The army was reduced from 90,000 to 15,000 troops, and former Contras were integrated into its ranks, although the leadership remained essentially unchanged. The armed forces continued to own a profitable network of businesses and property amassed under the Sandinistas.

Chamorro was forbidden by law to seek a second term. The 1996 elections were held under the auspices of the five-member Supreme Electoral Council, an independent branch of government. During the campaign, Daniel Ortega portrayed himself as a moderate committed to national unity and reconciliation. A former mayor of Managua, Arnoldo Aleman, ran on a platform that promised economic reforms, the dismantling of the Sandinista-era bureaucracy, the cleaning up of the army, and the return of property confiscated by the Sandinistas to its original owners. He defeated Ortega 51 to 38 percent, avoiding a runoff. Aleman's first priority as president was to reform the army and the police; he named a civilian minister of defense, and a new military code was adopted. The size of the National Police was reduced from 16,000 to 6,800.

Throughout his presidency, Aleman was dogged by charges that he enriched himself in office, although he never faced formal legal proceedings while in office. In 1999, Aleman's right-wing Liberal Constitutional Party (PLC) government and the opposition, led by Daniel Ortega, agreed to a governability pact. The reforms guaranteed Aleman a seat in both the Nicaraguan and the Central American parliaments, thus assuring him immunity from prosecution. In the November 4, 2001, elections, ruling PLC candidate Enrique Bolanos, a conservative businessman respected for his personal integrity, defeated Daniel Ortega, 54 to 45 percent, in a bitterly fought contest in which the two major parties stacked the deck against participation by smaller parties. Concurrent legislative elections gave the Liberal Alliance 53 seats, the FSLN 38, and the Conservative Party of Nicaragua (PCN) 1.

On January 10, 2002, Bolanos was sworn in as Nicaragua's third post–Sandinista-era president, with a mandate to tackle widespread and systemic corruption, fraud, and incompetence throughout government. One of the major challenges became the confrontation with Aleman, who, along with family members and cronies, was accused of having stolen $100 million. Aleman, as president of the National Assembly, had immunity from criminal prosecution, and this status was seen by many as an example of the widespread impunity of officials that makes a mockery of justice. The protracted effort to indict, prosecute, and convict Aleman for fraud and embezzlement exposed the weakness of the legal system in resisting political pressure, although the system ultimately worked as designed. Different appeals, including a regional one, were exhausted, and Aleman received a conviction of 20 years for money laundering; additional charges are pending.

Aleman loyalists have made countless efforts, including alliances with the FSLN, to have the former president released from prison. Bolanos himself has not escaped accusations of corruption launched by partisan members of the comptroller-general's office. The resulting political paralysis in the National Assembly has prevented significant and needed changes to the judicial system, as well as the rationalization of the government structure as a whole. A public opinion poll conducted in September of 2004 indicated that the majority of Nicaraguans see Ortega and Aleman as obstacles to democracy who should leave the political scene (79.9 percent for the former and 85.9 percent for the latter).

The government of Bolanos also faces major economic challenges. Nicaragua is the poorest country in Central America and the second poorest in the Western Hemisphere. About 70 percent of Nicaraguans live below the poverty line, and up to 50 percent of the population is unemployed or underemployed. The legacies of the civil war have proven difficult to overcome, particularly in terms of the ravaged infrastructure, which was also hit hard by Hurricane Mitch in 1998. A severe drought has further affected the ability of a third of the population to consume even the basic nutritional requirement of 2,200 calories a day. In August of 2004, the UN Food and Agriculture Organization announced that 29 percent of Nicaragua's population lacks "food security" or the food needed to live a healthy and active life.

In the November 7, 2004, local elections, the FSLN swept 90 of the country's 152 municipalities, including the capital of Managua, and 15 of the 17 departmental capitals. Bolanos's Alliance for the Republic (APRE) won in five mayoralties. The PLC took 41 mayoralties (53 less than in the previous elections) and only one departmental capital. Abstention reached an all-time high of 52 percent. Campaigns and party platforms did not focus on the fundamental problems of extreme poverty and unemployment.

The offer to send troops in support of U.S. actions in Iraq was somewhat of a surprise to many Nicaraguans and was seen as a result of pressure from Washington, DC. Nevertheless, the road to rapprochement between the two countries had been cultivated for some time. Popular support in Nicaragua for the troop deployment was limited.

Political Rights and Civil Liberties: Nicaraguans can change their government democratically. The constitution provides for a directly elected president and a 96-member National Assembly elected every five years.

Political and civic activities continue to be conditioned on occasional political violence, corruption, and drug-related crime. Nicaragua was ranked 97 out of 146 countries surveyed in Transparency International's 2004 Corruption Perceptions Index.

The print media are varied and partisan, representing hard-line and moderate Sandinista, as well as pro- and antigovernment, positions. Before leaving office, the Sandinistas privatized the national radio system, mostly to Sandinista loyalists. There are five television stations, three of which carry news programming with partisan political content. Media outlets covering government corruption have been intimidated and/or closed by the government. Journalists have also lost their lives in suspicious incidents. In January, an outspoken TV journalist was shot dead as he arrived at work; during the November elections, a journalist of *La Prensa* (The Press) was murdered by a former FSLN security officer. There is free access to the Internet.

Freedom of religion is respected, and academic freedom is generally honored.

Nongovernmental organizations are active and operate freely. As a whole, civic society has blossomed in the post-Sandinista era. Generally, public demonstrations are allowed. Labor rights are complicated by the Sandinistas' use of unions as violent instruments to influence government economic policy. By means of the public sector unions, the Sandinistas have managed to gain ownership of more than three dozen privatized state enterprises. The legal rights of non-Sandinista unions are not fully guaranteed. The Ministry of Labor has declared strikes illegal. Citizens have no effective recourse when labor laws are violated either by the government or by violent Sandinista actions.

The judiciary is independent but continues to be susceptible to political influence and corruption. Large case backlogs, long delays in trials, and lengthy pretrial detention have caused the Supreme Court and National Assembly to initiate comprehensive structural reforms of the judicial system. Nevertheless, both the PLC and the FSLN have blocked President Enrique Bolanos's efforts to professionalize the judicial system, leaving it in the control of party stalwarts who frequently rule in ways that necessarily appear partisan.

The Ministry of Government oversees the National Police, the agency that is formally charged with internal security; in practice, the police share this responsibility with the army in rural areas. The conduct of security forces, reflecting enhanced civilian control, continues to improve, although abuses of human rights still occur. Forced confessions to the police remain a problem, as do cases in which security forces arbitrarily arrest and detain citizens. Prison and police holding-cell conditions are poor.

Violent crime is increasing in Managua and other major Nicaraguan cities, although the country remains relatively tranquil compared with some of its Central American neighbors. With long coastlines on both the Atlantic and Pacific, a high volume of land cargo, and myriad jungle airstrips, Nicaragua is an important transshipment point for drugs making their way north from South America. The Pan-American Highway in Nicaragua's southwest region is a primary venue for narcotics traffickers; although smuggling by air is increasing and small aircraft are occasionally commandeered by traffickers for flights to other countries. An evident and violent presence of local chapters of regional gangs (*maras*) is creating a climate of fear. Bolanos has joined other regional leaders in promoting cross-border cooperation to face this growing threat, though Nicaragua has yet to pass the draconian legislation of its neighbors against this scourge.

Nicaragua nominally recognizes the rights of its indigenous communities in its constitution and laws, but in practice those rights have not been respected. Approximately 5 percent of the population is indigenous and lives mostly in the Northern Autonomous Atlantic Region (RAAN) and Southern Autonomous Atlantic Region (RAAS). These regions are 50 percent of the national territory, but account for only 10 percent of the population. The largest community is that of the Miskito, with 180,000 people, and the smallest is the Rama, with 1,000. The 2001 ruling of the Inter-American Commission for Human Rights over logging rights in favor of these communities has not been fully implemented, although the legislation has been passed. In July 2003, the National Assembly finally approved the codification of the 1987 Autonomy Law that created these areas.

Violence against women, including rape and domestic abuse, remains a serious problem. Nicaragua is a source, and transshipment staging point, for the trafficking of women and children for purposes of prostitution.

Niger

Population: 12,400,000 **Political Rights:** 3*
GNI/capita: $180   **Civil Liberties:** 3*
Life Expectancy: 45   **Status:** Partly Free
Religious Groups: Muslim (80 percent), other [including
indigenous beliefs and Christian] (20 percent)
Ethnic Groups: Hausa (56 percent), Djerma (22 percent), Fula
(9 percent), Tuareg (8 percent), Beri Beri (4 percent), other (1 percent)
Capital: Niamey
Ratings Change: Niger's political rights and civil liberties ratings improved from 4 to
3 due to the greater representation of minorities in government and modest improve-
ments in press freedom.

Ten-Year Ratings Timeline (Political Rights, Civil Liberties, Status)

1995	1996	1997	1998	1999	2000	2001	2002	2003	2004
3,5PF	7,5NF	7,5NF	7,5NF	5,5PF	4,4PF	4,4PF	4,4PF	4,4PF	3,3PF

Overview: President Mamadou Tandja was expected to win a second
term in the second round of presidential elections to be held
in December 2004. He led the first round of voting held in
November. Press freedom registered modest improvements during the year.

After gaining independence from France in 1960, Niger was governed for 30
years by one-party and military regimes dominated by leaders of Hausa or Djerma
ethnicity. After 13 years of direct military rule, Niger was transformed into a nominally civilian, one-party state in 1987 under General Ali Seibou. International pressure and pro-democracy demonstrations led by the umbrella organization Niger Union
of Trade Union Workers forced Niger's rulers to accede to the Africa-wide trend
toward democratization in 1990. An all-party national conference drafted a new constitution that was adopted in a national referendum in 1992.

Mahamane Ousmane, of the Alliance of Forces for Change, won a five-year term
as the country's first democratically elected president in 1993 in elections deemed to
be free and fair. General Ibrahim Bare Mainassara overthrew Ousmane in January
1996 and won fraudulent elections six months later. Parliamentary elections in November were held in an atmosphere of intense intimidation and were boycotted by
most opposition parties.

In April 1999, Mainassara was assassinated by members of the presidential
guard. The head of the guard led a transitional government that held a constitutional referendum in July and national elections in November. In the presidential election, Tandja won in a second round of polling with 60 percent of the vote, defeating
former president Ousmane. Tandja's party, the National Movement for a Developing
Society (NMDS), and its partner, the Democratic and Social Convention, achieved a
two-thirds majority in the National Assembly by winning 55 of the 83 seats. The
other coalition—the Nigerien Party for Democracy and Socialism (PNDS), and the
Rally for Democracy and Progress—won the remaining 28 seats. Both elections were
deemed to be free and fair by international observers.

Tandja was expected to win a second term in presidential elections held in December 2004. Tandja led the first round of voting in November and will face off against Mahamadou Issoufou of the PNDS. Tandja's party and its allies made a strong showing in local government elections in July 2004. Analysts say Tandja's rural development policies have received strong support from subsistence farmers, who account for the majority of the population.

Niger is working with the United States as part of the Pan Sahel Initiative to promote security and stem the growth of terrorist organizations across the vast Sahel region.

Niger is struggling to implement unpopular structural reforms in an economy based mainly on subsistence farming, small trading, herding, and informal markets. Uranium is the most important export, but world demand has declined. The IMF, in June 2004, praised Niger for its poverty-reduction efforts.

Political Rights and Civil Liberties: Citizens of Niger can change their government democratically. Both the presidential and legislative polls in November 1999 were considered to be free and fair. In the first round of voting for presidential elections in November 2004, President Mamadou Tandja of the NMDS led with 40.7 percent, followed by Mahamadou Issoufou of the PNDS with 24.6 percent and Mahamane Ousmane of the Democratic and Social Convention with 17.4 percent. Six candidates contested the first round of voting. Tandja and Issoufou faced a runoff in the second round in December, and Tandja was expected to win. The ruling party, backed by a coalition of four other parties, was to compete for 113 National Assembly seats against six other parties in December

In 2003, opposition parties, grouped in an alliance called the Coordination of Democratic Forces, criticized President Tandja for what they said was an attempt to drive through a revision of the country's electoral law without the consultation of opposition parties. A new law would no longer oblige government ministers to resign before seeking electoral office. It would also abolish a requirement that the head of the Independent National Electoral Commission be a judge or magistrate.

Niger's president is directly elected every five years. The country has a power-sharing presidential system, with the president as head of state and the prime minister as head of government. The president must choose the prime minister from a list of three persons presented by the majority party or coalition in the representative unicameral National Assembly.

Niger was ranked 122 out of 146 countries surveyed in Transparency International's 2004 Corruption Perceptions Index. Niger's Association for the Fight against Corruption broadcast a series of television sketches in 2001 about the problem of corruption to raise awareness of the issue. The Network of Malian Journalists against Corruption and Poverty has expressed dismay over the slow pace of prosecution once wrongdoers are exposed.

Constitutional protections for free expression are guaranteed, but these rights are not always respected in practice. Criminal penalties are exacted for violations such as slander. Members of the media acknowledge that financial difficulties and a lack of training make it difficult to stay independent. A government newspaper and several private publications circulate, and there are dozens of private radio stations, some of which broadcast in local languages. The government does not restrict Internet access.

Press freedom saw modest improvements in 2004, with only one journalist reportedly detained during the year, compared with several journalists who were arrested in 2003. The Media Foundation for West Africa, based in Accra, Ghana, reported that the director of the independent radio station Saraounia FM was arrested in August 2004 after an interview with the reputed leader of a rebel group was aired. Mamane Abou, director of Niger's private weekly newspaper *Le Republicain*, was released from prison in January 2004 after spending two months in jail for criminal defamation. An appeals court granted his provisional release pending a second criminal case that was brought against him for "theft of documents." He was arrested in November 2003 in connection with an article that accused several government ministers of using unauthorized government funds to pay for government contracts; a criminal court sentenced him to six months in jail and ordered him to pay a hefty fine.

Freedom of religion is respected, although Muslims have not always been tolerant of the rights of members of minority religions to practice their faith. Islam is practiced by 80 percent of the population. Academic freedom is guaranteed but is not always respected. Security forces used tear gas to break up demonstrations at Abdou Moumouni University in 2004, and some students were arrested. They had set up barricades, burned tires, and damaged vehicles while protesting against scholarship arrears, poor housing conditions, and a lack of transportation. The students were released within two weeks.

Constitutional guarantees of freedom of assembly and association are generally respected. Human rights and other nongovernmental organizations operate openly and freely in Niger and publish reports that are often highly critical of the government. Workers have the right to form unions and bargain for wages, although more than 95 percent of the workforce is employed in the non-unionized subsistence agricultural and small-trading sectors.

The constitution provides for an independent judiciary, and courts have shown signs of independence. However, the judiciary is overburdened, limited by scant training and resources, and occasionally subject to executive interference and other outside influences. Efforts at reform are under way, and respect for human rights has improved under Tandja's government. However, prolonged pretrial detention remains a problem. Prisons are characterized by overcrowding and poor health and sanitary conditions. The International Committee of the Red Cross and other humanitarian groups have unrestricted access to prisons and detention centers.

Discrimination against ethnic minorities persists despite constitutional protections. The Hausa and Djerma ethnic groups dominate government and business, although major ethnic groups are represented at all levels of government. The government has supported greater minority representation in the National Assembly by designating eight seats for representatives of "special constituencies," specifically ethnic minorities and nomadic populations.

Nomadic peoples, such as the Tuaregs and many Peul, continue to have less access to government services. Under pressure from human rights groups, the National Assembly in 2003 banned the keeping or trading of slaves. The local human rights group Timidria campaigns against the practice of slavery.

Women suffer extensive societal discrimination, especially in rural areas. Family law gives women inferior status in property, inheritance rights, and divorce. In the East, some women among the Hausa and Peul ethnic groups are cloistered and may leave their homes only if escorted by a male and usually only after dark. Domestic violence against women is reportedly widespread. Sexual harassment and performing female genital mutilation are criminal offenses. Several women's rights organizations operate in the country, and the government has begun a project aimed at improving gender equality.

Nigeria

Population: 137,300,000 **Political Rights:** 4
GNI/capita: $300 **Civil Liberties:** 4
Life Expectancy: 52 **Status:** Partly Free
Religious Groups: Muslim (50 percent),
Christian (40 percent), Indigenous beliefs (10 percent)
Ethnic Groups: Hausa and Fulani (29 percent),
Yoruba (21 percent), Ibo (18 percent), other (32 percent)
Capital: Abuja

Ratings Change: Nigeria received a downward trend arrow due to increased threats and attacks against the media, efforts by the government to restrict the power of labor unions, and greater violence in the Delta region.

Ten-Year Ratings Timeline (Political Rights, Civil Liberties, Status)

1995	1996	1997	1998	1999	2000	2001	2002	2003	2004
7,7NF	7,6NF	7,6NF	6,4NF	4,3PF	4,4PF	4,5PF	4,5PF	4,4PF	4,4PF

Overview:

Opposition to the government of President Olusegun Obasanjo grew in 2004 with protests and strikes against the government's elimination of fuel subsidies. Violence escalated in the Niger Delta with the increasing prominence of heavily armed ethnic militia. Religious violence claimed hundreds of lives, and a radical, armed Islamist group emerged in the North. Press freedom suffered a setback with numerous attacks on members of the media during the year.

The military has ruled Nigeria for all but 15 years since independence from Britain in 1960. Generals and their backers argued that they were the only ones who could keep a lid on simmering tensions among the country's 250 ethnic groups, as well as between religious communities; the North is largely Muslim, while the South is mainly Christian.

Nigeria initially appeared to be emerging from several years of military rule under General Ibrahim Babangida in 1993, when presidential elections were held. Moshood Abiola, a Muslim Yoruba from the South, was widely considered the winner, but the military annulled the results. It continued to rule behind a puppet civilian administration until General Sani Abacha, a principal architect of previous coups, took power in November 1993. A predominantly military Provisional Ruling Council (PRC) was appointed, and all democratic structures were dissolved and political parties banned. Abiola was arrested in June 1994 after declaring himself Nigeria's rightful president. He died in detention, after suffering from a lack of proper medical care, just five weeks after Abacha himself died suddenly in June 1998.

The departure of the two most significant figures on Nigeria's political landscape opened possibilities for democratic change. General Abdulsalami Abubakar, the army chief of staff, emerged as the PRC's consensus choice to be the country's next leader, and he promised to oversee a transition to civilian rule in 1999. However, Obasanjo—a former general who had led a military regime in Nigeria from 1976 to 1979 and had spent three years in prison under Abacha—won the presidential poll in February. In legislative elections held that year, Obasanjo's People's Democratic Party (PDP) won the most seats in both the Senate and House of Representatives.

Nigeria made its first peaceful transition from one democratically elected government to another in April 2003, when Obasanjo was reelected for a second term. Anticipated widespread unrest during the elections did not materialize, although there was violence leading up to the polls, which were marred by irregularities. Obasanjo faced 19 opposition candidates. However, the race ultimately was between the southern Christian Obasanjo and former general Muhammadu Buhari, a northern Muslim and member of the All Nigeria People's Party (ANPP). Obasanjo won the presidency with 62 percent of the vote compared with 32 percent for Buhari. Buhari filed a petition on behalf of some 20 opposition parties to nullify the election results.

In the April legislative poll, Obasanjo's PDP won 52 Senate seats and 170 House seats. The ANPP captured 25 seats in the Senate and 81 in the House, while the Alliance for Democracy won 5 Senate seats and 30 House seats. Smaller parties secured the remainder of seats.

Local and international observers witnessed serious irregularities during the 2003 elections. The Transition Monitoring Group, a coalition of Nigerian civic organizations, deployed some 10,000 monitors who reported ballot-box stuffing, multiple voting, falsification of results, and voter intimidation. They maintained that fraud and intimidation were particularly prevalent in the southeast of the country and in the Niger Delta.

In the weeks leading up to local elections in 2004, there were several apparently politically motivated assassinations. In some states, the prospect of local elections also reignited ongoing interethnic conflict. The largest number of deaths occurred during clashes between political thugs, according to human rights groups.

Opposition to Obasanjo's government swelled in 2004 with protests and strikes aimed at reversing the elimination of fuel subsidies—a measure that the government says is necessary for economic reform. Nigeria, a major oil-producing country, has for decades provided costly subsidies for domestic fuels. Strikes in October, led by the umbrella Nigeria Labor Congress, shut down major cities for several days. In an apparent attempt to reduce the power of organized labor, Obasanjo in April presented a bill to the National Assembly that aimed to curb the power of unions.

Violence escalated in the Niger Delta in 2004 with the increasing prominence of an ethnic militia. The Niger Delta People's Volunteer Force, led by Moujahid Dokubo-Asari, had threatened to kill foreign oil workers in September, sending world oil prices soaring to record highs. The group claims to be fighting for political autonomy and a bigger slice of oil revenues for the Ijaw ethnic group, the largest in the delta region. Clashes between the Ijaws and their rivals, the Itsekiris, have claimed hundreds of lives in the delta.

Religious clashes continued in 2004. In the town of Yelwa, in central Plateau state, more than 600 people were killed in May after armed members of the predominantly Christian Tarok ethnic group attacked members of the mainly Muslim Fulani ethnic group, apparently in reprisal for earlier attacks against Taroks. Taroks and Fulanis have been engaged in a prolonged conflict over land use as well as political and economic control. Obasanjo imposed a state of emergency in the region and suspended the civilian governor. A small, armed Islamic group emerged in northeastern Nigeria during the year and attacked police stations and police patrols.

The majority of Nigerians are engaged in small-scale agriculture, while most wealth is controlled by a small elite. The agriculture and manufacturing sectors have deteriorated considerably in the pursuit of oil, which accounts for more than 98 percent of the country's export revenues and almost all foreign investment.

Political Rights and Civil Liberties:

Nigerians can change their government democratically. International observers noted irregularities during the 2003 presidential vote that reelected Olusegun Obasanjo, including ballot-box stuffing and alteration of results. Obasanjo's PDP also dominated the year's legislative elections. Members of the bicameral National Assembly are elected for four-year terms to 109 seats in the Senate and 360 in the House of Representatives. At least 30 parties participated in the April 2003 National Assembly elections, and 19 parties had candidates in the presidential elections.

The constitution requires government offices to reflect the country's ethnic diversity. The Hausa-Fulani from northern Nigeria generally dominated the military and the government from independence until Obasanjo was elected in 1999. Obasanjo's government is both ethnically and religiously diverse.

Corruption has bled the country of billions of dollars in oil revenue. The government has taken steps to improve transparency and reduce corruption, including reforming procedures for contract procurements and bidding. Nigeria was ranked 144 out of 146 countries surveyed in Transparency International's 2004 Corruption Perceptions Index.

Freedom of speech and expression is constitutionally guaranteed and respected irregularly in practice. Several private radio and television stations broadcast throughout the country, and numerous print publications operate largely unhindered. However, criminal defamation laws are still used against journalists. Sharia (Islamic law) in 12 northern states imposes severe penalties for alleged press offenses. Local authorities regularly target journalists who criticize them, and the media in northern Nigeria were most at risk. The government does not impede Internet access.

Press freedom suffered a setback in 2004 with numerous attacks on members of the media. Reporters sans Frontieres (RSF) said that 7 journalists were detained, 15 were physically attacked by security forces, and at least 3 were publicly threatened, in one case by a governor, in 2004. More than 20 other journalists have been placed under surveillance, expelled, subjected to extortion, summoned to a police station, heavily fined, suspended from work, or subjected to other forms of harassment, RSF said. Authorities banned local radio and television from relaying foreign news broadcasts live. One foreign journalist was expelled. Many of these incidents reflect the widespread security problems in Nigeria and the increasing power of state governors to influence activities within their states.

Religious freedom is guaranteed by the constitution, but many, including government officials, often discriminate against those of a religion different from their own. Religious violence, often reflecting regional and ethnic differences and accompanying competition for resources, has become increasingly common. In January, authorities in Plateau state banned the Council of Ulama, or the Muslim Council of Elders, on grounds that the group preaches religious hatred and intolerance. At least 2,500 people fled Plateau in February following two weeks of violence between Christians and Muslims that left scores dead. The government admitted that three years of sectarian violence in Plateau have exacted a high toll in lives lost and people displaced. Academic freedom is guaranteed and honored in practice.

Freedom of assembly and association are generally respected in practice. Police in May fired tear gas to disperse an antigovernment demonstration in Lagos and briefly arrested dozens of protesters. New York–based Human Rights Watch (HRW) in May said police deployed to quell violence between Muslims and Christians in the northern city of Kano used excessive force and may have committed dozens of unlawful killings in the name of restoring law and order. They reported that police fired into a crowd, killing around 40 people and wounding numerous others. In past incidents, none of the security forces has been brought to justice for unlawful or extrajudicial killings.

Despite several statutory restrictions on the rights of trade unions, workers, except members of the armed forces and those considered essential employees, may join trade unions, and the right to bargain collectively is guaranteed. About 10 percent of the workforce is unionized. Oil unions in 2004 repeatedly brought the country to a standstill through general strikes against a hike in fuel prices, which the government argues is necessary to eliminate domestic fuel subsidies. In April, Obasanjo sought to amend the 1990 Trade Act by outlawing strikes in the aviation, health, and education sectors. Strikes in other sectors were to be limited strictly to wage disputes and could be called only by unions representing workers in the activities concerned. The Senate in September passed a modified version of the labor bill, but it amended the no-strike clause so that it applies only to those working in essential services. The bill was pending approval by the House of Representatives.

The judiciary is subject to political influence and is hampered by corruption and inefficiency. The National Judicial Council has dismissed at least 20 judges in the past five years for accepting bribes and making improper judgments, some of which were perceived to be in favor of the ruling party or the government. Defendants do not always have legal representation and are often ill-informed about procedures and their rights. Lengthy pretrial detention remains a problem. In the northern states where Sharia law is in effect, flogging and amputation have been carried out for violations such as adultery and theft. The country's prisons are overcrowded, unhealthy, and life-threatening. Nevertheless, the government has allowed international organizations to visit detention facilities, and some improvements have been made.

HRW said in September that Islamic law courts in the North had failed to respect due process rights; the result was harsh and discriminatory sentences. The report said that northern state governors have used Islamic law as a political tool while condoning serious abuses. Women have been especially affected in cases of adultery or extramarital sex, where standards of evidence differ for men and for women, and pregnancy is considered sufficient evidence to convict a woman.

Although the constitution prohibits ethnic discrimination, societal discrimination is widely practiced, and clashes frequently erupt among the country's many ethnic groups. A number of armed youth groups have emerged to defend their ethnic and economic interests. Ethnic minorities in the oil-rich Niger Delta feel particularly discriminated against, primarily with regard to receiving a share of the country's oil wealth. London-based Amnesty International in September said fighting in Port Harcourt had killed up to 500 people in a month because of clashes between armed gangs. An ambush on an oil company boat in April killed seven people, including two Americans.

Nigerian women face societal discrimination, although educational opportunities have eroded a number of barriers over the years. Women play a vital role in the country's informal economy. Women of some ethnic groups are denied equal rights to inherit property, and marital rape is not considered a crime. About 60 percent of Nigerian women are subjected to female genital mutilation. Women's rights have suffered serious setbacks in the northern states governed under Sharia.

North Korea

Population: 22,800,000 **Political Rights:** 7
GNI/capita: $440 **Civil Liberties:** 7
Life Expectancy: 63 **Status:** Not Free
Religious Groups: Buddhist, Confucian, other
Ethnic Groups: Korean
Capital: Pyongyang

Ten-Year Ratings Timeline (Political Rights, Civil Liberties, Status)

1995	1996	1997	1998	1999	2000	2001	2002	2003	2004
7,7NF	7,7NF	7,7NF	7,7NF	7,7NF	7,7NF	7,7NF	7,7NF	7,7NF	7,7NF

Overview:
North Korea's foreign relations continued in 2004 to center around the rest of the world's efforts to engage the isolated Asian nation in talks about its self-proclaimed nuclear weapons program. No real progress on the issue had been made as of late 2004, as several rounds of talks held throughout the year produced empty promises. In September, a huge explosion suspected of being a nuclear test was reported.

The Democratic People's Republic of Korea was established in the northern part of the Korea Peninsula in 1948 following three years of post–World War II Soviet occupation. At independence, North Korea's uncontested ruler was Kim Il-sung, a former Soviet army officer who claimed to be a guerrilla hero in the struggle against Japan, which had annexed Korea as a colony in 1910. North Korea invaded South Korea in 1950 in an attempt to reunify the peninsula under Communist rule. Drawing in China and the United States, the ensuing three-year conflict killed as many as two million people and ended with a ceasefire rather than a peace treaty. Since then, the two Koreas have been on a continuous war footing, and the border remains one of the most heavily militarized places in the world.

Kim Il-sung solidified his power base during the Cold War, purging rivals, throwing thousands of political prisoners into labor camps, and fostering a Stalinist personality cult that promoted him as North Korea's "Dear Leader." The end of the Cold War, however, brought North Korea's command economy to the brink of collapse, as Pyongyang lost crucial Soviet and East Bloc subsidies and preferential trade deals. Kim's death in 1994 ushered in even more uncertainty. Under his son, the reclusive Kim Jong-il, the regime has maintained its rigid political control but has taken modest steps to free up North Korea's centrally planned economy. During the initial years of Kim Jong-il's rule, the situation grew even bleaker as natural disasters, economic mismanagement, and restrictions on the flow of information combined to kill an estimated one to two million North Koreans between 1995 and 1997, according to the U.S. State Department.

The threat of acute famine has receded thanks in part to foreign food aid, but a 2002 UN study found that more than half the population suffers from malnutrition. Moreover, North Korea's state-run health system has all but collapsed, hospitals lack adequate medicine and equipment, and clean water is in short supply because of electricity and chlorine shortages.

Against this backdrop, the economic reforms launched in July 2002 have made life tougher for ordinary North Koreans by igniting inflation and increasing unemployment. While the regime eased price controls, many of the promised salary raises designed to offset the higher prices have not materialized. The government has given factories more autonomy and has also allowed farmers to set up small markets in cities, something it has quietly tolerated for decades in the countryside. These markets now sell consumer goods as well as food. There is no expectation, however, of more far-reaching market reforms. The regime is adamantly opposed to any measures that would grant North Koreans significantly greater control over their daily lives, for fear of undermining its tight grip on power.

In September 2004, U.S. President George W. Bush signed the North Korean Humanitarian Act of 2004, which bans non-humanitarian assistance to North Korea due to the country's dismal human rights record. North Korea criticized the bill the following month, claiming that it "will pose a bigger obstacle at the six-party talks to solve nuclear tensions on the Korean peninsula".

Tension over North Korea's nuclear weapons program was renewed in October 2002, when Pyongyang admitted to having a nuclear weapons program, and has remained unabated since then. In December 2002, North Korea threw out international inspectors monitoring its Yongbyon nuclear reactor. In 2003, Pyongyang not only made a series of boasts about its alleged nuclear capabilities and threatened to test a nuclear weapon, but also pulled out of the Nuclear Non-Proliferation Treaty.

International observers' worst fears seemed confirmed in September 2004 when a huge explosion was reported within the country. The North Korean foreign minister subsequently said that the explosion was merely the demolition of a mountain for a power project, not a nuclear test. Many analysts believe, however, that the greatest threat posed by North Korea is not an actual nuclear bomb, but the country's potential to sell plutonium to rogue states or terrorists for hard cash. In September 2004, North Korea postponed indefinitely the latest round of six-nation talks (including South Korea, the United States, Russia, China, and Japan) on the issue. No new date for the talks had been set as of November 2004, but North Korea did issue a statement in that month indicating that it would be "quite possible" to resolve the conflict if the U.S. agreed to cooperate with the Communist regime rather than try to destroy the entire system. The statement, the first since the reelection of U.S. President Bush in early November, was seen as something of a conciliatory gesture.

Political Rights and Civil Liberties: North Korea is a dictatorship and one of the most tightly controlled countries in the world. The regime denies North Koreans even the most basic rights, holds tens of thousands of political prisoners under brutal conditions, and controls nearly every facet of social, political, and economic life.

Kim Jong-il, the North Korean leader since 1997, and a handful of elites from the Korean Worker's Party (KWP) rule by decree, although little is known about the regime's inner workings. Kim is formally general secretary of the KWP, supreme commander of North Korea's 1.1 million–strong army, and chairman of the National Defense Commission. This last post has been the "highest office of state" since the office of president was abolished in 1998. North Korea's parliament, the Supreme People's Assembly, is a rubber-stamp institution and meets only a few days each year. Parliamentary and local assembly elections were held in 1990, 1998, and, most recently, in August 2004. The elections were not free, and in the most recent elections, the Central Election Committee reported that Kim received 100 percent of the vote of his constituency. The government has created a few minority parties for the sake of appearances, but they do not fulfill any real electoral role.

North Koreans are subjected to intense political and ideological indoctrination. According to the U.S. State Department's human rights report for 2003, released in February 2004, "the cult of personality of Kim Jong Il and his father and the official *juche* ideology has declined somewhat, but remained an important ideological underpinning of the regime, approaching the level of a state religion." Juche refers to a national ideology of self-reliance (the country is totally dependent on foreign aid); it is imparted to citizens through the school system, the state-controlled media, and work and neighborhood associations.

North Korea was not ranked by Transparency International in its 2004 Corruption Perceptions Index.

Press freedom does not exist in any sense. The KWP controls all cultural and media activities, and practices extensive censorship. Foreign media broadcasts are banned.

Freedom of religious belief guaranteed by the constitution does not exist in practice. Persons practicing unauthorized religious activity are subject to harsh punishment. Academic freedom is likewise nonexistent.

Although the constitution guarantees equal treatment to all citizens, the government maintains a highly developed system of official discrimination. Individuals are accorded security ratings, termed either "core," "wavering," or "hostile" in terms of their loyalty to the regime. Nearly all facets of life, including employment and educational opportunities, residence, access to medical facilities, and severity of punishment in case of legal infractions, are determined by the rating. The government rates its subjects on the basis of the reports of a huge network of informers. It monitors all correspondence and communication, and can subject entire communities to security checks.

The law bans independent civic, human rights, and social welfare groups. Unauthorized public meetings are forbidden, and there are no known associations or organizations other than those created by the government. The government controls all labor unions. Strikes, collective bargaining, and other basic organized-labor activities are illegal.

North Korea does not have an independent judiciary and does not acknowledge individual rights, emphasizing instead "socialist norms of life" and a "collective spirit." Little information is available about specific criminal justice practices, as outside observers are generally not tolerated. Security forces are known to commit the most serious human rights abuses. Reports of arbitrary detentions, disappearances, and extrajudicial killings are common; torture is widespread and severe. The crimes for which capital punishment is the mandatory penalty are so broadly defined—"opposing socialism," for example—as to render them effectively "subjective criteria" rather than actual crimes, in the words of the UN Human Rights Committee. Starvation, torture, and execution in prisons are common, and because the government prohibits live births in prisons, forced abortions and infanticide are standard practices. The government engages in collective punishment, whereby an entire family can be imprisoned if one member of the family is accused of a crime. The regime also runs a network of "re-education through labor" camps that are notorious for their brutal and degrading treatment of inmates. In November 2004, refugees fleeing the country reported the occurrence of systematic medical and scientific experimentation on political prisoners.

Freedom of movement does not exist. Although internal travel rules have been relaxed to the extent that citizens are now allowed to travel beyond their home village, this means little in practice because very few citizens have any means of transportation. Permission to enter Pyongyang is tightly controlled. Exit visas are issued only to officials and some artists, athletes, academics, and religious figures. Emigration is illegal, and defection and attempted defection are capital crimes.

Despite recent market reforms, North Korea's economy remains centrally planned. The government assigns all jobs, prohibits private property, and directs and controls nearly all economic activity. Besides being grossly mismanaged, the economy is hobbled by creaking infrastructure, shortages of energy and raw materials, and an inability to borrow on world markets or from multilateral banks because of sanctions and a past foreign debt default.

Little is known about how problems such as domestic violence or workplace discrimination may affect North Korean women. There were widespread reports of trafficking of women and girls among the tens of thousands of North Koreans who have recently crossed into China.

Norway

Population: 4,600,000
GNI/capita: $38,730
Life Expectancy: 80
Religious Groups: Evangelical Lutheran (86 percent),
other Christian [including Protestant and Roman
Catholic] (3 percent), other (11 percent)
Ethnic Groups: Norwegian, Sami (20,000)
Capital: Oslo

Political Rights: 1
Civil Liberties: 1
Status: Free

Ten-Year Ratings Timeline (Political Rights, Civil Liberties, Status)

1995	1996	1997	1998	1999	2000	2001	2002	2003	2004
1,1F	1,1F	1,1F	1,1F	1,1F	1,1F	1,1F	1,1F	1,1F	1,1F

Overview:

Issues concerning immigration and asylum and Norway's foreign policy continued to spur debate among Norwegians in 2004. In June, the government ordered the end to a labor dispute between oil workers and companies that had threatened to halt production. Thousands of journalists went on strike in May over disagreements regarding pension benefits.

Following Denmark's rule from 1450 to 1814, Norway enjoyed a brief spell of independence during which the Eisvold Convention, Norway's current constitution, was adopted. Subsequently, Norway became part of a Swedish-headed monarchy. Norway gained independence in 1905 and has since functioned as a constitutional monarchy with a multiparty parliamentary structure.

The current, center-right government took power in October 2001 after the Labor Party suffered its worst election result in 90 years. The ruling coalition is made up of the Conservative Party, the Christian Democratic Party, and the Liberal Party, which together hold 122 seats. Kjell Magne Bondevik, of the Christian Democratic Party, is in his second term as prime minister. However, the largest party in parliament remains the Labor Party, with 43 seats. The constitutional monarch, King Harald V, ascended to the throne in 1991.

Norwegian citizens narrowly rejected European Union (EU) membership in referendums in 1972 and 1994, despite government support for joining. In addition to wanting to preserve their sovereignty, Norwegians feared the threat that membership would pose to the country's energy, agriculture, and fishing industries. As part of the European Economic Area, Norway has nearly full access to European markets. Nevertheless, while 75 percent of Norwegian exports go to EU countries and Norway has adopted almost all EU directives, it has little power to influence EU decisions as long as it remains outside. To maintain the current ruling coalition, which includes pro- and anti-EU parties (the Conservatives and the Christian Democrats, respectively), the government agreed not to reopen the question of EU membership during the term of the current parliament, which is scheduled to end in September 2005. However, Labor Party leader and EU supporter Jens Stoltenberg provoked a parliamentary debate on the issue in March 2004. The public remains divided over this issue.

A founding member of NATO, Norway has an active foreign policy. The government has sent envoys and negotiators to help resolve some of the world's most contentious disputes, most recently the conflict in Sri Lanka. In November, Foreign Minister Jan Petersen visited Colombo in an attempt to revive stalled peace talks. Earlier in the year, in July, public concern about the security of 150 Norwegian engineering troops in Iraq led to their transfer to Afghanistan. Norway runs 10 percent of the world's charities and gives one of the highest levels of overseas development aid as a percentage of its gross domestic product, a policy that has the support of 80 percent of the Norwegian public.

Norway was ranked first in the UN Human Development Index for 2003 and 2004. Its high standard of living is due in large part to the discovery of energy deposits in the 1960s. The government has put 80 percent of oil revenues in a petroleum fund that is invested overseas, thus helping to ensure that the benefits are enjoyed for many years.

Political Rights and Civil Liberties: Norwegians can change their government democratically. The 165-member parliament, or Storting, is directly elected for a four-year term by a system of proportional representation. It then selects one-quarter of its members to serve as the upper chamber, or Lagting, while the remaining members make up the lower chamber, or Odelsting. Neither body is subject to dissolution. The leader of the majority party or majority coalition in the Storting is appointed prime minister by the constitutional monarch, currently King Harald V. Although officially the head of state and commander in chief of the armed forces, the monarch performs largely ceremonial duties.

The indigenous Sami population, in addition to participating in the national political process, have their own consultative constituent assembly, the Sameting, which has worked to protect the group's language and cultural rights and to influence the national government's decisions about Sami land and its resources.

Norway remains one of the least corrupt countries in the world, and Norway was ranked 8 out of 146 countries surveyed in Transparency International's 2004 Corruption Perceptions Index. However, a 2003 Gallup survey found that nearly half of all Norwegians believe that bribery in the business world will be an increasing problem in the coming years. In 2003, a police probe into the Iranian operations of the state oil company Statoil led to the resignations of the chairman, the chief executive, and the head of the company's international division amid allegations of bribery. In June, Statoil was found guilty of corruption charges and fined 20 million kroner ($2.9 million); no former executive was indicted. The next month brought news of two U.S. government investigations into the affair, as Statoil is listed on the New York Stock Exchange.

Freedom of the press is constitutionally guaranteed. The state subsidizes many newspapers, the majority of which are privately owned and openly partisan, in order to promote political pluralism. However, subsidies have been cut in recent years, and there are fears that some special-interest publications will be forced to close. A government ban on political commercials, designed to ensure equal opportunity to the media for all candidates regardless of varying resources, violates the European Convention on Human Rights, which Norway has signed. In May, nearly 40,000 journalists and 84 media companies went on strike after mediation failed to produce an agreement on pension benefits. Norway continues to ban hard-core pornography in movie theaters, on television, and on video and DVD.

The monarch is the constitutional head of the Evangelical Lutheran Church of Norway, the state church. One-half of the cabinet must belong to the church, whose adherents make up 86 percent of the population. Other denominations must register with the state to receive support, which is determined by size of membership. By law, a course on religion and ethics, which focuses on Christianity, is mandatory for students, with no exemptions. In July, members of the right-wing Progress Party in the city of Krisiansand advocated banning Islam in Norway. Academic freedom is ensured for all.

The constitution guarantees freedom of peaceful assembly and association, as well as the right to strike. Unions play an important role in consulting with the government on social and economic issues, and about 60 percent of the workforce belongs to unions. In June, the government ordered an end to a week-long labor dispute between offshore oil workers and oil companies, spurred by the prospect of a lockout that would halt production in the world's third-largest oil exporter. A state arbitrator was assigned to settle the dispute, which centered on worker demands for better pension rights and job security.

The judiciary is independent, and the court system, headed by the Supreme Court, operates fairly at the local and national levels. The king appoints judges under advisement from the Ministry of Justice. The police are under civilian control, and there were no reports of human rights abuses committed by any domestic law enforcement authorities. According to the U.S. State Department's 2004 report on human rights practices, prison conditions generally meet international standards.

The government helps protect the heritage of the Sami population through Sami language instruction, broadcast programs, and subsidized newspapers in their regions. A deputy minister in the national government deals specifically with Sami issues.

In November, authorities barred a group of Jewish citizens from participating in a public commemoration of the Nazi riot of Kristallnacht in Oslo. Citing safety concerns, a government mandate forbade the display of any Jewish symbols, including the Star of David and the Israeli flag, during the commemoration.

Although the majority of Norwegians have a positive attitude toward immigrants, citizens are increasingly in favor of a stricter immigration policy, according to Statistics Norway. In December 2003, the government announced that asylum seekers denied residence in Norway would no longer be able to remain at immigration reception centers after an earlier report found a record number of asylum seekers registered at these centers. Polls suggest that discrimination in housing and employment against ethnic minorities is widespread. In August, the government ordered all townships to provide language and job training to new immigrants.

A new marriage law, which includes a clause under which both people must vow that they are getting married voluntarily and have an equal right to a divorce, has been criticized by the Roman Catholic Church. The Gender Equality Act provides equal rights for men and women, and a Gender Equality Ombudsman enforces the law. Traditionally, 40 percent of the cabinet is female; 8 of the current 19 ministers are women, and women make up 36 percent of the Storting. A new law requires that at least 40 percent of a firm's board of directors be women; the figure currently stands at about 7 percent.

Oman

Population: 2,700,000
GNI/capita: $7,830
Life Expectancy: 74
Religious Groups: Ibadi Muslim (75 percent), other
[including Sunni Muslim, Shi'a Muslim, and Hindu]
(25 percent)
Ethnic Groups: Arab, Baluchi, South Asian, African
Capital: Muscat

Political Rights: 6
Civil Liberties: 5
Status: Not Free

Ten-Year Ratings Timeline (Political Rights, Civil Liberties, Status)

1995	1996	1997	1998	1999	2000	2001	2002	2003	2004
6,6NF	6,6NF	6,6NF	6,6NF	6,6NF	6,5NF	6,5NF	6,5NF	6,5NF	6,5NF

Overview:

Despite recent limited steps to introduce political reform, including a new law establishing regulations for setting up private radio and television stations and the appointment of three women as ministers in government, ruling authority in 2004 remained heavily concentrated in the hands of Sultan Qaboos bin Said Al Said.

Oman has been an independent nation since Sultan bin Seif's expulsion of the Portuguese in 1650, ending more than a century of Portuguese involvement in certain regions of Oman. After the expulsion of the Portuguese, the sultan conquered neighboring territories, building a small empire that included parts of the eastern coast of Africa and the southern Arabian Peninsula.

During the 1950s and 1960s, Oman experienced a period of internal unrest centered mostly on the interior regions of the country. In 1964, a group of separatists supported by Communist governments, such as that of the People's Democratic Republic of Yemen (South Yemen), started a revolt in Oman's Dhofar province. This insurgency was not completely quelled until the mid-1970s, with Oman's government receiving direct military from its traditional ally, the United Kingdom, as well as from Iran and Jordan.

Qaboos came to power more than 30 years ago, after overthrowing his father, Sultan Said bin Taimur, who had ruled for nearly four decades. The new sultan launched a program to modernize Oman's infrastructure, educational system, governmental structure, and economy.

In 1991, Qaboos established the Consultative Council, or Majlis Al-shura, an appointed body aimed at providing the sultan with a wider range of opinions on ruling the country. The 1996 basic law, promulgated by a royal decree, transformed the Consultative Council into an elected body, but the right to vote in these elections was not granted to all citizens; only a limited number of citizens selected by tribal leaders were allowed to participate in the first elections. The basic law granted certain civil liberties; banned discrimination on the basis of sex, religion, ethnicity, and social class; and clarified the process for royal succession.

This limited political reform in the 1990s was overshadowed by a stronger effort to reform Oman's oil-dependent economy. In 1995, Qaboos spearheaded an effort to liberalize the economy, reduce its dependence on oil exports, and attract international investments. In preparation for its accession to the World Trade Organization (WTO), Oman lifted restrictions on foreign investment and ownership of enterprises in the country. In July 2003, the Ministry of Labor launched a five-year plan aimed at recruiting more Omani people into governmental and nongovernmental sectors. Debate over privatization of government operations in power, water, and telecommunications took place in 2004.

Political reform lags behind economic reform, with Qaboos maintaining a strong grip on political authority in Oman. In October 2003, Oman held the first full election in its history, for its Consultative Council. Though the powers of the Consultative Council remain limited, the election marked the first time that Oman gave the right to vote to all adult citizens, both men and women. In 2004, Oman issued a new law by royal decree establishing regulations for setting up private radio and television stations, a first in Oman's history. Another modest sign of progress was the appointment of three women as ministers in government.

Political Rights and Civil Liberties:

Citizens of Oman do not have the right to elect their country's leaders democratically. Citizens can express their views only in a very limited way, by electing members to the Consultative Council, which has no legislative powers and may only recommend changes to new laws. The Consultative Council is half of a bicameral body known as the Council of Oman; the other half, the 57-member State Council, is appointed by the sultan, currently Sultan Qaboos bin Said Al Said. The sultan has absolute power and issues laws by decree. He serves as the country's prime minister, heads the ministries of Defense, Foreign Affairs, and Finance, and is the governor of Oman's central bank. Article 34 of the basic law, Oman's constitution states that citizens have the right to address public authorities on personal matters or on matters related to public affairs in a manner consistent with Omani law. Mechanisms for citizens to petition the government through local government officials exist, and certain citizens are afforded limited opportunities to petition the sultan in direct meetings. Political parties are banned, and no meaningful organized political opposition exists.

Oman was ranked 29 out of 146 countries surveyed in Transparency International's 2004 Corruption Perceptions Index.

Freedom of expression and democratic debate are limited in Oman, with laws prohibiting criticism of the sultan. In August, Oman promulgated the Private Radio and Television Companies Law, which established regulations for setting up private radio and television companies, a first for Oman. As with other countries in the Arab world, the number of households with access to satellite television has increased, leading to an expansion in the diversity of sources of information. However, this information is mostly focused on issues in the Middle East region, as opposed to domestic issues in Oman. Oman's government permits private print publications, although many of these publications accept government subsidies and practice self-censorship. Omanis have access to the Internet through the national telecommunications company, and the government censors politically sensitive and pornographic content.

Islam is the state religion, according to the basic law. Non-Muslims have the right to worship, although non-Muslim religious organizations must register with the government and non-Muslims are banned from proselytizing. The Ministry of Awqaf (Religious Charitable Bequests) and Religious Affairs distributes standardized texts for mosque sermons and expects imams to stay within the outlines of these texts. The government restricts academic freedom by preventing the publication of politically sensitive topics.

The basic law allows the formation of nongovernmental organizations, but civic and associational life remains quite limited in Oman. The government has not permitted the establishment of independent human rights organizations. Article 32 of the basic law provides for the right to peaceful assembly within the limits of the law. All public gatherings require government permission, and government authorities have the authority to prevent organized public meetings without any appeal process.

Workers do not have the right to organize unions, but they can select a representative committee to voice their demands and represent their interest. In April 2003, the government issued a decree that removed a previous prohibition on strikes. Complaints related to labor and working conditions are managed by the Ministry of Social Affairs and Labor and mediated by the Labor Welfare Board.

Although the basic law states that the judiciary is independent, it remains subordinate to the sultan and the Ministry of Justice. Sharia (Islamic law) is the source of all legislation, and Sharia courts are responsible for family law matters such as divorce and inheritance. In less populated areas, tribal laws and customs are frequently used to adjudicate disputes. According to the law, arbitrary arrest and detention are prohibited. In practice, the police are not required to obtain an arrest warrant in advance. Many of the civil liberties guarantees expressed in the basic law have not been implemented. Prisons were not accessible to independent monitors, but former prisoners report crowded cells. Government authorities must obtain court orders to hold suspects in pretrial detention, but the police and security services do not regularly follow these procedures.

Some citizens of African origin have reported employment discrimination. Although the basic law prohibits discrimination on the basis of sex, women suffer from legal and social discrimination. According to official statistics, women constitute only 10 percent of the total labor force in Oman. Only two women won seats on the Consultative Council in the 2003 national elections. However, Sultan Qaboos appointed three women as government ministers in 2004, a first for Oman. Raweyah el-Bouseidi became the first minister in the history of Oman when she was appointed minister of higher education. Rajihah Bint-Abd-al-Amir became minister of tourism, and Sharifa Bint Khalfan became the minister of social development.

⬇ Pakistan

Population: 159,200,000 **Political Rights:** 6
GNI/capita: $420 **Civil Liberties:** 5
Life Expectancy: 61 **Status:** Not Free
Religious Groups: Muslim (97 percent) [Sunni
(77 percent), Shia (20 percent)], Christian, other
[including Christian and Hindu] (3 percent)
Ethnic Groups: Punjabi, Sindhi, Pashtun, Baloch, Muhajir
Capital: Islamabad
Trend Arrow: Pakistan received a downward trend arrow due to the entrenchment
of the military's power over both political and economic life.

Ten-Year Ratings Timeline (Political Rights, Civil Liberties, Status)

1995	1996	1997	1998	1999	2000	2001	2002	2003	2004
3,5PF	4,5PF	4,5PF	4,5PF	7,5NF	6,5NF	6,5NF	6,5NF	6,5NF	6,5NF

Overview:
A military government headed by General Pervez Musharraf
continues to wield effective power in Pakistan, and as 2004
progressed, the influence of the military over political, ju-
dicial, and economic structures was further solidified. Despite facing sustained protest from both the secular and Islamist opposition parties, Musharraf was able to replace
a recalcitrant prime minister in June and to pass legislation establishing a powerful
National Security Council that cements the military's role in governance and allows
him in his position as president to dismiss parliament. Furthermore, after he reneged on a pledge to step down as army chief by the end of the year, his supporters in
parliament passed a bill enabling him to continue in both roles—as president and as
head of the army. In the absence of an independent legislature and judiciary, the
media remain one of the only forums that provide oversight of official actions and
policy. However, the government became less tolerant of such criticism as the year
progressed and, on a number of occasions, harassed or intimidated members of the
press. A range of other human rights violations, including egregious legal and societal discrimination against women and religious minorities, continued to be reported
in 2004.

Pakistan came into existence as a Muslim homeland with the partition of British
India in 1947. Following a nine-month civil war, East Pakistan achieved independence in 1971 as the new state of Bangladesh. Deposing civilian governments at
will, the army has directly or indirectly ruled Pakistan for 29 of its 56 years of independence. As part of his efforts to consolidate power, the military dictator General
Zia ul-Haq amended the constitution in 1985 to allow the president to dismiss elected
governments. After Zia's death in 1988, successive presidents cited corruption and
abuse of power in sacking elected governments headed by Benazir Bhutto of the
Pakistan People's Party (PPP) in 1990 and 1996, and Nawaz Sharif of the Pakistan
Muslim League (PML) in 1993.

After the PML decisively won the 1997 elections, Sharif, as prime minister, largely
ignored Pakistan's pressing economic and social problems while undermining every

institution capable of challenging him, including repealing the president's constitutional power to dismiss governments, forcing the resignations of the chief justice of the Supreme Court and of an army chief, and cracking down on the press. However, when he attempted to reshuffle the army's leadership, he was deposed in October 1999 in a bloodless coup. Chief of Army Staff Musharraf then appointed himself "chief executive," declared a state of emergency, and issued a Provisional Constitution Order suspending parliament, the provincial assemblies, and the constitution. In December 2000, 18 of Pakistan's political parties, including archrivals PML and PPP, joined to form the Alliance for the Restoration of Democracy (ARD), an umbrella group calling for an end to military rule. However, Musharraf was able to successfully neutralize Sharif and Bhutto, his primary political opponents, through a combination of court convictions and exile.

Musharraf's primary aim since gaining power has been to ensure a dominant role for the military after Pakistan made the nominal transition back to democratic rule. The controversial Legal Framework Order (LFO) announced in 2002 gave him effective control over parliament and restricted the ability of opposition parties to contest the elections. The regime also openly promoted pro-government political parties, such as the newly formed Pakistan Muslim League Quaid-i-Azam (PML-Q). In the October 2002 parliamentary elections, no single party won a majority of seats; the PML-Q won 126 seats, while the PPP won 81 and the PML, 19. A coalition of six religious parties, the Muttahida Majlis-i-Amal (MMA), performed unexpectedly strongly, winning 63 seats in the national parliament and a majority of seats in two provinces. With support from independents and deserters from the other main parties, the PML-Q was able to form a government in November, and Musharraf's nominee, Mir Zafrullah Jamali, became prime minister. The PML-Q consolidated its position by winning a majority of seats in elections to the Senate held in February 2003.

Parliament remained deadlocked throughout most of 2003, with the main opposition parties insisting that Musharraf rescind the LFO and relinquish his position as army chief if he wished to continue as president. The stalemate was broken in December 2003, when Musharraf brokered a deal with the MMA in which it would support a constitutional amendment legitimizing the coup and his actions since then, in return for his pledge not to serve in both offices after December 2004. The party also agreed to support a bill introduced in January 2004 that would establish a powerful National Security Council (NSC), headed by the president, which had the power to dismiss the parliament and prime minister. Despite the fact that the MMA amended its stance and came out in opposition to the bill, it was rammed through both houses of parliament amid much protest in April. In September, the government then announced that a changed "national situation" required General Musharraf to stay on in both roles. Following this announcement, his supporters in parliament passed legislation enabling him to stay on as army chief for a further three years.

Meanwhile, growing clashes between Musharraf and Jamali on policy issues led to Jamali's ouster in June; Musharraf consolidated his position by appointing loyalist technocrat and former finance minister Shaukat Aziz to the post in August. While managing to contain the secular opposition, Musharraf has been less willing to rein in Islamic fundamentalist groups. Although several groups have been banned since September 2001, when Musharraf pledged to support the United States in its war on terrorism, and hundreds of activists have been periodically arrested, more than 40 groups continue to function under new names and their leaders have generally not been prosecuted. The increased parliamentary presence of religious parties with ties to radical *madrasas* (religious schools) and to militant groups suggests that the influence of the Islamists will continue to be strong. However, official tolerance for the activities of these groups declined following several assassination attempts against Musharraf (two in December 2003) and one against Aziz in July 2004. Working closely with U.S. intelligence, Pakistani security forces captured a number of high-value al-Qaeda targets in July and August, and troops engaged militants sheltering in the tribal areas of South Waziristan throughout the year, killing or capturing hundreds of fighters.

Political Rights and Civil Liberties: Despite the election of a civilian National Assembly in October 2002, the Pakistani military, headed by General Pervez Musharraf, continues to wield control over the structures of government. The 1973 constitution provided for a lower National Assembly, which currently has 272 directly elected seats and 70 seats reserved for women and non-Muslim minorities, and a Senate, whose 100 members are appointed by the four provincial assemblies for six-year terms. Shortly after the coup, Musharraf suspended the provincial and national assemblies. In 2001, he declared himself president, and in April 2002 extended his term as president by five years with a rigged referendum. In preparation for national elections (the Supreme Court had mandated that they be held by October 2002), Musharraf further strengthened the powers of the presidency and formalized the military's role in governance. The LFO gave him the right to dismiss unilaterally the national and provincial parliaments, as well as provide for a National Security Council dominated by military figures that would supervise the work of the civilian cabinet.

The LFO also restricts certain individuals from standing for elected office, as well as restricting political parties in their choice of leadership. Some of these measures were explicitly aimed at preventing former prime ministers Benazir Bhutto and Nawaz Sharif from contesting the 2002 elections. Although the government lifted the long-standing ban on political rallies shortly before the elections, significant restrictions remained in place, and the ability of opposition parties to mount effective campaigns was circumscribed. In its statement on the elections, the independent Human Rights Commission of Pakistan (HRCP) noted that governmental machinery had been used to intimidate opposition candidates. The report of the European Union Election Observation Mission concluded that there had been "serious flaws" in the electoral process.

Since the election, secular opposition parties and their leaders have continued to face intimidation and harassment from intelligence agencies and other government organs. In October 2003, Javed Hashmi, the leader of the ARD alliance, was arrested and charged with treason after he publicly criticized the army (he read an anti-Musharraf letter at a news conference), and in April 2004, he was sentenced to 23 years in prison on sedition charges.

On the positive side, women and minorities now have enhanced representation in the parliament. After repeated complaints by religious minorities, the government abolished the system of separate electorates in January 2002, enabling them to vote alongside Muslims and thus participate more fully in the political system. In addition, 10 seats in the reconstituted National Assembly were reserved for minorities and 60 were reserved for women.

Pakistan's government operates with limited transparency and accountability. Over the past five years, military officers have assumed an increasing role in governance through "army monitoring teams" that oversee the functioning of many civilian administrative departments. The army now has a stake in continuing to influence both commercial and political decision-making processes, as well as maintaining its traditional dominance over foreign policy and security issues. Serving and retired officers receive top public sector jobs in ministries, state-run corporations, and universities, as well as being given a range of other privileges. During the past two years, because of ongoing opposition boycotts, parliament did not function effectively, and many pieces of legislation were pushed through with limited debate.

Corruption is pervasive at almost all levels of politics and government and appears to be worsening; Transparency International's 2004 Corruption Perceptions Index ranked Pakistan in a tie for 129 out of a total of 146 countries, in a drop from the previous year. Although Musharraf has publicly stated that eliminating official corruption is a priority, the National Anti-Corruption Strategy approved in October 2002 focuses on politicians, civil servants, and businessmen, while virtually ignoring the military and security personnel.

The constitution and other laws authorize the government to curb freedom of speech on subjects including the constitution, the armed forces, the judiciary, and religion; blasphemy laws have also been used to suppress the media. Islamic fundamentalists and thugs hired by feudal landlords or local politicians continue to harass journalists and attack newspaper offices; Sajid Tanoli, a writer for a regional daily, was killed by unidentified assailants in January as a result of his reporting. On numerous occasions, police or security forces also subjected journalists to physical attack, intimidation, or arbitrary arrest. While journalists practice some self-censorship, Pakistan continues to have some of the most outspoken newspapers in South Asia, and the broadcast sector has become somewhat more diversified. However, over the past two years, military authorities have used increasingly aggressive tactics to silence critical voices in the media, according to Human Rights Watch. A number of journalists have been pressured to resign from prominent publications, charged with sedition, or arrested and intimidated by intelligence officials while in custody. The Web site of an online newspaper established abroad by exiled editor Shaheen Sehbai remains blocked by Pakistani telecommunications authorities. Musharraf himself has contributed to an atmosphere that is inimical to free speech by making public threats against specific members of the press.

Pakistan is an Islamic republic, and there are numerous restrictions on religious freedom. Section 295-C of the penal code mandates the death sentence for defiling the name of the prophet Muhammad. Human rights groups say that instances of Muslims bribing low-ranking police officials to file false blasphemy charges against Ahmadis, Christians, Hindus, and occasionally other Muslims have been increasing in recent years. Ahmadis consider themselves to be Muslims, but the constitution classifies them as a non-Muslim minority, and the penal code severely restricts Ahmadi religious practice. According to the U.S. State Department's Report on International Religious Freedom, as of mid-2004 there were more than 100 blasphemy cases pending in the courts. To date, appeals courts have overturned all blasphemy convictions, but suspects are generally forced to spend lengthy periods in prison, where they are subject to ill-treatment, and they continue to be targeted by religious extremists after they are released. In June, a man accused of blasphemy was murdered by the police constable who was supposed to be guarding him in the hospital where he was undergoing treatment. Religious minorities also face unofficial economic and societal discrimination, and are occasionally subjected to violence and harassment. The government often fails to protect religious minorities from sectarian violence, and discriminatory legislation contributes to creating a general climate of religious intolerance.

The government generally does not restrict academic freedom. However, student groups, some of whom have ties to radical Islamist organizations, violently attack or otherwise intimidate students, teachers, and administrators at some universities, which contributes to a climate of intolerance.

The military government banned all public political meetings, strikes, and rallies in March 2000. Following the ban, authorities have forcibly dispersed some protests and arrested political activists to prevent other demonstrations. Some Islamist leaders have been held under house arrest or in preventive detention under the Maintenance of Public Order ordinance, which allows for three months' detention without trial. Laws governing sedition, public order, and terrorism have been used to raid party offices and detain political activists and leaders in Punjab and Sindh. Although the military regime generally tolerates the work of nongovernmental organizations (NGOs), in recent years, Islamic fundamentalists have issued death threats against prominent human rights defenders and against female NGO activists who work in rural areas.

Despite legislation outlawing bonded labor and canceling enslaving debts, illegal bonded labor continues to be widespread; a November BBC report estimated that at least five million laborers are bonded to their employers. Trade unions are independent. The law restricts the right to strike, and workers in certain essential industries face restrictions on bargaining collectively and generally cannot hold strikes. The enforcement of child labor laws continues to be inadequate; recent surveys indicate that there are at least eight million child workers in Pakistan.

The judiciary consists of civil and criminal courts and a special Sharia (Islamic law) court for certain offenses. Lower courts remain plagued by endemic corruption; intimidation by local officials, powerful individuals, and Islamic extremists; and heavy backlogs that lead to lengthy pretrial detentions. The military regime undermined the Supreme Court's reputation for independence in January 2000, when it ordered all high-ranking judges to swear to uphold the Provisional Constitutional Order issued by Musharraf. When the chief justice and a number of other judges refused, they were replaced. Since then, the courts have rejected subsequent challenges to the legality of military rule. An International Crisis Group (ICG) report released in November drew attention to the fact that the executive has extended its influence over the judiciary by using the appointments system to remove independent judges, fill key positions with political allies, and reward those who issue judgments favorable to the government.

Other parts of the judicial system, such as the antiterrorism courts, operate with limited due process rights. A November 1999 ordinance vested broad powers of arrest, investigation, and prosecution in a new National Accountability Bureau and established special courts to try corruption cases. Musharraf has used both to prosecute rival politicians and officials from previous civilian governments. The Sharia court enforces the 1979 Hudood Ordinances, which criminalize nonmarital rape, extramarital sex, and several alcohol, gambling, and property offenses, and provide for Koranic punishments, including death by stoning for adultery, as well as jail terms and fines. According to Human Rights Watch, an estimated 210,000 cases are currently being processed under the ordinances. In part because of strict evidentiary standards, authorities have never carried out the Koranic punishments. In 2003, the provincial assembly in the North-West Frontier Province passed a bill that declared Sharia the supreme law of the province and empowered the government to Islamize the economy, the legal system, and education.

The Federally Administered Tribal Areas (FATA) are under a separate legal system, the Frontier Crimes Regulation, which authorizes tribal leaders to administer justice according to Sharia and tribal custom. Feudal landlords and tribal elders throughout Pakistan continue to adjudicate some disputes and impose punishment in unsanctioned parallel courts called *jirgas*. A 2002 Amnesty International report raised concerns that the jirgas abuse a range of human rights and are particularly discriminatory towards women. In April, the Sindh High Court issued a ruling that banned all trials conducted under the jirga system in the province.

Anecdotal evidence suggested that police continue to engage routinely in crime; use excessive force in ordinary situations; arbitrarily arrest and detain citizens; extort money from prisoners and their families; accept money to register cases on false charges; rape female detainees and prisoners; commit extrajudicial killings; and torture detainees, often to extract confessions. According to Human Rights Watch, political opponents, former government officials, and other critics of the regime are particularly at risk of arbitrary arrest or abduction, torture, and denial of basic due process rights at the hands of military authorities. Prison conditions continue to be extremely poor. A November 2003 Amnesty International report noted that the Juvenile Justice System Ordinance of 2000 remains largely unimplemented and that several thousand children continue to be jailed alongside adults.

Press reports indicate that there may be as many as 200,000 armed militants currently active in Pakistan, and these extremists continue to carry out terrorist attacks both within Pakistan and in neighboring countries, including assassination attempts and suicide attacks on foreign, Shia, and Christian targets. A report released by Amnesty International in April suggested that security forces and Pakistani authorities had committed a number of human rights abuses during the course of their operations to flush out foreign militants from the tribal areas of South Waziristan, including arbitrary arrest and detention, the destruction of property and the displacement of civilians, and possible extrajudicial executions.

Sunni and Shia fundamentalist groups continue to engage in the exchange of retaliatory killings, mainly in Punjab and Karachi. In October, an attack on a Shia mosque in Sialkot left dozens dead, and a week later a Sunni mosque in Multan was bombed; the two attacks were followed by a spate of assassinations in which several high-profile religious leaders were killed. Shia professionals in Karachi, including a large number of doctors, continue to be targeted. The South Asia Terrorism Portal has estimated that almost 200 people were killed and more than 600 were injured as a result of sectarian violence in 2004, a substantial increase over the previous two years.

In an atmosphere where the rule of law is weakly enforced and the military has expanded its control over economic resources, land rights are at risk. According to a Human Rights Watch report, tenant farmers in the Okara district of Punjab who have refused to cede their land rights to the army have faced besiegement, arbitrary arrest and detention, torture, "forced divorce," and dismissal from employment

A combination of traditional norms and weak law enforcement continue to contribute to rape, domestic violence, acid attacks, and other forms of abuse against women. Although less frequently than in the past, women are still charged under the Hudood Ordinances with adultery or other sexual misconduct arising from rape cases or alleged extramarital affairs, and 20,000 are currently estimated to be in prison as a result of being wrongfully charged. The threat of being charged with adultery may prevent some women from reporting rape. The government-appointed National Commission on the Status of Women recommended in 2003 that the ordinances be repealed, but because of the influence of Islamist parties in parliament, the suggestion is unlikely to be acted on. Gang rapes sanctioned by village councils as a form of punishment for crimes committed by a woman's relatives continue to be reported, despite the fact that harsh sentences have been handed down in some cases.

According to the HRCP, at least 600 women were killed by family members in so-called honor killings in 2003. Usually committed by a male relative of the victim, honor killings punish women who supposedly bring dishonor to the family. In October 2004, the lower house of parliament passed government-backed legislation introducing stiffer sentences and the possibility of the death penalty for those convicted of honor killings. However, given a prevailing environment where authorities generally do not aggressively prosecute and convict the perpetrators of violence against women, activists questioned the effectiveness of the bill. Pakistani women face unofficial discrimination in educational and employment opportunities.

Palau

Population: 20,000
GNI/capita: $7,500
Life Expectancy: 70
Religious Groups: Roman Catholic (49 percent), other [including Protestant and indigenous beliefs] (51 percent)
Ethnic Groups: Paluan (70 percent), Asian (28 percent), white (2 percent)
Capital: Koror

Political Rights: 1
Civil Liberties: 1
Status: Free

Ten-Year Ratings Timeline (Political Rights, Civil Liberties, Status)

1995	1996	1997	1998	1999	2000	2001	2002	2003	2004
1,2F	1,2F	1,2F	1,2F	1,2F	1,2F	1,2F	1,2F	1,1F	1,1F

Overview:
In November 2004, Tommy Esang Remengesau Jr. was reelected president of Palau for another four years. Voters also

decided to hold a constitutional referendum in 2005 on several issues, including recognition of dual citizenship, a requirement that the president and vice president run on the same ticket, and a merger of the bicameral legislature into a unicameral body.

The United States administered Palau, which consists of 8 main islands and more than 250 smaller islands about 500 miles southeast of the Philippines, as a UN Trusteeship Territory from the end of World War II until Palau became self-governing in 1981. Full independence was achieved in 1994 under the Compact of Free Association with the United States. By the terms of the compact, the United States provides Palau with $442 million in aid over 15 years from 1994 on and shoulders responsibility for Palau's external defense. In return, the United States has the right to set up military bases in the island state.

Vice President Remengesau was elected president in a narrow victory over Senator Peter Sugiyama in November 2000. Esang officially succeeded President Kuniwo Nakamura in January 2001. In the November 2004 election, Remengesau won 66.5 percent of the votes against his opponent Polycarp Basilios, who took 33.5 percent.

In a referendum held concurrently with the November general elections, voters decided to support the formation of a constitutional convention in 2005 to consider amending the constitution. The convention will review a number of issues, including allowing dual citizenship. Currently, the constitution states that only citizens can vote and own land in Palau, and about 25 percent of all Paluans live and work in the United States. An amendment would allow Palauans living in the United States and elsewhere to acquire citizenship in their resident countries without losing their right to vote and own land in Palau. Other major proposals to be reviewed are: requiring the president and vice president to be on the same ticket, adopting a unicameral legislature to replace the current bicameral one, and imposing term limits in congress and making those offices part time. Proponents hoped these measures would reduce factional fighting and the cost of running a legislature for the country's small population.

The country has been plagued by reports of human and drug trafficking, prostitution, and money laundering by criminal groups in recent years. The escape of a foreign drug convict from prison also sparked strong public criticism of the government. The authorities responded that more resources would be needed to make the necessary improvements in law enforcement and the judiciary.

Political Rights and Civil Liberties:

Citizens of Palau can change their government democratically. A bicameral legislature, the Olbiil Era Kelulau, consists of the 9-member Senate and the 16-member House of Delegates. Legislators are elected to four-year terms by popular vote. The president and vice president are also elected to four-year terms by popular vote. There is no limit on the number of terms, except that the president may serve only two terms consecutively. President Tommy Esang Remengesau Jr. was elected to his first term in November 2000, and Senator Sandra S. Pierantozzi became the first woman vice president. Remengesau won a second four-year term and Camsek Chin was elected vice president in November 2004. Politically, the island republic is organized into 16 states, each of which is headed by a governor. In December 2003, several states held state elections, which were regarded as fair and free. The winners were sworn in on

January 1, 2004. There are no political parties but factions exist. Alliances are formed and dismantled with such frequency that it has had a destabilizing effect on politics and government.

Public dissatisfaction with government corruption pressured the government to charge two lawmakers with fraud in February. Freedom of speech and the press is respected. There are five privately owned radio stations and one television station. The Internet, though not in widespread use, is accessible with no government intervention. Greater diffusion is limited by cost and access outside the main islands.

Citizens of Palau enjoy freedom of religion, but the government regulates the establishment of religious organizations by requiring them to obtain charters as nonprofit organizations from the Office of the Attorney General; no group has been denied its application. There were no reports of restrictions on academic freedom.

Freedom of association is respected, and civic associations and nongovernmental groups can operate freely. Many such groups focus on youth, health, and women's issues. Palau has no trade unions, although there are no laws or government policy against their formation. Freedom of assembly is guaranteed in the constitution and respected by the government.

The judiciary is independent, and fair trials are carried out. Internal order is provided for by a 300-member police and first response force. Palau has no armed forces; external defense is the responsibility of the United States under the Compact of Free Association. The compact, which will end in 2009, also provides Palau with financial and other assistance in exchange for the right to maintain military bases in the island state until 2034. Prisons are stark and have not seen significant improvement over time.

According to a May 2000 census, foreign workers account for nearly 30 percent of the population and 73 percent of the workforce. Reports of discrimination and abuse against foreign workers have surfaced in recent years, and the government has instituted strict measures to keep out foreign workers who are not actively employed. In 2003, the government announced tighter supervision to prevent marriages of convenience between foreigners and Palauans. Foreigners are said to have used fake marriages to extend their stay in Palau and to enter the United States, which grants Palauan citizens visa-free entry and residence under the compact agreement. There have been reports of human trafficking from China, the Philippines, and Taiwan, with some seeking employment in Palau and others using it as a conduit to enter the United States.

The economy is heavily dependent on transfer payments from the United States under the compact agreement, as well as money sent back to the island by its citizens working overseas. Subsistence agriculture and fishing are widely practiced. The government and tourist industry are the main employers.

Customarily high regard for women in this matrilineal society has led many women to be active in both traditional and modern sectors of the economy, as well as in politics. A small number of domestic abuse cases, many linked to alcohol and drug abuse, have been reported. Civil society groups assert that the true number may be higher as a result of under-reporting due to shame, fear of reprisal, and family pressure. The law prohibits rape, including spousal rape. Prostitution and sexual harassment are illegal.

Panama

Population: 3,200,000   **Political Rights:** 1
GNI/capita: $4,020   **Civil Liberties:** 2
Life Expectancy: 74   **Status:** Free
Religious Groups: Roman Catholic (85 percent),
Protestant (15 percent)
Ethnic Groups: Mestizo (70 percent), West Indian
(14 percent), European (10 percent), Amerindian (6 percent)
Capital: Panama City

Ten-Year Ratings Timeline (Political Rights, Civil Liberties, Status)

1995	1996	1997	1998	1999	2000	2001	2002	2003	2004
2,3F	2,3F	2,3F	2,3F	1,2F	1,2F	1,2F	1,2F	1,2F	1,2F

Overview:
In Panama's May 2004 presidential elections, the Democratic Revolutionary Party's (PRD) Martin Torrijos defeated his nearest challenger, former president Guillermo Endara, and the PRD also enjoyed a decisive victory in concurrent parliamentary elections. Meanwhile, the country continued to be plagued by violence, including by armed guerrillas and other groups from neighboring Colombia.

Panama was part of Colombia until 1903, when a U.S.-supported revolt resulted in the proclamation of an independent Republic of Panama. A period of weak civilian rule ended with a 1968 military coup that brought General Omar Torrijos to power. After the signing of the 1977 canal treaties with the United States, Torrijos promised democratization. The 1972 constitution had been revised to provide for the direct election of the president and Legislative Assembly for five years.

After Torrijos's death in 1981, General Manuel Noriega emerged as Panamanian Defense Force (PDF) chief; he subsequently rigged the 1984 election that brought to power the PRD, which was then the political arm of the PDF. The Democratic Alliance of Civic Opposition (ADOC) won the 1989 election, but Noriega annulled the vote and declared himself head of state. He was removed during a U.S. military invasion, and ADOC's Endara became president.

In May 1999, the Arnulfista Party's (PA) Mireya Moscoso, the widow of three-time president Arnulfo Arias and herself an unsuccessful presidential candidate in 1994, won 44.8 percent of the vote, more than 7 percent above the amount garnered by her rival, Martin Torrijos. Moscoso's government was hampered by its inability to effectively reduce corruption and incompetence in the public sector. Toward the end of her administration, there was generalized discontent with the government's efforts to fight corruption and with its running of the state and handling of the economy. Though the economy began to pick up in 2004, 40 percent of Panamanians live below the poverty level, 14 percent are unemployed, and an additional 4 percent are underemployed.

The May 2, 2004, presidential and parliamentary elections may have marked a change in the composition of the party system. Martin Torrijos, son of former strongman Omar Torrijos, received 47 percent of the votes in the presidential poll, easily outdistancing runner-up and former president Endara (1989–1994) of the Solidarity Party (PS), who received 31 percent of the vote. Jose Miguel Aleman, representing the PA, the discredited party of outgoing president Moscoso, captured only 17 percent of the vote. In the legislative election, the PRD won a majority of 42 seats in the 78-seat National Assembly, followed by the PA with only 17 seats; several other parties captured fewer than 10 seats each. The trouncing of the PA was seen as a rejection of Moscoso's corrupt and failure-ridden rule of the party; significantly, Aleman immediately withdrew from politics.

Armed violence has increased significantly in Panama in the past several years. Weekend police checkpoints are now commonplace both in Panama City and in crime-ridden Colon, although the country remains relatively safe when compared with many of its regional neighbors. In her last months in office, President Moscoso failed to pass her own version of the Hard Hand (*Mano Dura*) policy adopted by other regional countries such as Honduras and El Salvador. President Torrijos has promised a new campaign of Integral Security with Force and Firmness that does not only depend on heavy prison sentences, but also on reducing the national poverty level and creating jobs.

Repeated incursions into Panamanian territory by Colombian guerrillas, self-defense armed irregulars, and drug traffickers continue to spark concerns in the region about the spillover effects of Colombia's civil war. Panama has no military and instead relies on the police to provide both internal security and defense of its borders. Dozens of confrontations between armed Colombian groups and the Panamanian police raised questions about whether the latter are up to the challenge provided by the seasoned Colombians.

Political Rights and Civil Liberties: Panama's citizens can change their government democratically. The 2004 national elections were considered free and fair by international observers. The president and deputies to the 78-seat unicameral National Assembly are elected by popular vote for five-year terms. The constitution guarantees freedom of political organizations. In early 1999, Panama's largest political parties agreed to ban anonymous campaign contributions in an effort to stem the infiltration of drug money into the political process. Nevertheless, the widespread corruption of the governmental apparatus indicates the difficulty in enforcing any such bans. In the early stages of President Martin Torrijos's campaign, Hugo, his cousin and campaign manager had to resign over allegations of corruption.

Even before taking office the president-elect proposed a number of constitutional amendments, providing for structural and functional changes in the three powers of the state, provisions on the Panama Canal Authority, and granting constitutional status to the office of the public ombudsman. He accomplished this on September 2, thus easing the eventual passage of these amendments, which requires amendments be approved by two successive sessions of congress. An additional amendment would shorten the period between the election of the president and the assumption office, from four to two months.

On taking office, the Torrijos administration established a National Anti-Corruption Commission and opened investigations throughout the government in an effort to root out corruption. Torrijos also made initial efforts to implement a Transparency Law intended to allow greater public access to information about various state entities, but has since acted to limit its scope. In November, the administration exempted cabinet meetings minutes from public release under the law, and in October, the solicitor general advised against the disclosure of officials' assets. Panama was ranked 62 out of 146 countries surveyed in Transparency International's 2004 Corruption Perceptions Index.

Panama's media include an assortment of radio and television stations, daily newspapers, and weekly publications. There are 5 national dailies, 4 private television stations, 2 educational television broadcasters, and 100 or so radio stations. Restrictive media laws dating back to the regime of General Manuel Noriega remain on the books. The law permits the government to prosecute individual reporters and media owners for criminal libel and calumny, and officials can remand anyone who defames the government to jail without trial. A censorship board can fine radio stations for use of abusive language. There is free access to the Internet.

Freedom of religion is respected, and academic freedom is generally honored.

The judicial system, headed by the Supreme Court, was revamped in 1990. However, it remains overworked and its administration is inefficient, politicized, and prone to corruption. An unwieldy criminal code and a surge in cases, many against former soldiers and officials of the military period, complicate the judicial process. About two-thirds of prisoners face delays of about 18 months in having their cases heard. Slow progress has been made in making the legal system more responsive and also in developing special skills, such as forensic auditing, which recently located accounts of indicted former Presidents Arnolfo Aleman of Nicaragua and Alfonso Portillo of Guatemala.

The PDF was dismantled after 1989, and the military was formally abolished in 1994. However, the civilian-run Panamanian Public Forces (the national police) that replaced the PDF, although accountable to civilian authorities through a publicly disclosed budget, are poorly disciplined and corrupt. There are four components: the Panamanian National Police, the National Maritime Service, the National Air Service, and the Institutional Protection Service. Criminal investigations are the responsibility of a semiautonomous Judicial Technical Police. Like the country's prison guards, officers frequently use excessive force. The penal system is marked by violent disturbances in decrepit facilities that are severely overcrowded.

Nongovernmental organizations are free to organize. Freedom of assembly is generally recognized. Labor unions are well organized, but only 10 percent of the labor force is unionized. However, labor rights were diluted in 1995 when President Ernesto Perez Balladares pushed labor code revisions through congress. Furthermore, the government has issued decrees that do not allow union organization in export processing zones.

Discrimination against darker-skinned Panamanians, especially those from Colon, is widespread. The country's Asian, Middle Eastern, and Indian populations are similarly singled out. The living conditions of the indigenous populations, who often do not speak Spanish, are significantly lower than those of the general population, and they face significant discrimination in employment. Since 1993, indigenous groups have protested the encroachment of illegal settlers on Indian lands and delays by the government in formally demarcating the boundaries of those lands. Indian communities do enjoy, however, a large degree of autonomy and self-government. Late in 2003, the president of the Supreme Court, Cesar Pereira Burgos proposed creating the establishment of indigenous tribunals for the country's indigenous districts. This proposal is a direct response to the lack of legal facilities in these communities to deal with local problems, such as land disputes and sexual violence.

Violence against women and children is widespread and common. Panama is both a destination and a transit point for human trafficking.

Papua New Guinea

Population: 5,700,000
GNI/capita: $530
Life Expectancy: 57
Religious Groups: Roman Catholic (22 percent), Protestant (44 percent), indigenous beliefs (34 percent)
Ethnic Groups: Melanesian, Papuan, Negrito, Micronesian, Polynesian
Capital: Port Moresby

Political Rights: 3
Civil Liberties: 3
Status: Partly Free

Ten-Year Ratings Timeline (Political Rights, Civil Liberties, Status)

1995	1996	1997	1998	1999	2000	2001	2002	2003	2004
2,4PF	2,4PF	2,4PF	2,3F	2,3F	2,3F	2,3F	2,3F	3,3PF	3,3PF

Overview:

A new Limited Preferential Voting system was introduced in Papua New Guinea (PNG) December 2003, which replaced the first-past-the-post system that critics had long alleged was open to bribery. Australia continued throughout the year to spearhead efforts, with the use of police and monetary assistance, to restore peace and order in PNG. Agreement was reached in October on a draft Bougainville constitution between the PNG national government and Bougainville province.

PNG, which consists of the eastern part of New Guinea and some 600 smaller islands, gained independence from Australia in 1975. In 1988, miners and landowners on Bougainville Island began guerrilla attacks against the Australian-owned Panguna copper mine, which provided 40 percent of the country's total export revenues. A ceasefire collapsed in 1996, and fighting resumed. A new peace treaty between the government and the Bougainville Revolutionary Army was signed in August 2001 to end a civil war that had claimed more than 10,000 lives and crippled the economy.

The last elections were held in June 2002 and April and May of 2003. The next election must be held no later than 2007. Prime Minister Michael Somare has been in office since August 2002. Of the 109 seats in the unicameral national parliament, 19 were won by the National Alliance Party of Somare, 14 by the United Resources Party, 13 by the People's Democratic Movement, 9 by the People's Progressive Party, 6 by the Papua and Niugini Union Party, 5 by the People's Action Party, 4 by the People's Labor Party, and 40 by others including independents.

Peace in Bougainville remains fragile, as Bougainville independence hard-liners announced just one day after the UN peace monitors left the country on July 1, 2003, that they would not participate in the peace process. The UN Observer Mission to Bougainville had asked the PNG government to hold elections for self-rule in Bougainville before the end of 2004. In October, agreement on a draft Bougainville constitution between the PNG national government and the Bougainville province was an important step toward elections, which look likely to occur in 2005.

The first Australian Federal Police officers arrived in Port Moresby in December 2003 to provide training to local law enforcement. Australia pledged $325 million over five years to tackle crime and unrest in "hot spots" in the country, namely, Port Moresby, Mt. Hagen, Bougainville, and Lae. Australia initially wanted immunity for its police officers, but strong opposition from PNG officials and public opinion forced it to back down. Canberra committed another $628 million and another police contingent for Bougainville. Australian police officers were expected to arrive in Bougainville before the end of 2004 to help restore law and order in the first phase of the war-torn region's recovery process. PNG police reported that in 2003, 158 murders occurred in the capital—the highest number recorded ever. About 300 Australian police and civil servants were planned for deployment to PNG to take up operational jobs to boost law and order and good governance.

A new Limited Preferential Voting system was introduced in December 2003. The system, which replaces the first-past-the-post system, allows voters to rank three preferred candidates. Critics had long seen the older system as being open to bribery. The new system was used in a by-election in Abau district. Dr. Puka Temu, a former secretary for health and a member of the ruling National Alliance Party of Prime Minister Michael Somare, was elected. Election observers said less than 2 percent of the ballots were spoiled—a dramatic improvement from previous years. In October, nine persons, including poll officials, were arrested for voter fraud in an election for a new parliament representative for Port Moresby. Prosecution of the alleged offenders offered hope of improved efforts to promote fair and free elections. A constitutional amendment to extend the grace period between no-confidence votes from the current 18 months to 36 months was twice defeated.

Political Rights and Civil Liberties: Citizens of PNG can change their government democratically. Voters elect a unicameral parliament with 109 members from all 19 provinces and the National Capital District. The last general election was held in June 2002, resulting in a coalition government headed by Prime Minister Michael Somare. PNG is a member of the Commonwealth, and Queen Elizabeth II is represented by a governor-general elected by the PNG parliament. Sir Paulias Matane was sworn in as the new governor-general in June 2004. The major political parties are the National Alliance Party of Prime Minister Somare, the United Resources Party, the People's Democratic Movement and the People's Progressive Party. However, association with political parties is fluid.

Papua New Guinea was ranked 102 out of 146 countries surveyed in Transparency International's 2004 Corruption Perceptions Index. Official corruption and abuses of power are significant hurdles to attracting investment and economic growth. Authorities have yet to push beyond political rhetoric and implement real reforms to increase transparency and strengthen the rule of law.

Freedom of speech is generally respected. Of the two weekly papers, one is published in English and one in Tok Pisin (Melanesian pidgin), the national lingua franca. There are two major daily newspapers and several other smaller local weekly and monthly publications. The government operates two FM radio stations and one AM radio station, as well as a television station. Several radio stations and two television stations are operated by private entities. Foreign newspapers are available, as are radio and television broadcasts from Australia and other countries. The media provide independent coverage and report on controversial issues such as alleged abuses by police, cases of alleged corruption by government officials, and the views of the political opposition. During 2004, there were concerns that media freedom was threatened when the government cautioned against the publication and broadcast of any "negative" comments about the country. There are no government controls on access to the Internet; however, usage is low at 13.7 persons per 1,000, according to 2002 data of the International Telecommunications Union. The main constraints are high cost and connectivity outside the capital.

The government generally respects freedom of religion. The perceived threat to media freedom applies to academics, as well as journalists, for their writing on the economy and the government.

The constitution provides for freedom of association, and the government generally respects this right in practice. However, the government continues to restrict freedom of assembly in the form of marches and demonstrations, which require a 14-day advance notice and police approval. In 2001, police fired on student demonstrators in Port Moresby, killing four and injuring 20 persons. The government recognizes workers' right to strike, organize and engage in collective bargaining.

The judiciary is independent, and the legal system is based on English common law. The Supreme Court is the final court of appeal and has original jurisdiction on constitutional matters. The National Court hears most cases and appeals from the lower district courts established at the provincial level. There are also village courts, which are headed by laypersons, to adjudicate minor offenses under both customary and statutory law. The government increased the number of full-time judges in 2002 and took steps to expand training of the judiciary.

Police and judicial reforms are much needed. Law enforcement officials have been implicated in unlawful killings, use of excessive force in arresting and interrogating suspects, and conducting excessively punitive and violent raids. There was little progress in cutting long delays for court hearings and improving prison conditions. Prison conditions are poor, and international observers did not report any significant improvement. The country maintains ground, naval, air, and special operations forces. Control and effectiveness of the military are complicated by lack of resources for training and equipment, low morale, low pay, corruption, and disciplinary issues. In 2001, some officers staged a mutiny when plans to downsize the military were leaked. In the past several years, an Australian-led multinational force has downsized the PNG army and offered training to improve capacity and morale.

Violence between native tribes is a serious problem rooted in a cultural tradition of revenge for perceived wrongs. Lack of police enforcement and the increased availability of guns have exacerbated this problem. Attacks on Chinese nationals and their businesses were reported in the past year in connection with a police crackdown on the operation of horse racing machines and on illegal immigration. In several cases, the police had allegedly led or participated in lootings of Chinese-owned businesses.

Discrimination and violence against women and children are serious problems. Domestic violence is punishable by law, but prosecutions are rare as police commonly treat it as a private matter and family pressure and fear of reprisal discourage victims from pressing charges. Critics added that polygamy and the custom of paying a bride price reinforce the view that women are property. Prime Minister Somare voiced support of the death penalty for men convicted of gang rape.

◢Paraguay

Population: 6,000,000   **Political Rights:** 3
GNI/capita: $1,170   **Civil Liberties:** 3
Life Expectancy: 71   **Status:** Partly Free
Religious Groups: Roman Catholic (90 percent), other
[including Mennonite and Protestant] (10 percent)
Ethnic Groups: Mestizo (95 percent), other [including
Amerindian and white] (5 percent)
Capital: Asuncion
Trend Arrow: Paraguay received a downward trend arrow due to increasing
lawlessness and street crime.

Ten-Year Ratings Timeline (Political Rights, Civil Liberties, Status)

1995	1996	1997	1998	1999	2000	2001	2002	2003	2004
4,3PF	4,3PF	4,3PF	4,3PF	4,3PF	4,3PF	4,3PF	4,3PF	3,3PF	3,3PF

Overview:

Despite efforts by the government of Nicanor Duarte Frutos to promote good governance, fight tax evasion, and adopt IMF reports, Paraguay continued to face endemic corruption, widespread poverty, and a growing crime wave in 2004. Former dictator Alfredo Stroessner, living in exile in Brazil, was ordered arrested by a Paraguayan court for his part in the disappearance of Paraguayan activists three decades earlier.

Paraguay, which achieved independence from Spain in 1811, has been wracked by a series of crises since civilian rule was restored in 1989 and the 35-year reign of Stroessner and the right-wing Colorado party was ended. The fragility of the country's democratic institutions has resulted in nearly 15 years of popular uprisings, military mutinies, antigovernment demonstrations, bitter political rivalries, and unbroken rule by the Colorados.

Luis Gonzalez Macchi assumed the presidency in 1999 after his predecessor fled the country amid charges that he had orchestrated the murder of his vice president. International concern about individuals and organizations with ties to Middle Eastern extremist groups operating in Ciudad del Este and along the tri-border area, where Paraguay, Brazil, and Argentina meet, followed the September 11, 2001, terrorist attacks on the World Trade Center and the Pentagon in the United States.

In December 2002, Gonzalez Macchi offered to leave office three months early, just a week after lawmakers voted to start impeachment hearings against him. Accused of buying an armor-plated BMW stolen from Brazil, mishandling millions of dollars in state revenues, and embezzling $16 million from two banks in the process of liquidation, Gonzalez Macchi barely survived an impeachment trial in early 2003. Even his supporters did not defend the president, who allegedly doubled his personal wealth during his four years in power, saying only that it was inadvisable to oust him so late in his term. Gonzalez Macchi and many in the Colorado Party were discredited, too, by their unsuccessful efforts to reverse the country's downward economic spiral.

Favoring populist, anti-globalization rhetoric during the 2003 presidential campaign, former education minister and journalist Duarte, an insurgent Colorado, emerged victorious in national elections held April 27. Duarte had promised to purge the public sector and the judiciary of corruption and inefficiency, create jobs, and return fiscal stability to the country. Although the Colorado Party lost ground in congress in the concurrent legislative elections, it retained a majority of the 17 state governorships. On taking office on August 15, Duarte quickly began to inaugurate the good-government agenda that he had promised during the campaign. Skeptics, however, questioned whether the new anticorruption regime would be selectively applied to Duarte's rivals inside and outside the Colorado Party, or whether the elections would truly usher in a new period in Paraguayan politics.

Duarte moved to take control of the tax, ports, and customs authorities to combat tax evasion and smuggling in the country with a highly dollarized banking system and a tax system in which two-thirds of what should be collected is never paid or is siphoned off, owing to corruption. In October 2003, his law enforcement minister, the commandant of the national police, and the head of customs were forced to resign following revelations about a smuggling and corruption scandal.

In 2004, Duarte's government won international praise for paying foreign debt arrearages and for adopting reforms demanded the previous year by the IMF as part of an agreement for a badly needed stand-by loan. However, it appeared near paralysis in the face of the increase in public insecurity, as well as a long-run economic recession, endemic public corruption, and a poverty rate of more than 60 percent.

Sometimes violent land seizures by armies of homeless people in and around the capital city, Asuncion, contributed to a growing debate about the distribution of wealth in the country. In 2004, the land invaders were occasionally killed by militias in the pay of landowners. One out of every three Paraguayans lives below the poverty line, and emigration to Argentina, the traditional escape of the poor, became unattractive in the aftermath of that country's own economic crisis.

Public opinion surveys showed that after 15 years of turbulent civilian rule and 50 years after he seized power, 62 percent of Paraguayans viewed with favor the once-discredited former dictator Stroessner, now 91 and living in exile in Brazil. The governing council of the ruling Colorado Party in July voted nearly unanimously that he be allowed to return to Paraguay. In September, a Paraguayan court ordered Stroessner and his former armed forces chief of staff to be arrested in connection with the disappearance of three Paraguayan activists in Argentina in the 1970s under a secret regional police action known as Operation Condor.

During the year, the country was shaken by a crime wave whose magnitude was symbolized by the seeming impunity with which criminals abducted the daughter of a former Paraguayan president in a blaze of gunfire. In October, Duarte had to fire his law enforcement minister and a senior police chief, and order 1,000 more police on the streets, after police found the mutilated body of a tobacco magnate's 10-year-old son, who had been kidnapped on leaving elementary school.

Political Rights and Civil Liberties: Citizens of Paraguay can change their government democratically. The 2003 national elections were considered to be free and fair. Disillusionment with the entire political system was evidenced by the scant participation in recent elections by young people, who constitute nearly three-fourths of the population. The 1992 constitution provides for a president, a vice president, and a bicameral congress consisting of a 45-member Senate and an 80-member Chamber of Deputies elected for five years. The president is elected by a simple majority vote, and reelection is prohibited. The constitution bans the active military from engaging in politics. The Colorado Party has ruled Paraguay for 50 years; the other major political groupings include the Authentic Radical Liberal Party, the Beloved Fatherland Movement, the National Union of Ethical Citizens, and the National Agreement Party.

Corruption cases languish for years in the courts, and most end without resolution. According to the comptroller-general, corruption has cost the Paraguayan treasury $5 billion since the country returned to democracy in 1989. In April 2003, the prosecutor who had almost single-handedly brought then-president Luis Gonzalez Macchi to justice himself faced removal from office by a judicial panel just hours after the prosecutor claimed that the head of the panel owned a stolen Mercedes-Benz. Transparency International consistently ranks Paraguay as the most corrupt country in Latin America. In its 2004 Corruption Perceptions Index, Paraguay was ranked 140 of 146 countries surveyed worldwide.

The constitution provides for freedom of expression and the press, and the government generally respects these rights in practice. There are a number of private television and radio stations and independent newspapers, but only one state-owned media outlet, Radio Nacional, which has a limited audience. However, in 2004, the Inter American Press Association noted that "the status of press freedom was marked by several attempts by government officials to interfere with the free practice of journalism, either by resorting directly to force or by using court rulings and legislation." In March, the Paraguayan Journalists Union announced that the newspaper *Popular* had been censored in order to stop the publication of a series of articles involving President Niconar Duarte Frutos, in which it was reported that the president had given a car as a birthday gift to the daughter of the then-Speaker of the Chamber of Deputies. Journalists investigating corruption or covering strikes and protests are often the victims of intimidation or violent attack by security forces, and even death threats from politicians. On April 21, 2004, radio reporter Samuel Roman was shot dead by two men riding on a motorcycle in a Paraguayan border town.

Free expression is threatened by vague, potentially restrictive laws that mandate "responsible" behavior by journalists and media owners. According to an Inter American Press Association report issued in October 2004, the legislature passed a law that did not include an article guaranteeing access to sworn statements on the assets of public officials. The government does not restrict use of the Internet, nor does it censor Internet content.

The government generally respects freedom of religion. All religious groups are required to register with the Ministry of Education and Culture, but no controls are imposed on these groups, and many informal churches exist. The government generally does not restrict academic freedom.

Although the constitution guarantees freedom of association and assembly, these rights have been undermined by the previous government's tolerance of threats and the use of force, including imprisonment, by its supporters against the opposition. In 2004, the police used force against illegal but nonviolent demonstrations, and in several instances, the government mobilized the military to assist the police in maintaining public order in the face of unrest and rural land invasions. There are numerous trade unions and two major union federations, although they are weak and riddled with corruption. The constitution gives public sector workers the right to organize, bargain collectively, and strike, and nearly all these workers belong to the ruling Colorado Party. A new labor code designed to protect workers' rights was adopted in October 1993.

The judiciary, under the influence of the ruling party and the military, is susceptible to the corruption pervading all public and governmental institutions. The constitution permits detention without trial until the accused completes the minimum sentence for the alleged crime. There have been continuing reports of illegal detention by police and torture during incarceration, including of minors, particularly in rural areas. Reportedly corrupt police officials, who are poorly paid, remain in key posts and are in a position to give protection to, or compromise law enforcement actions against, narcotics traffickers. Colombian drug traffickers continue to expand operations in Paraguay, and accusations of high official involvement in drug trafficking date back to the 1980s. Overcrowding, unsanitary living conditions, and mistreatment are serious problems in the country's prisons; more than 95 percent of those held are pending trial, many for months or years after arrest.

The lack of security in border areas, particularly in the tri-border region, has allowed large organized-crime groups to engage in piracy and in the smuggling of weapons, narcotics, and contraband. In the aftermath of the September 11, 2001, attacks, attention focused on the serious lack of governmental control over Paraguay's lengthy and undeveloped land borders, extensive river network, and numerous airstrips (both registered and unregistered). The Islamic extremist organization Hezbollah and other militant organizations are active in the so-called Iguazu triangle region, which is delineated by the cities of Ciudad del Este in Paraguay, Foz do Iguacu in Brazil, and Puerto Iguazu in Argentina. A joint intelligence center run by Argentina, Brazil, and Paraguay monitors the region, and all three countries use their air forces for surveillance and interdiction efforts.

The constitution provides indigenous people with the right to participate in the economic, social, political, and cultural life of the country. In practice, the indigenous population is unassimilated and neglected. Low wages, long work hours, infrequent payment or nonpayment of wages, job insecurity, lack of access to social security benefits, and racial discrimination are common. Peasant and Indian organizations that demand and illegally occupy land often meet with police crackdowns, death threats, detentions, and forced evictions by vigilante groups in the employ of landowners.

Paraguay's economy remains heavily based on agriculture and various forms of contraband. The country has one of the most unequal distributions of land in the world, and it has been the booming agri-business industry that has kept the country from bankruptcy in the past five years. According to the Ministry for Social Action, 66 percent of the country's land is held by 10 percent of the population, while nearly one-third of Paraguayans have no land of their own. The top 10 percent own 40 percent of the wealth.

Sexual and domestic abuse of women, which is both widespread and vastly underreported, continues to be a serious problem in Paraguay, and employment discrimination is pervasive. Spousal abuse is common. Trafficking in persons to, from, and within the country is proscribed by the constitution and criminalized in the penal code; however, there were occasional reports of the practice for sexual purposes.

⚓Peru

Population: 27,500,000   **Political Rights:** 2
GNI/capita: $2,020   **Civil Liberties:** 3
Life Expectancy: 69   **Status:** Free
Religious Groups: Roman Catholic (90 percent), other
(10 percent)
Ethnic Groups: Amerindian (45 percent), mestizo
(37 percent), white (15 percent), other (3 percent)
Capital: Lima
Trend Arrow: Peru received a downward trend arrow due to growing indications of corruption at the highest levels of government.
Ten-Year Ratings Timeline (Political Rights, Civil Liberties, Status)

1995	1996	1997	1998	1999	2000	2001	2002	2003	2004
5,4PF	4,3PF	5,4PF	5,4PF	5,4PF	3,3PF	1,3F	2,3F	2,3F	2,3F

Overview: In 2004, President Alejandro Toledo continued to be the victim of a dangerous paradox that was partly of his own making: the country's economic recovery continued its upward swing amid a climate of freedom, but his personal popularity plummeted and his Peru Posible Party appeared on the verge of disintegration. At mid-year, Peru Posible lost control of the leadership of congress. Meanwhile, the country's broad-based anticorruption drive appeared to run out of most of its steam, as opposition parties and others increasingly decried Toledo's alleged corruption.

Since independence in 1821, Peru has seen alternating periods of civilian and military rule, with elected civilians holding office since a 12-year dictatorship ended in 1980. However, that same year, the Maoist Shining Path guerrilla group launched its two-decades-long insurgency. Alberto Fujimori, a university rector and engineer, defeated the novelist Mario Vargas Llosa in the 1990 election.

In 1992, Fujimori, backed by the military, suspended the constitution and dissolved congress. In November, he held elections for an 80-member constituent assembly to replace the congress. The opposition made a strategic decision to boycott the election, thus ensuring an overwhelming victory for pro-Fujimori forces. The assembly created a constitution—which established a unicameral congress more closely under presidential control—that was approved in a state-controlled referendum following the capture of the Shining Path leader, Abimael Guzman. Congress passed a law in August 1996 allowing Fujimori to run for a third term, despite a constitutional provision limiting the president to two terms. The law evaded this restriction by defining Fujimori's current term as his first under the 1993 constitution.

In the April 9, 2000, presidential election, Fujimori defeated Toledo, a U.S.-educated economist who had been raised in one of the many urban squatter settlements of former peasants recently migrated from the countryside, by 49.9 to 40.2 percent. Since Fujimori fell short of an absolute majority, a runoff election was slated for May 28. Toledo refused to participate in the second round, saying that he had been victimized by election-day voting irregularities, repeatedly assaulted by Fujimori supporters in the earlier campaign, suffered constant death threats and phone taps, virtually blacked out from media coverage, and the target of smear campaigns in the press.

In early September, a videotape was released showing Vladimiro Montesinos, the de facto head of the national intelligence service, bribing an opposition congressman at the same time that the spy chief was also being linked to the illegal shipment of arms to Colombian guerrillas. After other similar videos (labeled "Vladivideos") were exposed, the scandal raised suspicions that Fujimori had secured a parliamentary majority—after having failed to win one outright in the April general elections—by bribing opposition congressmen to change sides. In addition, the scandal underscored the fact that official corruption had become systemic. As a result, in late November, Fujimori was driven from office; opposition forces assumed control of congress; and a respected opposition leader, Valentin Paniagua, was chosen as interim president.

Following Fujimori's overthrow, the new opposition-controlled congress began a process of renewing the constitutional tribunal, which had been gutted because some of its members had opposed the third-term law, and reforming the constitution. At the end of 2000, Fujimori announced that he was availing himself of his dual citizenship to remain in Japan (where he lived throughout 2004). In April 2001 parliamentary elections, Toledo's Peru Posible Party won 25 percent of the votes, compared to 19 percent garnered by its closest competitor, the Apristas. Running on the slogan "Toledo Trabajo" (Toledo Means Jobs), Toledo bested former Aprista president Alan Garcia (1985–1990) in runoff elections held on June. In August, Toledo sacked Peru's top military chiefs and promised to thoroughly restructure the armed forces.

The 2002 reform of Peru's highly centralized political structure gave new regional governments almost a quarter of the national budget and a range of powers that had long been the province of the central government. However, Toledo's standing suffered from a host of personal scandals. In June, antigovernment riots protesting the sell-off of state-owned companies left two people dead and nearly $100 million in damages. The Shining Path also made a small comeback, killing 10 people in a car bomb attack outside the U.S. Embassy in March and making a limited effort to disrupt the November 2002 regional elections. Toledo's government suffered a serious setback at the polls in those elections, as voters selected the main opposition party and a group of independents in contests for 25 new regional governments, whose establishment was meant to end Lima's top-down monopoly on political control.

In August 2003, Peru's Truth and Reconciliation Commission—which Paniagua had appointed in July 2001—presented its report on the scope and origins of the political violence that had wracked the country from 1980 to 2000. While it concluded that the Maoist Shining Path guerrilla group was the "principal perpetrator of the human rights violations," which included 69,000 people killed, the commission also accused the military and security forces of serious and repeated atrocities. The report shocked many observers by more than doubling the number of deaths estimated to have occurred during the protracted insurgency. The findings showed that nearly three-fourths of the victims of both the guerrillas and the military were residents of Andean highland villages, rural poor who have long suffered neglect at the hand of the central government. In the present political climate of doubt and suspicion, the commission has not fulfilled hopes that it would finally lay to rest all unanswered questions about these events.

Toledo's popularity appeared to decline further by late 2003, as angry Peruvians took to the streets in increasing numbers over his questionable ethics and failure to make good on campaign promises of more jobs. The popular disenchantment grew despite the country's posting an annual inflation rate of just 1.5 percent, the lowest in decades, and holding its position as Latin America's economic growth leader.

In 2004, the tenuous hold of Toledo's ruling coalition was weakened even more by Peru Posible's loss of control of congress, including the resignation from the party of two of its founding members, which reduced its parliamentary representation to 36, 11 fewer than in 2001. By midyear, one public opinion survey showed that 70 percent of those polled felt that Toledo—considered on the basis of comparative polling data to be the most unpopular president in Latin America—was himself personally corrupt, and half said they wanted him to leave office early. Some media observers, however, claim that, at least in part, the upswing in public complaints about corruption reflected a tendency by the press, newly freed from the controls and interference of the Fujimori era, to engage in *denuncialogia*—an obsession with denunciations—that trivializes investigative journalism and helps to poison both political debate and public confidence.

Popular discontent appeared to extend to the entire political process, probably in no small part as a result of the resurgence, as a possible presidential successor, of Garcia, whose own presidency collapsed amid economic chaos, guerrilla insurgency, and rampant rights abuses. However, control of congress by the hardly more popular opposition, and the increased spotlight on potential successors to Toledo in the 2006 presidential contest, appeared to work against the probability of any extra-legal efforts to seize power in the politically volatile country.

In June, a special anticorruption court found former intelligence chief Montesinos guilty on charges of corruption, sentencing him to 15 years in prison. Nonetheless, in September, the self-exiled Fujimori, wanted in Peru on charges including murder and kidnapping, declared that he would run for president in 2006—despite being legally banned from holding public office.

In November, old wounds were reopened with the retrial of Shining Path guerrilla leader Abimael Guzman. The new trial for Guzman was the result of a Supreme Court decision questioning the validity of previous trials of accused terrorists in military courts directed by "faceless" judges (whose identities had been concealed to protect them and their families against credible death threats by the Shining Path). The retrial was suspended, however, after the courtroom was wracked by chaotic scenes, including the trading of accusations between the judge and the prosecutor, that appeared to discredit an already unpopular justice system.

Political Rights and Civil Liberties: Peruvians can change their government democratically, and the November 2002 elections were held largely without incident. In preparation for the 2001 vote, congress reformed the constitution, replacing a single nationwide district for congressional elections with a system of multiple districts based on the departments (provinces) into which the country is divided for administrative purposes. The move provided fair representation for the almost 50 percent of the population who live outside the four largest cities and guaranteed them at least some attention from the state and from political parties, which traditionally have ignored them.

In March, the government announced that it was dissolving the national intelligence service in the aftermath of a series of scandals. However, witnesses against military wrongdoers, including human rights violators, face threats to their physical well-being. Peru was ranked 67 out of 146 countries surveyed in Transparency International's 2004 Corruption Perceptions Index.

The press is largely privately owned and is now considered to be free. Although the number of threats, including death threats, against journalists has fallen since Alberto Fujimori's presidency, the practice still persists, especially in the provinces. Radio and television are both privately and publicly owned. The government does not limit access to the Internet.

The constitution provides for freedom of religion, and the government generally respects this right in practice. However, the Roman Catholic Church receives preferential treatment from the state. Academic freedom is not restricted by the government.

The constitution provides for the right of peaceful assembly, and the authorities generally respect this right in practice. The human rights community has reported that the Alejandro Toledo administration continues to work toward strengthening relations between the government and civil society. The government permits numerous nongovernmental organizations dedicated to monitoring and advancing human rights to operate freely. In recent years, these groups reported no harassment or other attempts by the authorities to hinder their operations.

During his period in office, Fujimori conducted a purge of the judiciary that removed 70 percent of judges. He replaced them with new appointees having "provisional" status, meaning that they lacked job tenure and thus were potentially unduly responsive to the government in cases where it had an interest. Since Toledo assumed office in July 2001, the Ministry of Justice has worked to put into place a broad anticorruption effort. However, popular perceptions of the justice system— that it is an inefficient, overloaded bureaucracy riddled by political influence and greed—are hard to change. Scant resources have resulted in most of Peru's more than 3,000 judges being overworked and underpaid, and Toledo's unpopularity results in part from, yet also reinforces, continuing public skepticism about any possibility of institutional reform.

In a positive development, in August 2004, the Constitutional Court, the country's highest tribunal, ordered a full investigation of two notorious 1986 prison massacres. In October 2004, the judicial branch presented the Constitutional Court with a request that it be given budgetary autonomy and a direct subsidy by congress.

Crime is spiraling out of control, and the most obvious contributing factors are the country's economic woes. The National Statistics Institute reports that over half of the population still lives in poverty, which recent economic growth has done little to alleviate. Public safety, particularly in Lima, is threatened by gang warfare and an increase in violent crime; police estimate that there are now more than 1,000 criminal gangs in the capital alone. Conditions remain deplorable in prisons for common criminals. Torture and ill-treatment on the part of the military and security forces remain a concern.

Under Toledo, the government has retained firm control over the military but has yet to embark on many of the necessary reforms of armed institutions that are still suffering from the serious professional deformations promoted by Vladimiro Montesinos, their de facto head under Fujimori. Peru lacks the codified distinction between national defense and internal security that is characteristic of modern, democratic states, and responsibility for internal security is shared between the military and the Peruvian National Police.

Only about 5 percent of the formal sector workforce belong to labor unions, which reflects a legacy of hostility by the Fujimori regime, cuts in the public sector workforce, more flexible labor policies, and other market reforms. In July, national labor unions called the first general strike in Peru since 1999, in protest against alleged public corruption. It received only tepid support and failed to shut down commercial activity in Lima, as had been intended.

Racism against Peru's large Native American population has been prevalent among the middle and upper classes, although the Fujimori government made some effort to combat it. The election of Toledo, who boasted of his indigenous heritage, is considered a watershed. However, the provisions of the 1993 constitution, and subsequent legislation regarding the treatment of native lands, are less explicit about the lands' inalienability and protection from being sold off than were earlier constitutional and statutory laws. The failure of the government to codify aspects of customary law (*derecho consuetudinario*) into positive law has been accompanied by recent incidents of vigilante violence, including lynchings, in the predominantly largely indigenous highlands.

Spousal abuse is a serious problem, although recently the government has taken some steps to address the issue. Forced labor, including child labor, exists in the gold-mining region of the Amazon. Discrimination against gay and transgender people, including occasional acts of violence, is a problem.

Philippines

Population: 83,700,000
GNI/capita: $1,030
Life Expectancy: 70
Religious Groups: Roman Catholic (83 percent), Protestant (9 percent), Muslim (5 percent), other [including Buddhist] (3 percent)
Ethnic Groups: Christian Malay (91.5 percent), Muslim Malay (4 percent), Chinese (1.5 percent), other (3 percent)
Capital: Manila

Political Rights: 2
Civil Liberties: 3
Status: Free

Ten-Year Ratings Timeline (Political Rights, Civil Liberties, Status)

1995	1996	1997	1998	1999	2000	2001	2002	2003	2004
2,4PF	2,3F	2,3F	2,3F	2,3F	2,3F	2,3F	2,3F	2,3F	2,3F

Overview:

Gloria Macapagal-Arroyo won a second six-year term as president in elections held in May 2004. She is credited with boosting tax revenues and stabilizing the budget deficit, but has been less successful in tackling the Philippines' rampant crime and chronic corruption, whose burdens fall heaviest on poorer Filipinos. Her administration also has struggled to reign in armed Islamic groups making their bases in the southern jungles.

The Philippines won independence in 1946 after being ruled for 43 years by the United States and occupied by the Japanese during World War II. It held U.S. commonwealth status from 1935 until its independence. Once one of Southeast Asia's wealthiest nations, the Philippines has been plagued since the 1960s by insurgencies, economic mismanagement, and widespread corruption. The country's economic and political development was set back further by Ferdinand Marcos's 14-year dictatorship. Marcos was finally chased out of office in 1986; he was succeeded by Corazon Aquino, who had previously been cheated out of victory in an election rigged by the strongman's cronies. Though she came to symbolize the Philippines' emergence from authoritarian rule, Aquino managed few deep political or economic reforms while facing seven coup attempts. Her more forceful successor, former army chief Fidel Ramos, ended chronic power shortages, privatized many state firms, and trimmed bureaucratic red tape.

With the popular Ramos constitutionally barred from running for reelection, Estrada, who was vice president, won the 1998 presidential election behind pledges to help poor Filipinos. Almost from the outset, the Estrada administration was dogged by allegations that it was corrupt and that it gave favorable treatment to the business interests of well-connected tycoons. The House of Representatives impeached him on these and other grounds in November 2000, but Estrada's supporters blocked prosecutors from introducing key evidence during his trial in the Senate. The resulting massive street protests and public withdrawal of support by military leaders forced Estrada to resign in January 2001.

As vice president, Arroyo became president under the constitutional line of succession. In the first major test of her administration's popularity, Arroyo's coalition won 8 of 13 contested Senate seats and a majority in the House in the May 2001 legislative elections. Nevertheless, Arroyo was dogged by questions about the legitimacy of her unelected administration, while her establishment image—she is the daughter of a former president of the Philippines—made her an easy political target for populist backers of former president Estrada.

In the May 2004 presidential election, Arroyo eked out a narrow victory over her main rival, former film star Fernando Poe Jr. According to the official vote tally released in June, Arroyo won 12.9 million votes (40 percent of the total), compared to Poe's 11.8 million votes (37 percent). The other three candidates each garnered 10 percent or less of the total vote. Poe's supporters waged demonstrations after exit polls indicated his likely loss, alleging that Arroyo's party had rigged votes; these accusations were never proven true.

Far from the political bickering in Manila, the southern Philippines continues to be wracked by Islamic militancy. Abu Sayyaf continues to engage in terrorist activities, including bombings and kidnappings. Although it claims to be a Muslim secessionist group, its activities appear to be motivated mostly by the financial gains made by ransoms. Jemaah Islamiyah, a regional terrorist group with ties to al-Qaeda, is believed to have training grounds on the southern island of Mindanao.

Meanwhile, Arroyo's government has made little progress in reviving stalled talks with Communist rebels, who have been waging a low-grade rural insurgency since 1969. The Communists' extortion of local businesses and attacks on military and civilian targets in the countryside have helped cripple rural development. The general security problem is compounded by the high level of corruption in the security forces. The administration has been more successful on the economic front, however. Its program to combat tax evasion led to improvements at the Bureau of Customs and the Bureau of Internal Revenue. The higher tax receipts that resulted helped stabilize the budget deficit, which although still large, was running some PHP 1.5 billion (about US$27,000,000) below target in the first ten months of 2004.

Political Rights and Civil Liberties:

Citizens of the Philippines can change their government democratically. The Philippines has a presidential system of government, with the directly elected president limited to a single six-year term. The legislature is bicameral: the 24 members of the Senate are elected on a nationwide ballot and serve six-year terms. The 264 members of the House of Representatives serve three-year terms; 212 of them are elected by district and 52 of them are chosen by party list. The ruling People's Power Coalition is headed by Gloria Macapagal Arroyo's party, the National Union of Christian Democrats (Lakas); the main opposition party is the Struggle for a Democratic Philippines (Laban). Elections in the Philippines are free and fair.

Corruption, cronyism, and influence peddling are widely believed to be rife in business and government. Despite recent economic reforms, a few dozen powerful families continue to play an overarching role in politics and hold an outsized share of land and corporate wealth. The Philippines was ranked 102 out of 146 countries surveyed in Transparency International's 2004 Corruption Perceptions Index.

The private press (most print and electronic media) is vibrant and outspoken, although newspaper reports often consist more of innuendo and sensationalism than investigative reporting. Although many television and radio stations are government owned, they are still outspoken (though they too lack strict journalistic ethics). The international organization Human Rights Watch called the Movies and Television Review and Classification Board's threats against television broadcasts showing lesbian relations in June 2004 "a blatant assault on freedom of expression." Although the censorship board does have broad powers to edit or ban content, in general, government censorship is not a serious problem. However, the Philippines is one of the most dangerous places in the world for journalists to work, according to the National Union of Journalists in the Philippines. Several journalists were killed in 2003 and during the first ten months of 2004. Many were ostensibly victims of revenge killings after reporting on crimes committed by local government officials; some others had been outspoken supporters of the government's fight against illegal drugs or had criticized government officials for not doing enough to curb the drug trade. The government does not restrict Internet use.

Filipinos of all faiths can worship freely in this mainly Christian society, and church and state are separate. However, Muslims say that they face economic and social discrimination in mainstream society at the hands of the country's Roman Catholic majority. The general consensus, nevertheless, is that the discrimination is based on culture, not religion. There are also reports of reverse discrimination (against Christians) in areas such as Mindanao, where Muslims are in the majority; Muslim-majority provinces lag behind Christian-majority ones on most development indicators.

University professors and other teachers can lecture and publish freely.

Citizens can hold protests, rallies, and other demonstrations without government interference. The law requires that groups request a permit before holding a rally, but this law is often ignored in practice. The Philippines has many active environmental, human rights, social welfare, and other nongovernmental groups. Trade unions are independent, and they may align themselves with international trade union confederations or trade secretariats. Collective bargaining is widespread, and strikes may be called, though unions must provide notice and obtain majority approval from union membership before calling a strike.

Despite many gains since the Marcos era, the rule of law continues to be weak. The judiciary, while generally independent, is hampered by corruption and inefficiency. Low pay for judges and prosecutors is often cited as a major factor in perpetuating corruption such as bribery. The constitution sets time limits for court cases, but because of backlogs, and because these limits are not mandatory, they are mostly ignored. Independent observers do not believe that the judicial system adequately guarantees defendants' constitutional rights to due process and legal representation.

The rule of law is not necessarily respected in the Philippines. Reports of arbitrary and unlawful arrest or detention in harsh prison conditions, disappearances, kidnappings, extrajudicial killings, and abuse of suspects and detainees continue. Although torture is prohibited by the constitution, it remains "an ingrained part of the arrest and detention process," according to the U.S. State Department's human rights report for 2003, released in February 2004. Members of the poorly disciplined Philippine National Police (PNP) are regularly described by the official Commission on Human Rights as the country's worst rights abusers. Most notably, PNP officers continue to be accused of illegal killings of criminal suspects, although officials frequently allege that these killings occur during shootouts. The PNP is under the jurisdiction of the Armed Forces of the Philippines.

The long-running conflict between the government and the Moro Islamic Liberation Front (MILF), the separatist Islamic rebel group, has caused severe hardship for many of the 15 million Filipinos on southern Mindanao and nearby islands. Amnesty International in April accused Filipino forces of summary killings, disappearances, torture, and illegal arrests during counterinsurgency operations on Mindanao. MILF guerrillas are widely accused of killings and other abuses and have attacked many Christian villages. Separately, the smaller Abu Sayyaf group has kidnapped and tortured many civilians and beheaded some of its captives. Islamic militants are suspected in a string of bombings on Mindanao in recent years, including two bombings in Davao City in March and April 2003 that killed at least 38 people.

In the countryside, the 10,000-strong New People's Army (NPA), the military arm of the Communist insurgency, continues to engage in executions, torture, and kidnappings, according to the U.S. State Department report. The army and progovernment militias operating in Mindoro Oriental and other provinces are responsible for summary killings, disappearances, torture, and illegal arrests while fighting Communist rebels, according to Amnesty International.

Minorities have equal representation in the political system. However, members of the Philippines' indigenous minority have limited access to some basic government services and are far less integrated into mainstream society than other minorities. This is more the result of the geographical remoteness of the areas that they tend to inhabit, however, than of legal or entrenched societal discrimination. Because their preferred areas of the country are also favored by the militant rebels, indigenous people suffer disproportionately from the country's armed conflict.

Citizens may travel freely, and there are no restrictions on employment or place of residence. The government generally respects the privacy of its citizens. The poor security situation takes a serious toll on individuals' ability to operate private businesses, however. Street crime, drug trafficking, kidnappings, extortion, and terrorist violence all conspire against business interests.

Filipino women have the same rights as men according to the law, though this is not always borne out in practice. Women have made many social and economic gains in recent years, and more women than men now enter high school and university. In the job market, though, women face some discrimination in the private sector and have a higher unemployment rate than men, according to the U.S. State Department report. Rape, domestic violence, sexual harassment on the job, and trafficking of Filipino women and girls abroad and at home for forced labor and prostitution continue to be major problems despite government and civil efforts to protect women from violence and abuse. There are reports of bonded labor (especially of children) in underground sectors such as prostitution and drug trafficking. The NPA, MILF, and Abu Sayyaf have also been accused of using child soldiers.

Poland

Population: 38,200,000   **Political Rights:** 1
GNI/capita: $4,570   **Civil Liberties:** 1*
Life Expectancy: 75   **Status:** Free
Religious Groups: Roman Catholic (95 percent), other
[including Eastern Orthodox and Protestant] (5 percent)
Ethnic Groups: Polish (96.7 percent), German (0.4 percent),
other [including Ukrainian and Byelorussian] (2.9 percent)
Capital: Warsaw
Ratings Change: Poland's civil liberties rating improved from 2 to 1 due to the deepening of EU integration trends, resulting in greater conformity with EU human rights standards.
Ten-Year Ratings Timeline (Political Rights, Civil Liberties, Status)

1995	1996	1997	1998	1999	2000	2001	2002	2003	2004
1,2F	1,2F	1,2F	1,2F	1,2F	1,2F	1,2F	1,2F	1,2F	1,1F

Overview: Poland achieved its long-standing goal of joining the European Union (EU) on May 1, 2004. However, the government declined in popularity over the course of the year. The prime minister, Leszek Miller, announced his resignation in March, but this did not stop his ruling party from suffering a major defeat in the European Parliament elections in June under his caretaker successor.

From the fourteenth to the eighteenth centuries, Poland and Lithuania maintained a powerful state that Prussia, Austria, and Russia destroyed in three successive partitions. Poland enjoyed a window of independence from 1918 to 1939, but was invaded by Germany and the Soviet Union during World War II and was forced into the Communist sphere at the end of the war. Polish citizens endured decades of Soviet rule until 1989, the year Lech Walesa and the Solidarity trade union movement forced the government to accept democratic reforms.

Fundamental democratic and free market-oriented reforms were introduced during the 1989-1991 period. Later changes were stimulated by a need to adjust the Polish legal system to EU requirements. Political parties with a background in the Solidarity movement stayed in power from 1989 to 1993 (several coalitions) and from 1997 to 2001 (Solidarity Election Action, or AWS). In 1995, former Communist Alexander Kwasniewski replaced the previous president, Solidarity leader Lech Walesa, and was subsequently reelected by a large margin of votes in 2000.

In September 2001, voters handed the government of Prime Minister Jerzy Buzek a decisive defeat in parliamentary elections. Democratic Left Alliance (SLD) leader Leszek Miller became the new prime minister. In the election to the Sejm (lower house of parliament), a coalition of the center-left SLD and the Labor Union (UP) took 41.04 percent of the vote and 216 seats, but failed to win a majority. The two parties formed a government with the leftist Polish Peasants' Party (PSL), which had won 42 seats. Civic Platform (PO), a new centrist party, finished second in the election with 12.68 percent of the vote and 65 seats. The following parties divided the remaining seats: the leftist-popular agrarian Self-Defense Party (Samoobrona), 53 seats; the center-right Law and Justice (PiS), 44; the right-wing League of Polish Families (LPR), 38; and the German minority, 2. The Solidarity movement, now a looser coalition known as the Coalition Electoral Action Solidarity of the Right, and the Freedom Union (UW) failed to secure a single seat.

In a June 2003 referendum, Polish voters overwhelmingly approved joining the EU, with 77 percent voting in favor. On May 1, 2004, Poland formally joined, along with nine other (mostly post-Communist) countries. In subsequent negotiations over a new draft constitution for the EU, Poland fought unsuccessfully for the disproportionate voting clout it was given in the Treaty of Nice (which remains in effect until the constitution is ratified). Poland also tried and failed to include a reference to God or Europe's Christian heritage in the draft. With these disappointments, Poland is one of several countries that may fail to ratify the constitution, which would prevent it from coming into effect.

In March 2004, Miller announced that he would resign as prime minister, effective in May. His SLD-led government's popularity suffered from the effects of a weak economy, high unemployment, and high budget deficits, and was also dogged by allegations of corruption. The final blow was the defection of a group of SLD members of parliament, who announced their intention to form a new party, Social Democratic Party of Poland. Miller was replaced by the SLD's Marek Belka, who is expected to be a caretaker prime minister until elections can be held in 2005.

The SLD's weakness was confirmed by a drubbing in Poland's first European Parliament elections, in June. Just 20.4 percent of voters turned out, and the SLD took just 5 of 54 seats. The PO captured 15 seats; the LPR, 10 seats; the PiS, 7 seats; and Samoobrona, 6 seats. The LPR and Samoobrona are both highly skeptical of EU integration; if they do well in the 2005 Polish election, they will be in a strong position to pressure Poland's government and voters to reject the EU constitution.

Over the past several years, Poland has sought to carve out a twenty-first century leadership position for itself in Europe. This is most clearly symbolized by the prominent Polish role in the stabilization of Iraq following the ouster of Saddam Hussein's regime by U.S.-led forces. In charge of one of the four postwar stabilization zones in Iraq, Polish officers command 8,000 troops from some 20 countries, including 2,500 Polish troops. Poland's role in Iraq has generated consternation in a number of capitals in Western Europe that had opposed any military action in Iraq. In October, Prime Minister Belka announced that Poland would begin gradually withdrawing its troops after Iraqi elections, scheduled for January 2005.

Political Rights and Civil Liberties:

Polish citizens can change their government democratically. Voters elect the president and members of parliament. The president's appointment of the prime minister is subject to confirmation by the Sejm (the lower house of parliament, whose 460 members serve a four-year term). The 100-member Senate can delay legislation but has few other powers. The next parliamentary election must be held by September 2005 at the latest; presidential elections are scheduled for October 2005. The political party system is fragmented. Until recently, the largest and most coherent groups were the AWS and SLD, but the former has disappeared from parliament and the latter has split into rival factions. In addition, there are several small but vocal right-wing parties, including PiS, Samoobrona, the PSL and the LPR.

In 2003, the SLD-led government faced allegations of party figures' links to organized crime and corruption. The "Rywin affair," which involves allegations that film producer Lew Rywin sought a bribe from a major newspaper publisher in return for using his political connections to influence the shape of the draft media law, helped bring down Prime Minister Leszek Miller in 2004. New allegations of corruption surfaced during the year involving an alleged bribe by a Russian oil company to a Polish government minister for the sale of a Polish refinery to the Russian company. Poland was ranked 67 out of 146 countries surveyed in Transparency International's 2004 Corruption Perceptions Index.

Poland's membership in the European Union required it to meet the EU's so-called "Copenhagen criteria," including "stability of institutions guaranteeing democracy, the rule of law, human rights and respect for and protection of minorities." In its last report on Poland's progress, issued in 2003, the EU Commission said "Poland has reached a high level of alignment with the acquis [the body of EU laws] in most policy areas." The report did criticize slow progress on corruption, however. The 1997 constitution guarantees freedom of expression and forbids censorship. However, the country's libel law treats slander as a criminal offense, and journalists oppose the growing number of related lawsuits. Infringements on media freedom include gag orders and arbitrary judicial decisions concerning investigations of individuals affiliated with parties in power. The law requires the media to maintain "respect for Christian values."

The state respects freedom of religion and does not require religious groups to register. However, registered religious groups enjoy a reduced tax burden. In 2003, the Roman Catholic Church for the first time met with serious accusations of sexual impropriety by clerics. The Church responded with investigations and dismissals, including that of a bishop. Academic freedom is generally respected, though a law on the books threatens anyone who "publicly insults or humiliates a constitutional institution" with a fine or up to two years imprisonment.

Polish citizens can petition the government, assemble freely, organize professional and other associations, and engage in collective bargaining. Public demonstrations require permits from local authorities. Since the 1980s, when shipyard workers in Gdansk launched a national strike and formed the Solidarity labor union, Poland has had a robust labor movement. Although Solidarity's political strength has waned in recent years, labor groups remain active and influential.

Poland has an independent judiciary, but courts are notorious for delays in administering cases. In 1989, the country began a reform process that has sought to increase the efficiency and professionalism of the judiciary. In its 2002 accession report, the European Commission acknowledged "steady progress" and "improved efficiency" in this process, but noted that Poland should continue efforts to increase public access to justice, address public perceptions of corruption within the judiciary, and improve the treatment of detainees by the police. State prosecutors have proceeded slowly on investigations into graft and corruption, contributing to concerns that they are subject to considerable political pressure. Prison conditions are fairly poor by European standards.

Ethnic minorities generally enjoy generous protections and rights provided under Polish law, including funding for bilingual education and publications and privileged representation in parliament (they are not subject to a minimum threshold requiring 5 percent of the vote to achieve representation). Poland's once-vibrant Jewish community was reduced to a tiny minority by the Holocaust and subsequent emigration. Poland's other minority groups are small, but some, particularly the 30,000 Roma, suffer societal racism.

Women have made inroads in the professional sphere and are employed in a wide variety of professions and occupations. A number of women hold high positions in government and in the private sector, and the first nominee by Poland to the European Commission was a woman, Danuta Huebner. Domestic violence against women is a problem in Poland. As in several other formerly Communist countries, trafficking in women and girls remains a problem.

Portugal

Population: 10,500,000
GNI/capita: $10,720
Life Expectancy: 77
Religious Groups: Roman Catholic (94 percent), other
[including Protestant] (6 percent)
Ethnic Groups: Portuguese, African
and Eastern European minorities
Capital: Lisbon

Political Rights: 1
Civil Liberties: 1
Status: Free

Ten-Year Ratings Timeline (Political Rights, Civil Liberties, Status)

1995	1996	1997	1998	1999	2000	2001	2002	2003	2004
1,1F	1,1F	1,1F	1,1F	1,1F	1,1F	1,1F	1,1F	1,1F	1,1F

Overview:

Portugal's Prime Minister Jose Manuel Durao Barroso resigned as prime minister to become the new president of the European Commission in 2004. Lisbon mayor Pedro Santana Lopes replaced Barroso. The high-profile trial against seven people accused of forming a child sex ring in the Casa Pia children's home network began in November.

Portugal was proclaimed a republic in 1910, after King Manuel II abdicated during a bloodless revolution. Antonio de Oliveira Salazar became prime minister in 1932 and ruled the country as a fascist dictatorship until 1968, when his lieutenant, Marcello Caetano, replaced him. During the "Marcello Spring," repression and censorship were relaxed somewhat, and a liberal wing developed inside the one-party National Assembly. In 1974, a bloodless coup by the Armed Forces Movement, which opposed the ongoing colonial wars in Mozambique and Angola, overthrew Caetano.

A transition to democracy began with the election of a Constitutional Assembly that adopted a democratic constitution in 1976. A civilian government was formally established in 1982 after a revision of the constitution brought the military under civilian rule, curbed the president's powers, and abolished the unelected Revolutionary Council. Portugal became a member of the European Economic Community (later the EU) in 1986, and in early 2002, the euro replaced Portugal's currency, the *escudo*. In 1999, Portugal handed over its last overseas territory, Macao, to the Chinese, ending a long history of colonial rule.

In January 2001, the Socialist Party's Jorge Sampaio was reelected president to a second five-year term in office. Prime Minister Antonio Guterres resigned at the end of 2001 after his ruling Socialist Party (PS) suffered significant losses in municipal elections. The general election held on March 17, 2002, two years earlier than scheduled, produced a narrow victory for the Social Democratic Party (PSD), Portugal's center-right party, ending six years of Socialist Party government. However, the PSD—whose leader, Manuel Barroso, was named the new prime minister—fell well short of an absolute majority, which forced it to form a governing alliance with the small Popular Party, a populist, right-of-center party.

In July 2004, Barroso stepped down as prime minister to become president of the European Commission, succeeding the Italian Romano Prodi. Santana Lopes, the mayor of Lisbon and the new head of the Social Democrats, replaced Barroso. The country tightened security during the Euro 2004 soccer championships held in June. Such measures were aimed to prevent violence both by terrorists, like the attacks in Madrid only a few months before, and by groups of hooligan fans coming from other countries.

In November, a pedophilia trial began against seven people, including a TV presenter, a former top diplomat, and a former director of the Casa Pia children's home network. The case emerged from a series of allegations in 2003 of child abuse in the long-established state-run orphanages. The allegations went back 30 years and were considered the greatest upheaval in Portuguese society since the revolution of 1974. In June, a judge had thrown out the case against a key Socialist, Paulo Pedroso, who was previously charged with pedophilia offenses in the Casa Pia scandal. Barroso supported the U.S.-led invasion of Iraq, even hosting the Azores summit that effectively marked the declaration of hostilities. The country still maintains 128 elite police officers in Iraq, who are providing security as part of a multinational force under British command.

Political Rights and Civil Liberties: Citizens of Portugal can change their government democratically. The 230 members of the unicameral legislature, the Assembly of the Republic, are elected every four years by popular vote using a system of proportional representation. The president is popularly elected for a five-year term, renewable once. The president receives advice from the Council of State, which includes six senior civilian officers, former presidents elected under the 1976 constitution, five members chosen by the assembly, and five members selected by the president. While the president holds no executive powers, he can delay legislation with a veto and dissolve the assembly to call early elections. The constitution was amended in 1997 to allow immigrants to vote in presidential elections.

The Portuguese have the right to organize in different political parties and other political groupings of their choice, except for fascist organizations. During the last elections in 2002, more than five parties won seats. The PSD took the lead with 40 percent of the vote, the PS was second with 38 percent, the Popular Party had around 9 percent, and the Communists got 7 percent. The autonomous regions of Azores and Madeira are relatively independent, with their own political and administrative regimes, and their own legislation and executive powers.

Portugal was ranked 27 out of 146 countries surveyed in Transparency International's 2004 Corruption Perceptions Index.

Freedom of the press is guaranteed by the constitution, and laws against insulting the government or the armed forces are rarely enforced. Commercial television has been making gains in recent years, providing serious competition for the public broadcasting channels that lack funds. Internet access is not restricted.

Although the country is overwhelmingly Roman Catholic, the constitution guarantees freedom of religion and forbids religious discrimination. The Religious Freedom Act, which was adopted in 2001, provides religions that have been established in the country for at least 30 years (or recognized internationally for at least 60 years) with a number of benefits formerly reserved for the Catholic Church, such as tax exemptions, legal recognition of marriage and other rites, chaplain visits to prisons and hospitals, and respect for traditional holidays. Academic freedom is respected.

There is freedom of assembly, and citizens can participate in demonstrations and open public discussion. National and international NGOs, including human rights groups, operated in the country without government interference. However, according to the 2004 U.S. State Department report on human rights practices, many complained of slow investigations or remedial action by the state. Workers have the right to organize, bargain collectively, and strike for any reason, including political ones. For the second time in two years, public sector workers went on strike in January to protest a government austerity plan, which has involved a wage freeze for public sector workers. According to the BBC, the government defended the austerity plan as needed to achieve "public discipline."

The constitution provides for an independent court system. However, there is a considerable backlog of pending trials as a result of general inefficiency and a number of vacancies in the judicial system. A number of concerns were raised during the Casa Pia pedophilia scandal about the leaking of information about the case by the prosecution to the public.

Human rights groups have expressed concern about the number of human rights abuses in the country, including unlawful police shootings, deaths in police custody, and poor prison conditions that amount to cruel, inhuman, and degrading treatment. A Justice Ministry report released during the year cited a number of problems in the country's prison system, including overcrowding, poor sanitary conditions, and high rates of HIV/AIDS among prisoners. The prison population—as a percentage of the total population—is over the EU average. Citing problems of overcrowding and unsanitary conditions, a 2004 report by the country's Justice Ministry argued that Portuguese prisons are the "worst" in the European Union (EU).

The constitution guarantees equal treatment under the law and nondiscrimination. The government has taken a number of steps in the past few years to combat racism, including passing antidiscrimination laws and launching initiatives that seek to promote the integration of immigrants and Roma (Gypsies) into Portuguese society. However, there have been few prosecutions in cases involving racial or religious discrimination or the use of excessive force by the police toward immigrants and Roma.

The country is a destination and transit point for trafficked persons, particularly women from Eastern Europe and former Portuguese colonies in South America and Africa. In 2000, a law was introduced that makes domestic violence a public crime and obliges the police to follow through on reports. Abortion is illegal, unless under exceptional circumstances, such as when the mother's life is at risk. In August, the government refused a Dutch "abortion ship" to enter the country's territorial waters. The ship's crew allegedly intended to hand out pills that induce abortion to Portuguese women who wanted them once it returned to international waters and was under Dutch laws. Women hold about 19 percent of the 230 seats in the legislature.

Qatar

Population: 700,000
GNI/capita: $20,701
Life Expectancy: 72
Religious Groups: Muslim (95 percent), other (5 percent)
Ethnic Groups: Arab (40 percent), Pakistani (18 percent),
Indian (18 percent), Iranian (10 percent), other (14 percent)
Capital: Doha

Political Rights: 6
Civil Liberties: 5*
Status: Not Free

Ratings Change: Qatar's civil liberties rating improved from 6 to 5 due to modest improvements in academic freedom and women's rights.

Ten-Year Ratings Timeline (Political Rights, Civil Liberties, Status)

1995	1996	1997	1998	1999	2000	2001	2002	2003	2004
7,6NF	7,6NF	7,6NF	7,6NF	6,6NF	6,6NF	6,6NF	6,6NF	6,6NF	6,5NF

Overview:

Political reform moved at an unhurried pace with limited advances in 2004. Qatar promulgated its first written constitution in June 2004, more than one year after it was approved by the vast majority of the 71,406 Qataris who voted in an April 2003 referendum. The new constitution sets the stage for elections to a new parliament, tentatively scheduled for 2005.

For the first half of the nineteenth century, the Al Khalifa family of Bahrain dominated the territory now known as Qatar. The Ottoman Empire occupied Qatar from 1872 until World War I, when the United Kingdom recognized Sheikh Abdullah bin Jassim Al Thani as the ruler of Qatar and Sheikh Abdullah signed a series of treaties of friendship and commerce with the United Kingdom. After World War II, Qatar rapidly developed its oil production industry, and the oil wealth contributed to economic and social development in the country.

Qatar became formally independent in 1971. From 1971 to 1995, Emir Khalifa bin Hamad Al Thani ruled as an absolute monarch, with few government institutions checking his authority. In 1995, the emir was deposed by his son Hamad, who began a program to introduce gradual political, social, and economic reforms. Hamad dissolved the Information Ministry shortly after taking power, an action designed to demonstrate his commitment to expanding press freedom.

In 1996, Hamad permitted the creation of Al-Jazeera, which has become one of the most popular Arabic language satellite television channels. Al-Jazeera, however, generally does not cover Qatari politics and focuses instead on regional issues such as the situation in Iraq and the Arab-Israeli conflict. In the past few years, Sheikh Hamad accelerated a program to build Qatar's educational institutions, attracting foreign universities to establish branches in Qatar; Cornell Medical School opened a branch in Doha in 2002. In 1999, Qatar held elections for a 29-member municipal council and became the first state of the Gulf Cooperation Council (GCC) to introduce universal suffrage.

In 2002, a 38-member committee appointed by Hamad presented a draft constitution, which was refined and presented to the public in a referendum in April 2003.

This new constitution, which was approved by almost 97 percent of voters, slightly broadens the scope of political participation without eliminating the monopoly on power enjoyed by the Al Thani family. Most rights in the new constitution do not apply to the majority of people living in Qatar—noncitizen residents.

Though political reform moved ahead slightly and slowly in 2004, Qatar took steps to ostensibly demonstrate outward signs of openness to reform by hosting numerous regional conferences throughout the year, including training for women from the Arab world planning to run for political office, a regional conference on incorporating human rights into education curriculums, and a conference on human rights and Islam.

Political Rights and Civil Liberties:

Qataris do not have the power to change the top leadership in their government democratically. They possess only limited power to elect local government representatives with limited powers over local services. These representatives report to the minister of municipal affairs and agriculture, who is appointed by the emir. The head of state is the emir—currently Khalifa bin Hamad Al Thani—and the Al Thani family has a monopoly on political power in Qatar. The emir appoints a prime minister and the cabinet. The constitution states that the emir appoints an heir after consulting with the royal family and other notables. A new constitution, ratified by public referendum in 2003 and promulgated by the emir in 2004, provides for elections to 30 of the 45 seats in a new advisory council, and the government announced tentative plans to hold these elections in 2005. The government does not permit the existence of political parties.

Qatar was ranked 38 out of 146 countries surveyed in Transparency International's 2004 Corruption Perceptions Index. Critics allege a lack of transparency in government procurement, with few proper procedures in place to ensure fair competition for government contracts.

The new constitution guarantees freedom of expression, and the state has generally refrained from direct censorship. However, content in the print and broadcast media is influenced by leading families. The five leading daily newspapers are privately owned, but their owners and board members include royal family members and other notables. Although the satellite television channel Al-Jazeera is privately owned, the Qatari government has reportedly paid operating costs for the channel since its inception. Qataris have access to the Internet through a telecommunications monopoly that has recently been privatized, but the government censors content and blocks access to certain sites deemed pornographic or politically sensitive.

Islam is Qatar's official religion; however, the new constitution explicitly provides for freedom of worship. The Ministry of Islamic Affairs regulates clerical affairs and the construction of mosques. Converting to another religion from Islam is considered apostasy and is a capital offense, but there have been no reports of executions for apostasy. The new constitution provides for freedom of opinion and research, but scholars often practice self-censorship on politically sensitive topics.

The constitution provides for freedom of assembly and the right to form organizations, but these rights are limited in practice. Public protests and demonstrations are rare, with the government placing strict limits on the public's ability to organize demonstrations. All nongovernmental organizations need state permission to operate, and the government closely monitors the activities of these groups. There are no independent human rights organizations, but a National Committee for Human Rights (NCHR), consisting of members of civil society and government ministries, has done some work on investigating allegations of human rights abuses. The NCHR has a human rights hotline and presents regular reports to the government cabinet on the human rights situation.

The law prohibits labor unions, but allows joint consultative committees of employers and workers to deal with disputes. Foreign national workers, who make up most of the workforce in Qatar, face severe disadvantages in labor contract cases. Although foreign laborers have limited legal rights to appear before the same courts as Qatari citizens, fear of job loss and deportation prevents many workers from exercising even these limited rights.

Despite constitutional guarantees, the judiciary is not independent in practice. The majority of Qatar's judges are foreign nationals who are appointed and removed by the emir. The judicial system consists of two sets of courts that became unified under a Higher Judicial Council in 1997: Sharia (Islamic law) courts, which have jurisdiction over a narrow range of issues, such as family law; and civil law courts, which have jurisdiction over commercial and civil suits. These two sets of courts have been united under the Supreme Judiciary Council.

The constitution protects individuals from arbitrary arrest and detention and bans torture. Defendants are entitled to legal representation. There are no reports of widespread violations of human rights in Qatar. Prisons meet international standards, and the police generally follow proper procedures set in accordance with the law.

The government discriminated against noncitizen foreign nationals in education, housing, health care, and other services offered free of charge to citizens.

The new constitution treats women as full and equal persons. Article 35 of the constitution bans discrimination based on sex, country of origin, language, or religion. Despite legal guarantees of equality, women continue to face societal gender discrimination, and few legal mechanisms are available for women to contest instances of discrimination. Sharia law gives preference to men over women on a range of issues related to family law, including divorce, custody of children, and inheritance. Qatari women must receive permission from male guardians to obtain driver's licenses, and men sometimes prevent female relatives from traveling alone. Women have the right to participate in elections and run for office. In the April 2003 municipal elections, Sheikha Yousef Hassan al-Jufairi became the first woman elected to public office.

Romania

Population: 21,700,000   **Political Rights:** 3*
GNI/capita: $1,870   **Civil Liberties:** 2
Life Expectancy: 71   **Status:** Free
Religious Groups: Eastern Orthodox [including all
sub-denominations] (87 percent), Protestant
(6.8 percent), Catholic (5.6 percent), other (0.6 percent)
Ethnic Groups: Romanian (90 percent), Hungarian (7 percent),
Roma (2 percent), other (1 percent)
Capital: Bucharest
Ratings Change: Romania's political rights rating declined from 2 to 3 due to flaws
in the first round of the presidential and parliamentary election process.

Ten-Year Ratings Timeline (Political Rights, Civil Liberties, Status)

1995	1996	1997	1998	1999	2000	2001	2002	2003	2004
4,3PF	2,3F	2,2F	2,2F	2,2F	2,2F	2,2F	2,2F	2,2F	3,2F

Overview: Romania held parliamentary elections in November 2004.
Despite allegations of fraud, the results were accepted by
the electoral bureau. The first round of presidential elec-
tions were held as well; a runoff was scheduled for December between Prime Minister Adrian Nastase and opposition candidate Traian Basescu.

Throughout the latter half of the Cold War, Romania was ruled by Nicolae
Ceaucescu, one of Eastern Europe's most repressive dictators, with virtually no
opposition. In late 1989, popular dissatisfaction with Ceaucescu's rule led to his
overthrow and execution by disgruntled Communists. A provisional government
was formed under Ion Iliescu, a high-ranking Communist and the leader of the National Salvation Front (NSF). The 1992 parliamentary elections saw the NSF split
into neo-Communist and reformist factions. In November 1996, Emil Constantinescu
of the Democratic Convention of Romania (CDR) defeated Iliescu in presidential elections. However, the CDR too was prone to considerable instability and lack of unity.

In the November 2000 parliamentary elections, the former Communist Party, renamed the Party of Social Democracy (PSD), won 65 of the 140 seats in the Senate
(the upper house of parliament) and 155 of the 327 seats in the Chamber of Deputies
(the lower house). A surprising development in these elections, however, was the
extent of support for the nationalist Greater Romania Party (PRM) led by Vadim Tudor, which gained 37 seats in the upper house and 84 seats in the lower house; Tudor
himself came in second in the 2000 presidential elections. The remaining seats in
parliament were won by smaller parties. Since 2000, Nastase of the PSD served as
prime minister. Romania's 2000 presidential elections brought Iliescu back to power.
Romania's 2004 general elections were held on November 28 for both president and
parliament. While the elections were generally accepted as fair, they were plagued
by allegations of fraud and other irregularities. Final results had not been announced
by November 30. A runoff for the presidency was scheduled for December 2004.
Notably, the PRM appeared to have lost many seats in both houses.

Romania applied to join the European Union (EU) in 1995. Negotiations, which began in 2000, were due to be completed by the end of 2004. An encouraging report from the EU reiterated Romania's projected accession date of 2007 and for the first time designated Romania as a "functioning market economy." Nevertheless, the report also expressed many concerns, including over judicial and media independence; corruption; and police brutality. The EU may agree to conclude negotiations officially once Romania has laws and programs in place to address the worst failings, while following the country closely to ensure progress after negotiations are complete.

In 2004, Romania's policy on international adoptions became headline news. Romania had imposed a ban on international adoptions of Romanian children in 2001 after pressure from the EU, which was concerned about corruption and trafficking and has linked the issue to Romania's EU membership. Since then, the United States, which had been the recipient of many of the children, has lobbied for an end to the ban. At the beginning of 2004, Romania broke the moratorium and allowed 105 children to be adopted in Italy. However in June, with help from EU advisers, the Romanian parliament passed a law that severely restricts international adoptions.

Political Rights and Civil Liberties:

Romanians can change their government democratically. Elections since 1991 have been considered generally free and fair by international observers. According to international monitoring groups, election laws provide an adequate basis for democratic elections. The president is directly elected, but he does not have substantial powers beyond foreign policy. He appoints the prime minister, who remains the most powerful politician. The members of the bicameral parliament are elected for four-year terms.

Romania has four major political parties: the PSD, the Democratic Alliance of Hungarians in Romania (DAHR); the populist-nationalist PRM; and the new Truth and Justice Alliance (DA) of Centrist Democratic and Liberal Parties. A 5 percent electoral threshold favors big parties. The president is not permitted to be a member of a political party. Bureaucrats and businessmen who profited from the post-Communist privatization continue to wield power.

General elections for both president and parliament took place on November 28. The main opposition presidential candidate dropped out of the race suddenly in October, officially for health reasons, resulting in a hasty replacement by Traian Basescu of the DA. He ran against Prime Minister Adrian Nastase and 10 other official candidates from smaller parties. The elections were deemed democratic by Organization for Security and Cooperation in Europe observers, although some procedural concerns were raised. Control over the number of times each voter cast a ballot was weak, and the opposition accused the PSD of busing supporters to various poll locations to vote multiple times. Media coverage was seen as biased toward the ruling party. However, the election bureau rejected opposition calls for annulment of the results due to fraud. The presidential race was Romania's closest since 1989, with rural voters generally supporting the PSD and urban voters favoring the DA. As of November 30, the opposition alliance was expected to more than double its representation in parliament. Basescu and Nastase were scheduled to face each other in a runoff for the presidency on December 12.

The 1991 constitution provides for a seat to be allotted to each national minority that passes a special threshold lower than the 5 percent otherwise needed to enter parliament. The number of these seats varies according to the number of eligible minorities, thus changing the total number of seats in the Chamber of Deputies. In the 2004 elections, 18 such seats were allotted.

In February, the Hungarian Civic Union broke off from the DAHR on a platform of advocating for territorial and administrative autonomy for Transylvania's Hungarian minority, which makes up less than half of Romania's Hungarians. However, the Central Election Commission refused the union's registration for both the June local elections and November general elections. In June, a bill that would grant the group autonomy was rejected by parliament.

Despite anticorruption legislation passed in 2003 that has been condoned by the EU, corruption remains a serious problem in Romania. The PSD announced a new zero-tolerance policy on corruption in March 2004 that will include training programs in schools and for public officials. Some officials have been arrested on corruption charges, but some were acquitted. In the case of the mayor of Bucharest and 79 other senior officials, some observers suspect political motivation behind the August corruption charges against them. In general, Romania continues to be criticized for passing laws and making mid-level arrests with no genuine progress. Romania was ranked 87 out of 146 countries surveyed in Transparency International's 2004 Corruption Perceptions Index.

In April, the government amended the 2003 corruption laws, which already required public officials to declare their assets, and extended the requirement to those running for major office. Transparency and accountability measures are in place, but the laws are often ignored or circumvented. A scandal broke in early 2004 when the EU criticized the Romanian government's award of a $2.5 billion highway contract to an American company without a prior open tender. The United States and Romania defended the award on the grounds that the company was the most qualified.

The 1991 constitution enshrines freedom of expression and the press, and the media are characterized by considerable pluralism. However, there have been increasing concerns about the state of press freedom. The government controls the largest funding sources, and state-owned companies favor pro-government media with valuable advertising revenue. Self-censorship is common and reportedly increased as the 2004 elections approached. Prime-time broadcasts are basically devoid of criticism of the government and were accused of favoring the ruling party in election coverage. Moreover, a debate flared in the fall as journalists accused the foreign owners of newspapers *Evenimentul Zilei* and *Romania Libera* of pushing pro-government editorial content and a focus on uncontroversial subjects instead of political news; the owners denied any such policy. Violence against journalists reportedly increased in 2004. For example, in September two journalists were assaulted by company bodyguards while photographing the headquarters of oil consortium VGB from public property; police did nothing to intervene except to advise the journalists to leave the premises. On a more positive note, in June, an amendment to the penal code was passed making libel punishable by fines instead of imprisonment.

Religious freedom is generally respected, although "nontraditional" religious organizations sometimes encounter difficulties in registering with the state secretary of religions. Lack of registration denies adherents the right to exercise freely their religious beliefs and prevents them from building places of worship and cemeteries. The government formally recognizes 17 religions in the country, each of which is eligible for some level of state support for such activities as the building of houses of worship and salaries for the clergy. The government does not restrict academic freedom.

The constitution provides for freedom of assembly, and the government respects this right in practice. In general, the government does not place restrictions on the work of nongovernmental organizations (NGOs), which usually find government officials to be cooperative. Workers' rights to form unions and to strike are fairly well protected, although in practice workers have some difficultly forming independent unions.

As part of the reform process for EU membership, constitutional changes have aimed to make the judiciary independent of the government. However, executive institutions still exercise undue control over the judicial system, and the EU has severely criticized Romania for its lack of judicial independence. Public prosecutors are considered by many international observers to have excessive powers, although the ability of the prosecutor-general to appeal otherwise final court decisions was eliminated by an April change to the Penal Code. In June, the head of the country's highest court, who was close to the opposition, was pressured into retirement for what many consider to have been political reasons; his replacement is a personal friend of President Ion Iliescu.

Police have been accused of using excessive force and of occasionally beating detainees. Prisons are considered to be overcrowded, despite recent improvements. Amnesty International released a report in 2004 criticizing conditions in Romania's psychiatric hospitals, and some individuals have been denied a fair trial by being sent into psychiatric care. Children in particular are not adequately protected from police brutality. There have been charges that Roma are disproportionately targeted by law enforcement.

Romania has 18 recognized minorities, the largest being Hungarians and, far behind, Roma. Minorities have the right to use their native tongue in communicating with authorities in areas where they represent at least 20 percent of the population. Signs must also be written in minority languages, and local government decisions must be announced in those languages. Constitutional changes adopted in October 2003 allow ethnic minorities the right to use their native languages in court. Property rights are respected, although the ability of citizens to start businesses continues to be encumbered by red tape, corruption, and organized crime. Romania has lost at the European Court of Human Rights in attempts to keep nationalized property.

The constitution guarantees women equal rights with men, but gender discrimination remains widespread. Women were expected to hold about 10 percent of the seats in the new parliament. Trafficking in women and girls for purposes of forced prostitution has become a major problem. Parliament passed a law in 2001 outlawing trafficking in human beings, and the country is involved in an extensive public education effort to warn people about the dangers of trafficking.

Russia

Population: 144,100,000
GNI/capita: $2,130
Life Expectancy: 65
Religious Groups: Russian Orthodox, Muslim, other
Ethnic Groups: Russian (82 percent), Tatar (4 percent),
Ukrainian (3 percent), other (11 percent)
Capital: Moscow

Political Rights: 6*
Civil Liberties: 5
Status: Not Free

Ratings Change: Russia's political rights rating declined from 5 to 6, and its status from Partly Free to Not Free, due to the virtual elimination of influential political opposition parties within the country and the further concentration of executive power.

Ten-Year Ratings Timeline (Political Rights, Civil Liberties, Status)

1995	1996	1997	1998	1999	2000	2001	2002	2003	2004
3,4PF	3,4PF	3,4PF	4,4PF	4,5PF	5,5PF	5,5PF	5,5PF	5,5PF	6,5NF

Overview:

During 2004, President Vladimir Putin took further steps toward the consolidation of executive authority by increasing pressure on opposition political parties and civil society, strengthening state control over national broadcast media, and pursuing politically driven prosecutions of independent business leaders and academics. The government also announced constitutional changes that will make governors appointed rather than elected officials, and Putin advanced plans to take over direct control of the hiring and dismissal of judges. In the March 2004 presidential election, Putin easily defeated his closest challenger with more than 70 percent of the vote.

With the collapse of the Soviet Union in December 1991, the Russian Federation reemerged as an independent state under the leadership of Boris Yeltsin. In 1993, Yeltsin put down an attempted coup by hard-liners in parliament, and a new constitution creating a bicameral national legislature, the Federal Assembly, was approved. The December 1995 parliamentary elections, in which 43 parties competed, saw strong support for Communists and ultranationalist forces. In the 1996 presidential poll, Yeltsin easily defeated Communist Gennady Zyuganov. The August 1998 collapse of the ruble and Russia's financial markets ushered in a new government that returned to greater state spending and economic control. One year later, Putin, then the head of the Federal Security Service, was named prime minister.

Conflict with the separatist region of Chechnya, which included a brutal two-year war, from 1994 to 1996, was reignited in 1999. After a Chechen rebel attack on the neighboring republic of Dagestan in August and deadly apartment house bombings in several Russian cities blamed by the Kremlin on Chechen militants, Russia responded with an attack on the breakaway region. The second Chechen war dramatically increased Putin's popularity, and after the December 1999 elections to the Duma (lower house of parliament), pro-government forces were able to shape a majority coalition.

An ailing Yeltsin—who was constitutionally barred from a third presidential term—resigned on December 31, 1999. Yeltsin turned over power to Putin, who, in the March 2000 presidential election, secured a 53 percent first-round victory over Communist leader Zyuganov, who received 29 percent. After taking office, Putin moved to consolidate his power, including implementing legislation removing Russia's 89 governors from positions in the upper house of parliament (the Federation Council) and allowing the president to suspend them from office if they violated federal law. Putin also created seven new "super regions" headed by Kremlin appointees and introduced personnel changes that have considerably altered the composition of the ruling elite through the influx of personnel from the security and military services; they now represent more than 25 percent of the country's ministers, deputy ministers, legislators, governors, and "super governors." Putin also challenged the political clout of some economic magnates—through criminal investigations and legal proceedings claimed to be part of an anticorruption campaign, but which critics say are selective political persecutions.

The December 2003 Duma election was marred by extensive bias in media coverage. In the run up to the vote, opposition political parties widely criticized the distorted and unbalanced coverage of their campaigns and the limits placed on their ability to reach voters through the airwaves. Questions of vote manipulation were raised when two liberal opposition parties fell just short of the 5 percent threshold required for representation, despite exit polls that showed they had surpassed it. The Kremlin-controlled Unity Party captured 306 of the Duma's 450 seats.

With the national broadcast media and most print media uniformly favorable to incumbent President Putin, no challenger was able to mount a respectable challenge in the March 2004 presidential election. Putin, who refused to take part in debates with his challengers, received 71.4 percent of the vote to 13.7 for his closest rival, Communist Nikolai Kharitonov, in a first-round victory; voter turnout was 64.3 percent.

Strife in Chechnya continued throughout the year, with Russian counterinsurgency operations and guerrilla warfare, assassinations, and acts of terrorism by Chechen rebels inside and outside Russian territory. At the same time, the Russian-backed Chechen government, abetted by Russian Federation forces, engaged in widespread acts of brutality, including abductions, the killing of suspected Chechen separatists, and the intimidation of organizations not fully under the control of the Moscow-backed local authorities.

In August, there were major terrorist incidents involving "black widows," female suicide bombers from Chechnya; these terrorists were responsible for explosions at a Moscow metro station and for the destruction of two civilian passenger airplanes. The following month, in the town of Beslan in North Ossetia (an area that adjoins Chechnya), extremist fighters took over a school and held more than a thousand schoolchildren, teachers, and parents hostage. The occupation resulted in the deaths of hundreds, mostly children.

Using the Beslan tragedy as a pretext, Putin publicly put forward a plan, already long discussed in the upper reaches of government, to further centralize control over Russia's oblasts (regions) and affect the hiring and dismissal of judges. Proposed constitutional reforms will make the post of governor appointed by the president rather than elected. In the face of Putin's growing power, most governors publicly endorsed the curtailment of their autonomy despite well-known private unhappiness with the plan. The Duma, where Putin's Unity Party commands more than a two-thirds constitutional majority, is expected to vote in favor of these changes that reduce public voice.

The year saw the ongoing trial of billionaire oil magnate Mikhail Khodorkovsky and several of his key corporate associates on charges of tax evasion. Efforts were made to sell off and dismantle his Yukos energy company to meet huge tax assessments. The year was also marked by the government's support for the expansion of the economic power of the state-controlled Gazprom concern into a conglomerate with vast, varied interests including oil, gas, and media interests.

Russia continued its repressive campaign against scholars and academics throughout the year. In April, Igor Sutyagin, head of the Military-Technical and Military-Economic Policy subdivision of the Moscow-based Institute of U.S. and Canada Studies of the Russian Academy of Sciences, was sentenced to 15 years in prison on charges of passing state military secrets to British and U.S. intelligence. Sutyagin denied the charges, saying he made use only of declassified source materials in his research. Human rights groups widely condemned the sentence, asserting that it was based on spurious charges intended by the government to limit international cooperation among scholars. In November, physicist Valentin Danilov was sentenced to 14 years in a Siberian prison on charges of passing space secrets to China. Danilov had earlier been found innocent of the charges in a jury trial, but the Supreme Court had overturned the verdict and ordered a new trial in June 2004.

Political Rights and Civil Liberties:

Russians cannot change their government democratically, particularly in light of the state's far-reaching control of broadcast media and the growing harassment of opposition parties and their financial backers. In the parliamentary elections of December 2003, more than two-thirds of seats in the Duma were won by the Kremlin's Unity Party, while most of the remaining seats were captured by parties promoted by the Kremlin-controlled media. There was significant evidence that there had been an undercount in the vote for liberal opposition parties that kept them from attaining the 5 percent threshold required for parliamentary representation. The leader of the third largest legislative party, Motherland (Rodina), backed President Vladimir Putin in the March 2004 presidential race. The Liberal Democratic Party, the fourth largest group in the Duma, is an ultranationalist faction known for the long-standing ties of its leaders to intelligence circles. The Communists are the sole party in the legislature generally free of Kremlin influence. In the presidential election of March 2004, state dominance of the media was in full display, debate was absent, and Putin won a first-round victory with 71.4 percent of the vote, more than five times that of his closest rival.

The 1993 constitution established a strong presidency with the power to appoint, pending parliamentary confirmation, and dismiss the prime minister. The bicameral legislature consists of a lower chamber (the Duma) and an upper chamber (the Federation Council). The power of the president is likely to be strengthened in the coming months, when the president gains control over the appointment of regional governors, who until now have been elected officials.

Corruption throughout the government and business world is pervasive. Tough legislation to combat money laundering entered into force in 2002, leading the Financial Action Task Force of the Organization for Economic Cooperation and Development to remove Russia from its list of noncooperating countries. However, the ongoing trial of Yukos chairman Mikhail Khodorkovsky and his associates, as well as new tax assessments and pressures on other Russian magnates, coming on the heels of the persecution and prosecution of former media owners Vladimir Gusinsky and Boris Berezovsky, reaffirms the view held by many independent Russian analysts that Putin's anticorruption efforts are selectively applied and have often targeted critics and potential political adversaries. Russia was ranked 90 out of 145 countries surveyed in the 2004 Transparency International Corruption Perceptions Index.

Although the constitution provides for freedom of speech, the government continues to put pressure on the dwindling number of media outlets still critical of the Kremlin. Since June 2003, when the last independent national television network, TVS, was seized by the government, allegedly to settle the company's debts, all Russian national television networks have been controlled by the government or by economic interests that support the government and uniformly praise the president. The government routinely intimidates media outlets for unsanctioned reporting on issues related to terrorism and the war in Chechnya. While the independent Ekho Moskvy radio station airs a wide range of viewpoints, it is vulnerable because it is owned by the Kremlin-controlled Gazprom conglomerate.

Libel laws are used to intimidate independent media. In August 2004, Alfa Bank, a top financial institution owned by Roman Fridman—a magnate with strong Kremlin support—filed a lawsuit against the daily *Kommersant,* one of the country's few independent newspapers. The suit charged the newspaper with damage to the bank's reputation through its coverage of a summertime liquidity crisis. The suit demanded more than $11 million for libel in a move that the newspaper's owners believed was motivated by the government's vendetta against the newspaper, which is owned by exiled Russian businessman Boris Berezovsky and is sharply critical of Putin and the Kremlin's policies.

With print and broadcast media increasingly under government control, the Internet, where there is wider access to independent information, is used regularly by 4.2 percent of the population. This cohort of regular users is growing by 20 to 40 percent a year, according to a Russian Federation government report.

In the breakaway republic of Chechnya, the military continued to impose severe restrictions on Russian journalists' access to the war zone, issuing accreditation primarily to those of proven loyalty to the government.

Freedom of religion is respected unevenly in this predominantly Orthodox Christian country. A 1997 law on religion requires churches to prove that they have existed for at least 15 years before being permitted to register. As registration is necessary for a religious group to conduct many of its activities, new, independent congregations are consequently restricted in their functions. Regional authorities continue to harass nontraditional groups, with the Jehovah's Witnesses and Mormons among the frequent targets. In June 2004, Jehovah's Witnesses were banned from organized activity in Moscow. Foreign religious workers are often denied visas to return to Russia. In recent years, several Roman Catholic priests have been deported, barred from entry, or refused visa renewals.

Academic freedom is generally respected, although the academic system is marred by some corruption at the higher levels and by very low levels of pay for educators. The year's prosecutions of scientists and researchers on charges of treason created a chill in some research institutes, engendering a climate that is restrictive of international contacts.

The government provides some space for freedom of assembly and association. However, legislation passed in 2002 gives the authorities the right to suspend political parties or nongovernmental organizations (NGOs) whose members are accused of extremism. Critics argue that the law offers an excessively broad definition of extremism, giving the government great latitude to suppress legitimate opposition political activities. In his May 2004 state of the nation speech, Putin launched a stinging attack on NGOs that are "receiving funding from influential foreign foundations and serving dubious groups and commercial interests." In 2004, human rights groups were attacked on state-dominated media for working against Russia's interests, and the offices of some rights groups were raided. Officials called for a state investigation of the Committee of Soldiers' Mothers, one of the country's most respected rights organizations.

The nongovernmental sector is composed of thousands of diverse groups, with many of them dependent on funding from foreign sources. While there had earlier been trends among Russia's newly wealthy to support the NGO sector through charitable giving, the prosecution and repression of business magnates (including Mikhail Khodorkovsky, patron of the Open Russia charitable fund), who had earlier supported NGOs focused on democratic reform has had a chilling effect on such funding. In 2004, a series of nationwide commemorations of the terrorist attack in Beslan was organized nominally under the leadership of youth, civic, and labor groups, although in fact its slogans and agenda were determined by government officials.

While trade union rights are legally protected, they are limited in practice. Although strikes and worker protests occur, anti-union discrimination and reprisals for strikes are not uncommon, and employers often ignore collective bargaining rights. In a rapidly changing economy in transition from the former system of total state domination, unions have proved unable to establish a significant presence in much of the private sector. The largest labor federation works in close cooperation with the Kremlin and coordinated a mass rally in Moscow under the direct supervision of the authorities to protest terrorism after the Beslan tragedy.

The judiciary suffers from corruption, inadequate funding, and a lack of qualified personnel. After the judicial reforms of 2002, the government has made progress in implementing due process and holding timely trials. Since January 2003, Russia's reformed criminal procedure code has provided for jury trials throughout the country, but the legislature has voted to postpone introducing jury trials in certain areas by up to four years because of financial and technical difficulties. The new code also gives the right to issue arrest and search warrants to the courts instead of prosecutors, and it abolishes in absentia trials. After the Belsan attack, Putin declared his intention to establish full control over an office in the Supreme Court that supervises the hiring and removal of judges. Human Rights Watch called the proposal "another erosion of the independence of the judiciary."

Critics charge that Russia has failed to address ongoing problems, such as the widespread use of torture and ill-treatment by law enforcement officials to extract confessions, and that the courts will be unable or unwilling to handle their expanded duties. In June 2004, Vladimir Lukin, the legislature's human rights ombudsman, reported that police are guilty of widespread rights violations. "The most impermissible means of influence are used in temporary holding cells and police offices," Lukin charged. Among the "means" cited in his report were electric shock, choking, and severe beating.

While prisons suffer from overcrowding, inadequate medical attention, and poor sanitary conditions, authorities took steps in 2003 to reduce the prison population, including introducing alternative sentences to incarceration. The new criminal procedure code limits pretrial detention to six months and has reduced overcrowding in pretrial detention centers (known as SIZOs). In the spring of 2004, the penal system saw a wave of hunger strikes against what the rights ombudsman said was a system of prison guard "extortion...[of] food, money and valuables from prisoners and their families." Putin has disbanded the presidential pardons commission, which was viewed as a safeguard against the harsh penal system and had released about 60,000 inmates since its inception in 1991, and ordered the creation of commissions in each of the country's regions. Human rights groups are frequently denied access to prisoners.

Ethnic minorities, particularly those who appear to be from the Caucasus or Central Asia, are subject to governmental and societal discrimination and harassment. Racially motivated attacks by skinheads and other extremist groups occur occasionally. Fringe anti-Semitic and racist parties organize small public rallies, and periodicals with racist and anti-Semitic content are published but attract a small readership.

The government places some restrictions on freedom of movement and residence. All adults are legally required to carry internal passports while traveling, documents that they also need in order to obtain many government services. Some regional authorities impose residential registration rules that limit the right of citizens to choose their place of residence freely. Police reportedly demand bribes for processing registration applications and during spot checks for registration documents, and these demands often unfairly target the Caucasian and dark-skinned populations.

In recent years, property rights have been legally strengthened. A land code that established the legal framework for buying and selling nonagricultural land was adopted in late 2001. In June 2002, parliament passed a law allowing the sale of agricultural land to Russian citizens; such sales had been severely restricted since the 1917 Bolshevik Revolution. However, recent prosecutions of economic magnates that have criticized government policies and backed opposition politicians, coupled with large tax liens on select companies, have reinforced perceptions that property rights are being eroded and that the rule of law is subordinated to political considerations.

Widespread corruption remains a serious obstacle to an effective market economy and is an impediment to genuine equality of opportunity. According to a 2002 report by the Moscow-based INDEM Foundation, Russians spend an estimated $37 billion annually on bribes and kickbacks, ranging from small payments to traffic police to large kickbacks by companies to obtain lucrative state contracts. Members of the old Soviet elite have used insider information to gain control of key industrial and business enterprises.

Domestic violence remains a serious problem, while police are often reluctant to intervene in what they regard as internal family matters. Economic hardships contribute to widespread trafficking of women abroad for prostitution. There is credible evidence that women face considerable discrimination in the workplace, including lower pay than their male counterparts for performing similar work.

↓Rwanda

Population: 8,400,000 **Political Rights:** 6
GNI/capita: $230 **Civil Liberties:** 5
Life Expectancy: 40 **Status:** Not Free
Religious Groups: Roman Catholic (56.5 percent),
Protestant (26 percent), other (17.5 percent)
Ethnic Groups: Hutu (84 percent), Tutsi (15 percent),
Twa [Pygmy] (1 percent)
Capital: Kigali
Trend Arrow: Rwanda received a downward trend arrow due to government restrictions on the functioning of political and civil society.

Ten-Year Ratings Timeline (Political Rights, Civil Liberties, Status)

1995	1996	1997	1998	1999	2000	2001	2002	2003	2004
7,6NF	7,6NF	7,6NF	7,6NF	7,6NF	7,6NF	7,6NF	7,5NF	6,5NF	6,5NF

Overview: In 2004, the government of Rwanda continued to use the legacy of the 1994 genocide as grounds for limiting dialogue between Rwandans. It took several actions that had the effect of further constricting political space, including restricting nongovernmental organizations (NGOs). The leading opposition party remained inactive after threats to ban it. Steps were taken to reduce the backlog of legal cases resulting from the genocide.

Rwanda's ethnic divide is deeply rooted. National boundaries demarcated by Belgian colonists led to often violent competition for power within the fixed borders of a modern state. Traditional and Belgian-abetted Tutsi dominance ended with a Hutu rebellion in 1959 and independence in 1962. Hundreds of thousands of Tutsis were killed or fled the country in recurring violence during the next decades. In 1990, the Tutsi-dominated RPF (Rwandan Patriotic Front) launched a guerrilla war to force the Hutu regime, led by General Juvenal Habyarimana, to accept power sharing and the return of Tutsi refugees.

President Habyarimana and Burundian president Cyprien Ntaryamira were killed in a plane crash near Kigali in April 1994. While the perpetrators of this act have never been identified, many observers believe that Hutu extremists, angered by Habyrimana's negotiation with the RPF, committed the act. The Hutus' chauvinist solution to claims for land and power by Rwanda's Tutsi minority, which constituted approximately 15 percent of the population, was to pursue the complete elimination of the Tutsi people. The ensuing genocide was well plotted, with piles of imported machetes distributed and death lists broadcast by radio, but it did not stop the RPF from successfully taking over the country.

The Hutu-dominated army and militia, along with as many as two million Hutu refugees, fled into neighboring countries, especially the Democratic Republic of the Congo. International relief efforts that eased the suffering of these refugees also had the effect of allowing retraining and rearming of large numbers of the former army and militia forces. The United Nations, which had earlier ignored specific warnings of an impending genocide in 1994, failed to prevent such activities, and the RPF took direct action, overrunning the refugee camps in the Democratic Republic of Congo.

Nearly three million Rwandan refugees subsequently returned to Rwanda between 1996 and 1998. Security has improved considerably since 1997, although isolated killings and "disappearances" continue. The government, led by the RPF, closely directs the country's political life. In 2000, President Pasteur Bizimungu resigned and was replaced by Vice President Paul Kagame, who had already been the de facto leader of the country. A new prime minister, Bernard Makuza, was appointed.

Rwanda's extended postgenocide political transition period officially ended in 2003 with the holding of national elections. The RPF's preeminent position in Rwandan political life, combined with a short campaign period, the material advantages of incumbency, and the continuing effects of the genocide, which inhibit free expression of political will, ensured Kagame's victory and that of the RPF and its allies in August presidential and September parliamentary elections. The largest opposition party, the Hutu-based Democratic Republican Movement (MDR), was declared illegal by the authorities for allegedly sowing "divisionism," a code word for the fanning of ethnic hatred. In a sign of the extent of the RPF's influence, even the MDR parliamentary delegation voted to ban the party. A new constitution that officially permits political parties to exist, under certain conditions, was unveiled in 2003.

In early 2004 a parliamentary commission issued a report criticizing a number of NGOs with propagating "genocide ideology." Subsequently, under the threat of banning, these organizations significantly limited activities that involved criticism of the government and its policies. In June, Bizimungu, a Hutu who was the first president after the genocide, was sentenced to 15 years in prison on charges of inciting civil disobedience, creating a criminal gang, and embezzling state funds, although Amnesty International and other independent observers questioned the fairness of the trial. In July, the entire judiciary was fired, and the government appointed new magistrates. Many elected local officials have also been forced out of office on charges of incompetence and corruption.

Continued instability in the region, including tensions with neighboring Uganda, pose considerable challenges to the country's peaceful development and complicate efforts to improve the exercise of human rights and fundamental freedoms.

Political Rights and Civil Liberties:

Rwandans cannot change their government democratically. The 2003 presidential and parliamentary elections gave Rwandans a limited amount of political choice. The 2003 constitution includes provisions that give strong powers to the president, who has sole authority to appoint the prime minister and who can dissolve parliament. The constitution provides for a 26-member indirectly elected senate in addition to an 80-member directly elected lower house. Senators serve eight-year terms of office while members of the lower house serve maximum five-year terms.

The constitution officially permits political parties to exist, under certain conditions. Political parties closely identified with the 1994 massacres are banned, as are parties based on ethnicity or religion. The cabinet must consist of representatives from several different parties, and the largest party is not allowed to occupy more than half of the cabinet seats. The constitution also provides that the president, prime minister, and president of the lower house cannot all belong to the same party.

Hutus have some representation in the government, including Prime Minister Bernard Makuza, who was from the MDR prior to its banning.

The constitution restricts political campaigning at the grassroots level. Its emphasis on "national unity" as a priority and a provision outlawing the incitement of ethnic hatred could be interpreted to limit the legitimate exercise of political pluralism. The constitution also includes a "forum" of parties that is ostensibly designed to foster communication between parties, but which could also serve to control party actions.

The government has undertaken a number of anticorruption measures. Government institutions particularly focused on the corruption issue include the Office of the Ombudsman, the Auditor General, and the National Tender Board. Rwanda was not ranked by Transparency International in its 2004 Corruption Perceptions Index.

The media reflect the RPF's predominant role and are constrained by fear of reprisals. During the genocide, 50 journalists were murdered, while others broadcast incitements to slaughter. The 2004 Annual Report by Reporters Sans Frontieres, a Paris-based press watchdog group, concluded that press freedom is not assured in Rwanda, and the group's Third Annual Press Freedom Index ranked the country 113 out of 167 countries rated. Journalists interviewed for the report's section on Rwanda admitted that they censor their own writing and say that the authorities have made it clear that certain topics cannot be discussed. As a result, newspaper coverage is heavily pro-government. The broadcast media are government controlled, although a media bill passed in June 2002 paved the way for the licensing of private radio and TV stations. There are a growing number of newspapers in the country, and limited, although increasing, Internet access.

Religious freedom is generally respected in Rwanda. Clerics had been among both the victims and the perpetrators of the 1994 genocide. The fact that several Catholic clerics have been implicated in the genocide has complicated relations between the government and the Catholic Church. Academic freedom is generally respected.

Although the constitution codifies freedoms of association and assembly, in reality they are limited. For example, activities that the government defines as "divisive" are prohibited. In June, parliament accepted the recommendations of a parliamentary commission created to investigate the existence and spread of a "genocide ideology" in Rwanda. As a result, the parliament recommended that five NGOs and several religious groups be banned and also called for action against several international NGOs operating in Rwanda. These include groups such as CARE International and Norwegian People's Aid. International human rights organizations such as Human Rights Watch and Amnesty International expressed serious concern that these decisions were based on overly broad interpretations of the law, vague allegations, and insubstantial research. In September, the executive branch decided not to ban implicated organizations outright, but to refer cases to the court system for prosecution.

Constitutional provisions for labor rights include the right to form trade unions, engage in collective bargaining, and strike. There are 27 registered unions under two umbrella groups. The larger group is the Central Union of Rwandan Workers, which was closely controlled by the previous regime, but which now has relatively greater independence.

The near destruction of the legal system and the death or exile of most of the judiciary have dramatically impeded the government's ability to administer postgenocide justice. In July, 503 judges were fired in a reform intended to improve the performance of the judiciary. Constitutional and legal safeguards regarding arrest procedures and detention are unevenly applied.

About 120,000 genocide suspects are incarcerated in jails built for 10,000. To help address this problem, the traditional justice system of *gacaca* was reinstituted in 2002. In this system, local notables preside over community trials dealing with the less serious genocide offenses. Some observers have expressed concern about the potential for partiality or for the application of uneven or arbitrary standards. The process, which moved slowly in previous years, gained momentum in 2004 as thousands of gacaca courts began to formally try suspects.

The International Criminal Tribunal for Rwanda (ICTR) in Arusha, Tanzania, has taken several measures in an attempt to speed up its work. The tribunal, similar to that in The Hague dealing with those accused of genocide and crimes against humanity in the former Yugoslavia, is composed of international jurists. Relations between Rwanda and the court in Arusha have deteriorated in recent years, with Rwanda accusing the ICTR of incompetence and the court accusing Rwanda of refusing to cooperate in war crimes investigations involving its army. As of November 2004, the ICTR had rendered 20 guilty verdicts, with 20 suspects on trial and 23 suspects awaiting trial.

Despite legal protection for equal rights, there is ongoing de facto discrimination against women in a variety of areas. Economic and social dislocation has forced women to take on many new roles, especially in the countryside. Rwanda's parliament is composed of an unusually high percentage of women—49 percent.

St. Kitts and Nevis

Population: 50,000
GNI/capita: $6,880
Life Expectancy: 70
Religious Groups: Anglican, other Protestant, Roman Catholic
Ethnic Groups: Black (majority), British, Portuguese, and Lebanese
Capital: Basseterre

Political Rights: 1
Civil Liberties: 2
Status: Free

Ten-Year Ratings Timeline (Political Rights, Civil Liberties, Status)

1995	1996	1997	1998	1999	2000	2001	2002	2003	2004
1,2F	1,2F	1,2F	1,2F	1,2F	1,2F	1,2F	1,2F	1,2F	1,2F

Overview:

The most important development of 2004 was the continued impetus on the part of Nevis to secede from St. Kitts, after only 21 years of collective independence from the United Kingdom. National parliamentary elections in October returned Prime Minister Denzil Douglas to office for a third consecutive term.

European colonization of Nevis began in the seventeenth century with the arrival of English and French colonists. The English settled mostly on Nevis, while the French chose St. Kitts. Intermittent warfare led to changes in sovereignty, but the Treaty of Paris in 1783 awarded both islands to Britain. In 1967, together with Anguilla, they became a self-governing state in association with Great Britain; Anguilla seceded late that year and remains a British dependency. The Federation of St. Kitts and Nevis attained full independence on September 19, 1983. St. Kitts has 31,000 inhabitants on 68 square miles, while Nevis has a population of 10,000 and an area of roughly 58 square miles.

Going into the March 6, 2000, elections, Prime Minister Douglas was able to tout his government's efforts at promoting resort construction in St. Kitts, combating crime, and raising public employees' salaries. Critics of the St. Kitts and Nevis Labour Party (SKNLP) claimed that the country had accumulated $192 million in debt and that the government had failed to reinvigorate the islands' sugar economy. The SKNLP won a stronger parliamentary majority in elections, taking all 8 seats on St. Kitts, out of the 11-member National Assembly. Opposition leader Kennedy Simmonds's People's Action Movement (PAM), which had hoped to oust the SKNLP by winning 3 seats in St. Kitts and forming a coalition with the winners of seats in Nevis, instead lost its only seat on the island to the SKNLP, which had previously held 7 seats.

In 2002, the Financial Action Task Force removed the twin island federation from the list of jurisdictions that were uncooperative in the fight against money laundering and other financial crimes.

Prime Minister Douglas called early elections for October 25, 2004, and his SKNLP won 7 seats, while the opposition PAM took the remaining seat on St. Kitts. Douglas's call for early elections was seen as an (successful) effort to ensure that he and the SKNLP would serve a third consecutive term in office. On Nevis, the Concerned Citizens Movement (CCM), a major force behind Nevis's push for independence and led by the premier of the island's local assembly, Vance Amory, kept 2 seats, while the Nevis Reformation Party (NRP) held onto 1.

Momentum began to gather in mid-2003 for Nevis to secede from St. Kitts, a process that cast a shadow over the twentieth anniversary of independence from Great Britain, which was celebrated on September 19 of that year. Nevis Premier Vance Amory, whose party dominates the local assembly, declared he would move toward a referendum on independence following his party's success in the October 2004 national elections, in which it consolidated its hold on two of Nevis's three seats to the National Assembly. Nevis is accorded the constitutional right to secede if two-thirds of the elected legislators in its local assembly approve and two-thirds of Nevisian voters endorse secession in a referendum. Though a 1998 referendum on independence failed the required two-thirds majority, Nevisians continue to feel neglected. No Nevisian is a member of the governing cabinet, and the island is entitled to only 3 of 11 seats in the national legislature. There is little support for independence from the region or further afield.

Political Rights and Civil Liberties:

Citizens are able to change their government democratically. The 2004 elections were generally deemed free and fair. The St. Kitts and Nevis national government consists of the prime minister, the cabinet, and the National Assembly. Elected assembly members—

eight from St. Kitts and three from Nevis—serve five-year terms. Senators, not to exceed two-thirds of the elected members, are appointed—one by the leader of the parliamentary opposition for every two by the prime minister. Nevis also has a local assembly, composed of five elected and three appointed members, and pays for all of its own services except for those involving police and foreign relations. St. Kitts has no similar body. The country is a member of the Commonwealth with a governor-general appointed by the Queen of England.

Drug trafficking and money laundering have corrupted the political system. St. Kitts and Nevis was not surveyed in the 2004 Transparency International Corruption Perceptions Index.

Constitutional guarantees of free expression are generally respected. Television on St. Kitts is government owned, although managed by a Trinidadian company, and there are some government restrictions on opposition access to it. Prime Minister Denzil Douglas has kept pledges to privatize radio, with the selling off of the government radio station. There are eight radio stations and two daily newspapers on the island. In addition, each major political party publishes a weekly or fortnightly newspaper. Opposition publications freely criticize the government, and international media are available. There is free access to the Internet.

The free exercise of religion is constitutionally protected and academic freedom is generally honored.

The right to organize political parties, civic organizations, and labor unions is generally respected, as is the right of assembly. The main labor union, the St. Kitts Trades and Labour Union is associated with the ruling SKLP. The right to strike, while not specified by law, is recognized and generally respected in practice.

The judiciary is generally independent. The highest court is the West Indies Supreme Court in St. Lucia, which includes a court of appeals and a High Court. Under certain circumstances there is a right of appeal to the Privy Council in London. However, the traditionally strong rule of law has been tested by the increase in drug-related crime and corruption, and the intimidation of witnesses and jurors is a problem. The national prison is overcrowded, and conditions are abysmal. In July 1998, the government hanged a convicted murderer, ending a 13-year hiatus in executions and defying pressure from Britain and human rights groups to end the death penalty. The deportation of a number of felons from the United States under the U.S. Illegal Immigration Reform and Immigrant Responsibility Act of 1996 has contributed to local law enforcement agencies in the region feeling overwhelmed.

Reports suggest that the country's economic citizenship program, which allows for the purchase of passports through real estate investments with a minimum of $250,000 and a registration fee of $35,000, has facilitated the illegal immigration of persons from China and other countries into the United States and Canada.

Violence against women is a problem. The Domestic Violence Act of 2000 criminalizes domestic violence and provides penalties for abusers. The Department of Gender Affairs, a part of the Ministry for Social Development, Community, and Gender Affairs, has offered counseling for victims of abuse and conducted training on domestic and gender violence. There are no laws for sexual harassment.

St. Lucia

Population: 200,000
GNI/capita: $4,050
Life Expectancy: 72
Religious Groups: Roman Catholic (90 percent),
Protestant (7 percent), Anglican (3 percent)
Ethnic Groups: Black African (90 percent), mulatto (6
percent), East Indian (3 percent), white (1 percent)
Capital: Castries

Political Rights: 1
Civil Liberties: 2
Status: Free

Ten-Year Ratings Timeline (Political Rights, Civil Liberties, Status)

1995	1996	1997	1998	1999	2000	2001	2002	2003	2004
1,2F	1,2F	1,2F	1,2F	1,2F	1,2F	1,2F	1,2F	1,2F	1,2F

Overview:

After expressing strong opposition to a new law allowing abortions in certain cases, a measure supported by much of St. Lucia's younger population, the country's Gender Relations Minister was dismissed in early 2004.

St. Lucia, a member of the British Commonwealth, achieved independence in 1979. In May 1997, Kenny Anthony led the St. Lucia Labour Party (SLP) to victory in legislative elections. On taking office, Anthony began to address concerns of an electorate weary of economic distress and reports of official corruption. In 1999, his government faced a series of issues concerning the hotel and airline industries, both vital for the tourism industry. In 2000, Anthony and the SLP gave their approval for regulated casino gambling, brushing aside objections from religious groups and the United Workers Party, to seemingly focus even more of their energies on revitalizing the country's tourism trade.

In June 2001, Anthony announced a two-month crackdown on crime, including increased police patrols and heavy penalties for gun crimes. He maintained that these measures were necessary to combat a wave of murders and armed robberies that he blamed, in part, on a U.S. policy of deporting hardened criminals to the island.

The SLP swept to victory in the December 3, 2001, general elections, winning 14 of 17 seats in parliament, just short of the 16-1 majority it had achieved in 1997. However, in an election called six months ahead of schedule, constituencies dominated by banana farmers registered their discontent with Anthony's party, reflecting a measure of popular dissatisfaction with his efforts to keep the island's ailing banana industry afloat. The farmers were unhappy that the Anthony administration had not made efforts to reduce high production costs that made St. Lucian exports uncompetitive. Nevertheless, Anthony was the only party leader to survive the election. Although her United Workers Party (UWP) won the other 3 seats, Morella Joseph—the first woman to lead a party into a general election—lost her seat, and National Alliance leader George Odlum and former UWP Prime Minister Vaughan Lewis failed in their efforts to be elected.

In November 2003, the government and opposition announced the establishment of a Constitution Review Commission to examine St. Lucia's constitution as it relates to issues of law and order. The level of violence had increased noticeably, with police blaming much of the violence on drug-related gangs. The United States named St. Lucia as a principal transit point in the eastern Caribbean for South American cocaine. Local authorities are also troubled over the increasing number of travelers coming through the island with fraudulent passports.

A revised version of the Criminal Code's Clause 166, passed by parliament in February 2004, allows for abortion in a number of restricted cases, including rape or incest. The country is 90 percent Roman Catholic, and there has been some backlash against this provision at home and abroad. In January 2004, Gender Relations Minister Sarah Flood-Beaubrun was dismissed after expressing vocal opposition to the measure. Groups abroad have called for the censure of major St. Lucia government leaders by the Vatican and the recanting of honors bestowed on them, as well as the excommunication of the governor-general of the country, Calliopa Pearlette Louisy. Nonetheless, there is wide support for the measure among St. Lucia's younger population.

Political Rights and Civil Liberties: Citizens are able to change their government democratically. The 2001 legislative elections were considered free and fair, although fewer than 50 percent of those eligible actually voted; 60 percent of registered voters had turned out in 1997. A governor general represents the British monarchy. Under the 1979 constitution, a bicameral parliament consists of the 17-member House of Assembly, elected for five years, and an 11-member Senate. Six members of the Senate are appointed by the prime minister, three by the leader of the parliamentary opposition, and two in consultation with civic and religious organizations. The island is divided into eight regions; each with its own elected council and administrative services.

Two parties, the SLP, in power since 1997, and the UWP, the official opposition dominate politics, parties are free to organize.

There have been allegations of corrupt activities on the part of government officials. Concerns over accountability in government were underscored in 2004 when allegations surfaced over a suspicious transfer of government property in New York. St. Lucia was not surveyed in the 2004 Transparency International Corruption Perceptions Index.

The media carry a wide spectrum of views and are largely independent of the government. There are five privately owned newspapers, two privately held radio stations, and one partially government-funded radio station, as well as two privately owned television stations. There is free access to the Internet.

Constitutional guarantees of the free exercise of religion are respected. Academic freedom is generally honored. In August, the government proposed a credit facility to provide resources for students wishing to pursue higher education at home and abroad.

Constitutional guarantees regarding the right to organize political parties, civic groups, and labor unions and to assemble freely are generally respected. Civic groups are well organized and politically active, as are labor unions, which represent the majority of wage earners.

The judicial system is independent and includes a High Court under the West Indies Supreme Court (based in St. Lucia), with ultimate appeal under certain circumstances to the Privy Council in London. In July 2003, a treaty replacing the Privy Council with a Caribbean Court of Justice (CCJ), to be based in Trinidad and Tobago, was approved by St. Lucia. In November of that year, parliament passed the Caribbean Court of Justice 2003 agreement, with St. Lucia pledging to contribute $2.5 million towards the establishment of the regional court. The CCJ is to have an appellate function and will also interpret the Caribbean Community (Caricom) Treaty.

Traditionally, citizens have enjoyed a high degree of personal security, although there are episodic reports of police misuse of force. In recent years, an escalating crime wave—including drug-related offenses, violent clashes during banana farmers' strikes, and increased violence in schools—has created concern among citizens. Over the last five years the murder rate has more than doubled from 14 in 1998 to 33 each for 2002 and 2003; there were 37 homicides in 2004. The island's nineteenth century prison, built to house a maximum of 80 inmates, houses close to 500. In late 2002, the government finished construction of a new, $17 million prison facility on the eastern part of the island.

Though there are no official barriers to their participation, women are underrepresented in politics and the professions. A growing awareness of the seriousness of violence against women has led the government and advocacy groups to take steps to offer better protection for victims of domestic violence.

St. Vincent and the Grenadines

Population: 100,000   **Political Rights:** 2
GNI/capita: $3,300   **Civil Liberties:** 1
Life Expectancy: 72   **Status:** Free
Religious Groups: Anglican (47 percent), Methodist (28 percent), Roman Catholic (13 percent), other [including Hindu, Seventh-Day Adventist, other Protestant] (12 percent)
Ethnic Groups: Black (66 percent), other [including mulatto, East Indian, and white] (34 percent)
Capital: Kingstown

Ten-Year Ratings Timeline (Political Rights, Civil Liberties, Status)

1995	1996	1997	1998	1999	2000	2001	2002	2003	2004
2,1F	2,1F	2,1F	2,1F	2,1F	2,1F	2,1F	2,1F	2,1F	2,1F

Overview:
The second reading for a new constitution for St. Vincent and the Grenadines was held in late 2004. Meanwhile, the political opposition maintained an effective campaign against the government and its policies throughout the year.

St. Vincent and the Grenadines achieved independence in 1979, with jurisdiction over the northern Grenadine islets of Bequia, Canouan, Mayreau, Mustique, Prune Island, Petit St. Vincent, and Union Island. The country is a member of the Commonwealth, with the British monarchy represented by a governor-general.

In the March 2001 elections, the social-democratic United Labour Party (ULP) captured 12 of the 15 contested parliamentary seats and Ralph Gonsalves became prime minister. The incumbent conservative New Democratic Party (NDP) won only 3 seats. International observers monitored the election, which had been preceded by serious political unrest and popular mobilization, for the first time in the country's history.

In 2001, Gonsalves, a one-time radical opposition figure, led a successful initiative to save the financially ailing Organization of Eastern Caribbean States by relieving it of some administrative requirements now carried out by its individual members. After a controversial trip to Libya, also in 2001, Gonsalves was criticized for not revealing publicly that the Arab nation had promised to buy all the bananas that the Caribbean could produce.

In June 2003, the Paris-based Financial Action Task Force (FATF) removed St. Vincent and the Grenadines from its list of jurisdictions deemed noncooperative in the fight against money laundering. This move was regarded as a major victory by the government of Prime Minister Gonsalves. In the same month, the U.S. Coast Guard detained eight ships when it discovered that several officers had licenses that were improperly issued by St. Vincent and the Grenadines.

In October 2004, the second reading of a proposed new constitution for the country was held, one week after the Constitutional Review Commission (CRC) launched a new informational publication on the issue. Throughout the year, the opposition NDP, led by Arnhim Eustace, staged an effective publicity-based campaign against the prime minister's government and policies, culminating in a November 3 candlelight march. The protests were a response to perceived mismanagement and corruption by the Gonsalves administration.

The periodic destruction caused by tropical weather has further burdened the island's troubled economy and made efforts of diversification more difficult. Crime continues to discourage tourism, which had begun a slow recovery from the September 11, 2001, attacks in the United States.

Political Rights and Civil Liberties: Citizens can change their government democratically. The constitution provides for representatives to the 15-member unicameral House of Assembly to be elected for five years. In addition, six senators are appointed—four by the government and two by the opposition. The March 2001 election was considered free and fair by international observers.

There have been allegations of drug-related corruption within the government and the police force, and of money laundering through St. Vincent banks. In 1995, the U.S. government described St. Vincent as becoming a drug-trafficking center and alleged that high-level government officials are involved in narcotics-related corruption. Since then, St. Vincent has taken steps to cooperate with U.S. antidrug trade efforts, such as signing an extradition treaty in 1996 with Washington. St. Vincent and the Grenadines was not surveyed in Transparency International's 2004 Corruption Perceptions Index.

The press is independent, with two privately owned independent weeklies and several smaller, partisan papers. Some journalists believe that government advertising is used as a political tool. The only television station is privately owned and free from government interference. Satellite dishes and cable are available to those who can afford them. The radio station is government owned, and call-in programs are prohibited. Equal access to radio is mandated during electoral campaigns, but the ruling party takes advantage of state control over programming. There is free access to the Internet.

The right to freedom of religion is constitutionally protected and reflected in practice. Academic freedom is generally honored.

Civic groups and non-governmental organizations are free from government interference. There is freedom of assembly. Labor unions are active and permitted to strike.

The judicial system is independent. The highest court is the West Indies Supreme Court (based in St. Lucia), which includes a court of appeals and a High Court. A right of ultimate appeal reports, under certain circumstances, to the Privy Council in London. Murder convictions carry a mandatory death sentence; in November, Prime Minister Ralph Gonsalves publicly endorsed the death penalty as a partial response to the rise in violent crime on the islands.

The independent St. Vincent Human Rights Association has criticized long judicial delays and the large backlog of cases caused by personnel shortages in the local judiciary. It has also charged that the executive branch of government at times exerts inordinate influence over the courts. Prison conditions remain poor—one prison designed for 75 inmates houses more than 300—and prisons are the targets of allegations of mistreatment. In February 2004, the Human Rights Association called on the government to ratify the Declaration on Human Rights adopted by the UN General Assembly in 1998.

Violence against women, particularly domestic violence, is a major problem. The Domestic Violence Summary Proceedings Act that provides for protective orders offers some protection. The punishment for rape is generally 10 years in prison, while sentences of 20 years for sexual assaults against minors are handed down.

Samoa

Population: 200,000
GNI/capita: $1,420
Life Expectancy: 73
Religious Groups: Christian (99.7 percent), other (0.3 percent)
Ethnic Groups: Polynesian (93 percent), Euronesian [mixed] (7 percent)
Capital: Apia

Political Rights: 2
Civil Liberties: 2
Status: Free

Ten-Year Ratings Timeline (Political Rights, Civil Liberties, Status)

1995	1996	1997	1998	1999	2000	2001	2002	2003	2004
2,2F	2,2F	2,2F	2,3F	2,2F	2,2F	2,2F	2,2F	2,2F	2,2F

Overview: Samoa's parliamentary opposition accused the government in 2004 of stealing millions of dollars from the town of Salelologa by paying too little for its land.

Germany controlled this group of Pacific Islands, formerly known as Western Samoa, between 1899 and World War I. New Zealand occupied and subsequently administered the islands under a League of Nations mandate and then as a UN Trust Territory until Western Samoa became independent in 1962. In 1988, the country changed its name to Samoa.

The centrist Human Rights Protection Party (HRPP) has dominated politics since independence. Tofilau Eti Alesana, who became prime minister in 1982, resigned in 1998 for health reasons. He was replaced by Deputy Prime Minister Tuilaepa Aiono Sailele Malielegoai, who led the HRPP to another victory in March 2001 by winning 30 of the 49 parliamentary seats.

In August 2003, the number of government departments and ministries was reduced from 27 to 14, mainly through mergers and appointments of new executive heads, in order to streamline the government. The government also announced increased police efforts to battle growing youth crime, particularly drug use and violence.

Samoa decided to forgo $150,000 in annual military aid from the United States when it refused to sign a bilateral treaty with Washington by a July 2003 deadline. The treaty would have granted exemptions from the Rome Statute of the International Criminal Court to U.S. citizens, who are alleged to have committed an international offense and currently live in Samoa.

In July 2004, the parliamentary opposition accused the government of stealing millions of dollars from the town of Salelologa by paying too little—$1.4 million—for nearly 3,000 acres. An opposition leader said that an independent valuation put the price at more than $15 million. Three of the seven villages of Salelologa took the Minister of Lands, Survey, and Environment to court. The villagers claimed their traditional chiefs did not have authority to sign over their land for that price; the Supreme Court ruled the land agreement signed was legally binding. This decision sparked another public debate on whether new laws are needed to constrain the powers of traditional chiefs.

A cyclone hit the island early in the year, imposing an extra burden on a struggling economy that depends heavily on foreign aid and remittances from more than 100,000 Samoans working overseas.

Political Rights and Civil Liberties: Samoans can change their government democratically. Previously, only the *matai* (family chiefs) could vote. Executive authority is vested in the chief of state. The 90-year-old Chief Susuga Malietoa Tanumafili II holds this title for life; the Legislative Assembly will elect his successor for five-year terms. The chief of state appoints the prime minister, who heads the government and names his own cabinet. All laws passed by the 49-member unicameral legislature must receive approval from the chief of state to take effect. Although candidates are free to propose themselves for electoral office, approval of the *matai* is essential. Two parliament seats are reserved for "at large" voters, that is, Samoans of mixed European-Samoan and Chinese-Samoan heritage.

Official corruption and abuses do not appear as widespread or serious as in some other Pacific Island states. Nevertheless, there have been allegations of corruption over the years.

The government generally respects freedom of speech and the press. One of the two television stations is operated by the government. Five private radio stations and satellite cable television are available in parts of the capital. Three English-language and several Samoan newspapers are available. Journalists are legally required to reveal their sources in the event of a defamation suit against them, but this law has not been tested in court. In 2004, publishers, journalists, and civil society groups called on the government to abolish the Printers and Publishers Act of 1982 and the Law of Criminal Libel. Critics charge that these laws impose on the public legal fees incurred by government leaders, who are frequently intolerant of news reports about them. There are several Internet service providers, and Internet use is growing rapidly.

The government respects freedom of religion in practice, and relations among religious groups are generally amicable. In 2000, the Supreme Court ruled that the 1990 Village Fono (Council of Chiefs) Act, which gives legal recognition to fono decisions, could not be used to infringe on villagers' freedom of religion, speech, assembly, and association. This ruling followed a fono decision in the village of Saluilua to banish members of a Bible study group, which the fono regarded as illegal. Similar rulings followed in 2003 and 2004. In 2003, the government established the Law Reform Commissioner to address conflicts between traditional customs and Christianity. There were no reports of restrictions on academic freedom.

Freedom of assembly and association is respected in practice. Human rights groups operate freely. About 20 percent of wage earners belong to trade unions. Workers have the legal right to bargain collectively, but they rarely pursue this option. Government workers can strike, subject to certain conditions to assure public safety. More than 60 percent of adults work in subsistence agriculture.

The judiciary is independent and upholds the right to a fair trial. The Supreme Court is the highest court with full jurisdiction on civil, criminal, and constitutional matters. The chief of state, on the recommendation of the prime minister, appoints the chief justice. Prisons meet basic international standards. Human rights groups have not reported problems such as lengthy detentions before trial or corruption of the courts in adjudicating cases.

Samoa has no armed forces, and the small police force is under civilian control. The police have little impact in the villages, where most disputes are settled by the fono, and punishments usually involve fines in cash or kind. Banishment from the village is reserved for serious offenses. Fono vary considerably in their decision-making styles and in the number of matai involved. Abuses by some fono officials have caused the public to question the legitimacy of their actions and limits of their authority.

The constitution prohibits discrimination, but there are problems in the treatment of women and non-matai. Excesses of traditional chiefs, or fono, were brought to light and curbed in a landmark court ruling in 2003 that found the banishment of villagers by the fono for their religious practices was illegal.

The government generally respects freedom of movement. A new permanent resident permit was introduced in 2004 as part of the Immigration Act of 2004. The Cabinet is required to determine annually eligibility and residency requirements for the granting of permanent resident permits. The cabinet decided to provide 10 permanent resident permits, two of which were for applicants outside of Samoa as part of the government's effort to attract foreign investments.

Domestic violence against women and children is common, and spousal rape is not illegal. Domestic abuses typically go unreported because of social pressure and fear of reprisal. In October, 17 women graduated in a new class of 49 police officers, and a woman was named the top student.

San Marino

Population: 30,000
GNI/capita: $34,330
Life Expectancy: 80
Religious Groups: Roman Catholic
Ethnic Groups: Sanmarinese, Italian
Capital: San Marino

Political Rights: 1
Civil Liberties: 1
Status: Free

Ten-Year Ratings Timeline (Political Rights, Civil Liberties, Status)

1995	1996	1997	1998	1999	2000	2001	2002	2003	2004
1,1F	1,1F	1,1F	1,1F	1,1F	1,1F	1,1F	1,1F	1,1F	1,1F

Overview:
In 2004, the government of San Marino agreed to a controversial European Union (EU) directive that imposes a withholding tax on nonresident savings accounts. The directive is intended to reduce harmful tax practices by tax havens.

Founded in A.D. 301, San Marino is the world's oldest and second smallest republic (after Vatican City). Although the Sammarinesi are ethnically and culturally Italian, they have succeeded in maintaining their independence against great odds since the fourth century. The papacy recognized San Marino's independence in 1631, as did the Congress of Vienna after the Napoleonic Wars in 1815. In 1862, Italy and San Marino signed a treaty of friendship and cooperation, beginning a long period of closeness between the two countries. Despite its dependence on Italy, from which it currently receives budget subsidies, San Marino maintains its own political institutions. It became a member of the Council of Europe in 1988 and a member of the United Nations in 1992. Tourism and banking dominate the country's economy.

Early elections were called in June 2001, leading to the return of a coalition of the Christian Democrats (PDCS) and the Socialist Party (PSS). The PDCS won 25 seats, the PSS 15, the Democratic Party (PPDS) 12, the Popular Party (APDS) 5, the Communist Party (RC) 2, and the National Alliance (AN) 1. A government crisis late in 2003 was resolved in December of that year with the replacement of the minister of foreign affairs.

In September 2004, Giuseppe Arzilli and Roberto Raschi were elected as captains-regent—joint heads of state. The term of office for captains-regent is six months. A decision by the EU Council of Ministers finalized the controversial directive that intends to reduce the harmful tax practices of European tax havens in the EU and outside of it. By agreeing to the directive, the country will impose a withholding tax on non-resident savings accounts. Part of the revenue of the tax will go back to the investor's state of residence.

Political Rights and Civil Liberties:

The Sammarinesi can change their government democratically. The 60 members of the Great and General Council (a unicameral legislature) are elected every five years by proportional representation. The executive power of the country rests with the 10-member Congress of State (cabinet), which is headed by the two captains-regent elected every spring and fall. The Great and General Council selects two of its members to serve as the captains-regent (joint heads of state) for a six-month period. Although there is no official prime minister, the secretary of state for foreign affairs has assumed some of the position's prerogatives.

Freely elected representatives determine the policies of the government in San Marino, where there are few problems with corruption. San Marino was not ranked in Transparency International's 2004 Corruption Perceptions Index.

Freedom of speech and the press are guaranteed in San Marino. There are daily newspapers, a state-run broadcast system for radio and television called RTV, and a private FM station, Radio Titiano. The Sammarinesi have access to all Italian print media and certain Italian broadcast stations, and enjoy few infringements on press freedoms. Access to the Internet is unrestricted.

The country prohibits religious discrimination by law. Roman Catholicism is the dominant, but not state, religion. People can request a donation of 0.3 percent of their income through their taxes to be allocated to the Catholic Church, or other churches like the Waldesian Church or the Jehovah's Witnesses. Academic freedom is respected in the country.

People are free to assemble, demonstrate, and conduct open public discussions. Workers are free to organize into trade unions and bargain collectively with employers. They are also free to strike, if they do not work in military occupations. Approximately half of the country's workforce is unionized.

The judiciary in the country is independent. Lower court judges are required to be noncitizens—generally Italians—to assure impartiality. The final court of review is San Marino's Council of Twelve, a group of judges chosen for six-year terms from among the members of the Grand and General Council. The country's prison system generally met international standards and civilian authorities maintained effective control over the police and security forces.

The population is generally treated equally under the law, although the European Commission against Racism and Intolerance (ECRI) has raised some concerns in the past about the status of foreigners in the country. Most of the foreign-born population is made up of Italians; only about 2 percent—mostly women from Central and Eastern Europe who work as private nurses for the elderly and ill—come from outside the EU. San Marino has no formal asylum policy, and a foreigner has to live in the country for 30 years to be eligible for citizenship. The European Convention on Nationality recommends that the period of residence before a foreigner can apply for citizenship should not exceed 10 years. In 2001, San Marino ratified the international convention on the Elimination of All Forms of Racial Discrimination (ICERD).

Women are given legal protections from violence and spousal abuse, and gender equality exists in the workplace and elsewhere. There are, however, slight differences in the way men and women can transmit citizenship to their children.

Sao Tome and Principe

Population: 200,000   **Political Rights:** 2
GNI/capita: $290   **Civil Liberties:** 2
Life Expectancy: 69   **Status:** Free
Religious Groups: Christian [Roman Catholic,
Evangelical Protestant, Seventh-Day Adventist]
(80 percent), other (20 percent)
Ethnic Groups: Mestico [Portuguese-African], African minority
[primarily descendants of slaves and indentured servants from Angola and Mozambique],
European [primarily Portuguese]
Capital: São Tomé

Ten-Year Ratings Timeline (Political Rights, Civil Liberties, Status)

1995	1996	1997	1998	1999	2000	2001	2002	2003	2004
1,2F	1,2F	1,2F	1,2F	1,2F	1,2F	1,2F	1,2F	2,2F	2,2F

Overview:
Political uncertainty and in-fighting among the parties in Sao Tome's coalition government persisted in 2004, as revenues from the leasing of offshore oil fields to foreign companies began to roll in.

Sao Tome and Principe consists of two islands approximately 125 and 275 miles off the coast of Gabon in the Gulf of Guinea. Seized by Portugal in 1522 and 1523, they became a Portuguese Overseas Province in 1951. Portugal granted local autonomy in 1973 and independence in 1975. On independence, the Movement for the Liberation of Sao Tome and Principe (MLSTP), which was formed in 1960, took power and functioned as the only legal party until a 1990 referendum established multiparty democracy. In 1991, Miguel dos Anjos Trovoada, an independent candidate backed by the opposition Democratic Convergence Party, became the first democratically elected president.

In presidential elections in 2001, Fradique de Menezes, of the Independent Democratic Alliance (ADI), replaced Trovoada, who had ruled the country for 10 years. In the first round of voting, de Menezes won with 56 percent compared with 38 percent for Manuel Pinto da Costa of the MLSTP. In parliamentary elections in March 2002, the MLSTP captured 24 seats, the Democratic Movement of Forces for Change won 23 seats, and the remaining 8 seats went to the Ue Kadadji coalition. De Menezes called on parliament to introduce laws against vote buying, which he said had been rampant in the March parliamentary poll. Nevertheless, international observers declared the polls to be free and fair.

President de Menezes was briefly ousted by a military coup in July 2003, returning to power after one week with the backing of Portugal and numerous African countries. The coup was staged by officers disgruntled over persistent poverty in the country and allegations of state corruption.

Sao Tome slid into a new crisis in March 2004 when Prime Minister Maria das Neves blocked two foreign investment deals, charging that she had not been consulted. The showdown with de Menezes led to a reshuffle of the unity government that left the president's party in the opposition. Neves was finally dismissed in September, amid mounting charges of corruption, and replaced by Damiao Vaz de Almeida, deputy president of the MLSTP-Social Democratic Party. Neves is the fourth prime minister sacked by President Menezes since 2001. She and 400 others are now the focus of a tribunal investigating the alleged disappearance of tens of thousands of dollars from an anti-poverty fund.

The recent discovery of large offshore oil fields has been a major source of political tensions. After two years of wrangling, the government agreed to give 60 percent of the proceeds to Nigeria, with which it shares territorial waters in the Gulf of Guinea. The two countries have established a Joint Development Zone and pledged transparency on oil revenues. In April 2004, U.S. oil giants ChevronTexaco and ExxonMobil were awarded the first exploration contract, worth $123 million. Eight other fields remain on the auction block.

Sao Tome and Principe is in the process of strengthening its relationship with the United States, which has led military training exercises and plans to build a deepwater port on the archipelago for the U.S. Navy to patrol waters surrounding the country and protect its oil resources there. Sao Tome and Principe has mostly relied on external assistance to develop its economy. Unemployment is about 45 percent, and it is one of the poorest countries in Africa. The upcoming oil bonanza has drawn comparisons with Equatorial Guinea, where an influx of petroleum dollars failed to bring benefits to the vast majority of the population. However, Sao Tome has a stronger democratic tradition, and its government passed legislation in 2004 creating a closely monitored national petroleum fund to manage the country's oil revenues.

Political Rights and Civil Liberties:

The people of Sao Tome and Principe have the right to change their government democratically. Presidential and legislative elections in 1991 gave the country's citizens their first chance to elect their leader in an open, free, and fair contest. The single-chamber National Assembly has 55 seats. Members are elected by popular vote to serve four-year terms. There are three main political parties: the Movement for the Liberation of Sao Tome and Principe (MLSTP), the Force for Change Democratic Movement, and the Ue-Kedadji coalition.

The country's newfound oil wealth has brought accusations of corruption. In June, the government sacked two senior members of the Joint Development Authority with Nigeria for unspecified reasons, later issuing a statement that bribery of officials would not be tolerated. Sao Tome and Principe was not surveyed in Transparency International's 2004 Corruption Perceptions Index.

Constitutionally protected freedom of expression is respected in practice. One state run and three privately owned newspapers and newsletters are published. While the state controls a local press agency and the only radio and television stations, no law forbids independent broadcasting. Opposition parties receive free airtime, and newsletters and pamphlets criticizing the government circulate freely.

Freedom of religion is respected within this predominantly Roman Catholic country. The government does not restrict academic freedom.

Freedom of assembly is respected. Citizens have the constitutional right to gather and demonstrate with an advance notice of two days to the government. The rights to organize, strike, and bargain collectively are guaranteed and respected. Few unions exist, but independent cooperatives have taken advantage of the government land-distribution program to attract workers. Because of its role as the main employer in the wage sector, the government remains the key interlocutor for labor on all matters, including wages. Working conditions on many of the state-owned cocoa plantations are harsh.

An independent judiciary, including a Supreme Court with members designated by, and responsible to, the National Assembly, was established by the 1990 referendum on multiparty rule. The Supreme Court has ruled against both the government and the president, but is occasionally subject to manipulation. The court system is overburdened, understaffed, inadequately funded, and plagued by long delays in hearing cases. Prison conditions are harsh.

The constitution provides for equal rights for men and women, but women encounter significant societal discrimination. Most have fewer opportunities than men for education or formal (business) sector employment. However, several women have been appointed to cabinet positions, including that of prime minister. Domestic violence against women is reportedly common. Although legal recourse is available, many victims are reluctant to bring legal action against their spouses or are ignorant of their rights.

Saudi Arabia

Population: 25,100,000
GNI/capita: $8,530
Life Expectancy: 72
Religious Groups: Muslim (100 percent)
Ethnic Groups: Arab (90 percent), Afro-Asian (10 percent)
Capital: Riyadh

Political Rights: 7
Civil Liberties: 7
Status: Not Free

Ten-Year Ratings Timeline (Political Rights, Civil Liberties, Status)

1995	1996	1997	1998	1999	2000	2001	2002	2003	2004
7,7NF	7,7NF	7,7NF	7,7NF	7,7NF	7,7NF	7,7NF	7,7NF	7,7NF	7,7NF

Overview:
The Saudi government maintained strict limits on citizens' political rights and civil liberties in 2004, despite taking some steps forward in a slow and quiet process of political reform carefully managed from above by the royal family. The monarchy continued a series of national dialogues on reform and finalized plans for a series of limited municipal elections in certain parts of the country in early 2005, but it implemented few tangible changes directly affecting Saudi citizens' rights. Attacks on foreign oil companies and the Saudi government raised more questions about internal stability

and contributed to record-high global oil prices. After a brutal attack in May on a residential compound housing foreign oil workers in Khobar, the government ramped up its counterterrorism efforts, achieving some success and a relative degree of calm by the fall of 2004.

In the 72 years since its unification in 1932 by King Abdul Aziz Al Saud, Saudi Arabia has been controlled by the Al Saud family, with King Fahd bin Abd al-Aziz Al Saud, the current king, the fifth in the Al Saud ruling dynasty. The Saudi monarchy rules in accordance with a conservative school of Sunni Islam. In the early 1990s, King Fahd embarked on a limited program of political reform, introducing an appointed consultative council, or Majlis al-Shura. However, this step did not lead to any substantial shift in political power. In 1995, King Fahd suffered a stroke, and since 1997, Crown Prince Abdullah bin Abd al-Aziz Al Saud has taken control of most decision making. Succession questions loom on the horizon—Crown Prince Abdullah is 81 years old, and the next closest successors are also aged.

Saudi Arabia has been under intense scrutiny since the September 11, 2001, attacks against the United States—15 of the 19 hijackers were Saudi citizens, and Osama bin Laden, the leader of the terrorist group al-Qaeda, is from a wealthy Saudi family. The Saudi government continued efforts to stem the flow of financial support to terrorist groups, implementing new rules against money laundering and more closely monitoring charitable contributions and organizations suspected of financing terrorist operations in Saudi Arabia and globally.

Terrorist groups that have posed a threat to Saudi Arabia for the past decade escalated their attacks in 2003 in an effort to destabilize the autocratic monarchy. These assaults continued through 2004, culminating in an attack in Khobar on residential compounds where mostly foreign oil workers lived and resulting in the killing of 22 people. The government increased its counterterrorism efforts, killing dozens of suspected terrorists, detaining hundreds on suspicion of involvement with terrorism, and claiming to have destroyed five of six major terrorist networks operating in the kingdom. In addition, the government declared a 30-day amnesty in early June for those involved with terrorist attacks. Attacks on soft targets such as foreign workers decreased but continued, with the kidnapping and beheading of American defense contractor Paul Johnson in June.

Attacks on foreigners and oil companies sent shock waves through the global oil markets, contributing to escalating oil prices. The record oil prices filled Saudi Arabia's coffers and alleviated some recent economic woes; Saudi Arabia was on track for earning $100 billion in revenue from its oil wealth in 2004, which led to record increases in the market capitalization of the country's stock exchange.

With the largest proven oil reserves in the world, Saudi Arabia is the world's leading oil producer and exporter. The country's oil wealth and importance to the global economy are key features affecting the country's external relations, and the Al Saud dynasty uses this unmatched wealth to shape and control internal politics. The government's dominance of the economy, endemic corruption, and financial mismanagement have led to mounting economic woes, with the world's largest oil producer seeing a decline in real gross domestic product per person over the last decade. The government has not taken substantial steps to diversify its oil-dominated economy; nearly 90 percent of the country's export earnings come from oil, and oil earnings constitute 75 percent of budget revenues. Unemployment is estimated at 30 percent, and this year, the government recognized the growing problem of poverty by announcing a strategy to create jobs and build housing for the underprivileged.

Amid the political instability and increased access to outside sources of information through satellite television and the Internet, pressure for political change has mounted. The government has responded by taking initial steps toward political reform, though it has not yet effected any concrete changes in the status of political rights and civil liberties. In the summer of 2003, Saudi Arabia established the King Abdul Aziz Center for National Dialogue, which has sponsored a national dialogue involving professionals and academics handpicked by the regime. In June, the national dialogue sponsored a session on the role of women in Saudi society. Municipal elections, announced in October 2003 and now tentatively scheduled for spring 2005, will provide Saudi men with a very limited opportunity for political participation.

Political Rights and Civil Liberties: Saudi Arabia is an absolute monarchy, and its citizens have no power to change the government democratically. The country's 1992 Basic Law declares that the Koran is the country's constitution. A 120-member Majlis al-Shura (Consultative Council) is appointed by the monarch. This council has limited powers and does not affect decision making or power structures in a meaningful way. The Council of Ministers, an executive body appointed by the king, passes legislation that becomes law once ratified by royal decree. The monarchy has a tradition of consulting with select members of Saudi society, but this process is not equally open to all citizens.

Saudi Arabia does not have political parties, and the only semblance of organized political opposition exists outside of the country, with many Saudi opposition activists being based in London. The Al Saud dynasty dominates and controls political life in the kingdom.

Municipal elections, originally announced in October 2003, are tentatively scheduled to begin in Riyadh in February 2005 and take place in other parts of the country through the spring. These elections will afford Saudi men a limited opportunity to select some of their leaders at the local level. According to electoral regulations published in August, male citizens who are at least 21 years old, are not serving in the military, and have resided in a particular electoral district for at least 12 months will be allowed to vote. Half of the seats are open for election, and the other half will remain positions appointed by the monarchy. Officials in the Municipal and Rural Affairs Ministry and the Interior Ministry will screen candidates, and all results are subject to final approval from the government.

Corruption is one consequence of the closed nature of Saudi Arabia's government and society, with foreign companies reporting that they often pay bribes to middlemen and government officials to secure business deals. Saudi Arabia was ranked 71 out of 146 countries surveyed in the 2004 Transparency International Corruption Perceptions Index.

The government tightly controls content in domestic media outlets, but is unable to do much about regional satellite television coverage. Government authorities have banned or fired journalists and editors who publish articles deemed offensive to the country's powerful religious establishment or the ruling authorities. The

Saudi regime has taken steps to limit the impact of new media. Government officials reportedly banned mobile phones with cameras from the country.

Religious freedom does not exist in Saudi Arabia, the birthplace of Islam and the location of the two holiest cities of Islam—Mecca and Medina. Islam is Saudi Arabia's official religion, and all citizens are required by law to be Muslims. The government prohibits the public practice of any religions other than Islam. Although the government recognizes the right of non-Muslims to worship in private, it does not always respect this right in practice. Academic freedom is restricted in Saudi Arabia, and informers monitor classrooms for compliance with limits on curriculums, such as a ban on teaching Western philosophy and religions other than Islam. In 2004, the government began efforts to reform school curriculums to delete disparaging religious references in textbooks.

Saudi citizens do not enjoy freedom of association and assembly. The government approved the establishment of the National Human Rights Association, a semi-official organization charged with reviewing allegations of human rights violations and monitoring the country's compliance with international human rights agreements. Chaired by Shura council member Abdullah bin Saleh al-Obeid, the National Human Rights Association has 41 members, including 10 women. Saudi law does not address labor unions, but since 2001 the government has permitted the establishment of labor committees in local companies with more than 100 employees.

The judiciary lacks independence from the monarchy. The king appoints all judges on the recommendation of the Supreme Judicial Council, and the monarchy serves as the highest court of appeal. The rule of law is regularly flouted by the Saudi regime, with frequent trials falling short of international standards. Secret trials are common, and political opponents of the regime are often detained without charge and held for indefinite periods of time. Allegations of torture by police and prison officials are frequent, though access to prisoners by independent human rights and legal organizations is strictly limited.

In 2004, a number of democracy advocates in the kingdom mounted a petition campaign in favor of reforms. In March, the government arrested 13 reformers who had called for establishing a constitutional monarchy and holding parliamentary elections. Three—Ali al-Doumani, Dr. Matrouk al-Faleh, and Dr. Abdullah al-Hamed—were tried for creating political instability after refusing to sign a document renouncing their reform efforts. The trial got off to a rocky start in August, when the judge suspended initial hearings after hundreds of supporters of the defendants rallied outside the courtroom.

Although racial discrimination is illegal, substantial prejudice against ethnic, religious, and national minorities exists. Foreign workers from Asia and Africa are subject to formal and informal discrimination and have difficulty obtaining justice.

Citizens have the right to own property and establish private businesses, but much private enterprise activity is connected with members of the ruling family and the government. Although Saudi Arabia first joined the General Agreement on Tariffs and Trade in 1993, its slow process of privatization and economic reform has prevented it from becoming a member of the World Trade Organization.

Women are not treated as equal members of society. They may not legally drive cars, and their use of public facilities is restricted when men are present. By law and custom, women cannot travel within or outside of the country without a male relative. Laws discriminate against women in a range of matters including family law, and a woman's testimony is treated as inferior to a man's in court. The Committee to Prevent Vice and Promote Virtue, a semiautonomous religious police force commonly known as the *mutawa'een*, enforce a strict policy of segregation between men and women and often use physical punishment to ensure that women meet conservative standards of dress in public.

The government will not allow women to take part in the municipal elections scheduled for early 2005. Prince Mansour bin Muteb bin Abdul Aziz, head of the elections committee, announced in October that the country did not have sufficient time to prepare for both women and men to vote, indicating that Saudi Arabia would require separate polling stations run by female election judges before it allowed women to participate politically.

Education and economic rights for Saudi women have improved. Girls were not permitted to attend school until 1964, but now more than half of the country's university students are female. In May 2004, women won the right to hold commercial licenses, opening the door for greater economic participation. In addition, women have become more visible in a society that is deeply conservative and segregated along gender lines. In January, Saudi state television began using women as newscasters. Also in January, businesswomen appeared unveiled and mixed with men and participated at the Jeddah Economic Forum, prompting the Grand Mufti of Saudi Arabia, Sheikh Abdul Aziz al-Asheikh, to condemn the women and the media outlets that showed pictures of the women participating in the conference.

⬆Senegal

Population: 10,900,000 **Political Rights:** 2
GNI/capita: $470 **Civil Liberties:** 3
Life Expectancy: 56 **Status:** Free
Religious Groups: Muslim (94 percent), other [including Roman Catholic and indigenous beliefs] (6 percent)
Ethnic Groups: Wolof (43.3 percent), Pular (23.8 percent), Serer (14.7 percent), Jola (3.7 percent), Mandinka (3 percent), Soninke (1.1 percent), European and Lebanese (1 percent), other (9.4 percent)
Capital: Dakar
Trend Arrow: Senegal received an upward trend arrow due to improved security in the southern Casamance region.

Ten-Year Ratings Timeline (Political Rights, Civil Liberties, Status)

1995	1996	1997	1998	1999	2000	2001	2002	2003	2004
4,5PF	4,4PF	4,4PF	4,4PF	4,4PF	3,4PF	3,4PF	2,3F	2,3F	2,3F

Overview:

For the fourth time in as many years, President Abdoulaye Wade replaced his prime minister in 2004. Security improved in the southern Casamance region following two decades of a separatist rebellion.

Since independence from France in 1960, Senegal has escaped military or harshly authoritarian rule. President Leopold Senghor exercised de facto one-party rule under the Socialist Party for more than a decade after independence. Most political restrictions were lifted after 1981. Abdou Diouf, of the Socialist Party, succeeded Senghor in 1981 and won large victories in unfair elections in 1988 and 1993.

Wade's victory in the presidential poll in 2000—his fifth attempt to win the presidency—overturned four decades of rule by the Socialist Party. Wade captured 59.5 percent of the runoff vote, against 41.5 percent for Diouf. The election was judged to have been free and fair by international observers.

The people of Senegal adopted a new constitution by an overwhelming majority in January 2001, reducing presidential terms from seven to five years, setting the number of terms at two, and giving women the right to own land for the first time. President Wade dissolved the National Assembly, which had been dominated by the former ruling Socialist Party, and elections were held in April. A coalition led by Wade won 89 of the 120 seats available, followed by the Socialist Party with 10; smaller parties captured the remainder of seats.

Peace accords between the government and the separatist Movement of the Democratic Forces of Casamance (MFDC) were signed in 2001. Casamance is separated from much of the rest of Senegal by Gambia; its geographic isolation helped contribute to a feeling of marginalization that sparked the conflict in 1982. Ethnically, the people of Casamance identify more with their southern neighbors in Guinea-Bissau than with northern Senegalese. Although the conflict has not come to a definitive end, armed resistance has all but ceased. Security in the Casamance region improved in 2004, and efforts were under way at resuming development there.

Wade replaced Prime Minister Idrissa Seck in April 2004 with Macky Sall. Sall is a former interior minister and a leading figure in Wade's Senegalese Democratic Party.

Senegal's population is mostly engaged in subsistence agriculture. The country's economy has enjoyed modest growth since the mid-1990s. The World Bank and the IMF in April 2004 granted $850 million in debt service relief to Senegal because of the country's political stability and structural reform efforts.

Political Rights and Civil Liberties: Citizens of Senegal can change their government democratically. Changes to the 1992 Electoral Code lowered the voting age to 18, introduced secret balloting, and created a nominally fairer electoral framework. The National Observatory of Elections, which was created in 1997, performed credibly in overseeing the 1998 legislative polls and the presidential elections in 2000. There are more than 75 legally registered political parties in Senegal. Elections for the 120-seat unicameral National Assembly are held every five years. The president is elected by popular vote every five years. The prime minister is appointed by the president.

Senegal was ranked 85 out of 146 countries surveyed in Transparency International's 2004 Corruption Perceptions Index. Although the government has initiated reforms to strengthen the rule of law and improve transparency, corruption remains a problem.

Freedom of expression is generally respected, and members of the independent media are often highly critical of the government and political parties. There are about 20 independent radio stations, some of which broadcast in rural areas. The government does not carry out formal censorship, but some self-censorship is practiced because of laws against "discrediting the state" and disseminating "false news" that President Abdoulaye Wade has promised to repeal. International press freedom organizations maintain that media rights have become more restricted under Wade. It is not unusual for journalists to be detained for questioning by authorities and pressured to reveal confidential sources. There are no official impediments to Internet access.

Journalists in July 2004 conducted a news blackout to protest the jailing of the publications director of the independent daily newspaper *Le Quotidien*. Authorities arrested Madiambal Diagne and charged him with publishing confidential documents, spreading false information, and committing acts likely to cause public unrest. Most private radio stations played songs and extracts of interviews given by Diagne instead of their regular programs, and newspapers reprinted the two articles that led to Diagne's arrest that were about alleged fraud in the customs service and government interference in the judiciary. Diagne was granted provisional release after being held for two weeks. International press freedom groups called on the government to remove all criminal penalties for press offenses from Senegalese law.

Religious freedom in Senegal, which is 94 percent Muslim, is respected. Rivalries between Islamic groups have sometimes erupted into violence. Academic freedom is guaranteed and respected.

Freedom of association and assembly are guaranteed, but authorities have sometimes limited these rights in practice. Human rights groups working on local and regional issues are among many nongovernmental organizations that operate freely.

Although union rights to organize, bargain collectively, and strike are legally protected, there are some restrictions on freedom of association and the right to strike. Most workers are employed in the informal business and agricultural sectors. Nearly all of the country's small industrialized workforce is unionized, and workers are a potent political force.

Poor pay and lack of tenure protections create conditions for external influence on a judiciary that is, by statute, independent. In high-profile cases, there is often considerable interference from political and economic elites. Uncharged detainees are incarcerated without legal counsel far beyond the lengthy periods already permitted by law.

There are credible reports that authorities beat suspects during questioning and pretrial detention, despite constitutional protection against such treatment. Prison conditions are poor. Reports of disappearances and extrajudicial killings in connection with the conflict in Casamance occur less frequently than in previous years. Sidi Badji, one of the last remaining separatist hard-liners, died in 2003.

In December 2003, Amnesty International said the government should swiftly and impartially bring to justice those responsible for disappearances in Casamance. It reported that between 1992 and 2001, approximately 180 people had disappeared in Casamance. It blamed about 100 of the disappearances on the army and about 80 on the MFDC. Thousands of people were forced to flee their homes because of the rebellion; many have begun to return.

Constitutional rights afforded women are often not honored, especially in the countryside, and women have fewer opportunities than men for education and formal sector employment. Despite governmental campaigns, domestic violence against women is reportedly common. Many elements of Sharia (Islamic law) and local customary law, particularly those regarding inheritance and marital relations, discriminate against women. Although Senegal banned female genital mutilation in 1999, it is still practiced among some ethnic groups. The government and nongovernmental organizations have been working to educate the population about the health risks of the practice.

↑ Serbia and Montenegro

Population: 10,700,000   **Political Rights:** 3
GNI/capita: $1,140   **Civil Liberties:** 2
Life Expectancy: 73   **Status:** Free
Religious Groups: Orthodox (65 percent),
Muslim (19 percent), Roman Catholic (4 percent),
other (12 percent)
Ethnic Groups: Serb (63 percent), Albanian (17 percent),
Montenegrin (5 percent), Hungarian (3 percent), other (12 percent)
Capital: Belgrade
Trend Arrow: Serbia and Montenegro receives an upward trend arrow due to increasing stabilization of the political scene after last year's assassination of Prime Minister Zoran Djindjic, including the successful holding of presidential and parliamentary elections and a decrease in official pressure on the media.

Name Change: On February 5, 2003, the Yugoslav parliament adopted a constitutional charter establishing the state of Serbia and Montenegro. Unless specifically noted, references to Serbia and Montenegro in this chapter do not pertain to Kosovo.

Ten-Year Ratings Timeline (Political Rights, Civil Liberties, Status)

1995	1996	1997	1998	1999	2000	2001	2002	2003	2004
6,6NF	6,6NF	6,6NF	6,6NF	5,5PF	4,4PF	3,3PF	3,2F	3,2F	3,2F

Overview: Serbia and Montenegro receives an upward trend arrow due to increasing stabilization of the political scene after last year's assassination of Prime Minister Zoran Djindjic, including the successful holding of presidential and parliamentary elections and a decrease in official pressure on the media.

Serbia and Montenegro managed to achieve a significant stabilization of its political system in 2004 following almost two years of political tension, including the 2003 assassination of Serbian prime minister Zoran Djindjic. Following parliamentary elections in December 2003, a newly formed government chose Vojislav Kostunica as prime minister in March 2004. In June, Boris Tadic was elected president in a tight race.

In April 1992, the former Yugoslav republics of Serbia and Montenegro jointly proclaimed the formation of the Federal Republic of Yugoslavia (FRY) after Marshal Josip Broz Tito's Socialist Federal Republic of Yugoslavia (SFRY) disintegrated in 1991. Throughout the 1990s, Slobodan Milosevic's Socialist Party of Serbia (SPS) ruled the country by virtue of its control over the country's security forces, financial and monetary institutions, and state-owned media. During the wars accompanying the breakup of Yugoslavia, Serbia under Milosevic was extensively involved in the wars in both Bosnia-Herzegovina and Croatia. In 1998-99, an Albanian insurgency in Serbia's Kosovo province provoked increasingly violent reprisals by FRY forces against the guerrillas and the Albanian civilian population in regions affected by the fighting. Eventually, NATO launched a 78-day bombing campaign against the FRY to force the withdrawal of Yugoslav and Serbian paramilitary forces from the province. Since June 1999, a NATO-led force has de facto occupied the Serbian province. The end for the Milosevic regime came on October 5, 2000, when a botched attempt to steal the September presidential elections resulted in hundreds of thousands of people converging on Belgrade to overthrow the Milosevic regime.

The Democratic Opposition of Serbia (DOS), a coalition of 18 political parties and one independent trade union, took power following parliamentary elections in December 2000. Despite the DOS's victory, however, relations between Serbia and its federal partner, Montenegro, which deteriorated in the 1990s, have remained difficult. The new union continues to suffer from numerous problems, largely the result of the great disparity in size between the two republics. Montenegro is only one-tenth the size of Serbia in population and constitutes a negligible part of the overall Serbia and Montenegro economy, while at the same time enjoying parity representation in most organs of government. Further complicating relations between the two republics is their difference regarding cooperation with the International Criminal Tribunal for the former Yugoslavia (ICTY). Montenegro, at least rhetorically, has been more supportive of cooperating with the ICTY, while in Serbia cooperation has often been grudging, if not absent altogether. One notable exception, however, was former Serbian prime minister Zoran Djindjic's extradition of Milosevic to The Hague in June 2001.

In March 2002, the European Union (EU) brokered the so-called Belgrade Agreement (ratified in January 2003), creating a new state called "Serbia and Montenegro." The new union of the two republics preserves some vestiges of a common state but also provides each republic with its own central bank, customs and taxation system, and currency (the euro is the official currency in Montenegro, but not in Serbia; Serbia and Montenegro has no unified official currency). Over the past two years, the EU has begun voicing support for a stronger union of the two republics, but intransigence in both republics has made fulfillment of the Belgrade agreement difficult; Montenegro, for instance, refuses to agree to scheduling federal parliamentary elections as called for by the Belgrade agreement. In November 2004, the EU adopted a "two-track mechanism" to guide Serbia and Montenegro's road toward EU membership. By means of this mechanism, the EU recognizes the different political and economic realities in the two republics, but still insists on the country's eventual membership as a single state.

Although the future of Serbia and Montenegro remains unclear, there is reason to believe that time is working in favor of the union. While there is some debate within Serbia itself over whether it would be preferable for Serbia to go it alone in its efforts to gain EU accession (rather than maintaining ties with Montenegro), Serbian political parties advocating outright separation from Montenegro have faired poorly in recent elections. Similarly, in Montenegro there does not appear to be the necessary critical mass of people in favor of secession and independence to make such a move realistic, although the Djukanovic government continues to argue that a referendum on this matter be held by 2006.

Within Serbia itself, the dominant parties and political leaders of the DOS for most of the post-Milosevic period were the Democratic Party of Serbia (DSS), led by former law professor Vojislav Kostunica, and the Democratic Party (DS), led by the late Serbian premier Zoran Djindjic. On March 12, 2003, Djindjic was assassinated by a group of organized crime figures associated with members of Milosevic-era security structures. With Djindjic's killing, Serbia and the DS lost one of its most capable politicians, and over the summer of 2003, revelations emerged of the involvement of some members of the DS in a variety of corruption scandals, which led to a sharp drop in the DS's popularity. With the DS losing control of the political situation in the parliament, new elections were called for December.

The new parliament elected in December 2003 stabilized the Serbian political situation somewhat by eliminating a number of small, relatively weak parties from the ruling coalition. However, the elections were somewhat marred by the fact that some parties, such as the SPS and the Serbian Radical Party (SRS), actually ran indicted war criminals on their parliamentary lists. While the nationalist SRS won the most seats in the December 2003 parliamentary elections, the parties loosely considered to be "pro-democratic" or "pro-Western" were able to form a coalition government to keep the SRS from coming to power. This new Serbian government, formed in March 2004 after two months of wrangling, made Kostunica Serbia's new prime minister. The minority coalition was composed of the DSS (with 53 seats); the liberal, reformist G17 Plus party led by the economists Miroljub Labus and Mladjan Dinkic (31 seats); the center-right Serbian Renewal Movement—New Serbia coalition led by Vuk Draskovic and former Cacak mayor Velimir Ilic (18 seats), with tacit support from Milosevic's former party, the SPS (22 seats). However, the weakness of the minority coalition government made it difficult throughout the year to advance reforms, adopt necessary legislation, and attract foreign investment. In addition, the government found itself unable to meet its obligations to extradite indicted war criminals to the ICTY for fear of losing the support of the SPS.

Following three unsuccessful attempts to hold presidential elections during the course of 2002-2003, Serbia finally managed to elect a president in June 2004. Despite a tight race, Djindjic's successor as head of the DS, Boris Tadic, succeeded in gaining a victory over Tomislav Nikolic, the leader of the nationalist SRS. Importantly, despite the growing strength of Tadic's DS (and the subsequent increasing weakness of the DSS), Tadic has promised to support the Kostunica government for a period of one year for the sake of political stability. Indicative of the continuing volatility of Serbian politics, however, was the fact that the Milosevic-era business tycoon, Bogoljub Karic, was able to run in the race and gain 20 percent of the vote without having any previous experience in politics. In September, Serbia held municipal elections. The main winners throughout the republic were again the DS and the SRS, which confirmed their leading positions in Serbian politics. Turnout for the municipal elections was a meager 23 percent.

At the end of 2004, the DS and the SRS had become the most important political parties in Serbia, although Kostunica's personal popularity continues to make the DSS a force with which to be reckoned. The breakdown in the Serbian political spectrum shows that the coalition of parties that joined to topple Milosevic in October 2000 can continue to count on some 1.7 to 2 million votes, while the dominant parties from the Milosevic era, the SPS and the SRS, together retain the support of some 1 to 1.4 million voters. There is considerable concern, however, that a downturn in the economy, or a major foreign policy shock (such as the loss of Kosovo), could lead many people to start supporting more extreme parties such as the SRS.

In Montenegro, the republic's veteran strongman, Milo Djukanovic, who served as president from 1998 to 2002, decided to step down from his post in 2002 and become Montenegro's prime minister. Two attempts to elect a new Montenegrin president that year failed after the elections did not attract the required 50 percent voter turnout. In February 2003, a new presidential law that dropped the 50 percent rule came into force. Subsequently, in May, Filip Vujanovic, a Djukanovic ally, was elected. Vujanovic won 64 percent of the votes, with 48.3 percent of eligible voters participating. Opposition parties refused to field candidates, although the Organization for Security and Cooperation in Europe (OSCE) deemed the elections to be generally in line with international standards.

Montenegro remains split between the majority of the Orthodox Christian population that declares itself to be Montenegrin and/or Serb and wants to maintain ties with Belgrade, and a minority of the Orthodox Christian population, supported by ethnic Albanians in Montenegro, some Muslims in the mainly Muslim Sandzak region, and some Roman Catholics along Montenegro's Adriatic coast, who prefer independence. (Many Sandzak Muslims, however, prefer maintaining the union because separation would mean the division of the Sandzak region, their ethno-religious community, between two independent states.) The pro-independence cause suffered a setback in 2003 when a new census showed that 30 percent of the Montenegrin population declared itself to be Serb, an increase of some 21 percent over the past decade and a further indication of how strong ethnic and emotional ties between Serbia and Montenegro remain. Djukanovic's independence aspirations continued to suffer further blows in 2004 as public opinion surveys showed that support for independence was falling; a poll published in November showed that less than 43 percent of Montenegro's population favored independence, far short of what would be needed for a legitimate referendum on the issue to pass.

Serbia and Montenegro's economic situation is starting to show some signs of a turnaround after several years of a difficult transition—which itself was preceded by more than a decade of war and international sanctions. The gross domestic product in 2004 was forecast to grow by 8 percent, while the country scored an important victory in international financial markets in July when the London Club of international creditors agreed to write off 62 percent of Serbia and Montenegro's debt. FDI has slowed to a trickle.

Political Rights and Civil Liberties: Citizens of Serbia and Montenegro can change their government democratically. The latest national elections were conducted freely and fairly. The chief executive in the state union of Serbia and Montenegro is the president, elected by the unicameral Assembly of Serbia and Montenegro, which is composed of 126 deputies (91 from Serbia and 35 from Montenegro). A major point of contention between the two republics has been holding direct popular elections for the state union assembly as called for in the Belgrade Agreement (the current deputies have been nominated by their respective parliaments). Montenegro has consistently delayed scheduling elections in order to avoid the creation of popularly legitimized federal institutions.

Each republic elects its own president in direct popular elections, and each republican government also has its own prime minister. The Montenegrin National Assembly is a unicameral, 75-seat legislature, and the Serbian National Assembly is a unicameral, 250-seat legislature, with deputies in both assemblies elected to four-year terms of office.

Numerous political parties exist and compete for power in elections. As noted above, the main parties in Serbia currently are the DS, the DSS, and the SRS. In Montenegro, the main parties are Prime Minister Djukanovic's Democratic Party of Socialists (SDP), and the main opposition party, the Socialist People's Party of Montenegro (SNP-CG).

Corruption has decreased overall from the excesses of the Milosevic era. However, the popular perception is that corruption remains at very high levels, perhaps due to more open media coverage of the problem. Serbia and Montenegro was ranked 97 out of 146 countries surveyed in Transparency International's 2004 Corruption Perceptions Index.

Freedom of the press has improved significantly since the Milosevic period, when the regime controlled state-owned media and some prominent members of the independent media were assassinated by "unknown" assailants. The government of Zoran Djindjic (January 2001-March 2003) also exerted considerable pressure on the main electronic media to support the government. During the state of emergency imposed after Djindjic's assassination on March 12, 2003, many journalists and media watchdog groups criticized the government for going too far in censoring coverage of the government's crackdown on organized crime groups. In Montenegro, Dusko Jovanovic, the publisher of a major opposition daily highly critical of the government, was assassinated in May. Although the investigation into Jovanovic's death is ongoing, one person arrested in connection with the murder claimed that he has ties to Montenegro's security services.

Libel remains a criminal offense in Serbia punishable by up to six months imprisonment; media advocacy groups continued to call for libel to be decriminalized in 2004. In Montenegro as well, libel remains a criminal offense, but punishable by fines rather than prison terms. During the course of 2004, the Kostunica government drafted, and the Serbian National Assembly passed, a Law on Free Access to Information of Public Importance, although the OSCE has stated that improvements still need to be made to the law as it is now written. There were no reports of the government restricting access to the Internet.

According to the constitution, all citizens enjoy freedom of religious belief. However, with ethnic and religious identities closely intertwined in the region, increases in interethnic tensions often take on the appearance of religious intolerance. When Albanian extremists in Kosovo launched violent attacks against Serbs in Kosovo in March, mobs in Belgrade and Nis responded by torching two mosques in both cities. Restitution of church property nationalized by the Communists remains a point of dispute between church and state. There were no reports that the government attempted to restrict academic freedom during the year.

Citizens enjoy freedom of association and assembly. Foreign and domestic nongovernmental organizations enjoy the freedom to pursue their activities. New laws are currently being drafted to codify relations between trade unions and the government.

Legal and judicial reform is under way, although progress has been slow because of the complicated political situation in the country. The judicial system is still plagued by a large backlog of cases, underpaid judges and state prosecutors, and an excess of judges left over from the Milosevic era. There are reports that the system takes an excessively long time in filing formal charges against suspects. Moreover, the authority and independence of the judicial system continue to suffer as a result of the failure of legislative institutions to heed judicial rulings. Prison conditions generally meet international standards.

Serbia and Montenegro continues to have considerable difficulties in its relations with the ICTY because of a reluctance to hand over indicted war criminals. However, in October, Serbia handed over the former head of the Bosnian Serb intelligence service, who was accused of participating in the Srebrenica massacres, easing tensions somewhat.

Increasing concern was being raised about the independence of Montenegro's judicial system after details emerged about procedural irregularities in a case involving Montenegrin prime minister Milo Djukanovic. In a case filed in October 2003, Djukanovic claimed that an opposition party member had committed libel by claiming that Djukanovic was engaged in human-trafficking operations. The judge fined the opposition leader in question, Miodrag Zivkovic, 8,000 euros after prohibiting Zivkovic from submitting any evidence to the court on his own behalf. The judge also refused to accept as evidence reports from the OSCE and the U.S. State Department. Defense requests for access to earlier investigations into the sex-trafficking scandal were also turned down.

Post-Milosevic reform of the military and security services continues to be an ongoing problem, as many analysts believe there are close ties between Milosevic-era security officials, networks supporting war crimes indictees, extreme nationalist forces, and some organized crime groups. Many of these problems were highlighted in the still-unexplained deaths of two conscripts in a barracks outside of Belgrade. Claims quickly circulated that the two recruits had been killed because they had seen war crimes indictees hiding in the barracks, but these claims were never proven. Officially, Serbia and Montenegro officials maintain that one of their goals remains entering NATO's Partnership for Peace (PfP) program, and, ultimately, NATO itself, although these goals remain hotly debated in a country that was in conflict with NATO less than seven years ago.

Cultural and ethnic minorities have their own political parties, access to media in their mother tongue, and other types of associations. Nevertheless, the numbers of individuals from ethnic minorities participating in government do not represent their percentages in the entire population. An important constitutional and political challenge facing Serbia and Montenegro is to satisfy increasing demands from regions with large ethnic minorities, such as Kosovo, the Sandzak, and Vojvodina. Similarly, there are frequent complaints of unfair treatment and police harassment of the Roma

(Gypsy) community. During the March attacks against Serbs in Kosovo, mobs attacked mosques in Belgrade and Nis; however, senior government and political leaders quickly condemned the violence. Some incidents of violence also occurred during the year between various ethnic groups in Vojvodina, although these were primarily linked to small groups of thugs and barroom brawls rather than to any organized, coordinated campaign. In September, Kostunica announced the formation of a National Minorities Council within the government, whose task will be to protect religious, language, and other features of ethnic minorities living in Serbia.

Although women are legally entitled to equal pay for equal work, traditional patriarchal attitudes prevalent throughout the Balkans often limit women's roles in the economy. In general, women are under represented in higher levels of government. In October, the Serbian government set up a Council for Gender Equality to work on issues of importance to women. Domestic violence remains a serious problem. Some towns in southern Serbia have become an important part of the network trafficking women from the former Soviet Union to Western Europe for purposes of forced prostitution.

Seychelles

Population: 100,000
GNI/capita: $6,530
Life Expectancy: 71
Religious Groups: Roman Catholic (86.6 percent), Anglican (6.8 percent), other (6.6 percent)
Ethnic Groups: Seychellois [mixture of Asian, African, and European]
Capital: Victoria

Political Rights: 3
Civil Liberties: 3
Status: Partly Free

Ten-Year Ratings Timeline (Political Rights, Civil Liberties, Status)

1995	1996	1997	1998	1999	2000	2001	2002	2003	2004
3,3PF	3,3PF	3,3PF	3,3PF	3,3PF	3,3PF	3,3PF	3,3PF	3,3PF	3,3PF

Overview:
Vice President James Michel took office as president of Seychelles in April 2004, replacing retiring president France Albert Rene, who had been head of government and chief of state since 1977. Rene's Seychelles People's Progressive Front (SPPF) remained the dominant political party.

Seychelles, an archipelago of some 115 islands in the western Indian Ocean, was a French colony until 1810. It was then colonized by Britain until its independence in 1976. A member of the Commonwealth, Seychelles functioned as a multiparty democracy for only one year before Rene, then prime minister, seized power by ousting President James Mancham. Mancham and other opposition leaders operated parties and human rights groups in exile after Rene made his ruling SPPF the sole legal party. Rene and his party continue to control government jobs, contracts, and resources, and Rene won one-party "show" elections in 1979, 1984, and 1989.

By 1992, however, the SPPF had passed a constitutional amendment to legalize opposition parties, and many exiled leaders returned to participate in a constitutional commission and multiparty elections.

Rene won a legitimate electoral mandate in the country's first multiparty elections in 1993. The 1998 polls were accepted as generally legitimate by opposition parties, which had waged a vigorous campaign. The Seychelles National Party (SNP), led by the Reverend Wavel Ramkalawan, emerged as the strongest opposition group by espousing economic liberalization, which Rene had resisted.

The political dominance of Rene and the SPPF was further shaken in the August 2001 presidential election, when Rene won a narrow victory that engendered widespread opposition complaints of fraud. In October 2002, Rene dissolved parliament and called for early legislative elections. The SPPF won the elections, but the SNP made significant inroads, winning 43 percent of the vote and 11 of the 33 seats in parliament.

Given his age and the length of time he had served as president, Rene's resignation in April 2004 was not unexpected. He continues to wield considerable political influence as leader of the SPPF. Rene was replaced by Michel, who previously served in various senior-level government positions prior to his appointment as vice president in 1996. The next presidential elections are scheduled to take place in 2006.

Political Rights and Civil Liberties:

Citizens of Seychelles can change their government democratically. In presidential and legislative elections in March 1998, the Seychellois people were able to exercise their democratic right to choose their representatives. SPPF control, however, over state resources and most media gave ruling-party candidates significant advantages in the polls. In the 2001 presidential election, the opposition increased its vote total from 20 to 45 percent. President France Albert Rene's victory, however, was marred by widespread opposition claims that the government had cheated. An official observer delegation from the Commonwealth concluded that the elections were peaceful but not entirely free and fair.

The current constitution was drafted in 1993 by an elected constitutional commission. The president and the National Assembly are elected by universal adult suffrage for five-year terms. The head of government is the president, who appoints the Council of Ministers. As amended in 1996, the constitution provides for a 34-member National Assembly, with 25 members directly elected and 9 allocated on a proportional basis to parties with at least 10 percent of the vote. Other amendments have strengthened presidential powers, and President James Michel has assumed direct responsibility for 7 of the 17 ministerial portfolios. The SNP leadership claims that its sympathizers are harassed by police and are victims of public sector job-related security investigations, which are generally carried out by SPPF agents at the district level.

Seychelles had become a one-party state under the regime established following Rene's 1977 military coup, but opposition parties were legalized in 1992. The SNP and the Democratic Party have been two traditionally important opposition parties.

Concerns exist about the extent of governmental corruption. These have focused particularly on the lack of transparency in allocation of government-owned land and privatization. Seychelles was ranked 48 out of 146 countries surveyed in Transparency International's 2004 Corruption Perceptions Index.

Freedom of speech has improved since one-party rule was abolished in 1993. Independent and pro-opposition publications have spoken out despite tough libel laws, although some self-censorship persists. There is one daily government newspaper, *The Nation*, and at least two other newspapers support or are published by the SPPF. Independent newspapers are critical of the government, but government dominance and the threat of libel suits restrict media freedom. The opposition weekly *Regar* has been sued repeatedly for libel under broad constitutional restrictions on free expression. There is also a need for more equal presentation in the state media of national events and deliberations at the National Assembly. The officially multi-partisan Seychelles Broadcasting Corporation's board of directors includes only one opposition representative, although it does have several non-SPPF members. High licensing fees have discouraged the development of privately owned broadcast media.

Churches in this predominantly Roman Catholic nation have been strong voices for human rights and democratization, and they generally function without government interference. Private human rights–related organizations operate in the country along with other nongovernmental organizations. Public demonstrations are generally tolerated, although on occasion the government has impeded opposition party gatherings. Discrimination against foreign workers has been reported. The right to strike is formally protected by the 1993 Industrial Relations Act, but is limited by several regulations. The SPPF-associated National Workers' Union no longer monopolizes union activity; two independent unions are now active.

The judiciary includes the Supreme Court, the Constitutional Court, a court of appeals, an industrial court, and magistrates' courts. Judges generally decide cases fairly, but still face interference in cases involving major economic or political actors. There are no Seychellois judges, and the impartiality of the non-Seychellois magistrates can be compromised by the fact that their tenure is subject to contract renewal. Security forces have been accused of using excessive force, including torture and arbitrary detention, especially in attempting to curb crime.

Islanders of Creole extraction face de facto discrimination. Nearly all of the Seychellois political and economic life is dominated by people of European and South Asian origin. The government does not restrict domestic travel but may deny passports for reasons of "national interest."

The growth of the economy since independence in 1976 has depended mainly on development of the islands' potential as a tourist destination. Tourism produces 70 percent of the country's hard currency, and the tourist sector employs approximately 30 percent of the labor force. A shortage of foreign exchange, however, has led to the emergence of a large currency black market.

Women constitute 29.4 percent of the Seychelles parliament—one of the highest percentages in Africa; this has been achieved without the benefit of a quota system. In general, however, women are less likely than men to be literate, and they have fewer educational opportunities. While almost all adult females are classified as "economically active," most are engaged in subsistence agriculture. Domestic violence against women is reportedly widespread but is rarely prosecuted and only lightly punished.

♠Sierra Leone

Population: 5,200,000   **Political Rights:** 4
GNI/capita: $140   **Civil Liberties:** 3
Life Expectancy: 35   **Status:** Partly Free
Religious Groups: Muslim (60 percent), indigenous
beliefs (30 percent), Christian (10 percent)
Ethnic Groups: Temne (30 percent), Mende (30 percent),
other tribes (30 percent), Creole (10 percent)
Capital: Freetown
Trend Arrow: Sierra Leone received an upward trend arrow due to continued efforts
to bring to justice those responsible for atrocities committed during the civil war.

Ten-Year Ratings Timeline (Political Rights, Civil Liberties, Status)

1995	1996	1997	1998	1999	2000	2001	2002	2003	2004
7,6NF	4,5PF	7,6NF	3,5PF	3,5PF	4,5PF	4,5PF	4,4PF	4,3PF	4,3PF

Overview:

The trials of indicted war crimes suspects in Sierra Leone's decade-long civil war got under way in the Special Court for Sierra Leone in 2004. Meanwhile, UN troops ceded more control of the country to Sierra Leonean forces as part of a phased withdrawal of international peacekeepers.

Founded by Britain in 1787 as a haven for liberated slaves, Sierra Leone became independent in 1961. The Revolutionary United Front (RUF) launched a guerrilla campaign from neighboring Liberia in 1991 to end 23 years of increasingly corrupt one-party rule by President Joseph Momoh. Power fell into the lap of Captain Valentine Strasser in 1992, when he and other junior officers attempted to confront Momoh about poor pay and working conditions at the front. Momoh fled the country. The Strasser regime hired South African soldiers from the security company Executive Outcomes to help win back key diamond-rich areas. In January 1996, Brigadier Julius Maada-Bio quietly deposed Strasser. Elections proceeded despite military and rebel intimidation, and voters elected Ahmad Tejan Kabbah, a former UN diplomat, as president.

In 1997, Major Johnny Paul Koroma toppled the Kabbah government, established the Armed Forces Revolutionary Council, and invited the RUF to join the junta. Nigerian-led West African troops, backed by logistical and intelligence support from the British company Sandline, restored Kabbah to power in February 1998, but the country continued to be racked by war. A peace agreement in July 1999 led to the beginning of disarmament, but the process stopped in May 2000 with a return to hostilities and the taking of about 500 peacekeepers as hostages. British troops flew in to help, and disarmament resumed in May 2001.

In the May 2002 presidential poll, in which eight candidates competed, Kabbah was reelected with 70 percent of the vote, compared with 22 percent for Ernest Koroma of the All People's Congress (APC), who comes from the same region as Johnny Paul Koroma. The RUF candidate, Alimamy Pallo Bangura, lagged with barely 2 percent of the vote. Kabbah's Sierra Leone People's Party (SLPP) dominated parliamentary elections the same month, winning 83 of 112 available seats, followed by the APC with 27; Koroma's party won 2 seats.

Although Sierra Leone's war has ended, Kabbah, who was reelected to the presidency in 2002, still faces daunting problems, many of which contributed to causing the conflict. Entrenched corruption, a culture of impunity, rampant poverty, and unequal distribution of the country's diamond wealth must be adequately addressed if the country is to enjoy lasting peace.

The Sierra Leone Truth and Reconciliation Commission, modeled on South Africa's Truth and Reconciliation Commission, warned in October 2004 that poverty and corruption remained rampant. The commission, which includes members from Canada, South Africa, The Gambia, and Sierra Leone, said women, as well as men between the ages of 18 and 35, needed to participate more fully in society and public office.

The Special Court for Sierra Leone in 2004 began holding trials of those deemed primarily responsible for war crimes and human rights abuses committed during the civil war. Witnesses recounted ghastly stories about atrocities that were committed across the countryside. The court has indicted 13 people, including Charles Taylor, who stepped down as president of Liberia in August 2003 and accepted Nigeria's offer of asylum. Taylor was accused of backing the former rebel RUF with weapons in exchange for diamonds. Interpol has issued a warrant for his arrest but says it is up to individual governments to apprehend Taylor; the Liberian government has not pursued him.

The departure of Taylor and the growing prospect for peace in Liberia bodes well for lasting peace in Sierra Leone. However, insecurity along the borders of Liberia, Sierra Leone, Guinea, and Cote d'Ivoire is perilous for the entire region. A phased withdrawal of the 17,300-strong UN Mission in Sierra Leone, the world's largest peacekeeping mission, is scheduled to be completed in June 2005.

Sierra Leone has vast diamond resources, but smuggling and war have turned it into one of the world's poorest countries. A ban on rough-diamond imports from Sierra Leone does not include diamonds that carry proven certificates of origin from the government.

Political Rights and Civil Liberties:

Citizens of Sierra Leone can change their government democratically. Presidential and legislative elections in February and March 1996 were imperfect, but were considered legitimate. Politicians, former combatants, and civil society representatives joined together in a conference in 2001 and approved a new electoral system for polls scheduled for the following year. Despite some logistical problems, the May 2002 presidential and parliamentary elections were considered the country's fairest since independence. President Ahmad Tejan Kabbah and his SLPP enjoyed the advantage of incumbency and state resources for both elections. Sierra Leone has a 124-seat unicameral parliament, of which 112 seats are chosen by popular vote and 12 seats are filled by paramount chiefs chosen in separate elections. Parliamentary elections are held every five years. The president is elected by popular vote every five years and serves as both chief of state and head of government. Local elections were held in May 2004; there were complaints of intimidation and some voting irregularities.

Dozens of political parties have formed, but many revolve around a specific personality and have little following. The major political parties include the SLPP, the APC, and the Peace and Liberation Party.

An anticorruption commission was established by the National Assembly in 2000. It has already brought several cases to court. Sierra Leone was ranked 114 out of 146 countries surveyed in Transparency International's 2004 Corruption Perceptions Index. Sierra Leoneans have expressed increasing frustration over what they see as a continuation of corrupt, elitist politics and neglect of the country's impoverished population.

Freedom of speech and of the press is guaranteed, but the government at times restricts these rights. Criminal libel laws are used occasionally to jail journalists. Several government and private radio and television stations broadcast, and newspapers openly criticize the government and armed factions. Dozens of newspapers are printed in Freetown, but most are of poor quality and often carry sensational or undocumented stories. Internet access is not impeded.

International press freedom groups harshly criticized the government in 2004 following the imprisonment of a well-known Sierra Leonean journalist. Paul Kamara, editor and publisher of the independent newspaper *For Di People*, was sentenced in October to two years in prison because of articles that linked Kabbah to fraudulent activities in 1967, when he helped oversee the Sierra Leone Produce Marketing Board. The court found Kamara guilty on two counts of "seditious libel" under the 1965 Public Order Act. The judge also recommended a six-month ban on *For Di People*. The Independent Media Commission was to rule on the recommendation. Freedom of religion is guaranteed and respected in practice. Academic freedom is guaranteed.

The rights of freedom of assembly and association are guaranteed, and these rights are generally respected. Several national and international nongovernmental organizations and civic groups, including human rights groups, operate openly and freely. Workers have the right to join independent trade unions of their choice. About 60 percent of workers in urban areas, including government employees, are unionized. There is a legal framework for collective bargaining.

The judiciary is active, but corruption and a lack of resources are impediments. Despite these obstacles, the judiciary has demonstrated independence, and a number of trials have been free and fair. Local courts resumed sitting in all districts of the country in 2003. There are often lengthy pretrial detentions in harsh conditions. Eight judges—from Sierra Leone, Canada, Austria, The Gambia, the United Kingdom, and Nigeria—were appointed to sit on the UN-backed Special Court for Sierra Leone. The court made history as the first international war crimes tribunal to sit UN-appointed judges alongside local judges at a court in the country where the atrocities took place. Its goal was to deliver justice cheaper and faster than tribunals for Rwanda and Bosnia. Funding has been a key source of frustration. The police force is widely seen as corrupt and incompetent. Arbitrary arrest without charge is common. Prison conditions are harsh and sometimes life threatening.

Sierra Leone once had one of Africa's worst human rights records. Abduction, maiming, rape, forced conscription, and extrajudicial killing were commonplace. Although security has improved considerably, lack of equipment for security forces and poor infrastructure could hinder longer-term efforts to keep a lid on unrest in Sierra Leone, especially if demobilized combatants lack opportunities for employment. In February, a program to disarm and rehabilitate more than 70,000 fighters was completed.

Despite constitutionally guaranteed equal rights, women face extensive legal and de facto discrimination, as well as limited access to education and formal (business) sector jobs. Married women have fewer property rights than men, especially in rural areas, where customary law prevails. Abuse of women, including rape, sexual assault, and sexual slavery, were rampant during the war. Female genital mutilation is widespread and no law prohibits it.

Singapore

Population: 4,200,000 **Political Rights:** 5
GNI/capita: $20,690 **Civil Liberties:** 4
Life Expectancy: 79 **Status:** Partly Free
Religious Groups: Buddhist, Muslim, Christian, other
Ethnic Groups: Chinese (77 percent), Malay (14 percent),
Indian (8 percent), other (1 percent)
Capital: Singapore

Ten-Year Ratings Timeline (Political Rights, Civil Liberties, Status)

1995	1996	1997	1998	1999	2000	2001	2002	2003	2004
5,5PF	4,5PF	5,5PF	5,5PF	5,5PF	5,5PF	5,5PF	5,4PF	5,4PF	5,4PF

Overview: Lee Hsien Loong, the son of former prime minister Lee Kuan Yew, was sworn in as Singapore's new prime minister in August 2004, but he is not expected to alter significantly the government's current policies. Meanwhile, the country's economy rebounded during the year.

Located along major shipping routes in Southeast Asia, Singapore became a British colony in 1867. Occupied by the Japanese during World War II, the city-state became self-governing in 1959, entered the Malaysian Federation in 1963, and became fully independent in 1965 under Prime Minister Lee Kuan Yew. Under him, the ruling People's Action Party (PAP) transformed a squalid port city into a regional financial center and an exporter of high-tech goods. At the same time, Lee restricted individual freedoms and stunted political development.

In 1990, Lee Kuan Yew handed power to Goh Chok Tong, who largely continued Lee's conservative policies and kept the PAP dominant in parliament. In the nine general elections that have been held since independence, the PAP has never won fewer than 95 percent of parliamentary seats.

During the campaign for the last parliamentary elections, held in November 2001, opposition candidates criticized the government for not doing more to help Singaporeans hurt by the country's first recession since independence. The PAP campaigned on the theme that no other party had the skills and experience to revive the economy. Repeating a tactic from the 1997 election campaign, the PAP also linked priority for public housing upgrades to support for the ruling party. On election day, the PAP received 75 percent of the vote and won 82 of parliament's 84 seats. Opposition parties contested only 29 seats, with the leftist Workers' Party and centrist Singapore People's Party winning 1 seat apiece. Veteran opposition politician J. B. Jeyaretnam of the Workers' Party was barred from contesting the elections after the court of appeal declared him bankrupt for being one day late in paying an installment on a damages award to PAP politicians who had successfully sued him for defamation. As a bankrupt individual, Jeyaretnam was barred from practicing law, thrown out of parliament, and prevented from running for office.

Lee Hsien Loong, the son of former prime minister Lee Kuan Yew, became Singapore's new prime minister on August 12, 2004, as part of a planned handover of power. His inauguration ended the 14-year tenure of Goh Chok Tong, but he is not expected to alter significantly the government's current policies. His primary challenges will be maintaining Singapore's economic recovery and endearing himself to his electorate. Although he has made concerted efforts to appear more approachable, he is still regarded as being more conservative and potentially more authoritarian than his predecessor.

The economy rebounded strongly in 2004 after being hit hard in 2003 by the global economic downturn and the onset of severe acute respiratory syndrome (SARS) in Asia. It is expected to continue performing strongly, but factors such as continued high oil prices and rising global interest rates could undermine growth.

Singapore's most import foreign relations remain those with the United States and with neighboring Malaysia. Ties with Malaysia are expected to improve if only because of the accession to political leadership of new figures in both countries within the space of one year (in Malaysia, Abdullah Badawi replaced Mahathir Mohamad as prime minister in October 2003).

Political Rights and Civil Liberties: Citizens of Singapore cannot change their government democratically. Singapore's 1959 constitution created a parliamentary system of government and allowed for the right of citizens to change their government peacefully. Periodic elections are held on the basis of universal suffrage, and voting is compulsory. In practice, however, the ruling PAP dominates the government and the political process, and uses a variety of indirect methods to handicap opposition parties. The head of government is not chosen through elections; the prime minister, like the cabinet, is appointed by the president. Singapore has had only three prime ministers since it gained independence in 1965. Lee Kuan Yew governed for 31 years, after which he appointed Goh Chok Tong his successor. Goh named Lee's eldest son, Lee Hsien Loong, deputy prime minister in 2003; the younger Lee acceded to the post of prime minister in August 2004. The legislature has just one house, with 94 members. Members of parliament are either elected (84 in the current parliament), appointed by opposition political parties (up to three members; there is one in the current parliament), or appointed by the president (nine in the current parliament).

Though general elections are free from irregularities and vote rigging, the PAP's manipulation of the political system means that they cannot be termed fair. Opposition parties are constrained by the ban on political films and televised programs; the curtailing of expressions of political opinion by the threat of libel or slander suits; strict regulations and limitations on associations, including political associations;

and the PAP's influence of the media and in the courts, among other things. The net result is that there is no effective opposition. The ruling party is quick to counter that its success is due to its strong track record concerning the economy, as well as opposition parties' disorganization and lack of credible candidates and ideas.

The government is known for its transparency and its relative lack of corruption. Singapore was ranked 5 out of 146 countries surveyed in Transparency International's 2004 Corruption Perceptions Index.

Singapore's press is somewhat freer than in past years, although serious restrictions on freedom of speech and expression remain. Two companies own all newspapers in the city-state; one is government controlled, and the other, though private, has close ties to the government. Although editorials and news coverage generally reflect governmental policies, newspapers increasingly are carrying letters, columns, and editorials critical of governmental policies. Journalists face pressure from the ruling party not to oppose the government's goals, and so often avoid reporting on sensitive topics, including alleged government corruption or nepotism or on the supposed compliance of the judiciary. All television channels and all radio stations, except for the BBC World Service, are operated by government-linked companies. The Newspaper and Printing Presses Act allows authorities to restrict the circulation of any foreign periodical whose news coverage allegedly interferes in domestic politics. Foreign newspapers and magazines are available, although authorities at times have restricted the circulation of foreign publications that carried articles that the government found offensive.

The government screens and sometimes censors films, television programs, videos, music, books, and magazines, mainly for excessive amounts of sex, violence, and drug references. The PAP has, however, loosened some restrictions on the arts in recent years, and the censorship boards' standards were developed taking into account the views of a citizen advisory panel. In any case, censorship of sex and violence has strong public support. The government controls the Internet by licensing Internet service providers, which filter and may even block material that the government considers objectionable.

Singaporeans of most faiths can worship freely, but meetings of Jehovah's Witnesses are banned because the group's roughly 2,000 members refuse to perform compulsory military service. Jehovah's Witnesses adherents can still practice their faith, however. The Societies Act stipulates that all religious groups register with the government.

Faculty members of public universities and political research institutions are not entirely free from government influence, since all such institutions have direct government links. The PAP prohibits public discussion of sensitive racial and religious issues and closely regulates political speech.

The government restricts freedom of association through the strict provisions of the 1966 Societies Act, including one provision that permits only groups registered as political parties or associations to engage in organized political activities. The Societies Act covers most organizations of more than 10 people, and these groups are required to register with the government. Singaporeans must get police permits to hold public talks or to make political speeches, and public assemblies of more than five people must receive police approval. The government has historically denied registration to groups it considered a threat to public order. In March, the police rejected an application for public lectures by a gay rights organization on the grounds that "the content was contrary to public interest."

Unions are permitted under the Trade Unions Act, and restrictions on their formation are relatively narrow (government employees may not join unions, for example). Almost all unions are affiliated with the National Trade Unions Congress, which freely acknowledges that its interests are closely aligned with those of the PAP. Collective bargaining is commonplace, and strikes are legal—except for workers in the water, gas, and electricity sectors—but rare.

The judiciary's independence has been called into question by the government's overwhelming success in court proceedings, particularly defamation suits, against political opponents. It is not clear, however, whether the government pressures judges or simply appoints judges who share its conservative philosophy. Many judges have ties to the PAP and its leaders. In any case, the judiciary is efficient, and in criminal cases, defendants enjoy a presumption of innocence and the right to confront witnesses and other due process rights.

The government generally respects citizens' right to privacy, but the issue is not specifically addressed in the constitution, and the government does maintain the right to search a person or property without a warrant if it deems the search necessary to preserve evidence. The government is also believed to monitor telephone and Internet communications, though this is not confirmed.

The government has the power to detain suspects without trial under both the Internal Security Act (ISA) and the Criminal Law Act (CLA). The ISA historically has been applied mainly against suspected Communist security threats, but the government has recently used the law to detain suspected Islamic terrorists. It allows authorities to detain suspects without charge or trial for an unlimited number of two-year periods. A 1989 constitutional amendment prohibits judicial review of the substantive grounds of detentions under the ISA and of the constitutionality of the law itself.

The government uses the CLA to detain mainly organized crime and drug-trafficking suspects. Under the law, authorities may place a suspect in preventive detention for an initial one-year period, which the president can extend for additional one-year periods, subject to habeas corpus appeal to the courts. Meanwhile, the Misuse of Drugs Act allows authorities to commit without trial suspected drug users to rehabilitation centers for up to three years.

Security forces are not known to commit serious abuses. Police occasionally mistreat detainees, although the government has in recent years jailed officers convicted of such abuses. The Penal Code mandates caning, in addition to imprisonment, for about 30 offenses; it is discretionary for certain other crimes involving the use of force. Caning is reportedly common.

The government actively promotes racial harmony and equity in Singapore's multiethnic society, and there is no legal discrimination. All citizens enjoy freedom of movement; however, the government occasionally infringes on citizens' right to choose housing by enforcing its policy of assuring ethnic balance in public housing, in which most Singaporeans live. Men can be conscripted for two years of compulsory military service on turning 18. Despite government efforts to boost their educational achievement, ethnic Malays have not on average achieved the schooling and income levels of ethnic Chinese or Indians and reportedly face unofficial discrimination in private sector employment.

Women enjoy the same legal rights as men in most areas, and many are well educated and hold professional jobs. Relatively few women, however, hold top positions in government and the private sector.

Slovakia

Population: 5,400,000
GNI/capita: $3,970
Life Expectancy: 74
Religious Groups: Roman Catholic (60.3 percent), Protestant (8.4 percent), other (31.3 percent)
Ethnic Groups: Slovak (86 percent), Hungarian (11 percent), Roma (2 percent), others [including Czech] (31.3 percent)
Capital: Bratislava

Political Rights: 1
Civil Liberties: 1*
Status: Free

Ratings Change: Slovakia's civil liberties rating improved from 2 to 1 due to the deepening of EU integration trends, resulting in greater conformity with EU human rights standards

Ten-Year Ratings Timeline (Political Rights, Civil Liberties, Status)

1995	1996	1997	1998	1999	2000	2001	2002	2003	2004
2,3F	2,4PF	2,4PF	2,2F	1,2F	1,2F	1,2F	1,2F	1,2F	1,1F

Overview:

Slovakia achieved two major goals in 2004, formally joining NATO in April and the European Union (EU) in May. However, turnout was disappointing in the country's first European Parliament election. In April, Ivan Gasparovic won the presidency in an election against former prime minister Vladimir Meciar.

Anti-Communist opposition forces brought about the collapse of the Czechoslovak government in 1989, and the country held its first free elections the following year. After elections in June 1992, negotiations began on increased Slovak autonomy within the Czech and Slovak Federative Republic. These discussions eventually led to a peaceful dissolution of the federation and the establishment of an independent Slovak Republic on January 1, 1993.

From 1993 to 1998, Meciar—who served twice as prime minister during this period—and the Movement for a Democratic Slovakia (HZDS) dominated politics in newly independent Slovakia. Meciar battled with then-president Michal Kovac over executive and governmental powers, opposed direct presidential elections, flouted the rule of law, and intimidated independent media. His policies resulted in Slovakia's failure to meet the criteria necessary to open EU accession talks and to join NATO. In the 1998 parliamentary elections, voters supported a major shift in Slovakia's political orientation by rejecting Meciar's rule and electing a broad right-left coalition. The new parliament selected Mikulas Dzurinda as prime minister and pursued policies to enhance judicial independence, combat corruption, undertake economic reforms, and actively seek membership in the EU and NATO.

In September 2002, twenty-five parties competed in free and fair parliamentary elections, although only seven parties exceeded the 5 percent representation threshold. Meciar's HZDS obtained 19.5 percent of the vote, but his party did not receive sufficient support to form a new government. Prime Minister Dzurinda's Slovak Democratic and Christian Union (SDKU) finished second and succeeded in forming a center-right government in partnership with the Party of the Hungarian Coalition (SMK), the Christian Democratic Movement (KDH), and the Alliance of the New Citizen (ANO). Seventy percent of eligible voters participated in the election.

Slovak nongovernmental organizations were particularly active during the campaign, organizing get-out-the-vote initiatives, publishing voter education materials, and monitoring media coverage. By law, public television channels provided equal airtime to candidates during the official campaign period. While parties were free to advertise in newspapers, laws prohibited campaign advertising on private television.

In April 2003, parliament ratified Slovakia's accession to NATO, and in a binding national referendum that was held the following month, Slovaks voted overwhelmingly in favor of joining the EU, with 92 percent supporting membership. Turnout for the referendum was a disappointing 52 percent of eligible voters, just slightly above the 50 percent needed to make the vote valid. Slovakia duly joined NATO and the EU in April and May 2004, respectively.

In Slovakia's first election for the European Parliament, enthusiasm for participation lagged far behind the zeal for membership itself. Just 17 percent of eligible adults voted in the June 2004 elections, the lowest total in the 25-member EU. The SDKU, KDH, and HZDS each took around 17 percent of the vote, as did a new left-wing populist party, Smer. Each received three seats in the European Parliament. The Hungarian party, SMK, took two seats.

In April 2004, Slovakia held a two-round election for the presidency. Former prime minister Vladimir Meciar did best in the first round, winning 32.7 percent of the vote. He faced a runoff against his former right-hand man, Ivan Gasparovic, later in the month. In the second round, with turnout of just 43.5 percent, Gasparovic won with 59.9 percent as Slovaks rejected the man who had caused their international isolation in the 1990s.

Along with other countries that have made NATO and EU membership strategic objectives and which are eager to have solid relations both with the United States and the EU, Slovakia has sought to find an appropriate political and diplomatic balance in its relations with the United States and the EU. In late 2004, it had 102 soldiers in Iraq, mostly involved in de-mining operations.

Political Rights and Civil Liberties: Slovak citizens can change their government democratically. Voters elect the president and members of the 150-seat National Council. A 2001 law grants voting privileges to foreigners, allowing permanent residents to vote in elections for municipal and regional governments.

Slovakia was required to meet the "Copenhagen criteria" in order to join the EU; these standards include "stability of institutions guaranteeing democracy, the rule of law, human rights and respect for and protection of minorities." The European Commission, the EU's executive, issued a positive opinion on Slovakia's candidacy in November 2003 (allowing it to join in May 2004), saying Slovakia had "reached a high level of alignment with the aquis [the body of EU law] in most policy areas." However, the Commission noted that more work remained to be done in certain areas, including antidiscrimination law.

Corruption is a problem in Slovakia, especially in health care, education, the police and the judiciary, according to the European Commission. Slovakia was ranked 57 out of 146 countries surveyed in Transparency International's 2004 Corruption Perceptions Index. Slovakia began a program of reforms in 1999 that has centralized and increased staffing for government anticorruption efforts. Moreover, the Law on Free Access to Information has contributed to better transparency in government administration.

Slovakia's media are largely free but remain vulnerable to political interference. Prison terms for press abuses such as defamation were eliminated in a 2002 reform. In 2003, revelations that the Slovak Secret Service wiretapped the editorial offices of *SME*, one of the country's leading daily national newspapers, raised fears of more widespread illegal surveillance. The government does not limit access to the Internet.

The government respects religious freedom. Registered churches and religious organizations are eligible for tax exemptions and government subsidies. The Roman Catholic Church is the largest denomination in the country and consequently receives the largest share of government subsidies. Although Slovakia has not banned or impeded any groups from practicing their faith, the U.S. State Department notes the persistence of anti-Semitism among some parts of the population. The government respects academic freedom.

The government respects the right to assemble peacefully, petition state bodies, and associate in clubs, political parties, and trade unions. Judges, prosecutors, firefighters, and members of the armed forces may not strike.

The constitution provides for an independent judiciary and a Constitutional Court, and an independent Judicial Council oversees assignment and transfer of judges. The European Commission has noted the perception of a high level of corruption in the Slovak courts and expressed concern over the judiciary's perceived lack of impartiality. Corruption and a significant backlog of cases have raised questions about the judicial system's capacity to function at EU levels.

There are more than 10 recognized ethnic minorities in Slovakia. While minorities have a constitutional right to contribute to the resolution of issues that concern them, Roma (Gypsies) continue to experience widespread discrimination and inequality in education, housing, employment, public services, and the criminal justice system. In 2003, there were reports of coerced or forced sterilization of Roma women the year before, on the orders of local health officials. Roma also face the persistent threat of racially motivated violence. Even though the law criminalizes such acts, reports indicate that law enforcement officials do not always investigate crimes against Roma. In response to these problems, the government began a new program to improve Roma education and housing in 2002. The government has also established an informal advisory board to widen dialogue with the Roma community. In December 2003, Slovakia reached an agreement with Hungary on the application of Hungary's Status Law, which grants special health and educational benefits to ethnic Hungarians residing outside of Hungary. A foundation in Slovakia will administer the support for Hungarians living there.

Slovak citizens enjoy a range of personal rights and liberties, including the right to move and travel freely.

Slovakia has a market economy in which the private sector accounts for approximately 80 percent of gross domestic product and 75 percent of employment. Official unemployment remains high at approximately 14 percent, but the government contends that many of those who collect unemployment benefits may simultaneously be working on the black market.

Although women enjoy the same legal rights as men, they continue to be underrepresented in senior-level business positions and the government.

Slovenia

Population: 2,000,000　**Political Rights:** 1
GNI/capita: $10,370　**Civil Liberties:** 1
Life Expectancy: 76　**Status:** Free
Religious Groups: Roman Catholic [including Uniate
(2 percent)] (70.8 percent), Lutheran (1 percent),
Muslim (1 percent), other (27.2 percent)
Ethnic Groups: Slovene (88 percent), Croat (3 percent),
Serb (2 percent), Bosniak (1 percent), other (6 percent)
Capital: Ljubljana

Ten-Year Ratings Timeline (Political Rights, Civil Liberties, Status)

1995	1996	1997	1998	1999	2000	2001	2002	2003	2004
1,2F	1,2F	1,2F	1,2F	1,2F	1,2F	1,2F	1,1F	1,1F	1,1F

Overview:　Twelve years after gaining independence, Slovenia achieved one of its primary foreign policy goals in May 2004 when it became a member of the European Union (EU). Parliamentary elections held in October resulted in a surprise victory by Slovenia's conservative Slovenian Democratic Party (SDS). On a more worrisome note, an April referendum overwhelmingly rejected restoring a variety of rights to individuals who had been "erased" from official government registries after independence from the former Yugoslavia. The results of the referendum increased both domestic and international concern about the civil rights of non-Slovenians living in the country.

The territory now constituting Slovenia was part of the Hapsburg Empire from 1335 to 1918. At the end of World War I, Slovenia became a part of the new Kingdom of Serbs, Croats, and Slovenes (renamed the Kingdom of Yugoslavia in 1929), and after World War II, it became a constituent republic of the Socialist Federal Republic of Yugoslavia. In 1990, Slovenia held its first postwar, multiparty, democratic elections, in which the Democratic United Opposition (DEMOS) secured victory. Voters also elected former Communist leader Milan Kucan president. Kucan was reelected in Slovenia's first postindependence polls in 1992, and again in 1996.

Slovenian society has enjoyed remarkable consensus in the postindependence period in comparison with the other former Yugoslav republics. Citizens agree that foreign policy should focus on Slovenia's entering European and trans-Atlantic organizations, and domestic policy should focus on maintaining a social-democratic model. For most of this period, Slovenia has been ruled by center-left governments whose most important component has been Janez Drnovsek's Liberal Democratic Party (LDS).

Slovenia's latest presidential elections were held over two rounds in 2002. In the first round, held in November, Drnovsek gained 44.3 percent of the vote. He comfortably outdistanced his nearest rival, Slovenian state prosecutor, but political newcomer, Barbara Brezigar of the SDS, who gained 30.7 percent. In the second-round runoff in December, Brezigar secured surprisingly strong support, winning 43 percent of the vote, although that was not enough to defeat Drnovsek's 56 percent. Seventy-one percent of the electorate turned out to vote in the first round of the elections and 65 percent for the second round.

In 2004, the 12-year lock on power of Slovenia's left-of-center parties was broken after Prime Minister Anton Rop's LDS-led coalition suffered a number of defeats. April was an especially stormy month for the Rop government, which suffered a series of setbacks including a resounding rejection by referendum of its attempts to restore retroactive residency rights to non-Slovenes, the loss of one of the LDS's coalition partners (the Slovenian People's Party, SLS), and the dismissal of five cabinet members.

All of these problems eventually contributed to an LDS loss in October's parliamentary elections. Although Janez Jansa's center-right SDS succeeded in unseating the LDS and becoming Slovenia's most popular political party, the SDS still faced difficulties in forming a government. At year's end, by forming a coalition with two smaller parties (New Slovenia and the Slovenian People's Party), Jansa had only managed to obtain 45 out of the 90 seats in the National Assembly, still one short of a governing majority. Turnout for the parliamentary elections was 60 percent.

Perhaps the most pressing civil rights problem in 2004 was the fate of the "erased": some 18,000 non-Slovene citizens of the former Yugoslavia who remained in Slovenia after independence, but who were administratively removed from official records after they failed to apply for citizenship or permanent resident status during a brief period in 1992. The "erased" were subsequently denied driver's licenses, access to state health care, and pensions. Under pressure from the EU, in 2003, the Slovenian government began drafting legislation to restore these rights. In April 2004, the LDS suffered a serious political setback when its bill granting retroactive residency rights to the "erased" was rejected in a referendum called by the opposition; 95 percent of the electorate opposed the government-backed bill, albeit on a low turnout of only 31 percent of the electorate.

Political Rights and Civil Liberties: Citizens of Slovenia can change their government democratically. Voters directly elect the president and members of the 90-seat National Assembly (parliament), which chooses the prime minister. The 40-seat National Council, a largely advisory body, represents professional groups and local interests. The political opposition to the government plays a constructive, cooperative role in public policy making. Elections held in 1992, 1996, 2000, and 2002 have been considered free and fair.

Although Slovenia received a relatively favorable score in Transparency

International's 2004 Corruption Perceptions Index (ranked 31 out of 146 countries surveyed), and while Slovenia generally has the reputation of being the most corruption free of the East-Central European states entering the EU, corruption in Slovenia is a significant problem. The most general forms of corruption in the country involve conflicts of interest among government officials, an intertwining of the public and private sectors, and relying on official connections to obtain lucrative government contracts for private businesses.

The government respects the constitutional rights of freedom of speech and of the press, although insulting public officials is prohibited by law. Most print media outlets are privately owned and support themselves with advertising revenues. Some electronic media outlets, such as Slovenia Radio-Television (RTV), remain state owned. A major complaint against the various media is that they do not represent a wide range of political or ethnic interests. There are also reports of some degree of self-censorship resulting from indirect political or economic pressures on media outlets. The Slovenian media launched its first-ever general strike on election day in October to protest low wages. Many of Slovenia's main media outlets, including three of the four main daily newspapers and National Radio and Television, joined the action. The strike was suspended after three days when the Trade Union of Slovenian Journalists won a commitment for new negotiations to begin on a collective bargaining agreement with the Association for Press and Media in the Chamber of Commerce of Slovenia, which represents most of Slovenia's big media enterprises. There were no reports of government attempts to restrict access to the Internet during the year.

The constitution guarantees freedom of conscience and religion. While most Slovenians remain Roman Catholics, at the same time, the Roman Catholic Church appears to be suffering from a significant crisis among its members; between 1991 and 2002, the percentage of Slovenes who identified themselves as active Catholics dropped from 69.8 percent to 57.8 percent. The most outstanding religious freedom issue over the past several years has been the consistent refusal of Slovenian authorities for 30 years to allow the country's small Muslim community to build a mosque in Ljubljana. Some Slovenian officials have justified the foot-dragging on granting a building permit to the mosque out of fear that it would provide the "infrastructure for terrorism" in Slovenia. In July, the Slovenian Constitutional Court blocked a proposed referendum challenging zoning laws allowing construction on the mosque to proceed, ruling that fundamental, universal human rights can overrule the democratically expressed will of the population. Restitution of religious properties confiscated during the Communist period is nearing its end. According to published reports, 86 percent of claims filed by religious organizations for de-nationalization of their property were resolved by the end of September 2003. There were no reports of government restrictions on academic freedom during the year.

The government respects the right of individuals to assemble peacefully, to form associations, to participate in public affairs, and to submit petitions. Military and police personnel may not join political parties. Workers enjoy the right to establish and join trade unions, to strike, and to bargain collectively.

According to the EU, the Slovenian judiciary enjoys "a high degree of independence." The judiciary consists of the Supreme Court, an administrative court, regional and district courts, and an appeals court, along with a Constitutional Court.

A separation of powers is built into the political system, and the various branches of government generally respect each other's powers and authorities. The constitution guarantees individuals due process, equality before the law, and a presumption of innocence until proven guilty. The main problem facing the judicial system is the fact that it is overburdened, with some criminal cases taking two to five years. Prison conditions are in line with international standards, although some overcrowding has been reported.

Slovenia's treatment of ethnic minorities is generally considered to be good, although in December 2003, the Italian-minority member of Slovenia's parliament, Roberto Battelli, resigned from the presidential commission for minorities claiming that the Italian minority was being pressured to assimilate. Incitement to racial hatred is prohibited under the Criminal Code. The constitution entitles the Italian and Hungarian ethnic communities to one deputy each in the National Assembly. However, there have been persistent reports of police harassment of Roma (Gypsies) and of residents from other former Yugoslav republics, the so-called new minorities. International watchdog groups report some governmental and societal discrimination against Serbs, Croats, Bosnians, Kosovo Albanians, and Roma now living in Slovenia.

According to the constitution, Slovenian citizens enjoy all recognized personal rights and freedoms, including the freedom to travel and to choose one's place of residence and the right to own private property.

Women enjoy the same constitutional rights and freedoms as men under the law. In February, the Slovenian parliament adopted a measure requiring that 40 percent of the electoral lists for the European parliamentary elections must be female. A total of 59.8 percent of Slovenia's women are in the workforce, the largest proportion of any of the 10 countries joining the EU in 2004. Slovenia also fares well in comparison with other countries in the relative pay scales between men and women; on average, Slovenian women receive 89 percent of the pay of their male counterparts, which compares favorably with similar rates in Austria and Italy (79 and 73 percent, respectively). Nevertheless, women remain under-represented in political life. Currently, there are 12 women serving in the 90-seat parliament and 3 women in the 40-seat National Council. Countrywide, women make up only 13 percent of town council members and less than 6 percent of all local mayors. Domestic violence remains a concern. In recent years, Slovenia has become both a transit country and a country of destination for women and girls trafficked from other parts of Eastern Europe for purposes of prostitution.

Solomon Islands

Population: 500,000
GNI/capita: $570
Life Expectancy: 61
Religious Groups: Anglican (45 percent), Roman
Catholic (18 percent), other [including indigenous
beliefs] (37 percent)
Ethnic Groups: Melanesian (93 percent), Polynesian
(4 percent), Micronesian (1.5 percent), other (1.5 percent)
Capital: Honiara

Political Rights: 3
Civil Liberties: 3
Status: Partly Free

Ten-Year Ratings Timeline (Political Rights, Civil Liberties, Status)

1995	1996	1997	1998	1999	2000	2001	2002	2003	2004
1,2F	1,2F	1,2F	1,2F	1,2F	4,4PF	4,4PF	3,3PF	3,3PF	3,3PF

Overview:

The Australia-led Regional Assistance Mission to the Solomon Islands (RAMSI) was deemed a success in 2004 in helping to restore peace and stability to this war-torn island state. Meanwhile, several individuals implicated in the coup of 2000, as well as high-ranking officials alleged to have abused their powers, were arrested and brought to trial during the year.

The Solomon Islands, which consists of more than 27 islands and 70 language groups, gained independence in 1978 after having been a protectorate of the United Kingdom. Clan identity remains much stronger than national identity and is a deep source of ethnic rivalry. Tensions between the two largest groups—the Guadal-canalese, natives of the main island of Gaudalcanal, and the Malaitans, who come from the nearby province of Malaita—over jobs and land rights erupted into open warfare in 1998. The Isatambu Freedom Movement (IFM), claiming to represent native Guadalcanalese interests, forced the eviction of 30,000 Malaitans from Guadalcanal. Scores were injured or killed in the fighting that ensued between the IFM and the Malaita Eagle Force (MEF), a band of armed Malaitans.

Prime Minister Bartholomew Ulufa'alu, a Malaitan, was taken hostage in June 2000 by the MEF, which seized control of the capital, Honiara. Ulufa'alu was forced to resign and was replaced by Manasseh Sogavare. Fighting officially ended with the Townsville Peace Agreement of October 2000, which was brokered by Australia and New Zealand. The agreement provides for the "restructure of the police force, a weapons amnesty, and reconciliation." Both countries sent unarmed peacekeepers to supervise the collection of arms, many of which had been brought in from Bougainville in Papua New Guinea after civil violence ended there in 1998. However, a group of Malaitan militants rejected the peace treaty and, under its leader, Harold Keke, killed 50 people and burned entire villages in the Weather Coast region of Guadalcanal. Armed gangs terrorized other parts of the country, including the capital, eventually forcing the government to leave Honiara. Parliamentary elections in December 2001 brought a new government to power under Sir Allan Kemakeza.

Under RAMSI auspices, Australia and New Zealand have sent millions of dollars and some 2,000 personnel (200 police, 200 military, and 1,500 support staff) to assist the Solomon Islands in its recovery. The Australian-led program, also known as "Operation Help a Friend," was approved by Honiara in July 2003 and endorsed by the United Nations the following month. RAMSI continued where a UN mission left off in June 2003; the first personnel arrived on Guadalcanal Island on July 23. The goal is to help local police regain control and to help government structures and legal systems operate effectively. In December, 232 people returned to their village on the remote Weather Coast region of Guadalcanal; about 1,600 had fled the area at the height of the civil unrest in 1998.

Prime Minister Kemakeza has been waging an enormous uphill battle to reform government and rebuild institutions paralyzed by violence. In 2004, the country remained in dire financial straits, and pay was suspended for government employees for several months. Donors have been pressing the government to reform its police and judiciary and improve transparency to curb endemic corruption. Change has been slow, but some important progress was made in 2004. Several leaders of the civil war and rebels against the government were arrested and brought to trial during the year. Among these were Andrew Te'e, who was supreme commander of the IFM, Harold Keke of the Guadacanal Liberation Front, and Simon Mani, a leader of the MEF. Several senior officials also have been arrested and charged for their alleged crimes.

In May, the national parliament was called for the first time since the rebel coup took the capital in June 2000. Opposition leader John Garo joined the government of Prime Minister Kemakeza as the new minister of state following a cabinet shuffle in June, and Nathaniel Waena, a parliament member, succeeded Sir John Ini Lapli as the new governor-general.

RAMSI marked its first anniversary on July 24, 2004, and the operation was deemed to have been a success in restoring stability and peace to the country. However, this situation is by no means permanent, and as a follow-up action to RAMSI, Australia sent 1,700 military personnel to provide police training and support. Improved conditions quickly reduced the number of Australian troops, but about 100 remained by the end of August to head police forces in several provinces until Solomon Island police are ready to resume authority.

Political Rights and Civil Liberties:

Citizens of the Solomon Islands can change their government democratically. The country is a member of the Commonwealth, and the British monarch is the nominal head of state, represented by a governor-general who is chosen by parliament for a five-year term. Nathaniel Waena, the current governor-general, was elected to this office in July 2004. The government is a modified parliamentary system with a 50-member, single-chamber Legislative Assembly; members are elected for four-year terms. A parliamentary majority elects the prime minister, who appoints his own cabinet.

The leading political parties are the People's Alliance Party, led by Kemakeza, and the Solomon Islands Alliance for Change Coalition, headed by Ulufa'alu. Each holds 40 percent of the seats in parliament. However, politics in the Solomon Islands are driven less by parties than personalities, and there are frequent changes to party affiliations and alliances.

Corruption is a serious problem, resulting in public dissatisfaction and significant economic harm. Many and consistent allegations of official corruption and abuses of power have tied politicians and government officials to logging contracts, licensing, and public contracts, among other activities. Petty corruption among the lower ranks of government officials also appears widespread. Government efforts at reform and improved transparency have not occurred.

Freedom of expression and of the press is generally respected in practice. Reports on corruption and abuses by police and politicians appear in the local media. Those charged with wrongdoing sometimes use legal and extralegal means to intimidate journalists, but the government generally leaves matters to the courts for adjudication. Internet access is low, mainly because of the lack of telecommunications infrastructure and prohibitive costs.

Freedom of religion is generally respected in practice. Academic freedom is also respected despite serious disruptions in instruction and research as a result of the recent violence and a lack of government funding.

Many civil society groups operated freely, with the largest numbers of groups promoting development and religion. The constitution guarantees freedom of assembly, and the government generally recognizes this right. Laws require organizers of demonstrations to obtain permits, which are typically granted. Workers are free to organize, and strikes are permitted. Wage earners represent 10 to 15 percent of the workforce; the rest engage in subsistence farming and fishing.

Threats against judges and prosecutors have weakened the independence and rigor of the judiciary. Judges and prosecutors have also been implicated in corruption and abuse scandals. In October, the chief justice was dismissed for alleged misconduct. A lack of resources limits the government's ability to provide legal counsel and timely prosecutions and trials. Traditional chiefs have asked the government to provide more funds to rural, traditional courts to ease demand on the formal court system. Nevertheless, some important rulings were handed down in 2004: a cabinet member was sentenced to three years in prison for extorting money from a local newspaper, a deputy police commissioner was charged with facilitating false claims and abuse of office, and a former police superintendent was found guilty of larceny, assault, intimidation, and extortion.

The constitution provides for an ombudsman, with the power to subpoena and investigate complaints of official abuse, mistreatment, or unfair treatment. The ombudsman's office has potentially far-reaching powers but is limited by a lack of resources.

Law enforcement relies on a civilian-controlled police force of about a thousand persons, and there is no army. Factional and ethnic rivalries within the police since the 2000 coup have rendered the police virtually useless. Many Malaitan officers joined the MEF, and the hiring of about 1,200 untrained former militants as "special constables" to stop fighting also caused problems. Several of these former militants and the paramilitary Police Field Force were implicated in criminal activities. When the police chief attempted to demobilize 800 of the special police in 2003, about 300 of them protested to demand outstanding salaries and claims before termination.

The country continues to recover from recent violence between Malaitans and non-Malaitans, particularly the Guadacanalese. Tensions remain and reconciliation among the different groups has yet to occur.

Despite legal guarantees of equal rights, discrimination limits the economic and political roles of women. No law prohibits domestic violence, although rape and common assault are illegal. Reports of violence against adult and teenage women have increased since the coup in June 2000. In December 2003, a local woman, described as a middle-aged divorced mother, was arrested and charged with having sex with a person of the same gender. Homosexuality is illegal in the Solomon Islands. The woman was denied bail and kept in police custody on the grounds that she might interfere with witnesses.

↑ Somalia

Population: 8,300,000 **Political Rights:** 6
GNI/capita: $120 **Civil Liberties:** 7
Life Expectancy: 47 **Status:** Not Free
Religious Groups: Sunni Muslim, Christian minority
Ethnic Groups: Somali (85 percent), other
[including Bantu and Arab] (15 percent)
Capital: Mogadishu
Trend Arrow: Somalia received an upward trend arrow due to progress in establishing a central government.

Ten-Year Ratings Timeline (Political Rights, Civil Liberties, Status)

1995	1996	1997	1998	1999	2000	2001	2002	2003	2004
7,7NF	7,7NF	7,7NF	7,7NF	7,7NF	6,7NF	6,7NF	6,7NF	6,7NF	6,7NF

Overview: After 13 years of civil strife and anarchy, the final phase of Somalia's marathon peace talks drew to a close in 2004.

Under the guidance of the Intergovernmental Authority on Development, a grouping of seven Horn of Africa countries acting as mediators, Somali delegates concluded the contentious process of forming a 275-member parliament, the Transitional Federal Assembly (TFA), in August as part of the new Transitional Federal Government (TFG). In October, legislators elected Abdullahi Yusuf, an Ethiopian-backed career soldier and leader of the breakaway enclave of Puntland, to a five-year term as president of Somalia's TFG. Despite substantial progress in realizing the goals of the peace talks, intermittent clashes continue to erupt between various rival factions throughout the country, resulting in the deaths of hundreds of civilians.

Somalia, a Horn of Africa nation, gained independence in July 1960 with the union of British Somaliland and territories to the south that had been an Italian colony. Other ethnic Somali–inhabited lands are now part of Djibouti, Ethiopia, and Kenya. General Siad Barre seized power in 1969 and increasingly employed divisive clan politics to maintain power. While flood, drought, and famine racked the nation, the struggle to topple Barre has caused civil war, starvation, banditry, and brutality since the late 1980s. When Barre was deposed in January 1991, power was claimed and contested by heavily armed guerrilla movements and militias divided by traditional ethnic and clan loyalties.

Extensive television coverage of famine and civil strife that took approximately 300,000 lives in 1991 and 1992 prompted a U.S.-led international intervention. The armed humanitarian mission in late 1992 quelled clan combat long enough to stop the famine, but ended in urban guerrilla warfare against Somali militias. The last international forces withdrew in March 1995 after the combined casualty count reached into the thousands. Approximately 100 peacekeepers, including 18 U.S. soldiers, were killed. The $4 billion UN intervention effort had little lasting impact.

The Djibouti-hosted Conference for National Peace and Reconciliation in Somalia adopted a charter in 2000 for a three-year transition, established the Transitional National Government (TNG), and selected a 245-member Transitional National Assembly (TNA). The TNA elected Abdiqassim Salad Hassan as transitional president in August 2000. The TNG and more than 20 rival groups signed a ceasefire in October 2002 in Kenya as a first step toward establishing a federal system of government. However, over the next year, the talks deadlocked when some faction leaders dropped out to form their own parallel talks in Mogadishu.

The faltering peace process was revitalized at a national reconciliation conference in Nairobi in 2004. In August, the new TFG, consisting of the 275-member TFA, replaced the TNG. The country's four largest clans were each given 61 seats, and an alliance of minority clans took the remaining 31. The parliament chose a speaker who facilitated the presidential contest won by Abdullahi Yusuf; more than two dozen candidates competed for the post. However, ongoing lawlessness forced the fledgling parliament to convene across the border in Kenya.

Under the Somali National Charter adopted in 2003 and amended in early 2004, Yusef appointed Ali Muhammad Gedi, a prominent member of the political arm of the United Somali Congress, as his prime minister in November 2004. Under the interim charter, Gedi will lead a five-year central government based in the Somali capital of Mogadishu. That government will face the daunting tasks of enforcing a ceasefire among warring clan-based militias, forming a new police force and army, and rebuilding the economic infrastructure. Somali leaders have agreed to undertake a national census while a new constitution, which must be approved in an internationally supervised referendum, is being drafted. The new government must also address the question of autonomy for the neighboring region of Somaliland, whose leadership has boycotted the peace talks. The presence of rival militias with suspected links to al-Qaeda and other terrorist organizations further complicate the picture, although President Yusef is perceived as an ally of the U.S.-led war on terrorism.

The UN Security Council has extended its mandate in the country until 2005. Despite a 12-year-old arms embargo, the Security Council says that illegal weapons and ammunition continue to be sold openly in Somali markets, particularly in the capital.

Somalia is a poor country where most people survive as pastoralists or subsistence farmers. More than a decade of conflict and a persistent drought have devastated the country's agricultural and livestock production, leaving 1.3 million people in dire need of food aid. Since the freezing of assets in 2001 belonging to Somalia's Al-Barakaat telecommunications and money-transfer firm, which was accused of aiding terrorist groups, private remittance companies have taken steps to self-regulate the industry, including the creation of a new watchdog body, the Somali Financial Services Association. Together, the companies facilitate the transfer of $750 million into the country each year.

Political Rights and Civil Liberties: Somalis cannot change their government democratically. The 2000 elections marked the first time Somalis had an opportunity to choose their government on a somewhat national basis since 1969. Some 3,000 representatives of civic and religious organizations, women's groups, and clans came together under the Intergovernmental Authority on Development, following Djibouti-hosted peace talks, to elect a transitional parliament in August 2000. In August 2004, the new 275-member parliament, the TFA, came into existence. Abdullahi Yusuf, leader of the breakaway enclave of Puntland, was elected to a five-year term as president

The region of Somaliland has exercised de facto independence from Somalia since May 1991, although it has failed to gain international recognition. A clan conference led to a peace accord among its clan factions in 1997, establishing a presidency and bicameral parliament with proportional clan representation. Somaliland is far more cohesive than the rest of the country, although reports of some human rights abuses persist. A referendum on independence and a new constitution were approved in May 2001, opening the way for a multiparty system. Dahir Riyale Kahin of the ruling Unity of Democrats Party emerged as the winner of historic presidential elections in 2003. Kahin had been vice president under Mohamed Egal, who died of kidney failure in 2002. International observers from 14 countries declared the voting to be free and fair. Municipal elections in December 2002 also drew 440,000 people to the polls.

Puntland established a regional government in 1998, with a presidency and a single-chamber quasi-legislature known as the Council of Elders. Political parties are banned. The traditional elders chose Abdullahi Yusuf, now the new president of Somalia, as the region's first president for a three-year term. After Jama Ali Jama was elected to replace him in 2001, Abdullahi Yusuf refused to relinquish power, claiming he was fighting terrorism. Yusuf seized power in 2002, reportedly with the help of Ethiopian forces.

Somalia was not ranked by Transparency International in its 2004 Corruption Perceptions Index.

Somalia's charter provides for press freedom. The country has about 20 privately owned newspapers, a dozen radio and television stations, and several Internet Web sites. Most of the independent newspapers or newsletters that circulate in Mogadishu are linked to a specific faction. Although journalists face harassment, most receive the protection of the clan supporting their publication. The transitional government launched its first radio station, Radio Mogadishu, in 2001. Press freedom is very limited in the country's two self-declared autonomous regions. In January 2004, two radio journalists were briefly detained by authorities in Puntland for coverage of the escalating border dispute between Puntland and Somaliland. In April, the editor of an independent weekly newspaper, *War-Ogaal*, was arrested and jailed for more than a month without charge for publishing an article accusing a Puntland minister of corruption. In September, the editor of the Somaliland independent daily newspaper *Jamhuuriya* was arrested for the fifteenth time in ten years. Reporters Sans Frontieres described the incident as the latest in a long campaign of legal harassment.

Somalia is an Islamic state, and religious freedom is not guaranteed. The Sunni majority often views non-Sunni Muslims with suspicion. Members of the small Christian community face societal harassment if they proclaim their religion, but a number of international Christian aid groups operate without hindrance. Academic freedom faces some restrictions similar to those imposed on the media, and there is no organized higher education system in most of the country.

Several indigenous and foreign nongovernmental organizations operate in Somalia with varying degrees of latitude. A number of international aid organizations, women's groups, and local human rights groups operate in the country. The charter provides workers with the right to form unions and assemble freely, but civil war and factional fighting led to the dissolution of the single labor confederation, the government-controlled General Federation of Somali Trade Unions. Wages are established largely by ad hoc bartering and the influence of clan affiliation.

Somalia's charter provides for an independent judiciary, although a formal judicial system has ceased to exist. In Mogadishu, Sharia (Islamic law) courts have been effective in bringing a semblance of law and order to the city. Efforts at judicial reform are proceeding slowly. The Sharia courts in Mogadishu are gradually coming under the control of the transitional government. Most of the courts are aligned with various subclans. Prison conditions are harsh in some areas, but improvements are under way.

Human rights abuses, including extrajudicial killing, rape, torture, beating, and arbitrary detention by Somalia's various armed factions, remain a problem. Many violations are linked to banditry. Two aid workers with the German Development Agency were killed in Somaliland in 2004 when their car was ambushed. Police arrested five Somalis in connection with the murders. A member of the UN field security team was abducted by a militia group but was released unharmed nine days later.

Although more than 80 percent of Somalis share a common ethnic heritage, religion, and nomadic-influenced culture, discrimination is widespread. Clans exclude one another from participation in social and political life. Minority clans are harassed, intimidated, and abused by armed gunmen.

Women's groups were instrumental in galvanizing support for Somalia's peace process. However, delegates forming the new parliament flouted a provision requiring that 33 of the 275 seats be reserved for women, appointing only 23. Women legislators are now seeking a constitutional amendment to increase that number by 14. The country's new charter prohibits sexual discrimination, but women experience intense discrimination under customary practices and variants of Sharia. Infibulation, the most severe form of female genital mutilation, is routine, and women's groups launched a national campaign to discourage the practice in March. UN agencies and nongovernmental organizations are working to raise awareness about the health dangers of this practice. Various armed factions have recruited children into their militias.

South Africa

Population: 46,900,000
GNI/capita: $2,500
Life Expectancy: 53
Political Rights: 1
Civil Liberties: 2
Status: Free
Religious Groups: Christian (68 percent), Muslim
(2 percent), Hindu (1.5 percent), other [including
Jewish, indigenous beliefs, and animist] (28.5 percent)
Ethnic Groups: Black (75 percent), white (14 percent),
mixed (9 percent), Indian (2 percent)
Capital: Pretoria

Ten-Year Ratings Timeline (Political Rights, Civil Liberties, Status)

1995	1996	1997	1998	1999	2000	2001	2002	2003	2004
1,2F	1,2F	1,2F	1,2F	1,2F	1,2F	1,2F	1,2F	1,2F	1,2F

Overview:

In 2004, South Africa celebrated a decade of democracy with a third round of free and fair general elections. However, President Thabo Mbeki undermined the country's stature as a regional leader by refusing to publicly condemn growing repression in neighboring Zimbabwe. The government further damaged its credibility by failing to confront an HIV infection rate that is the world's highest.

South Africa's apartheid government, which came to power in 1948, reserved political power for the white minority. International economic sanctions and civil unrest eventually forced the South African government to negotiate with its adversaries. Momentum for change accelerated with the accession to power of Frederick de Klerk and global moves toward democratization in the late 1980s. In 1990, de Klerk freed from prison African National Congress (ANC) leader Nelson Mandela after the latter had served 27 years of a life sentence. De Klerk initiated a negotiation process that resulted in legitimate multiparty elections in 1994. These elections brought Mandela and the ANC to power at the national level.

The ANC's electoral primacy was confirmed in elections in 1999 and then again on April 14, 2004. The party won 70 percent of the vote—its best showing yet—claiming 279 of the 400 seats in parliament; Mbeki was sworn in for a second five-year term.

Since the ANC has come to power, tension has increased with trade unions, independent media, traditional leaders, and the white minority. Hundreds of thousands of public sector workers went on strike in September 2004 in the largest industrial action in the last decade. Key areas of disagreement between the ANC and labor have included the government's conservative economic policies and its approach to the AIDS epidemic.

The ANC leadership largely blames the country's problems on the former white-supremacist regime. However, this argument has begun to lose potency with the growing economic empowerment of a minority of black South Africans. Protests have taken place over the slow pace of essential-services delivery to disadvantaged people. Serious challenges exist regarding economic development, and although progress has been made, the government has not kept promises to vastly improve education, health care, and housing. The durability of the new democratic structures is uncertain, as South Africa remains deeply divided by ethnicity and class. Some 40 percent of South Africans live in poverty, which could eventually pose a risk to social stability.

More than one in nine South Africans is HIV-positive. The country has the highest infection rate in the world, which poses enormous political and social problems. Up to 360,000 South Africans die yearly from AIDS, which has orphaned more than 650,000 children. Besides overwhelming the health care system, the pandemic threatens the economy by depleting future generations of workers. After having spent considerable political capital trying to keep anti-HIV drugs from the public health system, arguing that the virus did not necessarily cause AIDS, Mbeki in 2003 yielded to international and domestic pressure to provide universal antiretroviral drug treatment. However, very little has been done to implement the program. In July 2004, in what AIDS campaigners saw as another obstacle, the government rejected giving pregnant HIV-positive women a single dose of the drug nevirapine, recommending instead a more complex 28-week regimen that would reach fewer people. Mbeki's slowness in tackling the epidemic and the country's astronomical crime rates have scared off much foreign investment.

South Africa is deemed a regional leader, but Mbeki lacks the moral authority of his predecessor, Mandela. Mbeki's pursuit of "quiet diplomacy" with the ANC's historic ally, Zimbabwe president Robert Mugabe, has been ineffectual in resolving authoritarianism and economic collapse in that country.

Political Rights and Civil Liberties: South Africans can change their government democratically. Three successful national elections have taken place since 1994, the last in April 2004. Elections for the 400-seat National Assembly and 90-seat National Council of Provinces are by proportional representation based on party lists. The National Assembly elects the president to serve concurrently with the five-year parliamentary term. The next local elections are scheduled for 2005. In general, the electoral process, including voter education, balanced state-media coverage, and reliable balloting and vote counting, has functioned properly.

The ANC dominates the South African political landscape, as evidenced by its sweeping electoral victory in April 2004. The Democratic Alliance, the party favored by most white South Africans, emerged as the main opposition group with 50 seats in parliament. The Inkatha Freedom Party came in third, with 28 seats, demonstrating that it is no longer a major force outside of the Kwa-Zulu Natal province. The New National Party, formerly the National Party that ruled during apartheid, has seen support erode dramatically to only six seats.

In 2000, the cabinet endorsed a code of ethics for politicians, covering items such as conflict of interest and disclosure of financial assets and large gifts. Corruption is not widespread, but concerns about increasing incidents led to the introduction into parliament of the 2002 Prevention of Corruption bill. South Africa was ranked 44 out of 146 countries surveyed in Transparency International's 2004 Corruption Perceptions Index.

Freedom of expression is generally respected, although the government is sensitive to criticism. The state-owned South African Broadcasting Corporation (SABC) suffers from self-censorship. However, a variety of newspapers and magazines publish opinions sharply critical of the government and the ANC. Scores of small community radio stations operate, as well as one commercial television station, e-TV. Internet access is growing rapidly but remains elusive for disadvantaged people, particularly in rural areas, where computers and electricity are scarce.

The final version of the Broadcasting Amendment Bill passed by parliament in 2002 reflects the maturity of the democratic processes. Original draft legislation contained a clause requiring that the SABC report to the minister of communications regarding editorial content. The legislation was revised after considerable debate; the constitutionally mandated Independent Communications Authority of South Africa will ensure that the SABC fulfills its mission of broadcasting in the public interest.

Religious and academic freedom thrive.

The government generally respects the rights of freedom of assembly and association, and a lively protest scene prevails. Non-governmental organizations operate freely. In recent years, the ANC has seen increased tension with its traditional political allies, the Congress of South African Trade Unions and the South African Communist Party. Labor rights codified under the 1995 Labor Relations Act (LRA) are respected, and more than 250 trade unions exist. The right to strike can be exercised after reconciliation efforts. The LRA allows employers to hire replacement workers. The ANC government has introduced several labor laws designed to protect the rights of workers, although it has taken other actions that weaken trade union positions in bargaining for job security, wages, and other benefits.

The country's independent judiciary functions well. South Africa's new constitution, which took effect in February 1997, is one of the most liberal in the world and includes a sweeping bill of rights. Parliament has passed more than 500 laws relating to the constitution, revamping the apartheid-era legal system. This legislation is now being implemented; for example, some lower courts have been designated "equality courts," with a particular mandate to review instances of unfair discrimination.

The 11-member Constitutional Court, created to enforce the rules of the new democracy, has demonstrated considerable independence. In its Treatment Action Campaign ruling in 2002, the court challenged President Thabo Mbeki by requiring the government to provide treatment to women with HIV or AIDS. Lower courts generally respect legal provisions regarding arrest and detention, although courts remain understaffed. The bill of rights prohibits detention without trial, but lengthy pretrial detentions are common as a result of an overwhelmed judiciary. The death penalty was abolished in 1995.

Efforts to end torture and other abuses by the national police force have been implemented, although incidents still occur. Deaths in police custody continue to be a problem. The constitutionally mandated Human Rights Commission was appointed by parliament to "promote the observance of, respect for, and the protection of fundamental rights." Prisons often do not meet international standards and are characterized by overcrowding, poor health conditions, and abuses of inmates by staff or other prisoners.

Through a series of open hearings, the now-concluded Truth and Reconciliation Commission sought to heal divisions created by the apartheid regime. From 1996 to 1998, the commission received more than 20,000 submissions from victims and nearly 8,000 applications for amnesty from perpetrators. In 1998, the commission released a report on human rights abuses during the apartheid years that largely focused on atrocities committed by the white-minority government, but which also criticized the ANC. The controversial issue of reparations for victims of apartheid is actively debated between civil society and the government.

The breakdown of law and order is a serious problem. An estimated four million illegal firearms circulate in South Africa, and in recent years, the country has ranked first in the world in the per capita number of rapes and armed robberies. Only 1 in 10 violent crimes results in conviction.

In response to the September 11, 2001, attacks in the United States, the South African government drafted a terrorism bill, which alarmed many members of civil society who remembered the days when the ANC was persecuted as a terrorist organization. In particular, trade union groups were concerned about clauses that appeared to criminalize certain types of industrial action. The bill was withdrawn before the 2004 elections, but an amended version, excluding many of the offending clauses, was approved by the National Assembly in November.

In 2000, parliament approved legislation outlawing discrimination on the basis of race, ethnicity, or sex.

South African society is characterized by ample personal freedom, and a small black middle class is emerging. However, the white minority retains most economic power. Some three-quarters of South Africans are black, yet they enjoy less than a third of the country's total income. Unemployment stands at about 40 percent among blacks and 4 percent for whites. The quality of schooling differs for the two groups, and blacks living on farms often fail to receive formal education. The government seeks to lessen these disparities by improving, although slowly, housing and health care in disadvantaged areas. It has launched initiatives such as the Mining Charter, negotiated in 2002, which requires 25 percent of that industry to be black-owned in five years.

Equal rights for women are guaranteed by the constitution and promoted by the constitutionally mandated Commission on Gender Equality. Laws such as the Maintenance Act and the Domestic Violence Act are designed to protect women in financially inequitable and abusive relationships. These laws, however, do not provide the infrastructure necessary for implementation. Discriminatory practices in customary law remain prevalent, as does sexual violence against women and minors. Forty percent of rape survivors are girls under 18. The Criminal Law (Sexual Offences) Amendment Bill, introduced to parliament in 2003, seeks to widen protection for sex-crimes victims, but human rights groups say that it does not go far enough.

South Korea

Population: 48,200,000   **Political Rights:** 1*
GNI/capita: $9,930   **Civil Liberties:** 2
Life Expectancy: 77   **Status:** Free
Religious Groups: Christian (26 percent), Buddhist
(26 percent), Confucian (1 percent), none (46 percent),
other (1 percent)
Ethnic Groups: Korean
Capital: Seoul
Ratings Change: South Korea's political rights rating improved from 2 to 1 due to the holding of free and fair parliamentary elections following a highly politicized impeachment process.

Ten-Year Ratings Timeline (Political Rights, Civil Liberties, Status)

1995	1996	1997	1998	1999	2000	2001	2002	2003	2004
2,2F	2,2F	2,2F	2,2F	2,2F	2,2F	2,2F	2,2F	2,2F	1,2F

Overview:

The South Korean president, Roh Moo-hyun, survived a political crisis in early 2004 when the opposition brought about a parliamentary vote to impeach him. South Koreans backed Roh's party, the Uri Party, in parliamentary elections in April, however, giving him a major victory and allowing him to return to power in May after the Constitutional Court overturned the impeachment vote. Nevertheless, the Uri Party holds only a narrow majority in parliament, and Roh's aggressive style continues to polarize.

The Republic of Korea was established in 1948, three years after the Allied victory in World War II ended Japan's 35-year colonization of Korea and led to the division of the Korean Peninsula between U.S. and Soviet forces. During the Cold War, South Korea's mainly military rulers crushed left-wing dissent and kept the nation on a virtual war footing in response to the continuing threat from the North following the Korean War in the early 1950s. They also led an industrialization drive that transformed a poor, agrarian land into the world's eleventh-largest economy.

South Korea's democratic transition began in 1987, when military strongman Chun Doo-hwan acceded to widespread student protests and allowed his successor to be chosen in a direct presidential election. In voting that December, Chun's protégé, Roh Tae-woo, defeated the country's best-known dissidents, Kim Young-sam and Kim Dae-jung.

After joining the ruling party in 1990, Kim Young-sam defeated Kim Dae-jung in the 1992 presidential election to become South Korea's first civilian president since 1961. As president, Kim cracked down on corruption, sacked hard-line military officers, curbed the domestic security services, and successfully prosecuted former presidents Chun and Roh for corruption and treason. However, the country was hit hard by the regional financial crisis of 1997-1998. Angry over the government's failure to better supervise the country's banks and business conglomerates, South Koreans in December 1997 elected as president former dissident Kim Dae-jung, who became the country's first opposition candidate to win a presidential election. Under Kim Dae-jung, South Korea's economy rebounded to become one of the most robust in Asia.

Public frustration with a series of corruption scandals, along with criticism that Kim Dae-jung's policy of engagement with North Korea had reaped few benefits, helped the opposition Grand National Party (GNP) take the most seats in the 2000 parliamentary elections. It captured 133 out of parliament's 273 seats, with Kim's Millennium Democratic Party (MDP) taking 115.

With Kim Dae-jung constitutionally barred from seeking a second term, Roh, 56, won the December 2002 presidential elections on the MDP ticket. Roh narrowly beat Lee Hoi-chang, the candidate of the main opposition GNP, after a campaign in which Roh mixed populist promises with anti-American rhetoric.

Roh took office in February 2003 facing an economic slowdown, an opposition-led parliament, and public moves by North Korea to revive its nuclear weapons program. A major fundraising scandal during the year added urgency to longstanding calls from many quarters for an overhaul of South Korea's campaign finance laws. Late in the year, prosecutors were investigating allegations that former top aides to Roh, as well as legislators from across the political spectrum, accepted millions of dollars in illegal corporate donations before and after the 2002 presidential election. The opposition-led parliament put off consideration of several bills as it remained at loggerheads with Roh over how to investigate the scandal. Roh vetoed a GNP bill in November calling for an independent counsel to investigate allegations of corruption in his administration. The president said that any independent investigation should wait until prosecutors currently investigating three of his former aides finished their work. Elected on pledges to improve corporate governance, bring greater transparency to state institutions, and engage, rather than contain, bellicose North Korea, Roh was forced to reshuffle his priorities.

In February 2004, Roh survived a political crisis when the opposition brought about a parliamentary vote to impeach him. Although the opposition had long been averse to his policies and his generally anti-establishment position, the actual charges on which the vote was based related to breach of election rules, economic mismanagement and corruption. South Korean voters, however, were more put off by this unprecedented action than by the charges (which were in any case inflated), and they demonstrated their distaste for the opposition's politically motivated maneuvering by supporting the president's party in parliamentary elections held in April 2004. Roh's party, the Uri Party, won 152 seats to become the majority ruling party. The Grand National Party and the Millennium Democratic Party (MDP), the main opposition parties and the instigators of the impeachment vote, won 121 seats and 9 seats, respectively. The MDP's loss was particularly severe, as the party had previously held over 60 seats, and it proved that the impeachment vote was an enormous miscalculation. Although Roh had stepped down from power following the impeachment vote, the Uri Party's victory in the parliamentary elections led the Constitutional Court to overturn the impeachment vote, and Roh was reinstated as president in May. Nevertheless, the Uri Party holds only a narrow majority in parliament, and Roh's aggressive style continues to polarize.

Though the Uri Party now controls parliament, the economy is still underperforming. Labor disputes are becoming more contentious, and so negotiations with South Korea's famously strident labor unions should be an ongoing preoccupation for the current administration. Meanwhile, Pyongyang has yet to be fully engaged in disarmament talks.

Political Rights and Civil Liberties: South Koreans choose their government through free and fair elections held on the basis of universal suffrage. The 1988 constitution vests executive powers in a directly elected president who is limited to a single five-year term. The unicameral National Assembly, comprising 299 members, is directly elected for a four-year term.

The April 2004 parliamentary elections were significant not only because they followed a vote to impeach the president, Roh Moo-hyun, but also because they brought about a shift in power in parliament for the first time in more than 40 years. Indeed, the Heritage Foundation, a U.S.-based think tank, went so far as to call the elections a "victory for the electoral and campaign process in South Korea"—citing the improvement since 2002 in campaigning rules and the reduction in electoral irregularities under the watch of the National Election Commission—and a victory for democracy in general, noting that voter turnout, at 60 percent, reached an unprecedented level. Political participation and pluralism is vigorous; Roh's Uri Party is itself a splinter of the MDP (the party of former president Kim Dae-jung) formed only in late 2003.

Nevertheless, bribery, influence peddling, and extortion by officials have not been eradicated from politics, business, and daily life. South Korea was ranked 47 out of 146 countries surveyed in Transparency International's 2004 Corruption Perceptions Index.

South Korea's press generally is competitive. Newspapers are privately owned and report fairly aggressively on governmental policies and alleged official and corporate wrongdoing. Aggressive reporting, however, has landed several journalists in jail in recent years under criminal libel laws, some for reports that were critical but factually accurate. State-owned media display "a considerable degree of editorial independence," according to the U.S. State Department's 2003 human rights report released in February 2004. The same report noted, however, that the South Korean government does still exert indirect influence on the news media through activities such as lobbying or initiating tax audits. In addition, the government directly censors films for sex and violence, though it has been increasingly liberal in recent years. Violent and sexually explicit Web sites are also censored.

The constitution provides for freedom of religion, and South Korea does not enforce any state religion. Academic freedom is also unrestricted. The only limits on freedom of expression concern ideas considered to be pro-Communist or supportive of the North Korean regime.

South Korea maintains freedom of association, and the Law on Assembly and Demonstrations requires only that the police be informed in advance of all demonstrations, including political rallies. Human rights, social welfare, and other nongovernmental groups are active and operate freely.

South Korea's independent labor unions strongly advocate workers' interests, often by organizing high-profile strikes and demonstrations that sometimes lead to arrests. At the end of November 2004, the Korea Confederation of Trade Unions led a one-day strike involving hundreds of thousands of workers to protest pending legislation that would increase flexibility in the labor market. The centerpiece of the proposed bill is a provision allowing companies to hire temporary workers. The law bars strikes by workers in government agencies, state-run enterprises, and defense firms. In addition, workers must observe notification and cooling-off provisions before striking and can be forced to submit to arbitration.

Beginning in 2006, multiple unions will be permitted at the company level, a change expected to give workers greater choice of representatives. The law, however, still bars defense industry and white-collar government workers from forming unions and bargaining collectively, although government workers can form more limited workplace councils. Even those federations not recognized by the government operate in practice without restriction, however. Collective bargaining is widespread among both legal and unrecognized labor federations.

South Korea's judiciary generally is considered to be independent, and the U.S. State Department report declared that it is "becoming increasingly so in practice." There is no trial by jury; judges render verdicts in all cases. The National Police Administration, under the Ministry of Government Administration and Home Affairs, is occasionally responsible for human rights abuses such as verbal and physical abuse of detainees. The police administration is generally considered well-disciplined and uncorrupt.

Laws concerning detention are often vague. Of particular concern is the broadly drafted National Security Law (NSL), which authorizes the arrest of South Koreans accused of espionage and/or viewed as supporting North Korea. Because there is wide latitude to interpret the wording of this law, several people are thought to have been arrested for nonthreatening expressions of political views that were ostensibly anti–South Korean or pro–North Korean. In August 2004 the Constitutional Court ruled that the law did not excessively restrict human rights, but in October, the ruling Uri Party introduced legislation to loosen or scrap the law, offering the country alternatives ranging from revisions of the existing law to the drafting of an entirely new law. The move was part of the government's broader reform drive, but thousands of people rallied in protest, asserting that the law in its current form was still a necessary safeguard against security threats from North Korea.

Because South Korean citizenship is based on parentage rather than place of birth, non-ethnic South Koreans face extreme difficulties obtaining citizenship. Lack of citizenship bars them from the civil service and makes it harder to be hired by some major corporations. The very few ethnic minorities face legal and societal discrimination.

The government generally respects citizens' right to privacy. An Anti-Wiretap Law sets out the conditions under which the government can monitor phone calls, mail, and e-mail. Under the NSL, South Koreans may not listen to North Korean radio or read North Korean books if they are thought to be doing so to help that regime. This provision is rarely enforced, however, and North Korean media are freely available in South Korea. Travel both within South Korea and abroad is unrestricted; the only exception is travel to North Korea, for which government approval is required.

Women continue to face societal discrimination in this conservative country. Rape, domestic violence, and sexual harassment of women continue to be serious problems despite recent legislation and other initiatives to protect women. Women's groups say that rape and sexual harassment generally are not prosecuted, in part because women are reluctant to bring cases, and convicted offenders often receive light sentences. According to the U.S. State Department report, South Korea is "a major origin, transit and destination point for trafficking in women and children destined for the sex trade and domestic servitude."

Spain

Population: 42,500,000
GNI/capita: $14,580
Life Expectancy: 79
Religious Groups: Roman Catholic (94 percent), other (6 percent)
Ethnic Groups: Mediterranean and Nordic
Capital: Madrid

Political Rights: 1
Civil Liberties: 1
Status: Free

Ten-Year Ratings Timeline (Political Rights, Civil Liberties, Status)

1995	1996	1997	1998	1999	2000	2001	2002	2003	2004
1,2F	1,2F	1,2F	1,2F	1,2F	1,2F	1,2F	1,1F	1,1F	1,1F

Overview:

After eight years of conservative rule, the Socialist Party won general elections in March 2004. The elections took place only a few days after the bombing of commuter trains in Madrid by al-Qaeda, the Islamic terrorist group, took the lives of nearly 200 people. The government's quick response in blaming Basque terrorists was largely seen as the reason for the conservatives' defeat at the polls. Keeping an election promise, the newly elected prime minister, Jose Luis Rodriguez Zapatero, pulled 1,300 Spanish soldiers out of Iraq, citing the lack of a UN mandate for the 2003 U.S.-led invasion. On the domestic front, the government began drafting a law to legalize same-sex marriage.

The unification of present-day Spain dates from 1512. After a period of colonial influence and wealth, the country declined as a European power and was occupied by France in the early nineteenth century. By the end of the century, after a number of wars and revolts, Spain lost its American colonies. The Spanish Civil War, from 1936 to 1939, led to the deaths of more than 350,000 Spaniards and the victory of Franco's Nationalists, who executed, jailed, and exiled the opposition Republicans. During Franco's long rule, many countries cut off diplomatic ties, and his regime was ostracized by the United Nations from 1946 to 1955. Euskadi Ta Askatasuna (ETA, or Basque Fatherland and Freedom) was formed in 1959 with the aim of creating an independent Basque homeland. After a transitional period on Franco's death in 1975, Spain emerged as a parliamentary democracy, joining the European Economic Community, the precursor to the European Union (EU), in 1986.

During the March 2004 parliamentary elections, the Spanish Socialist Workers' Party (PSOE) won more than 43 percent of the vote, capturing 164 seats in the Congress of Deputies (lower house). The PSOE toppled the conservative People's Party (PP), which had been in power for 11 years, and which took 148 seats. Other parties winning seats included the left Convergence and Union (CiU), Catalonia's Republican Left (ERC), the Basque Nationalist Party (PNV), the United Left (IU), and the Canarian Coalition (CC). Lacking an outright majority, the PSOE relied on the support of various regionalist parties to support its legislation. In the Senate, the PP led by winning 102 directly elected seats, while the PSOE took 81 directly elected seats.

The election came only three days after multiple terrorist bombings of commuter trains in Madrid that killed nearly 200 people. Shortly after the bombing, the conservative government blamed ETA, a factor that angered voters when it was discovered that the perpetrators were linked to al-Qaeda. The attacks allegedly came in response to the conservative government's staunch support of the U.S.-led war in Iraq. Shortly after his accession to the post of prime minister, Rodriguez Zapatero pulled the 1,300 Spanish troops out of Iraq. However, he also promised to double the Spanish peacekeeping force in Afghanistan. A 16-year old Spaniard accused of trafficking a significant amount of explosives used in the bombing admitted to his role in the attacks during a very quick trial in November 2004 and received a six year sentence.

Regionalist pressures continued during the year as the Basque regional government continued to make plans for an illegal referendum in early 2005 that would propose *de facto* political independence from Spain. In the Catalan region, a coalition of socialists and radical nationalists joined forces after elections in November 2003 to demand more autonomy for the region.

In October 2004, the government, in collaboration with the French police, arrested ETA's political leader, Mikel Albizu, as well as his girlfriend and 16 other members of the group, in southwest France. The arrests, which also netted a significant amount of firearms and explosives, dealt a serious blow to the separatist group, which has been waging a 30-war against the Spanish state for Basque independence. By the end of the year, over 70 ETA members and collaborators had been arrested by the police.

The new government introduced a number of socially liberal pieces of legislation, including a same-sex marriage bill. If approved by parliament, Spain will be the third EU country to allow same-sex marriage. The prime minister, who made women's rights and gender equality a centerpiece of his electoral campaign, also introduced a "gender violence" law that would confront the widespread problem of domestic violence in the country.

Political Rights and Civil Liberties: Citizens of Spain can change their government democratically. The Chamber of Deputies has 350 members that are elected from closed party lists in individual constituencies. There is also a Senate, which has 259 members, 208 of which are directly elected and 51 of which are appointed as regional representatives. The country is divided into 17 autonomous regions with varying degrees of power. People generally have the right to organize in different political parties and other competitive groups of their choice. However, the Basque-separatist Batasuna Party remains permanently banned since 2003 for its alleged ties to the armed group ETA.

Political corruption remains an issue in Spain. Spain was ranked 22 out of 146 countries surveyed in Transparency International's 2004 Corruption Perceptions Index.

Spain has a free and lively press with more than 100 newspapers that cover a wide range of perspectives and are active in investigating high-level corruption. Daily newspaper ownership, however, is concentrated within large media groups like Prisa and Zeta. A Syrian-born television reporter for the Qatar-based satellite network Al-Jazeera, Spanish citizen Tayseer Alouni, was arrested and placed in police custody again in November. Alouni was among 35 people arrested and charged with terror-related offenses in September 2003. Alouni, who has interviewed Osama bin Laden for Al-Jazeera, was charged with having links to al-Qaeda and using reporting trips to Kabul, Afghanistan, as a cover for fund-raising activities.

The Basque separatist group, ETA, continued its campaign of fear targeted against journalists that oppose its views on the political situation in the disputed region. Journalists and newspapers reported receiving threats by ETA in October 2004.

Freedom of religion is guaranteed in Spain through constitutional and legal protections. Roman Catholicism, however, is the dominant religion and enjoys privileges that other religions do not, such as financing through the tax system. Jews, Muslims, and Protestants have official status through bilateral agreements with the state, while other religions (for example, Jehovah's Witnesses and the Mormons) have no special agreements with the state.

The government does not restrict academic freedom. However, ETA and other Basque nationalists, through a campaign of street violence and vandalism in the region, continue to intimidate unsympathetic academics, journalists, and politicians. The constitution provides for freedom of assembly and the government respected this right. People are free to demonstrate and speak publicly. Domestic and international nongovernmental organizations (NGOs) operated within the country freely without government restrictions. With the exception of members of the military, workers are free to organize and join unions of their choice. Workers also have the right to strike, although there are limitations imposed on foreigners. The Basic Act on Rights and Freedoms of Foreigners in Spain, which went into force in 2001, limits the rights of foreign workers to organize and strike. The law, which forces foreigners to "obtain authorization for their stay or residence in Spain" before they can organize, strike, or freely assemble, is intended to distinguish between "legal" and "irregular" foreigners. The issue is currently before the Constitutional Court.

The constitution provides for an independent judiciary. However, there have been concerns about the functioning of the judicial system, including the impact of media pressure on sensitive issues like immigration and Basque terrorism. The Spanish government endorsed a judicial reform plan in 2003 that will enhance the transparency of judges and magistrates. The judiciary has also been affected by Basque terrorism as judicial officials and law enforcement officers have been targets of ETA. Prison conditions generally met international standards. There were, however, reports of police abuse of prisoners, especially immigrants. Police can also hold suspects of certain terror-related crimes for up to five days with access only to a public lawyer.

The constitution provides for an ombudsman (the People's Defender) whose duties include investigating alleged human rights abuses by government officials.

The country has tightened its immigration legislation in recent years to stem the influx of immigrants into the country. In May, two foreign nationals who were loosely tied to the March 11 bomb attacks in Madrid were expelled from the country because they were deemed a threat to national security. The country's Aliens Law allows for the expulsion of legal immigrants if they are involved in activities that are considered threatening to the country's national security.

A Spanish national, Hamed Abderrahman Ahmed, who was held in U.S. military custody in Guantanamo Bay, Cuba, was turned over to Spanish authorities in February.

Women enjoy legal protections against rape, domestic abuse, and sexual harassment in the workplace. Despite this, violence against women—particularly within the home—remains a serious problem in the country. The new prime minister has made the protection of women's rights and gender equality a centerpiece of his administration. A "gender violence" law was drafted only a week after the government was installed in April.

There are no quotas for women in national elective office. However, 35 percent of the seats in parliament during the elections in March were won by women, a 7 percent increase from the previous elections in 2000. Trafficking in women for the purpose of sexual exploitation remains a problem. The government targets traffickers as part of its larger plan to control immigration.

Sri Lanka

Population: 19,600,000 **Political Rights:** 3
GNI/capita: $850 **Civil Liberties:** 3
Life Expectancy: 72 **Status:** Partly Free
Religious Groups: Buddhist (70 percent),
Hindu (15 percent), Christian (8 percent),
Muslim (7 percent)
Ethnic Groups: Sinhalese (74 percent), Tamil (18 percent),
Moor (7 percent), other (1 percent)
Capital: Colombo

Ten-Year Ratings Timeline (Political Rights, Civil Liberties, Status)

1995	1996	1997	1998	1999	2000	2001	2002	2003	2004
4,5PF	3,5PF	3,4PF	3,4PF	3,4PF	3,4PF	3,4PF	3,4PF	3,3PF	3,3PF

Overview:
The uneasy cohabitation between Sri Lanka's two main political parties came to an end in 2004, as President Chandrika Kumaratunga dissolved parliament in February and called for fresh elections to be held in April. Strengthened by a strategic electoral alliance with a leftist Sinhalese party, Kumaratunga's coalition was able to form a minority government, failing as it did to win a majority of seats in parliament. Meanwhile, wrangling between the southern political factions continues to impede any meaningful progress on peace talks with the Tamil Tiger separatist rebels. The February 2002 ceasefire is still in place and has contributed to somewhat greater freedom of movement and a reduction in human rights violations by security forces in the north and east of the country. However, the Tigers continue to commit numerous abuses, including the forcible conscription of child soldiers, politically motivated killings, and restrictions on freedom of expression and of association.

Since independence from Britain in 1948, political power in this island nation has alternated between the conservative United National Party (UNP) and the leftist Sri Lanka Freedom Party (SLFP). While the country has made impressive gains in literacy, basic health care, and other social needs, its economic development has been stunted and its social fabric tested by a long-standing civil war that has killed an estimated 65,000 people. The conflict initially pitted several Tamil guerrilla groups against the government, which is dominated by the Sinhalese majority. The war, although triggered by anti-Tamil riots in 1983 that claimed hundreds of lives, came in the context of long-standing Tamil claims of discrimination in education and employment opportunities. By 1986, the Liberation Tigers of Tamil Eelam (LTTE, or Tamil Tigers), which called for an independent Tamil homeland in the Northeastern Province, had eliminated most rival Tamil guerrilla groups and was in control of much of the northern Jaffna Peninsula. At the same time, the government was also fighting an insurgency in the south by the leftist People's Liberation Front (JVP). The JVP insurgency, and the brutal methods used by the army to quell it in 1989, killed 60,000 people.

In 1994, Kumaratunga ended nearly two decades of UNP rule by leading the SLFP-dominated People's Alliance (PA) coalition to victory in parliamentary elections and then winning the presidential election. Early in her term, she tried to negotiate a peace agreement with the LTTE, but following a renewal of hostilities by the LTTE, she reverted to focusing on a military solution to the conflict. Kumaratunga won early presidential elections in 1999, but the UNP and its allies gained a majority in parliamentary elections held in December 2001, and UNP leader Ranil Wickremasinghe became prime minister.

In response to an LTTE ceasefire offer, the new government declared a truce with the rebels, lifted an economic embargo on rebel-held territory, and restarted Norwegian-brokered peace talks. A permanent ceasefire accord with provisions for international monitoring was signed in February 2002. Shortly before the first round of talks took place, the government lifted its ban on the LTTE, and by December 2002, the government and the Tigers had agreed to share political power in a federal system. Although the LTTE suspended its participation in peace talks in April 2003, it stated that it remained committed to a political solution. In June, bilateral and multilateral donors pledged a total of $4.5 billion over a four-year period to support Sri Lanka's reconstruction, although much of the aid was conditionally tied to further progress in reaching a settlement with the Tigers.

However, such progress has remained constrained by conflict between the two main political parties. In November 2003, President Kumaratunga declared a state of emergency, sacked three cabinet ministers and assumed their portfolios, and temporarily suspended parliament. In order to justify these steps, she expressed concern that LTTE proposals for the establishment of a Tiger-dominated Interim Self Governing Authority (IGSA) in the Northeastern Province were a threat to national security. However, analysts noted that an equally compelling impetus for her actions was the UNP's motion to initiate impeachment proceedings against the chief justice of the supreme court, whom the president views as a key ally.

Although the state of emergency was pulled back and parliament resumed functioning, Wickremasinghe claimed that his ability to govern had been severely curtailed by the fact that President Kumaratunga continued to hold the important defense portfolio. The impasse was broken when the president dissolved parliament in February 2004 and called for fresh elections to be held in April. Bolstered by the direct support of the Marxist JVP, Kumaratunga's new PA-led United People's Freedom Alliance (UPFA) coalition won 105 out of 225 seats and managed to form a minority government. Apart from the JVP, other extremist and ethnic-based parties also made inroads, including a new party formed by Buddhist clergy, the Jathika Hela Urumaya (JHU, or National Heritage Party), which won nine seats. The new government's tenuous grip on power became immediately apparent when it failed to secure the election of its candidate to the post of Speaker of parliament; instead, the UNP was able to win the position with the help of votes from members of the smaller ethnic parties.

Meanwhile, the ceasefire with the LTTE continued to hold, despite an increasing incidence of violations during the year. Of particular concern was a spate of assassinations by the LTTE of political opponents, suspected informants, and intelligence operatives in the northeast, and more unusually, in Colombo. Uncertainty was also created when the leader of the LTTE forces in the eastern part of the Northeastern Province, Colonel Karuna, who controlled an estimated 6,000 out of a total of 15,000 LTTE troops, formed a breakaway faction in March, alleging discrimination in the treatment of eastern Tamils by the LTTE leadership. However, his rebellion proved to be short lived; after fierce internecine fighting in April, Karuna disbanded his forces and went into hiding, although clashes and killings between the two groups continued throughout the year as both attempted to reassert their control over the east.

Though President Kumaratunga had repeatedly criticized the UNP government for making excessive concessions to the LTTE, she has indicated that she also remains committed to finding a political solution to the ethnic conflict. Nevertheless, progress in resuming meaningful peace talks has been complicated by the addition to the ruling coalition of the JVP, which adamantly opposes granting more powers to the provinces or to the LTTE, and by the presence of pro-Sinhalese forces such as the JHU in parliament. While the LTTE insists that any future talks include discussions on the formation of an IGSA, which would give them effective rule over the Northeastern Province, it is clear that the stability of the present coalition government would be at risk if Kumaratunga were to proceed with talks on this basis.

Political Rights and Civil Liberties: Sri Lankans can change their government through elections based on universal adult suffrage. The 1978 constitution vested strong executive powers in a president who is directly elected for a six-year term and can dissolve parliament. The 225-member unicameral parliament is directly elected for a five-year term through a mix of single-seat, simple-plurality districts and proportional representation. Elections are open to multiple parties, and fair electoral laws and equal campaigning opportunities ensure a competitive political process. While elections are generally free and fair, they continue to be marred by some irregularities, violence, and intimidation. However, the interim report issued by the independent Center for Monitoring Election Violence noted that with 368 incidents on election day, the 2004 elections were considerably less beleaguered by violence and malpractice than previous polls had been. The LTTE refuses to allow free elections in the areas under its control and continues to intimidate—and sometimes kill—members of rival non-militarized Tamil political parties.

In recent years, the fact that the executive and legislative branches of government have been controlled by competing parties headed by long-standing political rivals has led to a general unwillingness to effectively resolve issues and construct coherent state policies. Although President Chandrika Kumaratunga's coalition was able to unseat the UNP's Ranil Wickremasinghe in the April 2004 elections and form a minority government headed by her choice of prime minister, it lacks the mandate and parliamentary strength to accomplish meaningful change. Differences of opinion between the main political factions over the correct way to approach the peace process have led to an inability to formulate a united strategy toward the LTTE and its specific demands during the ongoing but currently stalled negotiations.

Official corruption is a growing concern, and the legal and administrative framework currently in force is inadequate in terms of either promoting integrity or punishing the corrupt behavior of public officials. No current or former politician has thus far been sentenced for bribery or corruption, although a number of cases are under investigation or prosecution. Sri Lanka was ranked 67 out of 146 countries surveyed in the 2004 Transparency International Corruption Perceptions Index.

Freedom of expression is provided for in the constitution, and independent media outlets can generally express their views openly. However, the LTTE does not permit free expression in the areas under its control and continues to terrorize a number of Tamil journalists and other critics. During the November 2003 state of emergency, President Kumaratunga briefly deployed troops outside government-run media outlets and sacked the chairman of the government-owned Lake House media group. In 2004, the Colombo-based Free Media Movement repeatedly condemned the manipulation of the state media by the president's party for political ends, including pressure on editors and biased election coverage. Reporters, particularly those who cover human rights issues or official misconduct, continued to face harassment and threats from the police and security forces, government officials, political activists, and the LTTE. A number of journalists and media outlets were attacked during the year, and three journalists were killed. The government controls the largest newspaper chain, two major television stations, and a radio station, while business interests wield some control over content in the form of selective advertising and bribery.

Religious freedom is respected and members of all faiths are generally allowed to worship freely, although the constitution gives special status to Buddhism and there is some discrimination and occasional violence against religious minorities. The LTTE discriminates against Muslims in the areas under its control and has attacked Buddhist sites in the past. The U.S. State Department's 2004 Report on International Religious Freedom notes that Christian missionaries are occasionally harassed by Buddhist clergy and others opposed to their work. Tensions between the island's Buddhist majority and the Christian minority—and in particular, evangelical Christian groups—appear to be worsening, according to a report released in August by the U.S.-based Jubilee Campaign, with a sharp increase in attacks against churches and individuals noted at the end of 2003 and the introduction of draft anti-conversion legislation in May and June 2004.

The government generally respects academic freedom. However, the LTTE has a record of repressing the voices of those intellectuals who criticize its actions, sometimes through murder or other forms of violent intimidation. Groups such as the University Teachers for Human Rights-Jaffna (UTHR-J) have faced particularly severe harassment at the hands of the LTTE.

Freedom of assembly is generally respected, although both main political parties occasionally disrupt each other's rallies and political events. Except in conflict-affected areas, human rights and social welfare nongovernmental organizations generally operate freely. However, the LTTE does not allow for freedom of association in the regions under its control and reportedly uses coercion to force civilians to attend pro-LTTE rallies.

Trade unions are independent and engage in collective bargaining. Except for civil servants, most workers can hold strikes. However, under the 1989 Essential Services Act, the president can declare a strike in any industry illegal. Kumaratunga has used the act to end several strikes. Employers on tea plantations routinely violate the rights of the mainly Tamil workforce.

Successive governments have respected the constitutional provision for an independent judiciary, and judges can generally make decisions in an atmosphere free of overt intimidation from the legislative or executive branches. However, there is growing concern about the perceived politicization of the judiciary, in particular regarding the conduct of the chief justice of the Supreme Court. According to the Colombo-based Free Media Movement, he has narrowed the scope of human rights litigation, dismissed a number of judges without holding an inquiry or disciplinary hearing, and consistently defended the president and her party in legal actions relating to political disputes. At the lower levels of the judiciary, corruption is fairly common among both judges and court staff, and those willing to pay bribes have more efficient access to the legal system.

Despite an overall reduction in the number of human rights abuses committed by police and security forces, the rule of law remains somewhat weak, and torture and prolonged detention without trial continue to be issues of concern. Such practices are facilitated by legislation such as the Prevention of Terrorism Act (PTA), under which security personnel can arrest and detain suspects indefinitely without court approval. Although over 1,000 detainees held under PTA legislation have been released since the February 2002 ceasefire, several dozen remained in custody at the end of 2003, according to Amnesty International. There has been little progress in reducing acts of torture by the security forces and police, particularly of detainees during routine interrogations. Cases of custodial death and custodial rape continue to be reported. A lack of aggressive prosecution of the majority of past abuses contributes to a climate of impunity for those who have overstepped the bounds of the law.

The LTTE has effective control on the ground in large sections of the north and east of the country and operates a parallel administration that includes schools, hospitals, courts, and police and other law enforcement personnel. The Tigers raise money through extortion, kidnapping, theft, and the seizure of Muslim property, and have used threats and attacks to close schools, courts, and government agencies in their self-styled Tamil homeland. Despite their involvement in the peace process, the rebels continue to be responsible for summary executions of civilians, disappearances, arbitrary abductions and detentions, torture, and the forcible conscription of children to be used as soldiers. Press reports as well as an exhaustive report issued by Human Rights Watch in November indicated that the Tigers continued to recruit thousands of teenage girls and boys in 2004 despite their signing of the "Action Plan for Children Affected by War" in June 2003, in which they pledged to release all children within their ranks. Recruitment efforts are at times so intense that parents keep their children home from school so they will not be forcibly abducted.

The LTTE has also targeted Tamil political parties that challenge its claim to represent the Tamil people, particularly the Eelam People's Democratic Party (EPDP), with over 100 political killings being attributed to the LTTE since the ceasefire was signed, according to Human Rights Watch. A statement issued by the Colombo-based Peace Support Group noted that during a four-month period from April to July 2004, at least 40 people were killed as a consequence of their political affiliation, including EPDP members, followers of the breakaway Karuna faction of the LTTE, military intelligence officers, elected officials, and members of civil society.

Tamils maintain that they face systematic discrimination in several matters controlled by the state, including government employment, university education, and access to justice. Thousands of Tamils whose ancestors were brought from India to work as indentured laborers in the nineteenth century did not qualify for Sri Lankan citizenship and faced discrimination and exploitation by the native Sinhalese. However, in October 2003, the parliament approved legislation granting citizenship to about 170,000 previously stateless "Indian" Tamils. Tensions between the three major ethnic groups (Sinhalese, Tamil, and Muslim), which lead to occasional violent clashes, remain a concern. Overall, almost half of an estimated 730,000 internally displaced refugees have returned to their homes following the February 2002 ceasefire, but an equal number remain unwilling or unable to return to the northeast and continue to live in government-run camps throughout the country, according to Refugees International.

Women are under represented in politics and the civil service. Female employees in the private sector face some sexual harassment as well as discrimination in salary and promotion opportunities. Rape and domestic violence against women remain serious problems, and authorities weakly enforce existing laws. Although women have equal rights under civil and criminal law, matters related to the family, including marriage, divorce, child custody, and inheritance, are adjudicated under the customary law of each ethnic or religious group, and the application of these laws sometimes results in discrimination against women.

Sudan

Population: 39,100,000
GNI/capita: $370
Life Expectancy: 57
Religious Groups: Sunni Muslim (70 percent), indigenous beliefs (25 percent), Christian (5 percent)
Ethnic Groups: Black (52 percent), Arab (39 percent), Beja (6 percent), other (3 percent)
Capital: Khartoum

Political Rights: 7
Civil Liberties: 7
Status: Not Free

Ten-Year Ratings Timeline (Political Rights, Civil Liberties, Status)

1995	1996	1997	1998	1999	2000	2001	2002	2003	2004
7,7NF	7,7NF	7,7NF	7,7NF	7,7NF	7,7NF	7,7NF	7,7NF	7,7NF	7,7NF

Overview:
A long-simmering conflict in Sudan's western Darfur region exploded into widespread acts of ethnic cleansing, massacre, rape, and forced displacement in 2004. The United

States classified the situation as genocide. Sudanese government forces and state-backed Arab militias killed at least 70,000 black Africans and created a massive refugee crisis affecting at least 1.5 million people. Despite a ceasefire between rebel groups and the government and the passage of UN Security Council resolutions against Khartoum, attacks against civilians continued throughout the year. The conflict in Darfur threatened to jeopardize progress toward a final resolution of the 22-year-long war in the country's South. The government carried out a broad security clampdown in response to an alleged coup attempt, re-arresting Hassan al-Turabi, a leading Sudanese Muslim cleric and former leader of the ruling political party.

Africa's largest country, which achieved independence in 1956 after nearly 80 years of British rule, has been embroiled in civil wars for 38 of its 48 years as an independent state. The Anyanya movement, representing mainly Christian and animist black Africans in southern Sudan, battled Arab Muslim government forces from 1956 to 1972. In 1969, General Jafar Numeiri toppled an elected government and ushered in a military dictatorship. The South gained extensive autonomy under a 1972 accord, and for the next decade, an uneasy peace prevailed. Then, in 1983, Numeiri restricted southern autonomy and imposed Sharia (Islamic law). Civil war resumed, and Numeiri was overthrown in 1985. Civilian rule was restored in 1986 with the election of a government led by Sadiq al-Mahdi of the moderate Islamic Ummah Party. War, however, continued. Lieutenant General Omar al-Bashir ousted al-Mahdi in a 1989 coup, and al-Mahdi spent seven years in prison or under house arrest before fleeing to Eritrea. Until 1999, al-Bashir ruled through a military-civilian regime backed by senior Muslim clerics including Hassan al-Turabi, who wielded considerable power as the ruling National Congress (NC) party leader and speaker of the 360-member National Assembly.

Tensions between al-Bashir and al-Turabi climaxed in December 1999; on the eve of a parliamentary vote on a plan by al-Turabi to curb presidential powers, al-Bashir dissolved parliament and declared a state of emergency. He fired al-Turabi as NC head, replaced the cabinet with his own supporters, and held deeply flawed presidential and parliamentary elections in December 2000, which the NC won overwhelmingly. In June 2000, al-Turabi formed his own party, the Popular National Congress (PNC), but he was prohibited from participating in politics. In January 2001, the Ummah Party refused to join al-Bashir's new government despite the president's invitation, declaring that it refused to support totalitarianism.

Al-Turabi and some 20 of his supporters were arrested in February 2001 after he called for a national uprising against the government and signed a memorandum of understanding in Geneva with the southern-based, rebel Sudanese People's Liberation Army (SPLA). In May 2001, al-Turabi and four aides were charged with conspiracy to overthrow the government, and al-Turabi was placed under house arrest. In September 2002, he was moved to a high-security prison and subsequently released in October 2003.

By sidelining al-Turabi, who was considered a leading force behind Sudan's efforts to export Islamic extremism, al-Bashir began to lift Sudan out of international isolation. Although Vice President Ali Osman Mohammed Taha—who replaced al-Turabi as Islamic ideologue—remains firmly committed to Sudan's status as an Islamic state and to the government's self-proclaimed jihad against non-Muslims, al-

Bashir has managed in recent years to repair relations with several countries, including the United States. After the September 11 terrorist attacks against the United States, al-Bashir offered his country's cooperation in combating terrorism. Sudan had previously provided a safe haven for Osama bin Laden and al-Qaeda, the terrorist network.

In March 2004, al-Turabi was again placed under house arrest, this time on suspicion of plotting a coup with sympathizers of rebel groups in Darfur; al-Turabi had been outspokenly critical of the government's tactics in the region. In September, al-Turabi was jailed amid a broad security crackdown after the government said it foiled a coup attempt by his supporters. Thirty members of al-Turabi's PNC were detained, and authorities said they uncovered weapons caches in several locations around Khartoum.

Sudan's international image was substantially tarnished in 2004 as events in Darfur reached horrific proportions. The conflict began in earnest in February 2003 when the Sudan Liberation Army (SLA) and the Justice and Equality Movement (JEM), representing black farmers and villagers in Darfur, attacked Sudanese military garrisons in the region. Darfur residents had long complained of official discrimination, a lack of economic and land rights, and occasional pogrom-style attacks by state-backed Arab militias known as "Janjaweed." By early 2004, government and Janjaweed attacks against villages in Darfur were well under way, creating mass casualties and an enormous refugee crisis. Sudanese jet fighters and helicopter gunships routinely bombed and strafed villages. Horse- and camel-mounted Janjaweed militiamen, in seeming coordination with airborne government forces, would often follow air strikes, massacring survivors, especially men and boys. Hundreds of thousands of people, their villages torched, were forcibly displaced, relegated to makeshift, government-run refugee camps. Tens of thousands escaped westward to neighboring Chad. Attacks seemed to focus on three black tribal groups—the Fur, Massalit, and Zhagawa—which led to charges of racial discrimination, ethnic cleansing, and genocide by international human rights organizations. Many independent refugee accounts described a systematic campaign of rape of women by Janjaweed and government soldiers. By November 2004, approximately 70,000 people were dead and 1.5 million displaced.

Government-run camps for internally displaced people (IDPs) set up throughout Darfur lacked adequate sanitation facilities, water, or feeding centers. The government also routinely blocked humanitarian workers from accessing the camps. To discourage villagers from returning home, Janjaweed militiamen dumped the corpses of executed civilians into village wells to poison the water. Male refugees generally avoided venturing outside refugee camps for fear of being murdered; women generally went out in search of firewood and water, often exposing themselves to rape. By the fall of 2004, the World Health Organization announced that at least 10,000 people were dying monthly in the substandard and fetid camps. The UN World Food Program announced that nearly 22 percent of children under age five in Darfur were malnourished.

An April 2004 ceasefire between Darfur's rebel groups and government and Janjaweed forces broke down amid renewed Janjaweed attacks and failure by the government to disarm the militias. In July, the United States declared that the situation in Darfur amounted to genocide, and the African Union dispatched 300 monitors to the region. The UN Security Council adopted a resolution imposing a 30-day deadline on Khartoum to restore stability by disarming the Janjaweed and allowing the safe return of refugees. The resolution did not outline penalties for failure to adhere to its terms, and the deadline passed without Sudanese government compliance. In August, the government and rebel groups began what would become on-and-off peace talks in Nigeria. Meanwhile, the United Nations reported that traumatized refugees were being forcibly returned to unsafe villages vulnerable to attack by the Janjaweed, in violation of the government's prior agreement with the UN. In September, reports of continued fighting and renewed refugee movements emerged. The UN Security Council authorized another resolution, but again declined to threaten specified sanctions.

In late October, in the face of mounting international pressure, the Sudanese government approved the dispatch of 3,500 additional African Union troops. Their mobilization was delayed, however, because of lack of funds; the United States provided air transport for some. Khartoum approved the dispatch of the additional troops on condition that they not assume a civilian protection role. Rebel groups reported fresh government air attacks after Khartoum signed a peace pact in November and agreed to ban military flights over Darfur.

The Darfur crisis threatened to derail progress made in finally resolving the 22-year-long civil war in the country's South. While hostilities in the South declined markedly in 2004, a final settlement to the conflict was not achieved by the end of the year. The war pitted government forces and government-backed, northern Arab Muslims against African animists and Christians in the country's oil-rich South. A convoluted mix of historical, religious, ethnic, and cultural tensions has made peace elusive, while competition for economic resources—most notably, oil—has fueled the conflict. Past ceasefire attempts have failed, with Khartoum insisting on an unconditional ceasefire and the SPLA demanding the establishment of a secular constitution first.

Throughout the war, the government regularly bombed civilian targets, including villages, churches, and humanitarian relief facilities. The government also denied humanitarian relief workers access to rebel-held areas or areas containing large concentrations of internal refugees. The SPLA also engaged in attacks on civilians and child soldier recruitment. Human Rights Watch has documented how the Sudanese government used roads, bridges, and airfields built by international oil companies to wage war in the South, especially in the oil rich Western Upper Nile region. Some of the companies were criticized for ignoring government attacks against civilian targets.

A peace plan proposed in December 2001 by former U.S. senator John Danforth called for "one country, two systems" in Sudan, with an Islamic government in the North and a secular system in the South. The international community stepped up its mediation efforts in the civil war in 2002, in part to prevent Sudan from becoming a breeding ground for terror, as Afghanistan had prior to September 11, 2001. In 2003, substantive peace talks under the auspices of the Intergovernmental Authority on Development (IGAD) finally resulted in a relaxation of hostilities and a high degree of optimism that a final resolution of the conflict was within reach. In December 2003, an agreement was reached on the sharing of oil wealth.

Talks continued in 2004, culminating in the June signing of the Nairobi Declaration. The agreement paved the way toward a comprehensive ceasefire and a six-year transition period leading to a referendum on southern secession, during which time the government would withdraw 80 percent of its troops from the South. However, continued negotiations in the summer broke down amid the worsening crisis in Darfur, effectively stalling the IGAD process. Several international nongovernmental organizations (NGOs) expressed concern that the West was neglecting the IGAD process while focusing almost exclusively on Darfur.

By October, the protocols signed in 2003 were still not in place. However, optimism was high that a peace accord would be signed early in the New Year.

While the United Nations has lifted sanctions against Sudan, the United States still maintains its own based on the country's human rights abuses and its alleged continuing support for terrorism.

Political Rights and Civil Liberties: Sudanese citizens cannot change their government democratically. December 2000 presidential and parliamentary elections cannot credibly be said to have reflected the will of the people. The major opposition parties, which are believed to have the support of most Sudanese, boycotted in protest of what they said were attempts by a totalitarian regime to impart the appearance of fairness. The European Union declined an invitation to monitor the polls to avoid bestowing legitimacy on the outcome. Omar al-Bashir, running against former president Jafar Numeiri and three relative unknowns, won 86 percent of the vote. NC candidates stood uncontested for nearly two-thirds of parliamentary seats. Voting did not take place in some 17 rebel-held constituencies, and government claims of 66 percent voter turnout in some states were denounced as fictitious. The president can appoint and dismiss state governors at his discretion.

Sudan was ranked 122 out of 146 countries surveyed in the 2004 Transparency International Corruption Perceptions Index.

There is little press freedom in Sudan. Journalists practice self-censorship to avoid harassment, arrest, and closure of their publications. However, there are several daily newspapers and a wide variety of Arabic- and English-language publications, and while all of these are subject to censorship, some do criticize the government. Radio and television stations are owned by the government and are required to reflect government policy in broadcasts. Penalties apply to journalists who allegedly harm the nation or economy or violate national security. A 1999 law imposes penalties for "professional errors." In recent years, several journalists have been detained without explanation, and newspapers have been arbitrarily shut down by the authorities. There were reports throughout the year that the government was preventing journalists from traveling to Darfur to cover the conflict there.

Islam is the state religion, and the constitution claims Sharia (Islamic law) as the source of its legislation. At least 75 percent of Sudanese are Muslim, though most southern Sudanese adhere to traditional indigenous beliefs or Christianity. The overwhelming majority of those displaced or killed by war and famine in Sudan have been non-Muslims, and many have starved under a policy of withholding food pending conversion to Islam. Officials have described their campaign against non-Muslims as a holy war. Under the 1994 Societies Registration Act, religious groups must register in order to legally gather. Registration is reportedly difficult to obtain.

The government denies permission to build churches and sometimes destroys Christian schools, centers, and churches. Roman Catholic priests face random detention and interrogation by police.

Emergency law severely restricts freedom of assembly and association. Students are forbidden to participate in political activities, according to the Acts of Student Codes, introduced in 2002 after several university students in Khartoum were suspended for engaging in human rights activities, including organizing symposiums on women's rights and attending a conference on democracy. Other students have been expelled for organizing political activities, and security forces have forcefully broken up demonstrations and periodically closed the University of Khartoum.

According to the *Los Angeles Times*, in April Janjaweed gunmen attacked a school in the Darfur town of Kailek, killing six teachers and 36 children. Many other villages reported similar attacks on schools, stemming from what was claimed to be a government policy of anti-black discrimination.

While many international NGOs operate in Sudan, the government at times restricts their movement and ability to carry out their work, which often includes providing essential humanitarian assistance. In early November, the UN World Food Program reported that Sudanese army and police had surrounded IDP camps in Darfur and were barring outside access to the camps' inhabitants. Humanitarian workers have also been targeted, and in some cases kidnapped and killed, by rebel groups.

There are no independent trade unions. The Sudan Workers Trade Unions Federation is the main labor organization, with about 800,000 members. Local union elections are rigged to ensure the election of government-approved candidates. A lack of labor legislation limits the freedom of workers to organize or bargain collectively.

The judiciary is not independent. The chief justice of the Supreme Court, who presides over the entire judiciary, is government appointed. Regular courts provide some due process safeguards, but special security and military courts, which are used to punish political opponents of the government, provide none. "Special courts" often deal with criminal matters, despite their use of military judges. Criminal law is based on Sharia and provides for flogging, amputation, crucifixion, and execution. Ten southern, predominantly non-Muslim states are officially exempted from Sharia, although criminal law allows for its application in the future if the state assemblies choose to implement it. Arbitrary arrest, detention, and torture are widespread, and security forces act with impunity. Prison conditions do not meet international standards.

Serious human rights abuses by nearly every faction involved in the country's long-standing civil war and in the Darfur conflict have been reported. Secret police reportedly have operated "ghost houses"—detention and torture centers—in several cities. Government forces are said to have routinely raided villages, burning homes, killing residents, and abducting women and children to be used as slaves in the North. Relief agencies have discovered thousands of people held captive in the North and have purchased their freedom so they could return to the South. In 2002, the International Eminent Persons Group—a fact-finding mission composed of humanitarian relief workers, human rights lawyers, academics, and former European and American diplomats—confirmed the existence of slavery in Sudan. The group also reported on abductions and forced servitude under the SPLA's authority. Although there has been no organized effort to compile casualty statistics in southern

Sudan since 1994, the total number of people killed by war, famine, and disease is believed to exceed two million, with millions more displaced as refugees.

In February, national security agency officials arrested Salih Mahmoud Osman, a lawyer and member of the Sudanese Organization Against Torture (SOAT), after he advocated publicly on behalf of civilians in Darfur. He reportedly began a hunger strike at the end of June while being held incommunicado and without having been formally charged. According to Amnesty International, in August several civilians in Darfur reported being imprisoned for speaking with foreign journalists and visiting dignitaries, including U.S. secretary of state Colin Powell and UN secretary general Kofi Annan. SOAT has reported on the arbitrary arrest and torture of several people, including students suspected of engaging in political activities or harboring SPLA sympathies.

An anonymously written book about ingrained discrimination in Sudan circulated widely during the year. Called the "Black Book," it laid out in succinct detail a broad system of favoritism of northern Arabs over other peoples in Sudan. The book states that Sudan's northern region, constituting roughly 5 percent of the country's population, is overly represented in government. Most of the national budget is devoted to northern development, with other, non-Arab regions notably neglected by Khartoum, the book says. Equality of opportunity and business and property rights are generally restricted to Sudan's Arab Muslim community.

Women face discrimination in family matters such as marriage, divorce, and inheritance, which are governed by Sharia. Women are represented in parliament and hold 35 of the assembly's 360 seats. Public order police frequently harass women and monitor their dress for adherence to government standards of modesty. Female genital mutilation occurs despite legal prohibition, and rape is reportedly widespread in war zones. In March, the BBC reported the mass rape of at least 100 women by militiamen in Darfur. UN High Commissioner for Human Rights Louise Arbour speculated during the year that the systematic raping of women in Darfur would constitute crimes against humanity. There was also evidence of official attempts to cover up the problem: police arrested a Darfur man filing a complaint with the African Union ceasefire commission about attacks against women at a camp in El Fasher. He was released only after UN intervention. According to Amnesty International, women have less access to legal representation than men. President al-Bashir announced in January 2001 that Sudan would not ratify the international Convention on Eradication of All Forms of Discrimination against Women because it "contradicted Sudanese values and traditions." Children are used as soldiers by government and opposition forces in the Darfur conflict, just as they were used in the civil war in the South.

Suriname

Population: 400,000
GNI/capita: $1,921
Life Expectancy: 70
Religious Groups: Hindu (27.4 percent),
Muslim (19.6 percent), Roman Catholic (22.8 percent),
Protestant (25.2 percent), indigenous beliefs (5 percent)
Ethnic Groups: East Indian (37 percent), Creole (31 percent),
Javanese (15 percent), other (17 percent)
Capital: Paramaribo

Political Rights: 1
Civil Liberties: 2
Status: Free

Ten-Year Ratings Timeline (Political Rights, Civil Liberties, Status)

1995	1996	1997	1998	1999	2000	2001	2002	2003	2004
3,3PF	3,3PF	3,3PF	3,3PF	3,3PF	1,2F	1,2F	1,2F	1,2F	1,2F

Overview:

Legislative elections scheduled for May 2005 dominated Suriname's political debate in 2004, with speculation over whether the ruling New Front (NF) would prevail in the face of the surprising popularity of the party of a former dictator of Suriname.

The Republic of Suriname achieved independence from The Netherlands in 1975, which had acquired it as a result of the Treaty of Breda with the British in 1667. Five years after independence, a military coup, which brought Desi Bouterse to power as the head of a regime that brutally suppressed civic and political opposition, initiated a decade of military intervention in politics. In 1987, Bouterse permitted elections that were won handily by the NF, a four-party coalition of mainly East Indian, Creole, and Javanese parties. The National Democratic Party (NDP), organized by the military, won just three seats.

In 1990, the army ousted President Ramsewak Shankar, and Bouterse again took power, this time in a bloodless putsch popularly known as the "telephone coup." International pressure led to new elections in 1991. The center-right NF won a majority, although the NDP increased its share to 12. The National Assembly selected the NF's candidate, Ronald Venetiaan, as president. Bouterse quit the army in 1992 in order to lead the NDP. In the May 25, 2000, legislative elections, the NF won the majority of 51 National Assembly seats—three times as many as its closest rival.

The May 2001 death of a labor leader who was to be the star witness in a trial against Bouterse and others accused of 15 political killings committed on December 8, 1982, initially appeared to rob the prosecution of key testimony. However, the government vowed that testimony given by the witness during a preliminary hearing would be submitted in the trial by the judge who questioned him. The death of the lone survivor of the December 1982 massacre came amid a renewed push by the Dutch to bring Bouterse to account for the murders and for his role in the 1982 coup. He had already been tried and convicted by a Dutch court in absentia on charges of having introduced more than two tons of cocaine into The Netherlands between 1989 and 1997. Suriname did not extradite Bouterse to The Netherlands because of a bilateral agreement not to extradite their own citizens to each other's country.

In October 2002, authorities from neighboring Guyana complained that Suriname is a major supply route for illegal arms used in a crime wave gripping the Guyanese capital of Georgetown. The spillover effects of narcotics trafficking and the drug trade's ties to top political leaders—including Bouterse—continued to make the news.

In October 2003, a judge gave more than 50 convicted cocaine traffickers light sentences in an effort by the government to reduce overcrowding in the country's jails. The UN Drug Control Agency estimates that 20 tons of cocaine are smuggled annually through Suriname to Europe alone. Also in October, Dino Bouterse—the son of Desi Bouterse—was acquitted by a military court of stealing more than 80 guns, including 21 AK-47 assault rifles, from the government's secret service compound. The court ruled that there was insufficient evidence to convict him.

In 2004, legislative elections scheduled for May 2005 dominated Suriname's political debate, with observers saying that the ruling NF coalition headed by President Venetiaan appeared posed to capitalize on the country's new-found price and exchange-rate stability. However, a July public opinion poll by the Institute for Demographic Research showed surprising strength for Bouterse's NDP, which placed less than 1 percent behind the NF. The relatively weak showing by the NF reflected voter discontent, in part, with the side effects of the government's fiscal austerity program, which helped to stabilize both prices and the economy generally.

Political Rights and Civil Liberties: Citizens of Suriname can change their government democratically. The 1987 constitution provides for a 51-seat National Assembly, directly elected by proportional representation, which serves a five-year term and selects the state president. A Council of State (Raad van State), consisting of the president and representatives of the major political groupings, including unions, business, the military, and the legislature, has veto power over legislation deemed to violate the constitution.

Political parties largely reflect the cleavages in Suriname's ethnically complex society, although political-racial discord is much less than in neighboring Guyana. A record number of 23 parties competed in the 2000 elections.

The Heritage Foundation/*Wall Street Journal 2004 Index of Economic Freedom* found that corruption is rampant in Suriname, regulations are applied randomly, and there is a general level of very high regulation. Favoritism, particularly at elite levels, is common in business and government. Suriname was ranked 49 out of 146 countries surveyed in Transparency International's 2004 Corruption Perceptions Index.

The government generally respects freedom of expression. Radio is both public and private. A number of small commercial radio stations compete with the government-owned radio and television broadcasting systems, which generally offer pluralistic viewpoints. The government does not restrict access to the Internet. Public access to government information is recognized in law; however, it is very limited in practice.

The government generally respects freedom of religion and does not restrict academic freedom.

Although civic institutions remain weak, human rights organizations function freely. Freedom of assembly and association are provided for in the constitution, and the government respects these rights in practice. Workers can join independent trade unions, and the labor movement is active in politics. Collective bargaining is legal and conducted fairly widely. Civil servants have no legal right to strike.

The judiciary is weak and susceptible to political influence and suffers from ineffectiveness, a significant shortage of judges, and a large backlog of cases. The courts and the prisons are seriously overburdened by the volume of people detained for narcotics trafficking. The civilian police abuse detainees, particularly during arrests; guards mistreat prisoners; and prisons are dangerously overcrowded. Military personnel generally are not subject to civilian criminal law.

Discrimination against indigenous and tribal peoples is widespread. Tribal peoples, called Maroons, are the descendants of escaped African slaves who formed autonomous communities in the rain forest in the seventeenth and eighteenth centuries. Their rights to their lands and resources, to cultural integrity, and to the autonomous administration of their affairs are not recognized in Surinamese law.

Constitutional guarantees of gender equality are not enforced. Several organizations specifically address violence against women and related issues. Despite their central role in agriculture and food production, 60 percent of rural women, particularly those in tribal communities, live below the poverty level. In the absence of a comprehensive law against trafficking in persons, the practice, including the sexual exploitation of women and children, remained a problem. In 2004, there were no convictions for such trafficking.

⬇ Swaziland

Population: 1,200,000   **Political Rights:** 7
GNI/capita: $1,240   **Civil Liberties:** 5
Life Expectancy: 43   **Status:** Not Free
Religious Groups: Zionist [a blend of Christianity and indigenous ancestral worship] (40 percent),
Roman Catholic (20 percent), Muslim (10 percent),
other (30 percent)
Ethnic Groups: African (97 percent), European (3 percent)
Capital: Mbabane
Trend Arrow: Swaziland received a downward trend arrow due to an increase in the autocratic powers of the king under the country's new constitution.

Ten-Year Ratings Timeline (Political Rights, Civil Liberties, Status)

1995	1996	1997	1998	1999	2000	2001	2002	2003	2004
6,5NF	6,5NF	6,5NF	6,4NF	6,5NF	6,5NF	6,5NF	6,5NF	7,5NF	7,5NF

Overview:
Public debate of Swaziland's controversial and long-delayed draft constitution concluded at a conference in September 2004 that was dominated by supporters of royal rule and largely ignored submissions by labor and human rights groups urging democratic reforms. In November, the parliament, a body with little independent authority, voted overwhelmingly to ratify the new constitution.

Swaziland's King Mswati III is the latest monarch of the Dlamini dynasty, under which the Swazi kingdom expanded and contracted in conflicts with neighboring groups. Britain declared the kingdom a protectorate to prevent Boer expansion in the 1880s and assumed administrative power in 1903. Swaziland regained its independence in 1968, and an elected parliament was added to the traditional kingship and chieftaincies. In 1973, Mswati's predecessor, Sobhuza II (who died in 1983) repealed the 1968 constitution, ended the multiparty system in favor of the *tinkhundla* (local council) system, and declared himself absolute monarch.

Voting in October 1998 legislative elections was marked by very low turnout and was neither open nor fair. It was based on the Swazi tinkhundla system of closely controlled nominations and voting that seeks to legitimatize the rule of King Mswati III and his Dlamini clan. Security forces arrested and briefly detained labor and other pro-democracy leaders before the elections and after a series of bomb blasts. The 55 elected members of the National Assembly were approved by the government and were joined by 10 royal appointees.

Parliamentary elections in October 2003 were preceded by calls by critics of royal rule to boycott the polls, which were not deemed credible by international observers. However, the number of women legislators increased to an impressive 30 percent, or a total of 16 of 55 seats.

The country's new constitution, a product of five years of work by the Constitutional Review Commission, was unveiled in May 2003. Drafted by two of King Mswati's brothers, the document maintains a ban on political opposition to royal rule and reaffirms the palace's absolute control over the cabinet, parliament, and the courts. Although it provides for limited freedom of speech, assembly, and association, as well as limited equality for women, King Mswati may waive these rights at his discretion. In September 2004, public debate of the constitution concluded at a conference dominated by supporters of royal rule; submissions by labor and human rights groups that pushed for democratic reforms were largely ignored. The king has set a November deadline for ratification of the new charter by the parliament, a body with little independent authority. A group called the National Constitutional Assembly—a coalition of trade unions, banned political parties, and other civil society groups—is seeking an order from the country's Supreme Court to block King Mswati from decreeing the new constitution into law. The document already has the approval of parliament.

Most Swazis remain engaged in subsistence agriculture. In addition, many families depend on income from men working in South African mines. The country has the world's highest rate of HIV infection, at 38.6 percent of all adults.

Political Rights and Civil Liberties: Citizens of Swaziland cannot change their government democratically. King Mswati III is an absolute monarch, and royal decrees carry the full force of law. Of the 65 members of the National Assembly, 55 are elected by popular vote and 10 are appointed by the king. The king also appoints 20 members of the Senate, with the remaining 10 selected by the National Assembly. Members of both houses serve five-year terms. Political parties are banned by the constitution, although there are political associations, the two largest being the People's United Democratic Movement (PUDEMO) and the Ngwane National Liberatory Congress (NNLC).

Swaziland was not surveyed in the 2004 Transparency International Corruption Perceptions Index. A private firm hired by the Finance Ministry estimates that the government is losing more than $6.5 million per month to corrupt practices. An Anti-Corruption Unit was established in 1998 but has failed to produce a single indictment.

Freedom of expression is severely restricted, especially regarding political issues or matters concerning the royal family. Legislation bans publication of any criticism of the monarchy, and self-censorship is widespread. However, broadcast and print media from South Africa are received in the country. There is one independent radio station, which broadcasts religious programming. In 2003, the new information minister, Abednego Ntshangase, announced that the state media would not be permitted to cover anything that has a "negative bearing" on the government. The ban affects the country's only television station and news-carrying radio channels. The government does not restrict access to the Internet.

Freedom of religion is respected, although there are no formal constitutional provisions protecting the practice. Academic freedom is limited by self-censorship. The government restricts freedom of assembly and association. Political parties are banned, and pro-democracy protests are sometimes violently broken up by police using tear gas and rubber bullets. The trade union movement remains a target of police and government repression. The Swaziland Federation of Trade Unions (SFTU), the country's largest labor organization, has been a leader in demands for democratization, but not successfully, given the absolute rule of the monarch. Jan Sithole, the SFTU general secretary, has been jailed several times in recent years, and he and his family have received death threats. In 2001, Sithole and five other union leaders were charged with contempt of court and brought to trial for organizing a strike that had been banned by the authorities; the case was eventually dismissed. Workers in all elements of the economy, including the public sector, can join unions, and 80 percent of the private workforce is unionized. Wage agreements are often reached by collective bargaining.

The judiciary, which is based on Western and traditional law, is generally independent in most civil cases, although the royal family and the government often refuse to respect rulings with which they disagree. Swaziland's judicial system became mired in crisis in November 2002, when six South African judges on the court of appeals resigned after the prime minister said that the government would ignore court judgments that curbed the king's power. The appeals court was reconstituted in November 2004, following assurances that the government would adhere to its decisions.

There are regular reports of police brutality, including torture, beatings, and suspicious deaths of suspects in custody. Security forces generally operate with impunity and have used heavy-handed tactics to break up pro-democracy rallies. Prisoners complain of beatings and overcrowding, and of neglect of inmates suffering from HIV and AIDS.

The legal code provides some protection against sexual harassment, but Swazi women encounter discrimination in both formal and customary law. Employment regulations requiring equal pay for equal work are obeyed unevenly. Married women are considered minors, requiring spousal permission to enter into almost any form of economic activity, and they are allowed only limited inheritance rights. Only men can pass on Swazi citizenship to their children. Violence against women is common despite traditional strictures against it, and rape frequently goes unpunished.

Sweden

Population: 9,000,000
GNI/capita: $25,970
Life Expectancy: 80
Religious Groups: Lutheran (87 percent), other
[including Roman Catholic, Orthodox, Baptist, Muslim,
Jewish and Buddhist] (13 percent)
Ethnic Groups: Swedish (majority), Finnish, Sami
Capital: Stockholm

Political Rights: 1
Civil Liberties: 1
Status: Free

Ten-Year Ratings Timeline (Political Rights, Civil Liberties, Status)

1995	1996	1997	1998	1999	2000	2001	2002	2003	2004
1,1F	1,1F	1,1F	1,1F	1,1F	1,1F	1,1F	1,1F	1,1F	1,1F

Overview:

In 2004, Swedes closely followed the trial and sentencing of the man responsible for the 2003 murder of Foreign Minister Anna Lindh. Elections to the European Parliament that were held in June resulted in a setback for the ruling Social Democrats and an increase in support for euro-skeptic parties.

After a series of monarchical alliances with Finland, Denmark, and Norway in the eleventh through nineteenth centuries, Sweden emerged as a modern democracy. Its tradition of neutrality, beginning with World War I, was altered somewhat by its admission to the European Union (EU) in 1995, and further eroded by a more pragmatic approach to security first presented in 2002. However, Sweden has retained its commitment to stay outside of military alliances, including NATO.

The Social Democrats, led by Prime Minister Goran Persson, have dominated politics since the 1920s. With their partners, the Left (formerly Communist) Party and the Greens, the Social Democrats won 191 out of 349 seats in the 2002 parliamentary elections, promising not to cut back the generous welfare system. An impressive 79 percent of eligible Swedes voted in the poll.

The population overwhelmingly rejected the adoption of the euro in a referendum in September 2003, despite strong support from government and business. The "no" vote was generally attributed to popular fears of deterioration in Sweden's generous welfare state benefits and damage to the Swedish economy. The "no" vote may also have been a reflection of skepticism about the EU as a whole.

On September 10, 2003, just days before the referendum, Foreign Minister Lindh was mortally wounded in a knife attack in a Stockholm department store. The killing sparked considerable debate about security in Sweden, where violence is very rare and politicians regularly travel without bodyguards in order to maintain direct contact with citizens.

In January 2004, Mijailo Mijailovic confessed to the murder, claiming it was a random attack motivated by "voices inside his head." In March, a Stockholm district court sentenced Mijailovic to life in prison, finding him mentally sound and guilty of murder. However, an appeals court overturned this verdict in June and ordered Mijailovic to a closed psychiatric ward after declaring him insane, a decision that rules out prison under Swedish law. The appeals court ruling was met with general dismay by the Swedish population and elicited widespread criticism of the Swedish psychiatric care system. The case was sent to the Supreme Court and was pending as of November 30.

Elections to the European Parliament in June saw only 37 percent of Swedes cast their ballots. Those that did vote gave a surprising 3 seats (of 19) to the euro-skeptic June List, a coalition that formed in the wake of the defeat of the referendum on the euro. The Social Democrats led all parties with 5 seats but garnered a lower percentage of votes than expected, a fate shared by their allies the Green Party (1 seat) and the Left Party (2 seats). The right-of-center opposition parties, who recent opinion polls show are gaining in popularity, earned the rest of the seats: the Moderates won 4 seats, the People's Party captured 2 seats, the Center Party took 1 seat, and the Christian Democrats secured 1 seat. In October, Prime Minister Persson reshuffled his cabinet in hopes of heading off the center-right ahead of the 2006 parliamentary elections.

Political Rights and Civil Liberties: Swedes can change their government democratically. The unicameral parliament, the Riksdag, has 349 members, 310 of whom are elected every four years in a proportional system. The remaining 39 seats are awarded on a national basis to further secure a proportional representation. A party must receive at least 4 percent of the votes in the entire country or 12 percent in a single electoral district to qualify for any seats. The prime minister is appointed by the Speaker of the Riksdag and confirmed by the Riksdag. King Carl XVI Gustaf, crowned in 1973, is head of state, but royal power is limited to official and ceremonial functions.

The principal religious, ethnic, and immigrant groups are represented in parliament. Since 1993, the Sami community elects its own parliament, which has significant powers over education and culture and serves as an advisory body to the government.

Corruption is very low. Transparency International ranked Sweden the sixth least corrupt country in the world in its 2004 Corruption Perceptions Index. However, recent instances of corporate graft have stained Sweden's image. In 2003, some 80 employees of the state-owned alcohol retail monopoly Systembolaget were brought to court on bribery charges. In December 2003, executives from the insurance group Skandia were investigated and found culpable of fraudulent accounting and reaping millions of kroner in excessive bonuses.

Sweden's media are independent. Most newspapers and periodicals are privately owned, and the government subsidizes daily newspapers regardless of their political affiliation. The Swedish Broadcasting Corporation and the Swedish Television Company broadcast weekly radio and television programs in several immigrant languages. The ethnic press is entitled to the same subsidies as the Swedish-language press. Reporters Sans Frontieres has reported that journalists who investigate extreme right-wing groups are regularly threatened and even physically attacked by neo-Nazi militants.

Religious freedom is constitutionally guaranteed. Although the country is 87 percent Lutheran, all churches, as well as synagogues and mosques, receive some state financial support. Academic freedom is ensured for all.

Freedom of assembly and association is guaranteed, as are the rights to strike and participate in unions. Trade union federations are strong and well organized and represent approximately 80 percent of the workforce.

Sweden's judiciary, which includes the Supreme Court, district courts, and a court of appeals, is independent. The government maintains effective control of the security and armed forces. No instances of human rights abuses by police were reported during the year. A series of highly publicized jail breaks in 2004 called into question the traditional leniency of the Swedish penal system.

The Swedish intelligence service reports that neo-Nazi activity is increasing in Sweden, which is one of the world's largest producers of racist and xenophobic Web sites. However, the movement's main political party, Sweden Democrats, won only 1.4 percent of the vote in the 2002 general election, not enough to win seats in the Riksdag. In December 2003, anti-Nazi demonstrators attempting to break up a neo-Nazi march clashed with police, resulting in 12 injuries. Anti-Semitic and anti-Muslim attacks are on the rise.

The first half of 2004 saw only 10 percent of refugees granted asylum in Sweden, a large drop-off from previous years and the result of stricter government policy toward refugees from Iraq and Bosnia-Herzegovina. Sweden is generally very welcoming of refugees, but its immigration policy has become more restrictive in recent years. In April, Swedish officials revealed that hundreds of asylum seekers were mutilating their fingerprints in order to avoid identification by EU officials, who use a Union-wide database to store asylum seekers' fingerprints. If identified as having already attempted to secure asylum status in another EU country, asylum seekers may be expelled from Sweden.

Despite the support of the ruling Social Democrats, in April the Riksdag rejected a proposal to temporarily maintain work permit requirements for nationals from the 10 new EU countries. The proposal aimed to head off an influx of workers from the new EU countries, and was opposed by a diverse coalition of the Left Party, the Green Party, the Center Party, and the Christian Democrats.

Sweden is a leader in gender equality. At 45 percent, the proportion of females in the Riksdag is the highest of any parliament in the world, and half of all government ministers are women. Although 79 percent of women work outside the home, women still make only 70 percent of men's wages in the public sector and 76 percent in the private sector. Prime Minister Goran Persson has announced that the government will tighten already strict laws on gender equality if the gap remains in two years. Women are under represented on company boards as well, and the government has threatened to introduce quotas if this does not change. Trafficking in women and children to and through Sweden from other countries is a problem, which the government is taking significant steps to deal with.

In April, the Riksdag established a commission to consider replacing the current law permitting same-sex civil unions with one allowing gay marriage. Sweden gave formal recognition to adoption by gay couples for the first time in February 2003; however, no foreign adoption agencies have agreed to send children to gay households.

Switzerland

Population: 7,400,000
GNI/capita: $36,170
Life Expectancy: 80
Religious Groups: Roman Catholic (46 percent),
Protestant (40 percent), other (14 percent)
Ethnic Groups: German (63.7 percent), French (19.2 percent),
Italian (7.6 percent), Romansch (0.6 percent), other (8.9 percent)
Capital: Bern

Political Rights: 1
Civil Liberties: 1
Status: Free

Ten-Year Ratings Timeline (Political Rights, Civil Liberties, Status)

1995	1996	1997	1998	1999	2000	2001	2002	2003	2004
1,1F	1,1F	1,1F	1,1F	1,1F	1,1F	1,1F	1,1F	1,1F	1,1F

Overview:

In 2004 there were tensions within the government over the inclusion for the first time, in late 2003, of the leader of a right-wing nationalist party. This leader, Christoph Blocher, pushed to tighten Switzerland's asylum laws. His role in government also complicated Switzerland's ongoing negotiation of a series of bilateral accords with the European Union (EU), a key goal of Swiss foreign policy.

Switzerland, which has been a loose confederation of cantons since 1291, emerged in its current borders after the Napoleonic wars, in 1815, where its tradition of neutrality was also sealed. The country's four official ethnic communities are based on language: German, French, Italian, and Romansh (the smallest community). Switzerland has stayed out of international wars and only joined the United Nations after a referendum in 2002.

For this reason, membership in international institutions has long been a controversial issue in Switzerland. The country is surrounded by members of the EU, but the Swiss, who fiercely value not only their military neutrality but their political independence, have resisted EU membership. The country has even resisted membership in the European Economic Area, a halfway-house to EU membership that has a trade agreement with the EU.

Hostility not only to EU membership, but also to immigration, has been a hallmark of the right-wing Swiss People's Party (SVP). The other main political parties are the center-left Social Democratic Party (SP) the right-wing Free Democratic Party (FDP), and the center-right Christian Democratic People's Party (CVP). Traditionally, these last three parties held two seats each in the seven-member Bundesrat (Federal Council), with the SVP holding just one. However, the SVP's vote share increased gradually over the 1990s—in correspondence with a rightward move by the party—as it poached voters initially from small far-right parties, and then increasingly from the FDP.

During the October 2003 legislative election, the SVP made blatantly xenophobic appeals, including running a newspaper advertisement blaming "black Africans" for crime. The SVP insisted that it had nothing against legal immigrants, who make up a fifth of Switzerland's population, and that it was merely opposed to illegal immigration and abuse of the asylum policy. The SVP won the biggest share of the vote, while the SP finished just behind the SVP. The CVP received just under 15 percent of the vote, barely half the total of the SVP.

With this success, the SVP's leader, Christoph Blocher, called for a second Bundesrat seat for his party. Blocher demanded that he and another minister be appointed to the council, with a seat being taken from the CVP. After extensive negotiations, the other parties agreed. In late 2003, Blocher joined the cabinet as head of the Federal Department of Justice and Police, and the CVP lost a cabinet seat. The inclusion of the SVP has brought new tensions into the Swiss cabinet, for example over a tightening of asylum laws pushed by Blocher and over justice and home-affairs cooperation with the EU, and could slow down the legislative process.

The success of the SVP, the Swiss party most hostile to Swiss entry into the EU, strained relations with the EU. This has slowed a package of bilateral accords between the two that would deepen cooperation on tax evasion, justice, and home affairs. The package was submitted to the legislature in November 2004, and most of the agreements are expected to be ratified in 2005.

Political Rights and Civil Liberties: The Swiss can change their government democratically. The constitution of 1848, significantly revised in 1874 and 2000, provides for two directly elected legislative chambers—the Council of States (in which each canton has two members and each half-canton, one) and the National Council. The Federal Council is a seven-person executive; the presidency is ceremonial and rotates annually among the Federal Council's members. Collegiality and consensus are hallmarks of Swiss political culture.

The Swiss institutional system is characterized by decentralization and direct democracy. The cantons and half-cantons have control over much of economic and social policy, with the federal government's powers largely limited to foreign affairs and some economic policy. The rights of cultural, religious, and linguistic minorities are strongly protected. Referendums are also a common feature; any measure that modifies the constitution must be put to a referendum. Any new or revised law must be put to a referendum if 50,000 signatures in favor of doing so can be gathered, and voters may even initiate legislation themselves with 100,000 signatures.

The government is free from pervasive corruption. However, the country has traditionally drawn criticism for its banking-secrecy laws, which financial watchdogs claim enable money laundering and other crimes. In the IMF's 2004 report on its annual consultation with Switzerland, the IMF praised Switzerland for a toughening of laws on money laundering and terrorist financing in 2003. Switzerland was ranked 7 out of 146 countries surveyed in Transparency International's 2004 Corruption Perceptions Index.

Switzerland has a free media environment. The Swiss Broadcasting Corporation dominates the broadcast market. The penal code prohibits racist or anti-Semitic speech. Consolidation of newspapers in large media conglomerates has forced the closure of some small and local newspapers. Internet access is unrestricted.

Freedom of religion is guaranteed by the constitution. Most cantons support one or several churches. The country is split about evenly between Roman Catholicism and Protestantism, although as there are now officially more than 300,000

Muslims (and perhaps many more undocumented), Muslims are the largest non-Christian minority. Religion is taught in public schools, depending on the predominant creed in the canton. Students are free to choose their creed of instruction or opt out of religious instruction. In 2001, a cantonal court ruled that the Church of Scientology could not be a "real church" because it does not advocate belief in God. Scientologists face other legal obstacles, such as difficulty establishing private schools. Academic freedom is respected.

There is freedom of assembly and association. The right to collective bargaining is respected, and approximately a third of the workforce is unionized.

The judiciary is independent, and the rule of law prevails in civil and criminal matters. Most judicial decisions are made at the cantonal level, except for the federal Supreme Court, which reviews cantonal court decisions when they pertain to federal law. Refusal to perform military service is a criminal offense for males. Prison conditions are generally acceptable.

Women were only granted universal suffrage at the federal level in 1971, and the half-canton Appenzell-Innerrhoden denied women the vote until 1990. Abortion laws were liberalized to decriminalize abortion in the first 12 weeks of pregnancy following a referendum in 2002, which 72 percent of voters supported. The law gives women 10 weeks of maternity leave but no salary guarantee.

Syria

Population: 18,000,000
GNI/capita: $1,130
Life Expectancy: 70
Religious Groups: Sunni Muslim (74 percent), other Muslim [including Alawite and Druze] (16 percent), Christian [various sects] (10 percent)
Ethnic Groups: Arab (90 percent), other [including Kurd and Armenians] (10 percent)
Capital: Damascus

Political Rights: 7
Civil Liberties: 7
Status: Not Free

Ten-Year Ratings Timeline (Political Rights, Civil Liberties, Status)

1995	1996	1997	1998	1999	2000	2001	2002	2003	2004
7,7NF	7,7NF	7,7NF	7,7NF	7,7NF	7,7NF	7,7NF	7,7NF	7,7NF	7,7NF

Overview:

Political and civil liberties in Syria continued to deteriorate palpably in 2004 for the fourth year in a row. Although President Bashar Assad freed several hundred aging political prisoners jailed during his father's 30-year reign, he showed no such clemency to those opposed to his own autocratic rule. Some 2,000 Kurds were jailed for weeks or months without charge following antigovernment riots in March, while dozens of intellectuals were detained during the year for peacefully expressing their opinions.

Located at the heart of the Fertile Crescent, the Syrian capital of Damascus is the oldest continuously inhabited city in the world and once controlled a vast empire extending from Europe to India. The modern state of Syria is a comparatively recent entity, established by the French after World War I and formally granted independence in 1946. The country's precarious democratic institutions survived nominally in the face of persistent military coups until 1963, when the pan-Arab Baath Party seized power and amended the constitution to guarantee itself "the leading role in society and in the state."

The Syrian government has been dominated by Alawites, adherents of an offshoot sect of Islam who constitute just 12 percent of the population, since a 1970 coup brought General Hafez Assad to power. For the next 30 years, the Assad regime managed to maintain control of Syria's majority Sunni Muslim population, brutally suppressing all dissent. In 1982, government forces stormed the northern town of Hama to crush a rebellion by the Muslim Brotherhood and killed as many as 20,000 insurgents and civilians in a matter of days.

In 2000, Assad's son and successor, Bashar, inherited control of a country with the region's most stagnant economy and highest rate of population growth, with unemployment estimated at well over 20 percent. In his inaugural speech, the young leader pledged to eliminate government corruption, revitalize the economy, and establish a "democracy specific to Syria." The first six months of Assad's tenure, known as the "Damascus Spring" witnessed dramatic changes. Informal networks of public figures from all sectors of civil society were allowed to openly discuss the country's social, economic, and political problems. Assad released more than 600 political prisoners, closed the notorious Mazzeh prison, allowed scores of exiled dissidents to return home, reinstated dissidents who had been fired from state-run media outlets and universities, and allowed the establishment of the country's first privately owned newspaper.

In February 2001, however, the regime abruptly reinstated restrictions on public freedoms and launched an escalating campaign of threats, intimidation, and harassment against the reform movement. Ten of the country's leading reformists were arrested during the year and eventually sentenced to heavy prison terms. Economic reform also fell by the wayside as dozens of reform laws remained unimplemented, were put into effect half-heartedly, or lacked supporting regulatory changes needed to attract international investment.

The regime's renewed assault on political and civil liberties initially elicited little criticism from Western governments, in part because of Assad's cooperation in the war against the al-Qaeda terrorist network. However, Assad's covert efforts to assist Saddam Hussein's rearmament prior to the March 2003 U.S.-led invasion of Iraq and his unwillingness to disrupt the flow of foreign terrorist infiltration into the country after the war led to rapid deterioration in his relations with the administration of U.S. president George W. Bush, culminating in the May 2004 imposition of American economic sanctions on Syria. Meanwhile, Assad's refusal to relax Syrian control over Lebanon severely alienated France, which co-sponsored a September 2004 UN Security Council resolution calling on Damascus to immediately end its lucrative occupation altogether and opened the way for tough diplomacy by the European Union (EU).

Scenes of Iraqis celebrating the downfall of a government so strikingly similar to the Assad regime inspired Syria's pro-democracy movement to reassert itself. After the fall of Baghdad, nearly 300 intellectuals signed a petition demanding the release of all political prisoners, the cancellation of the state of emergency, and other political reforms. However, while the regime was willing to adjust the manner in which its control over society is legitimized and reproduced—most notably by reducing the two-million-member Baath Party's oversight of policy decisions—it remained unwilling to substantially loosen its grip on power.

Notwithstanding its claim to be threatened by radical Islamists, the Assad regime's behavior indicated that it feels most threatened not by religious fundamentalists, but by secular opposition forces seen as prospective allies of the West. In March 2004, security forces fired on a crowd of Kurdish soccer fans who had hoisted posters of Bush, touching off eight days of riots throughout Kurdish-inhabited areas of the country. At least 30 people, mostly Kurds, were killed as security forces suppressed the riots and arrested some 2,000 people.

While hundreds of Islamists and radical leftist political prisoners were released during the year, secular liberal activists were subjected to a steadily intensifying crackdown. The president of the Committees for the Defense of Democratic Liberties and Human Rights (CDDLHR), Aktham Naisse, was arrested in April after he organized a petition and rally calling for the lifting of emergency law. In September, the security forces detained the outspoken leader of a newly established liberal movement, Nabil Fayyad, and held him for 33 days. Fayyad, who had condemned the country's political leaders as "intellectual terrorists" for their intolerance of free speech just months earlier, emerged from prison broken and subdued, praising Assad for "defending public liberties."

Political Rights and Civil Liberties: The Syrian people cannot change their government or exert influence over policy making through democratic means. Under the 1973 constitution, the president is nominated by the ruling Baath Party and approved by a popular referendum. In practice, these referendums are orchestrated by the regime, as are elections to the 250-member People's Assembly, which holds little independent legislative power. The only legal political parties are the Baath Party and its six small coalition partners in the ruling National Progressive Front (NPF). All 167 of the NPF's candidates won seats in the March 2003 parliamentary elections, with heavily vetted independent candidates taking the remaining 83 seats.

Syria was ranked 71 out of 146 countries surveyed in the 2004 Transparency International Corruption Perceptions Index. Key regime officials and their offspring monopolize many lucrative import markets and benefit from a range of other illicit economic activities.

Freedom of expression is heavily restricted. Vaguely worded articles of the Penal Code and Emergency Law give the government considerable discretion in punishing those who express views or publish information that "opposes the goals of the revolution" or tarnishes the image of the state. Apart from a handful of non-news radio stations licensed in 2003, the broadcast media are state owned. While there are a few privately owned newspapers and magazines, a press law enacted in September 2001 permits the government to arbitrarily deny or revoke publishing licenses for reasons "related to the public interest" and compels privately owned print media outlets to submit all material to government censors on the day of publication. The country's leading independent newspaper, *Al-Doumari*, closed in 2003 in the face of recurrent bureaucratic harassment. Satellite dishes are illegal, but generally tolerated.

Muhammad Ghanem, a Syrian journalist for two newspapers based in the United Arab Emirates (UAE), was detained for 13 days in March 2004 after he wrote an article arguing that all Syrian Kurds should be granted citizenship. Even local journalists who publish material in foreign publications under pseudonyms have been unable to escape prosecution because of the government's extensive surveillance of telephone and Internet communication. In July, three journalists who wrote articles using pseudonyms for a UAE-based online newspaper—Muhammad Quteish, Haytham Quteish, and Yahia al-Aws—were sentenced to prison terms ranging from two to four years. In June, Abdel Rahman Shaguri was sentenced to two and a half years in prison on charges of "harming the image and national security of Syria" for sending e-mail copies of a dissident newsletter to friends and relatives. In October, Masoud Hamid was sentenced to five years in prison for sending e-mail photos of a June 2003 Kurdish demonstration in Damascus to a number of dissident-run Web sites.

Syrians are permitted to access the Internet only through state-run servers, which block access to a wide range of Web sites. Shortly after the outbreak of the March 2004 Kurdish riots, the authorities blocked access to two Kurdish-language Web sites that carried news, photos, and video clips of the violence. E-mail correspondence is extensively monitored by the intelligence agencies.

Although the constitution requires that the president be a Muslim, there is no state religion in Syria, and freedom of worship is generally respected. The Alawite minority dominates the officer corps of the military and security forces. Since the eruption of an Islamist rebellion in the late 1970s, the government has tightly monitored mosques and controlled the appointment of Muslim clergy. Academic freedom is heavily restricted. University professors have been routinely dismissed from state universities in recent years because of their involvement in the pro-democracy movement, and some have been imprisoned.

Freedom of assembly is largely nonexistent. While citizens can ostensibly hold demonstrations with prior permission from the Interior Ministry, in practice only the government, the Baath Party, or groups linked to them are allowed to organize demonstrations. Security forces forcibly dispersed a small crowd of activists who staged a demonstration against the state of emergency on March 8, arresting six people and briefly detaining two foreign journalists and an American diplomat who attended the rally.

Freedom of association is restricted. All nongovernmental organizations must register with the government, which generally denies registration to reformist groups. Although a few unregistered human rights groups have been allowed to operate in Syria, individual leaders of these groups have been jailed for human rights related activities. In addition to Aktham Naisse, two other leaders of the CDDLHR were detained in 2004 for more than a month.

All unions must belong to the General Federation of Trade Unions (GFTU). Although ostensibly independent, the GFTU is headed by a member of the ruling Baath Party and is used by the government to control all aspects of union activity in Syria. Strikes in nonagricultural sectors are legal, but they rarely occur.

While regular criminal and civil courts operate with some independence and generally safeguard defendants' rights, most politically sensitive cases have been tried by two exceptional courts established under emergency law: the Supreme State Security Court (SSSC) and the Economic Security Court (ESC). Both courts deny or limit the right to appeal, limit access to legal counsel, try most cases behind closed doors, and admit as evidence confessions obtained through torture. The ESC was formally abolished in 2004; henceforth, economic crimes will be tried by criminal courts.

The state of emergency in force since 1963 gives the security agencies virtually unlimited authority to arrest suspects and hold them incommunicado for prolonged periods without charge. Many of the estimated 3,000 remaining political prisoners in Syria have never been tried for any offense. The security agencies, which operate independently of the judiciary, routinely extract confessions by torturing suspects and detaining members of their families. There were scores of reports of torture by the security services during the year, and according to local human rights groups, at least four people (all of them Kurds) died from suspected torture by the security services. At least four people who returned from exile in 2004 were arrested and detained on their arrival. The government carried out two major releases of political prisoners during the year—around 120 in January and more than 250 in late July and early August.

The Kurdish minority in Syria faces cultural and linguistic restrictions, and suspected Kurdish activists are routinely dismissed from schools and jobs. Some 200,000 Syrian Kurds are deprived of citizenship and unable to obtain passports, identity cards, or birth certificates, which in turn prevents them from owning land, obtaining government employment, or voting. The September 2001 press law requires that owners and editors in chief of publications be Arabs. Scores of Kurds arrested during and after the March 2004 riots remained in detention as of November 30. Following the riots, the authorities explicitly banned all major independent Kurdish political groups.

Although most Syrians do not face travel restrictions, prominent activists living in Syria, as well as relatives of exiled dissidents, are routinely prevented from traveling abroad. Many Kurds lack the requisite documents to leave the country. Equality of opportunity has been compromised by rampant corruption and conscious government efforts to weaken the predominantly Sunni urban bourgeoisie.

The government has promoted gender equality by appointing women to senior positions in all branches of government and providing equal access to education, but many discriminatory laws remain in force. A husband may request that the Interior Ministry block his wife from traveling abroad, and women are generally barred from leaving the country with their children unless they can prove that the father has granted permission. Syrian law stipulates that an accused rapist can be acquitted if he marries his victim, and it provides for reduced sentences in cases of "honor crimes" committed by men against female relatives for alleged sexual misconduct. Personal status law for Muslim women is governed by Sharia (Islamic law) and is discriminatory in marriage, divorce, and inheritance matters. Violence against women is widespread, particularly in rural areas.

Taiwan

Population: 22,600,000
GNI/capita: $13,392
Life Expectancy: 76
Religious Groups: Mixture of Buddhist, Confucian, Taoist (93 percent), Christian (4.5 percent) other (2.5 percent)
Ethnic Groups: Taiwanese [including Hakka] (84 percent), mainland Chinese (14 percent), Aboriginal (2 percent)
Capital: Taipei

Political Rights: 2
Civil Liberties: 1*
Status: Free

Ratings Change: Taiwan's civil liberties rating improved from 2 to 1 due to improvements in the rule of law, including the consolidation of judicial independence.

Ten-Year Ratings Timeline (Political Rights, Civil Liberties, Status)

1995	1996	1997	1998	1999	2000	2001	2002	2003	2004
3,3F	2,2F	2,2F	2,2F	2,2F	1,2F	1,2F	2,2F	2,2F	2,1F

Overview: Taiwan's presidential election in March 2004 thrust the country into political turmoil. The Democratic Progressive Party (DPP) incumbent Chen Shui-bian was reelected, but by a very slim margin and only after irregularities: Chen and his vice president were shot just hours before the polling began. A legislative commission was established in August to investigate the shooting. At the same time, recent judicial reforms have reduced corruption and political influence over the courts.

Located some 100 miles off the southeast coast of China, Taiwan became the home of the Koumintang (KMT), or Nationalist, government-in-exile in 1949, when Communist forces overthrew the Nationalists following two decades of civil war on the mainland. While Taiwan is independent in all but name, Beijing considers it to be a renegade province of China and has long threatened to invade if the island formally declares independence.

Taiwan's democratic transition began in 1987, when the KMT government lifted a state of martial law imposed 38 years earlier. The KMT's Lee Teng-hui became the first native Taiwanese president in 1988. His election broke a stranglehold on politics by mainland refugees, who, along with their descendants, make up 14 percent of Taiwan's population.

In his 12 years in office, Lee oversaw far-reaching political reforms including the holding of Taiwan's first multiparty legislative elections in 1991 and the first direct presidential elections in 1996. Lee also played down the KMT's historic commitment to eventual reunification with China, promoting instead a Taiwanese national identity that undermined Beijing's claim that there is only "one China."

With Lee barred by term limits from seeking reelection, Chen's victory in the 2000 presidential race, in which he ran as the standard-bearer of the pro-independence DPP, broke the KMT's grip on politics and signaled that Taiwan would continue promoting an independent identity. After his election, Chen continued to assert that Taiwan should eventually be independent—the DPP's core position.

Chen won reelection in the March 2004 presidential polls by a margin of only 0.2 percent. Hours before the vote, Chen and his vice presidential running mate, Annette Lu, were shot. The candidate of the opposition KMT, who was expected to win the election by a comfortable margin, alleged that the shooting was staged to gain sympathy votes. The parliament (Legislative Yuan), which is controlled by the KMT, passed a law in August to establish a commission to investigate the shooting. The DPP and its ally, the Taiwan Solidarity Union (TSU), boycotted the commission on the grounds that it was unconstitutional; under its current statute, for example, the commission may have the right to detain citizens without a warrant. The DPP-TSU union also feared that it would be ignored in the commission; commission seats have been allocated according to representation in the Legislative Yuan, and so the KMT dominates the commission. The Constitutional Court held hearings on the constitutionality of the law and the commission. Elections to the Legislative Yuan were scheduled for December 2004.

Since the DPP victory in March, the government has appeared to take a firmer pro-independence stance. In September, for example, the premier (the head of the Executive Yuan), Yu Shyi-kun, publicly advocated for the first time that Taiwan develop offensive missile capability. Less than a week later, Chen asserted that the country should hold a plebiscite to assert its preference for independence, following the example set in 1945 by Mongolia. It is more than likely, however, that these moves were just ploys to shore up support among DPP and other pro-independence voters ahead of the legislative elections in December 2004. Even if Chen's intention were to assert formal independence, he is far from having the means to actually achieve this, as his party lacks a parliamentary majority. In addition, the United States, which supplies most of Taiwan's arms, cannot provide the island with offensive weapons (the 1979 Taiwan Relations Act, which governs U.S. policy toward the island, stipulates that the U.S. can provide Taiwan only with arms "of a defensive character").

Political Rights and Civil Liberties: Taiwanese citizens can change their government democratically. The 1946 constitution, adopted while the KMT was in power on the mainland, created a hybrid presidential-parliamentary system. The president, who is directly elected for a four-year term, wields executive power, appoints the premier, and can dissolve the Legislative Yuan. The prime minister is responsible to the unicameral 225-seat legislature, which is directly elected for a three-year term.

The administration of President Chen Shui-bian has been fairly successful in its attempts to crack down on vote buying and on the links between politicians and organized crime that were widely believed to have flourished under KMT rule. Nevertheless, electoral irregularities remain; the most notable recent example was the shooting—possibly staged—of Chen and his vice presidential running mate just hours before the presidential election in March 2004. Police also investigated some 2,000 cases of alleged vote buying during the election, though they did specify that they did not believe either of the candidates to be personally responsible for the bribery. Taiwan was ranked 35 out of 146 countries surveyed in Transparency International's 2004 Corruption Perceptions Index.

The Taiwanese press is "vigorous and active," according to the 2003 human rights report issued by the U.S. State Department in February 2004. Print media are completely independent, but electronic media and broadcast television stations are still subject to government influence. Given that the government and political parties are barred by law from owning or running media organizations, and that most Taiwanese can access approximately 100 cable television stations, the state's influence on the media is, on balance, minimal.

Taiwanese of all faiths can worship freely. Religious organizations can choose to register with the government; those that do may operate tax-free. Taiwanese professors and other educators can write and lecture freely. Laws barring Taiwanese from advocating Communism or independence from China remain on the books, but they are no longer enforced.

Freedom of assembly and association is well respected. Permits are required for public meetings outdoors, but these are routinely granted. All civic organizations must register with the government, but registration is routinely granted. Taiwanese human rights, social welfare, and environmental nongovernmental groups are active and operate without harassment.

Trade unions are independent, though "a number of laws and regulations limit the right of association," according to the U.S. State Department report. Collective bargaining, though not widespread, is legal in most industries. Teachers, civil servants, and defense industry workers are barred from joining unions or bargaining collectively. Labor unions must submit their constitutions to authorities for review. Moreover, the law restricts the right to strike by, for example, allowing authorities to order mediation of labor disputes and ban work stoppages while mediation is in progress.

Taiwan's judiciary is largely independent, and trials are public and generally fair. There is no trial by jury; judges decide all cases. Recent judicial reforms have reduced corruption and political influence over the courts. In August, the Ministry of Justice established a task force to investigate corruption in the judiciary and brought several officials under investigation. In September, the government reasserted its intention to crack down on organized crime, corruption, and bribery, especially ahead of the legislative elections scheduled for December. Another significant reform took place in August: the Legislative Yuan approved constitutional changes outlining a full-scale overhaul of the legislature. The changes, effective from 2008, include halving the number of seats in the Legislative Yuan and extending all legislators' terms from three to four years. Arbitrary arrest and detention are not permitted, and security forces generally respected this ban. Police occasionally committed acts of physical abuse against detainees, and a "historical and cultural tradition of corruption hindered police effectiveness," according to the U.S. State Department report. Still, police remain under civilian control, and human rights abuses are not considered a problem. Suspects are allowed attorneys during interrogations specifically to prevent abuse during detention. Prison conditions are generally adequate and conform to international norms; overcrowding is the biggest problem.

Taiwan's constitution provides for the equality of all citizens. The rights of the Aboriginal descendants of Malayo-Polynesians are protected, and the government has instituted social and educational programs to help the population assimilate into mainstream ethnic Chinese society. A quota system concerning employment of Aborigines and people with disabilities applies to firms wishing to compete for government contracts. Despite these efforts, the Aborigines still feel discriminated against: in November, for example, about 1,000 Aborigines held a demonstration to protest the Executive Yuan's alleged failure to allocate enough money for reconstruction in flood-ravaged areas of the country. Societal discrimination against Aborigines has lessened somewhat in recent years.

Laws protecting privacy are generally adhered to. Searches without warrants are allowed only in particular circumstances, and a 1999 law imposed strict punishments for illicit wiretapping. Travel is generally not restricted.

Taiwanese women have made impressive gains in recent years in business, but reportedly continue to face job discrimination in the private sector. Rape and domestic violence remain serious problems despite government programs to protect women. Although the law allows authorities to investigate complaints of domestic violence and to prosecute rape suspects without the victims' formally pressing charges, cultural norms inhibit many women from reporting these crimes.

Tajikistan

Population: 6,600,000
GNI/capita: $180
Life Expectancy: 68
Religious Groups: Sunni Muslim (85 percent),
Shia Muslim (5 percent), other (10 percent)
Ethnic Groups: Tajik (65 percent), Uzbek (25 percent),
Russian (4 percent), other (6 percent)
Capital: Dushanbe

Political Rights: 6
Civil Liberties: 5
Status: Not Free

Ten-Year Ratings Timeline (Political Rights, Civil Liberties, Status)

1995	1996	1997	1998	1999	2000	2001	2002	2003	2004
7,7NF	7,7NF	6,6NF	6,6NF	6,6NF	6,6NF	6,6NF	6,5NF	6,5NF	6,5NF

Overview:

The government of President Imomali Rakhmonov continued throughout 2004 to consolidate its power by clamping down on the media and working to sideline perceived and actual political opponents in advance of the 2005 parliamentary and 2006 presidential elections. Although several opposition parties joined forces in a tactical coalition early in the year, their prospects for success in the forthcoming polls appear limited by the dominance of pro-government parties and the weakness and limited popularity of much of the opposition. Meanwhile, Russia strengthened its foothold in the region following a bilateral agreement with Dushanbe on a number of strategic and economic matters, including the establishment of a permanent Russian military base in Tajikistan.

Conquered by Russia in the late 1800s, Tajikistan was made an autonomous region within Uzbekistan in 1924 and a separate socialist republic of the U.S.S.R. in 1929. Tajikistan declared independence from the Soviet Union in September 1991, and two months later, former Communist Party leader Rakhman Nabiyev was elected president.

Long-simmering clan-based tensions, combined with various anti-Communist and Islamist movements, soon plunged the country into a five-year civil war for central government control. In September 1992, Communist hard-liners forced Nabiyev's resignation; he was replaced later that year by Rakhmonov, a leading Communist Party member. The following month, Rakhmonov launched attacks against antigovernment forces that caused tens of thousands to flee into neighboring Afghanistan.

As the fighting continued, Rakhmonov was elected president in November 1994 after most opposition candidates either boycotted or were prevented from competing in the poll. The March 1995 parliamentary elections, in which the majority of seats were won by pro-government candidates, were boycotted by the United Tajik Opposition (UTO), a coalition of various secular and Islamic opposition groups that emerged during the war as the main opposition force fighting against Rakhmonov's government.

Following a December 1996 ceasefire, Rakhmonov and UTO leader Said Abdullo Nuri signed a formal peace agreement in Moscow on June 27, 1997, officially ending the civil war, which had claimed tens of thousands of lives and left several hundred thousand as refugees. The accord called for the merging of opposition forces into the regular army; granted an amnesty for UTO members; provided for the UTO to be allotted 30 percent of senior government posts; and established a 26-member National Reconciliation Commission, with seats evenly divided between the government and the UTO. The commission was charged with implementing the peace agreements, including preparing amendments for a referendum on constitutional changes that would lead to fair parliamentary elections.

During the next two years, the government and the UTO took steps toward implementing the peace accord. In a September 1999 referendum, voters approved a series of constitutional amendments permitting the formation of religion-based political parties. This move paved the way for the legal operation of the Islamic opposition, including the Islamic Renaissance Party (IRP), which constituted the backbone of the UTO. The referendum also included an amendment extending the president's single term in office from five to seven years. In November, Rakhmonov was reelected with a reported 97 percent of the vote in a poll criticized by international election observers for widespread irregularities.

As the final stage in the implementation of the 1997 peace accord, Tajikistan held elections in February 2000 for the 63-seat lower house of parliament. Rakhmonov's People's Democratic Party (PDP) received nearly 65 percent of the vote, followed by the Communist Party with 20 percent, and the IRP with 7 percent. Although the participation of six parties and a number of independent candidates in the poll provided some political pluralism, international election observers, including a joint mission by the Organization for Security and Cooperation in Europe (OSCE) and the United Nations, cited serious problems, including the exclusion of certain opposition parties, biased state media coverage, and a lack of transparency in the tabulation of votes. In the March elections to the 33-seat upper house of parliament, in which local assemblies elected 25 members and Rakhmonov appointed the remaining 8, the PDP obtained the overwhelming majority of seats.

After the elections, the National Reconciliation Commission was formally disbanded, and a UN observer mission withdrew in May 2000 after nearly six years in

Tajikistan. However, important provisions of the peace accord remained unimplemented, with demobilization of opposition factions incomplete and the government failing to meet the 30 percent quota of senior government posts to be awarded to the UTO.

Rakhmonov's already substantial powers as president were further consolidated in a June 22, 2003, constitutional referendum. Voters approved by a reported 93 percent a package of 56 constitutional amendments, the most controversial of which permits the president to serve two additional seven-year terms beyond the next presidential election in 2006. (The constitution previously limited the president to a single seven-year term.) Rakhmonov, who argued that this change would better reflect post–civil war circumstances and bring the country continued stability, could theoretically remain in office until 2020. Critics charged that most voters were not fully aware of the proposed changes, which were not printed on the ballot papers and had not been given much media coverage. The opposition Democratic Party urged its supporters to boycott the vote, while the opposition Social Democratic Party (SDP) and the IRP adopted less openly confrontational positions.

With parliamentary elections due in February 2005 and presidential elections a year later, the government increased its pressure in 2004 on opposition figures and other perceived potential challengers to the president's authority. Early in the year, Shamsiddin Shamsiddinov, a deputy chairman of the IRP, was sentenced to 16 years in prison on charges that included setting up an armed group, illegally crossing the state border, and polygamy; while in pretrial detention, he was allegedly abused and denied access to legal counsel. The IRP insists that the conviction was politically motivated. The authorities have also targeted exiled opponents, including Yakub Salimov, a former interior minister and Rakhmonov ally, who fled the country in 1997. He was charged by the Tajik government with treason for involvement in a 1998 invasion and brief occupation of northern Tajikistan and was arrested in Moscow in 2003. In February 2004, Salimov was extradited from Moscow at the request of the Tajik government, a decision some observers speculate may have been linked to bilateral negotiations over security issues. Salimov's trial opened in late November.

In August 2004, Drug Control Agency head Ghaffor Mirzoyev was arrested on charges including abuse of power, tax evasion, and murder. Some observers believe that his arrest was politically motivated because of his close ties with the mayor of Dushanbe, a potential rival for the presidency. Also in August, a Taraqqiyot (Progress) party official was arrested on suspicion of various offenses, including insulting the honor and dignity of the president. The arrest occurred after authorities raided the party's offices and seized a letter to the International Court of Justice protesting the government's repeated refusal to officially register Taraqqiyot.

Although three opposition parties—the Socialist Party, SDP, and IRP—formed a tactical coalition in April of this year the opposition is likely to have few chances of gaining seats in the upcoming elections in the face of the government's overwhelming political dominance. While the stated goal of the coalition is to ensure the proper conduct of the election, the three parties announced that they would field separate candidates, weakening their chances of capturing enough votes to enter parliament. In addition, the IRP faced internal struggles during the year regarding the party's political agenda. A new electoral law signed by Rakhmonov in July was criticized by opposition groups and international observers for failing to ensure truly independent electoral commissions and imposing excessively high registration fees on candidates. After the approval of the electoral law, the Democratic Party reversed its earlier decision not to join the opposition coalition, saying that the new law did not reflect sufficient input from the opposition and international bodies.

On the international front, Russia and Tajikistan finally reached agreement in October on a number of issues that will solidify Russia's military presence in Tajikistan and increase bilateral economic relations. Under the terms of the agreement, Russia's 201st Motorized Rifle Division in Tajikistan will be upgraded to a full military base, even as responsibility for guarding the Tajik-Afghan border will be transferred from Russian to Tajik jurisdiction over the next two years (most of the border guard officers are Russian, while the troops are Tajik conscripts). Russia will gain control of the Okno space-monitoring system at Nurek in Tajikistan, and Moscow will forgive Dushanbe's massive debts and invest in infrastructure projects in Tajikistan, including a hydropower plant. While the conclusion of the agreement ended a period of prolonged, and often tense, bilateral negotiations, the living and working conditions of the several hundred thousand Tajik migrant workers in Russia, who often face official harassment and discrimination, remained a source of friction between the two countries.

Relations with Uzbekistan, its more powerful Central Asian neighbor, remained uneasy, with Tajik civilians continuing to be killed accidentally by land mines laid by Uzbekistan along the Uzbek-Tajik border. The mines had been designed to prevent renewed invasions by Islamic radical groups that had entered into Uzbekistan via Tajikistan several years earlier. Tajikistan continued to benefit from technical and financial assistance from the United States, which was in the process of constructing a permanent embassy in Dushanbe during the year.

Political Rights and Civil Liberties:

Citizens of Tajikistan cannot change their government democratically. The 1994 constitution provides for a strong, directly elected executive who enjoys broad authority to appoint and dismiss officials. Amendments to the constitution adopted in a 1999 referendum further increased the powers of the president by extending his term in office from five to seven years and creating a full-time, bicameral parliament: the Assembly of Representatives (lower chamber), whose 63 members are elected by popular vote to serve five-year terms; and the National Assembly (upper chamber), whose 33 members are indirectly elected, 25 by local assemblies and 8 by the president, all for five-year terms. Constitutional amendments adopted in a 2003 referendum allow the president to run for two additional seven-year terms in office. Neither the presidential polls in 1994 and 1999 nor the parliamentary elections of 1995 and 2000 were free and fair.

Patronage networks and regional affiliations are central to political life, with officials from the Kulyob region—the home of President Imomali Rakhmonov—dominant in government. The pro-Rakhmonov PDP is the dominant political party. Secular opposition parties, including the Democratic Party and SDP, are weak and enjoy minimal popular support. A 1998 ban on religious-based parties was lifted, leading to the registration of the IRP, currently the only legal religious-based party in Central Asia. While the IRP has limited political influence within government structures, it also faces opposition criticism of having been co-opted by the authorities.

Corruption is reportedly pervasive throughout society, with payments often required to obtain lucrative government positions. One of the conditions for Tajikistan's receipt of development assistance from the International Bank for Reconstruction and Development is the country's efforts to fight corruption. Tajikistan was ranked 133 out of 146 countries in Transparency International's 2004 Corruption Perceptions Index.

Despite constitutional guarantees of freedom of speech and the press, independent journalists continue to face harassment and intimidation, selective tax audits, and denial of access to state printing facilities. The penal code criminalizes publicly defaming or insulting a person's honor or reputation. Consequently, journalists often avoid reporting on sensitive political issues, including corruption, and directly criticizing the president and other senior officials. Most newspapers in this impoverished country are weeklies and suffer from low advertising revenues and poor circulation. Most television stations are state owned or only nominally independent, and the process of obtaining broadcast licenses is cumbersome and expensive. Although the government does not block access to the Internet, the high cost of Internet service puts it out of reach of most citizens.

Dozens of journalists were murdered during the country's five-year civil war in the 1990s, and most of the cases have not been solved. In January 2004, the prosecutor-general's office announced that it had established a special group to investigate the killings.

Independent and opposition journalists and media outlets faced growing government pressure in 2004 in advance of the February 2005 parliamentary elections. Dodojon Atovulloev, the editor of the opposition newspaper *Charogi Ruz,* which is banned in Tajikistan for it antigovernment stance, returned briefly to Tajikistan from exile in Russia in June after having fled the country more than a decade earlier. However, Atovulloev left Tajikistan just four days later out of concern that the authorities could not guarantee his safety after he received death threats. Rajabi Mirzo, the editor of the opposition weekly *Ruzi Nav*, was assaulted in July near his home for what may have been political reasons; the paper frequently printed articles critical of the Tajik authorities. As of November 30, no arrests had been made in connection with the case. In August, the authorities closed down Jiyonkhon, an independent printing house, for the alleged tax violations of one of the opposition newspapers it printed; the charges were believed to be politically motivated. Jiyonkhon had published several opposition newspapers, including *Ruzi Nav* and *Nerui Sukhan*, which the state printing house in Dushanbe refused to print, forcing the newspapers to cease publication or find alternative printing facilities abroad. After *Ruzi Nav* contracted with an independent printing house in neighboring Kyrgyzstan, tax authorities impounded copies of *Ruzi Nav* on their arrival at the Dushanbe airport in November. In October, the Russian-language newspaper *Vechernii Dushanbe* lost a libel case brought by Dushanbe's city court deputy chairman, who claimed that an article in the paper had defamed him.

The government generally respects religious freedom in this predominantly Muslim country, although it monitors the activities of religious institutions to prevent them from becoming overtly political. Religious communities must register with the State Committee on Religious Affairs (SCRA), a process that some local authorities have used to prevent the activities of certain groups, including Jehovah's Witnesses. In contrast to previous years, there were reportedly no mosques closed and no imams removed by the SCRA. Members of the banned Hizb ut-Tahrir, which calls for the establishment of an Islamic caliphate throughout the Muslim world, have been given lengthy prison sentences on charges including subversion, distribution of extremist literature, and inciting religious hatred.

According to the 2004 U.S. State Department's human rights report, the Tajik government does not restrict academic freedom. However, the country's educational system suffers from inadequate funding and resources, declining enrollments of pupils owing to poverty, and corruption in the grading system. Students are frequently conscripted to work on cotton plantations and have been forced to pay a fine or have been expelled from school if they do not comply.

Although a number of nongovernmental organizations (NGOs) operate in the country without restrictions, the state strictly controls freedom of association for organizations of a political nature. Registration requirements are often lengthy and cumbersome. Registered groups must obtain permits to hold public demonstrations, and organizers of protests have at times faced government reprisals. Citizens have the legal right to form and join trade unions and to bargain collectively, which they do in practice. Although the law does not restrict the right to strike, it is necessary to apply to local authorities to receive permission to organize a strike; no strikes occurred during the year.

The judiciary is directly influenced by the executive branch, on which most judges depend for their positions, as well as by some criminal groups. Many judges are poorly trained and inexperienced, and bribery is reportedly widespread. The government took some steps to address the problem during the year by arresting some corrupt judges and prosecutors. Police often conduct arbitrary arrests and beat detainees to extract confessions. Detainees are frequently refused access to legal counsel and face lengthy pretrial detention. Prisons are severely overcrowded and suffer from unsanitary conditions and rampant disease. In 2004, Rakhmonov signed a moratorium on the death penalty, replacing capital punishment with a 25-year prison term.

Since the collapse of the Taliban regime in neighboring Afghanistan, narcotics trafficking across the porous, mountainous border with Tajikistan is reportedly on the rise. Organized crime groups involved in the drug trade allegedly have connections with members of the country's security and police forces. A 2004 agreement to gradually transfer border guard service along the Tajik-Afghan border from Russian to Tajik control raised concerns about potential increases in cross-border drug trafficking, since Tajikistan's limited resources are likely to render it even less successful than Russia in stemming the flow of narcotics.

Most of the population live in poverty and survive on subsistence agriculture, remittances from relatives working abroad, mainly in Russia, and foreign humanitarian aid. Widespread corruption, patronage networks, regional affiliations, limited privatization of land and industry, and the growing narcotics trade restrict equality of opportunity and limit economic growth. According to the Tajik Center of Strategic Research, about 15 percent of the incomes of small and medium businesses go to bribery and payoff of officials. Child labor, particularly on cotton farms, is reportedly commonplace.

Although women are employed throughout the government and the business world, they continue to face traditional societal discrimination. Violence against women, including spousal abuse, is reportedly common, but cases reported to the authorities are rarely investigated. Tajikistan is a source and transit country for persons trafficked for prostitution. In 2004, Rakhmonov signed a new law against human trafficking that addresses prevention, protection of victims, and the prosecution of traffickers, and a Tajik court applied the law for the first time in a trafficking case in November. In August, the Council of Ulems, the highest religious body of Muslims in Tajikistan, issued an edict banning women from mosques that do not have the necessary facilities to allow men and women to pray separately; Rakhmonov stated in November that he would not interfere with the decision.

Tanzania

Population: 36,100,000
GNI/capita: $290
Life Expectancy: 45
Religious Groups: Christian (30 percent), Muslim
(35 percent), indigenous beliefs (35 percent); Zanzibar:
Muslim (more than 99 percent)
Ethnic Groups: African (99 percent), other [including Asian,
European, and Arab] (1 percent)
Capital: Dar-es-Salaam

Political Rights: 4
Civil Liberties: 3
Status: Partly Free

Ten-Year Ratings Timeline (Political Rights, Civil Liberties, Status)

1995	1996	1997	1998	1999	2000	2001	2002	2003	2004
5,5PF	5,5PF	5,5PF	5,4PF	4,4PF	4,4PF	4,4PF	4,3PF	4,3PF	4,3PF

Overview:

Local elections took place in November, won by the ruling Chama Cha Mapinduzi (CCM) party; opposition parties claimed that the legitimacy of the polls had been affected by violence from pro-government supporters and biased election administration. Meanwhile, there were delays in the implementation of reforms regarding the autonomous islands of Zanzibar and Pemba, which had been agreed on in 2001 between the opposition Civic United Front (CUF) and the CCM. The islands have been flashpoints of conflict between the government and the opposition.

After Tanzania gained independence from Britain in 1961, the Chama Cha Mapinduzi party (CCM), under President Julius Nyerere, dominated the country's political life. The Zanzibar and Pemba Islands were merged with Tanganyika to become the United Republic of Tanzania after Arab sultans who had long ruled the islands were deposed in a violent revolution in 1964.

For much of his presidency, Nyerere espoused a collectivist economic philosophy known in Swahili as *ujaama*. While it may have been useful in promoting a sense of community and nationality, this policy resulted in significant economic dislocation and decline. During Nyerere's tenure, Tanzania also played an important role as a "Front Line State" in the international response to white-controlled regimes in southern Africa. Nyerere retained strong influence after he officially retired in 1985, until his death in 1999. His successor, Ali Hassan Mwinyi, held the presidency from 1985 to 1995 and presided over a carefully controlled political liberalization process. The CCM's landslide legislative victory in the 1995 parliamentary elections was seriously tainted by poor organization of the electoral process, fraud, and administrative irregularities. In addition, extensive use of state broadcasting and other government resources during the campaign favored the ruling party. The CCM won 80 percent of the 232 directly elected seats in the National Assembly. The voting in Zanzibar was plainly fraudulent, with the island's high court summarily rejecting opposition demands for fresh polls.

Tanzania held legislative and presidential elections in October 2000, the second since the reintroduction of multiparty politics. Incumbent president Benjamin Mkapa was reelected with about 70 percent of the vote, and the CCM won an overwhelming victory in the parliamentary election. Although the conduct of these elections represented a modest improvement over that of the 1995 vote, the elections were nonetheless marred by fraudulent polls biased in favor of the ruling party in the federated semiautonomous islands of Zanzibar and Pemba; the status of these islands in relation to the mainland has long provoked tension. The opposition CUF and independent observers convincingly demonstrated that the ruling CCM had engaged in fraud to retain power. Subsequent rioting in Zanzibar in early 2001 resulted in the deaths of more than 40 people. In October 2001, the CCM and the CUF announced a reconciliation agreement designed to resolve the political crisis and allow for more transparent government.

Significant progress occurred in 2003 regarding Zanzibar, with elections that resulted in a parliamentary victory by the CUF. These elections raised hopes that 2005 parliamentary and presidential elections (at which President Benjamin Mkapa is not expected to stand) may represent a positive step forward.

Local elections took place in November, won by the ruling CCM party. The elections were marred by some violence and by claims from opposition parties that the government supported CCM candidates and that the election authorities at times acted in a biased fashion. By late 2004, however, there were delays in the implementation of reforms agreed on in 2001 between the CUF and the CCM. These reforms were to have been implemented in such fields as government jurisdiction of the electoral process, police oversight, publicly owned media institutions, and the Zanzibar Electoral Commission. Delays have included the postponement of voter registration on Zanzibar. The CUF has also complained that mainland Tanzanians are being fraudulently included in the Zanzibari voting rolls.

Tanzania is one of the poorest countries in the world. According to World Bank statistics, per capita income in 2004 is estimated to be at about $290. Life expectancy at birth dropped from 50 years in 1990 to only 43 years in 2002. Infant mortality remains relatively high with 99 per 1,000 in 2003, as compared with 102 per 1,000 in 1990.

Political Rights and Civil Liberties: Tanzanians cannot choose their government democratically. Although opposition parties were legalized in 1992, the ruling CCM continues to dominate the country's political life.

Executive power rests with the president, who is elected by direct popular vote for a five-year term. The president can serve a maximum of two terms. The constitution provides for legislative power to be held by a unicameral National Assembly with members serving a term of five years, and for universal adult suffrage. The legislative body, the Bunge, has 274 members, with 232 elected for a five-year term in single-seat constituencies. The remaining seats are reserved for women elected by their political parties on the basis of proportional representation among the political parties represented in the National Assembly.

Thirteen opposition parties have formal status. Some of them are active, but they tend to be divided and ineffectual. The opposition CUF has sought to establish significant support on the Tanzanian mainland. Another major opposition party, the National Convention for Constitution and Reform (NCCR-Mageuzi), whose leader, Augustine Mrema, was runner-up to Benjamin Mkapa in the 1995 presidential election, has split. Parties with parliamentary representation receive government subsidies, but they criticize the low level of funding and the formula by which it is allocated. In 2003, most opposition parties came together in an electoral alliance, but the CUF did not join.

Corruption remains a serious problem, although the government has made some attempts to address it, including developing a national anticorruption action plan. The Prevention of Corruption Bureau recorded an increase in the number of reported incidents of corruption from 432 cases in 1998 to 1,461 cases at the end of 2000. However, it is not clear whether this represents an increase in corruption or increased reporting and improved detection of corruption. Tanzania's police chief has publicly stated that corruption is entrenched in some sections of the police force, especially in traffic and investigation departments. Tanzania was ranked 90 out of 146 countries surveyed in Transparency International's 2004 Corruption Perceptions Index.

Print and electronic media are active, but media impact is largely limited to major urban areas. The country has more than 50 regular newspapers, including 17 dailies. The growth of the broadcast media has been hindered by the lack of capital investment needed to set up television and radio stations, both public and private. Nevertheless, dozens of private FM radio stations are on the air, most of them in urban areas. Internet access, while limited to urban areas, is growing.

The number of journalists has also increased from only 230 in 1991 to more than 4,000 currently, but journalists in general have serious concerns about press laws that could limit freedom of expression. Progress for independence in the media over the past year was "encouraging," according to a 2004 report of the Tanzania chapter of the Media Institute of Southern Africa (MISA).

Although the constitution provides for freedom of speech, it does not specifically do so for the freedom of the press. These rights are especially constrained in Zanzibar by the semiautonomous Zanzibar government. Press reforms contained in a 2001 media bill did not apply to the island. There are no private broadcasters or newspapers on Zanzibar, though many islanders can receive mainland broadcasts and read the mainland press. The Zanzibari government has used its powers to selectively limit press freedom. For example, the weekly newspaper *Dira* was banned in November 2003, with no reason being given.

The population is believed to be divided fairly evenly between Muslim and Christian faiths. Freedom of religion is generally respected, and relations between the various faiths are mainly peaceful. In recent years, however, religious-based tensions have increased. In addition, on Zanzibar, the 2001 Mufti Law allowed the Zanzibari government to appoint a mufti to oversee Muslim organizations. Some Muslims are critical of this law, contending that it permits an excessive government role in the religious sphere.

Many nongovernmental organizations (NGOs) are active, and some have been able to influence the public policy process. However, an NGO act passed by parliament in 2002 contains many serious flaws, including compulsory registration backed by criminal sanctions, lack of appeal to the courts, alignment of NGO activities with government plans, prohibition of national networks and coalitions of NGOs, and inconsistencies with other related existing legislation. The International Helsinki Federation for Human Rights and the World Organization Against Torture have criticized the legislation on the grounds that it contravenes the Tanzanian constitution, the Universal Declaration of Human Rights, and the International Covenant on Civil and Political Rights.

Academic freedom is respected. Constitutional protections for the right to freedom of assembly are generally, but not always, respected. Laws allow rallies only by officially registered political parties, which may not be formed on religious, ethnic, or regional bases and cannot oppose the union of Zanzibar and the mainland. Less than 5 percent of the Tanzanian labor force is unionized. Workers' rights are limited. Essential workers are barred from striking; other workers' right to strike is restricted by complex notification and mediation requirements. A labor law was passed early this year, which the government states will help safeguard the rights and welfare of workers. Approximately 85 percent of Tanzania's people survive through subsistence agriculture.

Tanzania's judiciary has displayed signs of autonomy after decades of subservience to the one-party CCM regime, but it remains subject to considerable political influence. Arrest and pretrial detention laws are often ignored. Prison conditions are harsh, and police abuses are said to be common. According to government estimates, there are approximately 45,000 inmates in the country's prisons although the prisons' collective capacity is only 21,000. Such overcrowding has caused widespread concern. Questions have been raised regarding the safety and health of prisoners, including minors and women, who have been subjected to sexual harassment and human rights abuses. The 2002 Prevention of Terrorism Act, which some NGOs have criticized for containing inconsistencies and anomalies, gives the government considerable latitude in that it does not clearly define the term "terrorism." Rather, the act merely lists acts of terrorism, which include, among other things, attacks upon a person's life, kidnapping, and serious damage to property. It gives the police and immigration officials sweeping powers to arrest suspected illegal immigrants or anyone thought to have links with terrorists.

Compared to many of its neighbors, Tanzania has enjoyed relatively tranquil relations between its many ethnic groups. The presence of refugees from conflicts in Burundi, Rwanda, and the Democratic Republic of Congo, however, has in the past raised tensions. Women's rights guaranteed by the constitution and other laws are not uniformly protected. Especially in rural areas and in Zanzibar, traditional or Islamic customs discriminatory toward women prevail in family law, and women have fewer educational and economic opportunities. Domestic violence against women is reportedly common and is rarely prosecuted. Human rights groups have sought laws to bar forced marriages, which are most common among Tanzania's coastal peoples.

Thailand

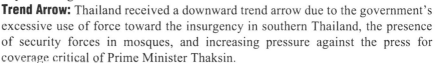

Population: 63,800,000
GNI/capita: $2,000
Life Expectancy: 71
Religious Groups: Buddhist (95 percent),
Muslim (3.8 percent), other (1.2 percent)
Ethnic Groups: Thai (75 percent), Chinese (14 percent),
other (11 percent)
Capital: Bangkok

Political Rights: 2
Civil Liberties: 3
Status: Free

Trend Arrow: Thailand received a downward trend arrow due to the government's excessive use of force toward the insurgency in southern Thailand, the presence of security forces in mosques, and increasing pressure against the press for coverage critical of Prime Minister Thaksin.

Ten-Year Ratings Timeline (Political Rights, Civil Liberties, Status)

1995	1996	1997	1998	1999	2000	2001	2002	2003	2004
3,4PF	3,3PF	3,3PF	2,3F	2,3F	2,3F	2,3F	2,3F	2,3F	2,3F

Overview:

With an eye to elections that must be called by January 2005, the administration of Thaksin Shinawatra continued to carry out the populist spending programs that had generated strong economic growth and high approval ratings in previous years. Thaksin's image as an effective CEO prime minister, however, has been tarnished by the government's incompetent handling of the outbreak of avian flu and the Muslim insurgency in the South, which had left 440 dead by the end of October. Allegations that Thaksin has used his official position to stifle critics and enrich his allies have for the first time led the administration to reverse policies in response to accusations of conflict of interest.

Known as Siam until 1939, Thailand is the only Southeast Asian nation never colonized by a European country. Beginning with a 1932 coup that transformed the kingdom into a constitutional monarchy, the army ruled periodically for the next six decades. The military last seized power in 1991. Thailand returned to civilian rule the following year when the country's revered monarch, King Bhumibol Alduyadej, convinced the military to appoint a civilian prime minister.

Thailand's export-led economy notched up strong growth in the decade prior to 1997, before being dragged down by the regional financial crisis. Amid noisy street protests by middle-class Thais in Bangkok against corruption and economic mismanagement, parliament voted no confidence in Tammany Hall style politician Chavalit Yongchaiyudh, replaced him with Democrat Party leader Chuan Leekpai, a former prime minister with a clean reputation, and approved a reformist constitution.

The new constitution created independent election and anticorruption bodies and introduced direct election of the Senate.

Criticizing the government for supposedly favoring the urban middle class over ordinary Thais, Thaksin, a former deputy prime minister who built his fortune in tele-communications, unseated Chuan in the January 2001 elections. During the campaign, Thaksin pledged to help poorer Thais hurt by the financial crisis by introducing cheap health care, a debt moratorium for farmers, and investment funds for each village. Thaksin's Thai (Loves) Thai (TRT) party won 248 out of parliament's 500 seats despite a December 2000 ruling by Thailand's new National Counter-Corruption Commission that Thaksin had deliberately falsified wealth-disclosure statements in 1997 as a cabinet minister. In what critics consider a controversial move, the Constitutional Court cleared Thaksin in August 2001.

Thaksin's government has won praise from many Thais for largely sticking to its electoral promises by introducing programs to help the poor and small businesses. Low interest rates and populist spending programs have fueled a consumption-driven economic growth spurt. Wanting to portray Thailand as a well-ordered country safe for foreign investors and tourists, the government has clamped down on negative news, such as the possible presence of terrorists in Thailand. In an attempt to protect the country's poultry industry, the government had long maintained that Thailand was safe from the deadly avian flu sweeping Asia. But in February 2004, the Thaksin administration was forced to confess that six million chickens had been culled and numerous human cases had been confirmed. The cover-up led Japan and the EU to ban Thai chicken imports and the Thai people to question the government's willingness to protect public safety when it conflicted with powerful private interests.

Many of Thaksin's moves run counter to the reformist spirit of the country's new constitution. While the constitution requires the prime minister and cabinet members to divest themselves of all business interests, many officials have simply transferred these holdings to family members. Critics contend that Thaksin and his associates have used government power to enrich themselves. For example, Shin Satellite, a subsidiary of Shin Corporation, a company in which Thaksin's family holds a significant stake, recently won an eight-year tax holiday worth $401 million from Thailand's Board of Investment. This was the first time that this state agency, historically charged with attracting foreign investment, had offered such incentives to a Thai-owned company, according to the *Far Eastern Economic Review*.

Thaksin's October 3, 2004, announcement of a new year-long war on drugs has raised fears of a new wave of extrajudicial killings. In the first three months of Thaksin's 2003 crackdown on narcotics, 2,245 people were killed, according to Amnesty International, and over 42,000 were blacklisted. Thailand has recently been deluged with methamphetamines and other narcotics from neighboring Burma, and many Thais support the government's attempt to eradicate drugs, even if they are uneasy with the means employed to do so.

Thailand's four southernmost provinces, home to most of the country's four million Muslims, erupted into violence in 2004. In January, more than 100 attackers raided a military depot, killing four soldiers and making off with 400 firearms in an operation whose meticulous planning and execution led to suspicions of outside involvement. In a series of coordinated attacks on 11 bases and checkpoints in April, insurgents killed five members of the Thai security forces, which responded with attacks that left more than 100 people dead. In October, 78 of 1,300 people arrested for demonstrating suffocated in security trucks while they were being transported to a detention center. The government declared martial law in most of Narathiwat, Pattani, and Yala provinces. Many fear that the government's hard-line approach will backfire by creating fertile recruiting ground for the international terrorist groups Jemaah Islamiah and al-Qaeda, both of which have past links to Thailand.

Much of Thailand's traditionally robust press encountered some type of political pressure in 2004. In such an environment, Thailand's revered monarch, King Bhumibol, used his annual December 5 birthday speech to criticize Thaksin for his arrogance, the insurgency in the South and the government cover-up of the bird flu.

Political Rights and Civil Liberties: Thais can change their government democratically, as evidenced by the August 2004 election of an opposition Democratic candidate as the governor of Bangkok. Thailand's constitution created a parliamentary system with a two-house legislature. The House of Representatives has 400 seats chosen by first-past-the-post balloting and 100 chosen by proportional representation, all directly elected for four-year terms. The Senate has 200 members, who are directly elected for six-year terms.

Anecdotal evidence suggests that official corruption is widespread, involving both bureaucrats demanding bribes in exchange for routine services and law enforcement officials being paid off to ignore trafficking and other illicit activities. Many critics allege that the nexus between politics and big business is strong and growing. Thaksin has responded to conflict-of-interest charges made by an opposition politician by filing criminal charges against him. According to the *Far Eastern Economic Review*, many Democratic Party legislators now spend more time defending themselves in court than scrutinizing policies in parliament. Thailand was ranked 64 out of 146 countries surveyed in Transparency International's 2004 Corruption Perceptions Index.

Thaksin's access to state-controlled media combined with the Shin Corporation's 50 percent interest in ITV, a formerly independent television station that have been established specifically to offer an alternative to state-dominated broadcast media, has narrowed the spectrum of opinion aired on television. The outspoken Nation Group lost is contract to produce news for ITV and was further pressured with advertising boycotts and spurious asset investigations, according to the *Nieman Reports*. Thaksin associate and current minister of industry Suriya Jungrungeangkit purchased 30 percent of the Nation Group's shares in 2004, leading many to fear that this economic stake will be used to suppress the voice of Thailand's most outspoken media source.

The print press also came under attack, not through formal censorship but through political intimidation, libel suits, and the threat of lost corporate and government advertising revenues, a potent threat to media companies that still carry large debts from the 1997 economic crisis. In February, the editor of the *Bangkok Post* lost his job when government officials pressured the paper's management about publishing stories deemed too critical of Thaksin. Three editors of the *Thai Post* and nongovernmental organization (NGO) media reformer Surpinya Klangnarong are currently being sued by the Shinawatra family's Shin Corporation for alleging that it had benefited under his administration. Foreign journalists are not immune to pressure from a government that increasingly uses approval of work permit and visa renewals as leverage. Four *Far Eastern Economic Review* journalists were named in a lese majesty case, *The Economist*'s annual report on Thailand was banned, and a reporter for the *International Herald Tribune* came under vocal attack for articles critical of Thaksin's economic programs.

Thais of all faiths have traditionally worshipped freely in this predominantly Buddhist society, although Muslims in the South have long complained of discrimination in jobs, education, and business opportunities. Recently, a heightened security interest in Islamic institutions has been deterring Muslims from visiting mosques. This discrimination is not limited to southern Thailand. Muslims in Chiang Mai province have complained that Thai security forces have been entering mosques for what locals claim are heavy-handed and religiously insensitive inspections. Professors and other educators can generally lecture and publish freely.

The constitution provides for freedom of assembly and association, and the government generally respected these rights in practice, according to the U.S. State Department human rights report for 2004. Permits are not required for gatherings unless held on public property or organized by foreign nationals, and these are granted routinely. Thailand civil society is dense with NGOs representing farmers, laborers, women, students, and human rights more broadly. Thailand is also home to many environmental groups. Private associations must register with the government, and such registrations are granted routinely. With the imposition of martial law in southern Thailand, the rights of assembly and association there have been severely circumscribed.

Thai trade unions are independent, though fewer than 2 percent of Thai workers are unionized. Private employers often breach the country's poorly enforced labor laws with violations that include using child and sweatshop labor and paying workers less than the minimum wage.

Though the judiciary is generally regarded as independent, it sometimes is subject to corruption, according to anecdotal evidence. Suspects frequently spend long periods in detention before trial because of heavy case backlogs, and trials often take years to complete. Security forces have been accused of using excessive force in dealing with unrest in the South. The suffocation deaths of 78 protestors in police custody occurred because they were piled on top of one another. Coming on the heels of the 2003 war on drugs that left 2,275 dead, this incident continues a trend in which Thailand's poorly trained police often are implicated in wrongful killings of criminal suspects as well as abuse of suspects and prison inmates. According to the U.S. State Department human rights report issued for 2004, conditions in prisons and some provincial immigration detention facilities are poor. Prolonged pretrial detention, including of aliens, is also a problem.

Attacks on civilians and government officials continue to occur almost daily, according to Amnesty International. During 2004, a number of prominent activists, including a Muslim lawyer campaigning against martial law in the South, were killed or disappeared.

Many of the estimated one million members of hill tribes have never been fully integrated into society. Reportedly, half of hill tribe members lack citizenship, rendering them ineligible to vote, own land, attend state schools, or be covered under labor laws. The government in 2000 made it easier for hill tribe members to gain citizenship, but corruption and inefficiency reportedly have slowed citizenship processing.

Reversing its long-standing policy of harboring refugees from neighboring Southeast Asian nations, in January, Thailand suspended screening of new refugee applicants from Burma by the UN High Commissioner for Refugees, according to Human Rights Watch. This followed a July 2003 decision to send all of the estimated 4,000 Burmese refugees and asylum seekers living in urban areas to border camps, despite the fear of cross-border violence and political and ethnic conflict in those camps. The government, which regularly expels as many as 10,000 Burmese migrants a month, also launched a new campaign to round up and deport more of the estimated one million Burmese migrant workers in Thailand. Citing systemic abuses in Burma, rights groups have criticized Thailand's toughened stance toward Burmese fleeing their country who are likely to face reprisals once they return.

Some 200,000 or more Thai women and children work as prostitutes, according to government and private estimates. Many prostitutes work under debt bondage, forced to repay loans by traffickers to their parents. Authorities prosecute relatively few traffickers, and many police, soldiers, local officials, and immigration officers reportedly either are involved in trafficking or take bribes to ignore it.

⬆Togo

Population: 5,600,000
GNI/capita: $270
Life Expectancy: 54
Religious Groups: Indigenous beliefs (51 percent),
Christian (29 percent), Muslim (20 percent)
Ethnic Groups: Native African (99 percent), European
and Syrian-Lebanese (1 percent)
Capital: Lome

Political Rights: 6
Civil Liberties: 5
Status: Not Free

Trend Arrow: Togo received an upward trend arrow due to the easing of criminal penalties against journalists.

Ten-Year Ratings Timeline (Political Rights, Civil Liberties, Status)

1995	1996	1997	1998	1999	2000	2001	2002	2003	2004
6,5NF	6,5NF	6,5NF	6,5NF	5,5PF	5,5PF	5,5PF	6,5NF	6,5NF	6,5NF

Overview: In an effort to win back foreign aid, Togo in 2004 eased criminal penalties against journalists and pledged to undertake more than 20 other reforms that officials say will demonstrate that the country is committed to improving its record on democracy and human rights. The European Union agreed to a partial resumption of aid in November 2004.

Togoland, a German colony for more three decades until France seized it at the outset of World War I, gained independence in 1960. The country's founding president, Sylvanus Olympio, was murdered in 1963 as Gnassingbe Eyadema, then a demobilized sergeant who had served in France's colonial wars, led an army coup to topple the country's democratically elected government. After assuming direct power in 1967, Eyadema suspended the constitution and extended his repressive rule through mock elections and a puppet political party.

In 1991, the organizing of free political parties was legalized, and multiparty elections were promised. The transition faltered, however, as soldiers and secret police harassed, attacked, or killed opposition supporters. Eyadema won fraudulent elections in 1993 and 1998.

Leading opposition parties boycotted the October 2002 legislative vote to protest preparations for the polls, which they said would prevent the holding of a free and fair election. The ruling Rally of the Togolese People party won 72 of 81 parliamentary seats.

Eyadema supporters in the National Assembly began setting the stage in 2002 for his victory in the June 2003 presidential election by changing the constitution to allow him to run for a third term. Lawmakers also altered the composition of the Independent National Electoral Commission, transferred responsibility for organizing the elections from the commission to the Ministry of the Interior, designated the ministry to select polling officers, and stipulated that presidential candidates were to reside in Togo for at least one year prior to elections. To help assure Eyadema's win, the Constitutional Court barred the president's main rival and opposition leader, Gilchrist Olympio, from participating in the polls. Earlier, the electoral commission had denied the candidacy of Olympio, who had been living in exile, on the grounds that he lacked a certificate of residency and could not prove that he had paid his taxes. Olympio appealed, but the commission's decision was upheld by the Constitutional Court.

Eyadema won another five-year term as president with 57 percent of the vote, compared with 34 percent for Emmanuel Bob-Akitani of Olympio's Union of Forces for Change (UFC) party. Four other candidates shared the remainder of the vote. The EU declined to send observers, saying it was unlikely that the vote would be fair. Monitors from the African Union and the Economic Community of West African States, however, claimed that the elections were free and fair. Opposition members maintained that they were intimidated or barred from polling stations, that ballot boxes were stuffed, that fictitious polling centers were created, and that some legitimate voting stations did not receive ballots.

The EU imposed sanctions on Togo a decade ago because of the government's resistance to democratic reform. In November 2004, it agreed to a partial resumption of aid but stated that full aid would not be restored until free and fair elections were held. International donors have partly conditioned a resumption of aid on political dialogue between the government and political opposition. Togolese authorities in 2004 eased travel restrictions against Olympio. The government also pardoned 500 prisoners, including several political prisoners. In April, the government pledged to undertake 22 reforms that would keep the country on what President Eyadema referred to as a "train" headed for democracy. The reforms included launching talks with the political opposition and amending press and communications laws.

Togo's economy is smarting from the EU sanctions, as well as from corruption and mismanagement. Corruption, military spending, and large, inefficient state-owned companies impede economic growth. Eighty percent of Togolese are engaged in subsistence agriculture.

Political Rights and Civil Liberties: The Togolese people cannot change their government democratically. Presidential elections in 1993 and 1998 were blatantly fraudulent. The National Assembly, which is dominated by President Eyadema's Rally of the Togolese People, amended the electoral code prior to the 2003 presidential election to favor Eyadema's candidacy. The measures reduced the power of the electoral commission and compromised its impartiality. The October 2002 legislative elections were neither free nor fair.

Togo was not ranked by Transparency International in its 2004 Corruption Perceptions Index. Corruption in Togo has been a serious impediment to development. Reporting about corruption has often landed Togolese journalists in jail.

At least 15 private newspapers publish in Lome. There are more than a dozen independent newspapers that publish sporadically and many private radio stations, most of which operate as pirate stations. Most of the independent broadcast media outlets, however, offer little vibrant local news coverage or commentary. Togo's watchdog groups include the Togolese Media Observatory, a nongovernmental organization made up of state-media and independent journalists, and which aims to protect press freedom and improve professionalism in journalism.

The National Assembly in 2004 amended the press and communications laws to remove prison terms for most offenses. International press freedom groups welcomed the move but said they would watch to see how the amended laws are applied. Prison sentences could still be imposed in cases of journalists found guilty of calling for theft, murder, racial hatred, or subverting security forces from "their duty to the country." Heavy fines of up to $9,000 remained in place for "defaming or insulting" the president, state institutions, courts, the armed forces, and public administration bodies. The previous laws had imposed jail terms of up to five years on reporters and were among the most repressive press laws in Africa.

Fewer journalists were threatened or jailed in 2004 than in previous years. Still, harassment remains a problem. Yves Kpeto, a reporter with Nana FM, and another journalist with the weekly newspaper *Le Combat du People* were roughed up by security forces in May 2004 at the University of Lome during a student demonstration.

Constitutionally protected religious freedom is generally respected. Academic freedom is not respected, and government informers and security forces maintain a presence on campuses. The University of Lome was closed for most of May following student demonstrations demanding better grants and living conditions. Several student leaders were jailed in connection with the protests.

Freedom of assembly is allowed, but is often restricted for the government's political opponents. Demonstrations are often banned or violently halted. Human rights groups are closely monitored and sometimes harassed. Togo's constitution includes the right to form and join unions, except for "essential" workers such as security forces. Nevertheless, only 20 percent of the labor force is unionized. Unions have the right to bargain collectively, but this right is restricted.

The judiciary is heavily influenced by the president. Traditional courts handle many minor matters. Courts are understaffed and inadequately funded, pretrial detentions are lengthy, and prisons are severely overcrowded. Extrajudicial killings, arbitrary arrests, and torture continue. Security forces commit abuses with impunity, and illegal detention is common. Amnesty International in 2004 cited Togo for malicious prosecution, arbitrary arrest, and excessive force against political demonstrations. Nine militants of the main opposition UFC party were sentenced in 2004 to between two and six years in prison in connection with disturbances during the 2003 presidential elections. They had been detained on what many believe were politically motivated charges following the destruction of a petrol station and the explosion of a handmade bomb in a French restaurant in Lome.

Ethnic discrimination is rife among the country's 40 ethnic groups. Political and military power is narrowly held by members of a few ethnic groups from northern Togo, especially Eyadema's Kabye ethnic group. Southerners dominate the country's commerce, and violence occasionally flares between the two groups.

Despite constitutional guarantees of equality, women's opportunities for education and employment are limited. A husband may legally bar his wife from working, or he may legally choose to receive her earnings. Customary law bars women's rights in divorce and denies inheritance rights to widows. Violence against women is common. Female genital mutilation is widely practiced by the country's northern ethnic groups, and a law prohibiting the practice is not enforced. Several organizations promote the rights of women.

Child trafficking for the purpose of slavery is a problem in Togo as it is in much of West Africa. The New York-based Human Rights Watch said in a 2003 report that hundreds of children each year were trafficked from, received in, or trafficked through Togo on false promises of education, professional training, and paid employment. The report said the children were transported at times under life-threatening conditions and were subjected to physical and mental abuse.

⬇Tonga

Population: 100,000
GNI/capita: $1,410
Life Expectancy: 71
Religious Groups: Christian (Free Wesleyan Church claims over 30,000 adherents)
Ethnic Groups: Polynesian, European (about 300)
Capital: Nuku'alofa

Political Rights: 5
Civil Liberties: 3
Status: Partly Free

Trend Arrow: Tonga received a downward trend arrow due to continuing government efforts to tighten controls over the media.

Ten-Year Ratings Timeline (Political Rights, Civil Liberties, Status)

1995	1996	1997	1998	1999	2000	2001	2002	2003	2004
5,3PF	5,3PF	5,3PF	5,3PF	5,3PF	5,3PF	5,3PF	5,3PF	5,3PF	5,3PF

Overview: The king of Tonga signed into law a controversial amendment to the constitution in December 2003 giving the government greater control over the media. This unpopular action was quickly followed by new media laws to curb foreign ownership and distribution of publications critical of the government. In October, the Supreme Court ruled that the media laws and parts of the amendments were null and void.

Tonga consists of 169 islands that King George Tupou I united under his rule in 1845. The country became a constitutional monarchy in 1875 and a British protectorate in 1900. In 1970, Tonga gained independence; it is a member of the British Commonwealth. The 85-year-old King Taufa'ahau Tupou IV has reigned since 1945.

Politics and the economy are dominated by the monarchy, hereditary nobles, and a few prominent commoners. The first strong show of public support for democratic reform was the election of pro-democracy candidates for seven of the nine directly elected seats reserved for commoners in the March 2002 elections. Soon afterward, the government initiated some public and economic sector reforms, which critics said were far from sufficient. Some voices for change have come from within the monarchy; Prince Tu'ipelehake, a nephew of the king's, had openly called on Australia to pressure Tonga to expand democracy in the kingdom. In October 2004, his proposal for a referendum to allow popular election of all representatives won a narrow approval from parliament after a similar proposal submitted as a people's petition in September 2004 was thrown out by parliament.

In December 2003, the government approved amendments to the constitution that—along with the controversial Newspaper Act and Media Operators Act that were passed by parliament in October 2003—give it licensing power over all publications in the kingdom, including foreign publications that circulate in Tonga. The Newspaper Act requires licenses for publishers, sellers, and importers, with violations carrying a $10,000 fine or imprisonment for a maximum of one year. The Media Operators Act limits foreign ownership of publications published in Tonga to 20 percent. The government said that these new laws were needed to address concerns about foreign entities entering the media market in Tonga and were not intended to curtail freedom of the press. In January 2004, 152 plaintiffs asked the Supreme Court for a judicial review of the media laws. In October, the Supreme Court ruled that the Media Operators Act, Newspaper Act, and parts of the constitutional amendment restricting freedom of speech were void and invalid.

In an attempt to deny its critics another favorable court ruling, the Tongan parliament abolished use of the British Civil Liberty Law by Tongan courts as part of a parcel of bills in December 2003. This law had been used to cover matters, like adoption, not addressed by Tongan law. In April 2004, Chief Justice Frederick Gordon Ward resigned to assume a new position as the chairman of the Court of Appeal in Fiji. There was speculation that Ward's resignation was prompted by the parliament's decision to abolish use of the British Civil Liberty Law.

In July, the parliament temporarily suspended two pro-democracy parliament members from attending sessions: 'Akilisi Pohiva was suspended for a day and a half, and 'Etuate Lvulavu for three days, for allegedly disrupting legislative proceedings with their questions about official corruption and abuses.

Political Rights and Civil Liberties: Tongan citizens cannot change their government democratically. The king, 33 hereditary nobles, and a few prominent commoners dominate politics and the economy through their majority in parliament and their substantial land holdings. King Taufa'ahau Tupou IV appoints his cabinet without election and for life terms, and the cabinet holds 12 of 30 seats in the unicameral legislature. Another nine parliament seats are reserved for the nobles, who are chosen by their peers, and cabinet members and nobles usually vote as one bloc. The remaining nine representatives are elected in general elections. The king appoints the prime minister and presides over the Privy Council, which makes major policy decisions. Prince Ulukalala Lavaka Ata, the king's third son, was appointed prime minister in 2000 over Crown Prince Tupoutoa Tupouto'a. Prince Ma'tau, the second son of the king, died in February 2004.

The number of seats held by prominent commoners has been shrinking in recent years, losing to pro-democracy candidates. In September, pro-democracy representatives proposed a referendum on directly electing all 30 representatives, while still allowing the king to appoint the prime minister and his cabinet from those elected. The parliament rejected this proposal, but put forth a similar one in October.

Official corruption and abuses are serious problems in Tonga, causing public dissatisfaction with the government and hindering economic growth. Nobles and others with connections to the political elite own large tracts of land and dominate big and medium-size businesses.

Despite constitutional guarantees for freedom of speech and the press, the government has a long history of suppressing criticism of the monarchy and government. The government owns shares in several private media companies and runs the country's television and radio stations. The government-owned Tonga Communications Corporation and the private Tonofon, with significant shareholding by members of the royal family, are the two Internet service providers. Internet diffusion in Tonga is limited by cost and technical access challenges.

In 2004, two church papers (the Roman Catholic Church's *Taumu'a Lelei* and the Tokaikolo Christian Fellowship's *'Ofa Ki Tonga*), the Tonga Chamber of Commerce's newsletter *Lali Buzz*, the government-owned weekly *Tonga Chronicle*, the Vula News Company, and the privately owned *Tonga Star* were granted new licenses. Vavau Press, publisher of the monthly *Matangi Tonga*, received a license in its third try and after one of its co-owners was granted Tongan citizenship. The *Tonga Times* and the opposition's *Ko e Kele'a* were both denied licenses. The government also arrested a New Zealand citizen of Tongan descent who entered the kingdom in February 2004 with 20 copies of the *Tonga Times*. In the last several years, the government has tried repeatedly to silence the *Tonga Times*, a particularly vocal critic of the government; the paper is independently owned by a New Zealand citizen of Tongan heritage and is published in New Zealand.

Freedom of religion is generally respected in this predominantly Christian society. However, the Tongan Broadcasting Commission requires that any references to religion on radio and television must conform to mainstream Christian beliefs. As such, there are limits on broadcasts about non-Christian religions as well as those, such as Mormonism, not considered mainstream. There were no reports of government restrictions on academic freedom, but self-censorship is practiced to avoid trouble with the government.

Freedom of assembly and association are generally respected for groups not involved in politics and not critical of government policies. In October 2003, nearly one-tenth of the country's population demonstrated against new media restrictions. Many civil society organizations are active in promoting education, public health, and children's and women's welfare. The 1963 Trade Union Act gives workers the right to form unions and strike, but regulations for union formation were never promulgated. The economy's substantial trade deficit is largely offset by remittances from Tongans working overseas, foreign aid, and tourism.

The judiciary is generally fair, efficient, and independent of the king and the executive branch. In 2004, the Supreme Court ruled that two prisoners suffered abuse in prison before their escape in January. The escapees voluntarily returned to prison after 11 days. It is not clear yet how the parliament's decision to abolish use of the British Civil Liberty Law will affect the judiciary. Traditional village elders also exercise considerable authority and frequently adjudicate local disputes. Prisons are sparse, but there were no reports of prisoner abuse. Suspects may exercise the right to an attorney and a court hearing.

Citizens enjoy freedom of travel, movement, and migration. Immigration laws were tightened after the illegal sale of Tongan passports, particularly to persons from China and Taiwan, became sore points in Tongan relations with major aid donors. Relations between Tongans and Chinese immigrants have worsened in recent years as evidenced by attacks against Chinese-owned shops.

Women face discrimination in almost every sphere of life and are frequent victims of domestic violence. There are few legal protections for women, and the police and courts generally consider domestic abuse better handled by families and village elders.

Trinidad and Tobago

Population: 1,300,000
GNI/capita: $6,750
Life Expectancy: 71
Political Rights: 3
Civil Liberties: 3
Status: Partly Free
Religious Groups: Roman Catholic (29.4 percent), Hindu (23.8 percent), Anglican (10.9 percent), Muslim (5.8 percent), Presbyterian (3.4 percent), other (26.7 percent)
Ethnic Groups: Black (40 percent), East Indian (40 percent), mixed (18 percent), other (2 percent)
Capital: Port-of-Spain

Ten-Year Ratings Timeline (Political Rights, Civil Liberties, Status)

1995	1996	1997	1998	1999	2000	2001	2002	2003	2004
1,2F	1,2F	1,2F	1,2F	1,2F	2,2F	3,3PF	3,3PF	3,3PF	3,3PF

Overview:
The government of Prime Minister Patrick Manning did not made any significant headway during 2004 in the struggle against dramatic increases in violent crime in Trinidad and Tobago. Meanwhile, the leader of a small radical group who had staged a coup attempt more than a decade earlier was rearrested in July on charges of conspiracy to murder.

Trinidad and Tobago, a member of the Commonwealth, achieved independence from Britain in 1962. In July 1991, Jamaat-al-Muslimeen, a small radical Muslim group, staged a coup attempt in Port-of-Spain. The prime minister and eight cabinet members were held hostage for four days, and 23 people died in bombings at the police headquarters, the state television station, and the parliamentary building.

After disputed elections in December 2001, Patrick Manning was appointed as prime minister. An ensuing stalemate in parliament, with 18 members of each party in a nine-month deadlock, led to street demonstrations and a legal challenge. Manning eventually called for legislative elections in October 2002. The polling was generally peaceful and saw the participation of six parties representing more than 100 candidates contesting the 36 open seats. Manning's People's National Movement (PNM) won 20 seats, while the United National Congress (UNC) had a heavy showing, reinforcing the domination of these two parties. Manning was sworn in for the third time since 1991, as the seventh prime minister of independent Trinidad and Tobago. His cabinet showed few changes and included his wife, Hazel, who again serves as minister of education; nepotism does not seem to be an issue for the electorate. In previous elections, there were concerns over the impartiality of the Elections and Boundaries Commission, but no major improprieties surfaced during the recent national or local polls. The UNC is, however, opposed to the redrawing of electoral districts as being partisan and favoring the PNM.

In local elections held in July 2003, the PNM won a majority of seats and took control of two districts that had been strongholds of the UNC, which won just 5 of 14 councils. Also during the year, the UNC became increasingly confrontational, forcing Manning's government to compromise when legislation required a two-thirds majority in parliament. Basdeo Panday, leader of the UNC, became increasingly confrontational, refusing to step down from the leadership of his party despite promising to do so when he turned 70 in May 2003.

Yasin Abu Bakr, the leader of Jamaat al-Muslimeen, a small radical Muslim group, was arrested in August 2003 on charges of conspiracy to murder, but was released on bail. He was rearrested in July of 2004 on charges that he was conspiring to murder two former members of his group, including his son-in-law. The group had staged a coup attempt in July 1991 in the capital, Port-of-Spain.

In August, a parliamentary integrity commission was established, an indication of the continuing effort to fight corruption. Meanwhile, growing crime was a critical problem throughout 2004; as of October of, there had been 222 murders, up from 175 in 2003.

Political Rights and Civil Liberties: Citizens of Trinidad and Tobago can change their government democratically. The 1976 constitution established the two-island nation as a republic, with a president, elected by a majority of both houses of parliament, replacing the former governor-general. Executive authority remains vested in the prime minister. The bicameral parliament consists of the 36-member House of Representatives, elected for five years, and the 31-member Senate, with 25 senators appointed by the prime minister and 6 by the opposition. Political parties are free to organize, but in practice, the dominance of the PNM and UNC has led to a two-party system.

In July 2001, then prime minister Basdeo Panday of the UNC lashed out at a Transparency International report that rated Trinidad, for the first time, as a country with high levels of official corruption. Panday, who was engaged in a long-running feud with prominent members of the local press, denied that there was corruption in his administration. Trinidad and Tobago was ranked 51 out of 146 countries surveyed in Transparency International's 2004 Corruption Perceptions Index. An Integrity Commission, established under the 2000 Integrity in Public Life Act, has the power to investigate the financial and ethical performance of public functionaries; Panday was the first person to be investigated by the commission.

Press outlets are privately owned and vigorous and offer pluralistic views. There are four daily newspapers and several weeklies. The broadcast media are both private and public. Panday refused, in 1998, to sign the Inter American Press Association's Declaration of Chapultepec on press freedom until it addressed instances of media dissemination of "lies, half-truths and innuendoes." Under Prime Minister Patrick Manning, the government did not interfere with freedom of speech and the press. There is free access to the Internet.

Freedom of religion is guaranteed under the constitution, and the government honors this provision. Foreign missionaries are free to operate, but the government limits representatives of a denomination to 35. Academic freedom is generally respected.

Freedom of association and assembly is respected. Labor unions are well organized, powerful, and politically active, although union membership has declined. Strikes are legal and occur frequently.

The judicial branch is independent, although subject to some political pressure and corruption. As a result of rising crime rates, the court system is severely backlogged, in some cases for up to five years, with an estimated 20,000 criminal cases awaiting trial. However, the government permits human rights monitors to visit prisons, which are severely overcrowded.

Street crime is on the rise, with the consumption and trafficking of illegal drugs considered to be largely responsible for the increase in violent crime. Drug corruption extends to the business community, and a significant amount of money is believed to be laundered through front companies. The Proceeds of Crime Act of 2000 provides severe penalties for money laundering and requires that major financial transactions be strictly monitored. The government works closely with U.S. law enforcement agencies to track drug shipments in and out of the country. In an indication of the seriousness of the country's crime wave, in January 2004, the Trinidad and Tobago Chamber of Industry and Commerce asked the government to strictly enforce laws, including the execution of convicted murderers.

Corruption in the police force, which is often drug related, is endemic, and law enforcement inefficiency results in the dismissal of some criminal cases. The police have won praise, however, for establishing a branch of Crime Stoppers, an international organization that promotes community involvement in preventing and informing on crime through a hotline.

The population is divided into three communities: Afro-Trinidadians, Indo-Trinidadians, and those of mixed race. The Indian community continues to edge towards numerical, and thus political, advantage. The most recent elections are emblematic of the racial tensions that continue to dominate electoral contests. In his speech opening parliament on September 10, 2004, President George Maxwell Richards highlighted the importance of not taking race issues for granted. Efforts to heal the wounds of the 1991 coup continue to characterize Trinidadian politics.

Violence against women is extensive and remains a low priority for police and prosecutors. While serious crimes such as murder and rape are reported, other instances of abuse go unreported. Women are present in the public and private sector, but men still dominate most leadership positions and pay differentials continue to favor the latter. Discrimination is forbidden under the constitution.

Tunisia

Population: 10,000,000   **Political Rights:** 6
GNI/capita: $1,990   **Civil Liberties:** 5
Life Expectancy: 73   **Status:** Not Free
Religious Groups: Muslim (98 percent),
Christian (1 percent), Jewish (1 percent)
Ethnic Groups: Arab (98 percent), other (2 percent)
Capital: Tunis

Ten-Year Ratings Timeline (Political Rights, Civil Liberties, Status)

1995	1996	1997	1998	1999	2000	2001	2002	2003	2004
6,5NF	6,5NF	6,5NF	6,5NF	6,5NF	6,5NF	6,5NF	6,5NF	6,5NF	6,5NF

Overview:

In October 2004, President Zine el-Abidine Ben Ali, who has ruled Tunisia with an iron fist for 17 years, won a fourth term as president in elections. These polls, as well as legislative elections held the same day, were marred by an opposition boycott and public apathy and were criticized for providing few opportunities for public participation in the political process. Tunisia's press freedoms remained restrictive, and the government continued to crack down on journalists and human rights defenders.

Nationalist pressures for Tunisian independence began in the 1930s under the leadership of Habib Bourguiba, leader of the Neo-Doustour party. Bourguiba became the country's first president when Tunisia gained independence in 1956 after more than 70 years as a French protectorate. Bourguiba's vision for Tunisia led to significant initiatives in the areas of social and economic development, including the promotion of one of the most liberal personal status codes in the Arab world; it ceded significant rights to women and remains unmatched in the Arab world today. He also furthered education and spending on economic development projects. However, political rights and civil liberties were severely restricted under Bourguiba's rule.

In 1987, Ben Ali, formerly the minister of the interior, led a bloodless coup, deposing the aging Bourguiba and promising to open up the political system. After an initial period of minor political reform, Ben Ali cracked down harshly on the Islamist opposition. Over time, the government's repressive practices extended beyond the Islamist opposition; hundreds of dissidents have been jailed over the last 15 years for peacefully exercising their civil liberties.

Tunisia's dismal human rights record has been attacked by international human rights groups, and more discreetly so by the international community. The European Union has quietly linked human rights and assistance in its agreements clauses with the North African state. The United States has recently been more openly critical, and during a visit to Tunis in December 2003, U.S. secretary of state Colin Powell praised Tunisia's partnership in the war against terrorism, but urged the government to pursue political reforms. However, the government's human rights record has not improved since Amnesty International issued, in 2003, a 40-page report describing how government opponents are subjected to arbitrary arrest, incommunicado detention, torture, and imprisonment.

The presidential election, which Ben Ali won with 94.52 percent of the vote, pointed to a likely continuation of that trend. Ben Ali ran against three other contenders, none of whom garnered more than 4 percent of the vote amid opposition boycotts and claims of manipulation, voter intimidation, and government restrictions. Ben Ali was backed by business groups, trade unions, and two opposition parties. Concurrent legislative elections initially featured 300 candidates from seven political parties competing for 182 seats. However, a major opposition party, the Progressive Democratic Party, pulled out its candidates at the last minute, arguing that the vote would be a sham.

The United States expressed disappointment, saying there had been little opportunity for public political participation. After Ben Ali's reelection, Amnesty International urged him to respect the country's obligations under Tunisian law and international human rights standards and put an end to human rights violations prevalent for the past decade.

Political Rights and Civil Liberties: Tunisians cannot change their government democratically. The 1959 constitution accords the president significant powers, including the right to select the prime minister and cabinet, to rule by decree when the legislature is not in session, and to appoint the governors of Tunisia's 23 provinces. The legislature, by contrast, serves as a rubber stamp for the president's policies and does not provide a check on executive power. Presidential elections lack any pretense of competition. A constitutional referendum in 2002 removed the three-term limit on the presidency and raised to 75 the maximum age to become president, which means that Ben Ali will be eligible to stand again for office in 2009. Although parliamentary elections are contrived to allow for the appearance of a multiparty legislature, the ruling Constitutional Democratic Rally (Rassemblement Constitutionnel Democratique, or RCD) holds a majority of the seats. After one opposition party, the Democratic Forum for Labor and Freedom was legalized last year—eight years after its formation—the number of authorized political parties in the country increased to seven.

Tunisia was ranked 39 out of 146 countries surveyed in Transparency International's 2004 Corruption Perceptions Index. Corruption in the government exists, including petty corruption and bribe taking by security forces. The government announced the creation of a body tasked with reducing corruption, but there were no public reports of its activities.

Tunisia's press freedoms are among the most restricted in the Arab world. The government controls domestic broadcasting and owns or controls six of the eight mainstream dailies. It also uses newsprint subsidies and financial control as means for indirect censorship of the private press. During the presidential and general election campaigns, state-run radio and television provided full coverage to the ruling

RCD but hardly any to the opposition candidates, according to local and international observers. Tunisian journalists critical of the regime continue to be harassed, threatened, imprisoned, physically attacked, and censored. In November 2003, journalist Zouhair Yahyaoui was released after almost a year and a half in prison. However, on the same day, Internet opposition journalist Naziha Rejiba received an eight-month suspended prison sentence on currency-exchange charges. In August 2004, plainclothes security men assaulted journalist Slim Boukhedr after he asked questions implying Ben Ali influenced the judiciary in a particular case. Abdallah Zouari, a journalist with the Islamist opposition newspaper *Al-Fajr*, was released in September 2004, after serving a 13-month sentence. The government restricted access to a number of Internet Web sites, including those belonging to Tunisian opposition and Islamist groups. In July 2004, six Internet users accused of being Islamist extremists and plotting terror attacks were each given a 13-year prison sentence, reportedly after confessions extracted under duress.

While Islam is the state religion, the government allows for the free practice of all religions as long as the public order is not disturbed. The government controls and subsidizes mosques and pays the salaries of prayer leaders. The 1988 law on mosques stipulates that only those appointed by the government may lead activities in the mosques, which are required to remain closed except during prayer times.

Academic freedom is severely restricted. The government closely monitored university staff and students for any Islamist activity, and used uniformed police on campuses to discourage expressions of dissent. Academic publications were submitted to the government prior to publication, and professors avoided teaching classes on sensitive subjects such as civil liberties and political systems.

Freedom of association and assembly is sharply curtailed. Politically oriented nongovernmental organizations remain unauthorized. The government refuses to legalize most independent human rights organizations.

Human rights defenders and democracy activists were subjected to increased government harassment during the year, including physical beatings, heavy police surveillance, and travel bans. In January, an assailant believed to be working with the state security services violently attacked prominent human rights activist and Internet journalist Sihem Bensedrine outside her home. The repression of dissidents increased around the elections period. Jallel Zoughlami, a known critic of Ben Ali and founder of an unauthorized monthly newspaper, and his brother Nejib were detained on September 22, shortly after they were attacked in the center of Tunis by several men. In October, two plainclothes policemen beat opposition activist Hamma Hammami in the street. Another activist, Moncef Marzouki, leader of the unauthorized political party Republican Congress (Congres pour la Republique, or CPR) was stopped and interrogated for three hours at Tunis airport when he was on his way to Paris in October to join a conference of the Tunisian opposition.

There is no independent judiciary; the government has used the courts to convict and imprison critics. Human Rights Watch released a report in July 2004 accusing the government of holding around 40 of the country's more than 500 political prisoners in solitary confinement, some for up to 13 years. They are all Islamist members of the banned Nahdha Party and were sentenced by military courts in 1992 in unfair trials. The government has denied the accusation. Amnesty International has expressed concern that a new antiterrorism law, passed in December 2003, would further erode human rights through its broad definition of terrorism and provisions for extended pretrial detention. The law came amid a climate of rampant abuse, including torture and ill-treatment of defendants, lack of guarantees for a free trial, harsh prison conditions, arbitrary arrest, and incommunicado detention.

Women enjoy substantial rights, and the government has worked to advance women's rights in the areas of property ownership and support to divorced women. However, inheritance law still discriminates against women. Unlike in many countries in the Arab world, a child's rights to citizenship are conveyed through either the mother or the father.

Turkey

Population: 71,300,000   **Political Rights:** 3
GNI/capita: $2,490   **Civil Liberties:** 3*
Life Expectancy: 69   **Status:** Partly Free
Religious Groups: Muslim [mostly Sunni] (99.8 percent), other (0.2 percent)
Ethnic Groups: Turkish (80 percent), Kurdish (20 percent)
Capital: Ankara

Ratings Change: Turkey's civil liberties rating improved from 4 to 3 due to the passage of another round of major reforms, including a complete overhaul of the penal code, greater civilian control of the military, the initiation of broadcasts in minority languages, and a decrease in the severest forms of torture.

Ten-Year Ratings Timeline (Political Rights, Civil Liberties, Status)

1995	1996	1997	1998	1999	2000	2001	2002	2003	2004
5,5PF	4,5PF	4,5PF	4,5PF	4,5PF	4,5PF	4,5PF	3,4PF	3,4PF	3,3PF

Overview: Turkey continued to pass monumental reforms in 2004 in preparation for European Union (EU) membership. May constitutional reforms improved gender equality and civilian oversight of the military, and September saw the first overhaul of the Turkish penal code in its 78-year history. A positive report from the EU Commission in October paved the way for a long-awaited date for the start of negotiations, expected to be set in December 2004.

Turkey emerged as a republic out of the breakup of the Ottoman Empire at the end of World War I. Its founder and the author of its guiding principles was Kemal Mustafa Ataturk ("Father of the Turks"), who declared that Muslim Turkey would be a secular state. Ataturk sought to modernize the country through measures such as the pursuit of Western learning, use of the Roman alphabet instead of Arabic script for writing Turkish, and abolishment of the Muslim caliphate.

Turkey stayed out of most of World War II, but joined the Allies in February 1945. After the war, the republic joined NATO in 1952 to guarantee its protection from the Soviet Union. However, modern Turkish political history has been unstable, and the army has overthrown civilian governments in three coups. The army, which sees itself as a bulwark against both Islamism and Kurdish separatism, has traditionally expressed opinions on the functioning of government that are rarely ignored.

The role of political Islam has been one of the defining questions of Turkish politics in the 1990s and early twenty-first century. In 1995, an Islamist party, Welfare, won the general election but failed to obtain a majority. Initially, two other parties formed a majority coalition without it, but the breakup of that coalition in 1996 led the Democratic Party to form a coalition with Welfare. The following year the army, ever protective of Turkey's secular roots, forced the coalition to resign. Welfare prime minister Necmettin Erbakan was replaced by a member of the Motherland Party. The Welfare party was banned in 1998 on the grounds that it was seeking to introduce Islamic rule.

The governments that followed failed to stabilize a shaky economy, which culminated in an economic crisis in 2001. In November 2002, the Justice and Development (AK) Party, whose roots lay in the then-disbanded Welfare, won a sweeping majority in the general election by promising to end government corruption and put the country on a firm path toward EU membership. The AK sought to distance itself from political Islamism, but its leader, Recep Tayyip Erdogan, a former mayor of Istanbul, had previously been banned from politics after he was convicted of crimes against secularism for reading a poem seeming to incite religious intolerance. Abdullah Gul served as prime minister until parliament changed the constitution to allow Erdogan to replace him in March 2003.

Erdogan has used his party's large parliamentary majority to push through successive wide-reaching reforms that are crucial to Turkey's application to join the EU. In 2004, the government passed further constitutional reforms and a thorough overhaul of the penal code. In October, Turkey's persistence paid off in a report from the European Commission, which recommended that in December 2004 the EU give Turkey a date to begin negotiations. However, the report cited continued shortcomings, including corruption, inequities in the status of women, and problems with the role of the military, and said that the EU should monitor Turkey to ensure progress. Turkey is not expected to join the EU for at least a decade.

Kurdish separatists fought a 15-year guerrilla war against Turkish forces in the southeast of the country that ended after the capture of their leader, Abdullah Ocalan, in 1999. The legacy of this conflict, in which more than 35,000 people were killed, remains in the form of discrimination and lingering tensions. In June, the Kurdish separatist PKK, now renamed Kongra-Gel, ended its five-year ceasefire with the government because, it claimed, not enough had been done to meet its demands. Clashes with government troops increased over the summer, with deaths on both sides. The EU added Kongra-Gel to its list of terrorist organizations in April 2004.

Turkey has also faced increasing violence from non-Kurdish terrorism. Bombs went off in Ankara and Istanbul ahead of visits by British prime minister Tony Blair in May and U.S. president George W. Bush in June, as well as at a Masonic lodge in March.

Political Rights and Civil Liberties: Turkish citizens can change their government democratically. The 1982 constitution provides for a 550-member parliament, the Grand National Assembly, which is elected to five-year terms. The prime minister is the head of government, but the assembly chooses a mostly symbolic president as head of state—currently Ahmet Necdet Sezer. Democratic choice has been undercut by the army in the past, the last time being in a "soft coup" that forced the government of the religious Welfare party out of office in 1997. Recep Tayyip Erdogan of the AK became prime minister in March 2003. The November 2002 elections were widely judged as free and fair.

In January 2003, new legal amendments loosened restrictions on party names and candidates and circumscribed the reasons for closure of a political party. However, a party can still be shut down if its program is not in agreement with the constitution, and the word "agreement" can be widely interpreted. In addition, a party must win at least 10 percent of the votes cast nationwide to have representation in parliament. As a result, although a large number and variety of parties participated in active campaigning in 2002, only two parties, AK and the Republican People's Party (CHP), won seats. Nevertheless, both of these parties had been in the opposition, thus attesting to the ability of the electorate to precipitate change.

Today, AK holds an overwhelming 367 parliamentary seats. The opposition has been in disarray since the 2002 elections, as confirmed by the tremendous victory of AK in March 2004 local elections. The AK Party appears to have abandoned its former Islamist aspirations. Although the party has supported some loosening of restrictions on religious activity, it has not made any attempt to undermine Turkey's secular underpinnings, but instead has steadfastly pursued a start to EU negotiations.

The National Security Council, once dominated by the military, had its policy-setting role downgraded to a purely advisory one in 2003. A civilian was chosen to head the council for the first time in August 2004, and constitutional reforms made military expenditures more accountable to parliament. Significantly, the military did not intervene when Erdogan was chosen prime minister, despite its known reservations. Nevertheless, the opinions of the top generals continue to generate press attention, and the possibility of military intervention in controversial policy making remains.

Turkey struggles with corruption in government and in daily life. The AK Party—"ak" means "pure" in Turkish—came to power amid promises to clean up governmental corruption, and since December 2003, Turkey has signed the Group of States Against Corruption (GRECO), the UN Convention against Corruption, and the European Convention on the Fight against Corruption. However, enforcement is lacking, and a culture of tolerance of corruption pervades among the general population. Transparency has improved through EU reforms, but here too implementation lags. Turkey was ranked 77 out of 146 countries surveyed in Transparency International's 2004 Corruption Perceptions Index.

While Turkey's constitution establishes freedom of the media and recent reforms have increased this freedom, some major impediments remain. Fines, arrests, and imprisonment are regularly allotted to media and journalists who, for example, criticize the military or portray the Kurds in too positive of a light. Turkey's Supreme Council of Radio and Television (RTUK) regularly sanctions broadcasters if they are not in compliance with a broadly defined set of principles. Furthermore, media organizations have an incentive to produce news of a certain political bent because they are nearly all owned by giant holding companies with interests in other sectors. Self-censorship therefore occurs. On the other hand, new laws were instituted allowing broadcasts for the first time in minority languages, and the first such broadcasts took place in June 2004. In addition, as of June 2004, a member of the military will no longer be part of the RTUK. The government does not restrict the Internet beyond the same censorship policies that apply to other media.

Turkey is a predominantly Muslim country, and much of its population is very devout. Three non-Muslim groups—Greek and Armenian Orthodox Christians, and Jews—are officially recognized. Other groups lack legal status, and their activities are subject to legal challenges. While the constitution protects freedom of religion, the Turkish republic was set up on the premise of secularism in which state and religious affairs are separated. In practice, this has meant considerable government control of religion. Women wearing headscarves are not allowed in public universities and government offices, and observant men are dismissed from the military. There are periodic protests against the headscarf ban, although the European Court of Human Rights ruled in June 2004 that the ban is legal, and AK dropped its attempt to introduce an easing of the ban in the 2004 penal code reforms. A much more vocal controversy erupted in spring 2004 over an AK proposal to allow graduates of vocational schools—including Islamic imam-*hatip* schools—to enroll in state universities. After the president vetoed the bill, AK allowed the matter to drop. The government does not otherwise restrict academic freedom, although self-censorship on sensitive topics like the role of Islam and the Kurdish problem are common.

The constitution protects freedom of association, but broad language leaves room for restrictions despite some tightening through recent reforms. Some local officials use bureaucracy to prevent registration of demonstrations, and police regularly disperse peaceful public gatherings, often using excessive force. Nevertheless, civil society plays an increasing role in Turkish politics. Regulation of the activities and membership of nongovernmental organizations (NGOs) has relaxed with recent reforms, although restrictions remain, particularly for pro-Kurdish groups. Employees have the right to join trade unions and cannot be discriminated against for doing so, but public employees do not have the right to strike.

The Turkish constitution establishes an independent judiciary, but the government can influence judges through its control of appointments, promotions, and financing. Recent reforms give all detainees the right to see a lawyer immediately, free of charge, although the law is not enforced in all instances, particularly in the southeast. The death penalty was fully abolished in 2004, as were State Security Courts, where many human rights abuses occurred. In September, parliament overhauled the penal code, making such fundamental changes as institutionalizing the concept that punishments should be in proportion to the crimes committed; there are accusations that residual ambiguities still allow judges to interpret some laws at will.

Leyla Zana and three other Kurdish former members of parliament, who were convicted of belonging to the PKK in 1994 in what was widely condemned as an unfair trial, were released in June pending an appeal. The four were considered by many to have been political prisoners, and the trial is considered symbolic both of Turkey's flawed judicial system and of the push for Kurdish rights. Their lawyers consider it unlikely that they will return to prison because of the amount of time they have already served.

The Erdogan government has a "zero-tolerance" policy concerning torture, backed up by new laws and training to improve implementation. However, while torture is widely reported as having decreased, particularly in its harshest forms, most rights groups agree that it still occurs and perpetrators are rarely punished. Prison conditions can be harsh, including measures such as solitary confinement and medical neglect. Most controversial are the F-type prisons, which are criticized for isolation of prisoners. An especially contentious imprisonment is that of Abdullah Ocalan, former leader of the Kurdish guerrilla movement, who is serving a life sentence in solitary confinement on an island off the Turkish coast; Ocalan allegedly has not had adequate access to his lawyer or to visitors.

Turkey claims that all Turkish citizens are treated equally, but its unwillingness to recognize Kurdish differences results in de facto unequal treatment under the law. Because minorities are defined solely by religion, Kurds are denied recognition, and a traditional emphasis on Turkishness over multiculturalism has left the Kurds facing restrictions on their language, culture, and freedom of expression. The situation has improved with the EU harmonization reforms, but official and informal discrimination remain.

Property rights are generally respected in Turkey. The most significant problem is the tens of thousands of Kurds who were driven from their homes by government forces during the conflict in the southeast. The government has initiated a project to compensate these people and return them to their villages. However, local paramilitary "village guards" have allegedly used intimidation and violence to prevent some from returning to their homes.

Constitutional amendments in the spring of 2004 included a provision granting women full equality before the law, building on earlier changes in the civil and penal codes. However, much of Turkey is socially conservative, and women have far lower status than men in practice. UNICEF has determined that in some rural provinces more than half of all girls under age 15 do not attend school. Women are also discriminated against in employment. "Honor crimes," including killings, in which family members punish women who "dishonor" the family by becoming pregnant out of wedlock or being raped, are a problem among traditional Muslim families. In February, the government instructed prayer leaders to state that honor killings are a sin against God, and the 2004 revisions to the penal code included an end to sentence reductions for these crimes. AK leaders attempted to include a law criminalizing adultery in the penal code amendments, which was ultimately excluded. Human trafficking for the purposes of prostitution is a problem in Turkey, although the government has been taking many steps to improve the situation.

Turkmenistan

Population: 5,700,000
GNI/capita: $1,200
Life Expectancy: 67
Political Rights: 7
Civil Liberties: 7
Status: Not Free

Religious Groups: Muslim (89 percent), Eastern
Orthodox (9 percent), other (2 percent)
Ethnic Groups: Turkmen (85 percent), Uzbek (5 percent),
Russian (4 percent), other (6 percent)
Capital: Ashgabat

Ten-Year Ratings Timeline (Political Rights, Civil Liberties, Status)

1995	1996	1997	1998	1999	2000	2001	2002	2003	2004
7,7NF	7,7NF	7,7NF	7,7NF	7,7NF	7,7NF	7,7NF	7,7NF	7,7NF	7,7NF

Overview:
The government of President Saparmurat Niyazov continued its campaign in 2004 against real and perceived opponents of the regime, including dismissing a number of se-
nior state officials. Despite limited gestures toward improving civil liberties, such as
the formal abolition of an exit-visa system and the easing of some restrictions on
nongovernmental organizations (NGOs) and religious groups, Turkmenistan remained one of the most repressive societies in the world. Meanwhile, the country's
strained relations with Russia and Uzbekistan appeared to show small signs of improvement during the year.

The southernmost republic of the former Soviet Union, Turkmenistan was conquered by the Mongols in the thirteenth century, seized by Russia in the late 1800s,
and incorporated into the U.S.S.R. in 1924. Turkmenistan gained formal independence in 1991 after the dissolution of the Soviet Union.

Niyazov, the former head of the Turkmenistan Communist Party, was the sole
candidate in elections to the newly created post of president in October 1990. After
the adoption of a new constitution in 1992, he ran unopposed again and was reelected for a five-year term with a reported 99.5 percent of the vote. The main opposition group, Agzybirlik, which was formed in 1989 by leading intellectuals, was
banned. In a 1994 referendum, Niyazov's tenure as president was extended for an
additional five years, until 2002, which exempted him from having to run again in
1997 as originally scheduled. In the December 1994 elections to the unicameral National Assembly (Mejlis), only Niyazov's Democratic Party of Turkmenistan (DPT),
the former Communist Party, was permitted to field candidates.

In the December 1999 Mejlis elections, every candidate was selected by the government and virtually all were members of the DPT. The Central Election Commission (CEC) claimed that voter turnout was 98.9 percent. The Organization for Security and Cooperation in Europe (OSCE), citing the lack of provision for nongovernmental parties to participate and the executive branch's control of the nomination of
candidates, refused to send even a limited assessment mission. In a further consolidation of his extensive powers, parliament unanimously voted in late December to
make Niyazov president for life. With this decision, Turkmenistan became the first

country in the Commonwealth of Independent States to formally abandon presidential elections.

Although Niyazov continued to exercise widespread power throughout the country in 2002, cracks in his regime became more visible during the year. Several high-level government defections, along with a purge by Niyazov of Turkmenistan's intelligence service, highlighted growing political tensions and challenges to the government. On November 25, Niyazov survived an alleged assassination attempt in Ashgabat when gunmen fired at the president's motorcade. The incident sparked a widespread crackdown against the opposition and perceived critics of the regime, drawing condemnation from foreign governments and international organizations, including the OSCE and the United Nations.

While some observers speculated that Niyazov himself had planned the shooting as an excuse to increase repression of his political enemies, others maintained that it was a failed attempt by certain members of the opposition to oust the president from power. According to the government, former foreign minister and prominent opposition leader Boris Shikhmuradov, along with three other former high-ranking officials living in exile, had organized the attack. He was alleged to have returned to Turkmenistan from exile in Russia with the help of the Uzbek authorities, an accusation that soured already strained relations with Uzbekistan. Shikhmuradov was arrested on December 25 and made a televised confession four days later that critics maintain had been coerced. On December 30, he was sentenced to life in prison following what human rights groups condemned as a Soviet-style show trial. Two of the alleged co-conspirators received life sentences in absentia, while many other suspects were given lengthy prison sentences.

The president subsequently announced early elections for the Halk Maslahaty (People's Council) in April 2003. The decision to hold the poll two years ahead of schedule was probably intended to eliminate any remaining opposition to Niyazov's government through a redistribution of legislative posts. There was no election campaign, and the state media did not provide information about the candidates, all of whom were nominated by the presidential administration. The CEC announced voter turnout of 99.8 percent, although the real figure is believed to be much lower.

A series of high-profile government reshuffles in 2004 highlighted ongoing political tensions and concerns about potential challengers to the regime. During the year, the minister of finance, the heads of two television channels, and several bank chairmen were dismissed on charges of corruption and nepotism. Other personnel changes involved the deputy mayor of Ashgabat, the head of the state border service, the country's ambassador to Belgium, and two regional governors. In a rare example of public opposition to the president, leaflets calling for Niyazov's overthrow were distributed in Ashgabat in July. No one claimed responsibility for the leaflets, and their distributors were not caught.

In the run-up to the December 19 Mejlis polls, the list of candidates was reportedly personally approved by Niyazov. The government refused to invite any international observers to monitor the election, which most analysts described as little more than a staged vote, given that all candidates will be approved by the authorities.

Relations with Russia appeared to improve in 2004 after having been strained the previous year. In April 2003, Ashgabat had unilaterally withdrawn from a 1993 dual citizenship agreement with Moscow, a decision that it decided to apply retroactively, thereby forcing dual citizenship holders to choose a nationality. The move provoked strong opposition from members of Russia's parliament and the media, who accused Moscow of having sold out the rights of ethnic Russians in Turkmenistan in exchange for a lucrative, long-term energy deal, which the two countries concluded in the same month. In 2004, Russian-Turkmen relations seemed to have stabilized with the February signing of a cooperation agreement covering economic, scientific, and cultural matters. Meanwhile, both Moscow and Ashgabat downplayed the citizenship issue as their economic relationship dominated the bilateral agenda.

The tense relationship between Uzbekistan and Turkmenistan, particularly after Ashgabat accused Tashkent of complicity in the 2002 assassination attempt against Niyazov, showed some signs of easing in late 2004. The presidents of the two countries met for the first time in four years on November 19 in the Uzbekistan city of Bukhara, where they signed a friendship treaty and an agreement simplifying travel for residents of their border areas. Nevertheless, serious problems remained over issues including border demarcation, the joint use of water resources, and the cross-border smuggling of gasoline and weapons.

Political Rights and Civil Liberties:

Citizens of Turkmenistan cannot change their government democratically. President Saparmurat Niyazov enjoys virtually absolute power over all branches and levels of government. In recent years, the government has undergone a rapid turnover of personnel as Niyazov has dismissed many officials whom he suspects may challenge his authority.

The country has two parliamentary bodies, neither of which enjoys genuine independence from the executive branch: the unicameral Mejlis (National Assembly), composed of 50 members elected by popular vote for five-year terms, and the approximately 2,500-member Halk Maslahaty (People's Council), composed of various elected and appointed members, which was officially made the country's supreme legislative body in August 2003. The 1994, 1999, and 2003 legislative elections were neither free nor fair.

Niyazov has established an extensive cult of personality, including erecting monuments to his leadership throughout the country. In 1994, he renamed himself Turkmenbashi, or leader of the Turkmen. He has enacted bizarre decrees, including ordering the renaming of the days of the week and months of the year after himself and his mother.

Only one political party, the Niyazov-led DPT, has been officially registered. Opposition parties have been banned, and their leading members face harassment and detention or have fled abroad. In September 2003, four prominent opposition groups in exile united to form the Union of Democratic Forces, whose stated goal is the replacement of Niyazov's government with one based on democratic principles. Some analysts have cited the wave of post-assassination attempt reprisals as the impetus for the long-divided opposition groups to put aside enough of their differences to join forces. Nevertheless, the opposition remains weak and unlikely to pose a serious challenge to the Niyazov regime.

Corruption is widespread, and the authorities have used anticorruption campaigns to remove potential rivals. Turkmenistan was ranked 133 out of 146 countries surveyed in Transparency International's 2004 Corruption Perceptions Index.

Freedom of speech and the press is severely restricted by the government, which controls all radio and television broadcasts and print media. Reports of dissenting political views are banned, as are even mild forms of criticism of the president. Subscriptions to foreign newspapers and magazines are forbidden, and foreign journalists have few opportunities to visit Turkmenistan. In July, the Turkmen government shut down broadcasts of Russia's Radio Mayak, the last foreign media outlet to reach Turkmenistan, ostensibly for technical reasons regarding the station's transmission equipment. A new Turkmen satellite television channel was launched by the government in October with the official purpose of promoting the country's image abroad. The state-owned Turkmen Telekom is the only authorized Internet provider in the country.

Two freelance journalists for Radio Free Europe/Radio Liberty (RFE/RL), Rakhim Esenov and Ashyrguly Bayryev, were detained in late February and early March, respectively, by agents from the National Security Ministry. Esenov was accused of smuggling copies of his novel from Russia into Turkmenistan, where it had been banned for ten years, and charged with instigating social, ethnic, and religious hatred. His son-in-law was also arrested as part of the government's policy of collectively punishing family members of the accused. The authorities did not specify the charges against Bayryev. Although both men were released in mid-March, the charges against them were not dismissed, and they were told to stop reporting for RFE/RL. Another RFE/RL correspondent, Mukhamed Berdiyev, was attacked by three men on April 30 and suffered serious head injuries.

The government restricts freedom of religion, and independent religious groups continue to face persecution. Members of religious groups not legally registered by the government, including Armenian Apostolic, Roman Catholic, and Pentecostal communities, have been fined, beaten, and imprisoned by security forces. The government controls access to Islamic education and restricts the number of Muslim mosques throughout the country. According to Forum 18, a religious freedom watchdog group based in Norway, the authorities demolished at least seven mosques in 2004, apparently to prevent unapproved Muslim services. The authorities have pressured houses of worship to display a copy of the *Rukhnama*, a quasi-spiritual guide allegedly authored by Niyazov.

A law on religion that came into effect in November 2003 criminalized the practice of religious groups not officially registered and prescribed up to one year of corrective labor against violators. The law effectively applied to all religions other than Sunni Islam and Russian Orthodoxy, the only two faiths that had successfully achieved registration. The registration fee was set at ten times the average monthly wage, and only clergymen with Turkmen citizenship and a university qualification in theology were authorized to lead a congregation. Under mounting international pressure, the government lifted some of its restrictions against religious organizations in 2004. The authorities eased registration requirements for religious groups in March by lowering from 500 to 5 the number of members required in each locality in which a group wished to register. In May, Niyazov decreed that practicing an unregistered religion would no longer be a criminal offense, although it remains illegal, with violators subject to fines. Although Seventh Day Adventist, Baha'i, Hare Krishna, and Baptist communities achieved formal registration shortly thereafter, other groups have experienced difficulties in attempting to register. Furthermore, members of independent religious congregations continued to face pressure from the authorities, including threats, detention, and confiscation of religious materials.

The government places significant restrictions on academic freedom, with schools increasingly being used to indoctrinate, rather than educate, students. The *Rukhnama* is required reading throughout the school system and has largely replaced many other traditional school subjects. All new textbooks must meet the government's strict ideological requirements. In February, Niyazov issued an order invalidating most higher education decrees received outside the country since 1993 and dismissing holders of such degrees from state jobs. Analysts view this decree as part of a broader effort to eliminate foreign influences from Turkmen society. Bribes are commonly required for admission to various schools and institutes.

The state security services regularly monitor the activities of citizens and foreign nationals, limiting open and free private discussion. Security officers use such surveillance techniques as wiretapping, the interception of mail, and the recruitment of informers. After the November 2002 assassination attempt, Niyazov reportedly directed law enforcement bodies to carefully monitor people's conversations in public places and called on people to assist the police by informing on their fellow citizens. In February 2004, Niyazov ordered the government to intensify video surveillance, including at all strategic economic facilities, public buildings, and government offices.

While the constitution guarantees peaceful assembly and association, these rights are severely restricted in practice. Public demonstrations against state policies are extremely rare. NGOs have faced increased harassment and threats for their activities as part of the post-November 2002 crackdown. In November 2003, a law on NGOs entered into force that effectively criminalized the activities of unregistered organizations and imposed penalties that include heavy fines, the confiscation of property, and imprisonment. In an apparent reversal, a new law was adopted in November 2004 that abolishes criminal penalties for unregistered NGOs. However, most observers suspect that the law is designed primarily to counter international criticism of the country's poor human rights record, rather than to genuinely improve the environment for Turkmenistan's civil society sector.

The government-controlled Colleagues Union is the only central trade union permitted. There are no legal guarantees for workers to form or join unions or to strike, although the constitution does not specifically prohibit these rights. Strikes in Turkmenistan are extremely rare.

The judicial system is subservient to the president, who appoints and removes judges for five-year terms without legislative review. The authorities frequently deny rights of due process, including public trials and access to defense attorneys. Police abuse and torture of suspects and prisoners, often to obtain confessions, is reportedly widespread. Those arrested and sentenced for complicity in the assassination attempt against Niyazov suffered ill-treatment or torture, had no access to legal counsel of their own choosing, and were convicted in closed trials; many of their friends and relatives were targeted for harassment and intimidation. In early 2003, the government broadened the definition of treason to cover a wide range of activities, including attempting to undermine the public's faith in the president's policies and failing to inform the authorities of a wide range of crimes. Prisons suffer from overcrowding and inadequate nutrition and medical care, and international organizations are not permitted to visit prisons.

Employment and educational opportunities for ethnic minorities are limited by the government's policy of promoting Turkmen national identity and its discrimination against those who are not ethnic Turkmen. Following the 2002 assassination attempt against Niyazov, which Turkmenistan openly accused Uzbekistan of supporting, the Turkmen authorities took a harder line against ethnic Uzbeks in Turkmenistan. The government has reportedly ordered the forced relocation of part of the Uzbek population living along the border with Uzbekistan and their replacement with ethnic Turkmen. Many ethnic Uzbek imams (Muslim religious leaders) have been dismissed and replaced by ethnic Turkmen, as have Uzbeks in other leadership positions in the country. In March 2004, the country's former chief mufti, Nasrullah ibn Ibadullah, an ethnic Uzbek, was sentenced to 22 years in prison on charges of treason; he had been removed from his post in January 2003 and was succeeded by an ethnic Turkmen. In April 2003, Ashgabat unilaterally abrogated its dual citizenship agreement with Russia. After Turkmen authorities set a deadline of June 22 of the same year for the selection of either Russian or Turkmen citizenship, many Russians holding dual citizenship reportedly frantically applied to leave Turkmenistan or risk automatically becoming Turkmen citizens. The authorities have ordered the closure of a variety of Russian-language institutions, including schools, throughout the country.

Freedom of movement and residence is severely restricted. Following the 2002 assassination attempt, travel within the country became more closely monitored, with travelers having to pass through various identity checkpoints. In March 2004, Niyazov formally abolished the country's exit-visa requirement—which had been eliminated in January 2002 but reintroduced the following year—to stave off trade restrictions by the United States. However, this decision is unlikely to ease travel abroad, which is extremely difficult for most Turkmen citizens and often requires the payment of bribes to government officials. In addition, the government is believed to maintain a lengthy blacklist of people—possibly thousands—who are not permitted to travel abroad, including those suspected of opposition to the authorities. In 2003, the State Service for the Registration of Foreign Citizens was established to monitor foreign visitors, whose activities are strictly regulated.

A continuing Soviet-style command economy and widespread corruption diminish equality of opportunity. Profits from the country's extensive energy exports rarely reach the general population, most of whom live in poverty. Police forcibly seize grain from farmers—who can only sell grain to a purchasing company that has a government monopoly—without providing compensation. In a move believed to stem from a government budget crisis, some 15,000 medical workers were dismissed in early 2004 and replaced with conscript soldiers, who essentially represent free labor. According to the Vienna-based International Helsinki Federation for Human Rights, the Turkmen government has engaged in "widespread violations of property rights" as part of a dramatic urban reconstruction project in Ashgabat that was launched in 2001. Hundreds of residents have reportedly been forced to vacate their homes on extremely short notice and have received little or no financial compensation or equivalent accommodation from the authorities.

The government restricts various personal social freedoms, including the wearing of long hair or beards by men. Traditional social and religious norms limit professional opportunities for women, and anecdotal reports suggest that domestic violence is common. A payment of $50,000 is required of foreign citizens wishing to marry Turkmen women; the money is ostensibly designed to provide for the couple's children if the marriage ends in divorce. Children are commonly used as forced labor during the annual fall cotton harvest.

Tuvalu

Population: 10,000
GNI/capita: $1,930
Life Expectancy: 66
Religious Groups: Church of Tuvalu [Congregationalist] (97 percent), other (3 percent)
Ethnic Groups: Polynesian (96 percent), Micronesian (4 percent)
Capital: Funafuti

Political Rights: 1
Civil Liberties: 1
Status: Free

Ten-Year Ratings Timeline (Political Rights, Civil Liberties, Status)

1995	1996	1997	1998	1999	2000	2001	2002	2003	2004
1,1F	1,1F	1,1F	1,1F	1,1F	1,1F	1,1F	1,1F	1,1F	1,1F

Overview: Tuvalu's frequent changes of government continued in 2004, when Prime Minister Saufatu Sopoanga was ousted in a no-confidence vote in August and replaced by Maatia Toafa.

The Gilbert and Ellice Islands became a British protectorate in 1892 and a British colony in 1916. This island state of nine atolls is situated in the central South Pacific Ocean. During World War II, the United States used the northernmost atoll of the Ellice Islands as a base to fight the Japanese. In 1974, as Britain was preparing the colony for independence, the Polynesian Ellice Islanders voted to separate themselves from the Micronesian Gilbertese, and the country attained independence on October 1, 1978, under the precolonial name of Tuvalu. (The Gilbert Islands, a group of 16 islands, form part of Kiribati.)

In Febraury 2001, Faimalaga Luka became prime minister after the sudden death from a heart attack of Ionatana Ionatana two months earlier. In December 2001, Luka was ousted in a no-confidence vote and replaced by Kolou Telake. In the July 2002 general elections, in which Telake failed to win a seat, Sopoanga was elected prime minister.

Intense political competition brought Tuvalu's parliament largely to a standstill in 2003. Sopoanga lost power after a by-election in May 2003 but refused to concede. In July 2003, the opposition took Sopoanga to court for refusing to convene parliament after the election of the new speaker in mid-June. Parliament eventually reconvened following by-elections in October, which gave Sopoanga a majority in parliament when opposition members agreed to join his cabinet.

Factional politics did not appear to have eased in 2004, with a no-confidence vote ousting Sopoanga in August. In October, an 8-7 vote elected Maatia Toafa as the new prime minister; Sopoanga was chosen for deputy prime minister. Frequent changes of government as a result of no-confidence votes in parliament have sustained a debate in the last decade over whether citizens should be allowed to choose their prime minister directly rather than through parliament.

The threats of climate change and rising sea levels continue to worry the population of these low-lying islands. Several years ago, the government asked Australia to agree to take its entire population in the event the islands are flooded, but Canberra refused.

Political Rights and Civil Liberties:

Citizens of Tuvalu can change their government democratically. Tuvalu is a member of the Commonwealth, and the head of state, Queen Elizabeth II, is represented by a governor-general who must be a citizen of Tuvalu. Governor-general Faimalaga Luka was appointed by parliament in September 2003. The prime minister, chosen by parliament, leads the government. The unicameral, 15-member parliament is elected to four-year terms. A six-person council administers each of the country's nine atolls. Council members are chosen by universal suffrage to four-year terms. There are no formal political parties, although there are no laws against their formation.

Tuvalu is one of the few places among Pacific Islands where corruption is not a serious problem.

The constitution provides for freedom of speech and the press, and the government generally respects these rights in practice. In 2001, the country's sole radio station, Radio Tuvalu, was privatized. The government voiced objections to some comments made on the station in 2001 but did not interfere with broadcasts. The sole television station, owned and operated by the government, went off the air in 2001 for financial reasons. Broadcast resumed in 2002 for several hours a day. Many residents use satellite dishes to access foreign programs. There is one fortnightly newspaper, *Tuvalu Echoes*. The first Internet connection was made in 1999. The government does not restrict access, but penetration is largely limited to the capital because of cost and connectively issues.

Religious freedom is generally respected in practice. The vast majority of the population, some 97 percent, is Congregational Protestant. Religion is a big part of life, and Sunday service is typically considered the most important weekly event. Academic freedom is also generally respected.

Nongovernmental groups across all levels of society provide a variety of health, education, and other services for women, youths, and the population at large. Public demonstrations are permitted, and workers are free to organize unions and choose their own representatives for collective bargaining. Being a largely subsistence economy with tiny service and manufacturing sectors, Tuvalu has only one registered trade union; the Tuvalu Seaman's Union has about 600 members who work on foreign merchant vessels. Workers have the right to strike, but no strikes have occurred in the island state's history. Public sector employees, who total fewer than 1,000, are members of professional associations that do not have union status.

The judiciary is independent and provides fair trials. Tuvalu has a two-tier judicial system. The higher courts include the Privy Council in London, the court of appeal, and the high court. The lower courts consist of senior and resident magistrates, the island courts, and the land courts. The chief justice, who is also the chief justice of Tonga, sits on the high court about once a year. A civilian-controlled, 70-

member constabulary force maintains internal order. Prisons are sparse but there were no reports of abuses.

Two-thirds of the population is engaged in subsistence farming and fishing. The country has no sub-surface fresh water, and increasing salinization of the soil is a serious concern. Geographical isolation limits options for economic development. Tuvalu generates income using various means, including the sale of coins and stamps, money sent back by islanders working overseas, sale of tuna fishing licenses to foreign fisheries, and lease of the country's Internet domain name, ".tv" to foreign firms. Another 10 percent of its annual budget is derived from the Tuvalu Trust Fund, a well-run overseas investment fund set up by the United Kingdom, Australia, and South Korea in 1987 to provide development assistance.

Although there is general respect for human rights, traditional customs and social norms condone discrimination against women and limit their roles in society. Violence against women is rare. Rape is a crime punishable by law, but spousal rape is not included in this definition. Prostitution is illegal, but no law specifically targets sexual harassment.

Uganda

Population: 26,100,000   **Political Rights:** 5
GNI/capita: $240   **Civil Liberties:** 4
Life Expectancy: 45   **Status:** Partly Free
Religious Groups: Roman Catholic (33 percent),
Protestant (33 percent), Muslim (16 percent),
indigenous beliefs (18 percent)
Ethnic Groups: Baganda (17 percent), Basogo (8 percent),
Ankole (8 percent), Iteso (8 percent), Bakiga (7 percent), Langi (6 percent),
Rwanda (6 percent), other (40 percent)
Capital: Kampala

Ten-Year Ratings Timeline (Political Rights, Civil Liberties, Status)

1995	1996	1997	1998	1999	2000	2001	2002	2003	2004
5,4PF	4,4PF	4,4PF	4,4PF	5,5PF	6,5PF	6,5PF	6,4PF	5,4PF	5,4PF

Overview:

During 2004, the Constitutional Court voided restrictions on the freedom of political parties to function. The government had also recommended to parliament that multiparty politics, which had been limited since 1986, be restored. The government, however, is also proposing lifting the two-term restriction on the presidency, which would allow incumbent Yoweri Museveni to be a candidate in elections scheduled for 2006. This change would require voters' approval in a 2005 referendum. Intermittent violence in the North continued throughout the year.

In the years following its independence from Britain in 1962, Uganda experienced considerable political instability. An increasingly authoritarian president, Milton

Obote, was overthrown by Idi Amin in 1971. Amin's brutality made world headlines as hundreds of thousands of people were killed. His 1978 invasion of Tanzania finally led to his demise, as Tanzanian forces and Ugandan exiles routed Amin's army. After Obote returned to power in 1980 in fraudulent elections, he and his backers from northern Uganda savagely repressed his critics, who were primarily from southern Ugandan ethnic groups.

Obote was ousted for a second time in a 1985 army coup. Conditions continued to worsen until the Museveni-led National Resistance Army entered the capital of Kampala in January 1986 and assumed power. The new government imposed a ban on most formal political party activities, including the sponsoring of candidates for elections and the staging of political rallies. In June 2000, a referendum was held on whether to lift the ban. Almost 90 percent of those voting supported continuation of the de facto single-party system; however, opposition parties had called for a boycott, and overall voter turnout was just over 50 percent.

Museveni and his National Resistance Movement (NRM) comfortably won presidential and legislative elections in 2001. However, the elections were held under conditions that called their legitimacy into question. Reports by human rights groups and donor countries concerning the March presidential election noted that state media and other official resources were mobilized in support of Museveni's successful candidacy, and that the ban on most formal party activities further hindered the opposition. Most observers believe, however, that Museveni would have won in an open contest and described the actual balloting and vote-tabulation processes as largely transparent. The opposition, which claimed that the elections were rigged, boycotted the subsequent parliamentary elections in June; the NRM's comfortable majority was buttressed by dozens of special-interest representatives nominated by the president.

In 2002, parliament passed the Political Parties and Organizations Act, putting forth the conditions under which political parties could be registered and could fully function. In 2003, the Constitutional Court ruled that parts of the law were unconstitutional, as they effectively prevented political parties from carrying out their activities. Despite the Constitutional Court's ruling, the NRM continues to dominate the nation's political life through direct and indirect means.

Regional tensions diminished somewhat in 2003, as Ugandan military forces withdrew from the eastern part of the Democratic Republic of Congo (DRC). These units had been sent to suppress rebels who had been perpetrating attacks across the border into Uganda.

International human rights groups, however, have criticized Uganda for continuing to support armed militias in eastern DRC in 2004. Tensions with Rwanda over influence in the region have remained high. In addition, a cult-based guerrilla movement, the Lord's Resistance Army (LRA), continued a gruesome insurgency in northern Uganda, with human rights violations committed on both sides.

Uganda has 1.5 million people living with HIV or AIDS. The latest records show that the rate of prevalence has gradually fallen from a national average of 30 percent in 1992 to about 6 percent today, the lowest in the sub-Saharan region.

Political Rights and Civil Liberties: Ugandans do not have the right to elect their government democratically. The only open multiparty elections were held in 1961 in preparation for the country's independence from Britain. In 1986, arguing that majoritarian democracy exacerbates religious and ethnic tensions in Africa, President Yoweri Museveni substituted a "no-party" system with only one, supposedly nonparty political organization—the NRM—allowed to operate unfettered. Uganda's 1995 constitution extended the ban for five years until the results of a 2000 referendum on the establishment of a multiparty system, in which the electorate approved the status quo. In 2004, the government sent to parliament its official recommendation that multiparty politics, which had been limited since 1986, be restored. At the same time, however, it also proposed lifting the two-term restriction on the presidency, which would allow incumbent president Museveni to be a candidate in elections scheduled for 2006. These proposals are subject to parliamentary approval and a referendum, which would be held in 2005.

Opposition parties have continued to protest about restrictive party registration requirements and the predominant status of the NRM. Other controversial issues include federalism, voter and candidate eligibility, the use of government resources to support NRM candidates, and the use of illegal paramilitary groups such as the Kalangala Action Plan to intimidate voters.

Parliament asserts some independence vis-à-vis the executive branch. High-level government officials have been censured, and several government actions and policies have been influenced or altered as a result of parliamentary oversight.

Some governmental corruption has been reported in the media. The inspector-general of government has accused the government and courts of frustrating the fight against corruption. He said cases took many years in court and culprits were not prosecuted. Under the 1995 constitution, new institutions were set up to investigate corruption and human rights violations and promote the return to democratic governance. These have made some headway in the fight against corruption and abuse of office by public officers, although a number of alleged corrupt acts by government officials have not been fully pursued and prosecuted. Uganda was ranked 102 out of 145 countries surveyed in the 2004 Transparency International Corruption Perceptions Index.

There is some freedom of expression. Independent print media outlets, including more than two dozen daily and weekly newspapers, are often highly critical of the government and offer a range of opposition views. Several private radio and television stations report on local political developments. Buttressed by legislation limiting press freedoms, however, the government at times selectively arrests or harasses journalists. A sedition law remains in force and is applied selectively to journalists and others who hold views that are at variance with those of the NRM. The largest newspapers and broadcasting facilities that reach rural areas remain state owned. Journalists have asked parliament to enact a freedom-of-information act.

There is no state religion, and freedom of worship is constitutionally protected and respected. Various Christian sects and the country's Muslim minority practice their creeds freely. The 2003 U.S. Department of State Report on International Religious Freedom commended the extent to which religious freedom is promoted in Uganda. Academic freedom is generally respected.

Freedom of association and assembly is officially recognized. The government has demonstrated increased respect for these rights in the constitution but continues to place some restrictions on them in practice. Nongovernmental organizations

(NGOs) currently make a significant contribution to Uganda's social, economic, cultural, and political life. They encourage the expression of different views and, significantly, have been willing to address politically sensitive issues. Local human rights organizations have shown an increasing interest in monitoring abuses and in conducting advocacy activities in comparison with their past focus on less controversial human rights education activities. The existence and activities of NGOs are, however, subject to stringent legal restrictions. The government continues to control civil society groups through the manipulation of their registration requirements, compelling NGOs to be nonsectarian and nonpolitical through the Non-Government Organizations Act. Security forces have halted numerous political rallies, some through force, and leading opposition activists have been harassed and, sometimes, subjected to arbitrary arrest.

The National Organization of Trade Unions, the country's largest labor federation, is independent of the government and political parties. An array of essential workers are barred from forming unions. Strikes are permitted only after a lengthy reconciliation process.

The judiciary is still influenced by the executive despite increasing autonomy. The Constitutional Court's interpretation that parts of the Political Parties and Organizations Act were unconstitutional showed considerable resolve to uphold independence and liberalism. However, sensitive human rights issues such as police brutality, rape, domestic violence, and vigilante justice remain serious concerns. Prolonged pretrial detention, inadequate resources, the army's occasional refusal to respect civilian courts, and poor judicial administration combine to impede the fair exercise of justice.

Prison conditions are difficult, especially in local jails. More than 500 prisoners die annually as a result of poor diet, sanitation, and medical care. Although there is registered progress toward the improvement of conditions in the prisons, conditions in both local administration and centrally administered prisons are poor. Pretrial detainees comprise more than half of the prison population.

The 2002 Suppression of Terrorism Bill, which defines any act of violence or threat of violence for political, religious, economic, or cultural ends as a terrorist act, imposes harsh penalties on suspected terrorists and has raised fears that it could be used against political opponents. The unlawful possession of arms is also defined as terrorism. Publishing news that is "likely to promote terrorism" can result in up to 10 years' imprisonment.

The Uganda Human Rights Commission 2003 report highlighted serious human rights violations by both rebel groups, including the LRA and the Uganda People's Defense Forces (UPDF). Torture by the security forces has continued despite the government's assurance that there is no institutionalized sanction of its use. The report also commended some elements of the security forces for protecting the rights to life and property amid challenges posed by armed robbers and the LRA. The northern part of the country has been racked by an LRA insurgency for more than 18 years. Nearly 1.6 million people have been displaced, 20,000 children have been abducted by the LRA, and thousands more have been caught up in the fighting between the UPDF and the LRA, which is thought to be composed of 80 percent children. Both the UPDF and the LRA have been accused of systematic human rights abuses.

Manipulation and exploitation of ethnic divisions pose a serious, continuing threat to peace in Uganda. Baganda people in the country's South continue to demand more recognition of their traditional kingdom. Proposed legislation, however, may make traditional chiefs subject to removal from office by the government. Northern ethnic groups complain of official neglect; that region especially is subject to continuing guerrilla activities.

Although the constitution enshrines the principle of equality between women and men, discrimination against women remains pronounced, especially in rural areas. Incidences of domestic violence and sexual abuse, including rape, are often not registered by police and are rarely investigated. There are no laws protecting women from domestic violence; draft laws such as the Domestic Relations Bill and the Sexual Offenses Act have been introduced in parliament but have not been approved. Cultural practices like female genital mutilation continue to exist. Up to 12,000 children in the conflict-affected districts of northern Uganda are estimated to have been abducted by the LRA since June 2002 alone. The Uganda Human Rights Commission and other NGOs indicate that sexual abuse of minors is increasing.

Uganda has legislated quotas for women officials in all elected bodies from village councils to the national parliament. Almost 20 percent of Uganda's parliament is female. One-third of local council seats must, by law, go to women.

Ukraine

Population: 47,400,000　**Political Rights:** 4
GNI/capita: $780　**Civil Liberties:** 3*
Life Expectancy: 68　**Status:** Partly Free
Religious Groups: Ukrainian Orthodox [Kiev Patriarchate (19 percent), Moscow Patriarchate (9 percent)], Ukrainian Greek Catholic (6 percent), Ukrainian
Ethnic Groups: Ukrainian (78 percent), Russian (17 percent), other (5 percent)
Capital: Kyiv
Ratings Change: Ukraine's civil liberties rating improved from 4 to 3 due to increases in media independence and associational rights resulting from widespread civic mobilization protesting fraudulent elections in November.

Ten-Year Ratings Timeline (Political Rights, Civil Liberties, Status)

1995	1996	1997	1998	1999	2000	2001	2002	2003	2004
3,4PF	3,4PF	3,4PF	3,4PF	3,4PF	4,4PF	4,4PF	4,4PF	4,4PF	4,3PF

Overview:　As 2004 drew to a close, opposition reformers led mass non-violent public demonstrations against voter fraud in the second round of Ukraine's November presidential election. The "Orange Revolution" protests involved as many as one million participants. The upsurge in public demonstrations also contributed to opening up Ukraine's media, particularly TV and radio, which formerly had been under the tight control of the executive branch.

In December 1991, Ukraine's voters ratified a declaration of independence from the U.S.S.R. and elected Leonid Kravchuk president. In 1994, Communists won a plurality in parliamentary elections, and Leonid Kuchma, a former director of the U.S.S.R.'s largest missile production facility, defeated Kravchuk in the presidential poll. In the first years of his presidency, Kuchma struggled against a Communist-influenced parliament to effect reforms. However, over time, his government became the target of domestic and international criticism for extensive and high-level corruption and for the erosion of political and free speech rights.

In the 1999 presidential election, Kuchma defeated Communist Party leader Petro Symonenko in the second round of voting with 56.21 percent of the vote; Symonenko received 37.5 percent. Observers declared the election unfair because of harassment of independent media, biased coverage by state media, intimidation of candidates and their supporters, and illegal campaigning by state officials. The murder in 2000 of independent journalist Heorhiy Gongadze, credible evidence that appeared to implicate Kuchma in the journalist's abduction, and revelations contained in secretly recorded conversations of the president's conversations all contributed to sparking mass public demonstrations and calls for the president's dismissal.

Despite polls showing that reform-minded Prime Minister Viktor Yushchenko had an approval rating of 63 percent, a coalition of the Communist Party and parties controlled by economic oligarchs ousted Yushchenko in April 2001; he was replaced by Anatoly Kinakh.

The Organization for Security and Cooperation in Europe declared that the March 2002 parliamentary elections had "brought Ukraine closer to meeting international commitments and standards for democratic elections." However, reformers and domestic election monitors accused government authorities of falsifying the vote—particularly in single-mandate districts, where opposition candidates did poorly and where pro-government candidates captured some three-quarters of all seats. Yushchenko's Our Ukraine bloc emerged as the single largest political force in the party-list vote, marking the first electoral success for the democratic opposition since independence. However, the pro-presidential For a United Ukraine bloc received enough post-election support from the Social Democratic Party of Ukraine–United, independent candidates—and even some members of Our Ukraine—to create a parliament majority. Nevertheless, the success of Yushchenko's electoral bloc in the party-list vote signaled the growing strength of democratic forces in the country and galvanized thousands who took to the streets during the year to demonstrate against Kuchma's growing authoritarianism and corruption.

After the election, Ukraine continued to be plagued by pervasive corruption and ongoing violations of basic rights. Kuchma came under increased scrutiny from Western and other democratic leaders because of evidence—believed to be credible by the U.S. government—that he had authorized the sale of a powerful radar system to Saddam Hussein's Iraq in violation of a UN embargo.

Kinakh remained prime minister until November 2002, when Kuchma dismissed him, ostensibly for failing to implement economic reforms. He was replaced by Viktor Yanukovych, a former convicted felon and representative of the Russian-speaking Donbas region, where economic oligarchs tightly controlled the local media and political life.

With the ascendancy in 2002 of Kuchma's chief of staff, Viktor Medvedchuk, authoritarian policies were reinforced amid unassailable evidence of pervasive government interference in the media through instructions, known as *temnyky* (theme directives). These directives were issued weekly, and failure to comply could result in various forms of harassment, such as tax audits, canceled licenses, and libel suits.

In 2003, Ukraine's reintegration with Russia appeared to be strengthened with the signing on September 19 of an agreement to create a Common Economic Space that could eventually link the two countries with Belarus and Kazakhstan in a common market and customs union. In April 2004, amid street protests, Ukraine's parliament ratified the agreement.

The main political events of 2004 revolved around the October-November presidential election. Despite high economic growth in 2003 and 2004, opinion polls showed that incumbent pro-government politicians were generally out of favor and that opposition reformer Yushchenko was by far the most popular candidate and the likely winner of the presidential vote.

To reduce the chances of an opposition victory, the government tightened control over radio and television broadcasting. In January 2004, a lower court order that a major opposition newspaper, *Silski Visti*, be shut down after it had published two anti-Semitic articles. Opposition leaders pressed the editors to apologize for the publication of the articles, but charged that the banning of the paper was a government effort to silence opposition media; the paper continued to publish as it challenged the court ruling. U.S.-sponsored Radio Liberty programs were removed from the radio airwaves in February, and in March, a court ordered that transmitting equipment be seized from opposition station Radio Kontynent. A national cable television station, Channel 5, with a national audience of approximately 3 percent, was subjected to tax inspections and frequently silenced in key urban centers.

In June, opposition members of parliament denounced the sale—for $800 million—of the Kryvorizhstal steelworks to a consortium headed by Donetsk industrialist Rinat Akhmetov (a financial supporter of Yanukovych) and Kuchma's son-in-law, Viktor Pinchuk. An alternative bid of $1.5 billion with a further $1 billion in capital improvements from a consortium led by Britain's LNM and U.S. Steel was turned down by the State Property Fund. Reformers claimed the bid process leading to privatization was rigged.

With Yushchenko and other opposition presidential candidates—including Socialist Party leader Oleksander Moroz—virtually banished from the national airwaves, opposition campaigning focused on mass meetings throughout the country. Once the election campaign moved into high gear in July, opposition candidates, especially front-runner Yushchenko, encountered harassment and obstacles to campaigning. Meeting halls were locked by local authorities at the last minute, public squares were blocked, and the campaign airplane was denied landing rights in nearby airports, creating delays as Yushchenko traveled from more distant airports to reach voters.

In September, with his grassroots campaign attracting large crowds around the country, Yushchenko took ill after a meeting with high-ranking State Security officials. His illness was life-threatening and debilitating, forcing the candidate off the campaign trail for several weeks. Forensic tests later determined the candidate had been poisoned with a large dose of dioxin in what was deemed an assassination attempt, only one of several attempts on his life.

In the first-round vote on October 31, which included significant evidence of voting irregularities, Yushchenko came in first among 24 candidates with 39.7 percent to 37.3 percent for Yanukovych, who enjoyed strong official backing from Russian president Vladimir Putin. Incumbent President Kuchma did not run as the Constitution precluded his seeking a third term.

In the November 21 runoff, Yushchenko faced off with Yanukovych. Exit polls conducted by a consortium of polling groups led by the Democratic Initiatives Foundation, found Yushchenko had won comfortably by a 10 percent margin. However, preliminary results from the Central Election Commission (CEC) showed Yanukovych the winner by less than 3 percent. The CEC's results, moreover, showed a near 100 percent voter turnout in Yanukovych's home region of Donetsk (well above the national average of 78 percent) as well as massive last-minute infusions of absentee ballots in southern and eastern Ukraine. Opposition politicians went public with tapes of high-ranking executive-branch officials indicating a conspiracy to commit massive voter fraud by tampering with the CEC's computer server. The opposition and international and domestic monitors denounced the results as tainted and the putative winner, Yanukovych, as "not legitimate."

As November 2004 drew to an end, millions massed peacefully in Kiev and other major Ukrainian cities to protest evidence of fraud in the second-round vote. Television journalists organized protests that helped surmount government censorship and content controls. There were signs that the Supreme Court and parliament would reexamine the results, which had not yet been officially published pending opposition court challenges. The "Orange Revolution" offered hope that the crisis would end in the eventual victory of due process, the likely election of Viktor Yushchenko, and an end to the corruption and criminality that had characterized the rule of President Leonid Kuchma.

Political Rights and Civil Liberties: Ukrainian voters are able to change their government democratically, although the bitterly disputed 2004 presidential election did not offer a level playing field in terms of legal protections, media access, and unfettered campaigning opportunities for opposition candidates. The elections were monitored by more than 4,000 foreign observers, the largest international mentoring effort in history, and 10,000 domestic monitors were deployed by the Committee of Voters of Ukraine. While some monitors faced impediments and hostility, monitors were generally able to collect significant data on election abuses. Despite the falsification of several million ballots and the rigging of the data coming to the computer server of the CEC, massive citizen protests offered hope that the attempt at voter fraud would fail and a democratically elected president would emerge from the process.

Citizens elect the president and delegates to the Verkhovna Rada, the 450-seat unicameral parliament. Under a 2001 election law adopted, half of parliament is elected in proportional voting and half in single-mandate constituencies. The president serves as the head of state and can appoint and dismiss the prime minister, who in turn appoints most other cabinet members in consultation with the president.

Ukraine has a number of political parties and coalitions, the most important of which are the pro-Yushchenko Our Ukraine bloc, the Yulia Tymoshenko bloc, the National Agrarian Party (linked to parliamentary speaker Yuri Lytvyn), the Socialist

Party, the Party of Regions (linked to Prime Minister Yanukovich), and the United Social Democrats (headed by President Kuchma's chief of staff, Viktor Medvedchuk). Corruption at the highest levels of the Kuchma administration was believed to be widespread, and there is significant petty corruption at the lower levels of authority. Ukraine was ranked 122 out of 146 countries surveyed in Transparency International's 2004 Corruption Perceptions Index.

The 1996 constitution guarantees freedom of speech and expression, but the government has frequently violated these rights through direct and well-documented interference in media content. In October and November, journalists organized protests and hunger strikes against state control of media content. After the second-round presidential vote and amid massive street protests, controls over journalists were removed at private national TV channels 1+1, Novy Kanal, and ICTV.

During the months leading up to the 2004 presidential election, two small independent television broadcasters, cable station Channel Five (with a 3 percent national audience in November 2004) and Era-TV (which broadcasts in the mornings and late evenings through a licensing arrangement with state television) were crucial independent sources of news and information. Independent and opposition newspapers were published throughout the year and appeared in enlarged editions during the weeks leading up to the presidential vote. The rural antigovernment newspaper *Silski Visti* challenged a court order to cease publication and expanded its circulation in special editions to six million copies during the period between the first and second round of the elections.

As 2004 ended, opposition figures, who throughout the year had been frequently subjected to unbalanced reporting on nationwide television, began to appear and speak directly to the public on news and interview programs. Until November, state media reflected a pro-government bias, while private media outlets typically reflected the views of their owners, usually pro-government oligarchs.

Journalists who report on corruption or criticize the government are particularly subject to harassment and violence, and press freedom groups noted numerous such cases in 2004. Nearly 40 journalists have been murdered, and the killing of investigative journalist Heorhiy Gongadze remained unresolved amid significant evidence of a government cover-up. Under a law in effect since 2001, libel no longer carries criminal charges.

The constitution and the Law on Freedom of Conscience and Religion define religious rights in Ukraine, and these are generally well respected. There are limited restrictions on the activities of foreign religious organizations, and all religious groups with more than 10 members must register with the state. Acts of anti-Semitism are consistently investigated and condemned by state authorities. In 2004, political divisions emerged between religious denominations with clerics from the Ukrainian Orthodox Church–Kiev Patriarchate, the Ukrainian Greek Catholic Church, and Protestant denominations generally critical of the ruling elite. Many hierarchs and clerics from the Ukrainian Orthodox Church (Moscow Patriarchate) actively campaigned for the ruling elite's candidate for president, Prime Minister Viktor Yanukovych.

Academic freedom was generally respected in most disciplines, although students who engaged in opposition political activity were subject to threats of expulsion or suspension. Students were pressed in numerous universities to vote for the government candidate. Often these pressures were exerted by university administrators, including rectors and deans, who threatened students with expulsion from dormitories if high levels of support for Yanukovych were not forthcoming. New private universities played an important role in augmenting state-supported higher education, and their students played a key role as volunteers in election-monitoring efforts and in protests of voter fraud.

Ukraine has several thousand nongovernmental organizations and an increasingly vibrant civil society. The constitution guarantees the right to peaceful assembly but requires advance notification to government authorities. As 2004 progressed, civic groups—many of them led by young activists—became increasingly active in nonpartisan voter-education efforts and in preparations for election monitoring. In November, the strength of civil society was demonstrated in massive protests of voter fraud in which the authorities did not use force to interfere.

Trade unions function, but strikes and worker protests are infrequent. The leader of the country's largest national labor federation was forced to withdraw from an opposition parliamentary faction as the result of an orchestrated threat to his union leadership organized by allies of the presidential administration. A smaller independent labor federation that includes miners and railway workers is closely linked with democratic opposition parties.

The judiciary consists of the Supreme Court, regional courts, and district courts, as well as a Constitutional Court. The constitution guarantees equality before the law, but the president, members of parliament, and judges are immune from criminal prosecution unless parliament consents. The judiciary is inefficient and subject to corruption. Although the Constitutional Court as a rule has often functioned independently, the retirement in 2003 of its well-regarded chief justice raised questions about its ongoing independence. However, as 2003 drew to an end, there were signs the Supreme Court would take an objective look at the massive array of evidence suggesting voting fraud and a stolen election. Other courts traditionally have lacked independence. Judges are often penalized for independent decision making, and there is significant evidence of routine interference in judicial decisions by the executive branch.

In 2002, the Council of Europe's Committee for the Prevention of Torture issued a report that criticized the Ukrainian police for using methods of interrogation, including electric shocks, cigarette burns, asphyxiation, and suspension by the arms or legs.

In response to ongoing allegations of criminal attacks on opposition figures, in 2003, the prosecutor-general in charge of investigating these cases was dismissed from office and replaced with an official analyst regarded to be more resolutely loyal to the president.

While the country's Roma population suffers from discrimination, the government has actively interceded to protect the rights of most ethnic and minorities, including the Jewish minority and the Turkic Crimean Tatar community.

The government generally respects personal autonomy and privacy, and the constitution guarantees individuals the right to own property, to work, and to engage in entrepreneurial activity. However, crime, corruption, and the slow pace of economic reform have effectively limited these rights. In 2001, the Constitutional Court struck down the country's Soviet-era *propiska* system, which had required individuals to register with the Interior Ministry in their place of residence. Opponents of the provision had long argued that the regulation violated freedom of movement. Property rights are generally respected, unless the interests of oligarch clans are involved. In such cases, cronyism and protection of insider interests prevail.

Gender discrimination is prohibited under the constitution, but women's rights were not a priority for government officials. In some settings, women face discrimination in employment, but there is little effective redress through existing antidiscrimination mechanisms. The sexual trafficking of women abroad for the purpose of prostitution remains a major problem and a threat to women's rights and security.

United Arab Emirates

Population: 4,200,000
GNI/capita: $20,217
Life Expectancy: 74
Political Rights: 6
Civil Liberties: 6
Status: Not Free
Religious Groups: Muslim [Shia (16 percent)] (96 percent), other (4 percent)
Ethnic Groups: Emirati (19 percent), other Arab and Iranian (23 percent), South Asian (50 percent), European and East Asian (8 percent)
Capital: Abu Dhabi

Ten-Year Ratings Timeline (Political Rights, Civil Liberties, Status)

1995	1996	1997	1998	1999	2000	2001	2002	2003	2004
6,5NF	6,5NF	6,5NF	6,5NF	6,5NF	6,5NF	6,5NF	6,5NF	6,6NF	6,6NF

Overview:
Sheikh Zayed bin Sultan Al Nahyan, president of the United Arab Emirates (UAE) since its founding, died in 2004, setting off a transition of power to the next generation in the ruling family.

For most of its history, the territory of the UAE—a federation of seven separate emirates formerly known as the Trucial States—was controlled by various competing tribal forces. Attacks on shipping in waters off the coast of this territory led British forces to conduct raids against the tribes in the nineteenth century. In 1853, the tribal leaders signed a treaty with the United Kingdom agreeing to a truce, which led to a decline in the raids on shipping. Though never formal British colonies, the territories were provided protection by the British, and tribal leaders of the emirates often referred their disputes to the United Kingdom for mediation.

In 1971, the United Kingdom announced that it was ending its treaty relationships with the seven emirates of the Trucial States, as well as Bahrain and Qatar. Six of the seven states entered into a federation called the United Arab Emirates, and Ras al-Khaimah, the seventh state, joined in 1972. The 1971 provisional constitution kept significant power in the hands of each individual emirate.

In contrast to many of its neighbors, the UAE has achieved some success in diversifying its economy beyond dependence on the petroleum sector, building a leading free-trade zone in Dubai and a major manufacturing center in Sharjah, as well as investing resources to develop its profile as a leading center for tourism in the region. In 2001, the government cracked down on corruption with arrests of senior officials. In the wake of the September 11, 2001, attacks on the World Trade Center and Pentagon, the government introduced reforms in its financial services and banking sectors to cut down on terrorist financing.

Economic reform has not been matched by political reform in the UAE, which has a closed political system in which the views of citizens are not taken into account. Recent reforms undertaken in the governance sector are generally more closely related to issues of trade, commerce, and the economy than to the enhancement of political rights and civil liberties. Political power remains in the hands of traditional tribal leaders.

After the death of President Sheikh Zayed in 2004, the UAE's Supreme Council of Rulers selected Zayed's oldest son, Khalifa bin Zayed Al Nahyan, as president. Mohammed bin Zayed Al Nahyan replaced Khalifa as crown prince. This shift in power to the new generation did not result in any meaningful and substantive changes in the UAE's power structure, with the ruling family maintaining a firm grip on its monopoly of political power.

Political Rights and Civil Liberties:

Citizens of the UAE cannot change their government democratically. The UAE has never held an election. All decisions about political leadership rest with the dynastic rulers of the seven separate emirates of the UAE in what is known as the Supreme Council of Rulers, the highest executive and legislative body in the country. These seven leaders select a president and vice president, and the president appoints a prime minister and cabinet. The UAE has a 40-member Federal National Council with delegates appointed by the seven leaders every two years. However, the council serves only as an advisory body, reviewing proposed laws and questioning federal government ministers.

The UAE does not have political parties. Rather, the allocation of positions in the government is largely determined by tribal loyalties and economic power. Abu Dhabi, the major oil producer in the UAE, has controlled the presidency of the UAE since its inception. Citizens have limited opportunities to express their interests through traditional consultative sessions.

The UAE is considered among the least corrupt countries in the region, with fewer reported cases of official corruption in 2004; it was ranked 29 out of 146 countries surveyed in Transparency International's 2004 Corruption Perceptions Index.

Although the UAE's constitution provides for some freedom of expression, in practice the government severely restricts this right. The Printing and Publishing Law (No. 15 of 1980) applies to all media and prohibits "defamatory material and negative material about presidents, friendly countries, [and] religious issues, and [prohibits] pornography." Laws prohibit criticism of the government, ruling families, and friendly governments, and they also include vague provisions against statements that threaten society. As a consequence, journalists commonly practice self-censorship, and the leading media outlets in the UAE frequently publish government statements without criticism or comment. However, Dubai has a "Media Free Zone," where few restrictions have been reported on print and broadcast media produced for audiences outside of the UAE. Internet access is widely available, though there were reports that a leading Internet service provider, the government-owned Etisalat, blocked sites deemed morally objectionable from time to time.

The UAE's constitution provides for freedom of religion. Islam is the official religion, and the majority of citizens are Sunnis. However, Shia minorities are free to worship without interference. The government controls content in nearly all Sunni mosques. Academic freedom is limited, with the Ministry of Education censoring textbooks and curriculums in both public and private schools.

The government places limits on freedom of assembly and association. Small discussions on politics in private homes are generally tolerated, but there are limits on citizens' ability to organize broader gatherings. Public meetings require government permits. All nongovernmental organizations (NGOs) must register with the Ministry of Labor and Social Affairs, and registered NGOs reportedly receive subsidies from the government.

The UAE has no labor unions, although the government has mediated labor disputes. Foreign nationals, who make up the vast majority of the UAE's workforce, are generally not offered labor protections. In July 2003, the government issued a ban on a long-standing practice of employers forcing foreign employees to surrender their passports as a condition of employment.

The judiciary is not independent, with court rulings subject to review by the UAE's political leadership. An estimated 40 to 45 percent of judges in the court system are noncitizen foreign nationals. Although the constitution bans torture, Sharia (Islamic law) courts sometimes impose flogging sentences for individuals found guilty of drug use, prostitution, and adultery. In July 2004, the UAE passed new legislation setting stricter punishments for crimes involving terrorism, including financing terrorism and harboring terrorists.

Discrimination against noncitizens, who make up the vast majority of the population and at least half of the workforce, occurs in many aspects of life, including employment, access to education, housing, and health care.

The constitution provides for equality before the law but does not specifically mention gender equality. In practice, women's social, economic, and legal rights are not always protected because of incomplete implementation of the law and traditional biases against women. Women are under represented in government, although there are small signs of limited openings for women, with women receiving appointments at various levels of government in 2004. Sheikha Lubna Al Qasimi became the first woman minister in the UAE when she was appointed minister of the economy and planning. In addition, Sheikh Sultan Al Qasimi, the ruler of Sharja, one of the seven emirates, appointed five women to Sharja's consultative council.

Human trafficking and forced labor remain problems in the UAE. Despite a July 2002 ban on using children under the age of 15 as jockeys in camel races, several human rights monitors report continued problems with young children from South Asia being kidnapped or sold by relatives into slavery and trafficked to the UAE for use as camel jockeys in races. There are numerous allegations of physical abuse and malnourishment aimed at keeping the children jockeys under desired weight levels.

United Kingdom

Population: 59,700,000 **Political Rights:** 1
GNI/capita: $25,510 **Civil Liberties:** 1
Life Expectancy: 78 **Status:** Free
Religious Groups: Anglican, Roman Catholic,
Muslim, Protestant, Sikh, Hindu, Jewish
Ethnic Groups: English (82 percent), Scottish (10 percent),
Irish (2 percent), Welsh (2 percent), other [including Indian
and Pakistani] (4 percent)
Capital: London

Ten-Year Ratings Timeline (Political Rights, Civil Liberties, Status)

1995	1996	1997	1998	1999	2000	2001	2002	2003	2004
1,2F	1,2F	1,2F	1,2F	1,2F	1,2F	1,2F	1,1F	1,1F	1,1F

Overview:
The Labour government of Prime Minister Tony Blair suffered erosion in its popularity in 2004 owing to difficult conditions in Iraq and the slower-than-promised improvements in public services on which Labour has campaigned. Labour did poorly in the June elections for the European Parliament, whereas a party hostile to Britain's European Union (EU) membership achieved its best-ever result. This was partly due to British voters' concerns about the EU's draft constitution, finalized shortly before the elections.

The English state emerged before the turn of the first millennium and was conquered by Norman French invaders in 1066. Celtic-speaking Wales and Ireland were incorporated into the kingdom over the course of the centuries; Scotland joined on more favorable terms with the creation of Great Britain in 1707. The Glorious Revolution of 1688-1689 began a gradual—but eventually total—assertion of the powers of parliament, as Britain became one of the world's first democracies, with a significant extension of voting rights in 1832.

Separatism has persisted in the Celtic lands; most of Ireland won independence after World War I, with Protestant-majority Northern Ireland remaining part of the United Kingdom. Most of Britain's global empire, the most important portion of which was India, became independent in the decades after World War II, although many of Britain's former colonies maintain links with the country through the Commonwealth. Significant powers were devolved to a Scottish Parliament (and fewer to a Welsh assembly) established by the current Labour Party government, which was first elected in 1997 and was reelected in 2001. Peace negotiations restored home rule to Northern Ireland in 1998, but home rule has since been suspended because of breakdowns in the peace process.

After nearly two decades of Conservative Party rule Blair's "New Labour," so called because of its radical shift from its socialist past, adopted Conservative-style positions on a number of issues and swept general elections in May 1997. In June 2001 parliamentary elections, the Labour Party secured a second term in office with another landslide victory, trouncing the opposition Conservative Party. The United

Kingdom's third largest party, the Liberal Democrats, increased its representation in Parliament.

Despite a promise to focus on public services, particularly the ailing health and transport systems, Blair's second term as prime minister has been dominated by his support of the U.S.-led war in Iraq. Blair supported George W. Bush, the U.S. president, in the UN Security Council and on the world stage, despite anger within his own Labour Party and demonstrations on the streets. After the end of the initial hostilities in Iraq, however, the government suffered renewed criticism surrounding the case it had made for the war in the run-up to the conflict. In particular, the government clashed with the BBC over a report that it had exaggerated the threat from Iraq's weapons of mass destruction. Though a report cleared the government of deception, the suicide of a government scientist who had been a source for the BBC damaged the government's reputation. At the same time, Michael Howard, who became leader of the Conservative Party in late 2003, was unable to offer a strong challenge to Blair and the Labour Party from the opposition benches in 2004.

In 2004, the EU completed negotiations on a new draft constitution. The British government claimed that it had successfully negotiated Britain's relatively Euroskeptic views into the draft. In particular, a proposal that could have seen EU foreign policy and tax policy be subjected to "qualified majority votes" (in which more populous countries have a larger vote) was not included; instead, Britain and the other 24 EU members will retain a veto in these areas. However, the opposition Conservative Party successfully pressured the government into promising to hold a referendum on the constitution, which Blair had initially resisted. There is a significant threat that Britain will vote no on the document when the referendum is held, preventing it from coming into force. British skepticism about the EU was further demonstrated by the European Parliament elections in June, in which the Conservatives beat Labour and the virulently anti-EU UK Independence Party came in third, winning 16 percent of the vote. Turnout at that election was just 38 percent.

Despite sustained increases in spending, the government has failed to deliver major improvements in public services, notwithstanding repeated promises to the electorate to do so. Some improvement has come, notably in health care. The Conservative Party, which failed to take advantage of the government's disappointing progress, was seen as lacking in fresh ideas and compelling leadership. Conservatives' support for the war in Iraq also made it difficult for the party to appear as a viable and meaningfully different alternative to Labour.

Northern Ireland's peace process, anchored by the Good Friday agreement of 1998, remains stalled since the suspension of the power-sharing government in Belfast in October 2002. This occurred after Sinn Fein, a hard-line Catholic nationalist party allied to the Irish Republican Army, was caught spying on ministers of the Northern Ireland government and on other parties. In new elections for the Northern Ireland Assembly in December 2003, Sinn Fein and the Protestant and loyalist Democratic Unionist Party did best, edging out their more moderate rivals on both sides. The two parties have not been able to work together to restore home rule to the province, which is run from London as long as the Northern Ireland government is suspended. Nonetheless, the two parties negotiated with each other through British and Irish government intermediaries in 2004, and a breakthrough on the subject of weapons decommissioning could lead to fresh elections in 2005.

Political Rights and Civil Liberties: The British can change their government democratically. Each of the 659 members of the House of Commons is elected in a single-member district. This procedure multiplies the power of the two largest parties, Labour and the Conservatives, at the expense of third parties. The Liberal Democrats are the most disadvantaged; although they won 16.8 percent of the vote in the 2001 election, they received only 7.9 percent of the seats in the House of Commons. The separation of powers is weak, with the prime minister and all members of his cabinet also being members of the legislature. The executive has in recent years become more powerful at the expense of the House of Commons. The monarch, currently Queen Elizabeth II, is the head of state but plays only a ceremonial role. The opposition party plays a crucial role in the Commons; although it is unable to block legislation, it holds ministers accountable in parliamentary debates that are widely covered in the press.

After a period of centralization under Conservative governments from 1979 to 1997, the Labour Party made constitutional reform a key part of its 1997 election platform. In government, it has delivered a far-reaching (though asymmetrical) devolution of power to Northern Ireland, Scotland, and Wales. The first elections to the Scottish Parliament and the Welsh Assembly were held in 1999. The Scottish body has more power (including some tax-raising powers) than its Welsh counterpart, largely because of stronger separatist sentiment in Scotland. Welsh nationalism is largely cultural; with official protection and encouragement, the number of Welsh-language speakers actually grew 17 percent from 1991 to 2001. The Northern Ireland Assembly was suspended in October 2002 after complications in the peace process.

The government is largely free of pervasive corruption. The United Kingdom was ranked 11 out of 146 countries surveyed in Transparency International's 2004 Corruption Perceptions Index.

The media market in Britain is free, lively, and competitive. Many daily newspapers across a broad spectrum of political opinions compete for readers. Although broadcasting is dominated by the state-owned BBC, the corporation is editorially independent of the government. In 2003, the BBC claimed that the government exaggerated evidence of Iraqi weapons of mass destruction, leading to an extensive inquiry that eventually exonerated the government. While the episode tarnished the reputations of both the government and the BBC, more generally, it was a sign of the healthy political debate that is possible in Britain. Internet access is not restricted by the government.

Although the Church of England and the Church of Scotland are established churches, the government both prescribes freedom of religion in law and protects it in practice. Scientology is not recognized as an official religion for charity purposes. Muslims and other religious minorities complain of discrimination. The government respects academic freedom.

Civic organizations and nongovernmental organizations are allowed to operate freely, and the freedom to assemble is respected, as demonstrated by massive protests against the government's participation in the Iraq war in February 2003. The right to organize in unions is protected. Trade unions have traditionally played a strong role in the Labour Party, though this is weakening as the party moves to the center and seeks a larger role for the private sector in traditional public sector areas, such as health care.

A historical oddity in the justice system was removed in 2003 when the post of

Lord Chancellor was abolished. The position, the second-oldest office in Britain after the monarchy, combined a legislative seat in the House of Lords, a senior executive position in the cabinet, and a powerful judicial position as, effectively, the top judge in the country. As such, it was a serious breach of the separation of powers (already weak in Britain), and the Labour government abolished it in 2003, creating the cabinet position of secretary for constitutional affairs. However, the top judges in the land remain the Law Lords, a combination of legislative and judicial authority that weakens judicial independence. The police maintain high professional standards, and prisons generally meet international standards.

Britain has large numbers of immigrants and second-generation children of immigrants, who receive equal treatment under the law. In practice, their living standards are lower than the national average. Women also receive equal treatment under the law, but are under-represented in politics and the top levels of business.

United States of America

Population: 293,600,000 **Political Rights:** 1
GNI/capita: $35,400   **Civil Liberties:** 1
Life Expectancy: 77   **Status:** Free
Religious Groups: Protestant (52 percent), Roman
Catholic (24 percent), Mormon (2 percent),
Jewish (1 percent), Muslim (1 percent), other (20 percent)
Ethnic Groups: White (77 percent), black (13 percent), Asian
(4 percent), Amerindian (1.5 percent), Pacific Islander (0.3 percent), other (4 percent)
Capital: Washington, DC

Ten-Year Ratings Timeline (Political Rights, Civil Liberties, Status)

1995	1996	1997	1998	1999	2000	2001	2002	2003	2004
1,1F	1,1F	1,1F	1,1F	1,1F	1,1F	1,1F	1,1F	1,1F	1,1F

Overview: In a year of intensified controversy over the domestic and international implications of the war in Iraq and the war on terrorism, the dominating political event of 2004 was the election of President George W. Bush to a second term. Bush won by a 3 percent margin, despite a series of investigations that called into question the administration's rationale for invading Iraq and criticized aspects of its conduct in the war on terrorism. There were, in addition, disturbing revelations of torture and prisoner abuse in U.S.-run facilities in Iraq and allegations of prisoner abuse at the U.S.-maintained detention camp in Guantanamo Bay, Cuba.

The United States of America was founded in 1776 during a revolution against British colonial rule. The current system of government began functioning in 1789, following the ratification of the country's constitution. Because the founders of the United States distrusted concentrated government power, they set up a system in which the federal government has three competing centers of power—executive, legislative, and judicial branches—and they left many powers with the state governments and the citizenry.

In 2000, George W. Bush of the Republican Party was certified as the forty-third president of the United States following one of the closest and most controversial elections in the country's history. Despite having lost the popular vote to the Democratic nominee, former vice president Al Gore, by 47.88 percent to 48.39 percent, Bush won the Electoral College—which under the U.S. system determines the presidential election—by a narrow margin of 271 to 266. A third candidate, Ralph Nader, representing the environmentally oriented Green Party, received slightly less than 3 percent of the popular vote. An even greater source of controversy during the election was the outcome of the vote in the state of Florida, which was ultimately decided in Bush's favor by a 5-4 vote of the U.S. Supreme Court.

Bush achieved reelection in 2004 after one of the country's most bitterly contested and polarized presidential campaigns. The Democratic Party nominee, Senator John Kerry, a decorated veteran of the Vietnam War, accused the president of having misled the country about the reasons for launching the war in Iraq in 2003 and asserted that the Bush administration was mishandling the postwar occupation, which had claimed the lives of 1,000 U.S. troops. Nevertheless, voters whose principal motivation was national security tended to favor Bush, as did those who were influenced by what came to be known as "moral values," an elastic concept that, in the context of the 2004 election, referred principally to a stance against abortion, same-sex marriage, and the perceived exclusion of religion from the public sphere.

Bush and his running mate, Vice President Dick Cheney, gained 51 percent of the national vote to 48 percent for Kerry and his running mate, Senator John Edwards. According to the Electoral College, Bush won with 286 electoral votes to Kerry's 252. The clear-cut nature of the outcome helped dispel some of the cloud that hung over the 2000 presidential contest. In contrast, the 2004 election was conducted without major controversy, although concerns lingered regarding the Ohio vote, and some voting districts reported problems with long lines on election day and malfunctioning equipment. The Organization for Security and Cooperation in Europe sent an observer mission to the United States to monitor the elections and issued a report that polling procedures adhered to international standards.

The 2004 contest was the first conducted since the adoption of legislation designed to curb the influence of financial contributions in presidential politics. However, the election was the most expensive in U.S. history, with tens of millions spent by the campaigns, parties, and advocacy groups on television advertising alone. Both parties conducted extensive drives to get their voters to the polls, with the result that the turnout figure, at 58 percent, was the highest since 1968.

In addition to winning the presidency, the Republican Party increased its majorities in the House of Representatives and the Senate. In the Senate, the Republicans added four members to their majority; they now control the 100-seat chamber by a 55-44 margin, with 1 independent. In the House, the Republicans enhanced their majority by 3; they now hold 232 seats, compared with the Democrats' 202. One seat is held by an independent who usually votes with the Democrats.

Aside from the election, the United States was mainly preoccupied with the conflict in Iraq, where insurgents operating primarily in the "Sunni triangle" continued to kill U.S. troops, foreign workers, and Iraqi security officials and civilians. In

April, news media outlets published reports that revealed that U.S. troops were responsible for acts of abuse, torture, and sexual humiliation of Iraqi prisoners at the Abu Ghraib prison in Baghdad. The revelations were accompanied by shocking photographs, taken by prison guards, that showed prisoners in physically and sexually humiliating positions. Several of the guards responsible for the abuse were subsequently charged and placed before court-martial hearings. There were also charges of abuse of prisoners detained during the 2001 conflict in Afghanistan and interned at a U.S.-controlled facility in Guantanamo Bay, Cuba.

The prisoner abuse scandals occurred in the context of a debate over whether the United States should strictly adhere to the Geneva Convention in its treatment of prisoners captured in the course of the war on terrorism. A series of memorandums from the White House and the Defense Department argued that the Geneva accords need not be applied in cases involving terrorists or enemy combatants. Critics contended that such arguments contributed to an environment in which lower-level officials believed they had sanction to apply torture to prisoners in Iraq, Afghanistan, and Guantanamo.

Another controversy to emerge involved what were called "ghost prisoners"— alleged terrorists detained in various parts of the world and held in unspecified locations outside any judicial system or congressional oversight. This issue also reflected differences between the administration—which claims that existing laws and international covenants are inadequate instruments in cases of terrorism—and civil libertarians, who contend that the administration is routinely violating American and international laws. The administration has also drawn fire for its policy of "renditions," in which foreign nationals accused of involvement in terrorism are sent to foreign countries that have a reputation for tolerating torture of prisoners.

In addition to the furor over the treatment of prisoners, the Bush administration faced other problems related to its domestic conduct of the war on terrorism. The USA Patriot Act, a measure adopted in the wake of the terrorist assaults on the United States on September 11, 2001, continued to be a source of controversy. Legislation to modify the law was introduced in Congress, and federal courts rolled back some of its provisions. The Supreme Court and lower federal courts also issued rulings asserting jurisdiction over prisoners held at Guantanamo and elsewhere, rejecting the administration's claim that the prisoners were "enemy combatants" rather than prisoners of war subject to the dictates of international law.

In two noteworthy cases, the administration asserted that Jose Padilla and Yasser Hamdi, both of whom had claims to U.S. citizenship, were enemy combatants and were thus not entitled to normal constitutional protections. Both Padilla and Hamdi were incarcerated without formal charges or access to attorneys. After the Supreme Court issued a ruling that asserted that U.S. citizens held in military custody had the right to have their cases heard by an independent authority, Hamdi was released and left the United States for Saudi Arabia.

Political Rights and Civil Liberties: Citizens of the United States can change their government democratically. The United States has a bicameral legislature. The upper chamber, the Senate, consists of 100 members—two from each of the 50 states. Senators are elected to six-year terms. The lower chamber, the House of Representatives, consists of 435 members elected for two-year terms. Members of this chamber are elected directly by voters in the districts they represent. The president and vice president are elected for four-year terms. By constitutional provision, the president is limited to two terms in office.

In the U.S. federal political system, a great deal of government responsibility devolves to the 50 individual states. Most law enforcement matters are dealt with at the state level, as is education, and states have been given wide powers to raise revenues through various forms of taxation. Some states give citizens wide powers to influence legislation through institutions of direct democracy, such as referendums on wide-ranging issues like same sex marriage, tax rates, and immigrant rights.

In electing a president, the United States uses a unique system that combines a popular vote and the ballots cast by an electoral college. The Electoral College apportions votes to each state on the basis of population and congressional representation. The electors in a particular state then usually cast all their ballots for the candidate who won the popular vote in their state, no matter what the margin. Two states, Maine and Nebraska, have chosen to apportion their electoral votes between the candidates according to the percentage of the state's votes each receives, and other states are considering similar changes. The Electoral College vote determines the winner of the election. Under this system, it is possible for a candidate to win the presidency even though an opposing candidate may have won a greater number of popular votes nationwide. In 2000, this system led to the anomalous situation in which the winning candidate, George W. Bush, actually received fewer popular votes than his main opponent, Vice President Al Gore, the Democratic nominee.

Presidential election campaigns in the United States are long and expensive. The various candidates for the Democratic nomination began campaign activities in early 2003, nearly two years before the actual polling day. In 2001, Congress passed a law, the McCain-Feingold bill, designed to limit the impact of moneyed interests on presidential politics. Nevertheless, the two parties and the constituency and interest groups that support them have drawn on various methods to circumvent the spirit of the legislation, and the 2004 race was the most expensive ever, with a total expenditure of $1.2 billion, much of which was spent by advocacy groups rather than by the parties themselves.

The United States has an intensely competitive political system dominated by two major parties, the Republicans and the Democrats. The U.S. electoral system is based on a "first past the post," or majoritarian, system for legislative seats, which tends to discourage a multiplicity of parties. In addition, the U.S. system is characterized by legal and other hurdles that act to discourage the rise of new, independent parties. Yet, on occasion, candidates representing third parties or particular causes have had a significant impact on presidential politics. In 2004, however, the most prominent third-party candidate, Ralph Nader, gained only approximately 1 percent of the national vote.

A serious problem for American democracy is the widespread practice of drawing districts for the House of Representatives and for state legislatures that are designed to guarantee the election of a particular party or to protect incumbent legislators, whatever their party. This practice, known as "gerrymandering," has been a part of the American system since its inception. Recently, however, sophisticated computer techniques have strengthened the ability of the dominant party in a state to carve out districts that considerably limit the competitive nature of legislative elections. In the 2004 election for the House of Representatives, only five incumbents were defeated and in only 35 races did the winner receive 55 percent or less of the total vote.

The federal government has a high degree of transparency. A substantial number of auditing and investigative agencies function independently of party influence or the influence of incumbent officials. The press is generally vigorous in covering stories of official corruption, as it was in the case of the governors of the states of New Jersey and Connecticut, both of whom were forced to resign as a result of allegations of corruption. The efforts of these entities are reinforced by a number of private watchdog organizations that focus on such disparate issues as political campaign spending, open government, the impact of business lobbying on the legislative process, and the defense budget. The press also plays a major role in investigating and publicizing allegations of improprieties by officials at all levels. Federal agencies regularly place information relevant to their mandate on Web sites to broaden public access. The United States also has in place strict measures to reduce the level of corruption in the private sector. The most recent corporate governance legislation, the Sarbanes-Oxley Act of 2002, was enacted after a series of scandals involving inflated earnings reports by major corporations.

The United States has a free, diverse, and constitutionally protected press. In recent years, a debate has arisen over the impact of media consolidation, accomplished through the purchase of large press entities—television networks, newspapers, and weekly magazines—by giant corporations with little or no previous interest in journalism. During 2004, controversy erupted over the attempts by federal prosecutors to compel journalists to divulge the names of confidential sources. In all, eight journalists were threatened with contempt-of-court citations. In the most noteworthy case, a special prosecutor demanded that reporters reveal the identity of administration officials who might have leaked the fact that the wife of Ambassador Joseph Wilson, a critic of the administration's Iraq policies, was an undercover employee of the CIA. Several reporters were threatened with imprisonment by a federal judge involved in the case. Internet access is widespread, and Internet journalists and "bloggers" have become an increasingly important force in political coverage and commentary.

The United States has a long tradition of religious freedom. Adherents of practically every major religious denomination, as well as many smaller groupings, can be found throughout the country, and religious belief and religious service attendance is high. There is an ongoing debate over the role of religion in public life, often centered on the question of whether government subsidies to schools sponsored by religious denominations meet constitutional standards. Issues such as same sex marriage and so-called partial-birth abortion and even the place of the words "under God" in the Pledge of Allegiance are heavily loaded with religious overtones and serve to mobilize evangelical Christians—and their political counterparts—to engage in the political process.

Although a contentious debate has emerged over the university's role in society, academic life is notable for a healthy level of intellectual freedom. In 2004, academics and students participated in vigorous debates over public policy issues, especially the war in Iraq, the global economy, and U.S. policy toward Israel and Palestine. Organizations opposed to Israel's treatment of the Palestinians have organized campaigns on a number of campuses to encourage university administrations to withdraw investments from corporations doing business in Israel. A number of the country's prestigious universities have adopted policies of "political correctness" intended to combat harassment against traditionally marginalized groups. However, such policies are controversial as they may restrict the expression of opinions, usually voiced by political conservatives, that diverge from mainstream campus views.

Private discussion and public debate are vigorous. In general, the right to public protest is observed by public officials. A controversy emerged during the 2004 Republican Party national convention, held in New York City, over restrictions placed on the location and timing of public protests and over what civil libertarians called overly aggressive police tactics aimed at demonstrators. Serious restrictions were also placed on protest groups at the Democratic Party national convention in Boston. Likewise, during the election campaign period, the Bush campaign was criticized for segregating Kerry supporters in attendance at rallies from the rest of the assemblage or excluding them altogether.

Trade unions by law are guaranteed the right to organize workers and engage in collective bargaining with employers. The right to strike is also guaranteed. Over the years, however, the strength of organized labor has declined, to the point where less than 9 percent of the private workforce is represented by unions, one of the lowest figures among stable, economically advanced democracies. An important factor in labor's decline is the country's labor code, which is regarded as an impediment to organizing efforts. Union organizing efforts are also impeded by strong resistance from employers and the federal government's failure to strictly enforce the law against labor code violators. Several attempts to modify core labor laws have been defeated in Congress over the years. At the same time, trade unions remain an important force in political life. In recent years, unions have become more directly involved in Democratic Party affairs, and unions served as a crucial source of campaign funds and volunteer workers for the Democrats in the 2004 presidential election.

Judicial independence is respected, though the influence of the court system has become a source of sometimes bitter contention over the years, with critics claiming that judicial authority has expanded into areas of governance that are best left to the legislative branch. Despite a strong rule-of-law tradition, a number of controversies have emerged over the treatment of poor and especially minority defendants in criminal law cases. African Americans and Hispanics constitute a large portion of defendants in criminal cases involving murder, rape, assault, and robbery. The police in a number of large cities have been accused of using unnecessary force in dealing with black and Hispanic criminal suspects, although the number and intensity of complaints have declined in the past few years, and most urban police departments mandate some form of human rights training for new officers.

Civil liberty and other groups have advanced a broad critique of the criminal justice system, contending that there are too many Americans (especially minority group Americans) in prison, that prison sentences are often excessive, and that too many people are prosecuted for minor drug offenses. There are movements in several states toward shorter prison sentences and earlier releases for convicted felons. Nevertheless, the most recent survey showed that more than 2.2 million Americans—44 percent of whom were African American—were in federal, state, or local prisons.

Concern has also been raised about prison conditions, especially the disturbing levels of violence and rape and the reportedly inadequate medical attention for prisoners with mental illness. The United States has the highest rate of legal executions in the democratic world. As evidence of a growing controversy over the death penalty, several states have announced a moratorium on capital punishment while studies are undertaken on the death penalty's fairness. During 2003, 144 persons were sentenced to death in federal and state courts, the lowest figure in 30 years.

Civil libertarians and Arab American organizations have expressed concerns that the Justice Department, as part of its offensive against domestic terrorism, has engaged in the "racial profiling" of men who have come to the United States from countries in the Middle East or South Asia. In response, Justice Department officials contend that a measure of profiling is essential in the war against terrorism given the Middle Eastern or South Asian origins of the majority of those involved in terrorist plots against the United States. In its most recent annual report, the Federal Bureau of Investigation listed 149 instances of hate crimes against Arab Americans, which is a reduction from the level of complaints immediately following September 11, 2001.

Citizens of the United States enjoy a high level of personal autonomy. The right to own property is protected by law and is a jealously guarded part of the American "way of life," and business entrepreneurship is encouraged as a matter of government policy.

The United States is one of the world's most racially and ethnically diverse societies. In recent years, the country's population dynamics have shifted in important ways, as Americans of Latin American ancestry have replaced African Americans as the leading minority group and the percentage of whites in the population has declined somewhat. A complex variety of policies and programs are designed to protect the rights of minorities, including laws to prevent discrimination on the job, affirmative action plans for university admissions, quotas to guarantee representation in the internal affairs of some political parties, and policies to ensure that minorities are not treated unfairly in the apportionment of government-assistance efforts. African Americans, however, continue to lag in economic standing, education, and other social indicators. Black Americans are more likely to live in poverty, less likely to own businesses, less likely to have gained a university degree, and more likely to have served time in prison than members of other groups, including many recent immigrant groups.

The United States has a long history of liberal immigration policies. In recent years, there has been some debate over the degree to which new immigrants are assimilating into American society. Most observers, however, believe that the country has struck a balance that both encourages assimilation and permits new immigrants to maintain certain religious or cultural customs. The United States has in recent years not faced the kind of controversy that has erupted in other countries over the wearing of the *hijab* (headscarf) by Muslim girls in public schools or women in public buildings.

The U.S. government has been less successful in devising a policy for dealing with undocumented immigrants, several million of whom live and work in the country at any one time. Many immigrants' rights advocates assert that the country would not be able to meet labor needs if illegal immigration were curbed. At the beginning of his first presidential administration, Bush indicated he was prepared to reach an agreement with Mexico to establish policies to regulate the flow of migrant workers who cross the border into the United States. After the events of September 11, 2001, negotiations with Mexico were dropped, and the administration adopted a tougher stance toward undocumented workers and visitors whose visas have expired. In 2004, the administration introduced legislation that would grant amnesty to many undocumented workers and establish a guest-worker program aimed primarily at immigrants from Mexico.

The Bush administration has drawn particular criticism for policies that, civil libertarians contend, discriminate against immigrants and visa applicants from countries in the Middle East and South Asia. These measures subject those from predominantly Muslim countries to special registration requirements, interviews by law enforcement officials, and lengthy visa application procedures. Concern has also been expressed about the federal government's policy of holding asylum seekers in detention facilities while their applications are being assessed. At the same time, the United States has not reduced the number of legal immigrants allowed into the country, which is high by global standards.

A major issue in 2004 was the right of homosexuals to marry. Referendums to define marriage as between a man and a woman, thus denying marriage rights to same sex couples, were adopted in 11 states.

Women have made important strides toward equality over the past several decades. Women are heavily represented in the law, medicine, and journalism, and predominate in the university programs that train students for these professions. Although the average compensation of female workers is 80 percent of that for male workers, women with recent university degrees have effectively attained parity with men. Nonetheless, there remain many female-headed families that live in conditions of poverty.

Uruguay

Population: 3,400,000
GNI/capita: $4,340
Life Expectancy: 75
Political Rights: 1
Civil Liberties: 1
Status: Free
Religious Groups: Roman Catholic (66 percent), Protestant (2 percent), Jewish (1 percent), other (31 percent)
Ethnic Groups: White (88 percent), mestizo (8 percent), black (4 percent)
Capital: Montevideo

Ten-Year Ratings Timeline (Political Rights, Civil Liberties, Status)

1995	1996	1997	1998	1999	2000	2001	2002	2003	2004
2,2F	1,2F	1,2F	1,2F	1,2F	1,1F	1,1F	1,1F	1,1F	1,1F

Overview:

On October 31, 2004, Uruguayans broke 170 years of political hegemony by the country's two traditional parties to elect former mayor of Montevideo, Tabare Vasquez, as president, aligning the country with a regional shift to the left. Although he promised to join neighboring Brazil and Argentina in seeking closer relations with Fidel Castro's Cuba, Vazquez nonetheless showed some signs of moving to the political center, appointing moderate senator Danilo Astori as his choice for finance minister. Vasquez's Broad Front coalition also captured a majority of seats in both houses of congress in concurrent legislative elections.

After gaining independence from Spain, the Oriental Republic of Uruguay was established in 1830. The Colorado Party dominated a relatively democratic political system throughout the 1960s. However, from 1973 to 1985, the country was dominated by a military regime whose viciousness earned Uruguay the nickname "The Torture Chamber of Latin America."

In 1998, the country's other traditional party, the centrist National Party, racked by mutual accusations of corruption, joined the opposition Colorado Party in supporting the latter's presidential nominee, Jorge Batlle Ibanez, a five-time presidential candidate whose father and great-uncle had been respected Colorado Party presidents. Faced with dismal economic prospects and a choice between presidential candidates representing the moderate right or an eclectic left, in 1999, Uruguayans gave Batlle 52 percent of the vote, to 40 percent obtained by Vazquez. On taking office, the new president incorporated several National Party members into his cabinet.

Batlle immediately sought an honest accounting of the human rights situation under the former military regime. Batlle also showed equally firm determination to reduce spending and taxes and to privatize state monopolies. In 2001, crises in the rural sector and an increase in violent crime, in what was still one of Latin America's safest countries, dominated much of the public's attention, as did growing labor unrest.

A currency devaluation and default in Argentina at the end of 2001 shrank Uruguay's international reserves 80 percent in six months, with the country losing its coveted investment-grade status on Wall Street. By midyear of 2002, the government was forced to impose a weeklong bank holiday, Uruguay's first in 70 years, to staunch a run on the country's banks. The spillover effect from Argentina's economic crisis was blamed for a day of violence in August, when looters ransacked businesses and labor unions staged antigovernment protests that brought much of Uruguay's capital, Montevideo, to a standstill. In October, the National Party withdrew its members from Batlle's government.

Disputes with neighboring Brazil over regional free trade, and with Argentina over specific human rights issues festering since the 1970s, dominated Uruguay's political debate in 2003. The economy had shrunk by 11 percent in two years, and one of every three Uruguayans lived below the poverty line in the worst economic crisis in the country's history. A bond restructuring that year avoided a potentially catastrophic economic default and was accompanied by small economic rally.

Batlle also remained the region's only vociferous opponent of Cuba's leader, Fidel Castro. However, the luster of Batlle's human rights record dimmed after he chose as a naval attaché to Buenos Aires a navy captain accused of responsibility for the deaths of two Argentines when both countries were ruled by military dictatorships.

The October 2004 presidential and parliamentary elections proved to be a crushing defeat for the Colorado Party, whose presidential candidate, Guillermo Stirling won just 10 percent of the vote, as well as for the National Party and its standard bearer Jorge Larranaga, who garnered 34 percent. Vazquez, whose Broad Front coalition ranged from Christian Democrats to former left-wing Tupamaro guerrillas, captured 51 percent in the first round of voting to be elected president. The Broad Front enjoyed a similar rout in both houses of congress, where for the first time in many years, the party in government could count on a majority.

After fiercely opposing the privatization of state companies and the shrinking of the state's role in Uruguay's economy, the newly elected Vazquez, who during the campaign had promised moderate economic policies and an emphasis on helping the poor, faced the challenge of creating a stable macroeconomic framework and attracting foreign capital. Astori, the new finance minister, sought to reassure the private sector by promising clear rules for investors, a free-floating exchange rate, fiscal discipline, and an inflation-targeted monetary policy. However, questions also remained about the personal ties maintained by the leftist Vazquez to the country's former rightist military dictatorship during the 1980s.

Political Rights and Civil Liberties: Citizens of Uruguay can change their government democratically. The 2004 elections were free and fair despite isolated acts of violence registered against several parties' local headquarters. The 1967 constitution established a bicameral congress consisting of the 99-member Chamber of Deputies and the 31-member Senate, with every member serving a five-year term. The president is also directly elected for a five-year term. In 1999, for the first time, Uruguayan parties selected a single presidential candidate in open primary elections. Previously, the parties had fielded a number of candidates, and the candidates with the most votes then accumulated the votes cast for the others.

Uruguay has three major political parties: the Colorado Party, the National Party, and the Broad Front. The Broad Front swept to victory in 2004 in coalition with the smaller left-wing social democratic New Space party headed by the son of Zelmar Michelini, a former senator assassinated in 1976 in Buenos Aires by a joint Argentine-Uruguayan military commando unit.

Uruguay, long a haven for anonymous foreign bank deposits as a result of its strict banking secrecy laws, has also taken measures to regulate financial activities in order to reduce the potential for money laundering. October 1998 saw the passage of antidrug legislation that made narcotics-related money laundering a crime. The Financial Investigations Unit (FIU) was established in order to present more complete evidence in narcotics-related prosecutions. On the request of the Central Bank, financial institutions must provide certain information, and banks (including offshore banks), currency exchange houses, and stockbrokers are required to report transactions of more than $10,000. The FIU also requires all entities under its jurisdiction to report suspicious financial transactions to a financial information analysis unit.

The Transparency Law (Ley Cristal) entered into force in January 1999. It criminalizes a broad range of potential abuses of power by governmental officeholders, including the laundering of funds related to public corruption cases. It also requires financial disclosure statements to be filed by high-ranking officials. Public officials who know of a drug-related crime or incident and do nothing about it may be charged with a "crime of omission" under the Citizen Security Law. Uruguay ranks near the top of public transparency ratings for Latin America issued annually by Transparency International and in 2004 was cited by the group for a "perceived. . . fall in corruption" compared to the previous year. Uruguay was ranked 28 out of 146 countries surveyed in Transparency International's 2004 Corruption Perceptions Index.

Constitutional guarantees regarding free expression are generally respected. The press is privately owned, and broadcasting is both commercial and public. Numerous daily newspapers publish, many associated with political parties; there are also a number of weeklies. In 1996, a number of publications ceased production because of a government suspension of tax exemptions on the import of newsprint. In addition, a June 1996 decree requires government authorization to import newsprint. Internet access is unrestricted.

Freedom of religion is a cherished political tenet of democratic Uruguay and is broadly respected. The government does not restrict academic freedom.

Civic organizations have proliferated since the return of civilian rule. Numerous women's rights groups focus on violence against women, societal discrimination, and other problems. Freedom of assembly and association are provided by law in Uruguay, and the government generally respected those rights in practice. Workers exercise their right to join unions, bargain collectively, and hold strikes. Unions are well organized and politically powerful. Strikes are sometimes marked by violent clashes and sabotage.

The judiciary is relatively independent, but has become increasingly inefficient in the face of escalating crime, particularly street violence and organized crime. The court system is severely backlogged, and suspects under arrest often spend more time in jail than they would were they to be convicted and serve the maximum sentence for their crime. Allegations of police mistreatment, particularly of youthful offenders, have increased; however, prosecutions of such acts are also occurring more frequently. Prison conditions do not meet international standards.

President Jorge Batlle's stance in favor of human rights appeared to waiver in 2003. In November, Batlle announced that the case of the daughter-in-law of Argentine poet Juan Gelman, detained in Buenos Aires in 1976 and later allegedly made to disappear in Uruguay, was included in a 1986 law that effectively granted amnesty to Uruguay's military and police accused of committing rights violations during the military's 12-year regime. Efforts by that regime in the mid-1970s to kill U.S. congressman Ed Koch, a fierce critic of the Uruguayan military, were also confirmed by independent investigators in 2003 after having been first reported in 1993.

The small black minority continues to face discrimination. Uruguay's continuing economic crisis has forced thousands of formerly middle-class citizens to join rural migrants in the shantytowns ringing Montevideo.

Violence against women continues to be a problem. However, the government generally protects children's rights and welfare, and has placed the education and health of children as a top priority.

Uzbekistan

Population: 26,400,000   **Political Rights:** 7
GNI/capita: $310   **Civil Liberties:** 6
Life Expectancy: 70   **Status:** Not Free
Religious Groups: Muslim [mostly Sunni] (88 percent),
Eastern Orthodox (9 percent), other (3 percent)
Ethnic Groups: Uzbek (80 percent), Russian (6 percent),
Tajik (5 percent), Kazakh (3 percent), other (6 percent)
Capital: Tashkent

Ten-Year Ratings Timeline (Political Rights, Civil Liberties, Status)

1995	1996	1997	1998	1999	2000	2001	2002	2003	2004
7,7NF	7,6NF	7,6NF	7,6NF	7,6NF	7,6NF	7,6NF	7,6NF	7,6NF	7,6NF

Overview: A series of suicide bombings and subsequent violent clashes in March and April and again in July 2004 underscored the tenuous nature of Uzbekistan's political stability, even as the government continued its repressive policies against perceived opponents of the regime. The authorities responded to the attacks with a wave of arrests and convictions, targeting suspected members of banned Islamic groups. Repression against media outlets and foreign-based nongovernmental organizations (NGOs) working in Uzbekistan intensified during the year, partly in an effort to stifle dissent in advance of the December parliamentary elections. Meanwhile, the European Bank for Reconstruction and Development (EBRD) and the U.S. government cut financial assistance to the Uzbek government as a result of the regime's failure to implement meaningful political and human rights reforms.

Located along the ancient trade route of the famous Silk Road, Uzbekistan was incorporated into Russia by the late 1800s. The Uzbekistan Soviet Socialist Republic was established in 1924, and its eastern region was detached and made the separate Tajik Soviet Socialist Republic five years later.

On December 29, 1991, more than 98 percent of the country's electorate approved a popular referendum on Uzbekistan's independence. In a parallel vote, Islam Karimov, former Communist Party leader and chairman of the People's Democratic Party (PDP), the successor to the Communist Party, was elected president with a reported 88 percent of the vote. The only independent candidate to challenge him, Erk (Freedom) Party leader Mohammed Solih, charged election fraud. Solih fled the country two years later, and his party was forced underground. The opposition group Birlik (Unity) was barred from contesting the election and was later refused legal registration as a political party, and the Islamic Renaissance Party (IRP) and other religious-based groups were banned entirely. Only pro-government parties were allowed to compete in elections to the first post-Soviet legislature in December 1994 and January 1995. A February 1995 national referendum to extend Karimov's first five-year term in office until the year 2000 was allegedly approved by 99 percent of the country's voters.

The government's repression of members of the political opposition and of Muslims not affiliated with state-sanctioned religious institutions intensified following a series of deadly bombings in Tashkent in February 1999. The authorities blamed the attacks, which they described as an assassination attempt against Karimov, on the Islamic Movement of Uzbekistan (IMU), an armed group seeking the overthrow of Uzbekistan's secular government and its replacement with an Islamic state. The state justified its increasing crackdowns on moderate secular and religious groups under the pretext of fighting violent Islamist organizations, including the IMU.

Of the five parties that competed in the December 1999 parliamentary election, which was strongly criticized by international election observers, all supported the president and differed little in their political platforms. In the January 2000 presidential poll, Karimov defeated his only opponent, Marxist history professor Abdulhasiz Dzhalalov, with 92 percent of the vote. The government refused to register genuinely independent opposition parties or permit their members to stand as candidates. Meanwhile, in August 2000, the IMU engaged in armed clashes with government troops; the following month, the U.S. government placed the IMU on its list of international terrorist organizations for its ties to Osama bin Laden's terrorist network, al-Qaeda, and to the Taliban. As part of its declared effort to prevent renewed invasions by the IMU, Uzbekistan subsequently placed land mines along portions of its borders with Kyrgyzstan and Tajikistan, leading to protests by both governments and reports of accidental deaths of civilians in the region.

After the September 11, 2001, terrorist attacks, Uzbekistan became a key strategic ally of the United States in its military operations in Afghanistan. Tashkent's decision to permit the deployment of U.S. troops on its territory for search-and-rescue and humanitarian operations was widely seen as an effort to obtain various concessions from the West, including economic assistance, security guarantees, and reduced criticism of its poor human rights record. In March 2002, the United States and Uzbekistan signed a Declaration on Strategic Partnership and Cooperation Framework, in which both countries agreed to cooperate on economic, legal, humanitarian, and nuclear proliferation matters. Uzbekistan's continued collaboration with the U.S.-led antiterrorism campaign led to American commitments of financial assistance in exchange for promises from Karimov of political reforms.

In March 2003, the EBRD set a one-year deadline for compliance with three broad benchmarks for reform in Uzbekistan: greater political openness and freedom of the media, free functioning of civil society groups, and implementation of the recommendations of the UN Special Rapporteur on Torture. The EBRD announced that it would limit investments in Uzbekistan if the benchmarks were not met. Two months later, the EBRD held its annual meeting in Tashkent, the first such large-scale function in Central Asia. In the weeks surrounding the meeting, police intensified harassment of human rights defenders and relatives of religious prisoners in an attempt to prevent them from staging public protests about government abuses.

For the January 2004 local elections, all candidates were vetted in advance by Karimov's administration. The government claimed a voter turnout of 97 percent. The elections were for local neighborhood committees (*mahallahs*), which the government uses to observe and control the general population.

The fragile state of Uzbekistan's political stability was highlighted by a series of suicide bomb attacks and related violent clashes in late March and early April in Bukhara and Tashkent, in which some 50 people lost their lives. Most media outlets provided limited coverage of the events and focused almost exclusively on official government accounts, which led to widespread rumors about the identities and motives of the attackers. The fact that police appeared to be the main targets of the violence prompted speculation that the bombings were acts of revenge carried out by relatives of those imprisoned for alleged religious extremism. The authorities maintained that the bombings were the work of radical international Islamist groups— singling out the banned Hizb-ut-Tahrir group and the IMU—and dismissed charges of any links between the violence and the government's repressive political and economic policies. Meanwhile, a previously unknown Islamist group called Jamoat, a successor to the IMU, claimed responsibility.

In the days following the attacks, law enforcement agencies detained and arrested hundreds of alleged suspects and increased security measures in the capital and other large cities. According to Human Rights Watch, they targeted Muslims practicing outside of state-controlled mosques, including women. Dozens of defendants were convicted in the second half of the year for their alleged roles in the attacks, and all received lengthy prison sentences in trials that did not meet basic standards of due process. On July 30, several people were killed when suicide bombers struck again, in coordinated attacks on the U.S. and Israeli embassies and the office of Uzbekistan's prosecutor-general. Several Islamic groups, including the IMU and Jamoat, claimed responsibility.

In April, the EBRD announced its decision to limit investment in Uzbekistan, citing the government's lack of progress on democratic and economic reform benchmarks established one year earlier. Similarly, in July, the United States suspended $18 million of the $55 million originally earmarked for Uzbekistan in 2004; U.S. aid had peaked at $220 million in 2002. The decision was based on the 2002 Strategic Partnership and Cooperation Framework, which makes U.S. assistance to the Uzbek government conditional on Tashkent's introduction of meaningful political reforms and curbs in human rights abuses.

In the run-up to the December 26, 2004, elections for the lower house of the new bicameral parliament, only the country's five legal parties, all of which are considered to be pro-presidential, were granted registration to participate in the elections. Several opposition groups, including Erk and Birlik, announced in November that they will boycott the vote after being unable to register candidates. The Organization for Security and Cooperation in Europe (OSCE) announced that it will send a limited observer mission to monitor the vote.

Political Rights and Civil Liberties:

Citizens of Uzbekistan cannot change their government democratically. President Islam Karimov and the executive branch dominate the legislature and judiciary, and the government severely represses all political opposition. The national legislature largely confirms decisions made by the executive branch. The 1994-1995 and 1999 parliamentary elections and the 2000 presidential poll, in which only pro-government candidates could participate, were neither free nor fair. In a January 2002 nationwide referendum, 91 percent of voters allegedly approved amending the country's constitution to extend the presidential term from five to seven years. Karimov's current term in office will therefore end in 2007, rather than in 2005. In a parallel vote, 93 percent of voters officially supported replacing the country's 250-member single-chamber legislature with a bicameral parliament consisting of a 120-seat lower house and a 100-member upper house (Senate). Independent observers raised serious doubts about the validity of the referendum, citing the presence of police at polling stations and the fact that some people had been able to vote on behalf of several individuals. In April 2003, parliament adopted legislation providing former presidents immunity from prosecution and lifelong state-funded security for them and their immediate family.

A 1997 law prohibits parties based on ethnic or religious affiliations and those advocating subversion of the constitutional order. Only five parties, all pro-government, have been registered, and no genuine political opposition groups function legally or participate in the government. Members of unregistered secular opposition groups, including Birlik and Erk, are subject to discrimination, and many are in exile abroad. Although the authorities allowed both Erk and Birlik to hold open meetings in Tashkent in 2003, neither group was allowed to register officially as a political party. In May 2004, several members of Erk and at least one member of Birlik were arrested or threatened with arrest in a move denounced by the opposition as politically motivated.

Corruption is reportedly widespread throughout various levels of government, with bribery a common practice to obtain lucrative positions. Uzbekistan was ranked 114 out of 146 countries surveyed in Transparency International's 2004 Corruption Perceptions Index.

The state imposes strict limits on freedom of speech and the press, particularly with regard to reports on the government and Karimov. The government controls major media outlets and newspaper printing and distribution facilities. The country's private broadcast and print media outlets generally avoid political issues, are largely regional in scope, and suffer from administrative and financial constraints. Although official censorship was abolished in May 2002, the responsibility for censoring material was transferred to newspaper editors, who were warned by the State Press Committee that they would be held personally accountable for what they publish. Self-censorship is widespread, while the few journalists who dare to produce probing or critical reports of the authorities face harassment, physical violence, and closure of their media outlets. The government has blocked a number of non-Uzbek news Web sites, and access to controversial information on the Internet remains extremely difficult.

Most Uzbek media were slow to report the March and April 2004 bomb attacks, and coverage of both those and the July bombings was limited largely to official government statements. In September, the authorities ordered the international media training and support organization Internews-Uzbekistan to be shut down for six months for alleged technical violations. According to media watchdog groups, the closure represented an attempt by the authorities to stifle criticism in advance of the December parliamentary elections. The previous month, five independent television channels linked to Internews were stripped of their broadcasting licenses.

In a case that attracted international attention, independent journalist and human rights activist Ruslan Sharipov, who had written widely on government corruption, was sentenced in August 2003 to five and a half years in prison on charges of homosexuality—which is a criminal offense in Uzbekistan—and of having sexual relations with a minor. Sharipov reportedly confessed to the charges under duress and was tortured while in custody. In September, an appeals court reduced his sentence to four years, and in March 2004, he was transferred from prison to house arrest. Following continuing international pressure, Sharipov's prison term was replaced in June 2004 with two years of community service in his hometown of Bukhara. In September, he was granted asylum in the United States.

The government exercises strict control over Islamic worship, including the content of imams' sermons, and is suspicious and intolerant of followers of Muslim organizations not sanctioned by the state. Many members of such groups have been arrested or imprisoned on charges of anti-constitutional activities, often under the pretext of the government's fight against militant Islamists. Muslim prisoners are frequently tortured for their religious convictions or to compel them to renounce their beliefs. Authorities have targeted members of the banned Hizb-ut-Tahrir (Islamic Party of Liberation), an international movement calling for the creation of an Islamic caliphate throughout the Muslim world. Suspected members have been forced to give confessions under torture, and their family members have been subjected to interrogation, arrest, and extortion. According to Forum 18, the authorities followed the wave of 2004 suicide bomb attacks with a new crackdown against religious Muslims, as well as believers of other faiths, including Protestants and Jehovah's Witnesses.

The government permits the existence of certain mainstream religions, including approved Muslim and Jewish communities, as well as the Russian Orthodox Church and some other Christian denominations. As of January 2004, the authorities had registered some 2,100 religious congregations and organizations. However, the activities of other congregations are restricted through legislation that requires all religious groups to comply with burdensome state registration criteria. Involvement in religious activities carried out by unregistered groups is punishable by fines or imprisonment, and meetings held by such groups have been raided and participants interrogated and arrested. The 1998 Law on Freedom of Conscience and Religious Organizations prohibits activities including proselytizing and private religious instruction, and requires groups to obtain a license to publish or distribute materials.

The government limits academic freedom, according to the 2003 U.S. State Department Country Reports on Human Rights Practices, published in 2004. While professors generally are required to have their lectures pre-approved, implementation of this restriction varies, the report stated, and university professors reportedly practice self-censorship. Corruption is widespread throughout the educational system, with bribes commonly required to gain entrance into exclusive universities and to obtain good grades.

Open and free private discussion is limited by the mahalla committees, a traditional neighborhood organization that the government has turned into an official system for public surveillance and control. According to a 2003 Human Rights Watch report, the mahalla committees maintain files on those considered to be overly pious in their religious expression and alert the police of so-called suspicious religious and other activities.

Freedom of association is restricted. Although nonpolitical associations and social organizations are generally allowed to register, complicated regulations and governmental bureaucracy make the process difficult. Unregistered nongovernmental organizations (NGOs), including the Human Rights Society of Uzbekistan (HRSU), do not exist as legal entities and can face difficulties operating. Regulations require NGOs to confer with the Ministry of Justice about holding meetings and to allow ministry representatives to attend such gatherings. In December 2003, the government prevented a conference on the death penalty from being held in Tashkent just one day before it was scheduled to take place. The meeting was organized by a local group, Mothers against the Death Penalty and Torture, and supported by the OSCE, the British Embassy, and Freedom House. The authorities cancelled the conference on the grounds that the local group was not a legally registered organization. On February 16, 2004, police arrested Muidinjon Kurbanov, chairman of a regional branch of the HRSU, on weapons and narcotics charges. Civil society workers maintain that the evidence was planted and that Kurbanov's arrest was politically motivated.

In 2004, the government moved against foreign NGOs working in Uzbekistan by beginning enforcement of a 1999 order requiring all foreign NGOs to reregister with the Ministry of Justice. The government refused to allow the Open Society Institute, funded by businessman and philanthropist George Soros, to renew its registration. While authorities accused the institute of funding educational materials seeking to discredit government political and economic policies, critics of the move charged that it was part of a wider government attempt to control foreign NGO activities throughout the country. New banking restrictions requiring government oversight on foreign grant transactions has led to lengthy delays in grant payments to local recipients; Uzbek NGOs rely largely on international assistance to fund their operations.

Despite constitutional provisions for freedom of assembly, the authorities severely restrict this right in practice. Law enforcement officials have used force to prevent demonstrations against human rights abuses in the country, and participants have been harassed, detained, and arrested. In recent years, there have been some small protests by human rights activists and family members of people jailed for allegedly being members of violent Islamic groups. In November, thousands of merchants rioted in the Fergana Valley region when police and tax officials began confiscating goods belonging to traders who were not complying with new controversial and onerous trade regulations. Demonstrators burned police cars and beat three tax inspectors and a police officer. The Council of the Federation of Trade Unions is dependent on the state, and no genuinely independent union structures exist. Organized strikes are extremely rare.

The judiciary is subservient to the president, who appoints all judges and can remove them from office at any time. Police routinely physically abuse and torture suspects to extract confessions, which are accepted by judges as evidence and often serve as the basis for convictions. Law enforcement authorities reportedly often plant narcotics, weapons, and banned religious literature on suspected members of Islamic groups or political opponents to justify their arrest. Executions are regarded as state secrets, and relatives are sometimes not informed until months after the execution has occurred. The authorities conducted waves of arrests of alleged suspects following the suicide bomb attacks in March-April and July. According to Human Rights Watch, the police in many cases made arrests without warrants, conducted unsanctioned searches of people's homes, and planted evidence. Detainees experienced incommunicado detention, limited access to attorneys, and mistreatment during the investigative phases, and their trials failed to meet basic standards of due process, Human Rights Watch reported.

Prisons suffer from severe overcrowding and shortages of food and medicine. The Jaslyk prison camp is notorious for its extremely harsh conditions and ill-treatment of religious prisoners. Inmates, particularly those sentenced for their religious beliefs, are often subjected to ill-treatment or torture, and Human Rights Watch has documented a number of torture-related deaths in custody during the last few years. An estimated 5,000 to 6,000 political prisoners are being held in Uzbekistan's penal institutions.

Although racial and ethnic discrimination is prohibited by law, the belief that senior positions in government and business are reserved for ethnic Uzbeks is widespread.

The government severely limits freedom of movement and residence within the country and across borders. There are restrictions on foreign travel, including the use of a system of exit visas, which are often issued selectively. Permission is required from local authorities to move to a new city, and the authorities rarely grant permission to those wishing to move to Tashkent. Bribes are often paid to obtain the necessary registration documents. In July, the mayor of Tashkent ordered residents of the capital without official residence permits expelled and dismissed from their jobs; he justified the move as necessary to guard against terrorist attacks by Islamist groups.

Widespread corruption, bureaucratic regulations, and the government's tight control over the economy limit most citizens' equality of opportunity. There has been little reform in the country's large and predominantly centrally planned agricultural sector, in which the state sets high production quotas and low purchase prices for farmers. A series of government regulations and decrees over the last few years have placed increasing restrictions on market traders and their ability to continue to operate.

Women's educational and professional prospects are restricted by traditional cultural and religious norms and by ongoing economic difficulties throughout the country. Victims of domestic violence are discouraged from pressing charges against their perpetrators, who rarely face criminal prosecution. The trafficking of women abroad for prostitution remains a serious problem. Local authorities frequently use schoolchildren as free or cheap labor to harvest cotton; many children work long hours under unhealthy conditions, often receiving inadequate food and water.

Vanuatu

Population: 200,000
GNI/capita: $1,080
Life Expectancy: 67
Political Rights: 2
Civil Liberties: 2
Status: Free
Religious Groups: Presbyterian (36.7 percent),
Anglican (15 percent), Roman Catholic (15 percent),
indigenous beliefs (7.6 percent), Seventh-Day Adventist
(6.2 percent), Church of Christ (3.8 percent), other (15.7 percent)
Ethnic Groups: Melanesian (98 percent), other [including French, Vietnamese, and
Chinese] (2 percent)
Capital: Port Vila

Ten-Year Ratings Timeline (Political Rights, Civil Liberties, Status)

1995	1996	1997	1998	1999	2000	2001	2002	2003	2004
1,3F	1,3F	1,3F	1,3F	1,3F	1,3F	1,3F	1,2F	2,2F	2,2F

Overview:

Following a snap general election in July 2004, parliament elected Kalkot Mataskelekele as the new president on August 16 and confirmed Serge Vohor as the new prime minister. In September, the parliamentary opposition led a failed no-confidence vote against Vohor. To promote greater political stability, Vohor proposed several constitutional amendments, which must be voted on in a public referendum in 2005.

Vanuatu is an archipelago of 83 islands lying 1,300 miles northeast of Sydney, Australia. The British and French jointly governed it as a unique Anglo-French "condominium" in 1906 until it achieved independence in 1980. The Anglo-French legacy continues to split society along linguistics lines in all spheres of life from politics to religion and economics.

The left-leaning Vanua'aku Party (VP) led the country from 1980 through 1991. A split within the party allowed Maxime Carlot Korman, leader of the francophone Union of Moderate Parties (UMP), to become Vanuatu's first French-speaking prime minister in 1991. Serge Vohor, who headed a dissident faction of the UMP, replaced Carlot Korman in 1995. Barak Sope of the Melanesian Progressive Party took power in 1999 when Vohor was ousted by a no-confidence vote. Edward Natapei of the VP became prime minister in 2001.

Faced with a possibly successful no-confidence vote, Natapei called for a snap election in June 2004, and the election was held a month later. Independent candidates won 6 of the 52 seats, reflecting widespread public frustration with party and factional politics. However, no party won a clear mandate. Negotiations led parliament to elect Kalkot Mataskelekele, a former Supreme Court justice and a drafter of the constitution, as president. Vohor was chosen as prime minister to lead a coalition government. However, the issues in question were not resolved; a no-confidence vote called in September to unseat Vohor failed.

In December 2004, parliament approved the holding of a referendum in early 2005 on amendments to the constitution. If approved, elected representatives would lose their seats if they move from one political party to another after an election, no-confidence votes would be limited to the 12 months after the general election and the last 12 months of the prime minister's four-year term, and parliamentary terms would be extended from four to five years. These amendments aim to restore stability to government, which has been severely compromised by intense rivalries between political parties and the frequent use of no-confidence votes to topple governments as power alignments shift.

Political Rights and Civil Liberties: Citizens of Vanuatu can change their government democratically. The constitution provides for parliamentary elections every four years. The prime minister, who appoints his own cabinet, is chosen from within the 52-member parliament to head the government. Members of parliament and the heads of the six provincial governments also form an electoral college to select the president for a five-year term. The president is the head of state, a largely ceremonial post. The National Council of Chiefs works in parallel with the parliament and exercises authority mainly over language and cultural matters.

No-confidence votes have forced several changes of government in recent years. Parliamentary coalitions have been formed and dissolved with increasing frequency since the 1990s, and fraud and bribery have become widespread in elections.

Many political parties are active. The leading parties are the VP and the National Union Party, which took eight and ten seats, respectively, in the last election in June 2004 and formed a coalition government. Another top vote getter was the UMP, which took nine seats. Other political parties are the Vanuatu Republic Party, the People's Democratic Party, the National United Party, the Melanesian Progressive Party, the Greens and the John Frum Movement, which is also a religious group. However, party loyalty is weak. Politicians frequently switch affiliations and rivalries are intense.

Corruption is a problem but not pervasive. In 2001, then-prime minister Barak Sope was forced to resign after allegations of corruption caused him to lose a parliamentary vote of no confidence. There have been individual reports of police corruption, but it does not appear widespread. Since 2003, the government has strengthened laws to stop money laundering and tax evasion in order to protect its offshore banking business, a significant source of revenue. These efforts helped persuade the Organization for Economic Cooperation and Development (OECD) to remove Vanuatu from the list of uncooperative tax havens in May 2003.

The government generally respects freedom of speech and of the press. The state-owned Television Blong Vanuatu broadcasts in English and French. The weekly *Port Vila Press* and the privately owned *Vanuatu Daily*, *Nasara*, and *Port Vila News* supply international, national, and local news. Most media outlets deliver information in Bismala (a pidgin used throughout the islands), English, and French. The number of mobile phone and Internet users, although rising, remains small because of high costs and limited access outside the capital of Port Vila.

The government generally respects freedom of religion in this predominantly Christian country. There were no reports of restrictions on academic freedom. Port Vila hosts the Emalus Campus of the University of the South Pacific.

There have been no reports of government restrictions on civil society groups, and nongovernmental organizations are active in a variety of spheres. Many receive support from foreign private foundations and bilateral aid donors. Public demonstrations are permitted by law and respected by the government in practice. Workers can organize unions, bargain collectively, and strike. There are five independent trade unions organized under the umbrella Vanuatu Council of Trade Unions, which represents about 40 percent of the country's 25,000-person workforce.

Although the judiciary is generally independent, it is weak and inefficient. Lack of resources has kept the government from hiring and retaining qualified judges and prosecutors. Criminal defendants are often held for long pretrial detentions, and prison conditions are poor. Vanuatu has no armed forces. The Vanuatu Mobile Force is a parliamentary wing of the small police force; both are under the command of a civilian police commissioner. There have been reports of police abuse, but such incidents appear to be infrequent and not widespread or severe.

The vast majority of the population is engaged in either subsistence farming or fishing. In January, parliament passed a new law to stop all mixed-race and naturalized citizens from farming kava, a native herb that has gained popularity among health supplement consumers in the West. Tourism, the civil service, and offshore banking provide employment in the service sector.

In September, the National Council of Chiefs passed a motion to require people to carry permits for movement between provinces because of concerns about crime in the capital.

Violence against women is common and particularly severe in rural areas. Spousal rape is not a crime, and no law prohibits wife beating or sexual harassment. Most cases go unreported because the victims fear reprisal or are discouraged by family pressure, and the police and courts generally hesitate to intervene or impose stronger punishment for offenders. Women's rights leaders consider village chiefs to be major obstacles to improving conditions for women. The traditional practice of "bride payment," or a dowry, is still widely used, which critics charge encourages the view of women as property.

Venezuela

Population: 26,200,000 **Political Rights:** 3
GNI/capita: $4,080 **Civil Liberties:** 4
Life Expectancy: 73 **Status:** Partly Free
Religious Groups: Roman Catholic (96 percent),
Protestant (2 percent), other (2 percent)
Ethnic Groups: Spanish, Italian, Portuguese, Arab,
German, African, indigenous people
Capital: Caracas

Ten-Year Ratings Timeline (Political Rights, Civil Liberties, Status)

1995	1996	1997	1998	1999	2000	2001	2002	2003	2004
3,3PF	2,3F	2,3F	2,3F	4,4PF	3,5PF	3,5PF	3,4PF	3,4PF	3,4PF

Overview: President Hugo Chavez consolidated his hold on power following the defeat of a presidential recall referendum in August 2004 that was held amid charges of ballot rigging. Although he faced an economy in ruins and high levels of street crime and unemployment, Chavez devoted considerable attention during the year to advancing his influence over the judicial system, media, and other institutions of civil society.

The Republic of Venezuela was established in 1830, nine years after independence from Spain. Long periods of instability and military rule ended with the establishment in 1961 of civilian rule and the approval of a constitution. Until 1993, the social-democratic Democratic Action Party (AD) and the Social Christian Party (COPEI) dominated politics. Former president Carlos Andres Perez (1989–1993) of the AD was nearly overthrown by Chavez and other nationalist military officers in two 1992 coup attempts in which dozens were killed. In 1993, Perez was charged with corruption and removed from office by congress. Rafael Caldera, a former president (1969–1974) of the COPEI and a populist, was elected president in late 1993 as head of the 16-party National Convergence, which included Communists, other leftists, and right-wing groups. With crime soaring, public corruption unabated, oil wealth drying up, and the country in its worst economic crisis in 50 years, popular disillusionment with politics deepened.

In 1998, Chavez made his antiestablishment, anticorruption, populist message a referendum on the long-ruling political elite—famous for its interlocking system of privilege and graft, but also for its consensual approach to politics—in that year's presidential contest. As the country's long-ruling political parties teetered at the edge of collapse, last-minute efforts to find a consensus candidate to oppose Chavez were unsuccessful. In February 1999, Chavez won with 57 percent of the vote, taking the reins of the world's fifth-largest oil-producing country.

A constituent assembly dominated by Chavez followers drafted a new constitution that strengthened the presidency and allowed Chavez to retain power until 2013. After Venezuelans approved the new constitution in a national referendum on December 15, 2000, congress and the Supreme Court were dismissed. Although he was reelected as president, new national elections held in July 2000 marked a resurgence of a political opposition that had been hamstrung in its efforts to contest Chavez's stripping of congress and the judiciary of their independence and power. Opposition parties won most of the country's governorships, about half the mayoralties, and a significant share of power in the new congress. Nevertheless, that November, Chavez's congressional allies granted him special fast-track powers that allowed him to decree a wide range of laws without parliamentary debate.

In April 2002, following the deaths of 19 people in a massive protest against the government, Chavez was deposed in a putsch by dissident military officers working with major opposition groups. However, he was reinstated two days later when loyalist troops and supporters gained the upper hand in the streets and in barracks around the country. Opponents of Chavez cited as giving them a right to rebel Article 350 of the 1999 constitution, which permits citizens not to recognize a government that infringes on human and democratic rights—an article that was included by Chavez to justify his own 1992 coup attempts.

Throughout the year, the country was wracked by protests by a broad spectrum of civil society and saw unprecedented discontent among military officers. In October, an estimated one million Venezuelans marched in Caracas demanding that

Chavez call either early elections or a referendum on his rule—and threatening a general strike if he did not accede. When Chavez did not respond, the opposition called for a general strike in February 2003. Although the strike lasted 62 days, it was unsuccessful in forcing Chavez's hand. During the remainder of 2003, Chavez appeared on a collision course with a political opposition that seemed determined to force his resignation before the end of his elected term. However, the opposition also faced questions about its own democratic commitment given the failed coup attempt and its promotion of the failed strike, as well as more practical concerns about its own cohesion and effectiveness.

Following Chavez's successful quashing of the strike, opponents quickly mobilized behind a recall referendum, which is allowed under the constitution. The first attempt to collect the necessary signatures succeeded in gathering 2.8 million at a time when polls showed 65 percent of Venezuelans would vote to oust Chavez, but it was declared invalid by the National Elections Council (CNE). Opponents then quickly mobilized to collect new signatures. The last half of 2003 was marked by a series of government social services initiatives, including urban health care and literacy programs supported by the Cuban government, that appeared to give Chavez a lift in popularity in the face of the potential referendum. An increase in political violence in the country came as a crime wave continued unabated.

In March 2004, the Inter-American Commission on Human Rights published a major country report highlighting serious and long-standing institutional issues related to the rule of law and the respect for civil and political rights. Meanwhile, congress, controlled by Chavez supporters, approved a measure allowing it to remove and appoint judges to the Supreme Court, which controls the rest of the judiciary. The Organic Law of the Supreme Court allowed Chavez to limit the tribunal's independence, while the body was expanded from 20 to 32 justices—appointed by a simple majority vote of the pro-government majority in parliament. The government also announced that it was studying a measure to unify municipal and state police forces into a single institution, thus wresting control from mayors and governors, many of whom oppose Chavez.

By midyear, more than four million people had signed petitions in favor of the recall vote against Chavez. The poll, which was the country's first-ever referendum to recall a president, was set for August 15. Chavez won the referendum with 58 percent of the vote. The European Union declined to monitor the referendum, saying that it had not been able to secure from Venezuelan officials "the conditions to carry out an observation in line with the Union's standard methodology." Other international observer groups that did monitor the vote issued findings that the election was legitimate, though flawed. Following the referendum, which was conducted in relative peace and characterized by a high turnout, domestic opposition groups continued to insist that there was a large discrepancy between the official results and their own exit polls. Independent observers said that there were credible reports of voter harassment, including physical intimidation and the reassignment of thousand of voters to far-away polling stations, and vote tampering; it was an open question, however, if these materially affected the overwhelming outcome. In October, regional and municipal elections, voters overwhelmingly backed pro-Chavez candidates.

In November, the assassination of a "super prosecutor" investigating the failed

2002 coup against Chavez gave the president an opportunity to blame Florida-based anti-Chavez "terrorists" for the crime; a lawyer suspected of participation in the crime was killed by police in what was described as a "shootout." In December, a law giving the government control over the content of radio and television programs was to go into effect, with Chavez claiming that the "Venezuelan people have begun to free themselves from. . .the dictatorship of the private media." The record high oil prices that in 2004 enabled the president to engage in spectacular social spending in poorer districts, his unbroken string of electoral victories, and the government's growing control over sectors of Venezuelan life all appeared to make Chavez largely unassailable in the 2006 presidential election.

Political Rights and Civil Liberties: Citizens can change their government democratically. Under the constitution approved in 1961, the president and a bicameral National Assembly are elected for five years. The Senate has at least two members from each of the 21 states and the federal district of Caracas. The Chamber of Deputies has 189 seats. On the national level, there are no independent government institutions. The military high command is loyal to a single person, the president, rather than to the constitution and the law. Hugo Chavez's party, the Fifth Republic Movement, controls the National Assembly (though narrowly), as well as the Supreme Justice Tribunal and the intelligence services. It also controls the Citizen Power branch of government created to fight corruption by the 1999 constitution. This branch is made up of the offices of the ombudsman (responsible for compelling the government to adhere to the constitution and laws), the comptroller-general (who controls the revenues and expenses incurred by the government), and the public prosecutor (who provides opinions to the courts on the prosecution of criminal cases and brings to the attention of the proper authorities cases of public employee misconduct and violations of the constitutional rights of prisoners or accused persons).

The Chavez government has done little to free the government from excessive bureaucratic regulations, registration requirements, and other forms of control that increase opportunities for corruption. It has relied instead on attacking persons and social sectors it considers to be corrupt and selectively enforcing good-government laws and regulations against its opponents. A 2003 study by the World Bank found that Venezuela has one of the most regulated economies in the world. New regulations and controls over the economy have ensured that public officials have retained ample opportunities for personal enrichment enjoyed under previous governments. A July 2004 ruling by the Overseas Private Investment Corporation, a U.S. government agency, held that Venezuela illegally expropriated the assets of a U.S. company involved in a joint venture with the country's state-owned oil company.

On April 7, 2003, the Law against Corruption was put into effect. It establishes a citizen's right to know, and sets out the state's obligations to provide a thrice-yearly rendition of public goods and expenses, except those security and national defense expenditures as exempted by law. The law also requires most public employees to present a sworn declaration of personal assets within 30 days of assuming a post, as well as 30 days after leaving it; allows for the extradition of corrupt officials and their prohibition from holding office in the future; and includes a prohibition on officials holding secret foreign bank accounts. Venezuela was ranked 114 out of 146 countries surveyed in Transparency International's 2004 Corruption Perceptions Index.

Although the constitution provides for freedom of the press, exercise of that right is becoming increasingly difficult in practice. In 2003, as the country moved toward a referendum on Chavez's presidency, the government proposed several measures to tighten its control over opposition newspapers and television and radio stations. A climate of intimidation and hostility against the press has been established in the past few years, in large part as a result of strong anti-media rhetoric by the government and a significant anti-Chavez slant on the part of media owners. The state allocates broadcast licenses in a biased fashion and engages in favoritism in the distribution of government advertising revenues. In July 2004, a new law was ratified that regulates the work of journalists, provides for compulsory registration with the national journalism association, and punishes reporters' "illegal" conduct with prison sentences of three to six months. A Supreme Court ruling upheld censorship laws that effectively declared that laws protecting public authorities and institutions from insulting criticism were constitutional. The Law on the Social Responsibility of Radio and TV, giving the government control over the content of radio and television programs, was to go into effect in December. The government does not restrict Internet access.

Freedom of religion, which the constitution guarantees on the condition that its practice not violate public morality, decency, or the public order, is generally respected by the government. Academic freedom traditionally is generally respected. However, government funding has been withheld from the country's universities, and the rectors of those institutions charged that the government did so to punish them; all of the major public university rectors were elected on antigovernment platforms.

Although professional and academic associations generally operate without official interference, the Supreme Court ruled in 2000 that nongovernmental organizations that receive funding from foreign governments or whose leaders are not Venezuelan are not part of "civil society." As a result, they may not represent citizens in court or bring their own legal actions. In January 2004, the Chavez government made an effort to undermine the legitimacy of reputable human rights organizations by questioning their ties to international organizations and making unsupported accusations of links to foreign governments. Freedom of peaceful assembly and association are guaranteed in the constitution, and the government generally respected these rights in practice. Public meetings and marches, the latter of which require government permits, were generally permitted without impediment, although government supporters often sought to disrupt these, frequently using violence.

The president and his supporters have sought to break what they term a "stranglehold" of corrupt labor leaders on the job market, a move that labor activists say tramples on the rights of private organizations. Opposition and traditional labor leaders say that challenges by insurgent workers' organizations mask Chavez's intent to create government-controlled unions; the president's supporters maintain that the old labor regime amounted to little more than employer-controlled workers' organizations. Security forces frequently break up strikes and arrest trade unionists, allegedly under the guidance of Cuban security officials. In early 2004, the government refused to recognize the elected leaders of the Confederation of Venezuelan Workers and ordered the arrest of its secretary-general, forcing him to flee the country.

Until Chavez took power, the judicial system was headed by a nominally independent Supreme Court that was nevertheless highly politicized, undermined by the chronic corruption (including the growing influence of narcotics traffickers) that permeates the entire political system, and unresponsive to charges of rights abuses. Under Chavez, the effectiveness and impartiality of the judicial branch remains tenuous. An unwieldy new judicial code, which has helped to reduce the number of people jailed while awaiting arraignment, has hampered some law enforcement efforts, resulting in low rates of conviction and shorter jail terms even for convicted murderers. Police salaries are inadequate.

Widespread arbitrary detention and torture of suspects, as well as dozens of extrajudicial killings by the often-corrupt military security forces and the police, have increased as crime continues to soar. Since the 1992 coup attempts, weakened civilian governments have had less authority over the military and the police, and overall rights abuses are committed with impunity.

Since Chavez's election, Venezuela's military, which is largely unaccountable to civilian rule, has become an active participant in the country's social development and delivery of public services. The 1999 constitution assigns the armed forces a significant role in the state but does not provide for civilian control over the military's budget or procurement practices, or for related institutional checks. A separate system of armed forces courts retains jurisdiction over members of the military accused of rights violations and common criminal crimes, and decisions cannot be appealed in civilian court.

Venezuela's indigenous peoples belong to 27 ethnic groups. The formal rights of Native Americans have improved under Chavez, although those rights, specifically the groups' ability to make decisions affecting their lands, cultures, and traditions, and the allocation of natural resources, are seldom enforced, as local political authorities rarely take their interests into account. Indigenous communities typically face deforestation and water pollution. Few Indians hold title to their land; many say that they do not want to, as they reject market concepts of individual property, preferring instead that the government recognize those lands traditionally held by them as native territories. At the same time, indigenous communities trying to defend their legal land rights are subject to abuses, including murder, by gold miners and corrupt rural police. The constitution creates three seats in the National Assembly for indigenous people and also provides for "the protection of indigenous communities and their progressive incorporation into the life of the nation." The lack of effective legal rights, however, has created an unprecedented migration by Indians to poverty-stricken urban areas.

Women are more active in politics than in many other Latin American countries and comprise the backbone of Venezuela's sophisticated grassroots network of nongovernmental organizations. However, there is substantial institutional and societal prejudice on issues of domestic violence and rape, and work-related sexual harassment is common.

Vietnam

Population: 81,500,000 **Political Rights:** 7
GNI/capita: $430 **Civil Liberties:** 6
Life Expectancy: 72 **Status:** Not Free
Religious Groups: Buddhist, Hoa Hao, Cao Dai,
Christian, indigenous beliefs, Muslim
Ethnic Groups: Vietnamese (85-90 percent), other
[including Chinese, Muong, Tai, Meo, Khmer, Man,
and Cham] (10-15 percent)
Capital: Hanoi

Ten-Year Ratings Timeline (Political Rights, Civil Liberties, Status)

1995	1996	1997	1998	1999	2000	2001	2002	2003	2004
7,7NF	7,7NF	7,7NF	7,7NF	7,7NF	7,6NF	7,6NF	7,6NF	7,6NF	7,6NF

Overview:

The Vietnamese government continued to deny its citizens basic freedoms in 2004, as evidenced by the adoption of a new law on religion that will further reinforce state control of religion and churches. Two trials—of a former academic and of a military historian— contributed to the ongoing political suppression of those who advocate political reform. The U.S. House of Representatives passed a bill to restrict official development assistance to Vietnam unless Hanoi improves its human rights record, beginning with the release of political and religious prisoners.

Vietnam won independence from France in 1954 after a century of colonial rule followed by Japanese occupation during World War II. At independence, the country was divided into the Western-backed Republic of South Vietnam and the Communist-ruled Democratic Republic of Vietnam in the North. A war erupted between the two sides, and U.S. military support for South Vietnam persisted for more than a decade. The violence and destruction killed tens of thousands of soldiers and civilians and maimed many more on both sides. Hostilities also spilled into neighboring countries. In 1975, the North claimed victory and united the country the following year.

Poor economic policies left the tattered country in deep poverty. In 1986, the government began to dismantle collectivized farms and encourage small-scale private enterprise. Economic reforms have since continued, spurring rapid economic growth. A stock exchange was set up in 2000, tourism became a major source of revenue, and the country has become a major exporter of foodstuff and manufactured products. Nevertheless, Vietnam's leadership continues to be divided over the pace and depth of privatization and other market reforms. Moderates see deep-rooted reforms as essential to modernizing the impoverished country and creating enough jobs to stave off social unrest. Hard-liners fear that further loosening of the state's control over the economy, including the privatization of state-owned businesses, will leave millions out of work and possibly lead to a social backlash.

Political reform has not followed economic change. Since 2001, after several thousand Montagnards held protests to demand greater religious freedom, increased land rights, and political autonomy for the region, Hanoi has cracked down on the group, an ethnic and religious minority (mainly Christian) in the central highlands. More than 70 Montagnards ("mountain dwellers" in French) are serving long jail sentences for participating in protests or trying to flee to Cambodia. Several Montagnards were arrested by the Vietnamese government in April at a rally in Dak Lak province to protest government seizure of their lands. Vietnam is fast becoming the top producer of coffee beans in the world, and land seized from the highland Montagnards are often turned over to lowland Vietnamese to grow commercial crops like coffee beans. To date, hundreds of Montagnards have escaped to Cambodia's Ratanakiri province in the northeast, and nearly 400 have been airlifted or made their way to UN safe houses in the Cambodian capital. However, the Cambodian government has asserted it will not allow the refugees to remain in Cambodia, and the UN High Commissioner for Refugees has stated it will not petition the Vietnamese government on the refugees' behalf and interfere with internal affairs in Vietnam.

In 2001, the Communist Party of Vietnam (CPV) elected Nong Duc Manh as its new leader. The following year, Phan Van Khai was chosen as prime minister and Tran Duc Luong as state president. The appointment of these three men from northern, central, and southern Vietnam preserved the leadership troika's traditional regional balance. In the May 2002 parliamentary elections, the CPV vetted all candidates for the legislature.

In July 2004, Tran Khue, a former academic held since December 2002, was given a 19-month prison sentence for "abusing the right to democracy and freedom" and breaking a house arrest order made in October 2001. Tran was initially accused of espionage after publishing numerous articles and open letters critical of government policies and advocating political reform. Also in July, Pham Que Duong, a 73-year-old military historian, faced trial for signing a petition calling for reforms and measures against graft.

The continued suppression of political rights and civil liberties by the Vietnamese government was condemned by the United States, which cited Vietnam as among the worst violators of religious freedom in 2004. The U.S. House of Representatives passed legislation to restrict development aid transfers to Vietnam—reaching some $40 million in 2003—until the country begins to release its political and religious prisoners. However, the U.S. Senate was not expected to pass its own version of the bill or turn the House bill into law.

SARS—severe acute respiratory syndrome—and the bird flu had an enormous impact on the economy. The government confirmed in August that three persons died form the latest attack of the bird flu.

Political Rights and Civil Liberties: Ruled by the CPV as a single-party state, Vietnam is one of the most tightly controlled countries in the world. The CPV's Central Committee is the top decision-making body in Vietnam. The National Assembly, whose 498 members are elected to five-year terms, generally follows the party's dictates in legislation. The party-controlled Fatherland Front vets all assembly candidates and allows only CPV cadres and some independents to run. However, delegates speak out for grassroots complaints, influence legislation, question state ministers, and debate legal, social, and economic issues—within limits set by the party. They also regularly criticize officials' performance and governmental corruption and inefficiency.

Senior party and government officials have publicly acknowledged growing public discontent with official abuses and corruption. However, in the last several years, the government has largely responded with high-profile prosecutions, rather than fundamental reforms at all levels of government. For example, a deputy trade minister was arrested in November for selling export quotas to Vietnamese garment makers, and a former deputy sports minister was sentenced to eight years in prison in October for raping a 13-year old girl. The announcement by the CPV in 2004 to begin scrutinizing alleged corruption in the Transportation, Industry, and Education Ministries was notable because results of a survey paid for by a Swedish government grant will be made publicly available in January 2005. Vietnam was ranked 102 out of 146 countries surveyed in the 2004 Transparency International Corruption Perceptions Index.

The Ministry of Culture and Information manages and supervises press and broadcasting activities. Officials have punished journalists who overstepped the bounds of permissible reporting by jailing or placing them under house arrest, taking away their press cards, or closing down newspapers. Publications deemed bad or inaccurate are subject to official bans. Government control also relies on a 1999 law that requires journalists to pay damages to groups or individuals found to be harmed by press articles, even if the reports are accurate. At least one suit has been filed under this law, although it was later withdrawn. While journalists cannot report on sensitive political or economic matters or openly question the CPV's single-party rule, they have reported on high-level governmental corruption and mismanagement, providing a small outlet for public grievances.

Television is the dominant medium. Vietnam Television broadcasts to the whole country, and there are many provincial television stations. Satellite television is officially restricted to senior officials, international hotels, and foreign businesses, but many Vietnamese homes and businesses pick up some foreign stations via satellite. About two million Vietnamese have access to the Internet, which is tightly controlled by the government. A 2003 law formally banned receipt and distribution of antigovernment e-mail messages, and Web sites considered "reactionary" are blocked. Owners of domestic Web sites are required to submit their Web content for official approval.

The regime sharply restricts religious freedom by regulating religious organizations and clergy and harassing independent religious groups and their leaders. All religious groups and most individual clergy must join a party-controlled supervisory body. One such body exists for each religion that the state officially recognizes—Buddhism; Roman Catholicism; Protestantism; Islam; Cao Daiism, a synthesis of several religions; and the Hoa Hao faith, a reformist Buddhist church. Religious groups must obtain permission to build or refurbish places of worship; run religious schools or do charitable work; hold conventions, training seminars, and special celebrations; and train, ordain, promote, or transfer clergy. These regulations hinder efforts by religious groups to expand schools, obtain teaching materials, publish religious texts, and increase the number of students training for the clergy.

Cao Daiists have largely been barred since 1975 from ordaining new priests. Protestants were largely prohibited from training new clergy until the government agreed in 2003 to allow Protestants in southern Vietnam to re-open a long-closed seminary. Reported abuses by local officials have been particularly severe: churchgoers were jailed, religious gatherings were prohibited, children of Protestant families were barred from attending school beyond the third grade, and food rations were withheld from believers.

A new law on religion, the Ordinance on Beliefs and Religions took effect on November 15. The new law expands state control over freedom of worship. The government claims that the new law will ensure people's basic right to beliefs and religious freedom.

Academic freedom is limited. University professors must adhere to party views when teaching or writing on political topics and refrain from criticizing government policies. Nevertheless, ordinary Vietnamese, particularly those living in major cities, are increasingly free of government intrusion into their daily lives. The regime continues to rely on informers, block wardens, and a household registration system to keep tabs on individuals, but this surveillance is now directed mainly at known dissidents rather than the general population.

Human rights organizations and other private groups with rights-oriented agendas are banned. However, the leadership increasingly allows farmers and others to hold small protests over local grievances, which often concern land seizures. Thousands of Vietnamese try to gain redress each year by writing letters to or personally addressing officials. In addition to land matters, citizens complain about official corruption, economic policies, government inefficiency, and opaque bureaucratic procedures.

Trade unions remain state controlled, but hundreds of independent "labor associations" are permitted to represent many workers at individual firms and in some service industries. Nevertheless, union membership is low given that most workers are small-scale farmers in rural areas. Enforcement of child labor, workplace safety, and other labor laws is poor.

Vietnam's judiciary is subservient to the CPV, which controls courts at all levels. Defense lawyers cannot call or question witnesses and sometimes are permitted only to appeal for leniency for their clients. While defendants have a constitutional right to counsel, scarcity of lawyers often makes this right impossible to enforce. Moreover, many lawyers reportedly are reluctant to take human rights and other sensitive cases because they fear harassment and retribution by the state.

Police at times beat suspects and detainees, and prison conditions are poor. Inmates generally are required to work, but receive little or no wages. The death penalty is applied mainly for violent crimes, but is sometimes also used against Vietnamese convicted of nonviolent crimes, including economic and drug-related offenses. The actual number of political prisoners is unknown. Since 2001, at least 10 Vietnamese Internet dissidents have been arrested, with 6 of them sentenced to long jail terms. The government denies holding any prisoners on political grounds.

Ethnic minorities face unofficial discrimination in mainstream society, and some local officials restrict minority access to schooling and jobs. Minorities generally have little input into development projects that affect their livelihoods and communities.

Economic opportunities have grown for women, but they continue to face discrimination in wages and promotion. Many women are victims of domestic violence, and thousands are trafficked internally and externally each year for the purpose of prostitution.

⬇️Yemen

Population: 20,000,000
GNI/capita: $490
Life Expectancy: 60
Religious Groups: Muslim [including Sunni and Shia], other
Ethnic Groups: Arab [majority], Afro-Arab, South Asian
Capital: Sanaa

Political Rights: 5
Civil Liberties: 5
Status: Partly Free

Trend Arrow: Yemen received a downward trend arrow due to governmental restrictions on press freedom, including closing newspapers and detaining journalists on questionable charges.

Ten-Year Ratings Timeline (Political Rights, Civil Liberties, Status)

1995	1996	1997	1998	1999	2000	2001	2002	2003	2004
5,6NF	5,6NF	5,6NF	5,6NF	5,6NF	5,6NF	6,6NF	6,5NF	5,5PF	5,5PF

Overview:

Troubling signs of a weakening government commitment to press freedom emerged in Yemen, as the government jailed a prominent journalist—Abdel Karim al-Khaiwani, editor of the opposition weekly newspaper *Al-Shoura*—and closed several newspapers in 2004. Some of the government actions to limit press freedom were related to a crackdown following a bloody three-month rebellion, led by cleric and former member of parliament Hussein Badreddin al-Hawthi, in the northern region of Saada.

As part of the ancient Minaean, Sabaean, and Himyarite kingdoms, Yemen has a long history stretching back nearly 3,000 years. For centuries, a series of imams controlled most of northern Yemen and parts of southern Yemen. The Ottoman Empire ruled many of the cities from the sixteenth to the nineteenth century, and the British Empire controlled areas in the southern part of the country in the first part of the twentieth century, including the port of Aden. Yemen was divided into two countries—the Yemen Arab Republic (North Yemen) and the People's Democratic Republic of Yemen (South Yemen)—that ultimately became unified in 1990 after decades of conflict and tension.

In the face of widespread poverty and illiteracy, tribal influences that limit the central government's authority in certain parts of the country, a heavily armed citizenry, and the threat of radical Islamist terrorism, Yemen has managed to take some limited steps to improve its record on political rights and civil liberties in the 14 years since unification.

In 1999, President Ali Abdullah Saleh won a five-year term in the country's first nationwide direct presidential election, gaining 96.3 percent of the vote. Saleh's only opponent came from within the ruling General People's Congress (GPC), and his term in office was extended from five to seven years in a 2001 referendum.

Yemen's April 2003 parliamentary election, its third in the last decade, took place despite concerns that popular unrest resulting from the war in Iraq might lead to a postponement. International election observers noted that Yemen had made substantial improvements in electoral management and administration. On the surface, the elections were competitive, with the opposition Islah party taking seats in constituencies that were former strongholds of the ruling party. However, there were numerous problems with the election. Voter registration was characterized by widespread fraud, and underage voting was a pervasive problem.

Yemen was plagued by continued economic woes in 2004, with price inflation in basic food staples such as flour, wheat, fruit, and vegetables causing hardship for many Yemenis. The World Bank criticized Yemen's slow pace of economic reform, saying that the government had failed to implement key reforms such as privatizing state-owned companies and reforming the civil service. In June, Saleh announced that the government would delay a proposed move to reduce diesel fuel subsidies.

Yemen has faced challenges from terrorist and secessionist movements over the past decade. In 2004, a Yemeni court convicted 15 men for their roles in plotting and conducting a series of terrorist attacks in Yemen over the last four years.

In June 2004, clashes broke out between government forces and supporters of Hussein Badreddin al-Hawthi, a prominent cleric in Yemen's Zaidi community in the northern region of Saada. Al-Hawthi, who formed an opposition group called Believing Youth, had become strongly critical of the Yemeni government's relationship with the United States, accusing the government of taking actions to please the United States at the expense of the Yemeni people. Hundreds of people were reportedly killed in the clashes, with several human rights organizations calling for inquiries into reports of extrajudicial killings, mass arrests, and incommunicado detentions by government forces. The government stamped out the rebellion by the fall of 2004. Saleh accused several opposition political parties of supporting al-Hawthi's insurgency.

Despite these worrying signs of backsliding on political reform, the government continued to take steps to present an image of a country moving forward on democratic reform, participating in numerous international conferences on democratic development and hosting an intergovernmental regional conference on democracy, human rights, and the role of the International Criminal Court in January 2004.

Political Rights and Civil Liberties: Citizens of Yemen cannot change their government democratically. On the surface, Yemen appears to have a relatively open democratic system, with citizens of Yemen voting for president and members of parliament. In reality, Yemen's politics is monopolized by the ruling party, the GPC, which has increased the number of parliament seats it holds from 145 in 1993 to 237 in the current parliament. Yemen's government suffers from the absence of any real system of checks and balances of power and any significant limits on the executive's authority.

Yemen is headed by a popularly elected president, with a bicameral parliament composed of a 301-seat, popularly elected House of Representatives and an 111-member Majlis al-Shura, or Consultative Council, appointed by the president. The House of Representatives has legislative authority, and the Majlis al-Shura serves in an advisory capacity. Yemen is one of the few countries in the Arab world to organize regular elections on national and local levels, with limited competition among the ruling GPC party; two main opposition parties, Islah and the Yemeni Socialist Party (YSP); and a handful of other parties. Although local council members are popularly elected—the most recent local election was held in 2001—President Ali Abdullah Saleh appoints all local council chairpersons, who wield most of the decision-making authority.

Corruption is an endemic problem at all levels of government and society. Despite recent efforts by the government to step up efforts to fight corruption and institute a civil service reform program, Yemen lacks most legal safeguards to protect against conflicts of interest. Chief auditing and investigative bodies charged with fighting corruption are not sufficiently independent of the executive authorities. Yemen was ranked 112 out of 146 countries surveyed in Transparency International's 2004 Corruption Perceptions Index.

The state maintains a monopoly over the media that reach the most people—television and radio. Access to the Internet is not widespread, and the government reportedly blocks Web sites it deems offensive.

Journalists face threats of violence and death, arbitrary arrest, and often unclear judicial processes. In February, unknown gunmen entered the house of Sadeq Nasher, editor of *Al-Khaleej* newspaper, and issued a death threat prompted by Nasher's investigations into the December 2002 assassination of political opposition leader Jarallah Omar. In February, Saleh ordered the release of Najeeb Yabli, who was detained for writing an article in *Al-Ayyam* daily newspaper critical of Saleh's policies. In March, a Yemeni court ordered the release of journalist Saeed Thabet, who was detained for publishing "false information" on an assassination attempt against the president's son, Colonel Ahmad Ali Abdullah Saleh. Thabet was later fined and banned from working as a journalist for six months by the Western Court of Sana'a. In April, Ahmed al-Hubaishy, editor of the weekly newspaper *May 22*, a newspaper that has been critical of Islamic militants, was beaten by unknown assailants.

Article 103 of the Press and Publications Law outlaws direct personal criticism of the head of state and publication of material that "might spread a spirit of dissent and division among the people" or "leads to the spread of ideas contrary to the principles of the Yemeni Revolution, [is] prejudicial to national unity or [distorts] the image of the Yemeni, Arab, or Islamic heritage."

Despite a call by Saleh in June to put an end to imprisonment penalties for press offenses, government authorities used the Press and Publications Law numerous times in 2004. In September, Abdel Karim al-Khaiwani, editor of the prominent opposition weekly *Al-Shoura*, was convicted of incitement, insulting the president, publishing false news, and encouraging divisions within society because of a series of opinion pieces criticizing the government's actions in Saada. Hundreds were killed in the three-month uprising, which was centered in the northern mountains along Yemen's border with Saudi Arabia. Al-Khaiwani was sentenced to one year in jail, and the government suspended *Al-Shoura* from publication for six months. While in prison, al-Khaiwani was attacked and severely beaten by another inmate in early November. The government took steps to withdraw the license of *Al-Hurriya* newspaper. The Information Ministry closed a new weekly, *Al-Neda*, for violating Article 37 of the Press and Publications Law, which requires a new newspaper or magazine to publish within six months of registration; *Al-Neda* had missed this deadline by two days.

Article 2 of the constitution states that Islam is the religion of state, and Article 3 declares Sharia (Islamic law) to be the source of all legislation. Yemen has few religious minority groups, and their rights are generally respected in practice. Strong politicization of campus life, including tensions between supporters of the ruling GPC and opposition Islah parties, places limits on academic freedom.

Yemenis have the right to form associations, according to Article 58 of the constitution. Yemen has several thousand nongovernmental organizations (NGOs), although some observers question the viability and independence of these groups. In October, a Social Affairs Ministry official announced plans to establish new controls on foreign funding for Yemeni NGOs and new regulations for registering NGOs. The government respects the right to form and join trade unions, but some critics claim that the government and ruling party elements have stepped up efforts to control the affairs of these organizations.

Yemenis enjoy some freedom of assembly and demonstration, though the government restricts this from time to time. In March, thousands demonstrated in major cities across Yemen to protest Israel's extrajudicial killing of Hamas leader Sheikh Ahmad Yassin. However, in September, the government prevented a demonstration planned by opposition parties in Sana'a against government actions in quelling the Saada rebellion. In October, government security forces arrested members of the opposition Liberation Party for conducting a public demonstration.

The judiciary is nominally independent, but in practice it is weak and susceptible to interference from the executive branch. Government authorities have a spotty record of enforcing judicial rulings, particularly those issued against prominent tribal or political leaders. The lack of a truly independent judiciary impedes progress in all aspects of democracy and good governance; without an independent arbiter for disputes, people often resort to tribal forms of justice or direct appeals to the executive branch of government.

The 2004 trials of suspects involved in terrorist attacks in Yemen were held in secret, and several human rights groups criticized the fairness of these proceedings, saying that defense attorneys were not permitted to meet with their clients in private and were not provided with full access to all of the evidence.

Arbitrary detention occurs, sometimes because of a lack of proper training of law enforcement officials and at other times because of a lack of political will at the most senior levels of government. In May, the Yemeni press reported that more than 50 government security officers were prosecuted for violating human rights. Prison conditions remain poor and overcrowded, though the government took steps to upgrade the quality of some prisons in 2004 and provided human rights groups with access to some prisons.

Yemen is relatively homogenous ethnically and racially. The Akhdam, a small minority group, lives in poverty and faces social discrimination.

Women are afforded most legal protections against discrimination and provided with guarantees of equality. In practice, women continue to face pervasive discrimination in several aspects of life. Women are vastly under-represented in elected office. Despite the best efforts of women's rights groups to increase the number of women in parliament, only one woman won a seat in the 2003 parliamentary elections, out of 301 total seats. The number of women registered to vote increased nearly sevenfold in the past decade, from half a million in the 1993 parliamentary elections to more than three million in the 2003 parliamentary elections.

A woman must obtain permission from her husband or father to receive a passport and travel abroad. Unlike men, women do not have the right to confer citizenship on a foreign-born spouse, and the process of obtaining Yemeni citizenship for a child of a Yemeni mother and a foreign-born father is in practice more difficult than that for a child born of a Yemeni father and a foreign-born mother.

Zambia

Population: 10,900,000   **Political Rights:** 4
GNI/capita: $340   **Civil Liberties:** 4
Life Expectancy: 35   **Status:** Partly Free
Religious Groups: Christian (50-75 percent), Muslim and Hindu (24-49 percent), indigenous beliefs (1 percent)
Ethnic Groups: African (99 percent), other [including European] (1 percent)
Capital: Lusaka

Ten-Year Ratings Timeline (Political Rights, Civil Liberties, Status)

1995	1996	1997	1998	1999	2000	2001	2002	2003	2004
3,4PF	5,4PF	5,4PF	5,4PF	5,4PF	5,4PF	5,4PF	4,4PF	4,4PF	4,4PF

Overview:
Friction escalated in 2004 between civil rights groups and President Levy Mwanawasa, whom they accused of dominating the country's constitutional reform process. The government's drive to punish graft under the previous administration showed signs of flagging, with just one conviction to date amid alleged mishandling of cases by the president's anticorruption task force.

President Kenneth Kaunda and the United National Independence Party (UNIP) ruled Zambia from independence from Britain in 1964 until the transition to a multiparty system in 1991. Kaunda's regime grew increasingly repressive and corrupt as it faced security and economic difficulties during the long guerrilla wars against white rule in neighboring Rhodesia (now Zimbabwe) and Portuguese-controlled Mozambique. UNIP's socialist policies, combined with a crash in the price of copper, Zambia's main export, precipitated an economic decline unchecked for two decades.

In the face of domestic unrest and international pressure, Kaunda permitted free elections in 1991. Former labor leader Frederick Chiluba and his Movement for Multiparty Democracy (MMD) won convincingly. By contrast, the November 1996 presidential and parliamentary polls lacked legitimacy, largely because of a series of repressive measures instituted by the government. State resources and media were mobilized extensively to support Chiluba and the ruling MMD, and serious irregularities plagued election preparations. Voter lists were incomplete or otherwise suspect; independent monitors estimated that more than two million people were effectively disenfranchised. Candidate eligibility requirements were changed, which resulted in the exclusion of Kaunda, the most credible opposition candidate. Most opposition parties boycotted the polls, in which the MMD renewed its parliamentary dominance.

International observer groups that did monitor the polls, along with independent domestic monitors and opposition parties, declared the process and the results to be fraudulent.

Prior to the December 2001 presidential elections, the incumbent Chiluba supported a move within his party to change the constitution so that he could run for a third term. Dissension within his party, the opposition, and civil society forced him to retreat from that plan. Instead, the MMD nominated Mwanawasa, who narrowly won the vote by only 29 percent against a divided opposition. Both domestic and international election monitors cited serious irregularities with the campaign and election. The country's high court has so far withheld judgment on a petition by opposition candidates to overturn Mwanawasa's victory. During concurrent parliamentary elections, the MMD captured 69 seats out of 150 elected members. Hotly contested by-elections in 2003 increased the number of seats held by the MMD to 75. The main opposition party rejected the results.

Although widely perceived as former president Chiluba's handpicked successor, Mwanawasa has backed wide-ranging legal inquiries into alleged corruption by Chiluba and his senior associates while they were in power. However, a lack of concrete results has started to erode public confidence in the process. Only one official, Chiluba's former aide Richard Sakala, has gone to prison for corruption (in 2003). The government's campaign was dealt a further blow in August 2004, when a court dismissed more than 100 counts of corruption and theft against Zambia's former intelligence chief and its former ambassador to the United States, who had fled the country and were deemed beyond the court's jurisdiction. The two were considered key players in the plundering of an estimated $40 million from state coffers during Chiluba's tenure.

Despite promises of greater transparency and inclusiveness in the country's constitutional reform process, the government has relied on a commission whose members were mostly appointed by Mwanawasa, who has final authority over its proposals. A coalition of religious and civil society groups called the Oasis Forum is seeking the creation of a more representative Constituent Assembly to steer the review process, which would involve a national referendum.

Zambia was suspended from World Bank and IMF programs in 2003 because of a $125 million budget deficit. In July 2004, after the government slashed spending and announced a six-month freeze on the salaries of civil servants, the IMF approved a new $320 million loan. However, it postponed a final decision on forgiving a large portion of Zambia's crushing $6.5 billion debt until December. Independent monitors said in February that some funding intended for poverty relief had been spent on contracts that enriched top officials. The government's privatization drive ground to a halt in 2004, with no new sales of state-owned companies. Some 25 out of the original 284 state-owned enterprises are in various stages of transfer.

The country is among those suffering most from the AIDS pandemic; government figures indicate that Zambia already has nearly 700,000 AIDS orphans. UNAIDS estimated infection rates in 2002 at 21.5 percent.

Political Rights and Civil Liberties: Zambians cannot change their government democratically. While Zambians' constitutional right to change their government freely was honored in the 1991 elections, both the

1996 and 2001 elections won by the ruling MMD were subjects of intense controversy. President Levy Mwanawasa, who was reprimanded by Acting Chief Justice Ernest Sakala in 2002 for intimidating witnesses during the 2001 presidential election, has said he intends to drag the case out until the next election. The president and parliament are elected to serve concurrent five-year terms. The National Assembly includes 150 elected members, as well as 8 members appointed by the president and the Speaker of the Assembly.

Although the opposition is fragmented, together the biggest parties—the United Party for National Development, the United National Independence Party, and the Forum for Democracy and Development—hold a majority of 73 seats in the National Assembly.

High levels of corruption have burdened development, although Mwanawasa has taken the initiative in rooting out state graft. He earned praise for banning cabinet ministers and senior officials from bidding on government contracts and for sacking his own vice president, Enoch Kavindele, for involvement in an irregular oil contract. However, the long-awaited corruption trial of former president Chiluba has been repeatedly delayed, and a multi-agency task force appointed in 2002 has been accused of wasting taxpayer money and failing to produce results. Zambia was ranked 102 out of 146 countries surveyed in Transparency International's 2004 Corruption Perceptions Index.

The constitution provides for freedom of speech and the press, although these rights are restricted in practice. The government dominates broadcasting, although an independent radio station, Radio Phoenix, presents nongovernmental views. The Public Order Act, among other statutes, has at times been used to harass and intimidate journalists. Other tools of harassment have included criminal libel suits and defamation suits brought by MMD leaders in response to stories on corruption.

A bill to expand the right of access to information and liberalize the broadcasting sector was abruptly withdrawn in November 2002 by Kavindele, who cited global security concerns after the September 11, 2001, terrorist attacks in the United States. Independent media organizations have since lobbied unsuccessfully for its passage. The government does not restrict access to the Internet.

Constitutionally protected religious freedom has been respected in practice. The government does not restrict academic freedom.

Nongovernmental organizations (NGOs) engaged in promoting human rights, such as the Zambian Independent Monitoring Team, the Zambian Civic Education Association, and the Law Association of Zambia, operate openly. In 1999, however, the government drafted a policy that would closely regulate NGOs. The police frequently denied rally permits to opposition and citizens' groups, and forcibly broke up demonstrations, resulting in one death in 2004.

Zambia's trade unions remain among Africa's strongest, and union rights are constitutionally guaranteed. The Zambia Congress of Trade Unions, an umbrella organization for Zambia's 19 largest unions, operates democratically without government interference. The 1993 Industrial and Labor Relations Act protects collective bargaining rights, and unions negotiate directly with employers. About two-thirds of the country's 300,000 formal (business) sector employees are union members.

The judicial system, which has at times been subject to political influence, is under considerable pressure, with several high-level cases pending. In late 2003,

Frederick Chiluba was formally charged with the theft of $41 million in state funds during his tenure as president, having lost his immunity from prosecution the year before. After nearly a year of delays, prosecutors dismissed the case against Chiluba in September 2004, only to re-arrest him hours later on six reduced charges that alleged the theft of $1 million. The change of strategy was due in part to the loss of two key witnesses and co-defendants who had fled the country in May. The new corruption trial of Chiluba and two businessmen is set for December.

The court system is severely overburdened. Pretrial detainees are sometimes held for years under harsh conditions before their cases reach trial. The Magistrates and Judges Association identified congestion in prisons and delayed trials as extremely serious problems; malnourishment and poor health care in prisons cause many deaths. Although Zambia technically has a death penalty, Mwanawasa is an outspoken opponent of capital punishment and has implemented a de facto moratorium. He has refused to sign any death warrants since taking office and has commuted the death sentences of dozens of death-row prisoners. The country's Constitutional Review Commission has taken up the issue of eliminating the death penalty altogether. Customary courts of variable quality and consistency, whose decisions often conflict with both national law and constitutional protections, decide many civil matters. The government human rights commission investigated frequent complaints about police brutality and denounced the torture of coup suspects, but it has no power to bring charges against alleged perpetrators.

The constitution prohibits discrimination based on race, tribe, gender, place of origin, marital status, political opinion, color, or creed. However, societal discrimination remains a serious obstacle to women's rights. A 1998 regional human development report noted that Zambia was one of the lowest-performing countries in southern Africa in terms of women's empowerment. Women are denied full economic participation and are discriminated against in rural land allocation. A married woman must have her husband's permission to obtain contraceptives. Discrimination against women is especially prevalent in traditional tribunals that are courts of first instance in most rural areas. Spousal abuse and other violence against women are reportedly common. An October 2004 survey by the U.S. Agency for International Development found that 48 percent of Zambian women have been subjected to physical or emotional abuse by their spouse or partner.

Zimbabwe

Population: 12,700,000
GNI/capita: $490
Life Expectancy: 41
Political Rights: 7*
Civil Liberties: 6
Status: Not Free
Religious Groups: Syncretic [part Christian, part indigenous beliefs] (50 percent), Christian (25 percent), indigenous beliefs (24 percent), other [including Muslim] (1 percent)
Ethnic Groups: Shona (82 percent), Ndebele (14 percent), other (4 percent)
Capital: Harare
Ratings Change: Zimbabwe's political rights rating declined from 6 to 7 due to government repression of political opponents, civil society activists, and independent media representatives.

Ten-Year Ratings Timeline (Political Rights, Civil Liberties, Status)

1995	1996	1997	1998	1999	2000	2001	2002	2003	2004
5,5PF	5,5PF	5,5PF	5,5PF	6,5PF	6,5PF	6,6NF	6,6NF	6,6NF	7,6NF

Overview: Zimbabwe descended further into crisis in 2004 as the authoritarian government of President Robert Mugabe continued to stifle dissent, and militia loyal to Mugabe attacked opposition supporters with impunity. Economic collapse, and with it serious food shortages, deepened as the government expanded its ruinous policy of expropriating white-owned commercial farmland, and as other economic mismanagement and corruption widened. The government further curtailed the freedom of journalists, opposition parties, and civil society organizations.

Zimbabwe gained independence in 1980 after a guerrilla war against a white-minority regime that had declared unilateral independence from Britain in 1965 in what was then Southern Rhodesia; Mugabe has ruled the country since then. For a few years, Zimbabwe was relatively stable, although from 1983 to 1987, the government suppressed resistance from the country's largest minority group, the Ndebele, to dominance by Mugabe's majority ethnic Shona group. Severe human rights abuses accompanied the struggle, which ended with an accord that brought Ndebele leaders into the government.

The 2000 parliamentary elections were deemed by observers to be fundamentally flawed prior to balloting. Candidates and supporters of the opposition Movement for Democratic Change (MDC) faced violence and intimidation, including the use of rape as a weapon. A constitutional provision empowering Mugabe and allied traditional leaders to appoint one-fifth of parliament's members helped to ensure the continued majority in parliament of the ruling Zimbabwe African National Union-Patriotic Front (ZANU-PF). Voter registration, identification procedures, and tabulation of results were judged highly irregular by some independent observers. The state-controlled media offered limited coverage of opposition viewpoints, and the ZANU-PF used state resources heavily in campaigning. Mugabe issued a pardon for thousands of people, most of them from ZANU-PF, for crimes committed during the election campaign, including assault, arson, kidnapping, torture, rape, and attempted murder. According to the Zimbabwe Human Rights Forum, the rights of more than 18,000 people were violated.

In 2002, Mugabe claimed victory in a deeply flawed presidential election that failed to meet minimum international standards for legitimacy. The election pitted Mugabe against the MDC's Morgan Tsvangirai, a popular trade union leader who was arrested and charged with treason in 2003 after organizing national strikes.

Parliamentary by-elections held in 2003 in two districts near the capital, Highfield and Kuwadzanaw, were marred by intimidation against the MDC, which nonetheless won the polls. Party members were prevented from undertaking normal campaign activities and were detained, beaten, and harassed.

The MDC announced in August 2004 that it would suspend its participation in parliamentary and local elections because it believed there was no hope of a fair poll. The move could backfire, however, by allowing ZANU-PF to gain the two-thirds majority necessary to rewrite the constitution and further restrict democratic rights. In September, ZANU-PF increased its seats in parliament to 98, versus the MDC's 51, after the opposition party boycotted by-elections. The next parliamentary poll is planned for March 2005.

In the biggest split in the ZANU-PF since independence, Information Minister Jonathon Moyo was reprimanded and six of the party's ten provincial chairmen were suspended after a failed revolt against the appointment of a new vice president, Joyce Mujuru.

In recent years, Mugabe has turned against student groups, nongovernmental organizations (NGOs), labor unions, and white landowners to create the country's worst crisis since independence. War veterans and government-supported youth militias have occupied or disrupted opposition strongholds and white-owned land, with the overt or complicit backing of the government. Arrests of opposition members and protestors continued throughout 2004.

The government's seizures of white-owned farmland, which began in 2000, have prompted economic collapse, particularly in commercial farming on which exports, foreign exchange, and 400,000 jobs depended. Much of the seized land has gone to ZANU-PF officials, who often have no farming background, instead of to the landless rural black Zimbabweans who were supposed to benefit. The gross domestic product has fallen 30 percent since the land reform began, with the result that Zimbabwe has become one of the world's fastest shrinking economies. Fewer than 500 white-owned farms remain out of the 4,500 that existed when land invasions started. Unemployment exceeds 70 percent. Inflation was 132.6 percent in December 2004, down from a record 622.8 percent in January 2004 but still one of the highest in the world. Aid agencies have warned that nearly half of Zimbabwe's 12 million people need emergency food aid, largely because of faults in the redistribution policy. Party officials handling distribution have manipulated food aid that arrives, withholding relief from suspected opposition supporters. The situation is likely to worsen, considering the government's announcement in June that it planned to nationalize all productive farmland in the country.

Severe shortages of drugs and equipment have pushed hospitals and clinics close to ruin. Infant mortality rates have risen, and the resource-starved health system cannot cope with an HIV epidemic—one of the worst in the world—that has infected one in four adults.

Zimbabwe is in arrears to internal and external creditors, which has led to suspension of disbursements and credit lines. This situation has created shortages of key imports, such as fuel. Concern about the land-reform program was one reason that the IMF suspended financial support to Zimbabwe.

Political Rights and Civil Liberties: Zimbabweans cannot change their government democratically. President Robert Mugabe and the ZANU-PF, which have dominated the political landscape since independence, manipulate political structures to ensure continued control. The party remains the predominant power through its control over the security forces, most of the media, and much of the economy. Since 1987, at least 15 amendments to the constitution— including scrapping the post of prime minister in favor of an executive president and abolishing the upper chamber of parliament, the Senate—have given the executive more power. In turn, popular opposition to Mugabe has deepened, with trade unions often at the forefront, and the opposition MDC has experienced rapid growth.

The last few years have seen political violence by ZANU-PF youth militias, which have disrupted meetings and campaigning by opposition members. Meanwhile, security forces have targeted church leaders and civic organizations. Mugabe has on several occasions invoked the Presidential Powers Act, which enables him to bypass normal governmental review and oversight procedures.

Corruption is rampant throughout the country, including at the highest levels of government. Charges of corruption emerged in the 1990s when Mugabe began to award government contracts to his relatives. Ruling party and government officials have been allocated extensive properties seized from white farmers. Reports of extensive corruption and nepotism have reduced public and investor confidence in Zimbabwe's economy. Zimbabwe was ranked 114 out of 146 countries surveyed in the 2004 Transparency International Corruption Perceptions Index.

Freedom of the press is severely restricted. No privately owned radio or television stations exist in Zimbabwe, and the state-controlled newspapers and radio and television stations serve as mouthpieces of the government. The Parliamentary Privileges and Immunities Act has been used to force journalists to reveal their sources, especially regarding reporting on corruption, before the courts and parliament. The government in June proposed to censor e-mail by requiring Internet service providers to turn over to the authorities "objectionable, obscene, unauthorized" messages.

The 2002 Access to Information and Protection of Privacy Act (AIPPA), which gives the information minister sweeping powers to decide who can work as a journalist, has been used to silence media critics of the government. The AIPPA created a governmental commission that hands out "licenses" for journalists, and those operating without a license face fines or prison. In 2004, authorities shut down Africa Tribune Newspapers, whose publisher had criticized AIPPA, for failing to inform them of title and format changes. The previous year, the government closed down *The Daily News*, an independent newspaper that had harshly criticized Mugabe, for failing to register for an AIPPA license. A subsequent application for a license was rejected, and five of the newspaper's directors were arrested. Several other Zimbabwean journalists have been assaulted or detained over the years. In May, the editor and a reporter of *The Standard,* an independent newspaper, were arrested for reporting on the murder of a mining boss. Foreign reporters face extreme difficulty gaining approval to work in or even visit the country, and several have been deported.

Freedom of religion is generally respected, but academic freedom is limited. Security forces and ruling party thugs harass dissident university students, who have been arrested or expelled from school for protesting against government policy.

The small nongovernmental sector is active, and several groups focus on human rights. However, NGOs report increased difficulty in operating due to intimidation and legal harassment. Public demonstrations and protests are essentially illegal under the 2002 Public Order and Security Act, which forbids criticism of the president, limits public assembly, and allows police to impose arbitrary curfews. Security forces often disrupt opposition meetings or declare them illegal or allow party militias to attack opposition activists with impunity. Intelligence agencies are among law enforcers empowered to disperse "illegal" assemblies and arrest participants. In 2004, the government drafted the Non-Governmental Organizations Bill, which would empower a government-appointed body to investigate and audit any group's activities and funding. The measure would ban foreign-funded organizations involved in governance and human rights issues.

The right to collective action is limited under the Labor Relations Act, which allows the government to veto collective bargaining agreements that it deems harmful to the economy. Strikes are allowed except for industries declared "essential" under the act. Mugabe has used his presidential powers to declare strikes illegal, and labor organizers are common targets of government harassment. Most notably, security forces arrested more than 400 people in response to a two-day general strike in 2003; many were beaten or tortured while in police custody. Because the labor movement provides the core of the most organized resistance to Mugabe's authoritarian rule, it has become a particular target for repression.

While some courts have struck down or disputed government actions, increasing pressure by the regime may soon end the judiciary's capacity to act independently. The high court in May quashed the defamation conviction of three journalists for a story that misreported facts surrounding the draft constitution. The government, however, has repeatedly refused to enforce court orders and has replaced senior judges or pressured them to resign. The judicial system has been burdened by the vacancy of nearly 60 magistrate posts, which has caused a backlog of 60,000 cases that require processing.

Security forces often ignore basic rights regarding detention, search, and seizure. With the decline in law and order, war veterans and ruling party militants have taken over traditional policing roles in land redistribution. The military has assumed more policing roles in food distribution and elections. The government has taken no clear action to halt the rising incidence of torture and mistreatment of suspects held by police or security services. In June, the government passed the Criminal Procedure and Evidence Amendment Act that allows police to hold suspects accused of economic crimes for up to four weeks without bail. Human rights activists assert this contravenes the constitutional right to be presumed innocent until proved guilty. The country's 47 prisons are bulging with 8,000 inmates above the nominal 16,600 capacity. This overcrowding has contributed to a rise in AIDS and TB infections and to food shortages. Deaths in prisons are often caused by poor health conditions or beatings by guards.

The ruling party that is dominated by the Shona majority ethnic group continues to encourage political and economic discrimination against the minority Ndebele people. A clash between the two ethnic groups in the 1980s culminated in the government's massacre of thousands of Ndebele. Today, the Ndebele tend to be marginalized politically and their region (Matabele, which is an opposition stronghold) lags behind in economic development.

In theory, the state does not control travel or residence. But in practice the land confiscations prevent whites from living on big farms, and foreign critics of the regime are expelled or prevented from entering the country.

The government controls the prices of many major commodities and food staples, and state-linked companies dominate many sectors. The current political turmoil and investment flight does not bode well for the business environment. In September, Mugabe announced that the government would seize half of the country's private mining companies. A profound lack of transparency in government tenders and other operations has allowed corruption to thrive.

Women enjoy extensive legal protections, but de facto societal discrimination and domestic violence persist. Youth militias supporting Mugabe use rape as a political weapon. The Supreme Court declared that women who marry under customary law must leave their original families and cannot therefore inherit their property. Married women cannot hold property jointly with their husbands. Access to education for women is especially limited in rural areas. Female heads of households have borne the brunt of the current economic hardships.

Armenia/Azerbaijan
Nagorno-Karabakh

Population: 150,000   **Political Rights:** 5
Religious Groups: Armenian **Civil Liberties:** 5
Apostolic [majority], other   **Status:** Partly Free
Ethnic Groups: Armenian [majority], other

Ten-Year Ratings Timeline (Political Rights, Civil Liberties, Status)

1995	1996	1997	1998	1999	2000	2001	2002	2003	2004
6,6NF	6,6NF	5,6NF	5,6NF	5,6NF	5,6NF	5,6NF	5,5PF	5,5PF	5,5PF

Overview: The year 2004 represented the 10-year anniversary of the end of the brutal war that was fought over the contested Nagorno-Karabakh region. Progress remained stalled in international efforts to bring about an enduring political resolution to the disputed territory. Though a fragile ceasefire is in force, the two sides are officially in a state of war. Armenian-backed forces and Azerbaijani troops continue to face each other across a demilitarized zone.

The Nagorno-Karabakh Autonomous Region, which is largely populated by ethnic Armenians and is located inside the former Soviet republic of Azerbaijan, was established in 1923. In February 1988, Nagorno-Karabakh's regional legislature adopted a resolution calling for union with Armenia. The announcement triggered the first mass violence related to the conflict with attacks against Armenians in the Azerbaijani city of Sumgait several days later.

Successive battles and counteroffensives were fought over the next several years between various Armenian, Azerbaijani, and Nagorno-Karabakh forces. At its inaugural session in January 1992, Nagorno-Karabakh's new legislature adopted a declaration of independence, which was not recognized by the international community. By the time a Russian-brokered ceasefire was signed in May 1994, Karabakh Armenians, assisted by Armenia, had captured essentially the entire territory, as well as six Azerbaijani districts surrounding the enclave. Nearly all ethnic Azeris had fled or been forced out of the enclave and its surrounding areas, and the fighting had resulted in thousands of casualties and an estimated one million refugees.

In December 1994, the head of Nagorno-Karabakh's state defense committee, Robert Kocharian, was selected by the territory's parliament for the newly established post of president. Parliamentary elections were held in April and May 1995, and Kocharian defeated two other candidates in a popular vote for president in November of the following year.

In September 1997, Foreign Minister Arkady Ghukasian was elected to replace Kocharian, who had been named prime minister of Armenia in March of that year. In the territory's June 2000 parliamentary vote, 123 candidates representing five parties competed for the assembly's 33 seats. The ruling Democratic Union Artsakh

(ZhAM), which supported Ghukasian, enjoyed a slim victory, winning 13 seats. The Armenian Revolutionary Federation–Dashnaktsutiun won 9 seats, the Armenakan Party captured 1 seat, and formally independent candidates, most of whom supported Ghukasian, won 10. International observers described the electoral campaign and voting process as calm and largely transparent, although problems were noted with the accuracy of some voter lists.

In February 2001, former defense minister Samvel Babayan was found guilty of organizing a March 2000 assassination attempt against Ghukasian and sentenced to 14 years in prison. His supporters insisted that the arrest was politically motivated, as Babayan had been involved in a power struggle with Ghukasian. Others, however, welcomed the arrest and conviction of Babayan, who had been accused of corruption and reportedly wielded considerable political and economic power in the territory.

Ghukasian was reelected to a second term as president on August 11, 2002, with 89 percent of the vote. His closest challenger, former Speaker of parliament Artur Tovmasian, received just 8 percent. Voter turnout was close to 75 percent. Observers from countries including the United States, the United Kingdom, and France reported no serious violations. While a number of domestic and international nongovernmental organizations (NGOs) concluded that the elections marked a further step in Nagorno-Karabakh's democratization, they did voice some criticisms, including the limited access for the opposition to state-controlled media. Azerbaijan's Foreign Ministry described the election as a violation of international norms, insisting that a legitimate vote could be held only after a peaceful resolution to the conflict.

With both Armenia's president, Robert Kocharian, and Azerbaijan's president, Heydar Aliyev, poised to seek reelection in 2003—and the domestic political risk associated with either leader's making significant public concessions over the territory during a campaign year—few observers expected any breakthroughs in the conflict during 2003. An upsurge in shooting incidents along the ceasefire line in the summer, which both Armenian and Azerbaijani officials accused the other side of instigating, fueled concerns of a further and more widespread escalation of violence.

The Organization for Security and Cooperation in Europe's Minsk Group—which was established a decade earlier to facilitate dialogue on a political settlement on Nagorno-Karabakh's status—continued to attempt to coax forward a resolution of the long-standing dispute but made little meaningful headway on this during 2004. While Armenia insists that Nagorno-Karabakh should be left outside Azeri jurisdiction, Azerbaijan maintains that the territory may be granted broad autonomy while remaining a constituent part of Azerbaijan. Azerbaijan also has refused to negotiate with Ghukasian, who has demanded direct representation in the peace process.

Nagorno-Karabakh held local elections in August, ignoring calls from the Council of Europe to cancel the balloting. The Azerbaijani Foreign Ministry issued a protest at the holding of these elections in the territory, which is internationally recognized as being part of Azerbaijan. The Armenian authorities in Karabakh, in turn, rejected the Azerbaijani claims.

Political Rights and Civil Liberties: Nagorno-Karabakh has enjoyed de facto independence from Azerbaijan since 1994 and retains close political, economic, and military ties with Armenia. Parliamentary elections in

1995 and 2000 were regarded as generally free and fair, as were the 1996 and 1997 presidential votes. However, the elections were considered invalid by most of the international community, which does not recognize Nagorno-Karabakh's independence. Nagorno-Karabakh's electoral law calls for a single-mandate system to be used in parliamentary elections; lawmakers have rejected the opposition's demands for the inclusion of party-based lists.

The territory officially remains under martial law, which imposes restrictions on civil liberties, including media censorship and the banning of public demonstrations. However, the authorities maintain that these provisions have not been enforced since 1995, a year after the ceasefire was signed.

The government controls many of the territory's broadcast media outlets, and most journalists practice self-censorship, particularly on subjects dealing with policies related to Azerbaijan and the peace process. Some observers maintain that the government used the attempted murder of President Arkady Ghukasian in 2000 as a pretext to intensify attacks against its critics. In 2004, *Demo*, the first independent nongovernmental publication, appeared in Nagorno-Karabakh. Printed in Armenian and Russian and provided with support by a British NGO, *Demo* was a small bright spot on an otherwise dismal media landscape.

The registration of religious groups is required under Nagorno-Karabakh's 1997 law on religion. The Armenian Apostolic Church, which is the territory's predominant religion, is the only faith registered with the territory. According to Forum 18, a religious-freedom watchdog group based in Norway, members of various minority faiths, including Pentecostals, Adventists, Baptists, and Jehovah's Witnesses, have faced restrictions on their activities.

Freedom of assembly and association is limited, although political parties and unions are allowed to organize.

The judiciary, which is not independent in practice, is influenced by the executive branch and powerful political and clan forces. Former defense minister Samvel Babayan alleged that he had been physically assaulted during his interrogation and detention as a suspect in the failed assassination attempt against Ghukasian in March 2000. The presiding judge in the case announced that the subsequent guilty verdict against Babayan was based on pretrial testimony in which Babayan confessed to the charges, although Babayan later retracted his admission of guilt, claiming that it had been obtained under duress. In 2003, the republic's authorities announced the replacement of the death penalty with life imprisonment.

The majority of Azeris who fled the fighting continue to live in squalid conditions in refugee camps in Azerbaijan, while international aid organizations are reducing direct assistance to the refugees. Land mine explosions continue to result in casualties each year, with children and teenagers among the most vulnerable groups. According to the International Committee of the Red Cross, at least 50,000 anti-personnel mines were laid during the war, although in many cases, records of minefield locations were never created or were lost. The HALO Trust, a British NGO, is the major de-mining group operating in the territory.

Nagorno-Karabakh's fragile peace has failed to bring significant improvement to the economy, particularly in the countryside, and pensioners are particularly hard hit. Widespread corruption, a lack of substantive economic reforms, and the control of major economic activity by powerful elites limit equality of opportunity for most residents.

China
Hong Kong

Population: 6,899,000   **Political Rights:** 5
Religious Groups: Mixture   **Civil Liberties:** 2*
of local religions (90 percent),   **Status:** Partly Free
Christian (10 percent)
Ethnic Groups: Chinese (95 percent), other (5 percent)
Ratings Change: Hong Kong's civil liberties rating
improved from 3 to 2 due to an increase in civic activism.

Ten-Year Ratings Timeline (Political Rights, Civil Liberties, Status)

1995	1996	1997	1998	1999	2000	2001	2002	2003	2004
--	--	6,3PF	5,3PF	5,3PF	5,3PF	5,3PF	5,3PF	5,3PF	5,2PF

Overview: In April 2004, the Chinese government intervened directly
in the affairs of Hong Kong (formally, the Hong Kong Spe-
cial Administrative Region, or SAR) for the second time since
the territory's 1997 handover from the United Kingdom, issuing a ruling on Hong Kong's
basic law that blocked the possibility of long-promised electoral reform. In response,
hundreds of thousands of protestors took to the streets in a mass civic action in July.
On the political rights side, democratic parties did not perform as well as expected in
legislative elections in September, and allegations of voter intimidation surfaced.

Located at the mouth of the Pearl River on the southern Chinese coast, Hong
Kong consists of Hong Kong Island and Kowloon Peninsula, both ceded in perpetuity to Britain by China in the mid-1800s, and the mainland New Territories, which
Britain "leased" for 99 years in 1898. Hong Kong's transition to Chinese rule began
in 1984, when Britain agreed to return the territory to China in 1997 in return for
Beijing's pledge to maintain the capitalist enclave's legal, political, and economic
autonomy for 50 years.

London and Beijing later drafted a mini-constitution for Hong Kong, the basic
law, that laid the blueprint for introducing direct elections for 18 seats in the territory's
60-member legislature, known as the Legislative Council (Legco), in 1991 and gradually expanding the number to 30 over 12 years. The remaining 30 seats are chosen by
"functional constituencies"—essentially interest groups that tend to support Beijing.
Hong Kong's last colonial governor, Christopher Patten, infuriated Beijing with his
attempt to deepen democracy by giving ordinary residents greater say in choosing
Legco's indirectly elected seats. After China took control of Hong Kong as planned
in 1997, Beijing retaliated by disbanding the partially elected Legco and installing,
for 10 months, a provisional legislature that repealed or tightened several of the
territory's civil liberties laws.

As chief executive since the handover, Tung Chee-hwa has seen his popularity
wane as Hong Kong's economy has suffered in the wake of the 1997-1998 regional
financial crisis and as Beijing has become increasingly heavy-handed in its rule over
the Hong Kong SAR. A Beijing-organized committee chose him for the top job in
1996 after Chinese leaders indicated that he was their preferred choice.

The vast majority of Hong Kong voters favor direct elections for the chief executive and for all of Legco's seats, and the basic law allows direct elections for the chief executive in 2007 and for the entire Legco in 2008. However, any changes would have to be approved by China's rubber-stamp National People's Congress (NPC), Hong Kong's chief executive, and the Legco. Tung, who was reelected to a second five-year term in 2002 by an 800-member committee of lawmakers, religious figures, and interest-group representatives, promised public consultations in 2004 or 2005 on changes to the electoral system.

In April 2004, however, the standing committee of the National People's Congress (China's legislature) issued a ruling preserving the status quo, in contravention of Tung's promise; it maintained that political reform in Hong Kong could not occur without the committee's prior approval. New York–based Human Rights Watch called the development a "serious setback for electoral reform" and claimed that "by adding additional procedural requirements, [Beijing] changed the rules of the game, essentially amending the Basic Law." The organization also warned that "if Beijing does not recognize reasonable limits to its powers under Article 158, [which allows the NPC to issue interpretations of the Basic Law]. . .the provision could become a vehicle for infringing civil and political rights safeguards in Hong Kong."

In July 2004, hundreds of thousands of people took part in a peaceful march and a rally to protest the ruling and to demand the right to elect directly the chief executive. The event was doubly significant because it also commemorated the one-year anniversary of the march protesting the government's attempt to introduce an anti-subversion bill that would have fallen short of international human rights standards (the bill was subsequently shelved and has not yet been reintroduced).

With popular support for increased political freedom running so high, a democratic victory in the September 2004 Legco elections—the first in which 30 of the 60 seats were directly elected—was expected. However, pro-Beijing parties retained control of the legislature, with pro-democracy parties winning a total of only 25 of the 60 seats in the Legco (18 of the 30 directly elected seats, and just 7 of the 30 seats chosen by functional constituencies). The elections were marred by voter intimidation, resulting in a vote that was decidedly not free. A report released by Human Rights Watch three days before the election detailed "how politicians, journalists and voters have faced political intimidation and criminal threats, much of it apparently emanating from Beijing with the aim of skewing election results to favor pro-Beijing candidates." In March, for example, two leading radio commentators resigned after receiving phone calls ordering them to stop broadcasting until after the elections. In May, voters phoned in to radio programs reporting that they faced pressure to vote for pro-Beijing candidates.

Political Rights and Civil Liberties: Hong Kong residents enjoy most basic rights, but voters cannot change their government through elections. The chief executive wields strong executive powers and is appointed rather than elected. The 800-member committee that reelected Tung in 2002 consisted of the 60 members of Hong Kong's Legco; Hong Kong's 36 delegates to China's NPC; 40 representatives of religious groups; 41 members of an official Chinese consultative body; and 623 interest group representatives chosen in July 2000 by a narrow electorate of just 180,000 voters. Those 180,000 voters, representing labor, business, and the professions, also chose 30 of the 60 seats in the 2000 Legco elections. Six other seats were chosen by the same 800 people who reelected Tung, leaving only 24 directly elected seats. The number of directly elected seats increased to 30 in the September 2004 Legco elections.

The territory's basic law restricts Legco's lawmaking powers, prohibiting legislators from introducing bills affecting Hong Kong's public spending, governmental operations, or political structure. Legco members can introduce bills concerning governmental policy, but only with the chief executive's prior approval. In certain cases, the government has used a very broad definition of "governmental policy" in order to exercise its right to block Legco bills. In addition, for an individual member's bill to pass, it must have separate majorities among Legco members who are directly elected and those who represent interest groups.

Beyond these formal limits on elections and legislative power, many Hong Kong residents have criticized what they see as collusion between the administration and a handful of powerful businessmen. They point, for example, to the government's decision in 2000 to bypass the routine bidding process in awarding a contract to develop the Cyberport industrial park to Richard Li, a son of Li Ka-shing, Hong Kong's wealthiest businessman.

Despite these concerns, even the government's staunchest critics generally acknowledge that Hong Kong residents enjoy the same basic rights that they had enjoyed before the handover. Many of these rights, however, are now on less solid legal footing. While the International Covenant on Civil and Political Rights continues to be formally incorporated into Hong Kong's 1991 bill of rights, the provisional legislature that served for 10 months after the handover watered down certain provisions of the bill of rights and rolled back certain laws protecting workers' rights. It also amended laws to give officials the power to cite national security concerns in denying registration to nongovernmental organizations (NGOs), de-registering existing groups, and barring public protests.

Hong Kong's press continues to be outspoken on many issues. There are 15 privately owned daily newspapers (though four of these are supported and guided editorially by Beijing), hundreds of magazines, four commercial television stations, and two commercial radio stations, and all operate virtually free from government control. No restrictions impede the international media. Although political debate is vigorous and the media represent multiple points of view, many media outlets practice some self-censorship when reporting on Chinese politics, powerful local business interests, and the issues of Tibetan and Taiwanese independence. Internet access and use is unrestricted.

Hong Kong fully respects religious freedom. Religious groups are specifically excluded from the Societies Ordinance, which requires NGOs to register with the government. Beijing does not interfere in religious matters in Hong Kong. University professors can write and lecture freely, and political debate on campuses is lively. Research is independent of the government.

The basic law guarantees freedom of assembly and association, and the government has never invoked its power to bar protests on national security grounds. The police merely must be notified in advance about demonstrations and marches. The July 2004 march protesting Beijing's interpretation of the basic law was the second major public assembly to draw international attention within the space of one year. A wide range of NGOs, including human rights groups, operate in Hong Kong without restrictions.

Hong Kong's trade unions are independent, and union membership is not restricted to a single trade, industry, or occupation. However, the law restricts some basic labor rights and does not protect others. The provisional legislature in 1997 removed both the legal basis for collective bargaining and legal protections against summary dismissal for union activity. The Employment Ordinance provides punishments for anti-union discrimination. Though strikes are legal in the territory, many workers have to sign employment contracts stating that job walkouts could be grounds for summary dismissal.

Hong Kong's common law judiciary is independent, and the judicial process is fair. Trials are by jury and are public. Courts address issues that fall within the limits of the SAR's autonomy and can interpret sections of the basic law that deal with the relationship between Beijing and the SAR. However, they must obtain an interpretation from the NPC's Standing Committee before making a final judgment. This effective limit of the power of final adjudication of Hong Kong's Court of Final Appeal "could be used to limit the independence of the judiciary or could degrade the courts' authority," according to the 2003 human rights report released by the U.S. State Department in February 2004.

Hong Kong's police force, which remains firmly under the control of civilian authorities, is well supervised and not known to be corrupt. The police are forbidden by law to employ torture and other forms of abuse. Arbitrary arrest and detention are also illegal; suspects must be charged within 48 hours of their arrest.

The basic law guarantees equality of all residents before the law. An Equal Opportunity Commission was established in 1996 to eradicate discrimination and promote equality of opportunity. Ethnic minorities are well represented in the civil service and many professions. Nevertheless, some minorities allege discrimination in renting apartments, landing private sector jobs, receiving treatment in public hospitals, and competing for public school and university slots. In mid-2004, the government issued a consultation paper on proposed legislation that would make various forms of racial discrimination and harassment illegal. The public was invited to comment on the proposal until the end of December 2004.

The government generally does not impose limits on personal autonomy and privacy. The Telecommunications Ordinance and the Post Office Ordinance permit the interception of communications, however. Wiretapping requires high-level authorization, but not a warrant. Residents enjoy freedom of movement within Hong Kong and abroad.

Women in Hong Kong enjoy equal access to schooling and are protected under the basic law, but nevertheless face discrimination in employment, salary, welfare, inheritance, and promotion, according to the U.S. State Department report. Violence against women remains a problem, partly because of light sentences for offenders and also because of cultural factors that result in many cases of violence and abuse going unreported. Traffickers bring women into Hong Kong for prostitution and to work as household help and use the territory to transit victims of trafficking.

China
Tibet

Population: 5,300,000*   **Political Rights:** 7
Religious Groups: Tibetan   **Civil Liberties:** 7
Buddhist [majority], other   **Status:** Not Free
(including Muslim and Christian)
Ethnic Groups: Tibetan, Chinese
* This figure from China's 2000 census includes 2.4 million
Tibetans living in the Tibet Autonomous Region (TAR) and
2.9 million Tibetans living in areas of Eastern Tibet that,
beginning in 1950, were incorporated into four Chinese provinces.

Ten-Year Ratings Timeline (Political Rights, Civil Liberties, Status)

1995	1996	1997	1998	1999	2000	2001	2002	2003	2004
7,7NF	7,7NF	7,7NF	7,7NF	7,7NF	7,7NF	7,7NF	7,7NF	7,7NF	7,7NF

Overview: China maintained its control over Tibet in 2004, jailing dissidents and managing the daily affairs in major Buddhist monasteries and nunneries. However, some positive signs were in evidence as well during the year, as the Chinese government indicated its willingness to allow a human rights delegation and nongovernmental organizations (NGOs) to visit in 2005.

China's occupation of Tibet has marginalized a Tibetan national identity that dates back more than 2,000 years. Beijing's modern-day claim to the region is based on Mongolian and Manchurian imperial influence over Tibet in the thirteenth and eighteenth centuries, respectively. Largely under this pretext, China invaded Tibet in late 1949 and, in 1951, formally annexed the Central Asian land. In an apparent effort to undermine Tibetan claims to statehood, Beijing split up the vast region that Tibetans call their traditional homeland. It incorporated roughly half of this region into four different southwestern Chinese provinces beginning in 1950. The rest of this traditional homeland was named the Tibet Autonomous Region (TAR) in 1965.

The defining event of Beijing's rule took place in 1959, when Chinese troops suppressed a local uprising by killing an estimated 87,000 Tibetans in the Lhasa area alone. The massacre forced the Tibetan spiritual and political leader, the fourteenth Dalai Lama, Tenzin Gyatso, to flee to Dharamsala, India, with 80,000 supporters. Mao Zedong's Cultural Revolution further devastated Tibet; China jailed thousands of monks and nuns, and nearly all of Tibet's 6,200 monasteries were destroyed. As resistance to Beijing's rule continued, Chinese soldiers forcibly broke up mainly peaceful protests throughout Tibet. Few large-scale protests against Chinese rule have occurred since 1989, when Beijing imposed martial law on Lhasa and the surrounding areas following three days of antigovernment protests and riots. Officials lifted martial law in 1990.

In addition to jailing dissidents, Chinese officials have stepped up their efforts to control religious affairs and undermine the exiled Dalai Lama's religious and political authority. In a flagrant case of interference with Tibet's Buddhist hierarchy,

China in 1995 detained six-year-old Gedhun Choekyi Nyima and rejected his selection by the Dalai Lama as the eleventh reincarnation of the Panchen Lama. The Panchen Lama is Tibetan Buddhism's second-highest religious figure. Officials then stage-managed the selection of another six-year-old boy as the Panchen Lama. Since the Panchen Lama identifies the reincarnated Dalai Lama, Beijing potentially could control the identification of the fifteenth Dalai Lama. The government has also tried to control the identification and education of other religious figures.

Political Rights and Civil Liberties: Under Chinese rule, Tibetans lack the right to determine their political future. The Chinese Communist Party rules the TAR and traditional Tibetan areas in nearby Qinghai, Sichuan, Gansu, and Yunnan provinces through appointed officials whose ranks include some Tibetans. No Tibetan, however, has ever held the peak post of TAR party secretary. Tibetans suffer the same lack of political freedom as their Han Chinese counterparts.

China controls the flow of information in Tibet, tightly restricting all media and regulating Internet use. The government blocks access to Tibetan-language broadcasts of Voice of America and Radio Free Asia (as well as the Norway-based Voice of Tibet), as it does for the Chinese-language broadcasts. Radio Free Asia reports that Tibetans who listen to foreign-language radio broadcasts may be liable for official intimidation or fines. In early 2004, the government banned a book written by a Tibetan that discussed religious issues and asserted that Tibetans revere the Dalai Lama.

Chinese officials permit Tibetans to take part in many religious practices, and most Tibetans practice some degree of Buddhism. However, since 1996, the government has also strengthened its control over monasteries under a propaganda campaign aimed largely at undermining the Dalai Lama's influence as a spiritual and political leader. Under this "patriotic education campaign," government-run "work teams" visit monasteries to conduct mandatory sessions on Beijing's version of Tibetan history and other political topics. Officials also require monks to sign a declaration agreeing to reject independence for Tibet, denounce the Dalai Lama, not listen to Voice of America radio broadcasts, and reject the boy whom the Dalai Lama identified as the eleventh Panchen Lama.

The government directly manages monasteries through Democratic Management Committees (DMCs) and local bureaus. Only "patriotic and devoted" monks and nuns may lead DMCs, and the government must in any case approve all committee members. According to the U.S. State Department's 2003 Human Rights Report, released in February 2004, "the government continue[s] to discourage the proliferation of monasteries, which it contend[s are] a drain on local resources and a conduit for political infiltration by the Tibetan exile community."

In universities, professors cannot lecture on politically sensitive topics, and many reportedly are required to attend political education sessions. The government also limits course materials to prevent campus-based political and religious activity, and bans ancient and/or religious texts from classrooms on political grounds.

Independent civic groups, human rights groups, and trade unions are illegal. However, in October, at a human rights conference in Australia, Chinese officials indicated that they would invite a human rights delegation to visit Tibet in 2005. Moreover, for the first time ever, Chinese officials invited NGOs to take part in the human rights discussion that will be held in China in 2005. Though improvements in the human rights situation thus far have been marginal at best, the observation made by the deputy secretary of the Australian Department of Foreign Affairs and Trade that China is being "increasingly forthcoming" in its response to Australian expressions of concern about the situation gives hope that conditions might begin to show more serious improvement in coming years.

Tibet is governed by China's corrupt, poorly developed, state-controlled legal system. Like the rest of China, it does not enjoy the rule of law. Human Rights Watch said in February that the government "is misusing criminal charges to repress political, cultural and religious expression in Tibetan communities." The organization was responding to the news that Tenzin Delek Rinpoche, a senior lama, was being held in a high-security prison. He had been sentenced to death in December 2002, but the sentence was suspended for two years and may be commuted to life in prison. Neither his trial nor any of the evidence against him—he was allegedly involved in a bombing—was made available to the public, on the grounds that "state secrets" were involved. In November 2004, the U.S. State Department renewed pressure on China to allow him a fair hearing before his stay of execution expired on December 2.

Tibetan political dissidents face particularly severe human rights abuses. Security forces routinely engage in arbitrary arrest and detention, torture, and execution, without due process, to punish even nonviolent protesters against Chinese rule. In March 2004, for example, security officials arrested a popular Tibetan singer and a composer because of the allegedly political content of their music. The previous month, security officials near Lhasa arrested a monk for possessing a photograph of the Dalai Lama and a Tibetan flag.

There are many political prisoners—strictly controlled access to the TAR makes it difficult to determine exactly how many, according to the 2003 U.S. State Department report—and they suffer beatings, physical and psychological torture, forced labor, and "political investigation" sessions that result in further punishment if detainees are not found to be loyal enough to the state. In October, the head of a Tibetan Buddhist monastery was shot and killed by the police; he and other monks had asked that the police repay them for medical treatment they had required after being beaten while in custody.

The issue of human rights scored an apparent victory in March, when one of the so-called "singing nuns" was released from prison after 15 years. Phuntsog Nyidron was detained in 1989 on charges of "counterrevolutionary propaganda and incitement" for her part in an independence march. She and 13 other imprisoned Tibetan women became known for smuggling a tape out of jail that had on it songs about their commitment to Tibet. However, Phuntsog Nyidron remains under constant government supervision, according to Human Rights Watch; at least two security officials out of the four assigned to her—two prison representatives and two public security officers—monitor her 24 hours a day. Calling China's strategy a "nasty game," the executive director of the organization's Asia Division remarked, "China tries to score points with other governments by opportunistically releasing activists, then keeping them isolated and under constant surveillance."

Because they belong to one of China's 55 recognized ethnic minority groups, Tibetans receive some preferential treatment in university admissions and governmental employment. Tibetans, however, generally need to learn Mandarin Chinese in order to take advantage of these preferences or to hold many private sector jobs. Many Tibetans are torn between a desire to learn Chinese in order to compete for university slots and jobs and the realization that increased use of Chinese threatens the survival of the Tibetan language and culture. Government development policies have helped most Tibetans to some extent, but the policies still benefit Han Chinese disproportionately.

Tibetans reportedly face difficulties obtaining passports. Up to 3,000 Tibetans, many without valid travel documents, cross the border into Nepal each year. Many seek to study or settle in India. The government restricts foreign travel to the TAR and restricts Tibetans' movements during particularly sensitive anniversaries or events.

In November 2004, however, the Russian government granted the Dalai Lama a visa for the first time in 13 years, risking the displeasure of China, with whom it has increasing political and military ties. The Dalai Lama led prayers in the Russian republic of Kalmykia, one of the largest centers of Buddhism in that country. China responded by indicating that it "opposes . . . visits by the Dalai Lama to countries with diplomatic relations with China" and expressing its hope that Russia would "strictly abide by . . . relevant political agreements between the two sides."

State employment policies are generally less restrictive for Tibetans than for Han Chinese. Officially, the government maintains the right to refuse an individual's application to take up religious orders, but this is not often exercised. In the private sector, employers favor Han Chinese for many jobs—especially in urban areas—and give them greater pay than Tibetans for the same work. Tibetans also find it more difficult than Han Chinese to obtain permits and loans to open businesses. Tibetans are limited in many areas because of their relatively poor command of Mandarin Chinese, the language that has become widespread in urban areas and many businesses.

China's restrictive family planning policies are somewhat more lenient toward Tibetans and other ethnic minorities than toward the Han Chinese majority. Officials generally limit urban Tibetans to two children and encourage—but do not require—rural Tibetans to stop at three children. These restrictions were in any case not enforced in 2004. As in other parts of China, prostitution is a growing problem in the TAR.

Cyprus
Northern (Turkish) Cyprus

Population: 229,000   **Political Rights:** 2
Religious Groups: Muslim   **Civil Liberties:** 2
(99 percent), other   **Status:** Free
[including Greek Orthodox] (1 percent)
Ethnic Groups: Turkish (99 percent), other [including Greek]
(1 percent)

Ten-Year Ratings Timeline (Political Rights, Civil Liberties, Status)

1995	1996	1997	1998	1999	2000	2001	2002	2003	2004
4,2PF	4,2PF	4,2PF	4,2PF	4,2PF	2,2F	2,2F	2,2F	2,2F	2,2F

Note: See Cyprus under Country Reports.

Overview:

Hopes were high in the Turkish part of the divided island of Cyprus as the two sides of the island came the closest yet to a settlement in 2004 through months of intervention and a proposed reunification plan by UN Secretary-General Kofi Annan. However, the Annan plan ultimately failed after the Turkish side voted yes but the Greek side voted no in a referendum on April 24. Mehmet Ali Talat, who became Turkish Cypriot prime minister following legislative elections in December 2003, resigned in November 2004 when his coalition lost its majority; fresh elections were expected in 2005.

Annexed by Britain in 1914, Cyprus gained independence in 1960 after a 10-year guerrilla campaign by partisans demanding union with Greece. In July 1974, Greek Cypriot National Guard members, backed by the military junta in power in Greece, staged an unsuccessful coup aimed at unification with Greece. Five days later, Turkey invaded northern Cyprus, seized control of 37 percent of the island, and expelled 200,000 Greeks from the North. Today the Greek and Turkish communities are almost completely separated in the South and North, respectively.

A buffer zone, called the Green Line, has divided Cyprus since 1974. The capital, Nicosia, which is located at the Green Line, is similarly divided. Tensions and intermittent violence between the Greek and Turkish populations have plagued the island since independence. UN resolutions stipulate that Cyprus is a single country in which the northern third is illegally occupied. In 1983, Turkish-controlled Cyprus declared its independence as the Turkish Republic of Northern Cyprus (TRNC), an entity recognized only by Turkey.

A major change occurred with the election in November 2002 of a new Turkish government, which has been much less indulgent of Turkish Cypriot president Rauf Denktash's opposition to reunification because Turkey's own chances of European Union (EU) membership have been linked to a resolution of the island's division. This, combined with significant pressure from the EU and the United States as well as UN intervention, has moved the two sides closer to settlement.

The latest and as yet most promising round of reunification negotiations began after the parliamentary elections in northern Cyprus in December 2003. These elections brought to power a new coalition led by Talat, the new prime minister. Talat's party, the Republican Turkish Party (CTP), partnered with its former rival, the Democratic Party—led by Serdar Denktash, son of the president—to form a pro-unification government. This represented the greatest upset ever for the largest party supporting President Rauf Denktash, the National Unity Party (UBP). With the side-lining of President Denktash, the way was cleared for the UN's Annan to propose a new path toward a settlement.

Annan led a series of negotiations that included the leaders of the Greek and Turkish Cypriot communities, followed by the inclusion of Greece and Turkey. When no consensus was reached, Annan himself proposed a plan that was put to a vote in simultaneous, separate referendums in northern and southern Cyprus on April 24. Prior to the Turkish Cypriot parliamentary elections, the international community had taken it for granted that the Turkish side would always oppose a settlement. However, with the Turkish Cypriot government fully on board, the Greek Cypriots began to express severe reservations about the plan. Ultimately, 76 percent of Greek Cypriots voted against the plan, while 65 percent of Turkish Cypriots voted in favor. With the island still divided, only Greek Cyprus joined the EU as planned on May 1.

However, the overwhelming approval of the Turkish Cypriots for reunification sparked profound efforts on the part of the international community to reward them by ending their isolation. Donors have pledged significant aid, including 259 million euros from the EU. There were also efforts to end trade and travel bans and to increase movement across the Green Line. Nevertheless, the southern Cypriots have worked against most direct contact between the North and the rest of the world, including picking over the specifics of the EU aid package, arguing that certain measures are equivalent to international recognition of the North. In addition, Talat has stated that the international community is not doing enough to move the South toward reconciliation with the North. Meanwhile, trade has increased between the two sides, and Greek Cypriots are no longer required to show a passport to cross into the North.

In October, Talal resigned as prime minister. In April, 3 representatives had left his coalition, leaving it with a minority of seats. When no party succeeded in forming a new government, legislators agreed to hold new elections in 2005.

Living standards in the North, which has an economy that depends heavily on the government of Turkey, are only about a third of those in the South. The public sector provides most jobs, although many Turkish Cypriots now cross the border to work on the Greek side. The suffering economy contributed substantially to support for reunification and the public turn against President Denktash. However, the economy showed signs of picking up toward the end of 2004.

Political Rights and Civil Liberties:

Turkish Cypriots can change the government of the TRNC democratically. The president and 50-seat legislature are elected to terms of not longer than five years. President Rauf Denktash's current term is set to expire by April 2005, and he has said that he will not run for reelection. The powers of the president are largely ceremonial, but Denktash has wielded influence through his status as the traditional leader of the Turkish Cypriot community. However, his role has diminished in favor of the prime minister since the election of pro-unification parties in 2003 and the yes vote in the unification referendum in 2004.

Some irregularities did occur in the December 2003 legislative elections. A group of independent election observers cited suspicions of inflated vote counts (presumably with Turkish settlers), pressure on voters to support specific parties, and biased reporting by the government television station. The observers said that electoral procedures were inadequate to ensure fair voting. During the subsequent referendum, some pro-reunification citizens were the target of vandalism and even violence; in Northern Nicosia, five Turkish Cypriot men were hospitalized after an attack by Turkey's extreme nationalist Grey Wolves. However, the incidents appeared to be isolated.

The 1,000-odd Greek and Maronite Christian residents of the North are disenfranchised, but many vote in elections in the Republic of Cyprus. Turkish Cypriots were allowed to cross the Green Line in order to vote in the European Parliament elections in June. However, only 97 Turkish Cypriots cast votes.

Corruption is not a severe problem in northern Cyprus. However, in 2004, the U.S. Treasury Department designated the First Merchant Bank of the TRNC as a financial institution of "primary money laundering concern."

The criminal code allows the government to jail journalists for what they write, and the government has been hostile to the independent press. Sener Levent, the editor of the outspoken daily newspaper *Afrika*, has faced hundreds of court summonses for his paper's criticism of Turkish and Turkish Cypriot officials, including many in 2004. Five journalists and the secretary of the Kibris Media Group received court summonses in 2004 for their articles on an antigovernment demonstration in Elia the previous year. The daily *Kibris* newspaper, which was in favor of reunification, was the target of death threats leading up to the referendum, and three small homemade bombs exploded outside its office just afterward. In contrast, President Denktash refused the UN's request for a news blackout during the reunification talks.

An agreement with Greek Cypriot authorities dating from 1975 provides for freedom of worship for both communities in both parts of the island. On September 1, the first church service since 1974 was held at Agia Mama church in Morphou, one of the most important places of worship for the Greek Orthodox faithful in Cyprus.

The government does not restrict academic freedom. In 2004, Turkish Cypriot schools began teaching a less partisan account of Cypriot history in favor of multiple perspectives, in accordance with Council of Europe recommendations.

There is freedom of assembly and association, although in July the government prevented peace activists from laying wreaths at the graves of Turkish Cypriots killed in the fighting in 1974 for fear that the action might spark confrontations. Civic groups and nongovernmental organizations generally operate without restrictions. Workers may form independent unions, bargain collectively, and strike. Charges against 30 members of the Turkish Cypriot Teachers Union for their 2001 criticism of the government were dropped in May.

The judiciary is independent, and trials generally meet international standards of fairness. Turkish Cypriot police, under the control of the Turkish military, sometimes abuse due process rights, and civilians are sometimes tried in military courts.

After the referendum on unification, the EU attempted to initiate direct trade and flights between northern Cyprus and the rest of the world, but it was unable to circumvent international regulations that control the ports and airports of the unrecognized state. However, trade between the two parts of the island did increase after restrictions were loosened. In addition, all EU citizens, including Greek Cypriots, can now travel to the North by presenting identity cards instead of passports. Conversely, Turkish Cypriot prime minister Mehmet Ali Talat rejected a Greek Cypriot proposal to open 11 new crossing points across the Green Line. Turkish Cypriots still have difficulty traveling because most governments do not recognize their travel documents.

Women are under-represented in government. There are legal provisions for equal pay for equal work, but these are often disregarded.

Georgia
Abkhazia

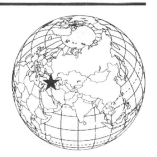

Population: 250,000
Religious Groups: Muslim [majority], Christian
Ethnic Groups: Abkhaz [majority], Georgian

Political Rights: 6
Civil Liberties: 5
Status: Not Free

Ten-Year Ratings Timeline (Political Rights, Civil Liberties, Status)

1995	1996	1997	1998	1999	2000	2001	2002	2003	2004
--	--	6,5NF	6,5NF	6,5NF	6,5NF	6,5NF	6,5NF	6,5NF	6,5NF

Overview: The breakaway republic of Abkhazia experienced a tumultuous year in 2004, including the murder of a leading opposition figure, Garri Aiba. A drawn-out leadership struggle followed on the heels of an intensely contested presidential election in October, the first openly contested presidential vote in the breakaway republic. Meanwhile, a final resolution to the long-standing conflict remained elusive throughout the year.

Annexed by Russia in 1864, Abkhazia became an autonomous republic of Soviet Georgia in 1930. The year after the 1991 collapse of the Soviet Union, Abkhazia declared its independence from Georgia, igniting a war that lasted nearly 14 months. In September 1993, Abkhaz forces, with covert assistance from Russia, seized control of the city of Sukhumi, ultimately defeating the Georgian army and winning de facto independence for the territory. As a result of the conflict, more than 200,000 residents, mostly ethnic Georgians, fled Abkhazia, while casualty figures were estimated in the thousands. An internationally brokered ceasefire was signed in Moscow in 1994, although a final decision on the territory's status remains unresolved. In the October 1999 elections for president of Abkhazia, Vladislav Ardzinba, the incumbent and the only candidate running for office, was reelected. The OSCE, the United Nations, and other international organizations refused to recognize the vote as legitimate. In a concurrent referendum on independence, the results of which were not accepted by any state, a reported 98 percent of voters supported independence for Abkhazia. Georgia denounced the polls as illegal and as an attempt to sabotage peace talks.

Tensions in the Kodori Gorge, an area controlled partly by Georgia and partly by Abkhazia, underscored the precariousness of the region's fragile peace. In October 2001, a group reportedly consisting of Chechen rebels and Georgian partisans clashed with Abkhaz troops following a deadly raid on a village in the gorge. The downing of a UN helicopter and the bombing of several Abkhaz villages by aircraft that Georgian authorities alleged had come from Russia intensified the conflict. Tbilisi responded by sending troops to the upper part of the gorge in what it said was an operation to protect ethnic Georgians living there from separatist attacks. Abkhaz officials insisted that despite a UN-brokered protocol calling for the withdrawal of Georgian forces, which was signed by Russia and Georgia in 2002, Georgia had not pulled all its troops out of the Kodori Gorge. Georgian authorities countered that the protocol did not require the withdrawal of other military detachments, including border guards.

Deputies loyal to Ardzinba won a landslide victory in the March 2002 parliamentary elections when the opposition Revival and People's Party withdrew most of its candidates in protest over the conduct of the campaign. Officially backed candidates, who won all 35 seats in the legislature, ran unopposed for 13 of them. Among the problems cited during the elections were that ethnic Georgians displaced by the war were not able to vote, official radio and television promoted pro-government candidates, and the head of the Central Election Commission had disqualified a number of candidates supported by the opposition. As it had for previous elections in Abkhazia, the international community declared the elections to be illegitimate.

On April 8, 2003, after just four months in office, the government of Prime Minister Gennady Gagulia, who had developed a reputation for political weakness and inefficiency, resigned. Gagulia stepped down following pressure from Amtsakhara, an increasingly powerful opposition political movement representing primarily veterans of the 1992-1993 war, which had threatened to organize a mass rally if he remained in office. On April 22, Defense Minister Raul Khajimba was named to succeed Gagulia as prime minister. Subsequently, Amtsakhara also called on Ardzinba to resign as president because of his poor health; Ardzinba, who was undergoing medical treatment in Moscow for an undisclosed illness and who was no longer actively involved in the daily running of the government, insisted that he had no intention of stepping down before the next presidential election, on October 3, 2004.

In advance of the presidential poll, a new political movement, called United Abkhazia (Yedinaya Abkhazia) took shape, with the hope of putting forward a single opposition candidate. However, all three of the new movement's leaders became presidential candidates: Sergei Shamba, the Abkhaz foreign minister; Nodar Khashba, a senior official in Russia's emergencies ministries; and Sergei Bagapsh, a former prime minister. The Central Election Commission barred one of the leading contenders, Alexander Ankvab, for allegedly failing to meet the residency requirement for presidential candidates. The commission also cited his refusal to take a full language test to evaluate his command of the state language of the Abkhaz Republic. Ankvab, who was the breakaway republic's interior minister during the Georgian-Abkhaz war of 1992-1993, has been among the most prominent opponents of President Ardzinba. The post-election period descended into a volley of charges and counter-charges between Bagapsh, whom elections officials declared to be the winner of the October 3 vote with 50.08 percent of the vote—more than the 50 percent threshold needed to avert a second-round runoff—and Khajimba, who had the backing of the Ardzinba administration, as well as that of Moscow. Meanwhile, outgoing president Ardzinba, who had handpicked Khajimba as his successor, refused to leave office, contesting Bagapsh's apparent victory. As of November 30, a clear solution for the dispute had not been realized.

Political Rights and Civil Liberties: Residents of Abkhazia can elect government officials, but the more than 200,000 displaced Georgians who fled the region during the war in the early to mid-1990s could not vote in the October 1999 presidential, March 2001 local, or March 2002 parliamentary elections. International organizations, including the OSCE, as well as the Georgian government, criticized the polls as illegitimate. Although the November 1994 constitution established a presidential-parliamentary system of government, the president exercises extensive control of the region.

The ethnic Georgian Abkhazian Supreme Council has been a government in exile in Tbilisi since being expelled from Abkhazia in 1993.

Opposition political parties include Aitara (Revival). Amtsakhara, a political group representing primarily veterans of the 1992–1993 war, has become a growing force in the territory's political life.

Several independent newspapers are published in the territory. Electronic media are controlled by the state and generally reflect government positions.

Reliable information on freedom of religion is difficult to obtain. Although a presidential decree bans Jehovah's Witnesses and members have been detained by the authorities in recent years, none were in detention at year's end, according to a representative of the group. Abkhazia's Ministry of Education prohibits instruction in the Georgian language in the territory's schools, the 2003 U.S. State Department's human rights report for Georgia stated. Local residents in the Gali district, whose population is largely ethnic Georgian, were denied access to education in their mother tongue.

Most nongovernmental organizations operating in Abkhazia rely on funding from outside the territory.

Defendants' limited access to qualified legal counsel, violations of due process, and the lengthiness of pretrial detentions are among the systemic problems in the territory's criminal justice system.

The human rights and humanitarian situation in Abkhazia continued to be a serious problem in 2004. A UN Security Council report issued on July 14, 2004, stated, "The precarious human rights situation . . . showed no signs of improvement. The rule of law, the administration of justice, as well as law enforcement mechanisms remained weak and did not provide adequate protection of the right to life and physical security."

Travel and choice of residence are limited by the ongoing conflict. Approximately 200,000 ethnic Georgians who fled Abkhazia during the early 1990s are living in western Georgia, most in the Zugdidi district bordering Abkhazia. Most of these internally displaced persons are unable or unwilling to return because of fears for their safety.

Equality of opportunity and normal business activities are limited by widespread corruption, the control by criminal organizations of large segments of the economy, and the continuing effects of the war. Abkhazia's economy is heavily reliant on Russia; the territory uses the Russian ruble as its currency.

India
Kashmir

Population: 11,000,000   **Political Rights:** 5
Religious Groups: Muslim   **Civil Liberties:** 5
(64.2 percent), Hindu   **Status:** Partly Free
(32.2 percent), Sikh (2.4 percent),
Buddhist (1.2 percent)
Ethnic Groups: Kashmiri [majority], Dogra, Ladakhi,
Gujjar, Bakerwal, Dard, Balti, other

Ten-Year Ratings Timeline (Political Rights, Civil Liberties, Status)

1995	1996	1997	1998	1999	2000	2001	2002	2003	2004
7,7NF	7,7NF	7,7NF	6,6NF	6,6NF	6,6NF	6,6NF	5,5PF	5,5PF	5,5PF

Overview: **Overall progress on finding a political solution to the conflict over the territory of Kashmir, where a continuing insurgency has killed at least 40,000 civilians, soldiers, and militants since 1989, remained slow throughout 2004. A reciprocal ceasefire between Indian and Pakistani troops declared in November 2003 was largely upheld in 2004, and the two national governments held several rounds of talks during the year.**

After centuries of rule in Kashmir by Afghan, Sikh, and local strongmen, the British seized control of the Himalayan land in 1846 and sold it to the Hindu maharajah of the neighboring principality of Jammu. The maharajah later incorporated Ladakh and other surrounding areas into what became the new princely state of Jammu and Kashmir. At the partition of British India into the new nations of India and Pakistan in 1947, Maharajah Hari Singh attempted to preserve Jammu and Kashmir's independence. However, after Pakistani tribesmen invaded, the maharajah agreed to Jammu and Kashmir's accession to India in return for promises of autonomy and eventual self-determination.

Within months of gaining their independence, India and Pakistan went to war in Kashmir. A UN-brokered ceasefire in January 1949 established the present-day boundaries, which gave Pakistan control of roughly one-third of Jammu and Kashmir, including the far northern and western areas. India retained most of the Kashmir Valley along with predominantly Hindu Jammu and Buddhist-majority Ladakh.

Under Article 370 of India's constitution and a 1952 accord, the territory received substantial autonomy. However, New Delhi began annulling the autonomy guarantees in 1953, and in 1957, India formally annexed the part of Jammu and Kashmir under its control. Seeking strategic roads and passes, China seized a portion of Kashmir in 1959. India and Pakistan fought a second, inconclusive war over the territory in 1965. Under the 1972 Simla accord, New Delhi and Islamabad agreed to respect the Line of Control (LOC), which demarcates the Indian- and Pakistani-held parts of Kashmir, and to resolve Kashmir's status through negotiation.

The armed insurgency against Indian rule gathered momentum after 1987, when the pro-India National Conference Party won state elections that were marred by widespread fraud and violence, and authorities began arresting members of a new, Muslim-based, opposition coalition. Militant groups with links to political parties assassinated several National Conference politicians and attacked government targets in the Kashmir Valley. The militants included the Jammu and Kashmir Liberation Front (JKLF) and other pro-independence groups consisting largely of indigenous Kashmiris, as well as Pakistani-backed Islamist groups that want to bring Kashmir under Islamabad's control.

As the violence escalated, New Delhi placed Jammu and Kashmir under federal rule in 1990 and attempted to quell the mass uprising by force. By the mid-1990s, the Indian army had greatly weakened the JKLF, which abandoned its armed struggle in 1994. The armed insurgency has since been dominated by Pakistani-backed extremist groups, which include in their ranks many non-Kashmiri fighters from elsewhere in the Islamic world. Although opposition parties joined together to form the All Parties Hurriyat Conference (APHC) in 1993, they boycotted the 1996 state elections, and the National Conference was able to form a government under party leader Farooq Abdullah.

In August 2000, Hizbul Mujahideen, the largest armed group in Kashmir, initiated a dialogue with the Indian government, but talks broke down when India refused to include Pakistan in the discussions. The two neighbors had engaged in a limited war in 1999 after Pakistan had seized strategic heights on the Indian side of the LOC. A summit held in 2001 failed to resolve the two countries' long-standing differences over Kashmir. Militants stepped up their attacks in the aftermath of the summit, with an increasing focus on targeting Hindu civilians in the southern districts of the state. In addition, a leading moderate separatist politician, Abdul Ghani Lone, was assassinated in May 2002, probably by a hard-line militant group.

Seeking legitimacy for the electoral process, New Delhi encouraged all political parties to participate in the fall 2002 state elections, but was unsuccessful in persuading the APHC to contest the polls. However, in a surprise result, the ruling National Conference lost 29 of its 57 assembly seats, while the Congress Party and the People's Democratic Party (PDP) made significant gains, winning 16 and 20 seats, respectively. In November, the two parties formed a coalition government headed by the PDP's Mufti Mohammad Sayeed. The new government promised to address issues of human rights violations, corruption, and economic development, and urged the central government to hold peace talks with separatist political groups. Sayeed also created a committee within the state assembly to study all autonomy-related issues.

After initial signs of improvement during the new government's honeymoon period, the incidence of both violence and human rights violations rose to previous levels in 2003. Nevertheless, the Indian government has shown a greater willingness to initiate a dialogue with various Kashmiri groups, including the APHC. In January 2004, talks were held for the first time between Kashmiri separatists and the highest levels of the Indian government. Numbers of fatalities decreased somewhat during the year; an estimated 1,800 people were killed during 2004, compared with more than 2,500 in 2003, according to the South Asia Terrorism Portal. The new central government announced in November that in response to an improved security situation, it planned to reduce troop numbers in the region, and in addition presented a four-year, $5 billion development package designed to improve infrastructure, education, and tourism.

Authorities in New Delhi also attempted to improve relations with Pakistan via a series of "confidence-building measures" announced in October 2003, including a resumption of transport links between the two countries. In November, Pakistan declared a ceasefire across the LOC, to which India reciprocated; the ceasefire was largely in place throughout 2004. After announcing the resumption of a "composite dialogue," including the Kashmir dispute, in January 2004, the two governments held several rounds of talks during the year. Although little substantive progress was made on finding a lasting solution to the conflict, the two sides did discuss a range of issues, including territorial control over the disputed Siachen glacier and the possibility of opening a bus route between the Indian and Pakistani portions of Kashmir, as well as affirming their commitment to solving the Kashmir dispute through peaceful negotiations.

Political Rights and Civil Liberties: India has never held a referendum on Kashmiri self-determination as called for in a 1948 UN resolution. The state's residents can nominally change the local administration through elections, but historically, elections have been marred by violence, coercion by security forces, and balloting irregularities. Militants commonly enforce boycotts called for by separatist political parties, threaten election officials and candidates, and kill political activists as well as civilians during the balloting. During the campaign period leading up to the 2002 elections for the 87-seat state assembly, over 800 people, including more than 75 political activists and candidates, were killed. However, the balloting process itself was carefully monitored by India's Election Commission, and turnout averaged just over 40 percent. Most independent observers judged the elections to be fair but not entirely free, largely because of the threat of violence.

Although Jammu and Kashmir was returned to local rule in 1996, many viewed the National Conference government as corrupt, incompetent, and unaccountable to the wishes and needs of Kashmiris. A report issued by the International Crisis Group noted that official corruption is "widespread" and corruption cases are seldom prosecuted. Much corrupt behavior and illegal economic activity can be traced directly to political leaders and parties and to militant groups. The new state government made a commitment to address issues of corruption and governance; however, progress in improving both has been slow, and government opacity remains a major concern.

The insurgency has forced Kashmiri media outlets to "tread carefully in their reporting," according to the Committee to Protect Journalists. Militant groups regularly threaten and sometimes kidnap, torture, or kill journalists, while authorities occasionally beat, detain, or otherwise harass journalists. Though it is generally not used, under India's 1971 Newspapers Incitements to Offenses Act (in effect only in Jammu and Kashmir), district magistrates can censor publications in certain circumstances. Other forms of pressure have also been employed against the media; in 2003, Reporters Sans Frontieres criticized a decision by the state government to stop placing official advertisements in the independent *Kashmir Observer* newspaper, thus depriving it of an important source of revenue. Despite these restrictions, however, newspapers do report on controversial issues such as alleged human rights abuses by security forces. Civilians' right to communicate was enhanced when the use of mobile phones was legalized in August 2003.

Freedom to worship and academic freedom are generally respected by Indian and local authorities. For the first time in over a decade, the state government granted permission to separatist groups who wished to organize a procession in order to mark the anniversary of the prophet Muhammad's birthday. However, Islamist militant groups do target Hindu and Sikh temples or villages for attack; a number of such instances, in which dozens of civilians were killed, occurred during the year.

Although local and national civil rights groups are permitted to operate, the Indian government has banned some international groups from visiting the state. Several human rights activists have been killed since 1989, and only a few individuals and groups continue to do human rights work. The APHC, an umbrella group of 23 secessionist political parties, is allowed to operate, although its leaders are frequently subjected to preventive arrest and its requests for permits for public gatherings are routinely denied. The Indian government has also denied permission for APHC leaders to travel to Pakistan. Politically motivated strikes, protest marches, and antigovernment demonstrations take place on a regular basis, although some are forcibly broken up by the authorities.

Under heavy pressure from both the government and militants, the judiciary barely functions, according to the U.S. State Department's 2003 human rights report. The government frequently disregards judicial orders quashing detentions, and security forces refuse to obey court orders, while militants routinely threaten judges, witnesses, and the families of defendants. Many judicial abuses are facilitated by the 1978 Public Safety Act and other broadly drawn laws that allow authorities to detain persons for up to two years without charge or trial. Although detentions under the security laws are nonrenewable, authorities frequently re-arrest suspects on new charges and impose new detentions; Amnesty International's 2003 report noted that hundreds of people remain held in preventive detention under such legislation. The new state government promised in November 2002 to review cases of detainees being held without trial and to release those against whom there were no charges. Although a screening committee met several times in 2003 and several political prisoners were released, progress in implementing this commitment remains slow.

In a positive step, the draconian 2002 Prevention of Terrorism Act (POTA), which gave authorities wide powers of interrogation and detention while expanding the definitions of punishable crimes and prescribing severe punishments for a broad range of criminal acts, was repealed by the new central government in September 2004. However, two other broadly written laws, the Armed Forces Special Powers Act and the Disturbed Areas Act, allow Indian forces to search homes and arrest suspects without a warrant, shoot suspects on sight, and destroy homes or buildings believed to house militants or arms. Moreover, the Special Powers Act requires New Delhi to approve any prosecution of Indian forces. While the state human rights commission examines some human rights complaints, it cannot directly investigate abuses by the army or other federal security forces or take action against those found guilty of violations. Efforts to bring soldiers to justice have been rare. However, the new state government did undertake several initiatives to improve accountability. In June 2003, it announced that 118 security force personnel had been punished for having committed rights violations.

In a continuing cycle of violence, several thousand militants, security force personnel, and civilians are killed each year. Approximately 500,000 Indian security forces based in Kashmir, including soldiers, federal paramilitary troops, and the police, carry out arbitrary arrests and detentions, torture, "disappearances," and custodial killings of suspected militants and alleged civilian sympathizers. From 3,000 to 8,000 people are estimated to have "disappeared" during the course of the insurgency. As part of the counterinsurgency effort, the government has organized and armed pro-government militias composed of former militants. Members of these groups act with impunity and have reportedly carried out a wide range of human rights abuses against pro-Pakistani militants as well as civilians. Local activists report that human rights violations continue to occur at levels similar to those of previous years.

Armed with increasingly sophisticated and powerful weapons, and relying to a greater degree on the deployment of suicide squads, militant groups backed by Pakistan continued to kill pro-India politicians, public employees, suspected informers, members of rival factions, soldiers, and civilians. Militants also engage in kidnapping, rape, extortion, and other forms of terror. Violence targeted against Kashmiri Hindus is part of a pattern since 1990 that has forced several hundred thousand Hindus to flee the region; many continue to reside in refugee camps near Jammu. Until the ceasefire declared in November 2003, shelling by Indian and Pakistani troops along the LOC killed numerous civilians during the year, displaced thousands more, and disrupted schools and the local economy.

Female civilians continue to be subjected to harassment and intimidation, including rape and murder, at the hands of both the security forces and militant groups. In recent years, women have also been targeted by militant groups. In 2001, the Lashkar-e-Jabbar group issued an ultimatum that all Muslim women wear the *burqa* (a head-to-toe covering); members of the group threw acid at and sprayed paint on several women who refused to comply with the directive. In late 2002, another militant group active in Rajouri district declared that no girls over the age of 12 should attend school.

♣ Israel
Israeli-Occupied Territories

Population: 3,762,000 (1,376,000: **Political Rights:** 6
Gaza; 2,386,000: West Bank). In **Civil Liberties:** 6
addition, there are some 220,000 **Status:** Not Free
Israeli settlers in the West Bank, 20,000 in the
Golan Heights, and 5,000 in the Gaza Strip. Approximately
177,000 Jews and 174,000 Arabs live in East Jerusalem.
Religious Groups: Muslim, Jewish, Christian
Ethnic Groups: Palestinian, Jewish, Bedouin
Trend Arrow: The Israeli-Occupied Territories received a downward trend arrow due
to an apparent increase in civilian deaths during Israeli Defense Forces (IDF)
incursions, and arrests and indictments of some soldiers and border police for
abuse of Palestinian civilians.

Note: The areas and total number of persons under Israeli jurisdiction changed
periodically during the year as a result the fluid nature of Israel's military presence in the West Bank and Gaza Strip.

Ten-Year Ratings Timeline (Political Rights, Civil Liberties, Status)

1995	1996	1997	1998	1999	2000	2001	2002	2003	2004
--	6,5NF	6,5NF	6,5NF	6,5NF	6,6NF	6,6NF	6,6NF	6,6NF	6,6NF

Overview: With the internationally backed "road map" to peace effectively in tatters and violence continuing, Israel in 2004 laid
the groundwork for a unilateral disengagement of its troops
and settlers from the Gaza Strip and parts of the West Bank. Israel continued construction of a security barrier in the West Bank, eliciting international condemnation. Israel maintained security roadblocks and checkpoints throughout the West Bank
and Gaza and carried out several armed operations against terrorist suspects. Palestinian Authority (PA) leader Yasser Arafat remained confined to his Ramallah compound until he fell ill; he died in November. Extensive and repeated raids in Gaza
killed many militants and, in several cases, civilians. Several Israeli troops were arrested during the year for alleged mistreatment of Palestinians, including one for
the unlawful killing of a teenage girl in Gaza.

After Palestinian rejection of a UN partition plan in 1947, Israel declared its independence on the portion of land allotted for Jewish settlement. The fledgling state
was jointly attacked by neighboring Arab states in Israel's 1948 War of Independence. While Israel maintained its sovereignty, Jordan seized East Jerusalem and
the West Bank, and Egypt took control of the Gaza Strip. In the 1967 Six-Day War,
Israel came to occupy the West Bank, Gaza, East Jerusalem, the Sinai Peninsula from
Egypt, and the Golan Heights from Syria. The Golan Heights had been used by Syria
to shell northern Israeli communities.

After 1967, Israel began establishing Jewish settlements in the West Bank and
Gaza Strip, an action regarded as illegal by most of the international community. Is-

rael maintains that these settlements are legal since under international law the West Bank and Gaza are in dispute, with their final legal status to be determined through direct bilateral negotiations based on UN Security Council Resolutions 242 and 338. The settlements have become a major sticking point in negotiations between Israel and the Palestinians and in relations between Israel and the international community. The PA- and U.S.-backed road map demands a freeze on settlements, a condition that Israel did not honor in 2004.

In what became known as the *intifada* (uprising), Palestinians living in the West Bank and Gaza began attacking mainly settlers and IDF troops in 1987 to protest Israeli rule. A series of secret negotiations between Israel and Arafat's Palestine Liberation Organization (PLO) conducted mainly in Oslo, Norway, produced an agreement in September 1993. The Declaration of Principles provided for a PLO renunciation of terrorism, PLO recognition of Israel, Israeli troop withdrawals, and gradual Palestinian autonomy in the West Bank and Gaza.

Most of Gaza and the West Bank town of Jericho were turned over to the PA in May 1994. Following the assassination of Israeli prime minister Yitzhak Rabin in November 1995 by a right-wing Jewish extremist opposed to the peace process, Israel, under the stewardship of Prime Minister Shimon Peres, began redeploying its forces from six major Palestinian cities in the West Bank and Gaza.

Under the Oslo provisions implemented so far, the Palestinians have had full or partial control of up to 40 percent of the territory of the West Bank and 98 percent of the Palestinian population. However, Palestinian jurisdiction eroded considerably after the eruption of the second intifada in September 2000, with the IDF temporarily reentering areas under PA control.

At the U.S. presidential retreat Camp David in July 2000 and at Taba, Egypt, in the fall and in early 2001, Israeli and Palestinian leaders engaged in negotiations under U.S. sponsorship. For the first time, Israel discussed compromise solutions on Jerusalem, agreeing to some form of Palestinian sovereignty over East Jerusalem and Islamic holy sites in Jerusalem's Old City. Israel also offered all of the Gaza Strip and more than 95 percent of the West Bank to the Palestinians. The Palestinian leadership rejected the Israeli proposals. Some analysts suggested that Arafat was not confident that Israeli offers guaranteed contiguity of Palestinian territory in the West Bank or that Israel would recognize a "right of return," allowing Palestinian refugees to live in Israel.

After the collapse of the talks, the Palestinians launched an armed uprising, and violence continued throughout the occupied territories in 2004. Insisting that the PA was not preventing terrorism, Israel responded to successive waves of Palestinian suicide bombings by staging incursions into Palestinian-ruled territory, destroying weapons factories, and killing several members of radical Islamist groups such as Hamas and Islamic Jihad, as well as members of the secular Tanzim and al-Aqsa Martyrs Brigade, both offshoots of Arafat's mainstream Fatah movement. No longer distinguishing between militants and political leaders of the groups, Israel assassinated Hamas leaders Sheikh Ahmed Yassin in March and Abdel Aziz Rantisi in April in helicopter strikes in Gaza.

The IDF staged several raids into the Gaza Strip in response to rocket fire from there into Israel. Israeli troops also tried to destroy arms-smuggling tunnels from Egypt into Gaza, killing civilians and razing many Palestinian homes and farming groves in the process; militants often operate in civilian areas and dig smuggling tunnels directly into private homes. In October, IDF forces staged Operation Days of Repentance, a 17-day mission in Gaza carried out to prevent rocket attacks against Israeli cities. At least 110 Palestinians were killed in the fighting, about half of whom were civilians, according to media reports. Israel denied the deliberate targeting of civilians, asserting that Palestinian gunmen and other militants were intentionally positioning themselves among civilian Palestinians, thus endangering them.

Israel and the PA took no meaningful steps during the year toward implementing a road map to peace put forward in April 2003 by the United States, Russia, the United Nations, and the European Union (EU). The multistage, performance-based plan demands concrete Palestinian moves against terrorist groups, to be followed by Israeli troop pullbacks and relaxation of curfews and travel restrictions. The plan also called for a freeze on Israeli settlement activity and the creation of an independent Palestinian state.

While attacks against Israel markedly decreased, isolated attacks, including suicide bombings, did take place. The PA continued to refuse to dismantle the terrorist groups.

Israel continued construction of a controversial security fence roughly along the West Bank side of the 1967 armistice line (Green Line). Composed of high-wire fencing, ditches, security sensors, watchtowers, and in some parts concrete slabs, the fence is designed to prevent terrorists from infiltrating Israel. In some areas, the fence juts farther east into the West Bank and restricts access to farming fields, schools, and jobs. For the most part, however, the fence is roughly close to the 1967 armistice line. Paradoxically, some media reports noted that the security fence provided a return to relative normalcy for some Palestinian communities; city officials in the West Bank town of Jenin reported a greater sense of security with fewer IDF incursions and increased commerce as a result of the barrier's construction. However, the barrier is seen by Palestinians as a means to expropriate West Bank land and collectively punish ordinary Palestinians for acts committed by terrorists. In July, the International Court of Justice in The Hague ruled that the security fence was illegal and that it should be dismantled. While Israel ignored the ruling, in August it re-routed a section of the fence after the country's high court ruled that the barrier cut off some Palestinian villagers from their land. The court issued its order after receiving a petition filed by Palestinians. Israel insists the fence is a temporary solution to an ongoing terrorist threat, not a permanent border.

During the year, in partial accordance with the road map, Israel dismantled some illegal West Bank settlement outposts built without permits. Outposts normally consist of a handful of trailer homes placed mainly by religious Jews on uninhabited land. However, new outposts reappeared shortly after others were dismantled. In late January, Prime Minister Ariel Sharon presented an initiative to withdraw Jewish settlements and Israeli troops from Gaza. The plan was not devised in conjunction with the Palestinians and was premised on being carried out unilaterally. It also included the dismantlement of four West Bank settlements. Palestinians voiced concern that the plan was part of a larger permanent settlement envisioned by Israel that would be imposed unilaterally and would stop short of a larger Israeli pullout from the West Bank.

In April, U.S. president George W. Bush publicly acknowledged that some large

West Bank settlements would remain intact as part of a final status resolution to the conflict, particularly heavily populated settlements close to the 1967 Green Line. Bush also rejected the right of Palestinian refugees to return to ancestral areas within Israel. Palestinians reacted very negatively to Bush's announcement. In August, the Israeli government issued tenders for 1,000 new housing units in existing West Bank settlements. The announcement came after the United States signaled that it would accept construction to accommodate the natural growth of settlement communities, but not entirely new settlements.

Israel confined Yasser Arafat to his Ramallah compound in 2003 and continued to do so throughout 2004. When he fell ill in early November he was permitted to fly to Paris for medical treatment. After Arafat's death on November 11, Sharon hinted that the Gaza plan could be implemented bilaterally.

Substantive peace talks between Israel and Syria, which in the past have centered on the status of the Golan Heights, did not take place during the year.

Political Rights and Civil Liberties: Palestinians in the West Bank and Gaza cannot vote in Israeli elections, as they are not citizens of Israel. They are permitted to vote in elections organized by the PA. Preparations for municipal and presidential elections began in mid-November, following Arafat's death, and voter registration was carried out smoothly.

After Israel's annexation of East Jerusalem in 1967, Arab residents there were issued Israeli identity cards and given the option of obtaining Israeli citizenship. However, by law, Israel strips Arabs of their Jerusalem residency if they remain outside the city for more than three months. Arab residents of East Jerusalem who do not choose Israeli citizenship have the same rights as Israeli citizens except the right to vote in national elections (they can vote in municipal elections). Many choose not to seek citizenship out of solidarity with Palestinians in the West Bank and Gaza Strip, believing East Jerusalem should be the capital of an independent Palestinian state. East Jerusalem's Arab population does not receive a share of municipal services proportionate to its numbers. Arabs in East Jerusalem have the right to vote in PA elections.

Druze and Arabs in the Golan Heights, who were formerly under Syrian rule, possess similar status to Arab residents of East Jerusalem. They cannot vote in Israeli national elections, but they are represented at municipal levels.

International press freedom groups regularly criticize Israel for preventing journalists from accessing conflict zones in the West Bank and Gaza, harming and sometimes killing them during armed battles, and harassing Palestinian journalists. Israel has long denied that it deliberately targets journalists and insists that reporters covering armed conflict in the West Bank and Gaza are in danger of getting caught in crossfire.

Early in the year, British photojournalist Tom Hurndall died after suffering a gunshot shot in the head by IDF troops as they battled gunmen in the West Bank. In March, IDF troops operating in the West Bank town of Jenin shot a Palestinian photographer covering clashes there. In May, an Agence-France Press photographer was shot in the leg while covering confrontations between Palestinians and IDF troops in Gaza. In June, the nongovernmental organization (NGO) Reporters Sans Frontieres lodged a complaint with Israeli defense minister Shaul Mofaz, alleging a pattern of harassment of journalists by IDF troops that included soldiers shooting at journalists with tear gas and detaining and threatening them. Also in June, Israeli helicopters fired missiles at a Gaza City building housing local and international media offices, causing some injuries. The IDF said the building was used by Hamas to communicate with terrorists and distribute incitement material.

Israel generally recognizes the right to freedom of worship and religion. On several occasions during the intifada, Israel has restricted Muslim men under 40 from praying on the Temple Mount compound in Jerusalem's Old City for fear of violent confrontations. Palestinians have deliberately damaged Jewish shrines and other holy places in the West Bank.

While academic freedom is generally respected, IDF closures, curfews, and the West Bank security barrier restrict access to Palestinian academic institutions. Israeli authorities have at times shut universities, and schools have been damaged during military operations. Throughout the intifada, schoolchildren have periodically been injured or killed during fighting.

Freedom of assembly is generally respected. However, Israel has imposed strict curfews in the West Bank at various times since September 2000. In December 2003, Israeli troops, reportedly fearing their lives were in danger, shot at demonstrators on the West Bank side of Israel's security fence.

There are many Palestinian NGOs and civic groups, whose activities are generally not restricted by Israel. Labor affairs in the West Bank and Gaza are governed by a combination of Jordanian law and PA decisions. Workers may establish and join unions without government authorization. Palestinian workers in Jerusalem are subject to Israeli labor law.

Palestinians accused by Israel of security offenses in Israeli-controlled areas are tried in Israeli military courts. Security offenses are broadly defined. Some due process protections exist in these courts, though there are limits on the rights to counsel, bail, and appeal. Administrative detention is widely used. Most convictions in Israeli military courts are based on confessions, sometimes obtained through physical pressure. In 2000, Israel outlawed the use of torture as a means of extracting security information, but milder forms of physical coercion are permissible in cases where the prisoner is believed to have immediate information about impending terrorist attacks. Human rights groups still criticize Israel for engaging in what they consider torture. Confessions are usually spoken in Arabic and translated into Hebrew for official records.

Israel holds approximately 7,000 Palestinians in jail. Many, suspected of involvement in terrorism, are held in administrative detention without charge or trial. Approximately 2,500 Palestinians were detained in 2004. In January, Israel released several hundred Palestinian prisoners as part of a swap with the radical Lebanon-based group Hezbollah, which released one Israeli hostage and the remains of three Israeli soldiers. In September, Israel released an additional 160 prisoners.

While Palestinians have recourse to Israel's highest civilian courts to protest home demolitions and Israel's tactics in carrying out targeted assassinations, decisions made in their favor are rare.

Several Israeli soldiers were arrested in 2004 for allegedly abusing and beating Palestinian civilians. In October, an IDF commander was arrested for the wrongful death of a 13-year-old girl in Gaza. According to the army, soldiers shot and wounded the girl as she walked in a restricted area carrying what was thought to be a bag of explosives. Carrying only books, the girl was again shot repeatedly by the IDF commander after he approached her. Although the IDF has disciplined some soldiers for apparent excessive use of force, Israeli human rights organizations have criticized the army for not being more vigilant in ensuring effective prosecution.

During the year, Israel continued its controversial policy of destroying the homes of families of suicide bombers, claiming that the policy serves as a deterrent. Throughout the Palestinian uprising, Israel has also destroyed many homes in the West Bank and Gaza Strip on the grounds that they provide cover for gunmen and bombers. Additionally, Israel has destroyed some Palestinian structures built without permits, especially in East Jerusalem.

Violence between Palestinians and settlers is not uncommon. Several Jewish settlers in the West Bank and Gaza Strip were ambushed and killed by Palestinian gunmen or attacked with mortar fire in 2004. Attacks by settlers against Palestinians also occasionally take place. In September, a Jewish settler in the West Bank who said he shot dead a Palestinian in self-defense was placed under house arrest.

Israel at times severely restricts freedom of movement in the West Bank and Gaza. The Israeli army maintained roadblocks and checkpoints throughout the West Bank and Gaza in 2004 to prevent terrorists from entering Israel. The security measures denied Palestinians easy passage from one town to another, making access to jobs, hospitals, and schools extremely difficult. Even senior Palestinian officials are subject to long delays and searches at Israeli checkpoints. The restrictions of movement between and among Palestinian towns and cities have been denounced as collective punishment. Travel for Palestinians between the West Bank and Gaza is extremely difficult. Israel exercises overall military control at border crossings between the West Bank and Jordan and between the Gaza Strip and Egypt. Construction of Israel's security barrier has also disconnected many Palestinians from their farming fields and has denied them and others easier access to other parts of the West Bank. All West Bank and Gaza residents must have identification cards in order to obtain entry permits into Israel, including East Jerusalem. Israel often denies permits to applicants with no explanation.

The Palestinian economy has been seriously affected by the intifida and the Israeli closures of the West Bank and Gaza; thousands of Palestinians rely on access to jobs in Israel. At various times during the year, Israel permitted several thousand Palestinian workers to enter the country, but not the nearly 200,000 who regularly crossed daily into Israel before the intifada. In November, the World Bank reported that nearly half the Palestinian population was living on less than two dollars per day.

While Palestinian women are under-represented in most professions and encounter discrimination in employment, they do have full entry access to universities and to many professions. Although Israel's occupation restricts the rights of women, Palestinian personal status law, derived in part from Sharia (Islamic law), puts women at a disadvantage in matters of marriage, divorce, and inheritance. Rape, domestic abuse, and "honor killings," in which unmarried women who are raped or who engage in premarital sex are murdered by a relative, are not uncommon. Since societal pressures prevent reporting of such incidents, the exact frequency of attacks is unknown. According to media reports, an average of one honor killing a week takes place in the West Bank and Gaza. These murders often go unpunished, or perpetrators serve extremely short prison sentences.

⬇ Israel
Palestinain Authority-Administered Territories

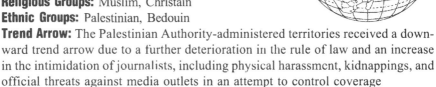

Population: 3,762,000
(1,376,000: Gaza;
2,386,000: West Bank).

Political Rights: 5
Civil Liberties: 6
Status: Not Free

Religious Groups: Muslim, Christain
Ethnic Groups: Palestinian, Bedouin

Trend Arrow: The Palestinian Authority-administered territories received a downward trend arrow due to a further deterioration in the rule of law and an increase in the intimidation of journalists, including physical harassment, kidnappings, and official threats against media outlets in an attempt to control coverage

Note: The areas and total number of persons under Palestinian jurisdiction changed periodically during the year as a result of the fluid nature of Israel's military presence and activities in the West Bank and Gaza Strip.

Ten-Year Ratings Timeline (Political Rights, Civil Liberties, Status)

1995	1996	1997	1998	1999	2000	2001	2002	2003	2004
--	5,6NF	5,6NF	5,6NF	5,6NF	5,6NF	5,6NF	5,6NF	5,6NF	5,6NF

Overview:

The year 2004 was marked by escalating disenchantment with Palestinian Authority (PA) leader Yasser Arafat's rule, Palestinian demands for political reform, and increasing internal and external pressure to end the armed uprising against Israel. Arafat died in November, ushering in a period of uncertainty. While an interim transition process took place immediately after Arafat's death, the lack of a chosen successor raised the specter of a destabilizing power struggle and presidential elections were called for January 2005. Much of 2004 was marked by the further erosion of law and order and growing vigilantism in Palestinian areas, and some Arafat critics were singled out for intimidation, including physical attack. Militias and PA officials also stepped up their threats against the media. Palestinians continued their *intifada* (uprising) in 2004, leading to Israeli incursions into areas previously ceded to Palestinian control. Israel intermittently reoccupied some West Bank towns and cities, carried out armed raids, and imposed strict curfews and roadblocks in and around Palestinian areas. The Israeli measures, sometimes resulting in Palestinian civilian deaths, generally followed terrorist attacks against Israelis by Palestinian Islamist groups and more secular groups such as Tanzim and the al-Aqsa Martyrs Brigade affiliated with Arafat's Fatah movement. No meaningful peace negotiations took place between the Palestinians and Israel during the year.

In the 1967 Six-Day War, Israel came to occupy Sinai, the West Bank, Gaza, East Jerusalem, and the Golan Heights. Israel annexed Jerusalem's Old City and East Jerusalem in 1967 and the Golan Heights in 1981.

In what became known as the intifada, Palestinians living in the West Bank and Gaza began attacking mainly targets of the Israel Defense Forces (IDF) in 1987 to protest Israeli rule. A series of secret negotiations between Israel and Arafat's Palestine Liberation Organization (PLO) conducted in Oslo, Norway, produced an agreement in September 1993. Premised on the land-for-peace formula articulated in UN Security Council Resolution 242 of November 1967, the Declaration of Principles provided for Israeli troop withdrawals and gradual Palestinian autonomy in the West Bank and Gaza in exchange for an end to Palestinian terrorism and for recognition of Israel.

Most of Gaza and the West Bank town of Jericho were turned over to the PA in May 1994, and over the next two years, Israel redeployed its forces in the West Bank and Gaza. Under the provisions of Oslo implemented so far, the PA has had full or partial control of up to 40 percent of the territory of the West Bank and 98 percent of the Palestinian population. However, the IDF has temporarily reentered some PA-controlled territory since the onset of the second intifada in September 2000.

At the U.S. presidential retreat Camp David in July 2000, and at Taba, Egypt, in the fall and in early 2001, Israeli Prime Minister Ehud Barak and U.S. president Bill Clinton engaged the Palestinian leadership in the most far-reaching negotiations ever. For the first time, Israel discussed compromise solutions on Jerusalem, agreeing to some form of Palestinian sovereignty over East Jerusalem and Islamic holy sites in Jerusalem's Old City. Israel also offered all of the Gaza Strip and more than 95 percent of the West Bank to the Palestinians. Arafat, however, rejected the offers. Some analysts have suggested that Arafat balked over Jewish claims to Jerusalem and Israel's refusal to recognize a "right of return," which would in principle allow Palestinian refugees to live in Israel. Following a controversial visit by then-Likud leader Ariel Sharon to the Temple Mount in Jerusalem in September 2000, the Palestinians launched an armed uprising. Sharon became prime minister in elections in February 2001.

Violence continued throughout Palestinian areas in 2004. In response to terrorist attacks inside Israel and to attacks against Jewish settlers and IDF personnel in the West Bank and Gaza, Israeli forces carried out several incursions into Palestinian-ruled territory, killing and arresting many suspected militants. Israel killed several top Hamas and Islamic Jihad figures and radical Islamists suspected of committing or preparing attacks against Israel. Hamas and Islamic Jihad reject Israel's right to exist and are committed to its destruction. Both groups routinely recruit Palestinians—including children and women—to carry out suicide attacks. Fatah's al-Aqsa Martyrs Brigade has also carried out several suicide attacks since 2000. Palestinians condemned Israel for the killings—often carried out by helicopter gunships or undercover units—and labeled them "assassinations." Israel also faced international criticism for what it termed "targeted killings." Israel justified the policy on the grounds that its repeated requests that the PA detain Palestinians suspected of planning or carrying out attacks had gone unheeded. Civilians were also killed during Israeli operations. Israel denied the deliberate targeting of civilians, insisting that Palestinian gunmen and other militants position themselves among civilian populations, thus putting them in harm's way.

Israel carried out several antiterrorism operations in the West Bank and Gaza, reimposing roadblocks and sending troops back into Palestinian areas from which it had previously withdrawn. Large-scale operations in Gaza, designed to stop rocket fire from there, resulted in many deaths of militants and some civilians.

Israel also continued construction of a controversial security fence inside the West Bank. While the barrier helped reduce the number of terrorist attacks inside

Israel, it did significantly disrupt the lives of many Palestinians living on or near the fence's route.

A "road map" toward peace with Israel, put forward by the United States, Russia, the United Nations, and the European Union (EU) in 2003, remained essentially dormant in 2004. The multistage, performance-based plan is premised on demonstrative Palestinian action at ending violence, to be followed by Israeli troop pullbacks and easing of curfews and travel restrictions on Palestinians. It also calls for a freeze of Israeli settlement activity once Palestinian terrorism ends.

Jewish settlements in the West Bank and Gaza represent a major sticking point in negotiations between Israel and the Palestinians. While Israel dismantled only some illegal outposts in the West Bank—composed mostly of small, makeshift trailers—it continued construction activity in existing settlements.

Much of 2004 was dominated by a deepening political crisis within the Palestinian community. Criticism mounted over perceived widespread corruption in the PA, and over Arafat's refusal to transfer meaningful authority to Prime Minister Ahmed Qurei, including relinquishing control over the various Palestinian security services, a key international demand. Though he threatened to resign, Qurei ultimately acquiesced to Arafat's continued exclusive authority. In 2003, Arafat had consolidated all security authority in a new national security council answerable solely to him.

In February 2004, in a direct challenge to Arafat, 400 members of his Fatah Party resigned in protest over corruption at the top levels of the PA. The World Bank threatened to cut off aid to the PA if it did not end its corrupt financial practices, including its refusal to cease paying civil servants and security chiefs in cash and not via a more accountable direct-deposit system. Estimates of the amount of money Arafat had deposited into private funds and offshore holdings ran into the billions of dollars. The Palestinian Center for Policy and Survey Research reported that 87 percent of Palestinians regarded PA institutions as corrupt.

By the summer, challenges to Arafat's rule peaked. In July, Arafat appointed his cousin, Moussa Arafat, as Gaza security chief. The move prompted mass and at times violent protests by various armed factions, including by the traditionally loyal al-Aqsa Martyrs Brigade and security forces loyal to former Gaza security chief Mahmoud Dahlan, who is widely considered a pragmatist. The protests seemed emblematic of deep disaffection felt by the younger, activist guard toward the older leadership establishment.

Growing lawlessness and acts of unpunished vigilantism in Palestinian-administered areas—including summary, public executions of Palestinians accused of collaborating with Israel—compounded the sense of disillusionment with the PA. In August, an inquiry by the Palestinian Legislative Council (PLC) blamed the PA and Arafat for the break down of law and order. The PLC announced that the Palestinian leadership had made no explicit political decision to end the escalating, random violence.

Arafat fell ill in November and was permitted to fly to Paris for medical treatment. He had been confined by Israel to his Ramallah compound since September 2003. After Arafat died on November 11, interim power effectively transferred to Prime Minister Ahmed Qurei and Arafat's PLO deputy and former PA prime minister Mahmoud Abbas. While the transition was relatively smooth, tensions among various Palestinian factions and militant groups became heightened. Gunmen loyal to

Arafat threatened Abbas while he attended a memorial service for Arafat in Gaza. According to the PA's basic law, the Speaker of the PLC assumed the PA presidency for 60 days. Presidential elections were called for January 9, 2005.

Political Rights and Civil Liberties: Palestinian residents of the West Bank, Gaza, and East Jerusalem chose their first popularly elected government in 1996. Independents won 35 of the 88 PLC (Legislative Council) seats, while members of Arafat's Fatah Party won the remainder. The PLC has complained of being marginalized by the executive authority; though it has debated hundreds of draft laws, few have been signed into law. The PA government indefinitely postponed local elections in May 1998, citing the threat of Israeli interference. As per agreements with Israel, the council has no real authority over borders or defense policy. Laws governing Palestinians in the occupied territories derive from Ottoman, British Mandate, Jordanian, Egyptian, and PA law, and Israeli military orders.

Arafat, who did not face meaningful opposition in the 1996 election, became PA chairman, or president, with 88 percent of the vote. Despite some irregularities, particularly in East Jerusalem, international observers regarded the vote as reasonably reflective of the will of the voters. Subsequent presidential elections were repeatedly postponed by Arafat. In November 2004, following Arafat's death, Palestinians registered to vote for the presidential elections scheduled to take place in the new year. According to Miftah, a Palestinian nongovernmental organization (NGOs), the number of registered voters increased 72 percent from registration efforts held over the summer.

Palestinian residents of the West Bank, Gaza, and East Jerusalem do not have the right to vote in national elections in Israel. Arabs in East Jerusalem who hold Israeli identity cards can vote in the city's municipal elections and can also vote in PA elections.

Rampant corruption within the PA, combined with the deterioration of civic order and the PA's ability to deliver basic services, have benefited Hamas, which operates an extensive private charitable social services network. Transparency and the consolidation of PA finances became priority issues in the wake of Arafat's death.

The media are not free in the West Bank and Gaza, and press freedom deteriorated further in 2004. Under a 1995 PA press law, journalists may be fined and jailed and newspapers closed for publishing "secret information" on Palestinian security forces or news that might harm national unity or incite violence. However, another press law, also signed in 1995, stipulates that Palestinian intelligence services do not reserve the right to interrogate, detain, or arrest journalists on the basis of their work. Nevertheless, several small media outlets are pressured by authorities to provide favorable coverage of the PA. Arbitrary arrests, threats, and the physical abuse of journalists critical of the PA are routine. Official Palestinian radio and television are government mouthpieces.

Journalists covering the Israeli-Palestinian conflict and Palestinian political affairs face harassment by the PA. PA officials reportedly threaten journalists who file stories deemed unfavorable. PA-affiliated militias have also warned Israeli journalists to stay out of Palestinian areas. International press freedom groups have called on the PA to cease harassment of journalists.

In January, the PA ordered all journalists in the West Bank and Gaza working for Arab satellite TV networks to refer to Palestinians killed by Israeli forces as "martyrs." Fatah activists also attacked Seif al-Din Shahin, a correspondent for the Al-Arabiya network, after he reported that several people were injured during a public rally where Fatah members fired their weapons in the air. Fatah went on to issue statements threatening journalists who had voiced criticism of the attack on Shahin. In February, masked gunmen stormed the Ramallah office of al-Quds Educational TV, demanding videotapes and beating employees. The same month, gunmen opened fire on the office of the Gaza weekly *Al-Daar*, a paper that had been outspoken on corruption in the PA. In May, gunmen in Gaza failed in their attempt to abduct *New York Times* bureau chief James Bennett.

In July, the PA-affiliated Palestinian Journalists' Syndicate issued an edict threatening Palestinian journalists with severe punishment if they reported on clashes between rival Palestinian groups and other forms of internal strife. Some journalists reported receiving death threats, and others admitted that they stopped covering the internecine Palestinian struggle.

Arafat never ratified a 1996 law passed by the PLC that guarantees freedom of expression. In December 2003, Muhammad Muqbel, director-general of the PA Ministry of Sports and Youth, was arrested and held for several hours after allegedly making critical remarks about Arafat at a conference in Ramallah focusing on democracy and reform.

The PA generally respects freedom of religion, though no law exists protecting religious expression. The basic law declares Islam the official religion of Palestine and also states that "respect and sanctity of all other heavenly religions [i.e., Judaism and Christianity] shall be maintained." The PA requires all Palestinians to be affiliated with a religion, which must be displayed on identification cards. Personal status law, which governs marriage and divorce, is based on religious law; for Muslims, it is derived from Sharia (Islamic law), and for Christians, from ecclesiastical courts. Some Palestinian Christians have experienced intimidation and harassment by radical Islamic groups and PA officials, leading many to emigrate from traditionally Christian towns like Bethlehem. In December 2003, the IDF reported that Palestinians fired on Jews visiting Joseph's tomb, a Jewish shrine in Nablus.

The PA has authority over all levels of education. Some Palestinian schools teach hatred of Israel, and some textbooks and curriculums promote Israel's destruction. IDF closures, curfews, and the West Bank security barrier restrict access to Palestinian academic institutions. Israeli authorities have at times shut universities, and schools have been damaged during military operations. Throughout the intifada, schoolchildren have periodically been injured or killed during fighting.

The PA requires permits for rallies and demonstrations and prohibits violence and racist sloganeering. Nonetheless, anti-Israel and anti-Semitic preaching and incitement to violence were regular features of mosque prayer services and official radio and television broadcasts in 2004. The PA has also operated military training summer camps for children, often named for suicide bombers. Violence against Jews is regularly praised and glorified at the camps. There are a broad range of Palestinian NGOs and civic groups. Many, though, do not actively criticize the PA.

Labor affairs in the West Bank and Gaza are governed by a combination of Jordanian law and PA decisions. Workers may establish and join unions without government authorization. Palestinian workers seeking to strike must submit to arbitration by the PA Ministry of Labor. There are no laws in the PA-ruled areas to protect the rights of striking workers. Palestinian workers in Jerusalem are subject to Israeli labor law.

The Palestinian judicial system is not independent. While the PA revealed a draft constitution in April 2003, Arafat never endorsed it. A constitution would strengthen the judiciary, one of the weakest Palestinian institutions. In August 2004, the Palestinian justice minister resigned after Arafat created a rival agency to the Justice Ministry.

Palestinian judges lack proper training and experience. Israeli demands for a Palestinian crackdown on terrorism have given rise to state security courts, which lack almost all due process rights. There are reportedly hundreds of administrative detainees currently in Palestinian jails and detention centers. The same courts are also used to try those suspected of collaborating with Israel or for drug trafficking. Defendants are not granted the right to appeal sentences and are often summarily tried and sentenced to death. Executions often take place immediately after sentencing and are carried out by firing squad. According to the Palestinian Human Rights Monitoring Group, alleged collaborators are routinely tortured in Palestinian jails and are denied the right to defend themselves in court. These practices are not prohibited under Palestinian law.

The limits of Palestinian justice and the further breakdown of the rule of law were underscored throughout the year. Offshoots of Arafat's Fatah Party controlled the seemingly anarchic West Bank cities of Jenin and Nablus with impunity. Gaza also became increasingly lawless. Many Palestinians accused of collaborating with Israel were summarily executed in public. These murders generally go unpunished. In July, gunmen in the West Bank shot and seriously wounded Palestinian legislator Nabil Amr. Gun battles between rival security forces were also a common feature during the year. A study released in April by the Palestinian Human Rights Monitoring Group showed that over 11 percent of Palestinians killed since 2000 died at the hands of fellow Palestinians. In October, gunmen attempted to assassinate Gaza security chief Moussa Arafat. In November, the *Jerusalem Post* reported that Arafat directed millions of dollars to the al-Aqsa Martyrs Brigade while police forces went unpaid, thereby increasing the militia group's strength over that of the police.

Palestinian security forces routinely failed to prevent terrorist attacks against Israelis, including stopping rocket or mortar attacks. There were increasing signs of cooperation between the security services and militant groups.

Violence between Palestinians and settlers is not uncommon. Several Jewish settlers in the West Bank and Gaza Strip were ambushed and killed by Palestinian gunmen. These attacks generally go unpunished by the PA. Settlers sometimes attack Palestinians, often without serious legal penalties.

The intifada and Israeli closures of the Palestinian territories have exacted a serious toll on the Palestinian economy. According to the World Bank, nearly half of the Palestinian population lives below the poverty line of two dollars' income per day. Economic output plunged as tens of thousands of Palestinians who normally work in Israel were denied entry into the country at various times during the year in response to terrorist attacks. The EU also cut its aid to Palestinians in half in February because of corruption and mismanagement in the PA.

While Palestinian women are under-represented in most professions and encounter discrimination in employment, they do have full access to universities and to many professions. Personal status law, derived in part from Sharia (Islamic law), puts women at a disadvantage in matters of marriage, divorce, and inheritance. Rape, domestic abuse, and "honor killings," in which unmarried women who are raped or who engage in premarital sex are murdered by a relative, are not uncommon. Since societal pressures prevent reporting of such incidents, the exact frequency of attacks is unknown. According to media reports, an average of one honor killing a week takes place in the West Bank and Gaza. These murders often go unpunished, or perpetrators serve extremely short prison sentences.

Moldova
Transnistria

Population: 619,000
Religious Groups: Christian
Orthodox (94 percent),
other [including Roman Catholic,
Protestant, and Muslim] (6 percent)
Ethnic Groups: Moldovan (40 percent), Ukrainian
(28 percent), Russian (23 percent), other (9 percent)

Political Rights: 6
Civil Liberties: 6
Status: Not Free

Ten-Year Ratings Timeline (Political Rights, Civil Liberties, Status)

1995	1996	1997	1998	1999	2000	2001	2002	2003	2004
--	6,6NF	6,6NF	6,6NF	6,6NF	6,6NF	6,6NF	6,6NF	6,6NF	6,6NF

Overview:
Joint mediation by Russia, Ukraine, and the Organization for Security and Cooperation in Europe (OSCE) in hopes of resolving the conflict between the Moldovan government and leaders in the breakaway region of Transnistria led to negotiations in 2004, but no settlement was reached. Tensions escalated over the summer, as the Transnistrian authorities forcibly closed schools teaching the Moldovan language in the Latin script, which led to each side imposing sanctions on the other.

The Dnestr Moldovan Republic (DMR), bounded by the Dniester River to the west and the Ukrainian border on the east, is a breakaway region in the eastern part of Moldova with a large population of ethnic Russians and ethnic Ukrainians. In Moldova, the region is called Transnistria. Historically distinct, Transnistria was attached to the territory that became Moldova when Stalin redrew borders in 1940. As the Soviet Union began to falter in the early 1990s, pro-Russian separatists in Transnistria feared that Romanian-speaking Moldova would join neighboring Romania. They reacted by declaring independence, establishing the DMR, and setting up an authoritarian presidential system.

With weapons and other assistance from the Russian army, the DMR leadership fought a military conflict with Moldova that ended in a 1992 ceasefire. A new

Moldovan constitution in 1994 gave the territory substantial autonomy, but the conflict remains unresolved. The separatist regime has been strong enough to resist absorption by Moldova yet too weak to gain outright international recognition. It is not recognized by any independent state.

Over the past several years, the OSCE, Russia, and Ukraine have attempted to mediate a final settlement between Moldova and the DMR. They also participate in the Joint Control Commission that monitors compliance with the 1992 ceasefire.

After Moldovan elections in 2001, in which Communist Party leader Vladimir Voronin was elected president, there were some hopes that a new resolution to the Transnistrian conflict would be achieved. However, negotiations have made little progress over the past several years. The lingering presence in Transnistria of more than 1,000 Russian soldiers and a supply of Russian weapons has further complicated matters. In 1999, Russia agreed to an OSCE initiative calling for the removal of all Russian weapons and troops by December 2002. However, as the withdrawal deadline approached, Russia announced that it would not meet its obligation and attempted to refashion the force as "guarantors" of any eventual diplomatic settlement. In response to this development, the OSCE extended the deadline by 12 months. During the course of 2003, some movement was seen on the issue, but ultimately Russia declared that it would not remove all of its troops until a final settlement was reached. Large quantities of armaments were evacuated in 2003 and 2004.

After Voronin rejected, in November 2003, a plan that would have created a "joint state," talks became deadlocked. Early in 2004, the five negotiators (from the OSCE, Russia, Ukraine, Moldova, and Transnistria) agreed to meet regularly, but talks in May and November had no results; Transnistria failed to send representatives to talks in June.

The situation was further hampered in July, when Transnistrian authorities decided to close the six schools on their territory teaching in Moldovan using the Latin script if the schools did not obtain a licensing permit. When the schools resisted, a militia took some of them by force, blocking entrances to teachers and students and evicting orphans who lived at one. As a result, the Moldovan government imposed economic sanctions on the territory and temporarily withdrew from negotiations. Transnistria responded by blockading rail links to Moldova.

In general, the Transnistrian authorities have been very effective in pursuing their short-term goals, and they currently see no reason to compromise on demands for wide-ranging autonomy or on contentious points such as developing a Transnistrian military and currency. The competing interests of Russia, Ukraine, and Western institutions, such as the European Union and the OSCE, further impede progress in finding a solution.

Political Rights and Civil Liberties: Residents of Transnistria cannot elect their leaders democratically, and they are unable to participate freely in Moldovan elections. While the DMR maintains its own legislative, executive, and judicial branches of government, no country recognizes the government's sovereignty. Igor Smirnov is now serving his third term as president, and he has said that he will not step down until Transnistria is independent. The various presidential and parliamentary elections that have been held since 1992 have generally been considered neither free nor fair by the international community, although they have not been monitored.

Candidates with genuine prospects of challenging Smirnov in 1996 and 2001 were banned from participation. The main opposition movement was also banned, and those opposition politicians who remain are harassed and threatened. Native Moldovan speakers are not represented in government and are under constant political pressure. The Ministry of State Security conducts Soviet-style interviews of citizens suspected of subversive activities and engages in brutality and heavy-handed threats.

The DMR government controls most print and electronic media in Transnistria and restricts freedom of speech. Independent newspapers and television stations do exist, but they frequently experience harassment when they criticize the DMR government. Authorities have confiscated copies of independent newspapers. A state editorial committee oversees the activity of all print and electronic media. The committee's members include the ministers of security, justice, foreign affairs, and information.

Religious freedom is restricted. Authorities have denied registration to some religious groups, such as Baptists and Methodists, and Jehovah's Witnesses are regularly harassed and arrested. The government also limits the ability of religious groups to rent space for prayer meetings. A Jewish cemetery was vandalized in April.

Although 4,000 students regularly attend schools that teach Moldovan in the Latin script, such activities are banned in Transnistria. In July, the Ministry of Education declared that such schools must obtain a licensing permit and adopt the official curriculum. Militias were subsequently sent to block entry to schools that did not comply. Parents and teachers who resisted the action were forcibly removed, and some were threatened by authorities. It is generally believed that the issue is not about language but about the politics of teaching in the official language of Moldova, rather than in Russian.

The authorities severely restrict freedom of assembly, and on the few occasions when permits have been granted for groups to protest, the organizers have been harassed. The authorities have also organized "spontaneous" counter-rallies on such occasions. Freedom of association is similarly circumscribed. Nongovernmental organizations (NGOs) have been harassed by police officials, who reportedly invite NGO leaders for "informational discussions" and pressure landlords of properties being used by NGOs not to renew leases. In July, the chairman of the Moldovan Helsinki Committee was attacked, allegedly by pro-government forces trying to prevent him from attending a human rights roundtable. Trade unions are holdovers from the Soviet era, and the United Council of Labor Collectives works closely with the government.

The judiciary is not independent but instead implements the will of the authorities. Politically motivated killings and police harassment have been reported, and political prisoners are frequently denied access to lawyers. Police can detain suspects for up to 30 days. The police continue to use torture and arbitrary arrest, especially against political opponents of the DMR government. Prison conditions are considered harsh, and prisons are severely overcrowded.

The so-called Ilascu group was imprisoned by Transnistria following what is widely considered to have been an unfair trial that found them guilty of crimes against the Transnistrian authorities during the 1992 armed conflict. They were imprisoned in inhumane conditions and tortured. One of the four members of the group was released in May 2001, and a second was released in June 2004. In July, the European Court of Human Rights ruled that Moldova and Russia were responsible for paying damages for infringement of the rights of the four and said that the remaining two must be released immediately. Moldova and Russia have paid compensation, but the two men still remain in jail.

Authorities discriminate against ethnic Moldovans, who constitute 40 percent of the region's population.

The Transnistria authorities are entrenched in the territory's economic activities, both legal and illegal. Transnistria is a major exporter of drugs and illicit arms. It is likely that revenues of the customs department, headed by the president's son, line official pockets. Russia also has interests in Transnistria's illegal activities, although Russia's economic influence over the territory is probably less than it once was.

Domestic violence against women is a problem, and women are under-represented in most positions of authority. Transnistria is a transit point for trafficking in women.

Morocco
Western Sahara

Population: 273,000
Religious Groups: Muslim
Ethnic Groups: Arab, Berber

Political Rights: 7
Civil Liberties: 6
Status: Not Free

Ten-Year Ratings Timeline (Political Rights, Civil Liberties, Status)

1995	1996	1997	1998	1999	2000	2001	2002	2003	2004
7,6NF	7,6NF	7,6NF	7,6NF	7,6NF	7,6NF	7,6NF	7,6NF	7,6NF	7,6NF

Overview: Hope for independence or self-determination for the Western Sahara people suffered numerous setbacks in 2004, starting with the resignation of UN special envoy James Baker and culminating in October, when a UN-backed plan for autonomy failed to win full approval of a key UN General Assembly committee. However, some encouraging signs of confidence-building emerged during the year as hundreds of families from the territory and from Sahrawi refugee camps visited one another, some for the first time in decades. The Polisario Front released 100 Moroccan POWs, but held on to some 400 more.

Western Sahara was a Spanish colony from 1884 until 1975, when Spanish forces withdrew from the territory following a bloody two-year conflict with the Polisario Front. Moroccan claims to the territory date to Moroccan independence in 1956. Mauritania also laid claim to the southern portion of the territory. In 1976, Morocco and Mauritania partitioned the territory under a tripartite agreement with Spain, but the Polisario declared the establishment of an independent Sahrawi Arab Democratic Republic (SADR) and fought to expel foreign forces. Mauritania renounced its claims to the land and signed a peace agreement with the Polisario in 1979, prompting Morocco to seize Mauritania's section of territory.

In 1991, the United Nations brokered an agreement between Morocco and the Polisario that called for a ceasefire and the holding of a referendum on independence to be supervised by the newly created Mission for a Referendum in Western Sahara (MINURSO). However, the referendum, initially scheduled for January 1992, was repeatedly postponed after Morocco insisted that the list of eligible voters include an additional 48,000 people who, according to the Polisario and most international observers, were Moroccan nationals.

In the ensuing years, Morocco has attempted to cement its hold on the Western Sahara by settling Moroccans in the territory and by offering incentives such as salaries and free housing to Sahrawis who relocated from the territory to Morocco. At the same time, the Moroccans have repeatedly rebuffed UN attempts to broker a lasting solution to the conflict. On ascending the Moroccan throne in 1999, King Muhammad made some important gestures toward reconciliation, including releasing prisoners and allowing limited activity for Sahrawi human rights groups. In 2003, he formed a special commission to resolve the question of hundreds of Sahrawis who were forcibly "disappeared" during his father's reign.

In his 2004 report to the UN Security Council, Secretary-General Kofi Annan expressed his regret over the resignation of UN special envoy Baker and the failure of the conflicting parties to have benefited from his experience. He appointed Alvaro de Soto to replace Baker, but said an agreement on self-determination for the Western Sahara appeared more distant than at the start of the year. He also registered concern over an escalation in rhetoric between the conflicting parties, as Morocco and Algeria, which hosts the Sahrawi refugee camps, traded accusations of blocking progress on a resolution. At the end of October, the UN Security Council granted a six-month extension to MINURSO's mandate.

In September, a special committee in the UN General Assembly failed to reach a consensus on a peace plan, proposed by Baker and backed by Algeria, that would make the territory a semiautonomous part of Morocco during a four- to five-year transition period. After that, a referendum would let residents choose independence, continued semiautonomy, or integration with Morocco. The UN vote, which is nonbinding but reflects international opinion, passed by 52-0, but a majority of the 191-member committee abstained. In April, the plan had won UN Security Council backing, but Morocco said it could not accept any eventual referendum that made independence an option; the Polisario had accepted the plan.

Despite the deadlock in peace plans, both Morocco and the Polisario went ahead with a package of confidence-building measures promoted by MINURSO and the UN High Commissioner for Refugees (UNHCR). The measures included family visits and limited telephone and personal mail services. By the end of August, some 1,200 persons from refugee camps in Algeria and the territory had exchanged visits, and more were planned for the rest of the year. Flown on UN planes and accompanied by UN civilian police officers, many Sahrawis were able to see their close relatives for the first time in 30 years.

During the year, the Polisario released 200 Moroccan POWs, who were repatriated under the auspices of the International Red Cross. The United Nations said another 412 prisoners remain in Polisario camps in Tindouf, Algeria, and in Polisario-controlled areas of Western Sahara, some for more than 20 years. The Polisario claims that Morocco holds, or withholds information on, some 150 combatants and supporters, but the Moroccan government officially denies holding any former Sahrawi fighters.

Political Rights and Civil Liberties: Sahrawis have never been able to elect their own government. The Moroccan government organizes and controls local elections in the Moroccan-held areas of the territory. Only Sahrawis whose views are consonant with the Moroccan government hold seats in the Moroccan parliament.

Freedom of expression remains very restricted both for Sahrawis and for foreign journalists covering the Western Sahara. In 2004, the authorities expelled five Norwegian and French journalists for meeting with Sahrawi activists. Moroccan security forces closely monitor the political views of Sahrawis, and police and paramilitary forces resort to repressive measures against those suspected of supporting the Polisario and independence. Private media and Internet access are virtually nonexistent.

The overwhelming majority of Sahrawis are Sunni Muslim, and the Moroccan authorities generally respect freedom of worship. Restrictions on religious freedom in Western Sahara are similar to those found in Morocco. Academic freedom is severely restricted.

Freedom to assemble or to form political organizations is restricted. For example, Sahrawis are largely unable to form political associations or politically oriented nongovernmental organizations. In January, King Muhammad pardoned some 20 political prisoners and detainees, among them activists working on human rights in the Western Sahara. Nonviolent demonstrations are often dispersed with excessive force by security forces, particularly in the form of beatings.

Little organized-labor activity occurs. The same labor laws that apply in Morocco are employed in Moroccan-controlled areas of the territory. Moroccan unions are present in these areas, but not active.

The civilian population living in Moroccan-controlled areas of Western Sahara is subject to Moroccan law. Activists in the territory and in Morocco suspected of opposing the government's Western Sahara policies have over the past decades been subject to particularly harsh treatment, including arbitrary killing, incommunicado detention, and torture.

Local and international human rights organizations say hundreds, if not more than 1,000, Sahrawis remain "disappeared." A new Equity and Reconciliation Commission, created in late 2003, has begun to investigate and document disappearances and other abuses that occurred between 1956 and 1999, but it has a limited mandate and no judicial authority. In a report issued in October, Human Rights Watch urged the commission to handle Western Sahara–related abuses "as thoroughly and fairly as those that occurred elsewhere." It said authorities "continue to persecute advocates of an independent Western Sahara, and are generally less tolerant of dissent in this region than elsewhere."

Freedom of movement within Western Sahara is limited in militarily sensitive areas, within both the area controlled by Morocco and the area controlled by the Polisario.

As in Morocco itself, women are subjected to various forms of legal and cultural discrimination. Female illiteracy is very high, especially in rural areas.

Pakistan
Kashmir

Population: 4,200,000
Religious Groups: Muslim
[Shia majority, Sunni minority]
(99 percent), other (1 percent)
Ethnic Groups: Kashmiri, Punjabi, Balti, Gujjar, Ladakhi, Shina, other

Political Rights: 7
Civil Liberties: 5
Status: Not Free

Ten-Year Ratings Timeline (Political Rights, Civil Liberties, Status)

1995	1996	1997	1998	1999	2000	2001	2002	2003	2004
--	--	--	--	--	--	--	7,5NF	7,5NF	7,5NF

Overview: Relations between archrivals India and Pakistan thawed further in 2004 as the two governments held several rounds of talks over the status of Kashmir and other issues. Although Pakistani leader General Pervez Musharraf continued to face international pressure to crack down on the Islamist militant groups that make incursions into Indian-administered Kashmir from Pakistani-administered Kashmir, some militant activity continued to be reported. Meanwhile, the Pakistani government faced demands from nationalist and pro-independence Kashmiri groups for increased political representation in Azad Kashmir and the Northern Areas. Sectarian tensions also remained high; when protests by the majority Shia population in the Northern Areas turned violent, a curfew was imposed in much of the territory in June.

For centuries, Kashmir was ruled by Afghan, Sikh, and local strongmen. In 1846, the British seized control of the territory and sold it to the Hindu maharajah of the neighboring principality of Jammu. The maharajah later incorporated Ladakh and other surrounding areas into the new princely state of Jammu and Kashmir. When British India was partitioned into India and Pakistan in 1947, Maharajah Hari Singh tried to maintain Jammu and Kashmir's independence. However, after Pakistani tribesmen invaded, he agreed to cede Jammu and Kashmir to India. In return, India promised autonomy and eventual self-determination for the territory.

India and Pakistan went to war over Kashmir within months of gaining their independence. As part of a UN-brokered ceasefire in January 1949 that established the present-day boundaries, Pakistan gained control of roughly one-third of Jammu and Kashmir, including the far northern and western areas, as well as a narrow sliver of land adjoining Indian-held Kashmir. India retained most of the Kashmir Valley along with Jammu and Ladakh.

Unlike India, Pakistan never formally annexed the portion of Kashmir under its control. The Karachi Agreement of April 1949 divided Pakistani-administered Kashmir into two distinct entities, Azad (free) Kashmir and the Northern Areas. The Northern Areas consist of the five districts of Gilgit, Ghizer, Ghanche, Diamer, and Baltistan. Pakistan retained direct administrative control over the Northern Areas, while Azad Kashmir was given a larger degree of nominal self-government.

For several decades, an informal council administered Azad Kashmir. A legislative assembly was set up in 1970, and the 1974 interim constitution established a parliamentary system headed by a president and a prime minister. However, the political process in Azad Kashmir has been suspended on several occasions by the military rulers of Pakistan. In 1977, General Zia ul-Haq dissolved the legislative assembly and banned all political activity for eight years, while in 1991, the prime minister of Azad Kashmir was dismissed, arrested, and imprisoned in Pakistan.

Chronic infighting among Azad Kashmir's various political factions has also allowed Islamabad to interfere with ease in the electoral process. In the 1996 state elections, Sultan Mahmud Chaudhary's Azad Kashmir People's Party (AKPP) emerged with a majority of seats. The outgoing Muslim Conference (MC) had boycotted the elections, accusing the AKPP of vote rigging and fraud. In elections held in July 2001, with a 48 percent turnout, the MC swept back into power, winning 30 out of 48 seats. However, Musharraf installed a serving general as the president of Azad Kashmir later that month, amid speculation that Islamabad intended to reassert its control over the territory.

The lack of political representation in the Northern Areas has fueled demands for both formal inclusion within Pakistan and self-determination. In 1988, Gilgit was wracked by unrest after the majority Shias demanded an independent state. The Pakistani army suppressed the revolt with the help of armed Sunni tribesmen from a neighboring province. In May 1999, the Pakistani Supreme Court directed the government to act within six months to give the Northern Areas an elected government with an independent judiciary. After the verdict, the Pakistani government announced a package that provided for an appellate court and an expanded and renamed Northern Areas Legislative Council (NALC). In August 2003, the NALC submitted a proposal to the Pakistani government that called for a more autonomous form of provincial government along the lines of what currently exists in Azad Kashmir. Elections to the NALC were held in October 2004, but the NALC continues to have few real financial and legislative powers.

Since early 2002, Musharraf has been under sustained international pressure to curb the activities of Pakistani-based militant groups. However, when Musharraf banned the movement of militants from the Pakistani portion of Kashmir into the Indian-held section of Kashmir in June 2003, hard-line Islamist groups in Azad Kashmir organized protest rallies denouncing his decision and vowed to continue their armed insurgency.

While the Pakistani authorities have readily provided support to armed militants fighting in India, they have been less tolerant of groups that espouse Kashmiri self-determination. In January 2001, 12 small Kashmiri separatist groups in Azad Kashmir and the Northern Areas announced the formation of the All Parties National Alliance, which committed itself to fighting for an independent Kashmir and demanded that both India and Pakistan release jailed members of the group. Nationalist and pro-independence groups in Pakistani-administered Kashmir have continued to agitate for increased political representation. In August 2003, Shabir Choudhury, the leader of the pro-independence Jammu and Kashmir Liberation Front (JKLF), accused the Pakistani government of denying human rights to the Kashmiri people.

Sectarian tension between the majority Shias and the Sunnis in the Northern Areas continues to be a concern. Violent protests erupted in 2003 among Shias in Gilgit over the government's decision to introduce a new educational curriculum. Attempts by Shias to campaign for changes to the curriculum led to the imposition of a curfew in Gilgit and several other parts of the Northern Areas in June 2004 after thousands of Shia protestors clashed with security forces and attacked government buildings, offices, and a state-run hotel.

Political Rights and Civil Liberties: The political rights of the residents of Pakistani-administered Kashmir remain severely limited. Neither the Northern Areas nor Azad Kashmir has representation in Pakistan's national parliament. The Northern Areas are directly administered by the Pakistani government and have no constitution guaranteeing them fundamental rights, democratic representation, or the separation of powers, according to Amnesty International. Executive authority is vested in the minister for Kashmir affairs, a civil servant appointed by Islamabad. An elected 29-seat NALC serves in an advisory capacity and has no authorization to change laws or spend revenue. Elections to the NALC were held in October 2004; candidates who won seats included independents as well as representatives of several national political parties.

Azad Kashmir has an interim constitution, an elected unicameral assembly headed by a prime minister who sits for five-year terms, and a president. However, Pakistan exercises considerable control over both the structures of governance and electoral politics. Islamabad's approval is required to pass legislation, and the minister for Kashmir affairs handles the daily administration of the state. Twelve of the 48 seats in the Azad Kashmir assembly are reserved for Kashmiri "refugees" in Pakistan, and the elections to these seats are the subject of some manipulation.

In addition, candidates in elections are required to support the accession of Kashmir to Pakistan. According to Human Rights Watch, authorities barred at least 25 candidates from the pro-independence JKLF from contesting the July 2001 elections after they refused to sign a declaration supporting the accession of all of Kashmir to Pakistan. Several hundred JKLF supporters, including its chief, Amanullah Khan, were arrested while protesting against the decision. Fifteen other nationalists who agreed to the "accession" clause competed in the elections, but none won a seat.

Azad Kashmir receives a large amount of financial aid from the Pakistani government, but successive administrations have been tainted by corruption and incompetence. A lack of official accountability has been identified as a key factor in the poor socioeconomic development of both Azad Kashmir and the Northern Areas.

The Pakistani government uses the constitution and other laws to curb freedom of speech on a variety of subjects, including the status of Kashmir. In recent years, authorities have banned several local newspapers from publishing and have detained or otherwise harassed Kashmiri journalists. In addition to pressure from the authorities, journalists face some harassment from other, nonstate actors. In June

2002, political party activists attacked the office of the weekly *Naqqara*, a Gilgit-based newspaper, and assaulted the staff. Azad Kashmir has 1 daily, 10 weeklies and 3 monthlies that publish regularly. While the Northern Areas have no local broadcast media, a local radio station was inaugurated in Azad Kashmir in 2002, and the government also announced plans to launch a satellite television station.

Pakistan is an Islamic republic, and there are numerous restrictions on religious freedom. In addition, religious minorities face unofficial economic and societal discrimination and are occasionally subject to violent attack. Shia Muslims, who form the majority of the population in the Northern Areas, include a large number of Ismailis, a group that follows the Aga Khan. Sectarian strife between the majority Shia population and the increasing number of Sunni Muslims (many of whom are migrants from elsewhere in Pakistan) continues to be a problem. In June, violence erupted in Gilgit between security forces and Shia protestors who were campaigning for changes to be made in religious textbooks, which they allege present only a Sunni version of Islamic history. The Aga Khan Rural Support Program, run by the Aga Khan Foundation, an international development organization that focuses on Ismaili Shia communities worldwide, has in recent years been subjected to harassment and violence from extremist Sunni religious leaders. Extremists have also targeted girls' schools; in February, the BBC reported that nine schools had been burned down or dynamited by suspected Islamists who oppose the educating of girls and women.

Freedom of association and assembly is restricted. The constitution of Azad Kashmir forbids individuals and political parties from taking part in activities prejudicial to the ideology of the state's accession to Pakistan. Political parties that advocate Kashmiri independence are allowed to operate, but not to participate in elections. According to Amnesty International, some people who do not support the accession of Azad Kashmir to Pakistan have been dismissed from their jobs and denied access to educational institutions. A number of nationalist political parties have been formed in the Northern Areas that advocate either self-rule or greater political representation within Pakistan. However, their leaders are subject to harassment, arbitrary arrest, and long jail terms. The Balawaristan National Front (BNF), which advocates for independence for the Northern Areas from Pakistan, estimates that more than 70 individuals are facing sedition or treason cases as a result of their political activities.

In recent years, police have suppressed antigovernment demonstrations, sometimes violently, in both Azad Kashmir and the Northern Areas, and have imposed lengthy curfews in order to forestall protestors from assembling. These have included rallies by nationalist political organizations, as well as student protests and demonstrations by the Shia or Sunni communities. A report by the independent Human Rights Commission of Pakistan (HRCP) noted that during the curfew imposed in June 2004, police used excessive force against civilians and arrested the leadership of the Shia community that had organized the protests and hunger strikes.

Nongovernmental organizations (NGOs) are generally able to operate freely. In July 2003, the HRCP established an office in Gilgit to monitor the human rights situation in the region. However, employees of NGOs that focus on women's issues are sometimes subjected to threats and other forms of harassment from religious leaders and Islamist militant groups.

The judiciary of the Northern Areas consists of district courts and a chief court, whose decisions are final. The Northern Areas Council Legal Framework Order of 1994 provides for a court of appeals, but this court has not yet been established. The territory continues to be governed by the colonial-era Frontier Crimes Regulations, under which residents are required to report to local police stations once a month. Law enforcement agencies have reportedly used torture on political activists who have been detained or imprisoned. Azad Kashmir has its own system of local magistrates and high courts, whose heads are appointed by the president of Azad Kashmir. Appeals are adjudicated by the Supreme Court of Pakistan.

A number of Islamist militant groups, including members of al-Qaeda, have bases in, and operate from, Pakistani-administered Kashmir with the tacit permission of Pakistani intelligence. Several militant groups that advocate the accession of Kashmir to Pakistan receive weapons and financial aid from the Pakistani government in support of their infiltrations into Indian-administered Kashmir. Under pressure from the United States, General Pervez Musharraf, Pakistan's president, undertook several steps to curb infiltrations across the line of control (LOC), such as banning the main militant groups and persuading them to close some of their training camps in Azad Kashmir. However, by 2003, militant activity had increased to previous levels. Tension between the Islamist, pro-Pakistan groups and the pro-independence Kashmiri groups has reportedly intensified. In April 2003, police in Azad Kashmir arrested more than a dozen Kashmiri militants over fears of a possible clash between two rival groups.

Until a bilateral ceasefire was declared in November 2003, shelling between Indian and Pakistani forces around the LOC in Kashmir killed or displaced numerous civilians; some of these people remain unable to return to their homes. In addition, the Azad Kashmir government manages relief camps for refugees from Indian-administered Kashmir, which are funded by the Pakistani government. The appropriation of land in the Northern Areas by non-Kashmiri migrants from elsewhere in Pakistan, which has been tacitly encouraged by the federal government and army, has led to dwindling economic opportunities for the local population as well as an increase in religious and ethnic tensions.

The status of women in Pakistani-administered Kashmir is similar to that of women in Pakistan. Domestic violence, rape, honor killings, and other forms of abuse continue to be issues of concern. Women are not granted equal rights under the law, and their educational opportunities and choice of marriage partner remain circumscribed. In February, a spate of attacks by suspected Islamist hard-liners opposed to women's education targeted girls' schools in the Northern Areas.

Russia
Chechnya

Population: 1,200,000
Religious Groups: Muslim
[majority], Russian Orthodox
Ethnic Groups: Chechen (83 percent), other [including
Russian and Ingush] (17 percent)

Political Rights: 7
Civil Liberties: 7
Status: Not Free

Ten-Year Ratings Timeline (Political Rights, Civil Liberties, Status)

1995	1996	1997	1998	1999	2000	2001	2002	2003	2004
--	--	--	6,6NF	7,7NF	7,7NF	7,7NF	7,7NF	7,7NF	7,7NF

Overview:

In 2004, the debilitating, long-term civil war in Chechnya continued to victimize civilians through acts of terrorism, "disappearances," and war crimes perpetrated by various parties to the conflict. Violence spread significantly outside the confines of Chechnya, as rebels and terrorists conducted strikes in neighboring regions and in the Russian heartland. Attacks included suicide bombings that brought down two Russian passenger airlines in August and an assault on a school in the town of Beslan in neighboring North Ossetia. The year also saw the assassination in May of Akhmad Kadyrov, the Kremlin's handpicked Chechen president. On August 29, after an election to fill the post of the assassinated president, the authorities declared the former interior minister, Alu Alkhanov, president.

A small, partly mountainous Northern Caucasus republic, Chechnya has been at war with Russia for much of its history since the late 1700s. In February 1944, the Chechens were deported en masse to Kazakhstan under the pretext of their having collaborated with Germany during World War II. Officially rehabilitated in 1957 and allowed to return to their homeland, they remained politically suspect and were excluded from the region's administration.

After being elected Chechnya's president in October 1991, former Soviet Air Force Commander Dzhokhar Dudayev proclaimed Chechnya's independence. Moscow responded with an economic blockade. In 1994, Russia began assisting Chechens opposed to Dudayev, whose rule was marked by growing corruption and the rise of powerful clans and criminal gangs. Russian president Boris Yeltsin sent 40,000 troops into Chechnya by mid-December and attacked the capital, Grozny, widening the conflict. As casualties mounted, Russian public opposition to the war increased, fueled by criticism from much of the country's then-independent media. In April 1996, Dudayev was killed by a Russian missile.

A peace deal was signed in August 1996, resulting in the withdrawal of most Russian forces from Chechnya. However, a final settlement on the republic's status was put off until 2001. In May 1997, Russia and Chechnya reached an accord recognizing the elected president, Aslan Maskhadov, as Chechnya's legitimate leader.

Following incursions into neighboring Dagestan by renegade Chechen rebels and deadly apartment bombings in Russia that the Kremlin blamed on Chechen militants, then-Russian prime minister Vladimir Putin launched a second military offensive on Chechnya in September 1999. Russian troops conquered the flat terrain in the north of the republic, but progress slowed considerably as they neared heavily defended Grozny. Amid hostilities, Moscow withdrew recognition of Maskhadov.

Russia's indiscriminate bombing of civilian targets caused some 200,000 people to flee Chechnya, most to the tiny neighboring Russian republic of Ingushetia. After federal troops finally captured Grozny in February 2000, the Russian military focused on rebel strongholds in the southern mountainous region. Russian security sweeps led to atrocities in which civilians were regularly beaten, raped, or killed. Russian forces were subject to almost daily guerrilla bomb and sniper attacks by rebels. The renewed campaign enjoyed broad popular support in Russia fueled by the media's now one-sided reporting favoring the official government position.

Following the September 11, 2001, terrorist attacks on the United States, Moscow defended its actions in Chechnya as part of the broader war on global terrorism, asserting a connection between Chechen separatists and terrorists linked to Osama bin Laden, leader of al-Qaeda, the terrorist network; no connections have been proven. As the war has persisted and atrocities have mounted, some Chechen fighters have engaged in terrorist acts. In an ordeal covered live by Russian television, a group of Chechen rebels stormed a Moscow theater on October 23, 2002, taking 750 people hostage. More than 120 hostages died, most from the effects of a sedative gas that Russian troops used to incapacitate the rebels. Russian authorities reported that all 41 of the rebels had been killed.

As part of a largely unsuccessful Russian campaign to build up the authority of pro-Moscow Chechen factions, a March 23, 2003, referendum on a new Chechen constitution took place in the absence of open and free media, with opponents of the referendum and its questions effectively silenced. Chechnya's Moscow-appointed administration claimed results indicated a voter turnout of 85 percent, with 96 percent of voters in favor of the Kremlin-backed constitution. However, an independent survey of voter sentiments by the Russian rights group Memorial found that 80 percent of the indigenous population opposed the referendum.

After the referendum, presidential and legislative elections, which were held on October 5, 2003, saw the victory of Kremlin-backed candidate Akhmad Kadyrov as president. The Organization for Security and Cooperation in Europe criticized the elections for not offering voters significant choice, and the U.S. government judged them as "seriously flawed."

Reliable estimates suggest that thousands of Chechens, mostly civilians, died in 2004 as a result of the conflict. Rights groups estimate that an average of 50 people disappear each month, usually as a result of abductions believed to originate with Russian forces. Increasingly women, children, and adolescent males from pro-rebel families are targeted. Pro-Russian Chechen officials this year admitted that more than 200,000 have died since war broke out in Chechnya in 1994, and hundreds of thousands have been wounded and displaced.

Officially more than 70,000 Russian troops and security forces remain in Chechnya. In 2004, Russia attempted to transfer increased responsibility for the counterinsurgency effort to Chechen units linked to criminal activities, torture, and gross rights violations.

Chechen fighters assassinated Kadyrov and a dozen others in May 2004 in an explosion that ripped through a stadium. The bomb had been planted in the concrete months earlier when the stadium was under repair. In August, female *shahid* (martyr) terrorists opposed to the Russian occupation blew up two Russian passenger airplanes that had left Moscow.

After Kadyrov's death, authorities scheduled a new election on August 29. Alu Alkanov, a graduate of the U.S.S.R.'s Academy of the Interior Ministry and Chechnya's interior minister since 2003, won with a reported 74 percent of the vote amid a claimed 85 percent voter turnout. Journalists observing the process pronounced the voter-turnout figure wildly inflated.

On September 1, anti-Russian terrorist guerrillas carried out a military assault in the neighboring republic of North Ossetia, taking over a school in the town of Beslan. Some 400 people—half of them children—died in the hostage situation, after local citizens moved to rescue their relatives.

Political Rights and Civil Liberties:

Residents of Chechnya do not have the means to change their government democratically. While the 1997 presidential elections—conducted by the region's separatist authorities—were characterized by international observers as reasonably free and fair, the resumption of war in the republic in 1999 led to the total evisceration of the political rights of Chechens. President Aslan Maskhadov fled the capital city in December 1999, and the parliament elected in 1997 ceased to function. In June 2000, Russian president Vladimir Putin enacted a decree establishing direct presidential rule over Chechnya.

Claims by the Russian government that they were returning the region to democratic rule by means of a March 2003 referendum lacked credibility. The referendum was orchestrated by the Kremlin, with no opportunity for debate, widespread vote rigging, and official results that indicated a voter turnout of 85 percent and nearly unanimous support for a new constitution.

In the subsequent presidential and parliamentary elections of October 5, 2003, candidates representing a genuine alternative were not on the ballot and real debate was stifled in an atmosphere of repression and censorship. After the assassination of the newly elected president, Akhmad Kadyrov, in May 2004, a new election was conducted under similarly undemocratic circumstances. Under the authoritarian rule of President Alu Alkhanov, as under Kadyrov, there is no party pluralism and politicians who advocate Chechen state independence are unable to work openly and freely. The current regime, which includes Ramzan Kadyrov, son of the assassinated president, is linked to a network of criminal Chechen groups and is denounced by Maskhadov and separatist Chechens as traitorous.

The disruptive effects of the war continue to severely hinder news production and the free flow of information. Russian state-run television and radio continue to broadcast in Chechnya, although much of the population remains without electricity. Alkhanov's administration effectively controls all other broadcast and most print media, which predominantly reflect official viewpoints. There are three licensed television broadcasters, whose content is pro-regime. The Chechen rebel government operates a Web site with reports about the conflict and other news from its perspective. The editors of an independent weekly, *Groznensky Rabochy,* left Chechnya in 1999. The paper is now edited in Moscow and has limited distribution in Chechnya amid increased government restrictions on media coverage of the conflict. The paper's editor reports that there is widespread self-censorship by reporters who fear violent reprisals from rebels and pro-government forces.

The Russian military imposes severe restrictions on journalists' access to the widening Chechen war zone, issuing accreditation primarily to those of proven loyalty to the Russian government. Few foreign reporters are allowed into the breakaway republic, and when they are allowed entry, access is restricted by military and police authorities, as journalists covering the war must be accompanied at all times by military officials. In 2004, Russian and Georgian journalists who traveled to the region to cover the aftermath of the siege at Beslan appear to have been drugged, presumably by Russian authorities. One Russian journalist employed by U.S.-funded Radio Liberty was detained by Russian authorities and prevented from covering the siege.

Most Chechens are Muslims who practice Sufism, a mystical form of Islam. The Wahhabi sect, with roots in Saudi Arabia and characterized by a strict observance of Islam, has been banned, although adherents to its radical fundamentalist Islamic teachings form an important core of those engaged in terrorism against civilians. Since the start of the last war in 1994, many of the republic's schools have been damaged or destroyed, and education in Chechnya has been sporadic. Most schools have not been renovated and continue to lack such basic amenities as textbooks, electricity, and running water.

Some charitable nongovernmental organizations (NGOs) working on humanitarian, cultural, and social issues are allowed to operate but are under increasing Russian government criticism and pressure. An important but small Western-supported NGO, the LAM Center for Complex Research and Popularization of Chechen Culture, conducts activities in Russia to promote intergroup understanding and makes small grants to a small network of embattled NGOs. However, associational and trade union life is dominated by pro-regime organizations, and any groups and NGO activists who are viewed as sympathetic to the cause of Chechen independence are subject to persecution.

Russian government officials threaten international NGOs active in the country. In May 2004, the official spokesman for the Russian Foreign Ministry, Alexander Yakovenko, told a press conference in Moscow that most humanitarian organizations in Chechnya are improperly involved in monitoring activities instead of giving humanitarian assistance. His remarks echoed those of Putin, who had broadly criticized Russian NGOs in his state of the nation address.

Occasional protests are held by family members pressing for action on the abduction and murder of their relatives. In March 2004, medical students in Grozny protested the forced abduction of a colleague. There have been occasional strikes including one by teachers and students protesting forced abductions and raids on schools by masked gunmen associated with the Russian occupation.

Amid widespread conflict, the rule of law is virtually nonexistent. Civilians are subject to harassment and violence, including torture, rape, and extrajudicial executions, at the hands of Russian soldiers. Senior Russian military authorities have shown disregard for these widespread abuses. The new police and security structures—some of them created by recruitment from private armies and militarized gangs loyal to Alkhanov's new regime—are engaged in widespread criminal activity and rights violations. Particularly notorious is the former Presidential Security Service—renamed the Akhmad Kadyrov Special Purpose Regiment in 2004—which is reportedly involved in extortion, adductions, trading in contraband, and the maintenance of unsanctioned prisons and torture chambers.

Extrajudicial killings, disappearances, and other war crimes are rarely investigated and even more rarely punished. In an unprecedented development, on July 25, 2003, a military court in Rostov-on-Don, Russia, found Russian Colonel Yuri Budanov guilty of kidnapping and murdering a Chechen woman and sentenced him to 10 years in a maximum security prison. In 2004, this sentence was upheld on appeal by higher Russian courts. In December 2003, a Russian military court initiated the trial of four soldiers for murders alleged to have been committed in the Shattoi region of Chechnya in January 2002.

Russian troops engage in so-called mopping-up operations in which they seal off entire towns and conduct house-to-house searches for suspected rebels. During these security sweeps, soldiers have been accused of beating and torturing civilians, looting, and extorting money. Thousands of Chechens have gone missing or been found dead after such operations. In 2002, Chechnya issued new rules for troops conducting sweeps, including identifying themselves and providing a full list of those detained. Rights activists have accused federal troops, as well as pro-Russian Chechen government forces, of widely ignoring these rules. Human rights groups report the ongoing operation of illegal filtration camps by Russian authorities and Alkhanov's security forces. The camps detain and "filter" out Chechens suspected of ties to rebel groups, with "filtration" often used as a euphemism for "murder."

While many external refugee camps have been closed and Chechens who fled the violence have been pressured to return to their homes, there are still tens of thousands of refugees outside of Chechnya. Many refugees who return live in appalling conditions in tent camps, abandoned buildings, or cramped quarters with friends or relatives. There are tens of thousands of additional internally displaced persons inside the region and well over 100,000 long-term homeless, many of them orphaned children and teens.

Travel to and from the republic and inside its borders is severely restricted. After the resumption of the war, the Russian military failed to provide safe exit routes from the conflict zones for noncombatants.

Widespread corruption and the economic devastation caused by the war severely limit equality of opportunity. Ransoms obtained from kidnapping and the lucrative illegal oil trade provide money for Chechens and members of the Russian military. Much of the republic's infrastructure and housing remains damaged or destroyed after years of war, with reconstruction funds widely believed to have been substantially misappropriated by corrupt local authorities. In the capital city of Grozny, the long-term conflict has devastated civilian life, with more than 60 percent of all buildings completely destroyed. Much of the population ekes out a living selling produce or other goods at local markets. Residents who have found work are employed mostly by the local police, the Chechen administration, or the oil and construction sectors, or at small enterprises, including cafés.

While women continue to face discrimination in a traditional, male-dominated culture, the war has resulted in many women becoming the primary breadwinners for their families. Russian soldiers reportedly rape Chechen women in areas controlled by federal forces. Increasing numbers of women were reported to have been abducted and have disappeared.

Serbia and Montenegro
Kosovo

Population: 1,970,000
Religious Groups: Muslim
(majority), Serbian
Orthodox, other
Ethnic Groups: Albanian (88 percent), Serb (7 percent),
other [including Montenegrin, Turk, Croat, and Roma] (5 percent)

Political Rights: 6*
Civil Liberties: 5
Status: Not Free

Ratings Change: Kosovo's political rights rating declined from 5 to 6, and its
status from Partly Free to Not Free, due to the Serbian community boycott of
parliamentary elections following an increase in ethnic violence.

Ten-Year Ratings Timeline (Political Rights, Civil Liberties, Status)

1995	1996	1997	1998	1999	2000	2001	2002	2003	2004
7,7 NF	7,7 NF	7,7 NF	7,7 NF	7,7 NF	6,6NF	6,6NF	5,5PF	5,5PF	6,5NF

Overview:

The year 2004 saw aggression against non-Albanian ethnic
communities in March, the international community's weak
response to the crisis, and elections in October boycotted by
99 percent of Kosovo's Serbian minority.

Control over Kosovo was a source of conflict between ethnic Albanians and
Serbs throughout the twentieth century. The current round of troubles began in the
early 1980s after the death of Yugoslav dictator Marshal Josip Broz Tito, when ethnic Albanians in the province began a series of demonstrations in favor of republic
status within the former Yugoslavia, and, in some case, outright independence from
Yugoslavia. Tensions increased after former Serbian strongman Slobodan Milosevic
came to power and began to revoke much of Kosovo's autonomy. For most of the
1990s, an uneasy status quo was maintained between the Yugoslav government
and the Kosovo Albanians, who developed an entirely parallel society in Kosovo,
replete with quasi-governmental institutions, hospitals, and school systems.

In late 1997, a guerrilla movement called the Kosovo Liberation Army (KLA)
began a series of attacks on Serb targets in the province, as well as against fellow
Albanians deemed to be collaborating with the Serbian government. These moves
provoked harsh reprisals from Yugoslav government forces and various forms of
political and social repression against Kosovo Albanians. In March 1999, NATO
launched a 78-day air campaign against the Federal Republic of Yugoslavia (FRY) to
force it to relinquish control over the province. During the war, Yugoslav military
forces and paramilitary gangs forced hundreds of thousands of ethnic Albanians
out of the province.

Under the terms of UN Security Council Resolution (UNSCR) 1244 of June 1999,
a NATO-led peacekeeping force (KFOR) assumed responsibility for security in
Kosovo. UNSCR 1244 turned Kosovo into a protectorate of the international community, while officially maintaining Yugoslav sovereignty over the province. Although in 2003 the FRY was officially transformed into the union of Serbia and

Montenegro (SCG), this did not affect Kosovo's international legal limbo as a province formally a part of the SCG but practically a protectorate of the international community.

Since international forces moved into Kosovo in mid-1999, tens of thousands of non-Albanians have been forced to flee the province. A large Serb population is concentrated in a triangle-shaped piece of territory north of the Ibar River, and there are smaller, scattered Serb enclaves in southern parts of the province. On a visit to a Serb enclave in October 2004, Soren Jessen-Petersen, who took over as head of the UN Interim Administration Mission in Kosovo (UNMIK) in June, decried the fact that in twenty-first-century Europe, human beings are forced to live in ghettoes enclosed by barbed wire.

Tensions in Kosovo exploded into two days of violent upheaval on March 17 and 18 of 2004. Although no one officially claimed responsibility for the riots, most analyses laid the blame on KLA successor groups, and claimed that the riots were both organized and systematic. During the violence, 20 people were killed, 800 homes and 30 churches were destroyed, and more than 4,000 Serbs and other non-Albanians were left homeless. UN Secretary-General Kofi Annan called the March events "an organized, widespread, and targeted campaign" against non-Albanian communities in Kosovo, and Human Rights Watch reported that international organizations in Kosovo "failed catastrophically in their mandate to protect minority communities during the March 2004 violence." In the aftermath of the violence, the chief of UNMIK, Harri Holkeri, resigned from his position, allegedly because of ill health, though most observers believe that he was forced out because of poor leadership in dealing with Kosovo's problems.

Elections for a provincial parliament, held on October 23, were marred by a boycott by the Serb community (99 percent of Serbs registered to vote in Kosovo refused to cast a ballot). The elections did not significantly alter the political balance of power in Kosovo, as Kosovo president Ibrahim Rugova's Democratic League of Kosovo (LDK) maintained its position as the Kosovo Albanians' leading political party, followed by Hashim Thaci's Democratic Party of Kosovo (PDK) and Ramush Haradinaj's Alliance for the Future of Kosovo (AAK). Further trouble with the ballot was seen a week after the elections, when Kosovo's Central Election Commission called for a recount of all the ballots cast in response to numerous complaints. Overall turnout for the elections was 53 percent.

Non-Albanian ethnic minorities have not been the only victims of persecution by extremists in the province. Over the past four years, criminal elements associated with the former KLA, Thaci's PDK, and Haradinaj's AAK have repeatedly been accused of murdering political opponents. In March, unknown attackers threw a hand grenade at the home of Kosovo president Ibrahim Rugova. Although no one was injured in the attack, it provided further confirmation of the violence plaguing Kosovo's political and social life.

The March violence and the failure of the Serb community to participate in the October parliamentary elections have created new uncertainties about the future of the province. In the aftermath of the March violence, many international officials began arguing that the official "standards before status" policy for Kosovo, in which Kosovo's political leaders and society at large had to achieve certain performance benchmarks on issues such as democratization, minority rights, and respect for neighboring states, was no longer tenable because of tensions building within the province for independence. According to this view, only a quick move toward final status for the province, to begin at some point in 2005, could alleviate the pressure from the ethnic Albanian majority for independence. There was significant fear that another round of violence would soon break out, this time aimed against the international community as well as against non-Albanians. The Serb boycott, however, means that there are no legitimate representatives of the Serb community in Kosovo to deal with; at year's end it was unclear whether the government Belgrade would consider Kosovo's new government legitimate.

Political Rights and Civil Liberties: According to UNSCR 1244, ultimate authority within Kosovo resides with the UN special representative in the province, who is appointed by the UN secretary-general. The special representative, who also serves as chief of UNMIK, is responsible for implementing civilian aspects of the agreement ending the war. Elections in Kosovo in the post-1999 period, organized by the international community, have been considered "generally free and fair," although, given the large role played by international officials in the administration of the province, and the lack of freedom of movement for ethnic minorities in Kosovo, in many ways the level of democratization in Kosovo remains quite low. In the October 2002 municipal elections, contested by more than 60 political entities, voter turnout was approximately 54 percent. There was a disproportionately low Serb turnout because of continuing complaints about the lack of freedom of movement to and from polling places.

Kosovo's government currently consists of what are called the Provisional Institutions of Self-Government (PISG), including a 120-seat Assembly whose members are popularly elected and serve three-year terms. Twenty seats in the Assembly are reserved for representatives of ethnic minorities. The Assembly elects a president (currently, Ibrahim Rugova of the LDK) who also serves a three-year term.

Throughout the post-1999 period, the main political parties in Kosovo have been Rugova's LDK, which enjoys anywhere between 45-60 percent of the popular vote in general and municipal elections; the PDK, led by former KLA leader Hashim Thaci, which garners between 25-30 percent; and the AAK, led by another former KLA leader, Ramush Haradinaj, which usually gains 7-8 percent. Serbs (when they have chosen to participate in elections) have generally voted for an umbrella organization named the "Return Coalition" which usually gets 5-10 percent of the vote.

Freedom of expression is limited because of the overall lack of security in the province. Although a wide variety of print and electronic media operate in Kosovo, journalists report frequent harassment and intimidation. A survey conducted by the Organization for Security and Cooperation in Europe (OSCE) Mission in Kosovo in December 2001 found that 78 percent of the journalists questioned did not feel free to do investigative journalism without fear of reprisal. In a report on the performance of Kosovo media during the violence in March, the OSCE noted that Kosovo's media had engaged in "reckless and sensationalist reporting," had displayed "an unacceptable level of emotion, bias, and carelessness," and was deserving of "the strongest criticism." New regulations imposed by the international community after the violence in March to prevent similar abuses have subsequently been criticized by local journalists. According to the executive director of the Association for Professional Journalists in Kosovo, the new regulations "have worsened the media's unprofessionalism." In September 2004, a Kosovo Albanian journalist known for her investigative reporting against corruption and nepotism was the victim of an assassination attempt. There were no reports of government attempts to restrict access to the Internet.

The Albanian population in Kosovo, which is predominantly Muslim, on the whole enjoys freedom of belief and religious association, but there have been consistent, systematic attacks on Orthodox churches and other holy sites associated with the Serb population. During the March violence, 30 Serbian Orthodox churches and monasteries were destroyed and/or damaged. Since NATO took control of Kosovo, in total more than 130 churches and other properties belonging to the Serbian Orthodox Church have been destroyed or damaged. There were also reports in 2003 from Kosovo's small Protestant community that "Islamic extremists" were attending services so as to be able to identify worshippers and later harass them. There were also several reported incidents of attacks on Protestant places of worship. Academic freedom, however, has not been restricted.

Freedom of assembly, especially in flashpoints for ethnic conflict such as the divided city of Mitrovica, is occasionally restricted by UNMIK and/or KFOR because of security concerns. Both domestic and foreign nongovernmental organizations (NGOs) generally function freely, although lack of donor funding in the past two years has forced a large number of NGOs to cease operations. Current UNMIK regulations governing workers' rights allow for workers to join unions, although there is no explicit right to association. Similarly, the law does not recognize the right to strike, although no attempt is made to prevent workers from striking. The largest union in Kosovo, BSPK, claims to represent some 100,000 workers.

Kosovo lacks a functioning criminal justice system. One report on the state of Kosovo's judicial system after five years of international rule claimed that Kosovo's justice system "is on the verge of collapse." Ethnic Albanian judges are generally unwilling to prosecute cases involving Albanian attacks on non-Albanians, and the physical safety of non-Albanian judges brought into Kosovo to try cases is difficult to guarantee. Criminal suspects who have been arrested under the UN special representative's power to order executive detentions are frequently released on the orders of local judges. Given the breakdown of normal legal and judicial institutions, international observers have noted an increase in the number of murders attributable to blood feuds and vendettas, carried out in accordance with a medieval Albanian legal code known as the Kanun of Lek Dukagjini. Since 1999, approximately 40 murders have been attributed to blood feuds in Kosovo.

Prison conditions in Kosovo are generally in line with international standards, although prison overcrowding remains a problem. Police are generally believed to act professionally. While many Kosovo Police Service (KPS) officers tried to protect ethnic minorities during the March riots, others were accused of actively participating in the violence. Also, KFOR arrest and detention procedures remain the object of criticism for their lack of transparency.

Several leading members of the former KLA are under investigation for war crimes by the International Criminal Tribunal for the Former Yugoslavia (ICTY) for actions committed before, during, and after the NATO intervention. The KLA's successor organization, the Kosovo Protection Force, has been widely implicated in numerous violent acts since its formation in 1999, and especially in the events of March 17 and 18. In October 2004, the chief prosecutor of the ICTY, Carla Del Ponte, criticized both international officials in Kosovo and local ethnic Albanian political leaders for their unwillingness to cooperate with the ICTY's efforts.

During 2003, Amnesty International issued a report noting that non-Albanians in Kosovo "find themselves subjected to both direct and indirect discrimination when seeking access to basic civil, political, social, economic and cultural rights." Freedom of movement continues to be a significant problem in Kosovo for ethnic minorities.

Gender inequality continues to be a serious problem in Kosovo. Patriarchal societal attitudes often limit a woman's ability to gain an education or to choose her own marriage partner. According to the results of a study published in 2004, only half of Kosovo women between the ages of 25 and 64 have received even basic elementary education. In some rural areas of Kosovo, this figure reaches 90 percent. Similarly, in many rural areas of Kosovo, women are effectively disenfranchised by "family voting," in which the male head of a household casts ballots for the entire family.

Trafficking is a major problem in Kosovo, which serves as a place of transit, a point of destination, and a source for women and children trafficked from Eastern to Western Europe for purposes of prostitution. The presence of a large international military force and of numerous civilian agencies provides a relatively affluent clientele for the trafficking trade in the province. NGOs estimate that 80 percent of the clients at brothels in Kosovo are locals and 20 percent are foreigners.

United States
Puerto Rico

Population: 3,917,000   **Political Rights:** 1
Religious Groups: Roman **Civil Liberties:** 2
Catholic (85 percent),   **Status:** Free
other [including Protestant] (15 percent)
Ethnic Groups: White [mostly Spanish origin] (80.5 percent),
black (8 percent), other (11.5 percent),

Ten-Year Ratings Timeline (Political Rights, Civil Liberties, Status)

1995	1996	1997	1998	1999	2000	2001	2002	2003	2004
1,2F	1,2F	1,2F	1,2F	1,2F	1,2F	1,2F	1,2F	1,2F	1,2F

Overview: Puerto Rico experienced the closest governor's race in the island's history during 2004, with the outcome undetermined one month after the November poll.

Puerto Rico acquired the status of a commonwealth of the United States following approval by plebiscite in 1952. Under its terms, Puerto Rico exercises approximately the same control over its internal affairs as do the 50 U.S. states. Although they are U.S. citizens, residents cannot vote in presidential elections and are represented in the U.S. Congress by a delegate to the House of Representatives who can vote in committee, but not on the floor.

The commonwealth's election commission was still tabulating results in the latest governor's race on November 30. Anibal Acevedo Vila, the candidate of the pro-commonwealth Popular Democratic Party (PDP) was slightly ahead of Pedro Rossello, who represented the New Progressive Party (NPP), which favors statehood status for the island. The margin was razor-thin: 48.38 to 48.18. Ruben Berrios, the candidate of the pro-independence Independence Party, received less than 5 percent of the vote.

The narrowness of the election results reflects divisions within the population over the principal issue confronting Puerto Ricans for years: its relationship with the United States. Several nonbinding referendums in the past have shown Puerto Ricans almost equally divided between those who support the current, commonwealth status, and those who prefer that the island formally become part of the United States as a state. Rossello had anchored his campaign on a proposal for the United States Congress to define the island's status, an action Rossello said would lead to a binding referendum on the issue. He advocated a referendum that would include only two options—statehood or independence—and exclude the commonwealth status quo, which he described as a "colonial" option.

The new governor will succeed Sila Maria Calderon, a member of the PDP. During Calderon's tenure, the U.S. military agreed to abandon the use of the small island of Vieques as a bombing range after several years of negotiations and civil disobedience. The United States also shut down the Roosevelt Roads naval base.

Political Rights and Civil Liberties: The commonwealth constitution, modeled after that of the United States, provides for a governor and a bicameral legislature, consisting of a 28-member Senate and a 54-member House of Representatives, elected for four years. As U.S. citizens, Puerto Ricans are guaranteed all civil liberties granted in the United States.

Puerto Rico has a varied and outspoken media. During 2004, a coalition of human rights and gay organizations formally complained about frequent anti-homosexual comments and jokes on radio and television. The coalition announced plans to ask the U.S. Federal Communications Commission and the U.S. Commission on Civil Rights to conduct investigations of attacks on gays in the media.

Freedom of religion is guaranteed in this predominantly Roman Catholic territory, and a substantial number of evangelical churches have been established on the island in recent years. Academic freedom is guaranteed.

There is a robust civil society, with numerous nongovernmental organizations representing the interests of different constituencies. Freedom of assembly is guaranteed by law, and Puerto Ricans frequently mount protest rallies against government policies or policies of the United States. Trade union rights are respected by the government, and unions are generally free to organize and strike. During 2004, a strike by workers at the island's water utility caused water shortages and polarized the population between supporters and opponents of the action.

The legal system is based on U.S. law, and a Supreme Court heads an independent judiciary. Crime is the most serious problem facing the island. More than 750 murders were committed in 2003, and the murder rate was three times the average for the United States. Puerto Rico is one of the Caribbean's main drug transshipment points, and a substantial percentage of murders are drug related. Governor Sila Maria Calderon made crime prevention a major priority of her administration. The effort, however, has been hampered by low police morale and an inadequate legal system.

A controversy has emerged over the issue of capital punishment. Although Puerto Rico prohibits the death penalty, Puerto Ricans are subject to the death penalty for crimes that violate U.S. federal law. In recent years, there has been an upsurge in attempts by illegal migrants from various Caribbean countries, many traveling in flimsy boats, to reach Puerto Rico. Many were brought to the island by smugglers, who encouraged their migration efforts by warning that new U.S. policies would make illegal immigration more difficult in the future.

Laws granting equal rights for women in education, at the workplace, and in other aspects of society have been adopted. Women's rights organizations, however, claim that women are still subject to widespread discrimination.

Survey Methodology—2005

INTRODUCTION

The *Freedom in the World* survey provides an annual evaluation of the state of global freedom as experienced by individuals. Freedom is the opportunity to act spontaneously in a variety of fields outside the control of the government and other centers of potential domination. Freedom House measures freedom according to two broad categories: political rights and civil liberties. Political rights enable people to participate freely in the political process, including through the right to vote, compete for public office, and elect representatives who have a decisive impact on public policies and are accountable to the electorate. Civil liberties allow for the freedoms of expression and belief, associational and organizational rights, rule of law, and personal autonomy without interference from the state.

Freedom House does not maintain a culture-bound view of freedom. The methodology of the survey established basic standards that are derived in large measure from the Universal Declaration of Human Rights. These standards apply to all countries and territories, irrespective of geographical location, ethnic or religious composition, or level of economic development.

The survey includes both analytical reports and numerical ratings for 192 countries and 14 select territories. Each country and territory is assigned a numerical rating, which is calculated based on the methodology described below, on a scale of 1 to 7. A rating of 1 indicates the highest degree of freedom and 7 the least amount of freedom.

The survey findings are reached after a multi-layered process of analysis and evaluation by a team of regional experts and scholars. Although there is an element of subjectivity inherent in the survey findings, the ratings process emphasizes intellectual rigor and balanced and unbiased judgments.

The survey does not rate governments or government performance per se, but rather the real-world rights and freedoms enjoyed by individuals. Freedoms can be affected by state actions, as well as by nonstate actors, including terrorists and other armed groups. Thus, the survey ratings generally reflect the interplay of a variety of actors, both governmental and nongovernmental.

In addition to country reports, *Freedom in the World* includes reports on a select group of territories based on their political significance and size. Freedom House divides territories into two categories: related territories and disputed territories. Related territories consist mostly of colonies, protectorates, and island dependencies of sovereign states that are in some relation of dependency to that state and whose relationship is not currently in serious legal or political dispute. Disputed territories are areas within internationally recognized sovereign states whose status is in serious political or violent dispute and whose conditions differ substantially from those of the relevant sovereign states. They are often outside of central government control and characterized by intense, longtime, and widespread insurgency or independence movements that enjoy popular support. This year, the territories of Macao (China), Northern Ireland (United Kingdom), West Papua (Indonesia), and Kurdistan (Iraq) are no longer being treated in separate reports because of a reduction in the intensity of civil or political conflict or due to greater integration of the territory's identity into that of the related sovereign state. Developments in these territories are now reflected in the relevant country reports and ratings. In addition, the territory of Cyprus, which was previously listed under Turkey, has been renamed Northern (Turkish) Cyprus and listed under Cyprus.

HISTORY OF THE SURVEY

Freedom House's first year-end reviews of freedom began in the 1950s as the *Balance Sheet of Freedom*. This modest report provided assessments of political trends and their implications for individual freedom. In 1972, Freedom House launched a new, more comprehensive annual study of freedom called *Freedom in the World*. Raymond Gastil, a Harvard-trained specialist in regional studies from the University of Washington at Seattle, developed the survey's methodology, which assigned countries political rights and civil liberties ratings and categorized them as Free, Partly Free, or Not Free. The findings appeared each year in Freedom House's *Freedom at Issue* bimonthly journal (later titled *Freedom Review*). The survey first appeared in book form in 1978 and continued to be produced by Gastil, with essays by leading scholars on related issues, until 1989, when a larger team of in-house survey analysts was established. Subsequent editions of the survey, including the 2005 edition, have followed essentially the same format.

OVERVIEW OF RESEARCH AND RATINGS REVIEW PROCESS

This year's survey covers developments from December 1, 2003, through November 30, 2004, in 192 countries and 14 territories. The research and ratings process involved nearly two dozen analyst/writers and 13 senior-level academic advisers. The eight members of the core research team headquartered in New York, along with 15 outside consultant writers, prepared the country and territory reports. The writers used a broad range of sources of information, including foreign and domestic news reports, academic analyses, nongovernmental organizations, think tanks, individual professional contacts, and visits to the region in preparing their reports.

The country and territory ratings were proposed by the writers of each related report. The ratings were reviewed on a comparative basis in a series of six regional meetings—Sub-Saharan Africa, Asia-Pacific, Central and Eastern Europe and the Former Soviet Union, Middle East and North Africa, Latin America and the Caribbean, and Western Europe—involving the writers and academic advisers with expertise in each region. The ratings were compared to the previous year's findings, and any major proposed numerical shifts or category changes were subjected to more intensive scrutiny. These reviews were followed by cross-regional assessments in which efforts were made to ensure comparability and consistency in the findings. Some of the key country reports were also reviewed by the academic advisors.

The survey's methodology is reviewed periodically by an advisory committee on methodological issues. Over the years, the committee has made a number of modest methodological changes to adapt to evolving ideas about political rights and civil liberties. At the same time, the time series data are not revised retroactively, and any changes to the methodology are introduced incrementally in order to ensure the comparability of the ratings from year to year.

RATINGS PROCESS

(*NOTE: see the full checklists and keys to political rights and civil liberties ratings and status at the end of the methodology essay.*)

Raw Points—The ratings process is based on a checklist of 10 political rights questions (grouped into three subcategories) and 15 civil liberties questions (grouped into four subcategories). Raw points are awarded to each of these questions on a scale of 0 to 4, where 0 points represents the smallest degree and 4 points the greatest degree of rights or liberties present. The only exception to the addition of 0 to 4 points per checklist item is Additional Discretionary Question B in the Political Rights Checklist, for which 1 to 4 points are subtracted depending on the severity of the situation. The highest number of points that can be awarded to the political rights checklist is 40 (or a total of up to 4 points for each of the 10 questions). The highest number of points that can be awarded to the civil liberties checklist is 60 (or a total of up to 4 points for each of the 15 questions).

To answer the political rights questions, Freedom House considers to what extent the system offers voters the opportunity to choose freely from among candidates and to what extent the candidates are chosen independently of the state. However, formal electoral procedures are not the only factors that determine the real distribution of power. In many countries, the military retains a significant political role, while in others, the king maintains considerable power over the elected politicians. In addition, elected governments must exhibit levels of accountability, openness, and transparency between elections.

In answering the civil liberties questions, Freedom House does not equate constitutional guarantees of human rights with the on-the-ground fulfillment of these rights. Both laws and actual practices are factored into the ratings decisions. For states and territories with small populations, particularly tiny island nations, the absence of trade unions and other forms of association is not necessarily viewed as a negative situation unless the government or other centers of domination are deliberately blocking their establishment or operation.

Political Rights and Civil Liberties Ratings—The total number of points awarded to the political rights and civil liberties checklists determines the political rights and civil liberties ratings. Each point total corresponds to a rating of 1 through 7, with 1 representing the highest and 7 the lowest level of freedom. (see tables 1 and 2).

Status of Free, Partly Free, Not Free—Each pair of political rights and civil liberties ratings is averaged to determine an overall status of "Free," "Partly Free," or "Not Free." Those whose ratings average 1.0 to 2.5 are considered Free, 3.0 to 5.0 Partly Free, and 5.5 to 7.0 Not Free (see table 3). [In previous years, countries or territories with a combined average score of 5.5 could be either Partly Free or Not Free, depending on the total number of raw points that they received.]

The designations of Free, Partly Free, and Not Free each cover a broad third of the available raw points. Therefore, countries and territories within any one category, especially those at either end of the category, can have quite different human rights situations. In order to see the distinctions within each category, a country or territory's political rights and civil liberties ratings should be examined. For example, countries at the lowest end of the Free category (2 in political rights and 3 in civil liberties, or 3 in political rights and 2 in civil liberties) differ from those at the upper end of the Free group (1 for both political rights and civil liberties). Also, a designation of Free does not mean that a country enjoys perfect freedom or lacks serious problems, only that it enjoys comparably more freedom than Partly Free or Not Free (or some other Free) countries.

Indications of Ratings and/or Status Changes—Each country or territory's political rights rating, civil liberties rating, and status is included in the statistics section that precedes each country or territory report. A change in a political rights or civil liberties rating since the previous survey edition is indicated with an asterisk next to the rating that has changed. A brief ratings change explanation is included in the statistics section.

Trend Arrows—Upward or downward trend arrows may be assigned to countries and territories. Trend arrows indicate general positive or negative trends since the previous survey that are not necessarily reflected in the raw points and do *not* warrant a ratings change. A country cannot receive both a numerical ratings change and a trend arrow in the same year. A trend arrow is indicated with an arrow next to the name of the country or territory that appears before the statistics section at the top of each country or territory report.

GENERAL CHARACTERISTICS OF EACH POLITICAL RIGHTS AND CIVIL LIBERTIES RATING

POLITICAL RIGHTS

Rating of 1—Countries and territories that receive a rating of 1 for political rights come closest to the ideals suggested by the checklist questions, beginning with free and fair elections. Those who are elected rule, there are competitive parties or other political groupings, and the opposition plays an important role and has actual power. Minority groups have reasonable self-government or can participate in the government through informal consensus.

Rating of 2—Countries and territories rated 2 in political rights are less free than those rated 1. Such factors as political corruption, violence, political discrimination against minorities, and foreign or military influence on politics may be present and weaken the quality of freedom.

Ratings of 3, 4, 5—The same conditions that undermine freedom in countries and territories with a rating of 2 may also weaken political rights in those with a rating of 3, 4, or 5. Other damaging elements can include civil war, heavy military involvement in politics, lingering royal power, unfair elections, and one-party dominance. However, states and territories in these categories may still enjoy some elements of political rights, including the freedom to organize quasi-political groups, reasonably free referenda, or other significant means of popular influence on government.

Rating of 6—Countries and territories with political rights rated 6 have systems ruled by military juntas, one-party dictatorships, religious hierarchies, or autocrats. These regimes may allow only a minimal manifestation of political rights, such as some degree of representation or autonomy for minorities. A few states are traditional monarchies that mitigate their relative lack of political rights through the use of consultation with their subjects, tolerance of political discussion, and acceptance of public petitions.

Rating of 7—For countries and territories with a rating of 7, political rights are absent or virtually nonexistent as a result of the extremely oppressive nature of the regime or severe oppression in combination with civil war. States and territories in this group may also be marked by extreme violence or warlord rule that dominates political power in the absence of an authoritative, functioning central government.

CIVIL LIBERTIES

Rating of 1—Countries and territories that receive a rating of 1 come closest to the ideals expressed in the civil liberties checklist, including freedom of expression, assembly, association, education, and religion. They are distinguished by an established and generally equitable system of rule of law. Countries and territories with this rating enjoy free economic activity and tend to strive for equality of opportunity.

Rating of 2—States and territories with a rating of 2 have deficiencies in a few aspects of civil liberties, but are still relatively free.

Ratings of 3, 4, 5—Countries and territories that have received a rating of 3, 4, or 5 range from those that are in at least partial compliance with virtually all checklist standards to those with a combination of high or medium scores for some questions and low or very low scores on other questions. The level of oppression increases at each successive rating level, including in the areas of censorship, political terror, and the prevention of free association. There are also many cases in which groups opposed to the state engage in political terror that undermines other freedoms. Therefore, a poor rating for a country is not necessarily a comment on the intentions of the government, but may reflect real restrictions on liberty caused by nongovernmental actors.

Rating of 6—People in countries and territories with a rating of 6 experience severely restricted rights of expression and association, and there are almost always political prisoners and other manifestations of political terror. These countries may be characterized by a few partial rights, such as some religious and social freedoms, some highly restricted private business activity, and relatively free private discussion.

Rating of 7—States and territories with a rating of 7 have virtually no freedom. An overwhelming and justified fear of repression characterizes these societies.

Countries and territories generally have ratings in political rights and civil liberties that are within two ratings numbers of each other. Without a well-developed civil society, it is difficult, if not impossible, to have an atmosphere supportive of political rights. Consequently, there is no country in the survey with a rating of 6 or 7 for civil liberties and, at the same time, a rating of 1 or 2 for political rights.

ELECTORAL DEMOCRACY DESIGNATION

In addition to providing numerical ratings, the survey assigns the designation "electoral democracy" to countries that have met certain minimum standards. In determining whether a country is an electoral democracy, Freedom House examines several key factors concerning how its national leadership is chosen.

To qualify as an electoral democracy, a state must have satisfied the following criteria:

> 1) A competitive, multiparty political system;
>
> 2) Universal adult suffrage for all citizens (with exceptions for restrictions that states may legitimately place on citizens as sanctions for criminal offenses);
>
> 3) Regularly contested elections conducted in conditions of ballot secrecy, reasonable ballot security, and in the absence of massive voter fraud that yields results that are unrepresentative of the public will;
>
> 4) Significant public access of major political parties to the electorate through the media and through generally open political campaigning.

The electoral democracy designation reflects a judgment about the last major national election or elections. In the case of presidential/parliamentary systems, both elections must have been free and fair on the basis of the above criteria; in parliamentary systems, the last nationwide elections for the national legislature must have been free and fair. The presence of certain irregularities during the electoral process does not automatically disqualify a country from being designated an electoral democracy. A country cannot be listed as an electoral democracy if it reflects the ongoing and overwhelming dominance of a single party or movement over the course of numerous national elections; such states are considered to be dominant party states. Nor can a country be an electoral democracy if significant authority for national decisions resides in the hands of an unelected power, whether a monarch or a foreign international authority. A country is removed from the ranks of electoral democracies if its last national election failed to meet the criteria listed above, or if changes in law significantly eroded the public's possibility for electoral choice.

Freedom House's term "electoral democracy" differs from "liberal democracy" in that the latter also implies the presence of a substantial array of civil liberties. In the survey, all Free countries qualify as both electoral and liberal democracies. By contrast, some Partly Free countries qualify as electoral, but not liberal, democracies.

POLITICAL RIGHTS AND CIVIL LIBERTIES CHECKLIST

POLITICAL RIGHTS
A. Electoral Process
1. Is the head of state and/or head of government or other chief authority elected through free and fair elections?

2. Are the legislative representatives elected through free and fair elections?

3. Are there fair electoral laws, equal campaigning opportunities, fair polling, and honest tabulation of ballots?

B. Political Pluralism and Participation

1. Do the people have the right to organize in different political parties or other competitive political groupings of their choice, and is the system open to the rise and fall of these competing parties or groupings?

2. Is there a significant opposition vote, de facto opposition power, and a realistic possibility for the opposition to increase its support or gain power through elections?

3. Are the people's political choices free from domination by the military, foreign powers, totalitarian parties, religious hierarchies, economic oligarchies, or any other powerful group?

4. Do cultural, ethnic, religious, and other minority groups have reasonable self-determination, self-government, autonomy, or participation through informal consensus in the decision-making process?

C. Functioning of Government

1. Do freely elected representatives determine the policies of the government?

2. Is the government free from pervasive corruption?

3. Is the government accountable to the electorate between elections, and does it operate with openness and transparency?

Additional discretionary Political Rights questions:

A. For traditional monarchies that have no parties or electoral process, does the system provide for consultation with the people, encourage discussion of policy, and allow the right to petition the ruler?

B. Is the government or occupying power deliberately changing the ethnic composition of a country or territory so as to destroy a culture or tip the political balance in favor of another group?

NOTE: For each political rights and civil liberties checklist question, 0 to 4 points are **added**, depending on the comparative rights and liberties present (0 represents the least, 4 represents the most). However, for additional discretionary question B only, 1 to 4 points are **subtracted**, when necessary.

CIVIL LIBERTIES
D. Freedom of Expression and Belief

1. Are there free and independent media and other forms of cultural expression?

(Note: in cases where the media are state controlled but offer pluralistic points of view, the survey gives the system credit.)

2. Are there free religious institutions, and is there free private and public religious expression?

3. Is there academic freedom, and is the educational system free of extensive political indoctrination?

4. Is there open and free private discussion?

E. Associational and Organizational Rights

1. Is there freedom of assembly, demonstration, and open public discussion?

2. Is there freedom of political or quasi-political organization? (Note: this includes political parties, civic organizations, ad hoc issue groups, etc.)

3. Are there free trade unions and peasant organizations or equivalents, and is there effective collective bargaining? Are there free professional and other private organizations?

F. Rule of Law

1. Is there an independent judiciary?

2. Does the rule of law prevail in civil and criminal matters? Are police under direct civilian control?

3. Is there protection from police terror, unjustified imprisonment, exile, or torture, whether by groups that support or oppose the system? Is there freedom from war and insurgencies?

4. Is the population treated equally under the law?

G. Personal Autonomy and Individual Rights

1. Is there personal autonomy? Does the state control travel, choice of residence, or choice of employment? Is there freedom from indoctrination and excessive dependency on the state?

2. Do citizens have the right to own property and establish private businesses? Is private business activity unduly influenced by government officials, the security forces, or organized crime?

3. Are there personal social freedoms, including gender equality, choice of marriage partners, and size of family?

4. Is there equality of opportunity and the absence of economic exploitation?

KEY TO RAW POINTS, POLITICAL RIGHTS AND
CIVIL LIBERTIES RATINGS, AND STATUS

Table 1		Table 2	
Political Rights (PR)		**Civil Liberties (CL)**	
Total Raw Points	**PR Rating**	**Total Raw Points**	**CL Rating**
36-40	1	53-60	1
30-35	2	44-52	2
24-29	3	35-43	3
18-23	4	26-34	4
12-17	5	17-25	5
6-11	6	8-16	6
0-5	7	0-7	7

Table 3

Combined Average of the PR and CL Ratings	**Country Status**
1.0 to 2.5	Free
3.0 to 5.0	Partly Free
5.5 to 7.0	Not Free

Tables and Ratings

Table of Independent Countries

Country	PR	CL	Freedom Rating	Country	PR	CL	Freedom Rating
Afghanistan	5▲	6	Not Free	Dominica	1	1	Free
Albania	3	3	Partly Free	Dominican	2▲	2	Free
Algeria	6	5	Not Free	Republic			
Andorra	1	1	Free	East Timor	3	3	Partly Free
Angola	6	5	Not Free	Ecuador	3	3	Partly Free
Antigua and	2▲	2	Free	Egypt	6	5▲	Not Free
Barbuda				El Salvador	2	3	Free
⬆ Argentina	2	2	Free	Equatorial Guinea	7	6	Not Free
Armenia	5▼	4	Partly Free	Eritrea	7	6	Not Free
Australia	1	1	Free	Estonia	1	1▲	Free
Austria	1	1	Free	Ethiopia	5	5	Partly Free
Azerbaijan	6	5	Not Free	Fiji	4	3	Partly Free
Bahamas	1	1	Free	Finland	1	1	Free
Bahrain	5	5	Partly Free	France	1	1	Free
⬇ Bangladesh	4	4	Partly Free	Gabon	5	4	Partly Free
Barbados	1	1	Free	The Gambia	4	4	Partly Free
Belarus	7▼	6	Not Free	Georgia	3▲	4	Partly Free
Belgium	1	1	Free	Germany	1	1	Free
Belize	1	2	Free	⬆ Ghana	2	2	Free
⬇ Benin	2	2	Free	Greece	1	2	Free
Bhutan	6	5	Not Free	Grenada	1	2	Free
Bolivia	3	3	Partly Free	Guatemala	4	4	Partly Free
Bosnia-Herzegovina	4	3▲	Partly Free	⬇ Guinea	6	5	Not Free
Botswana	2	2	Free	Guinea-Bissau	4▲	4	Partly Free
Brazil	2	3	Free	⬇ Guyana	2	2	Free
⬆ Brunei	6	5	Not Free	Haiti	7▼	6	Not Free
Bulgaria	1	2	Free	Honduras	3	3	Partly Free
Burkina Faso	5▼	4	Partly Free	Hungary	1	1▲	Free
Burma	7	7	Not Free	Iceland	1	1	Free
⬆ Burundi	5	5	Partly Free	⬆ India	2	3	Free
⬆ Cambodia	6	5	Not Free	⬆ Indonesia	3	4	Partly Free
Cameroon	6	6	Not Free	⬇ Iran	6	6	Not Free
Canada	1	1	Free	⬇ Iraq	7	5	Not Free
Cape Verde	1	1	Free	Ireland	1	1	Free
Central African	6▲	5	Not Free	Israel	1	3	Free
Republic				Italy	1	1	Free
Chad	6	5	Not Free	⬇ Jamaica	2	3	Free
Chile	1	1	Free	Japan	1	2	Free
China	7	6	Not Free	Jordan	5	4▲	Partly Free
⬇ Colombia	4	4	Partly Free	Kazakhstan	6	5	Not Free
Comoros	4▲	4	Partly Free	Kenya	3	3	Partly Free
Congo (Brazzaville)	5	4	Partly Free	Kiribati	1	1	Free
Congo (Kinshasa)	6	6	Not Free	Kuwait	4	5	Partly Free
Costa Rica	1	1▲	Free	Kyrgyzstan	6	5	Not Free
Cote d'Ivoire	6	6▼	Not Free	Laos	7	6	Not Free
⬆ Croatia	2	2	Free	Latvia	1	2	Free
Cuba	7	7	Not Free	Lebanon	6	5	Not Free
Cyprus	1	1	Free	Lesotho	2	3	Free
Czech Republic	1	1▲	Free	Liberia	5▲	4▲	Partly Free
Denmark	1	1	Free	Libya	7	7	Not Free
Djibouti	5	5	Partly Free	Liechtenstein	1	1	Free

Country	PR	CL	Freedom Rating
Lithuania	2▼	2	Free
Luxembourg	1	1	Free
🔻 Macedonia	3	3	Partly Free
Madagascar	3	3	Partly Free
Malawi	4▼	4	Partly Free
Malaysia	4▲	4	Partly Free
🔻 Maldives	6	5	Not Free
Mali	2	2	Free
Malta	1	1	Free
Marshall Islands	1	1	Free
Mauritania	6	5	Not Free
Mauritius	1	1▲	Free
Mexico	2	2	Free
Micronesia	1	1	Free
Moldova	3	4	Partly Free
Monaco	2	1	Free
Mongolia	2	2	Free
Morocco	5	4▲	Partly Free
Mozambique	3	4	Partly Free
Namibia	2	3	Free
Nauru	1	1	Free
Nepal	5	5▼	Partly Free
Netherlands	1	1	Free
New Zealand	1	1	Free
Nicaragua	3	3	Partly Free
Niger	3▲	3▲	Partly Free
🔻 Nigeria	4	4	Partly Free
North Korea	7	7	Not Free
Norway	1	1	Free
Oman	6	5	Not Free
🔻 Pakistan	6	5	Not Free
Palau	1	1	Free
Panama	1	2	Free
Papua New Guinea	3	3	Partly Free
🔻 Paraguay	3	3	Partly Free
🔻 Peru	2	3	Free
Philippines	2	3	Free
Poland	1	1▲	Free
Portugal	1	1	Free
Qatar	6	5▲	Not Free
Romania	3▼	2	Free
Russia	6▼	5	Not Free
🔻 Rwanda	6	5	Not Free
St. Kitts and Nevis	1	2	Free
St. Lucia	1	2	Free
St. Vincent and the Grenadines	2	1	Free
Samoa	2	2	Free
San Marino	1	1	Free
Sao Tome and Príncipe	2	2	Free
Saudi Arabia	7	7	Not Free
✿ Senegal	2	3	Free
✿ Serbia and Montenegro	3	2	Free

Country	PR	CL	Freedom Rating
Seychelles	3	3	Free
✿ Sierra Leone	4	3	Partly Free
Singapore	5	4	Partly Free
Slovakia	1	1▲	Free
Slovenia	1	1	Free
Solomon Islands	3	3	Partly Free
✿ Somalia	6	7	Not Free
South Africa	1	2	Free
South Korea	1▲	2	Free
Spain	1	1	Free
Sri Lanka	3	3	Partly Free
Sudan	7	7	Not Free
Suriname	1	2	Free
🔻 Swaziland	7	5	Not Free
Sweden	1	1	Free
Switzerland	1	1	Free
Syria	7	7	Not Free
Taiwan	2	1▲	Free
Tajikistan	6	5	Not Free
Tanzania	4	3	Partly Free
🔻 Thailand	2	3	Free
✿ Togo	6	5	Not Free
🔻 Tonga	5	3	Partly Free
Trinidad and Tobago	3	3	Partly Free
Tunisia	6	5	Not Free
Turkey	3	3▲	Partly Free
Turkmenistan	7	7	Not Free
Tuvalu	1	1	Free
Uganda	5	4	Partly Free
Ukraine	4	3▲	Partly Free
United Arab Emirates	6	6	Not Free
United Kingdom	1	1	Free
United States	1	1	Free
Uruguay	1	1	Free
Uzbekistan	7	6	Not Free
Vanuatu	2	2	Free
Venezuela	3	4	Partly Free
Vietnam	7	6	Not Free
🔻 Yemen	5	5	Partly Free
Zambia	4	4	Partly Free
Zimbabwe	7▼	6	Not Free

PR and CL stand for Political Rights and Civil Liberties. 1 represents the most free and 7 the least free rating.

✿ 🔻 up or down indicates a general trend in freedom.

▲▼ up or down indicates a change in Political Rights or Civil Liberties since the last survey.

The freedom ratings reflect an overall judgment based on survey results. See the essay on survey methodology for more details.

Note: The ratings in this table reflect global events from December 1, 2003, through November 30, 2004.

Table of Related Territories

Country	PR	CL	Freedom Rating
China			
Hong Kong	5	2▲	Partly Free
United States			
Puerto Rico	1	2	Free

Table of Disputed Territories

Country	PR	CL	Freedom Rating
Armenia/Azerbaijan			
Nagorno-Karabakh	5	5	Partly Free
China			
Tibet	7	7	Not Free
Cyprus			
Northern			
(Turkish) Cyprus	2	2	Free
Georgia			
Abkhazia	6	5	Not Free
India			
Kashmir	5	5	Partly Free
Israel			
Israeli-Occupied			
territories	6	6	Not Free
Palestinian Authority-			
Administered	5	6	Not Free
territories			
Moldova			
Transnistria	6	6	Not Free
Morocco			
Western Sahara	7	6	Not Free
Pakistan			
Kashmir	7	5	Not Free
Russia			
Chechnya	7	7	Not Free
Serbia &			
Montenegro			
Kosovo	6▼	5	Not Free

Combined Average Ratings: Independent Countries

FREE	Monaco	Paraguay	Algeria
1.0	Panama	Seychelles	Angola
Andorra	St. Kitts and Nevis	Solomon Islands	Azerbaijan
Australia	St. Lucia	Sri Lanka	Bhutan
Austria	St. Vincent and Grenadines	Trinidad and Tobago	Brunei
Bahamas	South Africa	Turkey	Cambodia
Barbados	South Korea		Central African
Belgium	Suriname	**3.5**	Republic
Canada	Taiwan	Bosnia-Herzegovina	Chad
Cape Verde		Fiji	Egypt
Chile	**2.0**	Georgia	Guinea
Costa Rica	Antigua and Barbuda	Indonesia	Kazakhstan
Cyprus	Argentina	Moldova	Kyrgyzstan
Czech Republic	Benin	Mozambique	Lebanon
Denmark	Botswana	Sierra Leone	Maldives
Dominica	Croatia	Tanzania	Mauritania
Estonia	Dominican Republic	Ukraine	Oman
Finland	Ghana	Venezuela	Pakistan
France	Guyana		Qatar
Germany	Israel	**4.0**	Russia
Hungary	Lithuania	Bangladesh	Rwanda
Iceland	Mali	Colombia	Tajikistan
Ireland	Mexico	Comoros	Togo
Italy	Mongolia	The Gambia	Tunisia
Kiribati	Samoa	Guatemala	
Liechtenstein	Sao Tome and Principe	Guinea-Bissau	**6.0**
Luxembourg	Vanuatu	Malawi	Cameroon
Malta		Malaysia	Congo (Kinshasa)
Marshall Islands	**2.5**	Nigeria	Cote d'Ivoire
Mauritius	Brazil	Tonga	Iran
Micronesia	El Salvador	Zambia	Iraq
Nauru	India		Swaziland
Netherlands	Jamaica	**4.5**	United Arab Emirates
New Zealand	Lesotho	Armenia	
Norway	Namibia	Burkina Faso	**6.5**
Palau	Peru	Congo (Brazzaville)	Belarus
Poland	Philippines	Gabon	China
Portugal	Romania	Jordan	Equatorial Guinea
San Marino	Senegal	Kuwait	Eritrea
Slovakia	Serbia and Montenegro	Liberia	Haiti
Slovenia	Thailand	Morocco	Laos
Spain		Singapore	Somalia
Sweden		Uganda	Uzbekistan
Switzerland	**PARTLY FREE**		Vietnam
Tuvalu	**3.0**	**5.0**	Zimbabwe
United Kingdom	Albania	Bahrain	
United States	Bolivia	Burundi	**7.0**
Uruguay	East Timor	Djibouti	Burma
	Ecuador	Ethiopia	Cuba
1.5	Honduras	Nepal	Libya
Belize	Kenya	Yemen	North Korea
Bulgaria	Macedonia		Saudi Arabia
Greece	Madagascar		Sudan
Grenada	Nicaragua	**NOT FREE**	Syria
Japan	Niger	**5.5**	Turkmenistan
Latvia	Papua New Guinea	Afghanistan	

Combined Average Ratings: Related Territories

FREE
1.5
Puerto Rico (US)

PARTLY FREE
3.5
Hong Kong (China)

Combined Average Ratings: Disputed Territories

FREE	PARTLY FREE	NOT FREE
2.0	**5.0**	**5.5**
Cyprus	Kashmir (India)	Abkhazia (Georgia)
[Northern Turkish]	Nagorno-Karabakh	Kosovo (Serbia and
(Cyprus)	(Armenia/Azerbaijan)	Montenegro)
		Palestinian Authority-
		Administered Territories
		(Israel)
		6.0
		Israeli-Occupied
		Territories (Israel)
		Kashmir (Pakistan)
		Transnistria (Moldova)
		6.5
		Western Sahara
		(Morocco)
		7.0
		Chechnya (Russia)
		Tibet (China)

Electoral Democracies (119)

Albania
Andorra
Antigua and Barbuda
Argentina
Australia
Austria
Bahamas
Bangladesh
Barbados
Belgium
Belize
Benin
Bolivia
Botswana
Brazil
Bulgaria
Canada
Cape Verde
Chile
Colombia
Comoros
Costa Rica
Croatia
Cyprus
Czech Republic
Denmark
Dominica
Dominican Republic
East Timor
Ecuador
El Salvador
Estonia
Finland
France
Georgia
Germany
Ghana
Greece
Grenada
Guatemala
Guyana
Honduras
Hungary
Iceland
India
Indonesia

Ireland
Israel
Italy
Jamaica
Japan
Kenya
Kiribati
Latvia
Lesotho
Liechtenstein
Lithuania
Luxembourg
Macedonia
Madagascar
Malawi
Mali
Malta
Marshall Islands
Mauritius
Mexico
Micronesia
Moldova
Monaco
Mongolia
Mozambique
Namibia
Nauru
Netherlands
New Zealand
Nicaragua
Niger
Nigeria
Norway
Palau
Panama
Papua New Guinea
Paraguay
Peru
Philippines
Poland
Portugal
Romania
St. Kitts and Nevis
St. Lucia
St. Vincent and the Grenadines
Samoa

San Marino
Sao Tome and Principe
Senegal
Serbia and Montenegro
Seychelles
Sierra Leone
Slovakia
Slovenia
Solomon Islands
South Africa
South Korea
Spain
Sri Lanka
Suriname

Sweden
Switzerland
Taiwan
Thailand
Trinidad and Tobago
Turkey
Tuvalu
Ukraine
United Kingdom
United States
Uruguay
Vanuatu
Venezuela

The Survey Team

CONTRIBUTING AUTHORS

Martin Edwin "Mick" Andersen is an investigative reporter and a historian. He has worked as a special correspondent for *Newsweek* and the *Washington Post* in Argentina, a staff member of the Senate Foreign Relations Committee, and senior adviser for policy planning with the Criminal Division of the U.S. Justice Department. He serves as the Latin America analyst for *Freedom in the World*.

Anjalika Bardalai is the Managing Editor of *Country Finance* and the Asian Regional Editor for the Economist Intelligence Unit. She has written for *The National Interest* and the *Far Eastern Economic Review*, and was a speaker at the China Forum sponsored by the Universidad de los Andes in Bogota, Colombia. She serves as an East and Southeast Asia analyst for *Freedom in the World*.

Gordon N. Bardos is Assistant Director of the Harriman Institute at Columbia University. His research interests focus on problems of nationalism and ethnic conflict, and he is a frequent commentator on the Balkans in the U.S. and European press. He serves as the Balkans analyst for *Freedom in the World*.

Gary C. Gambill is an adjunct professor at College of Mount Saint Vincent in New York City and former editor of the *Middle East Intelligence Bulletin*. He has written extensively on Lebanese and Syrian politics, authoritarianism in the Arab World, and American foreign policy in the region. He serves as a Middle East analyst for *Freedom in the World*.

Thomas W. Gold frequently teaches as an adjunct professor of political science at the City University of New York. He is a former Assistant Professor of Comparative Politics at Sacred Heart University and the author of *The Lega Nord and Contemporary Politics in Italy*. He earned his doctorate from the New School for Social Research and received a Fulbright Fellowship to conduct research in Italy in 1996 and 1997. He serves as a Western Europe analyst for *Freedom in the World*.

Michael Gold-Biss is Professor of National Security Policy at the Center for Hemispheric Defense Studies, National Defense University in Washington, DC. He is the author of *The Discourse on Terrorism: Political Violence and the Subcommittee on Security and Terrorism, 1981-1986* and coeditor with Richard Millett of *Beyond Praetorianism: The Latin American Military in Transition*. He holds a doctorate in international relations from American University. He serves as the Central America and Caribbean analyst for *Freedom in the World*.

Michael Goldfarb is Senior Press Officer at Freedom House. He has worked as a reporter in Israel for United Press International and as a writer for Time.com, the Web site of *Time* magazine. He serves as a Middle East analyst for *Freedom in the World*.

Robert Lane Greene writes for Economist.com and *The Economist* and is an adjunct lecturer in Global Affairs at New York University. Previously, he was the editor of country analyses at Economist.com. He holds a master's degree from Oxford University in European politics, where he was a Marshall Scholar. He serves as a Western Europe analyst for *Freedom in the World.*

Adrian Karatnycky is Senior Scholar and Counselor at Freedom House, advising the organization on programs, policy, and research. From 1996 until 2003, he served as president of Freedom House. He is co-author of three books on East European politics and editor or co-editor of 16 volumes of studies on global political rights, civil liberties, and political transitions. He serves as the Russia, Ukraine, and Belarus analyst for *Freedom in the World.*

Karin Deutsch Karlekar is a Senior Researcher at Freedom House and the editor of Freedom House's annual *Freedom of the Press* survey. She was the author of the Afghanistan and Sri Lanka reports for Freedom House's *Countries at the Crossroads 2004* survey of democratic governance. Ms. Karlekar holds a PhD in Indian history from Cambridge University and previously worked as a consultant for Human Rights Watch and an editor at the Economist Intelligence Unit. She serves as the South Asia analyst for *Freedom in the World.*

Brian M. Katulis is an analyst and public opinion research consultant who has worked on democracy and governance projects in the Middle East, Asia, Central and Eastern Europe, and Latin America. His experience includes work on the Policy Planning Staff at the Department of State and the Near East and South Asian Directorate of the National Security Council during the Clinton Administration. He serves as a Middle East analyst for *Freedom in the World.*

Judith Matloff is an Adjunct Professor at the Columbia Graduate School of Journalism. She worked as a foreign correspondent for 20 years and wrote a book about Angola, *Fragments of a Forgotten War.* Her last two assignments abroad were Africa Bureau Chief and Moscow Bureau Chief for the *Christian Science Monitor.* She serves as an Africa analyst for *Freedom in the World.*

Edward R. McMahon holds a joint appointment as Research Associate Professor in the Departments of Political Science and Community Development and Applied Economics at the University of Vermont. Previously, he was dean's professor of applied politics and the director of the Center on Democratic Performance at Binghamton University (SUNY). He has also served as regional director for West, East, and Central Africa at the National Democratic Institute for International Affairs and as a diplomat with the U.S. Department of State. He serves as an Africa analyst for *Freedom in the World.*

Ann Marie Murphy is an Assistant Professor at the John C. Whitehead School of Diplomacy and International Relations, Seton Hall University, and an adjunct research scholar at the Weatherhead East Asian Institute, Columbia University. Dr. Murphy's research interests include political change in Southeast Asia, international politics in the Asia-Pacific, and U.S. policy toward the region. She serves as a Southeast Asia analyst for *Freedom in the World*.

Aili Piano is a Senior Researcher at Freedom House and co-editor of *Freedom in the World*. She was a country report author for several editions of *Nations in Transit*, a Freedom House survey of democratization in East-Central Europe and Eurasia, and for Freedom House's *Countries at the Crossroads 2004* survey of governance. Before joining Freedom House, Ms. Piano worked as a diplomatic attaché at the Estonian Mission to the United Nations. She serves as the Central Asia analyst for *Freedom in the World*.

Arch Puddington is Director of Research at Freedom House and co-editor of *Freedom in the World*. He has written widely on American foreign policy, race relations, organized labor, and the history of the Cold War. He is the author of *Broadcasting Freedom: The Cold War Triumph of Radio Free Europe and Radio Liberty* and *Lane Kirkland: Champion of American Labor*. He serves as the United States and Canada analyst for *Freedom in the World*.

Sarah Repucci is a Researcher at Freedom House and co-editor of Freedom House's *Countries at the Crossroads* survey of governance. She has written articles on Turkey's bid for European Union membership and transatlantic cooperation. She serves as a Western and Southeastern Europe analyst for *Freedom in the World*.

Mark Yaron Rosenberg is a Research Assistant at Freedom House. He is a recent Phi Beta Kappa graduate of the University of California, Berkeley, where he earned a BA with highest honors in Political Economy, and was previously employed at the Export-Import Bank of the United States. He serves as the Scandinavia and Baltic states analyst for *Freedom in the World*.

Nejla Sammakia is Program Officer for the Middle East, North Africa with the Open Society Institute, Soros Foundation. She has worked as a researcher with Human Rights Watch and Amnesty International, and has extensive experience as a journalist in the Middle East with the Associated Press and Agence France Presses, and as free-lance journalist and consultant working on the Arab region out of Washington DC. She serves as the North Africa analyst for *Freedom in the World*.

Cindy Shiner is a freelance journalist who has spent much of her time in Africa. She has written for the *Washington Post*, done broadcasts for National Public Radio, and worked as a consultant on Africa issues for Human Rights Watch. She serves as an Africa analyst for *Freedom in the World*.

Yves Sorokobi is an award-winning journalist and human rights professional. An analyst and commentator on Africa's democratization process, he has worked as Africa program coordinator for the Committee to Protect Journalists and as a senior communications consultant with the International AIDS Vaccine Initiative. He serves as an Africa analyst for *Freedom in the World*.

Christopher Walker is Director of Studies at Freedom House and co-editor of Freedom House's *Countries at the Crossroads* survey of governance. He has written extensive analyses of European and Eurasian political and security affairs. He serves as the Caucasus analyst for *Freedom in the World.*

Anny Wong is a political scientist with the RAND Corporation. Her research covers science and technology policy, international development, homeland security, and U.S. relations with Asia-Pacific countries. She serves as the Pacific Islands analyst for *Freedom in the World.*

ACADEMIC ADVISORS

Adotei Akwei is Campaigns Director for Amnesty International USA.

Jon B. Alterman directs the Middle East Program at the Center for Strategic and International Studies.

David Becker is Associate Professor in the Department of Government, Dartmouth College.

Charles Gati is Senior Adjunct Professor in European Studies in the Paul H. Nitze School for Advanced International Studies, Johns Hopkins University.

Thomas Lansner is Adjunct Assistant Professor of International Affairs in the School of International and Public Affairs, Columbia University.

Peter M. Lewis is Associate Professor in the School of International Service, American University.

Thomas O. Melia is Director of Research at the Institute for the Study of Diplomacy at the Edmund A. Walsh School of Foreign Service, Georgetown University, where he is also an adjunct professor.

Alexander J. Motyl is Professor in the Department of Political Science and Deputy Director of the Center for Global Change and Governance, Rutgers University-Newark.

Andrew Moravcsik is Professor of Politics and Director of the European Union Program, Princeton University.

Andrew J. Nathan is Class of 1919 Professor of Political Science at Columbia University.

Phillip Oldenburg is an independent scholar. He currently serves as Senior Lecturer in the Department of Government, University of Texas at Austin, and as Adjunct Research Associate at the Southern Asian Institute, Columbia University.

Arturo Valenzuela is Professor of Government and Director of the Center for Latin American Studies in the Edmund A. Walsh School of Foreign Service, Georgetown University.

Bridget Welsh is Assistant Professor of Southeast Asian Studies in the Paul H. Nitze School for Advanced International Studies, Johns Hopkins University.

Linda Stern, copy editor
Ida Walker, proofreader
Mark Wolkenfeld, production coordinator
Alex Taurel, intern

Selected Sources

PUBLICATIONS/BROADCASTS

ABC Color [Paraguay], www.abc.com.py

Africa

Africa Confidential, www.africa-confidential.com

Africa Daily, www.africadaily.com

Africa Energy Intelligence, www.africaintelligence.com

AFRICAHOME dotcom, www.africahome.com

AfricaOnline.com, www.africaonline.com

Aftenposten Norway, www.aftenposten.no

Agence France Presse (AFP), www.afp.com

allAfrica.com, www.allafrica.com

Al-Ray Al-'am [Kuwait], www.alraialaam.com

Al-Raya [Qatar], www.raya.com

Al-Thawra [Yemen], www.althawra.gov.ye

Al-Watan [Qatar], www.al-watan.com

American Broadcasting Corporation News (ABC), www.abcnews.go.com

Andorra Times, www.andorratimes.com

Arab News [Saudi Arabia], www.arabnews.com

Asia Times, www.atimes.com

Associated Press (AP), www.ap.org

Australia Broadcasting Corporation News Online, www.abc.net.au/news

Bahrain Post, www.bahrainpost.com

Bahrain Tribune, www.bahraintribune.com

Baltic News Service, www.bns.lt

Bangkok Post, www.bangkokpost.co.th

British Broadcasting Corporation (BBC), www.bbc.co.uk

Cabinda.net, www.cabinda.net

Cable News Network (CNN), www.cnn.com

Cameroon Tribune, www.cameroon-tribune.cm

The Central Asia-Caucasus Analyst (Johns Hopkins University), www.cacianalyst.org

The Christian Science Monitor, www.csmonitor.com

CIA World Factbook, www.cia.gov/cia/publications/factbook

Civil Georgia, www.civil.ge

Daily Excelsior [India-Kashmir], www.dailyexcelsior.com

Daily Star [Bangladesh], www.dailystar.net

Danas [Serbia and Montenegro], www.danas.co.yu

Dani [Bosnia-Herzegovina], www.bhdani.com

Dawn [Pakistan], www.dawn.com

Der Standard [Austria], www.derstandard.at

Die Zeit [Germany], www.zeit.de

Deutsche Presse-Agentur [Germany], www.dpa.de

Deutsche Welle [Germany], www.dwelle.de

The East Africa Standard [Kenya], www.eastandard.net

East European Constitutional Review (New York University), www.law.nyu.edu/eedr

The Economist, www.economist.com

The Economist Intelligence Unit reports

EFE News Service [Spain], www.efenews.com

Election Watch, www.electionwatch.org

El Mercurio [Chile], www.elmercurio.cl

El Nuevo Herald [United States], www.miami.com/mld/elnuevo

El Pais [Uruguay], www.elpais.com.uy

El Tiempo [Colombia], www.eltiempo.com

El Universal [Venezuela], www.eluniversal.com.ve

Expreso [Peru], www.expreso.co.pe

Far Eastern Economic Review, www.feer.com

Federal Bureau of Investigation Hate Crime Statistics, www.fbi.gov/ucr/2003/03semimaps.pdf

The Financial Times, www.ft.com

Finnish News Agency, http://virtual.finland.fi/stt

Folha de Sao Paulo, www.folha.com.br

Foreign Affairs, www.foreignaffairs.org

Foreign Policy, www.foreignpolicy.com

Frankfurter Allgemeine Zeitung [Germany], www.faz.net

The Friday Times [Pakistan], www.thefridaytimes.com

The Frontier Post [Pakistan], www.frontierpost.com

Global News Wire, www.lexis-nexis.com

Globus [Croatia], www.globus.com.hr

The Good Friday Agreement [Northern Ireland], www.nio.gov.uk/issues/agreement.htm

The Guardian [Nigeria], www.ngrguardiannews.com

Gulf Daily News [Bahrain], www.gulf-daily-news.com

Gulf News Online [United Arab Emirates], www.gulf-news.com

Gulf Times [Qatar], www.gulf-times.com

Haveeru Daily [Maldives], www.haveeru.com.mv

The Hindustan Times [India], www.hindustantimes.com

Iceland Review, www.icelandreview.com

The Independent [United Kingdom], www.independent.co.uk

Index on Censorship, www.indexonline.org

India Today, www.india-today.com
The Indian Express, www.indian-express.com
Insight Magazine, www.insightmag.com
Integrated Regional Information Networks (IRIN), www.irinnews.org
Inter Press Service, www.ips.org
Interfax News Agency, www.interfax-news.com
International Herald Tribune, www.iht.com
Irish Independent, www.unison.ie/irish independent
Irish Times, www.ireland.com
The Jordan Times, www.jordantimes.com
Journal of Democracy, www.journalofdemocracy.org
Kashmir Times [India - Kashmir], www.kashmirtimes.com
Kathmandu Post, www.nepalnews.com.np/ktmpost.htm
Khaleej Times [United Arab Emirates], www.khaleejtimes.com
Kuensel [Bhutan], www.kuenselonline.com
Kurier [Austria], www.kurier.at
Kuwait Post, www.kuwaitpost.com
La Jornada [Mexico], www.jornada.uam.nx
La Nacion [Argentina], www.lanacion.com.ar
La Repubblica [Italy], www.repubblica.it
La Tercera [Chile], www.tercera.cl
Lanka Monthly Digest [Sri Lanka], www.lanka.net/LMD
Latin American Regional Reports, www.latinnews.com
Latin American Weekly Reports, www.latinnews.com
Le Figaro [France], www.lefigaro.fr
Le Monde [France], www.lemonde.fr
Le Temps [Switzerland], www.letemps.ch
Lexis-Nexis, www.lexis-nexis.com
The Los Angeles Times, www.latimes.com
The Messenger [Georgia], www.messenger.com.ge
The Miami Herald, www.miami.com/mld/miamiherald
Mirianas Variety [Micronesia], www.mvariety.com
Mopheme News [Lesotho], www.lesoff.co.za/news
The Moscow Times, www.themoscowtimes.com
Nacional [Croatia], www.nacional.hr
The Nation, www.thenation.org
The Nation [Thailand], www.nationmultimedia.com
The Nation Online [Malawi], www.nationmalawi.com
National Public Radio (NPR), www.npr.org
National Review, www.nationalreview.com

Neue Zurcher Zeitung [Switzerland], www.nzz.ch
The New York Times, www.nytimes.com
The New Yorker, www.newyorker.com
NIN [Serbia and Montenegro], www.nin.co.yu
Noticias [Argentina], www.noticias.uolsinectis.com.ar
Notimex [Mexico], www.notimex.com
Novi Reporter [Serbia and Montenegro]
O Estado de Sao Paulo, www.estado.com.br
O Globo [Brazil], www.oglobo.globo.com
OFFnews [Argentina], www.offnews.info
Oman Arabic Daily, www.omandaily.com
Oman Daily Observer, www.omanobserver.com
Oslobodjenje [Bosnia-Herzegovina], www.oslobodjenje.com.ba
Outlook [India], www.outlookindia.com
Pagina/12 [Argentina], www.pagina12.com.ar
PANAPRESS, www.panapress.com
The Pioneer [India], www.dailypioneer.com
Political Handbook of the World, http://phw.binghamton.edu
Politika [Serbia-Montenegro], www.politika.co.yu
The Post [Zambia], www.zamnet.zm/zamnet/post/post.html
Radio Australia, www.abc.net.au/ra
Radio France Internationale, www.rfi.fr
Radio Free Europe-Radio Liberty reports, www.rferl.org
Radio Lesotho, www.lesotho.gov.ls/radio/radiolesotho
Radio New Zealand, www.rnzi.com
Reporter [Serbia and Montenegro]
Reuters, www.reuters.com
Ritzau [Denmark], www.ritzau.dk
Semana [Colombia], www.semana.com
Slobodna Bosna [Bosnia-Herzegovina], www.slobodna-bosna.ba
Solomon Islands Broadcasting Corporation, www.sibconline.com.sb
The Somaliland Times, www.somalilandtimes.net
South Asia Tribune [Pakistan], www.satribune.com
South China Morning Post [Hong Kong], www.scmp.com
The Statesman [India], www.thestatesman.net
Straits Times [Singapore], www.straitstimes.asia1.com.sg
Suddeutsche Zeitung [Germany], www.sueddeutsche.de
Tageblatt [Luxembourg], www.tageblatt.lu
Tamilnet.com, www.tamilnet.com
Tax-News.com, www.tax-news.com

This Day [Nigeria], www.thisdayonline.com
The Tico Times [Costa Rica], www.ticotimes.net
Time, www.time.com
The Times of Central Asia, www.times.kg
The Times of India, www.timesofindia.net
Transcaucasus: A Chronology,
   www.anca.org/anca/transcaucasus.asp
Turkistan Newsletter
U.S. News and World Report,
   www.usnews.com
U.S. State Department Country Reports on
Human Rights Practices, www.state.gov/g/
   drl/rls/hrrpt
U.S. State Department Country Reports on
Human Trafficking Reports, www.state.gov/g/
   tip
U.S. State Department International
Religious Freedom Reports, www.state.gov/
   g/drl/irf
Venpres [Venezuela], www.venpres.gov.ve
Voice of America, www.voa.gov
The Wall Street Journal, www.wsj.com
The Washington Post,
   www.washingtonpost.com
The Washington Times,
   www.washingtontimes.com
The Weekly Standard,
   www.weeklystandard.com
World of Information Country Reports,
   www.worldinformation.com
Xinhua, www.xinhuanet.com
Yemen Observer, www.yobserver.com
Yemen Times, www.yementimes.com

ORGANIZATIONS

Afghan Independent Human Rights
Commission, www.aihrc.org.af
Afghanistan Research and Evaluation Unit,
   www.areu.org.pk
American Civil Liberties Union, www.aclu.org
Amnesty International, www.amnesty.org
Annan Plan for Cyprus, www.cyprus-un-
   plan.org
Asian Center for Human Rights [India],
   www.achrweb.org
Asian Human Rights Commission [Hong
Kong], www.ahrchk.net
Balkan Human Rights Web,
   www.greekhelsinki.gr
Bangladesh Center for Development,
Journalism, and Communication,
   www.bcjdc.org
British Helsinki Human Rights Group,
   www.oscewatch.org/default.asp
Cabindese Government in Exile,
   www.cabinda.org
Cambridge International Reference on
   Current Affairs, www.circaworld.com

The Carter Center, www.cartercenter.org
Centre for Monitoring Electoral Violence [Sri
Lanka], www.cpalanka.org/cmev.html
Centre for Policy Alternatives [Sri Lanka],
   www.cpalanka.org
Committee for the Prevention of Torture,
   www.cpt.coe.int
Committee to Protect Journalists,
   www.cpj.org
Council of Europe, www.coe.int
Ditshwanelo - The Botswana Centre for
   Human Rights, www.ditshwanelo.org.bw
Election Commission of India, www.eci.gov.in
Eurasia Group, www.eurasiagroup.net
European Bank for Reconstruction and
Development, www.ebrd.org
European Commission Against Racism and
Intolerance, www.ecri.coe.int
European Institute for the Media,
   www.eim.org
Forum 18, www.forum18.org
Forum for Human Dignity [Sri Lanka],
   www.fhd.8m.net
Forum of Federations/Forum des
   Federations, www.forumfed.org
Global Rights, www.globalrights.org
The Government of Botswana Web site,
   www.gov.bw
Habitat International Coalition, http://
   home.mweb.co.za/hi/hic/
Heritage Foundation, www.heritage.org
Hong Kong Human Rights Monitor,
   www.hkhrm.org.hk
Human Rights Center of Azerbaijan, http://
   mitglied.lycos.de/hrca
Human Rights Commission of Pakistan,
   www.hrcp-web.org
Human Rights First, www.humanrightsfirst.org
Human Rights Watch, www.hrw.org
INFORM (Sri Lanka Information Monitor)
Institute for Democracy in Eastern Europe,
   www.idee.org
Institute for Security Studies, www.iss.co.za
Institute for War and Peace Reporting,
   www.iwpr.net
Inter American Press Association,
   www.sipiapa.com
International Bar Association,
   www.ibanet.org
International Campaign for Tibet,
   www.savetibet.org
International Centre for Ethnic Studies,
   www.icescolombo.org
International Commission of Jurists,
   www.icj.org
International Confederation of Free Trade
   Unions, www.icftu.org
International Crisis Group, www.crisisweb.org

International Federation of Journalists, www.ifj.org

International Foundation for Electoral Systems, www.ifes.org

International Freedom of Expression Exchange, www.ifex.org

International Helsinki Federation for Human Rights, www.ihf-hr.org

International Institute for Democracy and Electoral Assistance, www.idea.int

International Labour Organization, www.ilo.org

International Legal Assistance Consortium, www.ilacinternational.org

International Monetary Fund, www.imf.org

International Press Institute, www.freemedia.at

International Republican Institute, www.iri.org

International Society For Fair Elections And Democracy [Georgia], www.isfed.ge

Jamestown Foundation, www.jamestown.org

Kashmir Study Group, www.kashmirstudygroup.net

Kyrgyz Committee for Human Rights, www.kchr.elcat.kg

Macedonian Information Agency, www.mia.mk

The Malawi Human Rights Commission

Malta Data, www.maltadata.com

Media Institute of Southern Africa, www.misa.org

National Democratic Institute for International Affairs, www.ndi.org

The National Endowment for Democracy, www.ned.org

National Human Rights Commission [India], www.nhrc.nic.in

National Peace Council of Sri Lanka, www.peace-srilanka.org

National Society for Human Rights [Namibia], www.nshr.org.na

Nicaragua Network, www.nicanet.org

Observatory for the Protection of Human Rights Defenders, www.omct.org

Odhikar [Bangladesh], www.odhikar.org

Office of the High Representative in Bosnia and Herzegovina, www.ohr.int

Open Society Institute, www.soros.org

Organization for Security and Cooperation in Europe, www.osce.org

Pacific Media Watch, www.pmw.c20.org

People's Forum for Human Rights [Bhutan]

Population Reference Bureau, www.prb.org

Refugees International, www.refugeesinternational.org

Reporters Sans Frontieres, www.rsf.org

Republic of Angola, www.angola.org

Royal Institute of International Affairs, www.riia.org

Save the Children, www.savethechildren.org

Shan Women's Action Network, www.shanwomen.org

South African Human Rights Commission, www.sahrc.org.za

South African Press Association, www.sapa.org.za

South Asia Analysis Group [India], www.saag.org

South Asia Terrorism Portal [India], www.satp.org

Tibet Information Network, www.tibetinfo.net

Transitions Online, www.tol.cz

Transparency International, www.transparency.org

Turkish Ministry of Foreign Affairs, www.mfa.gov.tr

United Nations Development Program, www.undp.org

United Nations High Commissioner on Human Rights, www.unhchr.ch

United Nations Interim Mission in Kosovo, www.unmikonline.org

United Nations Population Division, www.un.org/esa/population

U.S. Department of State, www.state.gov

University Teachers for Human Rights-Jaffna, www.uthr.org

Washington Office on Latin America, www.wola.org

The World Bank, www.worldbank.org

World Markets Research Centre, www.wmrc.com

World Press Freedom Committee, www.wpfc.org

ABOUT FREEDOM HOUSE

Founded in 1941 by Eleanor Roosevelt and others, Freedom House is the oldest nonprofit, nongovernmental organization in the United States dedicated to promoting and defending democracy and freedom worldwide. Freedom House supports the global expansion of freedom through its advocacy activities, monitoring and in-depth research on the state of freedom, and direct support of democratic reformers throughout the world.

Advocating Democracy and Human Rights: For over six decades, Freedom House has played an important role in identifying the key challenges to the global expansion of democracy, human rights, and freedom. Freedom House is committed to advocating a vigorous U.S. engagement in international affairs that promotes human rights and freedom around the world.

Monitoring Freedom: Despite significant recent gains for freedom, hundreds of millions of people around the world continue to endure dictatorship, repression, and the denial of basic rights. To shed light on the obstacles to liberty, Freedom House issues studies, surveys, and reports on the condition of global freedom. Our research is meant to illuminate the nature of democracy, identify its adversaries, and point the way for policies that strengthen and expand democratic freedoms. Freedom House projects are designed to support the framework of rights and freedoms guaranteed in the Universal Declaration of Human Rights.

Supporting Democratic Change: The attainment of freedom ultimately depends on the actions of courageous men and women who are committed to the transformation of their societies. But history has repeatedly demonstrated that outside support can play a critical role in the struggle for democratic rights. Freedom House is actively engaged in these struggles, both in countries where dictatorship holds sway and in those societies that are in transition from autocracy to democracy. Freedom House functions as a catalyst for freedom by working to strengthen civil society, promote open government, defend human rights, enhance justice, and facilitate the free flow of information and ideas.